13th EDITIO

BUSINESS LAW TODAY

STANDARD EDITION
TEXT & SUMMARIZED CASES

Roger LeRoy Miller
Institute for University Studies
Arlington, Texas

Cengage

Australia • Brazil • Canada • Mexico • Singapore • United Kingdom • United States

Cengage

***Business Law Today, Standard Edition, Text & Summarized Cases* 13th Edition**
Roger LeRoy Miller

SVP, Higher Education & Skills Product: Erin Joyner

VP, Higher Education & Skills Product:
Michael Schenk

Product Director: Joe Sabatino

Associate Product Manager: Abbie Schultheis

Senior Content Manager: Julia Chase

Cengage Subject Matter Expert: Lisa Elliott

Learning Designers: Cazzie Reyes and Liz Harnage

Digital Delivery Lead: Steven McMillian

Product Assistant: Nick Perez

Marketing Director: Kristen Hurd

Marketing Manager: Andrew Stock

Intellectual Property Analyst: Ashley Maynard

Intellectual Property Project Manager: Nick Barrows

Production Service: SPi Global

Designer: Erin Griffin

Cover Image Credits: Kolonko/ShutterStock.com

Interior Image Credits:
iStockPhoto.com/metamorworks;
Alexander Supertramp/ShutterStock.com;
Kolonko/ShutterStock.com; silvae/Shutterstock.com;
Orhan Cam/Shutterstock.com;
Kozlik/Shutterstock.com;
Hekla/Shutterstock.com;
Kamil Fazrin Rauf/Shutterstock.com;
Artem Samokhvalov/Shutterstock.com;
Yuriy Kulik/Shutterstock.com; winui/Shutterstock.com;
Creative Images/Shutterstock.com;
iDEARReplay/Shutterstock.com;
Gary Lanfer/Shutterstock.com;
Rawpixel.com/Shutterstock.com

Library of Congress Control Number: 2020949409

Soft-cover Edition ISBN: 978-0-357-63485-1
Loose-leaf Edition ISBN: 978-0-357-63486-8

Cengage
200 Pier 4 Boulevard
Boston, MA 02210
USA

Printed at CLDPC, USA, 11-23

Contents in Brief

Contents

Unit 1 The Legal Environment of Business 1

Unit 7 Property and Its Protection 845

Preface

The present world landscape poses numerous challenges for students planning careers in the business world. It also offers limitless opportunities. To take advantage of those opportunities, prospective entrepreneurs—whether they aspire to work on Wall Street or Main Street—need to have a solid understanding of business law and the legal environment of corporate America. The most up-to-date text on the market, *Business Law Today: Standard Edition*, Thirteenth Edition, provides the perfect platform to achieve this goal.

Instructors have come to rely on the coverage, accuracy, and applicability of *Business Law Today*. This best-selling text engages your students, solidifies their understanding of legal concepts, and provides the best teaching tools available. Working on this edition, my objective was to make its pages more interesting, to the point, and visually compelling than ever before. I put particular focus on pedagogical devices within the text that focus on legal, ethical, and corporate issues, while never losing sight of the course's core curriculum.

The Thirteenth Edition incorporates the latest legal developments, from United States Supreme Court decisions to state-level legislation. It also includes nearly forty new and updated features and more than thirty new cases from 2019 and 2020, over one hundred new *Examples* and *Case Examples*, along with an extensive array of exhibits, *Focus Questions*, margin definitions, and case problems.

New and Updated Features

The Thirteenth Edition of *Business Law Today: Standard Edition* is filled with stimulating new and updated features designed to cover current high-interest legal topics.

1. **Entirely new *Cybersecurity and the Law*** features shed light on the risks that go with the many rewards offered by technology in the global marketplace. These features recount how some of the most important brands in corporate America are protecting themselves and their customers from the threats lurking in cyberspace. Some topics include:
   - *Should Apple Help Law Enforcement?* (Chapter 2)
   - *Counter Strike: Global Offensive* (Chapter 9)
   - *The CLOUD Act* (Chapter 29)
2. **Entirely new hypotheticals in selected chapter introductions** provide a real-world link that generates student interest and highlights specific legal concepts that will be discussed in the chapter. These hypotheticals—often based on real cases or business situations—help to introduce and illustrate legal issues facing managers, companies, and even industries.
3. ***Business Web Log*** features underscore the importance of the text material to real-world businesses. Each of these features discusses a major U.S. company that is engaged in a dispute involving a topic covered in the chapter. Some topics include
   - *Samsung and Forced Arbitration* (Chapter 4)
   - *Johnson & Johnson Faces Continuing Lawsuits over Its Talcum Powder* (Chapter 6)
   - *Online Competition, Bankruptcy, and the "Retail Apocalypse"* (Chapter 22)

4. ***Adapting the Law to the Online Environment*** features examine cutting-edge cyberlaw topics, such as:
   - *The Problem of "Contract Cheating"* (Chapter 13)
   - *Open Banking* (Chapter 20)
   - *Big Tech's Monopoly Problem* (Chapter 31)
5. ***Business Law Analysis*** features appear in numerous chapters of the text. These features are useful tools to help students master the legal analysis skills that they will need to answer questions and case problems in the book, on exams, and in everyday business situations. Topics include:
   - *The Impact of Patent Time Limits* (Chapter 7)
   - *Deciding If a Court Would Impose a Quasi Contract* (Chapter 10)
   - *Workers' Compensation Claims* (Chapter 24)
6. ***Ethical Issue*** features focus on the ethical aspects of a topic being discussed in order to emphasize that ethics is an integral part of a business law course. Examples include:
   - *Even Though Corporation* Can *Restrict the Speech of Their Employees,* Should *They Do So?* (Chapter 2)
   - *Does the Gig Economy Take Advantage of Independent Contractors?* (Chapter 23)
   - *Does Corporate America Need Board Of Director Gender Quotas?* (Chapter 30)
7. ***Managerial Strategy*** features emphasize the management aspects of business law and the legal environment. Topics include:
   - *The Power of Precedents* (Chapter 1)
   - *The Stakeholder Capitalism Movement* (Chapter 3)
   - *Can a Person Who Is Not a Member of a Protected Class Sue for Discrimination?* (Chapter 28)
8. ***Landmark in the Law*** features discuss a landmark case, statute, or development that has significantly affected business law. Examples include:
   - *Palsgraf v. Long Island Railroad Co.* (Chapter 5)
   - *The Digital Millennium Copyright Act* (Chapter 8)
   - *Federal Trade Commission Rule 433* (Chapter 18)

Making Ethical Business Decisions—The IDDR Approach

The Thirteenth Edition of *Business Law Today* boasts its own framework for helping students (and businesspersons) make ethical decisions—the **IDDR Approach**, which is presented in Chapter 3. This systematic approach provides students with a clear step-by-step process to analyze the legal and ethical implications of decisions that are in everyday business operations. The IDDR Approach uses four logical steps:

- **Step 1: Inquiry**
- **Step 2: Discussion**
- **Step 3: Decision**
- **Step 4: Review**

Students can remember the first letter of each step easily by using the phrase "I Desire to Do Right." Material in **Chapter 3 (Ethics in Business)** details the goals of each IDDR step and then provides a Sample Scenario to show students how to apply this new approach to ethical decision making. The text now focuses on real-life application of ethical principles.

After Chapter 3, to reinforce the application of the IDDR Approach, students are asked to use its various steps when answering each chapter's *A Question of Ethics*. In addition, the Thirteenth Edition retains the *Ethical Issue* feature in most chapters, several of which have been refreshed with timely topics involving the ever-evolving technologies and trends in business.

New Cases and Case Problems

The Thirteenth Edition of *Business Law Today* has new cases and case problems from 2019 and 2020 in nearly every chapter. The new cases have been carefully selected to illustrate important points of law and to be of high interest to students and instructors. I have made it a point to find recent cases that enhance learning and are straightforward enough for business law students to understand. At the end of each chapter, additional scenarios are presented as case problems that require students to apply concepts learned from the text.

Certain cases and case problems have been carefully chosen as good teaching cases and are designated as ***Spotlight Cases*** and ***Spotlight Case Problems***. Some examples include *Spotlight on Gucci, Spotlight on Beer Labels, Spotlight on Nike*, and *Spotlight on the Seattle Mariners*. Instructors will find these Spotlight decisions useful to illustrate the legal concepts under discussion, and students will enjoy studying the cases because they involve interesting and memorable facts. Other cases have been chosen as ***Classic Cases*** because they establish a legal precedent in a particular area of law.

Each case concludes with a section, called *Critical Thinking*, which includes at least one question. Each question is labeled *Ethical, Economic, Legal Environment, Political, Social*, or *What If the Facts Were Different?* In addition, *Classic Cases* include an *Impact of This Case on Today's Law* section that clarifies how the case has affected the legal environment. Suggested answers to all case-ending questions can be found in the *Answers Manual* for this text.

Many New Highlighted and Numbered Case Examples

Many instructors use cases and examples to illustrate how the law applies to business. This edition of *Business Law Today* offers hundreds of new 2019 and 2020 highlighted and consecutively numbered ***Examples*** and ***Case Examples***. *Examples* illustrate how the law applies in a specific situation, and *Case Examples* present the facts and issues of an actual case and then describe the court's decision and rationale.

In addition, this edition presents ***Spotlight Case Examples,*** which deal with especially high-interest cases, and ***Classic Case Examples,*** which discuss older, landmark decisions. The numbered *Examples* and *Case Examples* features are integrated throughout the text to help students better understand how courts apply legal principles in the real world.

Critical Thinking and Legal Reasoning Elements

For this edition of *Business Law Today,* I have included a discussion of legal reasoning in Chapter 1. The *Business Law Analysis* features that can be found throughout the text emphasize legal reasoning skills as well. *Critical Thinking* questions conclude most of the features and cases in this text. At the end of each chapter, a ***Debate This*** question requires students to think critically about the rationale underlying the law on a particular topic.

Answers to all *Critical Thinking* questions, as well as to the ***Business Scenarios and Case Problems*** at the end of every chapter, are presented in the Thirteenth Edition's *Answers Manual*. In addition, the answers to one case problem in each chapter, called the ***Business Case Problem with Sample Answer***, appear in Appendix E.

The chapter-ending materials also include a separate section of questions that focus on critical thinking and writing. This section always includes a ***Time-Limited Group Assignment*** and may also include a ***Critical Legal Thinking*** question requiring students to think critically about some aspect of the law discussed in the chapter or a ***Business Law Writing*** question requiring students to compose a written response.

Other Pedagogical Devices within Each Chapter

- ***Focus Questions*** (questions listed at the beginning of each chapter and repeated in the margins of the text provide a framework of main chapter concepts for the student).
- **Margin definitions** of each boldfaced *Key Term.*
- ***Know This*** (margin features).
- **Exhibits** (in most chapters).
- **Photographs** (with critical-thinking questions).

Chapter-Ending Pedagogy

- ***Practice and Review*** (in every chapter).
- ***Debate This*** (a statement or question at the end of *Practice and Review*).
- ***Key Terms*** (with appropriate page references to their margin definitions).
- ***Chapter Summary*** (in table format).
- ***Issue Spotters*** (in every chapter with answers in *Appendix D*).
- ***Business Scenarios and Case Problems*** (including in every chapter, a *Business Case Problem with Sample Answer* that is answered in *Appendix E*; in selected chapters, a *Spotlight Case Problem*; and in every chapter, a *A Question of Ethics* that applies this textbook's unique ***IDDR Approach*** to business ethics).
- ***Critical Thinking and Writing Assignments*** (including a *Time-Limited Group Assignment* in every chapter, and a *Business Law Writing* or a *Critical Legal Thinking* question in selected chapters).

Unit-Ending Pedagogy

Each of the seven units in the Thirteenth Edition of *Business Law Today* concludes with a ***Task-Based Simulation.*** This feature presents a hypothetical business situation and then asks a series of questions about how the law applies to various actions taken by the firm. To answer the questions, the student must apply the laws discussed throughout the unit. (Answers are provided in the *Answers Manual.*)

Supplements

Business Law Today, Thirteenth Edition, provides a comprehensive supplements package designed to make the tasks of teaching and learning more enjoyable and efficient. The following supplements are available for instructors.

MindTap Business Law for *Business Law Today,* Thirteenth Edition

Today's leading digital platform, **MindTap**, gives you complete control of your course—equipping you to craft unique learning experiences that challenge students, build confidence and elevate performance.

Use MindTap as-is or customize it to meet your specific needs. You can even integrate it easily into your institution's Learning Management System (LMS).

A streamlined learning path and redesigned assessments minimize reader distraction, while dual-pane assignments for students pair readings side-by-side with assessments. MindTap presents complex concepts using a blend of engaging narrative and media assets clearly linked to assessments. So, students can start applying concepts to real-world situations from the beginning of your course with content that progresses from understanding core concepts to critical thinking and, ultimately, application.

Exclusive **Instructor Tools** allow you to customize course content to your needs and tailor assessments to match the specific language and style of your course. New **Instructor Reports** provide actionable insights into student performance and present opportunities for just-in-time intervention.

Product Features

MindTap's outcomes-based learning design propels students from memorization to mastery. It's the only platform today that gives you complete ownership of your course. With MindTap you can challenge every student, build confidence and empower today's learners to be unstoppable.

Anchor Learning With Improved Learning Path Design

MindTap helps students focus by dividing the **Learning Path** into groups of bite-size activities that are anchored to a single concept. MindTap presents concepts by pairing instructional content with assessment in a visually captivating side-by-side format.

Provide Learning on the Go

Offer your students the flexibility they need to fit learning into their day—wherever they are and using whatever approach works best for them. Bite-size content and activities that students can complete on a smartphone or tablet keep learning engaging, even on the go.

Quick Lesson Videos Present Complex Topics Visually

MindTap contains a variety of new and existing **Quick Lesson Videos**, placed within Learn It activities and in the **Additional Resources**, Quick Lessons folder in the MindTap, to reach all types of learners.

Access Everything You Need in One Place

Cut down on prep with preloaded, organized course materials in MindTap. Teach more efficiently with interactive multimedia, assignments, quizzes and focused resources all on one screen. With MindTap you give your students the power to read, listen and study on their phones—so they can learn on their own terms.

Empower Students to Reach Their Potentials

Gain actionable insights into student engagement with MindTap's twelve distinct metrics. Identify topics troubling your entire class and instantly communicate with struggling students. You can track your class' performance down to the learning objective and curate your lectures in real-time to respond to distinct class-wide needs. Students can track their scores and take the guesswork out of studying with performance reports and personalized study materials that help them progress toward their goals.

Control Your Course, Your Content

Only MindTap gives you complete control of your course. You have the flexibility to reorder textbook chapters, add your own notes and embed a variety of content, including OER. Personalize course content to your students' needs by editing question text or answer choices. They can even read your notes, add their own and highlight key text to aid their progress.

Count on Our Dedicated Team, Whenever You Need Them

MindTap is not simply a comprehensive tool—it's a network of support from a personalized team eager to further your success. We're ready to help—from setting up your course to tailoring MindTap resources to meet your specific objectives. You'll be ready to make an impact from day one. And, we'll be right here to help you and your students throughout the semester—and beyond.

MindTap Table of Contents

Why Does [Topic] Matter to Me?

Immediately engage students with new activities that connect the upcoming chapter to an authentic, real-world scenario designed to pique engagement and emphasize relevance. Use these activities to ensure students read material before class and to trigger lively in-class discussion.

Chapter-Level Ebook

Immediately engage students with a dynamic eBook that brings the value, concepts and applications of the printed text to life. Students open an active learning experience as each chapter provides opportunities to interact with content using the approach that's best for the individual learner.

Learn It Activities

Easily add multimedia instruction to your course to supplement textbook learning. MindTap's **Learn It** activities offer small sections of instruction in the form of narrative, images, and/or Quick Lesson Videos that highlight the most important concepts in each chapter. Learn It activities reinforce the text's instruction and even approach concepts in a different way to promote student choice and autonomy with personalizing learning. You can assign Learn It activities to ensure that students have read and understand key concepts before class.

Check Your Understanding—Chapter Quizzes

Use MindTap's **Check Your Understanding** quizzes to assess student performance and immediately identify class-wide learning needs.

Apply It Activities

Assign any of MindTap's carefully designed, practically focused application activities to ensure your students know how to make business decisions through the lens of the law.

- **Case Problem Analyses** offer a multi-step activity that asks students to identify the facts in a scenario through a series of questions that promote a critical-thinking process so that students can arrive at the decision of the court. In the second part, the facts are changed, and students apply the same critical-thinking process on their own.

- **Brief Hypotheticals** help students spot the issue and apply the law in the context of a short, fictional scenario.

Additional Resources (found at the part level)

- **Business Cases** develop students' skills to apply critical-thinking and legal reasoning through relevant real-world business scenarios.
- **Quick Lesson Videos** highlight the most important concepts in each chapter.
- **PowerPoint Slides** edited for student use offer visual outlines of each chapter.

Cengage Testing Powered by Cognero

Cengage Testing Powered by Cognero is a flexible online system that allows instructors to do the following:

- Author, edit, and manage *Test Bank* content from multiple Cengage Learning solutions.
- Create multiple test versions in an instant.
- Deliver tests from their Learning Management System (LMS), classroom, or wherever they want.

Start Right Away! *Cengage Testing Powered by Cognero* works on any operating system or browser.

- Use your standard browser; no special installs or downloads are needed.
- Create tests from school, home, the coffee shop—anywhere with Internet access.

What Instructors Will Find

- ***Simplicity at every step.*** A desktop-inspired interface features drop-down menus and familiar, intuitive tools that take instructors through content creation and management with ease.
- ***Full-featured test generator.*** Create ideal assessments with a choice of fifteen question types—including true/false, multiple choice, opinion scale/Likert, and essay. Multi-language support, an equation editor, and unlimited metadata help ensure instructor tests are complete and compliant.
- ***Cross-compatible capability.*** Import and export content into other systems.

Instructor Companion Website

The *Instructor's Companion Website* is an all-in-one resource for class preparation, presentation, and testing. Accessible through www.cengage.com/login with your faculty account, you will find available for download:

- ***Instructor's Manual.*** Includes activities and assessments for each chapter and their correlation to specific learning objectives, an outline, key terms with definitions, a chapter summary, and several ideas for engaging with students with discussion questions, ice breakers, case studies, and social learning activities that may be conducted in an on-ground, hybrid, or online modality.

- ***Answers Manual.*** Provides answers to all questions presented in the text, including the ***Focus Questions,*** the questions in each case and feature, the *Issue Spotters*, the *Business Scenarios and Case Problems*, *Critical Thinking and Writing Assignments*, and the unit-ending *Task-Based Simulation* features.
- ***Test Bank.*** A comprehensive test bank, offered in Blackboard, Moodle, Desire2Learn, and Canvas formats, contains learning objective-specific true-false, multiple-choice and essay questions for each chapter. Import the test bank into your LMS to edit and manage questions, and to create tests.
- ***PowerPoint Slides.*** Presentations are closely tied to the Instructor Manual, providing ample opportunities for generating classroom discussion and interaction. They offer ready-to-use, visual outlines of each chapter, which may be easily customized for your lectures.
- ***Guide to Teaching Online.*** Presents technological and pedagogical considerations and suggestions for teaching the Business Law course when you can't be in the same room with students.
- ***Transition Guide.*** Highlights all of the changes in the text and in the digital offerings from the previous edition to this edition.
- ***Educator Guide.*** Walks you through what the unique activities are in the MindTap, where you'll find them and how they're built for easier curriculum integration.

Acknowledgments

Since I began this project many years ago, numerous business law professors and users of *Business Law Today* have been kind enough to help me revise the book and digital offerings, including the following:

John J. Balek
Morton College, Illinois

John Jay Ballantine
University of Colorado, Boulder

Lorraine K. Bannai
Western Washington University

Marlene E. Barken
Ithaca College, New York

Laura Barnard
Lakeland Community College, Ohio

Denise A. Bartles, J.D.
Missouri Western State University

Daryl Barton
Eastern Michigan University

Merlin Bauer
Mid State Technical College, Wisconsin

Donna E. Becker
Frederick Community College, Maryland

Richard J. Bennet
Three Rivers Community College, Connecticut

Dr. Anne Berre
Schreiner University, Texas

Robert C. Bird
University of Connecticut

Bonnie S. Bolinger
Ivy Tech Community College, Wabash Valley Region, Indiana

Brad Botz
Garden City Community College, Kansas

Teresa Brady
Holy Family College, Pennsylvania

Dean Bredeson
University of Texas at Austin

Lee B. Burgunder
California Polytechnic University, San Luis Obispo

Thomas D. Cavenagh
North Central College, Illinois

Bradley D. Childs
Belmont University, Tennessee

Corey Ciocchetti
University of Denver, Colorado

Peter Clapp
St. Mary's College, California

Dale Clark
Corning Community College, New York

Tammy W. Cowart
University of Texas, Tyler

Stanley J. Dabrowski
Hudson County Community College, New Jersey

Sandra J. Defebaugh
Eastern Michigan University

Patricia L. DeFrain
Glendale College, California

M. Yvonne Demory, J.D., LL.M.
George Mason University

Julia G. Derrick
Brevard Community College, Florida

Joe D. Dillsaver
Northeastern State University, Oklahoma

Claude W. Dotson
Northwest College, Wyoming

Larry R. Edwards
Tarrant County Junior College, South Campus, Texas

Jacolin Eichelberger
Hillsborough Community College, Florida

George E. Eigsti
Kansas City, Kansas, Community College

Florence E. Elliott-Howard
Stephen F. Austin State University, Texas

Tony Enerva
Lakeland Community College, Ohio

Benjamin C. Fassberg
Prince George's Community College, Maryland

Joseph L. Flack
Washtenaw Community College, Michigan

Jerry Furniss
University of Montana

Joan Gabel
Florida State University

Elizabeth J. Guerriero
Northeast Louisiana University

Phil Harmeson
University of South Dakota

Nancy L. Hart
Midland College, Texas

Mo Hassan
Cabrillo College, California

Andy E. Hendrick
Coastal Carolina University, South Carolina

Janine S. Hiller
Virginia Polytechnic Institute & State University

Karen A. Holmes
Hudson Valley Community College, New York

Fred Ittner
College of Alameda, California

Susan S. Jarvis
University of Texas, Pan American

Jack E. Karns
East Carolina University, North Carolina

Sarah Weiner Keidan
Oakland Community College, Michigan

Richard N. Kleeberg
Solano Community College, California

Bradley T. Lutz
Hillsborough Community College, Florida

Diane MacDonald
Pacific Lutheran University, Washington

Darlene Mallick
Anne Arundel Community College, Maryland

John D. Mallonee
Manatee Community College, Florida

Joseph D. Marcus
Prince George's Community College, Maryland

Woodrow J. Maxwell
Hudson Valley Community College, New York

Diane May
Winona State University, Minnesota

Beverly McCormick
Morehead State University, Kentucky

William J. McDevitt
Saint Joseph's University, Pennsylvania

John W. McGee
Aims Community College, Colorado

James K. Miersma
Milwaukee Area Technical Institute, Wisconsin

Susan J. Mitchell
Des Moines Area Community College, Iowa

Jim Lee Morgan
West Los Angeles College, California

Jack K. Morton
University of Montana

Annie Laurie I. Myers
Northampton Community College, Pennsylvania

Solange North
Fox Valley Technical Institute, Wisconsin

Jamie L. O'Brien
South Dakota State University

Ruth R. O'Keefe
Jacksonville University, Florida

Robert H. Orr
Florida Community College at Jacksonville

George Otto
Truman College, Illinois

Thomas L. Palmer
Northern Arizona University

David W. Pan
University of Tulsa, Oklahoma

Victor C. Parker, Jr.
North Georgia College and State University

Jane Patterson
Ozarks Technical Community College and Missouri State University

Donald L. Petote
Genesee Community College, New York

Francis D. Polk
Ocean County College, New Jersey

Gregory Rabb
Jamestown Community College, New York

Brad Reid
Abilene Christian University, Texas

Anne Montgomery Ricketts
University of Findlay, Ohio

Donald A. Roark
University of West Florida

Joey Robertson
Sam Houston State University

Hugh Rode
Utah Valley State College

Gerald M. Rogers
Front Range Community College, Colorado

Dr. William J. Russell
Northwest Nazarene University, Idaho

William M. Rutledge
Macomb Community College, Michigan

Roberto Sandoval
University of Texas at El Paso

Martha Wright Sartoris
North Hennepin Community College, Minnesota

Kurt M. Saunders
California State University, Northridge

Anne W. Schacherl
Madison Area Technical College, Wisconsin

Edward F. Shafer
Rochester Community College, Minnesota

Lance Shoemaker, J.D., M.C.P., M.A.
West Valley College, California

Lou Ann Simpson
Drake University, Iowa

Anthony A. Smith
Ithaca College

Denise Smith
Missouri Western State College

Hugh M. Spall
Central Washington University

Elisabeth "Lisa" Sperow
California Polytechnic State University, San Luis Obispo

Catherine A. Stevens
College of Southern Maryland

Nicole Forbes Stowell, Esquire
University of Southern Florida, St. Petersburg

Andrea Studzinski
College of DuPage

Maurice Tonissi
Quinsigamond Community College, Massachusetts

James D. Van Tassel
Mission College, California

Russell A. Waldon
College of the Canyons, California

Frederick J. Walsh
Franklin Pierce College, New Hampshire

James E. Walsh, Jr.
Tidewater Community College, Virginia

Randy Waterman
Richland College, Texas

Jerry Wegman
University of Idaho

Edward L. Welsh, Jr.
Phoenix College, Arizona

Whitney B. Westrich
University of Cincinnati

Clark W. Wheeler
Santa Fe Community College, Florida

Lori Whisenant
University of Houston, Texas

Kay O. Wilburn
The University of Alabama at Birmingham

John G. Williams, J.D.
Northwestern State University, Louisiana

Shallin S. Williams
Tri-County Technical College

James L. Wittenbach
University of Notre Dame, Indiana

Abby A. Wood, Esq.
Mt. San Antonio College

Margaret M. Wright, J.D. LL.M.
University of Illinois, Urbana-Champaign

Eric D. Yordy
Northern Arizona University

Joseph Zavaglia, Jr.
Brookdale Community College, New Jersey

Alexandria Zylstra, J.D., LL.M.
George Mason University

In addition, I give my thanks to the staff at Cengage especially Abbie Schultheis, Associate Product Manager; Joe Sabatino, Product Director; Julia Chase, Senior Content Manager; Cazzie Reyes and Liz Harnage, Learning Designers; Lisa Elliot, Subject Matter Expert; Steven McMillian, Digital Delivery Lead; Nick Perez, Product Assistant; Ashley Maynard, Permissions Analyst; and Nick Barrows, Permissions Project Manager. I also thank Andrew Stock in Marketing. Additionally, I would like to thank my project manager Ann Borman at SPi Global, the compositor, for accurately generating pages for the text and making it possible for me to meet my ambitious schedule for the print and digital products.

I give special thanks to Katherine Marie Silsbee for managing the project and providing exceptional research and editorial skills. I also thank William Eric Hollowell, co-author of the *Answers Manual* for his excellent research efforts. I am grateful for the copyediting services of Beverly Peavler and proofreading services of Maureen Johnson. I also thank Vickie Reierson and Suzanne Jasin for their many efforts on this project.

Roger LeRoy Miller

Dedication

To Lorraine,

The journey continues to more delightful times.
It's nice to be part of it with you.

R.L.M.

Sergii Gnatiuk/Shutterstock.com

Unit 1 The Legal Environment of Business

1 Law and Legal Reasoning

Focus Questions

The four Focus Questions *below are designed to help improve your understanding. After reading this chapter, you should be able to answer the following questions:*

1. What are four primary sources of law in the United States?
2. What is a precedent? When might a court depart from precedent?
3. What is the difference between remedies at law and remedies in equity?
4. What are some important differences between civil law and criminal law?

"Laws should be like clothes. They should be made to fit the people they are meant to serve."

Clarence Darrow
1857–1938
(American lawyer)

In the chapter-opening quotation, Clarence Darrow asserts that law should be created to serve the public. Because you are part of that public, the law is important to you. In particular, those entering the world of business will find themselves subject to numerous laws and government regulations. A basic knowledge of these laws and regulations is beneficial—if not essential—to anyone contemplating a successful career in today's business environment.

Although the law has various definitions, all of them are based on the general observation that **law** consists of *enforceable rules governing relationships among individuals and between individuals and their society.* In some societies, these enforceable rules consist of unwritten principles of behavior. In other societies, they are set forth in ancient or contemporary law codes. In the United States, our rules consist of written laws and court decisions created by modern legislative and judicial bodies. Regardless of how such rules are created, they all have one feature in common: *they establish rights, duties, and privileges that are consistent with the values and beliefs of a society or its ruling group.*

Law A body of enforceable rules governing relationships among individuals and between individuals and their society.

In this introductory chapter, we look at how business law and the legal environment affect business decisions. For instance, suppose that Mototron, Inc., plans to introduce a driverless car equipped with lidar, a radar system that relies on lasers, and artificially intelligent cameras. Even if its technicians put the vehicles through two million miles of testing on closed courses and deem them low risk, Mototron cannot simply start selling rides to consumers. The company must first test the cars on public roads, which requires permission from state governments. It must also establish safety rules with federal regulators and negotiate sustainable insurance rates. At each step, Mototron will have to adjust its bottom line to take account of the legal costs of introducing cutting-edge but potentially dangerous technology into the American marketplace.

Our goal in this text is not only to teach you about specific laws, but also to teach you how to think about the law and legal environment, and to develop your critical-thinking and legal reasoning skills. The laws may change, but the ability to analyze and evaluate the legal (and ethical) ramifications of situations as they arise is an invaluable and lasting skill.

1-1 Business Activities and the Legal Environment

Laws and government regulations affect almost all business activities—from hiring and firing decisions to workplace safety, the manufacturing and marketing of products, business financing, and more. To make good business decisions, businesspersons need to understand the laws and regulations governing these activities.

Realize also that in today's business world, simply being aware of what conduct can lead to legal **liability** is not enough. Businesspersons must develop critical-thinking and legal reasoning skills so that they can evaluate how various laws might apply to a given situation and determine the best course of action. Businesspersons are also pressured to make ethical decisions. Thus, the study of business law necessarily involves an ethical dimension.

Liability The state of being legally responsible (liable) for something, such as a debt or obligation.

As you will note, each chapter in this text covers a specific area of the law and shows how the legal rules in that area affect business activities. Although compartmentalizing the law in this fashion facilitates learning, it does not indicate the extent to which many different laws may apply to just one transaction. Exhibit 1–1 illustrates the various areas of the law that may influence business decision making.

Exhibit 1–1 Areas of the Law That May Affect Business Decision Making

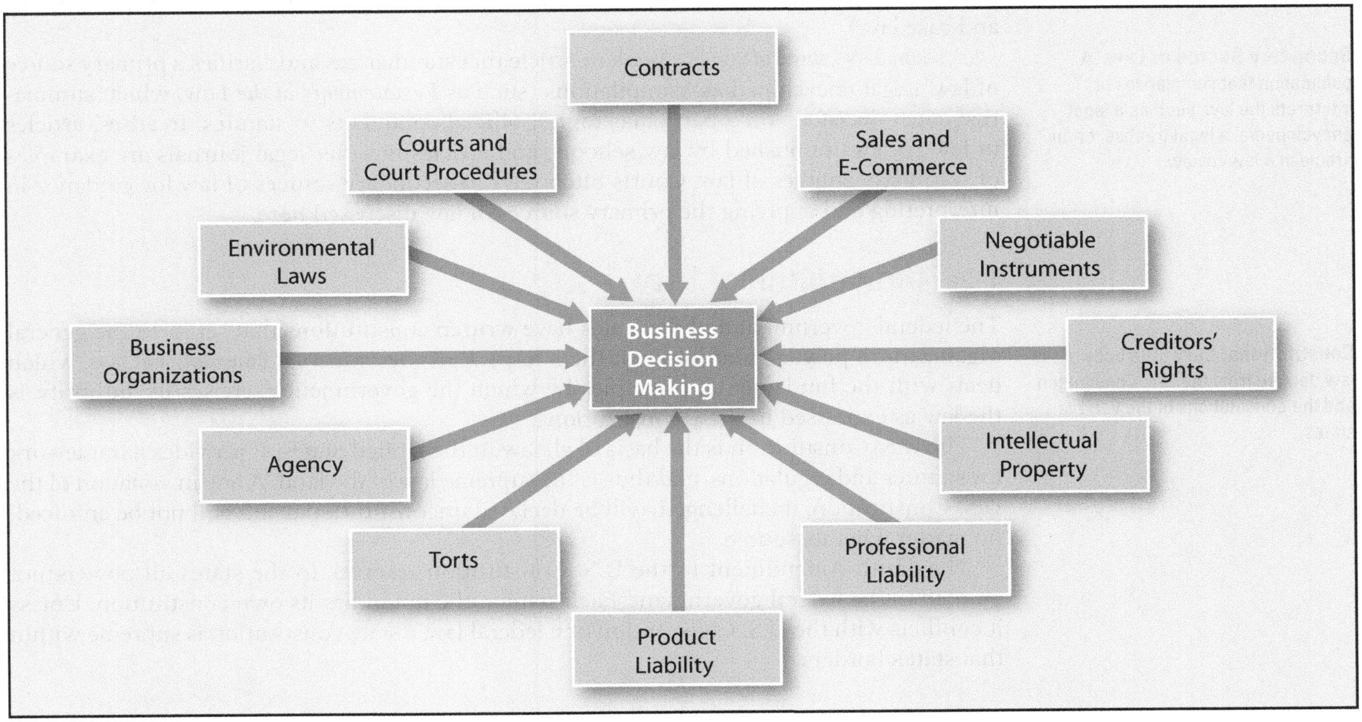

Example 1.1 Soon after it launched, YouTube faced a potentially catastrophic $1 billion copyright infringement lawsuit. Entertainment conglomerate Viacom claimed that the video-hosting platform was not taking sufficient steps to remove unlicensed use of Viacom's content on its site. A federal judge ensured YouTube's survival by ruling that the company was in compliance with federal copyright law as long as it responded reasonably to "take-down" requests from Viacom and other content providers.

Not surprisingly, with five hundred hours of video uploaded to its site each minute, YouTube has remained under constant legal pressure ever since. Liberal *and* conservative groups have sued the company for discriminating against their political viewpoints. It has faced regulatory scrutiny for, among other things, failing to protect users from sexual and racist harassment and hosting misleading election-related video content. At one point, the Federal Trade Commission fined the company $170 million for collecting personal information from children without their parents' consent. ■

1–2 Sources of American Law

Primary Source of Law A source that establishes the law on a particular issue, such as a constitution, a statute, an administrative rule, or a court decision.

There are numerous sources of American law. A source that establishes the law on a particular issue is called a **primary source of law**. Primary sources include the following:

- The U.S. Constitution and the constitutions of the various states.
- Statutory law—including laws passed by Congress, state legislatures, and local governing bodies.
- Regulations created by administrative agencies, such as the federal Food and Drug Administration.
- Case law (court decisions).

Focus Question 1

What are four primary sources of law in the United States?

We describe each of these important primary sources of law in the following pages. (See the appendix at the end of this chapter for a discussion of how to find statutes, regulations, and case law.)

Secondary Source of Law A publication that summarizes or interprets the law, such as a legal encyclopedia, a legal treatise, or an article in a law review.

A **secondary source of law** is a book or article that summarizes and clarifies a primary source of law. Legal encyclopedias, compilations (such as *Restatements of the Law*, which summarize court decisions on a particular topic), official comments to statutes, treatises, articles in law reviews published by law schools, and articles in other legal journals are examples of secondary sources of law. Courts often refer to secondary sources of law for guidance in interpreting and applying the primary sources of law discussed here.

1–2a Constitutional Law

Constitutional Law The body of law derived from the U.S. Constitution and the constitutions of the various states.

The federal government and the states have written constitutions that set forth the general organization, powers, and limits of their respective governments. **Constitutional law**, which deals with the fundamental principles by which the government exercises its authority, is the law as expressed in these constitutions.

The U.S. Constitution is the basis of all law in the United States. It provides a framework for statutes and regulations, and thus is the supreme law of the land. A law in violation of the U.S. Constitution, if challenged, will be declared unconstitutional and will not be enforced, no matter what its source.

The Tenth Amendment to the U.S. Constitution reserves to the states all powers not granted to the federal government. Each state in the union has its own constitution. Unless it conflicts with the U.S. Constitution or a federal law, a state constitution is supreme within that state's borders.

1–2b Statutory Law

Laws enacted by legislative bodies at any level of government, such as the statutes passed by Congress or by state legislatures, make up the body of law generally referred to as **statutory law**. When a legislature passes a statute, that statute ultimately is included in the federal code of laws or the relevant state code of laws.

Statutory Law The body of law enacted by legislative bodies (as opposed to constitutional law, administrative law, or case law).

Whenever a particular statute is mentioned in this text, we usually provide a footnote showing its **citation** (a reference to a publication in which a legal authority—such as a statute or a court decision—or other source can be found). In the appendix following this chapter, we explain how you can use these citations to find statutory law.

Citation A reference to a publication in which a legal authority—such as a statute or a court decision—or other source can be found.

Local Ordinances Statutory law also includes local ordinances. An **ordinance** is a regulation passed by a municipal or county governing unit to deal with matters not covered by federal or state law. Ordinances commonly have to do with city or county land use (zoning ordinances), building and safety codes, and other matters affecting only the local governing unit.

Ordinance A regulation enacted by a city or county legislative body that becomes part of that city's or county's statutory law.

Applicability of Statutes A federal statute, of course, applies to all states. A state statute, in contrast, applies only within the state's borders. State laws thus may vary from state to state. No federal statute may violate the U.S. Constitution, and no state statute or local ordinance may violate the U.S. Constitution or the relevant state constitution.

Example 1.2 The tension between federal, state, and local laws is evident in the national debate over so-called sanctuary cities—cities that limit their cooperation with federal immigration authorities. Normally, law enforcement officials are supposed to alert federal immigration authorities when they come into contact with an undocumented immigrant. Then, immigration officials request the state and local authorities to detain the individual for possible deportation.

But a number of cities across the United States have adopted either local ordinances or explicit policies that do not follow this procedure. Police in these cities often do not ask or report the immigration status of individuals with whom they come into contact. Other places refuse to detain undocumented immigrants who are accused of low-level offenses. ■

Michael Dwyer/Alamy

How have local "sanctuary cities" frustrated federal immigration procedures?

Uniform Laws During the 1800s, the differences among state laws frequently created difficulties for businesspersons conducting trade and commerce among the states. To counter these problems, a group of legal scholars and lawyers formed the National Conference of Commissioners on Uniform State Laws (NCCUSL, online at www.uniformlaws.org) in 1892 to draft **uniform laws** ("model statutes") for the states to consider adopting. The NCCUSL still exists today and continues to issue uniform laws.

Uniform Laws Model laws developed by the National Conference of Commissioners on Uniform State Laws for the states to consider enacting into statute.

Each state has the option of adopting or rejecting a uniform law. *Only if a state legislature adopts a uniform law does that law become part of the statutory law of that state.* Furthermore, a state legislature may choose to adopt only part of a uniform law or to rewrite the sections that are adopted. Hence, even though many states may have adopted a uniform law, those laws may not be entirely "uniform."

The Uniform Commercial Code (UCC) One of the most important uniform acts is the Uniform Commercial Code (UCC), which was created through the joint efforts of the NCCUSL and the American Law Institute.[1] The UCC was first issued in 1952 and has been adopted in all fifty states,[2] the District of Columbia, and the Virgin Islands.

The UCC facilitates commerce among the states by providing a uniform, yet flexible, set of rules governing commercial transactions. Because of its importance in the area of commercial law, we cite the UCC frequently in this text. From time to time, the NCCUSL revises the articles contained in the UCC and submits the revised versions to the states for adoption.

1–2c Administrative Law

Administrative Law The body of law created by administrative agencies in order to carry out their duties and responsibilities.

Administrative Agency A federal, state, or local government agency created by the legislature to perform a specific function, such as to make and enforce rules pertaining to the environment.

Another important source of American law is **administrative law**, which consists of the rules, orders, and decisions of administrative agencies. An **administrative agency** is a federal, state, or local government agency established to perform a specific function.

Rules issued by various administrative agencies affect almost every aspect of a business's operations. Regulations govern a business's capital structure and financing, its hiring and firing procedures, its relations with employees and unions, and the way it manufactures and markets its products.

Federal Agencies At the national level, numerous *executive agencies* exist within the cabinet departments of the executive branch. The Food and Drug Administration, for example, is an agency within the U.S. Department of Health and Human Services. Executive agencies are subject to the authority of the president, who has the power to appoint and remove their officers.

There are also major *independent regulatory agencies* at the federal level, including the Federal Trade Commission, the Securities and Exchange Commission, and the Federal Communications Commission. The president's power is less pronounced in regard to independent agencies, whose officers serve for fixed terms and cannot be removed without just cause.

State and Local Agencies There are administrative agencies at the state and local levels as well. Commonly, a state agency (such as a state pollution-control agency) is created as a parallel to a federal agency (such as the Environmental Protection Agency).

Just as federal statutes take precedence over conflicting state statutes, so do federal agency regulations take precedence over conflicting state regulations. Because the rules of state and local agencies vary widely, we focus here exclusively on federal administrative law.

Agency Creation Because Congress cannot possibly oversee the actual implementation of all the laws it enacts, it delegates such tasks to agencies. Congress creates an administrative agency by enacting **enabling legislation**, which specifies the name, composition, purpose, and powers of the agency being created.

Enabling Legislation A statute enacted by Congress that authorizes the creation of an administrative agency and specifies the name, composition, purpose, and powers of the agency being created.

Example 1.3 The Federal Trade Commission (FTC) was created in 1914 by the Federal Trade Commission Act.[3] This act prohibits unfair and deceptive trade practices. It also describes the procedures the agency must follow to charge persons or organizations with violations of the act, and it provides for judicial review (review by the courts) of agency orders.

Other portions of the act grant the agency powers to "make rules and regulations for the purpose of carrying out the Act," and to conduct investigations of business practices. In addition, the FTC can obtain reports from interstate corporations concerning their business practices, investigate possible violations of the act, publish findings of its investigations, and recommend new legislation. The act also empowers the FTC to hold trial-like hearings and to **adjudicate** (resolve judicially) certain kinds of disputes involving its regulations.

Adjudicate To render a judicial decision. Adjudication is the trial-like proceeding in which an administrative law judge hears and resolves disputes involving an administrative agency's regulations.

1. This institute was formed in the 1920s and consists of practicing attorneys, legal scholars, and judges.
2. Louisiana has adopted only Articles 1, 3, 4, 5, 7, 8, and 9.
3. 15 U.S.C. Sections 45–58.

Note that the powers granted to the FTC incorporate functions associated with the legislative branch of government (rulemaking), the executive branch (investigation and enforcement), and the judicial branch (adjudication). Taken together, these functions constitute the **administrative process**, which is the administration of law by administrative agencies. The administrative process involves rulemaking, enforcement, and adjudication.

Administrative Process The procedure used by administrative agencies in fulfilling their three basic functions: rulemaking, enforcement, and adjudication.

Rulemaking

A major function of an administrative agency is **rulemaking**—formulating new regulations or amending old ones. When Congress enacts an agency's enabling legislation, it confers the power to make **legislative rules**, or substantive rules, which are legally binding on all businesses.

The Administrative Procedure Act (APA)[4] imposes strict procedural requirements that agencies must follow in legislative rulemaking and other functions. **Example 1.4** The Occupational Safety and Health Act authorized the Occupational Safety and Health Administration (OSHA) to develop and issue rules governing safety in the workplace. When OSHA wants to formulate rules regarding safety in the steel industry, it has to follow specific procedures outlined by the APA. If an agency fails to follow the APA's rulemaking procedures, the resulting rule may not be binding.

TerryJ/iStock/Getty Images Plus

Which federal agency oversees worker safety?

Legislative Rules. Legislative rulemaking under the APA typically involves the following three steps (referred to as *notice-and-comment rulemaking*).

1. *Notice of the proposed rulemaking.* The notice must be published in the *Federal Register*, a daily publication of the U.S. government.
2. *A comment period.* The agency must allow ample time for interested parties to comment in writing on the proposed rule. The agency takes these comments into consideration when drafting the final version of the regulation.
3. *The final rule.* Once the agency has drafted the final rule, it is published in the *Federal Register*. (See the appendix at the end of this chapter for an explanation of how to find agency regulations.)

Rulemaking The process by which an administrative agency formally adopts a new regulation or amends an old one.

Legislative Rules Administrative agency rules that carry the same weight as congressionally enacted statutes.

Interpretive Rules. Administrative agencies also issue **interpretive rules** that are not legally binding but simply indicate how an agency plans to interpret and enforce its statutory authority. The APA does not apply to interpretive rulemaking. **Example 1.5** The Equal Employment Opportunity Commission periodically issues interpretive rules indicating how it plans to interpret the provisions of certain statutes, such as the Americans with Disabilities Act. These informal rules provide enforcement guidelines for agency officials.

Interpretive Rules Nonbinding rules or policy statements issued by an administrative agency that explain how it interprets and intends to apply the statutes it enforces.

Enforcement and Investigation

Agencies often enforce their own rules and have both investigatory and prosecutorial powers. Agencies investigate a wide range of activities, including coal mining, automobile manufacturing, and the industrial discharge of pollutants into the environment.

In an investigation, an agency can request that individuals or organizations hand over specified books, papers, electronic records, or other documents. In addition, agencies may conduct on-site inspections, although a search warrant is normally required for such inspections.[5] Sometimes, a search of a home, an office, or a factory is the only means of obtaining evidence needed to prove a regulatory violation.

After investigating a suspected rule violation, an agency may decide to take action against an individual or a business. Most administrative actions are resolved through negotiated

4. 5 U.S.C. Sections 551–706.
5. In some heavily regulated industries, such as the sale of firearms or liquor, agencies can conduct searches without obtaining a warrant.

settlement at their initial stages without the need for formal adjudication. If a settlement cannot be reached, though, the agency may issue a formal complaint and proceed to adjudication.

Administrative Law Judge (ALJ) One who presides over an administrative agency hearing and has the power to administer oaths, take testimony, rule on questions of evidence, and make determinations of fact.

Adjudication Agency adjudication involves a trial-like hearing before an **administrative law judge (ALJ)**. Hearing procedures vary widely from agency to agency. After the hearing, the ALJ renders a decision in the case. The ALJ can fine the charged party or prohibit the party from carrying on some specified activity.

Either the agency or the charged party may appeal the ALJ's decision to the commission or board that governs the agency. If the party fails to get relief there, appeal can be made to a federal court. Courts give significant weight (deference) to an agency's judgment and interpretation of its rules, though, and typically uphold the ALJ's decision unless it is unreasonable. If neither side appeals the case, the ALJ's decision becomes final.

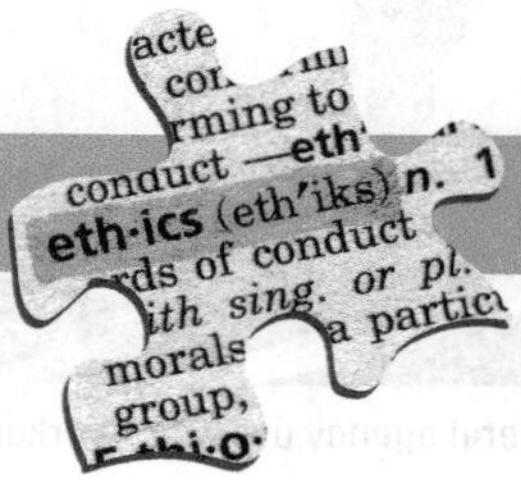

Ethical Issue

Do administrative agencies exercise too much authority? Administrative agencies, such as the Federal Trade Commission, combine in a single governmental entity functions normally divided among the three branches of government. They create rules, conduct investigations, and prosecute and pass judgment on violators. Yet administrative agencies' powers often go unchecked by the other branches. Some businesspersons have suggested that it is unethical for agencies—which are not even mentioned in the U.S. Constitution—to wield so many powers.

Although agency rulemaking must comply with the requirements of the Administrative Procedure Act (APA), the act applies only to legislative, not interpretive, rulemaking. In addition, the APA is largely procedural and aimed at preventing arbitrariness. It does little to ensure that the rules passed by agencies are fair or correct—or even cost-effective. On those rare occasions when an agency's ruling is challenged and later reviewed by a court, the court cannot reverse the agency's decision unless the agency exceeded its authority or acted arbitrarily. Courts typically are reluctant to second-guess an agency's rules, interpretations, and decisions. Moreover, once an agency has final regulations in place, it is difficult to revoke or alter them.

1–2d Case Law and Common Law Doctrines

The rules of law announced in court decisions constitute another basic source of American law. These rules of law include *interpretations* of constitutional provisions, of statutes enacted by legislatures, and of regulations created by administrative agencies.

Case Law The rules of law announced in court decisions. Case law interprets statutes, regulations, and constitutional provisions, and governs all areas not covered by statutory or administrative law.

Today, this body of judge-made law is referred to as **case law**. Case law—the doctrines and principles announced in cases—governs all areas not covered by statutory law or administrative law and is part of our common law tradition. We look at the origins and characteristics of the common law tradition in some detail in the discussion that follows.

1–3 The Common Law

Because of our colonial heritage, much American law is based on the English legal system. Knowledge of this system is crucial to understanding our legal system today because judges in the United States still apply common law principles when deciding cases.

1–3a Early English Courts

After the Normans conquered England in 1066, William the Conqueror and his successors began the process of unifying the country under their rule. One of the means they used to do this was the establishment of the king's courts, or *curiae regis*. Before the Norman Conquest, disputes had been settled according to the local legal customs and traditions in various regions of the country. The king's courts sought to establish a uniform set of rules for the country as a whole. What evolved in these courts was the beginning of the **common law**—a body of general rules that applied throughout the entire English realm. Eventually, the common law tradition became part of the heritage of all nations that were once British colonies, including the United States.

Common Law The body of law developed from custom or judicial decisions in English and U.S. courts, not attributable to a legislature.

Courts developed the common law rules from the principles underlying judges' decisions in actual legal controversies. Judges attempted to be consistent, and whenever possible, they based their decisions on the principles suggested by earlier cases. They sought to decide similar cases in a similar way and considered new cases with care because they knew that their decisions would make new law. Each interpretation became part of the law on the subject and served as a legal **precedent**—that is, a court decision that furnished an example or authority for deciding subsequent cases involving identical or similar legal principles or facts.

Focus Question 2

What is a precedent? When might a court depart from precedent?

Precedent A court decision that furnishes an example or authority for deciding subsequent cases involving identical or similar facts.

In the early years of the common law, there was no single place or publication where court opinions, or written decisions, could be found. Beginning in the late thirteenth and early fourteenth centuries, however, portions of significant decisions from each year were gathered together and recorded in *Year Books*. The *Year Books* were useful references for lawyers and judges. In the sixteenth century, the *Year Books* were discontinued, and other reports of cases became available. (See the appendix to this chapter for a discussion of how cases are reported, or published, in the United States today.)

1–3b *Stare Decisis*

The practice of deciding new cases with reference to former decisions, or precedents, eventually became a cornerstone of the English and U.S. judicial systems. The practice forms a doctrine called ***stare decisis***[6] (a Latin phrase meaning "to stand on decided cases").

Stare Decisis A common law doctrine under which judges are obligated to follow the precedents established in prior decisions.

Under the doctrine of *stare decisis*, judges are obligated to follow the precedents established within their jurisdictions. (The term *jurisdiction* refers to a geographic area in which a court or courts have the power to apply the law.) Once a court has set forth a principle of law as being applicable to a certain set of facts, that court must apply the principle in future cases involving similar facts. Courts of lower rank (within the same jurisdiction) must do likewise. Thus, *stare decisis* has two aspects:

1. A court should not overturn its own precedents unless there is a strong reason to do so.
2. Decisions made by a higher court are binding on lower courts.

Controlling Precedents Precedents that must be followed within a jurisdiction are known as controlling precedents. Controlling precedents are binding authorities. A **binding authority** is any source of law that a court must follow when deciding a case. Binding authorities include constitutions, statutes, and regulations that govern the issue being decided, as well as court decisions that are controlling precedents within the jurisdiction. United States Supreme Court case decisions, no matter how old, remain controlling until they are overruled by a subsequent decision of the Supreme Court, by a constitutional amendment, or by congressional legislation.

Binding Authority Any source of law that a court *must* follow when deciding a case.

Know This

Courts normally must follow the rules set forth by higher courts in deciding cases with similar fact patterns.

***Stare Decisis* and Legal Stability** The doctrine of *stare decisis* helps the courts to be more efficient because if other courts have carefully reasoned through a similar case, their legal

6. Pronounced *stahr*-ee dih-*si*-sis.

The Power of Precedent

Roberta owns and manages an independent auto repair shop in Boise City, Oklahoma. Over the past several years, business has been booming, thanks to an influx of people moving to Boise City from California. To take advantage of this population boom, Roberta is considering opening a used car dealership on an abandoned lot next to her repair shop.

Working Overtime

Knowing that used car dealerships operate on extremely thin margins, Roberta and her accountant attempt to come up with a list of all the costs to include in the new business plan. Roberta learns that other used car dealerships in the area are often open from 8 A.M. to 7 P.M., presumably to take advantage of customers who visit outside normal work hours. Most of the dealerships are also open on weekends, meaning that any salespeople that Roberta hires will work more than the normal forty-hour workweek. To determine her labor costs, Roberta needs to know if she must pay these employees overtime for the extra hours.

Relying on *Stare Decisis*

With auto repairs, the customer is charged a certain amount of "booked" hours per job, no matter how long the repair takes. Roberta's auto mechanics are paid per "booked" hour, also regardless of how long the actual repair takes. Consequently, the issue of overtime does not apply. Roberta knows she won't be able to pay her salespeople using this system. To get more information on her options, she calls Fran, a local labor lawyer, for advice.

Fran tells Roberta that, under the federal Fair Labor Standards Act (FLSA), employers are not required to pay overtime for any "sales[person] . . . primarily engaged in selling or servicing any automobiles." Furthermore, in a recent case, the United States Supreme Court upheld this segment of the FLSA, holding that the "plain language" of the federal law should determine the outcome of any overtime pay dispute. So, under federal law, the salespeople at Roberta's used car dealership would be exempt from overtime pay. Furthermore, explains Fran, thanks to the doctrine of *stare decisis*, should the salespeople sue Roberta seeking overtime pay, she could reasonably rely on the Supreme Court's decision as binding precedent on this matter.

Business Questions

1. *"When faced with a clearly erroneous precedent, my rule is simple," writes Supreme Court Justice Clarence Thomas. "We should not follow it." How do these words offer a cautionary tale for managers relying on* stare decisis *to make business decisions?*

2. *Should Roberta consider paying her salespeople overtime even though it is not required by federal law? Why or why not?*

reasoning and opinions can serve as guides. *Stare decisis* also makes the law more stable and predictable. If the law on a given subject is well settled, someone bringing a case to court can usually rely on the court to make a decision based on what the law has been. (See this chapter's *Managerial Strategy* feature to learn how this stability can help business managers in their decision-making process.)

Departures from Precedent Although courts are obligated to follow precedents, sometimes a court will depart from the rule of precedent. If a court decides that a precedent is simply incorrect or that technological or social changes have rendered the precedent inapplicable, the court may rule contrary to the precedent. Cases that overturn precedent often receive a great deal of publicity.

Classic Case Example 1.6 In *Brown v. Board of Education of Topeka*,[7] the United States Supreme Court expressly overturned precedent. The Court concluded that separate educational facilities for whites and blacks, which had previously been upheld as constitutional,[8] were inherently unequal. The Supreme Court's departure from precedent in the *Brown* decision received a tremendous amount of publicity as people began to realize the ramifications of this change in the law. ■

7. 347 U.S. 483, 74 S.Ct. 686, 98 L.Ed. 873 (1954).
8. See *Plessy v. Ferguson*, 163 U.S. 537, 16 S.Ct. 1138, 41 L.Ed. 256 (1896).

When There Is No Precedent Occasionally, courts must decide cases for which no precedents exist, called *cases of first impression*. For instance, as you will read throughout this text, the Internet and certain other technologies have presented many new and challenging issues for the courts to decide.

When deciding cases of first impression, courts often look at persuasive authorities. A **persuasive authority** is a legal authority that a court may consult for guidance but that is not binding on the court. A court may consider precedents from other jurisdictions, for instance, although those precedents are not binding. A court may also consider legal principles and policies underlying previous court decisions or existing statutes. Additionally, a court might look at fairness, social values and customs, and public policy (governmental policy based on widely held societal values). Federal courts can also look at unpublished opinions (those not intended for publication in a printed legal reporter) as sources of persuasive authority.[9]

Persuasive Authority Any legal authority or source of law that a court may look to for guidance but need not follow when making its decision.

***Stare Decisis* and Legal Reasoning** In deciding what law applies to a given dispute and then applying that law to the facts or circumstances of the case, judges rely on the process of **legal reasoning**. Through the use of legal reasoning, judges harmonize their decisions with those that have been made before, as the doctrine of *stare decisis* requires.

Legal Reasoning The process of reasoning by which judges harmonize their opinions with the judicial opinions in previous cases.

Students of business law and the legal environment also engage in critical thinking and legal reasoning. For instance, you may be asked to provide answers for some of the case problems that appear at the end of every chapter in this text. Each problem describes the facts of a particular dispute and the legal question at issue. If you are assigned a case problem, you will be asked to determine how a court would answer that question, and why. In other words, you will need to give legal reasons for whatever conclusion you reach.

Basic Steps in Legal Reasoning. At times, the legal arguments set forth in court opinions are relatively simple and brief. At other times, the arguments are complex and lengthy. Regardless of the length of a legal argument, however, the basic steps of the legal reasoning process remain the same. These steps, which you can also follow when analyzing cases and case problems, form what is commonly referred to as the *IRAC method* of legal reasoning. IRAC is an acronym formed from the first letters of the words *Issue, Rule, Application*, and *Conclusion*. To apply the IRAC method, ask the following questions:

1. Issue—*What are the key facts and issues?* This may sound obvious, but before you can analyze or apply the relevant law to a specific set of facts, you must clearly understand those facts. In other words, you should read through the case problem carefully—more than once, if necessary. Make sure that you understand the identities of the **plaintiff** (the one who initiates the lawsuit) and the **defendant** (the one being sued) in the case, and the progression of events that led to the lawsuit.

   Suppose that a plaintiff, Anna, comes before the court claiming *assault* (words or acts that wrongfully and intentionally make another person apprehensive of harmful or offensive contact). Anna claims that the defendant, Bryce threatened her while she was sleeping. Although the plaintiff was unaware that she was being threatened, her roommate, Jan, heard the defendant make the threat. So, in this scenario, the identities of the parties are obvious. Anna is the plaintiff, and Bryce is the defendant.

   The legal issue in this case is whether the defendant's action constitutes the tort of assault even though the plaintiff was unaware of that threat at the time it occurred. (A tort is a wrongful act brought under civil rather than criminal law.)

Plaintiff One who initiates a lawsuit.

Defendant One against whom a lawsuit is brought or the accused person in a criminal proceeding.

9. Rule 32.1 of the Federal Rules of Appellate Procedure.

2. **Rule**—*What rule of law applies to the case?* A rule of law may be a rule stated by the courts in previous decisions, by a state or federal statute, or by a state or federal administrative agency regulation. Often, more than one rule of law will be applicable to a case.

   In our hypothetical case, Anna and her attorney **allege** (claim) that Bryce committed a tort. Therefore, the applicable law is the common law of torts—specifically, tort law governing assault. Case precedents involving similar facts and issues thus would be relevant.

Allege To state, recite, assert, or charge.

3. **Application**—*How does the rule of law apply to the particular facts and circumstances of this case?* This step is often the most difficult because each case presents a unique set of facts, circumstances, and parties. Although cases may be similar, no two cases are ever identical in all respects.

   Normally, judges (and lawyers and law students) try to find previously decided cases that are as similar as possible to the one under consideration. Such a case is called a **case on point**. In this situation, there might be case precedents showing that if a victim is unaware of the threat of harmful or offensive contact, then no assault occurred. These would be cases on point that tend to prove that the defendant did not commit assault and should win the case.

   There might, however, also be cases showing that a sexual assault, at least, can occur even if the victim is asleep. These would be cases on point in the plaintiff's favor. You will need to carefully analyze if there are any missing facts in Anna's claim. For instance, you might want to know the specific threat that Bryce made (and Anna's roommate overheard). Did he threaten to rape, kill, or beat her? Did he know that she was asleep when he made the threat? Did he know that her roommate heard the threat and would relay it to her when she awoke? Sometimes, you will want to obtain additional facts before analyzing which case precedents should apply and control the outcome of the case.

Case on Point A previous case involving factual circumstances and issues that are similar to those in the case before the court.

4. **Conclusion**—*What conclusion should be drawn?* This step normally presents few problems. Usually, the conclusion is evident if the previous three steps have been followed carefully. In our sample problem, for instance, you may determine that Bryce did not commit a tort because Anna could not prove all of the required elements of assault.

There Is No One "Right" Answer. Many people believe that there is one "right" answer to every legal question. In many legal controversies, however, there is no single correct result. Good arguments can usually be made to support either side of a legal controversy. Quite often, a case does not involve a "good" person suing a "bad" person. In many cases, both parties have acted in good faith in some measure or in bad faith to some degree. Additionally, each judge has her or his own personal beliefs and philosophy. To some extent, these personal factors shape the legal reasoning process.

Remedy The relief given to an innocent party to enforce a right or compensate for the violation of a right.

1–3c Equitable Remedies and Courts of Equity

Focus Question 3

What is the difference between remedies at law and remedies in equity?

A **remedy** is the means given to a party to enforce a right or to compensate for the violation of a right. **Example 1.7** Elena is injured because of Rowan's wrongdoing. If Elena files a lawsuit and is successful, a court can order Rowan to compensate Elena for the harm by paying her a certain amount. The compensation is Elena's remedy. ■

The kinds of remedies available in the early king's courts of England were severely restricted. If one person wronged another, the king's courts could award either money or property, including land, as compensation. These courts became known as *courts of law*, and the remedies were called *remedies at law*. Even though this system introduced uniformity in the settling of disputes, when a person wanted a remedy other than property or economic compensation, the courts of law could do nothing, so "no remedy, no right."

Remedies in Equity *Equity* is a branch of law—founded on notions of justice and fair dealing—that seeks to supply a remedy when no adequate remedy at law is available. When individuals could not obtain an adequate remedy in a court of law, they petitioned the king for relief. Most of these petitions were referred to the *chancellor*, an adviser to the king who had the power to grant new and unique remedies. Eventually, formal chancery courts, or *courts of equity*, were established. The remedies granted by the chancery courts were called *remedies in equity*.

Plaintiffs (those bringing lawsuits) had to specify whether they were bringing an "action at law" or an "action in equity," and they chose their courts accordingly. A plaintiff might ask a court of equity to order the defendant to perform within the terms of a contract. A court of law could not issue such an order because its remedies were limited to the payment of money or property as compensation for damages.

A court of equity, however, could issue a decree for *specific performance*—an order to perform what was promised. A court of equity could also issue an *injunction*, directing a party to do or refrain from doing a particular act. In certain cases, a court of equity could allow for the *rescission* (cancellation) of the contract, thereby returning the parties to the positions that they held prior to the contract's formation. Equitable remedies will be discussed in greater detail in the chapters covering contracts.

The Merging of Law and Equity Today, in most states, the courts of law and equity have merged, and thus the distinction between the two courts has largely disappeared. A plaintiff may now request both legal and equitable remedies in the same action, and the trial court judge may grant either form—or both forms—of relief.

The distinction between legal and equitable remedies remains significant, however, because a court normally will grant an equitable remedy only when the remedy at law (property or monetary damages) is inadequate. To request the proper remedy, a businessperson (or her or his attorney) must know what remedies are available for the specific kinds of harms suffered. Exhibit 1–2 summarizes the procedural differences (applicable in most states) between an action at law and an action in equity.

Know This

Even though courts of law and equity have merged, the principles of equity still apply, and courts will not grant an equitable remedy unless the remedy at law is inadequate.

Equitable Maxims Over time, the courts have developed a number of **equitable maxims** that provide guidance in deciding whether plaintiffs should be granted equitable relief. Because of their importance, both historically and in our judicial system today, these maxims are set forth in this chapter's *Landmark in the Law* feature.

Equitable Maxims General propositions or principles of law that have to do with fairness (equity).

Exhibit 1–2 Procedural Differences between an Action at Law and an Action in Equity

PROCEDURE	ACTION AT LAW	ACTION IN EQUITY
Initiation of lawsuit	By filing a complaint	By filing a petition
Decision	By jury or judge	By judge (no jury)
Result	Judgment	Decree
Remedy	Monetary damages or property	Injunction, specific performance, or rescission

1–3d Schools of Legal Thought

How judges apply the law to specific cases, including disputes relating to the business world, depends on their philosophical approaches to law, among other things. The study of law, often referred to as **jurisprudence**, includes learning about different schools of legal thought and discovering how each school's approach to law can affect judicial decision making.

Jurisprudence The science or philosophy of law.

Natural Law The oldest school of legal thought, based on the belief that the legal system should reflect universal ("higher") moral and ethical principles that are inherent in human nature.

The Natural Law School According to the **natural law** theory, a higher, or universal, law exists that applies to all human beings. Each written law should reflect the principles inherent in natural law. If it does not, then it loses its legitimacy and need not be obeyed.

The natural law tradition is one of the oldest and most significant schools of jurisprudence. It dates back to the days of the Greek philosopher Aristotle (384–322 B.C.E.), who distinguished between natural law and the laws governing a particular nation. According to Aristotle, natural law applies universally to all humankind.

Science History Images/Alamy Stock Photo

What is the basic premise of Aristotle's natural law theory?

The notion that people have "natural rights" stems from the natural law tradition. Those who claim that certain nations, such as China and North Korea, are depriving many of their citizens of their human rights are implicitly appealing to a higher law that has universal applicability.

The question of the universality of basic human rights also comes into play in the context of international business operations. For instance, U.S. companies that have operations abroad often hire foreign workers as employees. Should the same laws that protect U.S. employees apply to these foreign employees? This question is rooted implicitly in a concept of universal rights that has its origins in the natural law tradition.

Legal Positivism *Positive law*, or national law, is the written law of a given society at a particular point in time. In contrast to natural law, it applies only to the citizens of that nation or society. Those who adhere to **legal positivism** believe that there can be no higher law than a nation's positive law.

According to the positivist school, there is no such thing as "natural rights." Rather, human rights exist solely because of laws. If the laws are not enforced, anarchy will result. Thus, whether a law is morally "bad" or "good" is irrelevant. The law is the law and must be obeyed until it is changed—in an orderly manner through a legitimate lawmaking process. A judge who takes this view will probably be more inclined to defer to an existing law than would a judge who adheres to the natural law tradition.

Legal Positivism A school of legal thought centered on the assumption that there is no law higher than the laws created by a national government. Laws must be obeyed, even if they are unjust, to prevent anarchy.

The Historical School The **historical school** of legal thought emphasizes the evolutionary process of law by concentrating on the origin and history of the legal system. This school looks to the past to discover what the principles of contemporary law should be. The legal doctrines that have withstood the passage of time—those that have worked in the past—are deemed best suited for shaping present laws. Hence, law derives its legitimacy and authority from adhering to the standards that historical development has shown to be workable. Followers of the historical school are more likely than those of other schools to adhere strictly to decisions made in past cases.

Historical School A school of legal thought that looks to the past to determine what the principles of contemporary law should be.

Legal Realism In the 1920s and 1930s, a number of jurists and scholars, known as *legal realists*, rebelled against the historical approach to law. **Legal realism** is based on the idea that law is just one of many institutions in society and that it is shaped by social forces and needs. This school reasons that because the law is a human enterprise, judges should look beyond the law and take social and economic realities into account when deciding cases.

Legal Realism A school of legal thought that holds that the law is only one factor to be considered when deciding cases, and that social and economic circumstances should also be taken into account.

Legal realists also believe that the law can never be applied with total uniformity. Given that judges are human beings with unique experiences, personalities, value systems, and

Equitable Maxims

In medieval England, courts of equity were expected to use discretion in supplementing the common law. Even today, when the same court can award both legal and equitable remedies, it must exercise discretion.

Students of business law and the legal environment should know that courts often invoke equitable maxims when making their decisions. Here are some of the most significant equitable maxims:

1. *Whoever seeks equity must do equity.* (Anyone who wishes to be treated fairly must treat others fairly.)
2. *Where there is equal equity, the law must prevail.* (The law will determine the outcome of a controversy in which the merits of both sides are equal.)
3. *One seeking the aid of an equity court must come to the court with clean hands.* (Plaintiffs must have acted fairly and honestly.)
4. *Equity will not suffer a wrong to be without a remedy.* (Equitable relief will be awarded when there is a right to relief and there is no adequate remedy at law.)
5. *Equity regards substance rather than form.* (Equity is more concerned with fairness and justice than with legal technicalities.)
6. *Equity aids the vigilant, not those who rest on their rights.* (Equity will not help those who neglect their rights for an unreasonable period of time.)

The last maxim has come to be known as the *equitable doctrine of laches.* The doctrine arose to encourage people to bring lawsuits while the evidence was fresh. If they failed to do so, they would not be allowed to bring a lawsuit. What constitutes a reasonable time, of course, varies according to the circumstances of the case.

Time periods for different types of cases are now usually fixed by *statutes of limitations*—that is, statutes that set the maximum time period during which a certain action can be brought. After the time allowed under a statute of limitations has expired, no action can be brought, no matter how strong the case was originally.

Application to Today's World *The equitable maxims listed here underlie many of the legal rules and principles that are commonly applied by the courts today—and that you will read about in this book.*

For instance, in the contracts materials, you will read about the doctrine of promissory estoppel. Under this doctrine, a person who has reasonably and substantially relied on the promise of another may be able to obtain some measure of recovery, even though no enforceable contract exists. The court will estop (bar) the one making the promise from asserting the lack of a valid contract as a defense. The rationale underlying the doctrine of promissory estoppel is similar to that expressed in the fourth and fifth maxims just listed.

intellects, different judges will obviously bring different reasoning processes to the same case. Female judges, for instance, might be more inclined than male judges to consider whether a decision might have a negative impact on the employment of women or minorities.

1–4 Classifications of Law

The law may be broken down according to several classification systems. One classification system divides law into **substantive law** (all laws that define, describe, regulate, and create legal rights and obligations) and **procedural law** (all laws that establish the methods of enforcing the rights established by substantive law).

Substantive Law Law that defines, describes, regulates, and creates legal rights and obligations.

Procedural Law Law that establishes the methods of enforcing the rights established by substantive law.

Example 1.8 A state law that provides employees with the right to workers' compensation benefits for any on-the-job injuries they sustain is a substantive law because it creates legal rights. Procedural laws, in contrast, establish the method by which an employee must notify the employer about an on-the-job injury, prove the injury, and periodically submit additional proof to continue receiving workers' compensation benefits. ■ Note that a law may contain both substantive and procedural provisions.

Other classification systems divide law into federal law and state law, and private law (dealing with relationships between persons) and public law (addressing the relationship

Cyberlaw An informal term used to refer to all laws governing electronic communications and transactions, particularly those conducted via the Internet.

between persons and their governments). Frequently, people use the term **cyberlaw** to refer to the emerging body of law that governs transactions conducted via the Internet, but cyberlaw is not really a classification of law. Rather, it is an informal term used to refer to both new laws and modifications of traditional legal principles that relate to the online environment.

Focus Question 4

What are some important differences between civil law and criminal law?

1–4a Civil Law and Criminal Law

Civil Law The branch of law dealing with the definition and enforcement of all private or public rights, as opposed to criminal matters.

Criminal Law The branch of law that defines and punishes wrongful actions committed against the public.

Civil law spells out the rights and duties that exist between persons and between persons and their governments, as well as the relief available when a person's rights are violated. Typically, in a civil case, a private party sues another private party who has failed to comply with a duty. Much of the law that we discuss in this text—including contract law and tort law—is civil law.

Criminal law has to do with wrongs committed against society for which society demands redress. Criminal acts are proscribed by local, state, or federal government statutes. Thus, criminal defendants are prosecuted by public officials, such as a district attorney (D.A.), on behalf of the state, not by their victims or other private parties.

Whereas in a civil case the object is to obtain a remedy (such as monetary damages) to compensate the injured party, in a criminal case the object is to punish the wrongdoer in an attempt to deter others from similar actions. Penalties for violations of criminal statutes consist of fines and/or imprisonment—and, in some cases, death.

1–4b Common Law and Civil Law Systems

Two types of legal systems predominate around the globe today. One is the common law system of England and the United States, which we discussed earlier. In a common law system, the body of law derives from custom and judicial decisions and depends on the importance of legal precedent.

Civil Law System A system of law derived from Roman law that is based on codified laws (rather than on case precedents).

The other, known as a **civil law system**, is based on Roman civil law, or "code law," which relies on legal principles enacted into law by a legislature or governing body. Thus, in a civil law system, the primary source of law is a statutory code, and case precedents are not judicially binding, as they normally are in a common law system. Although judges in a civil law system often refer to previous decisions as sources of legal guidance, those decisions are not binding. (Note that a *civil law system* is not the same as *civil law*, discussed in the previous section.)

Generally, countries that were once colonies of Great Britain have retained their English common law heritage. The civil law system, which is used in most continental European nations, has been retained in countries that were once colonies of those nations (see Exhibit 1–3). In the United States, the state of Louisiana, because of its historical ties to France, is heavily influenced by principles of civil law systems. A third, less prevalent legal system is widespread in Islamic countries, where the law is often influenced by *sharia*, the religious law of Islam.

1–4c National and International Law

U.S. businesspersons increasingly engage in transactions that extend beyond our national borders. For this reason, those who pursue a career in business today should have an understanding of the global legal environment.

National Law Law that pertains to a particular nation (as opposed to international law).

The law of a particular nation, such as Japan or Germany, is **national law**. National law, of course, varies from country to country because each country's law reflects the interests, customs, activities, and values that are unique to that nation's culture. Even though the laws and legal systems of various countries differ substantially, broad similarities do exist.

Exhibit 1–3 The Legal Systems of Selected Nations

CIVIL LAW		COMMON LAW	
Argentina	Indonesia	Australia	Nigeria
Austria	Iran	Bangladesh	Singapore
Brazil	Italy	Canada	United Kingdom
Chile	Japan	Ghana	United States
China	Mexico	India	Zambia
Egypt	Poland	Israel	
Finland	South Korea	Jamaica	
France	Sweden	Kenya	
Germany	Tunisia	Malaysia	
Greece	Venezuela	New Zealand	

In contrast, international law applies to more than one nation. **International law** can be defined as a body of written and unwritten laws observed by independent nations and governing the acts of individuals as well as governments. It is a mixture of rules and constraints derived from a variety of sources, including the laws of individual nations, customs developed among nations, and international treaties and organizations.

International Law Law that governs relations among nations.

The key difference between national law and international law is that government authorities can enforce national law. If a nation violates an international law, however, enforcement is up to other countries or international organizations, which may or may not choose to act. If persuasive tactics fail, the only option is to take coercive actions against the violating nation. Coercive actions range from the severance of diplomatic relations and boycotts to sanctions and, as a last resort, war.

Practice and Review

Suppose that the California legislature passes a law that severely restricts carbon dioxide emissions of automobiles in that state. A group of automobile manufacturers files a suit against the state of California to prevent enforcement of the law. The automakers claim that a federal law already sets fuel economy standards nationwide and that these standards are essentially the same as carbon dioxide emission standards. According to the automobile manufacturers, it is unfair to allow California to impose more stringent regulations than those set by the federal law. Using the information presented in the chapter, answer the following questions.

1. Who are the parties (the plaintiffs and the defendant) in this lawsuit?
2. Are the plaintiffs seeking a legal remedy or an equitable remedy? Why?
3. What is the primary source of the law that is at issue here?
4. Read through the appendix that follows this chapter, and then answer the following question: Where would you look to find the relevant California and federal laws?

Debate This

Under the doctrine of stare decisis, *courts are obligated to follow the precedents established in their jurisdiction unless there is a compelling reason not to do so. Should U.S. courts continue to adhere to this common law principle, given that our government now regulates so many areas by statute?*

Key Terms

adjudicate 6
administrative agency 6
administrative law 6
administrative law judge (ALJ) 8
administrative process 7
allege 12
binding authority 9
case law 8
case on point 12
citation 5
civil law 16
civil law system 16
common law 9
concurring opinion 27
constitutional law 4
criminal law 16
cyberlaw 16
defendant 11
dissenting opinion 27
enabling legislation 6
equitable maxims 13
historical school 14
international law 17
interpretive rules 7
jurisprudence 14
law 2
legal positivism 14
legal realism 14
legal reasoning 11
legislative rules 7
liability 3
majority opinion 27
national law 16
natural law 14
ordinance 5
***per curiam* opinion** 27
persuasive authority 11
plaintiff 11
plurality opinion 27
precedent 9
primary source of law 4
procedural law 15
remedy 12
rulemaking 7
secondary source of law 4
stare decisis 9
statutory law 5
substantive law 15
uniform laws 5

Chapter Summary: Law and Legal Reasoning

Sources of American Law	1. **Constitutional law**—The law as expressed in the U.S. Constitution and the various state constitutions. The U.S. Constitution is the supreme law of the land. State constitutions are supreme within state borders to the extent that they do not violate the U.S. Constitution or a federal law. 2. **Statutory law**—Laws or ordinances created by federal, state, and local legislatures. None of these laws can violate the U.S. Constitution, and no state statute or local ordinance can violate the relevant state constitution. Uniform laws, when adopted by a state legislature, become statutory law in that state. 3. **Administrative law**—The rules, orders, and decisions of federal or state government administrative agencies. Federal administrative agencies are created by enabling legislation enacted by the U.S. Congress. Agency functions include rulemaking, investigation and enforcement, and adjudication. 4. **Case law and common law doctrines**—Judge-made law, including interpretations of constitutional provisions, of statutes enacted by legislatures, and of regulations created by administrative agencies. Case law governs all areas not covered by statutory law or administrative law, and is part of our common law tradition.
The Common Law	1. **Common law**—Law that originated in medieval England with the creation of the king's courts, or *curiae regis*, and the development of a body of rules that were common to (or applied in) all regions of the country. 2. ***Stare decisis***—A doctrine under which judges "stand on decided cases"—or follow the rule of precedent—in deciding cases. *Stare decisis* is the cornerstone of the common law tradition. 3. ***Stare decisis* and legal reasoning**—Judges use legal reasoning to harmonize their decisions with those that have been made before, as required by the doctrine of *stare decisis*. The basic steps of legal reasoning form what is often referred to as the *IRAC method* of legal reasoning. IRAC stands for *Issue, Rule, Application,* and *Conclusion.* First, clearly grasp the relevant facts and identify the issue. Second, determine the rule of law that applies to the case. Third, analyze (using *cases on point*) how the rule of law applies to the particular facts of the dispute, and fourth, arrive at a conclusion.

4. **Remedies**—A remedy is the means by which a court enforces a right or compensates for a violation of a right. Courts typically grant legal remedies (monetary damages or property) but may also grant equitable remedies (specific performance, injunction, or rescission) when the legal remedy is inadequate or unavailable.
5. **Schools of legal thought**—Judges' decision making is influenced by their philosophy of law. The following are four important schools of legal thought, or legal philosophies:
   a. Natural law—One of the oldest and most significant schools of legal thought. Those who believe in natural law hold that there is a universal law applicable to all human beings and that this law is of a higher order than positive, or national, law.
   b. Legal positivism—A school of legal thought centered on the assumption that there is no law higher than the laws created by the government. Laws must be obeyed, even if they are unjust, to prevent anarchy.
   c. Historical school—A school of legal thought that stresses the evolutionary nature of law and looks to doctrines that have withstood the passage of time for guidance in shaping present laws.
   d. Legal realism—A school of legal thought that generally advocates a less abstract and more realistic approach to the law. This approach takes into account customary practices and the social and economic circumstances in which transactions take place.

Classifications of Law The law may be broken down according to several classification systems, such as substantive or procedural law, federal or state law, and private or public law. Three broad classifications are civil and criminal law, common law systems, and civil law systems, and national and international law. Cyberlaw is not really a classification of law but a term that refers to the growing body of case and statutory law that applies to Internet transactions.

Issue Spotters

1. The First Amendment to the U.S. Constitution provides protection for the free exercise of religion. A state legislature enacts a law that outlaws all religions that do not derive from the Judeo-Christian tradition. Is this law valid within that state? Why or why not? (See *Sources of American Law.*)
2. Apex Corporation learns that a federal administrative agency is considering a rule that will have a negative impact on the firm's ability to do business. Does the firm have any opportunity to express its opinion about the pending rule? Explain. (See *Sources of American Law.*)

—Check your answers to the *Issue Spotters* against the answers provided in Appendix D.

Business Scenarios and Case Problems

1–1. Binding versus Persuasive Authority. A county court in Illinois is deciding a case involving an issue that has never been addressed before in that state's courts. The Iowa Supreme Court, however, recently decided a case involving a very similar fact pattern. Is the Illinois court obligated to follow the Iowa Supreme Court's decision on the issue? If the United States Supreme Court had decided a similar case, would that decision be binding on the Illinois court? Explain. (See *The Common Law.*)

1–2. Sources of Law. This chapter discussed a number of sources of American law. Which source of law takes priority in the following situations, and why? (See *Sources of American Law.*)

1. A federal statute conflicts with the U.S. Constitution.
2. A federal statute conflicts with a state constitutional provision.
3. A state statute conflicts with the common law of that state.
4. A state constitutional amendment conflicts with the U.S. Constitution.

1–3. Remedies. Arthur Rabe is suing Xavier Sanchez for breaching a contract in which Sanchez promised to sell Rabe a Van Gogh painting for $150,000. (See *The Common Law.*)

1. In this lawsuit, who is the plaintiff, and who is the defendant?
2. If Rabe wants Sanchez to perform the contract as promised, what remedy should Rabe seek?
3. Suppose that Rabe wants to cancel the contract because Sanchez fraudulently misrepresented the painting as an original Van Gogh when in fact it is a copy. In this situation, what remedy should Rabe seek?
4. Will the remedy Rabe seeks in either situation be a remedy at law or a remedy in equity?

1–4. Philosophy of Law. After World War II ended in 1945, an international tribunal of judges convened at Nuremberg, Germany. The judges convicted several Nazi war criminals of "crimes against humanity." Assuming that the Nazis who were convicted had not disobeyed any law of their country and had merely been following their government's (Hitler's) orders, what law had they violated? Explain. (See *The Common Law.*)

1–5. Spotlight on AOL—Common Law. AOL, LLC, mistakenly made public the personal information of 650,000 of its members. The members filed a suit, alleging violations of California law. AOL asked the court to dismiss the suit on the basis of a "forum-selection" clause in its member agreement that designates Virginia courts as the place where member disputes will be tried. Under a decision of the United States Supreme Court, a forum-selection clause is unenforceable "if enforcement would contravene a strong public policy of the forum in which suit is brought." California has declared in other cases that the AOL clause contravenes a strong public policy. If the court applies the doctrine of *stare decisis*, will it dismiss the suit? Explain. [*Doe 1 v. AOL, LLC*, 552 F.3d 1077 (9th Cir. 2009)] (See *The Common Law.*)

1–6. Business Case Problem with Sample Answer—Reading Citations. Assume that you want to read the entire court opinion in the case of *Friends of Buckingham v. State Air Pollution Control Board*, 947 F.3d 68 (4th Cir. 2020).

Refer to the appendix to this chapter, and then explain specifically where you would find the court's opinion. (See *Finding Case Law.*)

—For a sample answer to Problem 1–6, go to Appendix E.

1–7. A Question of Ethics—The Doctrine of Precedent. Sandra White operated a travel agency. To obtain lower airline fares for her nonmilitary clients, she booked military-rate travel by forwarding fake military identification cards to the airlines. The government charged White with identity theft, which requires the "use" of another's identification. The trial court had two cases that represented precedents.

In the first case, David Miller obtained a loan to buy land by representing that certain investors had approved the loan when, in fact, they had not. Miller's conviction for identity theft was overturned because he had merely said that the investors had done something when they had not. According to the court, this was not the "use" of another's identification.

In the second case, Kathy Medlock, an ambulance service operator, had transported patients for whom there was no medical necessity to do so. To obtain payment, Medlock had forged a physician's signature. The court concluded that this was "use" of another person's identity. [*United States v. White*, 846 F.3d 170 (6th Cir. 2017)] (See *Sources of American Law.*)

1. Which precedent—the *Miller* case or the *Medlock* case—is similar to White's situation, and why?
2. In the two cases cited by the court, were there any ethical differences in the actions of the parties? Explain your answer.

Critical Thinking and Writing Assignments

1–8. Business Law Writing. John's company is involved in a lawsuit with a customer, Beth. John argues that for fifty years higher courts in that state have decided cases involving circumstances similar to his case in a way that indicates he can expect a ruling in his company's favor. Write at least one paragraph discussing whether this is a valid argument. Write another paragraph discussing whether the judge in this case must rule as those other judges did, and why. (See *The Common Law.*)

1–9. Time-Limited Group Assignment—Court Opinions. Go to the section entitled *Reading and Understanding Case Law* in the appendix at the end of this chapter, and read through the subsection entitled "Decisions and Opinions."

1. One group will explain the difference between a concurring opinion and a majority opinion.
2. Another group will outline the difference between a concurring opinion and a dissenting opinion.
3. The third group will explain why judges and justices write concurring and dissenting opinions, given that these opinions will not affect the outcome of the case at hand, which has already been decided by majority vote.

Appendix to Chapter 1

Finding and Analyzing the Law

This text includes numerous references, or *citations*, to primary sources of law—federal and state statutes, the U.S. Constitution and state constitutions, regulations issued by administrative agencies, and court cases. A citation identifies the publication in which a legal authority—such as a statute or court decision—can be found. In this appendix, we explain how you can use citations to find primary sources of law. Note that in addition to being published in sets of books, as described next, most federal and state laws and case decisions are available online.

Finding Statutory and Administrative Law

When Congress passes laws, they are collected in a publication titled *United States Statutes at Large*. When state legislatures pass laws, they are collected in similar state publications. Most frequently, however, laws are referred to in their codified form—that is, the form in which they appear in the federal and state codes. In these codes, laws are compiled by subject.

United States Code

The *United States Code* (U.S.C.) arranges all existing federal laws of a public and permanent nature by subject. Each of the fifty-two subjects into which the U.S.C. arranges the laws is given a title and a title number. For example, laws relating to commerce and trade are collected in "Title 15, Commerce and Trade." Titles are subdivided by sections.

A citation to the U.S.C. includes title and section numbers. Thus, a reference to "15 U.S.C. Section 1" means that the statute can be found in Section 1 of Title 15. ("Section" may be designated by the symbol §, and "Sections" by §§.) In addition to the print publication of the U.S.C., the federal government also provides a searchable online database of the *United States Code* at www.gpo.gov (click on "Libraries" and then "Core Documents of Our Democracy" to find the *United States Code*).

Commercial publications of these laws are available and are widely used. For example, Thomson Reuters publishes the *United States Code Annotated* (U.S.C.A.). The U.S.C.A. contains the complete text of laws included in the U.S.C., notes of court decisions that interpret and apply specific sections of the statutes, and the text of presidential proclamations and executive orders. The U.S.C.A. also includes research aids, such as cross-references to related statutes, historical notes, and other references. A citation to the U.S.C.A. is similar to a citation to the U.S.C.: "15 U.S.C.A. Section 1."

State Codes

State codes follow the U.S.C. pattern of arranging laws by subject. The state codes may be called codes, revisions, compilations, consolidations, general statutes, or statutes, depending on the state.

In some codes, subjects are designated by number. In others, they are designated by name. For example, "13 Pennsylvania Consolidated Statutes Section 1101" means that the statute can be found in Title 13, Section 1101, of the Pennsylvania code. "California Commercial Code Section 1101" means the statute can be found in Section 1101 under the subject heading "Commercial Code" of the California code. Abbreviations may be used. For example, "13 Pennsylvania Consolidated Statutes Section 1101" may be abbreviated "13 Pa. C.S. § 1101," and "California Commercial Code Section 1101" may be abbreviated "Cal. Com. Code § 1101."

Administrative Rules

Rules and regulations adopted by federal administrative agencies are initially published in the *Federal Register*, a daily publication of the U.S. government. Later, they are incorporated into the *Code of Federal Regulations* (C.F.R.).

Like the U.S.C., the C.F.R. is divided into titles. Rules within each title are assigned section numbers. A full citation to the C.F.R. includes title and section numbers. For example, a reference to "17 C.F.R. Section 230.504" means that the rule can be found in Section 230.504 of Title 17.

Finding Case Law

Before discussing the case reporting system, we need to look briefly at the court system. There are two types of courts in the United States: federal courts and state courts.

Both the federal and the state court systems consist of several levels, or tiers, of courts. *Trial courts*, in which evidence is presented and testimony is given, are on the bottom tier (which also includes lower courts handling specialized issues). Decisions from a trial court can be appealed to a higher court, which commonly is an intermediate *court of appeals*, or an *appellate court*. Decisions from these intermediate courts of appeals may be appealed to an even higher court, such as a state supreme court or the United States Supreme Court.

State Court Decisions

Most state trial court decisions are not published (except in New York and a few other states, which publish selected trial court opinions). Decisions from state trial courts are typically filed in the office of the clerk of the court, where the decisions are available for public inspection. (Increasingly, they can be found online as well.)

Written decisions of the appellate, or reviewing, courts, however, are published and distributed (in print and online). Many of the state court cases presented in this book are from state appellate courts. The reported appellate decisions are published in volumes called *reports* or *reporters*, which are numbered consecutively. State appellate court decisions are found in the state reporters of that particular state. Official reports are published by the state, whereas unofficial reports are published by nongovernment entities.

Regional Reporters State court opinions appear in regional units of the National Reporter System, published by Thomson Reuters. Most lawyers and libraries have these reporters because they report cases more quickly and are distributed more widely than the state-published reports. In fact, many states have eliminated their own reporters in favor of the National Reporter System.

The National Reporter System divides the states into the following geographic areas: Atlantic (A., A.2d, or A.3d), *North Eastern* (N.E., N.E.2d, or N.E.3d), *North Western* (N.W. or N.W.2d), *Pacific* (P., P.2d, or P.3d), *South Eastern* (S.E. or S.E.2d), *South Western* (S.W., S.W.2d, or S.W.3d), and *Southern* (So., So.2d, or So.3d). (The *2d* and *3d* in the abbreviations refer to *Second Series* and *Third Series*, respectively.) The states included in each of these regional divisions are indicated in Exhibit 1A–1, which illustrates the National Reporter System.

Exhibit 1A–1 The National Reporter System—Regional/Federal

Regional Reporters	Coverage Beginning	Coverage
Atlantic Reporter (A., A.2d, or A.3d)	1885	Connecticut, Delaware, District of Columbia, Maine, Maryland, New Hampshire, New Jersey, Pennsylvania, Rhode Island, and Vermont.
North Eastern Reporter (N.E., N.E.2d, or N.E.3d)	1885	Illinois, Indiana, Massachusetts, New York, and Ohio.
North Western Reporter (N.W. or N.W.2d)	1879	Iowa, Michigan, Minnesota, Nebraska, North Dakota, South Dakota, and Wisconsin.
Pacific Reporter (P., P.2d, or P.3d)	1883	Alaska, Arizona, California, Colorado, Hawaii, Idaho, Kansas, Montana, Nevada, New Mexico, Oklahoma, Oregon, Utah, Washington, and Wyoming.
South Eastern Reporter (S.E. or S.E.2d)	1887	Georgia, North Carolina, South Carolina, Virginia, and West Virginia.
South Western Reporter (S.W., S.W.2d, or S.W.3d)	1886	Arkansas, Kentucky, Missouri, Tennessee, and Texas.
Southern Reporter (So., So.2d, or So.3d)	1887	Alabama, Florida, Louisiana, and Mississippi.
Federal Reporters		
Federal Reporter (F., F.2d, or F.3d)	1880	U.S. Circuit Courts from 1880 to 1912; U.S. Commerce Court from 1911 to 1913; U.S. District Courts from 1880 to 1932; U.S. Court of Claims (now called U.S. Court of Federal Claims) from 1929 to 1932 and since 1960; U.S. Courts of Appeals since 1891; U.S. Court of Customs and Patent Appeals since 1929; U.S. Emergency Court of Appeals since 1943.
Federal Supplement (F.Supp., F.Supp.2d, or F.Supp.3d)	1932	U.S. Court of Claims from 1932 to 1960; U.S. District Courts since 1932; U.S. Customs Court since 1956.
Federal Rules Decisions (F.R.D.)	1939	U.S. District Courts involving the Federal Rules of Civil Procedure since 1939 and Federal Rules of Criminal Procedure since 1946.
Supreme Court Reporter (S.Ct.)	1882	United States Supreme Court since the October term of 1882.
Bankruptcy Reporter (Bankr.)	1980	Bankruptcy decisions of U.S. Bankruptcy Courts, U.S. District Courts, U.S. Courts of Appeals, and the United States Supreme Court.
Military Justice Reporter (M.J.)	1978	U.S. Court of Military Appeals and Courts of Military Review for the Army, Navy, Air Force, and Coast Guard.

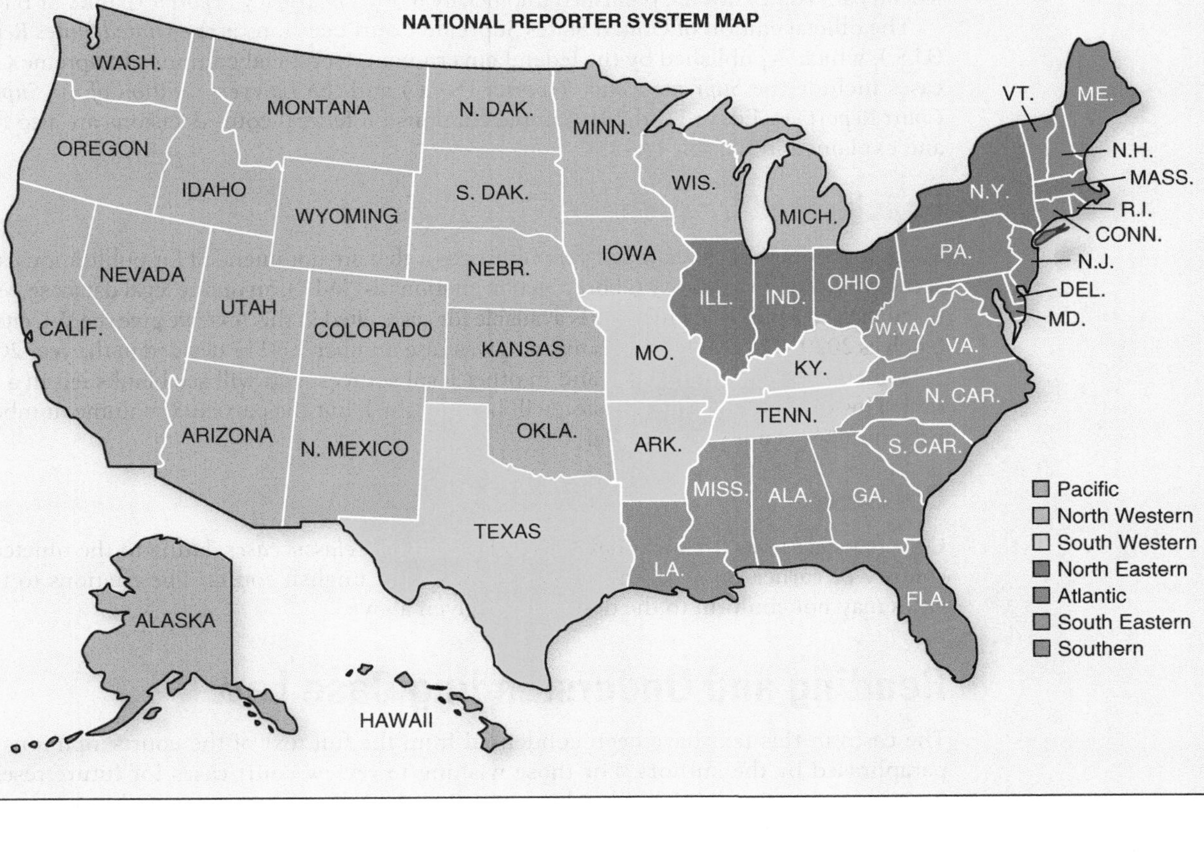

Case Citations After appellate decisions have been published, they are normally referred to (cited) by the name of the case and the volume, name, and page number of the reporter(s) in which the opinion can be found. The citation first lists information from the state's official reporter (if different from the National Reporter System), then the *National Reporter*, and then any other selected reporter. (Citing a reporter by volume number, name, and page number, in that order, is common to all citations.) When more than one reporter is cited for the same case, each reference is called a *parallel citation*.

Note that some states have adopted a "public domain citation system" that uses a somewhat different format for the citation. For example, in Oklahoma, an Oklahoma court decision might be designated "2020 OK 4," meaning that the decision was the 4th decision issued by the Oklahoma Supreme Court in 2020. A parallel citation to the *Pacific Reporter* is included after the public domain citation.

Consider the following citation: *NetScout Systems, Inc. v. Gartner, Inc.*, 334 Conn. 396, 223 A.3d 37 (2020). We see that the opinion in this case can be found in Volume 334 of the official *Connecticut Reports*, on page 396. The parallel citation is to Volume 223 of the *Atlantic Reporter, Third Series*, page 37.

When we present opinions in this text (starting in Chapter 2), in addition to the reporter, we give the name of the court hearing the case and the year of the court's decision. Sample citations to state court decisions are listed and explained in Exhibit 1A–2.

Federal Court Decisions

Federal district (trial) court decisions are published unofficially in the *Federal Supplement* (F.Supp., F.Supp.2d, or F.Supp.3d), and opinions from the circuit courts of appeals (federal reviewing courts) are reported unofficially in the *Federal Reporter* (F., F.2d, or F.3d). Cases concerning federal bankruptcy law are published unofficially in the *Bankruptcy Reporter* (Bankr. or B.R.).

The official edition of United States Supreme Court decisions is the *United States Reports* (U.S.), which is published by the federal government. Unofficial editions of Supreme Court cases include the *Supreme Court Reporter* (S.Ct.) and the *Lawyers' Edition of the Supreme Court Reports* (L.Ed. or L.Ed.2d). Sample citations for federal court decisions are also listed and explained in Exhibit 1A–2.

Unpublished Opinions

Many court opinions that are not yet published or that are not intended for publication can be accessed through Westlaw® (abbreviated in citations as "WL"), an online legal database. When no citation to a published reporter is available for cases cited in this text, we give the WL citation (such as 2020 WL 399117, which means it was case number 399117 decided in the year 2020).

Sometimes, both in this text and in other legal sources, you will see blanks left in a citation. This occurs when the decision will be published, but the particular volume number or page number is not yet available.

Old Cases

On a few occasions, this text cites opinions from old, *classic cases* dating to the nineteenth century or earlier. Some of these cases are from the English courts. The citations to these cases may not conform to the descriptions given above.

Reading and Understanding Case Law

The cases in this text have been condensed from the full text of the courts' opinions and paraphrased by the authors. For those wishing to review court cases for future research projects or to gain additional legal information, the following sections will provide useful insights into how to read and understand case law.

Exhibit 1A–2 How to Read Citations

STATE COURTS

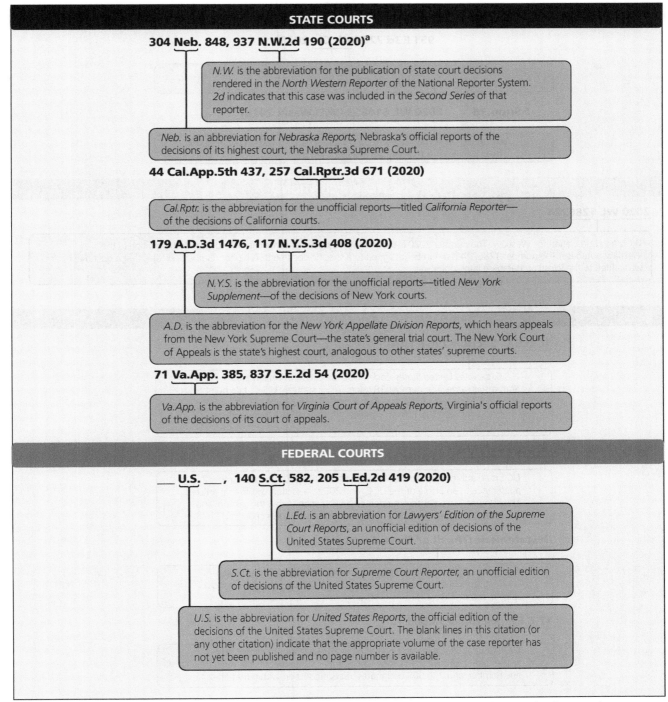

304 Neb. 848, 937 N.W.2d 190 (2020)[a]

N.W. is the abbreviation for the publication of state court decisions rendered in the *North Western Reporter* of the National Reporter System. *2d* indicates that this case was included in the *Second Series* of that reporter.

Neb. is an abbreviation for *Nebraska Reports,* Nebraska's official reports of the decisions of its highest court, the Nebraska Supreme Court.

44 Cal.App.5th 437, 257 Cal.Rptr.3d 671 (2020)

Cal.Rptr. is the abbreviation for the unofficial reports—titled *California Reporter*—of the decisions of California courts.

179 A.D.3d 1476, 117 N.Y.S.3d 408 (2020)

N.Y.S. is the abbreviation for the unofficial reports—titled *New York Supplement*—of the decisions of New York courts.

A.D. is the abbreviation for the *New York Appellate Division Reports,* which hears appeals from the New York Supreme Court—the state's general trial court. The New York Court of Appeals is the state's highest court, analogous to other states' supreme courts.

71 Va.App. 385, 837 S.E.2d 54 (2020)

Va.App. is the abbreviation for *Virginia Court of Appeals Reports,* Virginia's official reports of the decisions of its court of appeals.

FEDERAL COURTS

___ U.S. ___, 140 S.Ct. 582, 205 L.Ed.2d 419 (2020)

L.Ed. is an abbreviation for *Lawyers' Edition of the Supreme Court Reports,* an unofficial edition of decisions of the United States Supreme Court.

S.Ct. is the abbreviation for *Supreme Court Reporter,* an unofficial edition of decisions of the United States Supreme Court.

U.S. is the abbreviation for *United States Reports*, the official edition of the decisions of the United States Supreme Court. The blank lines in this citation (or any other citation) indicate that the appropriate volume of the case reporter has not yet been published and no page number is available.

a. The case names have been deleted from these citations to emphasize the publications. It should be kept in mind, however, that the name of a case is as important as the specific page numbers in the volumes in which it is found. If a citation is incorrect, the correct citation may be found in a publication's index of case names. In addition to providing a check on errors in citations, the date of a case is important because the value of a recent case as an authority is likely to be greater than that of older cases from the same court.

Exhibit 1A–2 How to Read Citations—Continued

FEDERAL COURTS (Continued)

951 F.3d 728 (6th Cir. 2020)

6th Cir. is an abbreviation denoting that this case was decided in the U.S. Court of Appeals for the Sixth Circuit.

___ F.Supp.3d ___, 2020 WL 614653 (W.D.Wash. 2020)

W.D.Wash. is an abbreviation indicating that the U.S. District Court for the Western District of Washington decided this case.

WESTLAW® CITATIONS[b]

2020 WL 1286224

WL is an abbreviation for Westlaw. The number 2020 is the year of the document that can be found with this citation in the Westlaw database. The number 1286224 is a number assigned to a specific document. A higher number indicates that a document was added to the Westlaw database later in the year.

STATUTORY AND OTHER CITATIONS

18 U.S.C. Section 1961(1)(A)

U.S.C. denotes *United States Code*, the codification of *United States Statutes at Large*. The number 18 refers to the statute's U.S.C. title number and 1961 to its section number within that title. The number 1 in parentheses refers to a subsection within the section, and the letter A in parentheses to a subsection within the subsection.

UCC 2–206(1)(b)

UCC is an abbreviation for *Uniform Commercial Code*. The first number 2 is a reference to an article of the UCC, and 206 to a section within that article. The number 1 in parentheses refers to a subsection within the section, and the letter b in parentheses to a subsection within the subsection.

***Restatement (Third) of Torts*, Section 6**

Restatement (Third) of Torts refers to the third edition of the American Law Institute's *Restatement of the Law of Torts*. The number 6 refers to a specific section.

17 C.F.R. Section 230.505

C.F.R. is an abbreviation for *Code of Federal Regulations*, a compilation of federal administrative regulations. The number 17 designates the regulation's title number, and 230.505 designates a specific section within that title.

b. Many court decisions that are not yet published or that are not intended for publication can be accessed through Westlaw, an online legal database.

Case Titles and Terminology

The title of a case, such as *Adams v. Jones*, indicates the names of the parties to the lawsuit. The *v.* in the case title stands for versus, which means "against." In the trial court, Adams was the plaintiff—the person who filed the suit. Jones was the defendant.

If the case is appealed, however, the appellate court will sometimes place the name of the party appealing the decision first, so the case may be called *Jones v. Adams*. Because some reviewing courts retain the trial court order of names, it is often impossible to distinguish the plaintiff from the defendant in the title of a reported appellate court decision. You must carefully read the facts of each case to identify the parties.

The following terms and phrases are frequently encountered in court opinions and legal publications. Because it is important to understand what these terms and phrases mean, we define and discuss them here.

Parties to Lawsuits The party initiating a lawsuit is referred to as the *plaintiff* or *petitioner*, depending on the nature of the action, and the party against whom a lawsuit is brought is the *defendant* or *respondent*. Lawsuits frequently involve more than one plaintiff and/or defendant.

When a case is appealed from the original court or jurisdiction to another court or jurisdiction, the party appealing the case is called the *appellant*. The *appellee* is the party against whom the appeal is taken. (In some appellate courts, the party appealing a case is referred to as the *petitioner*, and the party against whom the suit is brought or appealed is called the *respondent*.)

Judges and Justices The terms *judge* and *justice* are usually synonymous and are used to refer to the judges in various courts. All members of the United States Supreme Court, for instance, are referred to as justices. Justice is the formal title usually given to judges of appellate courts, although this is not always the case. In New York, a justice is a judge of the trial court (which is called the Supreme Court), and a member of the Court of Appeals (the state's highest court) is called a judge. The term *justice* is commonly abbreviated to J., and justices to JJ. A Supreme Court case might refer to Justice Sotomayor as Sotomayor, J., or to Chief Justice Roberts as Roberts, C.J.

Decisions and Opinions Most decisions reached by reviewing, or appellate, courts are explained in written *opinions*. The opinion contains the court's reasons for its decision, the rules of law that apply, and the judgment. You may encounter several types of opinions as you read appellate cases, including the following:

- When all the judges (or justices) agree, a *unanimous opinion* is written for the entire court.
- When there is not unanimous agreement, a **majority opinion** is generally written. It outlines the views of the majority of the judges deciding the case.
- A judge who agrees (concurs) with the majority opinion as to the result but not as to the legal reasoning often writes a **concurring opinion**. In it, the judge sets out the reasoning that he or she considers correct.
- A **dissenting opinion** presents the views of one or more judges who disagree with the majority view.
- Sometimes, no single position is fully supported by a majority of the judges deciding a case. In this situation, we may have a **plurality opinion**. This is the opinion that has the support of the largest number of judges, but the group in agreement is less than a majority.
- Finally, a court occasionally issues a ***per curiam* opinion** (*per curiam* is Latin for "of the court"), which does not indicate which judge wrote the opinion.

Majority Opinion A court opinion that represents the views of the majority (more than half) of the judges or justices deciding the case.

Concurring Opinion A court opinion by one or more judges or justices who agree with the majority but want to make or emphasize a point that was not made or emphasized in the majority's opinion.

Dissenting Opinion A court opinion that presents the views of one or more judges or justices who disagree with the majority's decision.

Plurality Opinion A court opinion that is joined by the largest number of the judges or justices hearing the case, but less than half of the total number.

***Per Curiam* Opinion** A court opinion that does not indicate which judge or justice authored the opinion.

A Sample Court Case

Knowing how to read and analyze a court opinion is an essential step in undertaking accurate legal research. The cases within this text have already been analyzed and briefed by the authors, and the essential aspects of each case are presented in a convenient format consisting of four sections: *Facts, Issue, Decision,* and *Reason*. This format is illustrated in the sample court case in Exhibit 1A–3, which is explained further in this chapter's *Business Law Analysis* feature.

In addition to this basic format, each case is followed by one or two critical-thinking questions regarding some issue raised by the case. We offer these questions as tools to help you develop your critical-thinking and legal reasoning skills. *What If the Facts Were Different?* questions alter the facts slightly and ask you to consider how this would change the outcome. A section entitled *Impact of This Case on Today's Law* concludes each *Classic Case* in this text to indicate the significance of the case for today's legal landscape.

Exhibit 1A–3 A Sample Court Case

Adelman's Truck Parts Corp. v. Jones Transport

United States Court of Appeals, Sixth Circuit, __ Fed.Appx. __, 2020 WL 238534 (2020).

Facts Don Jones, the owner and operator of Jones Transport, a small trucking company, ordered a used a Caterpillar C-7 motor from Adelman's Truck Parts Corporation. The purchase agreement did not specify the motor's horsepower. Expecting that it would be capable of 250 horsepower, Jones was disappointed to find that the motor delivered was capable of only 190 horsepower. Jones's mechanic also found a broken piston in the oil pan and a badly scored cylinder wall in the engine block. Jones contacted Adelman's and was told that it did not have a 250-horsepower Caterpillar C-7 motor in stock. Under the purchase agreement, Jones's only option was to return the motor for a refund, minus a 20 percent restocking fee, which Adelman's offered to waive. Jones refused the offer and filed a claim in a federal district court against Adelman's for breach of contract. The court issued a summary judgment in Adelman's favor. Jones appealed to the U.S. Court of Appeals for the Sixth Circuit, arguing that the remedy provision in the purchase agreement was unenforceable.

Issue Did Adelman's afford Jones the remedy that he was due?

Decision Yes. The U.S. Court of Appeals for the Sixth Circuit affirmed the lower court's judgment. "Because Jones was afforded the remedy that he was due . . . we agree with the district court."

Reason A seller may legitimately limit a buyer's remedies to the return of purchased goods and a repayment of the purchase price, or to the repair and replacement of goods that do not conform to the parties' contract. Here, the purchase agreement between Adelman's and Jones states, "BUYER'S EXCLUSIVE REMEDY RELATING TO THE GOODS SHALL BE LIMIITED SOLELY TO EITHER SELLER'S RETURN OF THE PURCHASE AMOUNT UPON [BUYER'S] RETURN OF THE NONCONFORMING GOODS OR SELLER'S REPAIR, CORRECTION AND/OR REPLACEMENT OF ANY OF THE GOODS WHICH ARE . . . NONCONFORMING." Adelman's gave Jones the remedy provided in the purchase agreement by offering Jones the opportunity to return the motor. The agreement's exclusive-remedy provision would have been unenforceable if it had deprived Jones of the value of the deal by leaving him without a remedy. But Jones was not left without a remedy—he could have returned the motor to Adelman's as the agreement specified. He chose not to.

Critical Thinking

- **Economic** *For a federal district court to hear a case, the "amount in controversy" must be at least $75,000. Jones paid $5,000 for the motor and $304 in freight charges. What other losses or injuries might Jones claim in order to cross the "amount in controversy" threshold? Explain.*

How to Brief Cases

Knowing how to read and understand court opinions and the legal reasoning used by the courts is an essential step in performing legal research. A further step is "briefing," or summarizing, the case. Briefing cases facilitates the development of critical-thinking skills that are crucial for businesspersons when evaluating relevant business law.

Legal researchers routinely brief cases by reducing the texts of the opinions to their essential elements. Generally, when you brief a case, you first summarize the background and facts of the case, as the authors have done for most of the cases presented in this text. You then indicate the issue (or issues) before the court. An important element in the case brief is, of course, the court's decision on the issue and the legal reasoning used by the court in reaching that decision.

There is a fairly standard procedure that you follow to "brief" any court case. You must first read the case opinion carefully. When you feel that you understand the case, you can prepare a brief of it. Although the format of the brief may vary, typically it will present the essentials of the case under headings such as the following:

1. **Citation**. Give the full citation for the case, including the name of the case, the court that decided it, and the year it was decided.
2. **Facts**. Briefly indicate (a) the reasons for the lawsuit, (b) the identity and arguments of the plaintiff(s) and defendant(s), respectively, and (c) the lower court's decision—if the decision is from a reviewing court.
3. **Issue**. Concisely phrase, in the form of a question, the essential issue before the court. (If more than one issue is involved, you may have two—or even more—questions.)
4. **Decision**. Indicate here—with a "yes" or "no," if possible—the court's answer to the question (or questions) in the *Issue* section.
5. **Reason**. Summarize as briefly as possible the reasons given by the court for its decision (or decisions) and the case or statutory law relied on by the court in arriving at its decision.

See this chapter's *Business Law Analysis* feature for a sample case brief and a discussion of how the brief relates to the IRAC method of legal reasoning.

Case Briefing and IRAC Legal Reasoning

Business Law Analysis

Here is a sample case brief of the opinion shown in Exhibit 1A–3.

1. **Citation**. *Adelman's Truck Parts Corp. v. Jones Transport*, United States Court of Appeals, Sixth Circuit, 797 Fed. Appx. 997, 2020 WL 238534 (2020). *Fed.Appx.* is the abbreviation for *Federal Appendix*, a case law reporter that includes judicial opinions of the U.S. courts of appeals that are not selected for publication in the *Federal Reporter*.
2. **Facts**. Don Jones, the owner and operator of Jones Transport, a small trucking company, ordered a used Caterpillar C-7 motor from Adelman's Truck Parts Corporation. The purchase agreement did not specify the motor's horsepower. Expecting that it would be capable of 250 horsepower, Jones was disappointed to find that the motor delivered was capable of only 190 horsepower. Jones's mechanic also found a broken piston in the oil pan and a badly scored cylinder wall in the engine block. Jones contacted Adelman's and was told that it did not have a 250-horsepower Caterpillar C-7

motor in stock. Under the purchase agreement, Jones's only option was to return the motor for a refund, minus a 20 percent restocking fee, which Adelman's offered to waive. Jones refused the offer and filed a claim in a federal district court against Adelman's for breach of contract. The court issued a summary judgment in Adelman's favor. Jones appealed to the U.S. Court of Appeals for the Sixth Circuit, arguing that the remedy provision in the purchase agreement was unenforceable.

3. **Issue**. Did Adelman's afford Jones the remedy that he was due?
4. **Decision**. Yes. The U.S. Court of Appeals for the Sixth Circuit affirmed the lower court's judgment. "Because Jones was afforded the remedy that he was due . . . we agree with the district court."
5. **Reason**. A seller may legitimately limit a buyer's remedies to the return of purchased goods and a repayment of the purchase price, or to the repair and replacement of goods that do not conform to the parties' contract. Here, the purchase agreement between Adelman's and Jones states, "BUYER'S EXCLUSIVE REMEDY RELATING TO THE GOODS SHALL BE LIMIITED SOLELY TO EITHER SELLER'S RETURN OF THE PURCHASE AMOUNT UPON [BUYER'S] RETURN OF THE NONCONFORMING GOODS OR SELLER'S REPAIR, CORRECTION AND/OR REPLACEMENT OF ANY OF THE GOODS WHICH ARE . . . NONCONFORMING." Adelman's gave Jones the remedy provided in the purchase agreement by offering Jones the opportunity to return the motor. The agreement's exclusive-remedy provision would have been unenforceable if it had deprived Jones of the value of the deal by leaving him without a remedy. But Jones was not left without a remedy—he could have returned the motor to Adelman's as the agreement specified. He chose not to.

Analysis: The sections in a case brief include the information necessary to perform IRAC legal reasoning. (IRAC stands for *Issue, Rule of Law, Application,* and *Conclusion.*) The first step in applying the IRAC legal reasoning method is to frame the issue. You need to understand the relevant facts, identify the parties, and determine the specific issue presented in the case. You will find this information in the first two sections of the brief. The *Facts* section identifies the plaintiff and the defendant. On the claim highlighted in this brief, the plaintiff is Don Jones, and Adelman's Truck Parts Corporation is the defendant. The *Facts* section also describes the events that underlie the parties' dispute and the allegations that one or both parties assert to support their request for a favorable resolution. Because this case is a decision of one of the U.S. courts of appeals, the lower court's ruling, the party appealing, and the appellant's contention on appeal are included.

It is important to carefully state the issue so that you can look for the appropriate *Rule of Law* that will guide the court's decision. In this case, the court considers whether Jones was afforded the remedy that he was due under the parties' agreement.

Result and Reasoning: The *Reason* section includes references to the relevant laws and judicial principles that the court applied in coming to the conclusion arrived at in the case. In this case, the *Rule of Law* included the principles of contract law that define the legitimate limits a seller may place on a buyer's remedies in their purchase agreement. The *Reason* section also explains the court's *Application* of the law to the facts in the case. The purchase agreement between Adelman's and Jones included a limit on the buyer's remedies to a refund of the price on a return of nonconforming goods to the seller. This provision would have been unenforceable if it had left Jones without a remedy, but the court reasoned that this was not the case. This reasoning led the court to arrive at the *Conclusion* that Adelman's had given Jones the remedy provided in the agreement by offering him the opportunity to return the motor for a full refund.

Janece Flippo/Shutterstock.com

2 Constitutional Law

"The United States Constitution has proved itself the most marvelously elastic compilation of rules of government ever written."

Franklin D. Roosevelt 1882–1945 (Thirty-second president of the United States, 1933–1945)

Focus Questions

The four Focus Questions *below are designed to help improve your understanding. After reading this chapter, you should be able to answer the following questions:*

1. What constitutional clause gives the federal government the power to regulate commercial activities among the states?
2. What is the Bill of Rights? What freedoms does the First Amendment guarantee?
3. Where in the Constitution can the due process clause be found?
4. Which constitutional amendments have been interpreted as implying a right to privacy?

The U.S. Constitution is brief. It contains only about seven thousand words—less than one-third as many as the average state constitution. Its brevity explains, in part, why the Constitution has proved to be so "marvelously elastic," as Franklin Roosevelt described it in the chapter-opening quotation. It might also explain why the U.S. Constitution has survived for more than two hundred years—longer than any other written constitution in the world.

Laws that govern business have their origin in the lawmaking authority granted by the Constitution. Neither Congress nor any state can enact a law that conflicts with the Constitution.

Disputes over constitutional rights frequently come before the courts. Suppose Rebecca visits the Boutique Bakery in Eugene, Oregon, to order a wedding cake for her upcoming marriage to Sheryl. Albert, who owns the bakery, refuses to take the order because of religious objections to same-sex marriage. Rebecca then sues Albert in a state court for violating an Oregon law that prohibits discrimination against customers based on their sexual orientation.

Albert counters that compelling him to bake the cake would violate his First Amendment right to freely exercise his religious beliefs. He also argues that the state cannot force him to express a message with which he disagrees—a message in favor of same-sex marriage. How should the court balance Rebecca's right to be free from discrimination against Albert's rights to freedom of religion and expression? In this chapter, we will examine the impact of the Constitution on America's business landscape, as well as the courts' role in resolving the conflicts that inevitably arise when constitutional rights are at stake.

2–1 The Constitutional Powers of Government

Following the Revolutionary War, the United States created a *confederal* form of government in which the states had the authority to govern themselves and the national government could exercise only limited powers. When problems arose because the nation was facing an economic crisis and state laws interfered with the free flow of commerce, a national convention was called. The delegates drafted the U.S. Constitution. This document, after its ratification by the states in 1789, became the basis for an entirely new form of government.

Federal Form of Government A system of government in which the states form a union and the sovereign power is divided between the central government and the member states.

Sovereignty The power of a state to do what is necessary to govern itself. Individual state sovereignty is determined by the U.S. Constitution.

Police Powers Powers possessed by the states as part of their inherent sovereignty. These powers may be exercised to protect or promote the public order, health, safety, morals, and general welfare.

2–1a A Federal Form of Government

The new government created by the Constitution reflected a series of compromises made by the convention delegates on various issues. Some delegates wanted sovereign power to remain with the states, whereas others wanted the national government alone to exercise sovereign power. The end result was a compromise—a **federal form of government** in which the national government and the states *share* sovereign power.

Federal Powers The Constitution sets forth specific powers that can be exercised by the national government, generally referred to as the federal government. It also provides that the federal government has the implied power to undertake actions necessary to carry out its expressly designated powers. All other powers are "reserved" to the states.

elenaleonova/iStock/Getty Images

Under the U.S. Constitution, states and municipalities have the power to regulate many types of local commercial activities, including the imposition of building codes. What is the general term used to describe these powers?

Regulatory Powers of the States As part of their inherent **sovereignty** (power to govern themselves), state governments have the authority to regulate certain affairs within their borders. This authority stems, in part, from the Tenth Amendment, which reserves all powers not delegated to the federal government to the states or to the people.

State regulatory powers are often referred to as **police powers**. The term encompasses more than just the enforcement of criminal laws. Police powers also give a state government broad rights to regulate private activities to protect or promote the public order, health, safety, morals, and general welfare. Fire and building codes, antidiscrimination laws, parking regulations, zoning restrictions, licensing requirements, and thousands of other state statutes have been enacted pursuant to states' police powers. Local governments, such as cities, also exercise police powers.

In the following case, the question was whether a pair of municipal ordinances regulating the rental of motorized scooters constituted a reasonable exercise of police powers.

Case 2.1

Classy Cycles, Inc. v. Panama City Beach

District Court of Appeal of Florida, First District, 44 Fla. L. Weekly D2729, _ So.3d _, 2019 WL 5945495 (2019).

Facts Panama City Beach, Florida, enacted two ordinances—the first to prohibit the overnight rental of motorized scooters, and the second to prohibit the rental of the scooters in the city effective at a future date. Both ordinances included an extensive rationale for their adoption, stating essentially that a geographically small city has the right to restrict a business from operating within the city when the restriction is for the safety of the city's citizens and visitors. Classy Cycles, Inc., filed a suit in a Florida state court against Panama City Beach, seeking to have the ordinances declared invalid. Classy Cycles argued that the city did not have the power to ban a business unless the business was a nuisance. Because the rental of scooters to the public was not a nuisance, the city could not completely prohibit it. The city countered that it could prohibit any activity, provided the reasoning supporting the prohibition was not arbitrary or unreasonable. The court entered a judgment in the city's favor. Classy Cycles appealed.

Issue Were the ordinances reasonably related to accomplishing the city's goal of protecting the safety of its citizens and visitors?

Decision Yes. A state intermediate appellate court affirmed the trial court's judgment. The city's ordinances regulating motorized scooters were a reasonable exercise of police powers.

Reason The appellate court recognized that municipalities have the authority to regulate activities affecting the public's health, safety, and welfare. To the extent that Classy Cycles argues otherwise, the "argument is without merit." Furthermore, explained the court, "our job is not to determine whether the City used the best method or least intrusive means" to regulate those activities, but whether the regulation was "reasonably related to accomplishing its goal." Under this analysis, a regulation must not be arbitrary or unreasonable, but needs to bear only a reasonable relationship to a legitimate state interest. In this case, the court noted that the rationale for the regulation is provided in the ordinances. They state that "the dangerous conditions" created by the irresponsible driving behavior of scooter renters, especially at night, amplified by the lack of training, supervision, and oversight practiced by the rental scooter businesses, "existed throughout the entire city." According to the court, this was sufficient to support a finding that the ordinances were neither arbitrary nor unreasonable.

Critical Thinking

- **Cultural** *What "dangerous conditions" might have prompted the city to enact the ordinances at issue in this case? Why?*
- **Economic** *What is the likely economic impact of the ordinances on the businesses in the city? Discuss*

2–1b Relations among the States

The U.S. Constitution also includes provisions concerning relations among the states in our federal system. Particularly important are the *privileges and immunities clause* and the *full faith and credit clause.*

The Privileges and Immunities Clause Article IV, Section 2, of the Constitution provides that the "Citizens of each State shall be entitled to all Privileges and Immunities of Citizens in the several States." This clause is often referred to as the interstate **privileges and immunities clause**. It prevents a state from imposing unreasonable burdens on citizens of another state—particularly with regard to means of livelihood or doing business.

Privileges and Immunities Clause Article IV, Section 2, of the U.S. Constitution requires states not to discriminate against one another's citizens. A resident of one state, when in another state, cannot be denied the privileges and immunities of citizens of that state.

When a citizen of one state engages in basic and essential activities in another state (the "foreign state"), the foreign state must have a *substantial reason* for treating the nonresident differently than its own residents. Basic activities include transferring property, seeking employment, and accessing the court system. The foreign state must also establish that its reason for the discrimination is *substantially related* to the state's ultimate purpose in adopting the legislation or regulating the activity. Thus, if Missouri wants to charge out-of-state real estate agents higher licensing fees than those required of Missouri resident agents, it will need to come up with a constitutionally acceptable reason for doing so.

The Full Faith and Credit Clause Article IV, Section 1, of the U.S. Constitution provides that "Full Faith and Credit shall be given in each State to the public Acts, Records, and judicial Proceedings of every other State." This clause, which is referred to as the **full faith and credit clause**, applies only to civil matters. It ensures that rights established under deeds, wills, contracts, and similar instruments in one state will be honored by other states. It also ensures that any judicial decision with respect to such property rights will be honored and enforced in all states.

Full Faith and Credit Clause A provision in Article IV, Section 1, of the U.S. Constitution that ensures that rights established under deeds, wills, contracts, and similar instruments in one state will be honored by other states and that judicial decisions will be honored and enforced in all states.

The full faith and credit clause has contributed to the unity of American citizens because it protects their legal rights as they move about from state to state. It also protects the rights of those to whom they owe obligations, such as persons who have been awarded monetary damages by courts. The ability to enforce such rights is extremely important for the conduct of business in a country with a very mobile citizenry.

2–1c The Separation of Powers

To make it difficult for the federal government to use its power arbitrarily, the Constitution divided the federal government's powers among three branches of government. The legislative branch makes the laws, the executive branch enforces the laws, and the judicial branch interprets the laws. Each branch performs a separate function, and no branch may exercise the authority of another branch.

Additionally, a system of **checks and balances** allows each branch to limit the actions of the other two branches, thus preventing any one branch from exercising too much power. The following are examples of these checks and balances:

Checks and Balances The system under which the powers of the federal government are divided among three separate branches—the executive, legislative, and judicial branches—each of which exercises a check on the actions of the others.

1. The legislative branch (Congress) can enact a law, but the executive branch (the president) has the constitutional authority to veto that law.
2. The executive branch is responsible for foreign affairs, but treaties with foreign governments require the advice and consent of the Senate.
3. Congress determines the jurisdiction of the federal courts, and the president appoints federal judges, with the advice and consent of the Senate. The judicial branch has the power to hold actions of the other two branches unconstitutional.

2–1d The Commerce Clause

To prevent states from establishing laws and regulations that would interfere with trade and commerce among the states, the Constitution explicitly gave the federal government the power to regulate interstate commerce. Article I, Section 8, of the U.S. Constitution expressly permits Congress "[t]o regulate Commerce with foreign Nations, and among the several States, and with the Indian Tribes." This clause, referred to as the **commerce clause**, has had a greater impact on business than any other provision in the Constitution.

Commerce Clause The provision in Article I, Section 8, of the U.S. Constitution that gives Congress the power to regulate interstate commerce.

Initially, the commerce power was interpreted as being limited to *interstate* commerce (commerce among the states) and not applicable to *intrastate* commerce (commerce within a state). In 1824, however, the United States Supreme Court decided the case of *Gibbons v. Ogden* (see this chapter's *Landmark in the Law* feature). The Court ruled that commerce within a state could also be regulated by the federal government as long as the commerce *substantially affected* commerce involving more than one state.

Focus Question 1

What constitutional clause gives the federal government the power to regulate commercial activities among the states?

The Expansion of Federal Powers under the Commerce Clause As the nation grew and faced new kinds of problems, the commerce clause became a vehicle for the additional expansion of the federal government's regulatory powers. Even activities that seemed purely local came under the regulatory reach of the federal government if those activities were

Gibbons v. Ogden (1824)

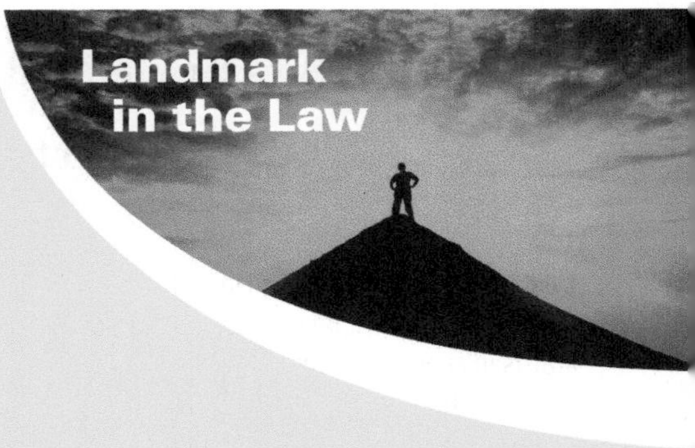

The commerce clause of the U.S. Constitution gives Congress the power "[t]o regulate Commerce with foreign Nations, and among the several States, and with the Indian Tribes." Before the commerce clause came into existence, states tended to restrict commerce within and beyond their borders, which made trade more costly and inefficient. The goal of the clause was to unify the states' commerce policies and improve the efficiency of exchanges.

The problem was that although the commerce clause gave Congress some authority to regulate trade among the states, the extent of that power was unclear. What exactly does "to regulate commerce" mean? What does "commerce" entail? These questions came before the United States Supreme Court in 1824 in the case of *Gibbons v. Ogden.*[a]

Background In 1803, Robert Fulton, the inventor of the steamboat, and Robert Livingston, who was the ambassador to France, secured a monopoly from the New York legislature on steam navigation on the waters in the state of New York. Their monopoly extended to interstate waters—waterways between New York and another state. Fulton and Livingston licensed Aaron Ogden, a former governor of New Jersey and a U.S. senator, to operate steam-powered ferryboats between New York and New Jersey.

Thomas Gibbons already operated a ferry service between New Jersey and New York, which had been licensed by Congress under a 1793 act regulating trade along the coast. Although the federal government had licensed Gibbons to operate boats in interstate waters, he did not have the state of New York's permission to compete with Ogden in that area. Ogden sued Gibbons. The New York state courts granted Ogden's request for an injunction—an order prohibiting Gibbons from operating in New York waters. Gibbons appealed the decision to the United States Supreme Court.

Marshall's Decision The issue before the Court was whether the law regulated commerce that was "among the several states." The chief justice on the Supreme Court was John Marshall, an advocate of a strong federal government. Marshall defined the word *commerce* as used in the commerce clause to mean all commercial intercourse—that is, all business dealings that affect more than one state. This broader definition included navigation.

In addition to expanding the definition of commerce, Marshall also validated and increased the power of the federal legislature to regulate commerce. Said Marshall, "What is this power? It is the power . . . to prescribe the rule by which commerce is to be governed."

Marshall held that the power to regulate interstate commerce is an exclusive power of the federal government. This power includes the power to regulate any intrastate commerce that substantially affects interstate commerce. Accordingly, the Court decided in favor of Gibbons.

Application to Today's World *Marshall's broad definition of the commerce power established the foundation for the expansion of federal powers in the years to come. Today, the federal government continues to rely on the commerce clause for its constitutional authority to regulate business activities.*

Marshall's conclusion that the power to regulate interstate commerce was an exclusive power of the federal government has also had significant consequences. By implication, it means that a state cannot regulate activities that extend beyond its borders, such as out-of-state online gambling operations that affect the welfare of in-state citizens. It also means that state regulations over in-state activities normally will be invalidated if the regulations substantially burden interstate commerce.

a. 22 U.S. (9 Wheat.) 1, 6 L.Ed. 23 (1824).

deemed to substantially affect interstate commerce. In 1942, the Supreme Court held that wheat production by an individual farmer intended wholly for consumption on his own farm was subject to federal regulation.[1]

The following *Classic Case* involved a challenge to the scope of the federal government's constitutional authority to regulate local activities.

1. *Wickard v. Filburn,* 317 U.S. 111, 63 S.Ct. 82, 87 L.Ed. 122 (1942).

Classic Case 2.2

Heart of Atlanta Motel v. United States

Supreme Court of the United States, 379 U.S. 241, 85 S.Ct. 348, 13 L.Ed.2d 258 (1964).

Facts In the 1950s, the United States Supreme Court ruled that racial segregation imposed by the states in school systems and other public facilities violated the Constitution. Privately owned facilities were not affected until Congress passed the Civil Rights Act of 1964, which prohibited racial discrimination in "establishments affecting interstate commerce."

LBJ Library photo by Cecil Stoughton

President Lyndon Johnson signs the 1964 Civil Rights Act.

The owner of the Heart of Atlanta Motel, in violation of the Civil Rights Act of 1964, refused to rent rooms to African Americans. The motel owner brought an action in a federal district court to have the Civil Rights Act declared unconstitutional on the ground that Congress had exceeded its constitutional authority to regulate commerce by enacting the statute.

The owner argued that his motel was not engaged in interstate commerce but was "of a purely local character." The motel, however, was accessible to state and interstate highways. The owner advertised nationally, maintained billboards throughout the state, and accepted convention trade from outside the state (75 percent of the guests were residents of other states).

The district court ruled that the act did not violate the Constitution and enjoined (prohibited) the owner from discriminating on the basis of race. The owner appealed. The case ultimately went to the United States Supreme Court.

Issue Did Congress exceed its constitutional power to regulate interstate commerce by enacting the Civil Rights Act of 1964?

Decision No. The United States Supreme Court upheld the constitutionality of the act.

Reason The Court noted that the act was passed to correct "the deprivation of personal dignity" accompanying the denial of equal access to "public establishments." Testimony before Congress leading to the passage of the act indicated that African Americans in particular experienced substantial discrimination in attempting to secure lodging while traveling. This discrimination impeded interstate travel and thus impeded interstate commerce.

As for the owner's argument that his motel was "of a purely local character," the Court said that even if this was true, the motel affected interstate commerce. According to the Court, "if it is interstate commerce that feels the pinch, it does not matter how local the operation that applies the squeeze." Therefore, under the commerce clause, "the power of Congress to promote interstate commerce also includes the power to regulate the local incidents thereof, including local activities."

Critical Thinking

- **What If the Facts Were Different?** *If this case had involved a small, private retail business that did not advertise nationally, would the result have been the same? Why or why not?*
- **Impact of This Case on Today's Law** *If the United States Supreme Court had invalidated the Civil Rights Act of 1964, the legal landscape of the United States would be much different today. The act prohibits discrimination based on race, color, national origin, religion, or gender in all "public accommodations," including hotels and restaurants. The act also prohibits discrimination in employment based on these criteria. Although state laws now prohibit many of these forms of discrimination as well, the protections available vary from state to state—and it is not certain whether such laws would have been passed had the outcome in this case been different.*

The Commerce Clause Today Today, at least theoretically, the power over commerce authorizes the federal government to regulate almost every commercial enterprise in the United States. The breadth of the commerce clause permits the federal government to legislate in areas in which Congress has not explicitly been granted power. Only occasionally has the Supreme Court curbed the federal government's regulatory authority under the commerce clause.

The Supreme Court has, for instance, allowed the federal government to regulate noncommercial activities relating to medical marijuana that take place wholly within a state's borders. **Spotlight Case Example 2.1** More than thirty states, including California, have adopted laws that legalize marijuana for medical purposes, and a significant number of states now permit the recreational use of marijuana. Marijuana possession, however, is illegal under the federal Controlled Substances Act (CSA).[2]

After the federal government seized the marijuana that two seriously ill California women were using on the advice of their physicians, the women filed a lawsuit. They argued that it was unconstitutional for the federal statute to prohibit them from using marijuana for medical purposes that were legal within the state.

The Supreme Court, though, held that Congress has the authority to prohibit the *intra*-state possession and noncommercial cultivation of marijuana as part of a larger regulatory scheme (the CSA).[3] In other words, the federal government may still prosecute individuals for possession of marijuana regardless of whether they reside in a state that allows the use of marijuana.

The "Dormant" Commerce Clause The United States Supreme Court has interpreted the commerce clause to mean that the federal government has the *exclusive* authority to regulate commerce that substantially affects trade and commerce among the states. This express grant of authority to the federal government, which is often referred to as the "positive" aspect of the commerce clause, implies a negative aspect—that the states do *not* have the authority to regulate interstate commerce. This negative aspect of the commerce clause is often referred to as the "dormant" (implied) commerce clause.

The dormant commerce clause comes into play when state regulations affect interstate commerce. In this situation, the courts normally weigh the state's interest in regulating a certain matter against the burden that the state's regulation places on interstate commerce. Because courts balance the interests involved, predicting the outcome in a particular case can be extremely difficult.

Case Example 2.2 Tennessee law imposed a two-year residency requirement on any business entity that wanted to acquire a state liquor license. As a result, Total Wine, a retail liquor chain, was blocked from opening a store in Nashville. Defending this action in court, Tennessee officials claimed that the residency requirement was justified under the Twenty-first Amendment, which gives states the responsibility of regulating alcohol for public benefit. The United States Supreme Court disagreed, finding that the law was primarily designed to shield state businesses from out-of-state competition. Without any realistic connection to health and safety measures, the Court ruled, the residency requirement did not "advance a legitimate local purpose" and therefore violated the dormant commerce clause.[4]

2–1e The Supremacy Clause

Article VI of the Constitution provides that the Constitution, laws, and treaties of the United States are "the supreme Law of the Land." This article, commonly referred to as the **supremacy clause**, is important in the ordering of state and federal relationships.

Supremacy Clause The provision in Article VI of the U.S. Constitution that the Constitution, laws, and treaties of the United States are "the supreme Law of the Land."

Preemption Under the supremacy clause, when there is a direct conflict between a federal law and a state law, the state law is rendered invalid. Because some powers are *concurrent* (shared by the federal government and the states), however, it is necessary to determine which law governs in a particular circumstance.

Preemption occurs when Congress chooses to act exclusively in a concurrent area. In this circumstance, a valid federal statute or regulation will take precedence over a conflicting state or local law or regulation on the same general subject.

Preemption A doctrine under which certain federal laws preempt, or take precedence over, conflicting state or local laws.

2. 21 U.S.C. Sections 801 *et seq.*
3. *Gonzales v. Raich*, 545 U.S. 1, 125 S.Ct. 2195, 162 L.Ed.2d 1 (2005).
4. *Tennessee Wine and Spirits Retailers Associations v. Thomas*, 588 U.S. _, 139 S.Ct. 2440, 204 L.Ed.2d 801 (2019).

Congressional Intent Often, it is not clear whether Congress, in passing a law, intended to preempt an entire subject area against state regulation. In these situations, the courts determine whether Congress intended to exercise exclusive power.

Generally, congressional intent to preempt will be found if a federal law regulating an activity is so pervasive, comprehensive, or detailed that the states have little or no room to regulate in that area. Also, when a federal statute creates an agency—such as the U.S. Food and Drug Administration (FDA)—to enforce the law, the agency's decisions in matters that come within its jurisdiction will likely preempt state laws.

Classic Case Example 2.3 A man who alleged that he had been injured by a faulty medical device (a balloon catheter that had been inserted into his artery following a heart attack) sued the manufacturer. The case ultimately came before the United States Supreme Court. The Court noted that the relevant federal law (the Medical Device Amendments) included a preemption provision.

Furthermore, the device had passed the FDA's rigorous premarket approval process. Therefore, the Court ruled that the federal regulation of medical devices preempted the man's state law claims for negligence, strict liability, and implied warranty.[5]

2–2 Business and the Bill of Rights

Focus Question 2

What is the Bill of Rights? What freedoms does the First Amendment guarantee?

Bill of Rights The first ten amendments to the U.S. Constitution.

The importance of having a written declaration of the rights of individuals eventually caused the first Congress of the United States to enact twelve amendments to the Constitution and submit them to the states for approval. The first ten of these amendments, commonly known as the **Bill of Rights**, were adopted in 1791.

The Bill of Rights embodies a series of protections for the individual against various types of conduct by the federal government.[6] Some constitutional protections apply to business entities as well. For example, corporations exist as separate legal entities, or legal persons, and enjoy many of the same rights and privileges as natural persons do.

Summarized next are the protections guaranteed by the first ten amendments:

1. The First Amendment guarantees the freedoms of religion, speech, and the press and the rights to assemble peaceably and to petition the government.
2. The Second Amendment guarantees the right to keep and bear arms.
3. The Third Amendment prohibits, in peacetime, the lodging of soldiers in any house without the owner's consent.
4. The Fourth Amendment prohibits unreasonable searches and seizures of persons or property.
5. The Fifth Amendment guarantees the rights to *indictment* (formal accusation) by a grand jury, to due process of law, and to fair payment when private property is taken for public use. The Fifth Amendment also prohibits compulsory self-incrimination and double jeopardy (prosecution for the same crime twice).
6. The Sixth Amendment guarantees the accused in a criminal case the right to a speedy and public trial by an impartial jury and with counsel. Accused defendants have the right to cross-examine witnesses against them and to solicit testimony from witnesses in their favor.
7. The Seventh Amendment guarantees the right to a trial by jury in a civil (noncriminal) case involving at least twenty dollars.[7]

---

5. *Riegel v. Medtronic, Inc.*, 552 U.S. 312, 128 S.Ct. 999, 169 L.Ed.2d 892 (2008); see also *Mink v. Smith & Nephew, Inc.*, 860 F.3d 1319 (11th Cir. 2017).
6. One of the proposed amendments was ratified more than two hundred years later (in 1992) and became the Twenty-seventh Amendment to the Constitution.
7. Twenty dollars was forty days' pay for the average person when the Bill of Rights was written.

8. The Eighth Amendment prohibits excessive bail and fines, as well as cruel and unusual punishment.
9. The Ninth Amendment establishes that the people have rights in addition to those specified in the Constitution.
10. The Tenth Amendment establishes that those powers neither delegated to the federal government nor denied to the states are reserved for the states.

We will look more closely at several of these amendments in a later chapter. In this chapter, we examine two important guarantees of the First Amendment—freedom of speech and freedom of religion. First, though, we look at how the Bill of Rights puts certain limits on government.

2–2a Limits on Federal and State Governmental Actions

As originally intended, the Bill of Rights limited only the powers of the federal government. Over time, however, the United States Supreme Court "incorporated" most of these rights into the protections against state actions afforded by the Fourteenth Amendment to the Constitution.

Know This
Although most of the rights in the Bill of Rights apply to actions of the states, some of them apply only to actions of the federal government.

The Fourteenth Amendment Passed in 1868 after the Civil War, the Fourteenth Amendment provides, in part, that "[n]o State shall . . . deprive any person of life, liberty, or property, without due process of law."

Starting in 1925, the Supreme Court began to define various rights and liberties guaranteed in the federal Constitution as constituting "due process of law," which was required of state governments under the Fourteenth Amendment. Today, most of the rights and liberties set forth in the Bill of Rights apply to state governments as well as to the federal government.

Judicial Interpretation The rights secured by the Bill of Rights are not absolute. Many of the rights guaranteed by the first ten amendments are described in very general terms. For instance, the Second Amendment states that people have a right to keep and bear arms, but it does not explain the extent of this right. As the Supreme Court once stated, the right does not extend so far that people can "keep and carry any weapon whatsoever in any manner whatsoever and for whatever purpose."[8] Legislatures can prohibit the carrying of concealed weapons or certain types of weapons, such as machine guns. Ultimately, the Supreme Court, as the final interpreter of the Constitution, gives meaning to constitutional rights and determines their boundaries.

2–2b The First Amendment—Freedom of Speech

A democratic form of government cannot survive unless people can freely voice their political opinions and criticize government actions or policies. Freedom of speech, particularly political speech, is thus a prized right, and traditionally the courts have protected this right to the fullest extent possible. (See this chapter's *Adapting the Law to the Online Environment* feature to learn how social media have flourished under the protection of the First Amendment.)

Symbolic speech—gestures, movements, articles of clothing, and other forms of expressive conduct—is also given substantial protection by the courts. The burning of the American flag to protest government policies, for instance, is a constitutionally protected form of expression. Similarly, wearing a T-shirt with a photo of a presidential candidate or taking a knee during the national anthem at a sporting event is a constitutionally protected form of expression.

Symbolic Speech Nonverbal expressions of beliefs. Symbolic speech, which includes gestures, movements, and articles of clothing, is given substantial protection by the courts.

8. *District of Columbia v. Heller*, 554 U.S. 570, 128 S.Ct. 2783, 171 L.Ed.2d 637 (2008).

Social Media and the Constitution

Adapting the Law to the Online Environment

Everyone, it seems, uses social media. And everyone, it seems, complains about social media. The complaints highlight a wide variety of objectionable content online, from hate speech to harassment to misinformation to offensive photos and videos. What steps, if any, should the U.S. government take to remedy the situation?

First Amendment Protections

In a business context, the term *social media* covers (1) those people or companies that generate opinions and other material, (2) those that consume this content, (3) those that host this content, and (4) those that sell advertising linked to this content. Except under very limited circumstances, the First Amendment protects the right of these groups to operate without government interference. This protection reflects the importance that Americans have always placed on allowing free speech in the public sphere.

The Communications Decency Act (CDA) offers an additional defense for social media speech. This federal law protects social media platforms from being held liable for user-generated content.[a] That is, Facebook cannot be sued or charged criminally for something that users do on their Facebook pages. Proponents of greater social media regulation have called for this section of the CDA to be repealed, but any such effort would certainly be challenged on First Amendment grounds.

Access Denied

In the face of government inaction, many social media companies have opted for self-regulation. Facebook, for example, bans attacks against people or groups based on race, ethnicity, sexual orientation, or religion affiliation. Similarly, Twitter prohibits statements that promote violence or hate, and YouTube tries to block any video that promotes a discriminatory ideology.

The targets of these efforts inevitably claim that they are being censored, but this is incorrect. Generally speaking, the Bill of Rights protects citizens against government measures, not those taken by private companies. So, while the exclusion policies of social medial giants such as Facebook and Twitter may frustrate and anger users, they do not violate those users' First Amendment rights.

Critical Thinking

One observer has said that the American legal system should evaluate social media companies based on how "they affect us as citizens, not only [on how] they affect us as consumers." What is your opinion of this statement?

a. 47 U.S.C. Section 230.

Alan Budman/Alamy Stock Photo

Is this inflatable rat an expression of symbolic speech?

The test is whether a reasonable person would interpret the conduct as conveying some sort of message. **Example 2.4** Union members set up an inflatable rat outside a construction site they are protesting for using non-union labor. If a reasonable person would interpret this conduct as conveying a message, then it will likely be a protected form of symbolic speech. ■

Reasonable Restrictions Expression—oral, written, or symbolized by conduct—is subject to reasonable restrictions. A balance must be struck between a government's obligation to protect its citizens and those citizens' exercise of their rights. Reasonableness is analyzed on a case-by-case basis. American courts have, for example, ruled that it is unreasonable for states to prohibit convicted sex offenders from accessing social media but reasonable for states to prohibit juvenile offenders from doing so.[9]

9. *Packingham v. North Carolina*, 582 U.S. _, 137 S.Ct. 1730, 198 L.Ed.2d. 273 (2017); and *In Re A.A.*, 30 Cal.App.5th 596 (2018).

Content-Neutral Laws. Laws that regulate the time, manner, and place, but not the content, of speech receive less scrutiny by the courts than do laws that restrict the content of expression. If a restriction imposed by the government is content neutral, then a court may allow it. To be content neutral, the restriction must be aimed at combating some secondary societal problem, such as crime, and not be aimed at suppressing the expressive conduct or its message.

Courts have often protected nude dancing as a form of symbolic expression. Nevertheless, the courts typically allow content-neutral laws that ban *all* public nudity. **Case Example 2.5** Ria Ora was charged with dancing nude at an annual "anti-Christmas" protest in Harvard Square in Cambridge, Massachusetts. Ora argued that the statute was overly broad and unconstitutional, and a trial court agreed. On appeal, a state appellate court reversed. The court found that the statute was constitutional because it banned public displays of open and gross lewdness in situations in which there was an unsuspecting or unwilling audience.[10]

Laws That Restrict the Content of Speech. If a law regulates the content of the expression, it must serve a compelling state interest and must be narrowly written to achieve that interest. Under the **compelling government interest** test, the government's interest is balanced against the individual's constitutional right to be free of government interference. For the statute to be valid, there must be a compelling governmental interest that can be furthered only by the law in question.

Compelling Government Interest A test of constitutionality that requires the government to have convincing reasons for passing any law that restricts fundamental rights, such as free speech, or distinguishes between people based on a suspect trait.

The United States Supreme Court has historically been dubious of government actions intended to restrict "offensive" speech. **Spotlight Case Example 2.6** The Consolidated Edison Company placed documents celebrating nuclear power in its billing envelopes. The New York Public Service Commission responded by barring all utilities from discussing public policy in communications with customers. The majority of the United States Supreme Court could not find any compelling reason for New York to restrict Consolidated Edison's free speech in this manner. The Court reasoned that the possibility that content may offend some customers does not justify its prohibition. This is particularly true, the Court noted, given how easy it is for customers to throw any offending documents in the trash.[11]

Corporate Political Speech

Political speech by corporations also falls within the protection of the First Amendment. Many years ago, the United States Supreme Court reviewed a Massachusetts statute that prohibited corporations from making political contributions or expenditures that individuals were permitted to make. The Court ruled that the Massachusetts law was unconstitutional because it violated the right of corporations to freedom of speech.[12]

Corporate political speech continues to be given significant protection under the First Amendment. **Classic Case Example 2.7** In *Citizens United v. Federal Election Commission*,[13] the Supreme Court overturned a twenty-year-old precedent on campaign financing. The case involved Citizens United, a nonprofit corporation.

Citizens United had produced a film called *Hillary: The Movie* that was critical of Hillary Clinton, who was seeking the Democratic presidential nomination. Campaign-finance law prohibited Citizens United from broadcasting the movie, however. The Court ruled that the restrictions were unconstitutional and that the First Amendment prevents limits from being placed on independent political expenditures by corporations.

10. *Commonwealth of Massachusetts v. Ora*, 451 Mass. 125, 883 N.E.2d 1217 (2008).
11. *Consolidated Edison Co. v. Public Service Commission*, 447 U.S. 530, 100 S.Ct. 2326, 65 L.Ed.2d 319 (1980).
12. *First National Bank of Boston v. Bellotti*, 435 U.S. 765, 98 S.Ct. 1407, 55 L.Ed.2d 707 (1978).
13. *Citizens United v. Federal Election Commission*, 558 U.S. 310, 130 S.Ct. 876, 175 L.Ed.2d 753 (2010).

Ethical Issue

Even though corporations *can* restrict the speech of their employees, *should* they do so? Federal law protects the right of workers to discuss some topics, such as forming a union, without fear of punishment from their employers. In general, however, while corporations may enjoy the protections of the First Amendment, their employees do not. (Remember, the Bill of Rights applies primarily to government actions, not those taken by private entities.) For years, such concerns seemed irrelevant at Google LLC. Indeed, the tech conglomerate told its 100,000 employees to "bring your whole self to work" and trumpeted "lively discussion" as a hallmark of its "workplace culture."

Eventually, however, Google managers began to worry about the impact of so much unpoliced speech at the company. A set of guidelines was instituted that required employees to refrain from discussing politics and other non-work-related issues at work. After that, Google fired a software engineer who posted an internal memo suggesting that men were better suited for tech work than women. Employees with conservative viewpoints were dismayed to learn that a manager had referred to them as "poisonous a**holes" who should be fired. Leftward leaning "Googlers" felt they had been retaliated against after protesting lucrative payouts to company executives who had been fired for sexual misconduct. "People need to be able to discuss what's going on in the world," said one skeptical management expert of the changes at Google. "Communities are where you do that and the community where people spend most of their waking time is at the office."

smontgom65/iStock Editorial/Getty Images

The U.S. Supreme Court decision in *Citizens United* allows corporations to spend to elect or defeat candidates for president and Congress. Why did this decision upset some people?

Commercial Speech The courts also give substantial protection to *commercial speech*, which consists of communications—primarily advertising and marketing—made by business firms that involve only their commercial interests. The protection given to commercial speech under the First Amendment is not as extensive as that afforded to noncommercial speech, however.

Generally, a restriction on commercial speech will be considered valid as long as it (1) seeks to implement a substantial government interest, (2) directly advances that interest, and (3) goes no further than necessary to accomplish its objective. A substantial government interest exists when the government has an important stake in the matter at hand.

A state may restrict certain kinds of advertising, for instance, in the interest of protecting consumers from being misled. States also have a legitimate interest in the beautification of roadsides, and this interest allows states to place restraints on billboard advertising. **Example 2.8** Café Erotica, a nude dancing establishment, sues the state after being denied a permit to erect a billboard along an interstate highway in Florida. Because of the state's legitimate interest in highway beautification and safety, a court will likely rule that it is not an unconstitutional restraint on commercial speech.

At issue in the following *Spotlight Case* was whether a government agency had unconstitutionally restricted commercial speech when it prohibited the use of a certain illustration on beer labels.

Spotlight on Beer Labels: Case 2.3

Bad Frog Brewery, Inc. v. New York State Liquor Authority

United States Court of Appeals, Second Circuit, 134F.3d 87 (1998).

Facts Bad Frog Brewery, Inc., makes and sells alcoholic beverages. Some of the beverages feature labels with a drawing of a frog making the gesture generally known as "giving the finger." Renaissance Beer Company was Bad Frog's authorized New York distributor. Renaissance applied to the New York State Liquor Authority (NYSLA) for brand label approval, as required by state law before the beer could be sold in New York. The NYSLA denied the application, in part, because "the label could appear in grocery and convenience stores, with obvious exposure on the shelf to children of tender age." Bad Frog filed a suit in a federal district court against the NYSLA, asking for, among other things, an injunction against the denial of the application. The court granted summary judgment in favor of the NYSLA. Bad Frog appealed to the U.S. Court of Appeals for the Second Circuit.

Eric Isselee/ShutterStock.com

Can a label be too offensive?

Issue Was the NYSLA's ban of Bad Frog's beer labels a reasonable restriction on commercial speech?

Decision No. The U.S. Court of Appeals for the Second Circuit reversed the judgment of the district court and remanded the case for judgment to be entered in favor of Bad Frog.

Reason The appellate court held that the NYSLA's denial of Bad Frog's application violated the First Amendment. The ban on the use of the labels lacked a "reasonable fit" with the state's interest in shielding minors from vulgarity. In addition, the NYSLA did not adequately consider alternatives to the ban. The court acknowledged that the NYSLA's interest "in protecting children from vulgar and profane advertising" was "substantial." The question was whether banning Bad Frog's labels "directly advanced" that interest. "In view of the wide currency of vulgar displays throughout contemporary society, including comic books targeted directly at children, barring such displays from labels for alcoholic beverages cannot realistically be expected to reduce children's exposure to such displays to any significant degree."

The court concluded that a commercial speech limitation must be "part of a substantial effort to advance a valid state interest, not merely the removal of a few grains of offensive sand from a beach of vulgarity." Finally, as to whether the ban on the labels was more extensive than necessary to serve this interest, the court pointed out that there were "numerous less intrusive alternatives." For example, the NYSLA could have placed restrictions on the permissible locations where the appellant's products could be displayed in stores.

Critical Thinking

- **Legal Environment** *Whose interests are advanced by the banning of certain types of advertising?*
- **What If the Facts Were Different?** *If Bad Frog had sought to use the label to market toys instead of beer, would the court's ruling likely have been the same? Explain your answer.*

Unprotected Speech The United States Supreme Court has made it clear that certain types of speech will not be given any protection under the First Amendment. Speech that harms the good reputation of another, or defamatory speech (defamation is discussed in the torts chapter), will not be protected. In addition, speech that violates criminal laws (such as threatening or obscene speech) is not constitutionally protected.

Threatening Speech. Note that in the case of threatening speech, the speaker must have posed a "true threat." In other words, the speaker must have meant to communicate a serious intent to commit an unlawful, violent act against a particular person or group. **Case Example 2.9** While awaiting trial on various firearm and drug charges, James Knox appeared in a YouTube music video called "F*** the Police." In the video, Knox identified two Pittsburgh law enforcement officers involved in his arrest and rapped that he was going to "jam this rusty knife" into one of the officer's "guts" and "chop his feet." Knox was eventually convicted of making terroristic threats. On appeal, he argued that his video was a piece of artistic expression protected by the First Amendment.

The Pennsylvania Supreme Court rejected this defense. Knox's lyrics, the court found, went well beyond a general animosity toward the police. Besides referring to the two law enforcement officers by name, Knox claimed to know when they went off duty. He also pledged to murder one of the officer's confidential informants and bragged about making fake 911 calls and killing any police officer who responded. According to the court, this level of specificity differentiated Knox's words from "mere" violent lyrics, which would have been protected speech. Instead, they were "true threats," which were not protected.[14]

Obscene Speech. The First Amendment, as interpreted by the Supreme Court, also does not protect obscene speech. Numerous state and federal statutes make it a crime to disseminate and possess obscene materials. Objectively defining obscene speech has proved difficult, however. It is even more difficult to prohibit the dissemination of obscenity and pornography online.

Most of Congress's attempts to pass legislation protecting minors from pornographic materials on the Internet have been struck down on First Amendment grounds when challenged in court. One exception is a law that requires public schools and libraries to install **filtering software** on computers to keep children from accessing adult content.[15] Such software is designed to prevent persons from viewing certain websites based on their Internet addresses or **meta tags**, or key words. This act does not unconstitutionally burden free speech because it is flexible and libraries can disable the filters for any patrons who ask.

Filtering Software A computer program that is designed to block access to certain websites, based on their content. The software blocks the retrieval of a site whose URL or key words are on a list within the program.

Meta Tags Key words in a document that can serve as index references to the document. On the Web, search engines return results based, in part, on the tags in Web documents.

2–2c The First Amendment—Freedom of Religion

The First Amendment states that the government may neither establish any religion nor prohibit the free exercise of religious practices. The first part of this constitutional provision is referred to as the *establishment clause*, and the second part is known as the *free exercise clause*. Government action, both federal and state, must be consistent with this constitutional mandate.

Establishment Clause The provision in the First Amendment that prohibits the government from establishing any state-sponsored religion or enacting any law that promotes religion or favors one religion over another.

The Establishment Clause

The **establishment clause** prohibits the government from establishing a state-sponsored religion, as well as from passing laws that promote (aid or endorse) religion or show a preference for one religion over another. Although the establishment clause involves the separation of church and state, it does not require a complete separation.

Applicable Standard. Establishment clause cases often involve such issues as the legality of allowing or requiring school prayers, using state-issued vouchers to pay tuition at religious schools, and teaching creation theories versus evolution in public schools. Federal or state laws that do not promote or place a significant burden on religion are constitutional even if they have some impact on religion. For a government law or policy to be constitutional, it must not have the primary effect of promoting or inhibiting religion.

Know This

The free exercise clause applies only to the actions of the state and federal governments, not to private employers. Private employers may nonetheless be required to accommodate their employees' religious beliefs.

Religious Displays. Religious displays on public property have often been challenged as violating the establishment clause. The United States Supreme Court has ruled on a number of such cases, often focusing on the proximity of the religious display to nonreligious symbols or on the balance of symbols from different religions. The Supreme Court eventually decided that public displays having historical, as well as religious, significance do not necessarily violate the establishment clause.

Case Example 2.10 Mount Soledad is a prominent hill near San Diego. There has been a forty-foot cross on top of Mount Soledad since 1913. In the 1990s, a war memorial was

14. *Commonwealth of Pennsylvania v. Knox*, 647 Pa. 593, 190 A.3d 1146 (2018).
15. Children's Internet Protection Act (CIPA), 17 U.S.C. Sections 1701–1741.

constructed next to the cross that included six walls listing the names of veterans. The site was privately owned until 2006, when Congress authorized the property's transfer to the federal government "to preserve a historically significant war memorial."

Steve Trunk and the Jewish War Veterans filed lawsuits claiming that the cross display violated the establishment clause because it endorsed the Christian religion. A federal appellate court agreed, finding that the primary effect of the memorial as a whole sent a strong message of endorsement and exclusion (of non-Christian veterans). The court noted that although not all cross displays at war memorials violate the establishment clause, the cross in this case physically dominated the site. Additionally, the cross was originally dedicated to religious purposes, had a long history of religious use, and was the only portion visible to drivers on the freeway below.[16]

To gain a better understanding of how courts analyze whether public displays violate the establishment clause, see this chapter's *Business Law Analysis* feature.

The Free Exercise Clause The **free exercise clause** guarantees that people can hold any religious beliefs they want or can have no religious beliefs. The constitutional guarantee of personal religious freedom restricts only the actions of the government, however, and not those of individuals or private businesses.

Free Exercise Clause The provision in the First Amendment that prohibits the government from interfering with people's religious practices or forms of worship.

Restrictions Must Be Necessary. The government must have a compelling state interest for restricting the free exercise of religion, and the restriction must be the only way to further that interest. **Case Example 2.11** Gregory Holt, an inmate in an Arkansas state prison, was a devout Muslim who wished to grow a beard in accord with his religious beliefs. The

16. *Trunk v. City of San Diego*, 629 F.3d 1099 (9th Cir. 2011).

Business Law Analysis

Determining When Public Religious Displays Violate the Establishment Clause

Judge James DeWeese hung a poster in his courtroom showing the Ten Commandments. The poster also included a number of editorial statements made by DeWeese, such as "God is the final authority, and we acknowledge His unchanging standards of behavior."

The American Civil Liberties Union (ACLU) filed a suit, alleging that the poster violated the establishment clause. DeWeese responded that his purpose was not to promote religion but to educate others about two conflicting legal philosophies—moral relativism and moral absolutism. DeWeese expressed his view that "our legal system is based on moral absolutes from divine law handed down by God through the Ten Commandments." Does displaying this poster in a courtroom violate the establishment clause?

Analysis: The establishment clause prohibits the government from passing laws or taking actions that promote religion or show a preference for one religion over another. In assessing a government action (in this case, displaying a religious poster in a courtroom), the courts look at the predominant purpose for the action and ask whether the action has the effect of endorsing religion. Although DeWeese claimed to have a nonreligious (educational) purpose for displaying the poster of the Ten Commandments, his own statements showed a religious purpose. DeWeese was trying to teach others to believe as he believed, that our legal system is based on moral truths handed down by God.

Result and Reasoning: DeWeese's statements reflected his views about "warring" legal philosophies and his belief that "our legal system is based on moral absolutes from divine law handed down by God through the Ten Commandments." Based on his statements, DeWeese's poster had the religious purpose of endorsing Judeo-Christian religious views, which violated the establishment clause.

Can prison policy prevent a devout Muslim from keeping a short beard?

menonsstocks/iStock/Getty Images

state corrections department prohibited inmates from growing beards. Holt asked for an exemption to grow a half-inch beard on religious grounds, and prison officials denied his request. Holt filed a suit in a federal court against Ray Hobbs, the director of the department, and others. A federal statute prohibits the government from taking any action that substantially burdens the religious exercise of a prisoner unless it is the least restrictive means of furthering a compelling governmental interest.

The defendants argued that beards compromise prison safety—a compelling government interest—because contraband can be hidden in them and because an inmate can quickly shave his beard to disguise his identity. The case ultimately reached the United States Supreme Court, which noted that "an item of contraband would have to be very small indeed to be concealed by a 1/2-inch beard." Furthermore, the Court reasoned, the department could simply search the beard, the way it already searched prisoners' hair and clothing. Therefore, the department's policy, which prevented Holt from growing a half-inch beard, violated his right to exercise his religious beliefs.[17]

Restrictions Must Not Be a Substantial Burden. To comply with the free exercise clause, a government action must not be a substantial burden on religious practices. A burden is substantial if it pressures individuals to modify their behavior and to violate their beliefs.

Case Example 2.12 The Affordable Care Act (ACA) requires employer-sponsored health plans to provide contraceptives and pregnancy "preventive services" to employees.[18] A company that objects to this rule for religious reasons can "opt out" by filing notice with the federal government. For Steven Hotze, the owner of Braidwood Management, the very act of filling out this paperwork went against the principles of his religious faith. To keep from having to do so, he and several other plaintiffs brought a lawsuit against the government claiming that their free exercise of religion was being violated.

A federal court in Texas agreed and issued an injunction against the ACA's contraception orders. The court found that as long as corporate entities or business owners sincerely believe that filling out paperwork makes them complicit in providing contraceptives, that belief can be considered religious. Therefore, to require them to complete the paperwork is a substantial burden on their free exercise rights. As a result of this decision, the government would have to find another, less restrictive, way to ensure employee access to contraceptives.[19]

Public Welfare Exception. When religious *practices* work against public policy and the public welfare, the government can act. For instance, the government can require that a child receive certain types of vaccinations or receive medical treatment when the child's life is in danger—regardless of the child's or parent's religious beliefs.

In other words, when public safety is an issue, an individual's religious beliefs often must give way to the government's interests in protecting the public. **Example 2.13** In public, a woman of the Muslim faith may choose to wear a scarf, known as a *hijab*, over her head. Nevertheless, due to public safety concerns, many courts today do not allow the wearing of any headgear (hats or scarves) in courtrooms.

---

17. *Holt v. Hobbs*, 574 U.S. 352, 135 S.Ct. 853, 190 L.Ed.2d 747 (2015).

18. Patient Protection and Affordable Care Act, Section 1001(a)(5), 42 U.S.C.A Section 300gg-13(a)(4). See also *Burwell v. Hobby Lobby Stores, Inc.*, 573 U.S. 682, 134 S.Ct. 2751, 189 L.Ed.2d 675 (2014).

19. *Deotte v. Azar*, 332 F.R.D. 173, 104 Fed. R. Serv. 3d 566 (N.D.Tex. 2019).

2–3 Due Process and Equal Protection

Two other constitutional guarantees of great significance to Americans are mandated by the due process clauses of the Fifth and Fourteenth Amendments and the equal protection clause of the Fourteenth Amendment.

Focus Question 3

Where in the Constitution can the due process clause be found?

2–3a Due Process

Both the Fifth and the Fourteenth Amendments provide that no person shall be deprived "of life, liberty, or property, without due process of law." The **due process clause** of each of these constitutional amendments has two aspects—procedural and substantive. Note that the due process clause applies to "legal persons," such as corporations, as well as to individuals.

Due Process Clause The provisions in the Fifth and Fourteenth Amendments that guarantee that no person shall be deprived of life, liberty, or property without due process of law. State constitutions often include similar clauses.

Procedural Due Process Procedural due process requires that any government decision to take life, liberty, or property must be made fairly. This means that the government must give a person proper notice and an opportunity to be heard. The government must also use fair procedures in determining whether individuals will be subjected to punishment or have some burden imposed on them.

Fair procedure has been interpreted as requiring that the person have at least an opportunity to object to a proposed action before a fair, neutral decision maker (who need not be a judge). **Example 2.14** Doyle, a nursing student in Kansas, poses for a photograph standing next to a placenta used as a lab specimen. Although she quickly deletes the photo from her library, it ends up on Facebook. When the director of nursing sees the photo, Doyle is expelled. She sues for reinstatement and wins. The school violated Doyle's due process rights by expelling her from the nursing program for taking a photo without giving her an opportunity to present her side to school authorities.

Substantive Due Process Substantive due process focuses on the content of the legislation rather than the fairness of the procedures. Substantive due process limits what the government may do in its legislative and executive capacities. Legislation must be fair and reasonable in content and must further a legitimate governmental objective.

If a law or other governmental action limits a fundamental right, the courts will hold that it violates substantive due process unless it promotes a compelling state interest. Fundamental rights include interstate travel, privacy, voting, marriage and family, and all First Amendment rights. Thus, for instance, a state must have a substantial reason for taking any action that infringes on a person's free speech rights.

In situations not involving fundamental rights, a law or action does not violate substantive due process if it rationally relates to any legitimate governmental end. It is almost impossible for a law or action to fail the "rationality" test. Under this test, almost any government regulation of business will be upheld as reasonable.

2–3b Equal Protection

Under the Fourteenth Amendment, a state may not "deny to any person within its jurisdiction the equal protection of the laws." The United States Supreme Court has used the due process clause of the Fifth Amendment to make the **equal protection clause** applicable to the federal government as well. Equal protection means that the government must treat similarly situated individuals in a similar manner.

Equal Protection Clause The provision in the Fourteenth Amendment that requires state governments to treat similarly situated individuals in a similar manner.

Equal protection, like substantive due process, relates to the substance of the law or other governmental action. When a law or action limits the liberty of all persons to do something, it may violate substantive due process. When a law or action limits the liberty of some persons but not others, it may violate the equal protection clause. **Example 2.15** If a law prohibits all advertising on the sides of trucks, it raises a substantive due process question. If the law makes an exception to allow truck owners to advertise their own businesses, it raises an equal protection issue.

In an equal protection inquiry, when a law or action distinguishes between or among individuals, the basis for the distinction—that is, the classification—is examined. Depending on the classification, the courts apply different levels of scrutiny, or "tests," to determine whether the law or action violates the equal protection clause. The courts use one of three standards: strict scrutiny, intermediate scrutiny, or the "rational basis" test.

Strict Scrutiny If a law or action prohibits or inhibits some persons from exercising a fundamental right, the law or action will be subject to "strict scrutiny" by the courts. A classification based on a *suspect trait*—such as race, national origin, or citizenship status—will also be subject to strict scrutiny. Under this standard, the classification must be necessary to promote a *compelling government interest*.

Compelling state interests include remedying past unconstitutional or illegal discrimination, but do not include correcting the general effects of "society's discrimination." **Example 2.16** For a city to give preference to minority applicants in awarding construction contracts, it normally must identify past unconstitutional or illegal discrimination against minority construction firms. Because the policy is based on suspect traits (race and national origin), it will violate the equal protection clause *unless* it is necessary to promote a compelling state interest. Generally, few laws or actions survive strict-scrutiny analysis by the courts.

Intermediate Scrutiny Another standard, that of "intermediate scrutiny," is applied in cases involving discrimination based on gender or legitimacy. Laws using these classifications must be substantially related to *important government objectives*. **Example 2.17** A state law prohibits the sale of low-alcohol beer (less than 0.5 percent "alcohol by volume") to any male under the age of eighteen and to any female under the age of twenty-one. Suppose a retail liquor chain challenges this law, claiming that it unfairly exposes the chain to sanctions and loss of liquor license. Because it does not seem to further any important government objective, the law would not survive intermediate scrutiny by a court.

The state also has an important objective in establishing time limits (called *statutes of limitation*) for how long after an event a particular type of action can be brought. Nevertheless, the limitation period must be substantially related to the important objective of preventing fraudulent or outdated claims. **Example 2.18** A federal law requires employees to file gender discrimination complaints within 180 days of the employer's discriminatory conduct. A court will likely reject a complaint that relies on evidence of discrimination that occurred outside this 180-day period, even if that discrimination directly caused low wages within the proper time frame. If this result is unfair, it will be up to the U.S. Congress, not the courts, to amend the statute of limitations.

The "Rational Basis" Test In matters of economic and social welfare, a classification will be considered valid if there is any conceivable "rational basis" on which the classification might relate to a *legitimate government interest*. It is almost impossible for a law or action to fail the rational basis test.

Case Example 2.19 A Chicago ordinance prohibits food trucks from parking within two hundred feet of the entrance of any "brick and mortar" establishment that serves food, including convenience stores with hot dog rollers. Violators of the ordinance face a fine of up to $2,000 for each day that the truck is parked within the restricted area. The owner of the Cupcakes for Courage food truck filed suit against the city, alleging that, contrary to the state constitution, the ordinance unfairly favored restaurants over "mobile food vehicles."

Applying the rational basis test, the Illinois Supreme Court rejected this claim. The court ruled that Chicago's ordinance was rationally related to the legitimate government interest of protecting the city's restaurants. To a greater degree than food trucks, the court found restaurants contribute to Chicago's economic well-being by paying property taxes and encouraging neighborhood retail activity.[20]

2–4 Privacy Rights

Focus Question 4
Which constitutional amendments have been interpreted as implying a right to privacy?

The U.S. Constitution does not explicitly mention a general right to privacy. In a 1928 Supreme Court case, *Olmstead v. United States*,[21] Justice Louis Brandeis stated in his dissent that the right to privacy is "the most comprehensive of rights and the right most valued by civilized men." The majority of the justices at that time, however, did not agree with Brandeis.

It was not until the 1960s that a majority on the Supreme Court endorsed the view that the Constitution protects individual privacy rights. In a landmark 1965 case, *Griswold v. Connecticut*,[22] the Supreme Court invalidated a Connecticut law that effectively prohibited the use of contraceptives on the ground that it violated the right to privacy. The Supreme Court held that a constitutional right to privacy was implied by the First, Third, Fourth, Fifth, and Ninth Amendments.

Today, privacy rights receive protection under various federal statutes as well as the U.S. Constitution. State constitutions and statutes also secure individuals' privacy rights, often to a significant degree. In addition, privacy rights are protected to an extent under tort law, consumer law, and employment law. This chapter's *Cybersecurity and the Law* feature explores the challenges of a corporate strategy that emphasizes privacy rights in an industry marked by cyber insecurity.

20. *LMP Services, Inc. v. City of Chicago*, 2019 IL 123123, _ N.E.3d _ (2019).
21. 277 U.S. 438, 48 S.Ct. 564, 72 L.Ed. 944 (1928).
22. 381 U.S. 479, 85 S.Ct. 1678, 14 L.Ed.2d 510 (1965).

Cybersecurity and the Law

Should Apple Help Law Enforcement?

In one of its company statements, Apple, Inc., emphasized that its products are designed "to protect your privacy and give you control over your information," but that this goal was "not always easy." The difficulty comes from a pressure that today's technology companies cannot avoid—the tension between the individual's desire for privacy and society's desire for security.

The Encryption Debate

Each iPhone produced by Apple is *encrypted* so that it can be unlocked only with a password. This encryption is so strong that even Apple's technicians cannot access an iPhone without the owner's consent. This level of privacy causes problems when law enforcement needs evidence from a smartphone whose owner will not, or cannot, provide the password.

For example, Mohammed Alshamrani was killed by sheriffs' deputies after fatally shooting three people at a naval base in Pensacola, Florida. The Federal Bureau of Investigation (FBI) wanted access to Alshamrani's two iPhones to determine whether he had been in contact with other potential domestic terrorists. Apple refused to help "break into" Alshamrani's devices. Similarly, the company has declined to build "backdoor" access into iPhones, for fear that any entry point will eventually be breached by hackers.

Apple's position angers those who believe that tech companies should prioritize helping law enforcement protect society from crime over protecting a phone user's privacy. Indeed, the U.S. Constitution allows the government to infringe on an individual's privacy to investigate a probable crime. Nevertheless, Apple's stance has earned the company a reputation for consumer advocacy. "It's brilliant marketing," says one observer. "They're so concerned with your privacy that they're willing to wave the finger at the FBI."

(Continues)

Continued

iPhones Can Be Hacked

Despite its air of invincibility, the iPhone is not hackproof. Several years before the Pensacola shooting, the FBI paid hackers to break into an iPhone owned by Syed Farook. (In tandem with his wife, Farook had fatally shot fourteen people in a terrorist attack in Southern California before being killed by law enforcement.) At least two software security companies, Cellebrite and Grayshift, have managed to bypass encryption codes on older iPhone models. On one occasion, Apple used federal copyright law to force Twitter to remove a tweet that contained a coded "key" that would unlock the company's encryption secrets. With each new iPhone, Apple closes these loopholes. Nonetheless, some in the security industry believe that it is fighting a "losing battle" against the twin privacy threats of individual hackers and government surveillance.

Critical Thinking

Tim Cook, Apple's chief operating officer, has suggested that the United States Congress should pass a law limiting the ability of Apple and other tech companies to keep consumer data private. Why would a business executive make such a request?

czardases/iStock/Getty Images

Most medical records are being put online. What law protects patients' right to privacy with respect to their online medical files?

2–4a Federal Privacy Legislation

Congress has enacted a number of statutes that protect the privacy of individuals in various areas of concern. Most of these statutes deal with personal information collected by governments or private businesses.

In the 1960s, Americans were sufficiently alarmed by the accumulation of personal information in government files that they pressured Congress to pass laws permitting individuals to access their files. Congress responded by passing the Freedom of Information Act, which allows individuals to request copies of any information on them contained in federal government files. Congress later enacted the Privacy Act, which also gives persons the right to access such information.

In the 1990s, responding to the growing need to protect the privacy of individuals' health records—particularly computerized records—Congress passed the Health Insurance Portability and Accountability Act (HIPAA).[23] This act defines and limits the circumstances in which an individual's "protected health information" may be used or disclosed by health care providers, health care plans, and others. These and other major federal laws protecting privacy rights are listed and briefly described in Exhibit 2–1.

2–4b The USA Patriot Act

The USA Patriot Act was passed by Congress in the wake of the terrorist attacks of September 11, 2001, and then reauthorized twice.[24] The Patriot Act has given government officials increased authority to monitor Internet activities (such as e-mail and website visits) and to gain access to personal financial information and student information. Law enforcement officials can track the telephone and e-mail communications of one party to find out the identity of the other party or parties. Privacy advocates argue that this law adversely affects the constitutional rights of all Americans, and it has been widely criticized in the media.

To gain access to these communications, the government must certify that the information likely to be obtained is relevant to an ongoing criminal investigation, but it does not need to provide proof of any wrongdoing. **Example 2.20** General David Petraeus, who ran the wars

23. HIPAA was enacted as Pub. L. No. 104-191 (1996) and is codified in 29 U.S.C.A. Sections 1181 *et seq.*

24. The Uniting and Strengthening America by Providing Appropriate Tools Required to Intercept and Obstruct Terrorism Act of 2001, also known as the USA Patriot Act, was enacted as Pub. L. No. 107-56 (2001), and last reauthorized by Pub. L. No. 112-114 (2011).

Exhibit 2–1 Federal Legislation Relating to Privacy

TITLE OF ACT	PROVISIONS CONCERNING PRIVACY
Freedom of Information Act (1966)	Provides that individuals have a right to access information about them collected in government files.
Family Educational Rights and Privacy Act (1974)	Limits access to computer-stored records of education-related evaluations and grades in private and public colleges and universities.
Privacy Act (1974)	Protects the privacy of individuals about whom the federal government has information. Regulates agencies' use and disclosure of data, and gives individuals access to and a means to correct inaccuracies.
Electronic Communications Privacy Act (1986)	Prohibits the interception of information communicated by electronic means.
Driver's Privacy Protection Act (1994)	Prevents states from disclosing or selling a driver's personal information without the driver's consent.
Health Insurance Portability and Accountability Act (1996)	Requires health care providers and health care plans to inform patients of their privacy rights and of how their personal medical information may be used. States that medical records may not be used for purposes unrelated to health care or disclosed without permission.
Financial Services Modernization Act (Gramm-Leach-Bliley Act) (1999)	Prohibits the disclosure of nonpublic personal information about a consumer to an unaffiliated third party unless strict disclosure and opt-out requirements are met.

in Iraq and Afghanistan, resigned as director of the Central Intelligence Agency after his extramarital affair with Paula Broadwell, his biographer, became public. Apparently, after Petraeus broke off the affair with Broadwell, she sent harassing e-mails to another woman, who reported the harassment. The FBI investigated, accessed Petraeus's e-mail accounts, and discovered that he had communicated with Broadwell via messages left in a draft folder on his e-mail account. Although there was no evidence that Petraeus had done anything illegal, he was urged to resign and did so. ■

Practice and Review

A state legislature enacted a statute that required any motorcycle operator or passenger on the state's highways to wear a protective helmet. Jim Alderman, a licensed motorcycle operator, sued the state to block enforcement of the law. Alderman asserted that the statute violated the equal protection clause because it placed requirements on motorcyclists that were not imposed on other motorists. Using the information presented in the chapter, answer the following questions.

1. Why does this statute raise equal protection issues instead of substantive due process concerns?
2. What are the three levels of scrutiny that the courts use in determining whether a law violates the equal protection clause?
3. Which level of scrutiny or test would apply to this situation? Why?
4. Under this standard or test, is the helmet statute constitutional? Why or why not?

Debate This

Legislation aimed at protecting people from themselves concerns the individual as well as the public in general. Protective helmet laws are just one example of such legislation. Should individuals be allowed to engage in unsafe activities if they choose to do so?

Key Terms

Bill of Rights 38
checks and balances 34
commerce clause 34
compelling government interest 41
due process clause 47
equal protection clause 47
establishment clause 44
federal form of government 32
filtering software 44
free exercise clause 45
full faith and credit clause 34
meta tags 44
police powers 32
preemption 37
privileges and immunities clause 33
sovereignty 32
supremacy clause 37
symbolic speech 39

Chapter Summary: Constitutional Law

The Constitutional Powers of Government	The U.S. Constitution established a federal form of government, in which government powers are shared by the national government and the state governments. At the national level, generally referred to as the federal level, government powers are divided among the legislative, executive, and judicial branches. The Tenth Amendment reserves to the states all powers not expressly delegated to the federal government. Under their police powers, state governments may regulate private activities in order to protect or promote the public order, health, safety, morals, and general welfare.
The Commerce Clause	1. **The expansion of federal powers**—The commerce clause expressly permits Congress to regulate commerce. Over time, courts expansively interpreted this clause, thereby enabling the federal government to wield extensive powers over the economic life of the nation. 2. **The commerce clause today**—Today, the commerce clause authorizes the federal government, at least theoretically, to regulate almost every commercial enterprise in the United States. 3. **The "dormant" commerce clause**—If state regulations substantially interfere with interstate commerce, they will be held to violate the "dormant" commerce clause of the U.S. Constitution. The positive aspect of the commerce clause, which gives the federal government the exclusive authority to regulate interstate commerce, implies a "dormant" aspect—that the states do not have this power.
The Supremacy Clause	The U.S. Constitution provides that the Constitution, laws, and treaties of the United States are "the supreme Law of the Land." Whenever a state law directly conflicts with a federal law, the state law is rendered invalid.
Business and the Bill of Rights	The Bill of Rights, which consists of the first ten amendments to the U.S. Constitution, embodies a series of protections for individuals—and, in some instances, business entities—against various types of interference by the federal government. Today, most of the protections apply against state governments as well. Freedoms guaranteed by the First Amendment that affect businesses include the following: 1. **Freedom of speech**—Speech, including symbolic speech, is given the fullest possible protection by the courts. Corporate political speech and commercial speech also receive substantial protection under the First Amendment. Certain types of speech, such as defamatory speech and obscene speech, are not protected under the First Amendment. Government attempts to regulate unprotected forms of speech in the online environment have, to date, met with numerous challenges. 2. **Freedom of religion**—Under the First Amendment, the government may neither establish any religion (the establishment clause) nor prohibit the free exercise of religion (the free exercise clause).

Due Process and Equal Protection	1. **Due process**—Both the Fifth and the Fourteenth Amendments provide that no person shall be deprived of "life, liberty, or property, without due process of law." Procedural due process requires that any government decision to take life, liberty, or property must be made fairly, using fair procedures. Substantive due process focuses on the content of legislation. Generally, a law that limits a fundamental right violates substantive due process unless the law promotes a compelling state interest, such as public safety. 2. **Equal protection**—Under the Fourteenth Amendment, a law or action that limits the liberty of some persons but not others may violate the equal protection clause. Such a law may be upheld, however, if there is a rational basis for the discriminatory treatment of a given group or if the law substantially relates to an important government objective.
Privacy Rights	The Constitution does not contain a specific guarantee of a right to privacy, but such a right has been derived from guarantees found in several constitutional amendments. A number of federal statutes protect privacy rights. Privacy rights are also protected by many state constitutions and statutes, as well as under tort law, consumer law, and employment law.

Issue Spotters

1. South Dakota wants its citizens to conserve energy. To help reduce consumer consumption of electricity, the state passes a law that bans all advertising by power utilities within the state. What argument could the power utilities use as a defense to the enforcement of this state law? (See *Business and the Bill of Rights.*)
2. Suppose that a state imposes a higher tax on out-of-state companies doing business in the state than it imposes on in-state companies. Is this a violation of the equal protection clause if the only reason for the tax is to protect the local firms from out-of-state competition? Explain. (See *Due Process and Equal Protection.*)

—Check your answers to the *Issue Spotters* against the answers provided in Appendix D.

Business Scenarios and Case Problems

2–1. The Free Exercise Clause. Thomas worked in the nonmilitary operations of a large firm that produced both military and nonmilitary goods. When the company discontinued the production of nonmilitary goods, Thomas was transferred to the plant producing military equipment. Thomas left his job, claiming that it violated his religious principles to participate in the manufacture of goods to be used in destroying life. In effect, he argued, the transfer to the military equipment plant forced him to quit his job. He was denied unemployment compensation by the state because he had not been effectively "discharged" by the employer but had voluntarily terminated his employment. Did the state's denial of unemployment benefits to Thomas violate the free exercise clause of the First Amendment? Explain. (See *Business and the Bill of Rights.*)

2–2. Spotlight on Plagiarism—Due Process. The Russ College of Engineering and Technology of Ohio University announced in a press conference that it had found "rampant and flagrant plagiarism" in the theses of mechanical engineering graduate students. Faculty singled out for "ignoring their ethical responsibilities" included Jay Gunasekera, chair of the department. Gunasekera was prohibited from advising students. He filed a suit against Dennis Irwin, the dean of Russ College, for violating his due process rights. What does due process require in these circumstances? Why? [*Gunasekera v. Irwin*, 551 F.3d 461 (6th Cir. 2009)] (See *Due Process and Equal Protection.*)

2–3. Business Case Problem with Sample Answer—Freedom of Speech. Mark Wooden sent an e-mail to an alderwoman for the city of St. Louis. Attached was a nineteen-minute audio that compared her to the biblical character Jezebel—she was a "bitch in the Sixth Ward," spending too much time with the rich and powerful and too little time with the poor. In a menacing, maniacal tone, Wooden said that he was "dusting off a sawed-off shotgun," called himself a "domestic terrorist," and referred to the assassination of President John F. Kennedy, the murder of a federal judge, and the shooting of Congresswoman Gabrielle Giffords. Feeling threatened, the alderwoman called the police. Wooden was convicted of harassment under a state criminal statute. Was this conviction unconstitutional under the First Amendment? Discuss. [*State of Missouri v. Wooden*, 388 S.W.3d 522 (Mo. 2013)] (See *Business and the Bill of Rights.*)

—For a sample answer to Problem 2-3, go to Appendix E.

2–4. Equal Protection. Abbott Laboratories licensed SmithKline Beecham Corp. to market an Abbott human immunodeficiency virus (HIV) drug in conjunction with one of SmithKline's drugs. Abbott then increased the price of its drug fourfold, forcing SmithKline to increase its prices and thereby driving business to Abbott's own combination drug. SmithKline filed a suit in a federal district court against Abbott. During jury selection, Abbott struck the only self-identified gay person among the potential jurors. (The pricing of HIV drugs is of considerable concern in the gay community.) Could the equal protection clause be applied to prohibit discrimination based on sexual orientation in jury selection? Discuss. [*SmithKline Beecham Corp. v. Abbott Laboratories*, 740 F.3d 471 (9th Cir. 2014)] (See *Due Process and Equal Protection.*)

2–5. Procedural Due Process. Robert Brown applied for admission to the University of Kansas School of Law. Brown answered "no" to questions on the application asking if he had a criminal history and acknowledged that a false answer constituted "cause for . . . dismissal." In fact, Brown had criminal convictions for domestic battery and driving under the influence. He was accepted for admission to the school. When school officials discovered his history, however, he was notified of their intent to dismiss him and given an opportunity to respond in writing. He demanded a hearing. The officials refused to grant Brown a hearing and then expelled him. Did the school's actions deny Brown due process? Discuss. [*Brown v. University of Kansas*, 599 Fed.Appx. 833 (10th Cir. 2015)] (See *Due Process and Equal Protection.*)

2–6. The Commerce Clause. Regency Transportation, Inc., operates a freight business throughout the eastern United States. Regency maintains its corporate headquarters, four warehouses, and a maintenance facility and terminal location for repairing and storing vehicles in Massachusetts. All of the vehicles in Regency's fleet were bought in other states. Massachusetts imposes a use tax on all taxpayers subject to its jurisdiction, including those that do business in interstate commerce, as Regency does. When Massachusetts imposed the tax on the purchase price of each tractor and trailer in Regency's fleet, the trucking firm challenged the assessment as discriminatory under the commerce clause. What is the chief consideration under the commerce clause when a state law affects interstate commerce? Is Massachusetts's use tax valid? Explain. [*Regency Transportation, Inc. v. Commissioner of Revenue*, 473 Mass. 459, 42 N.E.3d 1133 (2016)] (See *The Constitutional Powers of Government.*)

2–7. Freedom of Speech. Wandering Dago, Inc. (WD) operates a food truck in Albany, New York. WD brands itself and the food it sells with language generally viewed as ethnic slurs. Owners Andrea Loguidice and Brandon Snooks, however, view the branding as giving a "nod to their Italian heritage" and "weakening the derogatory force of the slur." Twice, WD applied to participate as a vendor in a summer lunch program in a state-owned plaza. Both times, the New York State Office of General Services (OGS) denied the application because of WD's branding. WD filed a suit in a federal district court against RoAnn Destito, the commissioner of OGS, contending that the agency had violated WD's right to free speech. What principles apply to the government's regulation of the content of speech? How do those principles apply in WD's case? Explain. [*Wandering Dago, Inc. v. Destito*, 879 F.3d 20 (2d Cir. 2018)] (See *Business and the Bill of Rights.*)

2–8. A Question of Ethics—Free Speech. Michael Mayfield, the president of Mendo Mill and Lumber Co., in California, received a "notice of a legal claim" from Edward Starski. The "claim" alleged that a stack of lumber had fallen on a customer as a result of a Mendo employee's "incompetence." The "notice" presented a settlement offer on the customer's behalf in exchange for a release of liability for Mendo. In a follow-up phone conversation with Mayfield, Starski said that he was an attorney—which, in fact, he was not. Starski was arrested and charged with violating a state criminal statute that prohibited the unauthorized practice of law. [*People v. Starski*, 7 Cal.App.5th 215, 212 Cal. Rptr.3d 622 (1 Dist. Div. 2 2017)] (See *Business and the Bill of Rights.*)

1. Starski argued that "creating an illusion" that he was an attorney was protected by the First Amendment. Is Starski correct? Explain.
2. Identify, discuss, and resolve the conflict between the right to free speech and the government's regulation of the practice of law.

Critical Thinking and Writing Assignments

2–9. Business Law Writing. Puerto Rico enacted a law that required specific labels on cement sold in Puerto Rico and imposed fines for any violations of these requirements. The law prohibited the sale or distribution of cement manufactured outside Puerto Rico that does not carry a required label warning and barred that cement from being used in government-financed construction projects.

Antilles Cement Corp., a Puerto Rican firm that imports foreign cement, filed a complaint in federal court. Antilles claimed that this law violated the dormant commerce clause. (The dormant commerce clause doctrine applies not only to commerce among the states and U.S. territories, but also to international commerce.) Write three paragraphs discussing whether the Puerto Rican law violates the dormant commerce clause. Explain your reasons. (See *The Constitutional Powers of Government.*)

2–10. Time-Limited Group Assignment—Free Speech and Equal Protection. For many years, New York City has had to deal with the vandalism and defacement of public property caused by unauthorized graffiti. In an effort to stop the damage, the city banned the sale of aerosol spray-paint cans and broad-tipped indelible markers to persons under twenty-one years of age. The new rules also prohibited people from possessing these items on property other than their own. Within a year, five people under age twenty-one were cited for violations of these regulations, and nearly nine hundred individuals were arrested for actually making graffiti.

Lindsey Vincenty and other artists wished to create graffiti on legal surfaces, such as canvas, wood, and clothing. Unable to buy supplies in the city or to carry them in the city if they were bought elsewhere, Vincenty and others filed a lawsuit on behalf of themselves and other young artists against Michael Bloomberg, the city's mayor, and others. The plaintiffs claimed that, among other things, the new rules violated their right to freedom of speech. (See *The Constitutional Powers of Government.*)

1. One group will argue in favor of the plaintiffs and provide several reasons why the court should hold that the city's new rules violate the plaintiffs' freedom of speech.
2. Another group will develop a counterargument that outlines the reasons why the new rules do not violate free speech rights.
3. A third group will argue that the city's ban violates the equal protection clause because it applies only to persons under age twenty-one.

3D generator/Shutterstock.com

3 Ethics in Business

Focus Questions

The five *Focus Questions* below are designed to help improve your understanding. After reading this chapter, you should be able to answer the following questions:

1. What are two different views of the role of business in society?
2. How do duty-based ethical standards differ from outcome-based ethical standards?
3. What is short-term profit maximization, and why does it lead to ethical problems?
4. What are the four steps in the IDDR approach to ethical decision making?
5. What ethical issues might arise in the context of global business transactions?

"New occasions teach new duties."

James Russell Lowell
1819–1891 (American editor, poet, and diplomat)

One of the most complex issues that businesspersons and corporations face is ethics. Ethics is not as clearly defined as the law, and yet it can substantially impact a firm's finances and reputation, especially when the firm is involved in a well-publicized scandal. Some scandals arise from conduct that is legal but ethically questionable. At other times, the conduct is both illegal and unethical. Business law and legal environment students must be able to think critically about both legal and ethical issues. As noted in the chapter-opening quotation, "New occasions teach new duties."

Suppose that Finn dropped out of Harvard University to start a company in Silicon Valley that developed and sold finger-prick blood-test kits. Finn raised millions from investors by claiming that his new technology would revolutionize blood testing by providing a full range of laboratory tests from a few drops of blood. The kits were marketed as a better alternative to traditional, more expensive lab tests ordered by physicians. They were sold at drugstores for a few dollars each and touted as a way for consumers to test their blood type and monitor their cholesterol, iron, and many other conditions. Within six years, Finn and his company were making millions. But complaints started rolling in that the test kits didn't work and the results were not accurate (because more blood was needed). Numerous consumers, drugstores, and government agencies sued the company for fraudulent and misleading marketing practices. Finn's profitable start-up now faces an uncertain future.

The goal of business ethics is not to stifle innovation. There is nothing unethical about a company selling an idea or technology that is still being developed. In fact, that's exactly what many successful start-ups do—take a promising idea and develop it into a reality. But businesspersons also need to consider what will happen if new technologies do not work. Do they go ahead with production and sales? What are the ethical problems with putting a product on the market that does not function as advertised? To be sure, there is not always one clear answer to an ethical question. What is clear is that rushing to production and not thinking through the ethical ramifications of decisions can be disastrous for a business.

3–1 Ethics and the Role of Business

Ethics Moral principles and values applied to social behavior.

At the most basic level, the study of **ethics** is the study of what constitutes right or wrong behavior. It is a branch of philosophy focusing on morality and the way moral principles are derived and implemented. Ethics has to do with the fairness, justness, rightness, or wrongness of an action.

Business Ethics The application of moral principles and values in a business context.

The study of **business ethics** typically looks at the decisions businesses make or have to make and whether those decisions are right or wrong. It has to do with how businesspersons apply moral principles in making their decisions. Those who study business ethics also evaluate what duties and responsibilities exist or should exist for businesses.

In this textbook, we include *Ethical Issues* in most chapters to emphasize the importance of ethics in business law. In addition, at the end of every chapter is a case problem, called *A Question of Ethics*, that relates to that chapter's contents.

3–1a The Relationship of Law and Ethics

The government has institutionalized some ethical rights and duties through the passage of laws and regulations. Many laws are designed to prevent fraudulent (misleading, deceptive) conduct in various contexts, including contracts, health care, financial reporting, mortgages, and sales. **Example 3.1** The Fraud Reduction and Data Analytics Act was passed by Congress in 2016 to identify and assess fraud risks in federal government agencies. The purpose of the law is to prevent, detect, and respond to fraud (including improper payments) in federal programs. ■ (This chapter's *Business Web Log* feature outlines a well-publicized fraud scandal.)

Sometimes, major legislation is passed after well-publicized ethical transgressions by industries or companies result in harm to the public. **Example 3.2** After alleged ethical lapses on Wall Street contributed to a financial crisis, Congress passed the Dodd-Frank Wall Street Reform and Consumer Protection Act.[1] Dodd-Frank made sweeping changes to the United States' financial regulatory environment in an attempt to promote financial stability and protect consumers from abusive financial services practices.

Similarly, Congress enacted the Sarbanes-Oxley Act[2] (SOX) after Enron, a major energy company, engaged in risky financial maneuvers that resulted in the loss of billions of dollars to shareholders. SOX was designed to help reduce corporate fraud and unethical management decisions by setting up accountability measures for publicly traded companies. Company heads must verify that they have read quarterly and annual reports and vouch for their accuracy. SOX also requires companies to set up confidential systems so that employees and others can "raise red flags" about suspected illegal or unethical auditing and accounting practices.[3] Laws cannot, however, codify all ethical requirements. ■

Gray Areas in the Law For a number of reasons, laws may sometimes be difficult to interpret and apply. When legislatures draft laws, they typically use broad language so that the provisions will apply in a variety of circumstances. It can be hard to determine how such broad provisions apply to specific situations. In addition, laws intended to address one situation may apply to other situations as well. And the legislative body that passes a law may not give clear guidance on the purpose of the law or the definition of terms in the law.

1. Pub. L. No. 111–203, 124 Stat. 1376, July 21, 2010, 12 U.S.C. Sections 5301 *et seq.*
2. 15 U.S.C. Sections 7201 *et seq.*
3. In one such system, employees can click on an on-screen icon that anonymously links them with NAVEX Global to report suspicious accounting practices, sexual harassment, and other possibly unethical behavior.

Business Web Log

Bogus Bank and Credit Card Accounts at Wells Fargo Bank

Wells Fargo Bank discovered that its employees had opened 2 million fake bank and credit card accounts for current customers without their authorization. The scam occurred over a period of five years. The bogus accounts generated extra fees for the bank and helped employees artificially inflate their sales figures to meet company goals and earn bonuses.

Wells Fargo fired 5,300 employees who were involved, paid $185 million in fines to the government, and refunded $5 million to customers. No executives were terminated initially, but the bank later fired four mid-level executives, and took stock awards and bonuses away from four other executives. Wells Fargo's accreditation rating with the Better Business Bureau dropped, and a number of state and local governments (as well as consumers) pulled their business from the bank. After an internal investigation, Wells Fargo announced that it would take back an additional $75 million in compensation from two top executives.

Angry customers filed lawsuits against Wells Fargo alleging fraud, invasion of privacy, negligence, and breach of contract. They claimed that Wells Fargo managers had acted unethically and pushed employees into committing fraud by requiring them to meet unreasonably high sales quotas. Federal and state governments and agencies continued to investigate the wrongdoing. Eventually, federal government regulators decided on an additional punishment: Until Wells Fargo makes significant improvements in its risk management and overall governance, the bank will operate under an "asset cap." That is, its growth will be limited by regulators.

Key Point

- *The employees' conduct was both unethical and illegal, but Wells Fargo's managers may not have acted illegally (assuming that they had no knowledge of the fraud). Nonetheless, management may have acted unethically by fostering a culture that encouraged questionable, and even illegal, sales practices. Not all unethical conduct is illegal.*

Know This: When it is not entirely clear how a law applies, a company's best defense to allegations of misconduct is to show that the firm acted honestly and responsibly under the circumstances.

Moral Minimum The minimum level of ethical behavior expected by society, which is usually defined as compliance with the law.

Other issues arise because laws are created through the political process. They therefore often involve compromises among competing interests and industries. As a result, a law's provisions may be ambiguous, may be weaker than intended by the original drafters, or may lack a means of enforcement. In short, the law is not always clear, and these "gray areas" in the law make it difficult to predict with certainty how a court will apply a given law to a particular action.

The Moral Minimum Compliance with the law is sometimes called the **moral minimum**. If people and entities merely comply with the law, they are acting at the lowest ethical level that society will tolerate.

Failure to meet the moral minimum can have significant consequences, especially in the context of litigation. A businessperson who fails to respond to a lawsuit can be held liable. **Case Example 3.3** Rick Scott deposited $2 million into an escrow account maintained by a company owned by Salvatore Carpanzano. Immediately after the deposit was made, the funds were withdrawn in violation of the escrow agreement. When Scott was unable to recover his money, he filed a suit against Salvatore Carpanzano and others. Salvatore failed to cooperate with discovery and did not respond to attempts to contact him by certified mail, regular mail, and e-mail. He also refused to make an appearance in court and did not finalize a settlement negotiated between the parties' attorneys. The court found that the defendant had intentionally failed to respond to the litigation and issued a judgment for more than $6 million in Scott's favor. On appeal, a federal appellate court affirmed the district court's judgment against Salvatore.[4]

4. *Scott v. Carpanzano,* 556 Fed.Appx. 288 (5th Cir. 2014).

Although the moral minimum is important, the study of ethics goes well beyond these legal requirements to evaluate what is right for society. *Businesspersons must remember that an action that is legal is not necessarily ethical.* For instance, a company can legally refuse to negotiate liability claims for injuries allegedly caused by a faulty product. But if the company's refusal is meant to increase the injured party's legal costs and force the party to drop a legitimate claim, the company is not acting ethically.

Private Company Codes of Ethics Most companies attempt to link ethics and law through the creation of internal codes of ethics. (We present the code of ethics of Costco Wholesale Corporation as an example in the appendix following this chapter.) Company codes are not laws. Instead, they are rules that the company sets forth and that it can enforce (by terminating an employee who does not follow them, for instance). Codes of conduct typically outline the company's policies on particular issues and indicate how employees are expected to act.

Example 3.4 Google's code of conduct starts with the motto "Don't be evil." The code then makes general statements about how Google promotes integrity, mutual respect, and the highest standard of ethical business conduct. Google's code also provides specific rules on a number of issues, such as privacy, drugs and alcohol, conflicts of interest, co-worker relationships, and confidentiality—it even includes a dog policy. The company takes a stand against employment discrimination that goes further than the law requires. It prohibits discrimination based on sexual orientation, gender identity or expression, and veteran status.

Industry Ethical Codes Numerous industries have also developed codes of ethics. The American Institute of Certified Public Accountants (AICPA) has a comprehensive Code of Professional Conduct for the ethical practicing of accounting. The American Bar Association (ABA) has model rules of professional conduct for attorneys, and the American Nurses Association (ANA) has a code of ethics that applies to nurses. These codes can give guidance to decision makers facing ethical questions. Violation of a code may result in the discipline of an employee or sanctions against a company from the industry organization. Remember, though, that these internal codes are not laws, so their effectiveness is determined by the commitment of the industry or company leadership to enforcing the codes.

3–1b The Role of Business in Society

Focus Question 1

What are two different views of the role of business in society?

Over the last two hundred years, public perception has moved toward expecting corporations to participate in society as corporate citizens. Originally, though, the only perceived duty of a corporation was to maximize profits and generate revenues for its owners. Although many people today may view this idea as greedy or ruthless, the rationale for the profit-maximization theory is still valid.

Business as a Pure Profit Maximizer In theory, if all firms strictly adhere to the goal of maximizing profits, resources flow to where they are most highly valued by society. Corporations can focus on their strengths. Other entities that are better suited to deal with social problems and perform charitable acts can specialize in those activities. The government, through taxes and other financial allocations, can shift resources to those other entities to perform public services. Thus, profit maximization can lead to the most efficient allocation of scarce resources.

Even when profit maximization is the goal, companies benefit by behaving ethically. For instance, customer satisfaction with a company is key to its profitability. Repeat customers are good for business. When customers are happy, word gets around, and it generates more business for the firm. Unsatisfied customers go elsewhere for the goods or services that the firm provides. When a business behaves badly, customers quickly report this online by posting bad reviews on such sites as Angie's List, Yelp, and TripAdvisor. Bad reviews obviously hurt a business's profits, while good reviews lead to higher profits.

Business as a Corporate Citizen Over the years, many people became dissatisfied with profit-maximization theory. Investors and others began to look beyond profits and dividends and to consider the **triple bottom line**—a corporation's profits, its impact on people, and its impact on the planet. Magazines and websites began to rank companies based on their environmental impacts and their ethical decisions. Corporations came to be viewed as "citizens" that were expected to participate in bettering communities and society.

Triple Bottom Line A measure that includes a corporation's profits, its impact on people, and its impact on the planet.

A Four-Part Analysis Whether one believes in profit-maximization theory or corporate citizenship, ethics is important in business decision making. When making decisions, a business should evaluate each of the following:

1. The legal implications of each decision.
2. The public relations impact.
3. The safety risks for consumers and employees.
4. The financial implications.

This four-part analysis will assist the firm in making decisions that not only maximize profits but also reflect good corporate citizenship.

3–1c Ethical Issues in Business

Ethical issues can arise in numerous aspects of doing business. A fundamental ethical issue for business is developing integrity and trust. Businesspersons should exhibit integrity in their dealings with other people in the company, other businesses, clients, and the community. By being honest and treating people fairly, businesspersons will earn their trust.

Businesses should also ensure that the workplace respects diversity and enforces equal opportunity employment and civil rights laws. In addition, businesses must comply with a host of federal and state laws and regulations, including those pertaining to the environment, financial reporting, and safety standards. Compliance with these rules can involve ethical issues. See this chapter's *Adapting the Law to the Online Environment* feature for a discussion of an ethical issue that has arisen from employees' work-related use of digital technology after work hours.

Should Employees Have a "Right of Disconnecting"?

Adapting the Law to the Online Environment

Almost all jobs today involve digital technology, whether it be e-mails, Internet access, or smartphone use. Most employees, when interviewed, say that digital technology increases their productivity and flexibility. The downside is what some call an "electronic leash"— employees are constantly connected and therefore end up working when they are not "at work." Over one-third of full-time workers, for example, say that they frequently check e-mails outside normal working hours.

Do Workers Have the Right to Disconnect?

Because the boundaries between being "at work" and being "at leisure" can be so hazy, some labor unions in other countries have attempted to pass rules that allow employees to disconnect from e-mail and other work-related digital communication during nonworking hours. For example, a French labor union representing high-tech workers signed an agreement with a large business association recognizing a "right of disconnecting."

In Germany, Volkswagen and BMW no longer forward e-mail to staff from company servers after the end of the working day. Other German firms have declared that workers are not expected to check e-mail on weekends and holidays. The government is considering legislating such restrictions nationwide.

The Thorny Issue of Overtime and the Fair Labor Standards Act

In the United States, payment for overtime work is strictly regulated under the Fair Labor Standards Act (FLSA). According to the Supreme Court, in this context, *work* is "physical or mental exertion (whether burdensome or not) controlled or required by the employer and pursued necessarily for the benefit of the employer and his business."[a] This definition was extended to off-duty work if such work is an "integral and indispensible part of [employees'] activities."[b] For example, a court ruled that Hormel Foods Corporation had to pay its factory workers for the time it took them to change into and out of the required white clothes before and after their shifts.[c]

Today's modern digital connectivity raises issues about the definition of *work*. Employees at several major companies, including Black & Decker, T-Mobile, and Verizon, have sued for unpaid overtime related to smartphone use. In another case, a police sergeant sued the city of Chicago, claiming that he should have been paid overtime for hours spent using his personal digital assistant (PDA). The police department had issued PDAs to officers and required them to respond to work-related communications even while off duty. The court agreed that some of the officers' off-duty PDA activities were compensable. Nevertheless, it ruled in favor of the city because the officers had failed to follow proper procedures for filing overtime claims.[d]

Not All Employees Demand the "Right to Disconnect"

In one Gallup poll, 79 percent of full-time employees had either strongly positive or somewhat positive views of using computers, e-mail, tablets, and smartphones to work remotely outside of normal business hours. According to the same poll, 17 percent of them report "better overall lives" because of constant online connectivity with their work. Working remotely after business hours apparently does not necessarily result in additional work-related stress.

Critical Thinking

From an ethical point of view, is there any difference between calling subordinates during off hours for work-related questions and sending them e-mails or text messages?

a. *Tennessee Coal, Iron & R. Co. v. Muscoda Local No. 123*, 321 U.S. 590, 64 S.Ct. 698, 8 L.Ed. 949 (1944). Although Congress later passed a statute that superseded the holding in this case, the statute gave the courts broad authority to interpret the FLSA's definition of *work*. 29 U.S.C. Section 251(a). See *Integrity Staffing Solutions, Inc. v. Busk*, 574 U.S. 27, 135 S.Ct. 513, 190 L.Ed.2d 410 (2014).

b. *Steiner v. Mitchell*, 350 U.S. 247, 76 S.Ct. 330, 100 L.Ed. 267 (1956).

c. *United Food & Commercial Workers Union, Local 1473 v. Hormel Food Corp.*, 367 Wis.2d 131, 876 N.W.2d 99 (2016).

d. *Allen v. City of Chicago*, 865 F.3d 167 (7th Cir. 2017).

The most difficult aspect of ethics that businesses face is in decision making, which is the focus of this text. Businesspersons must learn to recognize ethical issues, get the pertinent facts, evaluate the alternatives, and then make a decision. Decision makers should also test and reflect on the outcome of their decisions.

3–1d The Importance of Ethical Leadership

In ethics, as in other areas, employees take their cues from management. Talking about ethical business decision making is meaningless if management does not set standards. Furthermore, managers must apply the same standards to themselves as they do to the company's employees. This duty starts with top management.

Attitude of Top Management One of the most important ways to create and maintain an ethical workplace is for top management to demonstrate its commitment to ethical decision making. A manager who is not totally committed to an ethical workplace will rarely succeed in creating one. More than anything else, top management's behavior sets the ethical tone of a firm.

Managers have found that discharging even one employee for ethical reasons has a tremendous impact as a deterrent to unethical behavior in the workplace. This is true even if the company has a written code of ethics. If management does not enforce the company code, the code is essentially nonexistent.

The administration of a university may have had this concept in mind in the following case when it applied the school's professionalism standard to a student who had engaged in serious misconduct.

Know This: One of the best ways to encourage good business ethics at a workplace is to take immediate corrective action in response to any unethical conduct.

Case 3.1

Al-Dabagh v. Case Western Reserve University

United States Court of Appeals, Sixth Circuit, 777 F.3d 355 (2015).

Facts The curriculum at Case Western Reserve University School of Medicine identifies nine "core competencies." At the top of the list is professionalism, which includes "ethical, honest, responsible and reliable behavior." The university's Committee on Students determines whether a student has met the professionalism requirements. Amir Al-Dabagh enrolled at the school and did well academically. But he sexually harassed fellow students, often asked an instructor not to mark him late for class, received complaints from hospital staff about his demeanor, and was convicted of driving while intoxicated. The Committee on Students unanimously refused to certify him for graduation and dismissed him from the university. He filed a suit in a federal district court against Case Western, alleging a breach of good faith and fair dealing. The court ordered the school to issue a diploma. Case Western appealed.

ARLOU_ANDREI/Shutterstock.com

Under what circumstances can a medical school withhold a diploma from one of its students?

Issue Should a court defer to a university's determination that a student lacks the professionalism required to graduate?

Decision Yes. The U.S. Court of Appeals for the Sixth Circuit reversed the lower court's order to issue a diploma. The appellate court found nothing to indicate that Case Western had "impermissible motives," acted in bad faith, or dealt unfairly with Al-Dabagh.

Reason The Committee on Students' refusal to approve Al-Dabagh for graduation was an academic judgment. The court explained that it would overturn such a decision only if it substantially departed from accepted academic norms. There was nothing to indicate that such a departure occurred in Al-Dabagh's case. The plaintiff argued that the committee's decision was a "punitive disciplinary measure" unrelated to academics. But Case Western placed a high value on professionalism in the school's *academic* curriculum. Al-Dabagh also argued that the university defined professionalism too broadly and that it should be linked only to test scores and similar academic performance. "That is not how we see it or for that matter how the medical school sees it. . . . Our own standards indicate that professionalism does not end at the courtroom door. Why should hospitals operate any differently?"

Critical Thinking

- **What If the Facts Were Different?** *Suppose that Case Western had tolerated Al-Dabagh's conduct and awarded him a diploma. What impact might that have had on other students at the school? Why?*

Unrealistic Goals for Employees Certain types of behavior on the part of managers and owners contribute to unethical behavior among employees. Managers who set unrealistic production or sales goals increase the probability that employees will act unethically. If a sales quota can be met only through high-pressure, unethical sales tactics, employees will try to act "in the best interest of the company" and behave unethically. Managers who look the other way when they know about employees' unethical behavior also set an example—one indicating that ethical transgressions will be accepted.

Note that even when large companies have policies against sales incentives, individual branches may still promote them. **Case Example 3.5** The financial firm Morgan Stanley Smith Barney, LLC, has an internal policy barring sales contests. Nevertheless, Morgan Stanley branches in Massachusetts and Rhode Island held a sales contest in which brokers were given cash incentives of up to $5,000 for selling securities-based loans, or SBLs (loans that allow clients to borrow against their investments). Thirty financial advisers participated in the sales contest for almost a year until Morgan Stanley's compliance office noticed and halted the practice. One regional branch reportedly tripled its loans as a result of the contest. Eventually, Morgan Stanley paid a $1 million fine to the state of Massachusetts for, among other things, violating state securities rules and "failing to observe high standards of commercial honor."[5]

Fostering of Unethical Conduct Business owners and managers sometimes take more active roles in fostering unethical and illegal conduct, with negative consequences for their businesses. **Case Example 3.6** Rachel Maddox purchased a home on a hillside in Nashville. After heavy rains, Maddox noticed cracks in the basement. She also noticed that if a tennis ball was placed on the floor, it would roll toward the front of the house. Maddox contacted Olshan Foundation Repair and Waterproofing Co., who sent Kevin Hayman to inspect her property. Hayman—described on work orders as a "certified structural technician"—suggested $27,000 of repairs. Maddox agreed, in part because of Olshan's promise of a lifetime warranty.

Several years later, further rain caused new cracks in the foundation of the house, which had again begun to tilt. After several unsuccessful attempts to correct these problems, Olshan employees stopped coming to the property or returning Maddox's calls. An independent engineer told Maddox that Olshan's "repairs" had made the house foundation issues worse. Eventually, a local building inspector noted that the house appeared to be "sliding off the hill" and was unsafe for inhabitation. Maddox sued Olshan for fraud. At trial, a company executive admitted that Hayman's "certification" was based on a three-week course administered by the company. The court awarded Maddox $187,000 for the fair market value of her home, plus $15,000 in punitive damages because of Olshan's egregiously unethical behavior. This judgment was affirmed on appeal.[6]

3–2 Ethical Principles and Philosophies

How do business decision makers decide whether a given action is the "right" one for their firms? What ethical standards should be applied? Broadly speaking, **ethical reasoning**—the application of moral convictions or ethical standards to a situation—applies to businesses just as it does to individuals. As businesses make decisions, they must analyze the alternatives in a variety of ways, one of which is from an ethical perspective. In analyzing alternatives in this way, businesses may take one of two approaches.

Generally, the study of ethics is divided into two major categories—duty-based ethics and outcome-based ethics. **Duty-based ethics** is rooted in the idea that every person (and business) has certain duties to others, including humans and the planet. **Outcome-based ethics** determines what is ethical by looking at the consequences, or outcomes, of any given action. Most companies have written codes or policies that outline their approach to ethics.

Focus Question 2

How do duty-based ethical standards differ from outcome-based ethical standards?

Ethical Reasoning A reasoning process in which individuals link their moral convictions or ethical standards to the situation at hand.

Duty-Based Ethics An ethical philosophy rooted in the idea that every person (and every business) has certain duties to others, including both humans and the planet.

Outcome-Based Ethics An ethical philosophy that focuses on the consequences of any given action in order to maximize benefits and minimize harms.

3–2a Duty-Based Ethics

Duty-based ethics focuses on the obligations of the corporation. It deals with standards for behavior that traditionally were derived from revealed truths, religious authorities, and philosophical reasoning. These standards involve concepts of right and wrong, duties owed, and rights to be protected. Corporations today often describe these values or duties in their mission statements or strategic plans. Some companies base their statements on a nonreligious rationale. Others derive their values from religious doctrine.

Religious Ethical Principles Nearly every religion has principles or beliefs about how one should treat others. In the Judeo-Christian tradition, which is the dominant religious tradition in the United States, the Ten Commandments of the Old Testament establish these

5. *In re Morgan Stanley Smith Barney, LLC*, Docket No. E-2016-0055. www.sec.state.ma.us. 10 April 2017. Web.
6. *Maddox v Olshan Foundation Repair and Waterproofing Co. of Nashville, L.P.*, 2019 WL 4464816 (Tenn. Ct. App. 2019).

How can religious beliefs complicate or enhance a business owner's operations and decisions?

fundamental rules for moral action. The principles of the Muslim faith are set out in the Qur'an, and Hindus find their principles in the four Vedas.

Religious rules generally are absolute with respect to the behavior of their adherents. **Example 3.7** The commandment "Thou shalt not steal" is an absolute mandate for a person who believes that the Ten Commandments reflect revealed truth. Even a benevolent motive for stealing (such as Robin Hood's) cannot justify the act, because the act itself is inherently immoral and thus wrong. ■

For businesses, religious principles can be a unifying force for employees or a rallying point to increase employee motivation. They can also present problems, however, when owners, suppliers, employees, and customers have varying religious backgrounds. Taking an action based on religious principles, especially when those principles address socially or politically controversial topics, can lead to negative publicity and even to protests or boycotts.

Example 3.8 Bright Futures, a family-owned educational supply business in California, hires Jamie as a bookkeeper. When Jamie tells the owners that she is transgender, she is fired because of their religious beliefs. When Jamie's story is published in the local media, Bright Futures loses many customers. Eventually, Bright Futures closes down. ■

The Principle of Rights Another view of duty-based ethics focuses on basic rights. The principle that human beings have certain fundamental rights (to life, freedom, and the pursuit of happiness, for instance) is deeply embedded in Western culture. This view embraces the concept that certain actions (such as killing another person) are morally wrong because they violate the fundamental rights of others.

Principle of Rights The belief that human beings have certain fundamental rights.

Those who adhere to the **principle of rights**, or "rights theory," believe that a key factor in determining whether a business decision is ethical is how that decision affects the rights of others. These others include the firm's owners, its employees, the consumers of its products or services, its suppliers, the community in which it does business, and society as a whole.

Conflicting Rights. A potential dilemma for those who support rights theory is that they may disagree on which rights are most important. When considering all those affected by a business decision to downsize a firm, for instance, how much weight should be given to employees relative to shareholders? Which employees should be laid off first—those with the highest salaries or those who have worked for the firm for a shorter time (and have less seniority)? How should the firm weigh the rights of customers relative to the community, or of employees relative to society as a whole?

Resolving Conflicts. In general, rights theorists believe that whichever right is stronger in a particular circumstance takes precedence. **Example 3.9** Murray Chemical Corporation has to decide whether to keep a chemical plant in Utah open, thereby saving the jobs of a hundred and fifty workers, or shut it down. Closing the plant will prevent the contamination of a river with pollutants that would endanger the health of tens of thousands of people. In this situation, a rights theorist can easily choose which group to favor because the value of the right to health and well-being is obviously stronger than the basic right to work. Not all choices are so clear-cut, however. ■

Kantian Ethical Principles Duty-based ethical standards may be derived solely from philosophical reasoning. The German philosopher Immanuel Kant (1724–1804) identified some general guiding principles for moral behavior based on what he thought to be the fundamental nature of human beings. Kant believed that human beings are qualitatively different from other physical objects and are endowed with moral integrity and the capacity to reason and conduct their affairs rationally.

People Are Not a Means to an End. Based on his view of human beings, Kant said that when people are treated merely as a means to an end, they are being treated as the equivalent of objects and are being denied their basic humanity. For instance, a manager who treats subordinates as mere profit-making tools is less likely to retain motivated and loyal employees than a manager who respects subordinates. Management research has shown that employees who feel empowered to share their thoughts, opinions, and solutions to problems are happier and more productive.

The Categorical Imperative. When a business makes unethical decisions, it often rationalizes its actions by saying that the company is "just one small part" of the problem or that its decision would have "only a small impact." A central theme in Kantian ethics is that individuals should evaluate their actions in light of the consequences that would follow if everyone in society acted in the same way. This **categorical imperative** can be applied to any action.

Categorical Imperative An ethical guideline developed by Immanuel Kant under which an action is evaluated in terms of what would happen if everybody else in the same situation, or category, acted the same way.

Example 3.10 CHS Fertilizer is deciding whether to invest in expensive equipment that will decrease profits but will also reduce pollution from its factories. If CHS has adopted Kant's categorical imperative, the decision makers will consider the consequences if every company invested in the equipment (or if no company did so). If the result of purchasing the equipment would make the world a better place (less polluted), CHS's decision would be clear.

3–2b Outcome-Based Ethics: Utilitarianism

In contrast to duty-based ethics, outcome-based ethics focuses on the consequences of an action, not on the nature of the action itself or on any set of preestablished moral values or religious beliefs. Outcome-based ethics looks at the impacts of a decision in an attempt to maximize benefits and minimize harms.

The premier philosophical theory for outcome-based decision making is **utilitarianism**, a philosophical theory developed by Jeremy Bentham (1748–1832) and modified by John Stuart Mill (1806–1873)—both British philosophers. "The greatest good for the greatest number" is a paraphrase of the major premise of the utilitarian approach to ethics.

Utilitarianism An approach to ethical reasoning in which an action is evaluated in terms of its consequences for those whom it will affect. A "good" action is one that results in the greatest good for the greatest number of people.

Cost-Benefit Analysis

Under a utilitarian model of ethics, an action is morally correct, or "right," when, among the people it affects, it produces the greatest amount of good for the greatest number (or creates the least amount of harm). When an action affects the majority adversely, it is morally wrong. Applying the utilitarian theory thus requires the following steps:

1. A determination of which individuals will be affected by the action in question.
2. A **cost-benefit analysis**, which involves an assessment of the negative and positive effects of alternative actions on these individuals.
3. A choice among alternative actions that will produce maximum societal utility (the greatest positive net benefits for the greatest number of individuals).

Cost-Benefit Analysis A decision-making technique that involves weighing the costs of a given action against the benefits of that action.

For instance, assume that expanding a factory would provide hundreds of jobs but generate pollution that could endanger the lives of thousands of people. A utilitarian analysis would find that saving the lives of thousands creates greater good than providing jobs for hundreds.

Problems with the Utilitarian Approach

There are problems with a strict utilitarian analysis. In some situations, an action that produces the greatest good for the most people may not seem to be the most ethical.

Example 3.11 Phazim Company is producing a drug that will cure a disease in 99 percent of patients, but the other 1 percent will experience agonizing side effects and a horrible, painful death. A quick utilitarian analysis would suggest that the drug should be produced and marketed because the majority of patients will benefit. Many people, however, have significant concerns about manufacturing a drug that will cause serious harm to anyone. ■

3–2c Corporate Social Responsibility

In pairing duty-based concepts with outcome-based concepts, strategists and theorists developed the idea of the corporate citizen, which we touched on earlier, and the concept of corporate social responsibility. **Corporate social responsibility (CSR)** combines a commitment to good citizenship with a commitment to making ethical decisions, improving society, and minimizing environmental impact. CSR is not imposed on a corporation by law but is instead a form of self-regulation by the company.

Corporate Social Responsibility (CSR) The idea that corporations can and should act ethically and be accountable to society for their actions.

CSR is a relatively new concept in the history of business, but it is a concept that becomes more important every year. A survey of U.S. executives undertaken by the Boston College Center for Corporate Citizenship found that more than 70 percent of those polled agreed that corporate citizenship must be treated as a priority. More than 60 percent said that good corporate citizenship added to their companies' profits.

CSR can be a successful strategy for companies, but corporate decision makers must not lose track of the two descriptors in the title: *corporate* and *social*. The company must link the responsibility of citizenship with the strategy and key principles of the business. Incorporating both the social and the corporate components of CSR and making ethical decisions can help companies grow and prosper.

CSR is most successful when a company undertakes activities that are significant and related to its business operations. Some types of activities that businesses are practicing today include the following:

1. Environmental efforts, such as using efficient building materials and reducing the size of the firm's carbon footprint.
2. Ethical labor practices, including treating all employees fairly and ethically in international as well as domestic operations.
3. Charitable donations to local and national causes.
4. Volunteering for specific issues and organizations. As an incentive, many companies now pay employees to perform volunteer work.

Citizen of the Planet/Education Images/Universal Images Group/ Getty Images

What benefits are there to constructing a LEED-compliant office building?

The Corporate Aspects of CSR Arguably, any socially responsible activity will benefit a corporation. A corporation may see an increase in goodwill from the local community for creating a sports park, for instance. A corporation that is viewed as a good citizen may see a rise in sales. **Example 3.12** Sales have increased for Ben & Jerry's ice cream since the 1980s, when the company became known for its socially responsible business practices. The company uses only fair trade ingredients and opposes the use of growth hormones in cows. It promotes sustainability programs for dairy farmers and supports family farms. ■

At times, the benefit may not be immediate. It may cost more initially to construct a new plant that meets the high standards necessary to be certified as environmentally friendly by the LEED program, for example. (LEED stands for Leadership in Energy and Environmental Design.) Nevertheless, over the life of the building, the savings in maintenance and utilities may more than make up for the extra cost of construction.

Surveys of college students about to enter the job market confirm that young people are looking for socially responsible employers. While socially responsible activities may cost a corporation now, they may also lead to more talented and more committed employees. Corporations that engage in meaningful social activities retain workers longer, particularly younger ones. **Example 3.13** Google's focus on social responsibility attracts many young workers. Google has worked to reduce its carbon footprint and to make its products and services better for the environment. The company promotes green commuting, recycling, and reducing energy consumption at its data centers. ■

The Social Aspects of CSR Because business controls so much of the wealth and power in this country, it has a responsibility to use that wealth and power in socially beneficial ways. Thus, the social aspect requires that corporations demonstrate that they are promoting goals that society deems worthwhile and are moving toward solutions to social problems. Companies may be judged on how much they donate to social causes, as well as how they conduct their operations with respect to employment discrimination, human rights, environmental concerns, and similar issues. Millennials, in particular, are concerned about corporate social responsibility.

Some corporations publish annual social responsibility reports, which may also be called citizenship or sustainability reports. **Example 3.14** The multinational technology company Cisco Systems, Inc., issues corporate responsibility reports to demonstrate its focus on people, society, and the planet. In a recent report, Cisco outlined its commitment to developing its employees' skills, ethical conduct, and charitable donations (including matching employee contributions and giving employees time off for volunteer work). Cisco also reported on the social and economic impact of its business globally, in the areas of human rights, labor, privacy and data security, and responsible manufacturing. The report indicated that Cisco had completed more than a hundred energy-efficient projects and was on track to meet its goals of reducing emissions from its worldwide operations by 40 percent. ■

Stakeholders and CSR One view of CSR stresses that corporations have a duty not just to shareholders, but also to other groups affected by corporate decision making, called **stakeholders**. The rationale for this "stakeholder view" is that, in some circumstances, one or more of these groups may have a greater stake in company decisions than the shareholders do.

Stakeholders Groups that are affected by corporate decisions. Stakeholders include employees, customers, creditors, suppliers, and the community in which the corporation operates.

A corporation's stakeholders include its employees, customers, creditors, suppliers, and the community in which it operates. Advocacy groups, such as environmental groups and animal rights groups, may also be stakeholders. Under the stakeholder approach, a corporation considers the impact of its decision on these stakeholders, which helps it to avoid making a decision that may appear unethical and may result in negative publicity. In this chapter's *Managerial Strategy* feature, we take a closer look at an offshoot of CSR known as "stakeholder capitalism."

The most difficult aspect of the stakeholder analysis is determining which group's interests should receive greater weight if the interests conflict. For instance, companies that are struggling financially sometimes lay off workers to reduce labor costs. But some corporations have found ways to avoid slashing their workforces and to prioritize their employees' interests. Companies finding alternatives to layoffs include Dell (extended unpaid holidays), Cisco (four-day end-of-year shutdowns), Motorola (salary cuts), and Honda (voluntary unpaid vacation time). These alternatives not only benefit the employees who get to keep their jobs, but also the community as whole. Working people can afford to go out to local restaurants and shops and use local service providers. Thus, other businesses in the community benefit.

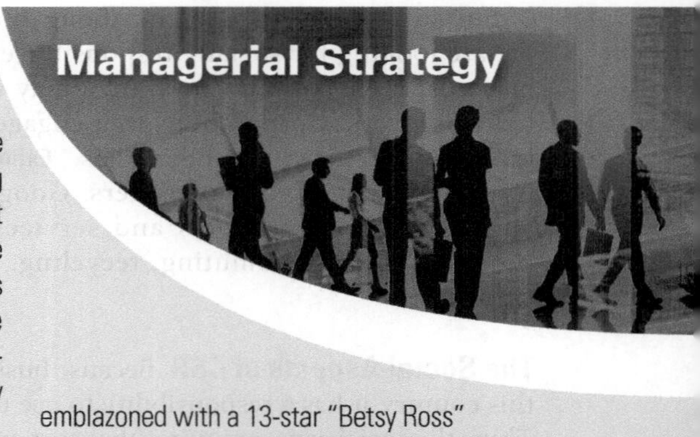

The Stakeholder Capitalism Movement

Fortune 500 companies are lining up help to fight climate change. PepsiCo has promised to cut carbon emissions from its business operations 20 percent by 2030. Amazon has pledged to become carbon neutral, with no emissions, by 2040. Not to be outdone, Microsoft has vowed to remove carbon from the atmosphere, erasing its entire "historical footprint" by 2050. These are examples of *stakeholder capitalism*, in which managers make decisions based not only on maximizing profits for investors, but also on contributing to the well-being of society.

Corporate Power

Managerial behavior impacts a wide array of stakeholders, as described in the text. Proponents of stakeholder capitalism believe that it is unethical to ignore these stakeholders in the corporate decision-making process, particularly given the benefits that corporations derive from operating in a stable society.

Critics of stakeholder capitalism point to some corporate laws that recognize the duty of directors, executives, and managers to act in the best interests of investors.[a] Managers, they say, should be hired because they are skilled at maximizing profits and minimizing losses, not at solving society's ills. "I don't want American capitalists [to define] the country's political and social values," says one executive. "I think the answers to these questions should be determined by the citizenry—publicly through debate and privately at the ballot box."

Star Power

The practical challenges of managerial activism are evident in Nike's decision to employ professional football player Colin Kaepernick as a commercial spokesperson. Kaepernick is a controversial figure because of his refusal to stand for the national anthem in protest of racial inequality. The day Nike announced his hiring, customers posted videos of themselves burning its products, and the company's stock price fell 3.17 percent.

Several years later, Kaepernick's comments caused Nike to recall a line of sneakers emblazoned with a 13-star "Betsy Ross" American flag, which he said was offensive because of its connections to the nation's slave era. Avoiding this kind of turmoil is what marketers had in mind when, in a poll, only one in five said it was appropriate for their brand to take a stance on politically charged issues.

Business Questions

1. *After a school shooting, Dick's Sporting Goods stopped selling certain firearms at its stores. What are the potential benefits and drawbacks of this form of corporate social responsibility?*
2. *Why might a state law require corporate managers to maximize company profits?*

a. See *eBay Domestic Holdings, Inc. v. Newmark*, 16 A.3d 1 (Court of Chancery of Delaware, 2010).

3–3 Sources of Ethical Issues in Business Decisions

A key to avoiding unethical conduct is to recognize how certain situations may lead individuals to act unethically. In this section, we first consider some specific areas in which ethical decisions may often arise. We then discuss some additional problems in making ethical business decisions.

Focus Question 3

What is short-term profit maximization, and why does it lead to ethical problems?

3–3a Short-Term Profit Maximization

Businesspersons often commit ethical violations because they are too focused on one issue or one needed result, such as increasing profits or outperforming the competition. Some studies indicate that top-performing companies may actually be more likely to behave unethically than less successful companies, because employees feel they are expected to continue performing at a high level. Thus, abnormally high profits and stock prices may lead to unethical behavior.

In attempting to maximize profits, corporate executives and employees have to distinguish between *short-run* and *long-run* profit maximization. In the short run, a company may increase its profits by continuing to sell a product even though it knows that the product is defective. In the long run, though, because of lawsuits, large settlements, and bad publicity, such unethical conduct will cause profits to suffer. An overemphasis on short-run profit maximization is perhaps the most common reason that ethical problems occur in business.

Case Example 3.15 Volkswagen's corporate executives were accused of cheating on the pollution emissions tests of millions of vehicles that were sold in the United States. Volkswagen (VW) eventually admitted that it had installed "defeat device" software in its diesel models. The software detected when the car was being tested and changed its performance to improve the test outcome. As a result, the diesel cars showed low emissions—a feature that made the cars more attractive to today's consumers.

Ultimately, Volkswagen agreed to plead guilty to criminal charges and pay $2.8 billion in fines. The company also agreed to pay $1.5 billion to the Environmental Protection Agency to settle the federal investigation into its "clean diesel" emissions fraud. Overall, the scandal has cost VW nearly $15 billion (in fines and to compensate consumers or buy back their vehicles). Even though the company has settled, six top executives at VW were charged with criminal wire fraud, conspiracy, and violations of the Clean Air Act. In the end, the company's focus on maximizing profits in the short run (with increased sales) led to unethical conduct that will hurt profits in the long run.[7]

In the following case, a drug manufacturer was accused of fabricating the "average wholesale prices" for its drugs to maximize its profits and receive an overpayment from Medicaid.

7. *In re Volkswagen "Clean Diesel" Marketing, Sales Practices, and Product Liability Litigation*, 229 F.Supp.3d 1052, 2017 WL 66281 (N.D.Cal. 2017).

Case 3.2

Watson Laboratories, Inc. v. State of Mississippi

Supreme Court of Mississippi, 241 So.3d 573, 2018 WL 372297 (2018).

Facts Watson Laboratories, Inc., makes generic drugs, which are provided by pharmacies to Medicaid patients. In the state of Mississippi, a claim is submitted for the cost of the drug to Mississippi Medicaid. The claim is paid according to a percentage of the drug's average wholesale price (AWP). Like other drug makers, Watson published its products' AWPs. But for more than a dozen years, Watson set each AWP to meet the requirements to obtain a generic designation for the drug, without regard to the actual price.

When Mississippi Medicaid learned that the actual prices were much lower than the published AWPs, the state filed a suit in a Mississippi state court against Watson. The court concluded that Watson caused the state to overpay for the drugs, and ordered the payment of more than $30 million in penalties, damages, and interest. Watson appealed.

Issue Did Watson commit fraud regarding the AWPs of its generic drugs?

Decision Yes. The Mississippi Supreme Court affirmed the lower court's order. Watson falsely misrepresented its AWPs, "knew that Mississippi Medicaid would rely on its false statements, and benefitted from this reliance."

Reason The elements of fraud are (1) the misrepresentation of facts with the knowledge that they are false, (2) an intent to induce another to rely on the misrepresentation, (3) justifiable reliance by the deceived party, (4) damage suffered as a result, and (5) a causal connection between the misrepresentation and the injury. The facts in this case established all of these elements. For years, Watson published AWPs that were fabricated numbers, knowing and intending that Mississippi Medicaid would rely on them to make its reimbursements. Mississippi Medicaid did not know that the numbers had no rational relationship to the actual prices and accepted the AWPs as a proper starting point for determining reimbursement rates. Evidence showed that determining reimbursements on this basis led to overpayment for the drugs in question. The evidence also supported the extent of the damage suffered at the expense of the taxpayers of the state of Mississippi.

Critical Thinking

- **Economic** *What marketing tool did Watson gain by inflating its AWPs?*
- **What If the Facts Were Different?** *Watson argued that AWP was a "term of art" in the pharmaceutical industry that meant "suggested price." Suppose that the court had accepted this argument. What might have been the effect of this decision?*

3–3b Social Media

Advancements in technology have created various new ethical issues for companies. Here, we focus on those involving social media. Most people think of social media—Facebook, Flickr, Instagram, Snapchat, Tumblr, Twitter, Pinterest, WhatsApp, LinkedIn, and the like—as simply ways to communicate rapidly. But everyone knows that they can quickly encounter ethical and legal disputes for posting statements that others interpret as harassing, inappropriate, insulting, or racist. Businesses often face ethical issues with respect to these social media platforms.

The Use of Social Media to Make Hiring Decisions In the past, to learn about a prospective employee, an employer would ask the candidate's former employers for references. Today, employers are likely to also conduct Internet searches to discover what job candidates have posted on their Facebook pages, blogs, and tweets.

On the one hand, job candidates may be judged by what they post on social media. On the other hand, though, they may be judged because they *do not participate* in social media. Given that the vast majority of younger people use social media, some employers have decided that the failure to do so raises a red flag. In either case, many people believe that judging job candidates based on what they do outside the work environment is unethical.

The Use of Social Media to Discuss Work-Related Issues Because so many Americans use social media daily, they often discuss work-related issues there. Numerous companies have strict guidelines about what is appropriate and inappropriate for employees to say when posting on their own or others' social media accounts. A number of companies have fired employees for such activities as criticizing other employees or managers through social media outlets. Until recently, such disciplinary measures were considered ethical and legal.

The Responsibility of Employers. A ruling by the National Labor Relations Board (NLRB—the federal agency that investigates unfair labor practices) has changed the legality of such actions. **Example 3.16** At one time, Costco's social media policy specified that its employees should not make statements that would damage the company, harm another person's reputation, or violate the company's policies. Employees who violated these rules were subject to discipline and could be fired.

The NLRB ruled that Costco's social media policy violated federal labor law, which protects employees' right to engage in "concerted activities." Employees can freely associate with each other and have conversations about common workplace issues without employer interference. This right extends to social media posts. Therefore, an employer cannot broadly prohibit its employees from criticizing the company or co-workers, supervisors, or managers via social media. ■

The Responsibility of Employees. While most of the discussion in this chapter concerns the ethics of business management, employee ethics is also an important issue. For instance, is it ethical for employees to make negative posts in social media about other employees or, more commonly, about managers? After all, negative comments about managers reflect badly on those managers, who often are reluctant to respond via social media to such criticism. Disgruntled employees may exaggerate the negative qualities of managers whom they do not like.

Some may consider the decision by the National Labor Relations Board outlined in *Example 3.16* to be too lenient toward employees and too stringent toward management. There is likely to be an ongoing debate about how to balance employees' right to free expression against employers' right to prevent the spreading of inaccurate negative statements online.

3–3c Awareness

Regardless of the context in which a decision is called for, sometimes businesspersons are not even aware that the decision has ethical implications. Perhaps they are focused on something else, for instance, or perhaps they do not take the time to think through their actions.

Case Example 3.17 Japanese airbag maker Takata Corporation manufactured some airbags that used an ammonium nitrate-based propellant without a chemical drying agent. It was later discovered that these airbags tended to deploy explosively, especially in higher temperatures, higher humidity, and older vehicles. When the airbags deployed, metal inflator cartridges inside them sometimes ruptured, sending metal shards into the passenger cabin.

lumen-digital/Shutterstock.com

Takata Corporation knew about its defective airbags, yet it continued to use them in production. How can business managers learn from Takata's situation?

By the beginning of 2017, these defective airbags had caused 11 deaths and 180 injuries in the United States. The federal government ordered recalls of the devices in nearly 42 million vehicles nationwide. Takata executives likely did not intend to hurt consumers and may not even have considered the ethics of their decision. Takata, however, continued to produce airbags with this defect for years. The company, which declared bankruptcy, agreed to pay $1 billion in fines and restitution and another $650 million to settle a class-action lawsuit that resulted from its actions.[8]

3–3d Rationalization

Sometimes, businesspersons make a decision that benefits them or their company that they know is ethically questionable. Afterward, they rationalize their bad behavior. For instance, a generally honest employee who normally does not steal might rationalize that it is acceptable to take company property for personal use or to lie to a client just this one time. An executive might rationalize that unethical conduct directed against a certain competitor is acceptable because that company deserves it. Individuals might rationalize that their conduct is simply a part of doing business and is not personal or unethical.

One suggestion that is useful in counteracting rationalization is for businesspersons to *first decide the right thing to do on an ethical level before making a business decision*. Then they can figure out how to mitigate the costs of doing the right thing. This works much better to prevent unethical conduct than making decisions based solely on a financial or business basis and then trying to make that result seem ethical (by rationalizing).

3–3e Uncertainty

One common denominator identified by businesspersons who have faced ethical problems is the feeling of uncertainty. They may be uncertain as to what they should do, what they should have done, or (as mentioned) whether there is even an ethical issue or ethical breach involved. Such uncertainty is practically unavoidable, but it should be treated as an indicator of a potential ethical problem.

When employees or executives express uncertainty about a particular decision, it is therefore best to treat the situation as involving an ethical issue. Decision makers should try to

8. *In re Takata Airbag Products Liability Litigation*, 255 F.Supp.3d 1241 (2017).

identify what the ethical dilemma is and why the individual or group is feeling uneasy. They should also take the time to think through the decision completely and discuss various options. They might want to consider whether the company would be pleased if the decision were reported to its clients or to the public. Building a process that supports and assists those facing ethical dilemmas can be key to avoiding unethical business practices (and any corresponding negative publicity).

3–4 Making Ethical Business Decisions

Even if officers, directors, and others in a company want to make ethical decisions, it is not always clear what is ethical in a given situation. Thinking beyond things that are easily measured, such as profits, can be challenging. Although profit projections are not always accurate, they may be more objective than considering the personal impacts of decisions on employees, shareholders, customers, and the community. But this subjective component of decision making can be equally important to a company's long-run profits.

Individuals entering the global corporate community, even in entry-level positions, must be prepared to make hard decisions. Sometimes, there is no "good" answer to the questions that arise. Therefore, it is important to have tools to help in the decision-making process and a framework for organizing those tools.

Several frameworks exist to help businesspersons make ethical decisions. Some frameworks, for instance, focus more on legal than ethical implications. This approach tends to be primarily outcome-based and, as such, may not be appropriate for a company that is values driven or committed to corporate social responsibility (or has a consumer or investor base that is focused on CSR). Other models, such as the Business Process Pragmatism™ procedure developed by ethics consultant Leonard H. Bucklin, set out a series of steps to follow. In this text, we present a modified version of this system that we call IDDR. ("I Desire to Do Right" is a useful mnemonic device for remembering the name.)

Focus Question 4
What are the four steps in the IDDR approach to ethical decision making?

3–4a A Systematic Approach: IDDR ("I Desire to Do Right")

Using the IDDR approach involves organizing the issues and approaching them systematically. This process can help eliminate various alternatives and identify the strengths and weaknesses of the remaining alternatives. Often, the best approach is for a group (rather than an individual) to carry out the process, which comprises the following steps. Thus, when individual employees face an ethical issue, they should talk with their supervisors, and then the parties should perform the following steps together.

Step 1: Inquiry The first step in making an ethical decision is to understand the problem. If an employee feels uneasy about a particular decision, decision makers should pay attention and ask questions. People generally know when something does not "feel" right, and this is often a good indicator that there may be an ethical problem. The decision makers must identify the ethical problem and all the parties involved—the stakeholders. It is important that they *not* frame the issue in a way that gives them the answer they might prefer. After gathering the relevant facts, the decision makers can also consider which ethical theories can help them analyze the problem thoroughly. Making a list of the ethical principles that will guide the decision may be helpful at this point.

Step 2: Discussion Once the ethical problem or problems have been clarified, a list of possible actions can be compiled. In discussing these alternatives, the decision makers should take time to think through each alternative completely and analyze its potential impact on various groups of stakeholders. They must evaluate the strengths and weaknesses of each option, along with its ethical and legal consequences. It is helpful to discuss with management the ultimate goals for the decision. At this point, too, the decision makers need to consider what they *should* do (what is the most ethical) before considering what they can or will do.

Step 3: Decision With all the relevant facts collected and the alternatives thoroughly analyzed and discussed, it's time to make a decision. Those participating in the decision-making process now work together to craft a consensus decision or plan of action for the company. Once the decision has been made, the decision makers should use the analysis from the discussion step to articulate the reasons they arrived at the decision. This results in documentation that can be shared with stakeholders to explain why the course of action is an ethical solution to the problem.

Step 4: Review After the decision has been made and implemented, it is important for the decision makers to review the outcome to determine whether the solution was effective. Did the action solve the ethical problem? Were the stakeholders satisfied with the result? Could anything have been handled better? The results of this evaluation can be used in making future decisions. Successful decision makers learn from their mistakes and continue to improve.

3–4b Applying the IDDR Approach—A Sample Scenario

To really understand the IDDR approach, it is helpful to work through the process by analyzing an ethical problem. Here, as a sample, we present a scenario that is based on a real story but contains fictional elements as well. The conversations and analyses included in the scenario are fictional. Because any discussions that may have happened took place behind closed doors, we cannot know if any ethical analysis or discussions about ethics occurred.

Example 3.18 Assume that you are an intern working on a social media campaign for Duane Reade, a New York pharmacy chain. As part of your internship, you follow several celebrity gossip Web pages and do regular Internet searches looking for any picture or mention of the stores. In the course of these searches, you find a picture of Katherine Heigl leaving a Duane Reade store carrying bags imprinted with the company logo. (Katherine Heigl is a recognizable actress from television's *Grey's Anatomy* and several major movies.) You can easily copy the picture to the company's Twitter account and add a caption about her shopping at one of the stores. Having customers or potential customers seeing this well-known person carrying Duane Reade bags and leaving the store could increase store visits and sales.

The question is this: Is it appropriate to use Heigl's photo without her permission as part of an advertising campaign? Use the IDDR approach to analyze what you should do. Assume that you, your supervisor, and a few other members of the marketing department engage in this analysis.

Step 1: Inquiry To begin, clarify the nature of the problem. You want to use a picture of Heigl from a celebrity gossip Web page to potentially increase profits for the company. The problem could be phrased in this way: "Is it ethical to use a picture of a famous person to try to improve sales without contacting her or the photographer first?" Note that the way you frame the question will affect how you answer it. For example, if the question was phrased, "Should we steal this picture?" the answer would be obvious. Remember *not* to frame the issue in a way that gives you the answer you might want.

You also need to identify the stakeholders. Here, the stakeholders include Heigl, the photographer who took the picture, Heigl's fans, and the potential customers of Duane Reade. Other stakeholders include your boss (who will get credit if sales increase due to the marketing campaign), Duane Reade stockholders, and store employees (who might see an increase in customers).

When gathering the facts, determine whether there are any legal issues. Given these facts, there may be state and federal laws that would guide a decision. For instance, reproducing a photograph without the owner's permission might violate federal copyright laws. In addition, most states have laws (sometimes called *right to publicity* laws) that protect a person's name, voice, or likeness (image or picture) from being used for advertising without the person's consent.

You can also consider which ethical theories can help you analyze the problem. The ethical theories may include religious values, rights theory, the categorical imperative, and utilitarianism. Ask yourself whether it is right, or ethical, to use Heigl's name or face without her permission as part of an advertising campaign.

Step 2: Discussion Several actions could be taken in this sample situation. Each action should be thoroughly analyzed using the various ethical approaches identified by the decision makers. The ultimate goals for the decision are to increase sales and do the least amount of harm to the business and its reputation without compromising the values of the business. We will analyze three alternatives here, though it is important as a decision maker to brainstorm and find as many options as possible. Exhibit 3–1 shows how our three alternatives could be analyzed.

It is important to note that different ethical perspectives will be more or less helpful in different situations. In the sample scenario, a strong argument can be made that Heigl's rights to privacy and to control her image are very important. Under other circumstances, however, the right to privacy might be outweighed by some other right, such as another person's right to safety. Using multiple theories will help ensure that the decision maker can work through the analytical process and find a result.

Step 3: Decision After a lively discussion concerning Heigl's rights to privacy and to compensation for the use of her image, the decisions makers come to a consensus. Given the potential for increased income, the company decides to use the picture. It will be posted on the company's Twitter account with a caption that reads, "Love a quick #DuaneReade run? Even @KatieHeigl can't resist shopping #NYC's favorite drugstore."

Make sure to articulate the reasons you arrived at the decision to serve as documentation explaining why the plan of action was ethical. In this meeting, the persuasive evidence was the projection for increased revenue balanced by the minimal harm to Heigl. Because the picture was taken on a public street, the people in the room did not feel that it involved a violation of any privacy right. The company would not have paid Heigl to do an advertisement. Also, because only people who followed Duane Reade on Twitter could view the tweet, the group felt the likelihood of any damage to Heigl was small. Most people felt that the worst that could happen would be that Heigl would ask them to remove it.

Step 4: Review You and the other decision makers at Duane Reade need to review the effectiveness of your decision. Assume that after the picture and caption are posted on Twitter, Heigl sees it and sues Duane Reade for "no less than $6 million." She argues that the company violated her rights by falsely claiming that she had endorsed its stores and that it misappropriated her name and likeness for a profit. The case is settled out of court, with Duane Reade paying an undisclosed amount to a foundation that Heigl created.

Here, the decision did not solve the ethical problem and, in fact, led to liability. Decision makers need to determine what they could have done better. Perhaps they should change

Exhibit 3–1 An Analysis of Ethical Approaches to the Sample Dilemma

ALTERNATIVE	LEGAL IMPLICATIONS	RELIGIOUS VALUES	CATEGORICAL IMPERATIVE	RIGHTS THEORY	UTILITARIANISM
1. Use the Picture without Permission	How does this alternative comply with copyright law? Are there any exceptions to copyright law that would allow this use?	Is this stealing? If so, it violates religious principles. Is it stealing to use a picture taken on a public street?	If everyone did this, then the images and names of famous people would often be used to promote products. Is this a good thing or not?	Using the picture may negatively impact the Webpage or Heigl's ability to make money using her image. It also may violate some right to privacy.	If we use the picture, we may see an increase in sales and an improvement in reputation. We may, however, be sued for using the image without permission.
2. Contact the Webpage and/or Heigl for Permission	Are there any laws that would make this alternative illegal? Are there any precautions we should take when asking for permission to avoid any appearance of threat or intimidation?	This alternative clearly is not stealing and thus would align with religious principles.	If everyone asked for permission, then such material would not be used without permission. This would seem to make the world a better place.	Getting permission would not seem to violate anyone's rights. In fact, giving someone the opportunity to decide might enhance that person's rights.	If we contact the parties for permission, we may be able to use the image, make more money, and improve our reputation. But the parties might refuse to give permission or demand payment, which would cost the company money.
3. Do Not Use the Picture	There are no legal implications to not using the picture.	This alternative clearly is not stealing and thus would align with religious principles.	If companies never used public, candid images of famous people, then all advertising would be staged. This might not make the world a better place.	Not using the picture may damage the stockholders' right to maximum income or the company's right to advertise as it sees fit.	If we do not use the picture, we avoid potential lawsuits. Alternatively, we won't have the potential increase in sales associated with the use of the famous face.

their practices and obtain legal counsel for their marketing department—or at least hire a legal consultant when ethical issues arise. Perhaps they need to establish an internal process for getting permission to use pictures from social media or other sources. In any event, it is likely that the company should change some of its policies and practices related to social media marketing.

The decision-making process is not easy or precise. It may entail repeating steps as decision makers recognize new alternatives or as unforeseen stakeholders appear. Sometimes, the analysis will lead to a clear decision, and other times it will not. Even if it does not, the process will allow decision makers to enter the public phase of the decision (action) with a better idea of what consequences to expect.

For more on the IDDR approach to ethical decision making, see the accompanying *Business Law Analysis* feature.

Applying the IDDR Framework

Business Law Analysis

Pfizer, Inc., developed a new antibiotic called Trovan (trovafloxacinmesylate). Tests in animals showed that Trovan had life-threatening side effects, including joint disease, abnormal cartilage growth, liver damage, and a degenerative bone condition. Pfizer was seeking approval from the Food and Drug Administration (FDA) to market Trovan for use in the United States when an epidemic of bacterial meningitis swept across Nigeria.

Pfizer sent three U.S. physicians to test Trovan on children who were patients in Nigeria's Infectious Disease Hospital. Pfizer's representatives obtained all necessary approvals from the Nigerian government and had Nigerian nurses explain the details of the study to parents and inform them that participation was voluntary. They did not, however, alert the parents or patients about the serious risks involved, or tell them about an effective conventional treatment that Doctors without Borders was providing at the same site. The results of the study showed that Trovan had a success rate of 94.4 percent in treating the children's condition. Nevertheless, eleven children died in the experiment, and others were left blind, deaf, paralyzed, or brain damaged. Rabi Abdullahi and other Nigerian children filed a suit in a U.S. federal court against Pfizer, alleging a violation of a customary international law norm prohibiting involuntary medical experimentation on humans.

Analysis: Pfizer could have applied the IDDR approach to review the ethical conflicts in a test of Trovan. (1) In the inquiry step, decision makers ask questions to understand the ethical dilemma, identify the stakeholders, gather relevant facts, and articulate the ethical principles at issue. (2) In the discussion step, the decision makers further explore potential actions and their effects. (3) The next step is to come to a consensus decision as to what to do. This consensus should withstand moral scrutiny and fulfill corporate, community, and individual values. (4) The last step is to review the outcome to determine whether it was effective and what the company could do better. In this instance, for example, fully informing the patients and their parents about the risks of the treatment would have been a better course of action.

Result and Reasoning: It seems unlikely that a proposed Trovan test on children, based on the facts described here, would have survived an IDDR analysis, under either a duty-based or an outcome-based ethical standard. It also would appear that Pfizer was rushing to test and market Trovan as soon as possible. This focus on short-run profit maximization took precedence over any ethical considerations. It is often easier to see ethical lapses in retrospect than it is to identify potential ethical problems in advance, however.

Focus Question 5

What ethical issues might arise in the context of global business transactions?

3–5 Business Ethics on a Global Level

Just as individual religions have different moral codes, individual countries and regions have different ethical expectations and priorities. Some of these differences are based on religious values, whereas others are cultural in nature. Such differences can make it even more difficult to determine what is ethical in a particular situation.

3–5a World Religions, Cultural Norms, and Ethics

Global businesses need to be conscious of the impact of different religious principles and cultural norms on ethics. For instance, in certain countries the consumption of alcohol is forbidden for religious reasons. It would be considered unethical for a U.S. business to produce alcohol in those countries and employ local workers to assist in alcohol production.

In other countries, women may not be treated as equals because of cultural norms or religion. In contrast, discrimination against employees on the basis of sex (or race, national origin, age, or disability) is prohibited in the United States. The varying roles of women can give rise to ethical issues regarding how women working for a U.S. company should dress or behave in certain regions of the world. Should female executives have to cover their heads? Should they avoid involvement in certain business transactions? How will various stakeholders react to whatever decisions companies make in these situations?

How far should companies go to cater to business partners in other nations? Going too far to please clients in another country can alienate a firm's employees and domestic customers and generate bad press. Decision makers in charge of global business operations should consider these ethical issues and make some decisions from the outset.

3–5b Outsourcing

Outsourcing is the practice by which a company hires an outside firm or individual to perform work rather than hiring employees to do it. Ethical problems involving outsourcing most often arise when global companies outsource work to other countries in an attempt to save on labor costs. This type of outsourcing elicits an almost automatic negative reaction in the U.S. public. Some people feel that companies should protect American jobs above all else. Furthermore, ethical questions often arise as to the employment practices of the foreign companies to which the work is outsourced.

Outsourcing The practice by which a company hires an outside firm or individual to perform work rather than hiring employees to do it.

Outsourcing covers a wide spectrum of ethical gray areas and is not always clearly unethical. Outsourcing domestically, for instance—such as when companies hire outside firms to transport goods—generally does not raise ethical issues. Nonetheless, companies involved in global operations need to be careful when outsourcing to make sure that employees in other nations are being treated fairly.

David Kashakhi/Alamy

Outsourcing cuts costs. But this nation's supply chain may suffer in a crisis, such as during the COVID 19 pandemic.

3–5c Avoiding Corruption

Another ethical problem in global business dealings has to do with corruption in foreign governments. Under the Foreign Corrupt Practices Act,[9] U.S. businesses are prohibited from making payments to (bribing) foreign officials to secure beneficial contracts, with certain exceptions. If such payments are lawful within the foreign country, then they are permitted. It is also acceptable to pay small amounts to minor officials to facilitate or speed up the performance of administrative services (such as approval of construction). Payments to private foreign companies or other third parties are also permissible.

Corruption is widespread in some nations, however, and it can be the norm in dealing with both government and private businesses in certain locations. Global companies must take special care when doing business in countries where corruption is common. Decision makers should discuss potential ethical problems with employees in advance and again when situations arise. The company's goal should be to ensure that it supports management and employees in doing the right thing and following the firm's anticorruption policies.

3–5d Monitoring the Employment Practices of Foreign Suppliers

Many businesses contract with companies in developing nations to produce goods, such as shoes and clothing, because the wage rates in those nations are significantly lower than those in the United States. But what if one of those contractors hires women and children at below-minimum-wage rates or requires its employees to work long hours in a workplace full of health hazards? What if the company's supervisors routinely engage in workplace conduct that is offensive to women? What if factories located abroad routinely violate U.S. labor and environmental standards?

Wages and Working Conditions Allegations that a business allows its suppliers to engage in unethical practices hurt the firm's reputation. **Example 3.19** Noi Supalai, a garment worker in Thailand, came forward with reports about how harshly she and other workers had been treated at Eagle Speed factory, which produced apparel for Nike Corporation. Because the

9. 15 U.S.C. Sections 78dd-1 *et seq.* This act will be discussed in more detail in the context of criminal law.

workers did not produce all of the "Just Do the Right Thing" line of products by a set deadline, Nike fined the factory and barred it from paying its workers. The factory then forced some two thousand employees to work sixteen-hour days or longer, and to take turns going home to shower. Workers eventually formed a union and named Supalai as president, but they were unsuccessful in getting the conditions improved. A meeting was set up between Supalai and a Nike representative, but Nike did not even show up. Supalai later learned that Nike chose to use other suppliers. ■

Corporate Watch Groups Given today's global communications network, few companies can assume that their actions in other nations will go unnoticed by "corporate watch" groups that discover and publicize unethical corporate behavior. As a result, U.S. businesses today usually take steps to avoid such adverse publicity—either by refusing to deal with certain suppliers or by arranging to monitor their suppliers' workplaces to make sure that employees are not being mistreated.

Example 3.20 A Chinese factory supplied parts for certain Apple products. After Apple discovered that the factory had violated labor and environmental standards, it began evaluating the practices at all the companies in its supply chain. Apple's audits revealed numerous violations, such as withholding worker pay as a disciplinary measure, falsifying pay records, and forcing workers to use unsafe machines. Apple terminated its relationship with one foreign supplier and turned over its findings to the Fair Labor Association, a nonprofit organization that promotes adherence to national and international labor laws, for further inquiry. ■

Practice and Review

James Stilton is the chief executive officer (CEO) of RightLiving, Inc., a company that buys life insurance policies at a discount from terminally ill persons and sells the policies to investors. RightLiving pays the terminally ill patients a percentage of the future death benefit (usually 65 percent) and then sells the policies to investors for 85 percent of the value of the future benefit. The patients receive the cash to use for medical and other expenses, and the investors are "guaranteed" a positive return on their investment. The difference between the purchase and sale prices is Right Living's profit. Stilton is aware that some sick patients may obtain insurance policies through fraud (by not revealing their illness on the insurance application). An insurance company that discovers such fraud will cancel the policy and refuse to pay. Stilton believes that most of the policies he has purchased are legitimate, but he knows that some probably are not. Using the information presented in this chapter, answer the following questions.

1. Would a person who adheres to the principle of rights consider it ethical for Stilton not to disclose the potential risk of cancellation to investors? Why or why not?
2. Using Immanuel Kant's categorical imperative, are the actions of RightLiving ethical? Why or why not?
3. Under utilitarianism, are Stilton's actions ethical? Why or why not? If most of the policies are, in fact, legitimate, does this make a difference in your analysis?
4. Using the IDDR approach, discuss the decision process Stilton should use in deciding whether to disclose the risk of fraudulent policies to potential investors.

Debate This

Executives in large corporations are ultimately rewarded if their companies do well, particularly as evidenced by rising stock prices. Consequently, shouldn't those who run corporations be able to decide what level of negative side effects is "acceptable" for their companies' products?

Key Terms

business ethics 57
categorical imperative 65
corporate social responsibility (CSR) 66
cost-benefit analysis 65
duty-based ethics 63
ethical reasoning 63
ethics 57
moral minimum 58
outcome-based ethics 63
outsourcing 77
principle of rights 64
stakeholders 67
triple bottom line 60
utilitarianism 65

Chapter Summary: Ethics in Business

Ethics and the Role of Business	**1. The relationship of law and ethics**—The government has created some ethical rights and duties through the passage of laws and regulations. Many laws are designed to prevent fraudulent conduct, including the Dodd-Frank Wall Street Reform and Consumer Protection Act and the Sarbanes-Oxley Act. **a. Gray areas in the law**—Sometimes legislation includes language that is overly broad or provisions that are ambiguous. Such gray areas make it difficult to predict how the law will apply or should be applied to a situation, complicating determinations of what is legal or ethical. **b. The moral minimum**—Lawful behavior is the moral minimum. The law has its limits, though, and some actions may be legal but not ethical. The study of ethics goes beyond legal requirements to evaluate what is right for society. **c. Codes of ethics**—Most large firms have internal ethical codes. Many industry associations also have codes of ethics for their members. Because these internal codes are not laws, their effectiveness is determined by the commitment of the company leadership or industry to enforcing the codes. **2. The role of business in society**—The public perception of corporations has changed from entities that primarily generate profits for their owners to entities that participate in society as corporate citizens. From either the profit maximization or corporate citizenship perspective, ethics is important in making business decisions. One ethical perspective looks to the *triple bottom line*, in which decision makers evaluate (a) the legal implications, (b) the public relations impact, (c) any safety risks, and (d) the financial implications of a decision. **3. Ethical issues in business**—A fundamental ethical issue for business is developing integrity and trust. Businesspersons should exhibit integrity in their dealings with other people in the company, other businesses, clients, and the community. **4. The importance of ethical leadership**—Management's commitment and behavior are essential in creating an ethical workplace. Management's behavior, more than anything else, sets the ethical tone of a firm and influences the behavior of employees.
Ethical Principles and Philosophies	**1. Duty-based ethics**—Ethics based on religious beliefs; the basic rights of human beings (the principle of rights); and philosophical reasoning, such as that of Immanuel Kant. A potential problem for those who support this ethical approach is deciding which rights are more important in a given situation. Management constantly faces ethical conflicts and trade-offs when considering all those affected by a business decision. **2. Outcome-based ethics (utilitarianism)**—Ethics based on philosophical reasoning, such as that of Jeremy Bentham and John Stuart Mill. Applying this theory requires a cost-benefit analysis, weighing the negative effects against the positive and deciding which course of action produces the better outcome. **3. Corporate social responsibility**—Corporate social responsibility (CSR) combines a commitment to good citizenship with a commitment to making ethical decisions, improving society, and minimizing environmental impact. Although there are different theories, the basic idea is that corporations can and should act ethically and be accountable to society for their actions. One view of CSR stresses that corporations have a duty not just to shareholders, but also to other groups affected by corporate decisions, called stakeholders.

Sources of Ethical Issues in Business Decisions	1. **Short-term profit maximization**—Executives should distinguish between short-run and long-run profit goals and focus on maximizing profits over the long run. An overemphasis on short-run profit maximization is perhaps the most common reason that ethical problems occur in business. 2. **Social media**—Advances in technology have created new ethical problems for companies. Issues involving social media include how to use social media in the hiring process and how to monitor employees' online activities. 3. **Awareness**—Whatever the context, businesspersons must be aware of the possibility that ethical issues will arise. 4. **Rationalization**—Sometimes, businesspersons make a decision that they know is not ethical but that will benefit them or their company. After the fact, they rationalize their unethical decision. 5. **Uncertainty**—When making a business decision, businesspersons may be uncertain as to what they should do, what they should have done, or whether an ethical issue or breach is even involved. Such uncertainty is unavoidable, but it should be treated as an indicator of a potential ethical problem.
Making Ethical Business Decisions	Making ethical business decisions is crucial in today's legal environment. Business decisions can be complex. Several frameworks exist to help businesspersons make ethical decisions. One such framework is the four-step IDDR ("I Desire to Do Right") approach. 1. ***I = Inquiry***—Involves identifying the ethical problem and all of the stakeholders, gathering the relevant facts, and considering which ethical theories can help in analyzing the problem. 2. ***D = Discussion***—Involves making a list of possible actions and evaluating the strengths and weaknesses of each option, including its ethical and legal consequences. 3. ***D = Decision***—Involves crafting a consensus decision or a company's plan of action. Decision makers should use the analysis from Step 2 to articulate the reasons behind the decision. 4. ***R = Review***—Involves reviewing the decision outcome to determine whether the solution was effective and satisfied the stakeholders. The results of this evaluation may be used in making future decisions.
Business Ethics on a Global Level	Global businesses need to be conscious of the impact of different religious principles and cultural norms on ethics. In addition, ethical concerns may arise in the areas of outsourcing, avoiding corruption, and monitoring the employment practices of foreign suppliers.

Issue Spotters

1. Acme Corporation decides to respond to what it sees as a moral obligation to correct for past discrimination by adjusting pay differences among its employees. Does this raise an ethical conflict between Acme and its employees? Between Acme and its shareholders? Explain your answers. (See *Ethical Principles and Philosophies.*)

2. Delta Tools, Inc., markets a product that under some circumstances is capable of seriously injuring consumers. Does Delta have an ethical duty to remove this product from the market, even if the injuries result only from misuse? Why or why not? (See *Making Ethical Business Decisions.*)

—Check your answers to the *Issue Spotters* against the answers provided in Appendix D.

Business Scenarios and Case Problems

3–1. Business Ethics. Jason Trevor owns a commercial bakery in Blakely, Georgia, that produces a variety of goods sold in grocery stores. Trevor is required by law to perform internal tests on food produced at his plant to check for contamination. On three occasions, tests of food products containing peanut butter were positive for salmonella contamination. Trevor was not required to report the results to U.S. Food and Drug Administration officials, however, so he did not. Instead, Trevor instructed his employees to simply repeat the tests until the results were negative. Meanwhile, the products that had originally tested positive for salmonella were eventually shipped out to retailers. Five people who ate Trevor's baked goods that year became seriously ill, and one person died from a salmonella infection. Even though Trevor's conduct was legal, was it unethical for him to sell goods that had once tested positive for salmonella? Why or why not? (See *Ethics and the Role of Business.*)

3–2. Ethical Conduct. Internet giant Zoidle, a U.S. company, generated sales of £2.5 billion in the United Kingdom (UK) in 2013 (roughly $4 billion in U.S. dollars). The U.K. corporate tax rate is usually between 20 percent and 24 percent, but Zoidle paid only 3 percent (£6 million). At a press conference, company officials touted how the company took advantage of tax loopholes and sheltered profits to avoid paying the full corporate income tax. They justified their practices as ethical, declaring that it would be verging on illegal to tell shareholders that the company paid more taxes than it should.

Zoidle receives significant benefits for doing business in the UK, including large sales tax exemptions and some property tax breaks. The UK relies on the corporate income tax to provide services to the poor and to help run the agency that regulates corporations. Is it ethical for Zoidle to avoid paying taxes? Why or why not? (See *Ethics and the Role of Business.*)

3–3. Consumer Rights. Best Buy, a national electronics retailer, offered a credit card that allowed users to earn "reward points" that could be redeemed for discounts on Best Buy goods. After reading a newspaper advertisement for the card, Gary Davis applied for, and was given, a credit card. As part of the application process, he visited a Web page containing Frequently Asked Questions as well as terms and conditions for the card. He clicked on a button affirming that he understood the terms and conditions. When Davis received his card, it came with seven brochures about the card and the reward point program. As he read the brochures, he discovered that a $59 annual fee would be charged for the card. Davis went back to the Web pages he had visited and found a statement that the card "may" have an annual fee. Davis sued, claiming that the company did not adequately disclose the fee. Is it unethical for companies to put terms and conditions, especially terms that may cost the consumer money, in an electronic document that is too long to read on one screen? Why or why not? Assuming that the Best Buy credit-card materials were legally sufficient, discuss the ethical aspects of businesses strictly following the language of the law as opposed to following the intent of the law. [*Davis v. HSBC Bank Nevada, N.A.*, 691 F.3d 1152 (9th Cir. 2012)] (See *Ethics and the Role of Business.*)

3–4. Business Ethics. Mark Ramun worked as a manager for Allied Erecting and Dismantling Co., where he had a tense relationship with his father, who was Allied's president. After more than ten years, Mark left Allied, taking 15,000 pages of Allied's documents on DVDs and CDs, which constituted trade secrets. Later, he joined Allied's competitor, Genesis Equipment & Manufacturing, Inc. Genesis soon developed a piece of equipment that incorporated elements of Allied equipment. How might business ethics have been violated in these circumstances? Discuss. [*Allied Erecting and Dismantling Co. v. Genesis Equipment & Manufacturing, Inc.*, 511 Fed.Appx. 398 (6th Cir. 2013)] (See *Making Ethical Business Decisions.*)

3–5. Ethical Principles. Stephen Glass made himself infamous as a dishonest journalist by fabricating material for more than forty articles for *The New Republic* magazine and other publications. He also fabricated supporting materials to delude *The New Republic's* fact checkers. At the time, he was a law student at Georgetown University. Once suspicions were aroused, Glass tried to avoid detection. Later, Glass applied for admission to the California bar. The California Supreme Court denied his application, citing "numerous instances of dishonesty and disingenuousness" during his "rehabilitation" following the exposure of his misdeeds. How do these circumstances underscore the importance of ethics? Discuss. [*In re Glass*, 58 Cal.4th 500, 316 P.3d 1199 (2014)] (See *Ethical Principles and Philosophies.*)

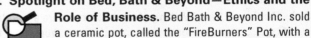

3–6. Business Case Problem with Sample Answer—Business Ethics. Operating out of an apartment in Secane, Pennsylvania, Hratch Ilanjian convinced Vicken Setrakian, the president of Kenset Corp., that he was an international businessman who could help turn around Kenset's business in the Middle East. At Ilanjian's insistence, Setrakian provided confidential business documents. Claiming that they had an agreement, Ilanjian demanded full, immediate payment and threatened to disclose the confidential information to a Kenset supplier if payment was not forthcoming. Kenset denied that there was a contract and filed a suit in a federal district court against Ilanjian, seeking return of the documents. During discovery, Ilanjian was uncooperative. Who behaved unethically in these circumstances? Explain. [*Kenset Corp. v. Ilanjian*, 600 Fed.Appx. 827 (3d Cir. 2015)] (See *Making Ethical Business Decisions.*)

—For a sample answer to Problem 3–6, go to Apppendix E.

3–7. Spotlight on Bed, Bath & Beyond—Ethics and the Role of Business. Bed Bath & Beyond Inc. sold a ceramic pot, called the "FireBurners" Pot, with a stainless steel fuel reservoir at its center and a bottle of gelled fuel for use with the fire pot called "FireGel." A red sticker on the fire pot warned, "DON'T REFILL UNTIL FLAME IS OUT & CUP IS COOL." "CARE AND USE INSTRUCTIONS" with the product cautioned, in a "WARNINGS" section, "Do not add fuel when lit and never pour gel on an open fire or hot surface." The label on the back of the fuel gel bottle instructed, "NEVER add fuel to a burning fire," and under a bold "WARNING" stated, "DANGER, FLAMMABLE LIQUID & VAPOR." M.H., a minor, was injured when a fire pot in one of the products—bought from Bed Bath & Beyond—was refueled with the gel and an explosion occurred. Safer alternatives for the design of the fire pot existed, but its manufacturer chose not to use them. In these circumstances, is Bed, Bath & Beyond ethically responsible for the injury to M.H.? Discuss. [*M.H. v. Bed, Bath & Beyond, Inc.*, 156 A.D.3d 33, 64 N.Y.S.3d 205 (1 Dept. 2017)] (See *Ethics and the Role of Business.*)

3–8. A Question of Ethics—Applying the IDDR Framework. Priscilla Dickman worked as a medical technologist at the University of Connecticut Health Center for twenty-eight years. Early in her career at the Health Center, Dickman sustained a back injury while at work. The condition eventually worsened, causing her significant back pain and disability. Her physician ordered restrictions on her work duties for several years. Then Dickman's supervisor received complaints that Dickman was getting personal phone calls and was frequently absent from her work area. Based on e-mails and other documents found on her work computer, it appeared that she had been running two side businesses (selling jewelry and providing travel agent services) while at work. The state investigated, and she was convicted of a civil ethics violation for engaging in "personal business for financial gain on state time utilizing state resources." Separate investigations resulted in criminal convictions for forgery and the filing of an unrelated fraudulent insurance claim. Dickman "retired" from her job (after she obtained approval for disability retirement) and filed a claim with the state of Connecticut against the health center. She alleged that her former employer had initiated the investigations to harass her and force her to quit. She claimed that the Health Center was unlawfully retaliating against her for being disabled and being put on workplace restrictions. [*Dickman v. University of Connecticut Health Center*, 162 Conn.App. 441, 132 A.3d 739 (2016)] (See *Making Ethical Business Decisions.*)

1. Assume that you are Dickman's supervisor and have been informed that she is frequently away from her desk and often makes personal phone calls. The first step of using the IDDR method is *inquiry*, so you start asking questions. Several people tell you that that Dickman has offered to sell them jewelry. Others say she has offered to make travel arrangements for them. You have not spoken to Dickman directly about the complaints and are not sure if you should. You know that the Health Center would need more evidence of wrongdoing to justify firing Dickman but are uncertain as to whether you can search her computer. Should you report your findings to management? Is there any ethical problem involved in investigating and possibly firing a long-term employee? Is it fair to terminate an employee who is under disability restrictions? How would you frame the ethical dilemma that the Health Center faced in this case, and who are the stakeholders? What ethical theories would you use to guide your decision?
2. Now suppose that you are Dickman. You have been a medical technologist for a long time but now experience severe back pain while at your desk at the Health Center. You find that you have less pain if you get up and move around during the day, rather than just sitting. That is why you are often away from your desk. You know that you will not be able to do this job much longer, and that is why you recently started a jewelry business and began providing travel services. Sure, you have made a few personal phone calls related to those businesses while at the Health Center, but other employees make personal calls, and they have not been fired. You feel that the Health Center's investigation was intended to force you to quit because you are disabled and cannot perform the tasks that you used to perform. Using the inquiry portion of the IDDR method, how might you frame the ethical issue you face, and who are the stakeholders? What ethical principles can help you analyze the problem thoroughly?

Critical Thinking and Writing Assignments

3–9. Business Law Writing. Assume that you are a high-level manager for a shoe manufacturer. You know that your firm could increase its profit margin by producing shoes in Indonesia, where you could hire women for $100 a month to assemble them. You also know that human rights advocates recently accused a competing shoe manufacturer of engaging in exploitative labor practices because the manufacturer sold shoes made by Indonesian women for similarly low wages. You personally do not believe that paying $100 a month to Indonesian women is unethical because you know that in their country, $100 a month is a better-than-average wage rate.

Write one page explaining whether you would have the shoes manufactured in Indonesia and make higher profits for the company, or avoid the risk of negative publicity and its potential adverse consequences for the firm's reputation. Are there other alternatives? Discuss fully. (See *Business Ethics on a Global Level.*)

3–10. Time-Limited Group Assignment—Corporate Social Responsibility. Methamphetamine (meth) is an addictive drug made chiefly in small toxic labs (STLs) in homes, tents, barns, and hotel rooms. The manufacturing process is dangerous, often resulting in explosions, burns, and toxic fumes. Government entities spend time and resources to find and destroy STLs, imprison meth dealers and users, treat addicts, and provide services for affected families.

Meth cannot be made without ingredients that are also used in cold and allergy medications. Arkansas has one of the highest numbers of STLs in the United States. To recoup the costs of fighting the meth epidemic, twenty counties in Arkansas filed a suit against Pfizer, Inc., which makes cold and allergy medications. They argued that it was Pfizer's ethical responsibility to either stop using ingredients in their cold and allergy medications that can be used to make meth or to compensate the government for the amount it spends closing down meth labs. (See *Ethics and the Role of Business, Ethical Principles and Philosophies,* and *Making Ethical Business Decisions.*)

1. The first group will outline Pfizer's ethical responsibility under the corporate social responsibility doctrine. To whom does Pfizer owe duties?
2. The second group will formulate an argument on behalf of Pfizer that the company has not breached any of its ethical responsibilities.
3. The third group will assume that they work for Pfizer and that the company is trying to determine the best course of action to prevent its medications from being used to make meth. The group will apply the IDDR approach and explain the steps in the reasoning used.
4. The fourth group will adopt a utilitarian point of view and perform a cost-benefit analysis to determine what the company should do. Specifically, should the company pay compensation to the state, or should it stop using certain ingredients in its medications?

Appendix to Chapter 3:

Costco Code of Ethics

Costco Wholesale Corporation takes a strong position on behaving ethically in all transactions and relationships. It also expects employees to behave ethically, according to domestic ethical standards, in any country in which it operates. Costco's Code of Ethics outlines its commitment to business ethics.

COSTCO

CODE OF ETHICS

By Jim Sinegal

OBEY THE LAW

The law is irrefutable! Absent a moral imperative to challenge a law, we must our business in total compliance with the laws of every community where we do business.

- Comply with all statutes.
- Cooperate with authorities.
- Respect all public officials and their positions.
- Avoid all conflict of interest issues with public officials.
- Comply with all disclosure and reporting requirements.
- Comply with safety and security standards for all products sold.
- Exceed ecological standards required in every community where we do business.
- Comply with all applicable wage and hour laws.
- Comply with all applicable anti-trust laws.
- Protect "inside information" that has not been released to the general public.

TAKE CARE OF OUR MEMBERS

The member is our key to success. If we don't keep our members happy, little else that we do will make a difference.

- Provide top-quality products at the best prices in the market.
- Provide a safe shopping environment in our warehouses.
- Provide only products that meet applicable safety and health standards.
- Sell only products from manufacturers who comply with "truth in advertising/packaging" standards.
- Provide our members with a 100% satisfaction guaranteed warranty on every product and service we sell, including their membership fee.
- Assure our members that every product we sell is authentic in make and in representation of performance.
- Make our shopping environment a pleasant experience by making our members feel welcome as our guests.
- Provide products to our members that will be ecologically sensitive.

Our member is our reason for being. If they fail to show up, we cannot survive. Our members have extended a "trust" to Costco by virtue of paying a fee to shop with us. We can't let them down or they will simply go away. We must always operate in the following manner when dealing with our members:

Rule #1 – The member is always right.

Rule #2 – In the event the member is ever wrong, refer to rule #1.

There are plenty of shopping alternatives for our members. We will succeed only if we do not violate the trust they have extended to us. We must be committed at every level of our company, with every once of energy and grain of creativity we have, to constantly strive to "bring goods to market at a lower price."

If we do these four things throughout our organization, we will realize our ultimate goal, which is to REWARD OUR SHAREHOLDERS.

TAKE CARE OF OUR EMPLOYEES

To claim "people are our most important asset" is true and an understatement. Each employee has been hired for a very important job. Jobs such as stocking the shelves, ringing members' orders, buying products, and paying our bills are jobs we would all choose to perform because of their importance. The employees hired to perform these jobs are performing as management's "alter egos." Every employee, whether they are in a Costco warehouse, or whether they work in the regional or corporate offices, is a Costco ambassador trained to give our members professional, courteous treatment.

Today we have warehouse managers who were once stockers and callers, and vice presidents who were once in clerical positions for Costco. We believe that Costco's future executive officers are currently working in our warehouses, depots, buying offices, and accounting departments, as well as in our home offices.

To that end, we are committed to these principles:

- Provide a safe work environment.
- Pay a fair wage.
- Make every job challenging, but make it fun!
- Consider the loss of any employee as a failure on the part of the company and a loss to the organization.
- Teach our people how to do their jobs and how to improve personally and professionally.
- Promote from within the company to achieve the goal of a minimum of 80% of management positions being filled by current employees.
- Create an "open door" attitude at all levels of the company that is dedicated to "fairness and listening."

RESPECT OUR VENDORS

Our vendors are our partners in business and for us to prosper as a company, they must proper with us. It is important that our vendors understand that we will be tough negotiators, but fair in our treatment of them.

- Treat all vendors and their representatives as you would expect to be treated if visiting their places of business.
- Pay all bills within the allocated time frame.
- Honor all commitments.
- Protect all vendor property assigned to Costco as though it were our own.
- Always be thoughtful and candid in negotiations.
- Provide a careful review process with at least two levels of authorization before terminating business with an existing vendor of more than two years.
- Do not accept gratuities of any kind from a vendor.

These guidelines are exactly that - guidelines, some common sense rules for the conduct of our business. Intended to simplify our jobs, not complicate our lives, these guidelines will not answer every question or solve every problem. At the core of our philosophy as a company must be the implicit understanding that not one of us is required to lie or cheat on behalf of PriceCostco. In fact, dishonest conduct will not be tolerated. To do any less would be unfair to the overwhelming majority of our employees who support and respect Costco's commitment to ethical business conduct.

If your are ever in doubt as to what course of action to take on a business matter that is open to varying ethical interpretations, take the high road and do what is right.

If you want our help, we are always available for advice and counsel. That's our job and we welcome your questions or comments.

Our continued success depends on you. We thank each of you for your contribution to our past success and for the high standards you have insisted upon in our company.

Courts and Alternative Dispute Resolution

4

"An eye for an eye will make the whole world blind."

Mahatma Gandhi
1869–1948 (Indian political and spiritual leader)

Every society needs to have an established method for resolving disputes. Without one, as Mahatma Gandhi implied in the chapter-opening quotation, the biblical "eye for an eye" would lead to anarchy. This is particularly true in the business world—almost all businesspersons will face a lawsuit at some time in their careers. For this reason, anyone involved in business needs to have an understanding of court systems in the United States, as well as the various methods of dispute resolution that can be pursued outside the courts.

Assume that QuickDoor, a food delivery service, is entangled in a labor dispute with 5,000 workers who feel they are owed back pay. If an individual worker were to go to court and win, the award would be about two thousand dollars—not enough to interest most labor lawyers. So the workers would like to combine their grievances into a single, multi-million-dollar *class action* lawsuit. QuickDoor's employment contract, however, prohibits such lawsuits. Instead, it requires an alternative dispute resolution method called *arbitration* to settle any labor disagreements between the workers and the company.

This contract provision means that QuickDoor might have to engage in 5,000 separate arbitration hearings, costing the company about $12 million, an amount greater than the cost of the underlying dispute. Which would be most fair for all concerned? Requiring QuickDoor and its workers to engage in thousands of alternative dispute resolution hearings? Or allowing a single class action lawsuit, despite the contracts? In this chapter, we will discuss how such legal disagreements are resolved, along with the benefits and drawbacks of the various methods of resolving them.

Focus Questions

The six Focus Questions *below are designed to help improve your understanding. After reading this chapter, you should be able to answer the following questions:*

1. What is judicial review? How and when was the power of judicial review established?
2. How are the courts applying traditional jurisdictional concepts to cases involving Internet transactions?
3. What is the difference between the focus of a trial court and that of an appellate court?
4. What is discovery, and how does electronic discovery differ from traditional discovery?
5. What is an electronic court filing system?
6. What are three alternative methods of resolving disputes?

4–1 The Judiciary's Role in American Government

The body of American law includes the federal and state constitutions, statutes passed by legislative bodies, administrative law, and the case decisions and legal principles that form the common law. These laws would be meaningless, however, without the courts to interpret and apply them. This is the essential role of the judiciary—the courts—in the American governmental system: to interpret and apply the law.

4–1a Judicial Review

As the branch of government entrusted with interpreting the laws, the judiciary can decide, among other things, whether the laws or actions of the other two branches are constitutional. The process for making such a determination is known as **judicial review**.

Judicial Review The process by which a court decides on the constitutionality of legislative enactments and actions of the executive branch.

The power of judicial review enables the judicial branch to act as a check on the other two branches of government, in line with the checks-and-balances system established by the U.S. Constitution. (Today, nearly all nations with constitutional democracies, including Canada, France, and Germany, have some form of judicial review.)

Focus Question 1

What is judicial review? How and when was the power of judicial review established?

4–1b The Origins of Judicial Review in the United States

The U.S. Constitution does not mention judicial review (although many constitutional scholars believe that the founders intended the judiciary to have this power). How was the doctrine of judicial review established? See this chapter's *Landmark in the Law* feature for the answer.

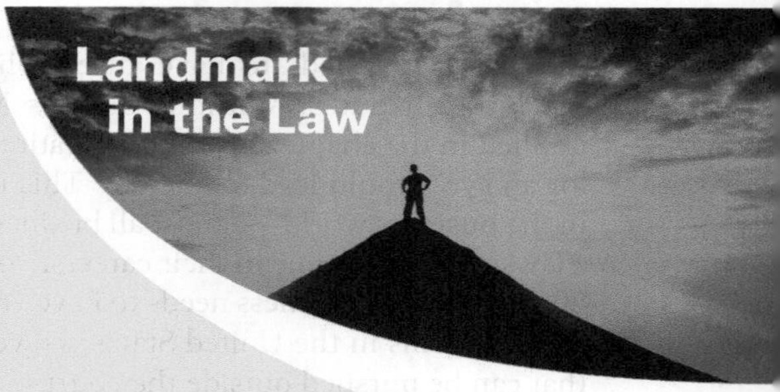

Marbury v. Madison (1803)

The power of judicial review was established in the Supreme Court's decision in the case of *Marbury v. Madison*.[a] Although the decision is widely viewed as a cornerstone of constitutional law, the case had its origins in early U.S. politics.

When Thomas Jefferson defeated the incumbent president, John Adams, in the presidential elections of 1800, Adams feared the Jeffersonians' antipathy toward business and toward a strong national government. Adams thus rushed to "pack" the judiciary with loyal Federalists (those who believed in a strong national government) by appointing what came to be called "midnight judges" just before he left office.

But Adams's secretary of state (John Marshall) was able to deliver only forty-two of the fifty-nine judicial appointment letters by the time Jefferson took over as president. Jefferson refused to order his secretary of state, James Madison, to deliver the remaining commissions.

Marshall's Dilemma William Marbury and three others to whom the commissions had not been delivered sought a writ of *mandamus* (an order directing a government official to fulfill a duty) from the United States Supreme Court, as authorized by the Judiciary Act in 1789.

As fate would have it, John Marshall had just been appointed as chief justice of the Supreme Court. Marshall faced a dilemma: If he ordered the commissions delivered, the new secretary of state (Madison) could simply refuse to deliver them—and the Court had no way to compel him to act. At the same time, if Marshall simply allowed the new administration to do as it wished, the Court's power would be severely eroded.

Marshall's Decision Marshall masterfully fashioned his decision to enlarge the power of the Supreme Court by affirming the Court's power of judicial review. He stated, "It is emphatically the province and duty of the Judicial Department to say what the law is. . . . If two laws conflict with each other, the Courts must decide on the operation of each. . . . [I]f both [a] law and the Constitution apply to a particular case, . . .the Court must determine which of these conflicting rules governs the case."

Marshall's decision did not require anyone to do anything. He concluded that the

a. 5 U.S. (1 Cranch) 137, 2 L.Ed. 60 (1803).

highest court did not have the power to issue a writ of *mandamus* in this particular case. Although the Judiciary Act specified that the Supreme Court could issue writs of *mandamus* as part of its original jurisdiction, Article III of the Constitution, which spelled out the Court's original jurisdiction, did not mention such writs. Because Congress did not have the right to expand the Supreme Court's jurisdiction, this section of the Judiciary Act was unconstitutional—and thus void. The *Marbury* decision stands to this day as a judicial and political masterpiece.

Application to Today's World *Since the* Marbury v. Madison *decision, the power of judicial review has remained unchallenged and today is exercised by both federal and state courts. If the courts did not have the power of judicial review, the constitutionality of Congress's acts could not be challenged in court—a congressional statute would remain law unless changed by Congress. The courts of other countries that have adopted a constitutional democracy often cite this decision as a justification for judicial review.*

4–2 Basic Judicial Requirements

Before a court can hear a lawsuit, certain requirements must be met. These requirements relate to jurisdiction, venue, and standing to sue. We examine each of these important concepts here.

4–2a Jurisdiction

In Latin, *juris* means "law," and *diction* means "to speak." Thus, "the power to speak the law" is the literal meaning of the term **jurisdiction**. Before any court can hear a case, it must have jurisdiction over the person or company against whom the suit is brought (the defendant) or over the property involved in the suit. The court must also have jurisdiction over the subject matter of the dispute.

Jurisdiction The authority of a court to hear and decide a specific case.

Jurisdiction over Persons or Property Generally, a court with jurisdiction over a particular geographic area can exercise personal jurisdiction (*in personam* jurisdiction) over any person or business that resides in that area. A state trial court, for instance, normally has jurisdictional authority over residents (including businesses) in a particular area of the state, such as a county or district. A state's highest court (often called the state supreme court)[1] has jurisdiction over all residents of that state.

A court can also exercise jurisdiction over property that is located within its boundaries. This kind of jurisdiction is known as *in rem* jurisdiction, or "jurisdiction over the thing." **Example 4.1** A dispute arises over the ownership of a boat in dry dock in Fort Lauderdale, Florida. The boat is owned by an Ohio resident, over whom a Florida court normally cannot exercise personal jurisdiction. The other party to the dispute is a resident of Nebraska. In this situation, because the boat is in Florida, a lawsuit concerning the boat could be brought in a Florida state court on the basis of the court's *in rem* jurisdiction.

Long Arm Statutes. Under the authority of a state **long arm statute**, a court can exercise personal jurisdiction over certain out-of-state defendants based on activities that took place within the state. Before exercising long arm jurisdiction over a nonresident, however, the court must be convinced that the defendant had sufficient contacts, or *minimum contacts*, with the state to justify the jurisdiction.[2] Generally, this means that the defendant must have enough of a connection to the state for the judge to conclude that it is fair for the state to exercise power over the defendant.

Long Arm Statute A state statute that permits a state to exercise jurisdiction over nonresident defendants.

1. As will be discussed shortly, a state's highest court is frequently referred to as the state supreme court, but there are exceptions. For example, in New York, the supreme court is a trial court.
2. The minimum-contacts standard was established in *International Shoe Co. v. State of Washington*, 326 U.S. 310, 66 S.Ct. 154, 90 L.Ed. 95 (1945).

If an out-of-state defendant caused an automobile accident or sold defective goods within the state, for instance, a court will usually find that minimum contacts exist to exercise jurisdiction over that defendant. **Spotlight Case Example 4.2** An Xbox game system caught fire in Bonnie Broquet's home in Texas and caused substantial personal injuries. Broquet filed a lawsuit in a Texas court against Ji-Haw Industrial Company, a nonresident company that made the Xbox components. Broquet alleged that Ji-Haw's components were defective and had caused the fire. Ji-Haw argued that the Texas court lacked jurisdiction over it, but a state appellate court held that the Texas long arm statute authorized the exercise of jurisdiction over the out-of-state defendant.[3]

Similarly, a state may exercise personal jurisdiction over a nonresident defendant who is sued for breaching a contract that was formed within the state. This is true even when that contract was negotiated over the phone or through online correspondence.

Corporate Contacts. Because corporations are considered legal persons, courts use the same principles to determine whether it is fair to exercise jurisdiction over a corporation. A corporation normally is subject to personal jurisdiction in the state in which it is incorporated, has its principal office, and is doing business. Courts apply the minimum-contacts test to determine if they can exercise jurisdiction over out-of-state corporations.

In the past, corporations were usually subject to jurisdiction in states in which they were doing business, such as advertising or selling products. The United States Supreme Court decided that this situation made questions of jurisdiction too unpredictable. After all, many corporations do business in multiple states, and the Court concluded that it was unfair to expose them to costly legal proceedings in numerous different locations. Now, a corporation is subject to jurisdiction only in states where it does such substantial and continuous business that it is "at home" in that state.[4] The courts look at the amount of business the corporation does within the state relative to the amount it does elsewhere.

Rusla Ruseyn/Shutterstock.com

Is the presence of a railroad company's tracks in one state enough to satisfy the minimum-contacts requirement?

Case Example 4.3 Norfolk Southern Railway Company is a Virginia corporation. Russell Parker, a resident of Indiana and a former employee of Norfolk, filed a lawsuit against the railroad in Missouri. Parker claimed that while working for Norfolk in Indiana he had sustained a cumulative injury. Norfolk argued that Missouri courts did not have jurisdiction over the company. The Supreme Court of Missouri agreed. Simply having train tracks running through Missouri was not enough to meet the minimum-contacts requirement. Norfolk also had tracks and operations in twenty-one other states. The plaintiff worked and was allegedly injured in Indiana, not Missouri. Even though Norfolk did register its corporation in Missouri, the amount of business that it did in Missouri was not so substantial that it was "at home" in that state.[5]

Jurisdiction over Subject Matter Jurisdiction over subject matter is a limitation on the types of cases a court can hear. In both the federal and the state court systems, there are courts of *general* (unlimited) *jurisdiction* and courts of *limited jurisdiction*. An example of a court of general jurisdiction is a state trial court or a federal district court.

Probate Court A state court of limited jurisdiction that conducts proceedings relating to the settlement of a deceased person's estate.

An example of a state court of limited jurisdiction is a **probate court**. Probate courts are state courts that handle only matters relating to the transfer of a person's assets and obligations after that person's death, including matters relating to the custody and guardianship of

3. *Ji-Haw Industrial Co. v. Broquet*, 2008 WL 441822 (Tex.App.—San Antonio 2008).
4. *Daimler AG v. Bauman*, 571 U.S. 117, 134 S.Ct. 746, 187 L.Ed. 624 (2014). See also *Frank v. P.N.K. (Lake Charles) LLC*, 947 F.3d. 331 (5th Cir. 2020).
5. *State ex rel. Norfolk Southern Railway Co. v. Dolan*, 512 S.W.3d 41 (Sup.Ct. Mo. 2017).

children and incompetent adults. An example of a federal court of limited subject-matter jurisdiction is a **bankruptcy court**. Bankruptcy courts handle only bankruptcy proceedings, which are governed by federal bankruptcy law.

Bankruptcy Court A federal court of limited jurisdiction that handles only bankruptcy proceedings, which are governed by federal bankruptcy law.

A court's jurisdiction over subject matter is usually defined in the statute or constitution creating the court. In both the federal and the state court systems, a court's subject-matter jurisdiction can be limited by any of the following:

1. The subject of the lawsuit.
2. The sum in controversy.
3. Whether the case involves a felony (a more serious type of crime) or a misdemeanor (a less serious type of crime).
4. Whether the proceeding is a trial or an appeal.

Original and Appellate Jurisdiction The distinction between courts of original jurisdiction and courts of appellate jurisdiction normally lies in whether the case is being heard for the first time. Courts having original jurisdiction are courts of the first instance, or trial courts—that is, courts in which lawsuits begin, trials take place, and evidence is presented. In the federal court system, the *district courts* are trial courts. In the various state court systems, the trial courts are known by various names, as will be discussed shortly.

The key point here is that any court having original jurisdiction is normally known as a trial court. Courts having appellate jurisdiction act as reviewing courts, or appellate courts. In general, cases can be brought before appellate courts only on appeal from an order or a judgment of a trial court or other lower court.

Jurisdiction of the Federal Courts Because the federal government is a government of limited powers, the jurisdiction of the federal courts is limited. Federal courts have subject-matter jurisdiction in two situations: those involving federal questions and diversity of citizenship.

Federal Questions. Article III of the U.S. Constitution establishes the boundaries of federal judicial power. Section 2 of Article III states that "[t]he judicial Power shall extend to all Cases, in Law and Equity, arising under this Constitution, the Laws of the United States, and Treaties made, or which shall be made, under their Authority." This clause means that whenever a plaintiff's cause of action is based, at least in part, on the U.S. Constitution, a treaty, or a federal law, then a **federal question** arises, and the federal courts have jurisdiction.

Federal Question A question that pertains to the U.S. Constitution, an act of Congress, or a treaty and provides a basis for federal jurisdiction in a case.

Any lawsuit involving a federal question, such as a person's rights under the U.S. Constitution, can originate in a federal court. Note that in a case based on a federal question, a federal court will apply federal law.

Diversity of Citizenship. Federal district courts can also exercise original jurisdiction over cases involving **diversity of citizenship**. The most common type of diversity jurisdiction requires *both* of the following:[6]

Diversity of Citizenship A basis for federal court jurisdiction over a lawsuit between citizens of different states or between a U.S. citizen and a citizen of a different country.

1. The plaintiff and defendant must be residents of different states.
2. The dollar amount in controversy must exceed $75,000.

For purposes of diversity jurisdiction, a corporation is a citizen of both the state in which it is incorporated and the state in which its principal place of business is located. A case involving diversity of citizenship can be filed in the appropriate federal district court. If the case starts in a state court, it can sometimes be transferred, or "removed," to a federal court. A large percentage of the cases filed in federal courts each year are based on diversity of citizenship.

6. Diversity jurisdiction also exists in cases between (1) a foreign country and citizens of a state or of different states and (2) citizens of a state and citizens or subjects of a foreign country. These bases for diversity jurisdiction are less commonly used.

The party seeking to move a case to federal court bears the burden of demonstrating that the grounds for diversity exist. **Case Example 4.4** Elijah Ratcliff was involved in a civil lawsuit with Greyhound Bus Lines over luggage theft on one of the company's busses. Greyhound is headquartered in Dallas, Texas. Ratcliff sought to have the civil trial removed to a federal court in New York. To do so, he needed to convince the federal court that he was a resident of New York so that the case would meet the requirements of diversity of jurisdiction.

The facts were not in his favor. First, he had filed a complaint against Greyhound in Texas. His mailing address was in Texas. The luggage was stolen on a return trip he took *to* Texas *from* New York. He indicated that voter registration forms and tax returns would prove his New York residency, but did not produce either. The U.S. district court concluded that Ratcliff was principally based in Texas and dismissed his case for lack of diversity jurisdiction. A federal appeals court affirmed.[7]

As noted, a federal court will apply federal law in cases involving federal questions. In a case based on diversity of citizenship, in contrast, a federal court will apply the relevant state law (which is often the law of the state in which the court sits).

Concurrent Jurisdiction Jurisdiction that exists when two different courts have the power to hear a case.

Exclusive Jurisdiction Jurisdiction that exists when a case can be heard only in a particular court or type of court.

Exclusive versus Concurrent Jurisdiction

When both federal and state courts have the power to hear a case, as is true in lawsuits involving diversity of citizenship, **concurrent jurisdiction** exists. When cases can be tried only in federal courts or only in state courts, **exclusive jurisdiction** exists.

Federal courts have exclusive jurisdiction in cases involving federal crimes, bankruptcy, most patent and copyright claims, suits against the United States, and some areas of admiralty law. State courts also have exclusive jurisdiction over certain subject matter—for instance, divorce and adoption.

When concurrent jurisdiction exists, a party may bring a suit in either a federal court or a state court. A number of factors can affect the decision of whether to litigate in a federal or a state court, such as the availability of different remedies, the distance to the respective courthouses, or the experience or reputation of a particular judge.

A resident of a state other than the one with jurisdiction might also choose a federal court over a state court if there is any concern that a state court might be biased against an out-of-state plaintiff. In contrast, a plaintiff might choose to litigate in a state court if it has a reputation for awarding substantial amounts of damages or if the judge is perceived as being pro-plaintiff. The concepts of exclusive and concurrent jurisdiction are illustrated in Exhibit 4–1.

7. *Ratcliff v. Greyhound Bus Lines,* 792 Fed.Appx. 121 (2nd Cir. 2020).

Exhibit 4-1 Exclusive and Concurrent Jurisdiction

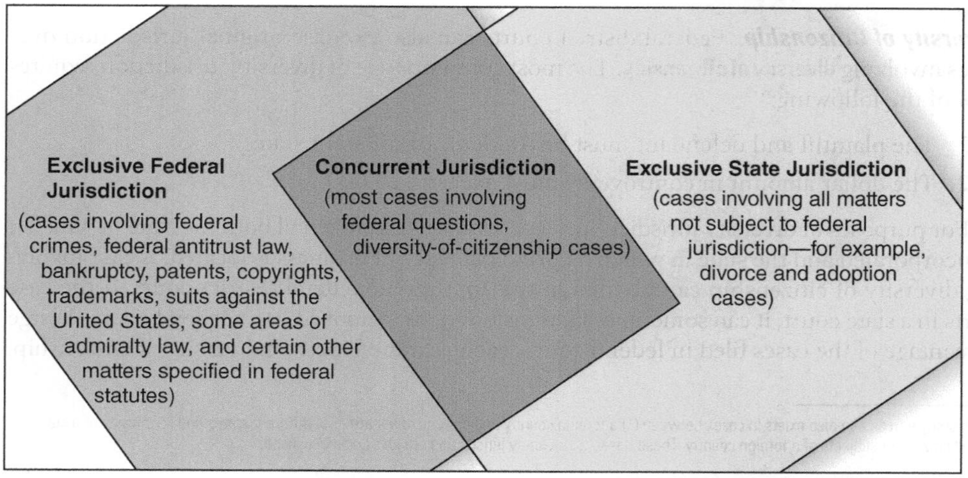
Exclusive Federal Jurisdiction
(cases involving federal crimes, federal antitrust law, bankruptcy, patents, copyrights, trademarks, suits against the United States, some areas of admiralty law, and certain other matters specified in federal statutes)
Concurrent Jurisdiction
(most cases involving federal questions, diversity-of-citizenship cases)
Exclusive State Jurisdiction
(cases involving all matters not subject to federal jurisdiction—for example, divorce and adoption cases)

4–2b Jurisdiction in Cyberspace

Focus Question 2

How are the courts applying traditional jurisdictional concepts to cases involving Internet transactions?

The Internet's capacity to bypass political and geographic boundaries undercuts the traditional basis on which courts assert personal jurisdiction. As already discussed, for a court to compel a defendant to come before it, there must be at least minimum contacts—the presence of a salesperson within the state, for example. Today, however, courts frequently have to decide what constitutes sufficient minimum contacts when a defendant's only connection to a jurisdiction is through an ad on a website.

The "Sliding-Scale" Standard The courts have developed a standard—called a "sliding-scale" standard—for determining when the exercise of jurisdiction over an out-of-state defendant is proper. The sliding-scale standard identifies three types of Internet business contacts and outlines the following rules of jurisdiction:

1. When the defendant conducts *substantial business* over the Internet (such as contracts and sales), jurisdiction is proper. This is true whether the business is conducted with traditional computers, smartphones, or other means of Internet access.
2. When there is *some interactivity* through a website, jurisdiction may be proper, depending on the circumstances. It is up to the courts to decide how much online interactivity is enough to satisfy the minimum-contacts requirement. **Case Example 4.5** Dr. Arthur Delahoussaye, a Louisiana resident, bought a special racing bicycle he saw listed on eBay from Frederick Boelter, who lived in Wisconsin. Later, while Delahoussaye was riding the bike, he had to "bunny hop" (jump) over a gap in the pavement. When he landed, the front wheel disconnected, pushing the forks of the bicycle into the ground and propelling him over the handlebars and onto the pavement. Delahoussaye suffered serious injuries. He sued Boelter in a Louisiana court, alleging that Boelter had negligently removed the secondary retention devices designed to prevent the detachment of the front wheel.

   The Louisiana court ruled that the state did not have jurisdiction over Boelter, and a state appellate court affirmed. Boelter did not have any prior relationship with Delahoussaye, did not initiate communications with Delahoussaye, and discussed the transaction with Delahoussaye only over the Internet. Payment was made through an intermediary, PayPal, and Boelter shipped the bicycle to Louisiana. The sale of a single bicycle to Delahoussaye over eBay was not enough to give Louisiana state jurisdiction over Boelter, so the plaintiff's case was dismissed.[8] ■
3. When a defendant merely engages in *passive advertising* on the Web, jurisdiction is never proper.[9]

International Jurisdictional Issues Because the Internet is global in scope, it raises international jurisdictional issues. The world's courts seem to be developing a standard that echoes the minimum-contacts requirement applied by U.S. courts.

Most courts are indicating that minimum contacts—doing business within the jurisdiction, for instance—are enough to compel a defendant to appear. The effect of this standard is that a business firm has to comply with the laws in any jurisdiction in which it targets customers for its products. This situation is complicated by the fact that many countries' laws on particular issues—such as free speech—are very different from U.S. laws.

The following case illustrates how federal courts apply a sliding-scale standard to determine if they can exercise jurisdiction over a foreign defendant whose only contact with the United States is through a website.

---

8. *Delahoussaye v. Boelter*, 199 So.3d 633 (La.App. 2016).
9. For a leading case on this issue, see *Zippo Manufacturing Co. v. Zippo Dot Com, Inc.*, 952 F.Supp. 1119 (W.D.Pa. 1997).

Spotlight on Gucci: Case 4.1

Gucci America, Inc. v. Wang Huoqing

United States District Court, Northern District of California, 2011 WL 30972 (2011).

Facts Wang Huoqing, a resident of the People's Republic of China, operated numerous websites. When Gucci discovered that Huoqing's websites were selling counterfeit goods—products that carried Gucci's trademarks but were not genuine Gucci articles—it hired a private investigator in San Jose, California, to buy goods from the websites. The investigator purchased a wallet that was labeled Gucci but was counterfeit.

narvikk/iStock Unreleased/Getty Images

Gucci luxury leather products are often counterfeited. Can Gucci sue an Asian company in the United States for selling counterfeit goods?

Gucci filed a trademark infringement lawsuit against Huoqing in a federal district court in California seeking damages and an injunction to prevent further infringement. Huoqing was notified of the lawsuit via e-mail but did not appear in court. Gucci asked the court to enter a default judgment—that is, a judgment entered when the defendant fails to appear. The court first had to determine whether it had personal jurisdiction over Huoqing based on the Internet sales.

Issue Could a U.S. federal court exercise personal jurisdiction over a resident of China whose only contact with the United States was through an interactive website that advertised and sold counterfeit goods?

Decision Yes. The U.S. District Court for the Northern District of California held that it had personal jurisdiction over the foreign defendant, Huoqing. The court entered a default judgment against Huoqing and granted Gucci an injunction.

Reason The court reasoned that the due process clause allows a federal court to exercise jurisdiction over a defendant who has had sufficient minimum contacts with the court's forum—the place where the court exercises jurisdiction. Specifically, jurisdiction exists when (1) the nonresident defendant engages in some act or transaction with the forum "by which he purposefully avails himself of the privilege of conducting activities in the forum, thereby invoking the benefits and protections of its laws; (2) the claim [is] one which arises out of or results from the defendant's forum-related activities; and (3) exercise of jurisdiction [is] reasonable."

To determine whether Huoqing had purposefully conducted business activities in California, the court used a sliding-scale analysis. Under this analysis, passive websites do not create sufficient contacts for such a finding, but interactive sites may do so. Huoqing's websites were fully interactive. In addition, Gucci presented evidence that Huoqing had advertised and sold the counterfeited goods within the court's district, and that he had made one actual sale within the district—the sale to Gucci's private investigator.

Critical Thinking

- **What If the Facts Were Different?** *Suppose that Gucci had not presented evidence that Huoqing made one actual sale through his website to a resident of the court's district (the private investigator). Would the court still have found that it had personal jurisdiction over Huoqing? Why or why not?*

4–2c Venue

Venue The geographic district in which a legal action is tried and from which the jury is selected.

Jurisdiction has to do with whether a court has authority to hear a case involving specific persons, property, or subject matter. **Venue**[10] is concerned with the most appropriate physical location for a trial. Two state courts (or two federal courts) may have the authority to exercise jurisdiction over a case, but it may be more appropriate or convenient to hear the case in one court than in the other.

Basically, the concept of venue reflects the policy that a court trying a suit should be in the geographic neighborhood (usually the county) where the incident leading to the lawsuit occurred or where the parties involved in the lawsuit reside. Venue in a civil case typically is where the defendant resides, whereas venue in a criminal case normally is where the

10. Pronounced *ven*-yoo.

crime occurred. Pretrial publicity or other factors, though, may require a change of venue to another community, especially in criminal cases when the defendant's right to a fair and impartial jury has been impaired.

Note that venue has lost some significance in today's world because of the Internet and 24/7 news reporting. Courts now rarely grant requests for a change of venue. Because everyone has instant access to the same information about a purported crime, courts reason that no community is more or less informed about the matter or prejudiced for or against the defendant.

4–2d Standing to Sue

Before a person can bring a lawsuit before a court, the party must have **standing to sue**, or a sufficient "stake" in the matter to justify seeking relief through the court system. Standing means that the party that filed the action in court has a legally protected interest at stake in the litigation. The party bringing the lawsuit must have suffered a harm, such as physical injury or economic loss, as a result of the action that will be the focus of the lawsuit. At times, a person can have standing to sue on behalf of another person, such as a minor (child) or a mentally incompetent person.

Standing to Sue The legal requirement that an individual must have a sufficient stake in a controversy in order to bring a lawsuit.

Case Example 4.6 Harold Wagner obtained a loan through M.S.T. Mortgage Group to buy a house in Texas. After the sale, M.S.T. transferred its interest in the loan to another lender, which assigned it to another lender, as is common in the mortgage industry. Eventually, when Wagner failed to make the loan payments, CitiMortgage, Inc., notified him that it was going to foreclose on the property and sell the house. Wagner filed a lawsuit claiming that the lenders had improperly assigned the mortgage loan. A federal district court ruled that Wagner lacked standing to contest the assignment. Under Texas law, only the parties directly involved in an assignment can challenge its validity. In this case, the assignment was between two lenders and did not directly involve Wagner.[11]

Another requirement to bring a lawsuit is that the controversy at issue be a **justiciable controversy**[12]—a controversy that is real and substantial, as opposed to hypothetical or academic. A court will not hear a case if the matter at issue is not justiciable.

Justiciable Controversy A controversy that is not hypothetical or academic but real and substantial. It is a requirement that must be satisfied before a court will hear a case.

4–3 The State and Federal Court Systems

Each state has its own court system. Additionally, there is a system of federal courts. Even though there are fifty-two court systems—one for each of the fifty states, one for the District of Columbia, and a federal system—similarities abound. Exhibit 4–2 illustrates the basic organizational structure characteristic of the court systems in many states. The exhibit also shows how the federal court system is structured.

Keep in mind that the federal courts are not superior to the state courts. They are simply an independent system of courts, which derives its authority from Article III, Sections 1 and 2, of the U.S. Constitution.

4–3a The State Court Systems

No two state court systems are exactly the same. Typically, a state court system will include several levels, or tiers, of courts. As indicated in Exhibit 4–2, state courts may include (1) trial courts of limited jurisdiction, (2) trial courts of general jurisdiction, (3) appellate courts, and (4) the state's highest court (often called the state supreme court).

11. *Wagner v. CitiMortgage, Inc.*, 995 F.Supp.2d 621 (N.D.Tex. 2014).
12. Pronounced jus-*tish*-uh-bul.

Exhibit 4–2 The State and Federal Court Systems

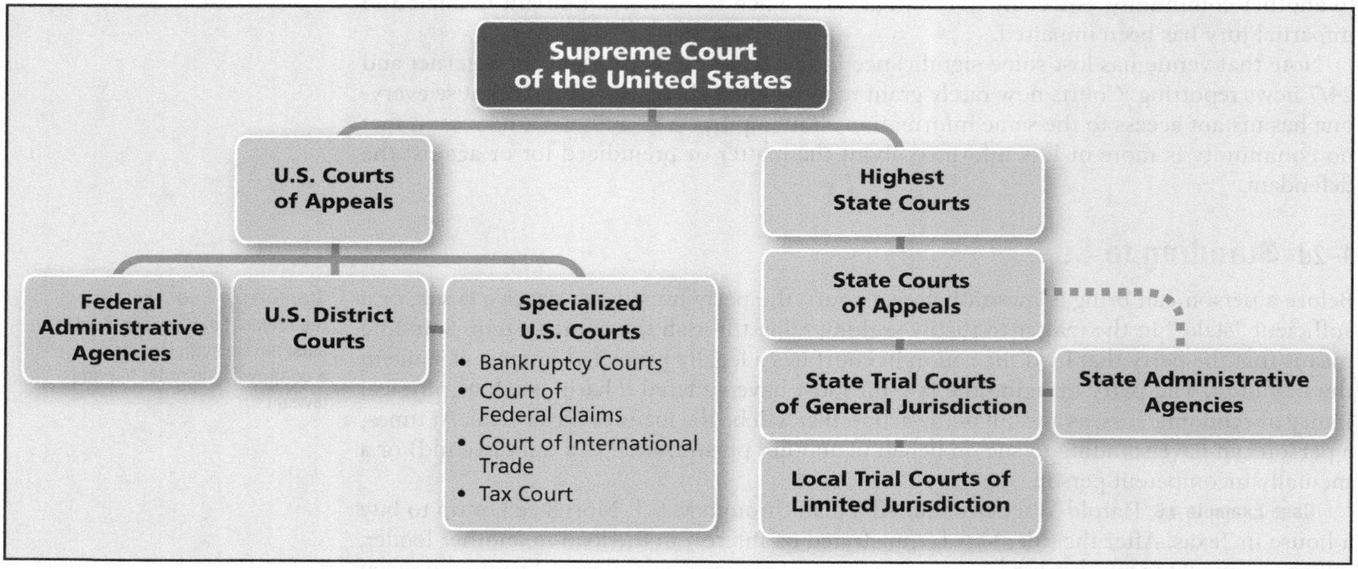

Generally, any person who is a party to a lawsuit has the opportunity to plead the case before a trial court and then, if that person loses, before at least one level of appellate court. If the case involves a federal statute or a federal constitutional issue, the decision of a state supreme court on that issue may be further appealed to the United States Supreme Court.

Trial Courts Trial courts are courts in which trials are held and testimony taken. State trial courts have either general or limited jurisdiction. Trial courts that have general jurisdiction as to subject matter may be called county, district, superior, or circuit courts.[13] These courts have jurisdiction over a wide variety of subjects, including both civil disputes and criminal prosecutions. (In some states, trial courts of general jurisdiction may hear appeals from courts of limited jurisdiction.)

Courts of limited jurisdiction may be called special inferior trial courts or minor judiciary courts. Limited jurisdiction courts might include local municipal courts (which could include separate traffic courts and drug courts) and domestic relations courts (which handle divorce and child-custody disputes). A **small claims court** is an inferior trial court that hears only civil cases involving claims of less than a certain amount, such as $5,000 (the amount varies from state to state). Suits brought in small claims courts are generally conducted informally, and lawyers are not required (in a few states, lawyers are not even allowed). Decisions of small claims courts and municipal courts may sometimes be appealed to a state trial court of general jurisdiction.

Small Claims Court A special court in which parties can litigate small claims without an attorney.

Focus Question 3

What is the difference between the focus of a trial court and that of an appellate court?

Appellate, or Reviewing, Courts Every state has at least one court of appeals (appellate court, or reviewing court), which may be an intermediate appellate court or the state's highest court. About three-fourths of the states have intermediate appellate courts. Generally, courts of appeals do not conduct new trials, in which evidence is submitted and witnesses are examined. Rather, an appellate court panel of three or more judges reviews the record of the case on appeal, which includes a transcript of the trial proceedings, and determines whether the trial court committed an error.

13. The name in Ohio is court of common pleas, and the name in New York is supreme court.

Focus on Questions of Law. Appellate courts generally focus on questions of law, not questions of fact. A **question of fact** deals with what really happened in regard to the dispute being tried—such as whether a party actually burned a flag. A **question of law** concerns the application or interpretation of the law—such as whether flag-burning is a form of speech protected by the First Amendment to the U.S. Constitution. Only a judge, not a jury, can rule on questions of law.

Question of Fact In a lawsuit, an issue that involves only disputed facts, and not what the law is on a given point.

Question of Law In a lawsuit, an issue involving the application or interpretation of a law.

Defer to the Trial Court's Findings of Fact. Appellate courts normally defer (give significant weight) to a trial court's findings on questions of fact, because the trial court judge and jury were in a better position to evaluate testimony. The trial court could directly observe witnesses' gestures, demeanor, and nonverbal behavior during the trial. An appellate court cannot. At the appellate level, the judges review the written transcript of the trial.

An appellate court will challenge a trial court's finding of fact only when the finding is clearly erroneous (that is, when it is contrary to the evidence presented at trial or when no evidence was presented to support the finding). In the following case, an appellate court reviewed the trial record of a case between a landlord and a business tenant.

Case 4.2

Oxford Tower Apartments, LP v. Frenchie's Hair Boutique

Superior Court of Pennsylvania, 2020 PA Super _, _ A.3d _, 2020 WL 119595 (2020).

Facts Frenchie's Hair Boutique sells hair extensions, clothing, and accessories. Rolande Christophe, the owner of Frenchie's, entered into a three-year commercial lease with Oxford Tower Apartments, LP, for a small storefront. Less than two years later, Oxford filed a suit in a Pennsylvania state court against Frenchie's and Christophe, alleging breach of contract and seeking unpaid rent. The defendants counterclaimed for damages. At the trial, Christophe testified that from the start of the lease, problems with the store, including a lack of heat in the building, interfered with her business. She complained to Oxford, to no avail. Fifteen months into the term, a pipe erupted, flooding the store with water and sewage. Frenchie's lost its inventory and was required to clear out so that the flooring could be replaced. Unable to reopen the store because of the lingering odor, Christophe stopped paying rent and gave Oxford the key. The court granted possession of the premises to Oxford and awarded damages for the loss of the inventory to Christophe. Oxford appealed, arguing that Christophe and Frenchie's were still obligated to pay the unpaid rent.

Iakov Filimonov/Shutterstock.com

Issue Were the decision and award of the trial court supported by competent evidence in the record?

Decision Yes. A state intermediate appellate court affirmed the lower court's order. Oxford retained possession of the premises, and Christophe and Frenchie's were entitled to damages for the cost of the lost inventory.

Reason An appellate court will not reverse a finding of fact by a trial court if the finding is supported by competent evidence in the record. Witness testimony and other forms of evidence are to be assessed and resolved by the trial court. It is not within the province of an appellate court to examine evidence or to substitute its judgment for that of the fact finder. Christophe testified about the problems that interfered with her ability to do business and that the landlord failed to remedy, despite frequent complaints. Oxford argued that Frenchie's and Christophe had not vacated the premises. In the appellate court's view, this claim was clearly contradicted by the record. After the pipe erupted, and the floors were replaced, Christophe could not reopen her store due to "the foul odor of waste emanating from the floor." She gave her key to the premises to Oxford. "The trial court concluded that the evidence presented supported a finding in favor of Appellees. We deem the trial court's determination to be well-supported by the record."

Critical Thinking

- **Economic** *Should an appellate court's review of the amount of damages awarded at trial be subject to the principle that limits appellate review of other evidence? Why or why not?*
- **Legal** *A judge or a jury can decide a question of fact, but only a judge can rule on a question of law. Why?*

Highest State Courts The highest appellate court in a state is usually called the supreme court but may be called by some other name. For instance, in both New York and Maryland, the highest state court is called the court of appeals. The decisions of each state's highest court are final on all questions of state law. Only when issues of federal law are involved can a decision made by a state's highest court be overruled by the United States Supreme Court.

Example 4.7 A city enacts an ordinance that prohibits citizens from engaging in door-to-door advocacy without first registering with the mayor's office and receiving a permit. A religious group sues the city, arguing that the law violates the freedoms of speech and religion guaranteed by the First Amendment. If the state supreme court upholds the law, the group could appeal the decision to the United States Supreme Court, because a constitutional (federal) issue is involved. ■

4–3b The Federal Court System

The federal court system is basically a three-tiered model consisting of (1) U.S. district courts (trial courts of general jurisdiction) and various courts of limited jurisdiction, (2) U.S. courts of appeals (intermediate courts of appeals), and (3) the United States Supreme Court.

Unlike state court judges, who are usually elected, federal court judges—including the justices of the Supreme Court—are appointed by the president of the United States and confirmed by the U.S. Senate. Under Article III, federal judges "hold their offices during Good Behavior." In the entire history of the United States, only seven federal judges have been removed from office through impeachment proceedings.

U.S. District Courts At the federal level, the equivalent of a state trial court of general jurisdiction is the district court. There is at least one federal district court in every state. The number of judicial districts can vary over time, primarily owing to population changes and corresponding caseloads. Today, there are ninety-four federal judicial districts.

U.S. district courts have original jurisdiction in federal matters. Federal cases typically originate in district courts. Federal courts with original, but specialized (or limited), jurisdiction include the bankruptcy courts and others that were shown in Exhibit 4-2.

U.S. Courts of Appeals In the federal court system, there are thirteen U.S. courts of appeals—also referred to as U.S. circuit courts of appeals. The federal courts of appeals for twelve of the circuits, including the U.S. Court of Appeals for the District of Columbia Circuit, hear appeals from the federal district courts located within their respective judicial circuits.

The Court of Appeals for the Thirteenth Circuit is called the Federal Circuit. It has national appellate jurisdiction over certain types of cases, such as cases involving patent law and cases in which the U.S. government is a defendant.

The decisions of the circuit courts of appeals are final in most cases, but appeal to the United States Supreme Court is possible. Exhibit 4–3 shows the boundaries of both the district courts and the U.S. courts of appeals within each circuit.

The United States Supreme Court At the highest level of the three-tiered model of the federal court system is the United States Supreme Court. According to Article III of the U.S. Constitution, there is only one national Supreme Court. All other courts in the federal system are considered "inferior." Congress is empowered to create inferior courts as it deems necessary. The inferior courts that Congress has created include the second tier in our model—the U.S. courts of appeals—as well as the district courts and any other courts of limited, or specialized, jurisdiction.

The United States Supreme Court consists of nine justices. Although the Supreme Court has original, or trial, jurisdiction in rare instances (set forth in Article III, Section 2), most

Exhibit 4-3 Boundaries of the U.S. Courts of Appeals and U.S. District Courts

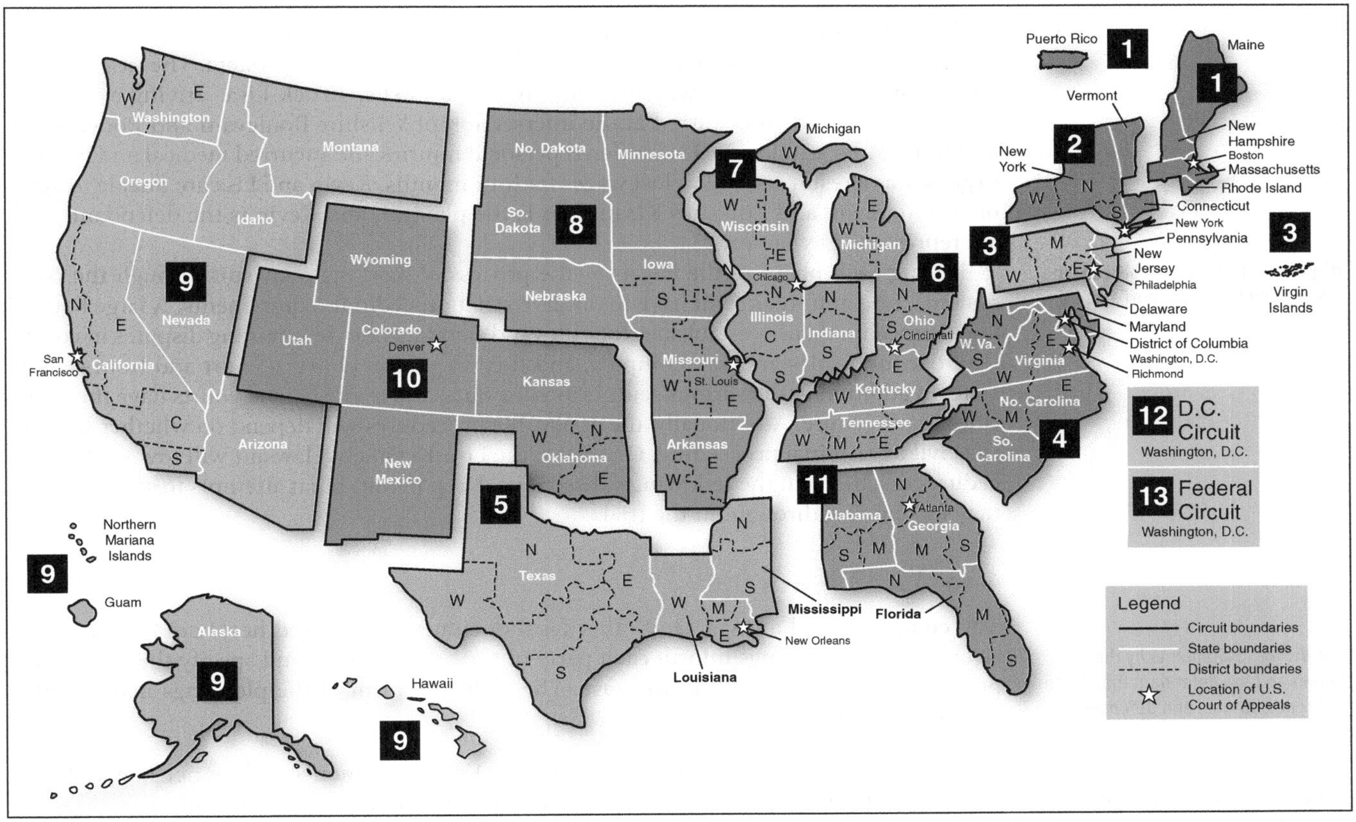

Source: Administrative Office of the United States Courts.

of its work is as an appeals court. The Supreme Court can review any case decided by any of the federal courts of appeals, and it also has appellate authority over some cases decided in the state courts.

Appeals to the Supreme Court. To bring a case before the Supreme Court, a party requests that the Court issue a writ of *certiorari*. A **writ of *certiorari*** [14] is an order issued by the Supreme Court to a lower court requiring that court to send the record of the case for review. Under the **rule of four**, the Court will not issue a writ unless at least four of the nine justices approve.

Whether the Court will issue a writ of *certiorari* is entirely within its discretion. The Court is not required to issue one, and most petitions for writs are denied. (Although thousands of cases are filed with the Supreme Court each year, it hears, on average, fewer than one hundred of these cases.)[15] A denial is not a decision on the merits of a case, nor does it indicate agreement with the lower court's opinion. Furthermore, a denial of the writ has no value as a precedent.

Petitions Granted by the Court. Typically, the Court grants petitions when cases raise important constitutional questions or when the lower courts are issuing conflicting decisions on a significant issue. The justices, however, never explain their reasons for hearing certain cases and not others, so it is difficult to predict which type of case the Court might select.

Writ of *Certiorari* A writ from a higher court asking a lower court for the record of a case.

Rule of Four A rule of the United States Supreme Court under which the Court will not issue a writ of *certiorari* unless at least four justices approve of the decision to issue the writ.

14. Pronounced sur-shee-uh-*rah*-ree.

15. From the mid-1950s through the early 1990s, the United States Supreme Court reviewed more cases per year than it has in the last few years. In the Court's 1982–1983 term, for instance, the Court issued opinions in 151 cases. In contrast, in its 2018–2019 term, the Court issued opinions in only 68 cases.

4–4 Following a State Court Case

To illustrate the procedures that would be followed in a civil lawsuit brought in a state court, we present a hypothetical case and follow it through the state court system. The case involves an automobile accident in which Kevin, driving a Lexus, struck Lisa, driving a Hyundai Genesis. The accident occurred at the intersection of Wilshire Boulevard and Rodeo Drive in Beverly Hills, California. Lisa suffered personal injuries and incurred medical and hospital expenses as a result, as well as lost wages for four months. Kevin and Lisa are unable to agree on a settlement, and Lisa sues Kevin. Lisa is the plaintiff, and Kevin is the defendant. Both are represented by lawyers.

Litigation The process of resolving a dispute through the court system.

During each phase of the **litigation** (the process of working a lawsuit through the court system), Lisa and Kevin will have to observe strict procedural requirements. A large body of law—procedural law—establishes the rules and standards for determining disputes in courts.

Procedural rules are very complex, and they vary from court to court and from state to state. In addition to the various sets of rules for state courts, the federal courts have their own rules of procedure. Additionally, the applicable procedures will depend on whether the case is a civil or criminal proceeding. Generally, the Lisa-Kevin civil lawsuit will involve the procedures discussed in the following subsections. Keep in mind that attempts to settle the case may be ongoing throughout the trial.

4–4a The Pleadings

Pleadings Statements by the plaintiff and the defendant that detail the facts, charges, and defenses of a case.

The complaint and answer (and other legal documents discussed here) are known as the **pleadings**. The pleadings inform each party of the other's claims and specify the issues (disputed questions) involved in the case. The style and form of the pleadings may be quite different in different states.

Complaint The pleading made by a plaintiff alleging wrongdoing on the part of the defendant. When filed with a court, the complaint initiates a lawsuit.

The Plaintiff's Complaint Lisa's suit against Kevin commences when her lawyer files a **complaint** with the appropriate court. The complaint contains statements alleging:

1. *Jurisdiction*. The facts necessary for the court to take *jurisdiction*.
2. *Legal theory*. A brief summary of the *facts* necessary to show that the plaintiff is entitled to relief (a remedy).[16]
3. *Remedy*. A statement of the *remedy* the plaintiff is seeking.

Complaints may be lengthy or brief, depending on the complexity of the case and the rules of the jurisdiction.

Service of Process The delivery of the complaint and summons to a defendant.

Summons A document informing defendants that a legal action has been commenced against them and that they must appear in court on a certain date to answer the plaintiffs' complaint.

Service of Process Before the court can exercise personal jurisdiction over the defendant (Kevin)—in effect, before the lawsuit can begin—the court must have proof that the defendant was notified of the lawsuit. Formally notifying the defendant of a lawsuit is called **service of process**. The plaintiff must deliver, or serve, a copy of the complaint and a **summons** (a notice requiring the defendant to appear in court and answer the complaint) to the defendant.

Default Judgment A judgment entered by a court against a defendant who has failed to appear in court to answer or defend against the plaintiff's claim.

The summons notifies Kevin that he must file an answer to the complaint within a specified time period (twenty days in the federal courts) or suffer a default judgment against him. A **default judgment** in Lisa's favor would mean that she would be awarded the damages alleged in her complaint because Kevin failed to respond to the allegations. In our legal system, no case can proceed to trial unless the plaintiff can prove that the defendant has been properly served.

16. The factual allegations in a complaint must be enough to raise a right to relief above the speculative level. They must plausibly suggest that the plaintiff is entitled to a remedy. See *Bell Atlantic Corp. v. Twombly*, 550 U.S. 544, 127 S.Ct. 1955, 167 L.Ed.2d 929 (2007).

Method of Service. How service of process occurs depends on the rules of the court or jurisdiction in which the lawsuit is brought. Under the Federal Rules of Civil Procedure, anyone who is at least eighteen years of age and is not a party to the lawsuit can serve process in federal court cases. In state courts, the process server is often a county sheriff or an employee of an independent company that provides process service in the local area.

Usually, the server hands the summons and complaint to the defendant personally or leaves it at the defendant's residence or place of business. In cases involving corporate defendants, the summons and complaint may be served on an officer or on a *registered agent* (representative) of the corporation. The name of a corporation's registered agent can usually be obtained from the secretary of state's office in the state where the company incorporated its business. Process can be served by mail in some states if the defendant consents (accepts service). When the defendant cannot be reached, special rules provide for alternative means of service, such as publishing a notice in the local newspaper.

In some situations, courts allow service of process via e-mail, as long as it is reasonably calculated to provide notice and an opportunity to respond. **Case Example 4.8** A county in New York filed a petition to remove a minor child, J.T., from his mother's care due to neglect. The child's father had been deported to Jordan, and the county sought to terminate the father's parental rights. Although the father's exact whereabouts were unknown, the county caseworker had been in contact with him via e-mail. Therefore, the court allowed the father to be served via e-mail because it was reasonably calculated to inform him of the proceedings and allow him an opportunity to respond.[17]

Today, some judges have allowed defendants to be served legal documents via social media, as discussed in this chapter's *Adapting the Law to the Online Environment* feature.

Ievgen Chabanov/Alamy Stock Photo

Usually, a summons is hand-delivered to the defendant. What other ways could a summons be served using today's technologies?

17. *In re J.T.*, 53 Misc.3d 888, 37 N.Y.S.3d 846 (2016).

Adapting the Law to the Online Environment

Using Social Media for Service of Process

Historically, when process servers failed to reach a defendant at home, they attempted to serve process at the defendant's workplace, by mail, or by publication. In our digital age, does publication via social media qualify as legitimate service of process?

Facebook has over 2 billion active users per month. Assume that a man has a Facebook account and so does his spouse. He has moved out and is intentionally avoiding service of a divorce summons. Even a private investigator has not been able to deliver that summons. What to do? According to some courts today, the lawyer for the woman can serve the divorce summons through a private message from her Facebook account.

An Increasing Use of Social Media for Service of Process

More and more courts are allowing service of process via Facebook and other social media. One New York City family court judge ruled that a divorced man could serve his ex-wife through her active Facebook account. She had moved out of the house and provided no forwarding address. A U.S. District Court in California recognized the service of process on a defendant on Facebook, partially because the defendant, who claimed to live in Costa Rica, responded to that service notice soon after it was posted.[a] A federal judge

a. *Elson v. Black*, 2019 WL 4673211 (U.S. District Court, C.D. California 2019).

(Continues)

Continued

in San Francisco allowed a plaintiff to use Twitter accounts to serve several defendants located in Kuwait who had allegedly financed terrorism using their Twitter accounts.[b]

The key requirement appears to be that the plaintiff has diligently and reasonably attempted to serve process by traditional means. Once the plaintiff has exhausted the usual means to effect service, then a court is likely to allow service via social media.[c]

Not All Courts Agree, Though

In spite of these examples, the courts have not uniformly approved of using social media to serve process. After all, it is relatively simple to create a fake Facebook account and nearly impossible to verify the true owner of that account. Some judges have voiced concerns that serving process via Facebook and other social media raises significant questions of whether that service comports with due process.[d]

Critical Thinking

In our connected world, is there any way a defendant could avoid service of process via social media?

b. *St. Francis Assisi v. Kuwait Finance House*, 2016 WL 5725002 (N.D.Cal. 2016).

c. *E.L.V.H., Inc. v. Bennett*, 2018 WL 3496105 (U.S. District Court, C.D. California 2018).

d. *FTC v. PCCare247, Inc.*, 2013 WL 841037 (S.D.N.Y. 2013); and *Asiacell Communications P.J.S.C. v. Doe*, 2018 WL3496105 (U.S. District Court, N.D. California 2018).

Waiver of Formal Service of Process. In many instances, the defendant is already aware that a lawsuit is being filed and is willing to waive (give up) the right to be served personally. The Federal Rules of Civil Procedure (FRCP) and many states' rules allow defendants to waive formal service of process, provided that certain procedures are followed.

In the Lisa-Kevin case, for instance, Lisa's attorney could mail a copy of the complaint to defendant Kevin, along with "Waiver of Service of Summons" forms for Kevin to sign. If he signs and returns the forms within thirty days, formal service of process is waived.

Under the FRCP, defendants who agree to waive formal service of process receive additional time to respond to the complaint (sixty days, instead of twenty days). Some states provide similar incentives to encourage defendants to waive formal service of process and thereby reduce associated costs and foster cooperation between the parties.

Answer Procedurally, a defendant's response to the plaintiff's complaint.

The Defendant's Answer

The defendant's **answer** either admits the statements or allegations set forth in the complaint or denies them and outlines any defenses that the defendant may have. If Kevin admits to all of Lisa's allegations in his answer, the court will enter a judgment for Lisa. If Kevin denies any of Lisa's allegations, the litigation will go forward.

Counterclaim A claim made by a defendant in a civil lawsuit against the plaintiff. In effect, the defendant is suing the plaintiff.

Reply Procedurally, a plaintiff's response to a defendant's answer.

Kevin can deny Lisa's allegations and set forth his own claim that Lisa was negligent and therefore owes him compensation for the damage to his Lexus. This is appropriately called a **counterclaim**. If Kevin files a counterclaim, Lisa will have to answer it with a pleading, normally called a **reply**, which has the same characteristics as an answer.

Kevin can also admit the truth of Lisa's complaint but raise new facts that may result in dismissal of the action. This is called raising an *affirmative defense*. For instance, Kevin could assert that Lisa was driving negligently at the time of the accident and thus was partially responsible for her own injuries. In some states, a plaintiff's contributory negligence operates as a complete defense, whereas in others it simply reduces the amount of damages that Lisa can recover.

Motion to Dismiss A pleading in which a defendant admits the facts as alleged by the plaintiff but asserts that the plaintiff's claim to state a cause of action has no basis in law.

Motion to Dismiss

A *motion* is a procedural request submitted to the court by an attorney on behalf of a client. A **motion to dismiss** requests the court to dismiss the case for stated reasons. Grounds for dismissal of a case include improper delivery of the complaint and summons, improper venue, and the plaintiff's failure to state a claim for which a court could grant relief. For instance, suppose that Lisa had suffered no injuries or losses as a result of Kevin's negligence. In that situation, Kevin could move to have the case dismissed because Lisa would not have stated a claim for which relief could be granted.

If the judge grants the motion to dismiss, the plaintiff generally is given time to file an amended complaint. If the judge denies the motion, the suit will go forward, and the defendant must then file an answer. Note that if Lisa wishes to discontinue the suit because, for instance, an out-of-court settlement has been reached, she can likewise move for dismissal. The court can also dismiss the case on its own motion.

Case Example 4.9 Espresso Disposition Corporation 1 entered into a contract with Santana Sales & Marketing Group, Inc. The agreement included a mandatory *forum-selection clause*, which was a provision designating that any disputes arising under the contract would be decided by a court in Illinois. When Santana Sales filed a lawsuit against Espresso in a Florida state court, Espresso filed a motion to dismiss based on the agreement's forum selection clause. Santana claimed that the forum-selection clause had been a mistake. The court denied Espresso's motion to dismiss. Espresso appealed. A state intermediate appellate court reversed the trial court's denial of Espresso's motion to dismiss and remanded the case to the lower court for the entry of an order of dismissal.[18]

4–4b Pretrial Motions

Either party may attempt to get the case dismissed before trial through the use of various pretrial motions. We have already mentioned the motion to dismiss. Two other important pretrial motions are the motion for judgment on the pleadings and the motion for summary judgment.

At the close of the pleadings, either party may make a **motion for judgment on the pleadings**, or on the merits of the case. The judge will grant the motion only when there is no dispute over the facts of the case and the sole issue to be resolved is a question of law. In deciding on the motion, the judge may consider only the evidence contained in the pleadings.

Motion for Judgment on the Pleadings A motion by either party to a lawsuit at the close of the pleadings requesting the court to decide the issue solely on the pleadings without proceeding to trial. The motion will be granted only if no facts are in dispute.

In contrast, in a **motion for summary judgment**, the court may consider evidence outside the pleadings, such as sworn statements (*affidavits*) by parties or witnesses, or other documents relating to the case. Either party can make a motion for summary judgment. Like the motion for judgment on the pleadings, a motion for summary judgment will be granted only if there are no genuine questions of fact and the sole question is a question of law. When a party appeals a court's grant or denial of a summary judgment motion, the appellate court engages in a *de novo* review, which means it applies the same standard that the trial court applied.

Motion for Summary Judgment A motion requesting the court to enter a judgment without proceeding to trial. The motion can be based on evidence outside the pleadings and will be granted only if no facts are in dispute.

4–4c Discovery

Before a trial begins, each party can use a number of procedural devices to obtain information and gather evidence about the case from the other party or from third parties. The process of obtaining such information is known as **discovery**. Discovery includes gaining access to witnesses, documents, records, and other types of evidence.

Discovery A method by which the opposing parties obtain information from each other to prepare for trial.

The Federal Rules of Civil Procedure and similar rules in the states set forth the guidelines for discovery. Generally, discovery is allowed regarding any matter that is not privileged and is relevant to the claim or defense of any party. Discovery rules also attempt to protect witnesses and parties from undue harassment and to safeguard privileged or confidential material from being disclosed.

Focus Question 4

What is discovery, and how does electronic discovery differ from traditional discovery?

If a discovery request involves privileged or confidential business information, a court can deny the request and can limit the scope of discovery in a number of ways. For instance, a court can require the party to submit the materials to the judge in a sealed envelope so that the judge can decide if they should be disclosed to the opposing party.

---

18. *Espresso Disposition Corp. 1 v. Santana Sales & Marketing Group, Inc.*, 105 So.3d 592 (Fla.App. 3 Dist. 2013).

Discovery prevents surprises at trial by giving parties access to evidence that might otherwise be hidden. This allows both parties to learn what to expect during a trial before they reach the courtroom. Discovery also gives parties the opportunity to file a motion for summary judgment based on the new information it reveals. Finally, discovery serves to narrow the issues so that trial time is spent on the main questions in the case.

Deposition The testimony of a party to a lawsuit or a witness taken under oath before a trial.

Interrogatories A series of written questions for which written answers are prepared by a party to a lawsuit, usually with the assistance of the party's attorney, and then signed under oath.

Depositions and Interrogatories Discovery can involve the use of depositions, interrogatories, or both. A **deposition** is sworn testimony by a party to the lawsuit or any witness. The person being deposed (the deponent) answers questions asked by the attorneys, and the questions and answers are recorded by an authorized court official and sworn to and signed by the deponent. (Occasionally, written depositions are taken when witnesses are unable to appear in person.) The answers given to depositions will, of course, help the attorneys prepare for the trial. They can also be used in court to impeach (challenge the credibility of) parties or witnesses who change their testimony at the trial. In addition, a witness's deposition can be used as testimony if that witness is not available for the trial.

Interrogatories are written questions for which written answers are prepared and then signed under oath. The main difference between interrogatories and written depositions is that interrogatories are directed to a party to the lawsuit (the plaintiff or the defendant), not to a witness, and the party can prepare answers with the aid of an attorney. In addition, the scope of interrogatories is broader because parties are obligated to answer the questions, even if that means disclosing information from their records and files (unless objected to).

Note that, as with other discovery requests, a court can impose sanctions on a party who fails to answer interrogatories. **Case Example 4.10** Construction Laborers Trust Funds for Southern California Administrative Company (the plaintiff), which administers various Southern California employee benefit plans, sued Mario Miguel Montalvo in a federal district court in California. The plaintiff alleged that the defendant, Montalvo, had failed to pay required benefit contributions for every hour that his employees worked (as required under federal law). The plaintiff also claimed that Montalvo had refused to allow an audit of his payroll and business records and had failed to submit monthly employment records needed to determine the amounts due.

Montalvo did not respond to plaintiff's interrogatories. On three occasions, the court ordered Montalvo to answer the interrogatories and produce the necessary documents. The defendant continued to disobey the court's orders and told the plaintiff's attorney that he was "too busy" to comply with the discovery requests. Eventually, the court entered a default judgment against Montalvo, noting that he had willfully disobeyed multiple court orders.[19]

Requests for Other Information A party can serve a written request on the other party for an admission of the truth on matters relating to the trial. Any matter admitted under such a request is conclusively established for the trial. For instance, Lisa can ask Kevin to admit that he was driving at a speed of forty-five miles an hour. A request for admission saves time at trial because the parties will not have to spend time proving facts on which they already agree.

Parties can also gain access to documents and other items not in their possession in order to inspect and examine them. Likewise, parties can gain "entry upon land" to inspect the premises. Kevin's attorney, for instance, normally can gain permission to inspect and photocopy Lisa's car repair bills.

When the physical or mental condition of one party is in question, the opposing party can ask the court to order a physical or mental examination, but the court will do so only if the need for the information outweighs the right to privacy of the person to be examined. If the court issues the order, the opposing party can obtain the results of the examination.

19. *Construction Laborers Trust Funds for Southern California Administrative Co. v. Montalvo*, 2011 WL 1195892 (C.D.Cal. 2011); see also, *Loop AI Labs Inc. v. Gatti*, 2017 WL 934599 (N.D.Cal. 2017).

Ethical Issue

Should the law require discovery on third-party litigation funding? Given the popularity of gambling in our society, it should come as no surprise that it's now possible to bet on lawsuits. Most of this "action" is placed by financing firms known as *third-party litigation funding groups*. For example, a third-party litigant might provide Plaintiff X with $300,000 to bring an age-discrimination suit against Company Z. If Plaintiff X prevails, the third-party litigant will get back its $300,000 plus a percentage of the settlement. If Plaintiff X fails, the third-party litigant loses its $300,000 "bet."

On the one hand, proponents of this multi-billion-dollar global enterprise insist that it provides individual plaintiffs and law firms with the funds they need to bring valid lawsuits. On the other hand, the U.S. Chamber of Commerce, among other critics, worries that plaintiffs with deep-pocketed third-party backers will force business defendants to settle frivolous lawsuits rather than pay the costs of litigating them. Also, there is the ethical question of control. With a large financial stake in a trial's outcome, the third-party litigant might try to dictate legal strategy or influence the settlement amount. For American civil courts to function properly, these decisions must rest solely with plaintiffs and their legal representatives.

Usually, plaintiffs are not obliged by law to disclose third-party litigants during discovery. Several states have passed laws requiring such disclosure, thus allowing courts and juries to determine for themselves the impact of outside funding on the legal proceedings. In the face of strong opposition from the third-party litigation industry, attempts to pass similar federal legislation have yet to succeed.

Electronic Discovery Any relevant material, including information stored electronically, can be the object of a discovery request. The federal rules and most state rules now specifically allow all parties to obtain electronic "data compilations." Electronic evidence, or **e-evidence**, includes all types of computer-generated or electronically recorded information. This might include e-mail, voice mail, tweets, blogs, social media posts, and spreadsheets, as well as documents and other data stored on computers.

E-Evidence A type of evidence that consists of computer-generated or electronically recorded information.

E-evidence can reveal significant facts that are not discoverable by other means. Computers, smartphones, cameras, and other devices automatically record certain information about files—such as who created a file and when, and who accessed, modified, or transmitted it—on their hard drives. This information is called **metadata**, which can be thought of as "data about data." Metadata can be obtained only from the file in its electronic format—not from printed-out versions.

Metadata Data that are automatically recorded by electronic devices and provide information about who created a file and when, and who accessed, modified, or transmitted the file. It can be described as data about data.

Example 4.11 John McAfee, the programmer responsible for creating McAfee antivirus software, was wanted for questioning in the murder of his neighbor in Belize. McAfee left Belize and was on the run from police, but he allowed a journalist to come with him and photograph him. When the journalist posted photos of McAfee online, some metadata were attached to a photo. The police used the metadata to pinpoint the latitude and longitude of the image and subsequently arrested McAfee in Guatemala.

E-Discovery Procedures. The Federal Rules of Civil Procedure deal specifically with the preservation, retrieval, and production of electronic data. Although parties may still use traditional means, such as interrogatories and depositions, to find out about the e-evidence, they must usually hire an expert to retrieve evidence in its electronic format. The expert uses software to reconstruct e-mail exchanges and establish who knew what and when they knew it. The expert can even recover files that the user thought had been deleted from a computer.

Advantages and Disadvantages. E-discovery has significant advantages over paper discovery. Back-up copies of documents and e-mail can provide useful—and often quite damaging—information about how a particular matter progressed over several weeks or months. E-discovery can uncover the proverbial smoking gun that will win the lawsuit, but it is also time consuming and expensive, especially when lawsuits involve large firms with multiple offices. Many companies have found it challenging to fulfill their duty to preserve electronic evidence from a vast number of sources. Failure to do so, however, can lead to sanctions and even force companies to agree to settlements that are not in their best interests.

A failure to provide e-evidence in response to a discovery request does not always arise from an unintentional failure to preserve documents and e-mail. The following case involved a litigant that delayed a response to gain time to intentionally alter and destroy data. At issue were the sanctions imposed for this spoliation. (*Spoliation of evidence* occurs when a document or information that is required for discovery is destroyed or altered significantly.)

Case 4.3

Klipsch Group, Inc. v. ePRO E-Commerce Limited

United States Court of Appeals, Second Circuit, 880 F.3d 620 (2018).

Facts Klipsch Group, Inc. makes sound equipment, including headphones. Klipsch filed a suit in a federal district court against ePRO E-Commerce Limited, a Chinese corporation. Klipsch alleged that ePRO had sold $5 million in counterfeit Klipsch products. ePRO claimed that the sales of relevant products amounted to less than $8,000 worldwide. In response to discovery requests, ePRO failed to timely disclose the majority of the responsive documents in its possession. ePRO also restricted Klipsch's access to its e-data. The court directed ePRO to hold the data to preserve evidence, but the defendant failed to do so. This failure led to the deletion of thousands of documents and significant quantities of data. Klipsch spent $2.7 million on a forensic examination to determine what had been blocked, what had been lost, and what might and might not be recovered. The court concluded that ePRO willingly engaged in spoliation of e-evidence. For this misconduct, the court imposed sanctions, including an order to pay Klipsch the entire $2.7 million for its restorative discovery efforts. ePRO appealed.

Issue Was it appropriate to impose on ePRO the cost of Klipsch's corrective discovery efforts?

Decision Yes. The U.S. Court of Appeals for the Second Circuit affirmed the imposition of the sanctions. "The district court's award properly reflects the additional costs ePRO imposed on its opponent by refusing to comply with its discovery obligations."

Reason ePRO failed to comply with its discovery obligations, which caused Klipsch to incur considerable additional expenses. A party's compliance with a discovery request is not optional. "The integrity of our civil litigation process requires that the parties . . . carry out their duties to maintain and disclose the relevant information in their possession in good faith." Discovery depends on the parties' voluntary preservation of evidence and disclosure of relevant information when asked. Noncompliance increases the cost of litigation. Discovery sanctions are appropriate to discourage delaying tactics and related misconduct. In this case, ePRO argued that the sanctions were "disproportionate." The court concluded, "The proportionality that matters here is that the amount of the sanctions was plainly proportionate—indeed, it was exactly equivalent—to the costs ePRO inflicted on Klipsch in its reasonable efforts to remedy ePRO's misconduct."

Critical Thinking

- **Economic** *Should the cost of corrective discovery efforts be imposed on an uncooperative party if those efforts turn up nothing of real value to the case? Explain.*
- **Legal Environment** *Should it be inferred from a business's failure to keep backup copies of its database that the business must therefore have destroyed the data? Discuss.*

4–4d Pretrial Conference

Either party or the court can request a pretrial conference, or hearing. Usually, the hearing consists of an informal discussion between the judge and the opposing attorneys after discovery has taken place. The purpose of the hearing is to explore the possibility of a settlement without a trial and, if this is not possible, to identify the matters that are in dispute and to plan the course of the trial.

4–4e Jury Selection

A trial can be held with or without a jury. The Seventh Amendment to the U.S. Constitution guarantees the right to a jury trial for cases in *federal* courts when the amount in controversy exceeds $20, but this guarantee does not apply to state courts. Most states have similar guarantees in their own constitutions (although the threshold dollar amount is higher than $20). The right to a trial by jury does not have to be exercised, and many cases are tried without a jury. In most states and in federal courts, one of the parties must request a jury in a civil case, or the judge presumes that the parties waive the right.

Before a jury trial commences, a jury must be selected. The jury selection process is known as ***voir dire***.[20] During *voir dire* in most jurisdictions, attorneys for the plaintiff and the defendant ask prospective jurors oral questions to determine whether a potential jury member is biased or has any connection with a party to the action or with a prospective witness. In some jurisdictions, the judge may do all or part of the questioning based on written questions submitted by counsel for the parties.

During *voir dire*, a party may challenge a prospective juror *peremptorily*—that is, ask that an individual not be sworn in as a juror without providing any reason. Alternatively, a party may challenge a prospective juror *for cause*—that is, provide a reason why an individual should not be sworn in as a juror. If the judge grants the challenge, the individual is asked to step down. A prospective juror may not be excluded from the jury by the use of discriminatory challenges, such as those based on racial criteria or gender.

Know This

Picking the "right" jury is often an important aspect of litigation strategy, and a number of firms now specialize in jury-selection consulting services.

Voir Dire A part of the jury selection process in which the attorneys question prospective jurors about their backgrounds, attitudes, and biases to ascertain whether they can be impartial jurors.

4–4f At the Trial

Once the trial begins, it follows the specific procedures discussed next.

Opening Arguments and Examination of Witnesses At the beginning of the trial, the attorneys present their opening arguments, setting forth the facts that they expect to prove during the trial. Then the plaintiff's case is presented. In our hypothetical case, Lisa's lawyer would introduce evidence (relevant documents, exhibits, and the testimony of witnesses) to support Lisa's position. The defendant has the opportunity to challenge any evidence introduced and to cross-examine any of the plaintiff's witnesses.

At the end of the plaintiff's case, the defendant's attorney has the opportunity to ask the judge to direct a verdict for the defendant on the ground that the plaintiff has presented no evidence that would justify the granting of the plaintiff's remedy. This is called a **motion for a directed verdict** (known in federal courts as a *motion for judgment as a matter of law*).

If the motion is not granted (it seldom is granted), the defendant's attorney then presents the evidence and witnesses for the defendant's case. At the conclusion of the defendant's case, the defendant's attorney has another opportunity to make a motion for a directed verdict. The plaintiff's attorney can challenge any evidence introduced and cross-examine the defendant's witnesses.

Motion for a Directed Verdict A motion for the judge to take the decision out of the hands of the jury and to direct a verdict for the party making the motion on the ground that the other party has not produced sufficient evidence to support a claim.

20. Pronounced vwahr *deehr*.

Closing Arguments and Awards After the defense concludes its presentation, the attorneys present closing arguments supporting their clients. The judge instructs the jury in the law that applies to the case (these instructions are often called *charges*), and the jury retires to the jury room to deliberate a verdict. Typically, jurors are instructed that they must decide the case based only on the information that they learned during the trial.

In the Lisa-Kevin case, the jury will decide in favor of either the plaintiff or the defendant. In addition, if the jury finds for the plaintiff, it will decide on the amount of the **award** (the monetary compensation to be paid to her).

Award The monetary compensation given to a party at the end of a trial or other proceeding.

4–4g Posttrial Motions

After the jury has rendered its verdict, either party may make a posttrial motion. If Lisa wins and Kevin's attorney has previously moved for a directed verdict, Kevin's attorney may make a **motion for judgment *n.o.v.*** (from the Latin *non obstante veredicto,* which means "notwithstanding the verdict"—called a *motion for judgment as a matter of law* in the federal courts). Such a motion will be granted only if the jury's verdict was unreasonable and erroneous. If the judge grants the motion, the jury's verdict will be set aside, and a judgment will be entered in favor of the opposite party (Kevin).

Motion for Judgment *n.o.v.* A motion requesting the court to grant judgment in favor of the party making the motion on the ground that the jury's verdict was unreasonable and erroneous.

Alternatively, Kevin could make a **motion for a new trial**, asking the judge to set aside the adverse verdict and to hold a new trial. The motion will be granted if, after looking at all the evidence, the judge is convinced that the jury was in error but does not feel that it is appropriate to grant judgment for the other side. A judge can also grant a new trial on the basis of newly discovered evidence, misconduct by the participants or the jury during the trial, or error by the judge.

Motion for a New Trial A motion asserting that the trial was so fundamentally flawed (because of error, newly discovered evidence, prejudice, or another reason) that a new trial is necessary to prevent a miscarriage of justice.

4–4h The Appeal

Assume here that any posttrial motion is denied and that Kevin appeals the case. (If Lisa wins but receives a smaller monetary award than she sought, she can appeal also.) Keep in mind, though, that a party cannot appeal a trial court's decision simply because of dissatisfaction with the outcome of the trial. A party must have legitimate grounds to file an appeal. In other words, the party must have a valid claim that the lower court committed an error. If Kevin has grounds to appeal the case, a notice of appeal must be filed with the clerk of the trial court within a prescribed time. Kevin now becomes the appellant, or petitioner, and Lisa becomes the appellee, or respondent.

Filing the Appeal Kevin's attorney files the record on appeal with the appellate court. The record includes the pleadings, the trial transcript, the judge's rulings on motions made by the parties, and other trial-related documents. Kevin's attorney will also provide the reviewing court with a *brief.* The **brief** is a formal legal document outlining the facts and issues of the case, the judge's rulings or jury's findings that should be reversed or modified, the applicable law, and arguments on Kevin's behalf (citing applicable statutes and relevant cases as precedents).

Brief A written summary or statement prepared by one side in a lawsuit to explain its case to the judge.

Lisa's attorney will file an answering brief. Kevin's attorney can file a reply to Lisa's brief, although it is not required. The reviewing court then considers the case.

Appellate Review As explained earlier, a court of appeals does not hear evidence. Instead, the court reviews the record for errors of law. Its decision concerning a case is based on the record on appeal and the attorneys' briefs. The attorneys can present oral arguments, after which the case is taken under advisement.

After reviewing a case, an appellate court has the following options:

1. The court can *affirm* the trial court's decision.
2. The court can *reverse* the trial court's judgment if it concludes that the trial court erred or that the jury did not receive proper instructions.
3. The appellate court can *remand* (send back) the case to the trial court for further proceedings consistent with its opinion on the matter.
4. The court might also affirm or reverse a decision in *part*. For instance, the court might affirm the jury's finding that Kevin was negligent but remand the case for further proceedings on another issue (such as the extent of Lisa's damages).
5. An appellate court can also *modify* a lower court's decision. If the appellate court decides that the jury awarded an excessive amount in damages, for instance, the court might reduce the award to a more appropriate, or fairer, amount.

thepixelchef/E+/Getty Images

Do parties to a trial decision always have a right to appeal that decision?

Appeal to a Higher Appellate Court If the reviewing court is an intermediate appellate court, the losing party may decide to appeal to the state supreme court (the highest state court). Such a petition corresponds to a petition for a writ of *certiorari* from the United States Supreme Court. Although the losing party has a right to ask (petition) a higher court to review the case, the party does not have a right to have the case heard by the higher appellate court.

Appellate courts normally have discretionary power and can accept or reject an appeal. Like the United States Supreme Court, state supreme courts generally deny most appeals. If the appeal is granted, new briefs must be filed before the state supreme court, and the attorneys may be allowed or requested to present oral arguments. Like the intermediate appellate court, the supreme court may reverse or affirm the appellate court's decision or remand the case. At this point, the case typically has reached its end (unless a federal question is at issue and one of the parties has legitimate grounds to seek review by a federal appellate court).

4–4i Enforcing the Judgment

The uncertainties of the litigation process are compounded by the lack of guarantees that any judgment will be enforceable. Even if a plaintiff wins an award of damages in court, the defendant may not have sufficient assets or insurance to cover that amount. Usually, one of the factors considered before a lawsuit is initiated is whether the defendant will be able to pay the damages sought, should the plaintiff win the case.

4–5 Courts Online

Most courts today have websites. Of course, each court decides what to make available at its site. Some courts display only the names of court personnel and office phone numbers. Others add court rules and forms. Many appellate court sites include judicial decisions, although the decisions may remain online for only a limited time. In addition, in some

Docket The list of cases entered on a court's calendar and thus scheduled to be heard by the court.

states, including California and Florida, court clerks offer information about the court's **docket** (its schedule of cases to be heard) and other searchable databases online.

Appellate court decisions are often posted online immediately after they are rendered. Recent decisions of the U.S. courts of appeals, for instance, are available online at their websites. The United States Supreme Court also has an official website and publishes its opinions there immediately after they are announced to the public. In fact, even decisions that are designated as "unpublished" opinions by the appellate courts are usually published (posted) online.

Focus Question 5

What is an electronic court filing system?

4–5a Electronic Filing

A number of state and federal courts allow parties to file litigation-related documents with the courts via the Internet or other electronic means. In fact, the federal court system has implemented its electronic filing system, Case Management/Electronic Case Files (CM/ECF), in nearly all federal courts. The system is available in federal district, appellate, and bankruptcy courts, as well as the U.S. Court of International Trade and the U.S. Court of Federal Claims. More than 41 million cases are on the CM/ECF system. Access to the electronic documents filed on CM/ECF is available through a system called PACER (Public Access to Court Electronic Records), which is a service of the U.S. courts.

A majority of the states have some form of electronic filing, although often it is not yet available in state appellate courts. Some states, including Arizona, California, Colorado, Delaware, Mississippi, New Jersey, New York, and Nevada, offer statewide e-filing systems. Generally, when electronic filing is made available, it is optional. Nonetheless, some state courts have now made e-filing mandatory in certain types of disputes, such as complex civil litigation.

4–5b Cyber Courts and Proceedings

Eventually, litigants may be able to use cyber courts, in which judicial proceedings take place only on the Internet. The parties to a case could meet online to make their arguments and present their evidence. Cyber proceedings might use e-mail submissions, video cameras, designated chat rooms, closed sites, or other Internet facilities. The promise of these virtual proceedings is greater efficiency and lower costs.

Electronic courtroom projects have already been developed in some federal and state courts. The state of Michigan has cyber courts that hear cases involving technology issues and high-tech businesses. Other states that have introduced cyber courts include California, Delaware, Louisiana, and North Carolina. The Federal Rules of Civil Procedure also authorize video conferencing, and some federal bankruptcy courts offer online chatting at their websites.

4–6 Alternative Dispute Resolution

Alternative Dispute Resolution (ADR) The resolution of disputes in ways other than those involved in the traditional judicial process, such as negotiation, mediation, and arbitration.

Litigation is expensive. It is also time consuming. Because of the backlog of cases pending in many courts, several years may pass before a case is actually tried. For these and other reasons, more and more businesspersons are turning to **alternative dispute resolution (ADR)** as a means of settling their disputes.

The great advantage of ADR is its flexibility. Methods of ADR range from the parties sitting down together and attempting to work out their differences to multinational corporations agreeing to resolve a dispute through a formal hearing before a panel of experts. Normally, the parties themselves can control how they will attempt to settle their dispute, what procedures will be used, whether a neutral third party will be present or make a decision, and whether that decision will be legally binding or nonbinding.

Today, more than 90 percent of cases filed with the courts are settled before trial through some form of ADR. Indeed, most states either require or encourage parties to undertake ADR prior to trial. Many federal courts have instituted ADR programs as well.

4–6a Negotiation

The simplest form of ADR is **negotiation**, in which the parties attempt to settle their dispute informally, with or without attorneys to represent them. Attorneys frequently advise their clients to negotiate a settlement voluntarily before they proceed to trial. Parties may even try to negotiate a settlement during a trial or after the trial but before an appeal.

Negotiation A process in which parties attempt to settle their dispute informally, with or without attorneys to represent them.

Negotiation traditionally involves just the parties themselves and (if attorneys are involved) their attorneys. The attorneys still act as advocates—they are obligated to put their clients' interests first. In contrast, other forms of ADR typically also involve neutral third parties.

4–6b Mediation

In **mediation**, a neutral third party acts as a mediator and works with both sides in the dispute to facilitate a resolution. The mediator talks with the parties separately as well as jointly and emphasizes their points of agreement in an attempt to help them evaluate their options. Although mediators may propose a solution (called a *mediator's proposal*), they do not make a decision resolving the matter. States that require parties to undergo ADR before trial often offer mediation as one of the ADR options or (as in Florida) the only option.

Mediation A method of settling disputes outside the courts by using the services of a neutral third party, who acts as a communicating agent between the parties and assists them in negotiating a settlement.

One of the biggest advantages of mediation is that it is not as adversarial as litigation. In a trial, the parties "do battle" with each other in the courtroom, trying to prove each other wrong, while the judge is usually a passive observer. In mediation, the mediator takes an active role and attempts to bring the parties together so that they can come to a mutually satisfactory resolution. The mediation process tends to reduce the hostility between the disputants, allowing them to resume their former relationship without bad feelings. For this reason, mediation is often the preferred form of ADR for disputes involving business partners, employers and employees, or other parties involved in long-term relationships.

Example 4.12 Two business partners, Mark and Charles, have a dispute over how the profits of their firm should be distributed. If the dispute is litigated, Mark and Charles will be adversaries, and their respective attorneys will emphasize how the parties' positions differ, not what they have in common. In contrast, if the dispute is mediated, the mediator will emphasize the common ground shared by Mark and Charles and help them work toward agreement. The two men can work out the distribution of profits without damaging their continuing relationship as partners. ■

Focus Question 6

What are three alternative methods of resolving disputes?

4–6c Arbitration

In **arbitration**, a more formal method of ADR, an arbitrator (a neutral third party or a panel of experts) hears a dispute and imposes a resolution on the parties. Arbitration differs from other forms of ADR in that the third party hearing the dispute makes a decision for the parties. Exhibit 4–4 outlines the basic differences among the three traditional forms of ADR.

Arbitration The settling of a dispute by submitting it to a disinterested third party (other than a court), who renders a decision.

Usually, the parties in arbitration agree that the third party's decision will be *legally binding*, although the parties can also agree to *nonbinding* arbitration. (Arbitration that is mandated by the courts often is nonbinding.) In nonbinding arbitration, the parties can go forward with a lawsuit if they do not agree with the arbitrator's decision.

In some respects, formal arbitration resembles a trial, although usually the procedural rules are much less restrictive than those governing litigation. In the typical arbitration, the parties present opening arguments and ask for specific remedies. Both sides present evidence and may call and examine witnesses. The arbitrator then renders a decision.

KLH49/E+/Getty Images

What are the steps in a typical arbitration proceeding?

Exhibit 4-4 Basic Differences in the Traditional Forms of ADR

	Type of ADR		
	Negotiation	**Mediation**	**Arbitration**
Description	Parties meet informally with or without their attorneys and attempt to agree on a resolution. This is the simplest and least expensive method of ADR.	A neutral third party meets with the parties and emphasizes points of agreement to bring them toward resolution of their dispute, reducing hostility between the parties.	The parties present their arguments and evidence before an arbitrator at a formal hearing. The arbitrator renders a decision to resolve the parties' dispute.
Neutral Third Party Present?	No	Yes	Yes
Who Decides the Resolution?	The parties themselves reach a resolution.	The parties, but the mediator may suggest or propose a resolution.	The arbitrator imposes a resolution on the parties that may be either binding or nonbinding.

The Arbitrator's Decision The arbitrator's decision is called an award. It is usually the final word on the matter. Although the parties may appeal an arbitrator's decision, a court's review of the decision will be much more restricted in scope than an appellate court's review of a trial court's decision. The general view is that because the parties were free to frame the issues and set the powers of the arbitrator at the outset, they cannot complain about the results. A court will set aside an award only in the event of one of the following:

1. The arbitrator's conduct or "bad faith" substantially prejudiced the rights of one of the parties.
2. The award violates an established public policy.
3. The arbitrator arbitrated issues that the parties did not agree to submit to arbitration.

Arbitration Clauses Just about any commercial matter can be submitted to arbitration. Parties can agree to arbitrate a dispute after it arises. Frequently, though, parties include an **arbitration clause** in a contract. The clause provides that any dispute that arises under the contract will be resolved through arbitration rather than through the court system.

Arbitration Clause A clause in a contract that provides that, in the event of a dispute, the parties will submit the dispute to arbitration rather than litigate the dispute in court.

Arbitration Statutes Most states have statutes (often based in part on the Uniform Arbitration Act) under which arbitration clauses will be enforced. Some state statutes compel arbitration of certain types of disputes, such as those involving public employees.

At the federal level, the Federal Arbitration Act (FAA) enforces arbitration clauses in contracts involving maritime activity and interstate commerce (though its applicability to employment contracts has been controversial, as discussed shortly). Because of the breadth of the commerce clause, arbitration agreements involving transactions only slightly connected to the flow of interstate commerce may fall under the FAA.

Case Example 4.13 Cable subscribers sued Cox Communications, Inc., in federal court. They claimed that Cox had violated antitrust law by tying premium cable service to the rental of set-top cable boxes. Cox filed a motion to compel arbitration based on an agreement it had sent to its subscribers. A district court granted the motion to compel, and the subscribers appealed. A federal appellate court affirmed, based on the Federal Arbitration Act. The subscribers' antitrust claims fell within the scope of the arbitration agreement.[21]

The Issue of Arbitrability The terms of an arbitration agreement can limit the types of disputes that the parties agree to arbitrate. Disputes can arise, however, when the parties do not specify limits or when the parties disagree on whether a particular matter is covered by their arbitration agreement.

When one party files a lawsuit to compel arbitration, it is up to the court to resolve the issue of *arbitrability*. That is, the court must decide whether the matter is one that must be resolved through arbitration. If the court finds that the subject matter in controversy is covered by the agreement to arbitrate, then it may compel arbitration. Usually, a court will allow the claim to be arbitrated if the court finds that the relevant statute (the state arbitration statute or the FAA) does not exclude such claims.

No party, however, will be ordered to submit a particular dispute to arbitration unless the court is convinced that the party has consented to do so. Additionally, the courts will not compel arbitration if it is clear that the arbitration rules and procedures are inherently unfair to one of the parties. (This chapter's *Business Web Log* feature deals with an arbitration clause Samsung sought to impose on buyers of its smartphones.)

21. *In re Cox Enterprises, Inc. Set-top Cable Television Box Antitrust Litigation*, 835 F.3d 1195 (10th Cir. 2016).

Samsung and Forced Arbitration

Business Web Log

Samsung, like other smartphone manufacturers, does not want to go to court to address every consumer complaint. Consequently, in each new smartphone box, it includes a Product Safety & Warranty Information brochure containing the following statement:

> ALL DISPUTES WITH SAMSUNG ARISING IN ANY WAY FROM THIS LIMITED WARRANTY OR THE SALE, CONDITION, OR PERFORMANCE OF THE PRODUCTS SHALL BE RESOLVED EXCLUSIVELY THROUGH FINAL AND BINDING ARBITRATION, AND NOT BY A COURT OR JURY.

In the same 101-page brochure, Samsung explains the procedures for arbitration and notes that purchasers can opt out of the arbitration agreement by calling a toll-free number or sending an e-mail within thirty days of purchase. The lead plaintiff in what became a class-action suit against Samsung did not take any steps to opt out.

The class-action suit alleged that the company misrepresented its smartphone's storage capacity and "rigged the phone to operate at a higher speed when it was being tested." Samsung moved to compel arbitration by invoking the arbitration provision in its Product Safety & Warranty Information brochure. A federal district court denied Samsung's motion to compel arbitration. On appeal, the trial court's reasoning was accepted. There was no evidence that the plaintiff had expressly agreed to submit to arbitration. The mere fact that an arbitration clause was included in the Product Safety & Warranty Information brochure did not create a binding contract between the plaintiff and Samsung. Further, even though the plaintiff had signed a Customer Agreement with the seller of the smartphone (Verizon Wireless), Samsung was not a signatory to that agreement.[a]

a. *Norcia v. Samsung Telecommunications America, LLC*, 845 F.3d 1279 (9th Cir. 2017).

Key Point

It is understandable that companies wish to avoid the high cost of going to court for every customer grievance. Binding arbitration offers businesses numerous advantages over litigation. A business must be certain, though, that a binding arbitration requirement is part of an actual contractual agreement between the business and its customers. Placing an arbitration clause, even in all capital letters, in a multi-page document that customers may never read is usually not sufficient.

Why would corporations such as Samsung want to settle disputes with consumers through arbitration rather than going to court?

Mandatory Arbitration in the Employment Context A significant question for businesspersons concerns mandatory arbitration clauses in employment contracts. Many employees claim they are at a disadvantage when they are forced, as a condition of being hired, to agree to arbitrate all disputes and thus waive their rights under statutes designed to protect employees. The United States Supreme Court, however, has held that mandatory arbitration clauses in employment contracts are generally enforceable.

Classic Case Example 4.14 In a landmark decision, *Gilmer v. Interstate/Johnson Lane Corp.*,[22] the Supreme Court held that a claim brought under a federal statute prohibiting age discrimination could be subject to arbitration. The Court concluded that the employee had waived his right to sue when he agreed, as part of a required registration application to be a securities representative with the New York Stock Exchange, to arbitrate "any dispute, claim, or controversy" relating to his employment.

Since the *Gilmer* decision, some courts have refused to enforce one-sided arbitration clauses. Nevertheless, the policy favoring enforcement of mandatory arbitration agreements remains strong.[23]

4–6d Other Types of ADR

The three forms of ADR just discussed are the oldest and traditionally the most commonly used. In addition, a variety of newer types of ADR have emerged, including those described here.

1. In *early neutral case evaluation*, the parties select a neutral third party (generally an expert in the subject matter of the dispute) and then explain their respective positions to that person. The case evaluator assesses the strengths and weaknesses of each party's claims.
2. In a *mini-trial*, each party's attorney briefly argues the party's case before the other party and a panel of representatives from each side who have the authority to settle the dispute. Typically, a neutral third party (usually an expert in the area being disputed) acts as an adviser. If the parties fail to reach an agreement, the adviser renders an opinion as to how a court would likely decide the issue.
3. Numerous federal courts now hold **summary jury trials (SJTs)**, in which the parties present their arguments and evidence and the jury renders a verdict. The jury's verdict is not binding, but it does act as a guide to both sides in reaching an agreement during the mandatory negotiations that immediately follow the trial.

Summary Jury Trial (SJT) A method of settling disputes by holding a trial in which the jury's verdict is not binding but instead guides the parties toward reaching an agreement during the mandatory negotiations that immediately follow.

4–6e Providers of ADR Services

ADR services are provided by both government agencies and private organizations. A major provider of ADR services is the American Arbitration Association (AAA), which handles more than 200,000 claims a year in its numerous offices worldwide. Most of the largest U.S. law firms are members of this nonprofit association. Cases brought before the AAA are heard by an expert or a panel of experts in the area relating to the dispute and are usually settled quickly. The AAA has a special team devoted to resolving large, complex disputes across a wide range of industries.

Hundreds of for-profit firms around the country also provide various dispute-resolution services. Typically, these firms hire retired judges to conduct arbitration hearings or otherwise assist parties in settling their disputes. The judges follow procedures similar to those

22. 500 U.S. 20, 111 S.Ct. 1647, 114 L.Ed.2d 26 (1991).
23. See, for example, *Cruise v. Kroger Co.*, 233 Cal.App.4th 390, 193 Cal.Rptr.3d 17 (2015).

of the federal courts and use similar rules. Usually, each party to the dispute pays a filing fee and a designated fee for a hearing session or conference.

4–6f Online Dispute Resolution

An increasing number of companies and organizations offer dispute-resolution services using the Internet. The settlement of disputes in these online forums is known as **online dispute resolution (ODR)**. The disputes have most commonly involved disagreements over the rights to domain names or over the quality of goods sold via the Internet, including goods sold through Internet auction sites.

Online Dispute Resolution (ODR) The resolution of disputes with the assistance of organizations that offer dispute-resolution services via the Internet.

Rules being developed in online forums may ultimately become a code of conduct for everyone who does business in cyberspace. Most online forums do not automatically apply the law of any specific jurisdiction. Instead, results are often based on general, universal legal principles. As with most offline methods of dispute resolution, any party may appeal to a court at any time.

ODR may be best suited for resolving small- to medium-sized business liability claims, which may not be worth the expense of litigation or traditional ADR. In addition, some local governments are using ODR to resolve claims. **Example 4.15** New York City has used Cybersettle.com to resolve auto accident, sidewalk, and other personal-injury claims made against the city. Parties with complaints submit their demands, and the city submits its offers confidentially online. If an offer exceeds a demand, the claimant keeps half the difference as a bonus.

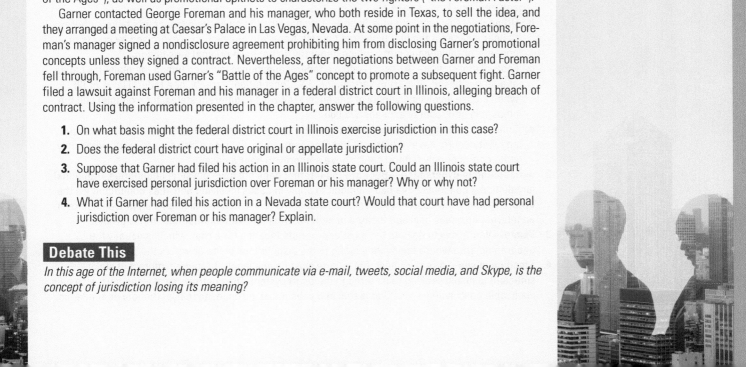

Practice and Review

Stan Garner resides in Illinois and promotes boxing matches for SuperSports, Inc., an Illinois corporation. Garner created the promotional concept of the "Ages" fights—a series of three boxing matches pitting an older fighter (George Foreman) against a younger fighter, such as John Ruiz or Riddick Bowe. The concept included titles for each of the three fights ("Challenge of the Ages," "Battle of the Ages," and "Fight of the Ages"), as well as promotional epithets to characterize the two fighters ("the Foreman Factor").

Garner contacted George Foreman and his manager, who both reside in Texas, to sell the idea, and they arranged a meeting at Caesar's Palace in Las Vegas, Nevada. At some point in the negotiations, Foreman's manager signed a nondisclosure agreement prohibiting him from disclosing Garner's promotional concepts unless they signed a contract. Nevertheless, after negotiations between Garner and Foreman fell through, Foreman used Garner's "Battle of the Ages" concept to promote a subsequent fight. Garner filed a lawsuit against Foreman and his manager in a federal district court in Illinois, alleging breach of contract. Using the information presented in the chapter, answer the following questions.

1. On what basis might the federal district court in Illinois exercise jurisdiction in this case?
2. Does the federal district court have original or appellate jurisdiction?
3. Suppose that Garner had filed his action in an Illinois state court. Could an Illinois state court have exercised personal jurisdiction over Foreman or his manager? Why or why not?
4. What if Garner had filed his action in a Nevada state court? Would that court have had personal jurisdiction over Foreman or his manager? Explain.

Debate This

In this age of the Internet, when people communicate via e-mail, tweets, social media, and Skype, is the concept of jurisdiction losing its meaning?

Key Terms

alternative dispute resolution (ADR) 108
answer 100
arbitration 109
arbitration clause 110
award 106
bankruptcy court 89
brief 106
complaint 98
concurrent jurisdiction 90
counterclaim 100
default judgment 98
deposition 102
discovery 101
diversity of citizenship 89
docket 108
e-evidence 103
exclusive jurisdiction 90
federal question 89
interrogatories 102
judicial review 89
jurisdiction 87
justiciable controversy 93
litigation 98
long arm statute 87
mediation 109
metadata 103
motion for a directed verdict 105
motion for a new trial 106
motion for judgment *n.o.v.* 101
motion for judgment on the pleadings 101
motion for summary judgment 101
motion to dismiss 100
negotiation 109
online dispute resolution (ODR) 113
pleadings 98
probate court 88
question of fact 95
question of law 95
reply 100
rule of four 97
service of process 98
small claims court 94
standing to sue 93
summary jury trial (SJT) 112
summons 98
venue 92
voir dire 105
writ of *certiorari* 97

Chapter Summary: Courts and Alternative Dispute Resolution

The Judiciary's Role in American Government	The role of the judiciary—the courts—in the American governmental system is to interpret and apply the law. Through the process of judicial review—determining the constitutionality of laws—the judicial branch acts as a check on the executive and legislative branches of government.
Basic Judicial Requirements	1. **Jurisdiction**—Before a court can hear a case, it must have jurisdiction over the person against whom the suit is brought or the property involved in the suit, as well as jurisdiction over the subject matter. **a.** Limited versus general jurisdiction—Limited jurisdiction exists when a court is limited to specific subject matter, such as probate or divorce. General jurisdiction exists when a court can hear any kind of case. **b.** Original versus appellate jurisdiction—Original jurisdiction exists when courts have authority to hear a case for the first time (trial courts). Appellate jurisdiction is exercised by courts of appeals, or reviewing courts, which generally do not have original jurisdiction. **c.** Federal jurisdiction—Arises (1) when a federal question is involved (when the plaintiff's cause of action is based, at least in part, on the U.S. Constitution, a treaty, or a federal law), or (2) when a case involves diversity of citizenship (citizens of different states, for example) and the amount in controversy exceeds $75,000. **d.** Concurrent versus exclusive jurisdiction—Concurrent jurisdiction exists when both federal and state courts have authority to hear the same case. Exclusive jurisdiction exists when only state courts or only federal courts have authority to hear a case. 2. **Jurisdiction in cyberspace**—Because the Internet does not have physical boundaries, traditional jurisdictional concepts have been difficult to apply in cases involving activities conducted via the Web. Gradually, the courts are developing standards to use in determining when jurisdiction over an Internet business operator located in another state (or even another country) is proper. 3. **Venue**—Venue has to do with the most appropriate location for a trial, which is usually the geographic area where the event leading to the dispute took place or where the parties reside. 4. **Standing to sue**—A requirement that a party must have a legally protected interest at stake sufficient to justify seeking relief through the court system. The controversy at issue must also be a justiciable controversy—one that is real and substantial, as opposed to hypothetical or academic.

The State and Federal Court Systems	**1. Trial courts**—Courts of original jurisdiction, in which legal actions are initiated. **a.** State—Courts of general jurisdiction can hear any case. Courts of limited jurisdiction include domestic relations courts, probate courts, traffic courts, and small claims courts. **b.** Federal—The federal district court is the equivalent of the state trial court of general jurisdiction. Federal courts of limited jurisdiction include the U.S. Tax Court, the U.S. Bankruptcy Court, and the U.S. Court of Federal Claims. **2. Appellate courts**—Courts of appeals, or reviewing courts, which generally do not have original jurisdiction. Every state has at least one court of appeals, and many have intermediate appellate courts. In the federal court system, the U.S. circuit courts of appeals are the intermediate appellate courts. **3. Supreme (highest) courts**—Each state has a supreme court, although it may be called by some other name. Appeal from the state supreme court to the United States Supreme Court is possible only if the case involves a federal question. As the highest court in the federal court system, the United States Supreme Court is the final arbiter of the U.S. Constitution and federal law.
Following a State Court Case	Rules of procedure prescribe the way in which disputes are handled in the courts. Rules differ from court to court, and separate sets of rules exist for federal and state courts, as well as for criminal and civil cases. A civil court case in a state court would involve the following procedures: **1. The pleadings**— **a.** Complaint—Filed by the plaintiff with the court to initiate the lawsuit. The complaint is served with a summons on the defendant. **b.** Answer—A response to the complaint in which the defendant admits or denies the allegations made by the plaintiff. The answer may assert a counterclaim or an affirmative defense. **c.** Motion to dismiss—A request to the court to dismiss the case for stated reasons, such as the plaintiff's failure to state a claim for which relief can be granted. **2. Pretrial motions (in addition to the motion to dismiss)**— **a.** Motion for judgment on the pleadings—May be made by either party. It will be granted if the parties agree on the facts and the only question is how the law applies to the facts. The judge bases the decision solely on the pleadings. **b.** Motion for summary judgment—May be made by either party. It will be granted if the parties agree on the facts and the sole question is a question of law. The judge can consider evidence outside the pleadings when evaluating the motion. **3. Discovery**—The process of gathering evidence concerning the case and obtaining information from the opposing party. Discovery involves depositions (sworn testimony by a party to the lawsuit or any witness), interrogatories (written questions and answers to these questions made by parties to the action with the aid of their attorneys), and various requests (for admissions, documents, and medical examinations, for instance). Discovery may also involve electronically recorded information, such as e-mail, voice mail, social media posts, and other data compilations. Although electronic discovery has significant advantages over paper discovery, it is also more time consuming and expensive and often requires the parties to hire experts. **4. Pretrial conference**—Either party or the court can request a pretrial conference to identify the matters in dispute after discovery has taken place and to plan the course of the trial. Also, the conference may explore the possibility of a settlement without a trial. **5. Trial**—Following jury selection (*voir dire*), the trial begins with opening statements from both parties' attorneys. The following events then occur: **a.** The plaintiff's introduction of evidence (including the testimony of witnesses) supporting the plaintiff's position. The defendant's attorney can challenge evidence and cross-examine witnesses. **b.** The defendant's introduction of evidence (including the testimony of witnesses) supporting the defendant's position. The plaintiff's attorney can challenge evidence and cross-examine witnesses. **c.** Closing arguments by the attorneys in favor of their respective clients, the judge's instructions to the jury, and the jury's verdict.

	6. Posttrial motions— **a.** Motion for judgment *n.o.v.* ("notwithstanding the verdict")—Will be granted if the judge is convinced that the jury's verdict was in error. **b.** Motion for a new trial—Will be granted if the judge is convinced that the jury's verdict was in error. The motion can also be granted on the grounds of newly discovered evidence, misconduct by the participants during the trial, or error by the judge. **7. Appeal**—Either party can appeal the trial court's judgment to an appropriate court of appeals. After reviewing the record on appeal, the abstracts, and the attorneys' briefs, the appellate court holds a hearing and renders its opinion.
Courts Online	Almost every court has a website offering information about the court and its procedures, and increasingly courts are publishing their opinions online. In the future, we may see cyber courts, in which all trial proceedings are conducted online. A number of state and federal courts allow parties to file litigation-related documents with the courts via the Internet or other electronic means. Nearly all of the federal appellate courts and bankruptcy courts and a majority of the federal district courts have implemented electronic filing systems.
Alternative Dispute Resolution	**1. Negotiation**—The parties come together, with or without attorneys to represent them, to try to reach a settlement without the involvement of a third party. **2. Mediation**—The parties themselves reach an agreement with the help of a neutral third party, called a mediator. The mediator may propose a solution but does not make a decision resolving the matter. **3. Arbitration**—The parties submit their dispute to a neutral third party, the arbitrator, who renders a decision. The decision may or may not be legally binding, depending on the circumstances. **4. Other types of ADR**—These include early neutral case evaluation, mini-trials, and summary jury trials (SJTs). **5. Providers of ADR services**—The leading nonprofit provider of ADR services is the American Arbitration Association. Hundreds of for-profit firms also provide ADR services. **6. Online dispute resolution**—A number of organizations and firms are now offering negotiation, mediation, and arbitration services through online forums. These forums have been a practical alternative for the resolution of domain name disputes and e-commerce disputes in which the amount in controversy is relatively small.

Issue Spotters

1. At the trial, after Sue calls her witnesses, offers her evidence, and otherwise presents her side of the case, Tom has at least two choices between courses of action. Tom can call his first witness. What else might he do? (See *Following a State Court Case.*)

2. Lexi contracts with Theo to deliver a quantity of computers to Lexi's Computer Store. They disagree over the amount, the delivery date, the price, and the quality. Lexi files a suit against Theo in a state court. Their state requires that their dispute be submitted to mediation or nonbinding arbitration. If the dispute is not resolved, or if either party disagrees with the decision of the mediator or arbitrator, will a court hear the case? Explain. (See *Alternative Dispute Resolution.*)

—Check your answers to the *Issue Spotters* against the answers provided in Appendix D.

Business Scenarios and Case Problems

4–1. Standing to Sue. Jack and Maggie Turton bought a house in Jefferson County, Idaho, located directly across the street from a gravel pit. A few years later, the county converted the pit to a landfill. The landfill accepted many kinds of trash that cause harm to the environment, including major appliances, animal carcasses, containers with hazardous content warnings, leaking car batteries, and waste oil. The Turtons complained to the county, but the county did nothing. The Turtons then filed a lawsuit against the county alleging violations of federal environmental laws pertaining to groundwater contamination and other pollution. Do the Turtons have standing to sue? Why or why not? (See *Basic Judicial Requirements.*)

4–2. Discovery. Advance Technology Consultants, Inc. (ATC), contracted with RoadTrac, LLC, to provide software and client software systems for products using global positioning satellite (GPS) technology being developed by RoadTrac. RoadTrac agreed to provide ATC with hardware with which ATC's software would interface. Problems soon arose, however, and RoadTrac filed a lawsuit against ATC alleging breach of contract. During discovery, RoadTrac requested ATC's customer lists and marketing procedures. ATC objected to providing this information because RoadTrac and ATC had become competitors in the GPS industry. Should a party to a lawsuit have to hand over its confidential business secrets as part of a discovery request? Why or why not? What limitations might a court consider imposing before requiring ATC to produce this material? (See *Following a State Court Case.*)

4–3. Arbitration. Horton Automatics and the Industrial Division of the Communications Workers of America—the union that represented Horton's workers—negotiated a collective bargaining agreement. If an employee's discharge for a workplace-rule violation was submitted to arbitration, the agreement limited the arbitrator to determining whether the rule was reasonable and whether the employee had violated it. When Horton discharged its employee Ruben de la Garza, the union appealed to arbitration. The arbitrator found that de la Garza had violated a reasonable safety rule, but "was not totally convinced" that Horton should have treated the violation more seriously than other rule violations. The arbitrator ordered de la Garza reinstated to his job. Can a court set aside this order from the arbitrator? Explain. [*Horton Automatics v. The Industrial Division of the Communications Workers of America, AFL-CIO,* 506 Fed. Appx. 253 (5th Cir. 2013)] (See *Alternative Dispute Resolution.*)

4–4. Discovery. Jessica Lester died from injuries suffered in an auto accident caused by the driver of a truck owned by Allied Concrete Co. Jessica's widower, Isaiah, filed a suit against Allied for damages. The defendant requested copies of all of Isaiah's Facebook photos and other postings. Before responding, Isaiah "cleaned up" his Facebook page. Allied suspected that some of the items had been deleted, including a photo of Isaiah holding a beer can while wearing a T-shirt that declared "I [heart] hotmoms." Can this material be recovered? If so, how? What effect might Isaiah's "misconduct" have on the result in this case? Discuss. [*Allied Concrete Co. v. Lester,* 736 S.E.2d 699 (Va. 2013)] (See *Following a State Court Case.*)

4–5. Electronic Filing. Betsy Faden worked for the U.S. Department of Veterans Affairs. Faden was removed from her position in April 2012 and was given until May 29 to appeal the removal decision. She submitted an appeal through the Merit Systems Protection Board's e-filing system seven days after the deadline. Ordered to show good cause for the delay, Faden testified that she had attempted to e-file the appeal while the board's system was down. The board acknowledged that its system had not been functioning on May 27, 28, and 29. Was Faden sufficiently diligent in ensuring a timely filing? Discuss. [*Faden v. Merit Systems Protection Board,* 553 Fed.Appx. 991 (Fed. Cir. 2014)] (See *Courts Online.*)

4–6. Business Case Problem with Sample Answer—Corporate Contacts. LG Electronics, Inc., a South Korean company, and nineteen other foreign companies participated in the global market for cathode ray tube (CRT) products. CRTs were components in consumer goods, including television sets, and sold for many years in high volume in the United States, including the state of Washington. The state filed a suit against LG and the others, alleging a conspiracy to raise prices and set production levels in the market for CRTs in violation of a state consumer protection statute. The defendants filed a motion to dismiss the suit for lack of personal jurisdiction. Should this motion be granted? Explain your answer. [*State of Washington v. LG Electronics, Inc.,* 185 Wash. App. 394, 341 P.3d 346 (2015)] (See *Basic Judicial Requirements.*)

—For a sample answer to Problem 4–6, go to Appendix E.

4–7. Appellate, or Reviewing, Courts. Angelica Westbrook was employed as a collector for Franklin Collection Service, Inc. During a collection call, Westbrook told a debtor that a $15 processing fee was an "interest" charge. This violated company policy, and Westbrook was fired. She filed a claim for unemployment benefits, which the Mississippi Department of Employment Security (MDES) approved. Franklin objected. At an MDES hearing, a Franklin supervisor testified that she had heard Westbrook make the false statement, although she admitted that there had been no similar incidents with Westbrook. Westbrook denied making the statement but added that, if she had said it, she did not remember it. The agency found that Franklin's reason for terminating Westbrook did not amount to the misconduct required to disqualify her for benefits and upheld the approval. Franklin appealed to a state intermediate appellate court. Is the court likely to uphold the agency's findings of fact? Explain. [*Franklin Collection Service, Inc. v. Mississippi Department of Employment Security,* 184 So.3d 330 (Miss.App. 2016)] (See *The State and Federal Court Systems.*)

4–8. Service of Process. Bentley Bay Retail, LLC, filed a suit in a Florida state court against Soho Bay Restaurant LLC, and its corporate officers, Luiz and Karine Queiroz, in their individual capacities. The charge against the Queirozes was for a breach of their personal guaranty for Soho Bay's debt to Bentley Bay. The plaintiff filed notices with the court to depose the Queirozes, who reside in Brazil. The Queirozes argued that they could not be deposed in Brazil. The court ordered them to appear in Florida to provide depositions in their *corporate* capacity. Witnesses appearing in court outside the jurisdiction of their residence are immune from service of process while in court.

On the Queirozes' appearance in Florida, can they be served with process in their *individual* capacities? Explain. [*Queiroz v. Bentley Bay Retail, LLC*, 43 Fla.L.Weekly D85, 27 So.3d 1108 (3 Dist. 2018)] (See *The State and Federal Court Systems*.)

4–9. A Question of Ethics—The IDDR Approach and Complaints. John Verble worked as a financial advisor for Morgan Stanley Smith Barney, LLC. After nearly seven years, Verble was fired. He filed a suit in a federal district court against his ex-employer. In his complaint, Verble alleged that he had learned of illegal activity by Morgan Stanley and its clients. He claimed that he had reported the activity to the Federal Bureau of Investigation, and that he was fired in retaliation. His complaint contained no additional facts. [*Verble v. Morgan Stanley Smith Barney LLC*, 676 Fed.Appx. 421 (6th Cir. 2017)] (See *Following a State Court Case*.)

1. To avoid a dismissal of his suit, does Verble have a *legal* obligation to support his claims with more facts? Explain.
2. Does Verble owe an *ethical* duty to back up his claims with more facts? Use the IDDR approach to express your answer.

Critical Thinking and Writing Assignments

4–10. Time-Limited Group Assignment—Access to Courts. Assume that a statute in your state requires that all civil lawsuits involving damages of less than $50,000 be arbitrated. Such a case can be tried in court only if a party is dissatisfied with the arbitrator's decision. The statute also provides that if a trial does not result in an improvement of more than 10 percent in the position of the party who demanded the trial, that party must pay the entire cost of the arbitration proceeding. (See *Alternative Dispute Resolution*.)

1. One group will argue that the state statute violates litigants' rights of access to the courts and trial by jury.
2. Another group will argue that the statute does not violate litigants' right of access to the courts.
3. A third group will evaluate how the determination on right of access would be changed if the statute was part of a pilot program that affected only a few judicial districts in the state.

Pixels/Shutterstock.com

5

Tort Law

> "Two wrongs do not make a right."
>
> **English Proverb**

Most of us agree with the chapter-opening quotation—two wrongs do not make a right. In this chapter, we consider a particular type of wrongful action called a **tort** (the word *tort* is French for "wrong").

Part of doing business today—and indeed, part of everyday life—is the risk of being involved in a lawsuit. The list of circumstances in which businesspersons can be sued is long and varied. Anytime one party's allegedly wrongful conduct causes injury to another, an action may arise under the law of torts. Through tort law, society compensates those who have suffered injuries as a result of the wrongful conduct of others.

The Apogee Health Center provides plant-based supplements and pharmaceuticals. It has just developed a cannabidiol (CBD) derived from hops rather than hemp or cannabis. Because hemp and cannabis are heavily regulated, while hops plants are not, Apogee Health's CBD is potentially extremely valuable. In a review on its website, PotTalk claims that it is scientifically impossible to produce a hops-derived CBD and condemns Apogee Health for "defrauding uninformed members of the alternative care community seeking pain relief." If PotTalk's accusation is false, has it committed a tort? As you will learn in this chapter, the tort of trade libel is one of many that can lead to liability for businesses. In this situation, Apogee Health could sue PotTalk—which also produces and sells CBD products—for intentionally interfering with its prospective economic advantage.

Focus Questions

The five Focus Questions *below are designed to help improve your understanding. After reading this chapter, you should be able to answer the following questions:*

1. What types of damages are available in tort lawsuits?
2. What is defamation? Name two types of defamation.
3. What conduct constitutes conversion?
4. Identify the five elements of negligence.
5. What is meant by strict liability? In what circumstances is strict liability applied?

5–1 The Basis of Tort Law

Two notions serve as the basis of all torts: wrongs and compensation. Tort law is designed to compensate those who have suffered a loss or injury due to another person's wrongful act. In a tort action, one person or group brings a personal suit against another person or group to obtain compensation (monetary damages) or other relief for the harm suffered.

Tort A wrongful act (other than a breach of contract) that results in harm or injury to another and leads to civil liability.

Focus Question 1

What types of damages are available in tort lawsuits?

5–1a The Purpose of Tort Law

Generally, the purpose of tort law is to provide remedies for the invasion of various *protected interests*. Society recognizes an interest in personal safety, and tort law provides remedies for acts that cause physical or emotional injury or interfere with physical or emotional security and freedom. Society also recognizes an interest in protecting property, and tort law provides remedies for acts that cause destruction of or damage to property.

Note that in legal usage, the singular noun *damage* is used to refer to harm or injury to persons or property. The plural noun **damages** is used to refer to monetary compensation for such harm or injury.

Damages A monetary award sought as a remedy for a breach of contract or a tortious action.

5–1b Damages Available in Tort Actions

Because the purpose of tort law is to compensate the injured party for the damage suffered, it is important to have a basic understanding of the types of damages that plaintiffs seek in tort actions.

Compensatory Damages A monetary award equivalent to the actual value of injuries or damage sustained by the aggrieved party.

Compensatory Damages Plaintiffs are awarded **compensatory damages** to compensate or reimburse them for actual losses. Thus, the goal is to make the plaintiffs whole and put them in the same position they would have been in had the tort not occurred. Compensatory damages awards are often broken down into *special damages* and *general damages*.

Special damages compensate plaintiffs for quantifiable monetary losses, such as medical expenses, lost wages and benefits (now and in the future), extra costs, the loss of irreplaceable items, and the costs of repairing or replacing damaged property. **General damages** compensate individuals (not companies) for the nonmonetary aspects of the harm suffered, such as pain and suffering. A court might award general damages for physical or emotional pain and suffering, loss of companionship, loss of consortium (losing the emotional and physical benefits of a spousal relationship), disfigurement, loss of reputation, or loss or impairment of mental or physical capacity.

Special Damages In a tort case, an amount awarded to compensate the plaintiff for quantifiable monetary losses, such as medical expenses, property damage, and lost wages and benefits (now and in the future).

General Damages In a tort case, an amount awarded to compensate individuals for the nonmonetary aspects of the harm suffered, such as pain and suffering. Not available to companies.

Case Example 5.1 While working as a seaman in Louisiana, Chedrick Starks was injured when a piece of equipment broke free and struck him. After undergoing several surgeries, Starks sued his employer for past and future medical expenses, and pain and suffering. At trial, a jury awarded him damages for past and future medical expenses and past pain and suffering, but did not award him damages for future pain and suffering. Starks appealed, claiming that the damages awarded were inadequate. A federal district court held that the jury's damages award was inconsistent. Starks had presented sufficient proof that his injuries and future medical treatment could result in future pain and suffering. Therefore, Starks was entitled to a new trial on the issue of damages.[1]

Punitive Damages Monetary damages that may be awarded to a plaintiff to punish the defendant and deter similar conduct in the future.

Punitive Damages Occasionally, the courts also award **punitive damages** in tort cases to punish the wrongdoers and deter others from similar wrongdoing. Punitive damages are appropriate only when the defendant's conduct was particularly egregious (flagrant) or reprehensible (blameworthy).

Thus, punitive damages are normally available mainly in intentional tort actions and only rarely in negligence lawsuits (*intentional torts* and *negligence* will be explained later in the chapter). They may be awarded, however, in suits involving *gross negligence*, which can be defined as an intentional failure to perform a manifest duty in reckless disregard of the effect on the life or property of another.

Courts exercise great restraint in granting punitive damages to plaintiffs in tort actions because punitive damages are subject to the limitations imposed by the due process clause of the U.S. Constitution. In a landmark decision, the United States Supreme Court held that

1. *Starks v. Advantage Staffing, LLC*, 217 F.Supp.3d 917 (E.D.La. 2016).

when an award of punitive damages is grossly excessive, it furthers no legitimate purpose and violates due process requirements.[2] Consequently, an appellate court will sometimes reduce the amount of punitive damages awarded to a plaintiff because the amount was excessive.

Legislative Caps on Damages State laws may limit the amount of damages—both punitive and general—that can be awarded to the plaintiff. More than half of the states have placed caps ranging from $250,000 to $750,000 on noneconomic general damages (such as for pain and suffering), especially in medical malpractice suits. More than thirty states have limited punitive damages, with some imposing outright bans.

Know This
Damage refers to harm or injury to persons or property. *Damages* is a legal term that refers to the monetary compensation awarded to a plaintiff who has suffered such harm or injury.

5–1c Classifications of Torts

There are two broad classifications of torts: *intentional torts* and *unintentional torts* (torts involving negligence). Intentional torts result from the intentional violation of persons or property (fault with intent). Negligence results from the breach of a duty to act reasonably (fault without intent). The classification of a particular tort depends largely on how the tort occurs (intentionally or negligently) and the surrounding circumstances.

5–1d Defenses

Even if a plaintiff proves all the elements of a tort, the defendant can raise a legally recognized **defense**—a reason why the plaintiff should not obtain damages. The defenses available may vary depending on the specific tort involved. A successful defense releases the defendant from partial or full liability for the tortious act.

Defense A reason offered by a defendant in an action or lawsuit as to why the plaintiff should not prevail.

A common defense to intentional torts against persons, for instance, is *consent*. When a person consents to the damaging act, there is generally no tort liability. The most widely used defense in negligence actions is *comparative negligence* (discussed later in this chapter).

Most states also have a *statute of limitations* that establishes the time limit (often two years from the date of discovering the harm) within which a particular type of lawsuit can be filed. After that time period, the plaintiff can no longer file a claim.

5–2 Intentional Torts against Persons

An **intentional tort**, as just mentioned, requires *intent*. The **tortfeasor** (the one committing the tort) must intend to commit an act, the consequences of which interfere with the personal or business interests of another in a way not permitted by law. An evil or harmful motive is not required—in fact, the person committing the action may even have a beneficial motive for committing what turns out to be a tortious act.

Intentional Tort A wrongful act knowingly committed.

Tortfeasor One who commits a tort.

In tort law, intent means only that the person intended the consequences of the act or knew with substantial certainty that certain consequences would result from the act. The law generally assumes that individuals intend the *normal* consequences of their actions. Thus, forcefully pushing another—even if done in jest and without any evil motive—is an intentional tort if injury results, because the object of a strong push can ordinarily be expected to fall down.

Intent can be transferred when a defendant intends to harm one individual but unintentionally harms a different person. This is called **transferred intent**. **Example 5.2** Alex swings a bat intending to hit Blake but misses and hits Carson instead. Carson can sue Alex for the tort of battery (discussed shortly) because Alex's intent to harm Blake can be transferred to Carson. ■

Transferred Intent A legal principle under which a person who intends to harm one individual, but unintentionally harms a different individual, can be liable to the second victim for an intentional tort.

2. *State Farm Mutual Automobile Insurance Co. v. Campbell*, 538 U.S. 408, 123 S.Ct. 1513, 155 L.Ed.2d 585 (2003).

5–2a Assault

Assault Any word or action intended to make another person fearful of immediate physical harm—a reasonably believable threat.

An **assault** is any intentional and unexcused threat of immediate harmful or offensive contact—words or acts that create in another person a reasonable apprehension of harmful contact. An assault can be completed even if there is no actual contact with the plaintiff, provided the defendant's conduct causes the plaintiff to have a reasonable apprehension of imminent harm. Tort law aims to protect individuals from having to expect harmful or offensive contact.

5–2b Battery

Battery Physical contact with another that is unexcused, harmful or offensive, and intentionally performed.

If the act that created the apprehension is *completed* and results in harm to the plaintiff, it is a **battery**, which is defined as an unexcused and harmful or offensive physical contact *intentionally* performed. **Example 5.3** Ivan threatens Jean with a gun and then shoots her. The pointing of the gun at Jean is an assault. The firing of the gun (if the bullet hits Jean) is a battery.

The contact can be harmful, or it can be merely offensive (such as an unwelcome kiss). Physical injury need not occur. The contact can be made by the defendant or by some force set in motion by the defendant, such as a rock thrown by the defendant. Whether the contact is offensive or not is determined by the *reasonable person standard*.[3]

If the plaintiff shows that there was contact, and the jury (or judge, if there is no jury) agrees that the contact was offensive, the plaintiff has a right to compensation. A plaintiff may be compensated for the emotional harm resulting from a battery, as well as for physical harm. Defendants may raise a number of legally recognized defenses to justify their conduct, including self-defense and defense of others.

5–2c False Imprisonment

False imprisonment is the intentional confinement or restraint of another person's activities without justification. False imprisonment interferes with the freedom to move without restraint. The confinement can be accomplished through the use of physical barriers, physical restraint, or threats of physical force. It is essential that the person under restraint does not wish to be restrained. (The plaintiff's consent to the restraint bars any liability.)

Businesspersons may face suits for false imprisonment after they have attempted to confine a suspected shoplifter for questioning. Under the "privilege to detain" granted to merchants in most states, a merchant can use *reasonable force* to detain or delay a person suspected of shoplifting the merchant's property. Although the details of the privilege vary from state to state, generally laws require that any detention be conducted in a *reasonable* manner and for only a *reasonable* length of time. Undue force or unreasonable detention can lead to liability for the business.

© Photobank gallery/Shutterstock.com

Under what circumstances can a person in jail sue for false imprisonment?

Case Example 5.4 Justin Mills was playing blackjack at the Maryland Live! Casino when two casino employees approached him, grabbed his arm, and led him into a back hallway. The employees (who were off-duty police officers moonlighting for the casino) accused Mills of counting cards and demanded his identification. They detained Mills and told him that they would not let him go unless he produced his ID so that the casino could ban him from the premises.

Mills gave the employees his passport and was eventually allowed to leave, but he secretly recorded the audio from the interaction using the smartphone in his pocket. Mills later filed a lawsuit alleging, in part, false

3. The reasonable person standard is an objective test of how a reasonable person would have acted under the same circumstances. See "The Duty of Care and Its Breach" later in this chapter.

imprisonment. A federal district court granted Mills a summary judgment on the false imprisonment claim, because the casino personnel had no legal justification for detaining him.[4] Cities and counties may also face liability for false imprisonment if they detain individuals without reason.

5–2d Intentional Infliction of Emotional Distress

The tort of *intentional infliction of emotional distress (IIED)* can be defined as extreme and outrageous conduct resulting in severe emotional distress to another. To be **actionable** (capable of serving as the ground for a lawsuit), the conduct must be so extreme and outrageous that it exceeds the bounds of decency accepted by society.

Actionable Capable of serving as the basis of a lawsuit. An actionable claim can be pursued in a lawsuit or other court action.

Outrageous Conduct Courts in most jurisdictions are wary of IIED claims and confine them to truly outrageous behavior. Generally, repeated annoyances (such as those experienced by a person who is being stalked), coupled with threats, are sufficient to support a claim. (See this chapter's *Business Law Analysis* feature for details of how courts analyze these types of claims.) Acts that cause indignity or annoyance alone usually are not enough.

Defenses to IIED In many instances, as noted throughout this text, courts will accept the legal fiction of corporate personhood to provide companies with the same rights before the law as individuals. It seems, however, that this fiction does not extend to IIED claims. **Case Example 5.5** Towerview Construction and Osprey Cove Real Estate worked out an agreement in which the real estate company loaned the construction company the funds to developed four residential lots. Once the lots were sold, Towerview would repay its loan. Eventually, Towerview came to believe that Osprey Cove was fraudulently taking steps to block the sale

4. *Mills v. PPE Casino Resorts Maryland, LLC*, 2017 WL 2930460 (D.Md. 2017).

Business Law Analysis

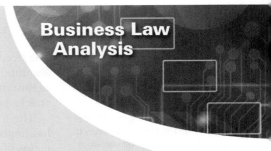

Analyzing Intentional Infliction of Emotional Distress Claims

While living in her home country of Tanzania, Sophia Kiwanuka signed an employment contract with Anne Bakilana, a Tanzanian living in the United States. Kiwanuka came to Washington, D.C., to work as a babysitter and maid in Bakilana's house. When Kiwanuka arrived, Bakilana confiscated her passport, held her in isolation, and forced her to work long hours under threat of having her deported. Kiwanuka worked seven days a week without breaks and was subjected to regular verbal and psychological abuse by Bakilana.

Kiwanuka filed a complaint against Bakilana for intentional infliction of emotional distress. Bakilana asked the court to dismiss the claim. Are Kiwanuka's allegations sufficient to show outrageous intentional conduct that resulted in severe emotional distress?

Analysis: In deciding whether the alleged conduct was sufficiently outrageous, a court would look at the repeated conduct of the purported tortfeasor. The complaint stated that Bakilana, on a daily basis, used her position of power and control over Kiwanuka to engage in an intentional pattern of outrageous verbal abuse against her. The complaint also alleged that Bakilana intentionally interfered with Kiwanuka's attempts to form relationships or acquaintances, which deepened Kiwanuka's suffering of isolation and distress.

Result and Reasoning: These allegations were sufficient to show extreme and outrageous conduct, intentionally committed, that resulted in severe emotional distress to Kiwanuka. Therefore, Kiwanuka was entitled to a trial on her claim for intentional infliction of emotional distress.

of the lots and filed suit for, among other claims, IIED. Affirming the ruling of a trial court, the Georgia Court of Appeals dismissed the claim. Both courts agreed that corporations cannot recover for IIED because they lack the ability to experience emotions.[5]

Other defenses to IIED are more straightforward. If the plaintiff gives consent to the outrageous conduct that leads to an IIED claim, the lawsuit is unlikely to proceed. Context also matters. Seemingly outrageous conduct that is normal under the circumstances is usually not actionable. Neither is outrageous speech when it is directed against a public figure. In most instances, such speech enjoys First Amendment protection.

Ethical Issue

Can someone be found liable for a tort if that person ruins the plaintiff's marriage? Many American courts once held that a wife was the property of her husband. A remnant of this principle exists in the tort law of six states: Hawaii, Mississippi, New Mexico, North Carolina, South Dakota, and Utah. In these jurisdictions, a spouse of either sex can bring a lawsuit for "alienation of affections," a variation on the tort of intentional infliction of emotional distress.

Examples of defendants who were found liable for this sort of unethical behavior include a wealthy businessman who allegedly "stole" the wife of a plumber and a female secretary who supposedly ruined a "fairy tale marriage." Although it may seem somewhat humorous that courts would involve themselves in such salacious and seemingly personal affairs, the consequences are no joke. A Mississippi jury awarded the plumber $750,000, and a North Carolina appeals court upheld a $1 million payment to the harmed spouse in the "fairy tale marriage."

Case law highlights several defenses to alienation of affections. The defendant can show that there was no affection left in the failing marriage to alienate. Alternatively, the defendant can prove, through text messages, phone calls, and "hook-up" locations, that the alienating conduct took place in a different state in which such behavior did not violate the state's tort law.

Focus Question 2

What is defamation? Name two types of defamation.

5–2e Defamation

The freedom of speech guaranteed by the First Amendment to the U.S. Constitution is not absolute. In interpreting the First Amendment, the courts must balance free speech rights against other strong social interests, including society's interest in preventing and redressing attacks on reputation.

Defamation Anything published or publicly spoken that causes injury to another's good name, reputation, or character.

Libel Defamation in writing or another permanent form (such as a digital recording).

Slander Defamation in oral form.

The tort of **defamation** involves wrongfully hurting a person's good reputation. The law has imposed a general duty on all persons to refrain from making false, defamatory statements of fact about others. Breaching this duty in writing or another permanent form (such as a digital recording) constitutes the tort of **libel**. Breaching the duty orally is the tort of **slander**. The tort of defamation also arises when a false statement of fact is made about a person's product, business, or legal ownership rights to property.

To establish defamation, a plaintiff normally must prove the following:

1. The defendant made a false statement of fact.
2. The statement was understood as being about the plaintiff and tended to harm the plaintiff's reputation.
3. The statement was published to at least one person other than the plaintiff.
4. In addition, plaintiffs who are public figures must prove *actual malice*.

5. *Osprey Cove Real Estate, LLC v. Towerview Construction, LLC*, 808 S.E.2d 425, 343 Ga.App. 436 (2017).

Statement of Fact Requirement Often at issue in defamation lawsuits (including online defamation) is whether the defendant made a *statement of fact* or *a statement of opinion*. Statements of opinion normally are not actionable because they are protected under the First Amendment. In other words, making a negative statement about another person is not defamation unless the statement is false and represents something as a fact. **Example 5.6** Vickie's statement "Lane cheats on his taxes," if false, can lead to liability for defamation because it is a statement of fact. The statement "Lane is a jerk" cannot constitute defamation because it is clearly an opinion.

Publication Requirement The basis of the tort of defamation is the publication of a statement or statements that hold an individual up to contempt, ridicule, or hatred. *Publication* here means that the defamatory statements are communicated to persons other than the defamed party. Publication can be made via the Internet.

The courts have generally held that even dictating a letter to a secretary constitutes publication, although the publication may be privileged (as discussed shortly). If a third party overhears defamatory statements by chance, the courts usually hold that this also constitutes publication. Note also that anyone who republishes or repeats defamatory statements is liable even if that person reveals the source of the statements.

Case Example 5.7 Eddy Ramirez, a meat cutter at Costco Wholesale Corporation, was involved in a workplace incident with a co-worker, and Costco gave him a notice of suspension. After an investigation in which co-workers were interviewed, Costco fired Ramirez. Ramirez sued, claiming that the suspension notice was defamatory. The court ruled in Costco's favor. Ramirez could not establish defamation, because he had not shown that the suspension notice was published to any third parties. Costco did nothing beyond what was necessary to investigate the events that led to Ramirez's termination.[6]

Damages for Libel Once a defendant's liability for libel is established, a plaintiff is normally entitled to general damages. General damages are designed to compensate the plaintiff for nonspecific harms such as disgrace or dishonor in the eyes of the community, humiliation, injured reputation, and emotional distress—harms that are difficult to measure. In other words, to recover general damages in libel cases, plaintiffs need not prove that they were actually harmed in any specific way as a result of the libelous statement.

In the following case, the plaintiff alleged defamation by e-mail and online reviews. She sought damages for harm to her reputation, lost income, and emotional distress.

6. *Ramirez v. Costco Wholesale Corp.*, 2014 WL 2696737 (Ct.Sup.Ct. 2014).

Case 5.1

Sky v. Van Der Westhuizen

Court of Appeals of Ohio, Fifth District, Stark County, 2019 -Ohio- 1960, 136 N.E.3d 820 (2019).

Facts Anastasia Sky, a psychotherapist, is a cat breeder and the owner of Skyhaven Birman Cattery. Sky exhibits her cats at shows, at which she has won many awards, and sells her cats to other breeders. Her cats and cattery are registered with the Cat Fanciers Association (CFA) in Ohio. E-mail purporting to be from Sky's employees and customers was sent to the CFA, alleging, among other things, that her cats were kept in deplorable conditions and treated cruelly and inhumanely. Reviews were posted online stating that Sky was "a crazy cat lady" whose medical license had been revoked due to drug abuse. The e-mail and posts were false. Sky filed a suit in an Ohio

(Continues)

Continued

state court, alleging defamation and emotional distress. A response to a subpoena identified the author of the e-mail and the reviews as Hilde Van Der Westhuizen, a competing breeder. The court entered a judgment in Sky's favor and awarded her damages for the harm to her reputation, loss of income, and emotional distress. Van Der Westhuizen appealed, arguing that the evidence did not support the award.

Issue Was Sky entitled to damages for defamation?

Decision Yes. A state intermediate appellate court affirmed the lower court's judgment. "In light of the testimony . . . , we find that the record contains competent, credible evidence to support the trial court's damage awards."

Reason The appellate court reviewed the testimony and other evidence presented to the trial court and found that it supported the judgment and award of damages for the harm to Sky's reputation as a breeder and a doctor. Sky testified that after the e-mail was sent, she was shunned in the breeding community and lost revenue as a result of a decrease in the sales of her kittens. She also lost ten patients as a result of the damaging reviews posted online and received fewer physician referrals. These losses undercut her current and future income. On the claim for emotional distress, testimony described the changes in Sky's appearance, mood, and emotional state following the defamatory e-mail and reviews. Evidence showed that she sought therapy, and she testified to her humiliation and mental suffering. In sum, the evidence supported the lower court's award.

Critical Thinking

- **Legal Environment** *Punitive damages may be awarded in a tort action when a defendant's actions show malice—that is, when a person's conduct is characterized by hatred, ill will, or a spirit of revenge. Would an award of punitive damages be appropriate in this case? Explain.*
- **Ethical** *Should Van Der Westhuizen make an effort to remove all of the false online statements and reviews of Sky that she posted? Why or why not?*

Damages for Slander In contrast to cases involving libel, in a case alleging slander, the plaintiff must prove *special damages* (defined earlier) to establish the defendant's liability. In other words, the plaintiff must show that the slanderous statement caused the plaintiff to suffer actual economic or monetary losses.

Unless this initial hurdle of proving special damages is overcome, a plaintiff alleging slander normally cannot go forward with the suit and recover any damages. This requirement is imposed in cases involving slander because slanderous statements have a temporary quality. In contrast, a libelous (written) statement has the quality of permanence, can be circulated widely, especially through social media, and usually results from some degree of deliberation on the part of the author.

Slander *Per Se* Exceptions to the burden of proving special damages in cases alleging slander are made for certain types of slanderous statements. If a false statement constitutes "slander *per se*," no proof of special damages is required for it to be actionable. The following four types of false utterances are considered to be slander *per se*:

1. A statement that another has a loathsome disease (such as a sexually transmitted disease) or a serious mental defect.
2. A statement that another has committed improprieties while engaging in a profession or trade.
3. A statement that another has committed or has been imprisoned for a serious crime.
4. A statement that a person is unchaste or has engaged in serious sexual misconduct. (This category of slander *per se* usually applies only to unmarried persons and sometimes only to women.)

Defenses to Defamation Truth is normally an absolute defense against a defamation charge. In other words, if the defendant in a defamation suit can prove that the allegedly defamatory statements were true, normally no tort has been committed.

Other defenses to defamation may exist if the statement is privileged or concerns a public figure. Note that the majority of defamation actions in the United States are filed in state courts, and the states may differ both in how they define defamation and in the particular defenses they allow, such as privilege.

Privileged Communications. In some circumstances, individuals will not be liable for defamatory statements because they enjoy a **privilege**, or immunity. Privileged communications are of two types: absolute and qualified.[7] Only in judicial proceedings and certain government proceedings is an absolute privilege granted. Thus, statements made in courtrooms by attorneys and judges during trials are absolutely privileged, as are statements made by government officials during legislative debate.

Privilege A special right, advantage, or immunity that enables a person or a class of persons to avoid liability for defamation.

In other situations, a person will not be liable for defamatory statements because that person has a *qualified*, or conditional, privilege. An employer's statements in written evaluations of employees are an example of a qualified privilege. Generally, if the statements are made in good faith and the publication is limited to those who have a legitimate interest in the communication, the statements fall within the area of qualified privilege. **Example 5.8** Jorge has worked at Google for five years and is being considered for a management position. His supervisor, Lydia, writes an e-mail about Jorge's performance to those evaluating him for the management position. The message contains certain negative statements, which Lydia honestly believes are true. If Lydia limits the disclosure of the contents of the message to company representatives, her statements will likely be protected by a qualified privilege.

Public Figures. Politicians, entertainers, professional athletes, and other persons who are in the public eye are considered *public figures*. In general, public figures are considered fair game, and false and defamatory statements about them that appear in the media will not constitute defamation unless the statements are made with **actual malice**.[8] To be made with actual malice, a statement must be made *with either knowledge of its falsity or a reckless disregard of the truth*.

Actual Malice The deliberate intent to cause harm that exists when a person makes a statement with either knowledge of its falsity or reckless disregard of the truth. It is required to establish defamation against public figures.

Statements about public figures, especially when made via a public medium, are usually related to matters of general interest. They are made about people who substantially affect all of us. Furthermore, public figures generally have some access to a public medium for answering disparaging falsehoods about themselves, whereas private individuals do not. For these reasons, public figures have a greater burden of proof in defamation cases (they must prove actual malice) than do private individuals.

Case Example 5.9 John Tiegen is a former U.S. Marine who defended the United States consulate in Benghazi, Libya, from a well-publicized terrorist attack. On leaving the military, Tiegen became a public speaker and a brand ambassador for several companies. Frederic Slice posted comments about Tiegen on websites operated by these companies, stating that the ex-Marine was a "liar" and had committed perjury by lying to Congress about Benghazi. Tiegen, admitting that he was a public figure, sued Slice for libel. A Texas appeals court dismissed the case because Tiegen could not show that Slice had acted with actual malice. Whether or not Slice's comments were true, Tiegen produced no evidence that Slice had known the statements were false or had acted with reckless disregard for the truth.[9]

---

7. Note that the term *privileged communication* in this context is *not* the same as privileged communication between professionals, such as attorneys, and their clients.

8. The landmark case establishing the actual malice requirement is *New York Times Co. v. Sullivan*, 376 U.S. 254, 84 S.Ct. 710, 11 L.Ed.2d 686 (1964).

9. *Tiegen v. Slice*, 2020 WL 728426 (Tex.App.—Dallas, 2020).

5–2f Invasion of the Right to Privacy and Appropriation

A person has a right to solitude and freedom from prying public eyes—in other words, to privacy. The Supreme Court has held that a fundamental right to privacy is implied by various amendments to the U.S. Constitution. Some state constitutions also explicitly provide for privacy rights. In addition, a number of federal and state statutes have been enacted to protect individual rights in specific areas.

Tort law also safeguards these rights through the torts of *invasion of privacy* and *appropriation*. Generally, to sue successfully for an invasion of privacy, a person must have a reasonable expectation of privacy, and the invasion must be highly offensive. (See this chapter's *Adapting the Law to the Online Environment* feature for a discussion of how invasion of privacy claims can arise when someone posts pictures or videos taken with digital devices.)

Invasion of Privacy Four acts qualify as an invasion of privacy:

1. *Intrusion into an individual's affairs or seclusion.* Invading someone's home or illegally searching someone's briefcase is an invasion of privacy. The tort has been held to extend to eavesdropping by wiretap, the unauthorized scanning of a bank account, compulsory blood testing, and window peeping. **Example 5.10** Sharon, a Walgreen's pharmacist, shares Luanna's prescription history with William, who is married to Sharon and used to date Luanna. If Luanna sues, she will likely win an invasion of privacy lawsuit against Sharon and her employer, Walgreen's. ■

Revenge Porn and Invasion of Privacy

Nearly every digital device today takes photos and videos and has software that allows the recording of conversations. Many couples immortalize their "private moments" using such digital devices. One partner may take a racy selfie and send it as an attachment to a text message to the other partner, for instance.

Occasionally, after a relationship ends, one partner seeks a type of digital revenge. The result, called revenge porn, involves the online distribution of sexually explicit images of a nonconsenting individual with the intent to humiliate that person.

State Statutes

Thirty-five states have enacted statutes that make revenge porn a crime. But these state laws differ. (In some states, it is a misdemeanor with less serious consequences, and in other states, it is a felony with more serious penalties.) In addition, most of these criminal statutes do not provide victims with a right to obtain damages. Therefore, victims have sued in civil courts on the basis of (1) invasion of privacy, (2) public disclosure of private facts, and (3) intentional infliction of emotional distress.

A Case Example

Nadia Hussain had dated Akhil Patel on and off for seven years. After they broke up, Patel hounded her with offensive and threatening phone calls, texts, and e-mails—often twenty to thirty per day. He did this for several years. He even came to her workplace a few times. Hussain filed police reports and changed her phone number multiple times, but the harassment continued. Patel also hacked or attempted to hack into her accounts (she had received alerts).

Eventually, Patel posted secretly recorded sexual videos of Hussain on the Internet. (He had recorded, without her consent, a Skype conversation they once had in which Hussain had undressed and masturbated.) Hussain sued Patel claiming invasion of privacy, public disclosure of private facts, and intentional infliction of emotional distress. A jury found in her favor and awarded $500,000 in damages for mental anguish and damage to her reputation. An appellate court affirmed but reduced the damages to $345,000 (because the intentional infliction of emotional distress claim was not supported by the evidence).[a]

Critical Thinking

Why might the appellate court have decided that the evidence did not support Nadia Hussain's intentional infliction of emotional distress claim?

a. *Patel v. Hussain*, 485 S.W.3d 153 (Tex.App.—Houston 2016); also see *Doe v. Doe*, 2017 WL 3025885 (S.D.N.Y. 2017).

2. *False light.* Publication of information that places a person in a false light is also an invasion of privacy. For instance, writing a story about a person that attributes ideas and opinions not held by that person is an invasion of privacy. (Publishing such a story could involve the tort of defamation as well.) **Case Example 5.11** Police received a report from a customer of West Gate Bank that his debit card had been stolen and used to withdraw funds from his account at the bank's ATM. The ATM video depicted a female walking up to an ATM and using a debit card to withdraw cash. To identify the person, the police posted still images from the video on the Crime Stoppers website and Facebook page. The caption said, "This young lady doesn't look like your typical crook, but she is! She used someone's stolen credit card.... If you know who she is, leave us a tip here."

   Police received tips that the woman in the video was Shayla Funk. Funk, as it turned out, was not a criminal and was simply withdrawing funds with her own card from her own bank account. Nevertheless, as a result of the posting, she lost her job as an occupational therapist. Funk sued the city and Crime Stoppers organization for defamation and for violating her privacy by representing her in a false light, and won. The court awarded Funk more than $259,000 in damages, which was affirmed on appeal by the state's highest court.[10]

3. *Public disclosure of private facts.* This type of invasion of privacy occurs when a person publicly discloses private facts about an individual that an ordinary person would find objectionable or embarrassing. A newspaper account about a private citizen's sex life or financial affairs could be an actionable invasion of privacy, even if the information revealed is true, because it should not be a matter of public concern.

4. *Appropriation of identity.* Under the common law, using a person's name, picture, or other likeness for commercial purposes without permission is a tortious invasion of privacy. Individuals' right to privacy normally includes the right to the exclusive use of their identity. **Example 5.12** An advertising agency asks a singer with a distinctive voice and stage presence to do a marketing campaign for a new automobile. The singer rejects the offer. If the agency then uses someone who imitates the singer's voice and dance moves in the ad, this would be actionable as an appropriation of identity.

Appropriation In tort law, the use by one person of another person's name, likeness, or other identifying characteristic without permission and for the benefit of the user.

Appropriation Most states today have codified the common law tort of appropriation of identity in statutes that establish the distinct tort of **appropriation**, or right of publicity. For example, the Illinois Right of Publicity Act (IRPA) defines a person's identity as "an attribute of an individual that serves to identify that individual to an ordinary, reasonable viewer or listener."[11] Under this law, a person's identity cannot be used for commercial purposes without consent.

Case Example 5.13 The online marketplace Groupon, Inc., uses an "Instagram Widget" to link publicly available photos from the social networking service to member businesses. All Instagram users identify themselves with a username. Christine Dancel took a photo of herself at Philly G's restaurant and posted it on Instagram. Because of the Widget, the photo and her username—"meowchristine"—automatically appeared on Philly G's Groupon page.

Dancel sued under the IRPA, claiming that she had not given consent to Groupon. She argued that a "reasonable viewer" would know that usernames are designed to identify individuals, just like actual names. The district court disagreed, holding that, in fact, many usernames, including "meowchristine," are too obscure to establish identity. A federal appellate court affirmed, noting that while *some* usernames might clearly identify an individual, it would place too great a burden on courts to determine if *each one* did under Illinois law.[12]

10. *Funk v. Lincoln-Lancaster County Crime Stoppers, Inc.*, 294 Neb. 715, 885 N.W.2d 1 (2016).
11. 765 I.L.C.S 1075/5, 30.
12. *Dancel v. Groupon, Inc.*, 949 F.3d 999 (7th Cir. 2019).

5–2g Fraudulent Misrepresentation

A misrepresentation leads another to believe in a condition that is different from the condition that actually exists. This is often accomplished through a false or incorrect statement. Although persons sometimes make misrepresentations accidentally because they are unaware of the existing facts, the tort of **fraudulent misrepresentation**, or fraud, involves *intentional* deceit for personal gain. The tort includes several elements:

Fraudulent Misrepresentation Any misrepresentation, either by misstatement or by omission of a material fact, knowingly made with the intention of deceiving another and on which a reasonable person would and does rely to that person's detriment.

1. The misrepresentation of facts or conditions with knowledge that they are false or with reckless disregard for the truth.
2. An intent to induce another to rely on the misrepresentation.
3. Justifiable reliance by the deceived party.
4. Damage suffered as a result of the reliance.
5. A causal connection between the misrepresentation and the injury suffered.

Puffery A salesperson's exaggerated claims concerning the quality of property offered for sale. Such claims involve opinions rather than facts and are not legally binding promises or warranties.

For fraud to occur, more than mere **puffery**, or *seller's talk*, must be involved. Fraud exists only when a person represents as a fact something that person knows is untrue. For instance, it is fraud to claim that a roof does not leak when one knows it does. Facts are objectively ascertainable, whereas seller's talk (such as "I am the best accountant in town") is not.

Case Example 5.14 Joseph Guido bought nine rental houses in Stillwater, New York. The houses shared a waste disposal system that was not functioning. Guido hired someone to design and install a new system. When town officials later discovered sewage on the property, Guido had the system partially replaced. He then represented to prospective buyers of the property, including Danny Revell, that the "Septic system [was] totally new—each field totally replaced." In response to a questionnaire from the buyers' bank, Guido denied any knowledge of environmental problems.

A month after the sale of the houses, the septic system failed and required substantial repairs. The buyers sued Guido for fraud. A jury found in favor of the plaintiffs and awarded damages. A state intermediate appellate court affirmed the judgment on appeal. Guido knew that the septic system was not totally new and that sewage had been released on the property (an environmental problem). He had misrepresented these facts to the buyers. The buyers' reliance on Guido's statements was justifiable because a visual inspection of the property did not reveal any problems.[13]

Petegar/E+/Getty Images

If a home seller claims that a new septic system was installed when it wasn't, does that constitute fraud?

Statement of Fact versus Opinion Normally, the tort of misrepresentation or fraud occurs only when there is reliance on a *statement of fact*. Sometimes, however, the tort may involve reliance on a *statement of opinion* if the individual making the statement has a superior knowledge of the subject matter. For instance, when a lawyer makes a statement of opinion about the law in a state in which the lawyer is licensed to practice, a court will treat it as a statement of fact.

Negligent Misrepresentation Sometimes, a tort action can arise from misrepresentations that are made negligently rather than intentionally. The key difference between intentional and negligent misrepresentation is whether the person making the misrepresentation had actual knowledge of its falsity. Negligent misrepresentation requires only that the person making the statement or omission did not have a reasonable basis for believing its truthfulness.

Liability for negligent misrepresentation usually arises when the defendant who made the misrepresentation owed a duty of care to the plaintiff to supply correct information. Statements or omissions made by attorneys and accountants to their clients, for instance, can lead to liability for negligent misrepresentation.

13. *Revell v. Guido*, 124 A.D.3d 1006, 2 N.Y.S.3d 252 (3d Dept. 2015).

5–2h Wrongful Interference

The torts known as **business torts** generally involve wrongful interference with another's business rights. Business torts involving wrongful interference are generally divided into two categories: wrongful interference with a contractual relationship and wrongful interference with a business relationship.

Business Torts Wrongful interference with another's business rights and relationships.

Wrongful Interference with a Contractual Relationship Three elements are necessary for wrongful interference with a contractual relationship to occur:

1. A valid, enforceable contract must exist between two parties.
2. A third party must know that this contract exists.
3. The third party must *intentionally* induce a party to breach the contract.

Classic Case Example 5.15 A classic case involved an opera singer, Johanna Wagner, who was under contract to sing for a man named Lumley for a specified period of years. A man named Gye, who knew of this contract, nonetheless "enticed" Wagner to refuse to carry out the agreement, and Wagner began to sing for Gye. Gye's action constituted a tort because it wrongfully interfered with the contractual relationship between Wagner and Lumley.[14] (Of course, Wagner's refusal to carry out the agreement also entitled Lumley to sue Wagner for breach of contract.)

The body of tort law relating to intentional interference with a contractual relationship has expanded greatly in recent years. In principle, any lawful contract can be the basis for an action of this type. The contract could be between a firm and its employees or a firm and its customers. Sometimes, for instance, a competitor draws away one of a firm's key employees. Only if the original employer can show that the competitor knew of the contract's existence, and intentionally induced the breach, can damages be recovered from the competitor.

GARWOOD & VOIGT Fine & Rare Books Maps & Prints

Opera singer Johanna Wagner is shown here in one of her many roles. She was under contract to sing for one person, but was enticed to break the contract and sing for someone else. Was a tort committed? If so, by whom?

Wrongful Interference with a Business Relationship Businesspersons devise countless schemes to attract customers, but they are prohibited from unreasonably interfering with another's business in their attempts to gain a share of the market. There is a difference between *competitive methods* and *predatory behavior*—actions undertaken with the intention of unlawfully driving competitors completely out of the market. Attempting to attract customers in general is a legitimate business practice, whereas specifically targeting the customers of a competitor is more likely to be predatory.

Example 5.16 A shopping mall contains two athletic shoe stores: Joe's and Ultimate Sport. Joe's cannot station an employee at the entrance of Ultimate Sport to divert customers by telling them that Joe's will beat Ultimate Sport's prices. This type of activity constitutes the tort of wrongful interference with a business relationship, which is commonly considered to be an unfair trade practice. If this activity were permitted, Joe's would reap the benefits of Ultimate Sport's advertising.

Defenses to Wrongful Interference A person will not be liable for the tort of wrongful interference with a contractual or business relationship if it can be shown that the interference was justified or permissible. Bona fide competitive behavior is a permissible interference even if it results in the breaking of a contract.

Example 5.17 If Antonio's Meats advertises so effectively that it induces Sam's Restaurant to break its contract with Burke's Meat Company, Burke's will be unable to recover against Antonio's Meats on a wrongful interference theory. After all, the public policy that favors free competition in advertising outweighs any possible instability that such competitive activity might cause in contractual relations.

14. *Lumley v. Gye*, 118 Eng.Rep. 749 (1853).

Know This
What society and the law consider permissible often depends on the circumstances.

5-3 Intentional Torts against Property

Intentional torts against property include trespass to land, trespass to personal property, conversion, and disparagement of property. These torts are wrongful actions that interfere with individuals' legally recognized rights with regard to their land or personal property. The law distinguishes real property from personal property. *Real property* is land and things "permanently" attached to the land. *Personal property* consists of all other items, which are basically movable. Thus, a house and lot are real property, whereas the furniture inside the house is personal property. Cash, stocks, and bonds are also personal property.

5-3a Trespass to Land

Trespass to Land Entry onto, above, or below the surface of land owned by another without the owner's permission or legal authorization.

A **trespass to land** occurs anytime a person, without permission, does any of the following:

1. Enters onto, above, or below the surface of land that is owned by another.
2. Causes anything to enter onto land owned by another.
3. Remains on land owned by another or permits anything to remain on it.

Actual harm to the land is not an essential element of this tort, because the tort is designed to protect the right of an owner to exclusive possession.

Common types of trespass to land include walking or driving on another's land, shooting a gun over the land, and throwing rocks at a building that belongs to someone else. Another common form of trespass involves constructing a building so that part of it is on an adjoining landowner's property.

Konstantin L/Shutterstock.com

What are some common types of trespass to land?

Establishing Trespass Before a person can be a trespasser, the real property owner (or other person in actual and exclusive possession of the property) must establish that person as a trespasser. For instance, "posted" trespass signs expressly establish as a trespasser a person who ignores these signs and enters onto the property. Any person who enters onto property to commit an illegal act (such as a thief entering a lumberyard at night to steal lumber) is established impliedly as a trespasser, without posted signs. In contrast, a guest in your home is not a trespasser unless that guest has been asked to leave but refuses.

Liability for Harm At common law, a trespasser is liable for any damage caused to the property and generally cannot hold the owner liable for injuries sustained on the premises. This common law rule is being abandoned in many jurisdictions in favor of a *reasonable duty of care* rule that varies depending on the status of the parties.

For instance, a landowner may have a duty to post a notice that guard dogs patrol the property. Also, if young children are likely to be attracted to the property by some object, such as a swimming pool or a sand pile, and are injured, the landowner may be held liable under the *attractive nuisance doctrine*. An owner can normally use reasonable force to remove a trespasser from the premises—or detain the trespasser for a reasonable time—without liability for damages, however.

Defenses against Trespass to Land One defense to a claim of trespass to land is to show that the trespass was warranted. This may occur, for instance, when the trespasser entered the property to assist someone in danger.

Another defense is for trespassers to show that they had a license to come onto the land. A *licensee* is one who is invited (or allowed to enter) onto the property of another for the licensee's benefit. A person who enters another's property to read an electric meter, for example, is a licensee. Another example of a licensee is someone who is camping on another person's land with the owner's permission but without paying for the privilege.

Note that licenses to enter are *revocable* by the property owner. If a property owner asks a meter reader to leave and the meter reader refuses to do so, the meter reader at that point becomes a trespasser.

5–3b Trespass to Personal Property

Whenever an individual wrongfully takes or harms the personal property of another or otherwise interferes with the lawful owner's possession of personal property, **trespass to personal property** (also called *trespass to chattels* or *trespass to personalty*[15]) occurs. In this context, harm means not only destruction of the property, but also anything that diminishes its value, condition, or quality.

Trespass to Personal Property Wrongfully taking or harming the personal property of another or otherwise interfering with the lawful owner's possession of personal property.

Trespass to personal property involves intentional meddling with a possessory interest (the right to possess), including barring an owner's access to personal property. **Example 5.18** Kelly takes Ryan's business law book as a practical joke and hides it so that Ryan is unable to find it for several days before the final examination. Here, Kelly has engaged in a trespass to personal property. (Kelly has also committed the tort of *conversion*—to be discussed next.)

If it can be shown that trespass to personal property was warranted, then a complete defense exists. Most states, for instance, allow automobile repair shops to retain a customer's car (under what is called an *artisan's lien*) when the customer refuses to pay for repairs already completed.

5–3c Conversion

Any act that deprives an owner of personal property or of the use of that property without the owner's permission and without just cause can constitute **conversion**. Even the taking of electronic records and data can form the basis of a conversion claim. Often, when conversion occurs, a trespass to personal property also occurs. The original taking of the personal property from the owner was a trespass, and wrongfully retaining the property is conversion.

Conversion Wrongfully taking or retaining possession of an individual's personal property and placing it in the service of another.

Focus Question 3
What conduct contitutes conversion?

Failure to Return Goods Conversion is the civil side of crimes related to theft, but it is not limited to theft. Even if the rightful owner consented to the initial taking of the property, so there was no theft or trespass, a failure to return the personal property may still be conversion. **Example 5.19** Chen borrows Mark's iPad Pro to use while traveling home from school for the holidays. When Chen returns to school, Mark asks for his iPad Pro back. Chen tells Mark that she gave it to her little brother for Christmas. In this situation, Mark can sue Chen for conversion, and Chen will have to either return the iPad Pro or pay damages equal to its replacement value.

Intention Conversion can occur even when people who possess the goods of others mistakenly believe that they are entitled to the goods. In other words, good intentions are not a defense against conversion. Someone who buys stolen goods, for instance, can be sued for conversion even if the buyer did not know that the goods were stolen. If the true owner of the goods sues the buyer and wins, the buyer must either return the property to the owner or pay the owner the full value of the property.

Know This
It is the *intent* to do an act that is important in tort law, not the motive behind the intent.

Case Example 5.20 Nicholas Mora worked for Welco Electronics, Inc., but had also established his own company, AQM Supplies. Mora used Welco's credit card without permission and deposited more than $375,000 into AQM's account, which he then transferred to his personal account. Welco sued. A California court held that Mora was liable for conversion. The court reasoned that when Mora misappropriated Welco's credit card and used it, he took part of Welco's credit balance with the credit-card company.[16]

15. Pronounced *per*-sun-ul-tee.
16. *Welco Electronics, Inc. v. Mora*, 223 Cal.App.4th 202, 166 Cal.Rptr.3d 877 (2014).

Richard Levine/Alamy

How can a portable credit-card terminal be used for conversion?

5–3d Disparagement of Property

Disparagement of property occurs when economically injurious falsehoods are made about another's product or property, rather than about another's reputation (as in the tort of defamation). Disparagement of property is a general term for torts specifically referred to as *slander of quality* or *slander of title*.

Disparagement of property An economically injurious falsehood about another's product or property.

Publication of false information about another's product, alleging that it is not what its seller claims, constitutes the tort of **slander of quality (trade libel)**. To establish trade libel, the plaintiff must prove that the improper publication caused a third party to refrain from dealing with the plaintiff and that the plaintiff sustained economic damages (such as lost profits) as a result. An improper publication may be both a slander of quality and a defamation of character. For instance a statement that disparages the quality of a product may also, by implication, disparage the character of the person who would sell such a product.

When a publication denies or casts doubt on another's legal ownership of property, and the property's owner suffers financial loss as a result, the tort of **slander of title** may exist. Usually, this is an intentional tort that occurs when someone knowingly publishes an untrue statement about property with the intent of discouraging a third party from dealing with the property's owner. For instance, a car dealer would have difficulty attracting customers if competitors publish a notice that the dealer's stock consists of stolen automobiles.

Slander of Quality (Trade Libel) The publication of false information about another's product, alleging that it is not what its seller claims.

Slander of Title The publication of a statement that denies or casts doubt on another's legal ownership of property, causing financial loss to that property's owner.

5–4 Negligence

The tort of **negligence** occurs when someone suffers injury because of another's failure to fulfill a required *duty of care*. In contrast to intentional torts, in torts involving negligence, the tortfeasor neither wishes to bring about the consequences of the act nor believes that they will occur. The person's conduct merely creates a risk of such consequences. If no risk is created, there is no negligence. Moreover, the risk must be foreseeable—that is, it must be such that a reasonable person engaging in the same activity would anticipate the risk and guard against it. In determining what is reasonable conduct, courts consider the nature of the possible harm.

Negligence The failure to exercise the standard of care that a reasonable person would exercise in similar circumstances.

Many of the actions giving rise to the intentional torts discussed earlier in the chapter constitute negligence if the element of intent is missing (or cannot be proved). **Example 5.21** Juan walks up to Maya and intentionally shoves her. Maya falls and breaks an arm as a result. In this situation, Juan has committed an intentional tort (assault and battery). If Juan carelessly bumps into Maya, however, and she falls and breaks an arm as a result, Juan's action will constitute negligence. In either situation, Juan has committed a tort. ■

To succeed in a negligence action, the plaintiff must prove each of the following:

Focus Question 4
Identify the five elements of negligence.

1. *Duty*. The defendant owed a duty of care to the plaintiff.
2. *Breach*. The defendant breached that duty.
3. *Causation in fact*. The plaintiff's injury would not have occurred without the defendant's breach.
4. *Proximate causation*. The connection between the defendant's breach and the plaintiff's injury is foreseeable and therefore justifies imposing liability.
5. *Damages*. The plaintiff suffered a legally recognizable injury.

We discuss each of these five elements of negligence next.

5–4a The Duty of Care and Its Breach

Central to the tort of negligence is the concept of a **duty of care**. The basic principle underlying the duty of care is that people in society are free to act as they please so long as their actions do not infringe on the interests of others. When someone fails to comply with the duty to exercise reasonable care, a potentially tortious act may result.

Duty of Care The duty of all persons, as established by tort law, to exercise a reasonable amount of care in their dealings with others. Failure to exercise due care, which is normally determined by the reasonable person standard, constitutes the tort of negligence.

Failure to live up to a standard of care may be an act (setting fire to a building) or an omission (neglecting to put out a campfire). It may be a careless act or a carefully performed but nevertheless dangerous act that results in injury. In determining whether the duty of care has been breached, courts consider several factors:

1. The nature of the act (whether it is outrageous or commonplace).
2. The manner in which the act was performed (cautiously versus heedlessly).
3. The nature of the injury (whether it is serious or slight).

Creating even a very slight risk of a dangerous explosion might be unreasonable, whereas creating a distinct possibility of someone getting burnt fingers on a stove might be reasonable.

The question in the following case was whether a fraternity's local chapter and its officers owed a duty of care to their pledges.

Case 5.2

Bogenberger v. Pi Kappa Alpha Corporation, Inc.

Supreme Court of Illinois, 2018 IL 120951, 104 N.E.3d 1110 (2018).

Facts David Bogenberger attended a pledge event at the Pi Kappa Alpha fraternity house at Northern Illinois University (NIU). The NIU Chapter officers planned an evening of hazing, during which the pledges were required to consume vodka provided by the members. By the end of the night, David's blood alcohol level was more than five times the legal limit. He lost consciousness. The NIU Chapter officers failed to seek medical attention. David died during the night. His father, Gary, filed a complaint in an Illinois state court against the NIU Chapter and its officers, on a theory of negligence. The plaintiff alleged that the defendants required the pledges, including David, to participate in the pledge event and to consume excessive and dangerous amounts of alcohol in violation of the state's hazing statute.[a] The court dismissed the complaint. A state intermediate appellate court reversed the dismissal. The defendants appealed to the Illinois Supreme Court.

Issue Did the NIU Chapter and its officers owe a duty of care to the pledges, including David, during the hazing event?

Decision Yes. The Illinois Supreme Court affirmed the intermediate appellate court's reversal of the trial court's dismissal. The plaintiff's "complaint . . . may proceed against the NIU Chapter [and] its officers."

Reason Each of us owes a duty of care to others to guard against injuries that are reasonably foreseeable consequences of our acts. The court reasoned that an injury due to hazing is reasonably foreseeable. This is indicated by the existence of the state's hazing statute, the university's rules, and the national Pi Kappa Alpha organization's policy against hazing. At hazing events involving the consumption of large amounts of alcohol, injuries are likely to occur. The magnitude of the burden of guarding against such injuries is small. In this case, then, it is reasonable to require the NIU Chapter and its officers to comply with the law and with the university's and fraternity's rules. It is further reasonable to place the consequences of that burden on the same parties—those who planned and carried out the pledge event. Thus "the NIU Chapter and the officers owed a duty to the pledges, including David, and plaintiff has sufficiently alleged a claim for negligence against them."

Critical Thinking

- **Legal Environment** *The NIU Chapter invited nonmember sorority women to participate in the hazing event by filling the pledges' cups with vodka and directing them to drink it. Did these women owe a duty of care to the pledges? Discuss.*
- **What If the Facts Were Different?** *Suppose that the pledges' attendance at the hazing event had been optional, and the NIU Chapter had furnished alcohol, but not required its consumption. Would the result have been different? Explain.*

---

a. As a result of the pledge event, the Pi Kappa Alpha national organization revoked the NIU Chapter's charter, and criminal charges were brought against those who participated in the hazing.

Reasonable Person Standard The standard of behavior expected of a hypothetical "reasonable person." It is the standard against which negligence is measured and that must be observed to avoid liability for negligence.

The Reasonable Person Standard Tort law measures duty by the **reasonable person standard**. In determining whether a duty of care has been breached, the courts ask how a reasonable person would have acted in the same circumstances. The reasonable person standard is said to be (though in an absolute sense it cannot be) objective. It is not necessarily how a particular person *would* act. It is society's judgment on how people *should* act. If the so-called reasonable person existed, that person would be careful, conscientious, even tempered, and honest.

The degree of care to be exercised varies, depending on the defendant's occupation or profession, relationship with the plaintiff, and other factors. Generally, whether an action constitutes a breach of the duty of care is determined on a case-by-case basis. The outcome depends on how the judge (or jury, in a jury trial) decides that a reasonable person in the position of the defendant would act in the particular circumstances of the case.

Note that the courts frequently use the reasonable person standard in other areas of law as well as in negligence cases. Indeed, the principle that individuals are required to exercise a reasonable standard of care in their activities is a pervasive concept in many areas of business law.

The Duty of Landowners Landowners are expected to exercise reasonable care to protect persons coming onto their property from harm. In some jurisdictions, landowners are held to owe a duty to protect even trespassers against certain risks. Landowners who rent or lease premises to tenants are expected to exercise reasonable care to ensure that the tenants and their guests are not harmed in common areas, such as stairways, entryways, and laundry rooms.

Duty to Warn Business Invitees of Risks. Retailers and other firms that explicitly or implicitly invite persons to come onto their premises have a duty to exercise reasonable care to protect these **business invitees**. The duty normally requires storeowners to warn business invitees of foreseeable risks, such as construction zones and wet floors, about which the owners knew or *should have known*.

Business Invitees Persons, such as customers or clients, who are invited onto business premises by the owner of those premises for business purposes.

Example 5.22 Liz enters a Crown Market, slips on a wet floor, and sustains injuries as a result. If there was no sign warning that the floor was wet when Liz slipped, the owner of Crown Market would be liable for damages. A court would hold that the business owner was negligent because the owner failed to exercise a reasonable degree of care in protecting the store's customers against foreseeable risks about which the owner knew or should have known. That a patron might slip on the wet floor and be injured was a foreseeable risk, and the owner should have taken care to avoid this risk or to warn the customer of it (by posting a sign or setting out orange cones, for instance). ■

The business owner also has a duty to discover and remove any hidden dangers that might injure a customer or other invitee. Hidden dangers might include uneven surfaces or defects in the pavement of a parking lot or walkway, or merchandise that has fallen off a store shelf.

© paichoom/Shutterstock.com

Does a "Wet Floor" sign relieve a restaurant owner from being held negligent if a customer slips?

Obvious Risks May Be an Exception. Some risks, of course, are so obvious that the owner need not warn of them. For instance, a business owner does not need to warn customers to open a door before attempting to walk through it. Other risks, however, may seem obvious to a business owner but may not be so to someone else, such as a child. In addition, even an obvious risk does not necessarily excuse a business owner from the duty to protect customers from foreseeable harm.

Case Example 5.23 During a trip to a Costco warehouse store in Nevada, Stephen Foster tripped and fell over a wooden pallet and sustained injuries. A Costco employee who was restocking the shelves had placed the pallet in the aisle without any barricades. When Foster sued Costco for negligence, Costco argued that it had not breached its duty by failing to warn customers because the pallet was open and obvious. A lower court agreed and granted a summary judgment in Costco's favor, but the Supreme Court of Nevada reversed. The court held that the open and obvious nature of a dangerous condition does not *automatically* relieve a business owner from the general duty of reasonable care. Every situation is different. Therefore, Foster was entitled to proceed to trial and argue that Costco should have used barricades or warnings to protect customers.[17]

The Duty of Professionals Persons who possess superior knowledge, skill, or training are held to a higher standard of care than others. Professionals—such as physicians, dentists, architects, engineers, accountants, and lawyers—are required to have a standard minimum level of special knowledge and ability. In determining what constitutes reasonable care, the law takes their training and expertise into account. Thus, an accountant's conduct is judged not by the reasonable person standard, but by the reasonable accountant standard.

If a professional violates the duty of care toward a client, the professional may be sued for **malpractice**, which is essentially professional negligence. For instance, a patient might sue a physician for *medical malpractice*. A client might sue an attorney for *legal malpractice*.

Malpractice Professional misconduct or the lack of the requisite degree of skill as a professional. Negligence on the part of a professional, such as a physician, is commonly referred to as malpractice.

5–4b Causation

Another element necessary in a negligence action is *causation*. If a person breaches a duty of care and someone suffers an injury, the wrongful act must have caused the harm for it to constitute the tort of negligence.

Courts Ask Two Questions In deciding whether there is causation, the court must address two questions:

1. *Is there causation in fact?* Did the injury occur because of the defendant's act, or would it have occurred anyway? If an injury would not have occurred without the defendant's act, then there is **causation in fact**.

   Causation in fact can usually be determined by the use of the *but for* test: "but for" the wrongful act, the injury would not have occurred. Theoretically, causation in fact is limitless. One could claim, for example, that "but for" the creation of the world, a particular injury would not have occurred. Thus, as a practical matter, the law has to establish limits, and it does so through the concept of proximate cause.

Causation in Fact An act or omission without which an event would not have occurred.

2. *Was the act the proximate cause of the injury?* **Proximate cause**, or legal cause, exists when the connection between an act and an injury is strong enough to justify imposing liability. Courts use proximate cause to limit the scope of the defendant's liability to a subset of the total number of potential plaintiffs that might have been harmed by the defendant's actions.

   Example 5.24 Ackerman carelessly leaves a campfire burning. The fire not only burns down the forest but also sets off an explosion in a nearby chemical plant that spills chemicals into a river, killing all the fish for a hundred miles downstream and ruining the economy of a tourist resort. Should Ackerman be liable to the resort owners? To the tourists whose vacations were ruined? These are questions of proximate cause that a court must decide.

Proximate Cause Legal cause. It exists when the connection between an act and an injury is strong enough to justify imposing liability.

Both questions concerning causation must be answered in the affirmative for tort liability to arise. If a defendant's action constitutes causation in fact but a court decides that the action was not the proximate cause of the plaintiff's injury, the causation requirement has not been met—and the defendant normally will not be liable to the plaintiff.

17. *Foster v. Costco Wholesale Corp.*, 128 Nev.Adv.Op. 71, 291 P.3d 150 (2012).

Know This

Proximate cause can be thought of in terms of social policy. Should the defendant be made to bear the loss instead of the plaintiff?

Foreseeability Questions of proximate cause are linked to the concept of foreseeability. It would be unfair to impose liability on a defendant unless the defendant's actions created a foreseeable risk of injury. Probably the most cited case on proximate cause is the *Palsgraf* case, which is discussed in this chapter's *Landmark in the Law* feature. In determining the issue of proximate cause, the court addressed the following question: Does a defendant's duty of care extend only to those who may be injured as a result of a foreseeable risk, or does it also extend to a person whose injury could not reasonably have been foreseen?

5–4c The Injury Requirement and Damages

For a tort to have been committed, the plaintiff must have suffered a *legally recognizable* injury. To recover damages (receive compensation), the plaintiff must have suffered some loss, harm, wrong, or invasion of a protected interest. If no harm or injury results from a given negligent action, there is nothing to compensate—and no tort exists. **Example 5.25** If you carelessly bump into a passerby, who stumbles and falls as a result, you may be liable in tort if the passerby is injured in the fall. If the person is unharmed, however, there normally cannot be a suit for damages because no injury was suffered.

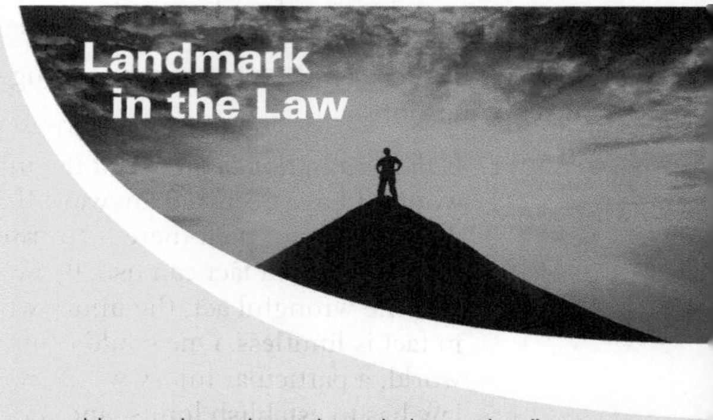

Palsgraf v. Long Island Railroad Co. (1928)

In 1928, the New York Court of Appeals (that state's highest court) issued its decision in *Palsgraf v. Long Island Railroad Co.*,[a] a case that has become a landmark in negligence law and proximate cause.

The Facts of the Case The plaintiff, Helen Palsgraf, was waiting for a train on a station platform. A man carrying a small package wrapped in newspaper was rushing to catch a train that had begun to move away from the platform. As the man attempted to jump aboard the moving train, he seemed unsteady and about to fall. A railroad guard on the train car reached forward to grab him, and another guard on the platform pushed him from behind to help him board the train. In the process, the man's package fell on the railroad tracks and exploded, because it contained fireworks. The repercussions of the explosion caused scales at the other end of the train platform to fall on Palsgraf, who was injured as a result. She sued the railroad company for damages in a New York state court.

The Question of Proximate Cause At the trial, the jury found that the railroad guards were negligent in their conduct. On appeal, the question before the New York Court of Appeals was whether the conduct of the railroad guards was the proximate cause of Palsgraf's injuries. In other words, did the guards' duty of care extend to Palsgraf, who was outside the zone of danger and whose injury could not reasonably have been foreseen?

The court stated that the question of whether the guards were negligent *with respect to Palsgraf* depended on whether her injury was *reasonably foreseeable* by the railroad guards. Although the guards may have acted negligently with respect to the man boarding the train, this had no bearing on the question of their negligence with respect to Palsgraf. This was not a situation in which a person committed an act so potentially harmful (for example, firing a gun at a building) that there would automatically be liability for any harm that resulted. The court stated that here "there was nothing in the situation to suggest to the most cautious mind that the parcel wrapped in newspaper would spread wreckage through the station." The court thus concluded that the railroad guards were not negligent with respect to Palsgraf, because her injury was not reasonably foreseeable.

Application to Today's World *The* Palsgraf *case established foreseeability as the test for proximate cause. Today, the courts continue to apply this test in determining proximate cause—and thus tort liability for injuries. Generally, if the victim of a harm or the consequences of a harm done are unforeseeable, there is no proximate cause. Note, though, that in the online environment, distinctions based on physical proximity, such as the "zone of danger" cited by the court in this case, are largely inapplicable.*

a. 248 N.Y. 339, 162 N.E. 99 (1928).

Essentially, the purpose of tort law is to compensate for legally recognized injuries resulting from wrongful acts. Thus, compensatory damages are the norm in negligence cases. As noted earlier, a court will award punitive damages only if the defendant's conduct was grossly negligent, reflecting an intentional failure to perform a duty with reckless disregard of the consequences to others.

5–4d Good Samaritan Statutes

Most states now have what are called **Good Samaritan statutes.**[18] Under these statutes, someone who is aided voluntarily by another cannot turn around and sue the "Good Samaritan" for negligence. These laws were passed largely to protect physicians and medical personnel who volunteer their services in emergency situations to those in need, such as individuals hurt in car accidents.

Good Samaritan Statutes A state statute stipulating that persons who provide emergency services to, or rescue, someone in peril cannot be sued for negligence unless they act recklessly and cause further harm.

5–4e Dram Shop Acts

Many states have also passed **dram shop acts,**[19] under which a bar owner or bartender may be held liable for injuries caused by a person who became intoxicated while drinking at the bar. The owner or bartender may also be held responsible for continuing to serve a person who was already intoxicated. Some states' statutes also impose liability on *social hosts* (persons hosting parties) for injuries caused by guests who became intoxicated at the hosts' homes. Under these statutes, it is unnecessary to prove that the bar owner, bartender, or social host was negligent. **Example 5.26** Monica hosts a Super Bowl party at which Brett, a minor, sneaks alcoholic drinks. Monica is potentially liable for damages resulting from Brett's drunk driving after the party, even if she was not negligent in serving the alcoholic beverages. ■

Dram Shop Acts A state statute that imposes liability on those who sell or serve alcohol for injuries resulting from accidents caused by intoxicated persons when the sellers or servers contributed to the intoxication.

5–4f Defenses to Negligence

Defendants often defend against negligence claims by asserting that the plaintiffs failed to prove the existence of one or more of the required elements for negligence. Additionally, there are three basic *affirmative* defenses in negligence cases (defenses that a defendant can use to avoid liability even if the facts are as the plaintiff states): (1) assumption of risk, (2) superseding cause, and (3) contributory or comparative negligence.

Assumption of Risk A plaintiff who voluntarily enters into a risky situation, knowing the risk involved, will not be allowed to recover. This is the defense of **assumption of risk**, which requires two elements:

1. Knowledge of the risk.
2. Voluntary assumption of the risk.

Assumption of Risk A defense to negligence that bars a plaintiff from recovering for injuries or damage suffered as a result of risks that were known and voluntarily assumed.

This defense is frequently asserted when a plaintiff is injured during recreational activities that involve known risk, such as skiing and skydiving. Courts do not apply the assumption of risk doctrine in certain situations, such as those involving emergencies, however.

Assumption of risk can apply not only to participants in sporting events, but also to spectators and bystanders who are injured while attending those events. In the following *Spotlight Case*, the issue was whether a spectator at a baseball game voluntarily assumed the risk of being hit by an errant ball thrown while the players were warming up before the game.

18. These laws derive their name from the Good Samaritan story in the Bible. In the story, a traveler who had been robbed and beaten lay along the roadside, ignored by those passing by. Eventually, a man from the region of Samaria (the "Good Samaritan") stopped to render assistance to the injured person.

19. Historically, a *dram* was a small unit of liquid, and spirits were sold in drams. Thus, a dram shop was a place where liquor was sold in drams.

Spotlight on the Seattle Mariners: Case 5.3

Taylor v. Baseball Club of Seattle, L.P.

Court of Appeals of Washington, 132 Wash.App. 32, 130 P.3d 835 (2006).

Facts Delinda Middleton Taylor went to a Mariners baseball game at Safeco Field with her boyfriend and two minor sons. Their seats were four rows up from the field along the right field foul line. They arrived more than an hour before the game began so that they could see the players warm up and get their autographs. When she walked in, Taylor saw that Mariners pitcher Freddy Garcia was throwing a ball back and forth with José Mesa right in front of their seats. As Taylor stood in front of her seat, she looked away from the field, and a ball thrown by Mesa got past Garcia and struck her in the face, causing serious injuries. Taylor sued the Mariners for the allegedly negligent warm-up throw. The Mariners filed a motion for a summary judgment in which they argued that Taylor, a Mariners fan, was familiar with baseball and the inherent risk of balls entering the stands, and had therefore assumed the risk of her injury. The trial court granted the motion and dismissed Taylor's case. Taylor appealed.

© Alan C. Heison/Shutterstock.com

Many fans arrive at baseball games early so they can watch the players warm up.

Issue Was the risk of injury from an errant baseball thrown during pregame warm-up foreseeable to a reasonable person with Taylor's familiarity with baseball?

Decision Yes. The state intermediate appellate court affirmed the lower court's judgment. Taylor, as a spectator in an unprotected area of seats, voluntarily undertook the risk associated with being hit by an errant baseball thrown during warm-ups before the start of the game.

Reason The court observed that there was substantial evidence that Taylor was familiar with the game. She was a seasoned Mariners fan, and both of her sons had played baseball for at least six years. "She attended many of her sons' baseball games, she witnessed balls entering the stands, she had watched Mariners' games both at the Kingdome [the Mariners' former stadium] and on television, and she knew that there was no screen protecting her seats, which were close to the field. In fact, as she walked to her seat she saw the players warming up and was excited about being in an unscreened area where her party might get autographs from the players and catch balls."

It was not legally relevant that the injury occurred during the pregame warm-up because "it is the normal, every-day practice at all levels of baseball for pitchers to warm up in the manner that led to this incident." The Mariners had satisfied their duty to protect spectators from balls entering the stands by providing a protective screen behind home plate. Taylor chose not to sit in the protected area and thus knowingly put herself at risk.

Critical Thinking

• **What If the Facts Were Different?** *Would the result in this case have been different if Taylor's minor son, rather than Taylor herself, had been struck by the ball? Should courts apply the doctrine of assumption of risk to children? Discuss.*

Superseding Cause An unforeseeable intervening event may break the connection between a wrongful act and an injury to another. If so, the event acts as a *superseding cause*—that is, it relieves a defendant of liability for injuries caused by the intervening event. **Example 5.27** While riding his bicycle, Derrick negligently hits Julie, who is walking on the sidewalk. As a result of the impact, Julie falls and fractures her hip. While she is waiting for help to arrive, a small plane crashes nearby and explodes, and some of the fiery debris hits her, causing her to sustain severe burns. Derrick will be liable for Julie's fractured hip because the risk of hitting her with his bicycle was foreseeable. Normally, though, Derrick will not be liable for the burns caused by the plane crash, because the risk of a plane's crashing nearby and injuring Julie was not foreseeable.

Contributory Negligence All individuals are expected to exercise a reasonable degree of care in looking out for themselves. In the past, under the common law doctrine of **contributory negligence**, a plaintiff who was also negligent (who failed to exercise a reasonable degree of care) could not recover anything from the defendant. Under this rule, no matter how insignificant the plaintiff's negligence was relative to the defendant's negligence, the plaintiff was precluded from recovering any damages. Today, only a few jurisdictions still follow this doctrine.

Contributory Negligence A rule in tort law, used in only a few states, that completely bars the plaintiff from recovering any damages if the harm suffered is partly the plaintiff's own fault.

Comparative Negligence In most states, the doctrine of contributory negligence has been replaced by a **comparative negligence** standard. Under this standard, both the plaintiff's and the defendant's negligence are computed, and the liability for damages is distributed accordingly.

Some jurisdictions have adopted a "pure" form of comparative negligence that allows a plaintiff to recover even if the extent of the plaitiff's fault is greater than that of the defendant. For instance, if a plaintiff was 80 percent at fault and the defendant 20 percent at fault, the plaintiff may recover 20 percent of the actual damages.

Many states' comparative negligence statutes, however, contain a "50 percent" rule that prevents a plaintiff who was more than 50 percent at fault from recovering any damages. Under this rule, a plaintiff who is 35 percent at fault could recover 65 percent of the actual damages, but a plaintiff who is 65 percent at fault could recover nothing.

Comparative Negligence A rule in tort law, used in the majority of states, that reduces the plaintiff's recovery in proportion to the plaintiff's degree of fault, rather than barring recovery completely.

5–5 Strict Liability

Another category of torts is called **strict liability**, or *liability without fault*. Intentional torts and torts of negligence involve acts that depart from a reasonable standard of care and cause injuries. Under the doctrine of strict liability, liability for injury is imposed for reasons other than fault.

Strict Liability Liability regardless of fault, which is imposed on those engaged in abnormally dangerous activities, on persons who keep dangerous animals, and on manufacturers or sellers that introduce into commerce defective and unreasonably dangerous goods.

5–5a Abnormally Dangerous Activities

Strict liability for damages proximately caused by an abnormally dangerous or exceptional activity is one application of this doctrine. Courts apply the doctrine of strict liability in such cases because of the extreme risk of the activity. For instance, even if blasting with dynamite is performed with all reasonable care, there is still a risk of injury. Because of the potential for harm, the person who is engaged in an abnormally dangerous activity—and benefits from it—is responsible for paying for any injuries caused by that activity. Although there is no fault, there is still responsibility because of the dangerous nature of the undertaking.

5–5b Other Applications of Strict Liability

The strict liability principle is also applied in other situations. Persons who keep wild animals, for instance, are strictly liable for any harm inflicted by the animals. In addition, an owner of domestic animals may be strictly liable for harm caused by those animals if the owner knew, or should have known, that the animals were dangerous or had a propensity to harm others.

A significant application of strict liability is in the area of *product liability*—liability of manufacturers and sellers for harmful or defective products. Liability here is a matter of social policy. Manufacturers and sellers can better bear the cost of injuries, and because they profit from making and selling the products, they should be responsible for the injuries the products cause.

Focus Question 5

What is meant by strict liability? In what circumstances is strict liability applied?

Practice and Review

Elaine Sweeney went to Ragged Mountain Ski Resort in New Hampshire with a friend. Elaine went snow tubing down a run designed exclusively for snow tubers. No Ragged Mountain employees were present in the snow-tube area to instruct Elaine on the proper use of a snow tube. On her fourth run down the trail, Elaine crossed over the center line between snow-tube lanes, collided with another snow tuber, and was injured. Elaine filed a negligence action against Ragged Mountain seeking compensation for the injuries that she sustained. Two years earlier, the New Hampshire state legislature had enacted a statute that prohibited a person who participates in the sport of skiing from suing a ski-area operator for injuries caused by the risks inherent in skiing. Using the information presented in the chapter, answer the following questions.

1. What defense will Ragged Mountain probably assert?
2. The central question in this case is whether the state statute establishing that skiers assume the risks inherent in the sport applies to Elaine's suit. What would your decision be on this issue? Why?
3. Suppose that the court concludes that the statute applies only to skiing and not to snow tubing. Will Elaine's lawsuit be successful? Explain.
4. Now suppose that the jury concludes that Elaine was partly at fault for the accident. Under what theory might her damages be reduced in proportion to how much her actions contributed to the accident and her resulting injuries?

Debate This

Each time a state legislature enacts a law that applies the assumption of risk doctrine to a particular sport, participants in that sport suffer.

Key Terms

actionable 123
actual malice 127
appropriation 129
assault 122
assumption of risk 139
battery 122
business invitee 136
business tort 131
causation in fact 137
comparative negligence 141
compensatory damages 120
contributory negligence 141
conversion 133
damages 120
defamation 124
defense 121
disparagement of property 134
dram shop act 139
duty of care 135
fraudulent misrepresentation 130
general damages 120
Good Samaritan statute 139
intentional tort 121
libel 124
malpractice 137
negligence 134
privilege 127
proximate cause 137
puffery 130
punitive damages 120
reasonable person standard 136
slander 124
slander of quality (trade libel) 134
slander of title 134
special damages 120
strict liability 141
tort 119
tortfeasor 121
transferred intent 121
trespass to land 132
trespass to personal property 133

Chapter Summary: Tort Law

Intentional Torts against Persons	1. **Assault and battery**—An assault is an unexcused and intentional act that causes another person to be apprehensive of immediate physical harm. A battery is an assault that results in actual physical contact. 2. **False imprisonment**—The intentional confinement or restraint of another person's movement without justification. 3. **Intentional infliction of emotional distress**—An extreme and outrageous act, intentionally committed, that results in severe emotional distress to another. 4. **Defamation (libel or slander)**—A false statement of fact, not made under privilege, that is communicated to a third person and that causes damage to a person's reputation. For public figures, the plaintiff must also prove actual malice. 5. **Invasion of the right to privacy**—Includes four types: wrongful intrusion into a person's private activities; publication of information that places a person in a false light; public disclosure of private facts that an ordinary person would find objectionable; and appropriation of identity, which involves the use of a person's name, likeness, or other identifying characteristic, without permission and for a commercial purpose. Most states have enacted statutes establishing appropriation of identity as the tort of *appropriation*, or right of publicity. Courts differ on the degree of likeness required. 6. **Fraudulent misrepresentation**—A false representation made by one party, through misstatement of facts or through conduct, with the intention of deceiving another and on which the other reasonably relies to the other's detriment. Negligent misrepresentation occurs when a person supplies information without having a reasonable basis for believing its truthfulness. 7. **Wrongful interference**—The knowing, intentional interference by a third party with an enforceable contractual relationship or an established business relationship between other parties for the purpose of advancing the economic interests of the third party.
Intentional Torts against Property	1. **Trespass to land**—The invasion of another's real property without consent or privilege. 2. **Trespass to personal property**—Unlawfully damaging or interfering with the owner's right to use, possess, or enjoy personal property. 3. **Conversion**—Wrongfully taking, retaining, or using the personal property of another without permission. 4. **Disparagement of property**—Any economically injurious falsehood that is made about another's product or property. The term includes the torts of *slander of quality* and *slander of title*.
Negligence	Negligence is the failure to exercise the standard of care that a reasonable person would apply in similar circumstances. A plaintiff must prove that a legal duty of care existed, that the defendant breached that duty, that the breach actually and proximately caused the plaintiff's injury, and that the plaintiff suffered a legally recognizable injury. 1. **Good Samaritan statutes**—State laws that protect those who voluntarily aid another from being sued for negligence. 2. **Dram shop acts**—State laws that impose liability on sellers and servers of alcohol for injuries caused by intoxicated persons when the sellers or servers contributed to the intoxication. 3. **Defenses to negligence**—The basic affirmative defenses in negligence cases are assumption of risk, superseding cause, and contributory or comparative negligence.
Strict Liability	Under the doctrine of strict liability, parties may be held liable, regardless of the degree of care exercised, for damages or injuries caused by their products or activities. Strict liability includes liability for harms caused by abnormally dangerous activities, by dangerous animals, and by defective products (product liability).

Issue Spotters

1. Jana leaves her truck's motor running while she enters a Kwik-Pik Store. The truck's transmission engages, and the vehicle crashes into a gas pump, starting a fire that spreads to a warehouse on the next block. The warehouse collapses, causing its billboard to fall and injure Lou, a bystander. Can Lou recover from Jana? Why or why not? (See *Negligence*.)

2. A water pipe bursts, flooding a Metal Fabrication Company utility room and tripping the circuit breakers on a panel in the room. Metal Fabrication contacts Nouri, a licensed electrician with five years' experience, to check the damage and turn the breakers back on. Without testing for short circuits, which Nouri knows that he should do, he tries to switch on a breaker. He is electrocuted, and his wife sues Metal Fabrication for damages, alleging negligence. What might the firm successfully claim in defense? (See *Negligence.*)

—Check your answers to the *Issue Spotters* against the answers provided in Appendix D.

Business Scenarios and Case Problems

5–1. Defamation. Richard is an employee of the Dun Construction Corp. While delivering materials to a construction site, he carelessly backs Dun's truck into a passenger vehicle driven by Green. This is Richard's second accident in six months. When the company owner, Dun, learns of this latest accident, a heated discussion ensues, and Dun fires Richard. Dun is so angry that he immediately writes a letter to the union of which Richard is a member and to all other construction companies in the community. In it, Dun states that Richard is the "worst driver in the city" and that "anyone who hires him is asking for legal liability." Richard files a suit against Dun, alleging libel on the basis of the statements made in the letters. Discuss. (See *Intentional Torts against Persons.*)

5–2. Liability to Business Invitees. Kim went to Ling's Market to pick up a few items for dinner. It was a stormy day, and the wind had blown water through the market's door each time it opened. As Kim entered through the door, she slipped and fell in the rainwater that had accumulated on the floor. The manager knew of the weather conditions but had not posted any sign to warn customers of the water hazard. Kim injured her back as a result of the fall and sued Ling's for damages. Can Ling's be held liable for negligence? Discuss. (See *Negligence.*)

5–3. Spotlight on Intentional Torts—Defamation. Sharon Yeagle was an assistant to the vice president of student affairs at Virginia Polytechnic Institute and State University (Virginia Tech). As part of her duties, Yeagle helped students participate in the Governor's Fellows Program. The *Collegiate Times,* Virginia Tech's student newspaper, published an article about the university's success in placing students in the program. The article's text surrounded a block quotation attributed to Yeagle with the phrase "Director of Butt Licking" under her name. Yeagle sued the *Collegiate Times* for defamation. She argued that the phrase implied the commission of sodomy and was therefore actionable. What is *Collegiate Times's* defense to this claim? [*Yeagle v. Collegiate Times,* 497 S.E.2d 136 (Va. 1998)] (See *Intentional Torts against Persons.*)

5–4. Business Case Problem with Sample Answer—Negligence. At the Weatherford Hotel in Flagstaff, Arizona, in Room 59, a balcony extends across thirty inches of the room's only window, leaving a twelve-inch gap with a three-story drop to the concrete below. A sign prohibits smoking in the room but invites guests to "step out onto the balcony" to smoke. Toni Lucario was a guest in Room 59 when she climbed out of the window and fell to her death. Patrick McMurtry, her estate's personal representative, filed a suit against the Weatherford. Did the hotel breach a duty of care to Lucario? What might the Weatherford assert in its defense? Explain. [*McMurtry v. Weatherford Hotel, Inc.,* 293 P.3d 520 (Ariz. App. 2013)] (See *Negligence.*)

—For a sample answer to Problem 5–4, go to Appendix E.

5–5. Negligence. Ronald Rawls and Zabian Bailey were in an auto accident in Bridgeport, Connecticut. Bailey rear-ended Rawls at a stoplight. Evidence showed it was more likely than not that Bailey failed to apply his brakes in time to avoid the collision, failed to turn his vehicle to avoid the collision, failed to keep his vehicle under control, and was inattentive to his surroundings. Rawls filed a suit in a Connecticut state court against his insurance company, Progressive Northern Insurance Co., to obtain benefits under an underinsured motorist clause, alleging that Bailey had been negligent. Could Rawls collect? Discuss. [*Rawls v. Progressive Northern Insurance Co.,* 310 Conn. 768, 83 A.3d 576 (2014)] (See *Negligence.*)

5–6. Negligence. Charles Robison, an employee of West Star Transportation, Inc., was ordered to cover an unevenly loaded flatbed trailer with a 150-pound tarpaulin. The load included uncrated equipment and pallet crates of different heights, about thirteen feet off the ground at its highest point. While standing on the load, manipulating the tarpaulin without safety equipment or assistance, Robison fell headfirst and sustained a traumatic head injury. He filed a suit against West Star to recover for his injury. Was West Star "negligent in failing to provide a reasonably safe place to work," as Robison claimed? Explain. [*West Star Transportation, Inc. v. Robison,* 457 S.W.3d 178 (Tex.App.—Amarillo 2015)] (See *Negligence.*)

5–7. Negligence. DSC Industrial Supply and Road Rider Supply are located in North Kitsap Business Park in Seattle, Washington. Both firms are owned by Paul and Suzanne Marshall. The Marshalls had outstanding commercial loans from Frontier Bank. The bank dispatched one of its employees, Suzette Gould, to North Kitsap to "spread Christmas cheer" to the Marshalls as an expression of appreciation for their business. Approaching the entry to Road Rider, Gould tripped over a concrete "wheel stop" and fell, suffering a broken arm and a dislocated elbow. The stop was not clearly visible, it had not been painted a contrasting color, and it was not marked with a sign. Gould had not been aware of the stop before she tripped over it. Is North Kitsap liable to Gould for negligence? Explain. [*Gould v. North Kitsap Business Park Management, LLC*, 192 Wash.App. 1021 (2016)] (See *Negligence*.)

5–8. Defamation. Jonathan Martin, an offensive lineman with the Miami Dolphins, abruptly quit the team and checked himself into a hospital seeking psychological treatment. Later, he explained that he left because of persistent taunting from other Dolphins players. The National Football League hired attorney Theodore Wells to investigate Martin's allegations of bullying. After receiving Wells's report, the Dolphins fired their offensive line coach, James Turner. Turner was a prominent person on the Dolphins team, and during his career he chose to thrust himself further into the public arena. He was the subject of articles discussing his coaching philosophy, and the focus of one season of HBO's "Hard Knocks," showcasing his coaching style. Turner filed a suit in a federal district court against Wells, alleging defamation. He charged that Wells had failed to properly analyze certain information. Is Turner likely to succeed on his claim? Explain. [*Turner v. Wells*, 879 F.3d 1254 (11th Cir. 2018)] (See *Intentional Torts against Persons*.)

5–9. A Question of Ethics—The IDDR Approach and Wrongful Interference. Julie Whitchurch was an employee of Vizant Technologies, LLC. After she was fired, she created a website falsely accusing Vizant of fraud and mismanagement to discourage others from doing business with the company. Vizant filed a suit in a federal district court against her, alleging wrongful interference with a business relationship. The court concluded that Whitchurch's online criticism of Vizant adversely affected its employees and operations, forced it to accept reduced compensation to obtain business, and deterred outside investment. The court ordered Whitchurch to stop her online efforts to discourage others from doing business with Vizant. [*Vizant Technologies, LLC v. Whitchurch*, 675 Fed.Appx. 201 (3d Cir. 2017)] (See *Intentional Torts against Persons*.)

1. How does the motivation for Whitchurch's conduct differ from that in other cases involving wrongful interference? What does this suggest about the ethics in this situation? Discuss.
2. Another group will argue that the statute does not violate litigants' right of access to the courts. Using the IDDR approach, analyze and evaluate Vizant's decision to file a suit against Whitchurch.

Critical Thinking and Writing Assignments

5–10. Time-Limited Group Assignment—Negligence. Donald and Gloria Bowden hosted a cookout at their home in South Carolina, inviting mostly business acquaintances. Justin Parks, who was nineteen years old, attended the party. Alcoholic beverages were available to all of the guests, even those who, like Parks, were between the ages of eighteen and twenty-one.

Parks consumed alcohol at the party and left with other guests. One of these guests detained Parks at the guest's home to give Parks time to "sober up." Parks then drove himself from this guest's home and was killed in a one-car accident. At the time of death, he had a blood alcohol content of 0.291 percent, which exceeded the state's limit for driving a motor vehicle. Linda Marcum, Parks's mother, filed a suit in a South Carolina state court against the Bowdens and others, alleging negligence. (See *Negligence*.)

1. The first group will present arguments in favor of holding the social hosts (Donald and Gloria Bowden) liable in this situation.
2. The second group will formulate arguments against holding the social hosts liable.
3. The states vary widely in assessing liability and imposing sanctions in the circumstances described in this problem. The third group will analyze the possible reasons why some courts treat social hosts who serve alcohol differently than parents who serve alcohol to their underage children.
4. The fourth group will decide whether the guest who detained Parks at his home to give Parks time to sober up could be held liable for negligence. What defense might this guest raise?

Evgeny Govoov/Shutterstock.com

6 Product Liability

Focus Questions

The four Focus Questions below are designed to help improve your understanding. After reading this chapter, you should be able to answer the following questions:

1. Can a manufacturer be held liable to any person who suffers an injury proximately caused by the manufacturer's negligently made product?
2. What are the elements of a cause of action in strict product liability?
3. What are three types of product defects?
4. What defenses to liability can be raised in a product liability lawsuit?

"You only have to do a very few things right in your life so long as you don't do too many things wrong."

Warren Buffett
1930–present (American businessman and the most successful investor in the twentieth century)

An area of tort law of particular importance to businesspersons is product liability. As Warren Buffett implies in the chapter-opening quote, to be successful, a business cannot make too many mistakes. This is especially true for businesses that make or sell products. The manufacturers and sellers of products may incur product liability when product defects cause injury or property damage to consumers, users, or bystanders (people in the vicinity of the product when it fails).

Suppose that Brandon is riding a Polaris all-terrain vehicle (ATV) that bursts into flame. Under product liability laws, he could sue Polaris. Indeed, Polaris is facing numerous product liability lawsuits from plaintiffs who were harmed when one of the company's ATVs caught fire. Despite claiming that riders contributed to their burns and other injuries by misusing its products, Polaris has recalled over 100,000 ATVs because of fire hazards.

In this chapter, you will learn about various theories of product liability under which plaintiffs can sue. Remember that although multimillion-dollar product liability lawsuits often involve big automakers, pharmaceutical companies, and the tobacco industry, many businesses face potential liability for the products they sell.

6–1 Product Liability Claims

Product Liability The legal liability of manufacturers, sellers, and lessors of goods for injuries or damage caused by the goods to consumers, users, or bystanders.

Those who make, sell, or lease goods can be held liable for physical harm or property damage caused by those goods to a consumer, user, or bystander. This is called **product liability**. Product liability claims may be based on the tort theories of negligence,

Business Web Log

Johnson & Johnson Faces Continuing Lawsuits Over Its Talcum Powder

In 1892, the director of scientific affairs of Johnson & Johnson (J&J) invented scented talcum powder. Talcum, or talc, is a soft mineral found in rock deposits. This invention quickly became J&J's Baby Powder, known throughout the world. Over time, the product expanded beyond being used on babies after a diaper change. In the early 1900s, women began applying the powder to their bodies and undergarments for a fresh scent.

In the 1970s, several studies suggested that using talc around the female genital area increased a woman's risk of ovarian cancer. Despite these studies, J&J denied the findings and did not include any warning labels on its talc-based products. The company has faced numerous setbacks in court, including one New Jersey case in which four plaintiffs were awarded almost $225 million—80 percent of which was in the form of punitive damages. Why punitive damages? Because the jury was convinced that J&J had withheld critical information about a possible relationship between cancer and talcum powder for more than four decades. Still facing thousands of lawsuits claiming that its talcum powder caused cancer, in 2020 J&J announced that it would stop selling the product in North America.

J&J maintains that "thousands of tests" have failed to show any connection between its products and cancer. (Even after federal researchers found traces of a carcinogen in J&J's Baby Powder, forcing the company to recall 33,000 containers of the product, the company responded by questioning the validity of the government's testing process.) Moreover, the International Agency for Research on Cancer classifies genital use of talc as only "possibly" carcinogenic—that is, having the potential to cause cancer. After all, talc is found in a wide variety of cosmetic products and has other uses, such as in paints and plastics.

Key Point

Product liability lawsuits are common for large corporations. Note that in the talcum powder cases, 90 percent or more of the jury awards were for "failure to warn." J&J could have warned consumers of a potential link between genital use of talcum powder and ovarian cancer, but it did not. Of course, sales of talc-based products would not have grown so rapidly had such a warning been evident on each J&J Baby Powder container.

fraudulent misrepresentation, and strict liability. Sometimes, a business faces multiple product liability lawsuits over the same product, as discussed in this chapter's *Business Web Log* feature.

6–1a Negligence

Negligence is the failure to exercise the degree of care that a reasonable, prudent person would have exercised under the circumstances. If a manufacturer fails to exercise "due care" to make a product safe, a person who is injured by the product may sue the manufacturer for negligence.

Due Care Must Be Exercised The manufacturer must exercise due care in all of the following areas:

1. Designing the product.
2. Selecting the materials.
3. Using the appropriate production process.
4. Assembling and testing the product.
5. Placing adequate warnings on the label to inform the user of dangers of which an ordinary person might not be aware.
6. Inspecting and testing any purchased components used in the final product.

Focus Question 1

Can a manufacturer be held liable to any person who suffers an injury proximately caused by the manufacturer's negligently made product?

Privity of Contract The relationship that exists between the promisor and the promisee of a contract.

Privity of Contract Not Required A product liability action based on negligence does not require privity of contract between the injured plaintiff and the defendant manufacturer. **Privity of contract** refers to the relationship that exists between the promisor and the promisee of a contract. Privity is the reason that normally only the parties to a contract can enforce that contract.

In the context of product liability law, privity is not required. A person who is injured by a defective product can bring a negligence suit even though that person was not the one who actually purchased the product—and thus is not in privity. A manufacturer is liable for its failure to exercise due care to *any person* who sustains an injury proximately caused by a negligently made (defective) product.

Relative to the long history of the common law, this exception to the privity requirement is a fairly recent development, dating to the early part of the twentieth century. A leading case in this area is *MacPherson v. Buick Motor Co.*, which is presented as this chapter's *Landmark in the Law* feature.

"Cause in Fact" and Proximate Cause In a product liability suit based on negligence, as in any action alleging that the defendant was negligent, the plaintiff must show that the defendant's conduct was the "cause in fact" of an injury. Cause in fact requires showing that but for the defendant's action, the injury would not have occurred. It must also be determined that the defendant's act was the *proximate cause* of the injury. This determination focuses on the foreseeability of the consequences of the act and whether the defendant should be held legally responsible.

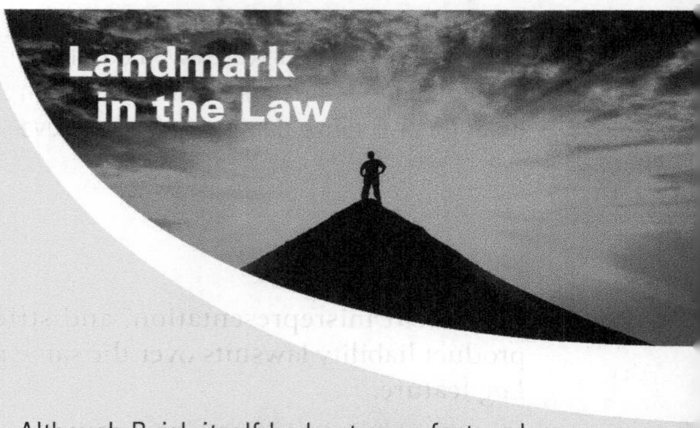

MacPherson v. Buick Motor Co. (1916)

In the landmark case of *MacPherson v. Buick Motor Co.*,[a] the New York Court of Appeals—New York's highest court—considered the liability of a manufacturer that had failed to exercise reasonable care in manufacturing a finished product.

Case Background Donald MacPherson suffered injuries while riding in a Buick automobile that suddenly collapsed because one of the wheels was made of defective wood. The spokes crumbled into fragments, throwing MacPherson out of the vehicle and injuring him.

MacPherson had purchased the car from a Buick dealer, but he brought a lawsuit against the manufacturer, Buick Motor Company. Buick itself had not made the wheel but had bought it from another manufacturer. There was evidence, though, that Buick could have discovered the defects by conducting a reasonable inspection and that no such inspection had taken place. MacPherson charged Buick with negligence for putting a human life in imminent danger.

The Issue Before the Court and the Court's Ruling The primary issue was whether Buick owed a duty of care to anyone except the immediate purchaser of the car—that is, the Buick dealer. In deciding the issue, Justice Benjamin Cardozo stated that "if the nature of a thing is such that it is reasonably certain to place life and limb in peril when negligently made, it is then a thing of danger. . . . If to the element of danger there is added knowledge that the thing will be used by persons other than the purchaser, and used without new tests, then, irrespective of contract, the manufacturer of this thing of danger is under a duty to make it carefully."

The court concluded that "beyond all question, the nature of an automobile gives warning of probable danger if its construction is defective. This automobile was designed to go 50 miles an hour. Unless its wheels were sound and strong, injury was almost certain." Although Buick itself had not manufactured the wheel, the court held that Buick had a duty to inspect the wheels and that Buick "was responsible for the finished product." Therefore, Buick was liable to MacPherson for the injuries he sustained when he was thrown from the car.

Application to Today's World *This landmark decision was a significant step in creating the legal environment of the modern world. As often happens, technological developments necessitated changes in the law. Today, automobile manufacturers are commonly held liable when their negligence causes automobile users to be injured.*

a. 217 N.Y. 382, 111 N.E. 1050 (1916).

At issue in the following case was whether the proximate cause of the injury to a product's user was the manufacturer's inadequate warnings or the purchaser's failure to follow the manufacturer's maintenance instructions.

Case 6.1

Primal Vantage Co. v. O'Bryan

Court of Appeals of Kentucky, __ S.W.3d __, 2019 WL 6044870 (2019).

Facts Dennis Martin owned a hunting stand (called a ladderstand) made by Primal Vantage Company. The stand consisted of a platform fifteen feet above the ground with an attached ladder. Five polypropylene straps secured the stand to a tree. On a hunting trip on Martin's property, Kevin O'Bryan climbed the stand's ladder. At that time, the stand had been affixed to the tree for five years without inspection or maintenance, and two of the straps had deteriorated and broken. When O'Bryan reached the platform, the remaining straps broke, and the stand collapsed. O'Bryan—seriously injured, paralyzed from the waist down, and suffering unremitting pain—filed a suit in a Kentucky state court against Primal Vantage, alleging product liability. A jury awarded O'Bryan damages on a finding that the warnings accompanying the stand were inadequate. The court ordered the damages to be paid to O'Bryan, and Primal Vantage appealed.

Issue Was the inadequacy of the warnings the proximate cause of the accident?

Decision Yes. A state intermediate appellate court affirmed the lower court's order. "Primal Vantage in the exercise of ordinary care should have been aware that the stand was unreasonably dangerous and failed to provide an adequate warning."

Reason Primal Vantage asserted that it was entitled to a verdict in its favor. A label on the stand told users to inspect the stand and not to use it if any parts were damaged or missing. Primal Vantage contended that even if these warnings were inadequate, that factor was not the proximate cause of O'Bryan's accident, because he admitted that he had never read them. "The real cause," the company argued, "was Martin's failure to inspect and maintain the ladderstand." The appellate court explained that the adequacy of a warning is measured not only by its content but also by its placement and visibility. This warning was on the back of the ladder. O'Bryan testified that if the warning had been visible, he would have read it and would not have climbed the ladder to the platform. Ultimately, the appellate court did not rule in Primal Vantage's favor. The court responded to the stand maker's argument by citing the principle that "except in extraordinary circumstances, the negligence of an intervening party does not relieve the manufacturer of the duty to warn adequately." If a product user's injury results from a manufacturer's breach of its duty of care, the manufacturer is liable for the harm.

Critical Thinking

- **Legal Environment** *In the initial trial, should the jury have found that O'Bryan was also at fault? How might this finding have affected the award of damages? Explain.*
- **Economic** *During* voir dire, *a potential juror asked whether the jury would be told how much Primal Vantage's insurance company would pay if O'Bryan was awarded damages. How should the court have responded? Why?*

6–1b Misrepresentation

When a user or consumer is injured as a result of a manufacturer's or seller's fraudulent misrepresentation, the basis of liability may be the tort of fraud. In this situation, the misrepresentation must have been made knowingly or with reckless disregard for the facts. The intentional mislabeling of packaged cosmetics, for instance, or the intentional concealment of a product's defects constitutes fraudulent misrepresentation.

The misrepresentation must be of a material fact, and the seller must have intended to induce the buyer's reliance on the misrepresentation. Misrepresentation on a label or advertisement is enough to show the intent to induce reliance. Of course, to bring a lawsuit on this ground, the buyer must have relied on the misrepresentation.

6–2 Strict Product Liability

Under the doctrine of strict liability, people may be liable for the results of their acts regardless of their intentions or their exercise of reasonable care. In addition, liability does not depend on privity of contract. The injured party does not have to be the buyer or a *third party beneficiary* (one for whose benefit a contract is made). In the 1960s, courts applied the doctrine of strict liability in several landmark cases involving manufactured goods, and this doctrine has since become a common method of holding manufacturers liable.

6–2a Strict Product Liability and Public Policy

The law imposes strict product liability as a matter of public policy. The public policy concerning strict product liability may be expressed in a statute or in the common law. This public policy rests on a threefold assumption:

1. Consumers should be protected against unsafe products.
2. Manufacturers and distributors should not escape liability for faulty products simply because they are not in privity of contract with the ultimate user of those products.
3. Manufacturers, sellers, and lessors of products are generally in a better position than consumers to bear the costs associated with injuries caused by their products. They can ultimately pass on these costs to all consumers in the form of higher prices.

gpointstudio/iStock/Getty Images

If a power tool is defective and injures a user, does the user sue under contract law or tort law?

California was the first state to impose strict product liability in tort on manufacturers. **Classic Case Example 6.1** William Greenman was injured when his Shopsmith combination power tool threw off a piece of wood that struck him in the head. He sued the manufacturer, claiming that he had followed the product instructions and that the product must be defective.

In a landmark decision, *Greenman v. Yuba Power Products, Inc.*,[1] the California Supreme Court set out the reason for applying tort law rather than contract law in cases involving consumers who were injured by defective products. According to the *Greenman* court, the "purpose of such liability is to [e]nsure that the costs of injuries resulting from defective products are borne by the manufacturers . . . rather than by the injured persons who are powerless to protect themselves." ■ Today, the majority of states recognize strict product liability, although some state courts limit its application to situations involving personal injuries (rather than property damage).

6–2b Requirements for Strict Product Liability

Focus Question 2

What are the elements of a cause of action in strict product liability?

After the *Restatement (Second) of Torts* was issued in 1964, Section 402A became a widely accepted statement of how the doctrine of strict liability should be applied to sellers of goods. These sellers include manufacturers, processors, assemblers, packagers, bottlers, wholesalers, distributors, retailers, and lessors.

The bases for an action in strict liability that are set forth in Section 402A can be summarized as the following six requirements. Depending on the jurisdiction, if these requirements are met, a manufacturer's liability to an injured party can be almost unlimited.

1. The product must have been in a *defective condition* when the defendant sold it.
2. The defendant must normally be engaged in the *business of selling* (or otherwise distributing) that product.
3. The product must be *unreasonably dangerous* to the user or consumer because of its defective condition.

1. 59 Cal.2d 57, 377 P.2d 897, 27 Cal.Rptr. 697 (1962); see also, *Okoye v. Bristol-Myers Squibb Co.*, 2017 WL 1435886 (N.D.Cal. 2017).

4. The plaintiff must incur *physical harm* to self or property by use or consumption of the product.
5. The defective condition must be the actual and legal cause of the injury or damage.
6. The *goods must not have been substantially changed* from the time the product was sold to the time the injury was sustained.

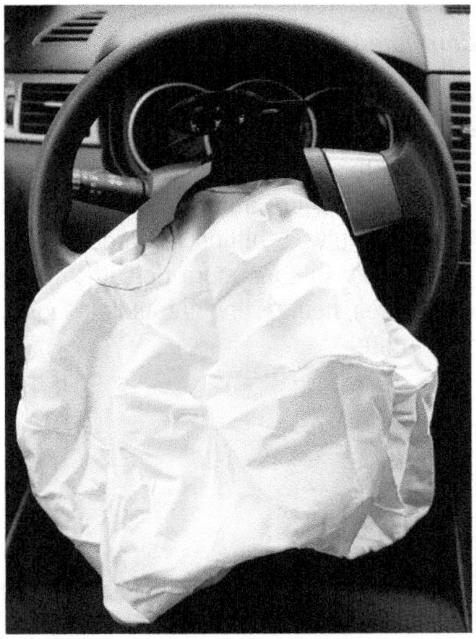

nikkytok/iStock/Getty Images

Does a person injured by a defective air bag have to prove that it was defective when the car was manufactured?

Proving a Defective Condition Under these requirements, in any action against a manufacturer, seller, or lessor, the plaintiff does not have to show why or how the product became defective. The plaintiff does, however, have to prove that the product was defective at the time it left the seller or lessor and that this defective condition made it "unreasonably dangerous" to the user or consumer.

Unless evidence can be presented that will support the conclusion that the product was defective when it was sold or leased, the plaintiff normally will not succeed. If the product was delivered in a safe condition and subsequent mishandling made it harmful to the user, the seller or lessor usually is not strictly liable.

Unreasonably Dangerous Products The *Restatement* recognizes that many products cannot possibly be made entirely safe for all uses. Thus, sellers or lessors of these products are held liable only when the products are *unreasonably* dangerous. A court may consider a product so defective as to be an **unreasonably dangerous product** in either of the following situations.

1. The product is dangerous beyond the expectation of the ordinary consumer.
2. A less dangerous alternative was economically feasible for the manufacturer, but the manufacturer failed to produce it.

Unreasonably Dangerous Product A product that is so defective that it is dangerous beyond the expectation of an ordinary consumer, or a product for which a less dangerous alternative was feasible but the manufacturer failed to produce it.

A product may be unreasonably dangerous due to a flaw in its manufacturing, design, or warning. As discussed in this chapter's *Cybersecurity and the Law* feature, the law is still unsettled when it comes to a manufacturer's strict liability if the flaw is in the product's security system.

Cybersecurity and the Law

The Internet of Things

The Internet of Things (IoT) refers to the online interconnection of computing devices imbedded in objects such as window shades, refrigerators, and health monitors. Each IoT device contains software that, like any computer software, is vulnerable to outside attack, or *hacking*. The inevitable harm caused by IoT hacking is likely to impact American business in the form of strict product liability lawsuits.

Unreasonably Dangerous?

If a defective oven catches fire, under strict product liability the manufacturer will most likely be held liable for any harm that results. But what if a cyber criminal gains control of a smart oven, causing it to catch fire and injure its owner? Does an ineffective IoT cybersecurity system make a product "unreasonably dangerous" to the consumer, leaving the manufacturer strictly liable? What if the problem was a glitch in the smart oven's software? Is software a "product" for the purposes of strict product liability?

As with any new legal issue caused by advancing technology, the answers to these questions will come from a combination of case law and legislation. California was the first state to regulate the IoT by requiring manufacturers of Internet-connected devices to equip them with "reasonable security features."[a] Ultimately, state courts

a. Cal. Civ. Code Section 1798.91.04(a).

(Continues)

Continued

will determine to what extent this law exposes manufacturers to strict product liability. It should not take long for the issue to arise, in California or elsewhere. Approximately 25 billion IoT products are in use, with billions more poised to enter workplaces, homes, and automobiles in the near future.

Critical Thinking

Security engineers discovered that faulty coding in the Chrysler Jeep's entertainment software made the car vulnerable to cyber attacks, conceivably enabling hackers to gain control of the vehicles. The United States Supreme Court has allowed a breach of warranty lawsuit against Chrysler by Jeep owners who contend that they would not have purchased the cars had they known about the security defect. Why might the outcome of this case be important for strict product liability law?

6–2c Product Defects

The *Restatement (Third) of Torts: Products Liability* defines the three types of product defects that have traditionally been recognized in product liability law—manufacturing defects, design defects, and inadequate warnings.

Focus Question 3

What are three types of product defects?

Manufacturing Defects According to Section 2(a) of the *Restatement (Third) of Torts: Products Liability*, a product "contains a manufacturing defect when the product departs from its intended design even though all possible care was exercised in the preparation and marketing of the product." Basically, a manufacturing defect is a departure from design specifications that results in products that are physically flawed, damaged, or incorrectly assembled. A glass bottle that is made too thin, causing it to explode in a consumer's face, is an example of a product with a manufacturing defect.

Quality Control. Usually, manufacturing defects occur when a manufacturer fails to assemble, test, or check the quality of a product adequately. In fact, the idea behind holding defendants strictly liable for manufacturing defects is to encourage greater investment in product safety and stringent quality control standards. Note that liability is imposed on a manufacturer (and on the wholesaler and retailer) regardless of whether the manufacturer's quality control efforts were "reasonable."

The Role of Expert Testimony. Cases involving allegations of a manufacturing defect are often decided based on the opinions and testimony of experts. **Case Example 6.2** Preston Cavner was seriously injured when the Cessna U206F plane he was piloting crashed shortly after takeoff. Cavner's wife, son, and a babysitter were also injured in the accident, and another son was killed. He filed a lawsuit against the manufacturer of the plane's engine, Continental Motors, Inc. (CMI), based on a manufacturing defect.

At trial, experts testified that there were "burrs," or sharp metal edges, in the Cessna's engine cylinders, a violation of CMI's design specifications. These burrs broke off and lodged in the engine's valves, leading to a loss of power and the resulting crash. A jury concluded that this manufacturing defect made the airplane unreasonably dangerous and awarded Cavner and the other injured parties more than $20 million in damages.[2] ■

Design Defects Unlike a product with a manufacturing defect, a product with a design defect is made in conformity with the manufacturer's design specifications. Nevertheless, it

2. *Cavner v. Continental Motors, Inc.*, 2019 WL 1254015 (8 Wash.App.2d 1001, 2019).

results in injury to the user because the design itself is flawed. The product's design creates an unreasonable risk to the user.

A product "is defective in design when the foreseeable risks of harm posed by the product could have been reduced or avoided by the adoption of a reasonable alternative design by the seller or other distributor, or a predecessor in the commercial chain of distribution, and the omission of the alternative design renders the product not reasonably safe."[3] See this chapter's *Business Law Analysis* feature for an example of how courts analyze design defects.

Test for Design Defects. To successfully assert a design defect, a plaintiff has to show that:

1. A reasonable alternative design was available.
2. As a result of the defendant's failure to adopt the alternative design, the product was not reasonably safe.

In other words, a manufacturer or other defendant is liable only when the harm was reasonably preventable.

Example 6.3 Gillespie accidentally cuts off several of his fingers while operating a table saw. He later files a lawsuit against the maker of the saw, claiming that the blade guards on the saw were defectively designed. At trial, however, an expert testifies that the alternative design for blade guards used for table saws could not have been used for the particular cut that Gillespie was performing at the time he was injured. In this situation, Gillespie's claim will likely fail because there is no proof that the "better" guard design would have prevented his injury.

According to the Official Comments accompanying the *Restatement (Third) of Torts*, a court can consider a broad range of factors in deciding claims of design defects. These

3. *Restatement (Third) of Torts: Products Liability*, Section 2(b).

How State Legislation Can Limit Recovery for Design Defects

Business Law Analysis

David Dobrovolny bought a new Ford F-350 pickup truck. A year later, the truck spontaneously caught fire in Dobrovolny's driveway. The truck was destroyed, but no other property was damaged, and no one was injured. Dobrovolny filed a suit in a Nebraska state court against Ford Motor Company on a theory of strict product liability to recover the cost of the truck. Nebraska limits the application of strict product liability to situations involving personal injuries. Will Dobrovolny's lawsuit succeed? Why or why not?

Analysis: The majority of states recognize strict product liability. The purpose of strict product liability is to ensure that the costs of injuries resulting from defective products are borne by the manufacturers rather than by the injured persons. The law imposes this liability as a matter of public policy. Some state courts limit the application of the tort theory of strict product liability to situations involving personal injuries rather than property damage.

Nebraska recognizes strict product liability, but the state's courts limit its application. The issue is whether these limits apply when a product self-destructs without causing damage to persons or other property.

Result and Reasoning: Because Nebraska limits strict product liability suits to situations involving personal injury, a court will most likely dismiss Dobrovolny's design defect claim. When a product injures only itself, the reasons for imposing strict product liability lose their significance. The consumer has not been injured, and the loss concerns the consumer's benefit of the bargain from the contract with the seller of the product. Although a consumer with only a damaged product may not recover in tort, the consumer is not without other remedies. Dobrovolny may attempt to recover for the loss of his truck under contract theories for breach of warranty.

factors include the magnitude and probability of the foreseeable risks, as well as the relative advantages and disadvantages of the product as it was designed and as it alternatively could have been designed.

Risk-Utility Analysis. Most courts engage in a risk-utility analysis, determining whether the risk of harm from the product as designed outweighs its utility to the user and to the public. **Case Example 6.4** Benjamin Riley, a county sheriff, was driving his Ford F-150 pickup truck near Ehrhardt, South Carolina, when it collided with another vehicle. The impact caused Riley's truck to leave the road and roll over. The driver's door of the truck opened in the collision, and Riley was ejected and killed. Riley's widow, Laura, as the representative of his estate, filed a product liability suit against Ford Motor Company. She claimed that the design of the door-latch system of the truck allowed the door to open in the collision. A state court held in her favor and awarded the estate $900,000 in damages.

Ford appealed, but the court found that a reasonable alternative design was available for the door-latch system. Evidence showed that Ford was aware of the safety problems presented by the current system (a rod-linkage system). After conducting a risk-utility analysis of a different system (a cable-linkage system), Ford had concluded that the alternative system was feasible and perhaps superior. The state's highest court affirmed the damages award.[4]

Robert Landau/Corbis Documentary/Getty Images

What creates a design defect in an umpire or catcher's facemask?

Consumer-Expectation Test. Instead of the risk-utility test, some courts apply the consumer-expectation test to determine whether a product's design was defective. Under this test, a product is unreasonably dangerous when it fails to perform in the manner that would reasonably be expected by an ordinary consumer.

Case Example 6.5 A representative from Wilson Sporting Goods Company gave Edwin Hickox an umpire's mask that was designed to be safer than other umpire's masks. The mask had a newly designed throat guard that angled forward instead of extending straight down. While Hickox was working as an umpire during a game and wearing the mask, he was was struck by a foul ball and injured. He suffered a concussion and damage to his inner ear, which caused permanent hearing loss. Hickox and his wife sued the manufacturer for product liability based on a defective design and won. A jury awarded $750,000 to Hickox and $25,000 to his wife. Wilson appealed.

The reviewing court affirmed the jury's verdict. The design was defective because "an ordinary consumer would have expected the mask to perform more safely than it did." The evidence presented to the jury had shown that Wilson's mask was more dangerous than comparable masks sold at the time. The new "masks could concentrate energy at the point of impact, rather than distribute energy evenly throughout the padded area of the mask," as an ordinary consumer would have expected a baseball mask to do.[5]

Inadequate Warnings A product may also be deemed defective because of inadequate instructions or warnings. A product will be considered defective "when the foreseeable risks of harm posed by the product could have been reduced or avoided by the provision of reasonable instructions or warnings by the seller or other distributor, or a predecessor in the commercial chain of distribution, and the omission of the instructions or warnings renders the product not reasonably safe."[6] Generally, a seller must also warn consumers of the harm that can result from the *foreseeable misuse* of its product.

Note that plaintiffs must show that inadequate warnings were the proximate cause of the injuries that they sustained. In the following case, a drug manufacturer argued that an injured plaintiff failed to prove that an inadequate warning was the cause of his injuries.

---

4. *Riley v. Ford Motor Co.*, 414 S.C. 185, 777 S.E.2d 824 (2015).
5. *Wilson Sporting Goods Co. v. Hickox*, 59 A.3d 1267 (D.C.App. 2013).
6. *Restatement (Third) of Torts: Products Liability*, Section 2(c).

Case 6.2

Stange v. Janssen Pharmaceuticals, Inc.

Superior Court of Pennsylvania,2018 PA Super 4, 179A.3d 45 (2018).

Facts Timothy Stange was twelve years old when his physician, Dr. Edward Kovnar, prescribed Risperdal, an antipsychotic drug, for Stange's Tourette's syndrome. (Tourette's syndrome is a neurological disorder characterized by repetitive behaviors and vocalizations, called tics.) Stange subsequently developed female breasts, a condition known as gynecomastia. Surgery successfully removed his breasts, but left him with permanent scars and pain. Risperdal is made by Janssen Pharmaceuticals, Inc. Janssen knew that gynecomastia was a frequent adverse event in children and adolescents who took Risperdal. But its label stated that the disorder's occurrence in those who took Risperdal was "rare." Stange filed a suit in a Pennsylvania state court against Janssen, alleging that the maker negligently failed to adequately warn of the risk of gynecomastia associated with Risperdal use. The court entered a judgment in favor of the plaintiff for more than $500,000. Janssen appealed to a state intermediate appellate court.

Issue Did Stange prove that an inadequate warning was the cause of his injuries?

Decision Yes. The appellate court affirmed the judgment in favor of Stange. "Due to Janssen's inadequate labeling and failure to warn, Dr. Kovnar was unaware of the specific heightened risks associated with the use of Risperdal."

Reason The court explained that in a case involving the failure to warn of a risk associated with a prescription drug, a plaintiff must prove that the manufacturer failed to exercise reasonable care to inform a physician of facts that make the drug likely to be dangerous. A physician must be fully aware of the drug's characteristics to properly decide whether to prescribe it. In this case, Janssen knew that gynecomastia was a frequent adverse event associated with Risperdal, not "rare." But the drug maker intentionally downplayed the risk of gynecomastia for adolescent boys using Risperdal. The drug label's "warnings were not accurate, strong, or clear. Instead, the warnings, to the extent they warned at all, were inaccurate and misleading about the risks." The court pointed out that Kovnar testified he would not have prescribed Risperdal to Stange if he had been aware of the increased risk.

Critical Thinking

- **Economic** *Why did Janssen downplay the risks of Risperdal in the warnings to physicians? Discuss.*
- **What If the Facts Were Different?** *Suppose that instead of suffering harm through a prescription drug's legitimate use, the plaintiff had been injured by a drug's illegal abuse. Would the result have been different? Explain.*

Content of Warnings. Important factors for a court to consider include the risks of a product, the "content and comprehensibility" and "intensity of expression" of warnings and instructions, and the "characteristics of expected user groups."[7] Courts apply a "reasonableness" test to determine if the warnings adequately alert consumers to the product's risks. For instance, children will likely respond more readily to bright, bold, simple warning labels, while educated adults might need more detailed information. For more on tips on making sure a product's warnings are adequate, see this chapter's *Managerial Strategy* feature.

Case Example 6.6 Jeffrey Johnson was taken to the emergency room for an episode of atrial fibrillation, a heart rhythm disorder. Dr. David Hahn used a defibrillator manufactured by Medtronic, Inc., to deliver electric shocks to Johnson's heart. The defibrillator had synchronous and asynchronous modes, and it reverted to the asynchronous mode after each use. Hahn intended to deliver synchronized shocks, which required him to select the synchronous mode for each shock. Hahn did not read the device's instructions, which Medtronic had provided both in a manual and on the device itself. As a result, he delivered one synchronized shock, followed by twelve asynchronous shocks that endangered Johnson's life.

---

7. *Restatement (Third) of Torts: Products Liability*, Section 2, Comment h.

When Is a Warning Legally Bulletproof?

A company can develop and sell a perfectly manufactured and designed product, yet still face product liability lawsuits for defective warnings. A product may be defective because of inadequate instructions or warnings when the foreseeable risks of harm posed by the product could have been reduced by reasonable warnings offered by the seller or other distributor. Manufacturers and distributors have a duty to warn users of any hidden dangers in their products. Additionally, they have a duty to instruct users in how to use the product to avoid any dangers. Warnings generally must be clear and specific. They must also be conspicuous.

When No Warning Is Required

Not all manufacturers have to provide warnings. People are expected to know that knives can cut fingers, for instance, so a seller need not place a bright orange label on each knife sold reminding consumers of this danger. Most household products are generally safe when used as intended.

In a New Jersey case, a ten-year-old boy was injured when he fell and struck his face on a Razor A kick scooter's handlebars. The padded end caps on the handlebars had deteriorated, and the boy's mother had thrown them away, exposing the handlebars' metal ends.

The boy and his mother sued, claiming that the manufacturer was required to provide a warning to prevent injuries of this type. The appellate court noted, however, that the plaintiffs were not able to claim that the Razor A was defective. "Lacking evidence that Razor A's end-cap design was defective, plaintiffs cannot show that Razor A had a duty to warn of such a defect, and therefore cannot make out their failure to warn claim."[a]

In an Indiana case, an employee of a concrete contractor was injured at a construction site when his head was struck by a sixteen-foot-long two-by-four board that had dislodged from a concrete formwork system. The employee sued the construction manager and the manufacturer of the formwork system for failure to warn. The court decided that the danger that lumber used in this formwork system could eject and strike a person was open and obvious. Therefore, neither the construction manager nor the manufacturer of the system was liable for failing to warn the employee.[b]

Medical Warnings

In a case involving a surgical procedure, a woman suffered severe damage to her pelvis that turned out to be permanent. Her lawsuit against the manufacturer of the mesh implant that caused the damage included a failure-to-warn claim. At trial, her physician testified that, if the manufacturer's "Instructions for Use" had informed him about the significant possibility of permanent damage, he would have chosen a different treatment plan. A federal appeals court upheld the jury's $20 million award, holding that the manufacturer's short, generic warning of risk did not provide enough information to either the plaintiff or her physician.[c]

The appeals court noted that, if the mesh implant manufacturer had provided ample warning, it might have been protected by the *learned intermediary doctrine*. Under this legal theory, a properly informed physician bears the responsibility to explain the risks of any drug or medical procedure to the patient. Opioid manufacturers have turned to the learned intermediary doctrine as a defense against product liability lawsuits stemming from the many thousands of fatal overdoses linked to their product in recent years. At least one court has rejected this approach, however, holding that an opioid manufacturer's aggressive marketing strategies negated any defense that proper label warnings would have provided.[d]

Business Questions

1. *To protect themselves, manufacturers have been forced to include lengthy safety warnings for their products. What might be the downside of such warnings?*

2. *Does a manufacturer have to create safety warnings for every product? Why or why not?*

a. *Vann v. Toys R Us*, 2014 WL3537937 (N.J.Sup.A.D. 2014).
b. *Gleaves v. Messer Construction Co.*, 77 N.E.3d 1244 (Ind. App. 2017).
c. *Kaiser v. Johnson & Johnson*, 947 F.3d 996 (7th Cir. 2020).
d. *Commonwealth v. Purdue Pharma, L.P. et al.*, 2019 WL 5495866 (36 Mass.L.Rptr. 56 2019).

Johnson and his wife filed a product liability suit against Medtronic asserting that Medtronic had provided inadequate warnings about the defibrillator and that the device had a design defect. A Missouri appellate court held that the Johnsons could not pursue a claim based on the inadequacy of Medtronic's warnings, but they could pursue a claim alleging a design defect. The court reasoned that in some cases, "a manufacturer may be held liable where it chooses to warn of the danger . . . rather than preclude the danger by design."[8]

8. *Johnson v. Medtronic, Inc.*, 365 S.W.3d 226 (Mo.App. 2012).

Obvious Risks. There is no duty to warn about risks that are obvious or commonly known. Warnings about such risks do not add to the safety of a product and could even detract from it by making other warnings seem less significant. As will be discussed later in this chapter, the obviousness of a risk and a user's decision to proceed in the face of that risk may be a defense in a product liability suit based on an inadequate warning.

Example 6.7 Sixteen-year-old Lana attempts to do a back flip on a trampoline and fails. She is paralyzed as a result. There are nine warning labels affixed to the trampoline, an instruction manual with safety warnings, and a placard attached at the entrance advising users not to do flips. If Lana sues the manufacturer for inadequate warnings, she is likely to lose. The warning labels are probably sufficient to make the risks obvious and insulate the manufacturer from liability for her injuries.

alexemanuel/iStock/Getty Images

How many and what types of warnings against doing back flips on this trampoline must be affixed to eliminate the manufacturer's liability?

Risks that may seem obvious to some users will not be obvious to all users. This is a particular problem when users are likely to be children. A young child may not be able to read or understand warning labels or comprehend the risk of certain activities. To avoid liability, the manufacturer would have to prove that the warnings it provided were adequate to make the risk of injury obvious to a young child.

State Laws and Constitutionality. An action alleging that a product is defective due to an inadequate label can be based on state law, but that law must not violate the U.S. Constitution. **Case Example 6.8** California once enacted a law imposing restrictions and a labeling requirement on the sale or rental of "violent video games" to minors. Although the video game industry had adopted a voluntary rating system for games, the legislators deemed those labels inadequate. The Video Software Dealers Association and the Entertainment Software Association immediately filed a suit in federal court to invalidate the law, and the law was struck down. The court found that the definition of a violent video game in California's law was unconstitutionally vague and violated the First Amendment's guarantee of freedom of speech.[9]

6–2d Market-Share Liability

Generally, in cases involving product liability, a plaintiff must prove that the defective product that caused the injury was made by a specific defendant. In a few situations, however, courts have dropped this requirement when a plaintiff cannot prove which of many distributors of a harmful product supplied the particular product that caused the injury. Under a theory of **market-share liability**, a court can hold each manufacturer responsible for a percentage of the plaintiff's damages that is equal to the percentage of its market share.

Market-Share Liability A theory under which liability is shared among all firms that manufactured and distributed a particular product during a certain period of time. This form of liability sharing is used only when the specific source of the harmful product is unidentifiable.

Case Example 6.9 Suffolk County Water Authority (SCWA) is a municipal water supplier in Suffolk County, New York. SCWA discovered the presence of a toxic chemical, perchloroethylene (PCE), used by dry cleaners and others in its local water. SCWA filed a product liability lawsuit against Dow Chemical Corporation and other companies that manufactured and distributed PCE. Dow filed a motion to dismiss the case for failure to state a claim, since SCWA could not identify each defendant whose allegedly defective product had caused the water contamination.

9. *Video Software Dealers Association v. Schwarzenegger*, 556 F.3d 950 (9th Cir. 2009); *Brown v. Entertainment Merchants Association*, 564 U.S. 786, 131 S.Ct. 2729, 180 L.Ed.2d 708 (2011).

A state trial court refused to dismiss the action, holding that SWCA's allegations were sufficient to invoke market-share liability. Under market-share liability, the burden of identification shifts to defendants if the plaintiff establishes a *prima facie* case on every element of the claim except identification of the specific defendant. (A *prima facie* case is one in which the plaintiff has presented sufficient evidence for the claim to go forward.)[10]

Courts in many jurisdictions do not recognize market-share liability, believing that it deviates too significantly from traditional legal principles. Jurisdictions that do recognize this theory of liability apply it only when it is difficult or impossible to determine which company made a particular product.

6–2e Other Applications of Strict Liability

Almost all courts extend the strict liability of manufacturers and other sellers to injured bystanders. **Example 6.10** A forklift that Trent is operating will not go into reverse, and as a result, it runs into a bystander. In this situation, the bystander can sue the manufacturer of the defective forklift under strict liability (and possibly bring a negligence action against the forklift operator as well).

Strict liability also applies to suppliers of component parts. **Example 6.11** Toyota buys brake pads from a subcontractor and puts them in Corollas without changing their composition. If those pads are defective, both the supplier of the brake pads and Toyota will be held strictly liable for injuries caused by the defects.

6–3 Defenses to Product Liability

Defendants in product liability suits can raise a number of defenses. One defense, of course, is to show that there is no basis for the plaintiff's claim. For instance, in a product liability case based on negligence, if a defendant can show that the plaintiff has not met the requirements (such as causation) for an action in negligence, generally the defendant will not be liable. A defendant may also assert that the *statute of limitations* for a product liability claim has lapsed.[11]

In a case involving strict product liability, a defendant can claim that the plaintiff failed to meet one of the requirements. If the defendant establishes that goods were altered after they were sold, for instance, the defendant normally will not be held liable.

6–3a Preemption

Focus Question 4

What defenses to liability can be raised in a product liability lawsuit?

A defense that has been successfully raised by defendants in recent years is preemption—that government regulations preempt claims for product liability. An injured party may not be able to sue a manufacturer of defective products that are subject to comprehensive federal regulatory schemes.

Medical devices, for instance, are subject to extensive government regulation and undergo a rigorous premarket approval process. **Case Example 6.12** The United States Supreme Court decided in *Riegel v. Medtronic, Inc.*, that a man who was injured by an approved medical device (a balloon catheter) could not sue its maker for product liability. The Court reasoned that Congress had created a comprehensive scheme of federal safety oversight for medical devices. The U.S. Food and Drug Administration is required to review the design, labeling, and manufacturing of medical devices before they are marketed to make sure that they are

---

10. *Suffolk County Water Authority v. Dow Chemical Co.*, 44 Misc.3d 569, 987 N.Y.S.2d 819 (N.Y.Sup. 2014).
11. Similar state statutes, called *statutes of repose*, place outer time limits on product liability actions.

safe and effective. Because premarket approval is a "rigorous process," it preempts all common law claims challenging the safety or effectiveness of a medical device that has been approved.[12]

Since the *Medtronic* decision, some courts have extended the preemption defense to other product liability actions.[13] Other courts have been unwilling to deny an injured party relief simply because the federal government was supposed to ensure the product's safety.

In the following *Spotlight Case*, the United States Supreme Court had to decide if the preemption defense barred a plaintiff's claim for injuries caused by vaccination.

12. *Riegel v. Medtronic, Inc.*, 552 U.S. 312, 128 S.Ct. 999, 169 L.Ed.2d 892 (2008).
13. See, for example, *Fortner v. Bristol-Myers Squibb Co.*, 2017 WL 3193928 (S.D.N.Y. 2017).

Spotlight on Injuries from Vaccinations: Case 6.3

Bruesewitz v. Wyeth, LLC

Supreme Court of the United States, 562 U.S. 223, 131 S.Ct. 1068, 179 L.Ed.2d 1 (2011).

Facts When Hannah Bruesewitz was six months old, her pediatrician administered a dose of the diphtheria, tetanus, and pertussis (DTP) vaccine according to the Centers for Disease Control and Prevention's recommended childhood immunization schedule. Within twenty-four hours, Hannah began to experience seizures. She suffered more than one hundred seizures during the next month. Her doctors diagnosed her with "residual seizure disorder" and "developmental delay."

Hannah's parents, Russell and Robalee Bruesewitz, filed a claim for relief in the U.S. Court of Federal Claims under the National Childhood Vaccine Injury Act (NCVIA). The NCVIA set up a no-fault compensation program for persons injured by vaccines. The claim was denied. The Bruesewitzes then filed a suit in a Pennsylvania state court against Wyeth, LLC, the maker of the vaccine, alleging strict product liability. The suit was moved to a federal district court. The court held that the claim was preempted by the NCVIA, which includes provisions protecting manufacturers from liability for "a vaccine's unavoidable, adverse side effects." A federal appellate court affirmed the district court's judgment. The Bruesewitzes appealed to the United States Supreme Court.

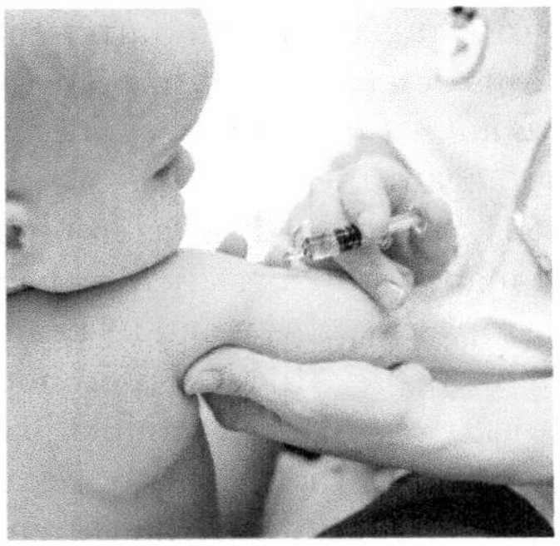
naumoid/iStock/Getty Images

What happens when a vaccine causes adverse side effects?

Issue Was the Bruesewitzes' strict product liability claim against Wyeth for the injuries that their child suffered from vaccination preempted by the National Childhood Vaccine Injury Act?

Decision Yes. The United States Supreme Court affirmed the lower court's judgment. The NCVIA preempted the Bruesewitzes' claim against Wyeth for injury to their daughter caused by the DTP vaccine's side effects.

Reason The Court reasoned that Congress enacted the NCVIA as a matter of public policy to stabilize the vaccine market and facilitate compensation. In the no-fault compensation program set up by the NCVIA, a person with a vaccine-related claim files a petition with the U.S. Court of Federal Claims. The court may award compensation for legal, medical, rehabilitation, counseling, special education, and vocational training expenses, as well as for diminished earning capacity, pain and suffering, and death. The awards are funded by a tax on the vaccine. In exchange for the "informal, efficient" compensation program, vaccine manufacturers that comply with the regulatory requirements are "immunized" from liability. The statute thus strikes a balance between paying victims harmed by vaccines and protecting the vaccine industry from collapsing under the costs of tort liability.

Critical Thinking

- **Political** *If the public wants to change the policy outlined in this case, which branch of the government—and at what level—should be lobbied to make the change? Explain.*
- **Economic** *What is the public policy expressed by the provisions of the NCVIA?*

6–3b Assumption of Risk

Assumption of risk can sometimes be used as a defense in a product liability action. To establish such a defense, the defendant must show that (1) the plaintiff knew and appreciated the risk created by the product defect and (2) the plaintiff voluntarily assumed the risk, even though it was unreasonable to do so.

dlewis33/E+/Getty Images

Under what circumstances can a tanning salon customer sue for injuries even though a release was signed?

Although assumption of the risk is a defense in product liability actions, some courts do not allow it to be used as a defense to strict product liability claims. **Case Example 6.13** When Savannah Boles became a customer of Executive Tans, she signed a contract. One clause stated that signers used the company's tanning booths at their own risk. It also released the manufacturer and others from liability for any injuries. Later, Boles's fingers were partially amputated when they came into contact with a tanning booth's fan. Boles sued the manufacturer, claiming strict product liability. The Colorado Supreme Court held that assumption of risk was not applicable because strict product liability is driven by public-policy considerations. The theory focuses on the nature of the product rather than the conduct of either the manufacturer or the person injured.[14]

6–3c Product Misuse

Similar to the defense of voluntary assumption of risk is that of product misuse, which occurs when a product is used for a purpose for which it was not intended. The courts have severely limited this defense. Today, product misuse is recognized as a defense *only when the particular use was not reasonably foreseeable*. If the misuse is foreseeable, the seller must take measures to guard against it.

Case Example 6.14 Steven Iliades was injured when he climbed into a press machine without placing it in manual mode, as he had been trained to do. Instead, he relied on a "light curtain," which stops the press when its beam is interrupted by the wave of a hand or arm. Because his body was stuck, Iliades could not engage the light curtain.

A trial court dismissed Iliades's product liability lawsuit against the press machine's manufacturer on the grounds that it was not reasonably foreseeable that an employee would disregard safety precautions to such an extreme degree. The Michigan Supreme Court eventually ordered a new trial, with instructions that the lower court focus not only on Iliades's misuse of the press machine, but also on whether such misuse, no matter how outrageous, was reasonably foreseeable by the manufacturer.[15]

6–3d Comparative Negligence (Fault)

Developments in the area of comparative negligence, or fault (discussed in the torts chapter), have also affected the doctrine of strict liability. Today, courts in many jurisdictions consider the negligent or intentional actions of both the plaintiff and the defendant when apportioning liability and awarding damages. A defendant may be able to limit at least some liability for injuries caused by a defective product if it can show that the plaintiff's misuse of the product contributed to the injuries.

When proved, comparative negligence differs from other defenses in that it does not completely absolve the defendant of liability. It can, however, reduce the amount of damages that will be awarded to the plaintiff. Note that some jurisdictions allow only intentional conduct to affect a plaintiff's recovery, whereas others allow ordinary negligence to be used as a defense to product liability.

---

14. *Boles v. Sun Ergoline, Inc.*, 223 P.3d 724 (Co.Sup.Ct. 2010).

15. *Iliades v. Dieffenbacher North America, Inc.*, 915 N.W.2d 338 (501 Mich. 326 2018).

6–3e Commonly Known Dangers

As mentioned, the dangers associated with certain products (such as sharp knives and guns) are so commonly known that manufacturers need not warn users of those dangers. If a defendant succeeds in convincing the court that a plaintiff's injury resulted from a *commonly known danger*, the defendant normally will not be liable.

Classic Case Example 6.15 In a case from 1957, Marguerite Jamieson was injured when an elastic exercise rope slipped off her foot and struck her in the eye, causing a detachment of the retina. Jamieson claimed that the manufacturer should be liable because it had failed to warn users that the exerciser might slip off a foot in such a manner.

The court stated that to hold the manufacturer liable in these circumstances "would go beyond the reasonable dictates of justice in fixing the liabilities of manufacturers." After all, stated the court, "almost every physical object can be inherently dangerous or potentially dangerous in a sense. . . . A manufacturer cannot manufacture a knife that will not cut or a hammer that will not mash a thumb or a stove that will not burn a finger. The law does not require [manufacturers] to warn of such common dangers."[16]

6–3f Knowledgeable User

A related defense is the *knowledgeable user* defense. If a particular danger (such as electrical shock) is or should be commonly known by particular users of the product (such as electricians), the manufacturer of electrical equipment need not warn these users of the danger.

Spotlight Case Example 6.16 The parents of a group of teenagers who had become overweight and developed health problems filed a product liability lawsuit against McDonald's. The plaintiffs claimed that the well-known fast-food chain should be held liable for failing to warn customers of the adverse health effects of eating its food products. The court rejected this claim, however, based on the knowledgeable user defense.

According to the court, it is well known that the food at McDonald's contains high levels of cholesterol, fat, salt, and sugar, and is therefore unhealthful. The court's opinion, which thwarted numerous future lawsuits against fast-food restaurants, stated, "If consumers know (or reasonably should know) the potential ill health effects of eating at McDonald's, they cannot blame McDonald's if they, nonetheless, choose to satiate their appetite with a surfeit of supersized McDonald's products."[17]

6–3g Statutes of Limitations and Repose

As mentioned previously, statutes of limitations restrict the time within which an action may be brought. The statute of limitations for product liability cases varies according to state law. Usually, the injured party must bring a product liability claim within two to four years. Often, **tolling** suspends the running of the prescribed period until the party suffering an injury has discovered it or should have discovered it.

To ensure that sellers and manufacturers will not be left vulnerable to lawsuits indefinitely, many states have passed statutes that place outer time limits on product liability actions. Such a statute is called a **statute of repose**, as mentioned earlier. For instance, a statute of repose may require that claims be brought within twelve years from the date of sale or manufacture of the defective product. If the plaintiff does not bring an action before the prescribed period expires, the seller cannot be held liable.

Tolling A legal doctrine that allows for the temporary suspension of the running of a prescribed time period, such as a statute of limitations.

Statute of Repose A statute that places outer time limits on product liability actions. Such statutes cut off absolutely the right to bring an action after a specified period of time following some event (often the product's manufacture or purchase) other than the occurrence of an injury.

---

16. *Jamieson v. Woodward & Lothrop*, 247 F.2d 23, 101 D.C.App. 32 (1957).
17. *Pelman v. McDonald's Corp.*, 237 F.Supp.2d 512 (S.D.N.Y. 2003).

Practice and Review

Shalene Kolchek bought a Great Lakes Spa from Val Porter, a dealer who was selling spas at the state fair. After Kolchek signed the contract, Porter handed her the manufacturer's paperwork and arranged for the spa to be delivered and installed for her. Three months later, Kolchek left her six-year-old daughter, Litisha, alone in the spa. While exploring the spa's hydromassage jets, Litisha got her index finger stuck in one of the jet holes.

Litisha yanked hard, injuring her finger, and then panicked and screamed for help. Kolchek was unable to remove Litisha's finger, and the local police and rescue team were called to assist. After a three-hour operation that included draining the spa, sawing out a section of the spa's plastic molding, and slicing the jet casing, Litisha's finger was freed. Following this procedure, the spa was no longer functional. Litisha was taken to the local emergency room, where she was told that a bone in her finger was broken in two places. Using the information presented in the chapter, answer the following questions.

1. Under which theories of product liability can Kolchek sue Porter to recover for Litisha's injuries?
2. Would privity of contract be required for Kolchek to succeed in a product liability action against Great Lakes? Explain.
3. For an action in strict product liability against Great Lakes, what six requirements must Kolchek meet?
4. What defenses to product liability might Porter or Great Lakes be able to assert?

Debate This

All liability suits against tobacco companies for causing lung cancer should be thrown out of court now and forever.

Key Terms

market-share liability 157
privity of contract 148
product liability 146
statute of repose 161
tolling 161
unreasonably dangerous product 151

Chapter Summary: Product Liability

Product Liability Claims	1. **Negligence**—The manufacturer must use due care in designing the product, selecting materials, using the appropriate production process, assembling and testing the product, placing adequate warnings on the label or product, and inspecting and testing its components. Privity of contract is not required. A manufacturer is liable for failure to exercise due care to any person who sustains an injury proximately caused by a negligently made (defective) product. 2. **Misrepresentation**—Fraudulent misrepresentation of a product may result in product liability based on the tort of fraud. The misrepresentation must have been made knowingly or with reckless disregard for the facts.

Strict Product Liability	1. **Requirements**— a. The defendant must have sold the product in a defective condition. b. The defendant must normally be engaged in the business of selling that product. c. The product must be unreasonably dangerous to the user or consumer because of its defective condition (in most states). d. The plaintiff must incur physical harm to self or property by use or consumption of the product. e. The defective condition must be the proximate cause of the injury or damage. f. The goods must not have been substantially changed from the time the product was sold to the time the injury was sustained. 2. **Product defects**—A product may be defective in three basic ways: in its manufacture, in its design, or in the instructions or warnings that come with it. 3. **Market-share liability**—When plaintiffs cannot prove which of many distributors of a defective product supplied the particular product that caused the plaintiffs' injuries, some courts apply market-share liability. All firms that manufactured and distributed the harmful product during the period in question are then held liable for the plaintiffs' injuries in proportion to the firms' respective shares of the market, as directed by the court. 4. **Other applications**—Manufacturers and other sellers are liable for harms suffered by bystanders as a result of defective products. Suppliers of component parts are strictly liable for defective parts that, when incorporated into a product, cause injuries to users.
Defenses to Product Liability	1. **Preemption**—An injured party may not be able to sue the manufacturer of a product that is subject to comprehensive federal safety regulations, such as medical devices. 2. **Assumption of risk**—The user or consumer knew of the risk of harm and voluntarily assumed it. 3. **Product misuse**—The user or consumer misused the product in a way unforeseeable by the manufacturer. 4. **Comparative negligence**—Liability may be distributed between the plaintiff and the defendant under the doctrine of comparative negligence if the plaintiff's misuse of the product contributed to the risk of injury. 5. **Commonly known dangers**—If a defendant succeeds in convincing the court that a plaintiff's injury resulted from a commonly known danger, such as the danger associated with using a sharp knife, the defendant will not be liable. 6. **Knowledgeable user**—If a particular danger is or should be commonly known by particular users of the product, the manufacturer of the product need not warn these users of the danger.

Issue Spotters

1. Rim Corporation makes tire rims and sells them to Superior Vehicles, Inc., which installs them on cars. One set of rims is defective, which an inspection would reveal. Superior does not inspect the rims. The car with the defective rims is sold to Town Auto Sales, which sells the car to Uri. Soon, the car is in an accident caused by the defective rims, and Uri is injured. Is Superior Vehicles liable? Explain your answer. (See *Product Liability Claims.*)
2. Bensing Company manufactures generic drugs for the treatment of heart disease. A federal law requires generic drug makers to use labels that are identical to the labels on brand-name versions of the drugs. Hunter Rothfus purchased Bensing's generic drugs in Ohio and wants to sue Bensing for defective labeling based on its failure to comply with Ohio state common law (rather than the federal labeling requirements). What defense might Bensing assert to avoid liability under state law? (See *Defenses to Product Liability.*)

—Check your answers to the *Issue Spotters* against the answers provided in Appendix D.

Business Scenarios and Case Problems

6–1. Product Liability. Carmen buys a television set manufactured by AKI Electronics. She is going on vacation, so she takes the set to her mother's house for her mother to use. Because the set is defective, it explodes, causing considerable damage to her mother's house. Carmen's mother sues AKI for the damage to her house. Discuss the theories under which Carmen's mother can recover from AKI. (See *Product Liability Claims.*)

6–2. Product Liability. Jason Clark, an experienced hunter, bought a paintball gun. Clark practiced with the gun and knew how to screw in the carbon dioxide cartridge, pump the gun, and use its safety and trigger. Although Clark was aware that he could purchase protective eyewear, he chose not to do so. Clark had taken gun safety courses and understood that it was "common sense" not to shoot anyone in the face. Clark's friend, Chris Wright, also owned a paintball gun and was similarly familiar with the gun's use and its risks.

Clark, Wright, and their friends played a game that involved shooting paintballs at cars whose occupants also had the guns. One night, while Clark and Wright were cruising with their guns, Wright shot at Clark's car but hit Clark in the eye. Clark filed a product liability lawsuit against the manufacturer of Wright's paintball gun to recover for the injury. Clark claimed that the gun was defectively designed. During the trial, Wright testified that his gun "never malfunctioned." In whose favor should the court rule? Why? (See *Product Liability Claims.*)

6–3. Product Misuse. Five-year-old Cheyenne Stark was riding in the backseat of her parents' Ford Taurus. Cheyenne was not sitting in a booster seat. Instead, she was using a seatbelt designed by Ford but was wearing the shoulder belt behind her back. The car was involved in a collision. As a result, Cheyenne suffered a spinal cord injury and was paralyzed from the waist down. The family filed a suit against Ford Motor Co., alleging that the seatbelt was defectively designed. Could Ford successfully claim that Cheyenne had misused the seatbelt? Why or why not? [*Stark v. Ford Motor Co.*, 365 N.C. 468, 723 S.E.2d 753 (2012)] (See *Defenses to Product Liability.*)

6–4. Business Case Problem with Sample Answer—Product Liability. While driving on Interstate 40 in North Carolina, Carroll Jett became distracted by a texting system in the cab of his tractor-trailer truck. He smashed into several vehicles that were slowed or stopped in front of him, injuring Barbara and Michael Durkee and others. The injured motorists filed a suit in a federal district court against Geologic Solutions, Inc., the maker of the texting system, alleging product liability. Was the accident caused by Jett's inattention or the texting device? Should a manufacturer be required to design a product that is incapable of distracting a driver? Discuss. [*Durkee v. Geologic Solutions, Inc.*, 502 Fed. Appx. 326 (4th Cir. 2013)] (See *Product Liability Claims.*)

—For a sample answer to Problem 6-4, go to Appendix E.

6–5. Strict Product Liability. Medicis Pharmaceutical Corp. makes Solodyn, a prescription oral antibiotic. Medicis warns physicians that "autoimmune syndromes, including drug-induced lupus-like syndrome," may be associated with use of the drug. Amanda Watts had chronic acne. Her physician prescribed Solodyn. Information included with the drug did not mention the risk of autoimmune disorders, and Watts was not otherwise advised of it. She was prescribed the drug twice, each time for twenty weeks. Later, she experienced debilitating joint pain and, after being hospitalized, was diagnosed with lupus. On what basis could Watts recover from Medicis in an action grounded in product liability? Explain. [*Watts v. Medicis Pharmaceutical Corp.*, 236 Ariz. 19, 365 P.3d 944 (2016)] (See *Strict Product Liability.*)

6–6. Strict Product Liability. Duval Ford, LLC, sold a new Ford F-250 pickup truck to David Sweat. Before taking delivery, Sweat ordered a lift kit to be installed on the truck by a Duval subcontractor. Sweat also replaced the tires and modified the suspension system to increase the towing capacity. Later, through Burkins Chevrolet, Sweat sold the truck to Shaun Lesnick. Sweat had had no problems with the truck's steering or suspension, but Lesnick did. He had the steering repaired and made additional changes, including installing a steering stabilizer and replacing the tires. Two months later, Lesnick was driving the truck when the steering and suspension suddenly failed, and the truck flipped over, causing Lesnick severe injuries. Could Lesnick successfully claim that Duval and Burkins had failed to warn him of the risk of a lifted truck? Explain. [*Lesnick v. Duval Ford, LLC*, 41 Fla.L.Weekly D281, 185 So.3d 577 (1 Dist. 2016)] (See *Product Liability Claims.*)

6–7. Spotlight on Pfizer, Inc.—Defenses to Product Liability. Prescription drugs in the United States must be approved by the Food and Drug Administration (FDA) before they can be sold. A drug maker whose product is approved through the FDA's "abbreviated new drug application" (ANDA) process cannot later change the label without FDA approval. Pfizer Inc. makes and sells by prescription Depo-T, a testosterone replacement drug classified as an ANDA-approved drug. Rodney Guilbeau filed a claim in a federal district court against Pfizer, alleging that he had experienced a "cardiovascular event" after taking Depo-T. He sought recovery on a state-law product liability theory, arguing that Pfizer had failed to warn patients adequately about the risks. He claimed that after the drug's approval its maker had become aware of a higher incidence of heart attacks, strokes, and other cardiovascular events among those who took it but had not added a warning to its label. What is Pfizer's best defense to this claim? Explain. [*Guilbeau v. Pfizer, Inc.*, 80 F.3d 304 (7th Cir. 2018)] (See *Defenses to Product Liability.*)

6–8. A Question of Ethics—The IDDR Approach and Product Liability. While replacing screws in a gutter, John Baugh fell off a ladder and landed head-first on his concrete driveway. He sustained a severe brain injury, which permanently limited his ability to perform routine physical and intellectual functions. He filed a suit in a federal district court against Cuprum S.A. de C.V., the company that designed and made the ladder, alleging a design defect under product liability theories. Baugh weighed nearly 200 pounds, which was the stated weight limit on this ladder. Kevin Smith, a mechanical engineer, testified on Baugh's behalf that the gusset (bracket) on the ladder's right front side was too short to support Baugh's weight. This caused the ladder's leg to fail and Baugh to fall. In Smith's opinion, a longer gusset would have prevented the accident. Cuprum argued that the accident occurred because Baugh climbed too high on the ladder and stood on its fourth step and pail shelf, neither of which were intended for the purpose. No other person witnessed Baugh using the ladder prior to his fall, however, so there was no evidence to support Cuprum's argument. [*Baugh v. Cuprum S.A. de C.V.*, 845 F.3d 838 (7th Cir. 2017)] (See *Strict Product Liability*.)

1. What is a manufacturer's legal and ethical duty when designing and making products for consumers? Did Cuprum meet this standard? Discuss.
2. Did the mechanical engineer's testimony establish that a reasonable alternative design was available for Cuprum's ladder? Explain.

Critical Thinking and Writing Assignments

6–9. Time-Limited Group Assignment. Bret D'Auguste was an experienced skier when he rented equipment to ski at Hunter Mountain Ski Bowl in New York. When D'Auguste entered an extremely difficult trail, he noticed immediately that the surface consisted of ice with almost no snow. He tried to exit the steeply declining trail by making a sharp right turn, but in the attempt, his left ski snapped off. D'Auguste lost his balance, fell, and slid down the mountain, striking his face and head against a fence along the trail. According to a report by a rental shop employee, one of the bindings on D'Auguste's skis had a "cracked heel housing." D'Auguste filed a lawsuit against the bindings' manufacturer on a theory of strict product liability. The manufacturer filed a motion for summary judgment. (See *Product Liability Claims*.)

1. The first group will take the position of the manufacturer and develop an argument why the court should *grant* the summary judgment motion and dismiss the strict product liability claim.
2. The second group will take the position of D'Auguste and formulate a basis for why the court should *deny* the motion and allow the strict product liability claim.
3. The third group will evaluate whether D'Auguste assumed the risk of this type of injury.
4. The fourth group will analyze whether the manufacturer could claim that D'Auguste's negligence (under the comparative negligence doctrine) contributed to his injury.

Alfa Photo/Shutterstock.com

7 Intellectual Property Rights

Focus Questions

The five Focus Questions *below are designed to help improve your understanding. After reading this chapter, you should be able to answer the following questions:*

1. Why is the protection of trademarks important?
2. How does the law protect patents?
3. What laws protect authors' rights in the works they create?
4. What are trade secrets, and what laws offer protection for this form of intellectual property?
5. How does the TRIPS agreement protect intellectual property worldwide?

Intellectual Property Property resulting from intellectual and creative processes.

"My words and my ideas are my property, and I'll keep and protect them as surely as I do my stable of unicorns."

Jarod Kintz
1982–present (American author)

Intellectual property is any property resulting from intellectual, creative processes—the products of an individual's mind, as suggested in the chapter-opening quotation. Although it is an abstract term for an abstract concept, intellectual property is nonetheless familiar to almost everyone. The apps for your iPhone or Samsung Galaxy, the movies you see, and the music you listen to are all forms of intellectual property.

More than two hundred years ago, the framers of the U.S. Constitution recognized the importance of protecting creative works in Article I, Section 8. Statutory protection of these rights began in the 1940s and continues to evolve to meet the needs of modern society.

Suppose that JD Beverage Company makes and sells a line of flavored vodkas called "Hot Lips Vodka." The name Hot Lips Vodka, along with an image of puckered lips, appears on the label of each bottle. The color of the lips logo depends on the vodka's flavor—red for chili pepper, green for apple, and so on. JD Beverage has registered trademarks for the name Hot Lips Vodka and the puckered lips logo, and the company heavily markets the vodka using hot lips as a theme. Sales of Hot Lips Vodka are at an all-time high.

Now another alcoholic beverage company begins to distribute a line of flavored vodkas called "Kiss Vodka." Like the Hot Lips label, the new vodka's label features the product's name and a puckered lips logo, and the company uses the lips in its marketing. JD Beverage believes that Kiss Vodka's use of the lips logo is diminishing the value of its Hot Lips brand and cutting into its sales. What can JD Beverage do? The answer lies in intellectual property law.

7–1 Trademarks

Focus Question 1

Why is the protection of trademarks important?

A **trademark** is a distinctive word, symbol, sound, or design that identifies the manufacturer as the source of particular goods and distinguishes its products from those made or sold by others. At common law, the person who used a symbol or mark to identify a business or product was protected in the use of that trademark. Clearly, if another company used the trademark, it could lead consumers to believe that its goods were made by the trademark owner. The law seeks to avoid this kind of confusion. (For information on how companies use trademarks and service marks, see this chapter's *Managerial Strategy* feature.)

Trademark A distinctive word, symbol, sound, or design that identifies the manufacturer as the source of particular goods and distinguishes its products from those made or sold by others.

Trademarks and Service Marks

Trademarks and service marks consist of much more than well-known brand names, such as Apple and Amazon. If you become a marketing manager, you will be involved in creating trademarks or service marks for your firm, protecting the firm's existing marks, and ensuring that you do not infringe on anyone else's marks. You will need to be aware that parts of a brand name or other forms of product identification may qualify for trademark protection. Some examples include:

1. **Catchy phrases**—Certain brands have established phrases that are associated with the brands, such as Nike's "Just Do It!" Take care to avoid using another brand's catchy phrase in your own program. Note, too, that not all phrases can become part of a trademark or service mark. When a phrase is extremely common, the courts normally will not grant it trademark or service mark protection.
2. **Abbreviations**—The public sometimes abbreviates a well-known trademark. For example, Budweiser beer is known as Bud and Coca-Cola as Coke. Do not use any name for a product or service that closely resembles a well-known abbreviation, such as Koke for a cola drink.
3. **Shapes**—The shape of a brand name, a service mark, or a container can take on exclusivity if the shape clearly aids in product or service identification. Just about everyone recognizes the shape of the fluid Coca-Cola bottle, for example. Avoid using a similar shape for competing products.
4. **Ornamental colors**—Sometimes, color combinations can become part of a service mark or trademark. For example, FedEx established its unique identity with the use of bright orange and purple. The courts have protected this color combination. The same holds for the black-and-copper color combination of Duracell batteries.
5. **Ornamental designs**—Symbols and designs associated with a particular mark are normally protected, so do not attempt to copy them. For instance, Levi's places a small tag on the left side of the rear pocket of its jeans. Cross uses a cut-off black cone on the top of its pens.
6. **Sounds**—Sounds can also be protected. For example, the familiar roar of the Metro-Goldwyn-Mayer (MGM) lion is protected.

When to Protect Trademarks and Service Marks

Once your company has established trademarks or service marks, it must decide how aggressively to protect those marks. If it fails to protect them, it faces the possibility that the marks will become generic. As discussed later, *aspirin, cellophane, thermos, dry ice, shredded wheat,* and many other familiar terms were once legally protected trademarks.

Protecting exclusive rights to a mark can be expensive, however, and a company must determine how much it is worth to protect its rights. Major expenditures to protect a small company's trademarks and service marks might not be cost-effective.

Business Questions

1. *The U.S. Patent and Trademark Office requires that a registered trademark or service mark be put into commercial use within six months. Extensions can be granted, but the mark must be put into commercial use within three years after the application has been approved. Why do you think the federal government established this requirement?*
2. *Should trademark protection apply to similarities between noncompeting products? Why or why not?*

In the following *Classic Case* concerning Coca-Cola, the defendants argued that the Coca-Cola trademark was not entitled to protection under the law because the term did not accurately represent the product.

Classic Case 7.1

Coca-Cola Co. v. Koke Co. of America

Supreme Court of the United States, 254 U.S. 143, 41 S.Ct. 113, 65 L.Ed. 189 (1920).

Facts John Pemberton, an Atlanta pharmacist, invented a caramel-colored, carbonated soft drink in 1886. His bookkeeper, Frank Robinson, named the beverage Coca-Cola after two of the ingredients, coca leaves and kola nuts. Asa Candler bought the Coca-Cola Company in 1891 and made the soft drink available throughout the United States and in parts of Canada and Mexico. Candler continued to sell Coke aggressively and to open up new markets in Europe and elsewhere, attracting numerous competitors, some of whom tried to capitalize directly on the Coke name.

The Coca-Cola Company brought an action in a federal district court to enjoin (prevent) other beverage companies from using the names Koke and Dope for their products. The defendants contended that the Coca-Cola trademark was a fraudulent representation and that Coca-Cola was therefore not entitled to any help from the courts. By using the Coca-Cola name, the defendants alleged, the Coca-Cola Company represented that the beverage contained cocaine (from coca leaves). The district court granted the injunction, but the federal appellate court reversed. The Coca-Cola Company appealed to the United States Supreme Court.

© Rob Wilson/ShutterStock.com

How is Coca-Cola protected?

Issue Did the marketing of products called Koke and Dope by the Koke Company of America and other firms constitute an infringement on Coca-Cola's trademark?

Decision Yes for Koke, but no for Dope. The United States Supreme Court enjoined the competing beverage companies from calling their products Koke but not from calling their products Dope.

Reason The Court noted that before 1900 the Coca-Cola beverage had contained a small amount of cocaine. This ingredient had been deleted from the formula by 1906 at the latest, however, and the Coca-Cola Company had advertised to the public that no cocaine was present in its drink. The court emphasized that Coca-Cola was a widely popular drink "to be had at almost any soda fountain." Because of the public's widespread familiarity with Coca-Cola, the retention of the name (referring to coca leaves and kola nuts) was not misleading: "Coca-Cola probably means to most persons the plaintiff's familiar product to be had everywhere rather than a compound of particular substances." The name Coke was found to be so common a term for the trademarked product Coca-Cola that the defendants' use of the similar-sounding Koke as a name for their beverages was disallowed. The Court could find no reason to restrain the defendants from using the name Dope, however.

Critical Thinking

- **What If the Facts Were Different?** *Suppose that Coca-Cola had been trying to make the public believe that its product contained cocaine. Would the result in the case likely have been different? Explain your answer.*
- **Impact of This Case on Today's Law** *In this early case, the United States Supreme Court made it clear that trademarks and trade names (and nicknames for those marks and names, such as "Coke" for "Coca-Cola") that are in common use receive protection under the common law. This holding is significant historically because it is the predecessor to the federal statute later passed to protect trademark rights (the Lanham Act, discussed next).*

7–1a Statutory Protection of Trademarks

Statutory protection of trademarks and related property is provided at the federal level by the Lanham Act of 1946.[1] The Lanham Act was enacted in part to protect manufacturers from losing business to rival companies that used confusingly similar trademarks. The Lanham Act incorporates the common law of trademarks and provides remedies for owners of trademarks who wish to enforce their claims in federal court. Many states also have trademark statutes.

1. 15 U.S.C. Sections 1051–1128.

Trademark Dilution The Federal Trademark Dilution Act[2] amended the Lanham Act to allow trademark owners to bring suits in federal court for **trademark dilution**. Later, Congress further amended the law on trademark dilution by passing the Trademark Dilution Revision Act (TDRA).[3]

Trademark Dilution The unauthorized use of a distinctive and famous mark in a way that impairs the mark's distinctiveness or harms its reputation.

Under the TDRA, to state a claim for trademark dilution, a plaintiff must prove the following:

1. The plaintiff owns a famous mark that is distinctive.
2. The defendant has begun using a mark in commerce that allegedly is diluting the famous mark.
3. The similarity between the defendant's mark and the famous mark gives rise to an *association* between the marks.
4. The association is likely to impair the distinctiveness of the famous mark or harm its reputation.

Trademark dilution laws protect "distinctive" or "famous" trademarks (such as Rolls-Royce, McDonald's, Starbucks, and Apple) from certain unauthorized uses. Such a mark is protected even when the unauthorized use is on noncompeting goods or is unlikely to confuse. More than half of the states have also enacted trademark dilution laws.

Know This

Trademark dilution laws protect the owners of distinctive marks from unauthorized uses even when the defendants' use involves noncompeting goods or is unlikely to cause confusion.

The Marks Need Not Be Identical A famous mark may be diluted not only by the use of an identical mark but also by the use of a *similar* mark, provided that it reduces the value of the famous mark. A similar mark is more likely to lessen the value of a famous mark when the companies using the marks provide related goods or compete against each other in the same market.

Spotlight Case Example 7.1 When Samantha Lundberg opened Sambuck's Coffeehouse in Astoria, Oregon, she knew that Starbucks was one of the largest coffee chains in the nation. Starbucks Corporation filed a dilution lawsuit, and a federal court ruled that use of the Sambuck's mark constituted trademark dilution because it created confusion for consumers. Not only was there a "high degree" of similarity between the marks, but also both companies provided coffee-related services through stand-alone retail stores. Therefore, the use of the similar mark (Sambuck's) reduced the value of the famous mark (Starbucks).[4]

7–1b Trademark Registration

Trademarks may be registered with the state or with the federal government. To register for protection under federal trademark law, a person must file an application with the U.S. Patent and Trademark Office in Washington, D.C. A mark can be registered (1) if it is currently in commerce or (2) if the applicant intends to put it into commerce within six months.

In special circumstances, the six-month period can be extended by thirty months. Thus, the applicant would have a total of three years from the date of notice of trademark approval to make use of the mark and to file the required use statement. Registration is postponed until the mark is actually used.

During this waiting period, applicants can legally protect their trademarks against third parties who have neither used the marks previously nor filed applications for them. Registration is renewable between the fifth and sixth years after the initial registration and every ten years thereafter (every twenty years for trademarks registered before 1990).

2. 15 U.S.C. Section 1125.
3. Pub. L. No. 103-312, 120 Stat. 1730 (2006).
4. *Starbucks Corp. v. Lundberg*, 2005 WL 3183858 (D.Or. 2005).

Ethical Issue

Should the law allow offensive trademark names? It is settled law that the First Amendment generally protects people's use of offensive words. Until recently, though, free speech did not necessarily extend to trademarking a word or name that some Americans find offensive. Under Section 2(a) of the Lanham Act (also known as the disparagement clause), the federal government could prohibit applicants from trademarking offensive (or disparaging) terms. The disparagement clause bars any trademark that "may disparage . . . or bring into contempt, or disrepute" any persons, institutions, beliefs, or national symbols. The U.S. Patent and Trademark Office (USPTO) used this clause to cancel the Washington Redskins football team's trademarks, which were deemed offensive to Native Americans.[5] Then came another case involving a musical group called The Slants, which consisted of only Asians.

dean bertoncelj/Shutterstock.com

Do trademarks that some people find offensive deserve First Amendment protection? Why or why not?

The members of The Slants picked the name because it was offensive. They claimed they wanted to turn the phrase upside down "to reappropriate it into something positive and empowering." When the trademark registration was reviewed by the USPTO, however, the USPTO cited Section 2(a) of the Lanham Act to deny registration. The band contested the ruling, noting that it could not get a record label deal unless it had a federally registered trademark. The case eventually was heard by the United States Supreme Court. In arguing before the Court, the band's attorney pointed out the numerous inconsistencies in the USPTO's decisions concerning potentially offensive names. For instance, the USPTO had approved a hip-hop group's registration of N.W.A.—which stands for Niggaz Wit Attitudes.

The United States Supreme Court eventually decided that the disparagement clause of the Lanham Act was an unconstitutional restraint on free speech. In a unanimous opinion, Justice Samuel Alito wrote, "It offends a bedrock First Amendment principle: Speech may not be banned on the ground that it expresses ideas that offend." Under this ruling, the federal government can no longer cancel or refuse to register trademarks—such as The Slants or the Redskins—that officials deem to be offensive or disparaging.[6]

7–1c Trademark Infringement

Registration of a trademark with the U.S. Patent and Trademark Office gives notice on a nationwide basis that the trademark belongs exclusively to the registrant. The registrant is also allowed to use the symbol ® to indicate that the mark has been registered. Whenever that trademark is copied to a substantial degree or used in its entirety by another, intentionally or unintentionally, the trademark has been *infringed* (used without authorization).

Know This

To prove trademark infringement, the trademark owner must show that the other party's use of the mark has created a likelihood of confusion about the origin of that party's goods or services.

When a trademark has been infringed, the owner has a cause of action against the infringer. To succeed in a lawsuit for trademark infringement, the owner must show that the defendant's use of the mark created a likelihood of confusion about the origin of the defendant's goods or services. The owner need not prove that the infringer acted intentionally or that the trademark was registered (although registration does provide proof of the date of inception of the trademark's use).

The most commonly granted remedy for trademark infringement is an *injunction* to prevent further infringement. Under the Lanham Act, a trademark owner that successfully proves

5. See *Pro-Football, Inc. v. Blackhorse*, 62 F.Supp.3d 498 (E.D.Va. 2014) and 112 F.Supp.3d 439 (E.D.Va. 2015).
6. *Matal v. Tam*, 582 U.S. ____, 137 S.Ct. 1744, 198 L.Ed.2d 366 (2017).

infringement can recover actual damages, plus the profits that the infringer wrongfully received from the unauthorized use of the mark. A court can also order the destruction of any goods bearing the unauthorized trademark. In some situations, the trademark owner may also be able to recover attorneys' fees.

7–1d Distinctiveness of the Mark

A central objective of the Lanham Act is to reduce the likelihood that consumers will be confused by similar marks. For that reason, only those trademarks that are deemed sufficiently distinctive from all competing trademarks will be protected.

To determine a mark's strength, courts classify it on a spectrum of five categories, ranging from strongest to weakest. *Fanciful* and *arbitrary marks* employ words and phrases with no commonly understood connection to the product. These are the two strongest categories and trigger the highest degree of trademark protection. *Suggestive marks*, which suggest a product's features and require consumers to use some imagination to associate the suggestive mark with the product, are in the middle of the spectrum. The two weakest categories are *descriptive* and *generic marks*. *Descriptive marks* define a particular characteristic of the product in a way that does not require any imagination. *Generic marks* describe the product in its entirety and are not entitled to trademark protection.

Strong Marks As the most distinctive (strongest) trademarks, fanciful and arbitrary marks receive automatic protection because they serve to identify a particular product's source, as opposed to describing the product itself. Fanciful trademarks often include invented words. Examples include *Xerox* for one company's copiers and *Google* for another company's search engine.

Arbitrary trademarks use words and phrases with no commonly understood connection to the product, such as *Dutch Boy* as a name for paint. Even a single letter used in a particular style can be an arbitrary trademark, such as the stylized X mark that Quiksilver, Inc., uses on its clothing.

Suggestive trademarks, representing the middle of the spectrum, indicate something about a product's nature, quality, or characteristics without describing the product directly. For instance, "Dairy Queen" suggests an association between its products and milk, but it does not directly describe ice cream. Suggestive marks can be transformed into strong marks by achieving a high degree of marketplace recognition, such as through substantial advertising.

Secondary Meaning Descriptive terms, geographic terms, and personal names are not inherently distinctive and do not receive protection under the law until they acquire a secondary meaning. Whether a secondary meaning becomes attached to a term or name usually depends on how extensively the product is advertised, the market for the product, the number of sales, and other factors.

A secondary meaning may arise when customers begin to associate a specific term or phrase (such as Calvin Klein) with specific trademarked items made by a particular company (designer clothing and goods). Once a secondary meaning is attached to a term or name, a trademark is considered distinctive and is protected. Even a color can qualify for trademark protection, such as the color schemes used by college sports teams.

Case Example 7.2 Federal Express Corporation (FedEx) provides transportation and delivery services worldwide using the logo FedEx in a specific color combination. FedEx sued a competitor, JetEx Management Services, Inc., for using the same color combination and a similar name and logo. JetEx also mimicked

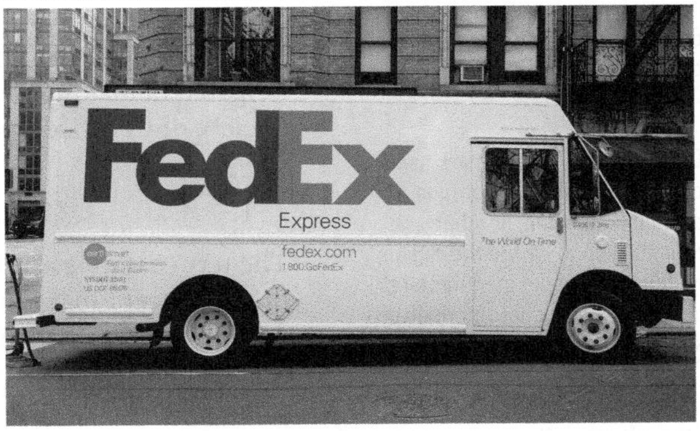

Leonard Zhukovsky/Shutterstock.com

Why should a company's distinctive colors, such those for FedEx, be protected under trademark law?

FedEx's trademarked slogan ("The World on Time" for FedEx, and "Keeping the World on Time" for JetEx). FedEx alleged trademark infringement and dilution, among other claims.

A federal district court in New York granted a permanent injunction to block JetEx from using the infringing mark in FedEx colors. When JetEx (now operating as JetEx Air Express) continued to use the infringing mark on its vehicles, FedEx went back to the court to enforce the injunction. The court entered a default judgment against JetEx and awarded FedEx an additional $25,000 in attorneys' fees and court costs.[7]

Generic Terms Generic terms that refer to an entire class of products, such as *bicycle* and *computer*, receive no protection, even if they acquire secondary meanings. A particularly thorny problem for a business arises when its trademark acquires generic use. For instance, *aspirin* and *thermos* were originally trademarked products, but today the words are used generically. Other trademarks that have acquired generic use include *escalator*, *trampoline*, *raisin bran*, *dry ice*, *lanolin*, *linoleum*, *nylon*, and *cornflakes*.

A trademark that is commonly used does not automatically become generic, though. **Case Example 7.3** David Elliot and Chris Gillespie sought to register numerous domain names (Internet addresses), including "googledisney.com" and "googlenewstvs.com." They were unable to register the names because all of them used the word *google*, a trademark of Google, Inc.

Elliot and Gillespie brought an action in federal court to have the Google trademark canceled because it had become a generic term. They argued that because most people now use *google* as a verb ("to google") when referring to searching the Internet with any search engine (not just Google), the term should no longer be protected. The court held that even if people do use the word *google* as a verb, it is still a protected trademark if consumers associate the noun with one company. The court concluded that "the primary significance of the word *google* to a majority of the public who utilize Internet search engines is a designation of the Google search engine."[8]

7–1e Service, Certification, and Collective Marks

Service Mark A trademark that is used to distinguish the services (rather than the products) of one person or company from those of another.

A **service mark** is essentially a trademark that is used to distinguish the services (rather than the products) of one person or company from those of another. For instance, each airline has a particular mark or symbol associated with its name. Titles and character names used in radio and television are frequently registered as service marks.

Certification Mark A mark used by one or more persons, other than the owner, to certify the region, materials, mode of manufacture, quality, or other characteristic of specific goods or services.

Other marks protected by law include certification marks and collective marks. A **certification mark** is used by one or more persons, other than the owner, to certify the region, materials, mode of manufacture, quality, or other characteristic of specific goods or services. Certification marks include such marks as "Good Housekeeping Seal of Approval" and "UL Tested."

Collective Mark A mark used by members of a cooperative, association, union, or other organization to certify the region, materials, mode of manufacture, quality, or other characteristic of specific goods or services.

When used by members of a cooperative, association, labor union, or other organization, a certification mark is referred to as a **collective mark**. **Example 7.4** Collective marks appear at the end of a movie's credits to indicate the various associations and organizations that participated in making the movie. The mark "CPA" is a collective mark used by members of the Society of Certified Public Accountants.

7–1f Trade Dress

Trade Dress The image and overall appearance of a product.

The term **trade dress** refers to the image and overall appearance of a product. Trade dress is a broad concept that can include all or part of the total image or overall impression created by a product or its packaging. **Example 7.5** The distinctive decor, menu, and style of service of a particular restaurant may be regarded as the restaurant's trade dress. Similarly, trade dress

7. *Federal Express Corp. v. JetEx Air Express, Inc.*, 2017 WL 816479 (E.D.N.Y. 2017).
8. *Elliot v. Google, Inc.*, 45 F.Supp.3d 1156 (D.Ariz. 2014).

can include the layout and appearance of a catalogue, the use of a lighthouse as part of a golf hole, the fish shape of a cracker, or the G-shaped design of a Gucci watch.

Basically, trade dress is subject to the same protection as trademarks. In cases involving trade dress infringement, as in trademark infringement cases, a major consideration is whether consumers are likely to be confused by the allegedly infringing use. **Example 7.6** Converse makes All-Star shoes, which were the first shoes ever endorsed by a famous basketball player, Chuck Taylor. Nike, Inc., which now owns Converse, sued thirty-one companies, including Ralph Lauren, for manufacturing very similar versions of these shoes, claiming that consumers were likely to be confused. The knockoffs used the same white rubber soles, rubber cap on the toes, canvas tops, and conspicuous stitching as used on All-Stars. Ralph Lauren ultimately agreed to settle its dispute with Nike by destroying all remaining fake All-Stars and paying Nike an undisclosed sum.

7–1g Counterfeit Goods

Counterfeit goods copy or otherwise imitate trademarked goods but are not genuine. The importation of goods bearing counterfeit trademarks poses a significant problem for U.S. businesses, consumers, and law enforcement (see the *Business Web Log* feature for an example). In addition to having negative financial effects on legitimate businesses, sales of certain counterfeit goods, such as pharmaceuticals and nutritional supplements, can present serious public health risks.

Stop Counterfeiting in Manufactured Goods Act The Stop Counterfeiting in Manufactured Goods Act[9] (SCMGA) was enacted to combat counterfeit goods. The act made it a crime to intentionally traffic in, or attempt to traffic in, counterfeit goods or services, or to knowingly use a counterfeit mark on or in connection with goods or services.

9. Pub. L. No. 109-181 (2006), which amended 18 U.S.C. Sections 2318–2320.

Amazon Faces Fake Products

The world's largest online retailer is facing at least one lawsuit alleging trademark infringement, copyright infringement, and other torts. Electronic cable designer and manufacturer Fuse Chicken, LLC, discovered that Amazon consumers were frequently being sold fake Fuse Chicken cables for their smartphones.

The reality today is that when any branded product becomes well known, cheap imitations become a problem. Amazon apparently did not do enough to prevent the sale of such inferior copies of Fuse Chicken's trademarked and copyrighted products. For example, Amazon sold Fuse Chicken's Bobine Auto iPhone Lightning Car Dock to a customer who gave it a one-star review because it broke within a week. The product was clearly a counterfeit version.

Fuse Chicken attempted to resolve the issue of counterfeit products with Amazon. When Fuse Chicken received little satisfaction, it filed suit.[a] In its lawsuit, Fuse Chicken pointed out that Amazon does not control the products sold via its "Sell Yours Here" listing site. Anybody can sell a trademarked or copyrighted product via this site. According to the lawsuit, "Amazon makes no effort to determine whether the products sold by such third-party sellers are authentic."

A much larger company, France's Chanel, has also taken legal action to protect itself against counterfeiters on Amazon.com. The company won a multimillion-dollar trademark infringement lawsuit against thirty vendors who were using Amazon to sell fake Chanel goods, such as bags, shirts, and cell phone cases. As part of the settlement, a federal judge in California ordered Amazon to disable the vendor sites and transfer any funds in their accounts to Chanel.[b]

a. *Fuse Chicken, LLC. v.* Amazon.com, *Inc.*, Case: 5:17-c-b-01538-SL Doc # 1 Filed July 21, 2017 in Northern District Ohio Court.

b. Kali Hays, "Chanel Scores Win Against Amazon Sellers in Counterfeit Fight." *www.wwd.com. WWD:* June 28, 2017, Web.

(Continues)

Continued

Key Point

Large-scale online retailing continues to grow, and Amazon continues to dominate this sector. The number of counterfeit products is growing, too. Amazon has decided to fight back. In tandem with its vendors, Amazon has filed numerous lawsuits against counterfeiters who take advantage of its platform.[c] It has also set up "Project Zero," a program in which sellers provide Amazon with trademarks, logos, and other protected data. Using this information, Amazon conducts a scan of billions of its product listings each day, searching for any possible infringements. Other online resellers, such as Alibaba and eBay, also face counterfeit issues. It's a multibillion-dollar problem that won't go away soon.

c. See *Amazon.com, Inc. v. Zhang et al*, W.D. Wash. 2020.

Before this act took effect, the law did not prohibit the creation or shipment of counterfeit labels that were not attached to products. Therefore, counterfeiters would make labels and packaging bearing a counterfeit trademark, ship the labels to another location, and then affix them to inferior products to deceive buyers. The SCMGA closed this loophole by making it a crime to traffic in counterfeit labels, stickers, packaging, and the like, whether or not they are attached to goods.

Penalties for Counterfeiting Persons found guilty of violating the SCMGA may be fined up to $2 million or imprisoned for up to ten years (or more, if they are repeat offenders). If a court finds that the statute was violated, it must order the defendant to forfeit the counterfeit products (which are then destroyed), as well as any property used in the commission of the crime. The defendant must also pay restitution to the trademark holder or victim in an amount equal to the victim's actual loss.

Case Example 7.7 Charles Anthony Jones pleaded guilty to trafficking in counterfeit prescription drugs for erectile dysfunction. The court sentenced Jones to thirty-seven months in prison and ordered him to pay more than $600,000 in restitution. Jones appealed, arguing that the amount awarded was more than the pharmaceutical companies' actual losses. The court agreed. The pharmaceutical companies were entitled only to their lost net profits rather than the retail price of the genuine drugs.[10] ■

Combating Online Sales of Counterfeit Goods The United States cannot prosecute foreign counterfeiters under U.S. laws, because our national laws do not apply to them. One effective tool that U.S. officials are using to combat online sales of counterfeit goods is to obtain a court order to close down the domain names of websites that sell such goods.

Example 7.8 U.S. agents have shut down hundreds of domain names on the Monday after Thanksgiving ("Cyber Monday"). Shutting down the websites, particularly on key shopping days, prevents some counterfeit goods from entering the United States. Europol, an international organization, has also used this tactic. ■

7–1h Trade Names

Trade Name A name that a business uses to identify itself and its brand. A trade name is directly related to a business's reputation and goodwill, and is protected under trademark law.

Trademarks apply to *products*. The term **trade name** refers to part or all of a *business's name*, whether the business is a sole proprietorship, a partnership, or a corporation. Generally, a trade name is directly related to a business and its goodwill.

A trade name may be protected as a trademark if the trade name is the same as the company's trademarked product—for instance, Coca-Cola. Unless it is also used as a trademark or service mark, a trade name cannot be registered with the federal government. Trade names

10. *United States v. Jones*, 616 Fed.Appx. 726 (5th Cir. 2015).

are protected under the common law, but only if they are unusual or fancifully used. The word *Safeway*, for instance, was sufficiently fanciful to obtain protection as a trade name for a grocery chain.

7–1i Licensing

One way to avoid litigation and still make use of another's trademark or other form of intellectual property is to obtain a license to do so. A **license** in this context is an agreement permitting the use of a trademark, copyright, patent, or trade secret for certain limited purposes. The party that owns the intellectual property rights and issues the license is the *licensor*, and the party obtaining the license is the *licensee*. Licensors often receive payments called **royalties** from licensees in return for permission to use the trademarked item.

License An agreement by the owner of intellectual property to permit another to use a trademark, copyright, patent, or trade secret for certain limited purposes.

A license grants only the rights expressly described in the license agreement. A licensor might, for instance, allow the licensee to use a trademark as part of its company or domain name, but not otherwise use the mark on any products or services. Disputes frequently arise over licensing agreements, particularly when the license involves Internet use.[11]

Royalties Payments made by a licensee to a licensor as part of an agreement for the ongoing use of the licensor's trademarked asset.

7–2 Patents

A **patent** is a grant from the government that gives an inventor the exclusive right to make, use, and sell an invention for a period of twenty years. Patents for designs, as opposed to inventions, are given for a fifteen-year period. The applicant must demonstrate to the satisfaction of the U.S. Patent and Trademark Office that the invention, discovery, process, or design is novel, useful, and not obvious in light of current technology. (See this chapter's *Business Law Analysis* for more about some fundamental patent issues.)

Patent A property right granted by the federal government that gives an inventor an exclusive right to make, use, and sell an invention for a limited time.

11. See, for instance, *Diebold Incorporated v. QSI, Inc.*, 2017 WL 3219866 (N.D. Ohio 2017).

The Impact of Patent Time Limits

Business Law Analysis

Stephen Kimble invented a toy made up of a glove equipped with a valve and a canister of pressurized foam. The patented toy allowed people to shoot fake webs like the Marvel Comics superhero Spider-Man. In 1990, Kimble tried to cut a deal with Marvel Entertainment concerning his toy, but he was unsuccessful. Then Marvel started selling its own version of the toy.

When Kimble sued Marvel for patent infringement, he won. The result was a settlement that involved a licensing agreement between Kimble and Marvel with a lump-sum payment plus a royalty to Kimble of 3 percent of all sales of the toy. The agreement did not specify an end date for royalty payments to Kimble, and Marvel later sued to have the payments stop after the twenty-year patent expired.

Analysis According to a United States Supreme Court case that was decided nearly sixty years ago, a licensee cannot be forced to pay royalties to a patent holder after the patent has expired. So, if a licensee signs a contract to continue to pay royalties after the patent has expired, the contract is invalid and thus unenforceable.

Result and Reasoning Applying its own precedent, the United States Supreme Court ruled in Marvel's favor. As Justice Elena Kagan said in the opinion, "Patents endow their holders with certain super powers, but only for a limited time." In a dissenting opinion, Justice Samuel A. Alito, Jr., countered, "The decision interferes with the ability of parties to negotiate licensing agreements that reflect the true value of a patent, and it disrupts contractual expectations." The majority did not necessarily disagree, noting that its decision was based on an outmoded understanding of economics and may serve to hinder competition and innovation. In this instance, however, the doctrine of *stare decisis* dictated the result.

Focus Question 2

How does the law protect patents?

Until recently, patent law in the United States differed from the laws of many other countries because the first person to invent a product or process obtained the patent rights, rather than the first person to file for a patent. It was often difficult to prove who invented an item first, however, which prompted Congress to change the system by passing the America Invents Act.[12] Now, the first person to file an application for a patent on a product or process will receive patent protection. In addition, the law established a nine-month limit for challenging a patent on any ground.

The period of patent protection begins on the date when the patent application is filed, rather than when the patent is issued, which can sometimes be years later. After the patent period ends (either fifteen or twenty years later), the product or process enters the public domain, and anyone can make, sell, or use the invention without paying the patent holder.

7–2a Searchable Patent Databases

A significant development relating to patents is the availability online of the world's patent databases. The website of the U.S. Patent and Trademark Office (www.uspto.gov) provides searchable databases covering U.S. patents granted since 1976. The website of the European Patent Office (www.epo.org) provides online access to 50 million patent documents in more than seventy nations through a searchable network of databases.

Businesses use these searchable databases in many ways. Companies may conduct patent searches to list or inventory their patents, which are valuable assets. Patent searches also enable companies to study trends and patterns in a specific technology or to gather information about competitors in the industry.

Know This

A patent is granted to inventions that are novel (new) and not obvious in light of prior discoveries.

7–2b What Is Patentable?

Under the Patent Act, "[w]hoever invents or discovers any new and useful process, machine, manufacture, or composition of matter, or any new and useful improvement thereof, may obtain a patent therefor, subject to the conditions and requirements of this title."[13] Thus, to be patentable, an invention must be *novel*, *useful*, and *not obvious* in light of current technology.

Almost anything is patentable, except the laws of nature, natural phenomena, and abstract ideas (including algorithms[14]). Even artistic methods and works of art, certain business processes, and the structures of storylines are patentable, provided that they are novel and not obvious.[15] Plants that are reproduced asexually (by means other than from seed), such as hybrid or genetically engineered plants, are patentable in the United States, as are genetically engineered (or cloned) microorganisms and animals.

As mentioned, abstract ideas (including theories and concepts) are not patentable. For this reason, ideas that involve analyzing information and displaying results have often been found ineligible for patents. Such an idea becomes patentable only if particular aspects or combinations of elements transform it into a patent-eligible claim. **Case Example 7.9** West View Research, LLC (WVR), holds numerous patents in a range of technologies, including speech recognition, wireless mobile devices, and medical devices. WVR filed a suit in federal court against several automakers, including Audi, Hyundai, Nissan, Tesla, and Volkswagen, alleging patent infringement.

12. The full title of this law is the Leahy-Smith America Invents Act, Pub. L. No. 112-29 (2011), which amended 35 U.S.C. Sections 1, 41, and 321.
13. 35 U.S.C. Section 101.
14. An *algorithm* is a step-by-step procedure, formula, or set of instructions for accomplishing a specific task. An example is the set of rules used by a search engine to rank the listings contained within its index in response to a particular query.
15. For a United States Supreme Court case discussing the obviousness requirement, see *KSR International Co. v. Teleflex, Inc.*, 550 U.S. 398, 127 S.Ct. 1727, 167 L.Ed.2d 705 (2007). For a discussion of business process patents, see *In re Bilski*, 545 F3d 943 (Fed. Cir. 2008).

WVR claimed that the carmakers had infringed two of its patents by selling vehicles with touch-screen displays that offered navigation, traffic, and weather information. A federal district court held in favor of the defendants, and a federal appellate court affirmed. The appellate court reasoned that the two patents simply described abstract ideas (analyzing information and displaying results) and lacked an inventive element that could transform them into patent-eligible inventions. WVR's two patents were thus invalid.[16]

oktay sonmez/Alamy

Why are abstract ideas, such as the in-dash navigation system in new cars, ineligible for patent protection?

7–2c Patent Infringement

If a firm makes, uses, or sells another's patented design, product, or process without the patent owner's permission, it commits the tort of patent infringement. Patent infringement may occur even though the patent owner has not put the patented product into commerce. Patent infringement may also occur even though not all features or parts of an invention are copied. (To infringe the patent on a process, however, all steps or their equivalent must be copied.)

Obviously, companies that specialize in developing new technology stand to lose significant profits if someone "makes, uses, or sells" devices that incorporate their patented inventions. Because these firms are the holders of numerous patents, they are frequently involved in patent infringement lawsuits (as well as other types of intellectual property disputes).

A complication in many such lawsuits is their global scope. Many companies that make and sell electronics and computer software and hardware are based in foreign nations (for instance, Sony is a Japanese firm). Foreign firms can apply for and obtain U.S. patent protection on items that they sell within the United States, just as U.S. firms can obtain protection in foreign nations where they sell goods. In the United States, however, no patent infringement occurs when a patented product is made and sold in another country.

Spotlight Case Example 7.10 Apple sued Samsung in federal court alleging that Samsung's Galaxy smartphones and tablets that use Google's HTC Android operating system infringed on Apple's patents. Apple had design patents that covered its devices' graphical user interface (the display of icons on the home screen), shell, and screen and button design. Apple had also patented the way information is displayed on iPhones and other devices, the way windows pop open, and the way information is scaled and rotated.

A jury found that Samsung had willfully infringed five of Apple's patents and awarded about $500 million in damages. The parties appealed. A judge later reduced the amount of damages awarded on the patent claims, but litigation continued. A federal appellate court held that elements of the physical design of these two manufacturers' mobile devices and their on-screen icons were not protected under the Lanham Act.

The United States Supreme Court reversed and remanded. The Court explained that the Patent Act provision governing damages for design patent infringement encompasses both a product sold to a consumer and a component of that product. Therefore, components of the infringing smartphones could be considered relevant to damages, even though the consumers could not purchase those components separately.[17] Eventually, the two parties settled for an undisclosed sum.

16. *West View Research, LLC v. Audi AG, Volkswagen AG*, 685 Fed.Appx. 923 (Fed.Cir. 2017).

17. *Apple, Inc. v. Samsung Electronics Co.*, 678 Fed.Appx. 1012 (Fed.Cir. 2017); *Samsung Electronics Co. v. Apple, Inc.*, 580 U.S. ___, 137 S.Ct. 429, 196 L.Ed.2d 363 (2016).

7–2d Remedies for Patent Infringement

If a patent is infringed, the patent holder may sue for relief in federal court. The patent holder can seek an injunction against the infringer and can also request damages for royalties and lost profits. In some cases, the court may grant the winning party reimbursement for attorneys' fees and costs. If the court determines that the infringement was willful, the court can triple the amount of damages awarded (treble damages).

In the past, permanent injunctions were routinely granted to prevent future infringement. Today, however, a patent holder must prove that it has suffered irreparable injury and that the public interest would not be *disserved* by a permanent injunction. Thus, courts have the discretion to decide what is equitable in the circumstances and to consider the public interest rather than just the interests of the parties.

Spotlight Case Example 7.11 Cordance Corporation developed some of the technology and software that automates Internet communications. Cordance sued Amazon.com, Inc., for patent infringement, claiming that Amazon's one-click purchasing interface infringed on one of Cordance's patents. After a jury found Amazon guilty of infringement, Cordance requested the court to issue a permanent injunction against Amazon's infringement or, alternatively, to order Amazon to pay Cordance an ongoing royalty.

The court refused to issue a permanent injunction, because Cordance had not proved that it would otherwise suffer irreparable harm. Cordance and Amazon were not direct competitors in the relevant market. Cordance had never sold or licensed the technology infringed by Amazon's one-click purchasing interface and had presented no market data or evidence to show how the infringement negatively affected Cordance. The court also refused to impose an ongoing royalty on Amazon.[18]

7–3 Copyrights

Copyright The exclusive right of an author or originator of a literary or artistic production to publish, print, sell, or otherwise use that production for a statutory period of time.

A **copyright** is an intangible property right granted by federal statute to the author or originator of certain literary or artistic productions. The 1976 Copyright Act,[19] as amended, governs copyrights. Works created after January 1, 1978, are automatically given statutory copyright protection for the life of the author plus 70 years. For copyrights owned by publishing companies, the copyright expires 95 years from the date of publication or 120 years from the date of creation, whichever is first. For works by more than one author, the copyright expires 70 years after the death of the last surviving author.

Focus Question 3

What laws protect authors' rights in the works they create?

Case Example 7.12 The popular character Sherlock Holmes originated in stories written by Arthur Conan Doyle and published from 1887 through 1927. Over the years, elements of the characters and stories created by Doyle have appeared in books, movies, and television series, including *Elementary* on CBS and *Sherlock* on BBC. Before 2013, those who wished to use the copyrighted Sherlock material had to pay a licensing fee to Doyle's estate. Then, in 2013, the editors of a book of Holmes-related stories filed a lawsuit in federal court claiming that the basic Sherlock Holmes story elements introduced before 1923 should no longer be protected. The court agreed and ruled that these elements have entered the public domain—that is, the copyright has expired, and they can be used without permission.[20]

18. *Cordance Corp. v. Amazon.com, Inc.*, 730 F.Supp.2d 333 (D.Del. 2010).
19. 17 U.S.C. Sections 101 *et seq.*
20. *Klinger v. Conan Doyle Estate, Ltd.*, 988 F.Supp.2d 879 (N.D.Ill. 2013).

7–3a Registration

Copyrights can be registered with the U.S. Copyright Office (www.copyright.gov) in Washington, D.C. Registration is not required, however. A copyright owner need not place a © or *Copr.* or *Copyright* on the work to have the work protected against infringement. Chances are that if somebody created it, somebody owns it.

Generally, copyright owners are protected against the following:

1. Reproduction of the work.
2. Development of derivative works.
3. Distribution of the work.
4. Public display of the work.

HARTSWOOD FILMS/BBC WALES/Album/Newscom

Why have the story elements from the famous Sherlock Holmes books entered the public domain?

7–3b What Is Protected Expression?

Works that are copyrightable include books, records, films, artworks, architectural plans, menus, music videos, product packaging, and computer software. To be protected, a work must be "fixed in a durable medium" from which it can be perceived, reproduced, or communicated. As noted, protection is automatic, and registration is not required.

To obtain protection under the Copyright Act, a work must be original and fall into one of the following categories:

1. Literary works (including newspaper and magazine articles, computer and training manuals, catalogues, brochures, and print advertisements).
2. Musical works and accompanying words (including advertising jingles).
3. Dramatic works and accompanying music.
4. Pantomimes and choreographic works (including ballets and other forms of dance).
5. Pictorial, graphic, and sculptural works (including cartoons, maps, posters, statues, and even stuffed animals).
6. Motion pictures and other audiovisual works (including multimedia works).
7. Sound recordings.
8. Architectural works.

Section 102 Exclusions Generally, something that is not an original expression will not qualify for copyright protection. Facts widely known to the public are not copyrightable. Page numbers are not copyrightable because they follow a sequence known to everyone. Mathematical calculations are not copyrightable.

In addition, it is not possible to copyright an idea. Section 102 of the Copyright Act specifically excludes copyright protection for any "idea, procedure, process, system, method of operation, concept, principle, or discovery, regardless of the form in which it is described, explained, illustrated, or embodied." Thus, others can freely use the underlying ideas or principles embodied in a work. What is copyrightable is the particular way in which an idea is *expressed*. Whenever an idea and an expression are inseparable, the expression cannot be copyrighted. An idea and its expression, then, must be separable to be copyrightable.

Compilations of Facts As mentioned, facts widely known to the public are not copyrightable. Compilations of facts, however, may be copyrightable. Under Section 103 of the Copyright Act, a compilation is a work formed by the collection and assembling of preexisting materials or of data that are selected, coordinated, or arranged in such a way that the resulting work as a whole constitutes an original work of authorship.

The key requirement for the copyrightability of a compilation is originality. For instance, a template form used by emergency room physicians to record patient information is not original and does not qualify for copyright protection. **Case Example 7.13** EC Design's LifePlanner is an elaborate spiral-bound daily planner, augmented by inspirational sayings, lists of goals, and plenty of space for personal entries. Craft Smith's Recollections Planner is a less expensive but still elaborate spiral-bound daily planner, augmented by inspirational sayings, lists of goals, and plenty of space for personal entries.

EC filed a copyright infringement lawsuit against Craft Smith based on the similarities between these two items. A federal court dismissed the suit for several reasons. First, the U.S. Copyright Office had rejected EC's attempt to register the LifePlanner layout because a layout is a "template of expression," not an original form of authorship. Second, as a compilation of materials gathered from other sources, the LifePlanner does not qualify as a protectable literary work. Third, the LifePlanner's utilitarian purpose—to help users plan and organize their lives—is not separate enough from the way it looks to earn protection under the law.[21]

7–3c Copyright Infringement

Whenever the form or expression of an idea is copied, an infringement of copyright occurs. The reproduction does not have to be exactly the same as the original, nor does it have to reproduce the original in its entirety. If a substantial part of the original is reproduced, copyright infringement has occurred.

Example 7.14 Ed Sheeran was accused of copyright infringement over his hit song "Photograph." Sheeran allegedly copied much of the song note for note from "Amazing," a single released a few years earlier by X Factor winner Matt Cardle. The songwriters of "Amazing" sued Sheeran, who reportedly settled the case for $20 million.

Note that when a copyright owner grants to another a license to use the work, the owner waives the right to sue that party (the licensee) for copyright infringement. In an action for copyright infringement, copying may be inferred when a plaintiff establishes that the defendant had access to the copyrighted work and that substantial similarities exist between it and the alleged copy. In the following case, involving two toy makers, the parties agreed that the plaintiff owned a valid copyright in certain toys and that the defendant had access to those products. The dispute was over the similarities between the respective products.

21. *Craft Smith, LLC v. EC Design, LLC*, 388 F.Supp.3d 1385 (D. Utah 2019).

Case 7.2

LEGO A/S v. ZURU Inc.

United States Court of Appeals, Federal Circuit, 799 Fed.Appx 823 (2020).

Facts LEGO A/S is an industry leader in designing and making toys, including construction toys. ZURU Inc. also designs, makes, and sells toys. When ZURU debuted its ZURU Action Figures in Walmart stores and on the Walmart website, LEGO filed a suit in a federal district court against ZURU, alleging infringement of LEGO's copyrights covering the appearance of its Minifigures, an iconic construction toy. LEGO posited that the Action Figures were substantially similar in overall look and feel to the Minifigures. The court agreed and granted LEGO a preliminary injunction. ZURU appealed, arguing that "a general sense of similarity is not sufficient" to support an injunction on the basis of copyright infringement. ZURU asked the court to "note specific differences in shape, expression, and proportions" between the toys.

Issue Were ZURU's Action Figures sufficiently similar to LEGO's Minifigures to infringe on LEGO's copyrights?

Decision Yes. The U.S. Court of Appeals for the Federal Circuit affirmed the lower court's findings and its entry of an injunction in LEGO's favor. The injunction restrained ZURU from manufacturing, selling, offering for sale, displaying, and importing products that allegedly infringe LEGO's copyrights.

Reason Contending that the designs of its figures were sufficiently different and distinct, ZURU argued that the lower court's failure to identify specific similarities in the two products' artistic expression rendered its findings "clearly erroneous." The appellate court reasoned that "such an analysis is fundamentally at odds" with the standard test for substantial similarity. The test is "whether an ordinary observer, unless he [or she] set out to detect the disparities" between two products, "would be disposed to overlook them, and regard the aesthetic appeal as the same." Under this standard, if the average person would recognize a copy as having been taken from an original, copyrighted work, the two items would be substantially similar. To make this assessment, a court must examine products for their whole concept and feel. The application of this principle "is especially appropriate in an infringement action involving children's works, because children's works are often less complex than those aimed at an adult audience." In this case, the lower court found the total concept and feel of the toys to be substantially similar. Because ZURU did not show otherwise, "we see no reason to disagree with the district court's finding on substantial similarity."

Critical Thinking

- **Legal Environment** *Accompanying LEGO's registration of its copyright are images depicting "Basic Minifigures." Rather than these images, the district court compared ZURU's Action Figures to actual LEGO Minifigures, which differ in facial expression and jacket color. Was this, as ZURU alleged, an improper comparison? Why or why not?*
- **Ethical** *On the eve of the trial, ZURU promised to recall its Action Figures from Walmart's stores in an effort to defeat LEGO's request for an injunction. Could this promise be considered ethical? Explain.*

Remedies for Copyright Infringement Those who infringe copyrights may be liable for damages or criminal penalties. These range from actual damages or statutory damages, imposed at the court's discretion, to criminal proceedings for willful violations. Actual damages are based on the harm caused to the copyright holder by the infringement, while statutory damages, not to exceed $150,000, are provided for under the Copyright Act. In addition, criminal proceedings may result in fines and/or imprisonment. In some instances, a court may grant an injunction against the infringer.

Spotlight Case Example 7.15 Rusty Carroll operated an online term paper business, R2C2, Inc., that offered up to 300,000 research papers for sale on nine different websites. Individuals whose work was posted on these websites without their permission filed a lawsuit against Carroll for copyright infringement. Because Carroll repeatedly failed to comply with court orders regarding discovery, the court found that the copyright infringement was likely to continue unless an injunction was issued. The court therefore issued a permanent injunction prohibiting Carroll and R2C2 from selling any term paper without sworn documentary evidence that the paper's author had given permission.[22]

The "Fair Use" Exception An exception to liability for copyright infringement is made under the "fair use" doctrine. In certain circumstances, a person or organization can reproduce copyrighted material without paying royalties. Section 107 of the Copyright Act provides as follows:

> [T]he fair use of a copyrighted work, including such use by reproduction in copies or phonorecords or by any other means specified by [Section 106 of the Copyright Act], for purposes such as criticism, comment, news reporting, teaching (including multiple

22. *Weidner v. Carroll*, 2010 WL 310310 (S.D.Ill. 2010).

copies for classroom use), scholarship, or research, is not an infringement of copyright. In determining whether the use made of a work in any particular case is a fair use the factors to be considered shall include—

(1) the purpose and character of the use, including whether such use is of a commercial nature or is for nonprofit educational purposes;
(2) the nature of the copyrighted work;
(3) the amount and substantiality of the portion used in relation to the copyrighted work as a whole; and
(4) the effect of the use upon the potential market for or value of the copyrighted work.

What Is Fair Use? Because the fair use guidelines are very broad, the courts determine whether a particular use is fair on a case-by-case basis. Thus, anyone reproducing copyrighted material may be committing a violation. In determining whether a use is fair, courts have often considered the fourth factor to be the most important. **Case Example 7.16** A number of research universities, in partnership with Google, Inc., agreed to digitize books from their libraries and create a repository for them. Eighty member institutions (including many colleges and universities) contributed more than 10 million works to the HathiTrust Digital Library. Some authors complained that this book scanning violated their rights and sued the HathiTrust and several associated entities for copyright infringement.

The court, however, sided with the defendants and held that making digital copies for the purposes of online search was a fair use. The library's searchable database enabled researchers to find terms of interest in the digital volumes—but not to read the volumes online. Therefore, the court concluded that the digitization did not provide a substitute that damaged the market for the original works.[23]

See this chapter's *Adapting the Law to the Online Environment* feature for a discussion of whether Beyoncé's use of three phrases written by another artist constituted fair use.

The First Sale Doctrine Section 109(a) of the Copyright Act provides that the owner of a particular item that is copyrighted can, without the authority of the copyright owner, sell or otherwise dispose of it. This rule is known as the first sale doctrine.

Kevin Winter/WireImage/Getty Images

Beyoncé sampled several phrases from another musician in one of her songs. Why might a court conclude that this use was not a fair use under copyright law?

Under this doctrine, once a copyright owner sells or gives away a particular copy of a work, the copyright owner no longer has the right to control the distribution of that copy. Thus, for instance, a person who buys a copyrighted book can sell it to someone else. The first sale doctrine also applies to copyrighted CDs and DVDs.

The United States Supreme Court has ruled that the first sale doctrine protects lawfully made copies no matter where in the world those copies were made. **Case Example 7.17** Supap Kirtsaeng, a citizen of Thailand, was a graduate student at the University of Southern California. He enlisted friends and family in Thailand to buy copies of textbooks there and ship them to him in the United States. Kirtsaeng resold the textbooks on eBay, where he eventually made about $100,000.

John Wiley & Sons, Inc., had printed some of those textbooks in Asia. Wiley sued Kirtsaeng in federal district court for copyright infringement. Kirtsaeng argued that Section

23. *Authors Guild, Inc. v. HathiTrust*, 755 F.3d 87 (2d Cir. 2014). See also *Authors Guild v. Google, Inc.*, 804 F.3d 202 (2d Cir. 2015).

Adapting the Law to the Online Environment

Beyoncé, Sampling, and a $20 Million Lawsuit

To date, Beyoncé's single "Formation" has been legally downloaded millions times. The video and the song itself were nominated for Grammy awards in the following categories: Record of the Year, Song of the Year, and Best Music Video.

What Does Sampling Involve?

In the song "Formation," Beyoncé sampled several phrases attributed to street performer and music artist Anthony Barré, popularly known as Messy Mya. (Sampling is taking a part of a sound recording and reusing it in a different recording.) Messy Mya became famous on YouTube by filming himself in New Orleans' gay, lesbian, and transgender communities in the aftermath of Hurricane Katrina. The three phrases that Beyoncé sampled are:

- "I like that."
- "What happened at the New Orleans."
- "Bitch, I'm back by popular demand."

Was It Fair Use?

Copyright law requires payment to copyright owners except for fair use. But what constitutes fair use? Typically, courts tend to measure fair use by looking at whether the use in question is of a commercial nature. Additionally, courts look at the amount and substantiality of the portion used in relation to the copyrighted work as a whole and the effect of the use on the potential market for the copyrighted work. Beyoncé claimed that her sampled use of Messy Mya's words fell under the fair use doctrine.

A Lawsuit Nonetheless

Messy Mya was shot and killed in 2010, and his estate would not accept the fair use doctrine defense offered by Beyoncé's attorneys. Rather, the estate sued for $20 million in back royalties, as well as proper credit for Messy Mya "as a writer, composer, producer, and performer." The suit alleged that "the verbatim copying of [Messy Mya's] voice and words by defendant is so blatant in both scale and degree that it raises this matter to an unusual level of striking similarity."

Are the three phrases that Beyoncé sampled worth $20 million? After losing a motion to dismiss the case based on a fair use defense in a federal district court, Beyoncé agreed to settle the case for the full $20 million.[a]

Critical Thinking

Beyoncé also used footage from a 2013 documentary called That B.E.A.T. *Why might international entertainment stars choose to use sampled words and sampled video footage without the permission of the copyright holders?*

a. *Estate of Barré v. Carter*, 272 F.Supp.3d 906 (E.D.La. 2017).

109(a) of the Copyright Act allows the first purchaser-owner of a book to sell it without the copyright owner's permission. The trial court held in favor of Wiley, and that decision was affirmed on appeal. Kirtsaeng then appealed to the United States Supreme Court, which ruled in Kirtsaeng's favor. The first sale doctrine applies even to goods purchased abroad and resold in the United States.[24]

7–3d Copyright Protection for Software

The Computer Software Copyright Act amended the Copyright Act to include computer programs in the list of creative works protected by federal copyright law. Generally, copyright protection extends to those parts of a computer program that can be read by humans, such as the high-level language of a source code. Protection also extends to the binary-language object code, which is readable only by the computer, and to such elements as the overall structure, sequence, and organization of a program.

24. *Kirtsaeng v. John Wiley & Sons, Inc.*, 568 U.S. 519, 133 S.Ct. 1351, 185 L.Ed.2d 392 (2013). See also *Geophysical Service, Inc. v. TGS-NOPEC Geophysical Co.*, 850 F.3d 785 (5th Cir. 2017).

Not all aspects of software are protected, however. Courts typically have not extended copyright protection to the "look and feel"—the general appearance, command structure, video images, menus, windows, and other screen displays—of computer programs. (Note that copying the "look and feel" of another's product may be a violation of trade dress or trademark laws, however.) Sometimes it can be difficult for courts to decide which particular aspects of software are protected.

Case Example 7.18 Oracle America, Inc., is a software company that owns numerous application programming interfaces, or API packages. Oracle grants licenses to others to use these API packages to write applications in the Java programming language. Java is open and free for anyone to use, but using it requires an interface.

When Google began using some of Oracle's API packages to run Java on its Android mobile devices, Oracle sued for copyright infringement. Google argued that the software packages were command structure, which are not protected under copyright law. Ultimately, a federal appellate court concluded that the API packages were source code and were entitled to copyright protection.[25] ■

The dispute in the following case was whether a third-party software support service infringed the copyright of the owner of the software that the service supported.

25. *Oracle America, Inc. v. Google, Inc.*, 750 F.3d 1339 (Fed.Cir. 2014).

Case 7.3

Oracle USA, Inc. v. Rimini Street, Inc.

United States Court of Appeals, Ninth Circuit, 879 F.3d 948 (2018).

Facts Oracle USA, Inc., licenses its proprietary enterprise software for a one-time payment. Oracle also sells its licensees maintenance contracts for the software. The maintenance work includes software updates. Rimini Street, Inc., provided third-party support for Oracle's enterprise software, in competition with Oracle's maintenance services. To compete effectively, Rimini also needed to provide software updates to its customers. Creating these updates required copying Oracle's copyrighted software.

Oracle filed a suit in a federal district court against Rimini, alleging copyright infringement. Oracle alleged that Rimini copied Oracle's software under the license of one customer for work for other customers, or for unknown or future customers, instead of restricting the copying to work for the licensee. A jury found in Oracle's favor. The court entered a judgment for Oracle, awarding damages of more than $50 million. Rimini appealed the judgment to the U.S. Court of Appeals for the Ninth Circuit.

Issue Did Rimini infringe Oracle's copyright?

Decision Yes. The U.S. Court of Appeals for the Ninth Circuit affirmed the judgment of the lower court. "Rimini's accused acts violated the exclusive right Oracle enjoys as owner of the software copyright."

Reason The appellate court acknowledged that software needs patches and updates to fix glitches. Enterprise software is customized to a user's specific purpose. To create updates for enterprise software requires copying the software so that it can be modified to develop and test the updates. Making this copy without a license violates the exclusive right of the copyright owner to copy the software. In this case, Oracle's licenses permitted its licensees to make copies for themselves to maintain the software. The licenses further allowed the licensees to outsource the maintenance work to others, such as Rimini. But the licenses limited the copying to support for the licensees. Work that Rimini performed under one customer's license for other customers was not in support of the licensee. The same reasoning applied to work performed for unknown or future customers.

Critical Thinking

- **Economic** *Rimini argued that Oracle was misusing the copyright in its proprietary software to stifle competition. Do you agree? Explain.*
- **What If the Facts Were Different?** *Suppose that Rimini had bought one of Oracle's licenses for itself. Would the result have been different? Why or why not?*

7–4 Trade Secrets

The law of trade secrets protects some business processes and information that are not or cannot be protected under patent, copyright, or trademark law. A **trade secret** is basically information of commercial value. A company's customer lists, plans, and research and development are trade secrets. Trade secrets may also include pricing information, marketing techniques, and production methods—anything that makes an individual company unique and that would have value to a competitor.

Trade Secret A formula, device, idea, process, or other information used in a business that gives the owner a competitive advantage in the marketplace.

Unlike copyright and trademark protection, protection of trade secrets extends both to ideas and to their expression. (For this reason, and because there are no registration or filing requirements for trade secrets, trade secret protection may be well suited for software.) Of course, the secret formula, method, or other information must be disclosed to some persons, particularly to key employees. Businesses generally attempt to protect their trade secrets by having all employees who use the process or information agree in their contracts, or in confidentiality agreements, never to divulge it.

Focus Question 4

What are trade secrets, and what laws offer protection for this form of intellectual property?

7–4a State and Federal Law on Trade Secrets

Under Section 757 of the *Restatement of Torts*, those who disclose or use another's trade secret, without authorization, are liable to that other party if either of the following is true:

1. They discovered the secret by improper means.
2. Their disclosure or use constitutes a breach of a duty owed to the other party.

Stealing of confidential business data by industrial espionage, as when a business taps into a competitor's computer, is a theft of trade secrets without any contractual violation and is actionable in itself.

Trade secrets have long been protected under the common law. Today, nearly every state has enacted trade secret laws based on the Uniform Trade Secrets Act. Additionally, the Economic Espionage Act made the theft of trade secrets a federal crime.

7–4b Trade Secrets in Cyberspace

Today's computer technology undercuts a business firm's ability to protect its confidential information, including trade secrets. For instance, a dishonest employee could e-mail trade secrets in a company's server to a competitor or a future employer. If e-mail is not an option, the employee might walk out with the information on a flash drive.

Case Example 7.19 Charles Furstenau was a manager at Radiant Global Logistics, a company that helps customers with shipping needs. Disgruntled with Radiant, Furstenau decided to join a competitor, BTX Logistics. Before doing so, he forwarded e-mails containing information on revenues, profit margins, preferred shippers, and financial projections from his Radiant account to his personal account. Learning this, Radiant sued Furstenau and BTX for misappropriation of trade secrets. A federal district court prohibited Furstenau from contacting clients he had worked with at Radiant for six months and indefinitely barred BTX from using the information in the e-mails to its advantage. A federal appeals court affirmed, with the caveat that Furstenau's "general knowledge" of the logistics trade, as opposed to the specific data in the e-mails, did not constitute a trade secret.[26]

For a summary of trade secrets and other forms of intellectual property, see Exhibit 7-1.

26. *Radiant Global Logistics v. Furstenau*, __ F.3d. __ (6th Cir. 2020).

Exhibit 7-1 Forms of Intellectual Property

	Definition	How Acquired	Duration	Remedy For Infringement
Trademark (service, certification, and collective marks, and trade dress)	Any distinctive word, symbol, sound, or design that an entity uses to distinguish its goods or services from those of others. The owner has the exclusive right to use that mark or trade dress.	1. At common law, ownership created by use of the mark. 2. Registration with the appropriate federal or state office gives notice and is permitted if the mark is currently in commercial use or will be within the next six months.	Unlimited, as long as it is in use. To continue notice by registration, the owner must renew by filing between the fifth and sixth years, and thereafter, every ten years.	1. Injunction prohibiting the future use of the mark. 2. Actual damages plus profits received by the party who infringed (can be increased under the Lanham Act). 3. Destruction of articles that infringed. 4. *Plus* attorneys' fees.
Patent	A grant from the government that gives an inventor exclusive rights to make, use, and sell an invention.	By filing a patent application with the U.S. Patent and Trademark Office and receiving its approval.	Twenty years from the date of the application; for design patents, fourteen years.	1. Injunction against infringer. 2. Possible monetary damages, including royalties and lost profits, plus attorneys' fees. 3. Damages may be tripled for intentional infringement.
Copyright	The right of an author or originator of a literary or artistic work, or other production that falls within a specified category, to have the exclusive use of that work for a given period of time.	Automatic (once the work or creation is put in tangible form). Only the *expression* of an idea (and not the idea itself) can be protected by copyright.	For authors: the life of the author plus 70 years. For publishers: 95 years after the date of publication or 120 years after creation.	Actual damages plus profits received by the party who infringed, *or* statutory damages under the Copyright Act. Courts may impose fines and/or imprisonment, as well as an injunction.
Trade Secret	Any information that a business possesses and that gives the business an advantage over competitors (including customer lists, plans, pricing information, and production methods).	Through the originality and development of the information and processes that constitute the business secret and are unknown to others.	Unlimited, so long as not revealed to others. Once revealed to others, it is no longer a trade secret.	Monetary damages for misappropriation (the Uniform Trade Secrets Act also permits punitive damages if willful), *plus* costs and attorneys' fees.

7–5 International Protections

For many years, the United States has been a party to various international agreements relating to intellectual property rights. For instance, the Paris Convention of 1883, to which about 180 countries are signatory, allows parties in one country to file for patent and trademark protection in any of the other member countries. Other international agreements include the Berne Convention, the Trade-Related Aspects of Intellectual Property Rights (known as the TRIPS agreement), the Madrid Protocol, and the Anti-Counterfeiting Trade Agreement.

7–5a The Berne Convention

Under the Berne Convention of 1886, if a U.S. citizen writes a book, every country that has signed the convention must recognize the writer's copyright in the book. Also, if a citizen of a country that has not signed the convention first publishes a book in one of the 169 countries that have signed, all other countries that have signed the convention must recognize that author's copyright. Copyright notice is not needed to gain protection under the Berne Convention for works published after March 1, 1989.

The European Union altered its copyright rules under the Berne Convention by agreeing to extend the period of royalty protection for musicians from fifty years to seventy years. This decision aids major record labels as well as performers and musicians. The profits of musicians and record companies have been shrinking in recent years because of the sharp decline in sales of compact discs and the rise in digital downloads (both legal and illegal).

7–5b The TRIPS Agreement

The Berne Convention and other international agreements have given some protection to intellectual property on a worldwide level. None of them, however, has been as significant and far reaching in scope as the Trade-Related Aspects of Intellectual Property Rights (TRIPS) agreement. Representatives from more than one hundred nations signed the TRIPS agreement in 1994.

Focus Question 5
How does the TRIPS agreement protect intellectual property worldwide?

Established Standards and Procedures The TRIPS agreement established, for the first time, standards for the international protection of intellectual property rights, including patents, trademarks, and copyrights for movies, computer programs, books, and music. The TRIPS agreement provides that each member country must include in its domestic laws broad intellectual property rights and effective remedies (including civil and criminal penalties) for violations of those rights.

Each member nation must ensure that legal procedures are available for parties who wish to bring actions for infringement of intellectual property rights. Additionally, a related document established a mechanism for settling disputes among member nations.

Prohibits Discrimination Generally, the TRIPS agreement forbids member nations from discriminating against foreign owners of intellectual property rights in the administration, regulation, or adjudication of such rights. In other words, a member nation cannot give its own nationals (citizens) favorable treatment without offering the same treatment to nationals of all member countries. **Example 7.20** A U.S. software manufacturer brings a suit for the infringement of intellectual property rights under Germany's national laws. Because Germany is a member of the TRIPS agreement, the U.S. manufacturer is entitled to receive the same treatment as a German manufacturer.

7–5c The Madrid Protocol

In the past, one of the difficulties in protecting U.S. trademarks internationally was that it was time consuming and expensive to apply for trademark registration in foreign countries. The filing fees and procedures for trademark registration vary significantly among individual countries. The Madrid Protocol, which was signed into law in 2003, may help to resolve these problems.

The Madrid Protocol is an international treaty that has been signed by about a hundred countries. Under its provisions, a U.S. company wishing to register its trademark abroad can submit a single application and designate other member countries in which it would like to register the mark. The treaty was designed to reduce the costs of obtaining international trademark protection by more than 60 percent.

Although the Madrid Protocol may simplify and reduce the cost of trademark registration in foreign nations, it remains to be seen whether it will provide significant benefits to trademark owners. Even with an easier registration process, the question of whether member countries will enforce the law and protect the mark still remains.

7–5d The Anti-Counterfeiting Trade Agreement

In 2011, Australia, Canada, Japan, Korea, Morocco, New Zealand, Singapore, and the United States signed the Anti-Counterfeiting Trade Agreement (ACTA), an international treaty to combat global counterfeiting and piracy. Other nations have since signed the agreement. Once a nation has adopted appropriate procedures, it can ratify the treaty.

Provisions and Goals The goals of the treaty are to increase international cooperation, facilitate the best law enforcement practices, and provide a legal framework to combat counterfeiting. The treaty has its own governing body.

The ACTA applies not only to counterfeit physical goods, such as medications, but also to pirated copyrighted works being distributed via the Internet. The idea is to create a new standard of enforcement for intellectual property rights that goes beyond the TRIPS agreement and encourages international cooperation and information sharing among signatory countries.

Border Searches Under ACTA, member nations are required to establish border measures that allow officials, on their own initiative, to search commercial shipments of imports and exports for counterfeit goods. The treaty neither requires nor prohibits random border searches of electronic devices, such as laptops and iPads, for infringing content.

If border authorities reasonably believe that any goods in transit are counterfeit, the treaty allows them to keep the suspect goods unless the owner proves that the items are authentic and noninfringing. The treaty allows member nations, in accordance with their own laws, to order online service providers to furnish information about (including the identity of) suspected trademark and copyright infringers.

Practice and Review

Two computer science majors, Trent and Xavier, have an idea for a new video game, which they propose to call "Hallowed." They form a business and begin developing their idea. Several months later, Trent and Xavier run into a problem with their design and consult with a friend, Brad, who is an expert in creating computer source codes. After the software is completed but before Hallowed is marketed, a video game called Halo 2 is released for both the Xbox and the PlayStation 3 systems. Halo 2 uses source codes similar to those of Hallowed and imitates Hallowed's overall look and feel, although not all the features are alike. Using the information presented in the chapter, answer the following questions.

1. Would the name Hallowed receive protection as a trademark or as trade dress?
2. If Trent and Xavier had obtained a business process patent on Hallowed, would the release of Halo 2 infringe on their patent? Why or why not?
3. Based only on the facts presented above, could Trent and Xavier sue the makers of Halo 2 for copyright infringement? Why or why not?
4. Suppose that Trent and Xavier discover that Brad took the idea of Hallowed and sold it to the company that produced Halo 2. Which type of intellectual property issue does this raise?

Debate This

Congress has amended the Copyright Act several times. Copyright holders now have protection for many decades. Was Congress justified in extending the copyright time periods? Why or why not?

Key Terms

certification mark 172
collective mark 172
copyright 178
intellectual property 166
license 175
patent 175
royalties 175
service mark 172
trade dress 172
trade name 174
trade secret 185
trademark 167
trademark dilution 169

Chapter Summary: Intellectual Property Rights

Trademarks	**1.** A **trademark** is a distinctive word, symbol, sound, or design that identifies the manufacturer as the source of the goods and distinguishes its products from those made or sold by others. **2.** The major federal statutes protecting trademarks and related property are the Lanham Act and the Federal Trademark Dilution Act. Generally, to be protected, a trademark must be sufficiently distinctive from all competing trademarks. **3. Trademark infringement** occurs when one party uses a mark that is the same as, or confusingly similar to, the protected trademark, service mark, certification mark, collective mark, or trade name of another party without permission when marketing goods or services.
Patents	**1.** A **patent** is a grant from the government that gives an inventor the exclusive right to make, use, and sell an invention for a period of twenty years (fourteen years for a design patent) from the date when the application for a patent is filed. To be patentable, an invention (or a discovery, process, or design) must be novel, useful, and not obvious in light of current technology. Computer software may be patented. **2.** Almost anything is patentable, except the laws of nature, natural phenomena, and abstract ideas (including algorithms). Even artistic methods and works of art, certain business processes, and the structures of storylines may be patentable. **3. Patent infringement** occurs when someone uses or sells another's patented design, product, or process without the patent owner's permission. The patent holder can sue the infringer in federal court and request an injunction, but must prove irreparable injury to obtain a permanent injunction against the infringer. The patent holder can also request damages and attorneys' fees. If the infringement was willful, the court can grant treble damages.
Copyrights	**1.** A **copyright** is an intangible property right granted by federal statute to the author or originator of certain literary or artistic productions. The Copyright Act, as amended, governs copyrights. Works created after January 1, 1978, are automatically given statutory protection for the life of the author plus seventy years. **2. Copyright infringement** occurs whenever the form or expression of an idea is copied without the permission of the copyright holder. An exception applies if the copying is deemed a "fair use." **3.** The Computer Software Copyright Act amended the Copyright Act to include computer programs in the list of creative works protected by federal copyright law.
Trade Secrets	**1. Trade secrets** are basically information of commercial value and include customer lists, plans, research and development, and pricing information. **2.** Trade secrets are protected under the common law and by statute in nearly all of the states against misappropriation by competitors. Unlike copyright and trademark protection, protection of trade secrets extends both to ideas and to their expression. The Economic Espionage Act made the theft of trade secrets a federal crime.
International Protections	Various international agreements provide international protection for intellectual property. A landmark agreement is the Trade-Related Aspects of Intellectual Property Rights (TRIPS) agreement, which provides for enforcement procedures in all countries signatory to the agreement.

Issue Spotters

1. Roslyn, a food buyer for Organic Cornucopia Food Company, decides to go into business for herself as Roslyn's Kitchen. She contacts Organic's suppliers, offering to buy their entire harvest for the next year. She also contacts Organic's customers, offering to sell her products for less than Organic. Has Roslyn violated any of the intellectual property rights discussed in this chapter? Explain. (See *Trade Secrets.*)

2. Global Products develops, patents, and markets software. World Copies, Inc., sells Global's software without the maker's permission. Is this patent infringement? If so, how might Global save the cost of suing World for infringement and at the same time profit from World's sales? (See *Patents.*)

—Check your answers to the *Issue Spotters* against the answers provided in Appendix D.

Business Scenarios and Case Problems

7–1. Patent Infringement. John and Andrew Doney invented a hard-bearing device for balancing rotors. Although they obtained a patent for their invention from the U.S. Patent and Trademark Office, it was never used as an automobile wheel balancer. Some time later, Exetron Corp. produced an automobile wheel balancer that used a hard-bearing device similar to the Doneys' device. Given that the Doneys had not used their device for automobile wheel balancing, does Exetron's use of a similar device infringe on the Doneys' patent? (See *Patents.*)

7–2. Fair Use. Professor Wise is teaching a summer seminar in business torts at State University. Several times during the course, he makes copies of relevant sections from business law texts and distributes them to his students. Wise does not realize that the daughter of one of the textbook authors is a member of his seminar. She tells her father about Wise's copying activities, which have taken place without her father's or his publisher's permission. Her father sues Wise for copyright infringement. Wise claims protection under the fair use doctrine. Who will prevail? Explain. (See *Copyrights.*)

7–3. Spotlight on Macy's—Copyright Infringement. United Fabrics International, Inc., bought a fabric design from an Italian designer and registered a copyright to the design with the U.S. Copyright Office. When Macy's, Inc., began selling garments with a similar design, United filed a copyright infringement suit against Macy's. Macy's argued that United did not own a valid copyright to the design and so could not claim infringement. Does United have to prove that the copyright is valid to establish infringement? Explain. [*United Fabrics International, Inc. v. C & J Wear, Inc.*, 630 F.3d 1255 (9th Cir. 2011)] (See *Copyrights.*)

7–4. Copyright Infringement. SilverEdge Systems Software hired Catherine Conrad to perform a singing telegram. SilverEdge arranged for James Bendewald to record Conrad's performance of her copyrighted song to post on the company's website. Conrad agreed to wear a microphone to assist in the recording, told Bendewald what to film, and asked for an additional fee only if SilverEdge used the video for a commercial purpose. Later, the company chose to post a video of a different performer's singing telegram instead. Conrad filed a suit in a federal district court against SilverEdge and Bendewald for copyright infringement. Are the defendants liable? Explain. [*Conrad v. Bendewald*, 500 Fed.Appx. 526 (7th Cir. 2013)] (See *Copyrights.*)

7–5. Business Case Problem with Sample Answer—Patents. The U.S. Patent and Trademark Office (PTO) denied Raymond Gianelli's application for a patent for a "Rowing Machine"—an exercise machine on which a user *pulls* on handles to perform a rowing motion against a selected resistance. The PTO considered the device obvious in light of a previously patented "Chest Press Apparatus for Exercising Regions of the Upper Body"—an exercise machine on which a user *pushes* on handles to overcome a selected resistance. On what ground might this result be reversed on appeal? Discuss. [*In re Gianelli*, 739 F.3d 1375 (Fed. Cir. 2014)] (See *Patents.*)

—For a sample answer to Problem 7–5, go to Appendix E.

7–6. Patents. Rodney Klassen was employed by the U.S. Department of Agriculture (USDA). Without the USDA's authorization, Klassen gave Jim Ludy, a grape grower, plant material for two unreleased varieties of grapes. For almost two years, most of Ludy's plantings bore no usable fruit, none of the grapes were sold, and no plant material was given to any other person. The plantings were visible from publicly accessible roads, but none of the vines were labeled, and the variety could not be identified by simply viewing the vines. Under patent law, an applicant may not obtain a patent for an invention that is in public use more than one year before the date of the application. Could the USDA successfully apply for patents on the two varieties given to Ludy? Explain. [*Delano Farms Co. v. California Table Grape Commission*, 778 F.3d 1243 (Fed.Cir. 2015)] (See *Patents.*)

7–7. Copyright Infringement. Savant Homes, Inc., is a custom home designer and builder. Using what it called the Anders Plan, Savant built a model house in Windsor, Colorado. This was a ranch house with two bedrooms on one side and a master suite on the other, separated by a combined family room, dining room, and kitchen. Ron and Tammie Wagner toured the Savant house. The same month, the Wagners hired builder Douglas Collins and his firm, Douglas Consulting, to build a house for them. After it was built, Savant filed a lawsuit in a federal district court against Collins for copyright infringement, alleging that the builder had copied the Anders Plan in the design and construction of the Wagner house. Collins showed that the Anders Plan consisted of standard elements and standard arrangements of elements. In these circumstances, has infringement occurred? Explain. [*Savant Homes, Inc. v. Collins*, 809 F.3d 1133 (10th Cir. 2016)] (See *Copyrights*.)

7–8. Patent Infringement. Finjan, Inc., owns a patent—U.S. Patent No. 7,418,731, or "the '731 patent"—for a system and method that protect computers from malicious software embedded in websites on the Internet. The system consists of a gateway that compares security profiles associated with requested files to the security policies of requesting users. The method includes scanning an incoming file to create the profile, which comprises a list of computer commands the file is programmed to perform. The '731 patent required "a list of computer commands." Blue Coat Systems, Inc., sold a competing product. Blue Coat's product scanned an incoming file for certain commands and created a new file called Cookie2 that contained a field showing whether, and how often, those commands appeared. Finjan filed a suit against Blue Coat, alleging patent infringement. Blue Coat argued that its profiles did not contain the '731 patent's required "list of computer commands." Did Blue Coat's product infringe Finjan's patent? Explain. [*Finjan, Inc. v. Blue Cost Systems, Inc.*, 879 F.3d 1299 (Fed. Cir. 2018)] (See *Patents*.)

7–9. Copyrights. The "Jimmy Smith Rap" is a copyrighted rap recording asserting the supremacy of jazz over other types of music. Released thirty years later, "Pound Cake" is a hip-hop song in which Aubrey Graham and Shawn Carter, professionally known as Drake and Jay-Z, rap about the greatness and authenticity of their work. At the beginning of the seven-minute-long "Pound Cake" is a sampling of thirty-five seconds of the "Jimmy Smith Rap." Criticizing jazz elitism, "Pound Cake" emphasizes that it is not the genre but the authenticity of the music that matters. The release of "Pound Cake" had no effect on the demand for the "Jimmy Smith Rap," for which there was no active market at the time. Did Drake and Jay-Z make "fair use" of the "Jimmy Smith Rap," or were they liable for copyright infringement? Explain. [*Estate of Smith v. Graham*, 799 FedAppx 36 (2d Cir. 2020)] (See *Copyrights*.)

7–10. A Question of Ethics—The IDDR Approach and Copyright Infringement. Usenet is an online bulletin board network. A user gains access to Usenet posts through a commercial service, such as Giganews, Inc. Giganews deletes or blocks posts that contain child pornography. Otherwise, the service does not monitor content. Perfect 10, Inc., owns the copyrights to tens of thousands of images, many of which have been illegally posted on Usenet through Giganews. When Perfect 10 notified Giganews of posts that contained infringing images, the service took them down. Despite these efforts, illegal posting continued. Perfect 10 filed a suit in a federal district court against Giganews, alleging copyright infringement. [*Perfect 10, Inc. v. Giganews, Inc.*, 847 F.3d 657 (9th Cir. 2017)] (See *Copyrights*.)

1. Is Giganews liable for copyright infringement? Do Internet service providers have an ethical duty to do more to prevent infringement? Why or why not?
2. Using the IDDR approach, decide whether a copyright owner has an ethical duty to protect against infringement.

Critical Thinking and Writing Assignments

7–11. Time-Limited Group Assignment—Patents. After years of research, your company has developed a product that might revolutionize the green (environmentally conscious) building industry. The product is made from relatively inexpensive and widely available materials combined in a unique way that can substantially lower the heating and cooling costs of residential and commercial buildings. The company has registered the trademark it intends to use for the product and has filed a patent application with the U.S. Patent and Trademark Office. (See *Patents*.)

1. One group will provide three reasons why this product does or does not qualify for patent protection.
2. A second group will develop a four-step plan for how the company can best protect its intellectual property rights (trademark, trade secret, and patent) and prevent domestic and foreign competitors from producing counterfeit goods or cheap knockoffs.
3. The third group will list and explain three ways in which the company can utilize licensing.

8 Internet Law, Social Media, and Privacy

Focus Questions

The five Focus Questions *below are designed to help improve your understanding. After reading this chapter, you should be able to answer the following questions:*

1. What is cybersquatting, and when is it illegal?
2. What law protects copyrights in the digital age?
3. Identify several ways that social media has affected American legal processes.
4. What law governs whether Internet service providers are liable for online defamatory statements made by users?
5. When does the law protect a person's electronic communications from being intercepted or accessed?

"The Internet is just the world passing around notes in a classroom."

Jon Stewart
1962–present (American comedian and former host of The Daily Show)

The Internet has changed our lives and our laws. Technology has put the world at our fingertips and now allows even the smallest business to reach customers around the globe. Because the Internet allows the world to "pass around notes" so quickly, as Jon Stewart joked in the chapter-opening quotation, it presents a variety of challenges for the law.

Courts are often in uncharted waters when deciding disputes that involve the Internet, social media, and online privacy. Judges may have no common law precedents to rely on when resolving cases. Long-standing principles of justice may be inapplicable. New rules are evolving, but often not as quickly as technology.

Suppose that one day Frank Smith, a law student, learns that someone has created a Facebook account called "Frank Smithsexfiendman." The Facebook page associated with this account is showing doctored photos and videos of Frank engaged in a number of sexually explicit acts. As if this were not bad enough, whoever set up the account has sent friend requests to many of Frank's family members and acquaintances, causing them to visit the embarrassing page. Frank reports the account to Facebook and requests that it be deleted because of the humiliating nature of its content. Twenty-four hours later, the Frank Smithsexfiendman page remains active.

Frank has no idea who is behind this elaborate prank. Can he succeed in a lawsuit against Facebook for defamation or invasion of privacy? Proving torts online can be difficult, particularly when the person who may be liable is impossible to identify. In this chapter, you will read about the rules pertaining to a number of online torts, as well as other legal challenges presented by the Internet and social media.

8–1 Internet Law

A number of laws specifically address issues that arise only on the Internet. These issues include unsolicited e-mail, domain names, cybersquatting, and meta tags, as we discuss here. We also discuss how the law is dealing with problems of trademark dilution online, as well as licensing.

8–1a Spam

Spam Bulk, unsolicited (junk) e-mail.

Businesses and individuals alike are targets of **spam.**[1] Spam is the unsolicited "junk e-mail" that floods virtual mailboxes with advertisements, solicitations, and similar communications. Considered relatively harmless in the early days of the Internet, spam has become a serious problem. By some estimates, it accounts for roughly 75 percent of all e-mails.

State Regulation of Spam In an attempt to combat spam, thirty-seven states have enacted laws that prohibit or regulate its use. Many state laws that regulate spam require the senders of e-mail ads to instruct the recipients on how they can "opt out" of further e-mail ads from the same sources. For instance, in some states, an unsolicited e-mail must include a toll-free phone number or return e-mail address that the recipient can use to ask the sender not to send unsolicited e-mails.

The Federal CAN-SPAM Act In 2003, Congress enacted the Controlling the Assault of Non-Solicited Pornography and Marketing (CAN-SPAM) Act.[2] The legislation applies to any "commercial electronic mail messages" that are sent to promote a commercial product or service. Significantly, the statute preempts state antispam laws except those provisions in state laws that prohibit false and deceptive e-mailing practices.

Generally, the act permits the sending of unsolicited commercial e-mail but prohibits certain types of spamming activities. Prohibited activities include the use of a false return address and the use of false, misleading, or deceptive information when sending e-mail. The statute also prohibits the use of "dictionary attacks"—sending messages to randomly generated e-mail addresses—and the "harvesting" of e-mail addresses from websites through the use of specialized software.

Case Example 8.1 Zoobuh provides "Safe E-mail for Kids and Families." Consequently, its customers were not pleased when they started receiving daily e-mails from the dating website xdating.com. These messages contained fake profiles of nonexistent xdating.com members supposedly living near the recipients. Furthermore, when recipients clicked the "unsubscribe" option in the e-mails, they unwittingly signed up to receive additional xdating.com marketing materials.

Alleging that these e-mails violated the CAN-SPAM Act, Zoobuh filed suit against the company that provided xdating.com access to its customer list. Zoobuh asserted that the spam caused lost time, as its employees worked to block the offending e-mails, and lost profits, as frustrated customers cancelled Zoobuh's e-mail service. Finding for Zoobuh, a federal judge awarded the company $3 million in damages.[3] Victories in court, however, have done little to curb spam, which continues to flow at a rate of many billions of messages per day.

1. The term *spam* is said to come from the lyrics of a Monty Python song that repeats the word *spam* over and over.
2. 15 U.S.C. Sections 7701 *et seq.*
3. *Zoobuh, Inc., v. Savicom, Inc.*, 2019 WL 1466285 (D. Utah, 2019).

The U.S. Safe Web Act After the CAN-SPAM Act took effect, spamming from servers located in other nations increased. These cross-border spammers generally were able to escape detection and legal sanctions because the Federal Trade Commission (FTC) lacked the authority to investigate foreign spamming.

Congress sought to rectify the situation by enacting the U.S. Safe Web Act (also known as the Undertaking Spam, Spyware, and Fraud Enforcement with Enforcers beyond Borders Act).[4] The act allows the FTC to cooperate and share information with foreign agencies in investigating and prosecuting those involved in spamming, spyware, and various Internet frauds and deceptions.

Internet Service Providers (ISP) A business or organization that offers users access to the Internet and related services.

The Safe Web Act also provides a "safe harbor" for **Internet service providers (ISPs)**—organizations that provide access to the Internet. The safe harbor gives ISPs immunity from liability for supplying information to the FTC concerning possible unfair or deceptive conduct in foreign jurisdictions.

8–1b Domain Names

Domain Name The series of letters and symbols used to identify a site operator on the Internet (an Internet address).

As e-commerce expanded worldwide, one issue that emerged involved the rights of a trademark owner to use the mark as part of a domain name. A **domain name** is part of an Internet address, such as "cengage.com."

Structure of Domain Names Every domain name ends with a top-level domain (TLD), which is the part of the name to the right of the period. This part of the name often indicates the type of entity that operates the site. For instance, com is an abbreviation for commercial, and edu is an abbreviation for education.

The second-level domain (SLD)—the part of the name to the left of the period—is chosen by the business entity or individual registering the domain name. Competition for SLDs among firms with similar names and products has led to numerous disputes. By using an identical or similar domain name, one company may attempt to profit from a competitor's **goodwill** (the intangible value of a business).

Goodwill In the business context, the valuable reputation of a business viewed as an intangible asset.

Domain Name Distribution System The Internet Corporation for Assigned Names and Numbers (ICANN), a nonprofit corporation, oversees the distribution of domain names and operates an online arbitration system. Due to numerous complaints, ICANN overhauled the domain name distribution system in 2012.

ICANN now sells new *generic top-level domain names* (gTLDs) for an initial price of $185,000 plus an annual fee of $25,000. Whereas TLDs previously had been limited to only a few terms (including com, net, and org), gTLDs can take any form. Many companies and corporations have acquired gTLDs based on their brands, such as aol, bmw, target, and walmart. Some companies have numerous gTLDs. Google's gTLDs, for instance, include android, chrome, gmail, goog, and YouTube.

Because gTLDs have greatly increased the potential number of domain names, domain name registrars have proliferated. Registrar companies charge a fee to businesses and individuals to register new names and to renew annual registrations (often through automated software). Many of these companies also buy and sell expired domain names.

Cybersquatting The act of registering a domain name that is the same as, or confusingly similar to, the trademark of another and then offering to sell that domain name back to the trademark owner.

8–1c Cybersquatting

One of the goals of the new gTLD system was to alleviate the problem of cybersquatting. **Cybersquatting** occurs when a party registers a domain name that is the same as, or confusingly similar to, the trademark of another and then offers to sell the domain name back to the

4. Pub. L. No. 109–455, 120 Stat. 3372 (2006), codified in various sections of 15 U.S.C. and 12 U.S.C. Section 3412.

trademark owner. **Example 8.2** Apple, Inc., has repeatedly sued cybersquatters that registered domain names similar to the names of its products, such as iphone8.com and ipods.com.

Focus Question 1

What is cybersquatting, and when is it illegal?

Anticybersquatting Legislation Because cybersquatting has led to so much litigation, Congress enacted the Anticybersquatting Consumer Protection Act (ACPA).[5] The act amended the Lanham Act—the federal law protecting trademarks. The ACPA makes cybersquatting illegal when both of the following are true:

1. The domain name is identical or confusingly similar to the trademark of another.
2. The one registering, trafficking in, or using the domain name has a "bad faith intent" to profit from that trademark.

Despite the ACPA, cybersquatting continues to present a problem for businesses. **Case Example 8.3** CrossFit, Inc., is a Delaware corporation that provides personal fitness services and products. CrossFit is well known in the fitness industry and licenses affiliates to operate individual CrossFit-branded programs. CrossFit granted a license to Andres Del Cueto Davalos to operate a location in Mexico and allowed him to use the domain name "CrossFitAlfa." Davalos later registered the domain name CrossFitBeta without CrossFit's permission and then used both of these domain names to redirect website visitors to a third website, www.woodbox.com. Davalos was attempting to siphon off CrossFit customers to another business that he co-owned, Woodbox Training Centers, which operated in twenty-five locations across Mexico. CrossFit sued under the ACPA. Because of Davalos's bad faith intent, the court awarded CrossFit the maximum amount of statutory damages available ($100,000 for each domain name), plus costs and attorneys' fees.[6]

Andrew Errington/Moment Mobile/Getty Images

How did the Anticybersquatting Consumer Protection Act affect a dispute involving the physical fitness program, CrossFit, and its affiliates?

Cybersquatting Proliferation All domain name registrars are supposed to relay information about registrations and renewals to ICANN and other companies that keep a master list of domain names, but this does not always occur. The speed at which domain names change hands and the difficulty in tracking mass automated registrations have created an environment in which cybersquatting can flourish.

Cybersquatters have also developed the tactic of **typosquatting**, or registering a name that is a misspelling of a popular brand name, such as googl.com or appple.com. Because many Internet users are not perfect typists, Web pages using these misspelled names may receive a lot of traffic, making them attractive to certain advertisers. If the misspelling that a typosquatter uses is significant, the trademark owner may have trouble gaining ACPA protection.

Typosquatting A form of cybersquatting that relies on mistakes, such as typographical errors, made by Internet users when entering information into a Web browser.

Applicability and Sanctions of the ACPA The ACPA applies to all domain name registrations of trademarks. Successful plaintiffs in suits brought under the act can collect actual damages and profits, or they can elect to receive statutory damages ranging from $1,000 to $100,000.

Although some companies have successfully sued under the ACPA, there are roadblocks to pursuing such lawsuits. Some domain name registrars offer privacy services that hide the true owners of websites, making it difficult for trademark owners to identify cybersquatters. Thus, before bringing a suit, a trademark owner has to ask the court for a subpoena to discover the identity of the owner of the infringing website. Because of the high costs of court proceedings, discovery, and even arbitration, many disputes over cybersquatting are settled out of court.

To facilitate dispute resolution, ICANN offers two dispute resolution forums: the Uniform Domain-Name Dispute-Resolution Policy (UDRP) and the Uniform Rapid

5. 15 U.S.C. Section 1129.
6. *CrossFit, Inc. v. Davalos*, 2017 WL 733213 (N.D.Cal. 2017).

Suspension (URS) system. More disputes are resolved through the UDRP, which allows common law trademark claims and has fewer procedural requirements. The newer URS system can be used by only registered trademark owners with clear-cut infringement claims. The URS has other limitations as well, but it is faster. **Example 8.4** IBM once filed a complaint with the URS against an individual who registered the domain names IBM.guru and IBM.ventures. A week later, the URS panel decided in IBM's favor and suspended the two domain names.

8–1d Meta Tags

Meta tags are key words that give Internet browsers specific information about a Web page. Meta tags can be used to increase the likelihood that a site will be included in search engine results, even if the site has nothing to do with the key words. In effect, one website can appropriate the key words of other sites with more frequent hits so that the appropriating site will appear in the same search engine results as the more popular sites.

Using another's trademark in a meta tag without the owner's permission normally constitutes trademark infringement. Some uses of another's trademark as a meta tag may be permissible, however, if the use is reasonably necessary and does not suggest that the owner authorized or sponsored the use.

Case Example 8.5 Nespresso USA, Inc., is a well-known espresso and coffee machine producer, and owner of the federally registered trademark "Nespresso." Nespresso also makes and sells espresso capsules for use with its machines. Africa America Coffee Trading Company, which does business as Libretto, makes espresso capsules that are compatible with Nespresso machines. Libretto's capsules are the same shape and size as Nespresso's, but they are made of plastic (not aluminum like Nespresso's). Libretto used Nespresso's trademark on its boxes and also used the word "Nespresso" as a meta tag in the source code for its website.

Nespresso attempted to contact Libretto and request that it stop producing and selling espresso capsules that infringed on its trademark, but Libretto did not respond. Nespresso filed a suit in a federal court in New York. The court concluded that Libretto had been infringing on Nespresso's trademark and permanently enjoined (prohibited) Libretto from using Nespresso's mark—including its meta tags.[7]

8–1e Trademark Dilution in the Online World

As previously explained, trademark *dilution* occurs when a trademark is used, without authorization, in a way that diminishes the distinctive quality of the mark. Unlike trademark infringement, a claim of dilution does not require proof that consumers are likely to be confused by a connection between the unauthorized use and the mark. For this reason, the products involved need not be similar, as the following *Spotlight Case* illustrates.

7. *Nespresso USA, Inc. v. Africa America Coffee Trading Co., LLC*, 2016 WL 3162118 (S.D.N.Y. 2016).

Spotlight on Internet Porn: Case 8.1

Hasbro, Inc. v. Internet Entertainment Group, Ltd.

United States District Court, Western District of Washington, 1996 WL 84853 (1996).

Facts Hasbro, Inc., the maker of Candy Land, a children's board game, owns the Candy Land trademark. The defendants, Brian Cartmell and the Internet Entertainment Group, Ltd., used candyland.com as a domain name for a sexually explicit Internet site. Any person who performed an online search for "candyland" was directed to this adult website. Hasbro filed a trademark dilution claim in a federal court, seeking a permanent injunction to prevent the defendants from using the CANDYLAND trademark.

Issue Did the defendants' use of the word *candyland* in connection with a sexually explicit website violate Hasbro's trademark rights?

Decision Yes. The district court granted Hasbro a permanent injunction and ordered the defendants to remove all content from the candyland .com website and to stop using the CANDYLAND mark.

digitalreflections/Shutterstock.com

Candy Land is a children's board game. Why did its parent company, Hasbro, Inc., sue a website?

Reason The court reasoned that Hasbro had shown that the defendants' use of the CANDYLAND mark and the domain name candyland. com in connection with their Internet site was causing irreparable injury to Hasbro. As required to obtain an injunction, Hasbro had demonstrated a likelihood that the defendants' conduct violated both the federal and the Washington State statutes against trademark dilution. "The probable harm to Hasbro from defendants' conduct outweighs any inconvenience that defendants will experience if they are required to stop using the CANDYLAND name."

Critical Thinking

- **What If the Facts Were Different?** *Suppose that the candyland.com website had not been sexually explicit but had sold candy. Would the result have been the same? Explain.*
- **Economic** *How can companies protect themselves from situations such as the one described in this case? What limits each company's ability to be fully protected?*

8–1f Licensing

Recall that a company may permit another party to use a trademark (or other intellectual property) under a license. A licensor might grant a license allowing its trademark to be used as part of a domain name, for instance.

Another type of license involves the use of a product such as software. This sort of licensing is ubiquitous in the online world. When you download an application on your smartphone or other mobile device, for instance, you are typically entering into a license agreement. You are obtaining only a *license* to use the software and not ownership rights in it. Apps published on Google Play, for instance, may use its licensing service to prompt users to agree to a license at the time of installation and use.

Licensing agreements frequently include restrictions that prohibit licensees from sharing the file and using it to create similar software applications. The license may also limit the use of the application to a specific device or give permission to the user for a certain time period.

8–2 Copyrights in Digital Information

Focus Question 2
What law protects copyrights in the digital age?

Copyright law is probably the most important form of intellectual property protection on the Internet. This is because much of the material on the Internet (including software and database information) is copyrighted, and in order for that material to be transferred online, it must be "copied." Generally, whenever a party downloads software, movies, or music into a computer's random access memory, or RAM, without authorization, a copyright is infringed.

In 1998, Congress passed additional legislation to protect copyright holders—the Digital Millennium Copyright Act (DMCA).[8] Because of its significance in protecting against the piracy of copyrighted materials in the online environment, this act is presented as this chapter's *Landmark in the Law* feature.

8. 17 U.S.C. Sections 512, 1201–1205, 1301–1332; and 28 U.S.C. Section 4001.

The Digital Millennium Copyright Act

The United States leads the world in the production of creative products, including books, films, videos, recordings, and software. Exports of U.S. creative products surpass those of every other U.S. industry in value.

Given the importance of intellectual property to the U.S. economy, the United States has actively supported international efforts to protect ownership rights in intellectual property, including copyrights. In 1996, to curb unauthorized copying of copyrighted materials, the member nations of the World Intellectual Property Organization (WIPO) adopted a treaty to upgrade global standards of copyright protection, particularly for the Internet.

Implementing the WIPO Treaty

Congress implemented the provisions of the WIPO treaty by enacting a new statute to update U.S. copyright law in 1998. The law—the Digital Millennium Copyright Act (DMCA)—is a landmark step in the protection of copyright owners. Because of the leading position of the United States in the creative industries, the law also serves as a model for other nations.

Among other things, the DMCA established civil and criminal penalties for anyone who circumvents (bypasses) encryption software or other technological antipiracy protection. Also prohibited are the manufacture, import, sale, and distribution of devices or services for circumvention.

Allowing Fair Use The act provides for exceptions to fit the needs of libraries, scientists, universities, and others. In general, the law does not restrict the "fair use" of circumvention methods for educational and other noncommercial purposes. For instance, circumvention is allowed to test computer security, conduct encryption research, protect personal privacy, and enable parents to monitor their children's use of the Internet. The exceptions are to be reconsidered every three years.

Limiting the Liability of Internet Service Providers The DMCA also includes a safe-harbor provision that limits the liability of Internet service providers (ISPs). Under the act, an ISP is not liable for any copyright infringement by a customer *unless* the ISP is aware of the subscriber's violation. An ISP may be held liable only if it fails to take action to shut the subscriber down after learning of the violation. A copyright holder has to act promptly, however, by pursuing a claim in court, or the subscriber has the right to be restored to online access.

Application to Today's World

Without the DMCA, copyright owners would have a more difficult time obtaining legal redress against those who, without authorization, decrypt or copy copyrighted materials. Nevertheless, problems remain, particularly because of the global nature of the Internet.

Donald Miralle/Getty Images

Was the use of a Prince song in a YouTube video considered a "fair use" under the DMCA? Why or why not?

8–2a Copyright Infringement

Technology has vastly increased the potential for copyright infringement. Even using a small portion of another's copyrighted sound recording (digital sampling) can constitute copyright infringement. Fair use can be asserted as a defense to copyright infringement. **Spotlight Case Example 8.6** Stephanie Lenz posted a short video on YouTube of her toddler son dancing with the Prince song "Let's Go Crazy" playing in the background. Universal Music Group (UMG) sent YouTube a take-down notice that stated that the video violated copyright law under the DMCA. YouTube removed the "dancing baby" video and notified Lenz of the allegations of copyright infringement, warning her that repeated incidents of infringement could lead it to delete her account.

Lenz filed a lawsuit against UMG claiming that accusing her of infringement constituted a material misrepresentation (fraud) because UMG knew that Lenz's video was a fair use of the song. The district court held that UMG should have considered the fair use doctrine before sending the take-down notice. UMG appealed, and the U.S. Court of Appeals for the Ninth Circuit affirmed. Lenz was allowed to pursue nominal damages from UMG for sending the notice without considering whether her use was fair.[9]

9. *Lenz v. Universal Music Group*, 815 F.3d 1145 (9th Cir. 2015).

Initially, criminal penalties for copyright violations could be imposed only if unauthorized copies were exchanged for financial gain. Then, Congress amended the law and extended criminal liability for the piracy of copyrighted materials to persons who exchange unauthorized copies of copyrighted works without realizing a profit.

See this chapter's *Adapting the Law to the Online Environment* feature for a discussion of copyright law in the context of video games.

8–2b File-Sharing Technology

Soon after the Internet became popular, a few enterprising programmers created software to compress large data files, particularly music files. The best-known compression and decompression system is MP3, which enables music fans to download songs or entire CDs onto

Riot Games, Inc., Protects Its Online Video Game Copyrights

The acronym LoL generally means "laugh out loud." But when it comes to the popular online video game *League of Legends*, owned by Riot Games, Inc., *LoL* means something much different. More than 100 million people use this free multiplayer video game online each month. Of course, competitors have eyed that large market for years.

Taking on a Chinese Competitor

To protect its *LoL* copyrights, U.S.-based Riot Games has filed a lawsuit against a Chinese company, Shanghai MoBai Computer Technology (Moby). Riot Games alleges that Moby has "blatantly and slavishly copied *LoL* in [Moby's online video game called] *Arena of Battle*."[a] In particular, Moby's copycat game features nearly sixty champions with similar names, sound effects, icons, and abilities as those used in *LoL*. Moby has marketed *Arena of Battle* through the Apple App Store as well as Google Play, and it has used alternative titles and aliases in order to sell its game.

Note that under current case law, video gameplay is not protected by copyright law. *Gameplay* describes how players interact with a video game, such as through its plot and its rules. Specific expressions of that gameplay, however—as measured by look, settings, stories, characters, and sound—are protected.

The Mobile Game Market in China

While *LoL* has been China's top computer desktop game for years, millions of Chinese online game players use only mobile platforms, such as smartphones and tablets. As a result, Tencent, the parent company of Riot Games, created a mobile version of *LoL* called *King of Glory*. It is almost an exact copy of *LoL*. *King of Glory* is now China's top-grossing Apple mobile game. Of course, there are no copyright issues with *King of Glory* because Tencent can copy its own video game.

Taking on a Cheating Software Developer

In addition to suing Moby, as mentioned earlier, Riot Games accused the makers of LeagueSharp of violating the Digital Millennium Copyright Act.[b] The plaintiff claimed that the defendants had violated the Digital Millennium Copyright Act[c] by circumventing *LoL*'s anti-cheating software. Customers had paid a monthly fee to use LeagueSharp. Among other things, the service enabled them to see hidden information, automate gameplay to perform with enhanced accuracy, and accumulate certain rewards at a rate not possible for a normal human player.

The obvious question is why anybody would have wanted to pay for LeagueSharp services—recall that *LoL* is a free online game. The reason is the advantage the cheating players gained over ordinary players. They could, for instance, more quickly and easily win "swords," which they could use to buy new characters with which to play. LeagueSharp's makers ultimately agreed to pay $10 million to Riot Games.[d]

Critical Thinking

If LoL is free to players, why would a Chinese company want to copy it?

a. *Riot Games, Inc., v. Shanghai MoBai Computer Technology Co., Ltd. et al*, Case No. 3:17-CV-00331 (N.D.Cal. 2017).

b. *Riot Games, Inc. v. Argote*, Case No. 2:16-CV-5871 (C.D.Cal. 2017).

c. Pub. L. No. 105–304, 112 Stat. 2860 (1998).

d. Chalk, Andy. "Riot awarded $10 million in Leaguesharp lawsuit settlement." pcgamer.com. 03 Mar. 2017. Web.

their computers or onto portable listening devices, such as smartphones. The MP3 system also made it possible for music fans to access other fans' files by engaging in file-sharing via the Internet.

Peer-to-Peer (P2P) Networking The sharing of resources among multiple computer or other devices without the requirement of a central network server.

Methods of File-Sharing File-sharing can be accomplished through **peer-to-peer (P2P) networking**. The concept is simple. Rather than going through a central network, P2P networking uses numerous computers or other devices that are connected to one another, often via the Internet.

A P2P network is a type of **distributed network,** which may include devices distributed all over the country or the world. Persons located almost anywhere can work together on the same project by using file-sharing programs on distributed networks.

Distributed Network A network that can be used by persons located (distributed) around the country or the globe to share computer files.

The predominant method of sharing files via the Internet is **cloud computing,** which is essentially a subscription-based or pay-per-use service that extends a computer's software or storage capabilities. Cloud computing can deliver a single application through a browser to multiple users. Alternatively, cloud computing might provide data storage and virtual servers that can be accessed on demand. Amazon, Facebook, Google, IBM, and Sun Microsystems are using and developing more cloud computing services.

Cloud Computing The delivery to users of on-demand services from third-party servers over a network.

The BitTorrent Protocol BitTorrent has become the most popular method of P2P file sharing in the world. Its popularity is based on the speed with which it can send multiple large, high-quality files without using a great deal of bandwidth. There is nothing inherently illegal about using BitTorrent. For instance, someone who uploads a *home* movie onto BitTorrent to share it with family members is most likely not breaking any law.

When BitTorrent is used to share recorded music files, however, copyright issues arise. Recording artists and their labels stand to lose large amounts of royalties and revenues if relatively few digital downloads are purchased and then made available on distributed networks. These concerns have prompted recording companies to pursue not only companies involved in file-sharing but also individuals who have file-shared copyrighted works.

In the following case, the owner of copyrights in musical compositions sought to recover from an Internet service provider, some of whose subscribers used BitTorrent to share the owner's copyrighted compositions without permission.

Case 8.2

BMG Rights Management (US), LLC v. Cox Communications, Inc.

United States Court of Appeals, Fourth Circuit, 881 F.3d 293 (2018).

Facts Cox Communications, Inc., is an Internet service provider (ISP) with 4.5 million subscribers. Some of the subscribers shared copyrighted files, including music files, without the copyright owners' permission, using BitTorrent. Cox's stated policy is to suspend or terminate subscribers who use the service to "infringe the . . . copyrights . . . of any party." Despite this policy, Cox declined to terminate infringing subscribers so as not to lose revenue.

BMG Rights Management (US), LLC, owns copyrights in some of the music shared by the subscribers. BMG sent millions of notices to Cox to alert the ISP to the infringing activity. Cox deleted the notices without acting on them. BMG filed a suit in a federal district court against Cox, seeking to hold the ISP liable under the Digital Millennium Copyright Act (DMCA) for its subscribers' infringement of BMG's copyrights. Cox claimed a "safe harbor" under the act. The court issued a judgment in BMG's favor. Cox appealed to the U.S. Court of Appeals for the Fourth Circuit.

Issue Was Cox liable for contributory copyright infringement?

Decision Yes. The U.S. Court of Appeals for the Fourth Circuit affirmed the judgment of the lower court. "Cox failed to qualify for the DMCA safe harbor because it failed to implement its [infringement] policy in any consistent or meaningful way."

Reason To qualify for a "safe harbor" under the DMCA, an ISP must implement a policy that provides for the termination of subscribers who repeatedly infringe copyrights. The court recognized that Cox had adopted such a policy. But, as shown by internal e-mails, Cox determined not to terminate subscribers who violated the policy. Although some subscribers were terminated, their service was always reactivated. Furthermore, when Cox decided to delete all infringement notices received from BMG, Cox dispensed with terminating subscribers who repeatedly infringed BMG's copyrights in particular. Cox argued that the DMCA requires termination of repeat infringers only in "appropriate circumstances." The court found no evidence that "appropriate circumstances" played any role in Cox's decisions to terminate (or not). Instead, those decisions were based on "one goal: not losing revenue from paying subscribers."

Critical Thinking

- **Technology** *Should an ISP be liable for copyright infringement by its subscribers regardless of whether the ISP is aware of the violation? Why or why not?*
- **Legal Environment** *Could Cox legitimately claim that it had no knowledge of subscribers who infringed BMG's copyrights, since the ISP was deleting all of BMG's infringement notices? Explain.*

Pirated Movies and Television File-sharing also creates problems for the motion picture industry, which loses significant amounts of revenue annually as a result of pirated DVDs. Numerous websites offer software that facilitates the illegal copying of movies. Popcorn Time, for example, is a BitTorrent site that offers streaming services that allow users to watch pirated movies and television shows without downloading them.

Case Example 8.7 UN4 Productions, Inc., creates and distributes a series of martial arts films called *Boyka Undisputed*. When the company determined that an unauthorized copy of *Boyka Undisputed 4* was being shared on BitTorrent, it tried to determine who was responsible for initially uploading the film. Failing in these efforts, UN4 subpoenaed a number of ISPs, requesting the "digital footprints" of anyone who had illegally downloaded *Boyka Undisputed 4* on BitTorrent.

This strategy identified five individuals, whom UN4 successfully sued for infringement of its copyrighted material. Because the defendants had not profited from these "minor" infringements, a federal judge determined that UN4 was only entitled to $750 in damages from each. The judge also ordered the defendants to destroy their downloaded files of the film.[10]

8–3 Social Media

Social media provide a means by which people can create, share, and exchange ideas and comments via the Internet. Social networking sites, such as Facebook, Google+, LinkedIn, Pinterest, and Tumblr, have become ubiquitous. Other social media platforms, including Instagram, Snapchat, and Twitter, have also gained popularity. Studies show that Internet users spend more time on social networks than at any other sites, and the amount of time people spend on social media is constantly increasing.

Social Media Forms of communication through which users create and share information, ideas, messages, and other content via the Internet.

8–3a Legal Issues

The emergence of Facebook and other social networking sites has affected the legal process in various ways. Here, we explain some uses of social media posts in the litigation process, as well as in the investigations that precede prosecutions or other actions. We also discuss what can happen when employees violate their employers' social media policies.

10. *UN4 Productions, Inc. v. Primozich*, 372 F.Supp.1129 (W.D. Wash. 2019).

Impact on Litigation Social media posts now are routinely included in discovery in litigation. Such posts can provide damaging information that establishes a person's intent or what that person knew at a particular time. Like e-mail, posts on social networks can be the smoking gun that leads to liability.

In some situations, social media posts have been used to reduce damages awards. **Example 8.8** Jil Daniels sues for injuries she sustained in a car accident, claiming that her injuries make it impossible for her to continue working as a hairstylist. The jury initially determines that her damages were $237,000, but when the jurors see Daniels's tweets and photographs of her partying in New Orleans and vacationing on the beach, they reduce the damages award to $142,000. ■

Impact on Settlement Agreements Social media posts have been used to invalidate settlement agreements that contained confidentiality clauses. **Case Example 8.9** Patrick Snay was the headmaster of Gulliver Preparatory School in Florida. When Gulliver did not renew Snay's employment contract, Snay sued the school for age discrimination. During mediation, Snay agreed to settle the case for $80,000 and signed a confidentiality clause that required he and his wife not to disclose the "terms and existence" of the agreement. Nevertheless, Snay and his wife told their daughter, Dana, that the dispute had been settled and that they were happy with the results.

Dana, a college student, had recently graduated from Gulliver and, according to Snay, had suffered retaliation at the school. Dana posted a Facebook comment that said, "Mama and Papa Snay won the case against Gulliver. Gulliver is now officially paying for my vacation to Europe this summer. SUCK IT." The comment went out to 1,200 of Dana's Facebook friends, many of whom were Gulliver students, and school officials soon learned of it. The school immediately notified Snay that he had breached the confidentiality clause and refused to pay the settlement amount. Ultimately, a state intermediate appellate court agreed and held that Snay could not enforce the settlement agreement.[11] ■

Criminal Investigations Law enforcement uses social media to detect and prosecute criminals. A surprising number of criminals boast about their illegal activities on social media. **Example 8.10** Paige Thompson, a former software engineer for Amazon, tweeted that "I've basically strapped myself with a bomb vest." Thompson was referring, metaphorically, to the punishment she was likely to receive for breaking into a server used by credit card company Capital One and compromising the financial data of more than 100 million people. The tweet resulted in her arrest and criminal charges that carry a maximum punishment of five years in prison and a $250,000 fine. ■

Police may also use social media to help them to locate a particular suspect or to determine the identity of other suspects within a criminal network. In fact, police officers in New York City and other locations have even assumed fake identities on Facebook in order to "friend" suspects and obtain information. According to at least one court, it is legally acceptable for law enforcement officers to set up a phony social media account to catch a suspect.[12]

Administrative Agencies Federal regulators also use social media posts in their investigations into illegal activities. **Example 8.11** Reed Hastings, the top executive of Netflix, stated on Facebook that Netflix subscribers had watched a billion hours of video the previous month. As a result, Netflix's stock price rose, which prompted a federal agency investigation. Under securities laws, such a statement is considered to be material information to investors. Thus, it must be disclosed to all investors, not just a select group, such as those who had access to Hastings's Facebook post.

11. *Gulliver Schools, Inc. v. Snay*, 137 So.3d 1045 (Fla.App. 2014).
12. *United States v. Gatson*, 2014 WL 7182275 (D.N.J. 2014). See also *United States v. Tutis*, 216 F.Supp.3d 467 (D.N.J. 2016).

The agency ultimately concluded that it could not hold Hastings responsible for any wrong-doing because the agency's policy on social media use was not clear. The agency then issued new guidelines that allow companies to disclose material information through social media if investors have been notified in advance.

Administrative law judges can base their decisions on the content of social media posts. **Case Example 8.12** Jennifer O'Brien was a tenured teacher at a public school in New Jersey when she posted two messages on her Facebook page. "I'm not a teacher—I'm a warden for future criminals!" and "They had a scared straight program in school—why couldn't I bring first graders?" Not surprisingly, outraged parents protested. The deputy superintendent of schools filed a complaint against O'Brien with the state's commissioner of education, charging her with conduct unbecoming a teacher.

After a hearing, an administrative law judge ordered that O'Brien be removed from her teaching position. O'Brien appealed to a state court, claiming that her Facebook postings were protected by the First Amendment and could not be used by the school district to discipline or discharge her. The court found that O'Brien had failed to establish that her Facebook postings were protected speech and that the seriousness of O'Brien's conduct did warrant removal from her position.[13]

Employers' Social Media Policies Many large corporations have established specific guidelines on using social media in the workplace. Employees who use social media in a way that violates their employer's stated policies may be disciplined or fired. Courts and administrative agencies usually uphold an employer's right to terminate a person based on violation of a social media policy.

Focus Question 3

Identify several ways that social media has affected American legal processes.

Case Example 8.13 Virginia Rodriquez worked for Walmart Stores, Inc., for almost twenty years and had been promoted to management. Then she was disciplined for violating the company's policies by having a fellow employee use Rodriquez's password to alter the price of an item that she purchased. Under Walmart's rules, another violation within a year would mean termination.

Nine months later, on Facebook, Rodriquez publicly chastised employees under her supervision for calling in sick to go to a party. The posting violated Walmart's "Social Media Policy," which was "to avoid public comment that adversely affects employees." Walmart terminated Rodriquez. She filed a lawsuit, alleging discrimination, but the court issued a summary judgment in Walmart's favor.[14] Note, though, that some employees' posts on social media may be protected under labor law.

8–3b Protection of Social Media Passwords

Employees and applicants for jobs or colleges have occasionally been asked to divulge their social media passwords. An employer or school may look at an individual's Facebook or other account to see if it includes controversial postings, such as racially discriminatory remarks or photos of parties where drugs were being used. Such postings can have a negative effect on a person's prospects even if they were made years earlier or are taken out of context.

More than half of the states have enacted legislation to protect individuals from having to disclose their social media passwords. These laws vary. Some states, such as Michigan, prohibit employers from taking adverse action against an employee or job applicant based on what the person has posted online. Michigan's law also applies to e-mail and cloud storage accounts.

---

13. *In re O'Brien*, 2013 WL 132508 (N.J.App. 2013). See also *Grutzmacher v. Howard County*, 851 F.3d 332 (4th Cir. 2017).
14. *Rodriquez v. Wal-Mart Stores, Inc.*, 2013 WL 102674 (N.D.Tex. 2013).

Legislation will not completely prevent employers and others from taking actions against employees or applicants based on their social network postings, though. Management and human resources personnel are unlikely to admit that they based a hiring decision on what they saw on someone's Facebook page. They may not even have to admit to looking at the Facebook page if they use private browsing, which enables people to keep their Web browsing activities confidential. How, then, would a person who does not get the job prove that the rejection occured because the employer accessed social media postings?

8–3c Company-wide Social Media Networks

Many companies, including Dell, Inc., and Nikon Instruments, have formed their own internal social media networks. Software companies offer a variety of systems, including Salesforce.com's Chatter, Microsoft's Yammer, and WebEx Meetings. Posts on these internal networks, or *intranets*, are quite different from the typical posts on Facebook, LinkedIn, and Twitter. Employees use them to exchange messages about topics related to their work, such as deals that are closing, new products, production flaws, how a team is solving a problem, and the details of customer orders. Thus, the tone is businesslike.

An important advantage to using an internal system for employee communications is that the company can better protect its trade secrets. The company usually decides which employees can see particular intranet files and which employees will belong to each "social group" within the company. Generally, the company will keep the data in its system on its own secure server.

Internal social media systems also offer additional benefits. They provide real-time information about important issues, such as production glitches, along with information about products, customers, and competitors. Another major benefit is a significant reduction in e-mail. Rather than wasting fellow employees' time on mass e-mailings, workers can post messages or collaborate on presentations via the company's social network.

8–4 Online Defamation

Cyber Tort A tort committed via the Internet.

A **cyber tort** is a tort that arises from online conduct. One of the most prevalent cyber torts is online defamation. Recall that defamation is wrongfully hurting a person's reputation by communicating false statements about that person to others. Because the Internet enables individuals to communicate with large numbers of people simultaneously (via tweets, for instance), online defamation is a common problem in today's legal environment.

Example 8.14 Ross sets up several websites asserting that, among other things, California real estate developer Bradley is a scam artist with a history of serious crimes including fraud and racketeering. As proof, the websites contain links to articles about a different Bradley, a convicted criminal from Pennsylvania. When the real estate developer sues for defamation, Ross admits that the online allegations are false and were intended to "inflict lots of pain" on Bradley, with whom he is engaged in a legal dispute. A federal jury in Nevada reacts to this admission by finding Ross liable and awards Bradley millions in damages. ■

8–4a Identifying the Author of Online Defamation

An initial issue raised by online defamation is simply discovering who is committing it. In the real world, identifying the author of a defamatory remark generally is an easy matter. Suppose, though, that a business firm has discovered that defamatory statements about its policies and products are being posted in an online forum. Such forums allow anyone—customers, employees, or crackpots—to complain about a firm that they dislike while remaining anonymous.

Therefore, a threshold barrier to anyone who seeks to bring an action for online defamation is discovering the identity of the person who posted the defamatory message. An Internet service provider (ISP) can disclose personal information about its customers only when ordered to do so by a court. Consequently, businesses and individuals are increasingly bringing lawsuits against "John Does" (John Doe, Jane Doe, and the like are fictitious names used in lawsuits when the identity of a party is not known or when a party wishes to remain anonymous for privacy reasons). Then, using the authority of the courts, the plaintiffs can obtain from the ISPs the identity of the persons responsible for the defamatory messages.

Note that courts have occasionally refused to order companies to disclose the identity of their users. **Case Example 8.15** Yelp, Inc., is a California company that operates a social networking website for consumer reviews. Seven users of Yelp posted negative reviews of Hadeed Carpet Cleaning, Inc., in Alexandria, Virginia. Hadeed brought a defamation suit against the "John Doe" reviewers in a Virginia state court, claiming that because these individuals were not actual customers, their comments were false and defamatory. Yelp failed to comply with a court order to reveal the users' identities and was held in contempt.

Yelp appealed, claiming that releasing the identities would violate the defendants' First Amendment right to free speech. A state intermediate appellate court affirmed the lower court's judgment, but that decision was reversed on appeal. The Supreme Court of Virginia ruled that even though the state trial court had jurisdiction, it did not have subpoena power over Yelp, a nonresident defendant. According to the court, "Enforcement of a subpoena seeking out-of-state discovery is generally governed by the courts and the law of the state in which the witness resides or where the documents are located."[15] ■

iPhone/Alamy

Can a business that receives poor reviews on Yelp force Yelp to disclose the reviewers' identities in a lawsuit for online defamation?

8–4b Liability of Internet Service Providers

Normally, those who repeat or otherwise republish a defamatory statement are subject to liability. Thus, newspapers, magazines, and television and radio stations are subject to liability for defamatory content that they publish or broadcast, even though the content was prepared or created by others.

Applying this rule to cyberspace, however, raises an important issue: Should ISPs be regarded as publishers and therefore be held liable for defamatory messages that are posted by their users in online forums or other arenas?

General Rule The Communications Decency Act (CDA) states that "no provider or user of an interactive computer service shall be treated as the publisher or speaker of any information provided by another information content provider."[16] Thus, under the CDA, ISPs usually are treated differently from publishers in print and other media and are not liable for publishing defamatory statements that come from a third party.

The CDA's broad protection for ISPs extends beyond republication of defamatory statements. This chapter's *Business Law Analysis* feature illustrates the CDA's general rule.

Focus Question 4

What law governs whether Internet service providers are liable for online defamatory statements made by users?

Exceptions Although the courts generally have construed the CDA as providing a broad shield to protect ISPs from liability for third party content, some courts have started establishing limits to this immunity. **Case Example 8.16** Roommate.com, LLC, operated an online roommate-matching website that helps individuals find roommates based on their descriptions of themselves and their roommate preferences. Users respond to a series of online questions, choosing from answers in drop-down and select-a-box menus. Some of the questions asked users to disclose their sex, family status, and sexual orientation—which is not permitted under the federal Fair Housing Act.

15. *Yelp, Inc. v. Hadeed Carpet Cleaning, Inc.*, 289 Va. 426, 770 S.E.2d 440 (2015).
16. 47 U.S.C. Section 230.

Business Law Analysis

Immunity of ISPs under the Communications Decency Act

CyberConnect, Inc., is an Internet service provider (ISP). Emma is a CyberConnect subscriber. Market Reach, Inc., is an online advertising company.

Using sophisticated software, Market Reach directs its ads to those users most likely to be interested in a particular product. When Emma receives one of the ads, she objects to the content. Furthermore, she claims that CyberConnect should pay damages for "publishing" the ad. Is CyberConnect liable for the content of Market Reach's ad?

Analysis: The Communications Decency Act (CDA) states that "no provider . . . of an interactive computer service shall be treated as the publisher or speaker of any information provided by another information content provider." In other words, under the CDA, CyberConnect and other ISPs are not liable for the content of published statements that come from a third party, such as the statements in Market Reach's ad.

Result and Reasoning: Because CyberConnect is not regarded as a publisher under the CDA, the company is not liable for the content of Market Reach's ad (even if Emma could prove that the content was defamatory). ISPs are not liable for third party content that they have no ability to control.

When a nonprofit housing organization sued Roommate.com, the company claimed it was immune from liability under the CDA. A federal appellate court disagreed and ordered Roommate.com to pay nearly $500,000. By creating the website and the questionnaire and answer choices, Roommate.com prompted users to express discriminatory preferences and matched users based on these preferences in violation of federal law.[17]

8–5 Privacy

In recent years, Facebook, Google, and Yahoo have all been accused of violating users' privacy rights. The right to privacy has been construed to be guaranteed by the Bill of Rights and some state constitutions. To maintain a suit for the invasion of privacy, though, a person must have a reasonable expectation of privacy in the particular situation.

8–5a Reasonable Expectation of Privacy

People clearly have a reasonable expectation of privacy when they enter their personal banking or credit-card information online. They also have a reasonable expectation that online companies will follow their own privacy policies. But it is probably not reasonable to expect privacy in statements made on Twitter—or photos posted on Twitter, Flickr, or Instagram, for that matter.

The collection and use of links included in the messages of Facebook users prompted some users to file a suit against the platform for violation of privacy. Facebook confirmed that it collects the "content and other information" that users provide when they "message or communicate with others" and that it may use that information. At issue in the following case was the remedy.

17. *Fair Housing Council of San Fernando Valley v. Roommate.com, LLC,* 666 F.3d 1216 (9th Cir. 2012).

Case 8.3

Campbell v. Facebook, Inc.

United States Court of Appeals, Ninth Circuit, __ F.3d __, 2020 WL 1023350 (2020).

Facts Facebook, Inc., operates a social media platform with over two billion active users, including seven of ten adults in the United States. One function allows a user to send a message that the platform describes as private because only the sender and recipient can view the contents. Matthew Campbell, Anna St. John, and other users filed a suit in a federal district court against Facebook, alleging that the company routinely captured, read, and used links contained in the messages without the users' consent, in violation of federal privacy law. The plaintiffs claimed that Facebook used the data to facilitate targeted advertising. After four mediation sessions, the parties reached a settlement. In the agreement, Facebook promised to add a disclosure to the "Help Center" page on its platform for a year revealing that "we use tools to identify and store links shared in messages." The court concluded that the plaintiffs were not likely to prevail if the case proceeded and approved the settlement. St. John appealed, arguing that the settlement was not fair because the plaintiffs received only "worthless" relief.

Issue Was requiring Facebook to post a notice on its platform a sufficient remedy for an alleged violation of privacy?

Decision Yes. The U.S. Court of Appeals for the Ninth Circuit affirmed the decision of the lower court. Given the unlikelihood that the plaintiffs would have succeeded if they had pursued their claim, "it was not unreasonable that the settlement gave [them] something of modest value."

Reason The court did not agree with St. John that the value of the relief accorded in the settlement was "worthless." Facebook was required to post a disclosure about the collection and possible use of its users' private data on a page that would be accessed by hundreds of thousands of the platform's users within a year. The post made it less likely that the users who read it would reveal private information to Facebook while using the platform.

In agreeing to the settlement, the plaintiffs gave up little, in the court's view. Under the federal statute on which the plaintiffs based their claim, they would have had to show that Facebook's practices included an unlawful "interception" of their messages. This would have required proof that Facebook read the messages in "transit" as opposed to in "storage," an uncertain legal issue. The plaintiffs would have had to show that they had not consented to Facebook's collection and use of their data. And they would have had to successfully argue that the activity did not occur in "the ordinary course of business." These obstacles amply supported the conclusion that the plaintiffs were "ultimately likely to have lost this entire case."

Critical Thinking

- **Legal Environment** *Is a violation of an individual's right to privacy, without more, enough to sustain a legal cause, or should additional consequences be required to maintain an action? Explain.*
- **Economic** *Should Facebook pay the platform's users for Facebook's use of their private data? Discuss.*

8–5b Data Collection and Cookies

Whenever a consumer purchases items online from a retailer, the retailer collects information about the consumer. A **cookie** is an invisible file that computers, smartphones, and other such devices create to track a user's Web browsing activities. Cookies provide detailed information to marketers about an individual's behavior and preferences, which is then used to personalize online services.

Cookie A small file sent from a website and stored in a user's Web browser to track the user's Web browsing activities.

Over time, a retailer can amass considerable data about a person's shopping habits. Does collecting this information violate the person's right to privacy? Should retailers be able to pass on the data they have collected to their affiliates? Should they be able to use the information to predict what a consumer might want and then create online "coupons" customized to fit the person's buying history?

Case Example 8.17 Any device connected to the Internet is capable of transmitting a multitude of information not only about the device but also about its use. Utilizing integrated software, smart TVs allow consumers to access the Internet and on-demand services, including Hulu, Netflix, and Pandora. Apparently, for three years, Vizio, Inc., which installs such software on smart TVs, was secretly tracking what viewers were watching on approximately 16 million of these devices. This information was then sold to advertisers, allowing them to specifically target advertising to Vizio smart TVs and to any computers, tablets, or smartphones connected to the same network.

A number of purchasers of Vizio smart TVs filed a class action data privacy lawsuit against the company for, at a minimum, violating the Video Privacy Protection Act.[18] Initially, Vizio insisted that by allowing advertisers to make "better-informed decisions," its actions actually benefited consumers. Eventually, however, the company reached a settlement that dispersed $11 million among more than 500,000 Vizio smart TV owners.[19]

8–5c The Electronic Communications Privacy Act

Focus Question 5

When does the law protect a person's electronic communications from being intercepted or accessed?

The Electronic Communications Privacy Act (ECPA)[20] amended federal wiretapping law to cover electronic forms of communications. Although Congress enacted the ECPA many years before the Internet existed, it nevertheless applies to communications that take place online.

The ECPA prohibits the intentional interception of any wire, oral, or electronic communication. It also prohibits the intentional disclosure or use of the information obtained by the interception.

Exclusions Excluded from the ECPA's coverage are any electronic communications through devices that an employer provides for its employee to use "in the ordinary course of its business." Consequently, if a company provides the electronic device (cell phone, laptop, tablet) to the employee for ordinary business use, the company is not prohibited from intercepting business communications made on it.

This "business-extension exception" to the ECPA permits employers to monitor employees' electronic communications made in the ordinary course of business. It does not permit employers to monitor employees' personal communications. Another exception allows an employer to avoid liability under the act if the employees consent to having the employer monitor their electronic communications.

Stored Communications Part of the ECPA is known as the Stored Communications Act (SCA).[21] The SCA prohibits intentional and unauthorized access to *stored* electronic communications, and sets forth criminal and civil sanctions for violators. A person can violate the SCA by intentionally accessing a stored electronic communication.

The SCA also prevents "providers" of communication services (such as cell phone companies and social media networks) from divulging private communications to certain entities and individuals. **Case Example 8.18** As part of an investigation into disability fraud, the New York County District Attorney's Office sought from Facebook the data and stored communications of 381 retired police officers and firefighters. The government suspected that these individuals had faked illness after 9/11 in order to obtain disability.

Facebook challenged the warrants in court, arguing that they were unconstitutional because they were overly broad and lacked particularity. The court ruled against Facebook and ordered it to comply. It also ordered the company not to notify the users that it was

---

18. 18 U.S.C. Section 2710(a).
19. *In Re Vizio, Inc. Consumer Privacy Litigation*, 2019 WL 3818854 (C.D. Calif. 2019).
20. 18 U.S.C. Sections 2510–2521.
21. 18 U.S.C. Sections 2701–2711.

disclosing their data to government investigators. Facebook complied but appealed the decision. The reviewing court held that only the individuals, not Facebook, could challenge the warrants as violations of privacy. Thus, the government was allowed to seize all of Facebook's digital data pertaining to these users.[22]

RidingMetaphor/Alamy

Why did a court rule that stored data from Facebook accounts of certain police officers and firefighters could be accessed by a third party?

8–5d Internet Companies' Privacy Policies

The Federal Trade Commission (FTC) investigates consumer complaints of privacy violations. The FTC has forced many companies, including Google, Facebook, and Twitter, to enter into agreements consenting to give the FTC broad power to review their privacy and data practices. It can then sue companies that violate the terms of the agreements.

At this chapter has pointed out, Facebook has had to deal with a number of complaints about its privacy policy and has changed its policy several times to satisfy its critics and ward off potential government investigations. Other companies, including mobile app developers, have also changed their privacy policies to provide more information to consumers. For the most part, companies—rather than courts or legislatures—have defined the privacy rights of online users. This situation, however, appears to be changing.

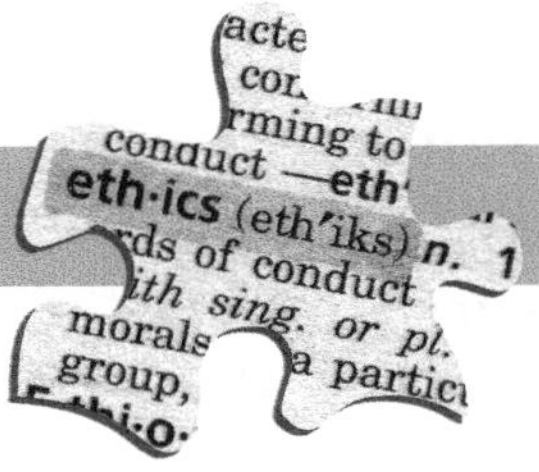

Ethical Issue

What are the privacy implications of the facial recognition industry? Using biometrics—the measurement and analysis of an individual's unique physical characteristics—facial recognition software can identify someone from a photo or video. The program is then able to compare this information with biometric details stored in a database to create a match. This technology has potential benefits, particularly in the arenas of national security and artificial intelligence. It also has one significant potential drawback: the loss of privacy. The idea of closed-circuit cameras scanning city streets or artificial intelligence applications scouring social media to pick out faces fills many with dread. "The right to participate in society anonymously is something we cannot lose," says one privacy advocate.

Nationwide, more than sixty university administrations have promised not to link facial recognition technology with their campus security cameras. Promoters of the Coachella Arts and Music Festival, an annual California event, and other large-scale events have made similar vows.

Several states already have comparable protections in place. Legislation passed many years ago in Illinois, for example, requires companies to obtain written permission before collecting a person's facial scan, fingerprints, or other biometrics.[23] Facebook ran afoul of this law with its Tag Suggestions photo-labeling service, which uses facial recognition software to connect faces with names on its social media platforms. The company paid $550 million to settle a class action lawsuit filed by Illinois residents who claimed that Tag Suggestions violated their right to privacy.[24]

---

22. *In re 381 Search Warrants Directed to Facebook, Inc.*, 29 N.Y.3d 231, 78 N.E.3d 141, 55 N.Y.S.3d 696 (2017).
23. The Illinois Biometric Information Privacy Act, 740 ILCS 14.
24. *Patel v. Facebook, Inc.*, 932 F.3d 1264 (9th Cir. 2019).

Practice and Review

While he was in high school, Joel Gibb downloaded numerous songs to his smartphone from an unlicensed file-sharing service. He used portions of the copyrighted songs when he recorded his own band and posted videos on YouTube and Facebook. He also used BitTorrent to download several movies from the Internet. Now Gibb has applied to Boston University. The admissions office has requested access to his Facebook password, and he has complied. Using the information presented in the chapter, answer the following questions.

1. What laws, if any, did Gibb violate by downloading music and videos from the Internet?
2. Was Gibb's use of portions of copyrighted songs in his own music illegal? Explain.
3. Can individuals legally post copyrighted content on their Facebook pages? Why or why not?
4. Did Boston University violate any laws when it asked Joel to provide his Facebook password? Explain.

Debate This

Internet service providers should be subject to the same defamation laws as newspapers, magazines, and television and radio stations.

Key Terms

cloud computing 200
cookie 207
cybersquatting 194
cyber tort 204
distributed network 200
domain name 194
goodwill 194
Internet service provider (ISP) 194
peer-to-peer (P2P) networking 200
social media 201
spam 193
typosquatting 195

Chapter Summary: Internet Law, Social Media, and Privacy

Internet Law

1. **Spam**—Unsolicited junk e-mail accounts for about three-quarters of all e-mails. Laws to combat spam have been enacted, but the flow of spam continues.
   a. The Controlling the Assault of Non-Solicited Pornography and Marketing (CAN-SPAM) Act prohibits false and deceptive e-mails originating in the United States.
   b. The U.S. Safe Web Act allows U.S. authorities to cooperate and share information with foreign agencies in investigating and prosecuting those involved in spamming, spyware, and various Internet frauds and deceptions. The act includes a "safe harbor" for Internet service providers.
2. **Domain names**—Trademark owners often use their mark as part of a domain name (Internet address). The Internet Corporation for Assigned Names and Numbers (ICANN) oversees the distribution of domain names. ICANN has expanded the available domain names to include new generic top-level domain names (gTLDs).
3. **Cybersquatting**—Registering a domain name that is the same as, or confusingly similar to, the trademark of another and then offering to sell the domain name back to the trademark owner is known as cybersquatting. Anticybersquatting legislation makes this practice illegal if the one registering, trafficking in, or using the domain name has a "bad faith intent" to profit from that mark.
4. **Meta tags**—Search engines compile their results by looking through a website's *meta tags*, or key words. Using another's trademark in a meta tag without the owner's permission normally constitutes trademark infringement.

	5. Trademark dilution—When a trademark is used online, without authorization, in a way that diminishes the distinctive quality of the mark, it constitutes trademark dilution. Unlike infringement actions, trademark dilution claims do not require proof that consumers are likely to be confused by a connection between the unauthorized use and the mark. **6. Licensing**—Many companies choose to permit others to use their trademarks and other intellectual property online through licensing. The purchase of software generally involves a license agreement. These agreements frequently include restrictions that prohibit licensees from sharing the file and using it to create similar software applications.
Copyrights in Digital Information	**1. Copyrighted works online**—Much of the material on the Internet (including software and database information) is copyrighted. In order for that material to be transferred online, it must be "copied." Generally, whenever a party downloads software or music without authorization, a copyright is infringed. **2. Digital Millennium Copyright Act**—The Digital Millennium Copyright Act (DMCA) protects copyrights online and establishes civil and criminal penalties for anyone who bypasses encryption software or other technologies. The DMCA provides exceptions for certain educational and nonprofit uses. It also limits the liability of Internet service providers for infringement unless the ISP is aware of the user's infringement and fails to take action. **3. File-sharing**—When file-sharing is used to download others' stored music files or illegally copy movies, copyright issues arise. Individuals who download music or movies in violation of copyright laws are liable for infringement. Companies that distribute file-sharing software or provide such services have been held liable for the copyright infringement of their users if the software or technology involved promoted copyright infringement.
Social Media	**1. Legal issues**—The emergence of Facebook and other social networking sites has had a number of effects on the legal process. Social media posts have had an impact on litigation and settlement agreements. Law enforcement and administrative agencies now routinely use social media to detect illegal activities and conduct investigations, as do many businesses. **2. Social media passwords**—Private employers and schools have sometimes looked at an individual's Facebook or other social media account to see if it included controversial postings. A number of states have enacted legislation that protects individuals from having to divulge their social media passwords. Such laws may not be completely effective in preventing employers from rejecting applicants or terminating workers based on their social media postings. **3. Company-wide social media networks**—Many companies today form their own internal social media networks through which employees can exchange messages about topics related to their work.
Online Defamation	Federal and state statutes apply to certain forms of cyber torts, or torts that occur in cyberspace, such as online defamation. Under the federal Communications Decency Act (CDA), Internet service providers generally are not liable for defamatory messages posted by their subscribers.
Privacy	**1. Expectation of privacy**—Numerous Internet companies have been accused of violating users' privacy rights. To sue for invasion of privacy, though, a person must have a reasonable expectation of privacy in the particular situation. It is often difficult to determine how much privacy can reasonably be expected on the Internet. **2. Data collection and cookies**—Whenever a consumer purchases items online from a retailer, the retailer collects information about the consumer through "cookies." Consequently, retailers have gathered large amounts of data about individuals' shopping habits. It is not always clear whether collecting such information violates a person's right to privacy. **3. The Electronic Communications Privacy Act (ECPA)**—The ECPA prohibits the intentional interception or disclosure of any wire, oral, or electronic communication. **a.** The ECPA includes a "business-extension exception" that permits employers to monitor employees' electronic communications made in the ordinary course of business (but not their personal communications). **b.** The Stored Communications Act (SCA) is part of the ECPA and prohibits intentional unauthorized access to stored electronic communications (such as backup data stored by an employer). **4. Internet companies' privacy policies**—Many companies establish Internet privacy policies, which typically inform users what types of data they are gathering and for what purposes it will be used.

Issue Spotters

1. Karl self-publishes a cookbook titled *Hole Foods*, in which he sets out recipes for donuts, Bundt cakes, tortellini, and other foods with holes. To publicize the book, Karl designs the website holefoods.com. Karl appropriates the key words of other cooking and cookbook sites with more frequent hits so that holefoods.com will appear in the same search engine results as the more popular sites. Has Karl done anything wrong? Explain. (See *Internet Law*.)
2. Eagle Corporation began marketing software in 2010 under the mark "Eagle." In 2019, Eagle.com, Inc., a different company selling different products, begins to use *eagle* as part of its URL and registers it as a domain name. Can Eagle Corporation stop this use of *eagle*? If so, what must the company show? (See *Internet Law*.)

—Check your answers to the *Issue Spotters* against the answers provided in Appendix D.

Business Scenarios and Case Problems

8–1. Privacy. See You, Inc., is an online social network. SeeYou's members develop personalized profiles to share information—photos, videos, stories, activity updates, and other items—with other members. Members post the information that they want to share and decide with whom they want to share it. SeeYou launched a program to allow members to share with others what they do elsewhere online. For example, if a member rents a movie through Netflix, SeeYou will broadcast that information to everyone in the member's online network. How can SeeYou avoid complaints that this program violates its members' privacy? (See *Privacy*.)

8–2. Copyrights in Digital Information. When she was in college, Jammie Thomas-Rasset wrote a case study on Napster, an online peer-to-peer (P2P) file-sharing network, and knew that it had been shut down because it was illegal. Later, Capitol Records, Inc., which owns the copyrights to a large number of music recordings, discovered that "tereastarr"—a user name associated with Thomas-Rasset's Internet protocol address—had made twenty-four songs available for distribution on KaZaA, another P2P network. Capitol notified Thomas-Rasset that she had been identified as engaging in the unauthorized trading of music. She replaced the hard drive on her computer with a new drive that did not contain the songs in dispute. Is Thomas-Rasset liable for copyright infringement? Explain. [*Capitol Records, Inc. v. Thomas-Rasset*, 692 F.3d 899 (8th Cir. 2012)] (See *Copyrights in Digital Information*.)

8–3. Privacy. Using special software, South Dakota law enforcement officers found a person who appeared to possess child pornography at a specific Internet protocol address. The officers subpoenaed Midcontinent Communications, the service that assigned the address, for the personal information of its subscriber. With this information, the officers obtained a search warrant for the residence of John Rolfe, where they found a laptop that contained child pornography. Rolfe argued that the subpoenas violated his "expectation of privacy." Did Rolfe have a privacy interest in the information obtained by the subpoenas issued to Midcontinent? Discuss. [*State of South Dakota v. Rolfe*, 825 N.W.2d 901 (S.Dak. 2013)] (See *Privacy*.)

8–4. File-Sharing. Dartmouth College professor M. Eric Johnson, in collaboration with Tiversa, Inc., a company that monitors peer-to-peer networks to provide security services, wrote an article titled "Data Hemorrhages in the Health-Care Sector." In preparing the article, Johnson and Tiversa searched the networks for data that could be used to commit medical or financial identity theft. They found a document that contained the Social Security numbers, insurance information, and treatment codes for patients of LabMD, Inc. Tiversa notified LabMD of the find in order to solicit its business. Instead of hiring Tiversa, however, LabMD filed a suit in a federal district court against the company, alleging trespass, conversion, and violations of federal statutes. What do these facts indicate about the security of private information? Explain. How should the court rule? [*LabMD, Inc. v. Tiversa, Inc.*, 2013 WL 425983 (11th Cir. 2013)] (See *Copyrights in Digital Information*.)

8–5. Business Case Problem with Sample Answer—Social Media. Mohammad Omar Aly Hassan and nine others were indicted in a federal district court on charges of conspiring to advance violent jihad (holy war against enemies of Islam) and other offenses related to terrorism. The evidence at Hassan's trial included postings he made on Facebook concerning his adherence to violent jihadist ideology. Convicted, Hassan appealed, contending that the Facebook items had not been properly authenticated (established as his own comments). How might the government show the connection between postings on Facebook and those who post them? Discuss. [*United States v. Hassan*, 742 F.3d 104 (4th Cir. 2014)] (See *Social Media*.)

—For a sample answer to Problem 8–5, go to Appendix E.

8–6. Social Media. Kenneth Wheeler was angry at certain police officers in Grand Junction, Colorado, because of a driving-under-the-influence arrest that he viewed as unjust. While in Italy, Wheeler posted a statement to his Facebook page urging his "religious followers" to "kill cops, drown them in the blood of their children, hunt them down and kill their entire bloodlines" and provided names. Later, Wheeler added a post to "commit a massacre in the Stepping Stones Preschool and day care, just walk in and kill everybody." Could a reasonable person conclude that Wheeler's posts were true threats? How might law enforcement officers use Wheeler's posts? Explain. [*United States v. Wheeler*, 776 F.3d 736 (10th Cir. 2015)] (See *Social Media*.)

8–7. Social Media. Irvin Smith was charged in a Georgia state court with burglary and theft. Before the trial, during the selection of the jury, the state prosecutor asked the prospective jurors whether they knew Smith. No one responded affirmatively. Jurors were chosen and sworn in, without objection. After the trial, during deliberations, the jurors indicated to the court that they were deadlocked. The court charged them to try again. Meanwhile, the prosecutor learned that "Juror 4" appeared as a friend on the defendant's Facebook page and filed a motion to dismiss her. The court replaced Juror 4 with an alternate. Was this an appropriate action, or was it an "abuse of discretion"? Should the court have admitted evidence that Facebook friends do not always actually know each other? Discuss. [*Smith v. State of Georgia*, 335 Ga.App. 497, 782 S.E.2d 305 (2016)] (See *Social Media*.)

8–8. Internet Law. Jason Smathers, an employee of America Online (AOL), misappropriated an AOL customer list with 92 million screen names. He sold the list for $28,000 to Sean Dunaway, who sold it to Braden Bournival. Bournival used it to send AOL customers more than 3 billion unsolicited, deceptive e-mail ads. AOL estimated the cost of processing the ads to be at least $300,000. Convicted of conspiring to relay deceptive e-mail in violation of federal law, Smathers was ordered to pay AOL restitution of $84,000 (treble the amount for which he had sold the AOL customer list). Smathers appealed, seeking to reduce the amount. He cited a judgment in a civil suit for a different offense against Bournival and others for which AOL had collected $95,000. Smathers also argued that his obligation should be reduced by restitution payments made by Dunaway. Which federal law did Smathers violate? Should the amount of his restitution be reduced? Explain. [*United States v. Smathers*, 879 F.3d 453 (2d. Cir. 2018)] (See *Internet Law*.)

8–9. A Question of Ethics—The IDDR Approach and Social Media. One August morning, around 6:30 A.M., a fire occurred at Ray and Christine Nixon's home in West Monroe, Louisiana. The Nixons told Detective Gary Gilley of the Ouachita Parish Sheriff's Department that they believed the fire was deliberately set by Matthew Alexander, a former employee of Ray's company. Ray gave Alexander's phone number to Gilley, who contacted the number's service provider, Verizon Wireless Services, L.L.C. Gilley said that he was investigating a house fire that had been started with the victims inside the dwelling, and wanted to know where the number's subscriber had been that day. He did not present a warrant, but he did certify that Verizon's response would be considered an "emergency disclosure." [*Alexander v. Verizon Wireless Services, L.L.C.*, 875 F.3d 243 (5th Cir. 2017)] (See *Social Media*.)

1. Using the *Inquiry* and *Discussion* steps in the IDDR approach, identify the ethical dilemma that Verizon faced in this situation and actions that the company might have taken to resolve that issue.
2. Suppose that Verizon gave Gilley the requested information, and that later Alexander filed a suit against the provider, alleging a violation of the Stored Communications Act. Could Verizon successfully plead "good faith" in its defense?

Critical Thinking and Writing Assignments

8–10. Time-Limited Group Assignment—File-Sharing. James, Chang, and Braden are roommates. They are music fans and frequently listen to the same artists and songs. They regularly exchange MP3 music files that contain songs from their favorite artists. (See *Copyrights in Digital Information*.)

1. One group of students will decide whether the fact that the roommates are transferring files among themselves for no monetary benefit protects them from being subject to copyright law.
2. The second group will consider whether it would be legal for each roommate to buy music on CD and then, after downloading a copy on to their hard drive, give the CD to the other roommates to do the same. Does this violate copyright law? Is it the same as file-sharing digital music? Explain.
3. A third group will consider streaming music services. If one roommate subscribes to a streaming service and the other roommates use the service for free, would this violate copyright law? Why or why not?

13_Phunkod/Shutterstock.com

9 Criminal Law and Cyber Crime

Focus Questions

The six Focus Questions below are designed to help improve your understanding. After reading this chapter, you should be able to answer the following questions:

1. How does the burden of proof differ in criminal versus civil cases?
2. What two elements normally must exist before a person can be held liable for a crime?
3. What are five broad categories of crimes? What is white-collar crime?
4. What defenses can be raised to avoid liability for criminal acts?
5. What constitutional safeguards exist to protect persons accused of crimes?
6. How has the Internet expanded opportunities for identity theft?

> "The crime problem is getting really serious. The other day, the Statue of Liberty had both hands up."
>
> **Jay Leno**
> 1950–present
> (American comedian and former television host)

The "crime problem" is of concern to all Americans, as suggested in the chapter-opening quotation. Not surprisingly, laws dealing with crime are an important part of the legal environment of business.

Society imposes a variety of sanctions to protect businesses from harm so that they can compete and flourish. These sanctions include damages for tortious conduct, damages for breach of contract, and various equitable remedies. Additional sanctions are imposed under criminal law.

Many statutes regulating business provide for criminal as well as civil sanctions. For instance, federal statutes that protect the environment often include criminal sanctions. Businesses that violate environmental laws can be criminally prosecuted. Walmart Inc., for example, was charged with illegally handling and disposing of hazardous materials (such as pesticides) at its retail stores across the nation. Walmart ultimately pleaded guilty to six counts of violating the Clean Water Act and was sentenced to pay over $81 million in fines as a result.

9-1 Civil Law and Criminal Law

Civil law pertains to the duties that exist between persons or between persons and their governments. Criminal law, in contrast, has to do with crime. A **crime** can be defined as a wrong against society proclaimed in a statute and, if committed, punishable by society through fines and/or imprisonment—and, in some cases, death.

Because crimes are *offenses against society* as a whole, they are prosecuted by a public official, such as a district attorney (D.A.) or an attorney general (A.G.), not by the crime victims. Once a crime has been reported, the D.A.'s office decides whether to file criminal charges and to what extent to pursue the prosecution or carry out additional investigation.

Crime A wrong against society proclaimed in a statute and, if committed, punishable by society through fines, imprisonment, or death.

9–1a Key Differences Between Civil Law and Criminal Law

Because the state has extensive resources at its disposal when prosecuting criminal cases, and because the sanctions can be so severe, there are numerous procedural safeguards to protect the rights of defendants. We look here at one of these safeguards—the higher burden of proof that applies in a criminal case—and at the sanctions imposed for criminal acts. Exhibit 9–1 summarizes these and other key differences between civil law and criminal law.

Burden of Proof In a civil case, the plaintiff usually must meet the *preponderance of the evidence* standard. That is, the plaintiff must convince the court that, based on the evidence presented by both parties, it is more likely than not that the plaintiff's allegation is true.

In a criminal case, in contrast, the state must prove its case **beyond a reasonable doubt.** If the jury views the evidence in the case as reasonably permitting either a guilty or a not guilty verdict, then the jury's verdict must be *not* guilty. In other words, the prosecutor must prove beyond a reasonable doubt that the defendant has committed every essential element of the alleged offense. If the jurors are not convinced of the defendant's guilt beyond a reasonable doubt, they must find the defendant not guilty.

Beyond a Reasonable Doubt The standard of proof used in criminal cases.

Focus Question 1

How does the burden of proof differ in criminal versus civil cases?

Note also that in a criminal case, the jury's verdict normally must be unanimous—agreed to by all members of the jury—to convict the defendant.[1] In a civil trial by jury, in contrast, typically only three-fourths of the jurors need to agree.

Criminal Sanctions The sanctions imposed on criminal wrongdoers are also harsher than those applied in civil cases. Remember that the purpose of tort law is to allow persons harmed by the wrongful acts of others to obtain compensation from the wrongdoer rather than to punish the wrongdoer.

In contrast, criminal sanctions are designed to punish those who commit crimes and to deter others from committing similar acts in the future. Criminal sanctions include fines as well as the much harsher penalty of the loss of liberty by incarceration in a jail or prison. Most criminal sanctions also involve probation and sometimes require restitution, community service, or an educational or treatment program. The harshest criminal sanction is, of course, the death penalty.

1. Note that two states, Louisiana and Oregon, used to allow jury verdicts that were not unanimous.

Exhibit 9-1 Key Differences between Civil Law and Criminal Law

ISSUE	CIVIL LAW	CRIMINAL LAW
Party who brings suit	The person who suffered harm.	The state.
Wrongful act	Causing harm to a person or to a person's property.	Violating a statute that prohibits some type of activity.
Burden of proof	Preponderance of the evidence.	Beyond a reasonable doubt.
Verdict	Three-fourths majority (typically).	Unanimous.
Remedy	Damages to compensate for the harm or a decree to achieve an equitable result.	Punishment (fine, imprisonment, or death).

9–1b Civil Liability for Criminal Acts

Some torts, such as assault and battery, provide a basis for a criminal prosecution as well as a tort action. **Example 9.1** Carlos is walking down the street, minding his own business, when suddenly a person attacks him. In the ensuing struggle, the attacker stabs Carlos several times, seriously injuring him. A police officer restrains and arrests the wrongdoer. In this situation, the attacker may be subject both to criminal prosecution by the state and to a tort lawsuit brought by Carlos. ■ Exhibit 9–2 illustrates how the same act can result in both a tort action and a criminal action against the wrongdoer.

9–1c Classification of Crimes

Felony A serious crime—such as arson, murder, rape, or robbery—that carries the most severe sanctions, ranging from more than one year in a state or federal prison to the death penalty.

Depending on their degree of seriousness, crimes are classified as felonies or misdemeanors. A **felony** is a serious crime punishable by death or by imprisonment for more than one year.[2] Many states also define several degrees of felony offenses and vary the punishment according to the degree.[3] For instance, most jurisdictions punish a burglary that involves forced entry into a home at night more harshly than a burglary that involves breaking into a nonresidential building during the day.

2. Federal law and most state laws use this definition, but there is some variation among states as to the length of imprisonment associated with a felony conviction.
3. Although the American Law Institute issued the Model Penal Code in 1962, it is not a uniform code, and each state has developed its own set of laws governing criminal acts. Thus, types of crimes and prescribed punishments may differ from one jurisdiction to another.

Exhibit 9-2 Tort Lawsuit and Criminal Prosecution for the Same Act

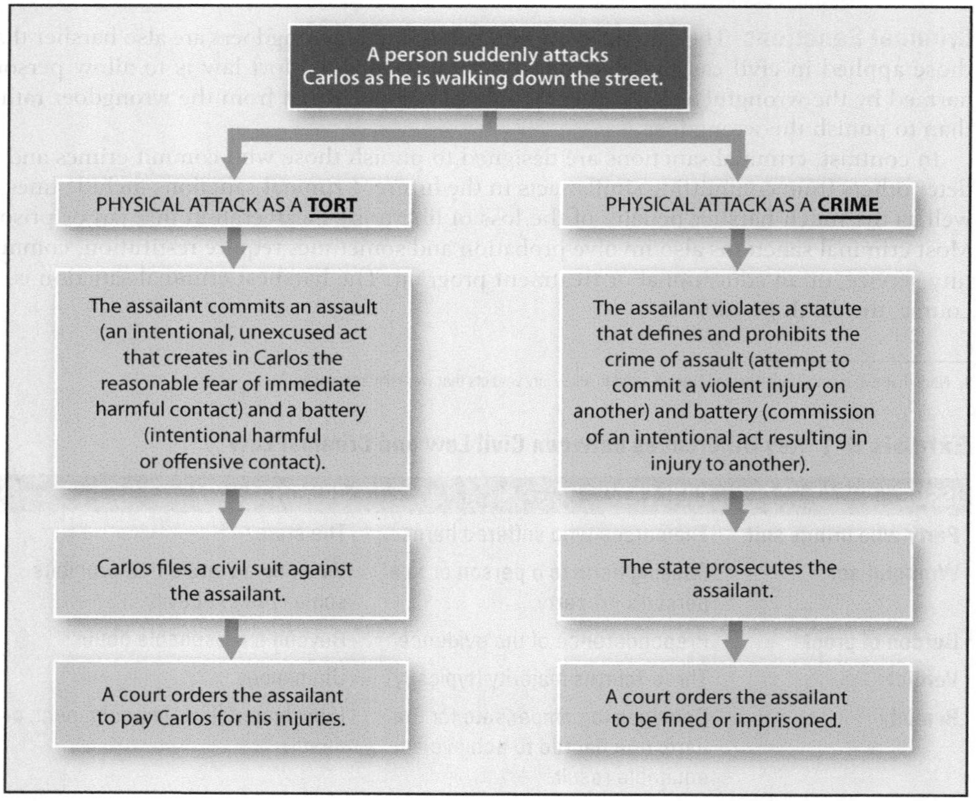

A **misdemeanor** is a less serious crime, punishable by a fine or by confinement in jail for up to a year. A **petty offense** is a minor violation, such as jaywalking or violating a building code, considered to be a subset of misdemeanors. Even for petty offenses, however, a guilty party can be put in jail for a few days, fined, or both, depending on state or local law. Whether a crime is a felony or a misdemeanor can determine in which court the case is tried and, in some states, whether the defendant has a right to a jury trial.

Misdemeanor A lesser crime than a felony, punishable by a fine or incarceration in jail for up to one year.

Petty Offense The least serious kind of criminal offense, such as a traffic or building-code violation.

9–2 Criminal Liability

Two elements normally must exist simultaneously for a person to be convicted of a crime:

1. The performance of a prohibited act (*actus reus*).
2. A specified state of mind or intent on the part of the actor (*mens rea*).

Focus Question 2

What two elements normally must exist before a person can be held liable for a crime?

9–2a The Criminal Act

Every criminal statute prohibits certain behavior. Most crimes require an act of *commission*. That is, a person must *do* something in order to be accused of a crime. In criminal law, a prohibited act is referred to as the ***actus reus***,[4] or guilty act. In some instances, an act of *omission* can be a crime, but only when a person has a legal duty to perform the omitted act, such as filing a tax return.

Actus Reus A guilty (prohibited) act. It is one of the two essential elements required to establish criminal liability.

The *guilty act* requirement is based on one of the premises of criminal law—that a person is punished for harm done to society. For a crime to exist, the guilty act must cause some harm to a person or to property. Thinking about killing someone or about stealing a car may be wrong, but the thoughts do no harm until they are translated into action. Of course, someone can be punished for *attempting* murder or robbery, but normally only if that person took substantial steps toward the criminal objective. Additionally, the person must have specifically intended to commit the crime to be convicted of an attempt. (Is a popular form of online currency causing so much harm to society that its use should be considered a criminal act? See this chapter's *Adapting the Law to the Online Environment* feature for a discussion.)

4. Pronounced *ak*-tuhs *ray*-uhs.

Should Bitcoin Be Illegal?

Bitcoin is a cryptocurrency, meaning that it only exists as a digital asset on the Internet. No central bank or government is involved with Bitcoin. Instead, a decentralized network of computers monitors all transactions, and the open market decides the value of each bitcoin. The cryptocurrency can be easily transferred by Internet users through the use of apps or other programs, sometimes called "wallets."

The Dark Web

The U.S. Congress, at the urging of many finance and law enforcement experts, has considered making Bitcoin illegal. The problem is that cryptocurrencies are tailor-made for criminal activity. Anyone can use Bitcoin without providing a name or identity, and it is very difficult to trace online purchases made using this form of trade.

Consequently, Bitcoin is the currency of choice on the *dark web*, a part of the Internet that can only be accessed through special methods designed to obscure the identity of providers and users. An estimated

(Continues)

(Continued)

$200 million in Bitcoin is spent on dark web markets each month. Law enforcement officials believe that the dark web is an important source of distribution for synthetic opioids, which cause thousands of deaths in the United States each year. In Park City, Utah, two thirteen-year-old boys overdosed on a synthetic opioid known as Pinky that they had purchased using Bitcoin on the dark web.

Stateless Currency

There is little evidence that a federal law banning Bitcoin, if passed, would have much effect. Buyers and sellers using Bitcoin are almost always able to remain anonymous. Furthermore, it can be difficult for law enforcement to determine the source not only of cryptocurrency-related crime but of any criminal activity that takes place online. As one expert puts it, "You can't prevent people from holding ones and zeros on a device in their pocket."

Critical Thinking

Despite Bitcoin's oversized presence on the dark web, only about 1 percent of all transactions using the cryptocurrency involve an illegal exchange of goods. How does this fact impact arguments in favor of banning Bitcoin?

9–2b State of Mind

Mens Rea A wrongful mental state ("guilty mind"), or intent. It is one of the two essential elements required to establish criminal liability.

A wrongful mental state ***(mens rea)***[5] is generally required to establish criminal liability. The required mental state, or intent, is indicated in the applicable statute or law. Theft, for example, involves the guilty act of taking another person's property. The guilty mental state involves both the awareness that the property belongs to another and the intent to deprive the owner of it. A court can also find that the required mental state is present when a defendant's acts are reckless or criminally negligent.

A criminal conspiracy exists when two or more people agree to commit an unlawful act, and then take some action toward its completion. The required intent involves purposely agreeing with others and intending to commit the underlying crime. In the following case, the issue was whether the evidence was sufficient to prove that the defendant had "knowingly and voluntarily" participated in a conspiracy to commit health-care fraud.

5. Pronounced *mehns ray*-uh.

Case 9.1

United States v. Crabtree

United States Court of Appeals, Eleventh Circuit, 878 F.3d 1274 (2018).

Facts Health Care Solutions Network, Inc. (HCSN), operated mental health centers to provide psychiatric therapy in a partial hospitalization program—a bridge between restrictive inpatient care and routine outpatient care. HCSN organized its business around procuring, retaining, and readmitting patients to maximize billing potential, without respect to their health needs. It ensured that patient files complied with strict Medicare requirements by editing intake information, fabricating treatment plans, and falsifying therapy and treatment notes. The scheme spanned seven years, and amounted to more than $63 million in fraudulent claims.

At one of HCSN's facilities, Doris Crabtree was responsible for patient therapy notes. The notes were systematically altered and falsified to support Medicare claims. Convicted in a federal district court of conspiracy to commit health-care fraud, Crabtree appealed to the U.S. Court of Appeals for the Eleventh Circuit. She argued that she had only been negligent and careless.

Issue Was the evidence sufficient to support Crabtree's conviction for conspiring to commit health-care fraud?

Decision Yes. The U.S. Court of Appeals for the Eleventh Circuit affirmed Crabtree's conviction. "A reasonable jury [could] conclude that Crabtree . . . had knowledge of the conspiracy at HCSN" and that she "voluntarily joined the conspiracy, given the substantial evidence of [her] role in furthering the fraud."

Reason A conspiracy, and a defendant's participation in it, can be proved by inferences drawn from the actions of the defendant and others, and from the circumstantial evidence of a scheme. In this case, the government provided "considerable" evidence that Crabtree was aware of the conspiracy. HCSN employees testified that, for example, she complied with their requests to doctor patient therapy notes to meet Medicare requirements. In conversation, Crabtree expressed awareness that some of the patients suffered from Alzheimer's, dementia, autism, and other conditions that were unsuitable for treatment at HCSN.

The government also proffered "substantial" evidence that she voluntarily joined the conspiracy. For example, Crabtree complied with requests to alter and fabricate notes for billing and Medicare purposes. In the notes, she would misrepresent the therapy that patients received. Thus, a patient's note might indicate full participation in a therapy session when, in fact, the patient was absent.

Critical Thinking

- **Legal Environment** *Could Crabtree have successfully avoided her conviction by arguing that her only "crime" was "naively trusting her co-workers"? Why or why not?*
- **Ethical** *It seems reasonable to assume that one of the purposes of any business is to "maximize billing potential." When does conduct to accomplish that purpose become unethical?*

Recklessness Defendants are *criminally reckless* if they consciously disregard a substantial and unjustifiable risk. **Example 9.2** A claustrophobic patient at the Vanderbilt University Medical Center in Nashville, Tennessee, was about to undergo a full body scan, which requires lying inside a large tube-like machine for about thirty minutes. A nurse, meaning to inject the patient with the anti-anxiety drug Versed, mistakenly injected her with vecuronium, a powerful narcotic used to keep patients from moving during surgery.

The mistake occurred, apparently, because both drugs start with "VE." After the patient died, state law enforcement officials charged the nurse with reckless homicide. When a medical professional does not read the label of a drug she is about to inject into a patient, she has arguably created a substantial and unjustifiable risk of severe harm or death. ■

Criminal Negligence *Criminal negligence* occurs when the defendant takes an unjustified, substantial, and foreseeable risk that results in harm. A defendant can be negligent even if the defendant was not actually aware of the risk but *should have been aware* of it.[6]

A homicide is classified as *involuntary manslaughter* when it results from an act of criminal negligence and there is no intent to kill. **Example 9.3** Demolition contractor Griffith Campbell was convicted of involuntary manslaughter after he caused a brick wall to collapse onto a Salvation Army store, leading to the deaths of six people in the thrift shop. The wall was unstable when it fell because Campbell had removed support beams and joists to sell for salvage. Furthermore, he had negligently conducted the demolition during business hours. ■

Strict Liability and Overcriminalization An increasing number of laws and regulations have imposed criminal sanctions for strict liability crimes—that is, offenses that do not require a wrongful mental state, or malice, to establish criminal liability. Critics say that such laws lead to overcriminalization.

Federal Crimes. The federal criminal code now lists more than four thousand criminal offenses, many of which do not require a specific mental state. In addition, several hundred thousand federal rules can be enforced through criminal sanctions, and many of these rules do not require intent. See this chapter's *Managerial Strategy* feature for a discussion of how these laws and rules affect American businesspersons.

Strict liability crimes are particularly common in environmental laws, laws aimed at combatting illegal drugs, and other laws affecting public health, safety, and welfare. **Case Example 9.4** Paul Kenner was a commercial cattle rancher in Nebraska. Due to a faulty fence, three hundred of Kenner's cattle wandered onto a national wildlife refuge, where they grazed for ten days. A Kenner ranch hand also drove an all-terrain vehicle onto the wildlife refuge, which is

6. Model Penal Code Section 2.02(2)(d).

prohibited by federal regulations. Kenner was convicted of four separate crimes involving failing to comply with the National Wildlife Refuge System.[7]

State Crimes. Many states have also enacted laws that punish behavior as criminal without the need to show criminal intent. **Example 9.5** In several states, a vendor who sells alcohol to someone under the age of twenty-one has committed a crime. Under these laws, vendors can be convicted of the crime regardless of their intent or their knowledge of the customer's actual age.

9–2c Corporate Criminal Liability

A *corporation* is a legal entity created under the laws of a state. At one time, it was thought that a corporation could not incur criminal liability because, although a corporation is a legal person, it can act only through its agents (corporate directors, officers, and employees). Therefore, the corporate entity itself could not "intend" to commit a crime. Over time, this view has changed. Obviously, corporations cannot be imprisoned, but they can be fined or denied certain legal privileges (such as necessary licenses).

7. *United States v. Kenner*, 238 F.Supp.3d 1157 (D.Neb. 2017).

The Criminalization of American Business

What do Bank of America, Citigroup, JPMorgan Chase, and Goldman Sachs have in common? All paid hefty fines for purportedly misleading investors about mortgage-backed securities. In fact, these companies paid the government a total of $50 billion in fines. The payments were made in lieu of criminal prosecutions.

Today, several hundred thousand federal rules that apply to businesses carry some form of criminal penalty. That is in addition to more than four thousand federal laws, many of which carry criminal sanctions for their violation. Each year, about 150 corporations either are convicted or plead guilty to violating federal statutes or rules.

Criminal Convictions

The first successful criminal conviction in a federal court against a company—the New York Central and Hudson River Railroad—was upheld by the Supreme Court in 1909 (the violation: cutting prices).[a] Many other successful convictions followed.

One landmark case developed the *aggregation test*, now called the Doctrine of Collective Knowledge.[b] This test aggregates the omissions and acts of two or more persons in a corporation, thereby constructing an *actus reus* and a *mens rea* out of the conduct and knowledge of several individuals.

Not all government attempts at applying criminal law to corporations survive. Courts have sometimes found insufficient evidence to show that a company acted with specific intent to commit a crime.[c] Often, however, companies choose to reach settlement agreements with the government rather than fight criminal indictments.

Many Pay Substantial Fines in Lieu of Prosecution

Under certain circumstances, corporations will reach so-called nonprosecution agreements with the government. These agreements typically involve multimillion- or multibillion-dollar fines. This number does not include fines paid to the Environmental Protection Agency or to the Fish and Wildlife Service.

According to law professors Margaret Lemos and Max Minzner, "Public enforcers often seek large monetary awards for self-interested reasons divorced from the public interest and deterrents. The incentives are strongest when enforcement agencies are permitted to retain all or some of the proceeds of enforcement."[d]

Business Questions

1. *Why might a corporation's managers agree to pay a large fine rather than to be indicted and proceed to trial?*

2. *How do managers determine the optimal amount of legal research to undertake to prevent their companies from violating the many thousands of federal regulations?*

a. *New York Central and Hudson River Railroad v. United States*, 212 U.S. 481, 29 S.Ct. 304, 53 L.Ed. 613 (1909).

b. *United States v. Bank of New England*, 821 F.2d 844 (1st Cir. 1987).

c. See, for example, *McGee v. Sentinel Offender Services, LLC*, 719 F.3d 1236 (11th Cir. 2013); *Golden v. FNF Servicing, Inc.*, 2015 WL 5302703 (M.D.Ga. 2015); and *United States ex rel. Salters v. American Family Care, Inc.*, 262 F.Supp.3d 1266 (N.D.Ala. 2017).

d. Margaret Lemos and Max Minzner, "For-Profit Public Enforcement," *Harvard Law Review 127*, 17 Jan. 2014.

Liability of the Corporate Entity Today, corporations are normally liable for the crimes committed by their agents and employees within the course and scope of their employment.[8] For liability to be imposed, the prosecutor typically must show that the corporation could have prevented the act or that a supervisor within the corporation authorized or had knowledge of the act. In addition, corporations can be criminally liable for failing to perform specific duties imposed by law (such as duties under environmental laws or securities laws).

Spotlight Case Example 9.6 A prostitution ring, the Gold Club, was operating out of motels in West Virginia. A motel manager, who was also an officer in the corporation that owned the motels, gave discounted rates to Gold Club prostitutes, and they paid him in cash. The corporation received a portion of the funds generated by the Gold Club's illegal operations. At trial, the jury found that the corporation was criminally liable because a supervisor within the corporation—the motel manager—had knowledge of the prostitution ring and profited from it, and the corporation allowed it to continue.[9]

Liability of Corporate Officers and Directors Corporate directors and officers are personally liable for the crimes they commit, regardless of whether the crimes were committed for their personal benefit or on the corporation's behalf. Additionally, corporate directors and officers may be held liable for the actions of employees under their supervision. Under the *responsible corporate officer doctrine*, a court may impose criminal liability on corporate officers regardless of whether they participated in, directed, or even knew about a given criminal violation.[10]

Case Example 9.7 Austin DeCoster owned and controlled Quality Egg, LLC, an egg-production and processing company with facilities across Iowa. His son, Peter DeCoster, was the chief operating officer. Due to unsanitary conditions in some of its facilities, Quality shipped and sold eggs that contained salmonella bacteria, which sickened thousands of people across the United States.

The federal government prosecuted the DeCosters under the responsible corporate officer doctrine, in part for Quality's failure to comply with regulations on egg-production facilities. The DeCosters ultimately pleaded guilty to violating three criminal statutes. But when they were ordered to serve three months in jail, the DeCosters challenged the sentence as unconstitutional. The court held that the sentence of incarceration was appropriate because the evidence suggested that the defendants knew about the unsanitary conditions in their processing plants.[11]

chaiwoot seetha/Shutterstock.com

If unsanitary conditions at an egg-production facility spark sickness among consumers, can the corporate owner be held criminally liable?

9–3 Types of Crimes

Federal, state, and local laws provide for the classification and punishment of hundreds of thousands of different criminal acts. Traditionally, though, crimes have been grouped into five broad categories: violent crime (crimes against persons), property crime, public order crime, white-collar crime, and organized crime. In addition, when crimes are committed in cyberspace rather than the physical world, we often refer to them as cyber crimes.

Focus Question 3

What are five broad categories of crimes? What is white-collar crime?

8. See Model Penal Code Section 2.07.
9. As a result of the convictions, the motel manager was sentenced to fifteen months in prison, and the corporation was ordered to forfeit the motel property. *United States v. Singh*, 518 F.3d 236 (4th Cir. 2008). For an example involving environmental laws, see *United States v. House of Raeford Farms, Inc.*, 2013 WL 179185 (M.D.N.C. 2013).
10. For a landmark case in this area, see *United States v. Park*, 421 U.S. 658, 95 S.Ct. 1903, 44 L.Ed.2d 489 (1975).
11. *United States v. Quality Egg, LLC*, 99 F.Supp.3d 920 (N.D. Iowa 2015).

9–3a Violent Crime

Robbery The act of forcefully and unlawfully taking personal property of any value from another.

Certain crimes are called *violent crimes*, or crimes against persons, because they cause others to suffer harm or death. Murder is a violent crime. So, too, is sexual assault. **Robbery**—defined as the taking of cash, personal property, or any other article of value from a person by means of force or fear—is another violent crime. Typically, states have more severe penalties for *aggravated robbery*—robbery with the use of a deadly weapon.

Assault and battery, which were discussed in the context of tort law, are also classified as violent crimes. **Example 9.8** Restaurateur Mario Batali was criminally charged with indecent assault and battery arising from an incident at a Boston restaurant. While taking a selfie with a fan, he allegedly kissed and groped her and, when she tried to escape his grasp, aggressively touched her face. ■

Each of these violent crimes is further classified by degree, depending on the circumstances surrounding the criminal act. These circumstances include the intent of the person committing the crime and whether a weapon was used. For crimes other than murder, the level of pain and suffering experienced by the victim is also a factor.

9–3b Property Crime

The most common type of criminal activity is property crime—crimes in which the goal of the offender is some form of economic gain or the damaging of property. Robbery is a form of property crime, as well as a violent crime, because the offender seeks to gain the property of another. We look here at a number of other crimes that fall within the general category of property crime.

Burglary The unlawful entry or breaking into a building with the intent to commit a felony.

Burglary Traditionally, **burglary** was defined under the common law as breaking and entering the dwelling of another at night with the intent to commit a felony. Originally, the definition was aimed at protecting an individual's home and its occupants. Most state statutes have eliminated some of the requirements found in the common law definition. The time of day at which the breaking and entering occurs, for example, is usually immaterial. State statutes frequently omit the element of breaking, and some states do not require that the building be a dwelling. When a deadly weapon is used in a burglary, the person can be charged with *aggravated burglary* and punished more severely.

Larceny The wrongful taking and carrying away of another person's personal property with the intent to permanently deprive the owner of the property.

Larceny Under the common law, the crime of **larceny** involved the unlawful taking and carrying away of someone else's personal property with the intent to permanently deprive the owner of possession. Put simply, larceny is stealing, or theft.

Whereas robbery involves force or fear, larceny does not. Therefore, picking pockets is larceny, not robbery. Similarly, an employee who takes company products and supplies home for personal use without authorization commits larceny.

Most states have expanded the definition of property that is subject to larceny statutes. Stealing computer programs may constitute larceny even though the "property" is not physical (see the discussion of cyber crime later in this chapter). The theft of natural gas, Internet access, and television cable service can also constitute larceny.

Obtaining Goods by False Pretenses Obtaining goods by means of false pretenses is a form of theft that involves trickery or fraud, such as using someone else's credit card number without permission. Statutes dealing with such illegal activities vary widely from state to state. They often apply not only to property, but also to services and cash.

Case Example 9.9 While Matthew Steffes was incarcerated, he devised a scheme to make free collect calls from prison. (A *collect call* is a telephone call in which the calling party places a call at the called party's expense.) Steffes had his friends and family members set up new phone number accounts by giving false information to AT&T. This information included fictitious business names, as well as personal identifying information stolen from a health-care clinic. Once a new phone number was working, Steffes made unlimited collect calls to it without paying the bill until AT&T eventually shut down the account. For nearly two years, Steffes used sixty fraudulently obtained phone numbers to make hundreds of collect calls. The loss to AT&T was more than $28,000.

Steffes was convicted in a state court of theft by fraud. He appealed, arguing that he had not made false representations to AT&T. The Wisconsin Supreme Court affirmed his conviction. The court held that Steffes had made false representations to AT&T by providing it with fictitious business names and stolen personal identifying information. He made these false representations so that he could make phone calls without paying for them, which deprived the company of its "property"—its electricity.[12]

Receiving Stolen Goods It is a crime to receive goods that a person knows or should have known were stolen or illegally obtained. To be convicted, the recipient of such goods need not know the true identity of the owner or the thief, and need not have paid for the goods. All that is necessary is that the recipient knows or should have known that the goods were stolen, which implies an intent to deprive the true owner of those goods.

Arson The willful and malicious burning of a building (and, in some states, vehicles and other items of personal property) is the crime of **arson.** At common law, arson traditionally applied only to burning down another person's house. The law was designed to protect human life. Today, arson statutes have been extended to cover the destruction of any building, regardless of ownership, by fire or explosion.

Arson The intentional burning of a building.

Every state has a special statute that covers the act of burning a building for the purpose of collecting insurance. **Example 9.10** Benton owns an insured apartment building that is falling apart. If he sets fire to it or pays someone else to do so, he is guilty not only of arson but also of defrauding the insurer, which is attempted larceny. Of course, the insurer need not pay the claim when insurance fraud is proved.

Forgery The fraudulent making or altering of any writing (including electronic records) in a way that changes the legal rights and liabilities of another is **forgery.** **Example 9.11** Without authorization, Severson signs Bennett's name to the back of a check made out to Bennett and attempts to cash it. Severson has committed the crime of forgery. Forgery also includes changing trademarks, falsifying public records, counterfeiting, and altering a legal document.

Forgery The fraudulent making or altering of any writing in a way that changes the legal rights and liabilities of another.

9–3c Public Order Crime

Historically, societies have always outlawed activities considered to be contrary to public values and morals. Today, the most common public order crimes include public drunkenness, prostitution, gambling, and illegal drug use. These crimes are sometimes referred to as victimless crimes because they normally harm only the offender. From a broader perspective, however, they are detrimental to society as a whole because they may create an environment that gives rise to property and violent crimes.

Example 9.12 A man is stumbling through a mall parking lot, screaming obscenities. A sheriff's deputy arrives on the scene and—noting that the man is slurring his speech, has bloodshot eyes, and smells of alcohol—arrests him for public intoxication. Under state law, this public order crime is a misdemeanor punishable by a fine of no more than $500.

9–3d White-Collar Crime

Crimes occurring in the business context are popularly referred to as *white-collar crimes*, although this is not an official legal term. Ordinarily, **white-collar crime** involves an illegal act or series of acts committed by an individual or business entity using some nonviolent means to obtain a personal or business advantage.

White-Collar Crime Nonviolent crime committed by individuals or business entities to obtain a personal or business advantage.

12. *State of Wisconsin v. Steffes*, 347 Wis.2d 683, 832 N.W.2d 101 (2013).

Usually, this kind of crime is committed in the course of a legitimate occupation. Corporate crimes fall into this category. In addition, certain property crimes, such as larceny and forgery, may also be white-collar crimes if they occur within the business context.

Embezzlement The fraudulent appropriation of funds or other property by a person who was entrusted with the funds or property.

Embezzlement When a person who is entrusted with another person's funds or property fraudulently appropriates it, embezzlement occurs. **Embezzlement** is not larceny, because the wrongdoer does not physically take the property from another's possession, and it is not robbery, because force or fear is not used.

Typically, embezzlement is carried out by an employee who steals funds. Banks are particularly prone to this problem, but embezzlement can occur in any firm. In a number of businesses, corporate officers or accountants have fraudulently converted funds for their own benefit and then "fixed" the books to cover up their crime. Embezzlement occurs whether the embezzler takes the funds directly from the victim or from a third person. If the financial officer of a corporation pockets checks from third parties that were given to her to deposit into the corporate account, she is embezzling.

Frequently, an embezzler takes relatively small amounts repeatedly over a long period. This might be done by underreporting income or deposits and embezzling the remaining amount, or by creating fictitious persons or accounts and writing checks to them from the corporate account. An employer's failure to remit state withholding taxes that were collected from employee wages can also constitute embezzlement.

The intent to return embezzled property—or its actual return—is not a defense to the crime of embezzlement, as the following *Spotlight Case* illustrates.

Spotlight on White-Collar Crime: Case 9.2

People v. Sisuphan

Court of Appeal of California, First District, 181 Cal.App.4th 800, 104 Cal.Rptr.3d 654 (2010).

Facts Lou Sisuphan was the director of finance at a Toyota dealership. Sisuphan complained repeatedly to management about another employee, Ian McClelland. The general manager, Michael Christian, would not terminate McClelland "because he brought a lot of money into the dealership." In an attempt to get McClelland fired, Sisuphan took and kept an envelope containing a payment of nearly $30,000 from one of McClelland's customers. McClelland believed the envelope had been deposited in the company safe's drop slot, but after it got stuck, Sisuphan wriggled the envelope free and kept it in the company's safe.

Later, Sisuphan told the dealership what he had done and returned the money, adding that he had "no intention of stealing the money." Christian fired Sisuphan the next day, and the district attorney later charged Sisuphan with embezzlement. After a jury trial, Sisuphan was found guilty. Sisuphan appealed.

Issue Did Sisuphan take the funds with the intent to defraud his employer?

tomeng/iStock Unreleased/Getty Images

A Toyota dealership employee committed embezzlement but returned the funds. Is this a crime?

Decision Yes. The appellate court affirmed Sisuphan's conviction for embezzlement. Sisuphan had the required intent at the time he took the funds, and the evidence that he repaid the dealership was properly excluded.

Reason The court reasoned that evidence of repayment is admissible only if it shows that a defendant's intent at the time of the taking was not fraudulent. In determining whether Sisuphan's intent was fraudulent at the time of the taking, the main issue was not whether he intended to spend the funds that he had taken, but whether he intended to use the payment "for a purpose other than that for which the dealership entrusted it to him." Sisuphan's stated purpose was to get McClelland fired. Because this purpose was beyond the scope of his responsibility, it was "outside the trust afforded him by the dealership" and indicated fraudulent intent.

Critical Thinking

- **Legal Environment** *Why was Sisuphan convicted of embezzlement instead of larceny? What is the difference between these two crimes?*

Mail and Wire Fraud One of the most potent weapons against white-collar criminals are the federal laws that prohibit mail fraud[13] and wire fraud.[14] These laws make it a federal crime to devise any scheme that uses the U.S. mail, commercial carriers (such as FedEx or UPS), or wire (including telegraph, telephone, television, e-mail, and online social media) with the intent to defraud the public. These laws are often applied when persons send untrue or misleading information via e-mail with the intent of obtaining a financial benefit under false pretenses.

Case Example 9.13 Donovan Davis and several associates launched Capital Blu Management to trade in the foreign currency marketplace. Over the course of several days, Capital Blu engaged in a disastrous series of trades, losing almost $3 million. Davis feared that if these losses were reported to investors, they would abandon the company, and his reputation in the financial community would suffer. So Capital Blu sent out a monthly report via mail and e-mail falsely reporting a 1.6 percent gain.

This monthly pattern of transmitting fraudulent reports continued until regulators shut Capital Blu down a year later. In a ruling upheld on appeal, a federal trial court found Davis responsible for $10 million in investor losses and convicted him on six counts of mail fraud and one count of wire fraud.[15]

The maximum penalty under these statutes is substantial. Persons convicted of mail or wire fraud may be imprisoned for up to twenty years and/or fined. If the violation affects a financial institution or involves fraud in connection with emergency disaster-relief funds, the violator may be fined up to $1 million, imprisoned for up to thirty years, or both.

Bribery The crime of bribery involves offering something of value to someone in an attempt to influence that person—who is usually, but not always, a public official—to act in a way that serves a private interest. Three types of bribery are considered crimes: bribery of public officials, commercial bribery, and bribery of foreign officials. As an element of the crime of bribery, intent must be present and proved. The bribe itself can be anything the recipient considers to be valuable, but the defendant must have intended it as a bribe. Realize that the *crime of bribery occurs when the bribe is offered*—it is not required that the bribe be accepted. *Accepting a bribe* is a separate crime.

Commercial bribery involves corrupt dealings between private persons or businesses. Typically, people make commercial bribes to obtain proprietary information, cover up an inferior product, or secure new business. Industrial espionage sometimes involves commercial bribes. **Example 9.14** Kent works at the firm of Jacoby & Meyers. He offers to pay Laurel, an employee in a competing firm, if she will give him her firm's trade secrets and pricing schedules. Kent has committed commercial bribery. So-called kickbacks, or payoffs for special favors or services, are a form of commercial bribery in some situations.

The Foreign Corrupt Practices Act In many foreign countries, government officials make the decisions on most major construction and manufacturing contracts. Side payments to government officials in exchange for favorable business contracts are not unusual in such countries. The Foreign Corrupt Practices Act[16] (FCPA) prohibits U.S. businesspersons from bribing foreign officials to secure beneficial contracts. Firms that violate the FCPA can be fined up to $2 million. Individuals can be fined up to $100,000 and imprisoned for up to five years.

Prohibition against the Bribery of Foreign Officials. The first part of the FCPA applies to all U.S. companies and their directors, officers, shareholders, employees, and agents. This part of the act prohibits the bribery of most officials of foreign governments if the purpose of the payment is to motivate the official to act in an official capacity to provide business opportunities.

The FCPA does not prohibit payments to minor officials whose duties are ministerial. A ministerial action is a routine activity, such as the processing of paperwork, with little or no discretion involved in the action. These payments, often referred to as "grease," are meant

13. The Mail Fraud Act of 1990, 18 U.S.C. Sections 1341–1342.
14. 18 U.S.C. Section 1343.
15. *United States v. Davis*, 789 Fed.Appx. 105 (11th Cir. 2019).
16. 15 U.S.C., Sections 78dd-1, *et seq.*

Rawpixel.com/Shutterstock.com

What type of payments to foreign officials are allowed under the Foreign Corrupt Practices Act?

to expedite the performance of administrative services. Thus, a firm that makes a payment to a minor official to speed up an import licensing process has not violated the FCPA.

Generally, the act also permits payments to foreign officials if such payments are lawful within the foreign country. Payments to private foreign companies or other third parties are permissible unless the U.S. firm knows that the payments will be passed on to a foreign government in violation of the FCPA.

Accounting Requirements. In the past, bribes were often concealed in corporate financial records. Thus, the second part of the FCPA is directed toward accountants. All companies must keep detailed accounting records that provide "reasonable assurance" that their transactions are accounted for and legal. The FCPA prohibits any person from making false statements to accountants or false entries in any record or account.

Case Example 9.15 Noble Corporation operated some offshore drilling rigs in Nigeria. Mark Jackson and James Ruehlen were officers at Noble. The U.S. government accused Noble of bribing Nigerian government officials and charged Jackson and Ruehlen individually with violating the FCPA's accounting provisions. Jackson and Ruehlen allegedly approved numerous "special handling" and "procurement" payments to the Nigerian government, knowing that those payments were actually bribes. Allowing illegal payments to be listed on the books as legitimate operating expenses violates the FCPA.[17]

Bankruptcy Fraud Federal bankruptcy law allows individuals and businesses to be relieved of oppressive debt through bankruptcy proceedings. Numerous white-collar crimes may be committed during the many phases of a bankruptcy proceeding. A creditor may file a false claim against the debtor. Also, a debtor may attempt to protect assets from creditors by fraudulently concealing property or by fraudulently transferring property to favored parties. For instance, a company-owned automobile may be "sold" at a bargain price to a trusted friend or relative.

Theft of Trade Secrets Trade secrets constitute a form of intellectual property that can be extremely valuable for many businesses. The Economic Espionage Act[18] made the theft of trade secrets a federal crime. The act also made it a federal crime to buy or possess the trade secrets of another person, knowing that the trade secrets were stolen or otherwise acquired without the owner's authorization.

Violations of the act can result in steep penalties. An individual who violates the act can be imprisoned for up to ten years and fined up to $500,000. A corporation or other organization can be fined up to $5 million. Additionally, any property acquired as a result of the violation, such as airplanes and automobiles, is subject to criminal forfeiture, or seizure by the government. Similarly, any property used in the commission of the violation, such as servers and other electronic devices, is subject to forfeiture. A theft of trade secrets conducted via the Internet, for instance, could result in the forfeiture of every computer or other device used to commit or facilitate the crime.

Insider Trading An individual who obtains "inside information" about the plans of a publicly listed corporation can often make stock-trading profits by purchasing or selling corporate securities based on the information. **Insider trading** is a violation of securities law. Generally, the rule is that a person who possesses inside information and has a duty not to disclose it to outsiders may not profit from the purchase or sale of securities based on that information until the information is made available to the public.

Insider Trading The purchase or sale of securities on the basis of information that has not been made available to the public.

17. *Securities Exchange Commission v. Jackson,* 908 F.Supp.2d 834 (S.D.Tex.—Houston 2012).
18. 18 U.S.C. Sections 1831–1839.

9–3e Organized Crime

As mentioned, white-collar crime takes place within the confines of the legitimate business world. *Organized crime*, in contrast, operates *illegitimately* by, among other things, providing illegal goods and services, such as illegal drugs, gambling, and prostitution. Today, organized crime is heavily involved in cyber crime.

Money Laundering

Organized crime and other illegal activities generate many billions of dollars in profits each year. Under federal law, banks and other financial institutions are required to report currency transactions involving more than $10,000. Consequently, those who engage in illegal activities face difficulties when they try to deposit their cash profits from illegal transactions.

As an alternative to simply storing cash from illegal transactions somewhere outside of the banking system, wrongdoers and racketeers often launder their "dirty" money through a legitimate business to make it "clean." **Money laundering** is engaging in financial transactions to conceal the identity, source, or destination of illegally gained funds.

Money Laundering Engaging in financial transactions to conceal the identity, source, or destination of illegally gained funds.

Example 9.16 Leo, a successful drug dealer, becomes a partner with a restaurateur. Little by little, the restaurant shows increasing profits. As a partner in the restaurant, Leo is able to report the "profits" of the restaurant as legitimate income on which he pays federal and state taxes. He can then spend those funds without worrying that his lifestyle may exceed the level possible with his reported income.

Racketeering

To curb the entry of organized crime into the legitimate business world, Congress enacted the Racketeer Influenced and Corrupt Organizations Act (RICO).[19] The statute makes it a federal crime to:

1. Use income obtained from racketeering activity to purchase any interest in an enterprise.
2. Acquire or maintain an interest in an enterprise through racketeering activity.
3. Conduct or participate in the affairs of an enterprise through racketeering activity.
4. Conspire to do any of the preceding activities.

Broad Application of RICO. The definition of racketeering is so inclusive—basically covering any attempt to earn illegal income involving more than one person—that it can be used against a broad range of criminal activity that has little to do with organized crime. RICO incorporates by reference twenty-six separate types of federal crimes and nine types of state felonies.[20] A person who commits two of these offenses is guilty of "racketeering activity."

Under the criminal provisions of RICO, any individual found guilty is subject to a fine of up to $25,000 per violation, imprisonment for up to twenty years, or both. Additionally, any assets (property or cash) that were acquired as a result of the illegal activity or that were "involved in" or an "instrumentality of" the activity are subject to government forfeiture.

SpeedKingz/Shutterstock.com

What might be some circumstances under which a shoplifter could be charged with racketeering?

Civil Liability. In the event of a RICO violation, the government can seek not only criminal penalties but also civil penalties, such as the divestiture of a defendant's interest in a business or the dissolution of the business. (Divestiture refers to the forfeiture and subsequent sale of the defendant's interest.)

Moreover, in some cases, the statute allows private individuals to sue violators and potentially to recover three times their actual losses (treble damages), plus attorneys' fees, for business injuries caused by a RICO violation. This is perhaps the most controversial aspect

19. 18 U.S.C. Sections 1961–1968.
20. See 18 U.S.C. Section 1961(1)(A).

of RICO and one that continues to cause debate in the nation's federal courts. The prospect of receiving treble damages in civil RICO lawsuits has given plaintiffs a financial incentive to pursue businesses and employers for violations.

9–4 Defenses to Criminal Liability

Focus Question 4

What defenses can be raised to avoid liability for criminal acts?

Persons charged with crimes may be relieved of criminal liability if they can show that their criminal actions were justified under the circumstances. In certain circumstances, the law may also allow someone to be excused from criminal liability because that person lacks the required mental state. We look at several of the defenses to criminal liability here.

Note that procedural violations, such as obtaining evidence without a valid search warrant, may also operate as defenses. Evidence obtained in violation of a defendant's constitutional rights normally may not be admitted in court. If the evidence is suppressed, then there may be no basis for prosecuting the defendant.

9–4a Justifiable Use of Force

Self-Defense The legally recognized privilege to do what is reasonably necessary to protect oneself, one's property, or someone else against injury by another.

Probably the best-known defense to criminal liability is **self-defense.** Other situations, however, also justify the use of force: the defense of one's dwelling, the defense of other property, and the prevention of a crime. In all of these situations, it is important to distinguish between deadly and nondeadly force. *Deadly force* is likely to result in death or serious bodily harm. *Nondeadly force* is force that appears reasonably necessary to prevent the imminent use of criminal force.

Generally speaking, people can use the amount of nondeadly force that seems necessary to protect themselves, their dwellings, or other property or to prevent the commission of a crime. Deadly force can be used in self-defense if the defender *reasonably believes* that imminent death or grievous bodily harm will otherwise result. In addition, normally the attacker must be using unlawful force, and the defender must not have initiated or provoked the attack.

Many states are expanding the situations in which the use of deadly force can be justified. Florida, for instance, allows the use of deadly force to prevent the commission of a "forcible felony," including robbery, carjacking, and sexual battery.

9–4b Necessity

Sometimes, criminal defendants are relieved of liability if they can show that a criminal act was necessary to prevent an even greater harm. **Example 9.17** Trevor is a convicted felon and, as such, is legally prohibited from possessing a firearm. While he and his wife are in a convenience store, a man draws a gun, points it at the cashier, and demands all the cash. Afraid that the man will start shooting, Trevor grabs the gun and holds on to it until police arrive. In this situation, if Trevor is charged with possession of a firearm, he can assert the defense of necessity. ■

9–4c Insanity

A person who suffers from a mental illness may be incapable of the state of mind required to commit a crime. Thus, insanity can be a defense to a criminal charge. Note that an insanity defense does not allow a person to avoid imprisonment. It simply means that a defendant who successfully proves insanity will be placed in a mental institution.

Example 9.18 Medina Espinosa of Beaver Dam, Wisconsin, was charged with first degree murder for shooting his ex-wife fifteen times. Ten days earlier, Espinosa apparently had been accidentally exposed to harmful chemicals at the Kraft Heinz factory where he worked.

According to Espinosa's attorney, these chemicals had caused neurological damage that left Espinosa unable to form the intent necessary to be held responsible for his ex-wife's murder. Consequently, he pleaded not guilty by reason of insanity.

Phonix_a Pk.sarote/Shutterstock.com

Suppose a defendant in a murder trial had been exposed to a chemical spill at work just before committing the alleged crime. How could the defendant's attorney use the workplace accident in the client's defense? What would the attorney have to prove?

9–4d Mistake

Everyone has heard the saying "ignorance of the law is no excuse." Ordinarily, ignorance of the law or a mistaken idea about what the law requires is not a valid defense. A *mistake of fact*, as opposed to a *mistake of law*, can excuse criminal responsibility if it negates the mental state necessary to commit a crime.

Example 9.19 If Oliver Wheaton mistakenly walks off with Julie Tyson's briefcase because he thinks it is his, there is no crime. Theft requires knowledge that the property belongs to another. (If Wheaton's act causes Tyson to incur damages, however, she may sue him in a civil action for the tort of trespass to personal property or conversion.)

9–4e Duress

Duress exists when the *wrongful threat* of one person induces another person to perform an act that would not otherwise have been performed. In such a situation, duress is said to negate the mental state necessary to commit a crime because the defendant was forced or compelled to commit the act.

Duress can be used as a defense to most crimes except murder. The states vary in how duress is defined and what types of crimes it can excuse, however. Generally, to successfully assert duress as a defense, the defendant must reasonably believe that an immediate danger exists, and the jury (or judge) must conclude that the defendant's belief was reasonable.

Know This

"Ignorance" is a lack of information. "Mistake" is a confusion of information, which can sometimes negate criminal intent.

9–4f Entrapment

Entrapment is a defense designed to prevent police officers or other government agents from enticing persons to commit crimes so that they can later be prosecuted for criminal acts. In the typical entrapment case, an undercover agent *suggests* that a crime be committed and pressures or induces an individual to commit it. The agent then arrests the individual for the crime.

For entrapment to succeed as a defense, both the suggestion and the inducement must take place. The defense is not intended to prevent law enforcement agents from setting a trap for an unwary criminal. Rather, its purpose is to prevent them from pushing the individual into a criminal act. The crucial issue is whether the person who committed a crime was predisposed to commit the illegal act or did so only because the agent induced it.

Duress Unlawful pressure that causes a person to perform an act that the person would not otherwise perform.

Entrapment A defense in which a defendant claims to have been induced by a public official to commit a crime that would otherwise not have been committed.

9–4g Statute of Limitations

With some exceptions, such as for the crime of murder, statutes of limitations apply to crimes just as they do to civil wrongs. In other words, the state must initiate criminal prosecution within a certain number of years. If a criminal action is brought after the statutory time period has expired, the accused person can raise the statute of limitations as a defense.

The running of the time period in a statute of limitations may be *tolled*—that is, suspended or stopped temporarily—if the defendant is a minor or is not in the jurisdiction. When the defendant reaches the age of majority or returns to the jurisdiction, the statutory time period begins to run again.

9–4h Immunity

Self-Incrimination Giving testimony in a trial or other legal proceeding that could expose the person testifying to criminal prosecution.

Accused persons are understandably reluctant to give information if it will be used to prosecute them, and they cannot be forced to do so. The privilege against **self-incrimination** is granted by the Fifth Amendment to the U.S. Constitution. The clause reads "nor shall [any person] be compelled in any criminal case to be a witness against himself."

When the state wishes to obtain information from a person accused of a crime, the state can grant *immunity* from prosecution or agree to prosecute for a less serious offense in exchange for the information. Persons who are granted immunity can no longer refuse to testify on Fifth Amendment grounds because they now have an absolute privilege against self-incrimination.

Plea Bargaining The process by which a criminal defendant and the prosecutor work out an agreement to dispose of the criminal case, subject to court approval.

Often, a grant of immunity from prosecution for a serious crime is part of the **plea bargaining** between the defendant and the prosecuting attorney. The defendant may be convicted of a lesser offense, while the state uses the defendant's testimony to prosecute accomplices for serious crimes carrying heavy penalties.

9–5 Constitutional Safeguards

Focus Question 5

What constitutional safeguards exist to protect persons accused of crimes?

Criminal law brings the power of the state, with all its resources, to bear against the individual. Criminal procedures are designed to protect the constitutional rights of individuals and to prevent the arbitrary use of power by the government.

The U.S. Constitution provides specific safeguards for those accused of crimes. Most of these safeguards protect individuals not only against federal government actions but also, by virtue of the due process clause of the Fourteenth Amendment, against state government actions. These protections are set forth in the Fourth, Fifth, Sixth, and Eighth Amendments.

9–5a Fourth Amendment Protections

Search Warrant An order granted by a public authority, such as a judge, that authorizes law enforcement personnel to search particular premises or property.

The Fourth Amendment protects the "right of the people to be secure in their persons, houses, papers, and effects." Before searching or seizing private property, law enforcement officers must obtain a **search warrant**—an order from a judge or other public official authorizing the search or seizure.

Advances in technology have allowed authorities to track phone calls and vehicle movements with greater ease and precision. The use of such technology can constitute a search within the meaning of the Fourth Amendment. **Spotlight Case Example 9.20** Antoine Jones owned and operated a nightclub in the District of Columbia. Government agents suspected that he was also trafficking in narcotics. As part of their investigation, agents obtained a warrant to attach a global positioning system (GPS) device to Jones's wife's car, which he used regularly. The warrant authorized installation in the District of Columbia and within ten days, but agents installed the device on the eleventh day and in Maryland.

The agents then tracked the vehicle's movement for about a month, eventually arresting Jones for possession and intent to distribute cocaine. Jones was convicted. He appealed, arguing that the government did not have a valid warrant for the GPS tracking. The United States Supreme Court held that the attachment of a GPS tracking device to a suspect's vehicle does constitute a Fourth Amendment search. The Court did not rule on whether the search in this case was unreasonable, however, and allowed Jones's conviction to stand.[21]

21. *United States v. Jones*, 565 U.S. 945, 132 S.Ct. 945, 181 L.Ed.2d 911 (2012).

Probable Cause To obtain a search warrant, law enforcement officers must convince a judge that they have reasonable grounds, or **probable cause,** to believe a search will reveal a specific illegality. Probable cause requires the officers to have trustworthy evidence that would convince a reasonable person that the proposed search or seizure is more likely justified than not.

Probable Cause Reasonable grounds for believing that a search or seizure should be conducted.

Classic Case Example 9.21 Based on a tip that Oscar Gutierrez was involved in drug trafficking, law enforcement officers went to his home with a drug-sniffing dog. The dog alerted officers to the scent of narcotics at the home's front door. Officers knocked for fifteen minutes, but no one answered. Eventually, they entered and secured the men inside the home. They then obtained a search warrant based on the dog's positive alert. Officers found eleven pounds of methamphetamine in the search, and Gutierrez was convicted. The evidence of the drug-sniffing dog's positive alert for the presence of drugs established probable cause for the warrant.[22]

The Fourth Amendment prohibits general warrants. It requires a particular description of what is to be searched or seized. General searches through a person's belongings are not permissible. The search cannot extend beyond what is described in the warrant. Although search warrants require specificity, if a search warrant is issued for a person's residence, items in that residence may be searched even if they do not belong to that individual.

Because of the strong governmental interest in protecting the public, a warrant normally is not required for seizures of spoiled or contaminated food. Nor are warrants required for searches of businesses in such highly regulated industries as liquor, guns, and strip mining.

Reasonable Expectation of Privacy The Fourth Amendment protects only against searches that violate a person's *reasonable expectation of privacy*. A reasonable expectation of privacy exists if (1) the individual actually expects privacy, and (2) the person's expectation is one that society as a whole would consider legitimate.

Classic Case Example 9.22 Jenny Stracner, an investigator with the Laguna Beach (California) Police Department, enlisted the aid of a local trash collector in gathering evidence on suspect Billy Greenwood. Instead of taking Greenwood's trash bags to be incinerated, the collector agreed to give them to Strancer. The officer found enough drug paraphernalia in the garbage to obtain a warrant to search Greenwood's home, where she found illegal drugs.

The United States Supreme Court upheld the search and Greenwood's subsequent arrest. People do not, the Court reasoned, have a reasonable expectation of privacy when it comes to their garbage bags. The Court noted that when we place our trash on a curb, we expose it to any number of intrusions by "animals, children, scavengers, snoops, and other members of the public." In other words, if Greenwood had truly intended to keep the contents of his garbage private, he would not have left it on the side of the road.[23]

Paul Vasarhelyi/Shutterstock.com

Do you feel that people have a reasonable expectation of privacy when it comes to the contents of garbage bags left on a curb? Why or why not?

9–5b Fifth Amendment Protections

The Fifth Amendment offers significant protections for accused persons. One is the guarantee that no one can be deprived of "life, liberty, or property without due process of law." Two other important Fifth Amendment provisions protect persons against double jeopardy and self-incrimination.

22. *United States v. Gutierrez,* 760 F.3d 750 (7th Cir. 2014).
23. *California v Greenwood,* 436 U.S. 35, 108 S.Ct. 1625, 100 L.Ed.2d 30 (1988).

Due Process of Law Remember that *due process of law* has both procedural and substantive aspects. Procedural due process requirements underlie criminal procedures. The law must be carried out in a fair and orderly way. In criminal cases, due process means that defendants should have an opportunity to object to the charges against them before a fair, neutral decision maker, such as a judge. Defendants must also be given the opportunity to confront and cross-examine witnesses and accusers, and to present their own witnesses.

Double Jeopardy The Fifth Amendment requirement that prohibits a person from being tried twice for the same criminal offense.

Double Jeopardy The Fifth Amendment also protects persons from **double jeopardy** (being tried twice for the same criminal offense). The prohibition against double jeopardy means that once a criminal defendant is acquitted (found "not guilty") of a particular crime, the government may not retry that defendant for the same crime.

The prohibition against double jeopardy does not preclude the crime victim from bringing a civil suit against that same defendant to recover damages, however. In other words, a person found "not guilty" of assault and battery in a state criminal case can be sued for damages by the victim in a civil tort case. Additionally, a state's prosecution of a crime will not prevent a separate federal prosecution relating to the same activity (and vice versa), provided the activity can be classified as a different crime.

Know This

The Fifth Amendment protection against self-incrimination does not cover partnerships or corporations.

Self-Incrimination The Fifth Amendment grants a privilege against self-incrimination. Thus, in criminal proceedings, accused persons cannot be compelled to give testimony that might subject them to criminal prosecution.

The Fifth Amendment's guarantee against self-incrimination extends only to natural persons. Because a corporation is a legal entity and not a natural person, the privilege against self-incrimination does not apply to it. Similarly, the business records of a partnership do not receive Fifth Amendment protection. When a partnership is required to produce these records, it must do so even if the information incriminates the persons who constitute the business entity.

Ethical Issue

Should police be able to force you to unlock your mobile phone? Today's cell phones can store countless pages of text, thousands of pictures, and hundreds of videos. Such data can remain on a mobile phone for years. Also, since the advent of the "cloud," much of the data viewable on a mobile phone is stored on a remote server. Should police nonetheless be able to force you to unlock your phone? Or does this practice violate the Fifth Amendment protection against self-incrimination?

In *Riley v. California*,[24] the United States Supreme Court unanimously held that warrantless search and seizure of digital contents of a mobile phone during an arrest is unconstitutional. Chief Justice John Roberts stated, "The fact that technology now allows for an individual to carry [the privacies of life] in his hand does not make the information any less worthy of the protection for which the Founders fought." Nevertheless, a number of federal courts have allowed evidence obtained from cell phones to be used against a defendant even when there was no search warrant.[25]

24 573 U.S. 373, 134 S.Ct. 2473, 189 L.Ed.2d 430 (2014). See also *United States v. Caballero*, 178 F.Supp.3d 1008 (S.D.Cal. 2016).
25 See, for instance, *Ly v. Beard*, 652 Fed.Appx. 550 (9th Cir. 2016); and *U.S. v. Miller*, 641 Fed.Appx. 242 (4th Cir. 2016).

9–5c The Exclusionary Rule

Under what is known as the **exclusionary rule,** any evidence obtained in violation of the constitutional rights spelled out in the Fourth, Fifth, and Sixth Amendments generally is not admissible at trial. All evidence derived from the illegally obtained evidence is known as the "fruit of the poisonous tree," and normally must also be excluded from the trial proceedings. For instance, if a confession is obtained after an illegal arrest, the arrest is the "poisonous tree," and the confession, if "tainted" by the arrest, is the "fruit."

Exclusionary Rule A rule that prevents evidence that is obtained illegally or without a proper search warrant from being admissible in court.

The purpose of the exclusionary rule is to deter police from conducting warrantless searches and engaging in other misconduct. The rule can sometimes lead to injustice, however. If evidence of a defendant's guilt was obtained improperly (without a valid search warrant, for instance), it normally cannot be used against the defendant in court.

Know This

Once suspects have been informed of their rights, anything they say can be used as evidence in a trial.

9–5d The *Miranda* Rule

In *Miranda v. Arizona*, a case decided in 1966, the United States Supreme Court established the rule that individuals who are arrested must be informed of certain constitutional rights. Suspects must be informed of their Fifth Amendment right to remain silent and their Sixth Amendment right to counsel. If the arresting officers fail to inform a criminal suspect of these constitutional rights, any statements the suspect makes normally will not be admissible in court. Because of its importance in criminal procedure, the *Miranda case* is presented as this chapter's *Landmark in the Law* feature.

Although the Supreme Court's *Miranda* ruling was controversial, the decision has survived attempts by Congress to overrule it. Over time, however, the Supreme Court has made a number of exceptions to the *Miranda* ruling. For instance, the Court has recognized a "public safety" exception that allows certain statements to be admitted even if the defendant was not given *Miranda* warnings. A defendant's statements that reveal the location of a weapon would be admissible under this exception.

Additionally, a suspect must unequivocally and assertively ask to exercise the right to counsel in order to stop police questioning. Saying, "Maybe I should talk to a lawyer" during an interrogation after being taken into custody is not enough.

9–6 Cyber Crime

The U.S. Department of Justice broadly defines **computer crime** as any violation of criminal law that involves knowledge of computer technology for its perpetration, investigation, or prosecution. Many computer crimes fall under the broad label of **cyber crime,** which describes any criminal activity occurring in the virtual community of the Internet.

Computer Crime Any violation of criminal law that involves knowledge of computer technology for its perpetration, investigation, or prosecution.

Cyber Crime A crime that occurs in the online environment.

Most cyber crimes are simply existing crimes, such as fraud and theft of intellectual property, in which the Internet is the instrument of wrongdoing. Here, we look at several types of activities that constitute cyber crimes against persons or property.

9–6a Cyber Fraud

Fraud is any misrepresentation knowingly made with the intention of deceiving another and on which a reasonable person would and does rely to her or his detriment. **Cyber fraud** is fraud committed over the Internet. Scams that were once conducted solely by mail or phone can now be found online, and new technology has led to increasingly creative ways to commit fraud.

Cyber Fraud Any misrepresentation knowingly made over the Internet with the intention of deceiving another for the purpose of obtaining property or funds.

Two widely reported forms of cyber crime are *advance fee fraud* and *online auction fraud*. In the simplest form of advance fee fraud, consumers order and pay for items, such as automobiles or antiques, that are never delivered. Online auction fraud is also fairly straightforward.

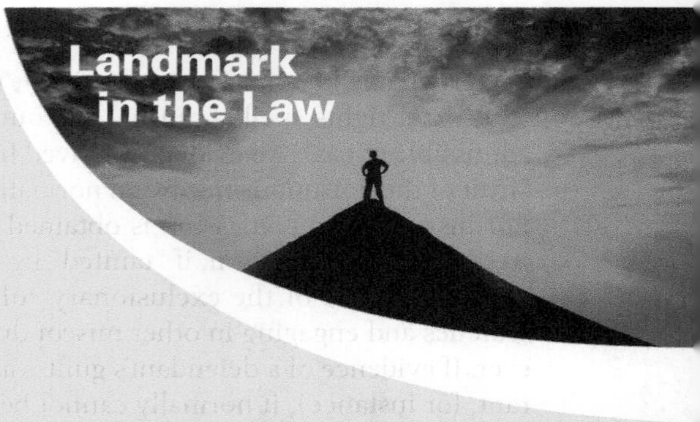

Miranda v. Arizona (1966)

The United States Supreme Court's decision in *Miranda v. Arizona*[a] has been cited in more court decisions than any other case in the history of U.S. law. Through television shows and other media, the case has also become familiar to most of the adult population in the United States.

The case arose after Ernesto Miranda was arrested in his home on March 13, 1963, for the kidnapping and rape of an eighteen-year-old woman. Miranda was taken to a police station in Phoenix, Arizona, and questioned by two police officers. Two hours later, the officers emerged from the interrogation room with a written confession signed by Miranda.

Rulings by the Lower Courts The confession was admitted into evidence at the trial, and Miranda was convicted and sentenced to prison for twenty to thirty years. Miranda appealed his conviction, claiming that he had not been informed of his constitutional rights. He did not assert that he was innocent of the crime or that his confession was false or made under duress. He claimed only that he would not have confessed if he had been advised of his right to remain silent and to have an attorney.

The Supreme Court of Arizona held that Miranda's constitutional rights had not been violated and affirmed his conviction. In its decision, the court emphasized that Miranda had not specifically requested an attorney.

The Supreme Court's Decision The *Miranda* case was subsequently consolidated with three other cases involving similar issues and reviewed by the United States Supreme Court. In its decision, the Court stated that whenever an individual is taken into custody, "the following measures are required: He must be warned prior to any questioning that he has the right to remain silent, that anything he says can be used against him in a court of law, that he has the right to the presence of an attorney, and that if he cannot afford an attorney one will be appointed for him prior to any questioning if he so desires." If the accused waives the rights to remain silent and to have counsel present, the government must be able to demonstrate that the waiver was made knowingly, intelligently, and voluntarily.

Application to Today's World *Today, both on television and in the real world, police officers routinely advise suspects of their "Miranda rights" on arrest. When Ernesto Miranda himself was later murdered, the suspected murderer was "read his Miranda rights." Interestingly, this decision has also had ramifications for criminal procedure in Great Britain. British police officers are required, when making arrests, to inform suspects, "You do not have to say anything. But if you do not mention now something which you later use in your defense, the court may decide that your failure to mention it now strengthens the case against you. A record will be made of everything you say, and it may be given in evidence if you are brought to trial."*

a. 384 U.S. 436, 86 S.Ct. 1602, 16 L.Ed.2d 694 (1966).

A person lists an expensive item for auction, on either a legitimate or a fake auction site, and then refuses to send the product after receiving payment. Or, as a variation, the wrongdoer may send the purchaser an item that is worth less than the one offered in the auction.

The larger online auction sites, such as eBay, try to protect consumers against such schemes by providing warnings or offering various forms of insurance. Nonetheless, it is nearly impossible to completely eliminate online fraud potential because users can assume multiple identities.

Case Example 9.23 A group of Romanians were arrested and brought to the United States to face charges for allegedly stealing millions of dollars from American victims on sites such as eBay, Craigslist, and Amazon. According to the federal government, one of the suspects, Ionut Ciobanu, created a fake Facebook profile calling himself Sgt. Judith Lane of the U.S. Air Force, a ruse designed to reassure potential purchasers of the nonexistent automobiles he was selling online.[26]

26. *United States v. Andrei-Catlin Stoica*, et al., E. D. Kentucky (2019).

9–6b Cyber Identity Theft

In cyberspace, thieves are not subject to the physical limitations of the "real" world. A thief can steal data stored in a networked computer with Internet access from anywhere on the globe. Only the speed of the connection and the thief's computer equipment limit the quantity of data that can be stolen.

Identity Theft

Identity theft occurs when the wrongdoer steals a form of identification—such as a name, date of birth, or Social Security number—and uses the information to access and steal the victim's financial resources. Widespread use of the Internet has caused a marked increase in identity theft, and many millions of Americans have been victimized.

Identity Theft The illegal use of someone else's personal information to access the victim's financial resources.

The Internet has provided relatively easy access to private data. Frequent Web surfers and social media users surrender a wealth of personal information. Websites use so-called "cookies" to collect data on their customers and visitors. Often, sites store information such as names, e-mail addresses, and credit card numbers. Identity thieves may be able to steal this information by fooling a website into thinking that they are the true account holders. Identity thieves may also be able to use personal information that people disclose on social media sites (such as birthdays, children's names, hometowns, employers) to gain access to financial information.

Focus Question 6

How has the Internet expanded opportunities for identity theft?

Stolen Credit Card Numbers. More than half of identity thefts involve the misappropriation of credit card accounts. In most situations, the legitimate holders of credit cards are not held responsible for the costs of purchases made with a stolen number. The loss is borne by the businesses and banks.

Example 9.24 The Northeast convenience store chain Wawa announced that a security breach in its computer system had allowed cyberthieves to obtain some of the company's stored credit card payment data. Two months later, someone going by the name of Joker Stash started posting these data for sale on the dark web, asking about $17 apiece for the credit card numbers of about 30 million Wawa customers. ■

Card Testing Online markets are particularly attractive for credit card thieves because the thieves can engage in a practice called "card testing." This involves using a stolen credit card number, or thousands of stolen credit card numbers, to make very small online purchases, perhaps no larger than two dollars. If the fraudulent transaction is successful, the criminal will raise the amount of the purchases until the issuing financial institution or the real owner notices. This chapter's *Cybersecurity and the Law* feature explores another tactic designed to "cash in" stolen credit card numbers online.

Password Theft

The more personal information a cyber criminal obtains, the easier it is to find a victim's online user name at a particular website. Once the online user name has been compromised, it is easier to steal the victim's password, which is often the last line of defense in protecting financial information.

Numerous software programs aid identity thieves in illegally obtaining passwords. A technique called *keystroke logging*, for instance, relies on software that embeds itself in a victim's computer and records every keystroke made on that computer. User names and passwords are then recorded and sold to the highest bidder. Internet users should also be wary of any links contained within e-mails sent from unknown sources. These links can sometimes be used to illegally obtain personal information.

Phishing

In a distinct form of identity theft known as **phishing,** the perpetrator "fishes" for financial data and passwords from consumers by posing as a legitimate business such as a bank or credit card company. The "phisher" may send an e-mail asking the recipient to "update" or "confirm" vital information. Often, the e-mail includes a threat that an account or some other service will be discontinued if the information is not provided. Once the

Phishing A form of identity theft in which the perpetrator sends e-mails purporting to be from a legitimate business to induce recipients to reveal their personal financial data, passwords, or other information.

Cybersecurity and the Law

Counter-Strike: Global Offensive

The online video game Counter-Strike: Global Offensive (CS:GO) involves two teams, each attempting to eliminate the other while carrying out objectives such as planting bombs or protecting hostages. CS:GO gamers, who number at around 20 million, also try to gain "loot boxes" that allow them to upgrade their avatars or weapons. Initially, the only way to open a loot box was to purchase a "container key" from Valve Corporation, which sells and operates CS:GO. Eventually, however, it became possible to trade loot boxes and container keys for "real" money on various Internet marketplaces.

The problem with this system became clear when Valve suspended all trading of container keys between players. Such activity, the company announced, had become "fraud sourced." In other words, the trading of container keys was being used to launder income from credit card fraud. Valve's actions highlight the opportunities presented to cyber criminals by online gaming markets. Cybercriminals can use their illicit earnings or stolen credit card numbers to buy virtual items and then sell those items—often at a discounted price—to other gamers in exchange for real money.

The Displacement Effect

According to "the displacement effect," as some parts of an economy become more highly regulated, tainted funds move to the less regulated parts of the economy. Under federal banking laws, only "convertible virtual currency" (CVC) is subject to regulation designed to combat money laundering. To fall under the definition of a CVC, the virtual currency must have a value in real currency or act as a substitute for real currency.[a] This definition does not cover CS:GO's container keys or, to give another example, the online survival contest Fortnite's V-bucks. Consequently, these online video games will continue to attract some players who are laundering money.

a. 31 U.S.C. Section 5330.

Critical Thinking

One suggestion for alleviating the problem of "fraud sourced" money is to require proof of identity from anyone who wants to trade virtual items on online gaming platforms. Do you think this strategy would be successful? Why or why not?

unsuspecting individual enters the information, the phisher can sell it or use it to masquerade as that person or to drain that person's bank or credit account.

Phishing scams have also spread to social networking sites and text messages. (Phishing via text messages is known as "smishing," because text messages use the Short Message Service, or SMS, format.) **Example 9.25** Customers of FedEx received an official-looking text informing them that they needed to set up delivery preferences for a package. The text included a link that, if clicked, took potential victims to a purported Amazon.com website promising them a reward if they filled out a customer satisfaction survey. To claim the reward, they had to provide their home address and a credit card number for shipping and handling. The FedEx texts and Amazon websites were fake. People who did provide their personal data, besides becoming susceptible to identify theft, were unwittingly signing up to pay $98.95 a month for additional nonexistent "rewards" in the future. ■

9–6c Hacking

Hacker A person who uses computers to gain unauthorized access to data.

Botnets Networks of compromised computers connected to the Internet that can be used to generate spam, relay viruses, or cause servers to fail.

A **hacker** is someone who uses one computer, smartphone, or other device to break into another. The danger posed by hackers has increased significantly because of **botnets,** or networks of computers that have been appropriated by hackers without the knowledge of their owners. A hacker may secretly install a program on thousands, if not millions, of personal computer "robots," or "bots."

Example 9.26 After Apple, Inc., introduced its mobile-payment system, cyber thieves began hacking into Apple mobile devices to make purchases with stolen credit card numbers. At about the same time, cyber criminals were stealing the credit card data of at least 60 million Home Depot customers and illegally accessing the financial information of 76 million

JPMorgan Chase clients. Hackers have also demonstrated that they can take over the dashboard computer systems that control cars. Additionally, the risk of takeover extends to numerous wireless-enabled medical devices, such as pacemakers and insulin pumps.

Malware Botnets are one form of **malware,** a term that refers to any program that is harmful to a computer or, by extension, its user. One type of malware is a **worm**—a software program that is capable of reproducing itself as it spreads from one computer to the next. The Conficker worm, for instance, spread to more than a million personal computers around the world within a three-week period. It was transmitted to some computers through the use of Facebook and Twitter.

A **virus,** another form of malware, is also able to reproduce itself but must be attached to an "infested" host file to travel from one computer network to another. For instance, hackers can corrupt banner ads that use Adobe's Flash Player or send bogus Flash Player updates. When an Internet user clicks on the banner ad or installs the update, a virus is installed. Worms and viruses can be programmed to perform a number of functions, such as prompting host computers to continually "crash" and reboot, or to otherwise infect the system.

Service-Based Hacking Today, many companies offer "software as a service." Instead of buying software to install on a computer, the user connects to Web-based software. The user can then write e-mails, edit spreadsheets, and the like using a Web browser.

Cyber criminals have adapted this method and now offer "crimeware as a service." Would-be thieves no longer have to be computer hackers to create botnets or steal banking information and credit card numbers. They can rent the online services of cyber criminals to do the work for a small price. The thieves can even target individual groups, such as U.S. physicians or British attorneys.

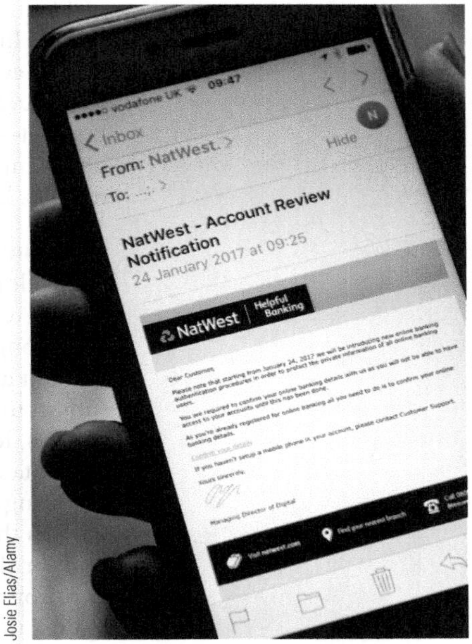

Josie Elias/Alamy

Hackers can potentially take over automobile computer systems. What other everyday products and services are susceptible to hacking?

Malware Malicious software programs, such as viruses and worms, that are designed to cause harm to a computer, network, or other device.

Worm A software program that automatically replicates itself over a network but does not alter files and is usually invisible to the user until it has consumed system resources.

Virus A software program that can replicate itself over a network and spread from one device to another, altering files and interfering with normal operations.

Cyberterrorists Criminals who use technology and the Internet to cause fear, violence, and extreme financial harm.

9–6d Cyberterrorism

Cyberterrorists use technology and the Internet to cause fear, violence, or extreme financial harm. Cyberterrorists, as well as hackers, may target businesses. The goals of a hacking operation might include a wholesale theft of data, such as a merchant's customer files, or the monitoring of a computer to discover a business firm's plans and transactions. A cyberterrorist might also insert false codes or data into a computer. For instance, the processing control system of a food manufacturer could be changed to alter the levels of ingredients so that consumers of the food would become ill.

A cyberterrorist attack on a major financial institution, such as the New York Stock Exchange or a large bank, could leave securities or money markets in flux. Such an attack could seriously affect the daily lives of U.S. citizens, business operations, and national security.

9–6e Prosecution of Cyber Crime

Cyber crime has raised new issues in the investigation of crimes and the prosecution of offenders. Determining the "location" of a cyber crime and identifying a criminal in cyberspace are two significant challenges for law enforcement.

Jurisdiction and Identification Challenges A threshold issue is, of course, jurisdiction. Jurisdiction is normally based on physical geography, and each state and nation has jurisdiction over crimes committed within its boundaries. But geographic boundaries simply do not apply in cyberspace. A person who commits an act against a business in California, where the act is a cyber crime, might never have set foot in California but might instead reside in, say, Canada, where the act may not be a crime.

Identifying the wrongdoer can also be difficult. Cyber criminals do not leave physical traces, such as fingerprints or DNA samples, as evidence of their crimes. Even electronic "footprints" (digital evidence) can be hard to find and follow. For instance, cyber criminals may employ software, such as Tor, to mask their IP addresses—codes that identify individual computers on the Internet—and the IP addresses of those with whom they communicate. Law enforcement must hire computer forensic experts to bypass the software and track down the criminals. For these reasons, laws written to protect physical property are often difficult to apply in cyberspace.

The Computer Fraud and Abuse Act Perhaps the most significant federal statute specifically addressing cyber crime is the Counterfeit Access Device and Computer Fraud and Abuse Act.[27] This act is commonly known as the Computer Fraud and Abuse Act, or CFAA.

Among other things, the CFAA provides that a person who accesses a computer online, without authority, to obtain classified, restricted, or protected data (or attempts to do so) is subject to criminal prosecution. Such data could include financial and credit records, medical records, legal files, military and national security files, and other confidential information. The data can be located in government or private computers. The crime has two elements: accessing a computer without authority and taking the data.

This theft is a felony if it is committed for a commercial purpose or for private financial gain, or if the value of the stolen information exceeds $5,000. Penalties include fines and imprisonment for up to twenty years. A victim of computer theft can also bring a civil suit against the violator to obtain damages, an injunction, and other relief.

---

27. 18 U.S.C. Section 1030.

Practice and Review

Edward Hanousek worked for Pacific & Arctic Railway and Navigation Company (P&A) as a roadmaster of the White Pass & Yukon Railroad in Alaska. As an officer of the corporation, Hanousek was responsible "for every detail of the safe and efficient maintenance and construction of track, structures, and marine facilities of the entire railroad," including special projects. One project was a rock quarry, known as "6-mile," above the Skagway River. Next to the quarry, and just beneath the surface, ran a high-pressure oil pipeline owned by Pacific & Arctic Pipeline, Inc., P&A's sister company. When the quarry's backhoe operator punctured the pipeline, an estimated one thousand to five thousand gallons of oil were discharged into the river. Hanousek was charged with negligently discharging a harmful quantity of oil into a navigable water of the United States in violation of the criminal provisions of the Clean Water Act (CWA). Using the information presented in the chapter, answer the following questions.

1. Did Hanousek have the required mental state (*mens rea*) to be convicted of a crime? Why or why not?
2. Which theory discussed in the chapter would enable a court to hold Hanousek criminally liable for violating the statute regardless of whether he participated in, directed, or even knew about the specific violation?
3. Could the backhoe operator who punctured the pipeline also be charged with a crime in this situation? Explain.
4. Suppose that, at trial, Hanousek argued that he could not be convicted because he was not aware of the requirements of the CWA. Would this defense be successful? Why or why not?

Debate This

Because of overcriminalization, particularly by the federal government, Americans may be breaking the law regularly without knowing it. Should Congress rescind many of the more than four thousand federal crimes now on the books?

Key Terms

actus reus 217
arson 223
beyond a reasonable doubt 215
botnets 236
burglary 222
computer crime 234
crime 214
cyber crime 234
cyber fraud 234
cyberterrorist 237
double jeopardy 232
duress 229
embezzlement 224
entrapment 229
exclusionary rule 233
felony 216
forgery 223
hacker 236
identity theft 235
insider trading 226
larceny 222
malware 237
mens rea 218
misdemeanor 217
money laundering 227
petty offense 217
phishing 236
plea bargaining 230
probable cause 231
robbery 222
search warrant 230
self-defense 228
self-incrimination 230
virus 237
white-collar crime 223
worm 237

Chapter Summary: Criminal Law and Cyber Crime

Civil Law and Criminal Law	1. **Civil law**—Pertains to the duties that exist between persons or between persons and their governments, excluding the duty not to commit crimes. 2. **Criminal law**—Has to do with crimes, which are wrongs against society proclaimed in statutes and, if committed, punishable by society through fines and/or imprisonment—or in some cases, death. Because crimes are *offenses against society as a whole*, they are prosecuted by a public official, not by the victims. 3. **Key differences**—An important difference between civil and criminal law is that the standard of proof is higher in criminal cases. 4. **Civil liability for criminal acts**—A criminal act may give rise to both criminal liability and tort liability. 5. **Classification of crimes**—Crimes may also be classified according to their degree of seriousness. Felonies are serious crimes usually punishable by death or by imprisonment for more than one year. Misdemeanors are less serious crimes punishable by fines or by confinement for up to one year.
Criminal Liability	1. **Guilty act**—In general, some form of harmful act to a person or property must be committed for a crime to exist. 2. **State of mind**—An intent to commit a crime, or a wrongful mental state, is also required for a crime to exist. 3. **Corporate criminal liability**—Corporations are normally liable for crimes committed by their agents or employees within the course and scope of their employment.
Types of Crimes	1. **Violent crimes**—Crimes that cause others to suffer harm or death, including murder, assault and battery, sexual assault, and robbery. 2. **Property crimes**—The most common form of crime. The offender's goal is to obtain some economic gain or to damage property. This category includes burglary, larceny, obtaining goods by false pretenses, receiving stolen property, arson, and forgery. 3. **Public order crimes**—Acts, such as public drunkenness, prostitution, gambling, and illegal drug use, that a statute has established are contrary to public values and morals. 4. **White-collar crimes**—Illegal acts committed by a person or business using nonviolent means to obtain a personal or business advantage. Usually, such crimes are committed in the course of a legitimate occupation. Examples include embezzlement, mail and wire fraud, bribery, bankruptcy fraud, theft of trade secrets, and insider trading. 5. **Organized crime**—A form of crime conducted by groups operating illegitimately to satisfy the public's demand for illegal goods and services (such as illegal drugs, gambling, and prostitution). Organized crime is heavily involved in cyber crime, money laundering, and racketeering (RICO) violations.
Defenses to Criminal Liability	Defenses to criminal liability include justifiable use of force, necessity, insanity, mistake, duress, entrapment, and the statute of limitations. In some cases, defendants may be relieved of criminal liability, at least in part, if they are given immunity.
Constitutional Safeguards	1. **Fourth Amendment**—Provides protection against unreasonable searches and seizures and requires that probable cause exist before a warrant for a search or seizure can be issued. 2. **Fifth Amendment**—Requires due process of law, prohibits double jeopardy, and protects against self-incrimination. 3. **Exclusionary rule**—A criminal procedural rule that prohibits the introduction at trial of all evidence obtained illegally or without a proper search warrant. 4. ***Miranda* rule**—A rule set forth by the Supreme Court in *Miranda v. Arizona* holding that individuals who are arrested must be informed of certain constitutional rights, including their right to counsel.

Cyber Crime

1. **Cyber fraud**—Misrepresentations are knowingly made over the Internet to deceive another. Two widely reported forms are online auction fraud and advance fee fraud.
2. **Cyber identity theft**—In cyberspace, identity theft is made easier by the fact that many e-businesses store information such as consumers' names, e-mail addresses, and credit card numbers. Password theft and phishing are variations of cyber identity theft.
3. **Hacking**—A hacker is a person who uses one computer to break into another. Malware is any program that is harmful to a computer or, by extension, a computer user. Worms and viruses are examples.
4. **Cyberterrorism**—A cyberterrorist attack on a major U.S. financial institution or telecommunications system could have serious repercussions, including jeopardizing national security.
5. **Prosecution of cyber crime**—Prosecuting cyber crime is more difficult than prosecuting traditional crime. Identifying the wrongdoer is complicated, and jurisdictional issues may arise. A significant federal statute addressing cyber crime is the Computer Fraud and Abuse Act.

Issue Spotters

1. Dana takes her roommate's credit card, intending to charge expenses that she incurs on a vacation. Her first stop is a gas station, where she uses the card to pay for gas. With respect to the gas station, has she committed a crime? If so, what is it? (See *Types of Crimes*.)
2. Without permission, Ben downloads consumer credit files from a computer belonging to Consumer Credit Agency. He then sells the data to Dawn. Has Ben committed a crime? If so, what is it? (See *Cyber Crime*.)

—Check your answers to the *Issue Spotters* against the answers provided in Appendix D.

Business Scenarios and Case Problems

9–1. Types of Cyber Crimes. The following situations are similar, but each represents a variation of a particular crime. Identify the crime and point out the differences in the variations. (See *Cyber Crime*.)

1. Chen, posing fraudulently as Diamond Credit Card Co., sends an e-mail to Emily, stating that the company has observed suspicious activity in her account and has frozen the account. The e-mail asks her to reregister her credit card number and password to reopen the account.
2. Claiming falsely to be Big Buy Retail Finance Co., Conner sends an e-mail to Dino, asking him to confirm or update his personal security information to prevent his Big Buy account from being discontinued.

9–2. Cyber Scam. Kayla, a student at Learnwell University, owes $20,000 in unpaid tuition. If Kayla does not pay the tuition, Learnwell will not allow her to graduate. To obtain the funds to pay the debt, she sends e-mails to people that she does not know asking them for financial help to send her child, who has a disability, to a special school. In reality, Kayla has no children. Is this a crime? If so, which one? (See *Cyber Crime*.)

9–3. Business Case Problem with Sample Answer—White-Collar Crime. Matthew Simpson and others created and operated a series of corporate entities to defraud telecommunications companies, creditors, credit reporting agencies, and others. Through these entities, Simpson and his confederates used routing codes and spoofing services to make long-distance calls appear to be local. They stole other firms' network capacity and diverted payments to themselves. They leased goods and services without paying for them. To hide their association with their corporate entities and with each other, they used false identities, addresses, and credit histories, and issued false bills, invoices, financial statements, and credit references. Did these acts constitute mail and wire fraud? Discuss. [*United States v. Simpson*, 741 F.3d 539 (5th Cir. 2014)] (See *Types of Crimes*.)

—For a sample answer to Problem 9–3, go to Appendix E.

9–4. Defenses to Criminal Liability. George Castro told Ambrosio Medrano that a bribe to a certain corrupt Los Angeles County official would buy a contract with the county hospitals. To share in the deal, Medrano recruited Gustavo Buenrostro. In turn, Buenrostro contacted his friend James Barta, the owner of Sav–Rx, which provides prescription benefit management services. Barta was asked to pay a "finder's fee" to Castro. He did not pay, even after frequent e-mails and calls with deadlines and ultimatums delivered over a period of months. Eventually, Barta wrote Castro a Sav–Rx check for $6,500, saying that it was to help his friend Buenrostro. Castro was an FBI agent, and the county official and contract were fictional. Barta was charged with conspiracy to commit bribery. At trial, the government conceded that Barta was not predisposed to commit the crime. Could he be absolved of the charge on a defense of entrapment? Explain. [*United States v. Barta*, 776 F.3d 931 (7th Cir. 2015)] (See *Defenses to Criminal Liability*.)

9–5. Fourth Amendment Protections. Federal officers obtained a warrant to arrest Kateena Norman on charges of credit card fraud and identity theft. Evidence of the crime included videos, photos, and a fingerprint on a fraudulent check. A previous search of Norman's house had uncovered credit cards, new merchandise, and identifying information for other persons. An Internet account registered to the address had been used to apply for fraudulent credit cards, and a fraudulently obtained rental car was parked on the property. As the officers arrested Norman outside her house, they saw another woman and a caged pit bull inside. They further believed that Norman's boyfriend, who had a criminal record and was also suspected of identify theft, could be there. In less than a minute, the officers searched only those areas within the house in which a person could hide. Would it be reasonable to admit evidence revealed in this "protective sweep" during Norman's trial on the arrest charges? Discuss. [*United States v. Norman*, 637 Fed. Appx. 934 (11th Cir. 2016)] (See *Constitutional Safeguards*.)

9–6. Types of Crimes. In Texas, Chigger Ridge Ranch, L.P., operated a 700-acre commercial hunting area called Coyote Crossing Ranch (CCR). Chigger Ridge leased CCR and its assets for twelve months to George Briscoe's company, VPW Management, LLC. The lease identified all of the vehicles and equipment that belonged to Chigger Ridge, which VPW could use in the course of business, but the lease did not convey any ownership interest. During the lease term, however, Briscoe told his employees to sell some of the vehicles and equipment. Briscoe did nothing to correct the buyers' false impression that he owned the property and was authorized to sell it. The buyers paid with checks, which were deposited into an account to which only Briscoe and his spouse had access. Which crime, if any, did Briscoe commit? Explain. [*Briscoe v. State of Texas*, 2018 WL 792255 (Tex.App.—Texarkana 2018)] (See *Types of Crimes*.)

9–7. A Question of Ethics—The IDDR Approach and Identity Theft. Heesham Broussard obtained counterfeit money instruments. To distribute them, he used account information and numbers on compromised FedEx accounts procured from hackers. Text messages from Broussard indicated that he had participated previously in a similar scam and that he knew the packages would be delivered only if the FedEx accounts were "good." For his use of the accounts, Broussard was charged with identity theft. In defense, he argued that the government could not prove he knew the misappropriated accounts belonged to real persons or businesses. [*United States v. Broussard*, 675 Fed.Appx. 454 (5th Cir. 2017)] (See *Cyber Crime*.)

1. Does the evidence support Broussard's assertion? From an ethical perspective, does it matter whether he knew that the accounts belonged to real customers? Why or why not?
2. Assuming that FedEx knew its customers' account information had been compromised, use the IDDR approach to consider whether the company had an ethical obligation to take steps to protect those customers from theft.

Critical Thinking and Writing Assignments

9–8. Critical Legal Thinking. Ray steals a purse from an unattended car at a gas station. Because the purse contains money and a handgun, Ray is convicted of grand theft of property (cash) and grand theft of a firearm. On appeal, Ray claims that he is not guilty of grand theft of a firearm because he did not know that the purse contained a gun. Can Ray be convicted of grand theft of a firearm even though he did not know that the gun was in the purse? Explain. (See *Types of Crimes*.)

9–9. Time-Limited Group Assignment—Cyber Crime. Cyber crime costs consumers millions of dollars every year. It costs businesses, including banks and other credit card issuers, even more. Nonetheless, when cyber criminals are caught and convicted, they are rarely ordered to pay restitution or sentenced to long prison terms. (See *Cyber Crime*.)

1. One group should formulate an argument that stiffer sentences would reduce the amount of cyber crime.
2. A second group should determine how businesspersons can best protect themselves from cyber crime and avoid the associated costs.
3. A third group should decide how and when a court should order cyber criminals to pay restitution to their victims. Should victims whose computers have been infected with worms or viruses be entitled to restitution, or only victims of theft who have experienced financial loss? What should the measure of restitution be? Should large companies that are victims of cyber crime be entitled to the same restitution as individuals?

Unit One—Task-Based Simulation

iStockPhoto.com/lisafx

CompTac, Inc., which is headquartered in San Francisco, California, is one of the leading software manufacturers in the United States. The company invests millions of dollars to research and develop new software applications and computer games that are sold worldwide. It also has a large service department and takes great pains to offer its customers excellent support services.

1. **Jurisdiction.** CompTac routinely purchases some of the materials necessary to produce its computer games from a New York firm, Electrotex, Inc. A dispute arises between the two firms, and CompTac wants to sue Electrotex for breach of contract. Can CompTac bring the suit in a California state court? Can CompTac bring the suit in a federal court? Explain.

2. **Negligence.** A customer at one of CompTac's retail stores stumbles over a crate in the parking lot and breaks her leg. Just moments earlier, the crate had fallen off a CompTac truck that was delivering goods from a CompTac warehouse to the store. The customer sues CompTac, alleging negligence. Will she succeed in her suit? Why or why not?

3. **Wrongful Interference.** Roban Electronics, a software manufacturer and one of CompTac's major competitors, has been trying to convince one of CompTac's key employees, Jim Baxter, to come to work for Roban. Roban knows that Baxter has a written employment contract with CompTac, which Baxter would breach if he left CompTac before the contract expired. Baxter goes to work for Roban, and the departure of its key employee causes CompTac to suffer substantial losses due to delays in completing new software. Can CompTac sue Roban to recoup some of these losses? If so, on what ground?

4. **Cyber Crime.** One of CompTac's employees in its accounting division, Alan Green, has a gambling problem. To repay a gambling debt of $10,000, Green decides to "borrow" from CompTac to cover the debt. Using his knowledge of Comp-Tac account numbers, Green electronically transfers $10,000 from a CompTac account into his personal checking account. A week later, he is luckier at gambling and uses the same electronic procedures to transfer funds from his personal checking account back to the CompTac account. Has Green committed any crimes? If so, what are they?

5. **Ethical Decision Making.** One of CompTac's best-selling products is a computer game that includes some extremely violent actions. Groups of parents, educators, and consumer activists have bombarded CompTac with letters and e-mail messages calling on the company to stop selling the product. CompTac executives are concerned about the public outcry, but at the same time, they realize that the game is CompTac's major source of profits. If it ceased marketing the game, the company could go bankrupt. If you were a CompTac decision maker, what would your decision be in this situation? How would you justify your decision from an ethical perspective?

6. **Intellectual Property.** CompTac wants to sell one of its best-selling software programs to An Phat Company, a firm located in Ho Chi Minh City, Vietnam. CompTac is concerned, however, that after an initial purchase, An Phat will duplicate the software without permission (and in violation of U.S. copyright laws) and sell the illegal bootleg software to other firms in Vietnam. How can CompTac protect its software from being pirated by An Phat Company?

7. **Social Media.** CompTac seeks to hire fourteen new employees. Its human resources (HR) department asks all candidates during their interview to disclose their social media passwords so that the company can access their social media accounts. Is it legal for employers to ask prospective employees for their social media passwords? Explain. If CompTac does not ask for passwords, can it legally look at a person's online posts when evaluating whether to hire or fire the person?

Sergii Gnatiuk/Shutterstock.com

Unit 2
Contracts and E-Contracts

10 Nature and Classification

Focus Questions

The five Focus Questions *below are designed to help improve your understanding. After reading this chapter, you should be able to answer the following questions:*

1. What is the objective theory of contracts?
2. What are the four basic elements necessary to the formation of a valid contract?
3. What is the difference between express and implied contracts?
4. When will a court impose a quasi contract?
5. What rules guide the courts in interpreting contracts?

Promise A declaration that binds the person who makes it (the promisor) to do or not to do a certain act.

Promisor A person who makes a promise.

Promisee A person to whom a promise is made.

"All sensible people are selfish, and nature is tugging at every contract to make the terms of it fair."

Ralph Waldo Emerson
1803–1882 (American poet)

As Ralph Waldo Emerson observed in the chapter-opening quotation, people tend to act in their own self-interest, and this influences the terms they seek in their contracts. Contract law must therefore provide rules to determine which contract terms will be enforced.

A contract is based on a **promise**—a declaration by a person (the **promisor**) that binds the person to do or not to do a certain act. As a result, the person to whom the promise is made (the **promisee**) has a right to expect or demand that something either will or will not happen in the future.

Like other types of law, contract law reflects our social values, interests, and expectations at a given point in time. It shows what kinds of promises our society thinks should be legally binding. For instance, licensing agreements that a person clicks on to download software on a smartphone are promises that should be legally binding. If Alicia agrees to Snapchat's terms of service but then reverse-engineers Snapchat's software to create competing software, she has breached her contract with Snapchat. Contract law also distinguishes between promises that create only moral obligations (such as a promise to take a friend to lunch) and promises that are legally binding (such as a promise to pay for items ordered online).

10–1 An Overview of Contract Law

Before we look at the numerous rules that courts use to determine whether a particular promise will be enforced, it is necessary to understand some fundamental concepts of contract law. In this section, we describe the sources and general function of contract law and introduce the objective theory of contracts.

10–1a Sources of Contract Law

The common law governs all contracts except when it has been modified or replaced by statutory law, such as the Uniform Commercial Code (UCC), or by administrative agency regulations. Contracts relating to services, real estate, employment, and insurance, for instance, generally are governed by the common law of contracts. Contracts for the sale and lease of goods, however, are governed by the UCC to the extent that the UCC has modified general contract law.

fstop123/E+/Getty Images

House purchases always are completed with explicit contracts. Why?

10–1b The Function of Contracts

No aspect of modern life is entirely free of contractual relationships. You acquire rights and obligations, for instance, when you borrow funds, buy or lease a house, obtain insurance, form a business, or purchase goods or services. Contract law is designed to provide stability and predictability, as well as certainty, for both buyers and sellers in the marketplace.

Contract law assures the parties to private agreements that the promises they make will be enforceable. Clearly, many promises are kept because the parties involved feel a moral obligation to keep them or because keeping a promise is in their mutual self-interest. Nevertheless, in business agreements, the rules of contract law are often followed to avoid potential disputes.

By supplying procedures for enforcing private agreements, contract law provides an essential condition for the existence of a market economy. Without a legal framework of reasonably assured expectations within which to make long-run plans, businesspersons would be able to rely only on the good faith of others. Duty and good faith are usually sufficient to obtain compliance with a promise. When price changes or adverse economic factors make contract compliance costly, however, these elements may not be enough. Contract law is necessary to ensure compliance with a promise or to entitle the innocent party to some form of relief.

10–1c The Definition of a Contract

A **contract** is an agreement that can be enforced in court. It is formed by two or more parties who agree to perform or to refrain from performing some act now or in the future.

Contract A set of promises constituting an agreement between parties, giving each a legal duty to the other and the right to seek a remedy for the breach of the promises or duties.

Generally, contract disputes arise when there is a promise of future performance. If the contractual promise is not fulfilled, the party who made it is subject to the sanctions of a court. That party may be required to pay damages for failing to perform the contractual promise. In a few instances, the party may be required to perform the promised act.

10–1d The Objective Theory of Contracts

In determining whether a contract has been formed, the element of intent is of prime importance. In contract law, intent is determined by what is referred to as the **objective theory of contracts.** Under this theory, a party's intention to enter into a contract is judged by outward, objective facts as interpreted by a *reasonable person*, rather than by the party's secret, subjective intentions. Objective facts may include:

Objective Theory of Contracts The view that contracting parties shall be bound only by terms that can be objectively inferred from promises made.

1. What the party said when entering into the contract.
2. How the party acted or appeared.
3. The circumstances surrounding the transaction.

Focus Question 1

What is the objective theory of contracts?

Case Example 10.1 The Leaf Clean Energy Company invested $30 million with Invenergy Wind, a wind energy developer. The investment contract prohibited Invenergy from conducting a "Material Partial Sale" without Leaf's consent. If such a sale occurred, Invenergy was required to pay Leaf a penalty. After Invenergy concluded a $1.8 billion "Material Partial Sale" without Leaf's consent, the investment company sued to obtain its penalty under the contract, which was about $126 million.

A lower court agreed that Invenergy had breached the contract but awarded Leaf only one dollar in damages. The court reasoned that, under the terms of the agreement, if Leaf *had* been notified and agreed to the sale, Leaf would not have received *any* payment. (That is, Leaf was entitled to a penalty only if Invenergy breached the contract.) It would have been unfair for Leaf to gain such a large amount when it had not suffered any actual harm. Applying the objective theory of contracts, the Delaware Supreme Court reversed and ordered Invenergy to pay Leaf the $126 million. The appellate court scolded the lower court for ignoring the "clear and unambiguous" terms of the contract, which were designed to prevent Invenergy from making any major financial decisions without Leaf's consent.[1]

10–2 Elements of a Contract

The many topics that will be discussed in the following chapters on contract law require an understanding of the basic elements of a valid contract and the way in which a contract is created. Also important is an understanding of the types of circumstances in which even legally valid contracts will not be enforced.

10–2a Requirements of a Valid Contract

The following list briefly describes the four requirements that must be met for a valid contract to exist. If any of these elements is lacking, no contract will have been formed. (Each item will be explained more fully in subsequent chapters.)

Focus Question 2

What are the four basic elements necessary to the formation of a valid contract?

1. *Agreement*. An agreement to form a contract includes an *offer* and an *acceptance*. One party must offer to enter into a legal agreement, and another party must accept the terms of the offer.
2. *Consideration*. Any promises made by the parties must be supported by legally sufficient and bargained-for consideration (something of value received or promised to convince a person to make a deal).
3. *Contractual capacity*. Both parties entering into the contract must have the contractual capacity to do so. The law must recognize them as possessing characteristics that qualify them as competent parties.
4. *Legality*. The contract's purpose must be to accomplish some goal that is legal and not against public policy.

An agreement to form a contract can modify the terms of a previous contract. When a dispute concerns whether this has occurred, the offer and acceptance of both agreements can be reviewed to determine their effect. If the terms are ambiguous, evidence outside the expression of an agreement can be considered to determine what the parties intended at the time.

Of course, as in every case involving a contract, the parties' *subjective* beliefs with respect to the terms are irrelevant, particularly in the absence of any evidence to support those beliefs. In the following case, the court applied the objective theory of contracts to determine the intent of parties who had agreed to a promissory note for the repayment of a student loan.

1. *Leaf Invenergy Company v. Invenergy Renewables LLC*, 210 A.3d 688 (Del. 2019).

Case 10.1

Credible Behavioral Health, Inc. v. Johnson

Court of Appeals of Maryland, 466 Md. 380, 220 A.3d 303 (2019).

Facts Credible Behavioral Health, Inc., provides software solutions to behavioral health and human services providers. Credible offers a tuition loan program to its employees who wish to pursue undergraduate, graduate, or postgraduate education. Emmanuel Johnson, a Credible employee, accepted the offer, and the parties memorialized their agreement in a promissory note. The terms provided that Johnson would repay the loan after completing his studies, with the percentage to be repaid depending on how long he remained with the company. Before Johnson obtained a degree, however, Credible fired him.

When he did not repay the loan, Credible filed a suit in a Maryland state court against him, seeking repayment. Johnson argued that the terms of the note required repayment only if he quit his employment, not if he was fired. The trial court ruled in his favor. Credible appealed. A state intermediate appellate court affirmed the ruling. Credible appealed to the state's highest court, the Maryland Court of Appeals.

Issue Did the parties intend the note to be repaid regardless of whether an employee quit or was fired?

Decision Yes. The Maryland Court of Appeals reversed the decision of the intermediate appellate court, which had upheld the ruling of the trial court. The lower courts "erred in construing the promissory note to require repayment only in situations where an employee quits."

Reason Credible argued that the terms of the note revealed that the parties intended the loan to be repaid on termination of employment whether an employee was fired or quit. The state's highest court applied the objective theory of contracts to determine the parties' intent in agreeing to the note and to interpret its terms to be consistent with that intent. This determination "is based on what a reasonable person in the position of the parties would have understood the language to mean and not the subjective intent of the parties at the time of formation." The note provided for the repayment of the loan, plus interest, "if you terminate employment with the company" less than thirty-six months after achieving a degree.

The note further provided that this amount was due and payable ninety days "after the termination of your employment, whether by you or the company." The court reasoned that this language "substantially uncloaks the intent underlying the promissory note. It makes clear that the parties intended the loan to be repaid . . . in situations where Credible fires an employee."

Critical Thinking

- **Legal Environment** *As a principle of contract interpretation, courts consistently strive to interpret contracts in accord with common sense. Does the application of this principle to the facts in this case support or undercut the decision of the Maryland Court of Appeals? Explain.*
- **Economic** *What consequences might Credible have suffered if the Maryland Court of Appeals had interpreted the terms of the note to require repayment only when an employee quit, not when that employee was fired? Discuss.*

10–2b Defenses to the Enforceability of a Contract

Even if all of the requirements listed above are satisfied, a contract may be unenforceable if the following requirements are not met. These requirements typically are raised as *defenses* to the enforceability of an otherwise valid contract.

1. *Voluntary consent.* The consent of both parties must be voluntary. For instance, if a contract was formed as a result of fraud, mistake, or duress (coercion), the contract may not be enforceable.
2. *Form.* The contract must be in whatever form the law requires. Some contracts must be in writing to be enforceable.

10–3 Types of Contracts

There are many types of contracts. They may be categorized based on legal distinctions as to their *formation*, *performance*, and *enforceability*.

10–3a Contract Formation

Contracts may be classified based on how and when they are formed. Exhibit 10–1 shows three such classifications, and the following subsections explain them in greater detail.

Offeror A person who makes an offer.

Offeree A person to whom an offer is made.

Bilateral Contract A type of contract that arises when a promise is given in exchange for a return promise.

Bilateral versus Unilateral Contracts Every contract involves at least two parties. The **offeror** is the party making the offer (promising to do or not to do something). The **offeree** is the party to whom the offer is made. A contract is classified as *bilateral* or *unilateral* depending on what the offeree must do to accept the offer and bind the offeror to a contract.

Bilateral Contracts. If the offeree can accept simply by promising to perform, the contract is a **bilateral contract.** Hence, a bilateral contract is a "promise for a promise." An example of a bilateral contract is a contract in which one person agrees to buy another person's automobile for a specified price. No performance, such as the payment of funds or delivery of goods, need take place for a bilateral contract to be formed. The contract comes into existence at the moment the promises are exchanged.

Example 10.2 Javier offers to buy Ann's smartphone for $200. Javier tells Ann that he will give her the cash for the phone on the following Friday, when he gets paid. Ann accepts Javier's offer and promises to give him the phone when he pays her on Friday. Javier and Ann have formed a bilateral contract.

Unilateral Contract A type of contract that results when an offer can be accepted only by the offeree's performance.

Unilateral Contracts. If the offer is phrased so that the offeree can accept only by completing the contract performance, the contract is a **unilateral contract.** Hence, a unilateral contract is a "promise for an act." In other words, the contract is formed not at the moment when promises are exchanged but rather when the contract is *performed.*

Example 10.3 Reese says to Kay, "If you drive my car from New York to Los Angeles, I'll give you $1,000." Only on Kay's completion of the act—bringing the car to Los Angeles—does she fully accept Reese's offer to pay $1,000. If she chooses not to accept the offer to drive the car to Los Angeles, there are no legal consequences.

Exhibit 10–1 Classifications Based on Contract Formation

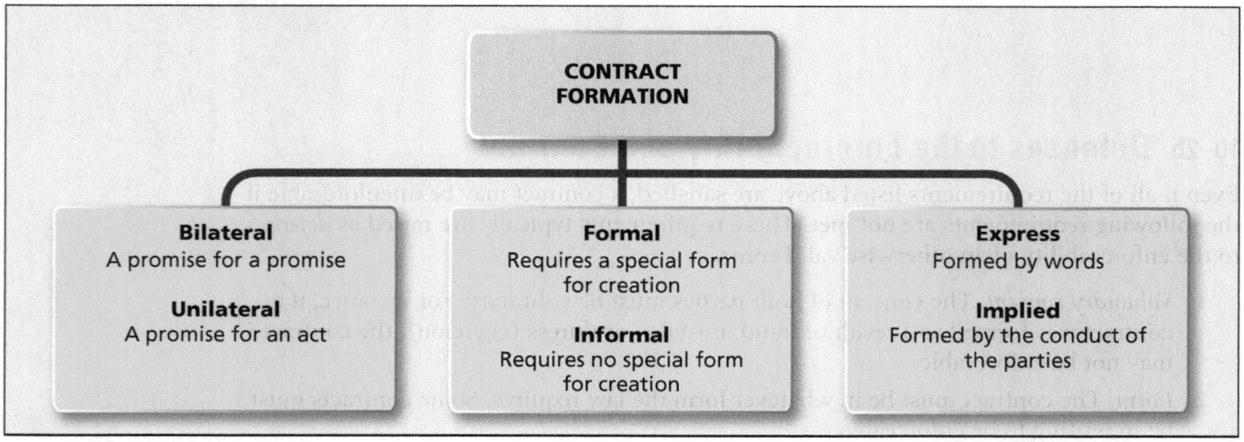

Contests, lotteries, and other competitions offering prizes are also examples of offers for unilateral contracts. If a person complies with the rules of the contest—such as by submitting the right lottery number at the right place and time—a unilateral contract is formed. The organization offering the prize is then bound to a contract to perform as promised in the offer. If the person fails to comply with the contest rules, however, no binding contract is formed.

Ethical Issue

Does a "You break it, you buy it" sign create a unilateral contract? It is not unusual to see posted in retail stores signs that say, "You break it, you buy it." The implication, of course, is that you are legally obligated to buy something if you break it while inspecting it prior to a potential purchase. This "rule" is often known as the "Pottery Barn Rule," even though that retailer has no such rule.

Some argue that posted signs of this nature create unilateral contracts. It is difficult to prove the validity of such contracts, however. After all, for a contract to be formed, the accepting party has to demonstrate acceptance of the terms purposed. Few courts would uphold the notion that every customer agrees to every proposition posted on the walls of retail establishments. Moreover, where is the consideration? That is, what does the retailer give customers in return for their acceptance of a unilateral contract that says, "You break it, you buy it"?

Consider also that every customer in a retail establishment is an *invitee*. Consequently, the retailer accepts the risk that customers may accidentally damage items on display, regardless of posted warnings. Simply stating that once a customer reads a sign and chooses to continue shopping constitutes an acceptance is not only legally problematic, it is ethically bothersome. Merchants cannot transfer the risk of breakage to customers just by posting notices.

Revocation of Offers for Unilateral Contracts. A problem arises in unilateral contracts when the promisor attempts to *revoke* (cancel) the offer after the promisee has begun performance but before the act has been completed. **Example 10.4** Seiko offers to buy Jin's sailboat, moored in San Francisco, on delivery of the boat to Seiko's dock in Newport Beach, three hundred miles south of San Francisco. Jin rigs the boat and sets sail. Shortly before his arrival at Newport Beach, Jin receives a message from Seiko withdrawing her offer. Is the offer terminated?

In contract law, offers are normally *revocable* (capable of being taken back, or canceled) until accepted. Under the traditional view of unilateral contracts, Seiko's revocation would terminate the offer. Because Seiko's offer was to form a unilateral contract, only Jin's delivery of the sailboat at her dock would have been an acceptance.

Natta Ang/Shutterstock.com

Can a party withdraw from an offer to buy a sailboat just before it is delivered to the agreed-upon location? Why or why not?

Because of the harsh effect on the offeree of the revocation of an offer to form a unilateral contract, the modern-day view is different. Today, once performance has been *substantially* undertaken, the offeror cannot revoke the offer. In fact, as illustrated by the following case, the rule in some states is that as soon as the offeree begins performing, the offeror is precluded from revoking or modifying the offer.

Case 10.2

Boswell v. Panera Bread Co.

United States Court of Appeals, Eighth Circuit, 879 F.3d 296 (2018).

Facts To recruit and retain managers for its restaurants, Panera Bread Company created a program under which managers were eligible to receive a one-time bonus. A manager who signed an agreement to participate in the program would be paid the bonus five years later, provided the manager was still working for Panera at that time. The amount of the bonus depended on the profitability of the manager's restaurant. Later, a change in general business conditions led Panera to conclude that the bonuses would be too costly. The employer set a $100,000 cap on the amount. Mark Boswell and sixty-six other managers filed a suit in a federal district court, maintaining that by imposing the cap, Panera committed breach of contract. The court issued a summary judgment in favor of the managers. Panera appealed to the U.S. Court of Appeals for the Eighth Circuit.

Issue Were the managers entitled to bonuses based on the offer's original terms?

Decision Yes. The U.S. Court of Appeals for the Eighth Circuit affirmed the judgment of the lower court. Panera's promise to pay bonuses in return for the managers' continued employment was an offer for a unilateral contract. "Panera was not entitled to move the goalposts on them by imposing a bonus cap, which was outside the contemplation of the . . . offer."

Reason The managers were at-will employees when they signed the bonus agreements, which provided that they would retain this status for the five-year period. Employment at will is a unilateral contract—the employer promises to pay if the employee works as directed. "An employer's promise to pay a bonus in return for an at-will employee's continued employment is an offer for a unilateral contract." To make an offer for a unilateral contract irrevocable, the offeree need only begin performance. The purpose of this rule is to protect the offeree's justifiable reliance on the offeror's promise. In this case, each of the managers had begun performing. Therefore, the offer had become irrevocable, and Panera could not modify its terms. Of course, "Panera could have terminated the managers if it chose and precluded them from receiving the bonus, but it did not."

Critical Thinking

- **Economic** *Could Panera have successfully argued that a drop in its revenue allowed it to impose the cap? Why or why not?*
- **Legal Environment** *Does the fact that the managers continued to work for Panera after it imposed the cap undercut their claim? Explain.*

Formal Contract An agreement that by law requires a specific form for its validity.

Informal Contract A contract that does not require a specific form or method of creation to be valid.

Express Contract A contract in which the terms of the agreement are stated in words, oral or written.

Formal versus Informal Contracts Another classification system divides contracts into formal contracts and informal contracts. A **formal contract** requires a special form or method of creation (formation) to be enforceable.[2] One example is *negotiable instruments*, which include checks, drafts, promissory notes, and certificates of deposit. Negotiable instruments are formal contracts because, under the Uniform Commercial Code, a special form and language are required to create them. *Letters of credit*, which are frequently used in international sales contracts, are another type of formal contract.

Any contract that is not a formal contract is an **informal contract** (also called a *simple contract*). No special form is required (except for certain types of contracts that must be in writing or evidenced by an electronic record). The contracts are usually based on their substance rather than their form. Typically, though, businesspersons put their contracts in writing (including electronic records) to ensure that there is some proof of a contract's existence should problems arise.

Express versus Implied Contracts Contracts may also be categorized as express or implied. In an **express contract**, the terms of the agreement are fully and explicitly

2. *See Restatement (Second) of Contracts*, Section 6. Remember that *Restatements of the Law* are books that summarize court decisions on a particular topic and that courts often refer to for guidance.

stated in words, oral or written. A signed lease for an apartment or a house is an express written contract. If a classmate accepts your offer to sell your textbooks from last semester for $200, an express oral contract has been made.

A contract that is implied from the conduct of the parties is called an **implied contract** (or sometimes an *implied-in-fact contract*). This type of contract differs from an express contract in that the *conduct* of the parties, rather than their words, creates and defines at least some of the terms of the contract. For an implied contract to arise, certain requirements must be met.

Implied Contract A contract formed in whole or in part from the conduct of the parties.

Requirements for Implied Contracts. Normally, if the following conditions exist, a court will hold that an implied contract was formed:

1. The plaintiff furnished some service or property.
2. The plaintiff expected to be paid for that service or property, and the defendant knew or should have known that payment was expected.
3. The defendant had a chance to reject the services or property and did not.

Focus Question 3
What is the difference between express and implied contracts?

Example 10.5 Ryan, a small business owner, needs an accountant to complete his tax return. He drops by a local accountant's office, explains his situation to the accountant, and learns what fees she charges. The next day, he returns and gives the receptionist all of the necessary documents to complete his tax return. Then he walks out without saying anything further. In this situation, Ryan has entered into an implied contract to pay the accountant the usual fees for her services. The contract is implied because of Ryan's conduct and hers. She expects to be paid for completing the tax return, and by bringing in the records she will need to do the job, Ryan has implied an intent to pay her.

Mixed Contracts with Express and Implied Terms. Note that a contract can be a mixture of an express contract and an implied contract. In other words, a contract may contain some express terms, while others are implied. During the construction of a home, for instance, the homeowner often asks the builder to make changes in the original specifications.

Spotlight Case Example 10.6 Lamar Hopkins hired Uhrhahn Construction & Design, Inc., for several projects in the construction of his home. For each project, the parties signed a written contract that was based on a cost estimate and specifications and that required changes to the agreement to be in writing. While the work was in progress, however, Hopkins repeatedly asked Uhrhahn to deviate from the contract specifications, which Uhrhahn did. None of these requests was made in writing.

One day, Hopkins asked Uhrhahn to use Durisol blocks instead of the cinder blocks specified in the original contract, indicating that the cost would be the same. Uhrhahn used the Durisol blocks but demanded extra payment when it became clear that the Durisol blocks were more complicated to install. Although Hopkins had paid for the other orally requested deviations from the contract, he refused to pay Uhrhahn for the substitution of the Durisol blocks. Uhrhahn sued for breach of contract. The court found that Hopkins, through his conduct, had waived the provision requiring written contract modification and created an implied contract to pay the extra cost of installing the Durisol blocks.[3]

jhorrocks/E+/Getty Images

Under what circumstances can an owner be liable for additional costs due to a request for a change in materials even though no written contract modification was created?

10–3b Contract Performance

Executed Contract A contract that has been fully performed by both parties.

Executory Contract A contract that has not yet been fully performed.

Contracts are also classified according to their state of performance. A contract that has been fully performed on both sides is called an **executed contract.** A contract that has not been fully performed by the parties is called an **executory contract.** If one party has fully performed but

3. *Uhrhahn Construction & Design, Inc. v. Hopkins,* 179 P.3d 808 (Utah App. 2008).

the other has not, the contract is said to be executed on the one side and executory on the other, but the contract is still classified as executory.

Example 10.7 Jackson, Inc., agreed to buy ten tons of coal from the Northern Coal Company. Northern has delivered the coal to Jackson's steel mill, but Jackson has not yet paid. At this point, the contract is executed on the part of Northern and executory on Jackson's part. After Jackson pays Northern, the contract will be executed on both sides. ■

10–3c Contract Enforceability

Valid Contract A contract that results when the elements necessary for contract formation (agreement, consideration, capacity, and legality) are present.

A **valid contract** has the four elements necessary to entitle at least one of the parties to enforce it in court. Those elements, as mentioned earlier, consist of (1) an agreement (offer and acceptance), (2) supported by legally sufficient consideration, (3) made by parties who have the legal capacity to enter into the contract, (4) for a legal purpose.

As you can see in Exhibit 10-2, valid contracts may be enforceable, voidable, or unenforceable. Additionally, a contract may be referred to as a *void contract*. We look next at the meaning of the terms *voidable*, *unenforceable*, and *void* in relation to contract enforceability.

Voidable Contract A contract that may be legally avoided at the option of one or both of the parties.

Voidable Contracts A **voidable contract** is a valid contract but one that can be avoided at the option of one or both of the parties. The party having the option can elect either to avoid any duty to perform or to *ratify* (make valid) the contract. If the contract is avoided, both parties are released from it. If it is ratified, both parties must fully perform their respective legal obligations.

For instance, contracts made by minors generally are voidable at the option of the minor (with certain exceptions). Contracts made by incompetent persons and intoxicated persons may also be voidable. Additionally, contracts entered into under fraudulent conditions are voidable at the option of the defrauded party. Contracts entered into under legally defined duress or undue influence are also voidable.

Unenforceable Contract A valid contract rendered unenforceable by some statute or law.

Unenforceable Contracts An **unenforceable contract** is one that cannot be enforced because of certain legal defenses against it. It is not unenforceable because a party failed to satisfy a legal requirement of the contract. Rather, it is a valid contract rendered unenforceable by some statute or law. For instance, some contracts must be in writing. If they are not, they will not be enforceable except in certain exceptional circumstances.

Exhibit 10–2 Enforceable, Voidable, Unenforceable, and Void Contracts

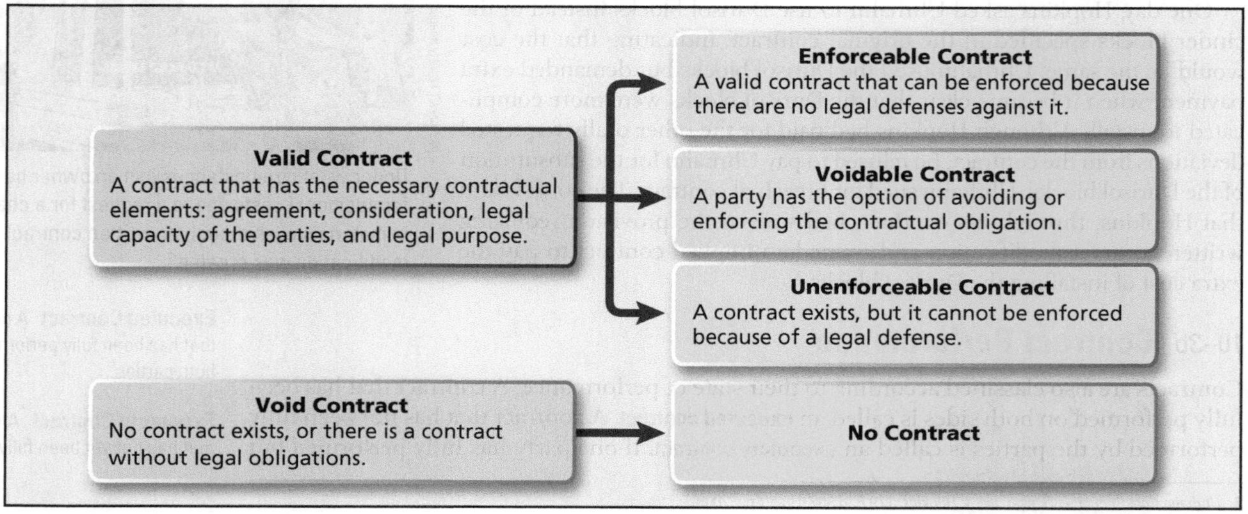

Void Contracts A **void contract** is no contract at all. The terms *void* and *contract* are contradictory. None of the parties has any legal obligations if a contract is void. A contract can be void because one of the parties was previously determined by a court to be mentally incompetent, for instance, or because the purpose of the contract was illegal.

Void Contract A contract having no legal force or binding effect.

10–4 Quasi Contracts

Express contracts and implied contracts are actual or true contracts formed by the words or actions of the parties. A **quasi contract**, or contract *implied in law*, is not an actual contract because it does not arise from any agreement, express or implied, between the parties themselves. Rather, it is a fictional contract that courts can impose on the parties "as if" the parties had entered into an actual contract. (The word *quasi* is Latin for "as if.")

Quasi Contract An obligation or contract imposed by law (a court), in the absence of an agreement, to prevent the unjust enrichment of one party.

Quasi contracts are equitable rather than legal contracts. Usually, they are imposed to avoid the *unjust enrichment* of one party at the expense of another. The doctrine of unjust enrichment is based on the theory that individuals should not be allowed to profit or enrich themselves inequitably at the expense of others. **Case Example 10.8** Chad Parker owned about an acre of property that had a trailer home on it. He sold the trailer to David and Alison Wilson for $1,000 and sold the property to them for $10,000. These agreements were made orally, and no title or deed transfers took place. The Wilsons lived in the trailer for seven years, making $11,228.19 of improvements to the structure and the property. After a falling out between Parker and David, Parker had the Wilsons evicted and moved back into the trailer.

Focus Question 4

When will a court impose a quasi contract?

A Pennsylvania appellate court found that, in the absence of any express contract, Parker had unjustly enriched himself at the Wilsons' expense. Enforcing a quasi contract, the court ordered Parker to pay the Wilsons $12,228.19 in damages. This amount represented the value of the improvements plus the $1,000 difference between how much the Wilsons actually paid Parker and how much they would have paid him had they rented the trailer and property for seven years.[4] For an example of when a court would most likely not impose a quasi contract, see this chapter's *Business Law Analysis* feature.

When the court imposes a quasi contract, a plaintiff may recover in ***quantum meruit***,[5] a Latin phrase meaning "as much as one deserves." *Quantum meruit* essentially describes the extent of compensation owed under a quasi contract.

Quantum Meruit A Latin phrase meaning "as much as one deserves." The expression describes the extent of compensation owed under a quasi contract.

10–4a Limitations on Quasi-Contractual Recovery

Although quasi contracts exist to prevent unjust enrichment, in some situations, the party who obtains a benefit is not liable for its fair value. Basically, a party who has conferred a benefit on someone else unnecessarily or as a result of misconduct or negligence cannot invoke the doctrine of quasi contract. The enrichment in those situations will not be considered "unjust."

Case Example 10.9 Michael Plambeck owned two chiropractic clinics in Kentucky that treated many patients injured in car accidents, including some who were customers of State Farm Automobile Insurance Company. All of the clinics' treating chiropractors were licensed to practice in Kentucky, but Plambeck (the owner) was not. Plambeck was a licensed chiropractor in another state but had allowed his Kentucky license to lapse because he was not treating any patients. Plambeck did not realize that Kentucky state law required him to be licensed as the owner of the clinics.

When State Farm discovered that Plambeck was not licensed in Kentucky, it filed a suit against the clinics seeking to recover payments it had made on behalf of its customers. The

4. *Wilson v. Parker*, 2020 PA Super 13, __ A.3d __ (2020).
5. Pronounced *kwahn*-tuhm *mehr*-oo-wit.

Deciding If a Court Would Impose a Quasi Contract

Business Law Analysis

American Commercial Lines (ACL) operates tow boats and barges. ACL entered into a contract with VCS Chemical Corp. to purchase a diesel fuel additive called LZ8411A, which was manufactured by Lubrizol. Following a dispute, VCS stopped distributing Lubrizol's LZ8411A. Instead of informing ACL of this development, VCS provided the tow boat company with a "counterfeit additive" of lower quality. When ACL found out, it filed a number of lawsuits, including one against Lubrizol under quasi contract theory.

Analysis: Federal judge Richard Posner explained quasi contract in these words: "The classic example is the physician who chances on a person lying unconscious on the ground and treats him. Because the patient is unconscious there can be no contractual negotiation regarding the physician's price for the treatment. Yet it is customary for physicians to be paid for the medical services they render, and so the law treats the situation as if the parties had contracted for treatment at the physician's normal rate."[a] A quasi contract is not, however, designed to reward a company such as ACL that *could have* entered into a contract with Lubrizol but did not.

Result and Reasoning: ACL cannot recover any damages from Lubrizol under quasi contract theory. Lubrizol did not manufacture the counterfeit additive or sell it to ACL. Nor was Lubrizol reasonably required to inform ACL about its dispute with VCS. If a corporation such as ACL is worried about being cheated in this manner, it should start entering into contracts with the manufacturers, and not just with the distributors, of the products it uses.

In this case, it is instructive to realize that VCS is a small company and Lubrizol is a large one. Thus, ACL was trying to access Lubrizol's "deep pockets" with a misguided reliance on quasi contract law.

a. *American Commercial Lines, LLC v. The Lubrizol Corp.*, 817 F.3d 548 (7th Cir. 2016). Also see *ConFold Pacific, Inc. v. Polaris Industries, Inc.*, 433 F.3d 952, 958 (7th Cir. 2006).

trial court awarded State Farm $577,124 in damages for unjust enrichment, but the appellate court reversed. The court reasoned that State Farm had a legal duty to pay for the chiropractic treatment of its customers and could not avoid paying for the services because the clinics' owner was not licensed. The payments did not constitute unjust enrichment, because the patients had, in fact, received treatment by licensed chiropractors.[6]

10–4b When an Actual Contract Exists

The doctrine of quasi contract generally cannot be used when an actual contract covers the area in controversy. In this situation, a party who claims that a nonperforming party was unjustly enriched already has a remedy. The nonbreaching party can sue the breaching party for breach of contract.

Case Example 10.10 R & M Trucking-Intermodal, Inc., is a trucking company in Illinois that provides transportation and warehousing services in the Chicago area. Richard Lombardi is a top executive at DRM Holdings, Inc., which, along with Dr. Miracle's, Inc., produces and distributes hair care products. Lombardi contracted with R & M to transport a large amount of inventory (773 pallets, or twenty full-size trailer loads) of hair relaxer kits for DRM. Lombardi then requested that R & M store the inventory until DRM could pick it up.

R & M agreed to store the goods for a weekly storage fee, but DRM never came to remove the pallets, despite repeated requests. DRM owed nearly $430,000 on the account, and payments were sporadic. Eventually, R & M filed a lawsuit, asserting a number of claims, including both breach of contract and quasi contract. Lombardi filed a motion to dismiss. The court held that R & M's quasi-contract claim must be dismissed under state law, because an express contract already existed that governed the parties' relationship.[7]

6. *State Farm Automobile Insurance Co. v. Newburg Chiropractic, P.S.C.*, 741 F.3d 661 (6th Cir. 2013).

7. *R & M Trucking-Intermodal, Inc. v. Dr. Miracle's, Inc.*, 2017 WL 3034673 (N.D.Ill. 2017).

10–5 Interpretation of Contracts

Parties may sometimes agree that a contract has been formed but disagree on its meaning or legal effect. One reason that this may happen is the technical legal terminology traditionally used in contracts, sometimes referred to as *legalese*. Today, many contracts are written in "plain," nontechnical language. Even then, though, a dispute may arise over the meaning of a contract simply because the rights or obligations under the contract are not expressed clearly—no matter how "plain" the language used.

In this section, we look at some common law rules of contract interpretation. These rules provide the courts with guidelines for deciding disputes over how contract terms or provisions should be interpreted. Exhibit 10–3 provides a brief graphic summary of how these rules are applied.

10–5a Plain Language Laws

The federal government and a majority of the states have enacted *plain language laws* to regulate legal writing and eliminate legalese. All federal agencies are required to use plain language in most of their forms and written communications. Plain language requirements have been extended to agency rulemaking as well. States frequently have plain language laws that apply to consumer contracts—contracts made primarily for personal, family, or household purposes. The legal profession has also moved toward plain English, and court rules in many jurisdictions require attorneys to use plain language in court documents.

10–5b The Plain Meaning Rule

When a contract's language is clear and unequivocal, a court will enforce it according to its obvious terms. The meaning of the terms must be determined from *the face of the instrument*—from the written document alone. This is sometimes referred to as the *plain meaning rule*. The words—and their plain, ordinary meanings—determine the intent of the parties at the time they entered into the contract. A court is bound to give effect to the contract according to this intent.

Know This

No one can avoid contractual obligations by claiming not to have read the contract. A contract normally is interpreted as if each party had read every word carefully.

Exhibit 10–3 Rules of Contract Interpretation

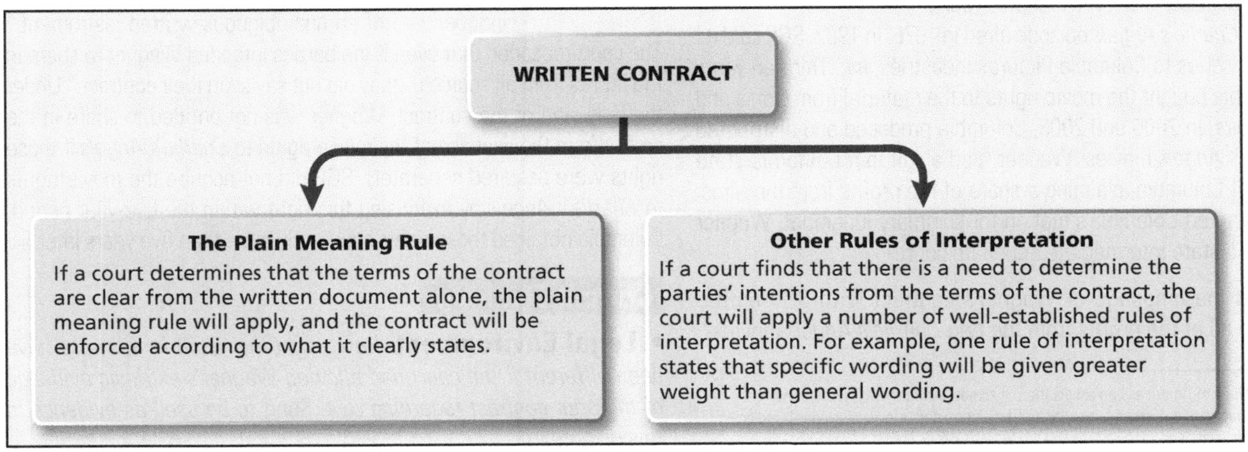

WRITTEN CONTRACT
The Plain Meaning Rule
If a court determines that the terms of the contract are clear from the written document alone, the plain meaning rule will apply, and the contract will be enforced according to what it clearly states.
Other Rules of Interpretation
If a court finds that there is a need to determine the parties' intentions from the terms of the contract, the court will apply a number of well-established rules of interpretation. For example, one rule of interpretation states that specific wording will be given greater weight than general wording.

Ambiguity What if a contract's language is not clear and unequivocal? A court will consider a contract to be unclear, or ambiguous, in the following situations:

1. When the intent of the parties cannot be determined from its language.
2. When it lacks a provision on a disputed issue.
3. When a term is susceptible to more than one interpretation.
4. When there is uncertainty about a provision.

Extrinsic Evidence If a contract term is ambiguous, a court may interpret the ambiguity against the party who drafted the contract term, as discussed shortly. Sometimes, too, a court may consider **extrinsic evidence**—evidence not contained in the document itself—in interpreting ambiguous contract terms. Such evidence may include the testimony of the parties, additional agreements or communications, or other information relevant to determining the parties' intent.

Extrinsic Evidence Any evidence not contained in the contract itself, which may include the testimony of the parties, additional agreements or communications, or other information relevant to determining the parties' intent.

The admissibility of extrinsic evidence can significantly affect the court's interpretation of ambiguous contractual provisions and thus the outcome of litigation. But when the contract is clear and unambiguous, a court normally cannot consider evidence outside the contract. The following *Spotlight Case* illustrates these points.

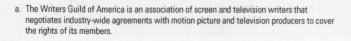

Spotlight on Columbia Pictures: Case 10.3

Wagner v. Columbia Pictures Industries, Inc.

California Court of Appeal, Second District, 146 Cal.App.4th 586, 52 Cal.Rptr.3d 898 (2007).

Facts Actor Robert Wagner entered into an agreement with Spelling-Goldberg Productions (SGP) "relating to *Charlie's Angels* (herein called the 'series')." The contract entitled Wagner to 50 percent of the net profits that SGP received from broadcasting the series and from all ancillary, music, and subsidiary rights in connection with the series. SGP hired Ivan Goff and Ben Roberts to write the series, under a contract subject to the Writers Guild of America Minimum Basic Agreement (MBA).[a] The MBA stipulated that the writer of a television show retains the right to make and market films based on the material, subject to the producer's right to buy this right if the writer decides to sell it within five years.

©Helga Esteb/Shutterstock.com

Actor Robert Wagner had the rights to the TV series Charlie's Angels.

The first *Charlie's Angels* episode aired in 1976. In 1982, SGP sold its rights to the series to Columbia Pictures Industries, Inc. Thirteen years later, Columbia bought the movie rights to the material from Goff's and Roberts's heirs. In 2000 and 2003, Columbia produced and distributed two *Charlie's Angels* movies. Wagner filed a suit in a California state court against Columbia, claiming a share of the profits from the films. The court granted Columbia's motion for summary judgment. Wagner appealed to a state intermediate appellate court.

Issue Did the language of Wagner's contract with SGP entitle Columbia to all of the profits from the two *Charlie's Angels* movies?

a. The Writers Guild of America is an association of screen and television writers that negotiates industry-wide agreements with motion picture and television producers to cover the rights of its members.

Decision Yes. The state intermediate appellate court affirmed the lower court's judgment.

Reason Wagner offered evidence to show that a previous contract with SGP involving a property titled *Love Song* had been intended to give him half of the net profits that SGP received from the property from all sources without limitation as to source or time. Wagner argued that because the profits provision in the *Charlie's Angels* agreement used identical language, the provision should be interpreted to give him the same share. The court stated that an "agreement is the writing itself." Extrinsic evidence is not admissible "to show intention independent of an unambiguous written instrument."

The court reasoned that even if the parties intended Wagner to share in the profits from all sources, "they did not say so in their contract." Under the language of the contract, Wagner was not entitled to share in the profits from the exercise of the movie rights to *Charlie's Angels* if those rights were acquired separately. SGP did not acquire the movie rights to *Charlie's Angels* by exercising this right within the five-year period. Columbia obtained those rights separately more than five years later.

Critical Thinking

- **Legal Environment** *How might the result in this case have been different if the court had allowed Wagner's extrinsic evidence of the prior contract regarding* Love Song *to be used as evidence in this dispute?*

10–5c Other Rules of Interpretation

Generally, as mentioned, a court will interpret contract language to give effect to the parties' intent *as expressed in the contract*. This is the primary purpose of the rules of interpretation—to determine the parties' intent from the language used in their agreement and to give effect to that intent. A court normally will not make or remake a contract, nor will it normally interpret the language according to what the parties *claim* their intent was when they made the contract.

Focus Question 5
What rules guide the courts in interpreting contracts?

Rules the Courts Use The courts use the following rules in interpreting contractual terms:

1. Insofar as possible, a reasonable, lawful, and effective meaning will be given to all of a contract's terms.
2. A contract will be interpreted as a whole. Individual, specific clauses will be considered subordinate to the contract's general intent. All writings that are a part of the same transaction will be interpreted together.
3. Terms that were the subject of separate negotiation will be given greater consideration than standardized terms and terms that were not negotiated separately.
4. A word will be given its ordinary, commonly accepted meaning, and a technical word or term will be given its technical meaning, unless the parties clearly intended something else.
5. Specific and exact wording will be given greater consideration than general language.
6. Written or typewritten terms prevail over preprinted terms.
7. Because a contract should be drafted in clear and unambiguous language, a party that uses ambiguous expressions is held to be responsible for the ambiguities. Thus, when the language has more than one meaning, it will be interpreted *against* the party that drafted the contract.
8. Evidence of *trade usage*, *prior dealing*, and *course of performance* may be admitted to clarify the meaning of an ambiguously worded contract. (We will define and discuss these terms in the chapter on sales and lease contracts.)

Express Terms Usually Given Most Weight In situations in which trade usage, prior dealing, and course of performance come into play, the courts observe certain priorities in interpreting contracts. Express terms (terms expressly stated in the contract) are given the greatest weight, followed by course of performance, course of dealing, and custom and usage of trade—in that order. When considering custom and usage, a court will look at the trade customs and usage common to the particular business or industry and to the locale in which the contract was made or is to be performed.

Case Example 10.11 E.I. du Pont de Nemours and Company's standard employment contract states that employees who "retire" keep any stock options provided by the company. According to the language of the contract, an employee can only "retire" after having been with the company for at least fifteen years. Employees who leave for other reasons must exercise the stock options by their last day of employment or lose them. (When a company offers stock options to its employees, it gives them the opportunity to buy a specified number of shares of the company's stock within a set time period and at a price established by the company on a prior date.)

After ten years with DuPont, James Bearden, at the age of sixty-seven, decided to stop working. Because Bearden did not exercise his stock options before leaving, DuPont allowed them to expire. Bearden sued, arguing that, going by the dictionary, "retirement" means exiting the workforce upon reaching a certain age. A federal appellate court rejected this reasoning. By the express language of the contract, the court held, Bearden had fallen short of the years-of-service requirement (fifteen years) and therefore had not "retired" from DuPont for stock option purposes.[8]

8. *Bearden v. E.I. du Pont de Nemours and Company*, 945 F.3d 1333 (11th Cir. 2019).

Practice and Review

Mitsui Bank hired Ross Duncan as a branch manager in one of its Southern California locations. At that time, Duncan received an employee handbook informing him that Mitsui would review his performance and salary level annually. In 2020, Mitsui decided to create a new lending program to help financially troubled businesses stay afloat. It promoted Duncan to be the credit development officer (CDO) and gave him a written compensation plan. Duncan's compensation was to be based on the new program's success and involved a bonus and commissions based on new loans and sales volume. The written plan also stated, "This compensation plan will be reviewed and potentially amended after one year and will be subject to such review and amendment annually thereafter."

Duncan's efforts as CDO were successful, and the business-lending program he developed grew to represent 25 percent of Mitsui's business in 2021 and 40 percent by 2023. Nevertheless, Mitsui refused to give Duncan a raise in 2021. Mitsui also amended Duncan's compensation plan to significantly reduce his compensation and to change his performance evaluation schedule to every six months. When he had still not received a raise by 2023, Duncan resigned as CDO and filed a lawsuit claiming breach of contract. Using the information presented in the chapter, answer the following questions.

1. What are the four requirements of a valid contract?
2. Did Duncan have a valid contract with Mitsui for employment as credit development officer? If so, was it a bilateral or a unilateral contract?
3. What are the requirements of an implied contract?
4. Can Duncan establish an implied contract based on the employment manual or the written compensation plan? Why or why not?

Debate This

Companies should be able to make or break employment contracts whenever and however they wish.

Key Terms

bilateral contract 248
contract 245
executed contract 251
executory contract 251
express contract 250
extrinsic evidence 256
formal contract 250
implied contract 251
informal contract 250
objective theory of contracts 245
offeree 248
offeror 248
promise 244
promisee 244
promisor 244
quantum meruit 253
quasi contract 253
unenforceable contract 252
unilateral contract 248
valid contract 252
voidable contract 252
void contract 253

Chapter Summary: Nature and Classification

An Overview of Contract Law	1. **Sources of contract law**—The common law governs all contracts except when it has been modified or replaced by statutory law, such as the Uniform Commercial Code (UCC), or by administrative agency regulations. The UCC governs contracts for the sale and lease of goods. 2. **The function of contracts**—Contract law establishes what kinds of promises will be legally binding and supplies procedures for enforcing legally binding promises, or agreements. 3. **The definition of a contract**—A contract is an agreement that can be enforced in court. It is formed by two or more parties who agree to perform or to refrain from performing some act now or in the future. Each party has a legal duty to the other and the right to seek a remedy for breach of the promise or duty. 4. **The objective theory of contracts**—In contract law, intent is determined by objective facts, not by the personal or subjective intent or belief of a party.
Elements of a Contract	1. **Requirements of a valid contract**—The four requirements of a valid contract are agreement, consideration, contractual capacity, and legality. 2. **Defenses to the enforceability of a contract**—Even if the four requirements of a valid contract are met, a contract may be unenforceable if it lacks voluntary consent or is not in the required form.
Types of Contracts	1. **Bilateral**—A promise for a promise. 2. **Unilateral**—A promise for an act (acceptance is the completed or substantial performance of the contract by the offeree). 3. **Formal**—Requires a special form for contract formation. 4. **Informal**—Requires no special form for contract formation. 5. **Express**—Formed by words (oral or written). 6. **Implied**—Formed at least in part by the conduct of the parties. 7. **Executed**—A fully performed contract. 8. **Executory**—A contract not yet fully performed. 9. **Valid**—A contract that has the four necessary contractual elements of agreement, consideration, capacity, and legality. 10. **Voidable**—A contract in which a party has the option of avoiding or ratifying the contractual obligation. 11. **Unenforceable**—A valid contract that cannot be enforced because of some statute or law. 12. **Void**—No contract exists.
Quasi Contracts	A quasi contract, or a contract implied in law, is a fictional contract that is imposed by a court to prevent unjust enrichment of one party at the expense of another.
Interpretation of Contracts	Increasingly, plain language laws require contracts to be written in nontechnical language so that the terms are clear and understandable to the parties. Under the plain meaning rule, a court will enforce the contract according to its obvious terms, the meaning of which must be determined from the written document alone. Other rules applied by the courts when interpreting contracts include giving greater consideration to specific wording and holding a party that uses vague terms responsible for the ambiguities.

Issue Spotters

1. Kerin sends a letter to Joli telling her that he has a book to sell at a certain price. Joli signs and returns the letter. When Kerin delivers the book, Joli sends it back, claiming that they do not have a contract. Kerin claims they do. What standard determines whether these parties have a contract? (See *An Overview of Contract Law*.)

2. Dyna tells Ed that she will pay him $1,000 to set fire to her store so that she can collect under a fire insurance policy. Ed sets fire to the store, but Dyna refuses to pay. Can Ed recover? Why or why not? (See *Types of Contracts*.)

—Check your answers to the *Issue Spotters* against the answers provided in Appendix D.

Business Scenarios and Case Problems

10–1. Unilateral Contract. Rocky Mountain Races, Inc., sponsors the "Pioneer Trail Ultramarathon," with an advertised first prize of $10,000. The rules require the competitors to run one hundred miles from the floor of Blackwater Canyon to the top of Pinnacle Mountain. The rules also provide that Rocky reserves the right to change the terms of the race at any time. Monica enters the race and is declared the winner. Rocky offers her a prize of $1,000 instead of $10,000. Did Rocky and Monica have a contract? Explain. (See *Types of Contracts.*)

10–2. Implied Contract. Janine was hospitalized with severe abdominal pain and placed in an intensive care unit. Her doctor told hospital personnel to order around-the-clock nursing care for Janine. At the hospital's request, a nursing services firm, Nursing Services Unlimited, provided two weeks of in-hospital care and, after Janine was sent home, two additional weeks of at-home care. During the at-home period of care, Janine was fully aware that she was receiving the benefit of the nursing services. Nursing Services later billed Janine $4,000 for the nursing care, but Janine refused to pay on the ground that she had never contracted for the services, either orally or in writing. In view of the fact that no express contract was ever formed, can Nursing Services recover the $4,000 from Janine? If so, under what legal theory? Discuss. (See *Types of Contracts.*)

10–3. Contract Classification. For employment with the Firestorm Smokejumpers—a crew of elite paratroopers who parachute into dangerous situations to fight fires—applicants must complete a series of tests. The crew chief sends the most qualified applicants a letter stating that they will be admitted to Firestorm's training sessions if they pass a medical exam. Jake Kurzyniec receives the letter and passes the exam, but a new crew chief changes the selection process and rejects him. Is there a contract between Kurzyniec and Firestorm? If there is a contract, what type of contract is it? (See *Types of Contracts.*)

10–4. Spotlight on Taco Bell—Implied Contract. Thomas Rinks and Joseph Shields developed Psycho Chihuahua, a caricature of a Chihuahua dog with a "do-not-back-down" attitude. They promoted and marketed the character through their company, Wrench, LLC. Ed Alfaro and Rudy Pollak, representatives of Taco Bell Corp., learned of Psycho Chihuahua and met with Rinks and Shields to talk about using the character as a Taco Bell "icon." Wrench sent artwork, merchandise, and marketing ideas to Alfaro, who promoted the character within Taco Bell. Alfaro asked Wrench to propose terms for Taco Bell's use of Psycho Chihuahua. Taco Bell did not accept Wrench's terms, but Alfaro continued to promote the character within the company.

Meanwhile, Taco Bell hired a new advertising agency, which proposed an advertising campaign involving a Chihuahua. When Alfaro learned of this proposal, he sent the Psycho Chihuahua materials to the agency. Taco Bell made a Chihuahua the focus of its marketing but paid nothing to Wrench. Wrench filed a suit against Taco Bell in a federal court claiming that it had an implied contract with Taco Bell and that Taco Bell breached that contract. Do these facts satisfy the requirements for an implied contract? Why or why not? [*Wrench, LLC. v. Taco Bell Corp.*, 256 F.3d 446 (6th Cir. 2001), *cert. denied*, 534 U.S. 1114, 122 S.Ct. 921, 151 L.Ed.2d 805 (2002)] (See *Types of Contracts.*)

10–5. Business Case Problem with Sample Answer—Implied Contracts. Ralph Ramsey insured his car with Allstate Insurance Co. He also owned a house on which he maintained a homeowner's insurance policy with Allstate. Bank of America had a mortgage on the house and paid the insurance premiums on the homeowner's policy from Ralph's account. After Ralph died, Allstate canceled the car insurance. Ralph's son Douglas inherited the house. The bank continued to pay the premiums on the homeowner's policy, but from Douglas's account, and Allstate continued to renew the insurance. When a fire destroyed the house, Allstate denied coverage, however, claiming that the policy was still in Ralph's name. Douglas filed a suit in a federal district court against the insurer. Was Allstate liable under the homeowner's policy? Explain. [*Ramsey v. Allstate Insurance Co.*, 514 Fed.Appx. 554 (6th Cir. 2013)] (See *Types of Contracts.*)

—For a sample answer to Problem 10–5, go to Appendix E.

10–6. Quasi Contracts. Lawrence M. Clarke, Inc., was the general contractor for construction of a portion of a sanitary sewer system in Billings, Michigan. Clarke accepted Kim Draeger's proposal to do the work for a certain price. Draeger arranged with two subcontractors to work on the project. The work provided by Draeger and the subcontractors proved unsatisfactory. All of the work fell under Draeger's contract with Clarke. Clarke filed a suit in a Michigan state court against Draeger, seeking to recover damages on a theory of quasi contract. The court awarded Clarke $900,000 in damages on that theory. A state intermediate appellate court reversed this award. Why? [*Lawrence M. Clarke, Inc. v. Draeger*, 2015 WL 205182 (Mich.App. 2015)] (See *Quasi Contracts.*)

10–7. Interpretation of Contracts. Lehman Brothers, Inc. (LBI), wrote a letter to Mary Ortegón offering her employment as LBI's "Business Chief Administrative Officer in Its Fixed Income Division." The offer included a salary of $150,000 per year and an annual "minimum bonus" of $350,000. The letter stated that the bonus would be paid unless Ortegón resigned or was terminated for certain causes. In other words, the bonus was not a "signing" bonus—it was clearly tied to her performance on the job. Ortegón accepted the offer. Before she started work, however, LBI rescinded it. Later, LBI filed for bankruptcy in a federal court. Ortegón filed a claim with the court for the amount of the bonus on the ground that LBI had breached its contract with her by not paying it. Can extrinsic evidence be admitted to interpret the meaning of the bonus term? Explain. [*Ortegón v. Giddens*, 638 Fed.Appx. 47 (2d Cir. 2016)] (See *Interpretation of Contracts.*)

10–8. Quasi Contracts. In New Jersey, a patient admitted to a medical care facility through the regular admissions process is responsible for applying to the state for assistance in paying the bill. In contrast, a patient admitted on an emergency basis is not responsible for applying to the state—the facility is. Of course, to obtain assistance, the patient must be indigent. D.B., a diagnosed schizophrenic, experienced a psychotic episode. The Warren County, New Jersey, psychiatric emergency screening service determined that he was a danger to himself and others. He was involuntarily committed to Newton Medical Center, a mental health-care facility. Newton did not apply to the state for financial assistance for D.B.'s treatment. Instead, Newton billed the patient $6,745.50. D.B., who was indigent, did not pay. Can Newton recover the amount of the unpaid bill from D.B. on a theory of quasi contract? Discuss. [*Newton Medical Center v. D.B.*, 452 N.J.Super. 615, 178 A.3d 1281, 2018 WL 480296 (App.Div. 2018)] (See *Quasi Contracts.*)

10–9. A Question of Ethics—The IDDR Approach and Contract Requirements. Mark Carpenter, a certified financial planner, contracted to recruit investors for GetMoni.com, which owned a defunct gold mine in Arizona. Carpenter then contracted with clients to invest their funds, sending more than $2 million to GetMoni.com. Only about 20 percent of the money went to developing the mine. The rest was used to run a Ponzi scheme. Carpenter collected another $1 million, but instead of sending it to GetMoni.com, he deposited it into his own account. A federal investigation unraveled the scheme. Carpenter was charged with two counts of fraud—one for his deal with GetMoni.com and one for his misrepresentations to clients after he stopped dealing with GetMoni.com. [*United States v. Carpenter*, 676 Fed.Appx. 397 (6th Cir. 2017)] (See *An Overview of Contract Law.*)

1. Which elements do Carpenter's contracts lack, preventing them from being enforced? Can he argue successfully that he acted ethically? Discuss.
2. Using the IDDR approach, discuss whether certified financial planners have an ethical obligation to contract in the best interests of their clients.

Critical Thinking and Writing Assignments

10–10. Time-Limited Group Assignment—Contracts. Review the basic requirements for a valid contract listed at the beginning of this chapter. Now consider the relationship entered into when a student enrolls in a college or university. (See *Elements of a Contract.*)

1. One group should analyze and discuss whether a contract has been formed between the student and the college or university.
2. A second group should assume that there is a contract and explain whether it is bilateral or unilateral.
3. The third group will consider the documents that each of you signed when enrolling in college. Did you read and understand the provisions? Would the plain meaning rule apply even if you did not understand some parts?

11 Agreement

Focus Questions

The four Focus Questions *below are designed to help improve your understanding. After reading this chapter, you should be able to answer the following questions:*

1. What three elements are necessary for an effective offer?
2. What elements are necessary for an effective acceptance?
3. How do click-on and shrink-wrap agreements differ?
4. What is the primary purpose of the Uniform Electronic Transactions Act?

Agreement A mutual understanding or meeting of the minds between two or more individuals regarding the terms of a contract.

Offer A promise or commitment to perform or refrain from performing some specified act in the future.

"It is necessity that makes laws."

Voltaire
1694–1778
(French intellectual and writer)

Voltaire's statement that it is "necessity that makes laws" is particularly true in regard to contracts. Contract law developed over time to meet society's need to know with certainty what kinds of promises, or contracts, will be enforced and the point at which a valid and binding contract is formed. For a contract to be considered valid and enforceable, four basic requirements—agreement, consideration, contractual capacity, and legality—must be met.

In this chapter, we look closely at the first of these requirements, **agreement**. The parties must agree on the terms of the contract and manifest to each other their *mutual assent* (agreement) to the same bargain. Ordinarily, agreement is evidenced by two events: an *offer* and an *acceptance*. One party offers a certain bargain to another party, who then accepts that bargain. An agreement does not necessarily have to be in writing. Both parties, however, must manifest their assent, or voluntary consent, to the same bargain.

Agreement is required to form a contract, whether it is formed in the traditional way (on paper) or online. In today's world, numerous contracts are formed via the Internet. When someone enters an online agreement with a cell phone company to purchase a smartphone and data plan, for instance, that person has entered into an electronic contract, or e-contract.

11–1 Offer

An **offer** is a promise or commitment to perform or refrain from performing some specified act in the future. The party making an offer is called the *offeror*, and the party to whom the offer is made is called the *offeree*.

Three elements are necessary for an offer to be effective:

1. There must be a serious, objective intention by the offeror.
2. The terms of the offer must be reasonably certain, or definite, so that the parties and the court can ascertain the terms of the contract.
3. The offer must be communicated to the offeree.

Focus Question 1

What three elements are necessary for an effective offer?

Once an effective offer has been made, the offeree's acceptance of that offer creates a legally binding contract (providing the other essential elements for a valid and enforceable contract are present).

11–1a Intention of the Offer

The first requirement for an effective offer is serious, objective intent on the part of the offeror. Intent is not determined by the *subjective* intentions, beliefs, or assumptions of the offeror. Rather, it is determined by what a reasonable person in the offeree's position would conclude that the offeror's words and actions meant. Offers made in obvious anger, jest, or undue excitement do not meet the requirement of serious, objective intent. Because these offers are not effective, an offeree's acceptance does not create an agreement.

Example 11.1 You ride to school each day with Spencer in his new automobile, which has a market value of $25,000. One cold morning, the car will not start. Spencer yells in anger, "I'll sell this car to anyone for $500!" You drop $500 in his lap. A reasonable person—taking into consideration Spencer's frustration and the obvious difference in value between the car's market price and the purchase price—would realize that Spencer's offer was not made with serious and objective intent. Therefore, no agreement is formed.

In the *Classic Case* presented next, the court considered whether an offer made "after a few drinks" met the serious-intent requirement.

Classic Case 11.1

Lucy v. Zehmer

Supreme Court of Appeals of Virginia, 196Va. 493, 84S.E.2d 516 (1954).

Facts W. O. Lucy and A. H. Zehmer had known each other for fifteen to twenty years. For some time, Lucy had wanted to buy Zehmer's farm, but Zehmer had always said that he was not interested in selling. One night, Lucy stopped in to visit with the Zehmers at a restaurant they operated. Lucy said to Zehmer, "I bet you wouldn't take $50,000 for that place." Zehmer replied, "Yes, I would, too; you wouldn't give fifty." Throughout the evening, the conversation returned to the sale of the farm. All the while, the parties were drinking whiskey.

dcwcreations/ShutterStock.com

Can an intoxicated person's offer to sell his farm for a specific price meet the serious-intent requirement?

Eventually, Zehmer wrote up an agreement on the back of a restaurant check for the sale of the farm, and he asked his wife, Ida, to sign it—which she did. When Lucy brought an action in a Virginia state court to enforce the agreement, Zehmer argued that he had been "high as a Georgia pine" at the time and that the offer had been made in jest: "two doggoned drunks bluffing to see who could talk the biggest and say the most." Lucy claimed that he had not been intoxicated and did not think Zehmer had been, either, given the way Zehmer handled the transaction. The trial court ruled in favor of the Zehmers, and Lucy appealed.

Issue Did the agreement meet the serious-intent requirement despite the claim of intoxication?

(Continues)

Continued

Decision Yes. The agreement to sell the farm was binding.

Reason The court held that the evidence given about the nature of the conversation, the appearance and completeness of the agreement, and the signing all tended to show that a serious business transaction, not a casual jest, was intended. The court had to look into the objective meaning of the Zehmers' words and acts: "An agreement or mutual assent is of course essential to a valid contract, but the law imputes to a person an intention corresponding to the reasonable meaning of his words and acts. If his words and acts, judged by a reasonable standard, manifest an intention to agree, it is immaterial what may be the real but unexpressed state of mind."

Critical Thinking

- **What If the Facts Were Different?** *Suppose that after Lucy signed the agreement, he decided he did not want the farm after all, and that Zehmer sued Lucy to perform the contract. Would this change in the facts alter the court's decision that Lucy and Zehmer had created an enforceable contract? Why or why not?*
- **Impact of This Case on Today's Law** *This is a classic case in contract law because it so clearly illustrates the objective theory of contracts with respect to determining whether an offer was intended. Today, the courts continue to apply the objective theory of contracts and routinely cite the* Lucy v. Zehmer *decision as a significant precedent in this area.*

Know This

An opinion is not an offer and not a contract term. Goods or services can be "perfect" in one party's opinion and "poor" in another's.

When Intent May Be Lacking The concept of intention can be further clarified by looking at statements that are *not* offers and situations in which the parties' intent to be bound might be questionable.

1. *Expressions of opinion.* An expression of opinion is not an offer. It does not indicate an intention to enter into a binding agreement.
2. *Statements of future intent.* A statement of an intention to do something in the future (such as "I plan to sell my Verizon stock") is not an offer.
3. *Preliminary negotiations.* A request or invitation to negotiate is not an offer. It only expresses a willingness to discuss the possibility of entering into a contract. Statements such as "Will you sell your farm?" or "I wouldn't sell my car for less than $8,000" are examples.
4. *Invitations to bid.* When a government entity or private firm needs to have construction work done, contractors are invited to submit bids. The invitation to submit bids is not an offer. The bids that contractors submit are offers, however, and the government entity or private firm can bind the contractor by accepting the bid.
5. *Advertisements and price lists.* In general, representations made in advertisements and price lists are treated not as offers to contract but as invitations to negotiate.[1] Only rarely are such materials construed as offers. On some occasions, courts have considered advertisements to be offers because they contained definite terms that invited acceptance. (An example is an ad offering a reward for a lost dog.)
6. *Live and online auctions.* In a live auction, a seller "offers" goods for sale through an auctioneer, but this is not an offer to form a contract. Rather, it is an invitation asking bidders to submit offers. In the context of an auction, a bidder is the offeror, and the auctioneer is the offeree. The offer is accepted when the auctioneer strikes the hammer.
   The most familiar type of auction today takes place online through websites like eBay and eBid. "Offers" to sell an item on these sites generally are treated as invitations to negotiate. Unlike live auctions, online auctions are automated. Buyers can enter incremental bids on an item (without approving each price increase) up to a specified amount or without a limit.

1. *Restatement (Second) of Contracts,* Section 26, Comment b.

Agreements to Agree Traditionally, agreements to agree—that is, agreements to agree to the material terms of a contract at some future date—were not considered to be binding contracts. The modern view, however, is that agreements to agree may be enforceable agreements (contracts) if it is clear that the parties intended to be bound by the agreements. In other words, under the modern view the emphasis is on the parties' intent rather than on form.

Spotlight Case Example 11.2 After a person was injured and nearly drowned on a water ride at one of its amusement parks, Six Flags, Inc., filed a lawsuit against the manufacturer that had designed the ride. The manufacturer claimed that the parties did not have a binding contract but had only engaged in preliminary negotiations that were never formalized in a construction contract.

The court, however, held that the evidence was sufficient to show an intent to be bound. The evidence included a faxed document specifying the details of the water ride, along with the parties' subsequent actions (having begun construction and written notes on the faxed document). The manufacturer was required to provide insurance for the water ride at Six Flags. In addition, its insurer was required to defend Six Flags in the personal-injury lawsuit that arose from the incident.[2]

Cassiohabib/Shutterstock.com

How did intention affect the outcome of a lawsuit between Six Flags and the manufacturer of a water ride?

Preliminary Agreements Increasingly, the courts are holding that a preliminary agreement constitutes a binding contract if the parties have agreed on all essential terms and no disputed issues remain to be resolved. In contrast, if the parties agree on certain major terms but leave other terms open for further negotiation, a preliminary agreement is binding only in the sense that the parties have committed themselves to negotiate the undecided terms in good faith in an effort to reach a final agreement.

In the following *Spotlight Case*, a dispute arose over an agreement to settle a case during the trial. One party claimed that the agreement, which was formed via e-mail, was binding. The other party claimed that the e-mail exchange was merely an agreement to work out the terms of a settlement in the future. Can an exchange of e-mails create a complete and unambiguous agreement?

2. *Six Flags, Inc. v. Steadfast Insurance Co.*, 474 F.Supp.2d 201 (D.Mass. 2007).

Spotlight on Amazon.com: Case 11.2

Basis Technology Corp. v. Amazon.com, Inc.

Appeals Court of Massachusetts, 71 Mass.App.Ct. 29, 878 N.E.2d 952 (2008).

Facts Basis Technology Corporation created software and provided technical services for a Japanese-language website operated by Amazon. com, Inc. The agreement between the two companies allowed for separately negotiated contracts for additional services that Basis might provide to Amazon. Later, Basis sued Amazon for various claims, including failure to pay for services not included in the original agreement. During the trial, the two parties appeared to reach an agreement to settle out of court via a series of e-mail exchanges outlining the settlement. When Amazon reneged, Basis served a motion to enforce the proposed settlement. The trial judge entered a judgment against Amazon, which appealed.

Issue Did the agreement that Amazon entered into with Basis via e-mail constitute a binding settlement contract?

Decision Yes. The Appeals Court of Massachusetts affirmed the trial court's finding that Amazon intended to be bound by the terms of the e-mail exchanges.

(Continues)

Continued

Reason The court examined the evidence consisting of e-mails between the two parties. It pointed out that in open court and on the record, counsel had "reported the result of the settlement without specification of the terms."

Amazon claimed that the e-mail terms were incomplete and were not definite enough to form an agreement. The court noted, however, that "provisions are not ambiguous simply because the parties have developed different interpretations of them." In the exchange of e-mails, the essential business terms were indeed resolved. Afterward, the parties were simply proceeding to record the settlement terms, not to create them. The e-mails constituted a complete and unambiguous statement of the parties' desire to be bound by the settlement terms.

Critical Thinking

• **What If the Facts Were Different?** *Assume that, instead of exchanging e-mails, the attorneys for both sides had had a phone conversation that included all of the terms to which they actually agreed in their e-mail exchanges. Would the court have ruled differently? Why or why not?*

11–1b Definiteness of the Offer

The second requirement for an effective offer involves the definiteness of its terms. An offer must have reasonably definite terms so that a court can determine if a breach has occurred and give an appropriate remedy.[3] The specific terms required depend, of course, on the type of contract. Generally, a contract must include the following terms, either expressed in the contract or capable of being reasonably inferred from it:

1. The identification of the parties.
2. The identification of the object or subject matter of the contract (also the quantity, when appropriate), including the work to be performed, with specific identification of such items as goods, services, and land.
3. The consideration to be paid.
4. The time of payment, delivery, or performance.

An offer may invite an acceptance to be worded in such specific terms that the contract is made definite. **Example 11.3** Nintendo of America, Inc., contacts your Play 2 Win Games store and offers to sell "from one to twenty-five Nintendo gaming systems for $75 each. State number desired in acceptance." You agree to buy twenty systems. Because the quantity is specified in the acceptance, the terms are definite, and the contract is enforceable. ■

When the parties have clearly manifested their intent to form a contract, courts sometimes are willing to supply a missing term in a contract, especially a sales contract. But a court will not rewrite a contract if the parties' expression of intent is too vague or uncertain to be given any precise meaning.

11–1c Communication of the Offer

A third requirement for an effective offer is communication—the offer must be communicated to the offeree. Ordinarily, one cannot agree to a bargain without knowing that it exists. **Case Example 11.4** Adwoa Gyabaah was hit by a bus owned by Rivlab Transportation Corporation. Gyabaah filed a suit in a New York state court against the bus company. Rivlab's insurer offered to tender the company's policy limit of $1 million in full settlement of Gyabaah's claims. On the advice of her attorney, Jeffrey Aronsky, Gyabaah signed a release (a contract forfeiting the right to pursue a legal claim) to obtain the settlement funds.

The release, however, was not sent to Rivlab or its insurer, National Casualty. Moreover, Gyabaah claimed that she had not decided whether to settle. Two months later, Gyabaah

3. *Restatement (Second) of Contracts*, Section 33. The UCC has relaxed the requirements regarding the definiteness of terms in contracts for the sale of goods. See UCC 2–204(3).

changed lawyers and changed her mind about signing the release. Her former attorney, Aronsky, filed a motion to enforce the release so that he could obtain his fees from the settlement funds. The court denied the motion, and Aronsky appealed. The reviewing court held that there was no binding settlement agreement. The release was never delivered to Rivlab or its insurer, nor was acceptance of the settlement offer otherwise communicated to them.[4]

(See this chapter's *Business Law Analysis* feature for an example of how courts deal with offers of a reward.)

11–1d Termination of the Offer

The communication of an effective offer to an offeree gives the offeree the power to transform the offer into a binding, legal obligation (a contract) by an acceptance. This power of acceptance does not continue forever, though. It can be terminated either by the *action of the parties* or by *operation of law*. Termination by the action of the parties can involve a revocation by the offeror or a rejection or counteroffer by the offeree.

Termination by Action of the Parties

An offer can be terminated by action of the parties in any of three ways: by revocation, by rejection, or by counteroffer.

Revocation. The offeror's act of withdrawing an offer is referred to as **revocation**. Unless an offer is irrevocable, the offeror usually can revoke the offer (even if there has been a promise to keep it open), as long as the revocation is communicated to the offeree before the offeree accepts. Revocation may be accomplished by either of the following:

Revocation The withdrawal of a contract offer by the offeror. Unless an offer is irrevocable, it can be revoked at any time prior to acceptance without liability.

1. Express repudiation of the offer (such as "I withdraw my previous offer of October 17").
2. Performance of acts that are inconsistent with the existence of the offer and are made known to the offeree (for instance, selling the offered property to another person in the offeree's presence).

4. *Gyabaah v. Rivlab Transportation Corp.*, 102 A.D.3d 451, 958 N.Y.S.2d 109 (2013).

Offers of a Reward

Business Law Analysis

The Baton Rouge Crime Stoppers (BCS) offered a reward for information about the "South Louisiana Serial Killer." The information was to be provided via a hotline. Dianne Alexander had survived an attack by a person suspected of being the killer. She identified a suspect in a police photo lineup and later sought to collect the reward. BCS refused to pay because she had not provided information to them via the hotline. Had Alexander complied with the terms of the offer?

Analysis: One of the requirements for an effective offer is communication, resulting in the offeree's knowledge of the offer. One of the requirements for an effective acceptance is also communication—in most situations, the offeror must be notified of the acceptance. In a unilateral contract, the full performance of some act is specified. If acceptance is evident, notification may be unnecessary, unless of course, the offeror asks for it.

Result and Reasoning: In this situation, the offer consisted of a reward. To obtain the reward, an offeree was asked to provide information regarding the "South Louisiana Serial Killer" to the Baton Rouge Crime Stoppers via a hotline. Alexander did not comply with the terms of this offer, and thus the offerors were not bound to pay her. She provided information to the police related to the arrest and indictment of the killer. But there was no indication in the offer that the police were the offerors or that they were authorized to accept the requested information on behalf of the offerors. Therefore, a court would not require BCS to pay the reward to Alexander.

The general rule followed by most states is that a revocation becomes effective when the offeree or the offeree's *agent* (a person acting on behalf of the offeree) actually receives it. Therefore, a statement of revocation sent via FedEx on April 1 and delivered at the offeree's residence or place of business on April 2 becomes effective on April 2. An offer made to the general public (such as through a website) may be revoked in the same manner in which it was originally communicated (through the same website).

Irrevocable Offers. Although most offers are revocable, some can be made irrevocable. Increasingly, courts refuse to allow an offeror to revoke an offer when the offeree has changed position because of justifiable reliance on the offer (under the doctrine of *promissory estoppel*). In some circumstances, "firm offers" made by merchants may also be considered irrevocable.

Option Contract A contract under which the offeror cannot revoke the offer for a stipulated time period (because the offeree has given consideration for the offer to remain open).

Another form of irrevocable offer is an option contract. An **option contract** is created when an offeror promises to hold an offer open for a specified period of time in return for a payment (consideration) given by the offeree. An option contract takes away the offeror's power to revoke an offer for the period of time specified in the option. If no time is specified, then a reasonable period of time is implied.

Option contracts are frequently used in conjunction with the sale of real estate. **Example 11.5** Tyler agrees to lease a house from Jackson, the property owner. The lease contract includes a clause stating that Tyler is paying an additional $15,000 for an option to purchase the property within a specified period of time at a specified price. If Tyler decides not to purchase the house after the specified period has lapsed, he loses the $15,000, and Jackson is free to sell the property to another buyer.

Termination by Action of the Offeree If the offeree rejects the offer, either by words or by conduct, the offer is terminated. Any subsequent attempt by the offeree to accept will be construed as a new offer, giving the original offeror (now the offeree) the power of acceptance.

Know This

The way in which a response to an offer is phrased can determine whether the offer is accepted or rejected.

Rejection. Like a revocation, a rejection is effective only when it is actually received by the offeror or the offeror's agent. **Example 11.6** Goldfinch Farms offers to sell specialty Maitake mushrooms to a Japanese buyer, Kinoko Foods. If Kinoko rejects the offer by sending a letter via U.S. mail, the rejection will not be effective (and the offer will not be terminated) until Goldfinch receives the letter.

Merely inquiring about an offer does not constitute rejection. **Example 11.7** Ray offers to buy Fran's digital pen for $100. Fran responds, "Is that your best offer?" A reasonable person would conclude that Fran has not rejected the offer but has merely made an inquiry. She could still accept and bind Ray to the $100 price.

Counteroffer An offeree's response to an offer in which the offeree rejects the original offer and at the same time makes a new offer.

Counteroffers. A **counteroffer** is a rejection of the original offer and the simultaneous making of a new offer. **Example 11.8** Burke, a beet farmer, offers to sell her product to Lang, the owner of the Lang's Roadside Veggie Stand, for $1.70 a pound. Lang responds, "Your price is too high. I'll offer to pay $1.30 a pound for your beets." Lang's response is a counteroffer because it rejects Burke's offer to sell her beets at $1.70 a pound and creates a new offer by Lang to purchase the beets at $1.30 a pound.

Mirror Image Rule A common law rule that requires that the terms of the offeree's acceptance adhere exactly to the terms of the offeror's offer for a valid contract to be formed.

At common law, the **mirror image rule** requires that the offeree's acceptance match the offeror's offer exactly. In other words, the terms of the acceptance must "mirror" those of the offer. If the acceptance materially changes or adds to the terms of the original offer, it will be considered not an acceptance but a counteroffer—which, of course, need not be accepted. The original offeror can, however, accept the terms of the counteroffer and create a valid contract.[5]

5. The mirror image rule has been greatly modified in regard to sales contracts. Section 2–207 of the UCC provides that a contract is formed if the offeree makes a definite expression of acceptance (such as signing the form in the appropriate location), even though the terms of the acceptance modify or add to the terms of the original offer.

Termination by Operation of Law The power of the offeree to transform the offer into a binding, legal obligation can be terminated by operation of law through the occurrence of any of the following events:

1. Lapse of time.
2. Destruction of the specific subject matter of the offer.
3. Death or incompetence of the offeror or the offeree.
4. Supervening illegality of the proposed contract.

Know This
When an offer is rejected, it is terminated.

Lapse of Time. An offer terminates automatically by law when the period of time *specified in the offer* has passed. If the offer states that it will be left open until a particular date, then the offer will terminate at midnight on that day. If the offer states that it will be left open for a number of days, this time period normally begins to run when the offer is actually *received* by the offeree, not when it is formed or sent.

If the offer does not specify a time for acceptance, the offer terminates at the end of a *reasonable* period of time. A reasonable period of time is determined by the subject matter of the contract, business and market conditions, and other relevant circumstances. An offer to sell farm produce, for instance, will terminate sooner than an offer to sell farm equipment because produce is perishable and subject to greater fluctuations in market value.

Destruction, Death, or Incompetence. An offer is automatically terminated if the specific subject matter of the offer (such as a smartphone or a house) is destroyed before the offer is accepted. An offeree's power of acceptance is also terminated when the offeror or offeree dies or becomes legally incapacitated, *unless the offer is irrevocable.* **Example 11.9** Sybil offers to sell commercial property to Westside Investments for $2 million. In June, Westside pays Sybil $5,000 in exchange for her agreement to hold the offer open for ten months (forming an option contract). If Sybil dies in July, her offer is not terminated, because it is irrevocable. Westside can purchase the property from Sybil's estate at any time within the ten-month period. ■

In contrast, a revocable offer is personal to both parties and cannot pass to the heirs, guardian, or estate of either party. This rule applies whether or not the other party had notice of the death or incompetence.

Jeff Greenberg/Universal Images Group/Getty Images

If the owner of a commercial property dies before the end of the time period specified in an option contract, what happens to the deal?

Supervening Illegality. A statute or court decision that makes an offer illegal automatically terminates the offer. **Example 11.10** Lee offers to lend Kim $10,000 at an annual interest rate of 15 percent. Before Kim can accept the offer, a law is enacted that prohibits interest rates higher than 8 percent. Lee's offer is automatically terminated. (If the statute is enacted after Kim accepts the offer, a valid contract is formed, but the contract may still be unenforceable.) ■

11–2 Acceptance

An **acceptance** is a voluntary act by the offeree that shows assent, or agreement, to the terms of an offer. The offeree's act may consist of words or conduct. The acceptance must be unequivocal and must be communicated to the offeror. Generally, only the person to whom the offer is made or that person's agent can accept the offer and create a binding contract. (See this chapter's *Adapting the Law to the Online Environment* feature for a discussion of how parties can sometimes inadvertently accept a contract via e-mail or text messages.)

Acceptance The act of voluntarily agreeing, through words or conduct, to the terms of an offer, thereby creating a contract.

Can Your E-Mails Create a Valid Contract?

The widespread use of e-mail as an informal means of communication is taken for granted in the business world. Not surprisingly, parties considering an agreement often exchange offers and counteroffers via e-mail. The parties may believe that these informal electronic exchanges are for negotiation purposes only. But such communications can lead to the formation of valid contracts.

E-Mails and Employment Contracts

As in so many areas of business communications, contract negotiations are often carried out using e-mail. Consider the case of Andrew Kolchins, a commodities trader who worked for the brokerage firm Evolution Markets. As Kolchins's employment contract was about to expire, Evolution Markets' chief executive officer (CEO) sent him an e-mail offering him a new agreement based on the same terms as his existing deal. Kolchins replied with an e-mail that stated, "I accept, pls send contract." The CEO responded with his own e-mail that read, "Mazel. Looking forward to another great run." ("Mazel" is shorthand for *mazel tov*, a Hebrew phrase used to express congratulations.)

Evolution Markets never presented Kolchins with a new written contract, and eventually terminated his employment. A New York trial court dismissed Kolchins's breach of contract lawsuit against his ex-employer but was overruled by the state court of appeals. The higher court found that the e-mails contained an offer, an acceptance, and a congratulatory exclamation with a forward-looking statement about a continued working relationship. As such, these communications could form the basis for a valid employment contract.[a]

"Accidental" Contracts via E-Mail

When a series of e-mails signal intent to be bound, a contract may be formed, even though some language in the e-mails may be careless or accidental. Even if a party later claims to have had unstated objections to the terms, the e-mails will prevail. What matters is whether a court determines that it is reasonable for the receiving party to believe that there is an agreement.

Indeed, e-mail contracting has become so common that only unusually strange circumstances will cause a court to reject such contracts.[b] Furthermore, under the Uniform Electronic Transactions Act, a contract "may not be denied legal effect solely because an electronic record was used in its formation." Most states have adopted this act, at least in part.

Critical Thinking

How can a company structure e-mail negotiations to avoid "accidentally" forming a contract?

a. *Kolchins v. Evolution Markets, Inc.*, 96 N.E.3d 784, 73 N.Y.3d 100 (2018).

b. See, for example, *Copano Energy, LLC v. Bujnoch*, __ S.W.3d __, 63 Tex. Sup. Ct. J 348 (2020).

Focus Question 2

What elements are necessary for an effective acceptance?

11–2a Unequivocal Acceptance

To exercise the power of acceptance effectively, the offeree must accept unequivocally. This is the mirror image rule previously discussed. An acceptance may be unequivocal even though the offeree expresses dissatisfaction with the contract. For instance, "I accept the offer, but can you give me a better price?" or "I accept, but please send a written contract" is an effective acceptance. (Notice how important each word is!)

An acceptance cannot impose new conditions or change the terms of the original offer. If it does, the acceptance may be considered a counteroffer, which is a rejection of the original offer. For instance, the statement "I accept the offer but only if I can pay on ninety days' credit" is a counteroffer and not an unequivocal acceptance.

Note that even when the additional terms are construed as a counteroffer, the other party can accept the terms by words or by conduct. **Case Example 11.11** Sonja Brown made a written offer to Lagrange Development to buy a particular house for $79,900. Lagrange's executive director, Terry Glazer, penciled in modifications to the offer—an increased purchase price of $84,200 and a later date for acceptance. Glazer initialed the changes and signed the document. Brown initialed the date change but not the price increase, and did not sign the revised contract. Nevertheless, Brown went through with the sale and received ownership of the property. When a dispute later arose as to the purchase price, a court found that Glazer's modification of the terms had constituted a counteroffer, which Brown had accepted by performance. Therefore, the contract was enforceable for the modified price of $84,200.[6]

11–2b Silence as Acceptance

Ordinarily, silence cannot constitute acceptance, even if the offeror states, "By your silence and inaction, you will be deemed to have accepted this offer." This general rule applies because an offeree should not be put under a burden of liability to act affirmatively in order to reject an offer. No consideration—that is, nothing of value—has passed to the offeree to impose such a liability.

In some instances, however, the offeree does have a duty to speak. If so, silence or inaction on the offeree's part will operate as an acceptance. Silence may be an acceptance when an offeree takes the benefit of offered services having had an opportunity to reject them and knowing that they were offered with the expectation of compensation.

Silence can also operate as an acceptance when the offeree has had prior dealings with the offeror. **Example 11.12** Marabel's restaurant routinely receives shipments of produce from a certain supplier. That supplier notifies Marabel's that it is raising its prices because its crops were damaged by a late freeze. If the restaurant does not respond in any way, the silence may operate as an acceptance, and the supplier will be justified in continuing regular shipments.

andresr/E+/Getty Images

Why can silence operate as an acceptance to changes in contract terms between a restaurant and its regular produce supplier?

11–2c Communication of Acceptance

Whether the offeror must be notified of the acceptance depends on the nature of the contract. In a unilateral contract, the full performance of some act is called for. Acceptance is usually evident, and notification is therefore unnecessary (unless the law requires it or the offeror asks for it). In a bilateral contract, in contrast, communication of acceptance is necessary, because acceptance is in the form of a promise. The bilateral contract is formed when the promise is made rather than when the act is performed.

Case Example 11.13 Mohammed Kutite sought to lease a gas station operated by Majors Management. The closing date for the lease agreement was October 1. On September 27, Majors sent Kutite five documents to sign and have notarized before the closing date. Kutite did so and returned the documents on September 28. Kutite refused, however, to sign a separate document acknowledging that he would continue using the ATM machine that was already at the gas station.

On October 2, Majors informed Kutite that if he did not sign the ATM agreement, then the deal was off. Kutite sued for breach of contract, claiming that the agreement had been formalized on September 28. A federal appellate court disagreed, holding that Kutite could not unilaterally establish a valid contract simply by returning the five signed and notarized forms. Rather, a final step was necessary—a Majors's representative needed to give some indication of assent. Communication of this acceptance never occurred, as was made clear by the blank lines on the five documents still awaiting Majors's signed approval.[7]

Know This

A bilateral contract is a promise for a promise, and a unilateral contract is performance for a promise.

6. *Brown v. Lagrange Development Corp.*, 2015 -Ohio- 133, 2015 WL 223877 (Ohio App. 2015).
7. *Kutite, LLC v. Excell Petroleum, LLC,* 780 Fed.Appx. 254 (6th Cir. 2019).

11–2d Mode and Timeliness of Acceptance

Acceptance in bilateral contracts must be timely. The general rule is that acceptance in a bilateral contract is timely if it is made before the offer is terminated. Problems may arise, though, when the parties involved are not dealing face to face. In such situations, the offeree should use an authorized mode of communication.

The Mailbox Rule. Acceptance takes effect, and thus completes formation of the contract, at the time the offeree sends or delivers the acceptance via the mode of communication expressly or impliedly authorized by the offeror. This is the so-called **mailbox rule**, also called the *deposited acceptance rule*, which the majority of courts follow. Under this rule, if the authorized mode of communication is the mail, then an acceptance becomes valid when it is dispatched (placed in the control of the U.S. Postal Service)—not when it is received by the offeror. (Note, however, that if the offer stipulates when acceptance will be effective, then the offer will not be effective until the time specified.)

Mailbox Rule A common law rule that acceptance takes effect, and thus completes formation of the contract, at the time the offeree sends or delivers the acceptance via the communication mode expressly or impliedly authorized by the offeror.

The mailbox rule does not apply to instantaneous forms of communication, such as when the parties are dealing face to face, by phone, by text, by video conferencing, or by e-mail. Under the Uniform Electronic Transactions Act (UETA—discussed later in this chapter), e-mail is considered sent when it either leaves the sender's control or is received by the recipient. This rule, which takes the place of the mailbox rule if the parties have agreed to conduct transactions electronically, allows an e-mail acceptance to become effective when sent.

Authorized Means of Communication. A means of communicating acceptance can be expressly authorized by the offeror or impliedly authorized by the facts and circumstances of the situation. An acceptance sent by means not expressly or impliedly authorized normally is not effective until it is received by the offeror.

When an offeror specifies how acceptance should be made, such as by overnight delivery, the contract is not formed unless the offeree uses that mode of acceptance. Both the offeror and the offeree are bound in contract the moment the specified means of acceptance is employed. **Example 11.14** Motorola Mobility, Inc., offers to sell 144 Moto G8 Power smartphones to Call Me Plus phone stores. The offer states that Call Me Plus must accept the offer via FedEx overnight delivery. The acceptance is effective (and a binding contract is formed) the moment that Call Me Plus gives the overnight envelope containing the acceptance to the FedEx driver. ■

If the offeror does not expressly authorize a certain mode of acceptance, then acceptance can be made by *any reasonable means*.[8] Courts look at the prevailing business usages and the surrounding circumstances to determine whether the mode of acceptance used was reasonable. Usually, the offeror's choice of a particular means in making the offer implies that the offeree can use the *same or a faster means* for acceptance. **Example 11.15** If the offer is made via USPS Priority Mail, it would be reasonable to accept the offer via Priority Mail or by a faster method, such as signed scanned documents sent as attachments via e-mail. ■

Substitute Method of Acceptance. Sometimes, the offeror authorizes a particular method of acceptance, but the offeree accepts by a different means. In that situation, the acceptance may still be effective if the substituted method serves the same purpose as the authorized means. Acceptance by a substitute method is not effective on dispatch, though. No contract will be formed until the acceptance is received by the offeror. **Example 11.16** Bennion's offer specifies acceptance via FedEx overnight delivery but the offeree accepts instead by overnight delivery from UPS. The substitute method of acceptance will still be effective, but not until the offeror (Bennion) receives the acceptance from UPS. ■

8. Note that UCC 2–206(1)(a) states specifically that an acceptance of an offer for the sale of goods can be made by any medium that is *reasonable* under the circumstances.

11-3 E-Contracts

E-Contract A contract that is formed electronically.

Numerous contracts are formed online. An electronic contract, or **e-contract**, must meet the same basic requirements (agreement, consideration, contractual capacity, and legality) as a paper contract. Disputes concerning e-contracts, however, tend to center on contract terms and whether the parties voluntarily agreed to those terms.

Online contracts may be formed not only for the sale of goods and services, but also for *licensing*. The "sale" of software generally involves a license, or a right to use the software, rather than the passage of title (ownership rights) from the seller to the buyer. **Example 11.17** When Lauren downloads an app on her smartphone, she has to select "I agree" several times to the terms and conditions under which she will use the software. After she agrees to these terms (the licensing agreement), she can use the application.

As you read through the following subsections, keep in mind that although we typically refer to the offeror and the offeree as a *seller* and a *buyer*, in many online transactions these parties would be more accurately described as a *licensor* and a *licensee*.

11-3a Online Offers

Sellers doing business via the Internet can protect themselves against contract disputes and legal liability by creating offers that clearly spell out the terms that will govern their transactions if the offers are accepted. All important terms should be conspicuous and easy to view.

Displaying the Offer The seller's website should include a hypertext link to a page containing the full contract so that potential buyers are made aware of the terms to which they are assenting. The contract generally must be displayed online in a readable format such as in a twelve-point typeface. All provisions should be reasonably clear.

Example 11.18 Netquip sells a variety of heavy equipment, such as trucks and trailers, online at its website. Because Netquip's pricing schedule is very complex, the schedule must be fully provided and explained on the website. In addition, the terms of the sale (such as any warranties and the refund policy) must be fully disclosed.

Provisions to Include An important rule to keep in mind is that the offeror (seller) controls the offer and thus the resulting contract. The seller should therefore anticipate any desired contractual terms and provide for them in the offer. In some instances, a standardized contract form may suffice. At a minimum, an online offer should include the following provisions:

1. *Acceptance of terms*. A clause that clearly indicates what constitutes the buyer's agreement to the terms of the offer, such as a box containing the words "I accept" that the buyer can click on to indicate acceptance. (Mechanisms for accepting online offers will be discussed later in this chapter.)
2. *Payment*. A provision specifying how payment for the goods (including any applicable taxes) must be made.
3. *Return policy*. A statement of the seller's refund and return policies.
4. *Disclaimer*. Disclaimers of liability for certain uses of the goods. For instance, an online seller of business forms may add a disclaimer that the seller does not accept responsibility for the buyer's reliance on the forms rather than on an attorney's advice.
5. *Limitation on remedies*. A provision specifying the remedies available to the buyer if the goods are found to be defective or if the contract is otherwise breached. Any limitation of remedies should be clearly spelled out.

6. *Privacy policy*. A statement indicating how the seller will use the information gathered about the buyer.
7. *Dispute resolution*. Provisions relating to dispute settlement, such as an arbitration clause.

Dispute-Settlement Provisions Online offers frequently include provisions relating to dispute settlement. For instance, the offer might include an arbitration clause specifying that any dispute arising under the contract will be arbitrated in a designated forum.

Case Example 11.19 Scott Rosendahl enrolled in an online college, Ashford University. He claimed that the school's adviser had told him that Ashford offered one of the cheapest undergraduate degree programs in the country. In fact, it did not. Rosendahl later sued the school, claiming that it had violated false advertising laws and had engaged in fraud and negligent misrepresentation. The university argued that the enrollment agreement clearly contained a requirement that all disputes be arbitrated. Rosendahl, like other students, had electronically assented to this agreement when he enrolled. Ashford presented the online application forms to the court, and the court dismissed Rosendahl's lawsuit. Rosendahl had agreed to arbitrate any disputes he had with Ashford.[9]

Forum-Selection Clause
A provision in a contract designating the court, jurisdiction, or tribunal that will decide any disputes arising under the contract.

Forum-Selection Clause. Many online contracts also contain a **forum-selection clause** indicating the forum, or location (such as a court or jurisdiction), for the resolution of any dispute arising under the contract. Significant jurisdictional issues can occur when parties are at a great distance, as they often are when they form contracts via the Internet. A forum-selection clause will help to avert future jurisdictional problems and also help to ensure that the seller will not be required to appear in court in a distant state.

Case Example 11.20 Rebecca Bextel developed a business plan to sell online greeting cards for the benefit of charitable organizations. She hired Tekstir, Inc., to develop the website for her venture, called Ecocards. Several months later, Bextel filed suit against Tekstir in a Wyoming state court, claiming the company had failed to meet its contractual obligations. Tekstir argued that the contract with Bextel included a forum-selection clause requiring any disputes to be ligated in Orange County, California. The Supreme Court of Wyoming held that the forum-selection clause was enforceable and granted Tekstir's motion to dismiss.[10]

Oleg Ribar/Shutterstock.com

The owner of a greeting card company in Wyoming sues a website designer in California. Is it fair to both parties if the forum-selection clause in their agreement requires that all disputes must be litigated in California? Why or why not?

Choice-of-Law Clause. Some online contracts may also include a *choice-of-law clause*, specifying that any dispute arising out of the contract will be settled in accordance with the law of a particular jurisdiction, such as a state or country. Choice-of-law clauses are particularly common in international contracts, but they may also appear in e-contracts to specify which state's laws will govern in the United States.

Sometimes, the same contract will include all three of these types of clauses (arbitration, forum-selection, and choice-of-law). **Case Example 11.21** Xlibris Publishing provides services to authors who wish to self-publish their work. It offers, through its website, a variety of publishing packages to facilitate editing, publishing, and marketing. Avis Smith, a New York resident, had previously

9. *Rosendahl v. Bridgepoint Education, Inc.*, 2012 WL 667049 (S.D.Cal. 2012).
10. *Ecocards v. Tekstir, Inc.*, 2020 WY 38, __ P.3d. __ (2020).

submitted his manuscript to Xlibris. Smith received an e-mail from Xlibris offering him a program at half price that would "provide the book what it deserves when it comes to exposure and publicity." Four days later, Smith contracted to purchase the Platinum Service Package from Xlibris for around $7,500 to be paid over three months.

A clause in the contract stated that any disputes between the parties would be arbitrated in Indianapolis, under the laws of Indiana. Communications between Smith and Xlibris deteriorated, and Smith ultimately filed a lawsuit against the company in a federal court in New York. Xlibris asked the court to compel arbitration in Indiana. The court ruled that Smith had consented to the arbitration, forum-selection, and choice-of-law clauses, which were enforceable. Smith was required to arbitrate the dispute in Indiana.[11]

11–3b Online Acceptances

The *Restatement (Second) of Contracts* states that parties may agree to a contract "by written or spoken words or by other action or by failure to act."[12] The Uniform Commercial Code (UCC), which governs sales contracts, has a similar provision. Section 2–204 of the UCC states that any contract for the sale of goods "may be made in any manner sufficient to show agreement, including conduct by both parties which recognizes the existence of such a contract." The courts have used these provisions in determining what constitutes an online acceptance.

Focus Question 3
How do click-on and shrink-wrap agreements differ?

Click-On Agreements The courts have concluded that the act of clicking on a box labeled "I accept" or "I agree" can indicate acceptance of an online offer. The agreement resulting from such an acceptance is often called a **click-on agreement** (sometimes, a *click-on license* or *click-wrap agreement*).

Click-on Agreement An agreement that arises when an online buyer clicks on "I agree" or otherwise indicates assent to be bound by the terms of an offer.

Generally, the law does not require that the parties have read all of the terms in a contract for it to be effective. Therefore, clicking on a box that states "I agree" to certain terms can be enough to bind a party to these terms. The terms may be contained on a website through which the buyer is obtaining goods or services, or they may appear on the screen of a computer, smartphone, or other device when software is downloaded from the Internet.

Case Example 11.22 Any person who agrees to work as an Uber driver must enter into a services agreement and driver addendum contract with Uber Technologies, Inc. The contracts include an arbitration provision. New drivers must click the "Yes, I agree" button to use the Uber App and to start working by picking up passengers.

A group of Chinese-speaking Uber drivers filed a breach of contract suit against the company. Uber responded with a motion to compel arbitration, which a federal district court granted. The plaintiffs had downloaded the Chinese version of the Uber App and could read the arbitration provision in their native language. Each had clicked on the button and agreed to arbitrate any disputes (whether or not they had actually read the clause). Thus, the arbitration clause was enforceable, and the lawsuit was dismissed.[13]

MikeDotta/Shutterstock.com

Does clicking on the "I agree" button of Uber's downloadable service agreement constitute acceptance of the arbitration clause in the agreement?

11. *Smith v. Xlibris Publishing*, 2016 WL 5678566 (E.D.N.Y. 2016).
12. *Restatement (Second) of Contracts*, Section 19.
13. *Kai Peng v. Uber Technologies, Inc.*, 237 F.Supp.3d 36 (E.D.N.Y. 2017).

In the following case, a lottery entrant claimed that the lottery breached its contract with him when it denied him the prize. The lottery acknowledged that he had accepted its offer to contract when he entered the contest online, and that his ticket had won the drawing. But it asserted that he was disqualified because he had failed to comply with the terms of the contract—that is, the rules of the contest.

Case 11.3

Bailey v. Kentucky Lottery Corp.

Kentucky Court of Appeals, 542 S.W.3d 305 (2018).

Facts Kentucky Lottery Corporation operates the Kentucky state lotteries. In a "second-chance" promotion, a scratch-off ticket that revealed an "FTP" ("Final Top Prize") symbol could be entered to win $175,000 in a drawing. The lottery operates a website at which individuals can register for an online account and enter the contest. The contest rules required an entrant to provide a valid phone number and mailing address, and keep them current. If the winner could not be reached within seven days after the drawing, disqualification would result.

Brett Bailey established an online account and entered several scratch-off tickets in the promotion. He provided a mailing address, but it was not correct, and before the drawing, he changed his phone number without notifying the lottery. Bailey's ticket won, but the lottery was unable to reach him—it could not contact him by phone, and a certified letter sent to the incorrect address was undeliverable. After expiration of the seven-day period, the prize was awarded to an eligible alternate. Later, Bailey filed a suit in a Kentucky state court against Kentucky Lottery Corporation, claiming breach of contract. The court granted a summary judgment to the defendant. Bailey appealed.

Issue Did Bailey accept the lottery's online contract terms and was he bound by those terms?

Decision Yes. A state intermediate appellate court affirmed the judgment of the lower court in favor of the lottery. "Bailey failed to comply with the requirements of the lottery's promotion, and the lottery had a contractual right to disqualify his entry from the drawing."

Reason Bailey entered the promotion by providing information on the lottery's website and by agreeing to the terms of use and to all other rules and regulations that applied to online account holders. The appellate court pointed out, "The purchase of a lottery ticket is the acceptance of an offer to contract and . . . the terms of the contract are the rules and regulations of the lottery." Here, Bailey agreed to the terms of the FTP promotion when he established an online account and entered his scratch-off tickets in the drawing. Those terms included requirements to provide and keep current a correct phone number and address. The rules further stated that a winner who could not be reached within a specific period after the drawing would be disqualified. Bailey did not provide a valid address, and he did not keep his phone number updated. Due to these omissions on Bailey's part, the lottery was unable to contact him when his ticket won the drawing, and the prize was awarded to another eligible entrant. "The court did not err when it granted summary judgment to the lottery."

Critical Thinking

- **Legal Environment** *The lottery's rules did not provide for entrants to be notified by e-mail, but contracts generally impose on the parties a duty to do everything necessary to carry them out. Did the lottery breach its contract with Bailey by failing to notify him by e-mail? Explain.*
- **What If the Facts Were Different?** *Suppose that Bailey had complied with the lottery's rules by keeping his address and phone number current, but that the lottery had not tried to notify him before the expiration of the seven-day period. Would the result have been different? Why or why not?*

Ethical Issue

How enforceable are click-on agreements to donate funds to a charity? Millions of online shoppers use PayPal as a convenient payment method. But PayPal can also be used to donate to a favorite charity. PayPal offers its users a Giving Fund platform. By going to PayPal's charity-giving platform, a potential contributor can choose from a list of charities. The Giving Fund platform requires two steps: clicking on the donation button for the charity and specifying the amount.

Many of the listed charities, though, have not yet actually signed up with PayPal to receive these donated funds. What happens when a contributor clicks on a listed charity that has not signed up? Apparently, neither the contributor nor the charity is notified, and PayPal sends the funds to other listed charities that are signed up with its service. Consequently, contributors' funds may go to charities that they did not choose, and charities may fail to receive donations meant for them. A number of individuals have filed a class-action lawsuit against PayPal based on this practice. The suit alleges that PayPal misled those making charitable contributions on its Giving Fund platform.[14]

Shrink-Wrap Agreements A **shrink-wrap agreement** (or *shrink-wrap license*) is an agreement whose terms are expressed inside a box in which goods are packaged. (The term *shrink-wrap* refers to the plastic that covers the box.) Usually, according to the agreement, the party who opens the box automatically accepts the terms by keeping the goods. Similarly, by opening a software package, the purchaser agrees to abide by the terms of the limited license agreement.

Shrink-Wrap Agreement An agreement whose terms are expressed in a document located inside a box in which goods (usually software) are packaged.

Example 11.23 Arial orders a new iPhone from Best Electronics, which ships it to her. Along with the iPhone, the box contains an agreement setting forth the terms of the sale, including what remedies are available. The document also states that Arial's retention of the iPhone for longer than thirty days will be construed as an acceptance of the terms.

In most instances, a shrink-wrap agreement is not between a retailer and a buyer, but is between the manufacturer of the hardware or software and the ultimate buyer-user of the product. The terms generally concern warranties, remedies, and other issues associated with the use of the product.

Shrink-Wrap Agreements and Enforceable Contract Terms. In some cases, the courts have enforced the terms of shrink-wrap agreements in the same way as the terms of other contracts. These courts have reasoned that by including the terms with the product, the seller proposed a contract that the buyer could accept by using the product after having an opportunity to read the terms. Thus, a buyer's failure to object to terms contained within a shrink-wrapped software package may constitute an acceptance of the terms by conduct.

Shrink-Wrap Terms That May Not Be Enforced. Sometimes, courts have refused to enforce certain terms included in shrink-wrap agreements because the buyer did not expressly consent to them. An important factor is when the parties form their contract.

If a buyer orders a product over the telephone, for instance, and the seller does not mention terms such as an arbitration clause or a forum-selection clause, clearly the buyer has not expressly agreed to these terms. If the buyer discovers the clauses *after* the parties entered into a contract, a court may conclude that those clauses were proposals for additional terms and not part of the contract.

Case Example 11.24 David Noble purchased a Samsung Smartwatch from an AT&T store after seeing ads saying that its battery life was twenty-four to forty-eight hours with typical use. But Noble's Smartwatch battery lasted only about four hours, so he returned the Smartwatch and received a new one. The second Smartwatch suffered from the same battery problem. Noble again went back to the AT&T store and, this time, was directed to ship the Smartwatch to Samsung. Samsung then sent Noble a third Smartwatch with equally poor battery life. Noble then filed a suit against Samsung in a federal district court. Samsung filed a motion to compel arbitration, which the district court denied. Samsung appealed.

14. *Friends for Health v. PayPal, Inc.*, 2017 WL 782249 (N.D.Ill. 2017).

Inside each of the Smartwatch boxes that Noble received was a tiny booklet titled "Health and Safety and Warranty Guide" that included a standard Limited Warranty. On page ninety-seven of the guide, a boldface question read "What is the procedure for resolving disputes?" Under that was a statement saying that any disputes would be resolved exclusively through binding arbitration, and not by a court or jury. The federal appellate court held that this language "tucked away in a brochure" was not sufficient to show that Noble had agreed to arbitration. Because consumers were not given reasonable notice of the arbitration clause (on the outside of the guide or somewhere obvious in the packaging), it was unenforceable.[15]

Browse-Wrap Terms Terms or conditions of use presented when an online buyer downloads a product but to which the buyer does not have to agree before installing or using the product.

Browse-Wrap Terms Like the terms of a click-on agreement, **browse-wrap term** can occur in a transaction conducted over the Internet. Unlike a click-on agreement, however, browse-wrap terms do not require the buyer or user to assent to the terms before, say, downloading or using certain software. **Case Example 11.25** James McCants bought dietary supplements over the Internet that allegedly seriously damaged his liver. When he sued the seller, Vitacost.com, Inc., the company moved for arbitration based on a clause in the browse-wrap terms. To see the arbitration clause, a purchaser would have had to scroll to the bottom of the seller's Web page and click on a hyperlink labeled "Terms and Conditions." The court held that these browse-wrap terms were not part of the sales agreement and were thus unenforceable.[16]

11–3c Federal Law on E-Signatures and E-Documents

E-Signature An electronic sound, symbol, or process attached to or logically associated with a record and adopted by a person with the intent to sign the record.

An **e-signature** has been defined as "an electronic sound, symbol, or process attached to or logically associated with a record and executed or adopted by a person with the intent to sign the record."[17] Electronic documents can be signed in a number of ways. Thus, e-signatures include encrypted digital signatures, names (intended as signatures) at the ends of e-mail messages, and "clicks" on a Web page if the clicks include some means of identification.

Under the Electronic Signatures in Global and National Commerce Act (E-SIGN Act),[18] no contract, record, or signature may be "denied legal effect" solely because it is in electronic form. An electronic signature is as valid as a signature on paper, and an e-document can be as enforceable as a paper one.

For an e-signature to be enforceable, however, the contracting parties must have agreed to use electronic signatures. For an electronic document to be valid, it must be in a form that can be retained and accurately reproduced.

The E-SIGN Act does not apply to all types of documents. Contracts and documents that are exempt include court papers, divorce decrees, evictions, foreclosures, health-insurance terminations, prenuptial agreements, and wills. Also, the only agreements governed by the UCC that fall under this law are those covered by Articles 2 and 2A and UCC 1–107 and 1–206. Despite these limitations, the E-SIGN Act significantly expanded contracting online.

11–3d Partnering Agreements

Partnering Agreement An agreement between a seller and a buyer who frequently do business with each other concerning the terms and conditions that will apply to all subsequently formed electronic contracts.

One way online sellers and buyers can prevent disputes over signatures in their e-contracts, as well as disputes over the terms and conditions of those contracts, is to form partnering agreements. In a **partnering agreement**, a seller and a buyer who frequently do business with each other agree in advance on the terms and conditions that will apply to all transactions subsequently conducted electronically. The partnering agreement can also establish special access and identification codes to be used by the parties when transacting business electronically.

---

15. *Noble v. Samsung Electronics Company, Inc.*, 682 Fed.Appx. 113 (3d Cir. 2017).
16. Vitacost.com, *Inc. v. McCants*, 210 So.3d 761 (Fla.App. 2017).
17. This definition is from the Uniform Electronic Transactions Act.
18. 15 U.S.C. Sections 7001 *et seq.*

A partnering agreement reduces the likelihood that disputes will arise under the contract because the buyer and the seller have agreed in advance to the terms and conditions that will accompany each sale. Furthermore, if a dispute does arise, a court or arbitration forum will be able to refer to the partnering agreement when determining the parties' intent.

11–4 The Uniform Electronic Transactions Act

Focus Question 4

What is the primary purpose of the Uniform Electronic Transactions Act?

The National Conference of Commissioners on Uniform State Laws and the American Law Institute promulgated the Uniform Electronic Transactions Act (UETA). The UETA has been adopted, at least in part, by forty-eight states.

The primary purpose of the UETA is to remove barriers to e-commerce by giving the same legal effect to electronic records and signatures as is given to paper documents and signatures. The UETA broadly defines an *e-signature* as "an electronic sound, symbol, or process attached to or logically associated with a record and executed or adopted by a person with the intent to sign the record."[19] A **record** is "information that is inscribed on a tangible medium or that is stored in an electronic or other medium and is retrievable in perceivable [visual] form."[20]

Record Information that is either inscribed on a tangible medium or stored in an electronic or other medium and is retrievable in visual form.

11–4a The Scope and Applicability of the UETA

The UETA does not create new rules for electronic contracts. Rather, it establishes that records, signatures, and contracts may not be denied enforceability solely due to their electronic form.

The UETA does not apply to all writings and signatures. It covers only electronic records and electronic signatures *relating to a transaction*. A *transaction* is defined as an interaction between two or more parties relating to business, commercial, or governmental activities.[21] The act specifically does not apply to wills or testamentary trusts or to transactions governed by the UCC (other than those covered by Articles 2 and 2A).[22] In addition, the provisions of the UETA allow the states to exclude its application to other areas of law.

11–4b The Federal E-SIGN Act and the UETA

Congress passed the E-SIGN Act a year after the UETA was presented to the states for adoption. Thus, a significant issue was to what extent the federal E-SIGN Act preempted the UETA as adopted by the states.

The E-SIGN Act[23] explicitly provides that if a state has enacted the uniform version of the UETA, it is not preempted by the E-SIGN Act. In other words, if the state has enacted the UETA without modification, state law will govern.

The problem is that many states have enacted nonuniform (modified) versions of the UETA, largely for the purpose of excluding other areas of state law from the UETA's terms. The E-SIGN Act specifies that those exclusions will be preempted to the extent that they are inconsistent with the E-SIGN Act's provisions.

19. UETA 102(8).
20. UETA 102(15).
21. UETA 2(12) and 3.
22. UETA 3(b).
23. 15 U.S.C. Section 7002(2)(A)(i).

The E-SIGN Act explicitly allows the states to enact alternative requirements for the use of electronic records or electronic signatures. Generally, however, the requirements must be consistent with the provisions of the E-SIGN Act, and the state must not give greater legal status or effect to one specific type of technology. Additionally, if a state enacts alternative requirements *after* the E-SIGN Act was adopted, the state law must specifically refer to the E-SIGN Act.

The relationship between the E-SIGN Act and the UETA is illustrated in Exhibit 11–1.

11–4c Highlights of the UETA

The UETA will not apply to a transaction unless the parties have agreed to conduct transactions by electronic means. The agreement may be explicit, or it may be implied by the conduct of the parties and the surrounding circumstances.[24] It may be reasonable, for instance, to infer that a person who gives out a business card with an e-mail address on it has consented to transact business electronically.[25] Agreement may also be inferred from a letter or other writing, as well as from verbal communication. Furthermore, a person who has previously agreed to an electronic transaction can withdraw this consent and refuse to conduct further business electronically.

Attribution Under the UETA, if an electronic record or signature is the act of a particular person, the record or signature may be attributed to that person. If someone types their name at the bottom of an e-mail purchase order, for instance, that name will qualify as a "signature" and be attributed to the person whose name appears.

Exhibit 11–1 The E-SIGN Act and the UETA

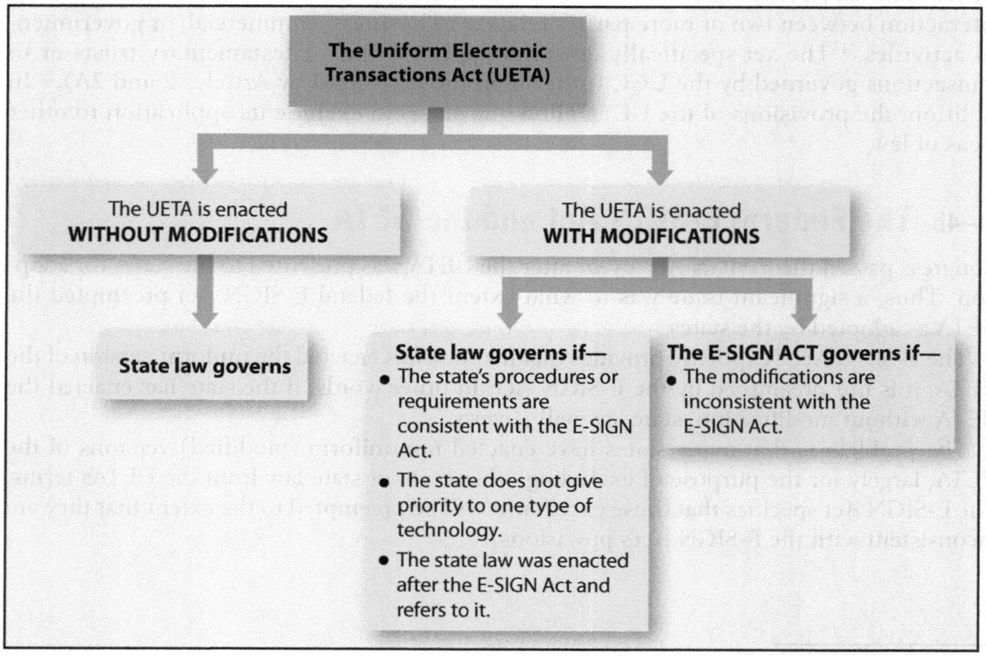

24. UETA 5(b).
25. UETA 5, Comment 4B.

The UETA contains no express provisions about what constitutes fraud or whether an agent is authorized to enter a contract. Under the UETA, other state laws control if any issues relating to agency, authority, forgery, or contract formation arise. If existing state law requires a document to be notarized, the electronic signature of a notary public or other person authorized to verify signatures satisfies this requirement.

The Effect of Errors The UETA encourages, but does not require, the use of security procedures (such as encryption) to verify changes to electronic documents and to correct errors. If the parties have agreed to a security procedure and one party does not detect an error because of failure to follow the procedure, the conforming party can legally avoid the effect of the change or error.

To avoid the effect of errors, a party must promptly notify the other party of the error and of the intent not to be bound by the error. In addition, the party must take reasonable steps to return any benefit received. Parties cannot avoid a transaction if they have benefited.

Timing An electronic record is considered *sent* when it is properly directed to the intended recipient in a form readable by the recipient's computer system. Once the electronic record leaves the control of the sender or comes under the control of the recipient, the UETA deems it to have been sent. An electronic record is considered *received* when it enters the recipient's processing system in a readable form—*even if no individual is aware of its receipt.*

Practice and Review

Shane Durbin wanted to have a recording studio custom-built in his home. He sent invitations to a number of local contractors to submit bids on the project. Rory Amstel submitted the lowest bid, which was $20,000 less than any of the other bids Durbin received. Durbin called Amstel to ascertain the type and quality of the materials that were included in the bid and to find out if he could substitute a superior brand of acoustic tiles for the same bid price. Amstel said he would have to check into the price difference. The parties also discussed a possible start date for construction.

Two weeks later, Durbin changed his mind and decided not to go forward with his plan to build a recording studio. Amstel filed a suit against Durbin for breach of contract. Using the information presented in the chapter, answer the following questions.

1. Did Amstel's bid meet the requirements of an offer? Explain.
2. Was there an acceptance of the offer? Why or why not?
3. Suppose that the court determines that the parties did not reach an agreement. Further suppose that Amstel, in anticipation of building Durbin's studio, had purchased materials and refused other jobs so that he would have time in his schedule for Durbin's project. Under what theory discussed in the chapter might Amstel attempt to recover these costs?
4. How is an offer terminated? Assuming that Durbin did not inform Amstel that he was rejecting the offer, was the offer terminated at any time described here? Explain.

Debate This

The terms and conditions in click-on agreements are so long and detailed that no one ever reads the agreements. Therefore, the act of clicking on "I agree" is not really an acceptance.

Key Terms

acceptance 269
agreement 262
browse-wrap terms 278
click-on agreement 275
counteroffer 268
e-contract 273
e-signature 278
forum-selection clause 274
mailbox rule 272
mirror image rule 268
offer 262
option contract 268
partnering agreement 278
record 279
revocation 267
shrink-wrap agreement 277

Chapter Summary: Agreement

Offer	1. **Intention**—There must be a serious, objective intent by the offeror to become bound by the offer. Nonoffer situations include (a) expressions of opinion; (b) statements of future intent; (c) preliminary negotiations; (d) invitations to bid; (e) advertisements and price lists; and (f) live and online auctions. 2. **Definiteness**—The terms of the offer must be sufficiently definite to be ascertainable by the parties or by a court. 3. **Communication**—The offer must be communicated to the offeree. 4. **Termination of the offer**—The offer can be terminated either by the action of the parties or by operation of law. a. The parties can either revoke or reject the offer. Some offers, such as a merchant's firm offer and option contracts, are irrevocable. A counteroffer is a rejection of the original offer and the making of a new offer. b. An offer terminates by operation of law through a lapse of time, destruction of the specific subject of the offer, death or incompetence of the parties, or the supervening illegality of the proposed contract.
Acceptance	1. Can be made only by the offeree or the offeree's agent. 2. Must be unequivocal. Under the common law (mirror image rule), if new terms or conditions are added to the acceptance, it will be considered a counteroffer. 3. Except in a few situations, an offeree's silence does not constitute an acceptance. 4. Communication of acceptance depends on the nature of the contract. In a unilateral contract, full performance is called for. In a bilateral contract, communication of acceptance is necessary because acceptance is in the form of a promise. 5. Acceptance in bilateral contracts must be timely and takes effect when the offeree sends or delivers the acceptance via the mode of communication authorized by the offeror.
E-Contracts	1. **Online offers**—The terms of a contract offer presented via the Internet should be as inclusive as the terms in an offer made in a written (paper) document. The offer should be displayed in an easily readable format and should include some mechanism, such as an "I agree" or "I accept" box, by which the customer can accept the offer. Because jurisdictional issues frequently arise with online transactions, the offer should include dispute-settlement provisions and may include a forum-selection clause. 2. **Online acceptances**— a. Click-on agreements are created when a buyer, completing an online transaction, is required to indicate assent to be bound by the terms of an offer by clicking on a box that says, for instance, "I agree." The terms of the agreement may appear on the website through which the buyer is obtaining goods or services, or they may appear on a computer screen when software is downloaded. b. The terms of a shrink-wrap agreement are expressed inside a box in which goods are packaged. The party who opens the box is informed that keeping the goods indicates agreement to the terms of the shrink-wrap agreement. c. Browse-wrap terms do not require the buyer or user to assent to the terms before, say, downloading or using certain software.

3. **Federal law on e-signatures and e-documents—**
   a. The Uniform Electronic Transactions Act (UETA) defines an e-signature as "an electronic sound, symbol, or process attached to or logically associated with a record and executed or adopted by a person with the intent to sign the record." E-signatures may include encrypted digital signatures, names at the ends of e-mail messages, and clicks on a Web page.
   b. The Electronic Signatures in Global and National Commerce Act (E-SIGN Act) gave validity to e-signatures by providing that no contract, record, or signature may be "denied legal effect" solely because it is in an electronic form.
4. **Partnering agreements**—A seller and a buyer who frequently do business with each other may agree in advance on the terms and conditions that will apply to all transactions subsequently conducted electronically.

The Uniform Electronic Transactions Act (UETA) The Uniform Electronic Transactions Act (UETA) has been adopted, at least in part, by most states, to create rules to support the enforcement of e-contracts. Under the UETA, contracts entered into online, as well as other electronic documents, are presumed to be valid. The UETA does not apply to certain transactions governed by the UCC or to wills or testamentary trusts.

Issue Spotters

1. Fidelity Corporation offers to hire Ron to replace Monica, who has given Fidelity a month's notice of her intent to leave the company. Fidelity gives Ron a week to decide whether to accept. Two days later, Monica decides not to leave and signs an employment contract with Fidelity for another year. The next day, Monica tells Ron of the new contract. Ron immediately e-mails a formal letter of acceptance to Fidelity. Do Fidelity and Ron have a contract? Why or why not? (See *Offer.*)
2. Applied Products, Inc., does business with Beltway Distributors, Inc., online. Under the Uniform Electronic Transactions Act, what determines the effect of the electronic documents evidencing the parties' deal? Is a party's "signature" necessary? Explain. (See *The Uniform Electronic Transactions Act.*)

—Check your answers to the *Issue Spotters* against the answers provided in Appendix D.

Business Scenarios and Case Problems

11–1. Offer. Ball writes to Sullivan and inquires how much Sullivan is asking for a specific forty-acre tract of land Sullivan owns. Ball then receives a letter from Sullivan stating, "I will not take less than $60,000 for the forty-acre tract as specified." Ball immediately sends Sullivan a fax stating, "I accept your offer for $60,000 for the forty-acre tract as specified." Discuss whether Ball can hold Sullivan to a contract for sale of the land. (See *Offer.*)

11–2. Shrink-Wrap Agreements. TracFone Wireless, Inc., sells phones and wireless service. The phones are sold for less than their cost, and TracFone recoups this loss by selling prepaid airtime for their use on its network. Software in the phones prohibits their use on other networks. The phones are sold subject to the condition that the buyer agrees "not to tamper with or alter the software." This condition is printed on the packaging. Bequator Corp. bought at least 18,616 of the phones, disabled the software so that they could be used on other networks, and resold them. Is Bequator liable for breach of contract? Explain. [*TracFone Wireless, Inc. v. Bequator Corp., Ltd.*, 2011 WL 1427635 (S.D.Fla. 2011)] (See *E-Contracts.*)

11–3. Online Acceptances. Heather Reasonover opted to try Internet service from Clearwire Corp. Clearwire sent her a confirmation e-mail that included a link to its website. Clearwire also sent her a modem. In the enclosed written materials, at the bottom of a page, in small type was the website URL. When Reasonover plugged in the modem, an "I accept terms" box appeared. Without clicking on the box, Reasonover quit the page. A clause in Clearwire's "Terms of Service," accessible only through its website, required its subscribers to submit any dispute to arbitration. Is Reasonover bound to this clause? Why or why not? [*Kwan v. Clearwire Corp.*, 2012 WL 32380 (W.D.Wash. 2012)] (See *E-Contracts.*)

11–4. Acceptance. Judy Olsen, Kristy Johnston, and their mother, Joyce Johnston, owned seventy-eight acres of real property on Eagle Creek in Meagher County, Montana. When Joyce died, she left her interest in the property to Kristy. Kristy wrote to Judy, offering to buy Judy's interest or to sell her own interest to Judy. She requested that Judy "please respond to Bruce Townsend." In a letter to Kristy—not to Bruce—Judy accepted the offer to buy Kristy's interest in the property. By that time, however, Kristy had offered to sell her interest to their brother, Dave, and he had accepted. Did Judy and Kristy have an enforceable binding contract, entitling Judy to specific performance? Or did Kristy's offer so limit its acceptance to one exclusive mode that Judy's reply was not effective? Discuss. [*Olsen v. Johnston*, 368 Mont. 347, 301 P.3d 791 (2013)] (See *Acceptance.*)

11–5. Acceptance. Amy Kemper was seriously injured when her motorcycle was struck by a vehicle driven by Christopher Brown. Kemper's attorney wrote to Statewide Claims Services, the administrator for Brown's insurer, asking for "all the insurance money that Mr. Brown had under his insurance policy." In exchange, the letter indicated that Kemper would sign a "limited release" on Brown's liability, provided that it did not include any language requiring her to reimburse Brown or his insurance company for any of their incurred costs. Statewide then sent a check and release form to Kemper, but the release demanded that Kemper "place money in an escrow account in regards to any and all liens pending." Kemper refused the demand, claiming that Statewide's response was a counteroffer rather than an unequivocal acceptance of the settlement offer. Did Statewide and Kemper have an enforceable agreement? Discuss. [*Kemper v. Brown*, 325 Ga.App. 806, 754 S.E.2d 141 (2014)] (See *Acceptance*.)

11–6. Business Case Problem with Sample Answer—Requirements of the Offer. Technical Consumer Products, Inc. (TCP), makes and distributes energy-efficient lighting products. Emily Bahr was TCP's district sales manager in Minnesota, North Dakota, and South Dakota when the company announced the details of a bonus plan. District sales managers who achieved 100 percent year-over-year sales growth and a 42 percent gross margin would earn 200 percent of their base salaries as a bonus. TCP retained absolute discretion to modify the plan. Bahr's base salary was $42,500. Her final sales results for the year showed 113 percent year-over-year sales growth and a 42 percent gross margin. She anticipated a bonus of $85,945, but TCP could not afford to pay the bonuses as planned, and Bahr received only $34,229. In response to Bahr's claim for breach of contract, TCP argued that the bonus plan was too indefinite to be an offer. Is TCP correct? Explain. [*Bahr v. Technical Consumer Products, Inc.*, 601 Fed. Appx. 359 (6th Cir. 2015)] (See *Offer*.)

—For a sample answer to Problem 11–6, go to Appendix E.

11–7. Acceptance. Altisource Portfolio Solutions, Inc., is a global corporation that provides real property owners with services that include property preservation—repairs, debris removal, and so on. Lucas Contracting, Inc., is a small trade contractor in Carrollton, Ohio. On behalf of Altisource, Berghorst Enterprises, LLC, hired Lucas to perform preservation work on certain foreclosed properties in eastern Ohio. When Berghorst did not pay for the work, Lucas filed a suit in an Ohio state court against Altisource. Before the trial, Lucas e-mailed the terms of a settlement. The same day, Altisource e-mailed a response that did not challenge or contradict Lucas's proposal and indicated agreement to it. Two days later, however, Altisource forwarded a settlement document that contained additional terms. Which proposal most likely satisfies the element of agreement to establish a contract? Explain. [*Lucas Contracting, Inc. v. Altisource Portfolio Solutions, Inc.*, 2016 -Ohio- 474 (2016)] (See *Acceptance*.)

11–8. Online Acceptances. Airbnb, Inc., maintains a website that lists, advertises, and takes fees or commissions for property rentals posted on the site. To offer or book accommodations on the site, a party must register and create an account. The sign-up screen states, "By clicking 'Sign Up' . . . you confirm that you accept the Terms of Service" (TOS). The TOS, which are hyperlinked, include a mandatory arbitration provision. Francesco Plazza registered with Airbnb and created an account but did not read the TOS. Later, Plazza filed a suit in a federal district court against Airbnb, alleging that the defendant was acting as an unlicensed real estate broker and committing deceptive trade practices in violation of New York state law. Airbnb filed a motion to compel arbitration, pursuant to the TOS. Can Plazza avoid arbitration? Explain. [*Plazza v. Airbnb, Inc.*, 289 F.Supp.3d 537 (S.D.N.Y. 2018)] (See *E-Contracts*.)

11–9. A Question of Ethics—The IDDR Approach and Intention. The Prince Hall Grand Lodge of Washington is a fraternal association incorporated in the state of Washington. The Grand Lodge Constitution provides that the Grand Master "shall decide all questions of . . . Masonic law." Grand Master Gregory Wraggs suspended the membership of Lonnie Traylor for "un-Masonic conduct." Traylor asked Wraggs to revoke the suspension and prepared a "Memo of Understanding." Wraggs agreed to talk but declined to revoke the suspension and did not sign the memo. Traylor filed a suit in a Washington state court against the Grand Lodge and Wraggs, alleging that the Grand Master's failure to revoke Traylor's suspension was a breach of contract. [*Traylor v. Most Worshipful Prince Hall Grand Lodge*, 197 Wash.App. 1026 (Div. 2 2017)] (See *Offer*.)

1. Was it ethical of Wraggs to agree to talk to Traylor but decline to revoke his suspension? Use the IDDR approach to decide.
2. On what basis would the court likely hold that there was no contract between Wraggs and Traylor? Is it unethical of Traylor to assert otherwise? Discuss, using the IDDR approach.

Critical Thinking and Writing Assignments

11–10. Time-Limited Group Assignment—E-Contracts. To download a specific app to your smartphone or tablet device, you usually have to check a box indicating that you agree to the company's terms and conditions. Most individuals do so without ever reading those terms and conditions. Print out a specific set of terms and conditions from a downloaded app to use in this assignment. All group members should print out the same set of terms and conditions. (See *E-Contracts*.)

1. One group will determine which of these terms and conditions are favorable to the company.
2. Another group will determine which of these terms and conditions could conceivably be favorable to the individual.
3. A third group will determine which terms and conditions, on net, favor the company too much.

Consideration, Capacity, and Legality

12

"Liberty of contract is not an absolute concept. It is relative to many conditions of time and place and circumstance."

Benjamin Cardozo
1870–1938
(Associate justice of the United States Supreme Court, 1932–1938)

Courts generally tend to enforce contracts, and much of the law is devoted to aiding the enforceability of contracts. Before a court will enforce a contractual promise, however, it must be convinced that there was some exchange of consideration underlying the bargain.

Furthermore, as indicated in the chapter-opening quotation, "liberty of contract" is not absolute. In other words, not all people can make legally binding contracts at all times. Contracts entered into by persons lacking the capacity to do so may be voidable. Similarly, contracts calling for the performance of an illegal act are illegal and thus void—they are not contracts at all.

Focus Questions

The five Focus Questions *below are designed to help improve your understanding. After reading this chapter, you should be able to answer the following questions:*

1. What are the two elements of consideration?
2. In what circumstances might a promise be enforced despite a lack of consideration?
3. Does a minor have the capacity to enter into an enforceable contract? What does it mean to disaffirm a contract?
4. Under what circumstances will courts enforce a covenant not to compete?
5. What are the consequences of entering an illegal agreement?

12–1 Consideration

In any legal system, some promises will be enforced, and other promises will not be enforced. The simple fact that a party has made a promise does not necessarily mean that the promise is enforceable.

Under the common law, a primary basis for the enforcement of promises is consideration. **Consideration** usually is defined as the value given in return for a promise. Often, consideration is broken down into two parts: (1) something of *legally sufficient value* must be given in exchange for the promise, and (2) there must be a *bargained-for exchange.*

Consideration The value given in return for a promise or performance in a contractual agreement.

Focus Question 1

What are the two elements of consideration?

Forbearance The act of refraining from an action that one has a legal right to undertake.

12–1a Legally Sufficient Value

To be legally sufficient, consideration must be something of value in the eyes of the law. The "something of legally sufficient value" may consist of any of the following:

1. A promise to do something that one has no prior legal duty to do.
2. The performance of an action that one is otherwise not obligated to undertake (such as providing accounting services).
3. The refraining from an action that one has a legal right to undertake (called a **forbearance**).

Consideration in bilateral contracts normally consists of a promise in return for a promise. In a contract for the sale of goods, for instance, the seller promises to ship specific goods to the buyer, and the buyer promises to pay for those goods when they are received. Each of these promises constitutes consideration for the contract.

In contrast, unilateral contracts involve a promise in return for a performance. **Example 12.1** Anita says to her neighbor, "If you paint my garage, I will pay you $800." Anita's neighbor paints the garage. The act of painting the garage is the consideration that creates Anita's contractual obligation to pay her neighbor $800. ■

What if, in return for a promise to pay, a person refrains from pursuing harmful habits, such as the use of tobacco and alcohol? Does such forbearance create consideration for the contract? This was the issue in the 1891 case *Hamer v. Sidway*, which we present as this chapter's *Landmark in the Law* feature.

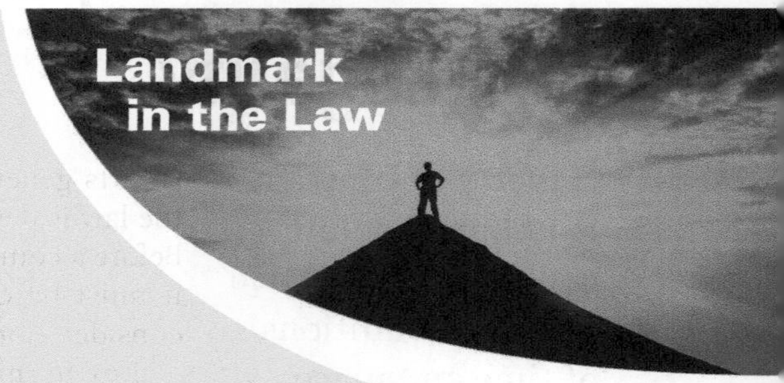

Hamer v. Sidway (1891)

In *Hamer v. Sidway*,[a] the issue before the court arose from a contract created in 1869 between William Story, Sr., and his nephew, William Story II. The uncle promised his nephew that if the nephew refrained from drinking alcohol, using tobacco, and playing billiards and cards for money until he reached the age of twenty-one, the uncle would pay him $5,000 (about $75,000 in today's dollars). The nephew, who indulged occasionally in all of these "vices," agreed to refrain from them and did so for the next six years.

Following his twenty-first birthday in 1875, the nephew wrote to his uncle that he had performed his part of the bargain and was thus entitled to the promised $5,000 (plus interest). A few days later, the uncle wrote the nephew a letter stating, "[Y]ou shall have the five thousand dollars, as I promised you." The uncle said that the money was in the bank and that the nephew could "consider this money on interest."

a. 124 N.Y. 538, 27 N.E. 256 (1891).

The Issue of Consideration The nephew left the money in the care of his uncle, who held it for the next twelve years. When the uncle died in 1887, however, the executor of the uncle's estate refused to pay the $5,000 (plus interest) claim brought by Hamer, a third party to whom the promise had been *assigned*. (The law allows parties to assign, or transfer, rights in contracts to third parties.) The executor, Sidway, contended that the contract was invalid because there was insufficient consideration to support it. The uncle had received nothing, and the nephew had actually benefited by fulfilling the uncle's wishes. Therefore, no contract existed.

The Court's Conclusion Although a lower court upheld Sidway's position, the New York Court of Appeals reversed and ruled in favor of the plaintiff, Hamer. "The promisee used tobacco, occasionally drank liquor, and he had a legal right to do so," the court stated. "That right he abandoned for a period of years upon the strength of the promise of the testator [one who makes a will] that for such forbearance he would give him $5,000. We need not speculate on the effort which may have been required to give up the use of those stimulants. It is sufficient that he restricted his lawful freedom of action within certain prescribed limits upon the faith of his uncle's agreement."

Application to Today's World *Although this case was decided more than a century ago, the principles enunciated by the court remain applicable to contracts formed today, including online contracts. For a contract to be valid and binding, consideration must be given, and that consideration must be something of legally sufficient value.*

12–1b Bargained-for Exchange

The second element of consideration is that it must provide the basis for the bargain struck between the contracting parties. The item of value must be given or promised by the promisor (offeror) in return for the promisee's promise or performance.

This element of bargained-for exchange distinguishes contracts from gifts. **Case Example 12.2** Rachel Thomas was admitted to a hospital emergency room with pregnancy-related complications. The attending physician, Dr. Archer, recommended that she be transported by medevac (helicopter) to a different facility. The woman and her husband informed the physician that they needed their insurer's preauthorization for that course of action or they could be personally liable for the costs. Dr. Archer allegedly promised to call the insurer and, if it would not approve the medevac, have the hospital bear the costs itself. But the physician failed to contact the insurer until much later, and the insurer declined coverage.

The couple sued the hospital, claiming breach of contract by Dr. Archer. The court ruled in favor of the hospital, and the case was appealed to the Alaska Supreme Court. The court held that the physician's alleged promise about insurance and payment did not give rise to an enforceable contract. There was no evidence that the hospital sought any consideration from the Thomases for the physician's alleged promise. Thus, there was no "bargained-for" consideration. The court affirmed the dismissal of the Thomases' contract claim (but remanded the case on the issue of promissory estoppel, a concept that will be discussed shortly).[1]

In the following case, the court was asked to consider whether a Major League Baseball team receives consideration from fans in exchange for promotional items that the fans receive when attending a game.

1. *Thomas v. Archer*, 384 P.3d 791 (Alaska 2016).

Case 12.1

Cincinnati Reds, L.L.C. v. Testa

Supreme Court of Ohio, 2018 -Ohio- 4669, 122 N.E.3d 1178 (2018).

Facts Faced with rising ticket prices and increasing entertainment options, Major League Baseball organizations have experienced challenges in getting fans to attend games. One way to attract fans is to offer them unique merchandise—such as bobbleheads, shirts, blankets, caps, player cards, tote bags, and bats—that they can obtain only by attending a game.

The Cincinnati Reds, L.L.C., often engages in these types of promotions. The Reds' home state, Ohio, imposes a sales tax on certain goods but exempts goods intended for resale. Concluding that the Reds' promotional items were purchased to give away, not to resell, the state board of tax appeals (BTA) denied the team's request for an exemption.

On appeal to the Ohio Supreme Court, the Reds argued that they resold the promotional items by promising to distribute them—that this promise creates a contractual expectation on the part of the fans, who buy tickets and attend games as consideration for receiving the items.

Issue Do ticket purchases and game attendance by Reds fans constitute consideration for receiving promotional items distributed by the Reds at the games?

Decision Yes. The Ohio Supreme Court reversed the decision of the BTA. "Consideration is given in exchange for the Reds' agreement to supply fans with . . . promotional items. The transfer of promotional items to fans thus constitutes a sale . . . and the promotional items are subject to the sale-for-resale exemption."

Reason The testimony of the Reds' chief financial officer, Doug Healy, contradicted the BTA's finding that the Reds intended to give away promotional items rather than sell them. Healy testified that

(Continues)

Continued

the Reds advertise in advance to notify fans which specific promotional items will be distributed at which games. Fans buy tickets to those games expecting to receive those items. If the Reds do not have enough of the items to provide one to each fan at the game, the Reds provide a different item, a ticket to a future game, or something else of equivalent value. Healy explained that the costs of the promotional items are included in the prices of the tickets, which are set before the season begins. The items are distributed at "less desirable" games for which tickets are not expected to be sold out.

The court reasoned that because the cost of the promotional item was included in the ticket price, part of the price paid for the right to attend the "less desirable" game and a separate part paid for the right to receive the promotional item. The court concluded, therefore, that the promotional items constituted things of value in exchange for which fans paid amounts included in the prices of the tickets.

Critical Thinking

- **Legal** *Fans sometimes catch and keep baseballs hit into the stands. How do these actions differ from the situation described in this case, in which the fans were promised and received promotional items for attending games? Does this distinction support or undercut the court's ruling?*

- **Economic** *What effect does the decision in this case have on the state's collection of revenue? Discuss.*

12–1c Adequacy of Consideration

Adequacy of consideration involves "how much" consideration is given. Essentially, adequacy of consideration concerns the fairness of the bargain.

The General Rule On the surface, when the items exchanged are of unequal value, fairness would appear to be an issue. Normally, however, a court will not question the adequacy of consideration based solely on the comparative value of the things exchanged.

In other words, the determination of whether consideration exists does not depend on the values of the things exchanged. Something need not be of direct economic or financial value to be considered legally sufficient consideration. In many situations, the exchange of promises and potential benefits is deemed to be sufficient consideration.

Under the doctrine of freedom of contract, courts leave it up to the parties to decide what something is worth, and parties are usually free to bargain as they wish. If people could sue merely because they had entered into an unwise contract, the courts would be overloaded with frivolous suits.

Know This
A consumer's signature on a contract does not always guarantee that the contract will be enforced. The contract must also comply with state and federal consumer protection laws.

When Voluntary Consent May Be Lacking Occasionally, an exception may be made to the general rule just discussed. A large disparity in the amount or value of the consideration exchanged may raise a red flag for a court to look more closely at the bargain. Shockingly inadequate consideration can indicate that fraud, duress, or undue influence was involved.

Example 12.3 Spencer pays $500 for an iPhone that he later discovers is a fake (counterfeit). Because the device is not authentic, he could claim that there was no valid contract because of inadequate consideration and fraud. ■ (Disparity in the consideration exchanged may also cause a judge to question whether the contract is so one-sided that it is *unconscionable*.[2])

2. Pronounced un-*kon*-shun-uh-bul.

12–1d Agreements That Lack Consideration

Sometimes, one or both of the parties to a contract may think that they have exchanged consideration when in fact they have not. Here, we look at some situations in which the parties' promises or actions do not qualify as contractual consideration.

Preexisting Duty

Under most circumstances, a promise to do what one already has a legal duty to do does not constitute legally sufficient consideration. A sheriff, for instance, cannot collect a reward for information leading to the capture of a criminal if the sheriff already has a legal duty to capture the criminal.

Likewise, if a party is already bound by contract to perform a certain duty, that duty cannot serve as consideration for a second contract. **Example 12.4** Bauman-Bache, Inc., begins construction on a seven-story office building and after three months demands an extra $75,000 on its contract. If the extra $75,000 is not paid, the firm will stop working. The owner of the land, finding no one else to complete construction, agrees to pay the extra $75,000. The agreement is not enforceable because it is not supported by legally sufficient consideration—Bauman-Bache had a preexisting contractual duty to complete the building.

Unforeseen Difficulties. The preexisting duty rule is intended to prevent extortion and the so-called holdup game. Nonetheless, if, during performance of a contract, extraordinary difficulties arise that were totally unforeseen at the time the contract was formed, a court may allow an exception to the rule. The key is whether the court finds that the modification is fair and equitable in view of circumstances not anticipated by the parties when the contract was made.[3]

© TFoxFoto/Shutterstock.com

Are there circumstances under which a contractor can legally demand a payment amount that is greater than what was stated in the contract?

Suppose that in *Example 12.4*, Bauman-Bache asked for the extra $75,000 because it encountered a rock formation that no one knew existed. Suppose, too, that the landowner agreed to pay the extra amount to excavate the rock. In this situation, if the court finds that it is fair to do so, it may enforce the agreement. If rock formations are common in the area, however, the court may determine that the contractor should have known of the risk. In that situation, the court may choose to apply the preexisting duty rule and prevent Bauman-Bache from obtaining the extra $75,000.

Rescission and New Contract. The law recognizes that two parties can mutually agree to rescind, or cancel, their contract, at least to the extent that it is *executory* (still to be carried out). **Rescission**[4] is the unmaking of a contract so as to return the parties to the positions they occupied before the contract was made.

Rescission A remedy whereby a contract is canceled and the parties are returned to the positions they occupied before the contract was made.

Sometimes, parties rescind a contract and make a new contract at the same time. When this occurs, it is often difficult to determine whether there was consideration for the new contract or whether the parties had a preexisting duty under the previous contract. If a court finds there was a preexisting duty, then the new contract will be invalid because there was no consideration.

Past Consideration

Promises made in return for actions or events that have already taken place are unenforceable. These promises lack consideration in that the element of bargained-for exchange is missing. In short, you can bargain for something to take place now or in the future but not for something that has already taken place. Therefore, **past consideration** is no consideration.

Past Consideration Something given or some act done in the past, which cannot ordinarily be consideration for a later bargain.

Spotlight Case Example 12.5 Jamil Blackmon became friends with Allen Iverson when Iverson was a high school student who showed tremendous promise as an athlete. Blackmon suggested that Iverson use "The Answer" as a nickname in the league tournaments,

3. *Restatement (Second) of Contracts,* Section 73.
4. Pronounced reh-*sih*-zhen.

and said that Iverson would be "The Answer" to the National Basketball Association's declining attendance. Later, Iverson said that he would give Blackmon 25 percent of any proceeds from the merchandising of products that used "The Answer" as a logo or a slogan. Because Iverson's promise was made in return for past consideration (Blackmon's earlier suggestion), it was unenforceable. In effect, Iverson stated his intention to give Blackmon a gift.[5]

Illusory Promises If the terms of the contract express such uncertainty of performance that the promisor has not definitely promised to do anything, the promise is said to be *illusory*—without consideration and unenforceable. **Example 12.6** The president of Tuscan Corporation says to his employees, "All of you have worked hard, and if profits remain high, a 10 percent bonus at the end of the year will be given—if management thinks it is warranted." This is an *illusory promise*, or no promise at all, because performance depends solely on the discretion of the president (the management). There is no bargained-for consideration. The statement declares merely that management may or may not do something in the future.

Option-to-cancel clauses in contracts for specified time periods sometimes present problems because of illusory promises. **Example 12.7** Abe contracts to hire Chris for one year at $5,000 per month, reserving the right to cancel the contract at any time. On close examination of these words, you can see that Abe has not actually agreed to hire Chris, because Abe can cancel without liability before Chris starts performance. Abe has not given up the opportunity of hiring someone else. This contract is therefore illusory.

But if, instead, Abe reserves the right to cancel the contract at any time *after* Chris has begun performance by giving Chris *thirty days' notice*, the promise is not illusory. Abe, by saying that he will give Chris thirty days' notice, is relinquishing the opportunity (legal right) to hire someone else instead of Chris for a thirty-day period. If Chris works for one month and Abe then gives him thirty days' notice, Chris has an enforceable claim for two months' salary ($10,000).

Exhibit 12–1 illustrates some common situations in which promises or actions do not constitute contractual consideration.

5. *Blackmon v. Iverson*, 324 F.Supp.2d 602 (E.D.Pa. 2003).

Exhibit 12–1 Examples of Agreements That Lack Consideration

PREEXISTING DUTY

When a person already has a legal duty to perform an action, a promise to perform that action is not legally sufficient consideration.

Example: A firefighter cannot receive a cash reward from a business owner for putting out a fire in a downtown commercial district. As a city employee, the firefighter had a duty to extinguish the fire.

PAST CONSIDERATION

When a person makes a promise in return for actions or events that have already taken place, there is no consideration.

Example: A real estate agent sells a friend's house without charging a commission, and in return, the friend promises to give the agent $1,000. The friend's promise is simply an intention to give a gift.

ILLUSORY PROMISES

When contract terms are so uncertain that there is no definite promise, the promise is illusory.

Example: A man promises to stop by soon to look at his neighbor's riding lawn mower. If he likes it, he will pay $900. The promise to purchase is simply a statement of something he might do in the future.

12–1e Settlement of Claims

Businesspersons and others often enter into contracts to settle legal claims. It is important to understand the nature of the consideration given in these settlement agreements. Commonly used settlement agreements include an *accord and satisfaction*, a *release*, and a *covenant not to sue*.

Accord and Satisfaction

In an **accord and satisfaction**, a debtor offers to pay, and a creditor accepts, a lesser amount than the creditor originally claimed was owed. The *accord* is the agreement. In the accord, one party undertakes to give or perform, and the other to accept, in satisfaction of a claim, something other than that on which the parties originally agreed. *Satisfaction* is the performance (usually payment) that takes place after the accord is executed.

A basic rule is that there can be no satisfaction unless there is first an accord. In addition, for accord and satisfaction to occur, the amount of the debt *must be in dispute*.

Accord and Satisfaction A common means of settling a disputed claim, whereby a debtor offers to pay a lesser amount than the creditor purports to be owed.

Liquidated Debt A debt whose amount has been ascertained, fixed, agreed on, settled, or exactly determined.

Liquidated Debts. If a debt is *liquidated*, accord and satisfaction cannot take place. A **liquidated debt** is one whose amount has been ascertained, fixed, agreed on, settled, or exactly determined. **Example 12.8** Barbara Kwan signs an installment loan contract with her banker. In the contract, Kwan agrees to pay a specified rate of interest on a specified amount of borrowed funds at monthly intervals for two years. Because both parties know the precise amount of the total obligation, it is a liquidated debt.

In the majority of states, a creditor's acceptance of a lesser sum than the entire amount of a liquidated debt is not satisfaction, and the balance of the debt is still legally owed. The reason for this rule is that the debtor has given no consideration to satisfy the obligation of paying the balance to the creditor. The debtor has a preexisting legal obligation to pay the entire debt. (Of course, even with liquidated debts, creditors often do negotiate debt settlement agreements with debtors for a lesser amount than was originally owed. Creditors sometimes even forgive or write off a liquidated debt as uncollectable.)

Know This

Even with liquidated debts, creditors will often enter into settlement agreements that allow debtors to pay a lesser amount than was originally owed.

Unliquidated Debts. An **unliquidated debt** is the opposite of a liquidated debt. The amount of the debt is not settled, fixed, agreed on, ascertained, or determined, and reasonable persons may differ over the amount owed. In these circumstances, acceptance of payment of the lesser sum operates as a satisfaction, or discharge, of the debt because there is valid consideration. The parties give up a legal right to contest the amount in dispute.

Unliquidated Debt A debt that is uncertain in amount.

Release

A **release** is a contract in which one party forfeits the right to pursue a legal claim against the other party. It bars any further recovery beyond the terms stated in the release.

A release will generally be binding if it meets the following requirements:

1. The agreement is made in good faith.
2. The release contract is in a signed writing (required in many states).
3. The contract is accompanied by consideration.[6]

Release An agreement in which one party gives up the right to pursue a legal claim against another party.

A person involved in an automobile accident may be asked to sign a release. Clearly, that person is better off knowing the extent of any injuries or damages before signing. **Example 12.9** Kara's car is damaged in an accident caused by Raoul's negligence. Raoul offers to give Kara $3,000 if she will release him from further liability resulting from the accident. Kara agrees and signs the release.

6. Under the Uniform Commercial Code (UCC), a written, signed waiver by an aggrieved party discharges any further liability for a breach, even without consideration.

gmnicholas/E+/Getty Images

Is it possible to limit one's liability after a car accident?

If Kara later discovers that the repairs will cost $4,200, she cannot recover the additional amount from Raoul. Kara is limited to the $3,000 specified in the release because a valid contract was formed. Kara and Raoul both voluntarily agreed to the terms in a signed writing, and sufficient consideration was present. The consideration was the legal right to recover damages that Kara forfeited should her damages be more than $3,000, in exchange for Raoul's promise to give her $3,000. ■

Covenant Not to Sue Unlike a release, a **covenant not to sue** does not always prevent further recovery. The parties simply substitute a contractual obligation for some other type of legal action based on a valid claim. Suppose in *Example 12.9* that Kara agrees not to sue Raoul for damages in a tort action if he will pay for the damage to her car. If Raoul fails to pay, Kara can bring an action for breach of contract.

As the following *Spotlight Case* illustrates, a covenant not to sue can form the basis for a dismissal of the claims of either party to the covenant.

Covenant Not to Sue An agreement to substitute a contractual obligation for another legal action based on a valid claim.

Spotlight on Nike: Case 12.2

Already, LLC v. Nike, Inc.

Supreme Court of the United States, 568 U.S. 85, 133 S.Ct. 721, 184 L.Ed.2d 553 (2013).

Facts Nike, Inc., designs, makes, and sells athletic footwear, including a line of shoes known as "Air Force 1." Already, LLC, also designs and markets athletic footwear, including the "Sugar" and "Soulja Boy" lines. Nike filed a suit in a federal district court against Already, alleging that Soulja Boys and Sugars infringed the Air Force 1 trademark. Already filed a counterclaim, contending that the Air Force 1 trademark was invalid.

While the suit was pending, Nike issued a covenant not to sue. Nike promised not to raise any trademark claims against Already based on Already's existing footwear designs or any future Already designs that constituted a "colorable imitation" of Already's current products. Nike then filed a motion to dismiss its own claims and to dismiss Already's counterclaim. Already opposed the dismissal of its counterclaim, but the court granted Nike's motion. The U.S. Court of Appeals for the Second Circuit affirmed. Already appealed to the United States Supreme Court.

Issue Did Nike's covenant not to sue Already over the Air Force 1 trademark prevent Already from suing to establish that Nike's trademark was invalid?

Decision Yes. The United States Supreme Court affirmed the judgment of the lower courts. Under the covenant not to sue, Nike could not file a trademark infringement claim against Already, and Already could not assert that Nike's trademark was invalid.

Reason The Supreme Court looked at the wording of the covenant not to sue to determine whether Already's counterclaim was *moot*. (A matter is moot if it involves no actual controversy for the court to decide, and federal courts will dismiss moot cases.) Nike had unconditionally and irrevocably promised not to assert any trademark infringement claims against Already relating to the mark used on any of Already's current footwear products and similar future designs. Under the covenant's broad language, the Court noted, "It is hard to imagine a scenario that would potentially infringe Nike's trademark and yet not fall under the covenant." Therefore, further litigation of the trademark dispute was unnecessary, and dismissal was proper.

Critical Thinking

- **Economic** *Why would any party agree to a covenant not to sue?*
- **Legal Environment** *Which type of contracts are similar to covenants not to sue?*

12–2 Promissory Estoppel

Sometimes, individuals rely on promises, and their reliance may form a basis for a court to infer contract rights and duties. Under the doctrine of **promissory estoppel** (also called *detrimental reliance*), a person who has reasonably and substantially relied on the promise of another can obtain some measure of recovery. Promissory estoppel allows a party to recover on a promise even though it was made *without consideration*. Under this doctrine, a court may enforce an otherwise unenforceable promise to avoid an injustice that would otherwise result.

Promissory Estoppel A doctrine that can be used to enforce a promise when the promisee has justifiably relied on the promise and when justice will be better served by enforcing the promise.

12–2a Requirements to Establish Promissory Estoppel

For the doctrine of promissory estoppel to be applied, the following elements are required:

1. There must be a clear and definite promise.
2. The promisor should have expected that the promisee would rely on the promise.
3. The promisee reasonably relied on the promise by acting or refraining from some act.
4. The promisee's reliance was definite and resulted in substantial detriment.
5. Enforcement of the promise is necessary to avoid injustice.

Focus Question 2

In what circumstances might a promise be enforced despite a lack of consideration?

If these requirements are met, a promise may be enforced even though it is not supported by consideration. In essence, the promisor (the offeror) will be **estopped** (barred or prevented) from asserting lack of consideration as a defense.

Estopped Barred, impeded, or precluded.

Promissory estoppel is similar in some ways to the doctrine of quasi contract that was discussed in a previous chapter. In both situations, a court acts in the interests of equity and imposes contract obligations on the parties to prevent unfairness even though no actual contract exists. The difference is that with quasi contract, no promise was made at all. In contrast, with promissory estoppel, an otherwise unenforceable promise was made and relied on.

12–2b Application of Promissory Estoppel

Promissory estoppel was originally applied to situations involving gifts (I promise to pay you $1,000 a week so that you will not have to work) and donations to charities (I promise to contribute $50,000 a year to the All Saints orphanage). Later, courts began to apply the doctrine in other situations, including business transactions, employment relationships, and disputes among family members.

Case Example 12.10 CBRE, Inc., was selling commercial real estate owned by API Foils, Inc. BH 329 NB, LLC, offered to buy the property for $7.5 million, which CBRE accepted. BH 329 NB signed a letter of intent setting forth the sale's terms, including the purchase price and an agreement to lease back the property to API for one year. API signed the letter of intent, showing its agreement in principle to the deal. The letter specified that it was not a sales contract.

CBRE promised it would not market or accept other purchase offers while the parties were closing the deal. Despite its promise, CBRE continued to market the property and eventually received a higher offer from a different buyer. CBRE then notified BH 329 NB that it no longer had a deal with API.

BH 329 NB sued CBRE for breach of contract and promissory estoppel. A federal district court dismissed the contract claim but allowed the promissory estoppel claim to go forward. CBRE clearly had promised not to market the property in exchange for the plaintiff's agreement not to lower its offer price. BH 329 NB reasonably relied on CBRE's promise by continuing to negotiate the deal with API, and by doing so, incurred costs and lost other business opportunities as a result.[7]

---

7. *BH 329 NB, LLC v. CBRE, Inc.*, 2017 WL 3641566 (D.N.J. 2017).

12–3 Contractual Capacity

Contractual Capacity The capacity required by the law for a party who enters into a contract to be bound by that contract.

Contractual capacity is the legal ability to enter into a contractual relationship. Courts generally presume the existence of contractual capacity, but in some situations, capacity is lacking or may be questionable. A person who has been determined by a court to be mentally incompetent, for instance, cannot form a legally binding contract. In other situations, a party may have the capacity to enter into a valid contract but may also have the right to avoid liability under it. For instance, minors—or *infants*, as they are commonly referred to in the law—usually are not legally bound by contracts.

In this section, we look at the effect of youth, intoxication, and mental incompetence on contractual capacity.

12–3a Minors

Age of Majority The age (eighteen years, in most states) at which a person is granted by law the rights and responsibilities of an adult.

Emancipation In regard to minors, the act of being freed from parental control.

Today, in almost all states, the **age of majority** (when a person is no longer a minor) for contractual purposes is eighteen years.[8] In addition, some states provide for the termination of minority on marriage.

Minority status may also be terminated by a minor's **emancipation**, which occurs when a child's parent or legal guardian relinquishes the legal right to exercise control over the child. Normally, minors who leave home to support themselves are considered emancipated. Several jurisdictions permit minors to petition a court for emancipation.

Focus Question 3

Does a minor have the capacity to enter into an enforceable contract? What does it mean to disaffirm a contract?

The general rule is that a minor can enter into any contract that an adult can, provided that the contract is not one prohibited by law for minors (such as a contract involving the sale of alcoholic beverages or tobacco products). A contract entered into by a minor, however, is voidable at the option of that minor, subject to certain exceptions (to be discussed shortly). To exercise the option to avoid a contract, a minor need only manifest (clearly show) an intention not to be bound by it. The minor "avoids" the contract by disaffirming it.

Disaffirmance The legal avoidance, or setting aside, of a contractual obligation.

Disaffirmance

The legal avoidance, or setting aside, of a contractual obligation is referred to as **disaffirmance**. To disaffirm, a minor must express, through words or conduct, the intent not to be bound to the contract. The minor must disaffirm the entire contract, not merely a portion of it. For instance, a minor cannot decide to keep part of the goods purchased under a contract and return the remaining goods.

Note that an adult who enters into a contract with a minor cannot avoid contractual duties on the ground that the minor can do so. Unless the minor exercises the option to disaffirm the contract, the adult party normally is bound by it.

Disaffirmance within a Reasonable Time. A minor can ordinarily disaffirm a contract at any time during minority[9] or for a reasonable time after reaching the age of majority. What constitutes a "reasonable" time may vary. If an individual fails to disaffirm an executed contract within a reasonable time after reaching the age of majority, a court will likely hold that the contract has been ratified (*ratification* will be discussed shortly).

A Minor's Obligations on Disaffirmance. All states' laws permit minors to disaffirm contracts (with certain exceptions), including executed contracts. However, state laws differ on the extent of a minor's obligations on disaffirmance.

Case Example 12.11 Ian Norred was a seventeen-year-old minor when he started working as a server at a Cotton Patch Café in Texas. Norred electronically signed a document titled "Notice to Employees" that contained a mutual arbitration agreement for all disputes arising out of his employment. Seven months later, Norred turned eighteen. Ten months after that,

8. The age of majority may still be twenty-one for other purposes, such as the purchase and consumption of alcohol.
9. In some states, however, minors who enter into a contract for the sale of land cannot disaffirm the contract until they reach the age of majority.

Norred left his job and filed a compensation lawsuit against Cotton Patch alleging violations of federal labor law. At the same time, Norred attempted to disaffirm the terms of his original employment contract. Citing Texas case law from 1889, the federal court ruled that, by waiting nearly a year after his eighteenth birthday, Norred had taken too long to disaffirm and was therefore bound by the arbitration agreement.[10]

Courts in most states hold that the minor need only return the goods (or other consideration) subject to the contract, provided the goods are in the minor's possession or control. Even if the minor returns damaged goods, the minor often is entitled to disaffirm the contract and obtain a refund of the purchase price.

A growing number of states place an additional duty on the minor to restore the adult party to the position that existed before the contract was made. These courts may hold a minor responsible for damage, ordinary wear and tear, and depreciation of goods that the minor used prior to disaffirmance. **Example 12.12** Sixteen-year-old Jay buys a truck for $5,900 from a used-car dealer. The truck develops mechanical problems nine months later, but Jay continues to drive it until the engine blows up and the truck stops running. Jay then disaffirms the contract and attempts to return the truck to the dealer for a refund of the full purchase price. In states that hold minors responsible for damage, Jay can still disaffirm the contract, but he may only recover the depreciated value—not the purchase price—of the truck.

Iakov Filimonov/Shutterstock.com

What factor could prevent a server who signed an employment contract as a minor from later disaffirming that contract?

Exceptions to a Minor's Right to Disaffirm State courts and legislatures have carved out several exceptions to the minor's right to disaffirm. Some contracts, such as marriage contracts and contracts to enlist in the armed services, cannot be avoided. These exceptions are made for reasons of public policy.

In addition, although ordinarily minors can disaffirm contracts even when they have misrepresented their age, a growing number of states have enacted laws to prohibit disaffirmance in such situations. Other states prohibit disaffirmance by minors who misrepresented their age while engaged in business as adults.

Finally, a minor who enters into a contract for necessaries may disaffirm the contract but remains liable for the reasonable value of the goods. **Necessaries** include whatever is reasonably needed to maintain the minor's standard of living. In general, food, clothing, shelter, and medical services are necessaries. What is a necessary for one minor, however, may be a luxury for another, depending on the minors' customary living standard. Contracts for necessaries are enforceable only to the level of value needed to maintain the minor's standard of living.

Necessaries Necessities required to maintain a standard of living, such as food, shelter, clothing, and medical attention.

Ratification The acceptance or confirmation of an act or agreement that gives legal force to an obligation that previously was not enforceable.

Know This

A minor's station in life (including financial position, social status, and lifestyle) is important in determining whether an item is a necessary or a luxury. For instance, clothing is a necessary, but if a minor from a low-income family contracts to purchase a $2,000 leather coat, a court may deem the coat a luxury. In this situation, the contract would not be for "necessaries."

Ratification In contract law, **ratification** is the act of accepting and giving legal force to an obligation that previously was not enforceable. A minor who has reached the age of majority can ratify a contract expressly or impliedly. *Express* ratification occurs when the individual, on reaching the age of majority, states orally or in writing an intention to be bound by the contract. *Implied* ratification takes place when the minor, on reaching the age of majority, behaves in a manner inconsistent with disaffirmance.

Example 12.13 Lindsay posts an ad on Craigslist offering to sell her grandmother's Yamaha grand piano for $6,000. Axel, who is seventeen years old, agrees to purchase the piano by making monthly payments of $200 over the next two and a half years. Axel does not disaffirm the contract, and six months into the agreement, he turns eighteen (the age of majority in his state). When Axel stops by Lindsay's house to make his seventh payment, he states, "I love the piano and will continue making payments." Axel's oral statement to Lindsay is an

10. *Norred v. Cotton Patch Café, LLC*, 2019 WL 5425479 (N.D. Texas 2019).

How can a minor imply ratification of an agreement to purchase a grand piano?

express ratification of their contract. He can no longer disaffirm it. Even if Axel never expressly tells Lindsay he will continue making payments but continues to do so well after reaching the age of majority, he has impliedly ratified the contract.

If a minor fails to disaffirm a contract within a reasonable time after reaching the age of majority, then a court must determine whether the conduct constitutes implied ratification or disaffirmance. Generally, courts presume that executed contracts are ratified and that executory contracts are disaffirmed.

Parents' Liability As a general rule, parents are not liable for the contracts made by minor children acting on their own, except contracts for necessaries, which the parents are legally required to provide. This is why businesses ordinarily require parents to cosign any contract made with a minor. The parents then become personally obligated to perform the conditions of the contract, even if their child avoids liability.

12–3b Intoxicated Persons

Intoxication is a condition in which a person's normal capacity to act or think is inhibited by alcohol or some other drug. A contract entered into by an intoxicated person can be either voidable or valid (and thus enforceable).

If the person was sufficiently intoxicated to lack mental capacity and the other party had reason to know it, then the transaction may be voidable at the option of the intoxicated person, even if the intoxication was purely voluntary. The intoxicated person has the option of disaffirming the contract while intoxicated or for a reasonable time after becoming sober. If, despite intoxication, the person understood the legal consequences of the agreement, the contract is enforceable. (Note that an intoxicated person may ratify a contract expressly or impliedly after becoming sober.)

Courts look at objective indications of intoxication to determine if a person possessed or lacked the required capacity. It is difficult to prove that a person's judgment was so severely impaired that the person could not comprehend the legal consequences of entering into a contract. Therefore, courts rarely permit contracts to be avoided due to intoxication.

12–3c Mentally Incompetent Persons

Contracts made by mentally incompetent persons can be void, voidable, or valid. If a court has previously determined that a person is mentally incompetent and has appointed a guardian to represent the person, any contract made by that person is *void*—no contract exists. Only the guardian can enter into a binding contract on behalf of the mentally incompetent person.

If a court has not previously judged a person to be mentally incompetent but the person was incompetent at the time the contract was formed, the contract is *voidable* in most states. A contract is voidable if the person was unaware of entering into the contract or lacked the mental capacity to comprehend its nature, purpose, and consequences. In such situations, the contract is voidable (or can be ratified) at the option of the mentally incompetent person but not at the option of the other party.

Case Example 12.14 Annabelle Duffie was mildly mentally retarded and, at age seventy, had the beginning of dementia. For her entire life, she had lived with her brother, Jerome. When Jerome died, he left Annabelle his property, including 180 acres of timberland near Hope, Arkansas, valued at more than $400,000. Less than three months later, Annabelle signed a deed granting her interest in the tract to Charles and Joanne Black. The Blacks agreed to pay Annabelle $150,000 in monthly payments of $1,000.

Later, Annabelle's nephew, Jack, was appointed to be her legal guardian. On her behalf, Jack filed a lawsuit in an Arkansas state court against the Blacks, seeking to void the land deal because of Annabelle's lack of mental competence. The court ordered the Blacks to return the property to Annabelle. They appealed. A state intermediate appellate court affirmed. The evidence showed that Annabelle had been incompetent her entire life. She lacked the cognitive ability to make the complex financial decisions involved in selling property. Therefore, the contract was voidable.[11]

A contract entered into by a mentally ill person (whom a court has not previously declared incompetent) may also be *valid* if the person had capacity *at the time the contract was formed.* Some people who are incompetent due to age or illness have *lucid intervals*—temporary periods of sufficient intelligence, judgment, and will. During such intervals, they will be considered to have legal capacity to enter into contracts in the majority of states.

12–4 Legality

Legality is the fourth requirement for a valid contract to exist. For a contract to be valid and enforceable, it must be formed for a legal purpose. A contract to do something that is prohibited by federal or state statutory law is illegal and, as such, is void from the outset and thus unenforceable. Additionally, a contract to commit a tortious act (such as engage in fraudulent misrepresentation) or to commit an action that is contrary to public policy is illegal and unenforceable.

12–4a Contracts Contrary to Statute

Statutes often prescribe the terms of contracts. Some statutes set forth rules specifying which terms and clauses may be included in certain contracts and which are prohibited. Others prohibit certain contracts on the basis of their subject matter, the status of the contracting parties, or other factors. Next, we examine several ways in which contracts may be contrary to statute.

Contracts to Commit a Crime Any contract to commit a crime is in violation of a statute. Thus, a contract to sell illegal drugs in violation of criminal laws is unenforceable, as is a contract to hide a corporation's violation of securities laws or environmental regulations.

Sometimes, the object or performance of a contract is rendered illegal by statute *after* the contract has been formed. In that situation, the contract is considered discharged (terminated) by law.

Usury Almost every state has a statute that sets the maximum rate of interest that can be charged for different types of transactions, including ordinary loans. A lender who makes a loan at an interest rate above the lawful maximum commits **usury**.

Usury Charging an illegal rate of interest.

Although usurious contracts are illegal, most states simply limit the interest that the lender may collect on the contract to the lawful maximum interest rate in that state. In a few states, the lender can recover the principal amount of the loan but no interest. In addition, states can make exceptions to facilitate business transactions. For instance, many states exempt corporate loans from the usury laws, and nearly all states allow higher interest rate loans for borrowers who could not otherwise obtain loans.

11. *Black v. Duffie,* 2016 Ark.App. 584, 508 S.W.3d 40 (2016).

Gambling Gambling is the creation of risk for the purpose of assuming it. Traditionally, the states have deemed gambling contracts illegal and thus void. Today, many states allow (and regulate) certain forms of gambling, such as horse racing, video poker machines, and charity-sponsored bingo. In addition, nearly all states allow state-operated lotteries and gambling on Native American reservations.

RosalreneBetancourt 9/Alamy

How can local licensing statutes affect a real estate transaction for high-end commercial property?

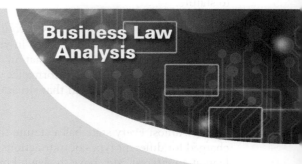

Licensing Statutes All states require members of certain professions—including physicians, lawyers, real estate brokers, accountants, architects, electricians, and stockbrokers—to have licenses. Some licenses are obtained only after extensive schooling and examinations, which indicate to the public that a special skill has been acquired. Others require only that the person obtaining the license be of good moral character and pay a fee.

Whether a contract with an unlicensed person is legal and enforceable depends on the purpose of the licensing statute. If the statute's purpose is to protect the public from unauthorized practitioners, then a contract involving an unlicensed practitioner generally is illegal and unenforceable. If the purpose is merely to raise government revenues, however, a contract with an unlicensed person may be enforced (and the unlicensed practitioner fined). See this chapter's *Business Law Analysis* feature for an example.

12–4b Contracts Contrary to Public Policy

Although contracts involve private parties, some are not enforceable because of the negative impact they would have on society. These contracts are said to be *contrary to public policy*. Examples include a contract to commit an immoral act, such as selling a child, and a contract that prohibits marriage (such as a contract to pay someone not to marry one's daughter). Business contracts that may be contrary to public policy include contracts in restraint of trade and unconscionable contracts or clauses.

Contracts in Restraint of Trade The United States has a strong public policy favoring competition in the economy. Thus, contracts in restraint of trade (anticompetitive agreements) generally are unenforceable because they are contrary to public policy. Typically, such contracts also violate one or more federal or state antitrust laws.

Business Law Analysis

Determining If a Contract with an Unlicensed Party Is Enforceable

PEMS Co. International, Inc., agreed to find a buyer for Rupp Industries, Inc., for a commission of 2 percent of the purchase price, which was to be paid by the buyer. Using PEMS's services, an investment group bought Rupp for $20 million and changed its name to Temp-Air, Inc. PEMS asked Temp-Air to pay a commission on the sale. Temp-Air refused, arguing that PEMS had acted as a broker in the deal without a license. The applicable statute defines a broker as any person who deals with the sale of a business. Can PEMS collect its commission?

Analysis: Whether a contract with an unlicensed person is legal and enforceable depends on the purpose of the statute. If the purpose is to protect the public from unauthorized practitioners, then a contract involving an unlicensed practitioner is generally illegal and unenforceable.

Result and Reasoning: The applicable statute defined a broker as any person who deals with the sale of a business. It seems clear that this definition covers PEMS. The purpose of this statute is to protect the public from potentially serious consequences related to having unlicensed parties handle business sales transactions that may involve millions of dollars.

PEMS's efforts toward the sale constituted the action of a broker. PEMS did not have a broker's license. Thus, if PEMS was acting as a broker, the unlicensed firm forfeited its right to collect a commission for its services. Using PEMS's services, an investment group made a successful purchase of Rupp. Therefore, PEMS is barred from maintaining this suit to collect the unpaid commission.

An exception is recognized when the restraint is reasonable and is an ancillary (secondary, or subordinate) part of the contract. Such restraints often are included in contracts for the sale of an ongoing business and employment contracts.

Covenants Not to Compete and the Sale of an Ongoing Business. Many contracts involve a type of restraint called a **covenant not to compete**, or a restrictive covenant (promise). A covenant not to compete may be created when a merchant who sells a store agrees not to open a new store in a certain geographic area surrounding the old store. Such an agreement enables the seller to sell, and the purchaser to buy, the goodwill and reputation of an ongoing business without having to worry that the seller will open a competing business a block away. Provided the restrictive covenant is reasonable and is an ancillary part of the sale of an ongoing business, it is enforceable.

Covenant Not to Compete A contractual promise of one party to refrain from conducting business similar to that of another party for a certain period of time and within a specified geographical area.

Covenants Not to Compete in Employment Contracts. Sometimes, an agreement not to compete (also referred to as a *noncompete agreement*) is included in an **employment contract**. People in middle-level and upper-level management positions commonly agree not to work for competitors and not to start a competing business for a specified period of time after terminating employment.

Employment Contract A contract between an employer and an employee in which the terms and conditions of employment are stated.

Noncompete agreements are generally legal in most states so long as the specified period of time (of restraint) is not excessive in duration and the geographic restriction is reasonable. To be reasonable, a restriction on competition must protect a legitimate business interest and must not be any greater than necessary to protect that interest. What constitutes a reasonable time period may be different in the online environment than in conventional employment contracts. Because the geographical restrictions apply worldwide, the time restrictions may be shorter.

Focus Question 4

Under what circumstances will courts enforce a covenant not to compete?

Companies sometimes use covenants not to compete as the starting point for lawsuits against competitors. **Case Example 12.15** Dana Clement was an administrator with Compassus, a hospice care provider in Houston. She left, taking a number of colleagues with her, to form a new branch of Crossroads Hospice in the same city. Compassus brought a number of claims, including conspiracy, against Crossroads, relying primarily on a covenant in Compassus's contract with Clement that forbade her from soliciting Compassus workers for employment elsewhere. A Texas appellate court dismissed the lawsuit, ruling that Crossroads could not be held responsible for Clement's actions. In large part, the court based its decision on the fact that Crossroads was unaware of the nonsolicitation covenant when it hired Clement and the other former Compassus employees.[12]

Ethical Issue

Are expansive noncompete agreements reducing worker mobility? You would probably expect workers to be asked to sign noncompete agreements that prevented them from, say, taking proprietary software code to a competitor. But would you expect a sandwich chain to require a worker to sign a noncompete agreement related to sandwich making? In the past, such agreements would not have been upheld in court. Today, they increasingly are. James Bessen, a writer for *The Atlantic*, has estimated that the number of lawsuits over noncompete agreements and trade secrets nearly tripled between 2000 and 2014.

Employees in high-tech firms seem to be the most affected. They often sign noncompete agreements that "freeze" them out of their industry for two years after they leave a high-tech employer, forcing them to seek jobs in other industries where they cannot use key skills and knowledge. The result is that noncompete agreements tend to limit job opportunities for highly skilled workers. In addition, noncompete agreements are increasingly being used with employees at lower levels (including blue-collar workers).

The negative impact of such agreements can be devastating on persons who lose or leave their jobs to find other employment. In other words, job mobility may be suffering from the pervasive use of noncompete agreements.

12. *Crossroads Hospice, Inc. v. FC Compassus, LLC*, __ S.W.3d __ 2020 WL 1264188 (1st Dist.—Houston 2020).

Enforcement Problems. The laws governing the enforceability of covenants not to compete vary significantly from state to state. California prohibits the enforcement of all covenants not to compete. In some states, such as Texas, such a covenant will not be enforced unless the employee has received some benefit in return for signing the noncompete agreement. This is true even if the covenant is reasonable as to time and area. If the employee receives no benefit, the covenant will be deemed void.

Reformation. Occasionally, depending on the jurisdiction, courts will *reform* covenants not to compete. If a covenant is found to be unreasonable in time or geographic area, the court may convert the terms into reasonable ones and then enforce the reformed covenant. This presents a problem, however, in that the judge has implicitly become a party to the contract. Consequently, courts usually resort to contract **reformation** only when necessary to prevent undue burdens or hardships.

Reformation A court-ordered correction of a written contract so that it reflects the true intentions of the parties.

In the following case, the court reformed a noncompete agreement by adding the words "current location." Was this modification reasonable given the facts of the case?

Case 12.3

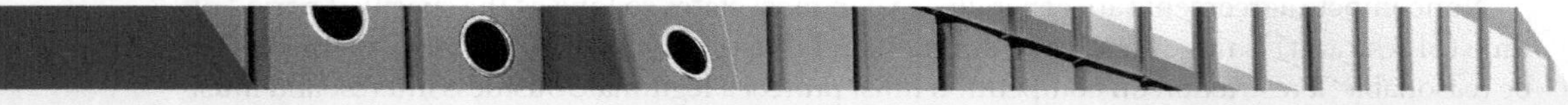

Kennedy v. Shave Barber Co.

Court of Appeals of Georgia, 822 S.E.2d 606 (2018).

Facts Patricia Kennedy worked as a master barber for The Shave, a barbershop in the Virginia-Highland neighborhood of Atlanta, Georgia. Under the terms of her employment contract, Kennedy agreed that, after leaving her employment, she would not work in the men's grooming industry "within a three (3) mile radius of any SHAVE location" for two years and would not solicit customers of The Shave for one year.

Less than a month after quitting her position, Kennedy opened a new salon, "PK Does Hair," two miles from The Shave. She solicited customers through social media accounts on which she posted photos originally posted on social media by The Shave.

The Shave filed a suit in a Georgia state court against Kennedy, alleging a breach of the noncompete provision of her employment contract. Kennedy argued that the geographic restriction in the noncompete provision was "unreasonable and uncertain." The court limited the geographic scope of the provision to a three-mile radius of The Shave's *current* location and issued an injunction in The Shave's favor. Kennedy appealed.

Issue Was the court's reformation of the geographic scope of the noncompete provision reasonable?

Decision Yes. A state intermediate appellate court affirmed the lower court's order in favor of The Shave. "Kennedy is in violation of . . . the restrictive covenants which where specifically designed to protect The Shave from competition from its former employees and loss of its client base. Therefore, the trial court did not err in finding the non-compete enforceable against Kennedy and in granting [an injunction] on this ground."

Reason The Shave had a legitimate business interest in protecting itself from the risk that Kennedy might appropriate customers by taking advantage of the contacts developed while she worked at The Shave.

The Shave had expended considerable resources in developing its name recognition and customer base. Most of The Shave's customers lived and worked within three miles of the Virginia-Highland location. The Shave had previously lost customers when two former employees opened competing barbershops within three miles. Based on the harm to The Shave's business if the noncompete provision was not enforced, the appellate court found the trial court's reformation of the provision's geographic scope to be reasonable. The appellate court also concluded that the trial court had eliminated any uncertainty by limiting the scope to three miles from The Shave's current location.

The appellate court also ruled, despite Kennedy's assertion to the contrary, that her social media posts of pictures of The Shave's customers constituted solicitation in further violation of the noncompete provision.

Critical Thinking

- **Legal** *What "legitimate business interests" justify the enforcement of a noncompete provision?*
- **Economic** *What sort of harm, particularly in Kennedy's situation, would support a court's refusal to enforce an employment contract's noncompete provision?*

Unconscionable Contracts or Clauses Ordinarily, a court does not look at the fairness or equity of a contract (or inquire into the adequacy of consideration). Persons are assumed to be reasonably intelligent, and the courts will not come to their aid just because they have made unwise or foolish bargains.

In certain circumstances, however, bargains are so oppressive that the courts relieve innocent parties of part or all of their duties. Such bargains are deemed **unconscionable**[13] because they are so unscrupulous or grossly unfair as to be "void of conscience."

Unconscionable Unscrupulous or grossly unfair. An unconscionable contract or clause is void on the basis of public policy because one party was forced to accept terms that are unfairly burdensome and that unfairly benefit the other party.

The Uniform Commercial Code (UCC) incorporates the concept of unconscionability in its provisions with regard to the sale and lease of goods.[14] A contract can be unconscionable on either procedural or substantive grounds, as discussed in the following subsections and illustrated graphically in Exhibit 12–2.

Procedural Unconscionability. Procedural unconscionability often involves inconspicuous print, unintelligible language ("legalese"), or the lack of an opportunity to read the contract or ask questions about its meaning. This type of unconscionability typically arises when a party's lack of knowledge or understanding of the contract terms deprives the party of any meaningful choice.

Procedural unconscionability can also occur when there is such a disparity in bargaining power between the two parties that the weaker party's consent is not voluntary. This type of situation often involves an **adhesion contract**, which is a standard-form contract written exclusively by one party (the dominant party) and presented to the other (the adhering party) on a take-it-or-leave-it basis. In other words, the adhering party (usually a buyer or borrower) has no opportunity to negotiate the terms of the contract. Not all adhesion contracts are unconscionable—only those that unreasonably favor the drafter.

Adhesion Contract A standard-form contract in which the stronger party dictates the terms.

13. Pronounced un-*kon*-shun-uh-bul.
14. See UCC 2–302 and 2–719.

Exhibit 12–2 Unconscionability

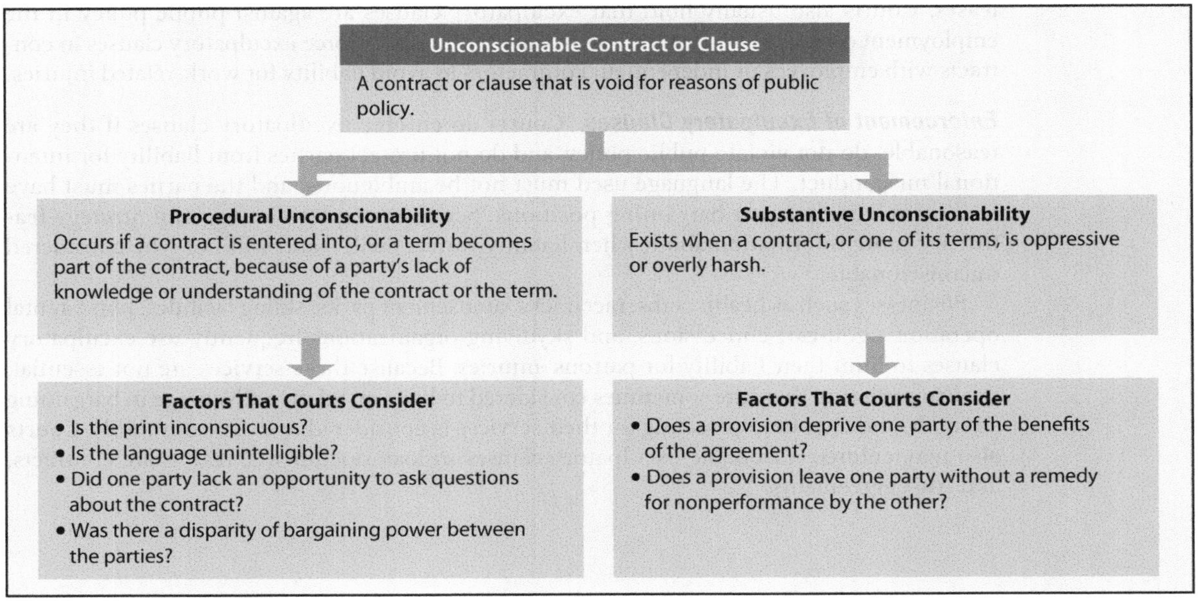

Unconscionable Contract or Clause
A contract or clause that is void for reasons of public policy.
Procedural Unconscionability
Occurs if a contract is entered into, or a term becomes part of the contract, because of a party's lack of knowledge or understanding of the contract or the term.
Substantive Unconscionability
Exists when a contract, or one of its terms, is oppressive or overly harsh.
Factors That Courts Consider
• Is the print inconspicuous?
• Is the language unintelligible?
• Did one party lack an opportunity to ask questions about the contract?
• Was there a disparity of bargaining power between the parties?
Factors That Courts Consider
• Does a provision deprive one party of the benefits of the agreement?
• Does a provision leave one party without a remedy for nonperformance by the other?

Case Example 12.16 Lianna Saribekyan placed diamonds, gold, and other collectibles in a safety deposit box at the Bank of America's (BANA's) Universal City, California, branch. A few months later, this branch was slated for closure. Without informing Saribekyan, bank employees drilled open her deposit box and placed its contents, unsecured, in storage for several days. Millions of dollars' worth of the items went missing, including four bags of diamonds inventoried by BANA as "beads" and a container full of gold that had been replaced with pennies.

The trial court found BANA liable but limited its payout to $2,460 because the bank's Safety Deposit Rules and Regulations capped damages for negligence at ten times the safety deposit box's annual rent. A California appellate court reversed, identifying a contract of adhesion. To support this conclusion, the court noted that the limitation of liability provision was "buried" in the small print of a five-page supplement to the original agreement, an addendum that Saribekyan was never shown. Furthermore, the court found BANA's negligence so grievous that to limit damages in such a way would "shock the conscience."[15]

Substantive Unconscionability. Substantive unconscionability occurs when contracts, or portions of contracts, are oppressive or overly harsh. Courts generally focus on provisions that deprive one party of the benefits of the agreement or leave that party without remedy for nonperformance by the other. Sometimes, courts will find that the same contract is both substantively and procedurally unconscionable.

Substantive unconscionability can arise in a wide variety of business contexts. For instance, a contract clause that gives a business entity unrestricted access to the courts but requires the other party to arbitrate any dispute with the firm may be unconscionable.

Exculpatory Clause A clause that releases a contractual party from liability in the event of monetary or physical injury, no matter who is at fault.

Exculpatory Clauses

Often closely related to the concept of unconscionability is the **exculpatory clause**, which releases a party from liability in the event of monetary or physical injury, *no matter who is at fault*. Indeed, courts sometimes refuse to enforce such clauses because they deem them to be unconscionable.

Violation of Public Policy. Most courts view exculpatory clauses with disfavor. Exculpatory clauses found in rental agreements for commercial property are frequently held to be contrary to public policy, and such clauses are almost always unenforceable in residential property leases. Courts also usually hold that exculpatory clauses are against public policy in the employment context. Thus, employers frequently cannot enforce exculpatory clauses in contracts with employees or independent contractors to avoid liability for work-related injuries.

Enforcement of Exculpatory Clauses. Courts do enforce exculpatory clauses if they are reasonable, do not violate public policy, and do not protect parties from liability for intentional misconduct. The language used must not be ambiguous, and the parties must have been in relatively equal bargaining positions. See this chapter's *Managerial Strategy* feature for more information about when liability waivers will—and will not—be considered unconscionable.

Businesses such as health clubs, racetracks, amusement parks, skiing facilities, horse-rental operations, golf-cart concessions, and skydiving organizations frequently use exculpatory clauses to limit their liability for patrons' injuries. Because these services are not essential, the firms offering them are sometimes considered to have no relative advantage in bargaining strength, and anyone contracting for their services is considered to do so voluntarily. Courts also may enforce reasonable exculpatory clauses in loan documents, real estate contracts, and trust agreements.

15. *Saribekyan v. Bank of America, NA*, 2020 WL 38676 (2nd Dist. Div. 3 Cal. 2020).

Managerial Strategy

Creating Liability Waivers That Are Not Unconscionable

Blanket liability waivers that absolve a business from virtually every event, even those caused by the business's own negligence, are usually unenforceable because they are unconscionable. Exculpatory waivers are common, nonetheless. We observe such waivers in gym memberships, on admissions tickets to sporting events, and in simple contracts for the use of campgrounds.

Typically, courts view liability waivers as voluntarily bargained for whether or not they have been read. Thus, a waiver included in the fine print on the back of an admission ticket or on an entry sign to a stadium may be upheld. In general, if such waivers are unambiguous and conspicuous, the assumption is that patrons have had a chance to read them and have accepted their terms.

Activities with Inherent Risks

Cases challenging liability waivers have been brought against skydiving businesses, ski resorts, bobsledding operations, white-water rafting companies, and health clubs. For example, in *Tuttle v Heavenly Valley, LP*,[a] an appellate court in California upheld a ski resort's liability waiver. In that case, the plaintiff collided with a snowboarder, which was "an inherent risk of skiing," and died. The court reasoned that, as a matter of public policy, if a ski resort is not *grossly* negligent, then reasonable liability waivers should usually be an absolute defense against liability. Because there was no gross negligence in this instance, the ski resort prevailed.

In a similar case, Teresa Brigance fell and broke her leg when her ski boot caught on the chairlift as she was attempting to get off the lift. She sued the owner, Vail Summit Resorts, Inc., for her injuries. Brigance had signed a liability waiver before taking ski lessons at the resort, however. The waiver stated that she understood the inherent dangers and risks of skiing, and it specifically mentioned lift loading and unloading. The court found the waiver was valid and enforceable, and therefore dismissed Brigance's suit against Vail Summit.[b]

Waivers Involving Minors

Liability waivers for inherently dangerous activities involving minors are often held to different legal standards. For instance, Kathy Miller signed a liability waiver warning of the risk of serious injury, paralysis, or death when she bought a ticket for her eleven-year-old daughter to visit House of Boom, a trampoline park. Miller's daughter broke her ankle in an accident involving another girl, and Miller sued to recoup the costs of the injury.

House of Boom, relying on the signed liability waiver, moved for the case to be dismissed. The Kentucky Supreme Court refused, finding that liability waivers between a parent and a for-profit entity involving the actions of a child are unenforceable. The court relied on two factors in making this decision. First, in Kentucky, parents have no right to enter into contracts on behalf of their children. Second, liability waivers in these cases are unacceptable in terms of public policy because they negate businesses' incentive to take "reasonable precautions to protect the safety of minor children."[c]

Business Questions

1. *What would be your strategy regarding liability waivers if you were managing a business that relied on minors engaging in inherently dangerous activities?*
2. *Under what circumstances would you, as a business owner, choose to aggressively defend your business against a customer's liability lawsuit?*

a. 2020 WL 563604 (4th Dis. Div. 3 Cal. 2020).

b. *Brigance v. Vail Summit Resorts, Inc.*, 883 F.Supp.3d 1243 (10th Cir. 2018).

c. *Miller v. House of Boom Kentucky, LLC*, 575 S.W.3d 656 (Ky, 2019).

Spotlight Case Example 12.17 Colleen Holmes participated in the Susan G. Komen Race for the Cure in St. Louis, Missouri. Her signed entry form included an exculpatory clause under which Holmes agreed to release the event sponsors from liability "for any injury or damages I might suffer in connection with my participation in this Event."

During the race, Holmes sustained injuries when she tripped and fell over an audiovisual box left on the ground by one of the sponsors. She filed a negligence suit against the sponsor whose employees had placed the box on the ground without barricades or warnings of its presence. The court held that the language used in the exculpatory clause clearly released all sponsors and their agents and employees from liability for future negligence. Holmes could not sue for the injuries she sustained during the race.[16]

Aceshot1/Shutterstock.com

Is a waiver of negligence liability that appears on an entry form for a foot race enforceable?

16. *Holmes v. Multimedia KSDK, Inc.*, 395 S.W.3d 557, (Mo.App.E.D. 2013).

Focus Question 5

What are the consequences of entering an illegal agreement?

12–5 The Effect of Illegality

In general, an illegal contract is void—that is, the contract is deemed never to have existed, and the courts will not aid either party. In most illegal contracts, both parties are considered to be equally at fault—*in pari delicto*.[17] If the contract is executory, neither party can enforce it. If it has been executed, neither party can recover damages.

The courts usually are not concerned if one wrongdoer in an illegal contract is unjustly enriched at the expense of the other. The main reason for this hands-off attitude is a belief that a plaintiff who has broken the law by entering into an illegal bargain should not be allowed to obtain help from the courts. Another justification is the hoped-for deterrent effect: a plaintiff who suffers a loss because of an illegal bargain will presumably be deterred from entering into similar illegal bargains in the future.

There are exceptions to the general rule that neither party to an illegal bargain can sue for breach and neither party can recover for performance rendered. We look at these exceptions here.

12–5a Justifiable Ignorance of the Facts

Sometimes, one of the parties to a contract has no reason to know that the contract is illegal and thus is relatively innocent. That party can often recover any benefits conferred in a partially executed contract. The courts will not enforce the contract but will allow the parties to return to their original positions.

A court may sometimes permit an innocent party who has fully performed under a contract to enforce the contract against the guilty party. **Example 12.18** A trucking company contracts with Gillespie to carry crates filled with goods to a specific destination for a normal fee of $5,000. The trucker delivers the crates and later finds out that they contained illegal goods. Although the shipment, use, and sale of the goods are illegal under the law, the trucker, being an innocent party, can normally still legally collect the $5,000 from Gillespie. ■

12–5b Members of Protected Classes

When a statute is clearly designed to protect a certain class of people, a member of that class can enforce a contract in violation of the statute even though the other party cannot. **Example 12.19** Statutes prohibit certain employees (such as flight attendants or pilots) from working more than a specified number of hours per month. An employee who is required to work more than the maximum can recover for those extra hours of service. ■

Other examples of statutes designed to protect a particular class of people are state statutes that regulate the sale of insurance. If an insurance company violates a statute when selling insurance, the purchaser can still enforce the policy and recover from the insurer.

12–5c Withdrawal from an Illegal Agreement

Image Source/DigitalVision/Getty Images

When two persons place an illegal bet on the outcome of a boxing match, can either withdraw from the wager?

If the illegal part of a bargain has not yet been performed, the party rendering performance can withdraw from the contract and recover the performance or its value. **Example 12.20** Marta and Andy decide to wager (illegally) on the outcome of a boxing match. Each deposits $1,000 with a stakeholder, who agrees to pay the winner of the bet. At this point, each party has performed part of the agreement. Before payment occurs, either party is entitled to withdraw from the agreement by giving notice to the stakeholder. ■

12–5d Severable, or Divisible, Contracts

A contract that is *severable*, or divisible, consists of distinct parts that can be performed separately, with separate consideration provided for each part. With an *indivisible* contract, in contrast, complete performance by each party is essential, even if the contract contains a number of seemingly separate provisions.

17. Pronounced in-*pah*-ree deh-*lick*-tow.

If a contract is divisible into legal and illegal portions, a court may enforce the legal portion but not the illegal one, so long as the illegal portion does not affect the essence of the bargain. This approach is consistent with the basic policy of enforcing the legal intentions of the contracting parties whenever possible.

Example 12.21 Cole signs an employment contract that is valid but includes an overly broad and thus illegal covenant not to compete. In that situation, a court might find the employment contract enforceable but reform the unreasonably broad covenant by converting its terms into reasonable ones. Alternatively, the court could declare the covenant illegal (and thus void) and enforce the remaining employment terms.

12–5e Fraud, Duress, or Undue Influence

Often, one party to an illegal contract is more at fault than the other. When one party uses fraud, duress, or undue influence to induce the other party to enter into an agreement, the second party will be allowed to recover for the performance or its value.

Practice and Review

Renee Beaver started racing go-karts competitively in 2020, when she was fourteen. Many of the races required her to sign an exculpatory clause to participate. She or her parents regularly signed such clauses. In 2022, right before her birthday, Renee participated in the annual Elkhart Grand Prix, a series of races in Elkhart, Indiana. During the event in which she drove, a piece of foam padding used as a course barrier was torn from its base and ended up on the track. A portion of the padding struck Beaver in the head, and another portion was thrown into oncoming traffic, causing a multikart collision during which she sustained severe injuries. Beaver filed an action against the race organizers for negligence. The organizers could not locate the exculpatory clause that Beaver had supposedly signed. Race organizers argued that she must have signed one to enter the race, but even if she had not signed one, her actions showed her intent to be bound by its terms. Using the information presented in the chapter, answer the following questions.

1. Did Beaver have the contractual capacity to enter into a contract with an exculpatory clause? Why or why not?
2. Assuming that Beaver did, in fact, sign the exculpatory clause, did she later disaffirm or ratify the contract? Explain.
3. Now assume that Beaver had stated that she was eighteen years old at the time she signed the exculpatory clause. How might this affect her ability to disaffirm or ratify the contract?
4. Suppose Beaver can prove that she did not actually sign an exculpatory clause and this fact convinces race organizers to pursue a settlement. They offer to pay Beaver one-half of the amount that she is claiming in damages if she now signs a release of all claims. Because Beaver is young and the full effect of her injuries may not yet be clear, what other type of settlement agreement might she prefer? What is the consideration to support any settlement agreement that Beaver enters into with the race organizers?

Debate This

After agreeing to an exculpatory clause or purchasing some item, minors often seek to avoid the contracts. Today's minors are far from naïve and should not be allowed to avoid their contractual obligations.

Key Terms

accord and satisfaction 291
adhesion contract 301
age of majority 294
consideration 285
contractual capacity 294
covenant not to compete 299
covenant not to sue 292
disaffirmance 294
emancipation 294
employment contract 297
estopped 293
exculpatory clause 302
forbearance 286
liquidated debt 291
necessaries 295
past consideration 289
promissory estoppel 293
ratification 295
reformation 300
release 291
rescission 289
unconscionable 301
unliquidated debt 291
usury 297

Chapter Summary: Consideration, Capacity, and Legality

Consideration	1. **Elements of consideration**— a. Something of *legally sufficient value* must be given in exchange for a promise. b. There must be a bargained-for exchange. The item of value must be given or promised in return for the other party's promise or performance. 2. **Legal sufficiency and adequacy of consideration**—Legal sufficiency means that something of legal value must be given in exchange for a promise. Adequacy relates to "how much" consideration is given and whether a fair bargain was reached. Courts will inquire into the adequacy of consideration only when fraud, undue influence, duress, or unconscionability may be involved. 3. **Contracts that lack consideration**—Consideration is lacking in the following situations: a. Preexisting duty—A promise to do what one already has a legal duty to do is not legally sufficient consideration for a new contract. b. Past consideration—Actions or events that have already taken place do not constitute legally sufficient consideration. c. Illusory promises—When the nature or extent of performance is too uncertain, the promise is rendered illusory (without consideration and unenforceable). 4. **Settlement of claims**—Disputes may be settled by the following, which are enforceable provided there is consideration: a. Accord and satisfaction—An *accord* is an agreement in which a debtor offers to pay a lesser amount than the creditor claims is owed. *Satisfaction* takes place when the accord is executed. b. Release—An agreement in which, for consideration, a party forfeits the right to seek further recovery beyond the terms specified in the release. c. Covenant not to sue—An agreement not to sue on a valid claim. A contractual obligation is substituted for some other type of legal action.
Promissory Estoppel	Under the equitable doctrine of promissory estoppel, a person who has reasonably and substantially relied on the promise of another can obtain some measure of recovery. The promise is binding, even though there is no consideration, if injustice can be avoided only by enforcement of the promise.
	CONTRACTUAL CAPACITY
Minors	1. **General rule**—Contracts with minors are voidable at the option of the minor. 2. **Emancipation**—Occurs when a child's parent or legal guardian relinquishes the legal right to exercise control over the child. Normally, minors who leave home to support themselves are considered emancipated. In some jurisdictions, minors are permitted to petition a court for emancipation. 3. **Disaffirmance**—The legal avoidance of a contractual obligation. a. Disaffirmance can take place (in most states) at any time during minority and within a reasonable time after the minor has reached the age of majority. b. The minor must disaffirm the entire contract, not just part of it. c. When disaffirming executed contracts, the minor has a duty to return the received goods if they are still in the minor's control or (in some states) to pay their reasonable value.

d. Minors who have misrepresented their age will be denied the right to disaffirm by some courts.
e. A minor may disaffirm a contract for necessaries but remains liable for the reasonable value of the goods.

4. **Ratification**—The acceptance, or affirmation, of a legal obligation.
   a. Express ratification—Occurs when the minor, in writing or orally, explicitly assumes the obligations imposed by the contract.
   b. Implied ratification—Occurs when the conduct of the minor is inconsistent with disaffirmance or when the minor fails to disaffirm an executed contract within a reasonable time after reaching the age of majority.
5. **Parents' liability**—Generally, except for contracts for necessaries, parents are not liable for the contracts made by minor children acting on their own.

Intoxicated Persons	1. A contract entered into by an intoxicated person is voidable at the option of the intoxicated person if the person was sufficiently intoxicated to lack mental capacity, even if the intoxication was voluntary. 2. A contract with an intoxicated person is enforceable if, despite being intoxicated, the person understood the legal consequences of entering into the contract.
Mentally Incompetent Persons	1. A contract made by a person previously judged by a court to be mentally incompetent is void. 2. A contract made by a person who is mentally incompetent, but has not been previously declared incompetent by a court, is voidable at the option of that person.
	LEGALITY
Contracts Contrary to Statute	1. **Usury**—Usury occurs when a lender makes a loan at an interest rate above the lawful maximum, which varies from state to state. 2. **Gambling**—Gambling contracts that violate state statutes are deemed illegal and thus void. 3. **Licensing statutes**—Contracts entered into by persons who do not have a license, when one is required by statute, will not be enforceable unless the underlying purpose of the statute is to raise government revenues (and not to protect the public from unauthorized practitioners).
Contracts Contrary to Public Policy	1. **Contracts in restraint of trade**—Contracts to restrain free competition are illegal and prohibited by statutes. An exception is a covenant not to compete. Such covenants usually are enforced by the courts if the terms are secondary to a contract (such as a contract for the sale of a business or an employment contract) and are reasonable as to time and area of restraint. Courts tend to scrutinize covenants not to compete closely and, at times, may reform them if they are overly broad rather than declaring the entire covenant unenforceable. 2. **Unconscionable contracts and clauses**—When a contract or contract clause is so unfair that it is oppressive to one party, it may be deemed unconscionable. As such, it is illegal and cannot be enforced. 3. **Exculpatory clauses**—An exculpatory clause releases a party from liability in the event of monetary or physical injury, no matter who is at fault. In certain situations, exculpatory clauses may be contrary to public policy and thus unenforceable.
	EFFECT OF ILLEGALITY
General Rule	In general, an illegal contract is void, and the courts will not aid either party when both parties are considered to be equally at fault (*in pari delicto*). If the contract is executory, neither party can enforce it. If the contract is executed, neither party can recover damages.
Exceptions	Several exceptions exist to the general rule that neither party to an illegal bargain will be able to recover. The court may grant recovery in the following situations: 1. **Justifiable ignorance of the facts**—When one party has no reason to know that the contract is illegal and so is relatively innocent. 2. **Members of protected classes**—When one party to the contract is a member of a group of persons protected by a particular statute. 3. **Withdrawal from an illegal agreement**—When either party seeks to recover consideration given for an illegal contract before the illegal act is performed. 4. **Severable, or divisible, contracts**—When the court can divide the contract into illegal and legal portions, and the illegal portion is not essential to the bargain. 5. **Fraud, duress, or undue influence**—When one party was induced by the other party to enter into an illegal bargain through fraud, duress, or undue influence.

Issue Spotters

1. Before Maria starts her first year of college, Fred promises to give her $5,000 when she graduates. She goes to college, borrowing and spending far more than $5,000. At the beginning of the spring semester of her senior year, she reminds Fred of the promise. Fred sends her a note that says, "I revoke the promise." Is Fred's promise binding? Explain. (See *Consideration.*)

2. Sun Airlines, Inc., prints on its tickets that it is not liable for any injury to a passenger caused by the airline's negligence. If the cause of an accident is found to be the airline's negligence, can it use the clause as a defense to liability? Why or why not? (See *Legality.*)

—Check your answers to the *Issue Spotters* against the answers provided in Appendix D.

Business Scenarios and Case Problems

12–1. Contracts by Minors. Kalen is a seventeen-year-old minor who has just graduated from high school. He is attending a university two hundred miles from home and has contracted to rent an apartment near the university for one year at $500 per month. He is working at a convenience store to earn enough income to be self-supporting. After living in the apartment and paying monthly rent for four months, he becomes involved in a dispute with his landlord. Kalen, still a minor, moves out and returns the key to the landlord. The landlord wants to hold Kalen liable for the balance of the payments due under the lease. Discuss fully Kalen's liability in this situation. (See *Contractual Capacity.*)

12–2. Spotlight on Kansas City Chiefs—Consideration. On Brenda Sniezek's first day of work for the Kansas City Chiefs Football Club, she signed a document that purported to compel arbitration of any disputes that she might have with the Chiefs. In the document, Sniezek agreed to comply at all times with and be bound by the constitution and bylaws of the National Football League (NFL). She agreed to refer all disputes to the NFL commissioner for a binding decision and to release the Chiefs and others from any related claims. Nowhere in the document did the Chiefs agree to do anything. Was there consideration for the arbitration provision? Explain. [*Sniezek v. Kansas City Chiefs Football Club*, 402 S.W.3d 580 (Mo.App. W.D. 2013)] (See *Consideration.*)

12–3. Consideration. Citynet, LLC, established an employee incentive plan "to enable the Company to attract and retain experienced individuals." The plan provided that participants who left Citynet's employment were entitled to "cash out" their entire vested balance. (When an employee's rights to a particular benefit become *vested*, they belong to that employee and cannot be taken away. The vested balance refers to the part of an account that goes with the employee on leaving the company.) When Citynet employee Ray Toney terminated his employment, he asked to redeem his $87,000.48 vested balance. Citynet refused, citing a provision of the plan that limited redemptions to no more than 20 percent annually. Toney filed a suit in a West Virginia state court against Citynet, alleging breach of contract. Citynet argued that the plan was not a contract but a discretionary bonus over which Citynet had sole discretion. Was the plan a contract? If so, was it bilateral or unilateral, and what was the consideration? [*Citynet, LLC v. Toney*, 235 W.Va.79, 772 S.E.2d 36 (2015)] (See *Consideration.*)

12–4. Business Case Problem with Sample Answer—Agreements That Lack Consideration. Arkansas-Missouri Forest Products, LLC (Ark-Mo), sells supplies to make wood pallets. Blue Chip Manufacturing (BCM) makes pallets. Mark Garnett, an owner of Ark-Mo, and Stuart Lerner, an owner of BCM, went into business together. Garnett and Lerner agreed that Ark-Mo would have a 30-percent ownership interest in their future projects. When Lerner formed Blue Chip Recycling, LLC (BCR), to manage a pallet repair facility in California, however, he allocated only a 5 percent interest to Ark-Mo. Garnett objected. In a "Telephone Deal," Lerner then promised Garnett that Ark-Mo would receive a 30 percent interest in their future projects in the Midwest, and Garnett agreed to forgo an ownership interest in BCR. But when Blue Chip III, LLC (BC III), was formed to operate a repair facility in the Midwest, Lerner told Garnett that he "was not getting anything." Ark-Mo filed a suit in a Missouri state court against Lerner, alleging breach of contract. Was there consideration to support the Telephone Deal? Explain. [*Arkansas-Missouri Forest Products, LLC v. Lerner*, 486 S.W.3d 438 (Mo.App. E.D. 2016)] (See *Consideration.*)

—For a sample answer to Problem 12–4, go to Appendix E.

12–5. Minors. Bonney McWilliam's father deeded a house in Norfolk County, Massachusetts, to Bonney and her daughter, Mechelle. Each owned a one-half interest. Described as "an emotionally troubled teenager," Mechelle had a history of substance abuse and a fractured relationship with her mother. At age sixteen, in the presence of her mother and her mother's attorney, Mechelle signed a deed transferring her interest in the house to Bonney. Later, still at odds with her mother, Mechelle learned that she did not have a right to enter the house to retrieve her belongings. Bonney claimed sole ownership. Mechelle filed a lawsuit in a Massachusetts state court against her mother to declare the deed void. Could the transfer of Mechelle's interest be disaffirmed? Explain. [*McWilliam v. McWilliam*, 46 N.E.3d 598 (Mass.App.Ct. 2016)] (See *Contractual Capacity.*)

12–6. Legality. Sue Ann Apolinar hired a guide through Arkansas Valley Adventures, LLC, for a rafting excursion on the Arkansas River. At the outfitter's office, Apolinar signed a release that detailed potential hazards and risks, including "overturning," "unpredictable currents," "obstacles" in the water, and "drowning." The release clearly stated that her signature discharged Arkansas Valley from liability for all claims arising in connection with the trip. On the river, while attempting to maneuver around a rapid, the raft capsized. The current swept Apolinar into a logjam where, despite efforts to save her, she drowned. Her son, Jesus Espinoza, Jr., filed a suit in a federal district court against the rafting company, alleging negligence. What are the arguments for and against enforcing the release that Apolinar signed? Discuss. [*Espinoza v. Arkansas Valley Adventures, LLC*, 809 F.3d 1150 (10th Cir. 2016)] (See *Legality*.)

12–7. Elements of Consideration. Carmen White signed a lease with Sienna Ridge Apartments in San Antonio, Texas. The lease required White to reimburse Sienna Ridge for any damage to the apartment not caused by the landlord's negligence or fault. After moving in, White received a new washer and dryer from her parents. She did not read the instruction manual before overloading the dryer with bedding, including an unwashed pillow, which started a fire. Sienna Ridge filed a claim for the resulting damage with Philadelphia Indemnity Insurance Company. Philadelphia paid the claim and filed a suit in a Texas state court against White, alleging that she had breached the lease by failing to reimburse Sienna Ridge for the damage. White argued that the lease was unenforceable for lack of consideration. Is White correct? Discuss. [*Philadelphia Indemnity Insurance Co. v. White*, 2017 WL 32899 (Tex.App.—San Antonio 2017)] (See *Consideration*.)

12–8. Contracts Contrary to Public Policy. P.M. and C.M. are married (the "Ms") and live in Iowa. Unable to conceive their own child, they signed a contract with T.B., who, in exchange for $13,000 and medical expenses, agreed to be impregnated with embryos fertilized with P.M.'s sperm and the ova (eggs) of an anonymous donor. T.B. agreed to carry the pregnancy to term, and she and her spouse D.B. (the "Bs") promised to deliver the baby at birth to the Ms. During the pregnancy, the relations between the parties deteriorated. When the baby was born, T.B. refused to honor the agreement to give up the child. Meanwhile, genetic testing excluded T.B. and D.B. as the biological parents and established P.M. as the father. Iowa exempts "surrogacy" from a state criminal statute that prohibits selling babies. There is no other state law on point. Is the contract between the Ms and the Bs enforceable? Discuss. [*P.M. v. T.B.*, 907 N.W.2d 522 (Iowa 2018)] (See *Legality*.)

12–9. A Question of Ethics—The IDDR Approach and Minors. Sky High Sports Nashville Operations, LLC, operated a trampoline park in Nashville, Tennessee. At the park, during a dodgeball tournament, Jacob Blackwell, a minor, suffered a torn tendon and a broken tibia. His mother, Crystal, filed a suit on his behalf in a Tennessee state court against Sky High, alleging negligence and seeking $500,000 to cover medical and other expenses. Sky High asserted that the claim was barred by a waiver of liability in a contract between the parties, which the defendant asked the court to enforce. The waiver released Sky High from liability for any "negligent acts or omissions." [*Blackwell v. Sky High Sports Nashville Operations, LLC*, 523 S.W.3d 624 (Tenn.App. 2017)] (See *Contractual Capacity*.)

1. Should Sky High offer a defense to the suit? What might Sky High argue as a reason for enforcing the waiver? Use the IDDR approach to answer these questions.
2. Would it be unethical to allow Jacob to recover? Apply the IDDR approach to explain.

Critical Thinking and Writing Assignments

12–10. Time-Limited Group Assignment—Preexisting Duty. Melissa Faraj owns a lot and wants to build a house according to a particular set of plans and specifications. She solicits bids from building contractors and receives three bids: one from Carlton for $160,000, one from Feldberg for $158,000, and one from Siegel for $153,000. She accepts Siegel's bid. One month after beginning construction of the house, Siegel contacts Faraj and tells her that because of inflation and a recent price hike for materials, his costs have gone up. He says he will not finish the house unless Faraj agrees to pay an extra $13,000. Faraj reluctantly agrees to pay the additional sum. (See *Consideration*.)

1. One group will evaluate whether a contractor can ever raise the price of completing construction based on inflation and the rising cost of materials.
2. A second group will assume that after the house is finished, Faraj refuses to pay the extra $13,000. The group will decide whether Faraj is legally required to pay this additional amount.
3. A third group will determine what types of extraordinary difficulties could arise during construction that would justify a contractor's charging more than the original bid.
4. A fourth group will consider what would happen if Faraj and Siegel had rescinded the initial contract and entered a new construction contract that included the extra $13,000. Would a court be likely to find that there was no consideration because of a preexisting duty? Explain.

Valeri Potapova/Shutterstock.com

13 Defenses to Contract Enforceability

Focus Questions

The five Focus Questions below are designed to help improve your understanding. After reading this chapter, you should be able to answer the following questions:

1. What is the difference between a unilateral and a bilateral mistake?
2. What are the elements of fraudulent misrepresentation?
3. What is the essential feature of undue influence?
4. What types of contracts must be in writing to be enforceable?
5. What is parol evidence? When is it admissible to clarify the terms of a written contract?

Voluntary Consent Knowledge of and genuine assent to the terms of a contract.

"Understanding is a two-way street."

Eleanor Roosevelt
1884–1962
(First Lady of the United States, 1933–1945)

An otherwise valid contract may still be unenforceable if the parties have not genuinely agreed to its terms. The lack of voluntary consent is a *defense* to the enforcement of a contract. As Eleanor Roosevelt stated in the chapter-opening quotation, "Understanding is a two-way street." If one party does not voluntarily consent to the terms of a contract, then there is no genuine "meeting of the minds," and the law will not normally enforce the contract, as we discuss in the first part of this chapter.

Voluntary consent (assent) may be lacking because of mistake, fraudulent misrepresentation, undue influence, or duress. Generally, parties who demonstrate that they did not genuinely agree to the terms of a contract can choose either to carry out the contract or to rescind (cancel) it and thus avoid the entire transaction.

A contract that is otherwise valid may also be unenforceable if it is not in the proper form. For instance, if a contract is required by law to be in writing and there is no written evidence or electronic record of it, the contract will not be enforced.

13–1 Mistakes

We all make mistakes, so it is not surprising that mistakes are made when contracts are created. In certain circumstances, contract law allows a contract to be avoided on the basis of mistake.

It is important to distinguish between *mistakes of fact* and *mistakes of value or quality*. Only a mistake of fact makes a contract voidable. Also, the mistake must involve some *material fact*—a fact that a reasonable person would consider important when determining a course of action.

Mistakes of fact occur in two forms—*unilateral* and *bilateral (mutual)*. A unilateral mistake is made by only one of the contracting parties, whereas a mutual mistake is made by both. We look at these two types of mistakes next and illustrate them graphically in Exhibit 13–1.

13–1a Unilateral Mistakes

Unilateral Mistake A mistake that occurs when one party to a contract is mistaken as to a material fact.

A **unilateral mistake** occurs when only one party is mistaken as to a material fact. Generally, a unilateral mistake does not give the mistaken party any right to relief from the contract. In other words, the contract normally is enforceable against the mistaken party.

Example 13.1 Elena intends to sell her jet ski for $2,500. When she learns that Chin is interested in buying a used jet ski, she sends him an e-mail offering to sell the jet ski to him. When typing the e-mail, however, she mistakenly keys in the price of $1,500. Chin immediately sends Elena an e-mail reply accepting her offer. Even though Elena intended to sell her jet ski for $2,500, she has made a unilateral mistake and is bound by the contract to sell it to Chin for $1,500.

This rule has at least two exceptions.[1] The contract may not be enforceable in either of the following situations.

1. The *other* party to the contract knows or should have known that a mistake of fact was made.
2. The error was due to a *substantial* mathematical mistake in addition, subtraction, division, or multiplication and was made inadvertently and without gross (extreme) negligence. If, for instance, a contractor's bid was significantly low because of a mistake in totaling the estimated costs, any contract resulting from the bid normally may be rescinded.

In both situations, the mistake must still involve some material fact.

13–1b Bilateral (Mutual) Mistakes

Bilateral Mistake A mistake that occurs when both parties to a contract are mistaken about the same material fact.

A **bilateral mistake** is a "mutual misunderstanding concerning a basic assumption on which the contract was made."[2] When both parties are mistaken about the same material fact, the contract can be rescinded, or canceled, by either party, although it is usually the adversely affected party that takes that step. Note that, as with unilateral mistakes, the mistake must be about a material fact.

1. The *Restatement (Second) of Contracts*, Section 153, liberalizes the general rule to take into account the modern trend of allowing avoidance in some circumstances even though only one party has been mistaken.
2. *Restatement (Second) of Contracts*, Section 152.

Exhibit 13–1 Mistakes of Fact

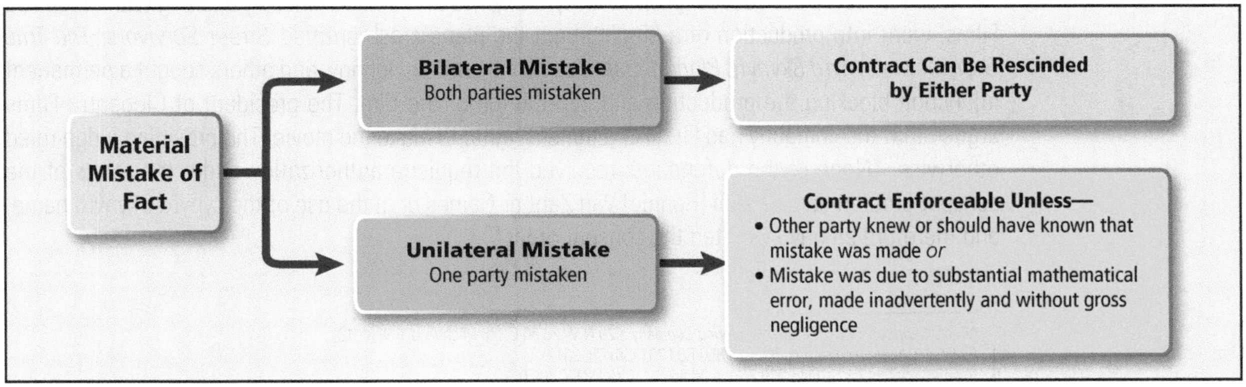

Focus Question 1

What is the difference between a unilateral and a bilateral mistake?

Contract May Be Reformed Rather than rescind a contract flawed by a bilateral mistake, judges often prefer to reform the agreement. Reformation allows a court, using its powers of equity, to restore the original goals of the parties who entered into the contract. **Case Example 13.2** Jason Allen was injured in a work-related automobile accident. Allen's employer had workers' compensation insurance with Accident Fund Insurance Company of America. After a series of disputes and negotiations, Allen and Accident Fund entered into a voluntary payment agreement (VPA) under which the insurance company consented to pay Allen $264.53 per week for 54.2 weeks.

Neither side noticed, however, that the arithmetic of the VPA was wrong. Accident Fund should have been paying Allen $264.53 per week for 131.7 weeks, not 54.2 weeks. A Michigan appellate court found that the faulty calculations had escaped the notice of both parties. To correct this bilateral mistake, the court ordered that the VPA be reformed with the correct figures, reflecting the intentions of Allen and Accident Fund at the time of their agreement.[3]

When the Parties Reasonably Interpret a Term Differently A word or term in a contract may be subject to more than one reasonable interpretation. If the parties to the contract attach materially different meanings to the term, their mutual misunderstanding may allow the contract to be rescinded or reformed. **Case Example 13.3** Offshore Energy Services (OES) contracted with companies to provide workers at offshore oil drilling operations. In its contract with rig operators, OES had an indemnity provision stating that it would insure the companies for tort claims filed against them by an OES employee. Raylin Richard, an OES employee, was injured while working on an oil rig. Richard filed a personal injury suit against Anadarko Petroleum, the head of that drilling project.

OES paid $2.5 million to Richard to settle the lawsuit, but OES's insurance company, Liberty Mutual, denied coverage. Liberty took the position that the indemnity clause in the contract between OES and Anadarko explicitly covered "subcontractors" but did not mention "contractors" like Anadarko. Both OES and Anadarko had thought that the indemnity provision applied to subcontractors and contractors, so they claimed that there had been a mutual mistake. The district court agreed and reformed the contract to include the word *contractors* as well as *subcontractors*. Thus, Liberty Mutual had to cover the amounts OES paid.[4]

Ethical Issue

Should a surviving member of Lynyrd Skynyrd abide by a thirty-year-old consent decree? One of the biggest songs of the 1970s was "Free Bird" by the southern rock group Lynyrd Skynyrd. Not too long after its release, the group's touring plane crashed, killing band members Ronnie Van Zant and Steve Gaines, among others. A decade later, all surviving band members became bound by a consent decree allowing the surviving musicians to tell only their personal *individual* stories rather than the story of the band. The order also prohibited the use of the group's name by any surviving member.

Flash forward three decades. Former Lynyrd Skynyrd drummer Artimus Pyle, along with Cleopatra Films, went into production of a biopic about the plane crash entitled *Street Survivors: The True Story of the Lynyrd Skynyrd Plane Crash.* Van Zant's brother, Johnny, and others sought a permanent injunction blocking the production and distribution of the film. The president of Cleopatra Films argued that the company had First Amendment rights to make the movie. The presiding judge ruled otherwise. "None of the defendants received the requisite authorization under the terms of the consent order in depiction of [Ronnie] Van Zant or Gaines or in the use of the Lynyrd Skynyrd name, and therefore all have violated the consent order."[5]

3. *Allen v Charlevoix Abstract & Engineering Company,* 929 N.W.2d 804, 326 Mich.App. 658 (2019).
4. *Richard v. Anadarko Petroleum Corp.,* 850 F.3d 701 (5th Cir. 2017).
5 *Ronnie Van Zant Inc. v. Pyle,* 270 F.Supp.3d 656 311C (S.D.N.Y. 2017).

13–1c Mistakes of Value

If a mistake concerns the future market value or quality of the object of the contract, the mistake is one of *value*, and the contract normally is enforceable. **Example 13.4** Pablo buys a violin from Bev for $250. Although the violin is very old, neither party believes that it is valuable. Later, however, an antiques dealer informs the parties that the violin is rare and worth thousands of dollars. Here, both parties were mistaken, but the mistake is a mistake of *value* rather than a mistake of *fact*. Because mistakes of value do not warrant contract rescission, Bev cannot rescind the contract.

The reason that mistakes of value do not affect the enforceability of contracts is that value is variable. Depending on the time, place, and other circumstances, the same item may be worth considerably different amounts. When parties form a contract, their agreement establishes the value of the object of their transaction—for the moment. Each party is considered to have assumed the risk that the value will change in the future or prove to be different from what was originally thought. Without this rule, almost any party who considered a bargain unfair could argue mistake.

Pictorial Press Ltd/Alamy

Ronnie Van Zant, the founder of the rock band Lynyrd Skynyrd, died in a plane crash in 1977. How did a consent decree limit how his story could be told in the future?

13–2 Fraudulent Misrepresentation

Although fraud is a tort, the presence of fraud also affects the authenticity of the innocent party's consent to a contract. When an innocent party is fraudulently induced to enter into a contract, the contract usually can be avoided because that party has not *voluntarily* consented to the terms.[6] Normally, the innocent party can either rescind the contract or enforce it and seek damages for any harms resulting from the fraud.

Generally, fraudulent misrepresentation refers only to misrepresentation that is consciously false and is intended to mislead another. That is, the person making a fraudulent misrepresentation knows or believes that the assertion is false or knows that there is no basis (stated or implied) for the assertion.[7]

Typically, fraud involves the following elements:

1. A misrepresentation of a material fact must occur.
2. There must be an intent to deceive.
3. The innocent party must justifiably rely on the misrepresentation.
4. To collect damages, a party must have been harmed as a result of the misrepresentation.

Focus Question 2
What are the elements of fraudulent misrepresentation?

13–2a Misrepresentation Has Occurred

The first element of proving fraud is to show that misrepresentation of a material fact has occurred. This misrepresentation can occur by words or actions. For instance, an art gallery owner's statement "This painting is a Picasso" is a misrepresentation of fact if the painting was done by another artist. Similarly, if a customer asks to see only Jasper Johns paintings and the owner immediately leads the customer over to paintings that were not done by Johns, the owner's actions can be a misrepresentation.

Know This
To collect damages in almost any lawsuit, there must be some sort of injury.

6. *Restatement (Second) of Contracts*, Sections 163 and 164.
7. *Restatement (Second) of Contracts*, Section 162.

Sometimes, a party agrees to enter into a contract on the basis of a promise that is not included in the document evidencing the agreement. Suppose that the document includes a *merger clause*, which states, "This agreement contains the entire agreement between the parties. There are no understandings or agreements between the parties except as expressly set forth." The issue in the following case concerned the effect of a merger clause on an allegation that the contract containing it was procured by fraud.

Case 13.1

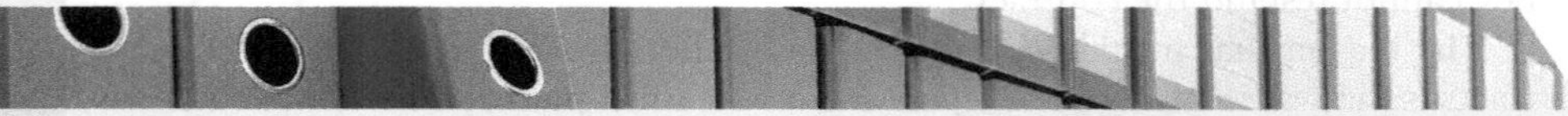

McCullough v. Allstate Property and Casualty Insurance Co.

Alabama Court of Civil Appeals, 256 So.3d 103 (2018).

Facts Allstate Property and Casualty Insurance Company issued a policy to Jerry McCullough, insuring his pickup truck. McCullough loaned the truck to an acquaintance, who returned it damaged. McCullough filed a claim on the policy. Allstate treated the claim as involving multiple different claims (each with a $250 deductible). Allstate also reported these claims to an insurance exchange, Verisk Analytics Automobile Property Loss Underwriting Service (A-PLUS).[a]

Contending that the damage had resulted from only one claim, McCullough filed a suit in a federal district court against Allstate. The insurer agreed to settle the suit for $8,000. McCullough agreed to this amount, but only if Allstate corrected the report to reflect that he was making only one insurance claim and that Allstate paid nothing on that claim. (McCullough did not feel that the $8,000 was a payment for the damage to his truck.) Allstate's lawyer sent McCullough an e-mail agreeing to these terms, but the promise was not included in the release and settlement agreement that the parties signed. The release had a merger clause saying that there were no other agreements, verbal or otherwise, between the parties except as set forth in the contract.

Later, McCullough learned that Allstate had reported to A-PLUS that it had paid $8,000 to him on his claim. He filed a suit in an Alabama state court against Allstate, seeking damages for fraud. Both parties filed motions for summary judgment. The court granted Allstate's motion and denied McCullough's. McCullough appealed.

Issue Should McCullough be allowed to present evidence that the release was procured by fraud?

Decision Yes. A state intermediate appellate court reversed the lower court's summary judgment in favor of Allstate, affirmed the court's denial of McCullough's motion for summary judgment, and remanded the case. Genuine issues of material fact precluded summary judgment on McCullough's claim for fraud.

Reason Allstate argued that McCullough's claim was barred by a merger clause in the release. The appellate court pointed out that under Alabama state law, a merger clause does not bar evidence of fraud in the inducement of a contract. "To hold otherwise is to encourage deliberate fraud." Thus, Allstate's motion for summary judgment should not have been granted.

McCullough's motion for summary judgment, however, was properly denied. McCullough asserted that he settled the federal lawsuit because he was promised that no payment on the claim would be on record. The release did not specify this promise, and Allstate later reported an $8,000 payment to A-PLUS. The court concluded that these allegations presented "a genuine issue of material fact as to whether Allstate, willfully to deceive, or recklessly without knowledge, agreed to report an amount of $0 on the claim and whether McCullough reasonably relied on any representation outside those contained in the release."

Critical Thinking

- **Legal Environment** *In most cases involving the interpretation and application of a contract, a party is not allowed to present evidence outside the document expressing the parties' agreement. Why not?*
- **What If the Facts Were Different?** *Suppose that under the law, a merger clause barred evidence of fraud in the inducement of a contract. How would this affect contract negotiations? Would the result in this case have been different? Discuss.*

---

a. A-PLUS reports information received from insurance companies regarding claims. The reports can affect a claimant's insurance costs.

Misrepresentation by Conduct Misrepresentation also occurs when a party takes specific action to conceal a fact that is material to the contract.[8] Therefore, if a seller's actions prevent a buyer from learning of some fact that is material to the contract, the seller's behavior constitutes misrepresentation by conduct. It would also be misrepresentation by conduct for a seller to untruthfully deny knowledge of facts that are material to the contract when a buyer requests such information.

Spotlight Case Example 13.5 Actor Tom Selleck contracted to purchase a horse named Zorro for his daughter from Dolores Cuenca. Cuenca acted as though Zorro were fit to ride in competitions, when in reality the horse was unfit for this use because of a medical condition. Selleck filed a lawsuit against Cuenca for wrongfully concealing the horse's condition, and a jury awarded Selleck more than $187,000 for Cuenca's misrepresentation by conduct.[9]

Statements of Opinion Statements of opinion and representations of future facts (predictions) are generally not subject to claims of fraud. Statements such as "This land will be worth twice as much next year" and "This car will last for years and years" are statements of opinion, not fact. Contracting parties should recognize them as opinions and not rely on them. A fact is objective and verifiable, whereas an opinion is usually subject to debate. Therefore, sellers are allowed to use *puffery* to sell their goods without being liable for fraud. Nevertheless, in certain situations, such as when a naïve purchaser relies on an opinion from an expert, the innocent party may be entitled to rescission or reformation.

Kathy Hutchins/Shutterstock.com

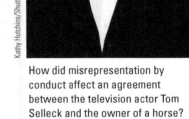

How did misrepresentation by conduct affect an agreement between the television actor Tom Selleck and the owner of a horse?

Misrepresentation of Law Misrepresentation of law *ordinarily* does not entitle a party to be relieved of a contract. **Example 13.6** Cameron has a parcel of property that she is trying to sell to Levi. Cameron knows that a local ordinance prohibits building anything higher than three stories on the property. Nonetheless, she tells Levi, "You can build a condominium one hundred stories high if you want to." Levi buys the land and later discovers that Cameron's statement is false. Levi generally cannot avoid the contract, because under the common law, people are assumed to know state and local laws.

Exceptions to this rule occur when the misrepresenting party is in a profession known to require greater knowledge of the law than the average citizen possesses. For instance, if Cameron, in *Example 13.6*, had been a lawyer or a real estate broker, her willful misrepresentation of the area's zoning laws probably would have constituted fraud.

Misrepresentation by Silence Ordinarily, neither party to a contract has a duty to come forward and disclose facts, and a contract normally will not be set aside because certain pertinent information has not been volunteered. **Example 13.7** Jude is selling a car that has been in an accident and has been repaired. He does not need to volunteer this information to a potential buyer. If, however, the buyer asks him if the car has had extensive bodywork and he lies, Jude has committed fraudulent misrepresentation.

In general, if the seller knows of a serious potential problem that the buyer cannot reasonably be expected to discover, the seller may have a duty to speak. Normally, the seller must disclose only a **latent defect**—that is, a defect that could not readily be ascertained. Because a buyer of a house could easily discover the presence of termites through an inspection, for instance, termites may not qualify as a latent defect. Also, when the parties are in a *fiduciary relationship*—one of trust, such as partners, physician and patient, or attorney and client—there is a duty to disclose material facts. Failure to do so may constitute fraud.

Latent Defect A defect that is not obvious or cannot readily be ascertained.

8. *Restatement (Second) of Contracts*, Section 160.
9. *Selleck v. Cuenca*, Case No. GIN056909, North County of San Diego, California, decided September 9, 2009.

13–2b Intent to Deceive

Scienter Knowledge on the part of a misrepresenting party that material facts have been falsely represented or omitted with an intent to deceive.

The second element of fraud is knowledge on the part of the misrepresenting party that facts have been misrepresented. This element, usually called ***scienter***,[10] or "guilty knowledge," generally signifies that there was an intent to deceive.

Scienter clearly exists if a party knows that a fact is not as stated. **Example 13.8** Richard applies for a position as a business law professor two weeks after his release from prison. On his résumé, he lies and says that he was a corporate president for fourteen years and taught business law at another college. After he is hired, his probation officer alerts the school to Richard's criminal history. The school immediately fires him. If Richard sues the school for breach of his employment contract, he is unlikely to succeed. Because Richard clearly exhibited an intent to deceive the college by not disclosing his personal history, the school can rescind his employment contract without incurring liability.

Scienter also exists if a party makes a statement believing that the statement is not true or makes a statement recklessly, without regard to whether it is true or false. Finally, this element is met if a party says or implies that a statement is made on some basis, such as personal knowledge or personal investigation, when it is not.

Innocent Misrepresentation A misrepresentation that occurs when a person makes a false statement of fact that the person believes is true.

Innocent Misrepresentation If a person makes a statement that the person believes to be true but that actually misrepresents material facts, the person is guilty only of an **innocent misrepresentation**, not of fraud. When an innocent misrepresentation occurs, the aggrieved party can rescind the contract but usually cannot seek damages. **Example 13.9** Bryant submits an application for no-fault automobile insurance with State Farm in which he states that he has not received any traffic citations for three years. State Farm accepts the application, and Bryant pays the premium.

Soon thereafter, State Farm discovers that, one year and eight months earlier, Bryant had been cited for operating a motor vehicle while impaired. Even if Bryant's misrepresentation on the application is an innocent mistake, State Farm can void the insurance contract and return the premium because the misrepresentation is material.

Negligent Misrepresentation A misrepresentation that occurs when a person makes a false statement of fact because the person did not exercise reasonable care or use the skill and competence required by the person's business or profession.

Negligent Misrepresentation Sometimes, a party will make a misrepresentation through carelessness, believing the statement is true. Such a misrepresentation may constitute **negligent misrepresentation** if the party did not exercise reasonable care in uncovering or disclosing the facts or did not use the skill and competence that the party's business or profession requires. **Example 13.10** Dirk, an operator of a weight scale, certifies the weight of Sneed's commodity. If Dirk knows that the scale's accuracy has not been checked for more than three years, his action may constitute negligent misrepresentation.

In almost all states, negligent misrepresentation is equal to *scienter,* or knowingly making a misrepresentation. In effect, negligent misrepresentation is treated as fraudulent misrepresentation, even though the misrepresentation was not purposeful. In negligent misrepresentation, culpable ignorance of the truth supplies the intention to mislead, even if the defendant can claim, "I didn't know."

13–2c Justifiable Reliance on the Misrepresentation

Know This

A statement of opinion is neither a contract offer, nor a contract term, nor fraud.

The third element of fraud is reasonably justifiable reliance on the misrepresentation of fact. The deceived party must have a justifiable reason for relying on the misrepresentation. Also, the misrepresentation must be an important factor (but not necessarily the sole factor) in inducing the deceived party to enter into the contract.

Reliance is not justified if the innocent party knows the true facts or relies on obviously extravagant statements (such as "this pickup truck will get fifty miles to the gallon"). The same rule applies to defects in property sold. If the defects would be obvious on inspection,

10. Pronounced sy-*en*-ter.

the buyer cannot justifiably rely on the seller's representations. If the defects are hidden or latent, however, the buyer is justified in relying on the seller's statements.

Case Example 13.11 Clifford Cronkelton negotiated with Patrick Shivley to buy a car wash in Ohio that had closed down due to bankruptcy. Cronkelton inspected the property and knew that he would have to replace some of the equipment, but he was concerned that the property needed to be winterized to protect it from damage. Shivley assured Cronkelton that the winterizing would be done.

Shivley contacted Guaranteed Construction Services, LLC, which hired Strayer Company to winterize the property. Strayer told Shivley that the only way to avoid problems was to leave the heat on at the car wash, but Shivley knew that the bank had shut off the heat. Later, the car wash was damaged by freezing. Although Shivley informed the bank about the damage, he did not tell Cronkelton, who did not become aware of the damages until after he had he bought the car wash. Cronkelton sued Guaranteed and Shivley for fraud and won. He was awarded more than $140,000 in damages. The defendants appealed. The reviewing court affirmed, holding that Cronkelton had justifiably relied on Shivley's representations that the car wash had been winterized.[11] ■

John de la Bastide/Shutterstock.com

Is it reasonable for the buyer of a car wash to rely on the seller's statements that the property has been properly winterized?

13–2d Injury to the Innocent Party

Most courts do not require a showing of harm in an action to rescind a contract. These courts hold that because rescission returns the parties to the positions they held before the contract was made, a showing of injury to the innocent party is unnecessary. In contrast, to recover damages caused by fraud, proof of harm is universally required. The measure of damages is ordinarily equal to the property's value had it been delivered as represented, less the actual price paid for the property.

In some situations, it may be difficult to identify an "innocent" party. Each year, for example, numerous essays are sold online to students who pass the work off as their own. To learn about the contractual ramifications of these transactions, in which neither party is entirely innocent, see this chapter's *Adapting the Law to the Online Environment* feature.

11. *Cronkelton v. Guaranteed Construction Services, LLC,* 2013-Ohio-328, 988 N.E.2d 656 (3d Dist. 2013).

The Problem of "Contract Cheating"

Adapting the Law to the Online Environment

"No matter what kind of academic paper you need, it is simple and secure to hire an essay writer for a price you can afford," the website promises. Further down, the site pledges that a "Built-in plagiarism checker" ensures that "the received paper is totally original with just one click." Such offers proliferate on the Internet, giving students the ability to choose among many competitors when purchasing made-to-order homework assignments for illicit (or at least unethical) purposes.

The Power of Disclaimers

The practice is popularly known as "contract cheating." Indeed, there is a contract for this work, just as there is for any other product that is bargained for, paid for, and delivered. But is it a valid contract, given the purpose of the product? Earlier, we noted that illegal contracts are void. Plagiarism, however, is not illegal. It is "merely" unethical. In most instances, if caught, the plagiarist will face a number of scholastic punishments, including possible expulsion. Plagiarists do not, for the most part, find themselves in civil or criminal court, however.

The online companies that sell these essays are also protected by carefully constructed legal disclaimers that inevitably

(Continues)

Continued

appear, in small print, near the bottom of their websites. The disclaimer will state that any product sold is for "research and reference purposes only" and is not intended to be presented as the student's own work.

How Effective Is a Disclaimer?

Generally speaking, parties to a contract cannot rely on a disclaimer to avoid legal responsibilities. For instance, a court will not accept a disclaimer that broadly states, "Company A is not responsible for any injuries" caused by a product. At the same time, parties are expected, "by the exercise of ordinary intelligence," to be aware of the nature of the transactions they enter into.[a] It would be difficult for either party in a contract cheating case to claim innocence as to the actual purpose of the transaction, or to allege misrepresentation by the other side. As a result, the courts have had very little to say about contract cheating. Instead, the burden has fallen on schools to combat the practice with student conduct pledges and anti-plagiarism software.

a. See *Rubin v. Sabharwal,* 171 A.D.3d 580, 99 N.Y.S.3d 17 (2019).

Critical Thinking

Josh pays AcademicShark.com $50 for an essay on the biblical references in Moby Dick. *The website promises "a top-notch grade" and includes a disclaimer as described above. Josh hands in the* Moby Dick *paper without making any changes and receives a C+. Does he have any recourse under contract law should he want a refund? Explain your answer.*

Because fraud actions necessarily involve wrongful conduct, courts may also award *punitive,* or *exemplary, damages,* which compensate a plaintiff over and above the amount of the actual loss. Because of the potential for punitive damages, which normally are not available in contract actions, plaintiffs often include a claim for fraudulent misrepresentation in their contract disputes.

13–3 Undue Influence and Duress

A contract lacks voluntary consent and is unenforceable if *undue influence* or *duress* is present.

13–3a Undue Influence

Undue Influence Persuasion that is less than actual force but more than advice and that induces a person to act according to the will or purposes of the dominating party.

Undue influence arises from relationships in which one party can greatly influence another party, thus overcoming that party's free will. A contract entered into under excessive or undue influence lacks voluntary consent and is therefore voidable.[12]

One Party Dominates the Other In various types of relationships, one party may have an opportunity to dominate and unfairly influence another party. Minors and elderly people, for instance, are often under the influence of guardians (persons who are legally responsible for them). If a guardian induces a young or elderly ward (the person whom the guardian looks after) to enter into a contract that benefits the guardian, the guardian may have exerted undue influence. Undue influence can arise from a number of confidential or fiduciary relationships, including attorney-client, physician-patient, guardian-ward, parent-child, husband-wife, and trustee-beneficiary.

Focus Question 3

What is the essential feature of undue influence?

The essential feature of undue influence is that the party being taken advantage of does not exercise free will in entering into a contract. It is not enough that a person is elderly or suffers from some mental or physical impairment. There must be clear and convincing evidence that the person did not act with free will. Similarly, the existence of a fiduciary relationship alone is insufficient to prove undue influence.

12. *Restatement (Second) of Contracts,* Section 177.

A Presumption of Undue Influence in Certain Situations The dominant party in a fiduciary relationship must exercise the utmost good faith in dealing with the other party. When the dominant party benefits from the relationship, a presumption of undue influence may arise. Thus, when a contract enriches the dominant party in a fiduciary relationship, the court will often *presume* that the contract was made under undue influence.

Example 13.12 Erik is the guardian for Kinsley, his ward. On her behalf, he enters into a contract from which he benefits financially. If Kinsley challenges the contract, the court will likely presume that the guardian has taken advantage of his ward. To rebut (refute) this presumption, Erik has to show that he made full disclosure to Kinsley and that consideration was present. He must also show that Kinsley received, if available, independent and competent advice before completing the transaction. Unless the presumption can be rebutted, the contract will be rescinded.

13–3b Duress

Agreement to the terms of a contract is not voluntary if one of the parties is *forced* into the agreement. The use of threats to force a party to enter into a contract constitutes *duress,* as does the use of blackmail or extortion to induce consent. Duress is both a defense to the enforcement of a contract and a ground for rescission of a contract.

To establish duress, there must be proof of a threat to do something that the threatening party has no right to do. Generally, for duress to occur, the threatened act must be wrongful or illegal, and it must render the person who receives the threat incapable of exercising free will. A threat to exercise a legal right, such as the right to sue someone, ordinarily does not constitute duress.

13–4 The Writing Requirement

Another defense to the enforceability of a contract is *form*—specifically, some contracts must be in writing. All states require certain types of contracts to be in writing or evidenced by a written memorandum or an electronic record. In addition, the party or parties against whom enforcement is sought must have signed the contract, unless certain exceptions apply (as discussed later in this chapter). In this text, we refer to these state statutes collectively as the **Statute of Frauds.**

Statute of Frauds A state statute that requires certain types of contracts to be in writing to be enforceable.

The following types of contracts are said to fall "within" or "under" the Statute of Frauds and therefore require a writing:

1. Contracts involving interests in land.
2. Contracts that cannot *by their terms* be performed within one year from the day after the date of formation.
3. Collateral, or secondary, contracts, such as promises to answer for the debt or duty of another.
4. Promises made in consideration of marriage.
5. Under the Uniform Commercial Code, contracts for the sale of goods priced at $500 or more.

Focus Question 4
What types of contracts must be in writing to be enforceable?

The actual name of the Statute of Frauds is misleading because it does not apply to fraud. Rather, in an effort to prevent fraud, the statute denies enforceability to certain contracts that do not comply with its requirements. The name derives from an English act passed in 1677 that was titled "An Act for the Prevention of Frauds and Perjuries."

13–4a Contracts Involving Interests in Land

A contract calling for the sale of land is not enforceable unless it is in writing or evidenced by a written or electronic memorandum. Land is *real property* and includes all physical objects that are permanently attached to the soil, such as buildings, fences, trees, and the soil itself. The Statute of Frauds operates as a defense to the enforcement of an oral contract for the sale of land. **Example 13.13** Skylar contracts orally to sell his property in Fair Oaks to Beth. If he later decides not to sell, under most circumstances, Beth cannot enforce the contract. ■

The Statute of Frauds also requires written evidence of contracts for the transfer of other interests in land, such as mortgage agreements and leases. Similarly, an agreement that includes an option to purchase real property must be in writing for the option to be enforced. The issue in the following case was whether a contract for a sale of land met this requirement.

Case 13.2

Sloop v. Kiker

Court of Appeals of Arkansas, Division III, 2016 Ark.App. 125, 484 S.W.3d 696 (2016).

Facts Russell and Sally Kiker owned a house in Newton County, Arkansas. Mona Sloop agreed to buy it for $850,000. The parties signed a contract that identified the property by its street address and stipulated a $350,000 down payment, which was nonrefundable if closing did not occur by August 31. On the same day, they executed a deed containing a formal, legal description of the property by metes and bounds. (Metes and bounds is a way of describing the boundary lines of property according to the distance between two points.) They also agreed that Sloop could live in the house as caretaker until the August 31 deadline.

When the closing had not occurred by September 6, the Kikers filed a suit in an Arkansas state court against Sloop, seeking an order to remove her from the property and a declaration that they were entitled to keep the down payment. Sloop filed a counterclaim for the return of the $350,000. She argued that their contract violated the Statute of Frauds. The court issued a summary judgment in the favor of the Kikers. Sloop appealed.

Issue Does a contract that describes the real property being sold by its street address satisfy the Statute of Frauds?

Decision Yes. A state intermediate appellate court affirmed the judgment of the lower court.

Reason Sloop argued that the contract did not satisfy the Statute of Frauds because it did not identify the Kikers as the sellers and it did not contain a sufficient description of the property. The court pointed out, however, that the deed the parties executed on the same day as the contract identified the Kikers as "grantors" and included a legal description of the property. "Generally, instruments executed at the same time by the same parties, for the same purpose, and in the course of the same transaction, are, in the eyes of the law, one instrument and will be read and construed together.

"Moreover, if a contract furnishes a means by which realty can be identified—a key to the property's location—the Statute of Frauds is satisfied." In this case, the designation in the contract of the premises by its street address met the requirement of the Statute of Frauds that the property being transferred be described with sufficient certainty for it to be identified.

Critical Thinking

- **Legal Environment** *Why does the Statute of Frauds require that a contract for a sale of land contain a sufficient description of the property?*
- **What If the Facts Were Different?** *Suppose that the court in the* Sloop *case had not construed the deed and the contract as one instrument but as separate documents. How might that have affected the result? Explain.*

13–4b The One-Year Rule

Contracts that cannot, *by their own terms,* be performed within one year *from the day after* the contract is formed must be in writing to be enforceable. The reason for this rule is that the parties' memory of their contract's terms is not likely to be reliable for longer than a year.

Time Period Starts the Day after the Contract Is Formed The one-year period begins to run *the day after the contract is made.* **Example 13.14** Superior University forms a contract with Kimi stating that she will teach three courses in history during the coming academic year (September 15 through June 15). If the contract is formed in March, it must be in writing to be enforceable—because it cannot be performed within one year. If the contract is formed in July, in contrast, it will not have to be in writing to be enforceable—because it can be performed within one year.

Contract Must Be Objectively Impossible to Perform within One Year The test for determining whether an oral contract is enforceable under the one-year rule is whether performance is *possible* within one year from the day after the date of contract formation. It does not matter whether the agreement is *likely* to be performed during that period.

When performance of a contract is objectively impossible during the one-year period, the contract must be in writing to be enforceable. **Example 13.15** A contract to provide five crops of tomatoes to be grown on a specific farm in Illinois would be objectively impossible to perform within one year. No farm in Illinois can produce five crops of tomatoes in a single year.

If performance is possible within one year under the contract's terms, the contract does not fall under the Statute of Frauds and need not be in writing. **Case Example 13.16** Robert and Lynette Knigge owned a B&L Food Store in Redfield, South Dakota. When Robert was diagnosed with brain cancer and given five months to live, he entered into an oral contract with his brother, David, to manage the store. Robert died five months after the date of the contract. Lynette terminated David's employment two months later. David filed a suit in a South Dakota state court against his sister-in-law. He claimed that, under his oral contract with Robert, he was entitled to a severance payment if he lost the job at the store. A state court dismissed David's suit, but the South Dakota Supreme Court reversed and remanded. Because the oral contract between David and Robert could have been performed within one year, it did not have to be in writing to be enforceable.[13] Exhibit 13–2 graphically illustrates the one-year rule.

Sorbis/Shutterstock.com

How did the one-year rule affect the outcome of a lawsuit regarding the management of a local food store?

13. *David Knigge v. B&L Food Stores, Inc.*, 2017 S.D. 4, 890 N.W.2d 570 (2017).

Exhibit 13–2 The One-Year Rule

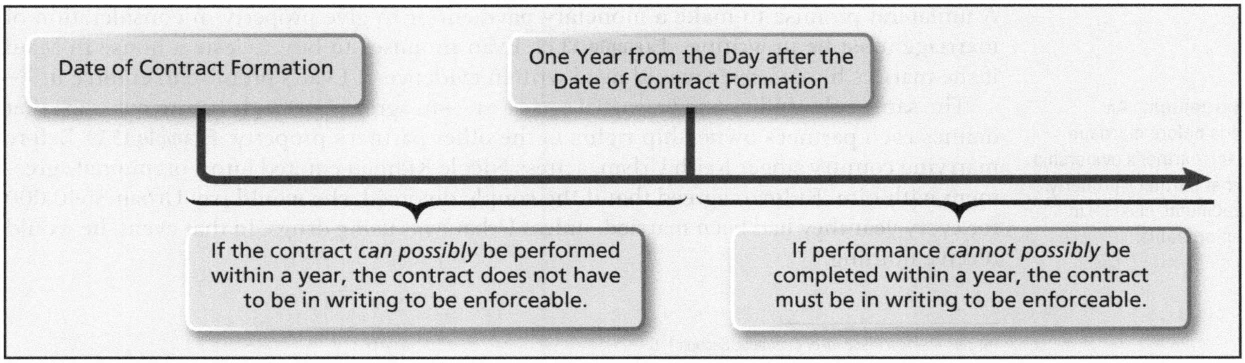
Date of Contract Formation
One Year from the Day after the Date of Contract Formation
If the contract *can possibly* be performed within a year, the contract does not have to be in writing to be enforceable.
If performance *cannot possibly* be completed within a year, the contract must be in writing to be enforceable.

13–4c Collateral Promises

Collateral Promise A secondary promise to a primary transaction, such as a promise made by one person to pay the debts of another if the latter fails to perform. A collateral promise normally must be in writing to be enforceable.

A **collateral promise**, or secondary promise, is one that is ancillary (subsidiary) to a principal transaction or primary contractual relationship. In other words, a collateral promise is one made by a third party to assume the debts or obligations of a primary party to a contract if that party does not perform. Any collateral promise of this nature falls under the Statute of Frauds and therefore must be in writing to be enforceable.

Primary versus Secondary Obligations An understanding of this concept requires the ability to distinguish between primary and secondary promises and obligations. A promise to pay another person's debt (or other obligation) that is *not conditioned on the person's failure to pay (or perform)* is a primary obligation. A promise to pay another's debt *only if that party fails to pay* is a secondary obligation. A contract in which a party assumes a primary obligation normally does not need to be in writing to be enforceable, whereas a contract assuming a secondary obligation does. **Example 13.17** Nigel tells Dr. Lu, an orthodontist, that he will pay for the services provided for Nigel's niece. Because Nigel has assumed direct financial responsibility for his niece's debt, this is a primary obligation and need not be in writing to be enforceable. In contrast, if Nigel commits to paying his niece's orthodontist bill only if her mother does not, it is a secondary obligation. In that situation, Lu must have a signed writing or record proving that Nigel assumed this obligation for it to be enforced. ■

An Exception—The "Main Purpose" Rule An oral promise to answer for the debt of another is covered by the Statute of Frauds *unless* the guarantor's purpose in accepting secondary liability is to secure a personal benefit. Under the "main purpose" rule, this type of contract need not be in writing.[14] The assumption is that a court can infer from the circumstances of a case whether a "leading objective" of the promisor was to secure a personal benefit.

Example 13.18 Carrie contracts with Custom Manufacturing Company to have some machines custom made for her factory. She promises Newform Supply, Custom's supplier, that if Newform continues to deliver the materials to Custom for the production of the custom-made machines, she will guarantee payment. This promise need not be in writing, even though the effect may be to pay the debt of another, because Carrie's main purpose is to secure a benefit for herself. ■

Another typical application of the main purpose doctrine occurs when one creditor guarantees a debtor's debt to another creditor to forestall litigation. The purpose is to allow the debtor to remain in business long enough to generate profits sufficient to pay *both* creditors. In this situation, the guaranty does not need to be in writing to be enforceable.

13–4d Promises Made in Consideration of Marriage

A unilateral promise to make a monetary payment or to give property in consideration of marriage must be in writing. **Example 13.19** Evan promises to buy Celeste a house in Maui if she marries him. Celeste would need written evidence of Evan's promise to enforce it. ■

Prenuptial Agreement An agreement made before marriage that defines each partner's ownership rights in the other partner's property. Prenuptial agreements must be in writing to be enforceable.

The same rule applies to a **prenuptial agreement**—an agreement made before marriage that defines each partner's ownership rights in the other partner's property. **Example 13.20** Before marrying country singer Keith Urban, actress Nicole Kidman entered into a prenuptial agreement with him. Kidman agreed that if the couple divorced, she would pay Urban $640,000 for every year they had been married, unless Urban was using drugs. In that event, he would receive nothing. ■

14. *Restatement (Second) of Contracts,* Section 116.

13–4e Contracts for the Sale of Goods

The Uniform Commercial Code (UCC) includes Statute of Frauds provisions that require written evidence or an electronic record of a contract for the sale of goods priced at $500 or more. (This low threshold amount may be increased in the future.)

A writing that will satisfy the UCC requirement need only state the quantity term (six thousand boxes of cotton gauze, for instance). The contract will not be enforceable for any quantity greater than that set forth in the writing.

Other agreed-on terms can be omitted or even stated imprecisely in the writing, as long as they adequately reflect both parties' intentions. A written memorandum or series of communications (including e-mail) evidencing a contract will suffice, provided that the writing is signed by the party against whom enforcement is sought.

13–4f Exceptions to the Statute of Frauds

Exceptions to the applicability of the Statute of Frauds are made in certain situations. We describe those situations in the following subsections.

Partial Performance When a contract has been partially performed and the parties cannot be returned to their positions prior to the contract's formation, a court may grant *specific performance.* Specific performance is an equitable remedy that requires that a contract be performed according to its precise terms. The parties still must prove that an oral contract existed, of course.

In cases involving oral contracts for the transfer of interests in land, courts usually look at whether justice is better served by enforcing the oral contract when partial performance has taken place. For instance, if the purchaser has paid part of the price, taken possession, and made valuable improvements to the property, a court may grant specific performance.

In some states, mere reliance on certain types of oral contracts is enough to remove them from the Statute of Frauds. Under the UCC, an oral contract for goods priced at $500 or more is enforceable to the extent that a seller accepts payment or a buyer accepts delivery of the goods.[15]

Case Example 13.21 Pacific Fruit, Inc., exports cargo from Ecuador. NYKCool, based in Sweden, provides maritime transportation. NYKCool and Pacific entered into a written contract with a two-year duration, under which NYKCool agreed to transport weekly shipments of bananas from Ecuador to California and Japan.

At the end of the period, the parties agreed to extend the deal, but a new contract was never signed. The parties continued making weekly shipments for four more years until a dispute arose over unused cargo capacity and unpaid freight charges. An international arbitration panel found that Pacific Fruit was liable to NYKCool for $8.7 million for breach of contract. Pacific Fruit appealed, arguing that there was no contract in place. The court affirmed the award in favor of NYKCool. "The parties' substantial partial performance on the contract weighs strongly in favor of contract formation."[16]

Admissions If a party against whom enforcement of an oral contract is sought "admits" under oath that a contract for sale was made, the contract will be enforceable.[17] The party's admission can occur at any stage of the court proceedings, such as during a deposition or other discovery, pleadings, or testimony.

---

15. UCC 2–201(3)(c).

16. *NYKCool A.B. v. Pacific Fruit, Inc.,* 2013 WL 163621 (2d Cir. 2013). The initials *A.B.* stand for *Aktiebolag,* which is the Swedish term for "limited company."

17. *Restatement (Second) of Contracts,* Section 133.

gerenme/Getty Images

If a seller admits under oath to a contract for $10,000 of commercial kitchen equipment, does the buyer owe more if additional equipment was installed?

If a party admits a contract subject to the UCC, the contract is enforceable, but only to the extent of the quantity admitted.[18] **Example 13.22** Rachel, the president of Bistro Corporation, admits under oath that an oral agreement was made with Commercial Kitchens, Inc., to buy certain equipment for $10,000. A court will enforce the agreement only to the extent admitted ($10,000), even if Commercial Kitchens claims that the agreement involved $20,000 worth of equipment. ■

Promissory Estoppel An oral contract that would otherwise be unenforceable under the Statute of Frauds may be enforced under the doctrine of *promissory estoppel.* Section 139 of the *Restatement (Second) of Contracts* provides that an oral promise can be enforceable, notwithstanding the Statute of Frauds, if the promisee has justifiably relied on the promise to the promisee's detriment. The promisee's reliance must have been foreseeable to the person making the promise, and enforcing the promise must be the only way to avoid injustice.

Note the similarities between promissory estoppel and the doctrine of partial performance discussed previously. Both require reasonable reliance and operate to estop, or prevent, a party from claiming that no contract exists.

Special Exceptions under the UCC Special exceptions to the applicability of the Statute of Frauds exist for sales contracts. Oral contracts for customized goods may be enforced in certain circumstances. Another exception has to do with oral contracts *between merchants* that have been confirmed in a written memorandum. We will examine this exception when we discuss the UCC's Statute of Frauds provisions.

Exhibit 13–3 graphically summarizes the types of contracts that fall under the Statute of Frauds and the various exceptions that apply.

13–4g Sufficiency of the Writing

A written contract will satisfy the writing requirement of the Statute of Frauds, as will a written memorandum or an electronic record that evidences the agreement and is signed by the party against whom enforcement is sought. The signature need not be placed at the end of the document but can be anywhere in the writing. A signature can consist of a typed name or even just initials rather than the full name.

18. UCC 2–201(3)(b).

Exhibit 13–3 Contracts Subject to the Statute of Frauds

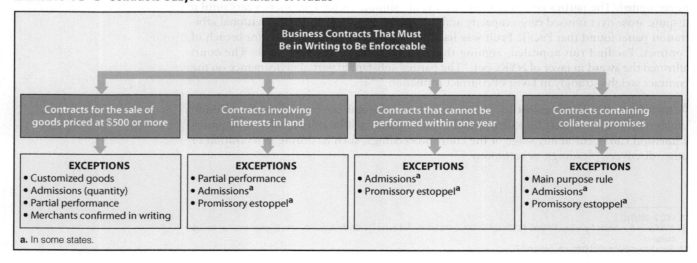

Business Contracts That Must Be in Writing to Be Enforceable

Contracts for the sale of goods priced at $500 or more	Contracts involving interests in land	Contracts that cannot be performed within one year	Contracts containing collateral promises
EXCEPTIONS • Customized goods • Admissions (quantity) • Partial performance • Merchants confirmed in writing	**EXCEPTIONS** • Partial performance • Admissions[a] • Promissory estoppel[a]	**EXCEPTIONS** • Admissions[a] • Promissory estoppel[a]	**EXCEPTIONS** • Main purpose rule • Admissions[a] • Promissory estoppel[a]

a. In some states.

What Constitutes a Writing? A writing can consist of any confirmation, invoice, sales slip, check, fax, or e-mail—or such items in combination. The written contract need not be contained in a single document to constitute an enforceable contract. One document may incorporate another document by expressly referring to it. Several documents may form a single contract if they are physically attached—such as by staple, paper clip, or glue—or even if they are only placed in the same envelope.

Example 13.23 Simpson orally agrees to sell some land next to a shopping mall to Terro Properties. Simpson gives Terro an unsigned memo that contains a legal description of the property, and Terro gives Simpson an unsigned first draft of their contract. Simpson sends Terro a signed letter that refers to the memo and to the first and final drafts of the contract. Terro sends Simpson an unsigned copy of the final draft of the contract with a signed check stapled to it. Together, the documents can constitute a writing sufficient to satisfy the Statute of Frauds and bind both parties to the terms of the contract as evidenced by the writings. ■

What Must Be Contained in the Writing? A memorandum or note evidencing an oral contract need only contain the essential terms of the contract, not every term. There must, of course, also be some indication that the parties voluntarily agreed to the terms. As mentioned, under the UCC, a writing evidencing a contract for the sale of goods need only state the quantity and be signed by the party against whom enforcement is sought.

Under most state laws, the writing must also name the parties and identify the subject matter, the consideration, and the essential terms with reasonable certainty. In addition, contracts for the sale of land usually must state the price and describe the property with sufficient clarity to allow these terms to be determined without reference to outside sources.

Note that because only the party against whom enforcement is sought must have signed the writing, a contract may be enforceable by one of its parties but not by the other. **Example 13.24** Rock orally agrees to buy Betty's lake house and lot for $350,000. Betty writes Rock a letter confirming the sale by identifying the parties and the essential terms of the sales contract—price, method of payment, and legal address—and signs the letter. Betty has made a written memorandum of the oral land contract. Because she signed the letter, she normally can be held to the oral contract by Rock. Betty cannot enforce the agreement against Rock, however. Because he has not signed or entered into a written contract or memorandum, Rock can plead the Statute of Frauds as a defense. ■

13–5 The Parol Evidence Rule

Sometimes, a written contract does not include—or contradicts—an oral understanding reached by the parties before or at the time of contracting. For instance, a landlord might tell a person who agrees to rent an apartment that cats are permitted, whereas the lease contract clearly states that no pets are allowed. In determining the outcome of such disputes, the courts look to a common law rule called the **parol evidence rule**.

Focus Question 5

What is parol evidence? When is it admissible to clarify the terms of a written contract?

Under this rule, if a court finds that a written contract represents the complete and final statement of the parties' agreement, then it will not allow either party to present parol evidence. *Parol evidence* is testimony or other evidence of communications between the parties that is not contained in the contract itself. Thus, a party normally cannot present evidence of the parties' "prior or contemporaneous agreements or negotiations" if that evidence contradicts or varies the terms of the parties' written contract.[19]

Parol Evidence Rule A rule of contracts under which a court will not receive into evidence prior or contemporaneous external agreements that contradict the terms of the parties' written contract.

The following case involved an alleged contract that appeared to be unenforceable for lack of consideration. One of the parties sought to present evidence outside the written terms of the deal to establish consideration. Could the court consider this evidence?

19. *Restatement (Second) of Contracts,* Section 213.

Case 13.3

Habel v. Estate of Capelli

Court of Appeals of Wisconsin, 2020 WI App 15, 391 Wis.2d 399, 941 N.W.2d 858 (2020).

Facts Alfred Habel operated a sports memorabilia business. John Capelli, a good customer, took some items for which he promised to pay later. When Habel sought payment, Capelli told him that he did not want his family to know how much he had spent and proposed that, in exchange for forbearance on the debt, Habel could sell Capelli's entire collection on his death and take a commission. Habel agreed, and they wrote out the terms, which gave Habel the choice not to perform the sale.

Sixteen years later, Capelli died. Habel showed the written agreement to Capelli's widow, Julie, who refused to let Habel sell the collection. Habel filed a suit in a Wisconsin state court against Capelli's estate, seeking specific performance or damages.

The estate argued that because the written terms gave Habel the option not to perform, there was no consideration on his part for the deal, making it unenforceable. The court agreed and granted a judgment in favor of the estate. Habel appealed, claiming that his forbearance was consideration.

Issue Did the parol evidence rule prevent Habel from presenting evidence of his purported forbearance?

Decision Yes. A state intermediate appellate court affirmed the judgment of the lower court. Habel's alleged agreement with Capelli was unenforceable for lack of consideration.

Reason When the written terms of an alleged contract are at issue, the parol evidence rule prevents a party from presenting evidence that contradicts or varies those terms.

In the terms of the alleged contract at issue in this case, Habel did not promise to do anything. Capelli "willed" Habel the right to sell Capelli's sports memorabilia collection. But the document provided that the parties' "agreement" could be terminated "in the event Habel shall not accept" to perform it. Under this provision, Habel assumed no obligation and could opt out of the deal. The alleged contract was thus rendered unenforceable for lack of consideration.

The court reasoned that it could not consider evidence of Habel's claim because the circumstances from which forbearance allegedly arose were not set out in the terms. The parol evidence rule barred the court's review of any such extrinsic evidence. "Habel's parol evidence cannot be used to vary or add terms, such as consideration—some detriment or obligation by Habel—when the document makes clear that all mutual promises are set forth therein."

Critical Thinking

- **Legal Environment** *Why is evidence of a prior negotiation or agreement that contradicts or varies the terms of a written agreement inadmissible in a court under the parol evidence rule?*
- **What If the Facts Were Different?** *Suppose that the written terms of the deal between Habel and Capelli had referred to other documents, such as unpaid invoices for Capelli's purchases, to be included as part of their alleged agreement. Would the result have been different? Discuss.*

13–5a Exceptions to the Parol Evidence Rule

Know This
The parol evidence rule and its exceptions relate to the rules concerning the *interpretation* of contracts.

Because of the rigidity of the parol evidence rule, courts make several exceptions. These exceptions include the following:

1. *Contracts subsequently modified.* Evidence of a *subsequent modification* (oral or written) of a written contract can be introduced in court. Oral modifications may not be enforceable, however, if they come under the Statute of Frauds (such as a modification that increases the price of the goods being sold to more than $500). Also, oral modifications will not be enforceable if the original contract provides that any modification must be in writing.[20]
2. *Voidable or void contracts.* Oral evidence can be introduced in all cases to show that the contract was voidable or void (for instance, induced by mistake, fraud, or misrepresentation). The reason is simple: if deception led one of the parties to agree

20. UCC 2–209(2), (3).

to the terms of a written contract, oral evidence indicating fraud should not be excluded. Courts frown on bad faith and are quick to allow the introduction at trial of parol evidence when it establishes fraud.

3. *Contracts containing ambiguous terms.* When the terms of a written contract are ambiguous, evidence is admissible to show the meaning of the terms. **Case Example 13.25** Howard and Eleanor Windows owned a home in Pennsylvania. When raw sewage backed up in the city's sewer system and infiltrated their home, they filed a claim with their homeowner's insurance company, Erie Insurance Exchange. Erie denied coverage under the insurance policy's general exclusion for water damage caused by "water or sewage which backs up through sewers and drains." The Windowses sued Erie for breach of contract.

   Erie claimed that the parol evidence rule applied and prevented the Windowses from presenting evidence that contradicted the water-damage exclusion in the policy. The court disagreed and allowed the Windowses to present their case to a jury, which awarded them more than $75,000 in damages. Erie appealed. The appellate court affirmed the jury's verdict, reasoning that the term "backs up" was not defined in the contract and was subject to more than one reasonable interpretation.[21]

4. *Incomplete contracts.* Evidence is admissible when the written contract is incomplete in that it lacks one or more of the essential terms. The courts allow evidence to "fill in the gaps" in the contract.

D_Townsend/Shutterstock.com

Which exception to the parol evidence rule applied in a dispute regarding an insurance claim for water and sewer damage?

5. *Prior dealing, course of performance, or usage of trade.* Under the UCC, evidence can be introduced to explain or supplement a written contract by showing a prior dealing, course of performance, or usage of trade.[22] This is because when buyers and sellers deal with each other over extended periods of time, certain customary practices develop. These practices are often overlooked in the writing of the contract, so courts allow the introduction of evidence to show how the parties have acted in the past. Usage of trade—practices and customs generally followed in a particular industry—can also shed light on the meaning of certain contract provisions, and thus evidence of trade usage may be admissible.

6. *Contracts subject to an orally agreed-on condition precedent.* Sometimes the parties agree that a condition must be fulfilled before a party is required to perform the contract. This is called a *condition precedent.* If the parties have orally agreed on a condition precedent and the condition does not conflict with the terms of a written agreement, then a court may allow parol evidence to prove the oral condition. The parol evidence rule does not apply here because the existence of the entire written contract is subject to an orally agreed-on condition. Proof of the condition does not alter or modify the written terms but affects the *enforceability* of the written contract.

7. *Contracts with an obvious or gross clerical (or typographic) error.* When an *obvious* or *gross* clerical (or typographic) error exists that clearly would not represent the agreement of the parties, parol evidence is admissible to correct the error. **Example 13.26** Davis agrees to lease office space from Stone Enterprises for $3,000 per month. The signed written lease provides for a monthly lease payment of $300 rather than the $3,000 agreed to by the parties. Because the error is obvious, Stone Enterprises would be allowed to admit parol evidence to correct the mistake.

---

21. *Windows v. Eric Insurance Exchange,* 161 A.3d 953 (Pa.Sup.Ct. 2017).
22. UCC 1–205, 2–202.

13–5b Integrated Contracts

In determining whether to allow parol evidence, courts consider whether the written contract is intended to be a complete and final statement of the terms of the agreement. If it is, the contract is referred to as an **integrated contract**, and extraneous evidence (evidence from outside the contract) is excluded.

Integrated Contract A written contract that constitutes the final expression of the parties' agreement. Evidence extraneous to the contract that contradicts or alters the meaning of the contract in any way is inadmissible.

Case Example 13.27 Volvo Trucks makes heavy-duty trucks. Andy Mohr Truck Center was one of its dealers for a few years, until the relationship soured and they ended up in litigation. Volvo sought to terminate Mohr's dealership, claiming that Mohr had misrepresented a material fact in connection with its dealership application.

Mohr supposedly had orally promised Volvo that it would build a new long-term facility for the dealership if Volvo awarded the contract to Mohr (the "new-facility claim"). Mohr claimed that Volvo had orally promised to give Mohr a Mack Truck dealership franchise because Volvo owned Mack Truck (the "Mack claim"). Neither of these alleged promises was written in the parties' contract, which contained an integration clause. A federal district court dismissed the new-facility claim and the Mack claim. A federal appellate court affirmed, noting that both Volvo and Mohr were sophisticated parties that had experience with franchises and dealer agreements. The existence of an integration clause in their contract made it unreasonable for them to rely on any representations made outside of the contract.[23]

A contract can be either completely or partially integrated. If it contains all of the terms of the parties' agreement, then it is completely integrated. If it contains only some of the terms and not others, it is partially integrated. If the contract is only partially integrated, evidence of consistent additional terms is admissible to supplement the written agreement.[24] Note that parol evidence is admitted only to add to the terms of a partially integrated contract. For both completely and partially integrated contracts, courts exclude any evidence that *contradicts* the writing.

Exhibit 13–4 illustrates the relationship between integrated contracts and the parol evidence rule.

23. *Andy Mohr Truck Center, Inc. v. Volvo Trucks North America*, 869 F.3d 598 (7th Cir. 2017).
24. *Restatement (Second) of Contracts*, Section 216.

Exhibit 13–4 The Parol Evidence Rule

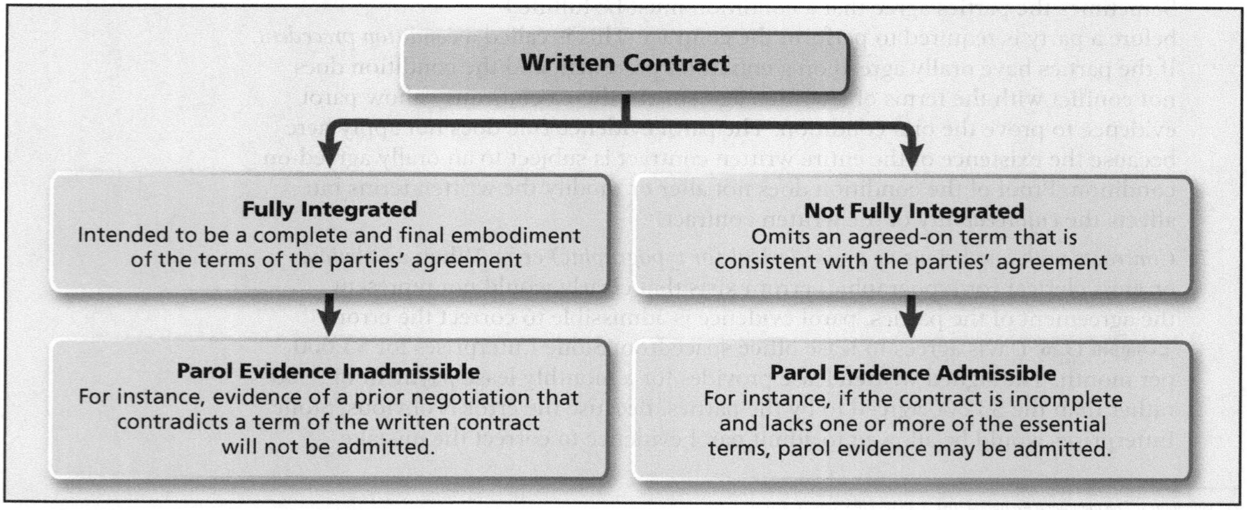

Written Contract
Fully Integrated
Intended to be a complete and final embodiment of the terms of the parties' agreement
Not Fully Integrated
Omits an agreed-on term that is consistent with the parties' agreement
Parol Evidence Inadmissible
For instance, evidence of a prior negotiation that contradicts a term of the written contract will not be admitted.
Parol Evidence Admissible
For instance, if the contract is incomplete and lacks one or more of the essential terms, parol evidence may be admitted.

Practice and Review

Chelene had been a caregiver for Marta's elderly mother, Janis, for nine years. Shortly before Janis passed away, Chelene convinced her to buy Chelene's house for Marta. Janis died before the papers were signed, however. Four months later, Marta used her inheritance to buy Chelene's house without having it inspected. The house was built in the 1950s, and Chelene said it was in "perfect condition." Nevertheless, one year after the purchase, the basement started leaking. Marta had the paneling removed from the basement walls and discovered that the walls were bowed inward and cracked. Marta then had a civil engineer inspect the basement walls, and he found that the cracks had been caulked and painted over before the paneling was installed. He concluded that the "wall failure" had existed "for at least thirty years" and that the basement walls were "structurally unsound." Using the information presented in the chapter, answer the following questions.

1. Can Marta avoid the contract on the ground that both parties made a mistake about the condition of the house? Explain.
2. Can Marta sue Chelene for fraudulent misrepresentation? Why or why not? What element (or elements) might be lacking?
3. Now assume that Chelene knew that the basement walls were cracked and bowed and that she hired someone to install paneling before offering to sell the house. Did she have a duty to disclose this defect to Marta? Could a court find that Chelene's silence in this situation constituted misrepresentation? Explain.
4. Can Marta obtain rescission of the contract based on undue influence? If the sale to Janis had been completed before her death, could Janis have obtained rescission based on undue influence? Explain.

Debate This

Many countries have eliminated the Statute of Frauds except for sales of real estate. The United States should do the same.

Key Terms

bilateral mistake 311
collateral promise 322
innocent misrepresentation 316
integrated contract 328
latent defect 315
negligent misrepresentation 316
parol evidence rule 325
prenuptial agreement 322
scienter 316
Statute of Frauds 319
undue influence 318
unilateral mistake 311
voluntary consent 310

Chapter Summary: Defenses to Contract Enforceability

Mistakes	1. **Unilateral**—Generally, the mistaken party is bound by the contract *unless* (a) the other party knows or should have known of the mistake or (b) the mistake is a substantial mathematical error—such as an error in addition or subtraction—made inadvertently and without gross negligence. 2. **Bilateral (mutual)**—When both parties are mistaken about the same material fact, such as identity, either party can avoid the contract.
Fraudulent Misrepresentation	When fraud occurs, the innocent party can usually enforce or avoid the contract. The following elements are necessary to establish fraud: 1. A misrepresentation of a material fact must occur. 2. There must be an intent to deceive. 3. The innocent party must justifiably rely on the misrepresentation. 4. To collect damages, a party must have been harmed as a result of the misrepresentation.

(Continues)

Undue Influence and Duress	1. **Undue influence**—Arises from special relationships, such as fiduciary relationships, in which one party's free will has been overcome by the undue influence exerted by the other party. The contract is voidable because it lacks voluntary consent. 2. **Duress**—The tactic of forcing a party to enter a contract under the fear of a threat—for instance, the threat of violence or serious economic loss. The party forced to enter the contract can rescind the contract.
The Writing Requirement	1. **Applicability**—The following types of contracts fall under the Statute of Frauds and must be in writing to be enforceable: **a.** Contracts involving interests in land, such as sales, leases, or mortgages. **b.** Contracts that cannot by their terms be fully performed within one year from the day after the contract's formation. **c.** Collateral promises, such as contracts made between a guarantor and a creditor whose terms make the guarantor secondarily liable. *Exception:* the "main purpose" rule. **d.** Promises made in consideration of marriage, including promises to make a monetary payment or give property in consideration of a promise to marry and prenuptial agreements made in consideration of marriage. **e.** Contracts for the sale of goods priced at $500 or more under the Statute of Frauds provision in Section 2–201 of the Uniform Commercial Code. 2. **Exceptions**—Partial performance, admissions, and promissory estoppel. Oral contracts for customized goods may be enforced in certain circumstances. Another exception concerns oral contracts between merchants that have been confirmed in writing. 3. **Sufficiency of the writing or electronic record**—To constitute an enforceable contract under the Statute of Frauds, under most state laws a writing must be signed by the party against whom enforcement is sought, name the parties, identify the subject matter and the consideration, and state with reasonable certainty the essential terms of the contract. Under the UCC, a contract for a sale of goods is not enforceable beyond the quantity of goods shown in the contract.
The Parol Evidence Rule	The parol evidence rule prohibits the introduction at trial of evidence of the parties' prior or contemporaneous negotiations or agreements if this evidence contradicts or varies the terms of the parties' written contract. The written contract is assumed to be the complete embodiment of the parties' agreement. Because of the rigidity of the parol evidence rule, courts make a number of exceptions. For instance, courts may allow parol evidence when a contract is void or voidable, contains ambiguous terms, or is incomplete.

Issue Spotters

1. In selling a house, Matt tells Ann that the wiring, fixtures, and appliances are of a certain quality. Matt knows nothing about the quality, but it is not as specified. Ann buys the house. On learning the true quality, Ann confronts Matt. He says he wasn't trying to fool her, he was only trying to make a sale. Can she rescind the deal? Why or why not? (See *Fraudulent Misrepresentation.*)

2. Paula orally agrees to work with Next Corporation in New York City for two years. Paula moves her family to the city and begins work. Three months later, Paula is fired for no stated cause. She sues for reinstatement and back pay. Next Corporation argues that there is no written contract between them. What will the court say? (See *The Writing Requirement.*)

—Check your answers to the *Issue Spotters* against the answers provided in Appendix D.

Business Scenarios and Case Problems

13–1. Voluntary Consent. Jerome is an elderly man who lives with his nephew, Philip. Jerome is totally dependent on Philip's support. Philip tells Jerome that unless Jerome transfers a tract of land he owns to Philip for a price 30 percent below market value, Philip will no longer support and take care of him. Jerome enters into the contract. Discuss fully whether Jerome can set aside this contract. (See *Undue Influence and Duress.*)

13–2. Statute of Frauds. Gemma promises a local hardware store that she will pay for a lawn mower that her brother is purchasing on credit if the brother fails to pay the debt. Must this promise be in writing to be enforceable? Why or why not? (See *The Writing Requirement*).

13–3. The Parol Evidence Rule. Rimma Vaks and her husband, Steven Mangano, executed a written contract with Denise Ryan and Ryan Auction Co. to auction their furnishings. The six-page contract provided a detailed summary of the parties' agreement. It addressed the items to be auctioned, how reserve prices would be determined, and the amount of Ryan's commission. When a dispute arose between the parties, Vaks and Mangano sued Ryan for breach of contract. Vaks and Mangano asserted that, before they executed the contract, Ryan had made various oral representations that were inconsistent with the terms of their written agreement. Assuming that their written contract was valid, can Vaks and Mangano recover for breach of an oral contract? Why or why not? [*Vaks v. Ryan,* 2014 Mass.App.Div. 37 (2014)]. (See *The Parol Evidence Rule.*)

13–4. Promises Made in Consideration of Marriage. After twenty-nine years of marriage, Robert and Mary Lou Tuttle were divorced. They admitted in court that before they were married, they had signed a prenuptial agreement. They both acknowledged that the agreement had stated that both would keep their own property and anything derived from that property. Robert came into the marriage owning farmland, while Mary Lou owned no real estate. During the marriage, ten different parcels of land, totaling about six hundred acres, were acquired, and two corporations, Tuttle Grain, Inc., and Tuttle Farms, Inc., were formed. A copy of the prenuptial agreement could not be found. Can the court enforce the agreement without a writing? Why or why not? [*In re Marriage of Tuttle,* 2013 WL 164035 (Ill.App. 5 Dist. 2013)] (See *The Writing Requirement.*)

13–5. Business Case Problem with Sample Answer—Fraudulent Misrepresentation. Joy Pervis and Brenda Pauley worked together as talent agents in Georgia. When Pervis "discovered" actress Dakota Fanning, Pervis sent Fanning's audition tape to Cindy Osbrink, a talent agent in California. Osbrink agreed to represent Fanning in California and to pay 3 percent of Osbrink's commissions to Pervis and Pauley, who agreed to split the payments equally. Six years later, Pervis told Pauley that their agreement with Osbrink had expired and there would be no more payments. Nevertheless, Pervis continued to receive payments from Osbrink. Each time Pauley asked about commissions, however, Pervis replied that she was not receiving any. Do these facts evidence fraud? Explain. [*In re Pervis,* 512 Bankr. 348 (N.D.Ga. 2014)] (See *Fraudulent Misrepresentation.*)

—For a sample answer to Problem 13–5, go to Appendix E.

13–6. Promises Made in Consideration of Marriage. Before their marriage, Linda and Gerald Heiden executed a prenuptial agreement. The agreement provided that "no spouse shall have any right in the property of the other spouse, even in the event of the death of either party." The description of Gerald's separate property included a settlement from a personal injury suit. Twenty-four years later, Linda filed for divorce. The court ruled that the prenuptial agreement applied only in the event of death, not divorce, and entered a judgment that included a property division and spousal support award. The ruling disparately favored Linda, whose monthly income with spousal support would be $4,467, leaving Gerald with only $1,116. Did the court interpret the Heidens' prenuptial agreement correctly? Discuss. [*Heiden v. Heiden,* 2015 WL 849006 (Mich.App. 2015)] (See *The Writing Requirement.*)

13–7. Exceptions to the Writing Requirement. Madeline Castellotti was the sole shareholder of Whole Pies, Inc., which owns John's Pizzeria in New York City. Her other assets included a 51 percent interest in a real estate partnership, a residence on Staten Island, and various bank accounts. When Madeline's son, Peter Castellotti, was going through a divorce, Madeline wanted to prevent Peter's then-wife Rea from benefiting from any of Madeline's assets. With this purpose in mind, she removed Peter from her will, leaving her daughter, Lisa Free, as the sole beneficiary. Lisa orally agreed to provide Peter with half of the income generated by the assets after their mother's death if his divorce was still pending and to transfer half of the assets after the divorce was final. In reliance on those promises, Peter agreed to pay the property taxes for the estate. Madeline died and Peter paid the taxes, but Lisa reneged on the deal. Peter filed a suit in a New York state court against his sister to recover. Should the court enforce the promise? On what legal theory? [*Castellotti v. Free,* 138 A.D.3d 198, 27 N.Y.S.3d 507 (1 Dept. 2016)] (See *The Writing Requirement.*)

13–8. The Statute of Frauds. Michael Brannon filed a suit in an Ohio state court against Derrick and Nancy Edman, claiming breach of an alleged oral contract for the sale of certain real property in Akron. Brannon asserted that he had moved onto the property and made significant improvements to the house, investing time and money in anticipation of receiving ownership of the property after all of the payments had been made. Brannon also said that he had diligently made the payments, and the Edmans had accepted them, crediting each against the remaining balance, until about half of the price had been paid. But when he attempted to make a payment in the third year of his occupancy, the Edmans refused it and threatened him with eviction. The Edmans argued that the Statute of Frauds barred Brannon's claim. Is this alleged contract enforceable? Explain. [*Brannon v. Edman,* 2018 -Ohio- 70, (9th Dist. 2018)] (See *The Writing Requirement.*)

A Question of Ethics—The IDDR Approach and Fraudulent Misrepresentation. Data Consulting Group contracted with Weston Medsurg Center, PLLC, a health-care facility in Charlotte, North Carolina, to install, maintain, and manage Weston's computers and software. At about the same time, Ginger

Blackwood began to work for Weston as a medical billing and coding specialist. Soon, she was submitting false time reports and converting Weston documents and data to her own purposes. On her request, Data Consulting manager Nasko Dinev removed evidence of her actions from her work computer. [*Weston Medsurg Center, PLLC v. Blackwood*, 795 S.E.2d 829 (2017)] (See *Fraudulent Misrepresentation*.)

1. What should Weston do when it learns of these activities? With respect to this situation, identify and consider the firm's primary ethical dilemma using the IDDR approach.
2. Suppose that despite Dinev's efforts, Weston is later able to recover the data that was removed from Blackwood's work computer. How might this affect Weston's choices? Discuss.

Critical Thinking and Writing Assignments

13–9. Time-Limited Group Assignment—The Writing Requirement. Jason Novell, doing business as Novell Associates, hired Barbara Meade as an independent contractor. The parties orally agreed on the terms of employment, including payment of a share of the company's income to Meade, but they did not put anything in writing. Two years later, Meade quit. Novell then told Meade that she was entitled to $9,602—25 percent of the difference between the accounts receivable and the accounts payable as of Meade's last day of work. Meade disagreed and demanded more than $63,500—25 percent of the revenue from all invoices, less the cost of materials and outside processing, for each of the years that she had worked for Novell. Meade filed a lawsuit against Novell for breach of contract. (See *The Writing Requirement*.)

1. The first group will evaluate whether the parties had an enforceable contract.
2. The second group will decide whether the parties' oral agreement falls within any exception to the Statute of Frauds.
3. The third group will discuss how the lawsuit would be affected if Novell admitted that the parties had an oral contract under which Meade was entitled to a share of the company's income, but claimed that they had agreed she would receive only 15 percent of the income from invoices, not 25 percent.

Third Party Rights and Discharge

14

"The laws of a state change with the changing times."

Aeschylus
525–456 B.C.E.
(Greek dramatist)

Once it has been determined that a valid and legally enforceable contract exists, attention can turn to the rights and duties of the parties to the contract. A contract is a private agreement between the parties who have entered into it, and traditionally these parties alone have rights and liabilities under the contract. This principle is referred to as **privity of contract,** and it establishes the basic principle that third parties have no rights in contracts to which they are not parties.

You may expect by now that for every rule of contract law, there is an exception. As times change, so must the laws, as indicated in the chapter-opening quotation. When justice cannot be served by adherence to a rule of law, exceptions to the rule must be made. For instance, privity of contract is not required for an injured person to recover damages under product liability laws.

In this chapter, we look at some exceptions to the rule of privity of contract: namely, *assignments*, *delegations*, and *third party beneficiary contracts*. We also examine how contractual obligations can be *discharged* and the degree of performance required to discharge a contract.

Focus Questions

The four Focus Questions *below are designed to help improve your understanding. After reading this chapter, you should be able to answer the following questions:*

1. What is an assignment?
2. In what situations is the delegation of duties prohibited?
3. What factors indicate that a third party beneficiary is an intended beneficiary?
4. When is a breach considered material, and what effect does that have on the other party's obligation to perform?

Privity of Contract The relationship that exists between the promisor and the promisee of a contract.

14–1 Assignments

In a bilateral contract, the two parties have corresponding rights and duties. One party has a *right* to require the other to perform some task, and the other has a *duty* to perform it. Sometimes, though, a party will transfer contractual rights to someone else.

Assignment The transfer to another of all or part of one's rights arising under a contract.

Focus Question 1
What is an assignment?

The transfer of contract *rights* to a third person is known as an **assignment.** (The transfer of contract duties is a *delegation*, as will be discussed later in this chapter.)

Assignments are important because they are often used in business financing. Lending institutions, such as banks, frequently assign the rights to receive payments under their loan contracts to other firms, which pay for those rights. **Example 14.1** Kendra obtains a loan from a bank to finance an online business venture. Later, she receives a notice from the bank stating that it has transferred (assigned) its rights to receive payments on the loan to another firm. When it is time to repay the loan, Kendra must make the payments to that other firm. ■

Note also that lenders that make *mortgage loans* (loans that enable prospective home buyers to purchase real estate) often assign their rights to collect the mortgage payments to a third party. Following an assignment, the home buyer is notified that future payments must be made to the third party, rather than to the original lender. Billions of dollars change hands daily in the business world in the form of assignments of rights in contracts. If it were not possible to transfer contractual rights, many businesses could not continue to operate.

14–1a Effect of an Assignment

Assignor A party who transfers (assigns) rights under a contract to another party (the *assignee*).

Assignee A party to whom rights under a contract are transferred, or assigned.

Obligee One to whom an obligation is owed.

Obligor One who owes an obligation to another.

In an assignment, the party assigning the rights to a third party is known as the **assignor,**[1] and the party receiving the rights is the **assignee.**[2] Other terms traditionally used to describe the parties in assignment relationships are **obligee** (the person to whom a duty, or obligation, is owed) and **obligor** (the person who is obligated to perform the duty).

In general, an assignment can take any form, oral or written, although it is advisable to put all assignments in writing. Of course, assignments covered by the Statute of Frauds—such as an assignment of an interest in land—must be in writing to be enforceable. In addition, most states require contracts for the assignment of wages to be in writing.[3] There are other assignments that must be in writing as well.

Extinguishes the Rights of the Assignor When rights under a contract are assigned unconditionally, the rights of the assignor are extinguished.[4] The assignee has a right to demand performance from the other original party to the contract, the obligor.

Example 14.2 Brenda is obligated by contract to pay Alex $1,000. Brenda is the obligor because she owes an obligation, or duty, to Alex. Alex is the obligee, the one to whom the obligation is owed. If Alex then assigns his right to receive the $1,000 to Charles, Alex is the assignor and Charles is the assignee. Charles now becomes the obligee because Brenda owes Charles the $1,000. Here, a valid assignment of a debt exists. Charles (the assignee-obligee) is entitled to enforce payment in court if Brenda (the obligor) does not pay him the $1,000. (Alex is no longer entitled to enforce payment because the assignment extinguished his original contract rights.) ■ These concepts are illustrated in Exhibit 14–1.

Assignee Takes Rights Subject to Defenses The assignee obtains only those rights that the assignor originally had. In addition, the assignee's rights are subject to the defenses that the obligor has against the assignor.

Example 14.3 Returning to *Example 14.2*, suppose that Brenda owes Alex the $1,000 under a contract in which she agreed to buy Alex's Microsoft Surface Pro. When Brenda decided to purchase the tablet, she relied on Alex's fraudulent misrepresentation that it had an Intel Core i7 processor. When Brenda discovers that its processor is an Intel i3, she tells Alex that she

1. Pronounced uh-*sye*-nore.
2. Pronounced uh-*sye-nee.*
3. See, for example, California Labor Code Section 300.
4. *Restatement (Second) of Contracts,* Section 317.

Exhibit 14–1 Assignment Relationships

In the assignment relationship illustrated here, Alex assigns his *rights* under a contract that he made with Brenda to a third party, Charles. Alex thus becomes the *assignor* and Charles the *assignee* of the contractual rights. Brenda, the *obligor*, now owes performance to Charles instead of Alex. Alex's original contractual rights are extinguished after assignment.

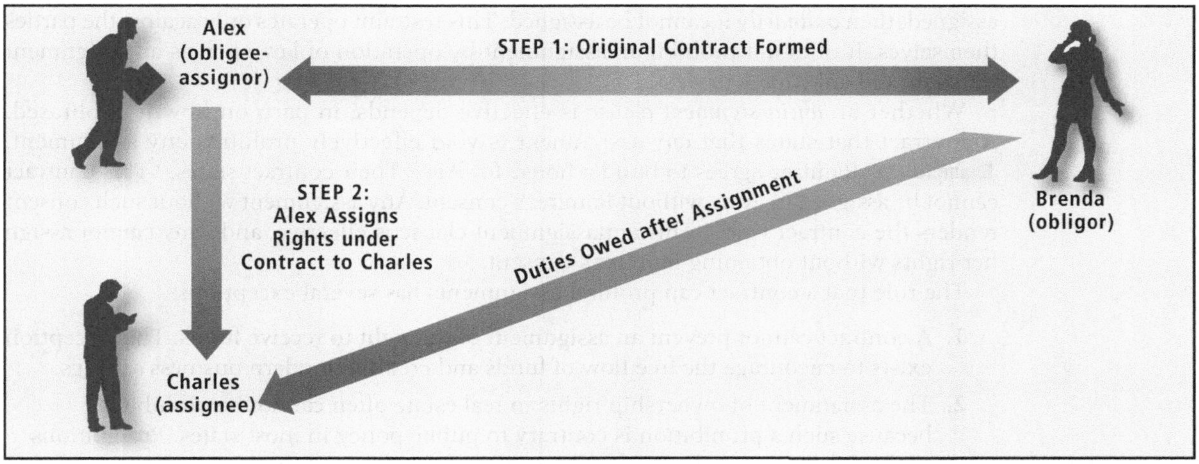

is going to return the device to him and cancel the contract. Even though Alex has assigned his "right" to receive the $1,000 to Charles, Brenda need not pay Charles the $1,000. Brenda can raise the defense of Alex's fraudulent misrepresentation to avoid payment.

14–1b Rights That Cannot Be Assigned

As a general rule, all rights can be assigned. Exceptions are made, however, in the following special circumstances.

When a Statute Expressly Prohibits Assignment If a statute expressly prohibits assignment, the right in question cannot be assigned. For instance, in many states, workers' compensation statutes prohibit an employee who is receiving benefits from assigning them to another.

When a Contract Is Personal in Nature When a contract is for personal services, the rights under the contract normally cannot be assigned unless all that remains is a monetary payment.[5] **Example 14.4** Anton signs a contract to be a tutor for Marisa's children. Marisa then attempts to assign to Roberto her right to Anton's services. Roberto cannot enforce the contract against Anton. Roberto's children may be more difficult to tutor than Marisa's. Thus, if Marisa could assign her rights to Anton's services to Roberto, it would change the nature of Anton's obligation. Because personal services are unique to the person rendering them, rights to receive personal services are likewise unique and cannot be assigned.

When an Assignment Will Significantly Change the Risk or Duties of the Obligor A right cannot be assigned if assignment will significantly alter the risks or the duties of the obligor.[6] **Example 14.5** Alice has a hotel, and to insure it, she takes out a policy with Northwest Insurance Company. The policy insures against fire, theft, floods, and vandalism. Alice attempts to assign the insurance policy to Carmen, who owns a hotel in another city.

The assignment is ineffective because it may substantially alter the insurance company's duty of performance and the risk that the company undertakes. An insurance company

5. *Restatement (Second) of Contracts*, Sections 317 and 318.
6. See Section 2–210(2) of the Uniform Commercial Code (UCC).

evaluates the particular risk associated with a specific party and tailors its policy to fit that risk. If the policy were assigned to a third party, the insurance risk could be materially altered.

When the Contract Prohibits Assignment If a contract stipulates that the right cannot be assigned, then *ordinarily* it cannot be assigned. This restraint operates only against the parties themselves. It does not prohibit an assignment by operation of law, such as an assignment pursuant to bankruptcy or death.

Whether an *antiassignment clause* is effective depends, in part, on how it is phrased. A contract that states that *any* assignment is void effectively prohibits any assignment. **Example 14.6** Ramirez agrees to build a house for Amy. Their contract states, "This contract cannot be assigned by Amy without Ramirez's consent. Any assignment without such consent renders the contract void." This antiassignment clause is effective, and Amy cannot assign her rights without obtaining Ramirez's consent.

The rule that a contract can prohibit assignments has several exceptions:

1. A contract cannot prevent an assignment of the right to receive funds. This exception exists to encourage the free flow of funds and credit in modern business settings.
2. The assignment of ownership rights in real estate often cannot be prohibited because such a prohibition is contrary to public policy in most states. Prohibitions of this kind are called restraints against **alienation** (the voluntary transfer of land ownership).
3. The assignment of negotiable instruments (such as checks and promissory notes) cannot be prohibited.
4. In a contract for the sale of goods, the right to receive payments on an account or damages for breach of contract may be assigned even though the sales contract prohibits such an assignment.[7]

Alienation The transfer of title to real property (which "alienates" the real property from the former owner).

14–1c Notice of Assignment

Once a valid assignment of rights has been made to a third party, the third party should notify the obligor of the assignment (for instance, in *Example 14.2*, Charles should notify Brenda). Giving notice is not legally necessary to establish the validity of the assignment because an assignment is effective immediately, whether or not notice is given. Two major problems arise, however, when notice of the assignment is *not* given to the obligor.

Priority Issues If the assignor assigns the same right to two different persons, the question arises as to which one has priority—that is, which one has the right to the performance by the obligor. The rule most often observed in the United States is that the first assignment in time is the first in right. Some states, though, follow the English rule, which basically gives priority to the first assignee who gives notice.

Example 14.7 Jason owes Alexis $5,000 under a contract. Alexis first assigns the claim to Louisa, who does not give notice to Jason. Then Alexis assigns it to Dorman, who notifies Jason. In most states, Louisa would have priority because the assignment to her was first in time. In some states, however, Dorman would have priority because he gave first notice.

Potential for Discharge by Performance to the Wrong Party Until the obligor has notice of an assignment, the obligor can discharge any obligations by performance to the assignor, and this performance constitutes a discharge to the assignee. Once the obligor receives proper notice, only performance to the assignee can discharge the obligor's obligations.

7. UCC 2–210(2).

Example 14.8 Recall that Alexis, the obligee in *Example 14.7*, assigned to Louisa her right to collect $5,000 from Jason, and Louisa did not give notice to Jason. What will happen if Jason later pays Alexis the $5,000? Although the assignment was valid, Jason's payment to Alexis will discharge the debt. Louisa's failure to notify Jason of the assignment will cause her to lose the right to collect the $5,000 from Jason. (Note that Louisa will still have a claim against Alexis for the $5,000.) If Louisa had given Jason notice of the assignment, Jason's payment to Alexis would not have discharged the debt.

14–2 Delegations

Just as a party can transfer rights to a third party through an assignment, a party can also transfer duties. Duties are not assigned, however. They are *delegated*. Normally, a **delegation of duties** does not relieve the party making the delegation (the **delegator**) of the obligation to perform in the event that the party to whom the duty has been delegated (the **delegatee**) fails to perform.

No special form is required to create a valid delegation of duties. As long as the delegator expresses an intention to make the delegation, it is effective. The delegator need not even use the word *delegate*. Exhibit 14–2 illustrates delegation relationships.

Delegation of Duties The transfer to another of a contractual duty.

Delegator A party who transfers (delegates) obligations under a contract to another party (the *delegatee*).

Delegatee A party to whom contractual obligations are transferred, or delegated.

14–2a Duties That Cannot Be Delegated

As a general rule, any duty can be delegated. This rule has some exceptions, however. Delegation is prohibited in the following circumstances:

1. When performance depends on the personal skill or talents of the obligor.
2. When special trust has been placed in the obligor.
3. When performance by a third party will vary materially from that expected by the obligee.
4. When the contract expressly prohibits delegation.

Focus Question 2
In what situations is the delegation of duties prohibited?

Exhibit 14–2 Delegation Relationships

In the delegation relationship illustrated here, Brower delegates her *duties* under a contract that she made with Horton to a third party, Kuhn. Brower thus becomes the *delegator* and Kuhn the *delegatee* of the contractual duties. Kuhn now owes performance of the contractual duties to Horton. Note that a delegation of duties normally does not relieve the delegator (Brower) of liability if the delegatee (Kuhn) fails to perform the contractual duties.

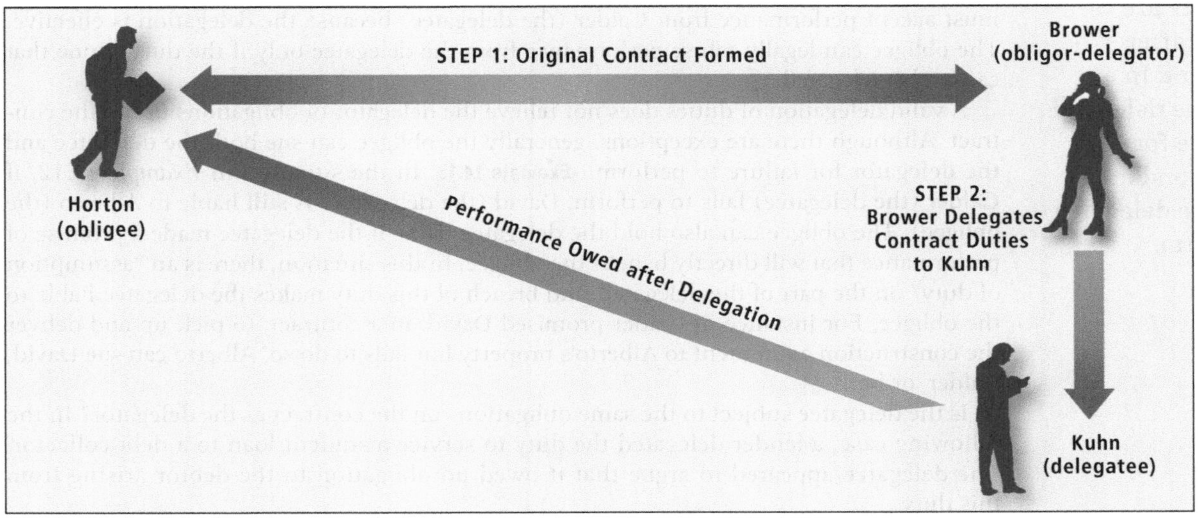

When the Duties Are Personal in Nature When special trust has been placed in the obligor or when performance depends on the obligor's personal skill or talents, contractual duties cannot be delegated. **Example 14.9** O'Brien, who is impressed with Brodie's ability to perform veterinary surgery, contracts with Brodie to have her perform surgery on O'Brien's prize-winning stallion in July. Brodie later decides that she would rather spend the summer at the beach, so she delegates her duties under the contract to Lopez, who is also a competent veterinary surgeon. The delegation is not effective without O'Brien's consent, no matter how competent Lopez is, because the contract is for *personal* performance.

In contrast, nonpersonal duties may be delegated. Suppose that, in *Example 14.9*, Brodie contracts with O'Brien to pick up a large horse trailer and deliver it to O'Brien's property. Brodie delegates this duty to Lopez, who owns a towing business. This delegation is effective because the performance required is of a *routine* and *nonpersonal* nature.

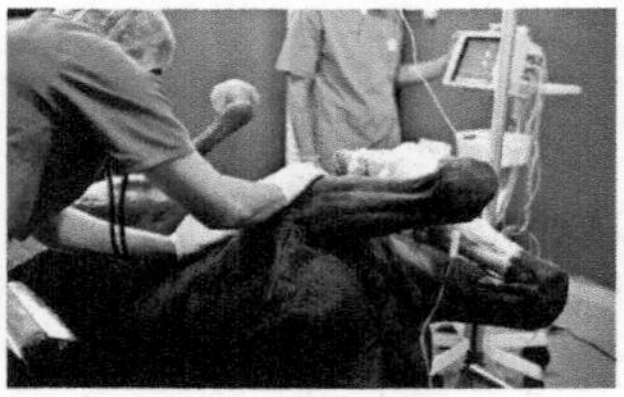

Under what circumstances may a veterinary surgeon delegate her duties to another veterinarian?

When Performance by a Third Party Will Vary Materially from That Expected by the Obligee When performance by a third party will vary materially from that expected by the obligee under the contract, contractual duties cannot be delegated. **Example 14.10** Jared, a wealthy investor, establishes the company Heaven Sent to provide grants of capital to struggling but potentially successful businesses. Jared contracts with Merilyn, whose judgment Jared trusts, to select the recipients of the grants. Later, Merilyn delegates this duty to Donald. Jared does not trust Donald's ability to select worthy recipients. This delegation is not effective because it materially alters Jared's expectations under the contract with Merilyn.

When the Contract Prohibits Delegation When the contract expressly prohibits delegation by including an *antidelegation clause*, the duties cannot be delegated. **Example 14.11** Dakota Company contracts with Belisario, a certified public accountant, to perform its audits. Because the contract prohibits delegation, Belisario cannot delegate the duty to perform the audits to another accountant—not even an accountant at the same firm.

14–2b Effect of a Delegation

Know This
In an assignment, the assignor's original contract rights are extinguished after the assignment. In a delegation, the delegator remains liable for performance under the contract if the delegatee fails to perform.

If a delegation of duties is enforceable, the obligee (the one to whom performance is owed) must accept performance from the delegatee (the one to whom the duties are delegated). **Example 14.12** David has a duty to pick up and deliver heavy construction machinery to Alberto's property. David delegates his duty to Calder. In this situation, Alberto (the obligee) must accept performance from Calder (the delegatee) because the delegation is effective. The obligee can legally refuse performance from the delegatee only if the duty is one that cannot be delegated.

A valid delegation of duties does not relieve the delegator of obligations under the contract. Although there are exceptions, generally the obligee can sue both the delegatee and the delegator for failure to perform. **Example 14.13** In the situation in *Example 14.12*, if Calder (the delegatee) fails to perform, David (the delegator) is still liable to Alberto (the obligee). The obligee can also hold the delegatee liable if the delegatee made a promise of performance that will directly benefit the obligee. In this situation, there is an "assumption of duty" on the part of the delegatee, and breach of this duty makes the delegatee liable to the obligee. For instance, if Calder promised David, in a contract, to pick up and deliver the construction equipment to Alberto's property but fails to do so, Alberto can sue David, Calder, or both.

Is the delegatee subject to the same obligations on the contract as the delegator? In the following case, a lender delegated the duty to service a student loan to a debt collector. The delegatee appeared to argue that it owed no obligation to the debtor arising from this duty.

Case 14.1

Mirandette v. Nelnet, Inc.

United States Court of Appeals, Sixth Circuit, 720 Fed.Appx. 288 (2018).

Facts To pay for his daughter's education, Kurt Mirandette borrowed the funds. As a condition of the loan, Mirandette signed a "Master Promissory Note" (MPN). The MPN did not specify when payments on the loan were to be credited. The loan was serviced by Nelnet, Inc., and Nelnet Servicing, LLC, which credited Mirandette's payments ten to thirty days after he mailed the checks. Mirandette filed a suit in a federal district court against the Nelnet companies, claiming breach of contract. He alleged that the defendants manipulated the date on which they credited the payments, resulting in the wrongful accrual of interest and late fees. The defendants responded that the MPN did not obligate them to credit payments as of a certain date. The court dismissed the suit. Mirandette appealed.

Issue Without proof to the contrary, does a delegatee of a duty to service a loan owe any obligation to the debtor?

Decision Yes. The U.S. Court of Appeals for the Sixth Circuit reversed the district court's dismissal of Mirandette's suit and remanded the case.

Reason The defendants argued first that Mirandette contracted with a third-party lender—not the defendants—to obtain the loan. The lender delegated the duty to service the loan to the defendants. The appellate court concluded that this argument "fails" because the defendants did not show that they had "no obligation to the debtor arising from their acceptance of the asserted delegation of the duty to service the loan."

The defendants also contended that they could credit Mirandette's payments on the loan whenever they chose because the MPN did not specify when the payments were to be credited. The court found this contention to be "untenable." Under this interpretation, the defendants could avoid crediting the payments indefinitely and charge interest on the full principal for the entire period of the loan. "Such an absurdity cannot have been intended by the parties signing this contract." Mirandette theorized that his payments should be credited on receipt. Because the lower court had not addressed this theory, the appellate court remanded the case for its consideration.

Critical Thinking

- **Legal Environment** *The MPN stated that "applicable state law . . . may provide for certain borrower rights." The Nelnet companies are based in Nebraska. Nebraska's commercial code provides that the delivery of a check marks the date of payment. How might this provision affect the decision of the lower court on remand?*
- **Economic** *According to the defendants' reasoning, borrowers would have no contract remedies if loan servicers overcharged them. What effect might this circumstance have in the market for credit? Discuss.*

14–2c "Assignment of All Rights"

Sometimes, a contract provides for an "assignment of all rights." This wording may create both an assignment of rights and a delegation of duties.[8] Typically, this situation occurs when general words are used, such as "I assign the contract" or "I assign all my rights under the contract." A court normally will construe such words as implying both an assignment of rights and a delegation of any duties of performance. Thus, the assignor remains liable if the assignee fails to perform the contractual obligations.

14–3 Third Party Beneficiaries

Another exception to the doctrine of privity of contract arises when the contract is intended to benefit a third party. The original parties to a contract can agree that the contract performance should be rendered to or directly benefit a third person. When this happens, the third

8. See UCC 2-210(1), (4); and *Restatement (Second) of Contracts*, Section 328.

Third Party Beneficiary One who is not a party to the contract but who stands to benefit from the contract's performance.

Intended Beneficiary A third party for whose benefit a contract is formed. An intended beneficiary can sue the promisor if the contract is breached.

person becomes an *intended* **third party beneficiary** of the contract. As the **intended beneficiary** of the contract, the third party has legal rights and can sue the promisor directly for breach of the contract.

14–3a Who Is the Promisor?

Who, though, is the promisor? In a bilateral contract, both parties to the contract make promises that can be enforced, so the court has to determine which party made the promise that benefits the third party. That person is the promisor.

In effect, allowing a third party to sue the promisor directly circumvents the "middle person" (the promisee) and thus reduces the burden on the courts. Otherwise, the third party would sue the promisee, who would then sue the promisor.

Classic Case Example 14.14 The classic case that gave third party beneficiaries the right to bring a suit directly against a promisor was decided in 1859. The case involved three parties—Holly, Lawrence, and Fox. Holly had borrowed $300 from Lawrence. Shortly thereafter, Holly loaned $300 to Fox, who in return promised Holly that he would pay Holly's debt to Lawrence on the following day. When Lawrence failed to obtain the $300 from Fox, he sued Fox to recover the funds. The court had to decide whether Lawrence could sue Fox directly (rather than suing Holly). The court held that when "a promise [is] made for the benefit of another, he for whose benefit it is made may bring an action for its breach."[9]

In the following case, the third party beneficiary was the former lead singer for a 1980s New Wave band. The promisor was the band's recording company and distributor. The promisee was a corporation formed by the band members to receive the band's royalties. The contract involved the payment of those royalties. The question before the court was whether the third party beneficiary could sue for breach of contract when the promisee lacked the capacity to bring the suit.

9. *Lawrence v. Fox*, 20 N.Y. 268 (1859).

Case 14.2

Bozzio v. EMI Group, Ltd.

United States Court of Appeals, Ninth Circuit, 811 F.3d 1144 (2016).

Facts In the 1980s, Dale Bozzio was the front woman of a Los Angeles–based New Wave band, Missing Persons. The members of the band formed Missing Persons, Inc. (MPI), a "loan-out" corporation through which to provide their artistic services.[a] Capitol Records (the promisor) entered into a contract with MPI (the promisee) to produce and market the band's recordings. The band members agreed to look solely to MPI for payment of all royalties and not to bring any claims against Capitol Records. After the group disbanded, MPI's corporate status was suspended for nonpayment of state corporate taxes.

Two decades later, Bozzio filed a suit in a federal district court against Capitol Records and others (including EMI Group, Ltd.), seeking royalties on their licensing for sale of "digital downloads, ringtones . . . , and streaming music" featuring the recordings of Missing Persons. Bozzio asserted that she was a third party beneficiary of the contract between Capitol Records and MPI with a right to sue directly for its enforcement.

The court dismissed the complaint on the ground that MPI, as a suspended corporation, lacked the capacity to sue. Bozzio appealed.

Issue Could Bozzio sue Capitol Records as a third party beneficiary even though MPI's corporate status had been suspended for nonpayment of state taxes?

Decision Yes. The U.S. Court of Appeals for the Ninth Circuit reversed the lower court's dismissal of the complaint and remanded the case. The appellate court concluded that MPI's

a. A *loan-out corporation* is a corporation formed for the financial benefit of artists and entertainers. Normally, its only function is to provide the services of an artist to producers and others.

status was irrelevant with respect to Bozzio's right to bring her third party claim.

Reason The court based its decision on controlling case law. "The California Supreme Court has not decided whether a promisee corporation's suspended status precludes suit by a third-party beneficiary of the contract, but . . . the California Court of Appeal [has] suggested that a third-party beneficiary suit may go forward notwithstanding the promisee's incapacity to sue."

Two issues that remained to be resolved on remand were whether Bozzio was, in fact, a third party beneficiary of the contract between MPI and Capitol Records, and if so, whether she forfeited the right to sue to enforce that contract when she agreed to look solely to MPI for payment of all royalties and not to bring any claims against Capitol Records.

Critical Thinking

- **Legal Environment** *Capitol Records will, of course, contend that Bozzio's agreement to look solely to MPI for payment of all royalties and not to bring any claims against Capitol Records bars her suit in this case. What would be Bozzio's best response to this contention? Discuss.*
- **E-Commerce** *What effect might an ultimate decision in the plaintiff's favor in this case have on the licensing and sale of digital music? Explain.*

14–3b Types of Intended Beneficiaries

Intended beneficiaries can be further classified as *creditor beneficiaries* or *donee beneficiaries.*

Creditor Beneficiary Like the plaintiff in *Classic Case Example 14.14*, a *creditor beneficiary* benefits from a contract in which one party (the promisor) promises another party (the promisee) to perform a duty that the promisee owes to a third party (the creditor beneficiary). As an intended beneficiary, the creditor beneficiary can sue the promisor directly to enforce the contract.

Case Example 14.15 Sharmalee Goonewardene filed a breach of contract lawsuit against ADP, a company that provided payroll services to her ex-employer, a travel agency called Altour. Goonewardene claimed that ADP was potentially liable for her unpaid wages under the third party beneficiary doctrine. A California appeals court concurred, reasoning that ADP had contracted with Altour to perform a duty—the payment of salary—owed to Goonewardene. Therefore, she could sue ADP as a third party beneficiary.

The California Supreme Court reversed, citing a fatal flaw in the lower court's analysis. That is, ADP did not pay Goonewardene's salary, Altour did. ADP's primary function was to relieve Altour of a time-consuming and complicated task that, if done improperly, can result in significant tax penalties. Evidently, the contract between Altour and ADP was meant to benefit ADP, not Goonewardene. Thus, the court found, she was *not* a third party beneficiary of that contract, and her suit against APD could not move forward.[10]

Donee Beneficiary When a contract is made for the express purpose of giving a *gift* to a third party, the third party is a *donee beneficiary*. A donee beneficiary can sue the promisor directly to enforce the promise.

The most common donee beneficiary contract is a life insurance contract. **Example 14.16** Ben (the promisee) pays premiums to Standard Life, a life insurance company, and Standard Life (the promisor) promises to pay a certain amount on Ben's death to anyone Ben designates as a beneficiary. The designated beneficiary is a donee beneficiary under the life insurance policy and can enforce the payout promise made by the insurance company on Ben's death.

10. *Goonewardene v. ADP, LLC*, 434 P.3d 124, 243 Cal.Rptr.3d 299 (2019).

14–3c When the Rights of an Intended Beneficiary Vest

An intended third party beneficiary cannot enforce a contract against the original parties until the third party's rights have *vested*, meaning that the rights have taken effect and cannot be taken away. Until these rights have vested, the original parties to the contract—the promisor and the promisee—can modify or rescind the contract without the consent of the third party.

When do the rights of third parties vest? Generally, the rights vest when any of the following occurs:

1. When the third party demonstrates express consent to the agreement, such as by sending a letter, a note, or an e-mail acknowledging awareness of, and consent to, the contract.
2. When the third party materially changes position in detrimental reliance on the contract, such as when a donee beneficiary contracts to have a home built in reliance on the receipt of funds promised in a donee beneficiary contract.
3. When the conditions for vesting are satisfied. For instance, the rights of a beneficiary under a life insurance policy vest when the insured person dies.

14–3d Incidental Beneficiaries

Incidental Beneficiary A third party who benefits from a contract even though the contract was not formed for that purpose. An incidental beneficiary has no rights in the contract and cannot sue to have it enforced.

Sometimes, a third person receives a benefit from a contract even though that person's benefit is not the reason the contract was made. Such a person is known as an **incidental beneficiary.** Because the benefit is *unintentional*, an incidental beneficiary cannot sue to enforce the contract. Only intended beneficiaries acquire legal rights in a contract.

Classic Case Example 14.17 Spectators who attended an automobile race (the Grand Prix) sued the organizations that presented the event. The spectators were upset because fourteen of the twenty cars that were supposed to race dropped out at the last minute due to tire failures. The plaintiffs claimed that they were third party beneficiaries of the contract between the teams of drivers and the race promoters. They sought compensation for traveling to and attending the race. The court dismissed the plaintiffs' claims, however. "A failure to satisfy the subjective expectations of spectators at a sporting event is not actionable." The defendants did not have a contract with the spectators, and the spectators could not sue as third party beneficiaries.[11]

14–3e Identifying Intended versus Incidental Beneficiaries

In determining whether a party is an intended or an incidental beneficiary, the courts focus on the parties' intent, as expressed in the contract language and implied by the surrounding circumstances. Any beneficiary who is not deemed an intended beneficiary is considered incidental. Exhibit 14–3 graphically illustrates the distinction between intended and incidental beneficiaries.

Focus Question 3

What factors indicate that a third party beneficiary is an intended beneficiary?

Although no single test can embrace all possible situations, courts often apply the *reasonable person* test: Would a reasonable person in the position of the beneficiary believe that the promisee intended to confer on the beneficiary the right to enforce the contract? In addition, the presence of one or more of the following factors strongly indicates that the third party is an intended beneficiary of the contract:

1. Performance is rendered directly to the third party.
2. The third party has the right to control the details of performance.
3. The third party is expressly designated as a beneficiary in the contract.

---

11. *Bowers v. Federation Internationale de L'Automobile*, 461 F.Supp.2d 855 (S.D.Ind. 2006).

Exhibit 14–3 Third Party Beneficiaries

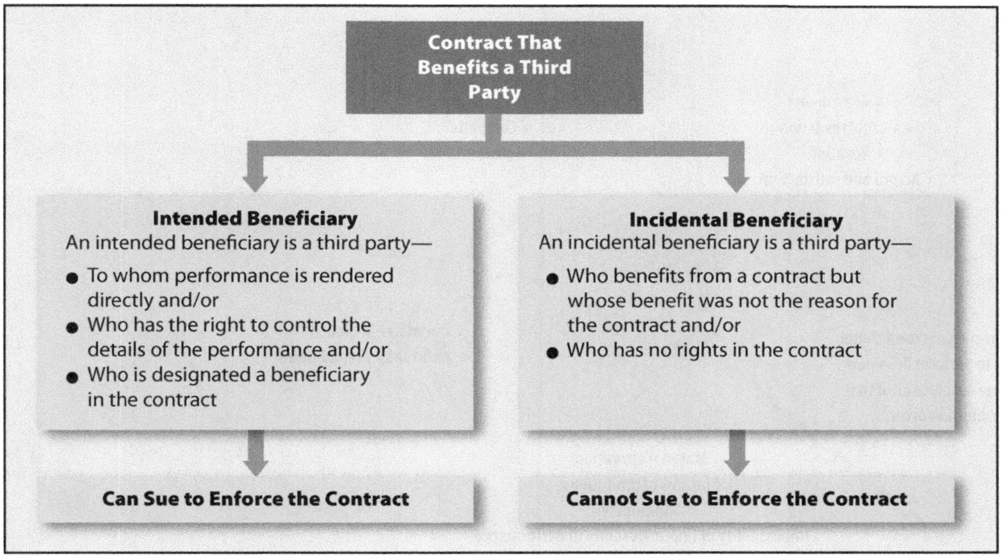

Case Example 14.18 New York City decided to build a fifteen-story forensic biology (DNA testing) laboratory next to Bellevue Hospital in Manhattan. The city turned the project over to the Dormitory Authority of the State of New York (DASNY), which oversees public projects. DASNY contracted with Perkins Eastman Architects, P.C., which hired Samson Construction Company to excavate the site and lay the foundation. Unfortunately, Samson's excavation of the site caused adjacent structures, including a building, sidewalks, roadbeds, sewers, and water systems, to "settle," causing about $37 million in damage.

DASNY and the city sued Samson and Perkins, alleging breach of contract. Even though the city was not named in the contract between Samson and Perkins, a state appellate court held that the city was an intended third party beneficiary. "The contract expressly states that a City agency will operate the DNA laboratory, and the City retained control over various aspects of the project."[12]

14–4 Contract Discharge

The most common way to **discharge**, or terminate, contractual duties is by the **performance** of those duties. The duty to perform under a contract may be *conditioned* on the occurrence or nonoccurrence of a certain event, or the duty may be *absolute*. As shown in Exhibit 14–4, in addition to performance, a contract can be discharged in numerous other ways, including discharge by agreement of the parties and discharge by operation of law.

Discharge The termination of an obligation, such as occurs when the parties to a contract have fully performed their contractual obligations.

Performance The fulfillment of one's duties under a contract—the normal way of discharging one's contractual obligations.

14–4a Conditions of Performance

In most contracts, promises of performance are not expressly conditioned or qualified. Instead, they are *absolute promises*. They must be performed, or the party making the promise will be in breach of contract. **Example 14.19** Paloma Enterprises contracts to sell a truckload of organic produce to Tran for $10,000. The parties' promises are unconditional: Paloma will deliver the produce to Tran, and Tran will pay $10,000 to Paloma. The payment does not have to be made if the produce is not delivered.

12. *Dormitory Authority of the State of New York v. Samson Construction Co.*, 137 A.D.3d 433, 27 N.Y.S.3d 114 (1 Dept. 2016).

Exhibit 14–4 Contract Discharge

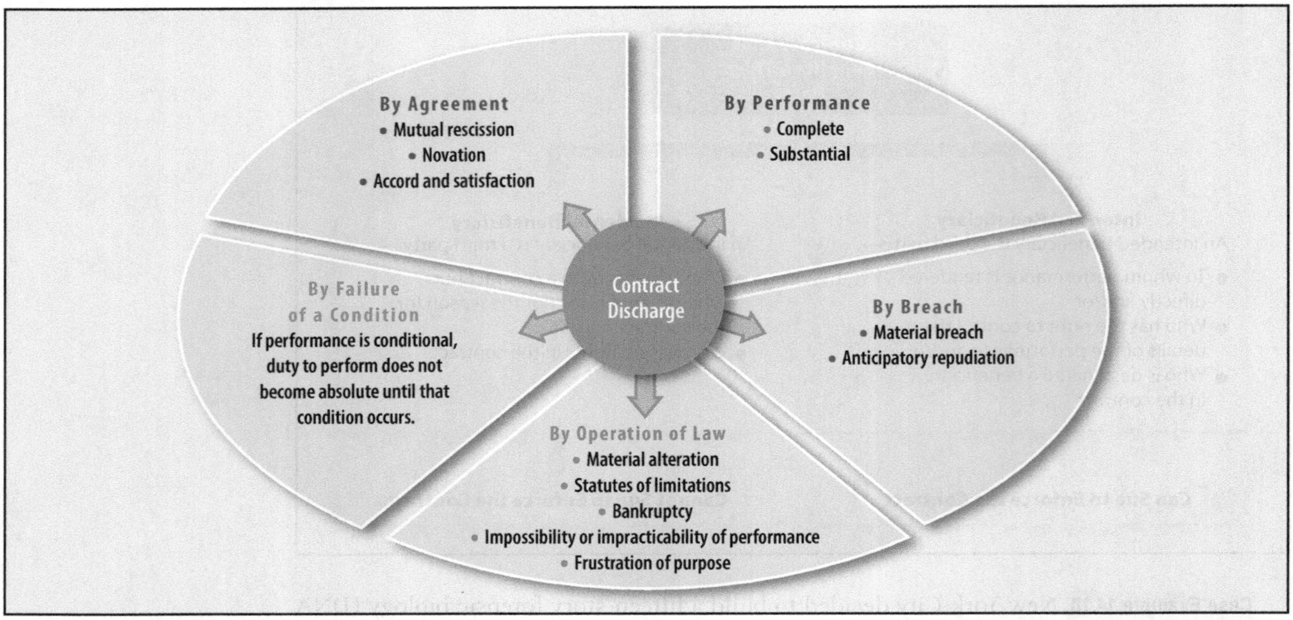

Condition A qualification, provision, or clause in a contractual agreement, the occurrence or nonoccurrence of which creates, suspends, or terminates the obligations of the contracting parties.

In some situations, however, contractual promises are conditioned. A **condition** is a qualification in a contract based on a possible future event, the occurrence or nonoccurrence of which will trigger or suspend the performance of a legal obligation or terminate an existing obligation under a contract. If the condition is not satisfied, the obligations of the parties are discharged.

Three types of conditions can be present in a contract: *conditions precedent*, *conditions subsequent*, and *concurrent conditions*.

Condition Precedent A condition in a contract that must be met before a party's promise becomes absolute.

Conditions Precedent A condition that must be fulfilled before a party's promise becomes absolute is called a **condition precedent.** The condition precedes the absolute duty to perform. Life insurance contracts frequently specify that certain conditions, such as passing a physical examination, must be met before the insurance company will be obligated to perform under the contract. A contract to lease university housing may be conditioned on the lessee's being a student at the university.

Many contracts are conditioned on an independent appraisal of value. **Example 14.20** Restoration Motors offers to buy Charlie's 1959 Thunderbird only if an expert appraiser estimates that it can be restored for less than a certain price. Thus, the parties' obligations are conditioned on the outcome of the appraisal. If the condition is not satisfied—that is, if the appraiser deems the cost to be significantly above the specified price—their obligations are discharged. ■

Condition Subsequent A condition in a contract that, if it occurs, operates to terminate a party's absolute promise to perform.

Conditions Subsequent When a condition operates to terminate a party's absolute promise to perform, it is called a **condition subsequent.** The condition follows, or is subsequent to, the absolute duty to perform. If the condition occurs, the party need not perform any further. **Example 14.21** A law firm hires Julia, a recent law school graduate. Their contract provides that the firm's obligation to continue employing Julia is discharged if she fails to pass the bar exam by her second attempt. This is a condition subsequent because a failure to pass the exam—and thus to obtain a license to practice law—will discharge a duty (employment) that has already arisen. ■

Generally, conditions precedent are common, and conditions subsequent are rare. The *Restatement (Second) of Contracts* omits the terms *condition subsequent* and *condition precedent* and refers to both simply as "conditions."[13]

Concurrent Conditions Conditions that must occur or be performed at the same time—they are mutually dependent. No obligations arise until these conditions are simultaneously performed.

Concurrent Conditions

When each party's absolute duty to perform is conditioned on the other party's absolute duty to perform, **concurrent conditions** are present. These conditions exist only when the parties expressly or impliedly are to perform their respective duties *simultaneously*.

Example 14.22 If Janet promises to pay for goods when HP, Inc., delivers them, the parties' promises to perform are mutually dependent. Janet's duty to pay for the goods does not become absolute until HP either delivers or tenders the goods. Likewise, HP's duty to deliver the goods does not become absolute until Janet tenders or actually makes payment. Therefore, neither can recover from the other for breach without first tendering performance.

David McNew/Getty Images

If HP agrees to sell and deliver goods to someone who agrees to pay for them, what are the concurrent conditions?

14–4b Discharge by Performance

The contract comes to an end when both parties fulfill their respective duties by performing the acts they have promised. Performance can also be accomplished by tender. **Tender** is an unconditional offer to perform by a person who is ready, willing, and able to do so. Therefore, a seller who places goods at the disposal of a buyer has tendered delivery and can demand payment according to the terms of the agreement. A buyer who offers to pay for goods has tendered payment and can demand delivery of the goods.

Once performance has been tendered, the party making the tender has done everything possible to carry out the terms of the contract. If the other party then refuses to perform, the party making the tender can consider the duty discharged and sue for breach of contract.

Tender An unconditional offer to perform an obligation by a person who is ready, willing, and able to do so.

Complete Performance

When a party performs exactly as agreed, there is no question as to whether the contract has been performed. When a party's performance is perfect, it is said to be complete.

Normally, conditions expressly stated in the contract must fully occur in all aspects for complete performance (strict performance) of the contract to take place. Any deviation breaches the contract and discharges the other party's obligations to perform.

For instance, most construction contracts require the builder to meet certain specifications. If the specifications are conditions, complete performance is required to avoid material breach. (*Material breach* will be discussed shortly.) If the conditions are met, the other party to the contract must then fulfill the obligation to pay the builder.

If the parties to the contract did not expressly make the specifications a condition, however, and the builder fails to meet the specifications, performance is not complete. What effect does that failure have on the other party's obligation to pay? The answer is part of the doctrine of *substantial performance*.

Substantial Performance

A party who in good faith performs substantially all of the terms of a contract can enforce the contract against the other party under the doctrine of substantial performance. Note that good faith is required. Intentionally failing to comply with the terms is a breach of the contract.

13. *Restatement (Second) of Contracts*, Section 224. Note that a plaintiff must prove a condition precedent, whereas the defendant normally proves a condition subsequent.

The basic requirements for performance to qualify as substantial performance are as follows:

1. The party must have performed in good faith. Intentional failure to comply with the contract terms is a breach of the contract.
2. The performance must not vary greatly from the performance promised in the contract. An omission, variance, or defect in performance is considered minor if it can easily be remedied by compensation (monetary damages).
3. The performance must create substantially the same benefits as those promised in the contract.

Courts decide whether performance was substantial on a case-by-case basis, examining all of the facts of the particular situation. **Case Example 14.23** Magic Carpet Ride (MCR) purchased a used airplane from Rugger Investment Group. The contract required the airplane to be free from liens, or legal claims against it. In fact, though, the airplane was burdened with a lien at the time of the sale. The two sides amended their contract, giving Rugger an additional ninety days to remove the lien or pay MCR a $90,000 penalty.

Rugger obtained the lien release eight days too late. MCR sued for breach of contract to recover the $90,000 penalty. A California appeals court found that (1) Rugger had tried in good faith to meet the ninety-day deadline and that (2) MCR had received all bargained-for benefits. As it would be unfair for MCR to get the airplane *and* an additional $90,000, the court decided that the eight-day delay did not bar Rugger from claiming substantial performance under the terms of the amended contract.[14] ■

Effect on Duty to Perform. If one party's performance is substantial, the other party's duty to perform—for instance, to make payment—remains absolute. In other words, the parties must continue performing under the contract. In contrast, if performance is not substantial, there is a material breach, and the nonbreaching party is excused from further performance.

Damages. Because substantial performance is not perfect, the other party is entitled to damages to compensate for the failure to comply with the contract. The measure of the damages is the cost to bring the object of the contract into compliance with its terms, if that cost is reasonable under the circumstances. If the cost is unreasonable, the measure of damages is the difference in value between the performance that was rendered and the performance that would have been rendered if the contract had been performed completely.

Performance to the Satisfaction of Another Contracts often state that completed work must personally satisfy one of the parties or a third person. The question is whether this satisfaction becomes a condition precedent, requiring actual personal satisfaction or approval for discharge, or whether the test of satisfaction is performance that would satisfy a *reasonable person* (substantial performance).

When the subject matter of the contract is *personal*, a contract to be performed to the satisfaction of one of the parties is conditioned, and performance must actually satisfy that party. For instance, contracts for portraits and works of art are considered personal. Therefore, only the personal satisfaction of the party fulfills the condition (unless a court finds that the party is expressing dissatisfaction to avoid payment or otherwise is not acting in good faith).

Most other contracts need be performed only to the satisfaction of a reasonable person unless they *expressly state otherwise*. When such contracts require performance to the satisfaction of a third party (such as "to the satisfaction of Robert Ames, the supervising engineer"), the courts are divided. A majority of courts require the work to be satisfactory to a reasonable person. But some courts do require the personal satisfaction of the third party designated in the contract (here, Robert Ames). Again, the personal judgment must be made honestly, or the condition will be excused.

14. *Magic Carpet Ride LLC v. Rugger Investment Group, L.L.C.*, 41 Cal.App.5th 357, 254 Cal.Rptr.3d 313 (2019).

Material Breach of Contract A **breach of contract** is the nonperformance of a contractual duty. A breach is *material* when performance is not at least substantial.[15] If there is a material breach, the nonbreaching party is excused from the performance of contractual duties and can sue for damages caused by the breach.

Breach of Contract The failure, without legal excuse, of a promisor to perform the obligations of a contract.

If the breach is *minor* (not material), the nonbreaching party's duty to perform may sometimes be suspended until the breach is remedied, but the duty is not entirely excused. Once the minor breach is cured (corrected), the nonbreaching party must resume performance of the contractual obligations.

Focus Question 4

When is a breach considered material, and what effect does that have on the other party's obligation to perform?

Any breach entitles the nonbreaching party to sue for damages, but only a material breach discharges the nonbreaching party from the contract. The policy underlying these rules is that contracts should go forward when only minor problems occur, but that contracts should be terminated if major problems arise.

Case Example 14.24 The Yuma County (Arizona) Airport Authority (YCAA) leased commercial space to Lux Air for the purpose of refuelling airplanes. On September 4, YCAA sent Lux Air a letter warning that certain outstanding debts must be covered by October 1 or YCAA would "exercise all of its remedies" under the lease agreement. Lux Air acknowledged receipt of the letter but failed to pay rent on October 1, as required. Three weeks later, YCAA evicted Lux Air.

Lux Air sued YCAA for breach of contract. In Arizona, a landlord may terminate a lease *only* if there has been a material breach by the tenant. Lux Air claimed that its breach was not material because YCAA, in the September 4 letter, did not clearly state the consequences of failure to pay rent. An Arizona appeals court rejected this excuse, finding that, given the communications between the two companies and the inherent contractual importance of rent, Lux Air "knew or should have known" what steps were necessary to avoid the termination of its lease.[16] (See this chapter's *Business Law Analysis* feature for further explanation of how courts determine whether there has been a material breach.)

15. *Restatement (Second) of Contracts*, Section 241.
16. *DBT Yuma LLC v. Yuma County Airport Authority*, 2019 WL 439290, Ariz. Ct. App. (1st Div. 2019).

Determining When a Breach Is Material

Business Law Analysis

The Northeast Independent School District in Bexar County, Texas, hired STR Constructors, Ltd., to renovate a middle school. STR subcontracted the tile work in the school's kitchen to Newman Tile, Inc. (NTI). The project had already fallen behind schedule. As a result, STR allowed its workers and other subcontractors' employees to walk on and damage the newly installed tile before it had cured, forcing NTI to constantly redo its work.

Despite NTI's requests for payment, STR remitted only half the amount due under their contract. When the school district refused to accept the kitchen, including the tile work, STR told NTI to quickly make repairs. A week later, STR terminated their contract. Did STR breach the contract with NTI?

Analysis: A breach of contract is the nonperformance of a contractual duty. A breach is *material* when performance is not at least substantial. On a material breach, the nonbreaching party is excused from performance. If a breach is *minor*, the nonbreaching party's duty to perform can sometimes be suspended until the breach has been remedied, but the duty to perform is not entirely excused. Once a minor breach has been cured, the nonbreaching party must resume performance. Any breach—material or minor—entitles the nonbreaching party to sue for damages.

Result and Reasoning: Yes, STR breached the contract with NTI. Because STR permitted its employees and other subcontractors to walk over and damage the newly installed tile, NTI had to redo its work constantly. Furthermore, despite NTI's requests for payment, STR remitted only half the amount due under the contract. Therefore, STR's performance was not substantial, and its breach was material.

Although NTI could have chosen to stop performing the contract right away and sue STR for breach, it did not. In fact, NTI continued to perform until STR terminated the contract. The termination apparently was done wrongfully and without good cause. The tile work would have been completed satisfactorily if STR had not allowed other workers to trample the newly installed tile before it had cured.

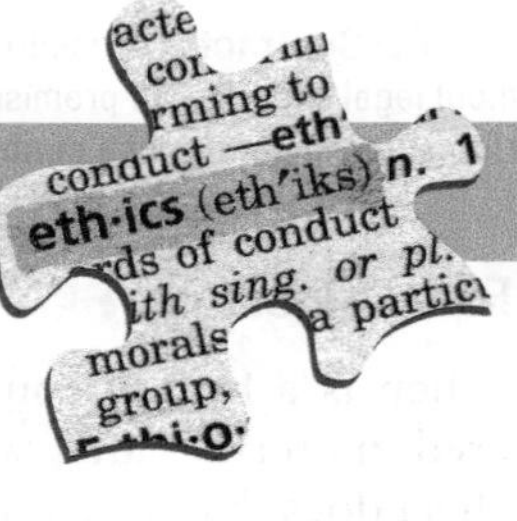

Ethical Issue

Is it a material breach of contract for a hospital to accept a donation and then refuse to honor part of its commitment? Country singer Garth Brooks was born in Yukon, Oklahoma, and has made generous contributions to charities in that town. When his mother, Colleen Brooks, died, he donated $500,000 to Integris Rural Health, Inc., in that town. Brooks believed that he and the hospital's president had agreed verbally that the donation would be used to build a new women's health center in Yukon, which would be named after his mother. Several years passed, but the health center was not built. Integris claimed that it intended to do something to honor Colleen Brooks but insisted that it had never promised to build a new health center. When Integris refused to return the $500,000, Garth Brooks sued for breach of contract.

Was the hospital's failure to build a women's health center and name it after Brooks's mother a material breach of the verbal contract between Brooks and hospital management? A jury in Rogers County, Oklahoma, thought so and awarded Brooks $500,000 in actual damages for breach of contract. The jury also awarded Brooks another $500,000 because it found the hospital guilty of reckless disregard and intentional malice.

Anticipatory Repudiation of a Contract Before either party to a contract has a duty to perform, one of the parties may refuse to perform that party's contractual obligations. This action is called **anticipatory repudiation.**[17]

Anticipatory Repudiation An assertion or action by a party indicating that the party will not perform a contractual obligation.

Repudiation Is a Material Breach. When anticipatory repudiation occurs, it is treated as a material breach of the contract, and the nonbreaching party is permitted to bring an action for damages immediately. The nonbreaching party can file suit even though the scheduled time for performance under the contract may still be in the future. Until the nonbreaching party treats this early repudiation as a breach, however, the breaching party can retract the anticipatory repudiation by proper notice and restore the parties to their original obligations.[18]

An anticipatory repudiation is treated as a present, material breach for two reasons. First, the nonbreaching party should not be required to remain ready and willing to perform when the other party has already repudiated the contract. Second, the nonbreaching party should have the opportunity to seek a similar contract elsewhere. Indeed, that party may have the duty to do so to minimize loss.

When does a landlord's refusal to perform a duty under a lease constitute a material breach entitling the tenant to bring an action for damages? That was the question in the following case.

17. *Restatement (Second) of Contracts,* Section 253; and UCC 2–610.
18. See UCC 2–611.

Case 14.3

Chalk Supply LLC v. Ribbe Real Estate LLC

Court of Appeals of Michigan, __ Mich.App. __, __ N.W.2d __, 2020 WL 39991 (2020).

Facts Chalk Supply LLC buys paints and other products, which it repackages and sells to consumers. Chalk Supply agreed to lease a warehouse from Ribbe Real Estate LLC (RRE) for eighteen months. Chalk Supply prepaid twelve and a half months' rent.

At Chalk Supply's request, the lease provided that a fire suppression system would be installed if required, with the cost to be "divided by 84 months (7 years) of which Tenant will pay in like equal installments during the term of the lease." A local ordinance required a fire suppression system. On receiving an estimate of the cost, however, RRE e-mailed Chalk Supply, before the tenant had moved onto the property, that RRE was not willing to pay for the system without a longer lease term.

Chalk Supply filed a suit in a Michigan state court against RRE, claiming breach of contract. The court ruled in Chalk Supply's favor and ordered RRE to return the money the tenant had paid in advance of the lease term. The landlord appealed.

Issue Was RRE's e-mail an anticipatory repudiation of the parties' lease entitling Chalk Supply to bring an action for breach of contract?

Decision Yes. A state intermediate appellate court affirmed the judgment of the trial court. RRE was in material breach of the parties' contract, and Chalk Supply could recover the money that it had paid in advance.

Reason Anticipatory repudiation occurs when a party states an intention not to perform a duty owed under a contract except on a condition that goes beyond the contract.

RRE and Chalk Supply executed a lease for a warehouse, and the tenant paid a substantial amount of the rent in advance. In their contract, the parties agreed that the landlord would pay the cost for a fire suppression system if required, and the tenant would repay that amount over eighty-four months. Under a local ordinance, a fire suppression system was required. RRE later refused to pay for the system unless the tenant agreed to negotiate a new, longer term for the lease. "This was, then, an anticipatory repudiation of the lease: . . . RRE would not perform a duty under the contract (pay for fire suppression if required) unless Chalk Supply extended the lease (a condition that went beyond the contract)."

RRE argued that its refusal to perform was not an anticipatory repudiation because it "was not unequivocal and was conditioned on the requirement of fire suppression." The court found this argument to be "meritless. . . . Saying that RRE would not pay for fire suppression if it was required was disavowing the very thing that RRE agreed to do."

Critical Thinking

- **Legal Environment** *The lease between RRE and Chalk Supply required a security deposit to cover any default on a month's rent by the tenant. Chalk Supply did not pay the deposit. Should the court have ruled that this breach prevented Chalk Supply from prevailing on its claim against RRE? Discuss.*
- **What If the Facts Were Different?** *Suppose that RRE had received an estimate of the cost of the fire suppression system before the parties executed the lease and had then insisted on conditioning its payment on a longer term. Would the result in this case have been different? Explain.*

Repudiation May Occur When Market Prices Fluctuate. Quite often, an anticipatory repudiation occurs when performance of the contract would be extremely unfavorable to one of the parties because of a sharp fluctuation in market prices.

Example 14.25 Mobile X enters into an e-contract to manufacture and sell 100,000 smartphones to Best Com, a global telecommunications company. Delivery is to be made two months from the date of the contract. One month later, three inventory suppliers raise their prices to Mobile X. Because of these higher prices, Mobile X stands to lose $500,000 if it sells the smartphones to Best Com at the contract price.

Mobile X immediately sends an e-mail to Best Com, stating that it cannot deliver the 100,000 phones at the contract price. Even though you may sympathize with Mobile X, its e-mail is an anticipatory repudiation of the contract. Best Com can treat the repudiation as a material breach and immediately pursue remedies, even though the contract delivery date is still a month away.

Know This

The risks that prices will fluctuate and values will change are ordinary business risks for which the law does not provide relief.

Bloomberg/Getty Images

A smartphone manufacturer learns its supply costs will suddenly increase and cancels its upcoming delivery to clients. What is this action called?

14–4c Discharge by Agreement

Any contract can be discharged by agreement of the parties. The agreement can be contained in the original contract, or the parties can form a new contract for the express purpose of discharging the original contract.

Discharge by Mutual Rescission Recission occurs when the parties cancel their contract and are returned to the positions they occupied prior to the contract's formation. For *mutual rescission* to take place, the parties must make another agreement that also satisfies the legal requirements for a contract—there must be an *offer*, an *acceptance*, and *consideration*. Ordinarily, if the parties agree to rescind the original contract, their promises not to perform the acts promised in the original contract will be legal consideration for the second contract.

Generally, a rescission agreement may be written or oral. Oral agreements to rescind most executory contracts are enforceable even if the original agreement was in writing. A writing (or electronic record) is required to rescind a contract for the sale of goods under the Uniform Commercial Code when the contract requires a written rescission. Also, agreements to rescind contracts involving transfers of realty must be evidenced by a writing or record.

When one party has fully performed, an agreement to rescind the original contract usually is not enforceable unless additional consideration or restitution is made. Because the performing party has received no consideration for the promise to call off the original bargain, additional consideration is necessary.

Novation The substitution, by agreement, of a new contract for an old one, with the rights under the old one being terminated.

Discharge by Novation The process of **novation** substitutes a third party for one of the original parties. Essentially, the parties to the original contract and one or more new parties get together and agree to the substitution. The requirements of a novation are as follows:

1. A previous valid obligation.
2. An agreement by all of the parties to a new contract.
3. The extinguishing of the old obligation (discharge of the prior party).
4. A new, valid contract.

Example 14.26 Union Corporation contracts to sell its pharmaceutical division to British Pharmaceuticals, Ltd. Before the transfer is completed, Union, British Pharmaceuticals, and a third company, Otis Chemicals, execute a new agreement to transfer all of British Pharmaceuticals' rights and duties in the transaction to Otis Chemicals. As long as the new contract is supported by consideration, the novation will discharge the original contract (between Union and British Pharmaceuticals) and replace it with the new contract (between Union and Otis Chemicals). ■

A novation expressly or impliedly revokes and discharges a prior contract. The parties involved may expressly state in the new contract that the old contract is now discharged. If the parties do not expressly discharge the old contract, it will be impliedly discharged if the new contract's terms are inconsistent with the old contract's terms.

Discharge by Accord and Satisfaction In an *accord and satisfaction*, the parties agree to accept performance different from the performance originally promised. An *accord* is a contract to perform some act to satisfy an existing contractual duty that has not yet been discharged. A *satisfaction* is the performance of the accord agreement. An accord and its satisfaction discharge the original contractual obligation.

Once the accord has been made, the original obligation is merely suspended until the accord agreement is fully performed. If it is not performed, the party to whom performance is owed can bring an action on the original obligation or for breach of the accord. **Example 14.27** Shea obtains a judgment of $8,000 against Marla. Later, both parties agree that the judgment can be satisfied by Marla's transfer of her automobile to Shea. This agreement to accept the auto in lieu of $8,000 in cash is the accord. If Marla transfers her automobile to Shea, the accord agreement is fully performed, and the $8,000 debt is discharged. If Marla refuses to transfer her car, the accord is breached. Because the original obligation is merely suspended, Shea can sue to enforce the judgment for $8,000 in cash or bring an action for breach of the accord. ■

14–4d Discharge by Operation of Law

Under specified circumstances, contractual duties may be discharged by operation of law. These circumstances include material alteration of the contract, an applicable statute of limitations, bankruptcy, impossibility or impracticability of performance, and frustration of purpose.

Material Alteration To discourage parties from altering written contracts, the law allows an innocent party to be discharged from a contract that has been materially altered. If one party alters a material term of the contract—such as the quantity term or the price term—without the other party's knowledge, the party who was unaware of the alteration can treat the contract as discharged or terminated.

Statutes of Limitations Statutes of limitations limit the period during which a party can sue on a particular cause of action. After the applicable limitations period has passed, a suit can no longer be brought.

The period for bringing lawsuits for breach of oral contracts is usually two to three years and for written contracts, four to five years. Lawsuits for breach of a contract for the sale of goods must be brought within four years after the cause of action has accrued.[19] In their original contract, the parties can agree to reduce this four-year period to not less than one year. They cannot, however, agree to extend it beyond four years.

Bankruptcy A proceeding in bankruptcy attempts to allocate a debtor's assets to the creditors in a fair and equitable fashion. Once the assets have been allocated, the debtor receives a *discharge in bankruptcy*. A discharge in bankruptcy ordinarily prevents the creditors from enforcing most of the debtor's contracts. Partial payment of a debt *after* discharge in bankruptcy will not revive the debt.

Impossibility of Performance After a contract has been made, supervening events (such as a fire) may make performance impossible in an objective sense. This so-called **impossibility of performance** can discharge the contract. The doctrine of impossibility of performance is applied only when the parties could not have reasonably foreseen, at the time the contract was formed, the event or events that rendered performance impossible.

Impossibility of Performance A doctrine under which a party to a contract is relieved of the duty to perform when performance becomes objectively impossible or totally impracticable.

Objective impossibility ("It cannot be done") must be distinguished from subjective impossibility ("I'm sorry, I personally cannot do it"). An example of subjective impossibility occurs when a person cannot deliver goods on time or make payment on time because the person has to have an emergency surgery. In effect, the nonperforming party is saying, "It is impossible for *me* to perform" rather than "It is impossible for *anyone* to perform." Accordingly, such excuses do not discharge a contract, and the nonperforming party is normally held in breach of contract.

©Elnur/Shutterstock.com

This dancer has a contract to dance the lead role in a ballet that will run for a month. What happens if he breaks a leg before the shows start?

When Performance Is Impossible. Three basic types of situations may qualify as grounds for the discharge of contractual obligations based on impossibility of performance:[20]

1. *When a party whose personal performance is essential to the completion of the contract dies or becomes incapacitated prior to performance.* **Example 14.28** Fred, a famous dancer, contracts with Ethereal Dancing Guild to play a leading role in its new ballet. Before the ballet can be performed, Fred becomes ill and dies. His personal performance was essential to the completion of the contract. Thus, his death discharges the contract and his estate's liability for his nonperformance.
2. *When the specific subject matter of the contract is destroyed.* **Example 14.29** A-1 Farm Equipment agrees to sell Gunther the green tractor on its lot and promises to have the tractor ready for Gunther to pick up on Saturday. On Friday night, however, a truck veers off the nearby highway and smashes into the tractor, destroying it beyond repair. Because the contract was for this specific tractor, A-1's performance is rendered impossible owing to the accident.

19. See UCC 2-725.
20. *Restatement (Second) of Contracts*, Sections 261–266; and UCC 2–615.

3. *When a change in the law renders performance illegal.* **Example 14.30** Russo contracts with Playlist, Inc., to create a website through which users can post and share movies, music, and other forms of digital entertainment. Russo commences the work. Before the site is operational, however, Congress passes the No Online Piracy in Entertainment (NOPE) Act. The NOPE Act makes it illegal to operate a website on which copyrighted works are posted without the copyright owners' consent. In this situation, the contract is discharged by operation of law. The purpose of the contract has been rendered illegal, and contract performance is objectively impossible.

Temporary Impossibility. An occurrence or event that makes performance temporarily impossible operates to suspend performance until the impossibility ceases. Once the temporary event ends, the parties ordinarily must perform the contract as originally planned.

Example 14.31 Mindy and Lyn contract to rent a sailboat from Key West Rentals for a month-long trip. The day before their trip is scheduled to begin, Hurricane Irma hits the coast where the boat is docked, causing damage. The hurricane makes performance temporarily impossible, and Mindy and Lyn postpone their trip. Once repairs are made to the dock and the boat, however, Key West Rentals will be required to perform the contract as originally planned. Mindy and Lyn have a right to rent the boat for a month for the previously agreed-on price.

Know This
The doctrine of commercial impracticability does not provide relief from such events as ordinary price increases or easily predictable changes in the weather.

Sometimes, however, the lapse of time and the change in circumstances surrounding such a contract make it substantially more burdensome for the parties to perform the promised acts. In that situation, the contract may be discharged. **Classic Case Example 14.32** In 1942, actor Gene Autry was drafted into the U.S. Army. Being drafted rendered his contract with a Hollywood movie company temporarily impossible to perform, and it was suspended until the end of World War II in 1945. When Autry got out of the army, the purchasing power of the dollar had declined so much that performance of the contract would have been substantially burdensome to him. Therefore, the contract was discharged.[21]

Commercial Impracticability

Courts may also excuse parties from their performance obligations when the performance becomes much more difficult or expensive than the parties originally contemplated. In one classic case, for instance, a court held that a contract could be discharged because a party would have to pay ten times more than the original estimate to excavate a certain amount of gravel.[22]

Commercial Impracticability A doctrine that may excuse the duty to perform a contract when performance becomes much more difficult or costly due to forces that neither party could have controlled or foreseen at the time the contract was formed.

For someone to invoke the doctrine of **commercial impracticability** successfully, however, the anticipated performance must become *extremely difficult or costly*.[23] Furthermore, the added burden of performing *must not have been foreseeable by the parties when the contract was made*.

Frustration of Purpose

Frustration of Purpose A court-created doctrine under which a party to a contract will be relieved of the duty to perform when the objective purpose of performance no longer exists due to reasons beyond that party's control.

Closely allied with the doctrine of commercial impracticability is the doctrine of **frustration of purpose.** In principle, a contract will be discharged if supervening circumstances make it impossible to attain the purpose both parties had in mind when making the contract. As with commercial impracticability, the supervening event must not have been foreseeable at the time of contracting.

There are some differences between the doctrines, however. Commercial impracticability usually involves an event that increases the cost or difficulty of performance. In contrast, frustration of purpose typically involves an event that decreases the value of what a party receives under the contract.

21. *Autry v. Republic Productions*, 30 Cal.2d 144, 180 P.2d 888 (1947).
22. *Mineral Park Land Co. v. Howard*, 172 Cal. 289, 156 P. 458 (1916).
23. *Restatement (Second) of Contracts*, Section 264.

Practice and Review

Val's Foods signs a contract to buy 1,500 pounds of basil from Sun Farms, a small organic herb grower, if an independent organization inspects the crop and certifies that it contains no pesticide or herbicide residue. Val's has a contract with several restaurant chains to supply pesto and intends to use Sun Farms' basil in the pesto to fulfill these contracts. When Sun Farms is preparing to harvest the basil, an unexpected hailstorm destroys half the crop. Sun Farms attempts to purchase additional basil from other farms, but it is late in the season, and the price is twice the normal market price. Sun Farms is too small to absorb this cost and immediately notifies Val's that it will not fulfill the contract. Using the information presented in the chapter, answer the following questions.

1. Suppose that Sun Farms supplies the basil that survived the storm but the basil does not pass the chemical-residue inspection. Which concept discussed in the chapter might allow Val's to refuse to perform the contract in this situation?
2. Under which legal theory or theories might Sun Farms claim that its obligation under the contract has been discharged by operation of law? Discuss fully.
3. Suppose that Sun Farms contacts every basil grower in the country and buys the last remaining chemical-free basil anywhere. Nevertheless, Sun Farms is able to ship only 1,475 pounds to Val's. Would this fulfill Sun Farms' obligations to Val's? Why or why not?
4. Now suppose that Sun Farms sells its operations to Happy Valley Farms. As part of the sale, all three parties agree that Happy Valley will provide the basil as stated under the original contract. What is this type of agreement called?

Debate This

The doctrine of commercial impracticability should be abolished.

Key Terms

alienation 336
anticipatory repudiation 348
assignee 334
assignment 334
assignor 334
breach of contract 347
commercial impracticability 352
concurrent conditions 345
condition 344
condition precedent 344
condition subsequent 344
delegatee 337
delegation of duties 337
delegator 337
discharge 343
frustration of purpose 352
impossibility of performance 351
incidental beneficiary 342
intended beneficiary 340
novation 350
obligee 334
obligor 334
performance 343
privity of contract 333
tender 345
third party beneficiary 340

Chapter Summary: Third Party Rights and Discharge

THIRD PARTY RIGHTS	
Assignments	**1.** An assignment is the transfer of rights under a contract to a third party. The person assigning the rights is the *assignor,* and the party to whom the rights are assigned is the *assignee.* The assignee has a right to demand performance from the other original party to the contract, the *obligor.* **2.** Generally, all rights can be assigned *unless:* **a.** A statute expressly prohibits assignment. **b.** The contract is for personal services. **c.** The assignment will significantly alter the obligor's risk or duties. **d.** The contract prohibits assignment. (Exception: Contracts cannot generally prohibit assignment of the right to receive funds, of ownership rights in real property, of negotiable instruments, or of certain payments on account or damages for breach of contract.) **3.** The assignee should notify the obligor of the assignment. Although not legally required, notification avoids two potential problems: **a.** If the assignor assigns the same right to two different persons, the first assignment in time is generally the first in right, but in some states the first assignee to give notice takes priority. **b.** Until the obligor is notified of the assignment, the obligor can tender performance to the assignor. If the assignor accepts the performance, the obligor's duties under the contract are discharged without benefit to the assignee.
Delegations	**1.** A delegation is the transfer of duties under a contract to a third party (the *delegatee*), who then assumes the obligation of performing the contractual duties previously held by the one making the delegation (the *delegator*). **2.** As a general rule, any duty can be delegated *unless:* **a.** Performance depends on the obligor's personal skills or talents. **b.** Special trust has been placed in the obligor. **c.** Performance by a third party will vary materially from that expected by the obligee. **d.** The contract expressly prohibits delegation. **3.** A valid delegation of duties does not relieve the delegator of obligations under the contract. If the delegatee fails to perform, the delegator is still liable to the obligee. **4.** An "assignment of all rights" is often construed to mean that both the rights and the duties arising under the contract are transferred to a third party.
Third Party Beneficiaries	A third party beneficiary contract is one that benefits a third party. **1. Intended beneficiary**—A third party for whose benefit a contract is created. When the promisor (the one making the contractual promise that benefits a third party) fails to perform as promised, the intended beneficiary can sue the promisor directly. Types of intended beneficiaries are creditor and donee beneficiaries. **2. Incidental beneficiary**—A third party who indirectly (incidentally) benefits from a contract but for whose benefit the contract was not specifically intended. Incidental beneficiaries have no rights to the benefits received and cannot sue to have the contract enforced.
CONTRACT DISCHARGE	
Conditions of Performance	Contract obligations may be subject to the following types of conditions: **1. Condition precedent**—A condition that must be fulfilled before a party's promise becomes absolute. **2. Condition subsequent**—A condition that, if it occurs, operates to terminate a party's absolute promise to perform. **3. Concurrent conditions**—Conditions that must be performed simultaneously. Each party's absolute duty to perform is conditioned on the other party's absolute duty to perform.
Discharge by Performance	A contract may be discharged by complete (strict) performance or by substantial performance. In some instances, performance must be to the satisfaction of another. Totally inadequate performance constitutes a material breach of the contract. An anticipatory repudiation of a contract allows the other party to sue immediately for breach of contract.

Discharge by Agreement	Parties may agree to discharge their contractual obligations in several ways: 1. **By rescission**—The parties mutually agree to rescind (cancel) the contract. 2. **By novation**—A new party is substituted for one of the primary parties to a contract. 3. **By accord and satisfaction**—The parties agree to render and accept performance different from that on which they originally agreed.
Discharge by Operation of Law	Parties' obligations under contracts may be discharged by operation of law owing to one of the following: 1. Material alteration. 2. Statutes of limitations. 3. Bankruptcy. 4. Impossibility of performance. 5. Commercial impracticability. 6. Frustration of purpose.

Issue Spotters

1. Eagle Company contracts to build a house for Frank. The contract states that "any assignment of this contract renders the contract void." After Eagle builds the house, but before Frank pays, Eagle assigns its right to payment to Good Credit Company. Can Good Credit enforce the contract against Frank? Why or why not? (See *Assignments*.)
2. C&D Services contracts with Ace Concessions, Inc., to service Ace's vending machines. Later, C&D wants Dean Vending Services to assume the duties under a new contract. Ace consents. What type of agreement is this? Are Ace's obligations discharged? Why or why not? (See *Contract Discharge*.)

—Check your answers to the *Issue Spotters* against the answers provided in Appendix D.

Business Scenarios and Case Problems

14–1. Third Party Beneficiaries. Wilken owes Rivera $2,000. Howie promises Wilken that he will pay Rivera the $2,000 in return for Wilken's promise to give Howie's children guitar lessons. Is Rivera an intended beneficiary of the Howie-Wilken contract? Explain. (See *Third Party Beneficiaries*.)

14–2. Assignment. Aron, a college student, signs a one-year lease agreement that runs from September 1 to August 31. The lease agreement specifies that the lease cannot be assigned without the landlord's consent. In late May, Aron decides not to go to summer school and assigns the balance of the lease (three months) to a close friend, Erica. The landlord objects to the assignment and denies Erica access to the apartment. Aron claims that Erica is financially sound and should be allowed the full rights and privileges of an assignee. Discuss fully whether the landlord or Aron is correct. (See *Assignments*.)

14–3. Conditions of Performance. Russ Wyant owned Humble Ranch in Perkins County, South Dakota. Edward Humble, whose parents had previously owned the ranch, was Wyant's uncle. Humble held a two-year option to buy the ranch. The option included specific conditions. Once it was exercised, the parties had thirty days to enter into a purchase agreement, and the seller could become the buyer's lender by matching the terms of the proposed financing. After the option was exercised, the parties engaged in lengthy negotiations, but Humble did not respond to Wyant's proposed purchase agreement nor advise him of available financing terms before the option expired. Six months later, Humble filed a suit against Wyant to enforce the option. Is Humble entitled to specific performance? Explain. [*Humble v. Wyant,* 843 N.W.2d 334 (S.Dak. 2014)] (See *Contract Discharge*.)

14–4. Discharge by Operation of Law. Dr. Jake Lambert signed an employment agreement with Baptist Health Services, Inc., to provide cardiothoracic-surgery services to Baptist Memorial Hospital–North Mississippi, Inc., in Oxford, Mississippi. Complaints about Lambert's behavior arose almost immediately. He was evaluated by a team of doctors and psychologists, who diagnosed him as suffering from obsessive-compulsive personality disorder and concluded that he was unfit to practice medicine. Based on this conclusion, the hospital suspended his staff privileges. Citing the suspension, Baptist Health Services claimed that Lambert had breached his employment contract. What is Lambert's best defense to this claim? Explain. [*Baptist Memorial Hospital–North Mississippi, Inc. v. Lambert,* 157 So.3d 109 (Miss.App. 2015)] (See *Contract Discharge*.)

14–5. Business Case Problem with Sample Answer—Conditions of Performance. H&J Ditching & Excavating, Inc., was hired by JRSF, LLC, to perform excavating and grading work on Terra Firma, a residential construction project in West Knox County, Tennessee. Cornerstone Community Bank financed the project with a loan to JRSF. As the work progressed, H&J received payments totaling 90 percent of the price on its contract. JRSF then defaulted on the loan from Cornerstone, and Cornerstone foreclosed and took possession of the property. H&J filed a suit in a Tennessee state court against the bank to recover the final payment on its contract. The bank responded that H&J had not received its payment because it had failed to obtain an engineer's certificate of final completion, a condition under its contract with JRSF. H&J responded that it had completed all the work it had contracted to do. What type of contract condition does obtaining the engineer's certificate represent? Is H&J entitled to the final payment? Discuss. [*H&J Ditching & Excavating, Inc. v. Cornerstone Community Bank*, 2016 WL 675554 (Tenn.App. 2016)] (See *Contract Discharge.*)

—For a sample answer to Problem 14–5, go to Appendix E.

14–6. Third Party Beneficiaries. The Health Care Providers Self Insurance Trust (the trust) provided workers' compensation coverage to the employees of its members, including Accredited Aides Plus, Inc. The trust contracted with Program Risk Management, Inc. (PRM), to serve as the program administrator. The contract obligated PRM to reimburse the trust for "claims, losses, and liabilities . . . arising out of" PRM's acts or omissions. When the trust became insolvent, the state of New York assessed the trust's employer-members for some of its debts. These employer-members filed a suit against PRM for breach of contract. Were the trust's employer-members third party beneficiaries of the trust's contract with PRM? If so, could the employer-members maintain this action against PRM? Explain. [*Accredited Aides Plus, Inc. v. Program Risk Management, Inc.*, 147 A.D.3d 122, 46 N.Y.S.3d 246 (N.Y.A.D. 3 Dept. 2017)] (See *Third Party Beneficiaries.*)

14–7. Assignments. State Farm Insurance Co. issued a policy to David Stulberger to insure a Nissan Rogue for collision damage. The policy provided, "No assignment . . . is binding upon us unless approved by us." When the Nissan was involved in an accident, State Farm agreed that the vehicle should be repaired. M.V.B. Collision Inc. performed the repairs at a cost of $14,101.80. State Farm offered to pay $9,960.36. Stulberger assigned to M.V.B. the right to pursue State Farm for the difference, or $4,141.44. The assignee filed a suit in a New York state court against the insurer to recoup this amount. The defendant responded with a motion to dismiss, arguing that the plaintiff lacked the capacity to sue because the defendant had not consented to the transfer by Stulberger. Is the assignment valid? Why or why not? [*M.V.B. Collision Inc. v. State Farm Insurance Co.*, 59 Misc.3d 406, 72 N.Y.S.3d 407 (N.Y.C. Dist. 2018)] (See *Assignments.*)

14–8. A Question of Ethics—The IDDR Approach and Discharge by Operation of Law. Lisa Goldstein reserved space for a marriage ceremony in a building owned by Orensanz Events, LLC, in New York City. The rental agreement provided that on cancellation of the event "for any reason beyond Owner's control," the client's sole remedy was another date for the event or a refund. Shortly before the wedding, the New York City Department of Buildings found Orensanz's building to be structurally unstable and ordered it vacated. The owner closed it and told Goldstein to find another venue. She filed a suit in a New York state court against Orensanz for breach of contract, arguing that the city's order had been for a cause within the defendant's control. [*Goldstein v. Orensanz Events, LLC*, 146 A.D.3d 492, 44 N.Y.S.3d 437 (1 Dept. 2017)] (See *Contract Discharge.*)

1. Is the owner of a commercial building ethically obligated to keep it structurally sound? Apply the IDDR approach in the context of the *Goldstein* case to answer this question.
2. Is a contracting party ethically obligated to "relax" the terms of the deal if the other party encounters "trouble" in performing them? Discuss.

Critical Thinking and Writing Assignments

14–9. Critical Legal Thinking. The concept of substantial performance permits parties to be discharged from contracts even though they have not fully performed their contractual obligations. Is this fair? Why or why not? What policy interests are at issue here? (See Contract Discharge.)

14–10. Time-Limited Group Assignment—Anticipatory Repudiation. ABC Clothiers, Inc., has a contract with John Taylor, owner of Taylor & Sons, a retailer, to deliver one thousand summer suits to Taylor's place of business on or before May 1. On April 1, John receives a letter from ABC informing him that ABC will not be able to make the delivery as scheduled. John is very upset, as he had planned a big ad campaign. (See *Contract Discharge.*)

1. The first group will decide whether John Taylor can immediately sue ABC for breach of contract (on April 2).
2. Now suppose that John Taylor's son, Tom, tells his father that they cannot file a lawsuit until ABC actually fails to deliver the suits on May 1. The second group will determine who is correct, John or Tom.
3. Assume that Taylor & Sons can either file immediately or wait until ABC fails to deliver the goods. The third group will evaluate which course of action is better, given the circumstances.

CONT
RACT
Company Limited in the world
123/45 XYZ Building, Abc Street,
Province State Country 12345678
Sir Mr. or Miss
Contract information
A contract is a voluntary arrangement between two or more parties that is enforceable at law as a
legal agreement. Contract is a branch of the law of obligations in jurisdictions of the civil law tradition.

YP_Studio/Shutterstock.com

15

Breach and Remedies

> "There's a remedy for everything except death."
>
> **Miguel de Cervantes**
> 1547–1616
> (Spanish author)

When one party breaches a contract, the other party—the nonbreaching party—can choose one or more of several remedies. A *remedy* is the relief provided to an innocent party when the other party has breached the contract. It is the means employed to enforce a right or to redress an injury. Although it may be an exaggeration to say there is a remedy for "everything" in life, as Cervantes claimed in the chapter-opening quotation, there is a remedy available for nearly every contract breach.

The most common remedies available to a nonbreaching party under contract law include damages, rescission and restitution, specific performance, and reformation. Courts distinguish between *remedies at law* and *remedies in equity*. Today, the remedy at law is normally monetary damages. Usually, a court will not award an equitable remedy unless the remedy at law is inadequate.

Suppose Daren, an orthodontist, is having a new office built for his orthodontic practice. He contracts with Bryan, doing business as Desert Sun Landscaping, to build a fountain in front of the new office for $14,000. Desert Sun installs the fountain while the office building is still under construction. Three weeks later, the fountain stops working properly. Desert Sun repairs the problem, which Bryan claims was caused by dirt and debris coming from the office construction.

The fountain continues to have problems, however. Within a month, the concrete slab underneath it irreparably cracks, and a pipe leading to the spray nozzles comes loose. Daren hires another landscaper to remove the defective fountain. Can Daren sue Bryan for breach of contract? If he sues and is successful, can he recover the $14,000 he paid for the fountain, as well as the cost of removing the fountain? These are the kinds of issues concerning breach and damages that we consider in this chapter.

Focus Questions

The four Focus Questions below are designed to help improve your understanding. After reading this chapter, you should be able to answer the following questions:

1. What is the standard measure of compensatory damages when a contract is breached?
2. When do courts grant specific performance as a remedy?
3. What remedy is available when a court imposes a quasi contract?
4. What is a limitation-of-liability clause, and when will courts enforce it?

Know This
The terms of a contract must be sufficiently definite for a court to determine the amount of damages to award.

15–1 Damages

A breach of contract entitles the nonbreaching party to sue for monetary damages. In contract law, damages compensate the nonbreaching party for the loss of the bargain (whereas in tort law, damages compensate for harm suffered as a result of another's wrongful act). Often, courts say that innocent parties are to be placed in the position they would have occupied had the contract been fully performed.[1]

15–1a Types of Damages

There are basically four broad categories of damages:

1. Compensatory (to cover direct losses and costs).
2. Consequential (to cover indirect and foreseeable losses).
3. Punitive (to punish and deter wrongdoing).
4. Nominal (to recognize wrongdoing when no monetary loss is shown).

Compensatory and punitive damages were discussed in the context of tort law. Here, we look at these types of damages, as well as consequential and nominal damages, in the context of contract law.

Compensatory Damages Damages that compensate the nonbreaching party for the *loss of the bargain* are known as *compensatory damages*. These damages compensate the injured party only for damages actually sustained and proved to have arisen directly from the loss of the bargain caused by the breach of contract. They simply replace what was lost because of the wrong or damage, and, for this reason, are often said to "make the person whole."

Example 15.1 Jane wires Roy, her financial advisor, $34,980 to purchase an allocation of FluidCoin's initial cryptocurrency offering. Roy does not invest these funds as agreed, instead commingling them with funds used for his personal acquisition of FluidCoin. Jane sues Roy, seeking $34,980 in compensatory damages. Finding breach of contract, a court awards Jane the $34,980 plus attorney's fees and litigation costs, with interest. ■

There is a two-step process to determine whether a breach of contract has resulted in compensatory damages. Initially, it must be established that there is a contract between the parties and that the contract has been breached. Next, it must be proved that the breach caused damages.

Case Example 15.2 Owens Community College lost its accreditation from the National League for Nursing Accreditation Commission (NLNAC) in July. The college did not inform its nursing students of this development until after classes had started in the fall. Carianne Baird and sixty-one other students from the program filed a breach of contract suit against Owens.

An Ohio appeals court determined that a contract existed in which the students paid their fees in exchange for a degree from an NLNAC-accredited institution. By losing that accreditation, Owens breached the contract. The court also recognized the probability that this breach would harm the plaintiffs' career prospects. Therefore, compensatory damages could be determined by measuring the difference between their future earnings capacity as graduates of an NLNAC-accredited nursing college and their future earnings capacity as graduates of now-unaccredited Owens.[2] ■ This chapter's *Cybersecurity and the Law* feature examines contractual issues, including potential damages, that arose when a popular fast food chain suffered a significant data breach.

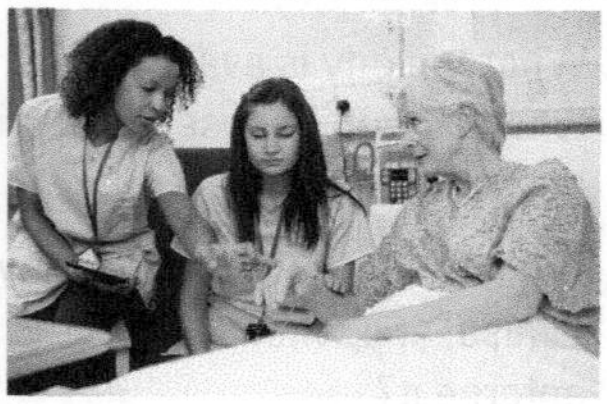
Monkey Business Images/shutterstock.com

How might a court determine the compensatory damages for students whose contract with a nursing school has been breached?

1. *Restatement (Second) of Contracts,* Section 347.
2. *Baird v. Owens Community College,* 2016 -Ohio- 537, Ohio Ct. App. (10th Dis. 2016).

Cybersecurity and the Law

Arby's Restaurant Group, Inc.

The restaurant chain Arby's was the target of third-party hackers who breached its credit card point-of-sale machines and stole the personal information of hundreds of thousands of customers. A group of these customers sued the company. The plaintiffs claimed that, despite being aware of other high-profile data breaches in the business world, Arby's failed to make meaningful improvements to the security of its point-of-sale network. The plaintiffs contended that any modern business transaction involves an implied contract in which, in return for a consumer's patronage, the retailer promises to take sufficient measures to protect the consumer's private information.

Arby's countered that the plaintiffs could not unilaterally impose a contractual obligation to safeguard credit card data. The company insisted that its only responsibility was to provide food in return for payment for the food. Rejecting these arguments, a federal court in Georgia ruled that a reasonable jury could find that an implied contract existed between Arby's and the plaintiffs. When customers use a credit card, the court concluded, they intend to share their financial information only with the merchant. If the customers had known that this information was at risk of being stolen, they likely would have taken their business elsewhre.[a]

a. *In Re Arby's Restaurant Group Litigation*, 2018 WL 2128441 (N.D. Georgia—Atlanta Div., 2018).

Critical Thinking

Suppose a court rules that Arby's weak point-of-sale security system does constitute a breach of contract. What might be some of the compensatory damages due to customers whose credit card information was stolen by hackers?

Standard Measure. The standard measure of compensatory damages is the difference between the value of the breaching party's promised performance under the contract and the value of that party's actual performance. This amount is reduced by any loss that the injured party has avoided.

Example 15.3 Randall contracts to perform certain services exclusively for Hernandez during the month of March for $4,000. Hernandez cancels the contract and is in breach. Randall is able to find another job during March but can earn only $3,000. He can sue Hernandez for breach and recover $1,000 as compensatory damages. Randall can also recover from Hernandez the amount that he spent to find the other job. ■ Expenses that are directly incurred because of a breach of contract—such as those incurred to obtain performance from another source—are called **incidental damages.**

Note that the measure of compensatory damages often varies by type of contract. Certain types of contracts deserve special mention and are discussed next.

Sale of Goods. In a contract for the sale of goods, the usual measure of compensatory damages is the difference between the contract price and the market price.[3] **Example 15.4** Medik Laboratories contracts to buy ten model UTS 400 network servers from Cal Industries for $4,000 each, but Cal Industries fails to deliver the servers. The market price of the servers at the time Medik learns of the breach is $4,500. Therefore, Medik's measure of damages is $5,000 (10 × $500), plus any incidental damages (expenses) caused by the breach. ■

Sometimes, the buyer breaches when the seller has not yet produced the goods. In that situation, compensatory damages normally equal the seller's lost profits on the sale, not the difference between the contract price and the market price.

Focus Question 1

What is the standard measure of compensatory damages when a contract is breached?

Incidental Damages Damages that compensate for expenses directly incurred because of a breach of contract, such as those incurred to obtain performance from another source.

3. This amount is the difference between the contract price and the market price at the time and place at which the goods were to be delivered or tendered. See Sections 2–708, 2–713, and 2–715(1) of the Uniform Commercial Code (UCC).

Sale of Land. Ordinarily, because each parcel of land is unique, the remedy for a seller's breach of a contract for a sale of real estate is specific performance, in which the buyer is awarded the bargained-for parcel of property. (Specific performance will be discussed more fully later in the chapter.) The majority of states follow this rule.

A minority of states apply a different rule when the seller breaches a land-sale contract unintentionally (for instance, when the seller cannot deliver good title to the land for an unforeseeable reason). In these states, a prospective buyer is limited to a refund of any down payment made plus any expenses incurred (such as fees for title searches, attorneys, and escrows). Thus, the minority rule effectively returns purchasers to the positions they occupied prior to the sale, rather than giving them the benefit of the bargain.

When the *buyer* is the party in breach, the measure of damages is typically the difference between the contract price and the market price of the land. The same measure is used when specific performance is not available (because the seller has sold the property to someone else, for instance).

Construction Contracts. The measure of damages in a building or construction contract depends on which party breaches and when the breach occurs.

1. *Breach by owner.* The owner may breach at three different stages—before performance has begun, during performance, or after performance has been completed. If the owner breaches *before performance has begun,* the contractor can recover only the profits that would have been made on the contract. (Profits equal the total contract price less the cost of materials and labor.) If the owner breaches *during performance,* the contractor can recover the profits plus the costs incurred in partially constructing the building. If the owner breaches *after construction has been completed,* the contractor can recover the entire contract price, plus interest.
2. *Breach by contractor.* When the contractor breaches the contract—either by failing to begin construction or by stopping work partway through the project—the measure of damages is the cost of completion. The cost of completion includes reasonable compensation for any delay in performance. If the contractor finishes late, the measure of damages is the loss of use. **Case Example 15.5** To remodel his home in Connecticut, Richard Viola hired J. S. Benson of J. S. Benson Woodworking & Design as his contractor. Over a period of five years, Viola paid Benson more than $500,000 to fabricate and install windows and doors, nearly $50,000 for the purchase of lumber, $10,000 to ship and store the lumber, as well as $111,000 toward the contract price. Nevertheless, Benson failed to complete the project and would not give Viola the lumber that he had purchased despite repeated requests. Viola eventually sued Benson for breaching the contract. A state court held that Benson had breached the contract and ordered him to pay $848,000 in damages. The damages awarded included additional amounts to reimburse Viola for attorneys' fees, rental costs (because he was unable to live in the home), and property taxes.[4]

Vasily Pindyurin/fStop/Getty Images

When a woodworking contractor breaches a contract, how is the measure of damages calculated?

3. *Breach by both owner and contractor.* When the performance of both parties—the construction contractor and the owner—falls short of what their contract required, the courts attempt to strike a fair balance in awarding damages.

Exhibit 15–1 summarizes the rules for the measure of damages in breached construction contracts.

4. *Viola v. J. S. Benson,* 2017 WL 2817404 (Ct. 2017).

Exhibit 15–1 Measure of Damages—Breach of Construction Contracts

PARTY IN BREACH	TIME OF BREACH	MEASURE OF DAMAGES
Owner	Before construction has begun	Profits (contract price less cost of materials and labor)
Owner	During construction	Profits plus costs incurred up to time of breach
Owner	After construction is completed	Full contract price, plus interest
Contractor	Before construction has begun	Cost in excess of contract price to complete work
Contractor	Before construction is completed	Generally, all costs incurred by owner to complete

Consequential Damages Foreseeable damages that result from a party's breach of contract are called **consequential damages,** or *special damages.* They differ from compensatory damages in that they are caused by special circumstances beyond the contract itself. They flow from the consequences, or results, of a breach. When a seller fails to deliver goods, knowing that the buyer is planning to use or resell those goods immediately, a court may award consequential damages for the loss of profits from the planned resale. In the following case, an advertising company sought to recover consequential damages consisting of lost profits that the company claimed had been caused by a delay in the delivery of a customized truck.

Consequential Damages Foreseeable damages that result from a party's breach of contract but are caused by special circumstances beyond the contract itself.

Case 15.1

HDAV Outdoor, LLC v. Red Square Holdings, LLC

Court of Appeals of Nevada,[a] __ P.3d __, 2019 WL 6974770 (2019).

Facts HDAV Outdoor, LLC, contracted with Red Square Holdings, LLC, to customize an Isuzu Diesel Eco Max box truck with LED light displays that would allow Red Square to use the truck for mobile advertising. HDAV Outdoor agreed to complete the customization within eight weeks after Red Square delivered the truck. HDAV Outdoor did not finish the job, however, until four and a half months after the eight-week completion date.

Red Square filed a suit in a Nevada state district court against HDAV Outdoor, alleging breach of contract and seeking damages. Mohamood Razack, Red Square's sales manager, testified that, based on the company's record of past profits, it had lost $12,000 per month in profits because of HDAV's "untimely" work.

The district court ruled in Red Square's favor and awarded damages in the amount of $45,000 in lost profits for the delay. HDAV Outdoor appealed, challenging the award.

Issue Did the district court abuse its discretion by awarding Red Square $45,000 in lost profits?

Decision No. The Nevada Court of Appeals affirmed the lower court's ruling and award. "HDAV Outdoor's challenge to the award of lost profits fails."

Reason The appellate court acknowledged that damages resulting from a breach of contract must be reasonably foreseeable at the time of the contract. The court recognized that those damages could include an award of lost profits that result from "an inability to timely use equipment as long as the delay is attributable to the breaching party."

In this case, HDAV Outdoor did not deliver the truck by the promised delivery date. Red Square claimed that its inability to use the truck until it was delivered resulted in lost profits. The appellant argued that Red Square had not provided evidence of its costs to offset against the sought-after lost profits. The appellate court explained, however, that an award of delay damages does not require the consideration of such an offset. "Obviously, Red Square was not incurring any costs specifically related to operating the truck because it did not have the truck to operate."

Finally, the court pointed out, "Red Square specifically notified HDAV Outdoor that it intended to commence advertising with the truck, and thus it was reasonably foreseeable that any delay in delivering the truck would adversely affect Red Square's profitability."

Critical Thinking

- **Legal Environment** *What might explain the difference between Razack's estimate and the district court's award of Red Square's lost profits for the delay in the delivery of the truck? Discuss.*
- **Economic** *Instead of being awarded as consequential damages, should "lost profits" be considered a risk in the change of value to the object of a contract assumed by the nonbreaching party? Why or why not?*

---

a. The Nevada Court of Appeals hears cases assigned to it by the Nevada Supreme Court, which otherwise hears all appeals from the state's district courts. This is similar to court systems in Idaho, Iowa, and Mississippi.

Know This
To avoid the risk of consequential damages, a seller can limit the buyer's remedies via contract.

For the nonbreaching party to recover consequential damages, the breaching party must know (or have reason to know) that special circumstances will cause the nonbreaching party to suffer an additional loss.[5] See this chapter's *Landmark in the Law* feature for a discussion of the nineteenth-century English case that established this rule on consequential damages.

Punitive Damages Punitive damages generally are not awarded in lawsuits for breach of contract. Because punitive damages are designed to punish the wrongdoer and set an example to deter similar conduct in the future, they have no legitimate place in contract law. A contract is simply a civil relationship between the parties. The law may compensate one party for the loss of the bargain—no more and no less. In a few situations, when a person's actions cause both a breach of contract and a tort, punitive damages may be available.

Nominal Damages A small monetary award (often one dollar) granted to a plaintiff when no actual damage was suffered.

Nominal Damages When no actual damage or financial loss results from a breach of contract and only a technical injury is involved, the court may award **nominal damages** to the innocent party. Nominal damages awards are often small, such as one dollar, but they do

5. UCC 2–715(2).

Hadley v. Baxendale (1854)

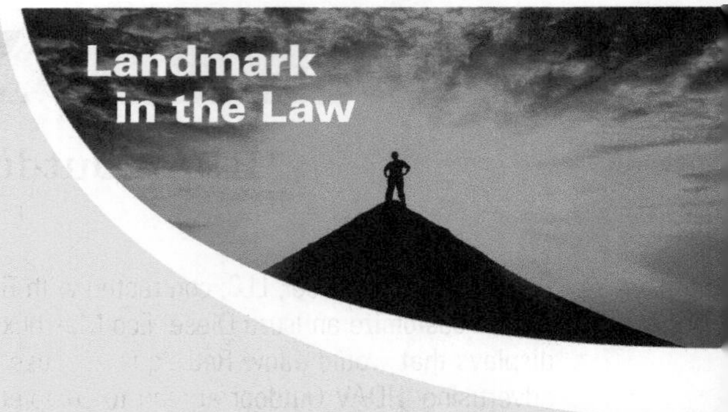

The rule that requires a breaching party to have notice of special ("consequential") circumstances that will result in additional loss to the nonbreaching party before consequential damages can be awarded was first enunciated in *Hadley v. Baxendale*,[a] a landmark case decided in 1854.

Case Background The case involved a broken crankshaft used in a flour mill run by the Hadley family in Gloucester, England. The crankshaft attached to the steam engine in the mill broke, and the shaft had to be sent to a foundry in Greenwich so that a new shaft could be made to fit the engine.

The Hadleys hired Baxendale, a common carrier, to transport the shaft from Gloucester to Greenwich. Baxendale received payment in advance and promised to deliver the shaft the following day. It was not delivered for several days, however. The Hadleys had no extra crankshaft on hand to use, so they had to close the mill during those days. The Hadleys sued Baxendale to recover the profits they lost during that time. Baxendale contended that the loss of profits was "too remote."

In the mid-1800s, it was common knowledge that large mills, such as that run by the Hadleys, normally had more than one crankshaft in case the main one broke and had to be repaired. It is against this background that the parties presented their arguments on whether the damages resulting from the loss of profits while the crankshaft was out for repair were "too remote" to be recoverable.

The Issue Before the Court and the Court's Ruling The crucial issue for the court was whether the Hadleys had informed the carrier, Baxendale, of the special circumstances surrounding the crankshaft's repair. Specifically, did Baxendale know at the time of the contract that the mill would have to shut down while the crankshaft was being repaired?

In the court's opinion, the only circumstances communicated by the Hadleys to Baxendale at the time the contract was made were that the item to be transported was a broken crankshaft of a mill and that the Hadleys were the owners and operators of that mill. The court concluded that these circumstances did not reasonably indicate that the mill would have to stop operations if the delivery of the crankshaft was delayed.

Application to Today's World
Today, the rule enunciated by the court in this case still applies. When damages are awarded, compensation is given only for those injuries that the defendant could reasonably have foreseen as a probable result of the usual course of events following a breach. If the alleged injury is outside the usual and foreseeable course of events, the plaintiff must show specifically that the defendant had reason to know the facts and foresee the injury.

This rule applies to contracts in the online environment as well. For example, suppose that an online merchant loses business (and profits) due to a computer system's failure. If the failure was caused by malfunctioning software, the merchant normally may recover the lost profits from the software maker if these consequential damages were foreseeable.

a. 9 Exch. 341, 156 Eng.Rep. 145 (1854).

establish that the defendant acted wrongfully. Most lawsuits for nominal damages are brought as a matter of principle under the theory that a breach has occurred and some damages must be imposed regardless of actual loss.

Example 15.6 Hernandez contracts to buy potatoes from Stanley at fifty cents a pound. Stanley breaches the contract and does not deliver the potatoes. Meanwhile, the price of potatoes falls. Hernandez is able to buy them in the open market at half the price he agreed to pay Stanley. Hernandez is clearly better off because of Stanley's breach. Thus, if Hernandez sues for breach of contract and wins, the court will likely award only nominal damages.

15–1b Mitigation of Damages

In most situations, when a breach of contract occurs, the injured party is held to a duty to mitigate, or reduce, the damages suffered. Under this doctrine of **mitigation of damages,** the required action depends on the nature of the situation.

Mitigation of Damages The requirement that a plaintiff do whatever is reasonable to minimize the damages caused by the defendant's breach of contract.

Employment Contracts In the majority of states, a person whose employment has been wrongfully terminated has a duty to mitigate damages incurred because of the employer's breach of the employment contract. In other words, a wrongfully terminated employee has a duty to take a similar job if one is available.

If the employee fails to do this, the damages received will be equivalent to the person's former salary less the income that person would have received in a similar job obtained by reasonable means. The employer has the burden of proving that such a job existed and that the employee could have been hired. Normally, a terminated employee is under no duty to take a job that is not of the same type and rank.

Example 15.7 Susan works as a librarian at Barnett University. When Susan is fired, she claims that she has been terminated in retaliation for filing an employment discrimination claim. Suppose that Susan succeeds in her employment discrimination claim but that Barnett can show that she has failed to take another librarian position when several comparable positions were available. Barnett can assert that she has failed to mitigate damages. In that situation, any compensation she is awarded for wrongful termination will be reduced by the amount she *could have obtained* from other employment.

Rental Agreements Some states require a landlord to use reasonable means to find a new tenant if a tenant abandons the premises and fails to pay rent. If an acceptable tenant becomes available, the landlord is required to lease the premises to this tenant to mitigate the damages recoverable from the former tenant.

The former tenant is still liable for the difference between the amount of the rent under the original lease and the rent received from the new tenant. If the landlord has not taken reasonable steps to find a new tenant, a court will likely reduce any award by the amount of rent the landlord could have received had this step been taken.

15–1c Liquidated Damages versus Penalties

A **liquidated damages** provision in a contract specifies that a certain dollar amount is to be paid in the event of a *future* default or breach of contract. (*Liquidated* means determined, settled, or fixed.)

Liquidated Damages An amount, stipulated in a contract, that the parties to the contract believe to be a reasonable estimation of the damages that will occur in the event of a breach.

Liquidated damages differ from penalties. Although a **penalty** also specifies a certain amount to be paid in the event of a default or breach of contract, it is designed to penalize the breaching party, not to make the innocent party whole. Liquidated damages provisions normally are enforceable. In contrast, if a court finds that a provision calls for a penalty, the agreement as to the amount will not be enforced, and recovery will be limited to actual damages.

Penalty A sum specified in a contract not as a measure of compensation for its breach but rather as a punishment for a default. The agreement as to the amount will not be enforced, and recovery will be limited to the actual damages.

Enforceability To determine whether a particular provision is for liquidated damages or a penalty, the court must answer two questions:

1. At the time the contract was formed, was it apparent that damages would be difficult to estimate in the event of a breach?
2. Was the amount set as damages a reasonable estimate and not excessive?[6]

If the answers to both questions are yes, the provision normally will be enforced. If either answer is no, the provision usually will not be enforced.

In the following *Spotlight Case*, the court had to decide whether a clause in a contract was an enforceable liquidated damages provision or an unenforceable penalty.

6. *Restatement (Second) of Contracts,* Section 356(1).

Spotlight on Liquidated Damages: Case 15.2

Kent State University v. Ford

Court of Appeals of Ohio, Eleventh District, Portage County 2015-Ohio-41, 26 N.E.3d 868, (2015).

Facts Gene Ford signed a five-year contract with Kent State University in Ohio to work as the head coach for the men's basketball team. The contract provided that if Ford quit before the end of the contract term, he would pay to the school liquidated damages in an amount equal to his salary ($300,000), multiplied by the number of years remaining on the contract. Laing Kennedy, Kent State's athletic director, told Ford that the contract would be renegotiated within a few years.

©Debby Wong/Shutterstock.com

If a college coach quits before the end of his contract, can the university recover liquidated damages?

Four years before the contract expired, however, Ford left Kent State and began to coach for Bradley University at an annual salary of $700,000. Kent State filed a suit in an Ohio state court against Ford, alleging breach of contract. The court enforced the liquidated damages clause and awarded the university $1.2 million. Ford appealed, arguing that the liquidated damages clause in his employment contract was an unenforceable penalty.

Issue Was the liquidated damages clause in Ford's contract enforceable?

Decision Yes. A state intermediate appellate court affirmed the lower court's award. The clause was not a penalty. "There was justification for seeking liquidated damages to compensate for Kent State's losses" on Ford's breach.

Reason At the time the contract was entered into, determining the damages that would result from a breach was "difficult, if not impossible." The resignation of a head coach from a university's basketball team may cause a loss in ticket sales and a drop in community and alumni support for the team. The university's ability to recruit players may also be affected. Of course, a search for a new coach and coaching staff will be required. These effects are not easy to measure before they happen, especially considering that such results may be different at different times in a coach's tenure. Kennedy's statement that the contract would be renegotiated indicated that Kent State was interested in the stability of these factors. And in this case, "based on the record, . . . the damages were reasonable." The salary that Bradley was willing to pay Ford showed the cost to Kent State of finding a new coach with his skill and experience. "There was also an asserted decrease in ticket sales, costs associated with the trip for the coaching search, and additional potential sums that may be expended."

Critical Thinking

- **Cultural** *How does a college basketball team's record of wins and losses, and its ranking in its conference, support the court's decision in this case?*

Common Uses of Liquidated Damages Provisions Liquidated damages provisions are frequently used in construction contracts. For instance, a provision requiring a construction contractor to pay $300 for every day the contractor is late in completing the project is a liquidated damages provision. Such provisions are also common in contracts for the sale of goods[7] and in certain loan contracts (see the example discussed in this chapter's *Business Law Analysis*). In addition, contracts with entertainers and professional athletes often include liquidated damages provisions.

15–2 Equitable Remedies

Sometimes, damages are an inadequate remedy for a breach of contract. In these situations, the nonbreaching party may ask the court for an equitable remedy. Equitable remedies include rescission and restitution, specific performance, and reformation.

---

7. Section 2–718(1) of the UCC specifically authorizes the use of liquidated damages provisions.

Business Law Analysis

Enforceability of Liquidated Damages Provisions

Planned Pethood Plus, Inc. (PPP), is a veterinarian-owned clinic. It borrowed $389,000 from KeyBank at an interest rate of 9.3 percent per year for ten years. The loan had a "prepayment penalty" clause that clearly stated that if the loan was repaid early, a specific formula would be used to assess a lump-sum payment to extinguish the obligation. The sooner the loan was paid off, the higher the prepayment penalty.

After a year, the veterinarians decided to pay off the loan. KeyBank invoked a prepayment penalty of $40,525.92, which was equal to 10.7 percent of the balance due. PPP sued, contending that the prepayment requirement was unenforceable because it was a penalty. The bank countered that the amount was not a penalty but liquidated damages and that the sum was reasonable. Was the loan's prepayment penalty clause enforceable?

Analysis: A liquidated damages provision in a contract specifies a certain amount of money to be paid in the event of a future default or breach of contract. In contrast, a penalty provision specifies a certain amount to be paid in the event of a default or breach of contract and is designed to penalize the breaching party. Liquidated damages provisions normally are enforceable, but penalty provisions are not.

To determine whether a provision is for liquidated damages or a penalty, ask (1) when the contract was formed, were the potential damages that would be incurred on its breach difficult to estimate, and (2) was the amount set as damages a reasonable estimate of those potential damages? If both answers are yes, the provision is for liquidated damages. If either answer is no, the provision is a penalty.

Result and Reasoning: PPP's loan included a prepayment penalty clause common to many loan agreements. If PPP decided to repay its loan early, an amount would be added to the balance due according to a specific formula. When the contract was formed, the potential loss to the lender on the loan's prepayment was difficult to estimate because the time of the prepayment could not be reasonably foreseen. The formula provided a reasonable estimate of that loss.

In other words, the answers to both questions in the Analysis section are yes. Thus, the provision in PPP's loan was for liquidated damages and enforceable.

15–2a Rescission and Restitution

As previously discussed, rescission is essentially an action to undo, or cancel, a contract—to return nonbreaching parties to the positions that they occupied prior to the transaction.[8] When fraud, mistake, duress, undue influence, lack of capacity, or failure of consideration is present, rescission is available. Rescission may also be available by statute.[9] The failure of one party to perform under a contract entitles the other party to rescind the contract. The rescinding party must give prompt notice to the breaching party.

Rescission of a contract on the basis of a breach is appropriate where the breach is found to be material and willful. A party seeking rescission must also show that the contracting parties can be restored to the *status quo*. In the following case, a landlord overcharged a tenant certain fees and did not explain how the amount was calculated, as the lease required. The question was whether these circumstances entitled the tenant to rescind the lease.

---

8. The rescission discussed here refers to *unilateral* rescission, in which only one party wants to undo the contract. In *mutual* rescission, both parties agree to undo the contract. Mutual rescission discharges the contract, whereas unilateral rescission is generally available as a remedy for breach of contract.

9. Many states have laws that allow individuals who enter into "home solicitation contracts" to rescind these contracts within three business days for any reason. See, for example, California Civil Code Section 1689.5.

Case 15.3

Cipriano Square Plaza Corp. v. Munawar

Maryland Court of Special Appeals, 2018 WL 1040020 (2018).

Facts Haseeb and Razia Munawar entered into a lease to rent space in a shopping center in Greenbelt, Maryland, owned by Cipriano Square Plaza Corporation. The lease obligated the Munawars to pay a pro rata (proportionate) share of the real estate taxes. The new tenants were assessed with property tax charges shortly after occupying the leased space. Asserting that the amount was excessive, they asked Cipriano for an explanation. The lease required the landlord to provide certain documents (such as tax bills) and explain how the tenants' share was calculated. After repeated requests, the Munawars received a partial reduction but no explanation. They filed a suit in a Maryland state court against Cipriano, alleging a breach of the lease. The court rescinded the deal. Cipriano appealed.

Issue Were the Munawars entitled to rescind their lease?

Decision Yes. A state intermediate appellate court affirmed the judgment of the trial court. The landlord had materially breached the lease, and its rescission was an appropriate remedy.

Reason Cipriano breached its duties to the Munawars regarding payment of their share of the real estate taxes. Cipriano's breach consisted of its overcharges of the Munawars' share of the taxes and the landlord's refusal to explain the calculation of this assessment. Cipriano had "ample opportunities" to make this explanation and failed to do so. The overbilling and the failure to explain it were voluntary and intentional. The breach was material—the overcharges were about 130 percent of the Munawars' actual pro rata share. And rescission would restore the parties to their status quo before the lease.

Cipriano argued that it would lose the benefit of its lease with the Munawars. But the purpose of rescission "is not to give the breaching party the benefit of the bargain that it would have had but for its breach." Here, before the lease, Cipriano had an empty store. As a result of the rescission, the landlord would once again have an empty store that it could lease to another party.

Critical Thinking

- **Legal Environment** *Cipriano designated Nicholas Vassello to testify on its behalf. Vassello was unable to explain how the Munawars' share of the property taxes was calculated. What effect might this testimony have had on the trial court's decision?*
- **Economic** *The lease provided that any monetary judgment in favor of the tenant could be recovered only on the landlord's sale of the shopping center. As a practical matter, how might this provision have affected the result in the* Cipriano *case?*

Restitution To rescind a contract, both parties generally must make **restitution** to each other by returning goods, property, or funds previously conveyed.[10] If the property or goods can be returned, they must be. If the property or goods have been consumed, restitution must be made in an equivalent dollar amount. Essentially, restitution involves the recapture of a benefit conferred on a defendant who has been unjustly enriched by that benefit.

Restitution An equitable remedy under which persons are restored to their original position prior to loss or injury, or placed in the position they would have been in had the breach not occurred.

Example 15.8 Katie contracts with Mikhail to design a house for her. Katie pays Mikhail $9,000 and agrees to make two more payments of $9,000 (for a total of $27,000) as the design progresses. The next day, Mikhail calls Katie and tells her that he has taken a position with a large architectural firm in another state and cannot design the house. Katie decides to hire another architect that afternoon. Katie can obtain restitution of the $9,000.

Restitution Is Not Limited to Rescission Cases Restitution may be required when a contract is rescinded, but the right to restitution is not limited to rescission cases. Because an award of restitution basically returns something to its rightful owner, a party can seek restitution in actions for breach of contract, tort actions, and other types of actions.

Restitution can be obtained when funds or property has been transferred by mistake or because of fraud or incapacity. Similarly, restitution might be available when there has been misconduct by a party who has a special relationship with the other party. Even in criminal cases, a court can order restitution of funds or property obtained through embezzlement, conversion, theft, or copyright infringement.

Know This

Restitution offers several advantages over traditional damages. First, restitution may be available in situations when damages cannot be proved or are difficult to prove. Second, restitution can be used to recover specific property. Third, restitution sometimes results in a greater overall award.

Case Example 15.9 Clara Lee contracted to purchase Rosalina Robles's dental practice in Chicago, Illinois, for $267,000. Nearly half of the practice's market value was attributed to the business's good reputation. After Lee took over the practice, however, *Chicago Magazine* and other local media revealed that one of the dentists at Robles's practice had treated underage prostitutes in the offices after hours. Federal authorities were investigating that dentist for this and other misconduct.

Lee sued Robles for fraud, alleging that she had deliberately withheld information about the dentist and the investigation. An Illinois state court awarded rescission, and the holding was affirmed on appeal. The appellate court reasoned that the parties' agreement for the sale of the dental practice required Robles to disclose "any material information." The duty to disclose included actions by a "governmental agency that materially alters the desirability or economic potential of the assets."[11]

15–2b Specific Performance

The equitable remedy of **specific performance** calls for the performance of the act promised in the contract. This remedy is attractive to a nonbreaching party because it provides the exact bargain promised in the contract. It also avoids some of the problems inherent in a suit for monetary damages, such as collecting a judgment and arranging another contract. Moreover, the actual performance may be more valuable (to the promisee) than the monetary damages.

Specific Performance An equitable remedy in which a court orders the parties to perform as promised in the contract. This remedy normally is granted only when the legal remedy (monetary damages) is inadequate.

Normally, however, specific performance will not be granted unless the party's legal remedy (monetary damages) is inadequate.[12] For this reason, contracts for the sale of goods rarely qualify for specific performance. Monetary damages ordinarily are adequate in sales contracts because substantially identical goods can be bought or sold in the market. Only if the goods are unique will a court grant specific performance. For instance, paintings, sculptures, and rare books and coins are often unique, and monetary damages will not enable a buyer to obtain substantially identical substitutes in the market.

Focus Question 2

When do courts grant specific performance as a remedy?

10. *Restatement (Second) of Contracts*, Section 370.
11. Clara Wonjung Lee, *DDS, Ltd. v. Robles*, 2014 WL 976776 (Ill.App. 2014). *DDS* stands for Doctor of Dental Surgery.
12. *Restatement (Second) of Contracts*, Section 359.

Sale of Land A court may grant specific performance to a buyer in an action for a breach of contract involving the sale of land. In this situation, the legal remedy of monetary damages may not compensate the buyer adequately because every parcel of land is unique. The same land in the same location obviously cannot be obtained elsewhere. Only when specific performance is unavailable (such as when the seller has sold the property to someone else) will damages be awarded instead.

Case Example 15.10 Harmony Development agreed to sell seven acres of a planned subdivision to Jerry Davis for $1.5 million. The contract required Harmony to spend $1.85 million improving the property so that Davis could construct a health club on it. After Harmony made the improvements, Davis informed the company that the subdivision no longer "fit in harmony" with his plans and refused to complete the purchase. Harmony sued for breach of contract. The Wyoming Supreme Court granted specific performance, calling the remedy "a means of compelling [Davis] to do precisely what he should have done without being coerced by a court."[13]

Contracts for Personal Services Contracts for personal services require one party to work personally for another party. Courts normally refuse to grant specific performance of personal-service contracts. One reason is that ordering parties to perform personal services against their will would amount to a type of involuntary servitude.[14]

Moreover, the courts do not want to monitor contracts for personal services, which usually require the exercise of personal judgment or talent. **Example 15.11** Nicole contracts with a surgeon to remove a tumor on her brain. If he refuses to perform the surgery, the court will not compel (nor would Nicole want) him to perform. A court cannot ensure meaningful performance in such a situation.[15]

If a contract is not deemed personal, the remedy at law of monetary damages may be adequate if a substantially identical service (for instance, lawn mowing) is available from other persons.

15–2c Reformation

Reformation is an equitable remedy used when the parties have *imperfectly* expressed their agreement in writing. Reformation allows a court to rewrite the contract to reflect the parties' true intentions.

kadmy/iStock/Getty Images

What happens when a contract mistakenly specifies a crane instead of a forklift?

Fraud or Mutual Mistake Courts order reformation most often when fraud or mutual mistake is present. **Example 15.12** If Carson contracts to buy a forklift from Yoshie but the written contract refers to a crane, a mutual mistake has occurred. Accordingly, a court could reform the contract so that the writing conforms to the parties' original intention as to which piece of equipment is being sold.

Incorrect Written Statement of the Parties' Oral Agreement A court will also reform a contract when two parties enter into a binding oral contract but later make an error when they attempt to put the terms into writing. Usually, the court will allow into evidence the correct terms of the oral contract, thereby reforming the written contract.

Covenants Not to Compete Courts also may reform contracts involving written covenants not to compete, or restrictive covenants. Such covenants are often included in contracts for the sale of ongoing businesses and in employment contracts. The agreements restrict the area and time in which one party can directly compete with the other party.

13. *Davis v. Harmony Development LLC*, 2020 WY 39, __ P.3d __ (2020).
14. Involuntary servitude, or slavery, is contrary to the public policy expressed in the Thirteenth Amendment to the U.S. Constitution.
15. Similarly, courts often refuse to order specific performance of construction contracts because courts are not set up to operate as construction supervisors or engineers.

Exhibit 15–2 Remedies for Breach of Contract

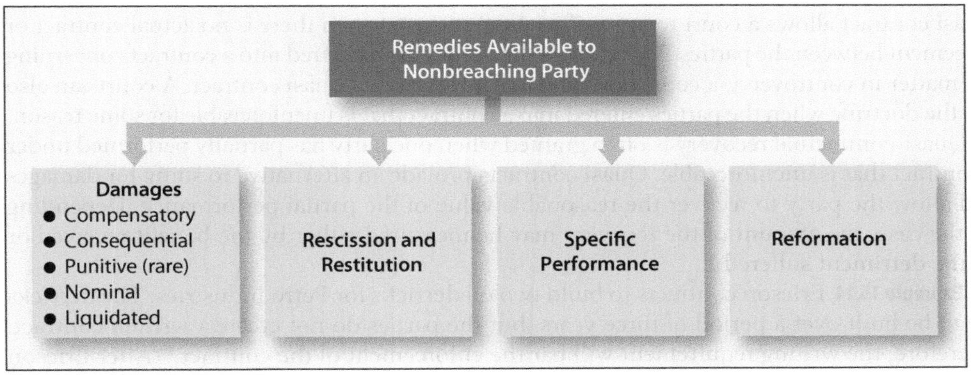

If a covenant not to compete is for a valid and legitimate purpose, but the area or time restraints are unreasonable, some courts will reform the restraints by making them reasonable and will then enforce the entire contract as reformed. Other courts will throw out the entire restrictive covenant as illegal. Thus, when businesspersons create restrictive covenants, they must make sure that the restrictions imposed are reasonable.

Case Example 15.13 Cardiac Study Center, Inc., a medical practice group, hired Dr. Robert Emerick. Later, Emerick became a shareholder of Cardiac and signed an agreement that included a covenant not to compete. The covenant stated that a physician who left the group promised not to practice competitively in the surrounding area for a period of five years. After Cardiac began receiving complaints from patients and other physicians about Emerick, it terminated his employment.

Emerick sued Cardiac, claiming that the covenant not to compete that he had signed was unreasonable and should be declared illegal. Ultimately, a state appellate court reformed the geographic and temporal restraints, and held that the covenant as reformed was both reasonable and enforceable. Cardiac had a legitimate interest in protecting its existing client base and prohibiting Emerick from taking its clients.[16]

Exhibit 15–2 graphically presents the remedies that are available to the nonbreaching party.

15–3 Recovery Based on Quasi Contract

Focus Question 3
What remedy is available if a court imposes a quasi contract?

In some situations, when no actual contract exists, a court may step in to prevent one party from being unjustly enriched at the expense of another party. As previously discussed, *quasi contract* is a legal theory under which an obligation is imposed in the absence of an agreement.

The legal obligation arises because the law considers that the party accepting the benefits has made an implied promise to pay for them. Generally, when one party has conferred a benefit on another party, justice requires that the party receiving the benefit pay the reasonable value for it. The party conferring the benefit can recover in *quantum meruit*, which means "as much as one deserves."

16. *Emerick v. Cardiac Study Center, Inc.*, 189 Wash.App. 711, 357 P.3d 696 (2015).

15–3a When Quasi Contract Is Used

Quasi contract allows a court to act as if a contract exists when there is no actual contract or agreement between the parties. Therefore, if the parties have entered into a contract concerning the matter in controversy, a court normally will not impose a quasi contract. A court can also use the doctrine when the parties entered into a contract that is unenforceable for some reason.

Quasi-contractual recovery is often granted when one party has partially performed under a contract that is unenforceable. Quasi contracts provide an alternative to suing for damages and allow the party to recover the reasonable value of the partial performance. Depending on the case, the amount of the recovery may be measured either by the benefit received or by the detriment suffered.

Know This
The function of a quasi contract is to impose a legal obligation on a party who made no actual promise.

Example 15.14 Ericson contracts to build two oil derricks for Petro Industries. The derricks are to be built over a period of three years, but the parties do not create a written contract. Therefore, the writing requirement will bar the enforcement of the contract.[17] After Ericson completes one derrick, Petro Industries informs him that it will not pay for the derrick. Ericson can sue Petro Industries under the theory of quasi contract. ■

15–3b The Requirements of Quasi Contract

To recover on a quasi contract theory, the party seeking recovery must show the following:

1. The party conferred a benefit on the other party.
2. The party conferred the benefit with the reasonable expectation of being paid.
3. The party did not act as a volunteer in conferring the benefit.
4. The party receiving the benefit would be unjustly enriched if allowed to retain the benefit without paying for it.

shotbydave/E+/Getty Images

Assume that it takes several years to build two oil derricks, but no written contract exists. If one is built, does the purchaser have to pay for it?

Applying these requirements to *Example 15.14*, Ericson can sue in quasi contract because all of the conditions for quasi-contractual recovery have been fulfilled. Ericson conferred a benefit on Petro Industries by building the oil derrick. Ericson built the derrick with the reasonable expectation of being paid. He did not intend to act as a volunteer. Petro Industries would be unjustly enriched if it was allowed to keep the derrick without paying Ericson for the work. Therefore, Ericson should be able to recover in *quantum meruit* the reasonable value of the oil derrick that was built, which is ordinarily equal to the fair market value.

15–4 Contract Provisions Limiting Remedies

A contract may include provisions stating that no damages can be recovered for certain types of breaches or that damages will be limited to a maximum amount. A contract may also provide that the only remedy for breach is replacement, repair, or refund of the purchase price. In addition, a contract may provide that one party can seek injunctive relief if the other party breaches the contract. Provisions stating that no damages can be recovered are called *exculpatory clauses*. Provisions that affect the availability of certain remedies are called *limitation-of-liability clauses*.

17. Contracts that by their terms cannot be performed within one year from the day after the date of contract formation must be in writing to be enforceable under the Statute of Frauds.

Ethical Issue **Can contracts for mixed martial arts fighters limit a fighter's right to stop fighting?** If you are a mixed martial arts champion, the highest-profile league to work for is the Ultimate Fighting Championship, or UFC. But a contract with UFC's parent company, Zuffa, LLC, includes numerous restrictions on your behavior.

The UFC's exclusivity clause, for instance, prevents you from competing in other mixed martial arts leagues. Another clause states that if you refuse a fight—or are injured or disabled—Zuffa can choose to extend the term of your contract. The term may be extended for any period when a fighter is unable or unwilling to compete or train for any reason. Zuffa can even retain the rights to a fighter who wants to retire from mixed martial arts.

You probably also signed an agreement that has a "champions clause." That means that if you become a champion, your contract with the UFC is automatically extended. If you get really famous, you do not even have rights to your likeness. You have signed those away to the UFC. So if a video game is based on your likeness, the UFC obtains the profits, and you do not. Therefore, you will have trouble negotiating with sponsors outside of the UFC, because you really do not own much of yourself to "sell."

A group of current and former mixed martial arts fighters have filed a lawsuit against Zuffa. They claim that these contract limitations are fundamentally unfair. Because the contracts prevent fighters from working with other promoters, profiting from individual marketing deals, and signing with outside sponsors, the suit alleges that the UFC is violating antitrust laws. Litigation is ongoing.[18]

15–4a Sales Contracts

The Uniform Commercial Code (UCC) provides that remedies can be limited in a contract for the sale of goods. We will examine the UCC provisions on limitation-of-liability clauses again in the context of the remedies available on the breach of a contract for the sale or lease of goods.[19]

15–4b Enforceability of Limitation-of-Liability Clauses

Focus Question 4

What is a limitation-of-liability clause, and when will courts enforce it?

Whether a limitation-of-liability clause in a contract will be enforced depends on the type of breach that is excused by the provision. Clauses that normally will not be enforced include provisions excluding liability for fraudulent or intentional injury or for illegal acts or other violations of law. Clauses excluding liability for negligence may be enforced in certain situations, however. When an exculpatory clause for negligence is contained in a contract made between parties who have roughly equal bargaining positions, the clause usually will be enforced.

Case Example 15.15 2010-1 SFG Venture, LLC, was the main lender on a commercial real estate loan for $15 million to fund construction of a hotel in Wisconsin. Lee Bank & Trust Co. purchased a 3.36 percent interest in the loan. Lee Bank signed a contract with SFG that included a clause limiting SFG's liability "except in the case of gross negligence or willful misconduct."

When the borrower made payments on the loan, SFG remitted 3.36 percent of each payment to Lee Bank. Eventually, however, the borrower stopped making payments, and litigation followed. Lee Bank sued SFG, which argued that it was protected by the contract provisions limiting its liability. The lower court refused to enforce the limitation-of-liability clause, but a state appellate court reversed. The court held that the clause was enforceable. It was sufficiently prominent in the contract and represented a reasonable allocation of risks in an arms-length business transaction.[20]

Bloomberg/Getty Images

Why did a court enforce the limitation-of-liability clause in a dispute over a hotel construction contract?

18. See *Cung Le v. Zuffa*, 2017 WL 2803171 (D.Nev. 2017); and *Le v. Zuffa*, 216 F.Supp.3d 1154 (D.Nev. 2016).
19. UCC 2–719.
20. *2010-1 SFG Venture, LLC v. Lee Bank & Trust Co.*, 332 Ga.App. 894, 775 S.E.2d 243 (2015).

Practice and Review

Kyle Bruno enters into a contract with X Entertainment to be a stuntman in a movie. Bruno is widely known as the best motorcycle stuntman in the business, and the movie, *Xtreme Riders*, has numerous scenes involving high-speed freestyle street-bike stunts. Filming is set to begin August 1 and end by December 1 so that the film can be released the following summer. Both parties to the contract have stipulated that the filming must end on time in order to capture the profits from the summer movie market.

The contract states that Bruno will be paid 10 percent of the net proceeds from the movie for his stunts. The contract also includes a liquidated damages provision, which specifies that if Bruno breaches the contract, he will owe X Entertainment $1 million. In addition, the contract includes a limitation-of-liability clause stating that if Bruno is injured during filming, X Entertainment's liability is limited to nominal damages. Using the information presented in the chapter, answer the following questions.

1. One day, while Bruno is preparing for a difficult stunt, he gets into an argument with the director and refuses to perform any stunts. Can X Entertainment seek specific performance of the contract? Why or why not?
2. Suppose that while performing a high-speed wheelie on a motorcycle, Bruno is injured by an intentionally reckless act of an X Entertainment employee. Will a court be likely to enforce the limitation-of-liability clause? Why or why not?
3. What factors would a court consider to determine if the $1 million liquidated damages clause is valid or is a penalty?
4. Suppose that there was no liquidated damages clause (or the court refused to enforce it) and X Entertainment breached the contract. The breach caused the release of the film to be delayed by many months. Could Bruno seek consequential (special) damages for lost profits from the summer movie market in that situation? Explain.

Debate This

Courts should always uphold limitation-of-liability clauses, whether or not the two parties to the contract had equal bargaining power.

Key Terms

consequential damages 361
incidental damages 359
liquidated damages 363
mitigation of damages 363
nominal damages 362
penalty 363
restitution 367
specific performance 367

Chapter Summary: Breach and Remedies

Damages	In contract law, the legal remedy designed to compensate the nonbreaching party for the loss of the bargain. The nonbreaching party frequently has a duty to *mitigate* (lessen or reduce) the damages suffered. There are four broad categories of damages. In addition, a contract may contain a provision for liquidated damages. 1. **Compensatory damages**—Damages that compensate the nonbreaching party for injuries actually sustained and proved to have arisen directly from the loss of the bargain resulting from the breach of contract.

a. In breached contracts for the sale of goods, the usual measure of compensatory damages is the difference between the contract price and the market price.
b. In a seller's breach of a contract for the sale of land, the measure of damages is ordinarily specific performance. For a buyer's breach, the measure of damages is typically the same as in contracts for the sale of goods.
c. In breached construction contracts, the measure of damages depends on which party breaches and at what stage of construction the breach occurs.

2. **Consequential damages**—Foreseeable damages that result from special circumstances beyond the contract itself (also called *special damages*). The damages flow only from the consequences of a breach. For a party to recover consequential damages, the breaching party must have known at the time the contract was formed that special circumstances existed that would cause the nonbreaching party to incur additional loss on breach of the contract.
3. **Punitive damages**—Damages awarded to punish the breaching party. Usually not awarded in an action for breach of contract unless a tort is involved.
4. **Nominal damages**—Damages small in amount (such as one dollar) that are awarded when a breach has occurred but no actual injury has been suffered. Awarded only to establish that the defendant acted wrongfully.
5. **Mitigation of damages**—In most situations, when a breach of contract occurs, the injured party is held to a duty to mitigate, or reduce, the damages suffered.
6. **Liquidated damages**—Damages specified in a contract as the amount to be paid to the nonbreaching party in the event the contract is breached. Clauses providing for liquidated damages are enforced if the damages were difficult to estimate at the time the contract was formed and if the amount stipulated is reasonable. If the amount is construed to be a penalty, the clause will not be enforced.

Equitable Remedies

1. **Rescission**—A remedy whereby a contract is canceled and the parties are restored to the original positions that they occupied prior to the transaction. Available when fraud, mistake, duress, undue influence, lack of capacity, or failure of consideration is present. The rescinding party must give prompt notice of the rescission to the breaching party.
2. **Restitution**—When a contract is rescinded, both parties must make restitution to each other by returning the goods, property, or funds previously conveyed. Restitution prevents the unjust enrichment of the parties.
3. **Specific performance**—An equitable remedy calling for the performance of the act promised in the contract. This remedy is available only in special situations—such as those involving contracts for the sale of unique goods or land—when monetary damages would be an inadequate remedy. Specific performance is not available as a remedy for breached contracts for personal services.
4. **Reformation**—An equitable remedy allowing a contract to be "reformed," or rewritten, to reflect the parties' true intentions. Available when an agreement is imperfectly expressed in writing.

Recovery Based on Quasi Contract

An equitable theory imposed by the courts to obtain justice and prevent unjust enrichment in a situation in which no enforceable contract exists. The party seeking recovery must show the following:

1. A benefit was conferred on the other party.
2. The party conferring the benefit did so with the expectation of being paid.
3. The party conferring the benefit did not volunteer the benefit.
4. The party receiving the benefit would be unjustly enriched if allowed to retain the benefit without paying for it.

Contract Provisions Limiting Remedies

A contract may provide that no damages (or only a limited amount of damages) can be recovered in the event the contract is breached. Under the Uniform Commercial Code, remedies may be limited in contracts for the sale of goods. Clauses excluding liability for fraudulent or intentional injury or for illegal acts cannot be enforced. Clauses excluding liability for negligence may be enforced if both parties hold roughly equal bargaining power.

Issue Spotters

1. Greg contracts to build a storage shed for Haney. Haney pays Greg in advance, but Greg completes only half the work. Haney pays Ipswich $500 to finish the shed. If Haney sues Greg, what will be the measure of recovery? (See *Damages*.)
2. Lyle contracts to sell his ranch to Marley, who is to take possession on June 1. Lyle delays the transfer until August 1. Marley incurs expenses in providing for cattle that he bought for the ranch. When they made the contract, Lyle had no reason to know of the cattle. Is Lyle liable for Marley's expenses in providing for the cattle? Why or why not? (See *Damages*.)

—Check your answers to the *Issue Spotters* against the answers provided in Appendix D.

Business Scenarios and Case Problems

15–1. Liquidated Damages. Carnack contracts to sell his house and lot to Willard for $100,000. The terms of the contract call for Willard to make a deposit of 10 percent of the purchase price as a down payment. The terms further stipulate that if the buyer breaches the contract, Carnack will retain the deposit as liquidated damages. Willard makes the deposit, but because her expected financing of the $90,000 balance falls through, she breaches the contract. Two weeks later, Carnack sells the house and lot to Balkova for $105,000. Willard demands her $10,000 back, but Carnack refuses, claiming that Willard's breach and the contract terms entitle him to keep the deposit. Discuss who is correct. (See *Damages*.)

15–2. Measure of Damages. Before buying a house, Dean and Donna Testa hired Ground Systems, Inc. (GSI), to inspect the sewage and water disposal system. GSI reported a split system with a watertight septic tank, a wastewater tank, a distribution box, and a leach field. The Testas bought the house. Later, Dean saw that the system was not as GSI described—there was no distribution box or leach field, and there was only one tank, which was not watertight. The Testas arranged for the installation of a new system and sold the house. Assuming that GSI is liable for breach of contract, what is the measure of damages? [*Testa v. Ground Systems, Inc.*, 206 N.J. 330, 20 A.3d 435 (App. Div. 2011)] (See *Damages*.)

15–3. Consequential Damages. After submitting the high bid at a foreclosure sale, David Simard entered into a contract to purchase real property in Maryland for $192,000. Simard defaulted (failed to pay) on the contract, so a state court ordered the property to be resold at Simard's expense, as required by state law. The property was then resold for $163,000, but the second purchaser also defaulted on his contract. The court then ordered a second resale, resulting in a final price of $130,000. Assuming that Simard is liable for consequential damages, what is the extent of his liability? Is he liable for losses and expenses related to the first resale? If so, is he also liable for losses and expenses related to the second resale? Why or why not? [*Burson v. Simard*, 35 A.3d 1154 (Md. 2012)] (See *Damages*.)

15–4. Liquidated Damages. Cuesport Properties, LLC, sold a condominium in Anne Arundel County, Maryland, to Critical Developments, LLC. As part of the sale, Cuesport agreed to build a wall between Critical Developments' unit and an adjacent unit within thirty days of closing. If Cuesport failed to do so, it was to pay $126 per day until completion. This was an estimate of the amount of rent that Critical Developments would lose until the wall was finished and the unit could be rented. Actual damages were otherwise difficult to estimate at the time of the contract. The wall was built on time, but without a county permit, and it did not comply with the county building code. Critical Developments did not modify the wall to comply with the code until 260 days after the date of the contract deadline for completion of the wall. Does Cuesport have to pay Critical Developments $126 for each of the 260 days? Explain. [*Cuesport Properties, LLC v. Critical Developments, LLC*, 209 Md.App. 607, 61 A.3d 91 (2013)] (See *Damages*.)

15–5. Business Case Problem with Sample Answer—Limitation-of-Liability Clauses. Mia Eriksson was a seventeen-year-old competitor in horseback-riding events. Her riding coach was Kristi Nunnink. Eriksson signed an agreement that released Nunnink from all liability except for damages caused by Nunnink's "direct, willful and wanton negligence." During an event at Galway Downs in Temecula, California, Eriksson's horse struck a hurdle. She fell from the horse and the horse fell on her, causing her death. Her parents, Karan and Stan Eriksson, filed a suit in a California state court against Nunnink for wrongful death. Is the limitation-of-liability agreement that Eriksson signed likely to be enforced in her parents' case? If so, how would it affect their claim? Explain. [*Eriksson v. Nunnink*, 233 Cal.App.4th 708, 183 Cal. Rptr.3d 234 (4 Dist. 2015)] (See *Contract Provisions Limiting Remedies*.)

—For a sample answer to Problem 15–5, go to Appendix E.

15–6. Damages. Robert Morris was a licensed insurance agent working for his father's independent insurance agency when he contacted Farmers Insurance Exchange in Alabama about becoming a Farmers agent. According to Farmers' company policy, Morris was an unsuitable candidate due to his relationship with his father's agency. But no Farmers representative told Morris of this policy, and none of the documents that he signed expressed it. Farmers trained Morris and appointed him its agent. About three years later, however, Farmers terminated the appointment for "a conflict of interest because his father was in the insurance business." Morris filed a suit in an Alabama state court against Farmers, claiming that he had been fraudulently induced to leave his father's agency to work for Farmers. If Morris was successful, what type of damages was he most likely awarded? What was the measure of damages? Discuss. [*Farmers Insurance Exchange v. Morris*, 228 So.3d 971 (Ala. 2016)] (See *Damages*.)

15–7. Reformation. Dr. John Holm signed a two-year employment agreement with Gateway Anesthesia Associates PLLC. During negotiations for the agreement, Gateway's president, Dr. Jon Nottingham, told Holm that on completion of the contract he would become a partner in the firm, and during the term he would be paid "like a partner." The written agreement did not reflect this promise—the contract read that Holm would be paid based on "net collections" for his services and did not state that at the end of the term he would become a partner. Later, Gateway told Holm that it did not intend to make him a partner. Holm filed a complaint in an Arizona state court against Gateway, alleging breach. Before the trial, Holm filed a motion to reform the contract to express what he had been told. Nottingham did not dispute Holm's account. What is the basis for the reformation of a contract? Is it appropriate in this case? Why or why not? [*Holm v. Gateway Anesthesia Associates PLLC*, 2018 WL 770503 (Ariz. Div. 1 2018)] (See *Equitable Remedies*.)

15–8. A Question of Ethics—The IDDR Approach and Damages. Dr. John Braun conceived a cutting-edge device to treat adolescent scoliosis, a severe deformity of the spine. As consideration for the assignment of his intellectual property in the invention, Medtronic Sofamor Danek, Inc., a medical device manufacturer, offered Braun a higher-than-typical royalty and upfront payment. Medtronic also promised to fund expensive human trials for the device to obtain Food and Drug Administration (FDA) approval. But Medtronic never applied for permission to conduct human clinical studies. Finally, frustrated with the lack of performance on the contract, Braun filed a suit in a federal district court against Medtronic, seeking damages for breach. [*Braun v. Medtronic Sofamor Danek, Inc.* 2017 WL 6388810 (10th Cir. 2017)] (See *Damages*.)

1. Why would Medtronic make expensive promises and fail to perform? Is this ethical? Discuss, using the IDDR approach.
2. What would be the measure of damages that Braun seeks? Do the circumstances warrant an award of punitive damages? Explain.

Critical Thinking and Writing Assignments

15–9. Critical Legal Thinking. Review the discussion of the doctrine of mitigation of damages in this chapter. What are some of the advantages and disadvantages of this doctrine? (See *Damages*.)

15–10. Time-Limited Group Assignment—Remedies. Frances Morelli agreed to sell Judith Bucklin a house in Rhode Island for $177,000. The sale was supposed to be closed by September 1. The contract included a provision that "if Seller is unable to convey good, clear, insurable, and marketable title, Buyer shall have the option to (a) accept such title as Seller is able to convey without reduction of the Purchase Price, or (b) cancel this Agreement and receive a return of all Deposits."

An examination of the public records revealed that the house did not have marketable title. Bucklin offered Morelli additional time to resolve the problem, and the closing did not occur as scheduled. Morelli decided that "the deal was over" and offered to return the deposit. Bucklin refused and, in mid-October, decided to exercise her option to accept the house without marketable title. She notified Morelli, who did not respond. She then filed a lawsuit against Morelli in a state court. (See *Equitable Remedies*.)

1. One group will discuss whether Morelli has breached the contract and will decide in whose favor the court should rule.
2. A second group will assume that Morelli did breach the contract and will determine what the appropriate remedy is in this situation.
3. A third group will list some possible reasons why Bucklin wanted to go through with the transaction even when faced with not receiving marketable title.

Unit Two—Task-Based Simulation

Alberto Corelli offers to pay $2,500 to purchase a painting titled *Moonrise* from Tara Shelley, an artist whose works have been causing a stir in the art world. Shelley accepts Corelli's offer. Assuming that the contract has met all of the requirements for a valid contract, answer the following questions.

1. **Minors.** Corelli is a minor when he purchases the painting. Is the contract void? Is it voidable? What is the difference between these two conditions? A month after his eighteenth birthday, Corelli decides that he would rather have the $2,500 than the painting. He informs Shelley that he is disaffirming the contract and requests that Shelley return the $2,500 to him. When she refuses to do so, Corelli brings a court action to recover the $2,500. What will the court likely decide in this situation? Why?
2. **Statute of Frauds.** Both parties are adults, the contract is oral, and the painting is still in progress. Corelli pays Shelley the $2,500 in return for her promise to deliver the painting to his home when it is finished. A week later, after Shelley finishes the painting, a visitor to her gallery offers her $3,500 for it. Shelley sells the painting to the visitor and sends Corelli a signed letter explaining that she is "canceling" their contract for the sale of the *Moonrise* painting. Corelli sues Shelley to enforce the contract. Is the contract enforceable? Explain.
3. **Capacity.** Both parties are adults, and the contract, which is in writing, states that Corelli will pay Shelley the $2,500 the following day. In the meantime, Shelley allows Corelli to take the painting home with him. The next day, Corelli's son returns the painting to Shelley, stating that he is canceling the contract. He explains that his father has been behaving strangely lately, that he seems to be mentally incompetent at times, and that he clearly was not acting rationally when he bought the painting, which he could not afford. Is the contract enforceable? Discuss fully.
4. **Impossibility of Performance.** Both parties are adults, and the contract is in writing. The contract calls for Shelley to deliver the painting to Corelli's gallery in two weeks. Corelli has already arranged to sell the painting to a third party for $4,000 (a $1,500 profit), but it must be available for the third party in two weeks, or the sale will not go through. Shelley knows this but does not deliver the painting at the time promised. Corelli sues Shelley for $1,500 in damages. Shelley claims that performance was impossible because her mother fell seriously ill and required Shelley's care. Who will win this lawsuit, and why?
5. **Agreement in E-Contracts.** Both parties are adults. Shelley, on her website, offers to sell the painting for $2,500. Corelli accepts the offer by clicking on an "I accept" box on the computer screen displaying the offer. Among other terms, the online offer includes a forum-selection clause stating that any disputes under the contract are to be resolved by a court in California, the state in which Shelley lives. After Corelli receives the painting, he notices a smear of paint across the lower corner that was not visible in the digitized image that appeared on Shelley's website. Corelli calls Shelley, tells her about the smear, and says that he wants to cancel the contract and return the painting.

   When Shelley refuses to cooperate, Corelli sues her in a Texas state court, seeking to rescind the contract. Shelley claims that any suit against her must be filed in a California court in accordance with the forum-selection clause. Corelli maintains that the forum-selection clause is unconscionable and should not be enforced. What factors will the court consider in deciding this case? What will the court likely decide? Would it matter whether Corelli read the terms of the online offer before clicking on "I accept"?

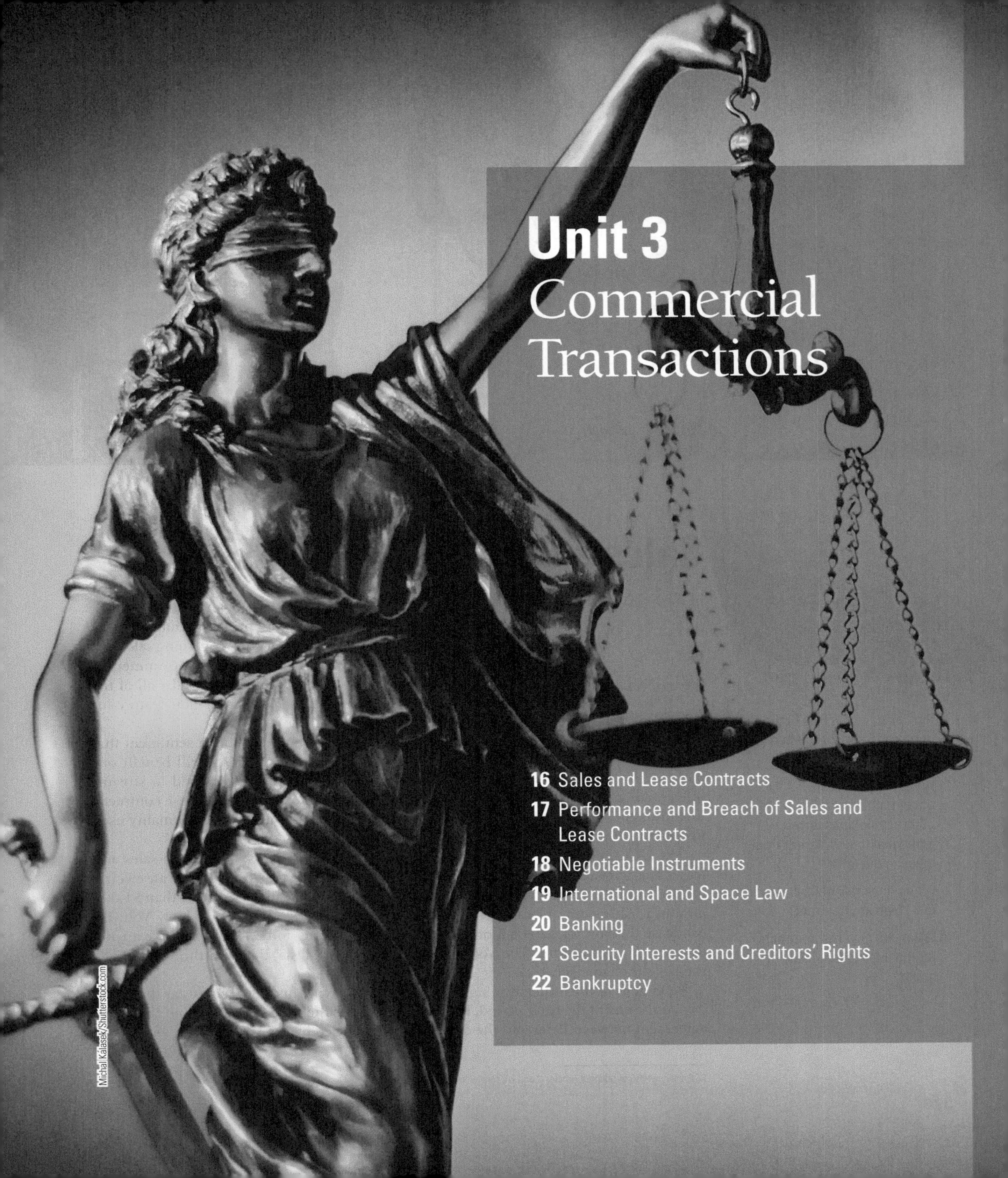

Michal Kalasek/Shutterstock.com

Unit 3
Commercial Transactions

16 Sales and Lease Contracts

Focus Questions

The four Focus Questions *below are designed to help improve your understanding. After reading this chapter, you should be able to answer the following questions:*

1. If a contract involves both goods and services, when does the UCC apply?
2. What happens if an acceptance to a sales contract includes terms additional to or different from those in the offer?
3. When does risk of loss pass in a shipment contract?
4. What law governs contracts for the international sale of goods?

"I am for free commerce with all nations."

George Washington
1732–1799
(First president of the United States, 1789–1797)

When we turn to contracts for the sale and lease of goods, we move away from common law principles and into the area of statutory law. State statutory law governing sales and lease transactions is based on the Uniform Commercial Code (UCC), which has been adopted as law by all of the states.[1] (See this chapter's *Landmark in the Law* feature for more information on the UCC.)

The chapter-opening quotation echoes a sentiment that most Americans believe—free commerce will benefit our nation. The UCC seeks to promote commerce. Its goal is to simplify and to streamline commercial transactions. The UCC allows parties to form sales and lease contracts, including those entered into online, without observing the same degree of formality used in forming other types of contracts.

The UCC applies not only to transactions between merchants, but also to sales and leases that consumers enter into with merchants. Suppose that Peter wants an electric car. He would like a Tesla Model S, but a lease on a Tesla typically costs more than $1,000 a month. After some research, Peter is considering the less expensive Chevy Volt. He can lease the Volt for $294 a month for thirty-nine months and only has to make a $500 down payment up front. The Volt is not as sleek as the Tesla, but with the Volt, he has the benefit of an electric car.

Peter goes to the dealership, signs a lease, and is driving his new electric car that same day. At the end of the lease period, Peter simply returns the car to the dealership. The lease agreement between Peter and the dealership is governed by the UCC.

1. Louisiana has not adopted Articles 2 and 2A, however.

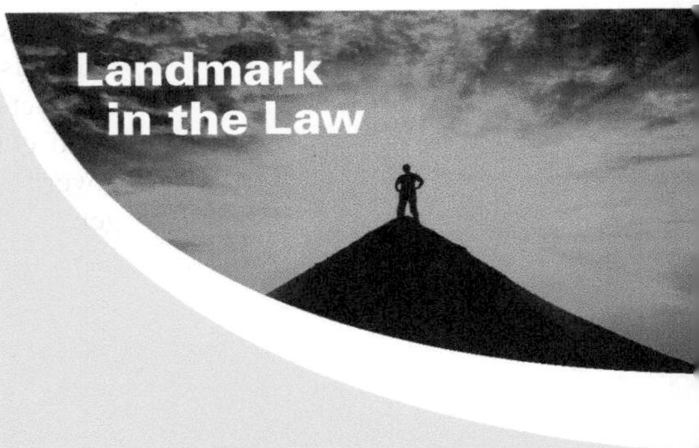

The Uniform Commercial Code

Of all the attempts to produce a uniform body of laws relating to commercial transactions in the United States, none has been as successful or comprehensive as the Uniform Commercial Code (UCC).

The Origins of the UCC In the early years of this nation, sales law varied from state to state, and this lack of uniformity complicated the formation of multistate sales contracts. To remedy this situation, the National Conference of Commissioners on Uniform State Laws (NCCUSL) began drafting the UCC in 1945. The most significant individual involved in the project was its chief editor, Karl N. Llewellyn of the Columbia University Law School. Llewellyn's intellect, continuous efforts, and ability to compromise made the first version of the UCC—completed in 1949—a legal landmark. Over the next several years, the UCC was substantially accepted by almost every state in the nation.

Comprehensive Coverage The concepts of *good faith* and *commercial reasonableness* permeate the UCC. It attempts to provide a consistent, integrated framework of rules to deal with all phases ordinarily arising in a commercial sales or lease transaction. For instance, consider the following events, all of which may occur during a single transaction:

1. *A contract for the sale or lease of goods is formed and executed.* Article 2 and Article 2A of the UCC provide rules governing all aspects of this transaction.
2. *The transaction may involve a payment—by check, electronic fund transfer, or other means.* Article 3 (on negotiable instruments), Article 4 (on bank deposits and collections), Article 4A (on fund transfers), and Article 5 (on letters of credit) cover this part of the transaction.
3. *The transaction may involve a bill of lading or a warehouse receipt that covers goods when they are shipped or stored.* Article 7 (on documents of title) deals with this subject.
4. *The transaction may involve a demand by the seller or lender for some form of security for the remaining balance owed.* Article 9 (on secured transactions) covers this part of the transaction.

Periodic Changes and Updates Various articles and sections of the UCC are periodically changed or supplemented to clarify certain rules or to establish new rules when changes in business customs render the existing UCC provisions inapplicable.

For instance, when leases of goods in the commercial context became important, Article 2A governing leases was added to the UCC. To clarify the rights of parties to commercial fund transfers, particularly electronic fund transfers, Article 4A was issued. Articles 3 and 4, on negotiable instruments and banking relationships, have undergone significant revisions. The NCCUSL also substantially revised Article 9 on secured transactions, and the revised Article 9 has been adopted by all of the states.

Application to Today's World *By periodically revising the UCC's articles, the NCCUSL has been able to adapt its provisions to changing business customs and practices. UCC provisions governing sales and lease contracts have also been extended to contracts formed in the online environment.*

16–1 The Scope of Articles 2 and 2A

Article 2 of the UCC sets forth the requirements for *sales contracts*, as well as the duties and obligations of the parties involved in the sales contract. Article 2A covers similar issues for *lease contracts*. Bear in mind, however, that the parties to sales or lease contracts are free to agree to terms different from those stated in the UCC.

16–1a Article 2—Sales

Article 2 of the UCC governs **sales contracts**, or contracts for the sale of goods. To facilitate commercial transactions, Article 2 modifies some of the common law contract requirements that were discussed in previous chapters.

Sales Contracts Contracts for the sale of goods.

To the extent that it has not been modified by the UCC, however, the common law of contracts also applies to sales contracts. In other words, the common law requirements for a valid contract—agreement, consideration, capacity, and legality—are also applicable to sales contracts.

In general, the rule is that when a UCC provision addresses a certain issue, the UCC governs, but when the UCC is silent, the common law governs. The relationship between general contract law and the law governing sales of goods is illustrated in Exhibit 16–1.

In regard to Article 2, keep two points in mind.

1. Article 2 deals with the sale of *goods*. It does not deal with real property (real estate), services, or intangible property such as stocks and bonds. Thus, if the subject matter of a dispute is goods, the UCC governs. If it is real estate or services, the common law applies.
2. In some situations, the rules can vary depending on whether the buyer or the seller is a *merchant*.

Sale The passing of title to property from the seller to the buyer for a price.

What Is a Sale? The UCC defines a **sale** as "the passing of title [evidence of ownership rights] from the seller to the buyer for a price" [UCC 2–106(1)]. The price may be payable in cash (or its equivalent) or in other goods or services. **Case Example 16.1** Blasini, Inc., contracted to buy the business assets of the Attic Bar & Grill in Omaha, Nebraska, from Cheran Investments, LLC. Blasini obtained insurance and was making monthly payments on the assets. A fire broke out and damaged the business assets (such as furniture and equipment) involved in the sale. Because the purchase price had not yet been fully paid, a dispute arose concerning who was entitled to the insurance proceeds for the damage.

The insurance company asked a Nebraska state court to resolve the matter. Ultimately, a state appellate court held that the sale of the Attic's business assets involved goods, and thus the agreement was governed by the UCC. Under UCC 2–401, title to the goods passed to Blasini at the time the contract was formed, regardless of whether the entire purchase price had been paid. Therefore, Blasini was entitled to the insurance proceeds.[2] ■

2. *Nautilus Insurance Co. v. Cheran Investments, LLC*, 2014 WL 292809 (Neb.Ct.App. 2014).

Exhibit 16–1 The Law Governing Contracts

This exhibit graphically illustrates the relationship between general contract law and statutory law (UCC Articles 2 and 2A) governing contracts for the sale and lease of goods. Sales contracts are not governed exclusively by Article 2 of the UCC but are also governed by general contract law whenever it is relevant and has not been modified by the UCC.

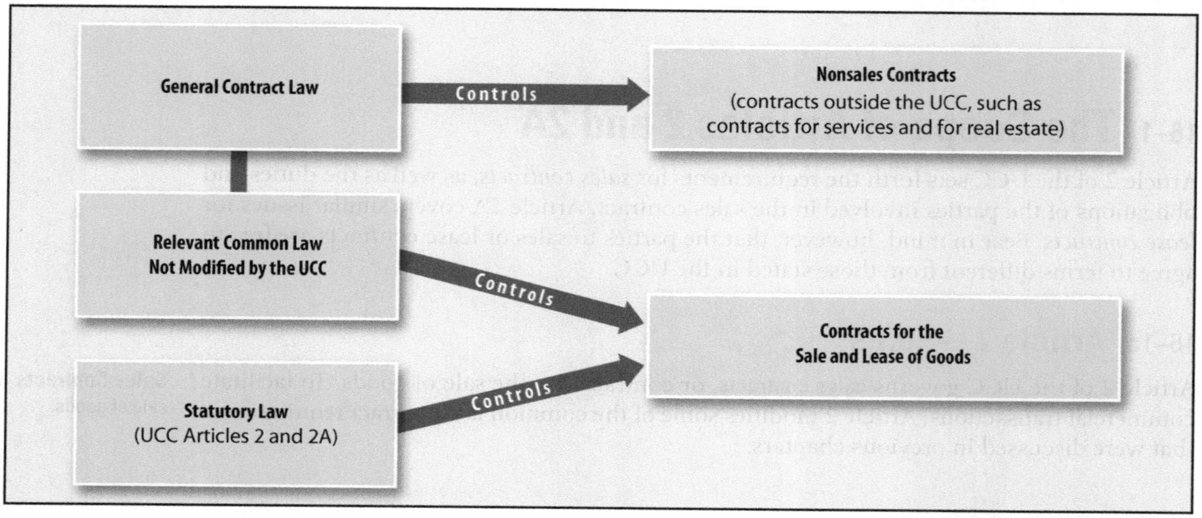

For a discussion of how states can impose taxes on online sales, see this chapter's *Adapting the Law to the Online Environment* feature.

What Are Goods? To be characterized as a *good,* the item of property must be *tangible,* and it must be *movable.* **Tangible property** has physical existence—it can be touched or seen. **Intangible property**—such as corporate stocks and bonds, patents and copyrights, and ordinary contract rights—has only conceptual existence and thus does not come under Article 2. A *movable* item can be carried from place to place.

Tangible Property Property that has physical existence and can be distinguished by the senses of touch and sight.

Intangible Property Property that cannot be seen or touched but exists only conceptually, such as corporate stocks. Such property is not governed by Article 2 of the UCC.

Goods Associated with Real Estate. Because real estate cannot be carried from place to place, it is excluded from Article 2. Goods *associated* with real estate often fall within the scope of Article 2, however [UCC 2–107]. For instance, a contract for the sale of minerals, oil, or natural gas is a contract for the sale of goods if *severance, or separation, is to be made by the seller.* In contrast, a contract for the sale of growing crops or timber to be cut is a contract for the sale of goods *regardless of who severs them from the land.*

Taxing Web Purchases

In 1992, the United States Supreme Court ruled that an individual state cannot compel an out-of-state business that lacks a substantial physical presence within that state to collect and remit state taxes.[a] Congress has the power to pass legislation requiring out-of-state corporations to collect and remit state sales taxes, but it has not yet done so.

South Dakota Steps Up

Taking matters into its own hands, the South Dakota legislature enacted a statute that required certain out-of-state sellers to collect and remit sales tax "as if the seller had a physical presence in the state." The law applied only to sellers that annually sell more than $100,000 worth of goods or services within the state. South Dakota then sued three large retailers, Wayfair, Inc., Overstock.com, Inc., and Newegg, Inc., for failing to collect taxes as required under this law. The lower courts and the state's highest court ruled in favor of the retailers because of the Supreme Court's precedent requiring physical presence.

The Supreme Court Changes Course

When the case reached the Supreme Court, however, the justices reexamined the earlier decision and—in *South Dakota v. Wayfair, Inc.*[b]— five out of nine of them chose to overrule it. The majority found that the case's focus on physical presence created an "online sales tax loophole" that gave out-of-state businesses an advantage. The justices concluded that in today's online environment, physical presence in a taxing state is not necessary for the seller to have a substantial connection with the state.

Chief Justice John Roberts wrote the dissenting opinion. He noted, "E-Commerce has grown into a significant and vibrant part of our national economy against the backdrop of established rules, including the physical-presence rule. Any alteration to those rules with the potential to disrupt the development of such a critical segment of the economy should be undertaken by Congress."

Such sentiments did little to dampen the enthusiasm of state legislatures eager to take advantage of the new online tax landscape and bolster their revenues. Within eighteen months of the Court's *Wayfair* decision, forty-three states had changed their laws to collect sales taxes on Internet purchases.

Critical Thinking

Does the Supreme Court's decision in South Dakota v. Wayfair, Inc., *make it more or less likely that Congress will enact legislation that requires out-of-state corporations to collect and pay taxes to states for a online sales?*

a. *Quill Corp. v. North Dakota,* 504 U.S. 298, 112 S.Ct. 1904, 119 L.Ed.2d 91 (1992).

b. 582 U.S.___, 138 S.Ct. 2080, 201 L.Ed.2d 403 (2018).

Predominant-Factor Test A test courts use to determine whether a contract is primarily for the sale of goods or for the sale of services.

Focus Question 1

If a contract involves both goods and services, when does the UCC apply?

Goods and Services Combined. When contracts involve a combination of goods and services, courts generally use the **predominant-factor test** to determine whether a contract is primarily for the sale of goods or for the sale of services. If a court decides that a mixed contract is primarily a goods contract, *any* dispute, even a dispute over the services portion, will be decided under the UCC.

Case Example 16.2 Paper City, a microbrewery, entered into a contract with La Resistance, a beer distribution company, under which La Resistance would purchase beer from Paper City and distribute it to retailers. Almost five years after La Resistance allegedly breached the contract, Paper City sued. Under Article 2 of the UCC, the statute of limitations for disputes involving contracts for the sale of goods is four years. As a result, the trial court dismissed Paper City's lawsuit.

Paper City appealed, claiming that its contract with La Resistance was for services, not goods, and was therefore not covered by Article 2. Paper City argued that, under the contract and according to "industry standards," La Resistance provided services such as managing Paper City's accounts and representing Paper City at trade shows. The only financial transactions on record between the two companies, however, were those in which La Resistance paid Paper City for beer. Accordingly, a Massachusetts appeals court concluded that the sale of goods (beer) was the predominant factor in the two parties' distribution agreement and affirmed the lower's court decision.[3]

Who Is a Merchant? Article 2 governs the sale of goods in general. It applies to sales transactions between all buyers and sellers. In a limited number of instances, though, the UCC presumes that certain special business standards ought to be imposed on merchants because of their relatively high degree of commercial expertise.[4] Such standards do not apply to the casual or inexperienced seller or buyer (consumer).

Section 2–104 sets out three ways in which merchant status can arise:

1. A merchant is a person who *deals in goods of the kind* involved in the sales contract. Thus, a retailer, a wholesaler, or a manufacturer is a merchant of those goods sold in the business. A merchant for one type of goods is not necessarily a merchant for another type. For instance, a sporting equipment retailer is a merchant when selling tennis rackets but not when selling a used iPad.
2. A merchant is a person who, by occupation, *holds himself or herself out as having special knowledge and skill* related to the practices or goods involved in the transaction. This broad definition may include banks or universities as merchants.
3. A person who *employs a merchant as a broker, agent, or other intermediary* has the status of merchant in that transaction. Hence, if an art collector hires a broker to purchase or sell art for her, the collector is considered a merchant in the transaction.

Merchant Under the UCC, a person who deals in goods of the kind involved in the sales contract or who holds herself or himself out as having skill or knowledge peculiar to the practices or goods being purchased or sold.

In summary, a **merchant** is someone who is in the business of buying or selling particular goods and who possesses or uses an expertise specifically related to those goods. This basic distinction is not always clear-cut. For instance, state courts appear to be split on whether farmers should be considered merchants.

16–1b Article 2A—Leases

Lease Under Article 2A of the UCC, a transfer of the right to possess and use goods for a period of time in exchange for payment.

Leases of personal property (goods such as automobiles and industrial equipment) have become increasingly common. In this context, a **lease** is a transfer of the right to possess and use goods for a period of time in exchange for payment. Article 2A of the UCC was created to fill the need for uniform guidelines in this area.

3. *Paper City Brewery Co., Inc. v. La Resistance, Inc.*, 124 N.E.3d 159, 95 Mass.App.Ct. 1103 (2019).
4. The provisions that apply only to merchants deal principally with the Statute of Frauds, firm offers, confirmatory memoranda, warranties, and contract modifications. These special rules reflect expedient business practices commonly known to merchants in the commercial setting. They will be discussed later in this chapter.

Article 2A covers any transaction that creates a lease of goods, as well as subleases of goods [UCC 2A–102, 2A–103(1)(k)]. Article 2A is essentially a repetition of Article 2, except that it applies to leases of goods rather than sales of goods and thus varies to reflect differences between sales and lease transactions. (Note that Article 2A does not apply to leases of real property, such as land or buildings.)

Definition of a Lease Agreement Article 2A defines a **lease agreement** as the bargain between a lessor and a lessee with respect to the lease of goods, as found in their language and as implied by other circumstances, including course of dealing and usage of trade or course of performance [UCC 2A–103(1)(k)]. A **lessor** is one who transfers the right to the possession and use of goods under a lease [UCC 2A–103(1)(p)]. A **lessee** is one who acquires the right to the temporary possession and use of goods under a lease [UCC 2A–103(1)(o)]. In other words, the lessee is the party who is leasing the goods from the lessor.

Article 2A applies to all types of leases of goods, including commercial leases and consumer leases. Special rules apply to certain types of leases, however, including consumer leases.

Lease Agreement An agreement in which one party (the lessor) agrees to transfer the right to the possession and use of property to another party (the lessee) in exchange for rental payments.

Lessor A party who transfers the right to the possession and use of goods to another in exchange for rental payments.

Lessee A party who acquires the right to the possession and use of another's goods in exchange for rental payments.

Consumer Leases Under UCC 2A–103(1)(e), a *consumer lease* involves three elements:

1. A lessor who regularly engages in the business of leasing or selling.
2. A lessee (except an organization) who leases the goods "primarily for a personal, family, or household purpose."
3. Total lease payments that are less than a dollar amount set by state statute.

To ensure special protection for consumers, certain provisions of Article 2A apply only to consumer leases. For instance, one provision states that a consumer may recover attorneys' fees if a court finds that a term in a consumer lease contract is unconscionable [UCC 2A–108(4)(a)].

16–2 The Formation of Sales and Lease Contracts

As mentioned, Article 2 and Article 2A of the UCC modify common law contract rules in several ways. Remember, though, that parties to sales contracts are normally free to establish whatever terms they wish. The UCC comes into play only when the parties have failed to provide in their contract for a contingency that later gives rise to a dispute. The UCC makes this clear time and again by using such phrases as "unless the parties otherwise agree" and "absent a contrary agreement by the parties."

16–2a Offer

In general contract law, the moment a definite offer is met by an unqualified acceptance, a binding contract is formed. In commercial sales transactions, the verbal exchanges, correspondence, and actions of the parties may not reveal exactly when a binding contractual obligation arises. The UCC states that an agreement sufficient to constitute a contract can exist even if the moment of its making is undetermined [UCC 2–204(2), 2A–204(2)].

Open Terms Remember that under the common law of contracts, an offer must be definite enough for the parties (and the courts) to ascertain its essential terms when it is accepted. In contrast, the UCC states that a sales or lease contract will not fail for indefiniteness even if one or more terms are left open as long as *both* of the following are true:

1. The parties intended to make a contract.
2. There is a reasonably certain basis for the court to grant an appropriate remedy [UCC 2–204(3), 2A–204(3)].

Know This
Under the UCC, it is the actions of the parties that determine whether they intended to form a contract.

The UCC provides numerous *open-term* provisions (discussed shortly) that can be used to fill the gaps in a contract. Thus, if a dispute occurs, all that is necessary to prove the existence of a contract is an indication (such as a purchase order) that there is a contract. Missing terms can be proved by evidence, or a court can presume that the parties intended whatever is reasonable under the circumstances.

Keep in mind, though, that if too many terms are left open, a court may find that the parties did not intend to form a contract. In addition, the *quantity* of goods involved must be expressly stated in the contract. If the quantity term is left open, the courts will have no basis for determining a remedy.

In the following case, one company orally agreed to store another company's goods in anticipation of forming a contract, but they did not agree on how long that arrangement would last. The question was whether the open term in their agreement rendered the contract unenforceable.

Case 16.1

Toll Processing Services, LLC v. Kastalon, Inc.

United States Court of Appeals, Seventh Circuit, 880 F.3d 820 (2018).

Facts Toll Processing Services, a subsidiary of International Steel Services, Inc., was formed to own and operate a pickle line. A pickle line is an operation used in the steel industry to process hot-rolled steel coil through acid tanks to remove rust and impurities. Toll Processing purchased a used pickle line from Ryerson & Sons that had been serviced by Kastalon, Inc., which provides equipment and repairs for the steel industry. Toll Processing was planning to reinstall the used pickle line somewhere else but did not have a facility. Kastalon agreed to move the pickle rolls to its facility and store them, at no cost, until Toll Processing could issue a purchase order to Kastalon to recondition the rolls. Both parties believed that Toll Processing would complete its plan to reinstall the pickle line within months, but they did not discuss the time frame.

Kastalon moved fifty-seven pickle rolls to its facility over a period of three months, but then had no further contact with Toll Processing for two years. Believing that the pickle rolls were of little value and that Toll Processing had gone out of business, Kastalon eventually scrapped the rolls and received $6,300 from a recycler. The following year, Toll Processing contacted Kastalon and requested a price quote for reconditioning the rolls, at which point Kastalon informed Toll that the rolls had been scrapped. Toll sued Kastalon for breach of contract (in addition to several other claims). A district court granted summary judgment in favor of Kastalon, finding that the oral agreement between the parties did not have a specific duration and lacked consideration. Toll Processing appealed.

Issue Did the fact that the parties' oral storage agreement lacked a specific duration render the contract unenforceable?

Decision Yes. A federal appellate court affirmed the judgment of the district court on the breach of contract claim. Although the parties may have attempted to form a contract, they did not reach a mutual understanding that Kastalon would store the pickle rolls for any certain period of time. Because there was no meeting of the minds on this term, the agreement was unenforceable. The appellate court reversed and remanded the district court's decision on Toll Processing's other claims, however.

Reason The court found that Kastalon's expectation that Toll Processing would hire it to repair and refurbish the pickle rolls constituted consideration. Nevertheless, the court concluded that the evidence showed that the parties did not have a mutual understanding that Kastalon would store the rolls indefinitely. The duration of the agreement was to be determined by the date on which Toll Processing issued a purchase order to Kastalon to repair and refurbish the rolls for use in the newly installed pickle line. When Kastalon agreed to store the rolls, Toll Processing did not know when—or even if—it would issue that purchase order. Because the parties' oral storage agreement was not sufficiently definite as to duration, a material term of the oral agreement, it was unenforceable.

Critical Thinking

- **What If the Facts Were Different?** *Suppose that the parties admitted that they had agreed Kastalon would store the rolls for up to one year. How would this have affected the court's decision on breach of contract?*
- **Ethical** *Was it unethical for Kastalon to scrap the rolls without attempting to contact Toll Processing? Explain.*

Open Price Term. If the parties have not agreed on a price, the court will determine a "reasonable price at the time for delivery" [UCC 2–305(1)]. If either the buyer or the seller is to determine the price, the price is to be fixed (set) in good faith [UCC 2–305(2)]. Under the UCC, *good faith* means honesty in fact and the observance of reasonable commercial standards of fair dealing in the trade [UCC 2–103(1)(b)].

Sometimes, the price fails to be fixed through the fault of one of the parties. In that situation, the other party can treat the contract as canceled or fix a reasonable price. **Example 16.3** Perez and Merrick enter into a contract for the sale of unfinished doors and agree that Perez will determine the price. Perez refuses to specify the price. Merrick can either treat the contract as canceled or set a reasonable price [UCC 2–305(3)].

Know This

The common law requires that the parties make their terms definite before they have a contract. The UCC applies general commercial standards to make the terms of a contract definite.

Open Payment Term. When parties do not specify payment terms, payment is due at the time and place at which the buyer is to receive the goods [UCC 2–310(a)]. The buyer can tender payment using any commercially normal or acceptable means, such as a check or credit card. If the seller demands payment in cash, the buyer must be given a reasonable time to obtain it [UCC 2–511(2)].

Example 16.4 Max agrees to purchase hay from Wagner's farm. Max leaves his truck and trailer at the farm for the seller to load the hay. Nothing is said about when payment is due, and the parties are unaware of the UCC's rules. Nevertheless, because the parties did not specify when payment was due, UCC 2–310(a) controls, and payment is due at the time Max picks up the hay. Therefore, Wagner can refuse to release the hay (or the vehicles on which the hay is loaded) to Max until he pays for it.

Open Delivery Term. When no delivery terms are specified, the buyer normally takes delivery at the seller's place of business [UCC 2–308(a)]. If the seller has no place of business, the seller's residence is used. When goods are located in some other place and both parties know it, delivery is made there. If the time for shipment or delivery is not clearly specified in the sales contract, the court will infer a "reasonable" time for performance [UCC 2–309(1)].

emholk/iStock/Getty Images

If no time for payment for hay is specified in a sales contract, when is payment due?

Duration of an Ongoing Contract. A single contract might specify successive performances but not indicate how long the parties are required to deal with each other. In this situation, either party may terminate the ongoing contractual relationship. Principles of good faith and sound commercial practice call for reasonable notification before termination, however, to give the other party time to make substitute arrangements [UCC 2–309(2), (3)].

Options and Cooperation Regarding Performance. When the contract contemplates shipment of the goods but does not specify the shipping arrangements, the *seller* has the right to make these arrangements in good faith, using commercial reasonableness in the situation [UCC 2–311].

When a sales contract omits terms relating to the assortment of goods, the *buyer* can specify the assortment. **Example 16.5** Petry Drugs, Inc., enters an e-contract to purchase one thousand toothbrushes from Marconi's Dental Supply. The toothbrushes come in a variety of colors, but the contract does not specify color. Petry, the buyer, has the right to take six hundred blue toothbrushes and four hundred green ones, if it wishes. Petry, however, must exercise good faith and commercial reasonableness in making its selection [UCC 2–311].

Open Quantity Terms. Normally, if the parties do not specify a quantity, no contract is formed. A court will have no basis for determining a remedy because there is almost no way for a court to determine objectively what is a reasonable quantity of goods for someone to buy. (In contrast, a court can objectively determine a reasonable price for particular goods by looking at the market for like goods.) Nevertheless, the UCC recognizes two exceptions to this rule in *requirements* and *output contracts* [UCC 2–306(1)].

Requirements Contract An agreement in which a buyer agrees to purchase and a seller agrees to sell all or up to a stated amount of what the buyer needs or requires.

1. *Requirements Contracts.* Requirements contracts are common in the business world and normally are enforceable. In a **requirements contract**, the buyer agrees to purchase and the seller agrees to sell all or up to a stated amount of what the buyer *needs* or *requires*. **Example 16.6** Umpqua Cannery forms a contract with Al Garcia. The cannery agrees to purchase from Garcia, and Garcia agrees to sell to the cannery, all of the green beans that the cannery needs or requires during the following summer. There is implicit consideration in this contract because the buyer (the cannery) gives up the right to buy goods (green beans) from any other seller. This forfeited right creates a legal *detriment*—that is, consideration.

   If, however, the buyer promises to purchase only if the buyer *wishes* to do so, the promise is illusory (without consideration) and unenforceable by either party. Similarly, if the buyer reserves the right to buy the goods from someone other than the seller, the promise is unenforceable (illusory) as a requirements contract.

Output Contract An agreement in which a seller agrees to sell and a buyer agrees to buy all or up to a stated amount of what the seller produces.

2. *Output Contracts.* In an **output contract**, the seller agrees to sell and the buyer agrees to buy all or up to a stated amount of what the seller *produces*. **Example 16.7** Ruth has planted two acres of organic tomatoes. Bella Union, a local restaurant, agrees to buy all of the tomatoes that Ruth produces that year to use at the restaurant. Again, because the seller essentially forfeits the right to sell goods to another buyer, there is implicit consideration in an output contract.

The UCC imposes a *good faith limitation* on requirements and output contracts. The quantity under such contracts is the amount of requirements or the amount of output that occurs during a *normal* production year. The actual quantity purchased or sold cannot be unreasonably disproportionate to normal or comparable prior requirements or output [UCC 2–306(1)].

Merchant's Firm Offer Under regular contract principles, an offer can be revoked at any time before acceptance. The major common law exception is an *option contract,* in which the offeree pays consideration for the offeror's irrevocable promise to keep the offer open for a stated period. The UCC creates a second exception for firm offers made by a merchant to sell, buy, or lease goods.

Firm Offer An offer (by a merchant) that is irrevocable without the necessity of consideration for a stated period of time or, if no definite period is stated, for a reasonable time (neither period to exceed three months).

A **firm offer** arises when a merchant-offeror gives *assurances* in a *signed writing* that the offer will remain open. A merchant's firm offer is irrevocable without the necessity of consideration[5] for the stated period or, if no definite period is stated, a reasonable period (neither period to exceed three months) [UCC 2–205, 2A–205].

Example 16.8 Osaka, a used-car dealer, e-mails Saucedo on January 1, stating, "I have a used 2020 Toyota RAV4 on the lot that I'll sell you for $26,000 any time between now and January 31." This e-mail creates a firm offer, and Osaka will be liable for breach if he sells that Toyota RAV4 to someone other than Saucedo before January 31.

Know This

The UCC provides that acceptance can be made by any means that is reasonable under the circumstances—including prompt shipment of the goods.

16–2b Acceptance

Acceptance of an offer to buy, sell, or lease goods generally can be made in any reasonable manner and by any reasonable means. The UCC permits acceptance of an offer to buy goods "either by a prompt *promise* to ship or by the prompt or current shipment of conforming or nonconforming goods" [UCC 2–206(1)(b)]. *Conforming goods* accord with the contract's terms, whereas *nonconforming goods* do not.

5. If the offeree pays consideration, then an option contract (not a merchant's firm offer) is formed.

Shipment of Nonconforming Goods The prompt shipment of nonconforming goods constitutes both an acceptance, which creates a contract, and a breach of that contract. This rule does not apply if the seller **seasonably** (within a specified time period or a reasonable amount of time) notifies the buyer that the nonconforming shipment is offered only as an *accommodation*, or a favor. The notice of accommodation must clearly indicate to the buyer that the shipment does not constitute an acceptance and that, therefore, no contract has been formed.

Seasonably Within a specified time period or, if no period is specified, within a reasonable time.

Example 16.9 McCleary orders one thousand blue smart fitness watches from Halderson. Halderson ships one thousand *black* smart fitness watches to McCleary. If Halderson notifies McCleary that it has only black watches in stock, and the black watches are being sent as an accommodation, then the shipment is an offer. A contract will be formed only if McCleary accepts the black watches.

If, however, Halderson ships black watches *without* notifying McCleary that the goods are being sent as an accommodation, the shipment is both an acceptance and a breach of the resulting contract. McCleary can sue Halderson for any appropriate damages.

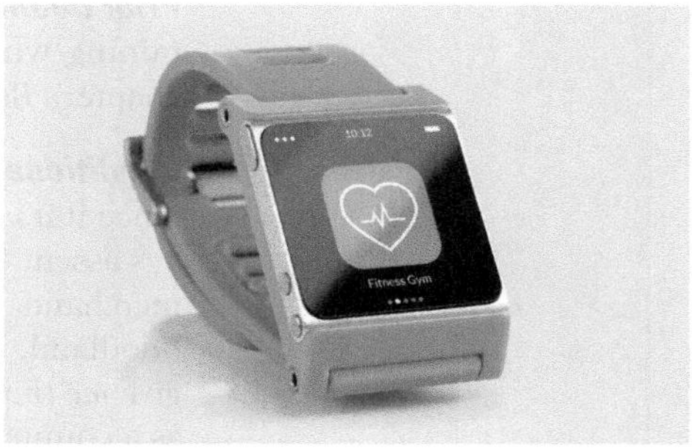

Alexey Boldin/Shutterstock.com

If a retailer orders blue smart fitness watches, but instead the seller sends black ones, is this an acceptance, a breach, or an accommodation?

Communication of Acceptance Required Under the common law, a unilateral offer can be accepted by beginning performance. The offeree need not notify the offeror of performance unless the offeror would not otherwise know about it. Under the UCC, however, the offeror must be notified within a reasonable time that the offeree has accepted the contract by beginning performance. Otherwise, the offeror can treat the offer as having lapsed before acceptance [UCC 2–206(2), 2A–206(2)].

Additional Terms Recall that under the common law, the *mirror image rule* requires that the terms of the acceptance exactly match those of the offer. **Example 16.10** Adderson e-mails an offer to sell twenty Samsung Galaxy Tab A 10.1 tablets to Beale. If Beale accepts the offer but changes it to require Tab S5e tablets, then there is no contract if the mirror image rule applies.

To avoid such situations, the UCC dispenses with the mirror image rule. Under the UCC, a contract is formed if the offeree's response indicates a *definite* acceptance of the offer, *even if the acceptance includes terms additional to or different from those contained in the offer* [UCC 2–207(1)]. Whether the additional terms become part of the contract depends, in part, on whether the parties are nonmerchants or merchants.

Focus Question 2

What happens if an acceptance to a sales contract includes terms additional to or different from those in the offer?

When One Party or Both Parties Are Nonmerchants. If one (or both) of the parties is a *nonmerchant*, the contract is formed according to the terms of the original offer submitted by the original offeror and not according to the additional terms of the acceptance [UCC 2–207(2)]. **Example 16.11** BettyBloom.com sells plants and gardening supplies online. Employees of a school district in Oregon order $10,000 worth of goods for a school project—without the authority or approval of their employer—from the website. The invoices that accompany the goods contain a *forum-selection clause* requiring all disputes to be resolved in California.

When the school district fails to pay, BettyBloom.com files suit in a California court. The court is likely to find that the forum-selection clause is unenforceable. The clause is an additional term included in invoices delivered to a nonmerchant buyer (the school district) with the purchased goods. The clause cannot become part of the contract unless the school district expressly agrees to it.

When Both Parties Are Merchants. The drafters of the UCC created a special rule for merchants to avoid the "battle of the forms," which occurs when two merchants exchange separate standard forms containing different contract terms. Under UCC 2–207(2), in contracts *between merchants,* the additional terms *automatically* become part of the contract unless one of the following conditions exists:

1. The original offer expressly limited acceptance to its terms.
2. The new or changed terms materially alter the contract.
3. The offeror objects to the new or changed terms within a reasonable period of time.

When determining whether an alteration is material, courts consider several factors. Generally, if the modification does not involve an unreasonable element of surprise or hardship for the offeror, the court will hold that the modification did not materially alter the contract.

Prior Dealings between Merchants. Courts also consider the parties' prior dealings in determining whether the added terms become part of contracts between merchants. See this chapter's *Business Law Analysis* feature for an example.

Conditioned on Offeror's Assent. The offeree's expression cannot be construed as an acceptance if it contains additional or different terms that are explicitly conditioned on the offeror's assent to those terms [UCC 2–207(1)]. This rule applies whether or not the parties are merchants. **Example 16.12** Philips offers to sell ninety boxes of peaches at a specified price to Foodland. Dawn, Foodland's owner, responds, "I accept your offer *on the condition that you give me thirty more boxes.*" Foodland's response will be construed not as an acceptance but as a counteroffer, which Philips may or may not accept.

Additional Terms between Merchants

Business Law Analysis

B.S. International (BSI), makes costume jewelry. Jayco, Inc., is a wholesaler of costume jewelry. Jayco sent BSI a letter outlining the terms for orders, including the necessary procedure for obtaining credit for items that customers rejected. The letter stated, "By signing below, you agree to the terms." Steven Brown, BSI's owner, signed the letter and returned it. For six years, BSI made jewelry for Jayco, which resold it. Items rejected by customers were sent back to Jayco but never returned to BSI.

BSI eventually filed a suit against Jayco, claiming $41,000 for the unreturned items. BSI showed the court a copy of Jayco's terms. Across the bottom had been typed a "P.S." (postscript) requiring the return of rejected merchandise. Was this P.S. part of the contract?

Analysis: Under the common law, variations in terms between the offer and the acceptance violate the mirror image rule, which requires that the terms of an acceptance exactly mirror the terms of the offer. The UCC dispenses with this rule. Under the UCC, a contract is formed if the offeree makes a definite expression of acceptance even though the terms of the acceptance modify or add to the terms of the offer.

When both parties to a sales contract are merchants, the additional terms become part of their contract unless (1) the original offer expressly requires acceptance of its terms, (2) the new or changed terms materially alter the contract, or (3) the offeror rejects the new or changed terms within a reasonable time.

In this situation, the original offer stated, "By signing below, you agree to the terms." This statement could be construed to expressly require acceptance of the terms to make the offer a binding contract. The contract stated that Jayco was to receive credit for any rejected merchandise. Nothing indicated that the merchandise would be returned to BSI.

Result and Reasoning: When Brown (BSI's owner and the offeree) signed Jayco's (the offeror's) letter, it indicated BSI's agreement to the terms. Thus, BSI made a definite expression of acceptance. The practice of the parties—for six years rejected items were not returned—supports the conclusion that their contract did not contemplate the return of those items. The P.S. could be interpreted as materially altering the contract. Therefore, the P.S. is not part of the contract, and a court should dismiss BSI's lawsuit.

Additional Terms May Be Stricken. The UCC provides yet another option for dealing with conflicting terms in the parties' writings. Section 2–207(3) states that conduct by both parties that recognizes the existence of a contract is sufficient to establish a contract for the sale of goods. This is so even if the parties' writings contain different terms. In this situation, "the terms of the particular contract will consist of those terms on which the writings of the parties agree, together with any supplementary terms incorporated under any other provisions of this Act."

In a dispute over contract terms, this provision allows a court simply to strike from the contract those terms on which the parties do not agree. **Example 16.13** SMT Marketing orders goods over the phone from Brigg Sales, Inc., which ships the goods with an acknowledgment form (confirming the order) to SMT. SMT accepts and pays for the goods. The parties' writings do not establish a contract, but there is no question that a contract exists. If a dispute arises over the terms, such as the extent of any warranties, UCC 2–207(3) provides the governing rule.

TatyanaMishchenko/iStock/Getty Images

Should prior dealings between a costume jewelry manufacturer and a buyer be considered if a contract dispute arises over additional terms? Why or why not?

As noted previously, the fact that a merchant's acceptance frequently contains terms that add to or even conflict with those of the offer is often referred to as the "battle of the forms." Although the UCC tries to eliminate this battle, the problem of differing contract terms still arises in commercial settings, particularly when standard forms for placing and confirming orders are used.

16–2c Consideration

The common law rule that a contract requires consideration also applies to sales and lease contracts. Unlike the common law, however, the UCC does not require a contract modification to be supported by new consideration. An agreement modifying a contract for the sale or lease of goods "needs no consideration to be binding" [UCC 2–209(1), 2A–208(1)]. Of course, a contract modification must be sought in good faith [UCC 1–304].

In some situations, an agreement to modify a sales or lease contract without consideration must be in writing to be enforceable. If the contract itself prohibits any changes to the contract unless they are in a signed writing, for instance, then only those changes agreed to in a signed writing are enforceable.

Sometimes, when a consumer (nonmerchant buyer) is dealing with a merchant, the merchant supplies the form that contains a clause prohibiting oral modification. In those situations, the consumer must sign a separate acknowledgment of the clause for it to be enforceable [UCC 2–209(2), 2A–208(2)]. Also, any modification that brings a sales contract under Article 2's Statute of Frauds provision usually must be in writing to be enforceable.

16–2d The Statute of Frauds

The UCC contains Statute of Frauds provisions covering sales and lease contracts. Under these provisions, sales contracts for goods priced at $500 or more and lease contracts requiring payments of $1,000 or more must be in writing to be enforceable [UCC 2–201(1), 2A–201(1)]. E-mails and other electronic records satisfy the writing requirement.

Know This

It has been proposed that the UCC be revised to eliminate the Statute of Frauds.

Sufficiency of the Writing A writing will be sufficient to satisfy the UCC's Statute of Frauds as long as it meets the following requirements:

1. It indicates that the parties intended to form a contract.
2. It is signed by the party (or agent of the party) against whom enforcement is sought. (Remember that a typed name can qualify as a signature.)

The contract normally will not be enforceable beyond the quantity of goods shown in the writing. All other terms can be proved in court by oral testimony. For leases, the writing or record must reasonably identify and describe the goods leased and the lease term.

Special Rules for Contracts between Merchants Once again, the UCC provides a special rule for merchants in sales transactions. (There is no corresponding rule that applies to leases under Article 2A.) Merchants can satisfy the Statute of Frauds if, after the parties have agreed orally, one of the merchants sends a signed written confirmation to the other merchant within a reasonable time.

The communication must indicate the terms of the agreement, and the merchant receiving the confirmation must have reason to know of its contents. Unless the merchant who receives the confirmation gives written notice of objection to its contents within ten days after receipt, the writing or record is sufficient, even though that merchant has not signed anything [UCC 2–201(2)].

Example 16.14 Alfonso is a merchant-buyer in Cleveland. He contracts over the telephone to purchase $6,000 worth of spare aircraft parts from Maria, a merchant-seller in New York City. Two days later, Maria e-mails a signed confirmation detailing the terms of the oral contract, and Alfonso receives it. Alfonso does not notify Maria in writing of any objection to the contents of the confirmation within ten days of receipt. Therefore, Alfonso cannot raise the Statute of Frauds as a defense against the enforcement of the oral contract. ■

Exceptions In addition to the special rules for merchants, the UCC defines three exceptions to the writing requirements of the Statute of Frauds. An oral contract for the sale of goods priced at $500 or more—or the lease of goods involving total payments of $1,000 or more—will be enforceable despite the absence of a writing in the circumstances described next [UCC 2–201(3), 2A–201(4)].

Specially Manufactured Goods. An oral contract for the sale or lease of custom-made goods will be enforceable if the following conditions exist:

1. The goods are *specially manufactured* for a particular buyer or specially manufactured or obtained for a particular lessee.
2. The goods are *not suitable for resale or lease* to others in the ordinary course of the seller's or lessor's business.
3. The seller or lessor has *substantially started to manufacture* the goods or has made commitments for the manufacture or procurement of the goods.

Under these conditions, once the seller or lessor has taken action, the buyer or lessee cannot repudiate the agreement claiming the Statute of Frauds as a defense. **Example 16.15** Womach orders custom window treatments from Hunter Douglas to use at her day spa business. The contract is oral, and the price is $6,000. When Hunter Douglas manufactures the window coverings and tenders delivery to Womach, she refuses to pay for them, even though the job is completed on time. Womach claims that she is not liable because the contract is oral. If the unique style, size, and color of the window treatments make it improbable that Hunter Douglas can find another buyer, Womach is liable to Hunter Douglas. ■

Admissions. An oral contract for the sale or lease of goods is enforceable if the party against whom enforcement of the contract is sought admits in pleadings, testimony, or other court proceedings that a contract for sale or lease was made. In this situation, the contract will be enforceable even though it was oral, but enforceability will be limited to the quantity of goods admitted.

Example 16.16 Gerald, a farmer, agrees by phone to sell his crops to Great Plains Cooperative. The parties reach two oral agreements for the delivery of corn. Gerald then reneges on the deal and sells his corn to another dealer. Great Plains pays a higher price to buy corn elsewhere and then sues Gerald for breach of contract. In court, Gerald acknowledges the first oral agreement but not the second. The court will apply the admissions exception to enforce the agreement admitted by Gerald, but the other agreement will be unenforceable under this exception.

Partial Performance. An oral contract for the sale or lease of goods is enforceable if payment has been made and accepted or goods have been received and accepted. This is the "partial performance" exception. The oral contract will be enforced at least to the extent that performance *actually* took place.

Example 16.17 Jamal orally contracts to lease to Opus Enterprises one thousand chairs at $2 each to be used during a one-day concert. Before delivery, Opus sends Jamal a check for $1,000, which Jamal cashes. Later, when Jamal attempts to deliver the chairs, Opus refuses delivery, claiming the Statute of Frauds as a defense, and demands the return of its $1,000.

Under the UCC's partial performance rule, Jamal can enforce the oral contract by tender of delivery of five hundred chairs for the $1,000 accepted. Similarly, if Opus had made no payment but had accepted the delivery of five hundred chairs from Jamal, the oral contract would have been enforceable against Opus for $1,000, the lease payment due for the five hundred chairs delivered.

These exceptions and other ways in which sales law differs from general contract law are summarized in Exhibit 16–2.

ghornephoto/E+/Getty Images

Can two oral agreements for delivery of corn be enforced if the seller admits that only the first agreement occurred?

Exhibit 16–2 Major Differences between Contract Law and Sales Law

TOPIC	CONTRACT LAW	SALES LAW
Contract Terms	The contract must contain all material terms.	Open terms are acceptable, if the parties intended to form a contract, but the quantity term normally must be specified, and the contract is not enforceable beyond the quantity term.
Acceptance	Mirror image rule applies. If additional terms are added in acceptance, a counteroffer is created.	Additional terms will not negate acceptance unless acceptance is made expressly conditional on assent to the additional terms.
Contract Modification	Modification requires consideration.	Modification does not require consideration.
Irrevocable Offers	Option contracts (with consideration) are irrevocable.	Merchants' firm offers (without consideration) are irrevocable.
Statute of Frauds Requirements	All material terms must be included in the writing.	Writing is required only for the sale of goods priced at $500 or more, but the contract is not enforceable beyond the quantity specified. Merchants can satisfy the requirement by a confirmatory memorandum evidencing their agreement. Exceptions exist for (1) specially manufactured goods, (2) admissions, and (3) partial performance.

16–2e Parol Evidence

Recall that *parol evidence* consists of evidence outside the contract, such as evidence of the parties' prior negotiations, prior agreements, or oral agreements made at the time of contract formation. When a contract completely sets forth all the terms and conditions agreed to by the parties and is intended as a final statement of their agreement, it is considered *fully integrated*. The terms of a fully integrated contract cannot be contradicted by evidence outside the contract.

If, however, the writing (or record) contains some of the terms the parties agreed on but not others, the contract is *not fully integrated*. In this situation, a court may allow evidence of *consistent additional terms* to explain or supplement the terms stated in the contract. The court may also allow the parties to submit evidence of *course of dealing, usage of trade*, or *course of performance* [UCC 2–202, 2A–202]. A court will not under any circumstances allow the parties to submit evidence that contradicts the contract's stated terms, however. (This is also the rule under the common law.)

Course of Dealing and Usage of Trade Under the UCC, the meaning of any agreement, evidenced by the language of the parties and by their actions, must be interpreted in light of commercial practices and other surrounding circumstances. In interpreting a commercial agreement, the court will assume that the course of prior dealing between the parties and the usage of trade were taken into account when the agreement was phrased.

Course of Dealing Prior conduct between the parties to a contract that establishes a common basis for their understanding.

Course of Dealing. A **course of dealing** is a sequence of actions and communications between the parties to a particular transaction that establishes a common basis for their understanding [UCC 1–303(b)]. A course of dealing is restricted to the sequence of conduct between the parties in their transactions prior to the agreement. Under the UCC, a course of dealing between the parties is relevant in ascertaining the meaning of the parties' agreement. It "may give particular meaning to specific terms of the agreement, and may supplement or qualify the terms of the agreement" [UCC 1–303(d)].

Usage of Trade Any practice or method of dealing that is so regularly observed in a place, vocation, or trade that parties justifiably expect it will be observed in their transaction.

Usage of Trade. Any practice or method of dealing that is so regularly observed in a place, vocation, or trade as to justify an expectation by the parties that it will be observed in their transaction is a **usage of trade** [UCC 1–303(c)].

Example 16.18 United Loans, Inc., hires Fleet Title Review to search the public records for prior claims on potential borrowers' assets. Fleet's invoice states, "Liability limited to amount of fee." In the search industry, liability limits are common. After conducting many searches for United, Fleet reports that there are no claims with respect to Main Street Autos. United loans $100,000 to Main, with payment guaranteed by Main's assets.

When Main defaults on the loan, United learns that another lender has priority to Main's assets under a previous claim. If United sues Fleet Title for breach of contract, Fleet's liability will normally be limited to the amount of its fee. The statement in the invoice was part of the contract between United and Fleet Title, according to the usage of trade in the industry and the parties' course of dealing. ■

Course of Performance The conduct that occurs under the terms of a particular agreement, which indicates what the parties to that agreement intended the agreement to mean.

Course of Performance A **course of performance** is the conduct that occurs under the terms of a particular agreement [UCC 1–303(a)]. Presumably, the parties themselves know best what they meant by their words. Thus, the course of performance actually carried out under their agreement is the best indication of what they meant [UCC 2–208(1), 2A–207(1)].

Example 16.19 Janson's Lumber Company contracts with Lopez to sell Lopez a specified number of two-by-fours. The lumber in fact does not measure exactly 2 inches by 4 inches but rather 1⅞ inches by 3¾ inches. Janson's agrees to deliver the lumber in five deliveries, and Lopez, without objection, accepts the lumber in the first three deliveries. On the fourth delivery, however, Lopez objects that the two-by-fours do not measure 2 inches by 4 inches.

The course of performance in this transaction—that is, Lopez's acceptance of three deliveries without objection under the agreement—is relevant in determining that here the term *two-by-four* actually means "1⅞ by 3¾." Janson's can also prove that *two-by-fours* need not be exactly 2 inches by 4 inches by applying course of prior dealing, usage of trade, or both. Janson's can, for example, show that in previous transactions, Lopez took 1⅞-by-3¾-inch lumber without objection. In addition, Janson's can show that in the lumber trade, two-by-fours are commonly 1⅞ inches by 3¾ inches.

billnoll/E+/Getty Images

Do two-by-fours actually measure 2 inches by 4 inches?

Rules of Construction The UCC provides *rules of construction* for interpreting contracts. Express terms, course of performance, course of dealing, and usage of trade are to be construed to be consistent with each other whenever reasonable. When such a construction is unreasonable, however, the UCC establishes the following order of priority [UCC 1–303(e), 2–208(2), 2A–207(2)]:

1. Express terms.
2. Course of performance.
3. Course of dealing.
4. Usage of trade.

16–2f Unconscionability

As previously discussed, an unconscionable contract is one that is so unfair and one-sided that it would be unreasonable to enforce it. Under the UCC, if a court deems a contract or a clause to have been unconscionable *at the time it was made*, the court can do any of the following [UCC 2–302, 2A–108]:

1. Refuse to enforce the contract.
2. Enforce the remainder of the contract without the unconscionable part.
3. Limit the application of the unconscionable term to avoid an unconscionable result.

The following *Classic Case* illustrates an early application of the UCC's unconscionability provisions.

Classic Case 16.2

Jones v. Star Credit Corp.

Supreme Court of New York, Nassau County 59 Misc.2d 189, 298 N.Y.S.2d 264 (1969).

Facts The Joneses, the plaintiffs, agreed to purchase a freezer for $900 as the result of a salesperson's visit to their home. Tax and financing charges raised the total price to $1,234.80. After making payments totaling $619.88, the plaintiffs brought a suit in a New York state court to have the purchase contract declared unconscionable under the UCC. At trial, the freezer was found to have a maximum retail value of approximately $300.

Issue Could this contract be denied enforcement on the ground of unconscionability?

Decision Yes. The court held that the contract was not enforceable and reformed the contract so that the Joneses were not required to make further payments on the freezer.

Reason The court relied on UCC 2–302(1), which states that if "the court as a matter of law finds the contract or any clause of the contract to have been unconscionable at the time it was made, the court may . . . so limit the application of any unconscionable clause as to avoid any unconscionable result."

(Continues)

The court then considered the disparity between the $900 purchase price and the $300 retail value, as well as the fact that the credit charges alone exceeded the retail value. These excessive charges were exacted despite the seller's knowledge of the plaintiffs' limited resources. The court reformed the contract so that the plaintiffs' payments, amounting to more than $600, were regarded as payment in full.

Critical Thinking

- **Social** *Why would the seller's knowledge of the buyers' limited resources support a finding of unconscionability?*
- **Impact of This Case on Today's Law** *This early case illustrates the approach that many courts today take when deciding whether a sales contract is unconscionable—an approach that focuses on excessive price and unequal bargaining power.*

16–3 Title and Risk of Loss

Before the creation of the UCC, *title*—the right of ownership—was the central concept in sales law and controlled all issues of rights and remedies of the parties to a sales contract. In some situations, title is still relevant under the UCC, and the UCC has special rules for determining who has title. (These rules do not apply to leased goods, obviously, because title remains with the lessor, or owner, of the goods.) In most situations, however, the UCC focuses less on title than on the concepts of *identification, risk of loss*, and *insurable interest*.

16–3a Identification

Identification In a sale of goods, the express designation of the goods provided for in the contract.

Before any interest in specific goods can pass from the seller or lessor to the buyer or lessee, the goods must exist and must be identified as the specific goods designated in the contract. **Identification** takes place when specific goods are designated as the subject matter of a sales or lease contract.

Identification allows title to pass from the seller to the buyer. (Remember, though, that title to leased goods does not pass to the lessee.) In addition, it allows risk of loss to pass from the seller or lessor to the buyer or lessee. This is important because it gives the buyer or lessee the right to insure the goods and the right to recover from third parties who damage the goods.

For goods already in existence, the parties can agree in their contract on when identification will take place. If the parties do not so specify, the UCC provisions discussed here determine when identification takes place [UCC 2–501(1), 2A–217].

Existing Goods If the contract calls for the sale or lease of specific goods that are already in existence, identification takes place at the time the contract is made. **Example 16.20** Litco Company contracts to lease a fleet of five cars designated by their vehicle identification numbers (VINs). Because the cars are identified by their VINs, identification has taken place, and Litco acquires an insurable interest in the cars at the time of contracting.

Future Goods Any goods that are not in existence at the time of contracting are known as *future goods*. Various rules apply to identification of future goods, depending on the goods.

- If a sale or lease involves unborn animals to be born within twelve months after contracting, identification takes place when the animals are conceived.
- If a sale involves crops that are to be harvested within twelve months (or the next harvest season occurring after contracting, whichever is longer), identification takes place when the crops are planted. Otherwise, identification takes place when the crops begin to grow.
- In a sale or lease of any other future goods, identification occurs when the goods are shipped, marked, or otherwise designated by the seller or lessor as the goods to which the contract refers.

Goods That Are Part of a Larger Mass As a general rule, goods that are part of a larger mass are identified when the goods are marked, shipped, or somehow designated by the seller or lessor as the particular goods that are the subject of the contract. **Example 16.21** Carlos orders 10,000 pairs of men's jeans from a lot that contains 90,000 articles of clothing for men, women, and children. Until the seller separates the 10,000 pairs of men's jeans from the other items, title and risk of loss remain with the seller.

A common exception to this rule involves fungible goods. **Fungible goods** are goods that are alike naturally, by agreement, or by trade usage. Typical examples include specific grades or types of wheat, petroleum, and cooking oil, which usually are stored in large containers. If the owners of these goods hold title as *tenants in common* (owners with undivided shares of the whole), a seller-owner can pass title and risk of loss to the buyer without actually separating the goods. The buyer replaces the seller as an owner in common [UCC 2–105(4)]. It is important to emphasize that what makes goods fungible is not simply that they are alike, but that they are of an *identical* grade or type.

Fungible Goods Goods that are alike by physical nature, agreement, or trade usage.

16–3b Passage of Title

Once goods are identified, the provisions of UCC 2–401 apply to the passage of title. Parties can expressly agree when and how title will pass. Throughout UCC 2–401, the words "unless otherwise explicitly agreed" appear, meaning that any explicit understanding between the buyer and the seller determines when title passes. Without an explicit agreement to the contrary, *title passes to the buyer at the time and the place the seller performs by delivering the goods* [UCC 2–401(2)]. For instance, if a person buys cattle at a livestock auction, title will pass to the buyer on physical delivery of the cattle (unless, of course, the parties agree otherwise).

Spotlight Case Example 16.22 Timothy Allen contracted with Indy Route 66 Cycles, Inc., to have a motorcycle custom built for him. Indy built the motorcycle and issued a "Certificate of Origin." Two years later, federal law enforcement officers arrested Allen on drug charges and seized his home and other property. The officers also seized the Indy-made motorcycle from the garage of the home of Allen's sister, Tena. Indy filed a claim against the government, arguing that it owned the motorcycle because it still possessed the "Certificate of Origin."

The court applied UCC Section 2–401(2) and ruled in favor of the government. Testimony by Indy's former vice president was "inconclusive" but implied that Indy had delivered the motorcycle to Allen. Because Indy had given up possession of the cycle to Allen, this was sufficient to pass title even though Indy had kept a "Certificate of Origin."[6]

Shipment Contract A contract for the sale of goods in which the seller is required or authorized to ship the goods by carrier. The seller assumes liability for any losses or damage to the goods until they are delivered to the carrier.

In the future, the delivery of goods may sometimes be accomplished by drones. This chapter's *Managerial Strategy* feature discusses the use of drones in commerce.

Hirkophoto/Stock Unreleased/Getty Images

When does title pass to the buyer of a motorcycle?

Shipment and Destination Contracts Unless otherwise agreed, delivery arrangements can determine when title passes from the seller to the buyer. In a **shipment contract,** the seller is required or authorized to ship goods by carrier, such as a trucking company. Under a shipment contract, the seller is required only to deliver conforming goods into the hands of a carrier, and title passes to the buyer at the time and place of shipment [UCC 2–401(2)(a)]. Generally, *all contracts are assumed to be shipment contracts if nothing to the contrary is stated in the contract.*

6. *United States v. 2007 Custom Motorcycle,* 2011 WL 232331 (D.Ariz. 2011).

Destination Contract A contract for the sale of goods in which the seller is required or authorized to ship the goods by carrier and tender delivery of the goods at a particular destination. The seller assumes liability for any losses or damage to the goods until they are tendered at the destination specified in the contract.

Document of Title A paper exchanged in the regular course of business that evidences the right to possession of goods (for example, a bill of lading or a warehouse receipt).

In a **destination contract,** the seller is required to deliver the goods to a particular destination, usually directly to the buyer, but sometimes to another party designated by the buyer. Title passes to the buyer when the goods are *tendered* at that destination [UCC 2–401(2) (b)]. *Tender of delivery* occurs when the seller places or holds conforming goods at the buyer's disposal (with any necessary notice), enabling the buyer to take possession [UCC 2–503(1)].

Delivery without Movement of the Goods When the sales contract does not call for the seller to ship or deliver the goods (when the buyer is to pick up the goods), the passage of title depends on whether the seller must deliver a **document of title,** such as a bill of lading or a warehouse receipt, to the buyer. A *bill of lading* is a receipt for goods that is signed by a carrier and serves as a contract for the transport of the goods. A *warehouse receipt* is a receipt issued by a warehouser for goods stored in a warehouse.

Commercial Use of Drones

The United States lags behind many other nations when it comes to the commercial use of small, pilotless aerial vehicles known as drones. These devices can be used for a variety of tasks, such as taking real estate videos and making airborne railroad track inspections, but their greatest business potential seems to lie in package delivery.

Not surprisingly, Amazon has been a leader in this field. As part of its Prime Air program, the company is making thirty-minute drone deliveries in England and has conducted numerous tests in controlled settings in the United States. Google's Wing drone delivery service operates in Australia and Finland, and UPS has extensively tested drone deliveries on American medical campuses.

The Federal Aviation Administration Rules

Efforts by Amazon, Google, UPS, and other American companies to provide drone delivery services to consumers have been held up by Federal Aviation Administration (FAA) regulations. The FAA has authority to regulate *all* unmanned aircraft systems (UASs). It first proposed rules on commercial drone use in 2015, and these rules were not finalized until 2016.[a] The FAA did not designate a drone company as a certified air carrier until 2019, when Google's Wing was given that classification, allowing the company to make short-distance deliveries in the small town of Christiansburg, Virginia.

The FAA's rules require operators to apply for a license to use drones commercially. Drone flights are limited to daylight hours, and drones are not allowed to go above four hundred feet or fly faster than one hundred miles per hour. The rules also require that licensed drone operators maintain a continuous visual line of sight with the drones during operation. The latest challenge for the FAA is to approve a drone identification and tracking system. Without these safeguards, law enforcement agencies have resisted widespread commercial applications of the technology, worrying that unidentified drones will be used for crimes such as terrorism and drug smuggling.

Court Actions

The FAA has attempted to fine other-than-recreational users of drones. One case involved Texas EquuSearch, a group that searches for missing persons. The organization requested an emergency injunction after receiving an e-mail from an FAA employee indicating that its drone use was illegal. A federal appellate court in the District of Columbia refused to grant an injunction. The court found that the FAA's e-mail was not subject to judicial review.[b]

In another relevant case, Michael Singer sued to block the city of Newton, Massachusetts, from enforcing a local drone ordinance. Singer, a physician who hopes to deliver medical supplies via drone, claimed that local businesses should not have to comply with both Newton's rules *and* existing FAA regulations. A federal court struck down the parts of Newton's ordinance that mirrored federal law but refused to limit local governments' ability to co-regulate drone use more generally, when appropriate.[c]

Business Questions

1. *What benefits can delivery by commercial drone provide to consumers?*
2. *Why might the United States be slow to adopt commercial drone delivery in comparison with some other nations?*

a. 14 C.F.R. Part 107.

b. *Texas EquuSearch Mounted Search and Recovery Team, RP Search Services, Inc., v. Federal Aviation Administration,* 2014 WL 2860332 (D.C. Cir. 2014).

c. *Singer v. City of Newton,* 284 F.Supp.3d 125 (D.Mass 2017).

When a document of title is required, title passes to the buyer *when and where the document is delivered*. Thus, if the goods are stored in a warehouse, title passes to the buyer when the appropriate documents are delivered to the buyer. The goods never move. In fact, the buyer can choose to leave the goods at the same warehouse for a period of time, and the buyer's title to those goods will be unaffected.

When no documents of title are required and delivery is made without moving the goods, title passes at the time and place the sales contract is made, if the goods have already been identified. If the goods have not been identified, title does not pass until identification occurs [UCC 2–401(3)].

Example 16.23 Greg sells lumber to Bodan. They agree that Bodan will pick up the lumber at the lumberyard. If the lumber has been identified (segregated, marked, or in any other way distinguished from all other lumber), title passes to Bodan when the contract is signed. If the lumber is still in large storage bins at the lumberyard, title does not pass to Bodan until the particular pieces of lumber to be sold under this contract are identified.

16–3c Risk of Loss

Under the UCC, risk of loss does not necessarily pass with title. When risk of loss passes from a seller or lessor to a buyer or lessee is generally determined by the contract between the parties. Sometimes, the contract states expressly when the risk of loss passes. At other times, it does not, and a court must interpret the performance and delivery terms of the contract to determine whether the risk has passed.

ProjectB/iStock/Getty Images

When does the risk of loss pass to the buyer in the sale of a horse, when the horse is paid for in monthly installments?

Like risk of loss, the risk of liability that arises from the goods does not necessarily require the passage of title. In addition, as with risk of loss, when this risk passes from a seller to a buyer is generally determined by the contract between the parties. **Case Example 16.24** Tammy Herring contracted to buy a horse named Toby from Stacy and Gregory Bowman, who owned Summit Stables in Washington. The contract required Herring to make monthly payments until she paid $2,200 in total for Toby. Additionally, Herring agreed to pay Toby's monthly boarding fee at Summit Stables until the purchase price balance was paid. The Bowmans were to provide Toby's registration papers to Herring only when she had paid in full.

One day, another stable boarder, Diana Person, was injured when she was thrown from a buggy drawn by Toby and driven by Herring's daughter. Person sued the Bowmans to recover for her injuries, but the court held that Herring (not the Bowmans) owned Toby at the time of the accident. Herring argued that she did not own the horse because she did not yet have its registration papers, but the court found that the contract clearly showed that Herring owned Toby. Therefore, the Bowmans were not liable for the injuries that Toby caused.[7]

Delivery with Movement of the Goods—Carrier Cases When the contract involves movement of the goods through a common carrier but does not specify when risk of loss passes, the courts first look for specific delivery terms in the contract. The terms that have traditionally been used in contracts within the United States are listed and defined in Exhibit 16–3. *Unless the parties agree otherwise*, these terms determine which party will pay the costs of delivering the goods and who bears the risk of loss. If the contract does not include these terms, then the courts must decide whether the contract is a shipment or a destination contract.

7. *Person v. Bowman*, 173 Wash.App. 1024 (2013).

Exhibit 16–3 Contract Terms—Definitions

These contract terms help to determine which party will bear the costs of delivery and when risk of loss will pass from the seller to the buyer.

TERM	DEFINITION
F.O.B. (free on board)	Indicates that the selling price of goods includes transportation costs to the specific F.O.B. place named in the contract. The seller pays the expenses and carries the risk of loss to the F.O.B. place named [UCC 2–319(1)]. If the named place is the place from which the goods are shipped (for example, the seller's city or place of business), the contract is a shipment contract. If the named place is the place to which the goods are to be shipped (for example, the buyer's city or place of business), the contract is a destination contract.
F.A.S. (free alongside ship)	Requires that the seller, at the seller's own expense and risk, deliver the goods alongside the carrier before risk passes to the buyer [UCC 2–319(2)]. An F.A.S. contract is essentially an F.O.B. contract for ships.
C.I.F. or **C.&F.** (cost, insurance, and freight, or just cost and freight)	Requires, among other things, that the seller "put the goods in the possession of a carrier" before risk passes to the buyer [UCC 2–320(2)]. (These are basically pricing terms, and the contracts remain shipment contracts, not destination contracts.)
Delivery ex-ship (delivery from the carrying vessel)	Means that risk of loss does not pass to the buyer until the goods are properly unloaded from the ship or other carrier [UCC 2–322].

Focus Question 3

When does risk of loss pass in a shipment contract?

Shipment Contracts. In a shipment contract, the seller or lessor is required or authorized to ship goods by carrier but is not required to deliver them to a particular final destination. The risk of loss in a shipment contract passes to the buyer or lessee when the goods are delivered to the carrier [UCC 2–319(1)(a), 2–509(1)(a), 2A–219(2)(a)].

Example 16.25 Pitman, a seller in Texas, sells five hundred cases of grapefruit to a buyer in New York, F.O.B. Houston (free on board in Houston—see Exhibit 16–3). The contract authorizes shipment by carrier. It does not require that the seller tender the grapefruit in New York. Risk passes to the buyer when conforming goods are properly placed in the possession of the carrier in Houston. If the goods are damaged in transit, the loss is the buyer's. (Actually, buyers have recourse against carriers, subject to certain limitations, and buyers usually insure the goods from the time the goods leave the seller.)

Destination Contracts. In a destination contract, the risk of loss passes to the buyer or lessee when the goods are tendered to the buyer or lessee at the specified destination [UCC 2–319(1) (b), 2–509(1)(b), 2A–219(2)(b)]. In *Example 16.25*, if the contract had been F.O.B. New York, the risk of loss during transit to New York would have been the seller's. Risk of loss would not have passed to the buyer until the carrier tendered the grapefruit to the buyer in New York.

The following case involves the interpretation and application of two stated contract conditions for passing the risk of loss from a carrier to the buyer—delivery of the goods to the buyer and the buyer's signature on a bill of lading.

Case 16.3

Total Quality Logistics, LLC v. Balance Transportation, LLC

Court of Appeals of Ohio, Twelfth District, Clermont County, 2020 -Ohio- 620, __ Ohio App.3d __, __ N.E.3d __, 2020 WL 877795 (2020).

Facts C&C North America, Inc., paid Total Quality Logistics, LLC (TQL), a freight broker, to arrange for the shipment of a truckload of granite to Sun City Granite. Balance Transportation, LLC, signed an agreement with TQL to transport the load.

Balance's driver, Adrian Bernal, delivered the granite in good condition to Sun City, whose representative signed, dated, and returned the bill of lading accompanying the shipment. As a Sun City employee unloaded the first block of granite, other slabs fell off the truck and were damaged.

TQL paid C&C for the cost of the damage and filed a complaint in an Ohio state court against Balance, seeking to recover the amount on a claim of breach of its contract with TQL. The court issued a summary judgment in Balance's favor. TQL appealed, asserting that the judgment should have been in its favor.

Issue Did the damage to the goods occur after the risk of loss passed from the carrier to the buyer?

Decision Yes. A state intermediate appellate court affirmed the judgment of the lower court. "The loss of cargo occurred after the risk of loss had shifted from Balance. This finding is dispositive [definitively resolves the issue] as to all claims raised by TQL."

Reason The agreement between TQL and Balance provided that the carrier's responsibility for the condition of the freight would end with its delivery and the buyer's signature on a bill of lading. On appeal, TQL argued that, although Sun City's representative had signed the bill of lading, Balance had not yet successfully delivered the cargo. Balance's driver, Bernal, still had to move his truck, park it, and unstrap the granite.

The court acknowledged that the Sun City representative had signed and dated the bill of lading, and returned it to Bernal, before instructing him to move his truck and park it. After doing as he was told, Bernal unstrapped the load from the trailer. "Up until this point," added the court, "there is no dispute that the cargo was in good condition."

During the unloading process, undertaken by Sun City's employee, the granite was badly damaged, however. "Since the damage occurred subsequent to delivery and receipt of the signed bill of lading, we agree with the trial court that Balance was no longer responsible for the risk of loss."

Critical Thinking

- **Legal Environment** *Generally, a broker who only arranges for shipment is not liable for damage or loss to goods during their transport. Why did TQL decide to pay C&C for the cost of the damage to the granite? Discuss.*
- **Economic** *Should a risk-of-loss provision be included in a contract for the sale or transport of goods? Why or why not?*

Delivery without Movement of the Goods The UCC also addresses situations in which the contract does not require the goods to be shipped or moved. Frequently, the buyer or lessee is to pick up the goods from the seller or lessor, or the goods are held by a bailee.

A **bailment** is a temporary delivery of personal property, without passage of title, into the care of another, called a *bailee*. Under the UCC, a *bailee* is a party who, by a bill of lading, warehouse receipt, or other document of title, acknowledges possession of goods and/or contracts to deliver them. For instance, a warehousing company or a trucking company may be a bailee.

Bailment A situation in which the personal property of one person (a bailor) is entrusted to another (a bailee), who is obligated to return the bailed property to the bailor or dispose of it as directed.

Goods Held by the Seller. When the seller keeps the goods for pickup, a document of title usually is not used. If the seller is a merchant, risk of loss to goods held by the seller passes to the buyer when the buyer *actually takes physical possession of the goods* [UCC 2–509(3)]. In other words, the merchant bears the risk of loss between the time the contract is formed and the time the buyer picks up the goods. **Case Example 16.26** Roger Adams bought a preassembled table saw that weighed 288 pounds from Sears Roebuck and Company. When Adams went to the loading area to pick up the saw, a Sears employee used a hydraulic lift to elevate it to the height of Adams's pickup bed. Adams then pulled the saw onto the truck, and the employee went back inside the store (and did not secure the saw).

Adams, who was standing in the bed of his truck, took a step and lost his balance. He grabbed the saw to steady himself. Both he and the saw fell off the truck, and he was injured. Adams sued Sears, alleging negligence, but the court granted summary judgment in favor of Sears. Sears was under no duty to help Adams secure the saw in the truck, so the employee had not been negligent. Once the truck was loaded, the risk of loss (or injury) passed to Adams under the UCC because he had taken physical possession of the goods.[8]

8. *Adams v. Sears Roebuck and Co.*, 2014 WL 670630 (D.Utah 2014).

While securing his purchases in his truck bed at a store's loading area, a customer falls and is injured. Who is liable, and why?

If the seller is not a merchant, the risk of loss to goods held by the seller passes to the buyer on *tender of delivery* [UCC 2–509(3)]. This means that a seller bears the risk of loss until the seller makes the goods available to the buyer and notifies the buyer that the goods are ready to be picked up.

With respect to leases, similar rules apply. The risk of loss passes to the lessee on the lessee's receipt of the goods if the lessor is a merchant. Otherwise, the risk passes to the lessee on tender of delivery [UCC 2A–219(2)(c)].

Goods Held by a Bailee. When a bailee is holding goods for a person who has contracted to sell them and the goods are to be delivered without being moved, the goods are usually represented by a document of title. The title document may be written, such as a bill of lading or a warehouse receipt, or evidenced by an electronic record.

When goods are held by a bailee, risk of loss passes to the buyer when one of the following occurs:

1. The buyer receives a negotiable document of title for the goods.
2. The bailee acknowledges the buyer's right to possess the goods.
3. The buyer receives a nonnegotiable document of title, *and* the buyer has a *reasonable time* to present the document to the bailee and demand the goods. If the bailee refuses to honor the document, the risk of loss remains with the seller [UCC 2–503(4)(b), 2–509(2)].

With respect to leases, if goods held by a bailee are to be delivered without being moved, the risk of loss passes to the lessee on acknowledgment by the bailee of the lessee's right to possession of the goods [UCC 2A–219(2)(b)].

Risk of Loss When the Contract Is Breached When a sales or lease contract is breached, the transfer of risk operates differently depending on which party breaches. Generally, the party in breach bears the risk of loss.

When the Seller or Lessor Breaches. If the seller or lessor breaches by supplying goods that are so nonconforming that the buyer has the right to reject them, the risk of loss does not pass to the buyer. **Example 16.27** A buyer orders ten stainless steel refrigerators from a seller, F.O.B. the seller's plant. The seller ships white refrigerators instead. The white refrigerators (nonconforming goods) are damaged in transit. The risk of loss falls on the seller. Had the seller shipped stainless steel refrigerators (conforming goods) instead, the risk would have fallen on the buyer [UCC 2–510(1)].

With nonconforming goods, the risk of loss does not pass to the buyer until one of the following occurs:

Cure The right of a party who tenders nonconforming performance to correct the nonconforming performance within the contract period.

1. The seller is able to **cure** the defects (that is, the goods are repaired, replaced, or discounted in price by the seller).
2. The buyer accepts the goods in spite of their defects (thus waiving the right to reject).

If a buyer accepts a shipment of goods and later discovers a defect, acceptance can be revoked. Revocation allows the buyer to pass the risk of loss back to the seller, at least to the extent that the buyer's insurance does not cover the loss [UCC 2–510(2)]. Article 2A provides similar rules for leases.

When the Buyer or Lessee Breaches. The general rule is that when a buyer or lessee breaches a contract, the risk of loss immediately shifts to the buyer or lessee. This rule has three important limitations:

1. The seller or lessor must already have identified the contract goods.

2. The buyer or lessee bears the risk for only a commercially reasonable time after the seller or lessor has learned of the breach.
3. The buyer or lessee is liable only to the extent of any deficiency in the seller's insurance coverage [UCC 2–510(3), 2A–220(2)].

16–3d Insurable Interest

Parties to sales and lease contracts often obtain insurance coverage to protect against damage, loss, or destruction of goods. Any party purchasing insurance must have a sufficient interest in the insured item to obtain a valid policy. Insurance laws—not the UCC—determine sufficiency. The UCC is helpful, however, because it contains certain rules regarding insurable interests in goods.

Insurable Interest of the Buyer or Lessee A buyer or lessee has an **insurable interest** in *identified* goods. The moment the contract goods are identified by the seller or lessor, the buyer or lessee has a property interest in them. That allows the buyer or lessee to obtain necessary insurance coverage for those goods even before the risk of loss has passed [UCC 2–501(1), 2A–218(1)]. When the parties do not explicitly agree on identification in their contract, then the UCC provisions on identification discussed earlier in this chapter apply.

Insurable Interest A property interest in goods being sold or leased that is sufficiently substantial to permit a party to insure against damage to the goods.

Insurable Interest of the Seller or Lessor A seller has an insurable interest in goods as long as the seller retains title to the goods. Even after title passes to the buyer, a seller who has a *security interest* in the goods (a right to secure payment) still has an insurable interest [UCC 2–501(2)]. Thus, both a buyer and a seller can have an insurable interest in the same goods at the same time. Of course, the buyer or seller must sustain an actual loss to recover from an insurance company. In regard to leases, the lessor retains an insurable interest in leased goods until the lessee exercises an option to buy and the risk of loss has passed to the lessee [UCC 2A–218(3)].

16–4 Contracts for the International Sale of Goods

Today, businesses often engage in sales and lease transactions on a global scale. International sales contracts between firms or individuals located in different countries are governed by the 1980 United Nations Convention on Contracts for the International Sale of Goods (CISG). The CISG governs international contracts only if the countries of the parties to the contract have ratified the CISG and if the parties have not agreed that some other law will govern their contract. As of 2021, the CISG had been adopted by eighty-four countries, including the United States, Canada, some Central and South American countries, China, most European nations, Japan, and Mexico. That means that the CISG is the uniform international sales law of countries that account for more than two-thirds of all global trade.

Focus Question 4

What law governs contracts for the international sale of goods?

16–4a Applicability of the CISG

Essentially, the CISG is to international sales contracts what Article 2 of the UCC is to domestic sales contracts. As discussed earlier, in domestic transactions the UCC applies when the parties to a contract for a sale of goods have failed to specify in writing some important term concerning price, delivery, or the like. Similarly, whenever the parties subject to the CISG have failed to specify in writing the precise terms of a contract for the international sale of goods, the CISG will be applied.

Unlike *the UCC, the CISG does not apply to consumer sales*. Neither the UCC nor the CISG applies to contracts for services.

16–4b A Comparison of CISG and UCC Provisions

The provisions of the CISG, although similar for the most part to those of the UCC, differ from them in certain respects. If the CISG and the UCC conflict, the CISG applies (because it is a treaty of the U.S. national government and therefore takes precedence over state laws under the U.S. Constitution). We look here at some differences with respect to contract formation.

Statute of Frauds Unlike the UCC, the CISG does not include any Statute of Frauds provisions. Under Article 11 of the CISG, an international sales contract does not need to be evidenced by a writing or to be in any particular form.

Offers UCC 2–205 provides that a merchant's firm offer is irrevocable, even without consideration, if the merchant gives assurances in a signed writing or record. In contrast, under the CISG, an offer can become irrevocable without a signed writing or record. Article 16(2) of the CISG provides that an offer will be irrevocable in either of the following circumstances:

1. The offeror states orally that the offer is irrevocable.
2. The offeree reasonably relies on the offer as being irrevocable.

In both of these situations, the offer will be irrevocable without a writing or record and without consideration.

Another difference is that, under the UCC, if the price term is left open, the court will determine "a reasonable price at the time for delivery" [UCC 2–305(1)]. Under the CISG, however, the price term must be specified, or at least provisions for its specification must be included in the agreement. Otherwise, normally no contract will exist.

Acceptances Under the UCC, a definite expression of acceptance that contains additional terms can still result in the formation of a contract, unless the additional terms are conditioned on the assent of the offeror. In other words, the UCC does away with the mirror image rule in domestic sales contracts.

Article 19 of the CISG provides that a contract can be formed even though the acceptance contains additional terms, unless the additional terms materially alter the contract. Under the CISG, however, a "material alteration" includes almost any change in the terms. If an additional term relates to payment, quality, quantity, price, time and place of delivery, extent of one party's liability to the other, or the settlement of disputes, the CISG considers the added term a material alteration. In effect, then, the CISG requires that the terms of the acceptance mirror those of the offer.

Toronto-Images.Com/Shutterstock.com

How did Article 19 of the CISG affect the court's decision regarding a dispute over the international sale of potatoes?

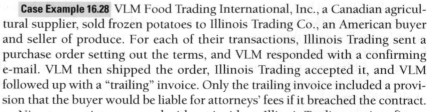

Case Example 16.28 VLM Food Trading International, Inc., a Canadian agricultural supplier, sold frozen potatoes to Illinois Trading Co., an American buyer and seller of produce. For each of their transactions, Illinois Trading sent a purchase order setting out the terms, and VLM responded with a confirming e-mail. VLM then shipped the order, Illinois Trading accepted it, and VLM followed up with a "trailing" invoice. Only the trailing invoice included a provision that the buyer would be liable for attorneys' fees if it breached the contract.

Nine transactions occurred without incident. Illinois Trading ran into financial difficulties, however, and did not pay for the next nine shipments. VLM filed a suit in a federal district court against the buyer, seeking to recover the unpaid amount plus attorneys' fees. Illinois Trading admitted that it owed the price for the potatoes but contested liability for the attorneys' fees. A federal appellate court agreed with Illinois Trading that under the CISG, the attorneys' fee provision in the trailing invoice did not become part of the parties' contract. The attorneys' fee provision was a material alteration to the contract terms, and Illinois Trading did not agree to the additional term.[9] ■

9. *VLM Food Trading International, Inc. v. Illinois Trading Co.*, 811 F.3d 247 (7th Cir. 2016).

Practice and Review

Guy Holcomb owns and operates Oasis Goodtime Emporium, an adult entertainment establishment. Holcomb wanted to create an adult Internet system for Oasis that would offer customers adult theme videos and live chat room programs using performers at the club. On May 10, Holcomb signed a work order authorizing Thomas Consulting Group (TCG) "to deliver a working prototype of a customer chat system, demonstrating the integration of live video and chatting in a Web browser." In exchange for creating the prototype, Holcomb agreed to pay TCG $64,697. On May 20, Holcomb signed an additional work order in the amount of $12,943 for TCG to install a customized firewall system. The work orders stated that Holcomb would make monthly installment payments to TCG, and both parties expected the work would be finished by September.

Due to unforeseen problems largely attributable to system configuration and software incompatibility, the project required more time than anticipated. By the end of the summer, the website was still not ready, and Holcomb had fallen behind in the payments to TCG. TCG was threatening to cease work and file suit for breach of contract unless the bill was paid. Rather than make further payments, Holcomb wanted to abandon the website project. Using the information presented in the chapter, answer the following questions.

1. Would a court be likely to decide that the transaction between Holcomb and TCG was covered by the Uniform Commercial Code (UCC)? Why or why not?
2. Would a court be likely to consider Holcomb a merchant under the UCC? Why or why not?
3. Did the parties have a valid contract under the UCC? Explain.
4. Suppose that Holcomb and TCG meet in October in an attempt to resolve their problems. At that time, the parties reach an oral agreement that TCG will continue to work without demanding full payment of the past-due amounts and Holcomb will pay TCG $5,000 per week. Assuming that the contract falls under the UCC, is the oral agreement enforceable? Why or why not?

Debate This

The UCC should require the same degree of definiteness of terms, especially with respect to price and quantity, as general contract law does.

Key Terms

bailment 399
course of dealing 392
course of performance 392
cure 400
destination contract 396
document of title 396
firm offer 386
fungible goods 395
identification 394
insurable interest 401
intangible property 381
lease 382
lease agreement 383
lessee 383
lessor 383
merchant 382
output contract 386
predominant-factor test 382
requirements contract 386
sale 380
sales contracts 379
seasonably 387
shipment contract 395
tangible property 381
usage of trade 392

Chapter Summary: Sales and Lease Contracts

The Scope of Articles 2 and 2A	1. **The Uniform Commercial Code (UCC)**—Attempts to provide a consistent, uniform, and integrated framework of rules to deal with all phases ordinarily arising in a commercial sales or lease transaction, including contract formation, passage of title, and risk of loss. The concepts of good faith and commercial reasonableness permeate the UCC. 2. **Article 2 (sales)**—Governs contracts for the sale of goods (tangible, movable personal property). Rules can vary if the buyer or seller is a merchant. The common law of contracts also applies to sales contracts to the extent that the common law has not been modified by the UCC. If there is a conflict between a common law rule and the UCC, the UCC controls. 3. **Article 2A (leases)**—Governs contracts for the lease or sublease of goods. Except that it applies to leases, instead of sales, of goods, Article 2A is essentially a repetition of Article 2 and varies only to reflect differences between sales and lease transactions.
The Formation of Sales and Lease Contracts	1. **Offer**— **a.** Not all terms have to be included for a contract to be formed (only the subject matter and quantity term normally must be specified). **b.** The price does not have to be included for a contract to be formed. **c.** Particulars of performance can be left open. **d.** A written and signed offer by a *merchant*, covering a period of three months or less, is irrevocable without payment of consideration. 2. **Acceptance**— **a.** Acceptance may be made by any reasonable means of communication. It is effective when dispatched. **b.** An offer can be accepted by a promise to ship or by prompt shipment of conforming goods, or by prompt shipment of nonconforming goods if accompanied by a notice of accommodation. **c.** Acceptance by performance requires notice within a reasonable time. Otherwise, the offer can be treated as lapsed before acceptance. **d.** A definite expression of acceptance creates a contract even if the terms of the acceptance differ from those of the offer, unless the additional or different terms in the acceptance are expressly conditioned on the offeror's assent to those terms. 3. **Consideration**—A modification of a contract for the sale of goods does not require consideration. 4. **The Statute of Frauds**— **a.** All contracts for the sale of goods priced at $500 or more, and lease contracts requiring payments of $1,000 or more, must be in writing. A writing is sufficient as long as it indicates the parties' intention to form a contract and is signed by the party against whom enforcement is sought. A contract normally is not enforceable beyond the quantity shown in the writing. **b.** When written confirmation of an oral contract *between merchants* is not objected to in writing by the receiver within ten days, the contract is enforceable. **c.** For exceptions to the Statute of Frauds, see Exhibit 16–2. 5. **Parol evidence rule**— **a.** The terms of a clear and complete written contract cannot be contradicted by evidence of prior agreements or contemporaneous oral agreements. **b.** Evidence is admissible to clarify the terms of a writing if the contract terms are ambiguous or if evidence of course of dealing, usage of trade, or course of performance is necessary to learn or to clarify the parties' intentions. 6. **Unconscionability**—An unconscionable contract is one that is so unfair and one-sided that it would be unreasonable to enforce it. If the court deems a contract or a clause in a contract to have been unconscionable at the time it was made, the court can (a) refuse to enforce the contract, (b) refuse to enforce the unconscionable clause, or (c) limit the application of any unconscionable clauses to avoid an unconscionable result.

Title and Risk of Loss

1. **Shipment contract**—In the absence of an agreement, title and risk pass on the seller's or lessor's delivery of conforming goods to the carrier [UCC 2–319(1)(a), 2–401(2)(a), 2–509(1)(a), 2A–219(2)(a)].
2. **Destination contract**—In the absence of an agreement, title and risk pass on the seller's or lessor's *tender* of delivery of conforming goods to the buyer or lessee at the point of destination [UCC 2–319(1)(b), 2–401(2)(b), 2–509(1)(b), 2A–219(2)(b)].
3. **Delivery without movement of the goods**—In the absence of an agreement, if the goods are not represented by a document of title, title passes on the formation of the contract, and risk passes on the buyer's or lessee's receipt of the goods if the seller or lessor is a merchant or on the tender of delivery if the seller or lessor is a nonmerchant.
4. **Risk of loss when the contract is breached**—
   a. If the seller or lessor breaches by tendering nonconforming goods that are rejected by the buyer or lessee, the risk of loss does not pass to the buyer or lessee until the defects are cured (unless the buyer or lessee accepts the goods in spite of their defects, thus waiving the right to reject) [UCC 2–510(1), 2A–220(1)].
   b. If the buyer or lessee breaches the contract, the risk of loss immediately shifts to the buyer or lessee for goods that are identified to the contract. The buyer or lessee bears the risk for only a commercially reasonable time after the seller or lessor has learned of the breach [UCC 2–510(3), 2A–220(2)].

Contracts for the International Sale of Goods

International sales contracts are governed by the United Nations Convention on Contracts for the International Sale of Goods (CISG) if the countries of the parties to the contract have ratified the CISG and if the parties have not agreed that some other law will govern their contract. Essentially, the CISG is to international sales contracts what Article 2 of the UCC is to domestic sales contracts. Unlike the UCC, however, the CISG does not apply to consumer sales. Whenever parties who are subject to the CISG have failed to specify in writing the precise terms of a contract for the international sale of goods, the CISG will be applied.

Issue Spotters

1. E-Design, Inc., orders 150 computer desks. Fav-O-Rite Supplies, Inc., ships 150 printer stands. Is this an acceptance of the offer or a counteroffer? If it is an acceptance, is it a breach of the contract? What if Fav-O-Rite told E-Design it was sending the printer stands as "an accommodation"? (See *The Formation of Sales and Lease Contracts.*)
2. Truck Parts, Inc. (TPI), often sells supplies to United Fix-It Company (UFC), which services trucks. Over the phone, they negotiate for the sale of eighty-four sets of tires. TPI sends a letter to UFC detailing the terms and two weeks later ships the tires. Is there an enforceable contract between them? Why or why not? (See *The Formation of Sales and Lease Contracts.*)

—Check your answers to the *Issue Spotters* against the answers provided in Appendix D.

Business Scenarios and Case Problems

16–1. Additional Terms. Strike offers to sell Bailey one thousand shirts for a stated price. The offer declares that shipment will be made by Dependable Truck Line. Bailey replies, "I accept your offer for one thousand shirts at the price quoted. Delivery to be by Yellow Express Truck Line." Both Strike and Bailey are merchants. Three weeks later, Strike ships the shirts by Dependable Truck Line, and Bailey refuses to accept delivery. Strike sues for breach of contract. Bailey claims that there never was a contract because his reply, which included a modification of carriers, did not constitute an acceptance. Bailey further claims that even if there had been a contract, Strike would have been in breach because Strike shipped the shirts by Dependable, contrary to the contract terms. Discuss fully Bailey's claims. (See *The Formation of Sales and Lease Contracts.*)

16–2. Spotlight on Goods and Services—The Statute of Frauds. Fallsview Glatt Kosher Caterers ran a business that provided travel packages, including food, entertainment, and lectures on religious subjects, to customers during the Passover holiday at a New York resort. Willie Rosenfeld verbally agreed to pay Fallsview $24,050 for the Passover package for himself and his family. Rosenfeld did not appear at the resort and never paid the money owed. Fallsview sued Rosenfeld for breach of contract. Rosenfeld claimed that the contract was unenforceable because it was not in writing and violated the UCC's Statute of Frauds. Is the contract valid? Explain. [*Fallsview Glatt Kosher Caterers, Inc. v. Rosenfeld*, 794 N.Y.S.2d 790 (N.Y. Super. 2005)] (See *The Formation of Sales and Lease Contracts.*)

16–3. Goods Held by the Seller or Lessor. Douglas Singletary bought a manufactured home from Andy's Mobile Home and Land Sales. The contract stated that the buyer accepted the home "as is where is." Singletary paid the full price, and his crew began to ready the home to relocate it to his property. The night before the home was to be moved, however, it was destroyed by fire. Who suffered the loss? Explain. [*Singletary, III v. P&A Investments, Inc.*, 712 S.E.2d 681 (N.C.App. 2011)] (See *Title and Risk of Loss.*)

16–4. Risk of Loss. Ethicon, Inc., a pharmaceutical company, entered into an agreement with UPS Supply Chain Solutions, Inc., to transport pharmaceuticals. The drivers were provided by International Management Services Co. under a contract with a UPS subsidiary, Worldwide Dedicated Services, Inc. During the transport of a shipment from Ethicon's facility in Texas to buyers "F.O.B. Tennessee," one of the trucks collided with a concrete barrier near Little Rock, Arkansas, and caught fire, damaging the goods. Who was liable for the loss? Why? [*Royal & Sun Alliance Insurance, PLC v. International Management Services Co.*, 703 F.3d 604 (2d Cir. 2013)] (See *Title and Risk of Loss.*)

16–5. Business Case Problem with Sample Answer—Goods and Services Combined. Allied Shelving and Equipment, Inc., sells and installs shelving systems. National Deli, LLC, contracted with Allied to provide and install a parallel rack system (a series of large shelves) in National's warehouse. Both parties were dissatisfied with the result. National filed a suit in a Florida state court against Allied, which filed a counterclaim. Each contended that the other had materially breached the contract. The court applied common law contract principles to rule in National's favor on both claims. Allied appealed, arguing that the court should have applied the UCC. When does a court apply common law principles to a contract that involves both goods and services? In this case, why might an appellate court rule that the UCC should be applied instead? Explain. [*Allied Shelving and Equipment, Inc. v. National Deli, LLC*, 40 Fla.L.Weekly D145, 154 So.3d 482 (Dist.App. 2015)] (See *The Scope of Articles 2 and 2A.*)

—For a sample answer to Problem 16-5, go to Appendix E.

16–6. Acceptance. New England Precision Grinding, Inc. (NEPG), sells precision medical parts in Massachusetts. NEPG agreed to supply Kyphon, Inc., with certain medical parts. NEPG contracted with Simply Surgical, LLC, to obtain the parts from Iscon Surgicals, Ltd. The contract did not mention Kyphon or require Kyphon's acceptance of the parts. Before shipping, Iscon would certify that the parts conformed to NEPG's specifications. On receiving the parts, NEPG would certify that they conformed to Kyphon's specifications. On delivery, Kyphon would also inspect the parts.

After about half a dozen transactions, NEPG's payments to Simply Surgical lagged, and the seller refused to make further deliveries. NEPG filed a suit in a Massachusetts state court against Simply Surgical, alleging breach of contract. NEPG claimed that Kyphon had rejected some of the parts, which gave NEPG the right not to pay for them. Do the UCC's rules with respect to acceptance support or undercut the parties' actions? Discuss. [*New England Precision Grinding, Inc. v. Simply Surgical, LLC*, 89 Mass.App.Ct.176, 46 N.E.3d 590 (2016)] (See *The Formation of Sales and Lease Contracts.*)

16–7. When Title Passes. James McCoolidge, a Nebraska resident, saw a used Honda Element for sale online. He contacted the seller, Daniel Oyvetsky, who offered to sell the vehicle for $7,500 on behalf of Car and Truck Center, LLC, a dealership in Nashville, Tennessee. McCoolidge paid the price and received the car and a certificate of title. Before he registered the certificate with the Nebraska Department of Motor Vehicles, he learned that the state of Tennessee had issued numerous certificates of title to the Element. Based on these documents, title could ultimately be traced to McCoolidge. But he chose to file a suit in a Nebraska state court against Oyvetsky, claiming that he had not received "clear" title. What does the UCC provide with respect to the passage of title under a sales contract? How does that rule impact McCoolidge's claim? Discuss. [*McCoolidge v. Oyvetsky*, 292 Neb. 955, 874 N.W.2d 892 (2016)] (See *Title and Risk of Loss.*)

16–8. Requirements Contracts. Medalist Golf, Inc., a high-end golf course builder, was working on a new golf course project in Missouri. Chris Williams, doing business as Cane Creek Sod, submitted a bid with Medalist to provide Meyer Zoysia grass sod for the project. Williams and Medalist executed a "grass supplier agreement" that specified the type and quality of grass to be used, stated the price, and gave Medalist a right to inspect and reject the sod. The parties estimated the quantity of sod needed for the project to be twenty-one acres. Williams had approximately sixty-five acres of Meyer Zoysia growing at the time. The agreement did not specify the amount of sod that Medalist would purchase from Williams, nor did it say that Medalist would buy Williams's sod exclusively. Later, when Medalist had an expert inspect Williams's sod (before it was harvested), the expert concluded that it did not meet the quality standards required for the project. Medalist therefore rejected the sod. Williams sued for breach of contract. Was the "grass supplier agreement" enforceable as a requirements contract? Why or why not? [*Williams v. Medalist Golf, Inc.*, 2018 WL 1046889 (E.D.Mo. 2018)] (See *The Formation of Sales and Lease Contracts.*)

16–9. A Question of Ethics—The IDDR Approach and Sales and Lease Contracts. Camal Terry signed a "Sales Contract" to buy a 1995 BMW 3 Series from Robin Drive Auto, a car dealership in Delaware. Terry agreed to pay $4,995, and Robin Drive agreed to hold the BMW on layaway for him in contemplation of a sale within twenty-one days. Also specified were a down payment of $1,200 and the timing of other payments. But under the payment schedule, Terry was to pay $100 a week for six weeks (forty-two days) even though the sale was to take place twenty-one days later. In addition, the contract provided that the payments were fees for storage and "prep" and were not deductible from the price of the car. Terry paid more than $1,000 before asking Robin Drive to refund the money. When the dealership refused, Terry filed a suit in a Delaware state court against Robin Drive. Testimony about the mismatched contract terms was conflicting. [*Terry v. Robin Drive Auto*, 2017 WL 65842 (Del. Com. Pl. 2017)] (See *The Formation of Sales and Lease Contracts.*)

1. Ethically, what is wrong with this deal? Explain.
2. Using the IDDR approach, consider whether Robin Drive has an ethical obligation to use a different contract in its sales to consumers.

Critical Thinking and Writing Assignments

16–10. Time-Limited Group Assignment—Parol Evidence. Mountain Stream Trout Co. agreed to buy "market size" trout from trout grower Lake Farms, LLC. Their five-year contract did not define *market size.* At the time, in the trade, *market size* referred to fish of one-pound live weight. After three years, Mountain Stream began taking fewer, smaller deliveries of larger fish, claiming that *market size* varied according to whatever its customers demanded and that its customers now demanded larger fish. Lake Farms filed a suit for breach of contract. (See *The Formation and of Sales and Lease Contracts.*)

1. The first group will decide whether parol evidence is admissible to explain the terms of this contract. Are there any exceptions that could apply?
2. A second group will determine the impact of course of dealing and usage of trade on the interpretation of contract terms.
3. A third group will discuss how parties to a commercial contract can avoid the possibility that a court will interpret the contract terms in accordance with trade usage.

13_Phunkod/Shutterstock.com

17 Performance and Breach of Sales and Lease Contracts

Focus Questions

The five Focus Questions *below are designed to help improve your understanding. After reading this chapter, you should be able to answer the following questions:*

1. What is the perfect tender rule? What are some important exceptions to this rule?
2. When will a buyer or lessee be deemed to have accepted the goods?
3. What remedies are available to a seller or lessor when the buyer or lessee breaches the contract?
4. When can a buyer or lessee revoke acceptance?
5. What implied warranties arise under the UCC?

"Gratitude is as the good faith of merchants: it holds commerce together."

François de la Rochefoucauld
1613–1680
(French author)

The performance required of the parties under a sales or lease contract consists of the duties and obligations each party has under the terms of the contract. The basic obligation of the seller or lessor is to *transfer and deliver conforming goods.* The basic obligation of the buyer or lessee is to *accept and pay for conforming goods* in accordance with the contract [UCC 2–301, 2A–516(1)]. Overall performance of a sales or lease contract is controlled by the agreement between the parties. If Reyes contracts with Nike to buy five shipments of soccer balls for his store, he is obligated to pay for them according to the terms of his contract (within thirty days of receiving each shipment, for instance).

When the contract is unclear and disputes arise, the courts look to the UCC and impose standards of good faith and commercial reasonableness. The obligations of good faith and commercial reasonableness underlie every sales and lease contract. The UCC's good faith provision, which can never be disclaimed, reads as follows: "Every contract or duty within this Act imposes an obligation of good faith in its performance or enforcement" [UCC 1–304]. *Good faith* means honesty in fact. For a merchant, it means both honesty in fact and the observance of reasonable commercial standards of fair dealing in the trade [UCC 2–103(1)(b)]. In other words, merchants are held to a higher standard of performance or duty than are nonmerchants.

Sometimes, circumstances make it difficult for a party to carry out the promised performance, leading to a breach of the contract. When a breach occurs, the aggrieved (wronged) party looks for remedies. At other times, a problem arises concerning the goods that are purchased or leased. In those situations, the buyer or lessee may sometimes be able to recover against the seller or lessor under a warranty.

fizkes/Shutterstock.com

How does the Uniform Commercial Code's good faith provision affect everyday business transactions?

17–1 Obligations of the Seller or Lessor

The major obligation of the seller or lessor under a sales or lease contract is to deliver or tender delivery of conforming goods to the buyer or lessee. **Conforming goods** are goods that conform to the contract description in every way.

Conforming Goods Goods that conform to contract specifications.

17–1a Tender of Delivery

Tender of delivery occurs when the seller or lessor makes conforming goods available to the buyer or lessee and provides whatever notification is reasonably necessary to enable the buyer or lessee to take delivery [UCC 2–503(1), 2A–508(1)].

Tender of Delivery A seller's or lessor's act of placing conforming goods at the disposal of the buyer or lessee and providing whatever notification is reasonably necessary to enable the buyer or lessee to take delivery.

Tender must occur at a *reasonable hour* and in a *reasonable manner.* In other words, a seller cannot call the buyer at 2:00 A.M. and say, "The goods are ready. I'll give you twenty minutes to get them." Unless the parties have agreed otherwise, the goods must be tendered for delivery at a reasonable hour and kept available for a reasonable period of time to enable the buyer to take possession of them [UCC 2–503(1)(a)].

Normally, all goods called for by a contract must be tendered in a single delivery, unless the parties have agreed that the goods may be delivered in several lots or *installments* [UCC 2–307, 2–612, 2A–510]. **Example 17.1** An order for one thousand Under Armour men's shirts cannot be delivered two shirts at a time. If, however, the parties agree that the shirts will be delivered in four orders of 250 each as they are produced (for summer, fall, winter, and spring inventory), then tender of delivery may occur in this manner.

17–1b Place of Delivery

The UCC provides for the place of delivery under a contract only if the contract does not indicate the place where the buyer or lessee will take possession. If the contract does not indicate where the goods will be delivered, then the place for delivery will be one of the following:

1. The *seller's place of business.*
2. The *seller's residence*, if the seller has no business location [UCC 2–308(a)].
3. The *location of the goods*, if both parties know at the time of contracting that the goods are located somewhere other than the seller's business [UCC 2–308(b)].

Example 17.2 Jihoo and Boyd both live in Los Angeles. Jihoo contracts to sell to Boyd five shipping containers that both parties know are located in San Francisco. If nothing more is specified in the contract, the place of delivery for the shipping containers is San Francisco. Jihoo may tender delivery by giving Boyd a negotiable or nonnegotiable document of title. Alternatively, Jihoo may obtain the bailee's (warehouser's) acknowledgment that the buyer is entitled to possession.[1]

1. Unless the buyer objects, the seller may also tender delivery by instructing the bailee in writing to release the goods to the buyer without a bailee's acknowledgment of the buyer's rights [UCC 2–503(4)]. Risk of loss, however, does not pass until the buyer has a reasonable amount of time in which to present the document or to give the bailee instructions for delivery.

Know This

Documents of title include bills of lading, warehouse receipts, and any other documents that, in the regular course of business, entitle a person holding these documents to obtain possession of, and title to, the goods covered.

17–1c Delivery via Carrier

In many instances, circumstances or delivery terms in the contract (such as F.O.B. or F.A.S. terms) make it apparent that the parties intended the goods to be moved by a carrier. In carrier contracts, the seller fulfills the obligation to deliver the goods through either a shipment contract or a destination contract.

Shipment Contracts Recall that a *shipment contract* requires or authorizes the seller to ship goods by a carrier, rather than to deliver them at a particular destination [UCC 2–319, 2–509(1)(a)]. Under a shipment contract, unless otherwise agreed, the seller must do the following:

1. Put the goods into the hands of the carrier.
2. Make a contract for their transportation that is reasonable according to the nature of the goods and their value. (For instance, certain types of goods require refrigeration in transit.)
3. Obtain and promptly deliver or tender to the buyer any documents necessary to enable the buyer to obtain possession of the goods from the carrier.
4. Promptly notify the buyer that shipment has been made [UCC 2–504].

If the seller fails to make a reasonable contract for transportation or notify the buyer of the shipment, the buyer can reject the shipment, but only if the seller's failure results in a *material loss* or a *significant delay*. **Example 17.3** Zigi's Organic Fruits sells strawberries to Lozier under a shipment contract. If Zigi's does not arrange for refrigerated transportation and the berries spoil during transport, a material loss to Lozier will likely result. ■ Of course, the parties can agree in their contract that a lesser amount of loss or delay will be grounds for rejection.

Destination Contracts In a *destination contract,* the seller agrees to deliver conforming goods to the buyer at a particular destination. The seller must give the buyer appropriate notice about the delivery and hold the goods at the buyer's disposal for a reasonable length of time. The seller must also provide the buyer with any documents of title necessary to enable the buyer to obtain delivery from the carrier [UCC 2–503].

Focus Question 1

What is the perfect tender rule? What are some important exceptions to this rule?

17–1d The Perfect Tender Rule

As previously noted, the seller or lessor has an obligation to ship or tender *conforming goods*. The buyer or lessee is then required to accept and pay for the goods according to the terms of the contract [UCC 2–507]. Under the common law, the seller was not necessarily obligated to deliver goods that conformed to the terms of the contract in every detail. Minor defects in performance were compensable under the substantial performance doctrine.

Perfect Tender Rule The legal right of a buyer or lessee of goods to insist on perfect tender by the seller or lessor. If the goods fail to conform to the contract, the buyer may accept the goods, reject the goods, or accept part and reject part of the goods tendered.

In contrast, the UCC adopted the perfect tender rule. The **perfect tender rule** states that if the goods or tender of delivery fail *in any respect* to conform to the contract, the buyer or lessee has the right to accept the goods, reject the entire shipment, or accept part and reject part [UCC 2–601, 2A–509].

Case Example 17.4 First Technology Capital, Inc., contracted to purchase a McDonnell Douglas DC-9-83 aircraft from Airborne, Inc. A technical summary report was attached and incorporated into the parties' contract. The report listed specifications for the plane that First Technology intended to buy, which, as it turned out, described a McDonnell Douglas MD-83 rather than the aircraft Airborne was selling. When First Technology refused to accept the DC-9-83 aircraft, Airborne sued for breach of contract.

A federal district court in New York held in First Technology's favor and dismissed the case. The specifications listed in the contract (the technical summary report) were clear. The DC-9-83 did not comply with those specifications. Therefore, under the perfect tender rule, the buyer had a right to reject the goods.[2]

(Note that the corollary to this rule is that if the goods conform in every respect, the buyer or lessee does not have a right to reject the goods.)

In the following case, a company ordered a custom-built tow truck from a manufacturer, but when it was delivered, the truck did not function properly. The question was whether the seller's tender of a truck that did not function properly gave the buyer a right to reject the truck under the perfect tender rule.

Photo 12/Alamy

How did the perfect tender rule affect a dispute over a sales contract involving a McDonnell Douglas aircraft?

2. *First Technology Capital, Inc. v. Airborne, Inc.*, 261 F.Supp.3d 371 (W.D.N.Y. 2017).

Case 17.1

All the Way Towing, LLC v. Bucks County International, Inc.

Superior Court of New Jersey, Appellate Division, 452N.J.Super. 565, 178A.3d 97 (2018).

Facts After extensive discussions, Bucks County International, Inc., contracted with All the Way Towing, LLC, to manufacture and sell a tow truck with particular specifications. The contract specified that the custom-made truck would be "an International 7300 4×4 with a Dynamic 801 tow body mounted." The truck was supposed to be delivered by April 15, but the first attempt at delivery occurred months later, in October. At that time, the tow truck's forks did not move correctly, and there were other significant problems. Bucks made two more attempts at delivery in October, but the towing function was not operational, and the truck spewed hydraulic fluid. The fourth attempt at delivery occurred in November. At that time, metal fell out from beneath the truck, and the wheel lift failed to close properly.

All the Way rejected the truck and, believing that Bucks would never be able to deliver a properly functioning truck, demanded return of the $10,000 deposit. When Bucks did not refund the deposit, All the Way sued. The trial court granted summary judgment to the defendant, dismissing the complaint because Bucks had tendered a tow truck as specified in the contract. All the Way appealed.

Issue Does delivering a truck that meets the contract specifications but does not function properly constitute a perfect tender?

Decision No. The state intermediate appellate court reversed the lower court's decision and remanded the case for a trial. Because there was a factual dispute concerning whether the tow truck conformed to the contract, summary judgment was not proper.

Reason The reviewing court noted that the lower court should have considered plaintiffs' allegations that the defendant had failed to deliver a truck that adequately performed its essential functions. "If plaintiffs' allegations regarding the tow truck's apparent problems, which were identified at each of four attempted deliveries, are ultimately proven, plaintiffs would have demonstrated the tow truck was nonconforming." If the truck was nonconforming, then All the Way Towing had a right to reject it under the perfect tender rule and to pursue the remedies available under the UCC.

Critical Thinking

- **What If the Facts Were Different?** *Suppose that Bucks had completely fixed the truck by the fourth time it was tendered. Could All the Way continue to reject delivery of the truck? Why or why not?*
- **Legal Environment** *What provisions might the parties in this situation have included in their contract to protect themselves from this type of dispute?*

17–1e Exceptions to the Perfect Tender Rule

Because of the rigidity of the perfect tender rule, several exceptions to the rule have been created, some of which are discussed here.

Agreement of the Parties Exceptions to the perfect tender rule may be established by agreement. If the parties have agreed, for instance, that defective goods or parts will not be rejected if the seller or lessor is able to repair or replace them within a reasonable period of time, the perfect tender rule does not apply.

The Right to Cure The UCC does not specifically define the term *cure,* but it refers to the right of the seller or lessor to repair, adjust, or replace defective or nonconforming goods [UCC 2–508, 2A–513]. The seller or lessor can attempt to cure a defect when the following are true:

1. A delivery is rejected because the goods were nonconforming.
2. The time for performance has not yet expired.
3. The seller or lessor provides timely notice to the buyer or lessee of the intention to cure.
4. The cure can be made within the contract time for performance.

Know This
If goods never arrive, the buyer or seller usually has at least some recourse against the carrier. Also, a buyer normally insures the goods from the time they leave the seller's possession.

Reasonable Grounds. Even if the contract time for performance has expired, sellers or lessors can still cure if they have *reasonable grounds to believe that the nonconforming tender will be acceptable to the buyer or lessee* [UCC 2–508(2), 2A–513(2)]. **Example 17.5** In the past, Reddy Electronics frequently allowed Topps Company to substitute gray keyboards when the silver keyboards that Reddy ordered were not available. Under a new contract for silver keyboards, Reddy rejects a shipment of gray keyboards. In this situation, Topps had reasonable grounds to believe Reddy would accept a substitute. Therefore, Topps can cure within a reasonable time even if conforming delivery will occur after the contract time for performance has ended. ■

A seller or lessor may tender nonconforming goods with a price allowance (discount). This may also serve as "reasonable grounds" for the seller or lessor to believe that the buyer or lessee will accept the nonconforming tender.

Limits the Right to Reject Goods. The right to cure substantially restricts the right of the buyer or lessee to reject goods. To reject, the buyer or lessee must inform the seller or lessor of the particular defect. If the defect is not disclosed, and if it is one that the seller or lessor could have cured, the buyer or lessee cannot later assert the defect as a defense. Generally, buyers and lessees must act in good faith and state specific reasons for refusing to accept goods [UCC 2–605, 2A–514].

Substitution of Carriers An agreed-on manner of delivery (such as the use of a particular carrier) may become impracticable or unavailable through no fault of either party. In that situation, if a commercially reasonable substitute is available, this substitute must be used and will constitute sufficient tender to the buyer [UCC 2–614(1)]. The seller or lessor is required to arrange for the substitute carrier and normally is responsible for any additional shipping costs (unless the contract states otherwise).

Example 17.6 A sales contract calls for a large generator to be delivered via Roadway Trucking Corporation on or before June 1. The contract terms clearly state the importance of the delivery date. The employees of Roadway Trucking go on strike. The seller must make a reasonable substitute tender, by another trucking company or perhaps by rail, if it is available. The seller normally will be responsible for any additional shipping costs. ■

Installment Contract A contract that requires or authorizes delivery in two or more separate lots to be accepted and paid for separately.

Installment Contracts An **installment contract** is a single contract that requires or authorizes delivery in two or more separate lots to be accepted and paid for separately. With an installment contract, a buyer or lessee can reject an installment *only if the nonconformity substantially impairs the value* of the installment and cannot be cured [UCC 2–307, 2–612(2), 2A–510(1)]. **Example 17.7** A seller, Emmy's Appliances, is to deliver fifteen freezers in lots of five each. In the first lot, four of the freezers have defective cooling units that cannot be repaired. In these circumstances, the buyer can reject the entire lot. If the buyer or lessee fails to notify the seller or lessor of the rejection, however, and subsequently accepts a nonconforming installment, the contract is reinstated [UCC 2–612(3), 2A–510(2)].

Unless the contract provides otherwise, the entire installment contract is breached only when one or more nonconforming installments *substantially* impair the value of the *whole contract*. The point to remember is that the UCC significantly alters the right of the buyer or lessee to reject the entire contract if the contract requires delivery to be made in several installments. The UCC strictly limits rejection to cases of *substantial* nonconformity.

Commercial Impracticability Occurrences unforeseen by either party when a contract was made may make performance commercially impracticable. When this occurs, the rule of perfect tender no longer applies. The seller or lessor must, however, notify the buyer or lessee as soon as practicable that there will be a delay or nondelivery.

The doctrine of commercial impracticability does not extend to problems that could have been foreseen, such as an increase in cost resulting from inflation. The nonoccurrence of the contingency must have been a basic assumption on which the contract was made [UCC 2–615, 2A–405].

Classic Case Example 17.8 Maple Farms, Inc., entered a contract to supply a school district in New York with milk for one school year. The contract price was the market price of milk in June, but by December, the price of raw milk had increased by 23 percent. Maple Farms stood to lose $7,350 on this contract (and more on similar contracts with other school districts).

To avoid performing the contract, Maple Farms filed a suit and claimed that the unanticipated increases in its costs made performance "impracticable." A New York trial court disagreed. Because inflation and fluctuating prices could have been foreseen, they did not render performance of this contract impracticable. The court ruled in favor of the school district.[3]

princessdlaf/E+/Getty Images

School districts often make long-term contracts for milk deliveries. Under what circumstances can a milk supplier claim commercial impracticability when it fails to deliver the milk?

Commercial Impracticability and Partial Performance Sometimes, an unforeseen event only *partially* affects the capacity of the seller or lessor to perform. Therefore, the seller or lessor can *partially* fulfill the contract but cannot tender total performance. In this situation, the seller or lessor is required to distribute any remaining goods or deliveries fairly and reasonably among the parties to whom it is contractually obligated to deliver the goods [UCC 2–615(b), 2A–405(b)]. The buyer or lessee must receive notice of the allocation and has the right to accept or reject it [UCC 2–615(c), 2A–405(c)].

Example 17.9 A Florida orange grower, Best Citrus, Inc., contracts to sell this season's crop to a number of customers, including Martin's grocery chain. Martin's contracts to purchase two thousand crates of oranges. Best Citrus has sprayed some of its orange groves with a chemical called Karmoxin. When studies show that persons who eat products sprayed with Karmoxin may develop cancer, the Department of Agriculture issues an order prohibiting the sale of these products. Best Citrus picks only those oranges not sprayed with Karmoxin, but there are not enough to meet all the contracted-for deliveries.

In this situation, Best Citrus is required to allocate its production. It notifies Martin's that it cannot deliver the full quantity specified in the contract and indicates the amount it will be able to deliver. Martin's can either accept or reject the allocation, but Best Citrus has no further contractual liability.

3. *Maple Farms, Inc. v. City School District of Elmira*, 76 Misc.2d 1080, 352 N.Y.S.2d 784 (1974).

Destruction of Identified Goods Sometimes, an unexpected event, such as a fire, totally destroys goods through no fault of either party and before risk passes to the buyer or lessee. In such a situation, *if the goods were identified at the time the contract was formed,* the parties are excused from performance [UCC 2–613, 2A–221]. If the goods are only partially destroyed, however, the buyer or lessee can inspect them and either treat the contract as void or accept the goods with a reduction of the contract price.

Example 17.10 Atlas Sporting Equipment agrees to lease to River Bicycles sixty bicycles of a particular model that has been discontinued. No other bicycles of that model are available. River specifies that it needs the bicycles to rent to tourists. Before Atlas can deliver the bicycles, they are destroyed by a fire. In this situation, Atlas is not liable to River for failing to deliver the bicycles. The goods were destroyed through no fault of either party, before the risk of loss passed to the lessee. The loss was total, so the contract is avoided. Clearly, Atlas has no obligation to tender the bicycles, and River has no obligation to make the lease payments for them.

Assurance and Cooperation If one party has "reasonable grounds" to believe that the other party will not perform as contracted, that party may *in writing* "demand adequate assurance of due performance" from the other party. Until such assurance is received, the doubting party may "suspend" further performance (such as payments due under the contract) without liability. What constitutes "reasonable grounds" is determined by commercial standards. If such assurances are not forthcoming within a reasonable time (not to exceed thirty days), the failure to respond may be treated as a *repudiation* of the contract [UCC 2–609, 2A–401].

Sometimes, the performance of one party depends on the cooperation of the other. The UCC provides an exception to the perfect tender doctrine if one party fails to cooperate. When cooperation is not forthcoming, the other party can suspend performance without liability and hold the uncooperative party in breach or proceed to perform the contract in any reasonable manner [UCC 2–311(3)].

Example 17.11 Aman is required by contract to deliver 1,200 Samsung washing machines to various locations in California on or before October 1. Farrell, the buyer, is to specify the locations for delivery. Aman repeatedly requests the delivery locations, but Farrell does not respond. The washing machines are ready for shipment on October 1, but Farrell still refuses to give Aman the delivery locations. If Aman does not ship on October 1, he cannot be held liable. Aman is excused for any resulting delay of performance because of Farrell's failure to cooperate.

17–2 Obligations of the Buyer or Lessee

The main obligation of the buyer or lessee under a sales or lease contract is to pay for the goods tendered in accordance with the contract. Once the seller or lessor has adequately tendered delivery, the buyer or lessee is obligated to accept the goods and pay for them according to the terms of the contract.

17–2a Payment

In the absence of any specific agreement, the buyer or lessee must make payment at the time and place the goods are *received* [UCC 2–310(a), 2A–516(1)]. When a sale is made on credit, the buyer is obligated to pay according to the specified credit terms (for instance, 60, 90, or 120 days), not when the goods are received. The credit period usually begins on the *date of shipment* [UCC 2–310(d)]. Under a lease contract, a lessee must make the lease payment that was specified in the contract [UCC 2A–516(1)].

Payment can be made by any means agreed on by the parties—cash or any other method generally acceptable in the commercial world. If the seller demands cash, the seller must give the buyer reasonable time to obtain it [UCC 2–511].

17–2b Right of Inspection

Unless the parties otherwise agree, or for C.O.D. (collect on delivery) transactions, the buyer or lessee has an absolute right to inspect the goods before making payment. This right allows the buyer or lessee to verify, before making payment, that the goods tendered or delivered are what were contracted for or ordered. If the goods are *not* what were ordered, the buyer or lessee has no duty to pay. *An opportunity for inspection is therefore a condition precedent to the right of the seller or lessor to enforce payment* [UCC 2–513(1), 2A–515(1)].

Inspection can take place at any reasonable place and time and in any reasonable manner. Generally, what is reasonable is determined by custom of the trade, past practices of the parties, and the like. The buyer bears the costs of inspecting the goods (unless otherwise agreed), but if the goods are rejected because they are not conforming, the buyer can recover the costs of inspection from the seller [UCC 2–513(2)].

17–2c Acceptance

Focus Question 2

When will a buyer or lessee be deemed to have accepted the goods?

After having had a reasonable opportunity to inspect the goods, the buyer or lessee can demonstrate acceptance in any of the following ways:

1. The buyer or lessee indicates (by words or conduct) to the seller or lessor that the goods are conforming or that the buyer or lessee will retain them in spite of their nonconformity [UCC 2–606(1)(a), 2A–515(1)(a)].
2. The buyer or lessee *fails to reject* the goods within a reasonable period of time [UCC 2–602(1), 2–606(1)(b), 2A–515(1)(b)].
3. In sales contracts, the buyer *performs any act inconsistent with the seller's ownership.* For instance, any use or resale of the goods—except for the limited purpose of testing or inspecting the goods—generally constitutes an acceptance [UCC 2–606(1)(c)].

Case Example 17.12 Hemacare Plus, Inc., ordered more than $660,000 in specialty pharmaceutical products from Cardinal Health 108, LLC. Cardinal supplied the products, which Hemacare used and did not reject or return. When Hemacare did not pay the invoices for the goods delivered, Cardinal filed a breach action in a federal district court. Because Hemacare had used the pharmaceutical products it received, the court found it had accepted the goods. Therefore, the court granted summary judgment to Cardinal, awarding $688,920 in damages (including interest, attorneys' fees, and costs).[4]

17–2d Partial Acceptance

If some of the goods delivered do not conform to the contract and the seller or lessor has failed to cure, the buyer or lessee can make a *partial* acceptance [UCC 2–601(c), 2A–509(1)]. The same is true if the nonconformity was not reasonably discoverable before acceptance. (In the latter situation, the buyer or lessee may be able to revoke the acceptance, as will be discussed later in this chapter.)

A buyer or lessee cannot accept less than a single commercial unit, however. The UCC defines a *commercial unit* as a unit of goods that, by commercial usage, is viewed as a "single

4. *Cardinal Health 108, LLC v. Hemacare Plus, Inc.*, 2017 WL 114405 (S.D.Ala. 2017).

whole" that cannot be divided without material impairment of the character of the unit, its market value, or its use [UCC 2–105(6), 2A–103(1)(c)]. A commercial unit can be a single article (such as a machine), a set of articles (such as a suite of furniture or an assortment of sizes), a quantity (such as a bale, a gross, or a carload), or any other unit treated in the trade as a single whole for purposes of sale.

17–2e Anticipatory Repudiation

What if, before the time for contract performance, one party clearly communicates to the other the intention not to perform? As discussed earlier in this text, such an action is a breach of the contract by anticipatory repudiation.

Possible Responses to Repudiation When anticipatory repudiation occurs, the nonbreaching party has a choice of two responses:

1. Treat the repudiation as a final breach by pursuing a remedy.
2. Wait to see if the repudiating party will decide to perform the contract despite the avowed intention to renege [UCC 2–610, 2A–402].

In either situation, the nonbreaching party may *suspend performance.*

A Repudiation May Be Retracted The UCC permits a breaching party to "retract" a repudiation (subject to some limitations). This retraction can be done by any method that clearly indicates the party's intent to perform. Once retraction is made, the rights of the repudiating party under the contract are reinstated. There can be no retraction, however, if since the time of the repudiation the other party has canceled or materially changed position or otherwise indicated that the repudiation is final [UCC 2–611, 2A–403].

Example 17.13 On April 1, Lyn, who owns a small inn, purchases a suite of furniture from Horton, proprietor of Horton's Furniture Warehouse. The contract states that "delivery must be made on or before May 1." On April 10, Horton informs Lyn that he cannot make delivery until May 10 and asks her to consent to the modified delivery date.

In this situation, Lyn has two options. She can either treat Horton's notice of late delivery as a final breach of contract and pursue a remedy or agree to the later delivery date. Suppose that Lyn does neither for two weeks. On April 24, Horton informs Lyn that he will be able to deliver the furniture by May 1 after all. In effect, Horton has retracted his repudiation, reinstating the rights and obligations of the parties under the original contract. Note that if Lyn had told Horton that she was canceling the contract after he repudiated, he would not have been able to retract his repudiation. ■

krsmanovic/Shutterstock.com

An inn owner buys new bedroom furniture, but the seller modifies the delivery date of the shipment. What are the inn owner's options?

17–3 Remedies of the Seller or Lessor

Remedies under the UCC are *cumulative,* meaning that the aggrieved (wronged) party is not limited to one exclusive remedy. (Of course, a party may not recover twice for the same harm.) When the buyer or lessee is in breach, the remedies available to the seller or lessor depend on the circumstances existing at the time of the breach. The most pertinent considerations are which party has possession of the goods, whether the goods are in transit, and whether the buyer or lessee has rejected or accepted the goods.

17–3a When the Goods Are in the Possession of the Seller or Lessor

If the breach occurs *before the goods have been delivered to the buyer or lessee,* the seller or lessor has the right to pursue a number of remedies, which are listed below and discussed in the following subsections.

1. Cancel (rescind) the contract.
2. Withhold delivery of the goods.
3. Resell or dispose of the goods and sue to recover damages.
4. Sue to recover the purchase price or lease payments due.
5. Sue to recover damages for the buyer's nonacceptance.

Focus Question 3

What remedies are available to a seller or lessor when the buyer or lessee breaches the contract?

The Right to Cancel the Contract If the buyer or lessee breaches the contract, the seller or lessor can choose to cancel (rescind) the contract [UCC 2–703(f), 2A–523(1)(a)]. The seller must notify the buyer or lessee of the cancellation, and at that point all remaining obligations of the seller or lessor are discharged. The buyer or lessee is not discharged from all remaining obligations, however. The buyer or lessee is in breach, and the seller or lessor can pursue remedies available under the UCC for breach.

The Right to Withhold Delivery In general, sellers and lessors can withhold or discontinue performance of their obligations under sales or lease contracts when the buyers or lessees are in breach. This is true whether a buyer or lessee has wrongfully rejected or revoked acceptance of contract goods (rejection and revocation of acceptance will be discussed later), failed to make a payment, or repudiated the contract [UCC 2–703(a), 2A–523(1)(c)]. The seller or lessor can also refuse to deliver the goods to a buyer or lessee who is insolvent (unable to pay debts as they become due), unless the buyer or lessee pays in cash [UCC 2–702(1), 2A–525(1)].

Know This

A buyer or lessee breaches a contract by wrongfully rejecting the goods, wrongfully revoking acceptance, refusing to pay, or repudiating the contract.

The Right to Resell or Dispose of the Goods When a buyer or lessee breaches or repudiates the contract while the seller or lessor is still in possession of the goods, the seller or lessor can resell or dispose of the goods. Any resale of the goods must be made in good faith and in a commercially reasonable manner. The seller must give the original buyer reasonable notice of the resale, unless the goods are perishable or will rapidly decline in value [UCC 2–706(2), (3)].

The seller or lessor can retain any profits made as a result of the sale or disposition and can hold the buyer or lessee liable for any loss [UCC 2–703(d), 2–706(1), 2A–523(1)(e), 2A–527(1)]. In sales transactions, the seller can recover any deficiency between the resale price and the contract price, and can also recover *incidental damages,* defined as the costs to the seller resulting from the breach [UCC 2–706(1), 2–710]. In lease transactions, the lessor can lease the goods to another party and recover damages from the original lessee. Damages include any unpaid lease payments up to the time the new lease begins. The lessor can also recover any deficiency between the lease payments due under the original lease and those due under the new lease, along with incidental damages [UCC 2A–527(2)].

When the goods are unfinished at the time of breach, the seller or lessor can do either of the following:

1. Cease manufacturing the goods and resell them for scrap or salvage value.
2. Complete the manufacture, resell or dispose of the goods, and hold the buyer or lessee liable for any difference between the contract price and the sale price.

In choosing between these two alternatives, the seller or lessor must exercise reasonable commercial judgment to mitigate the loss and obtain maximum value from the unfinished goods [UCC 2–704(2), 2A–524(2)].

The Right to Sue to Recover the Purchase Price or the Lease Payments Due Under the UCC, an unpaid seller or lessor can bring an action to recover the purchase price or payments due under the lease contract, plus incidental damages [UCC 2–709(1), 2A–529(1)]. If a seller or lessor is unable to resell or dispose of goods and sues for the contract price or lease payments due, the goods must be held for the buyer or lessee. The seller or lessor can resell or dispose of the goods at any time before collecting the judgment from the buyer or lessee. If the goods are resold, the net proceeds from the sale must be credited to the buyer or lessee because of the duty to mitigate damages.

Example 17.14 Canyonville Academy contracts with Stickme.com to purchase ten thousand bumper stickers with the school's name and logo on them. Stickme tenders delivery of the stickers, but Canyonville wrongfully refuses to accept them. In this situation, Stickme can bring an action for the purchase price. Stickme has delivered conforming goods, and Canyonville has refused to accept or pay for the goods. Obviously, Stickme will not likely be able to resell the stickers, so this situation falls under UCC 2–709. Stickme is required to make the bumper stickers available for Canyonville. In the unlikely event that it can find another buyer, it can sell the stickers at any time prior to collecting the judgment from Canyonville. ■

monkeybusinessimages/iStock/Getty Images

If a school orders special merchandise with its school name printed on it and then refuses the shipment of conforming goods, what can the seller do to recoup payment?

The Right to Sue to Recover Damages for the Buyer's Nonacceptance If a buyer or lessee repudiates a contract or wrongfully refuses to accept the goods, a seller or lessor can bring an action to recover the damages sustained. Ordinarily, the amount of damages equals the difference between the contract price or lease payments and the market price or lease payments at the time and place of tender of the goods, plus incidental damages [UCC 2–708(1), 2A–528(1)].

When the ordinary measure of damages is insufficient to put the seller or lessor in the same position as the buyer's or lessee's performance would have, the UCC provides an alternative. In that situation, the proper measure of damages is the lost profits of the seller or lessor, including a reasonable allowance for overhead and other expenses [UCC 2–708(2), 2A–528(2)].

17–3b When the Goods Are in Transit

If the seller or lessor has delivered the goods to a carrier or a bailee, but the buyer or lessee has not yet received them, the goods are said to be *in transit*. In limited situations, the seller or lessor can prevent goods in transit from being delivered to the buyer or lessee.

Effect of Insolvency and Breach If the seller or lessor learns that the buyer or lessee is insolvent, the seller or lessor can stop the carrier or bailee from delivering the goods regardless of the quantity of goods shipped. If the buyer or lessee is in breach but is not insolvent, however, the seller or lessor can stop delivery of goods in transit only if the quantity shipped is at least a carload, a truckload, a planeload, or a larger shipment [UCC 2–705(1), 2A–526(1)].

Example 17.15 Arturo orders a truckload of lumber from Timber Products, Inc., to be shipped to him six weeks later. Arturo, who owes payment to Timber Products for a past shipment, promises to pay the debt immediately and to pay for the current shipment as soon as it is received. After the lumber has been shipped, a bankruptcy court judge notifies Timber Products that Arturo has filed a petition in bankruptcy and listed Timber Products as one of his creditors. If the goods are still in transit, Timber Products can stop the carrier from delivering the lumber to Arturo. ■

Requirements for Stopping Delivery To stop delivery, the seller or lessor must *timely notify* the carrier or other bailee that the goods are to be returned or held for the seller or lessor. If the carrier has sufficient time to stop delivery, it must hold and deliver the goods according to the instructions of the seller or lessor. The seller or lessor is liable to the carrier for any additional costs incurred [UCC 2–705(3), 2A–526(3)].

The seller or lessor has the right to stop delivery of the goods under UCC 2–705(2) and 2A–526(2) until the time when the following occurs:

1. The buyer or lessee obtains possession of the goods.
2. The carrier or the bailee acknowledges the rights of the buyer or lessee in the goods (by reshipping or holding the goods for the buyer or lessee, for instance).
3. A negotiable document of title covering the goods has been properly transferred to the buyer (in sales transactions only), giving the buyer ownership rights in the goods [UCC 2–702].

Once the seller or lessor reclaims the goods in transit, any remedies allowed to sellers and lessors when the goods are in their possession can be pursued.

17–3c When the Goods Are in the Possession of the Buyer or Lessee

When the buyer or lessee breaches the contract while in possession of the goods, the seller or lessor can sue. The seller or lessor can sue to recover the purchase price of the goods or the lease payments due, plus incidental damages [UCC 2–709(1), 2A–529(1)].

Know This
Incidental damages include all reasonable expenses incurred because of a breach of contract.

In some situations, a seller may also have a right to reclaim the goods from the buyer. For instance, in a sales contract, if the buyer has received the goods on credit and the seller discovers that the buyer is insolvent, the seller can demand return of the goods [UCC 2–702(2)]. Ordinarily, the demand must be made within ten days of the buyer's receipt of the goods.[5] The seller's right to reclaim the goods is subject to the rights of a good faith purchaser or other subsequent buyer in the ordinary course of business who purchases the goods from the buyer before the seller reclaims them.

A lessor may also have a right to reclaim goods. If the lessee is in default (fails to make payments that are due, for instance), the lessor may reclaim leased goods that are in the lessee's possession [UCC 2A–525(2)].

17–4 Remedies of the Buyer or Lessee

When the seller or lessor breaches the contract, the buyer or lessee has numerous remedies available under the UCC. Like the remedies available to sellers and lessors, the remedies of buyers and lessees depend on the circumstances existing at the time of the breach. Relevant factors include whether the seller has refused to deliver conforming goods or has delivered nonconforming goods.

17–4a When the Seller or Lessor Refuses to Deliver the Goods

If the seller or lessor refuses to deliver the goods, or the buyer or lessee has rightfully rejected the goods, the remedies available to the buyer or lessee include the right to:

1. Cancel (rescind) the contract.
2. Obtain goods that have been paid for if the seller or lessor is insolvent.

5. The seller can demand and reclaim the goods at any time, though, if the buyer misrepresented his or her solvency in writing within three months prior to the delivery of the goods.

Know This
A seller or lessor breaches a contract by wrongfully failing to deliver the goods, delivering nonconforming goods, making an improper tender of the goods, or repudiating the contract.

3. Sue to obtain specific performance if the goods are unique or damages are an inadequate remedy.
4. Buy other goods (obtain *cover*), and obtain damages from the seller.
5. Sue to obtain identified goods held by a third party (*replevy* goods).
6. Sue to obtain damages.

The Right to Cancel the Contract When a seller or lessor fails to make proper delivery or repudiates the contract, the buyer or lessee can cancel, or rescind, the contract. On notice of cancellation, the buyer or lessee is relieved of any further obligations under the contract but retains all rights to other remedies against the seller [UCC 2–711(1), 2A–508(1)(a)]. (The right to cancel the contract is also available to a buyer or lessee who has rightfully rejected goods or revoked acceptance, as will be discussed shortly.)

The Right to Obtain the Goods on Insolvency If a buyer or lessee has made a partial or full payment for goods that are in the possession of a seller or lessor who is or becomes insolvent, the buyer or lessee has a right to obtain the goods. For this right to be exercised, the goods must be identified to the contract, and the buyer or lessee must pay any remaining balance of the price to the seller or lessor [UCC 2–502, 2A–522].

The Right to Obtain Specific Performance A buyer or lessee can obtain specific performance when the goods are unique and the remedy at law is inadequate [UCC 2–716(1), 2A–521(1)]. Ordinarily, monetary damages are sufficient to place buyers or lessees in the position they would have occupied if the sellors or lessors had fully performed. When the contract is for the purchase of a particular work of art or a similarly unique item, however, monetary damages may not be sufficient. Under these circumstances, equity requires that the seller or lessor perform exactly by delivering the goods identified to the contract (a remedy of specific performance).

Spotlight Case Example 17.16 Doreen Houseman and Eric Dare together bought a house and a pedigreed dog. When the couple separated, they agreed that Dare would keep the house (and pay Houseman for her interest in it) and Houseman would keep the dog. Houseman allowed Dare to take the dog for visits. After one such visit, Dare failed to return the dog. Houseman filed a lawsuit seeking specific performance of their agreement. The court found that because pets have special, subjective value to their owners, a dog can be considered a unique good. Thus, an award of specific performance was appropriate.[6]

fotojagodka/iStock/Getty Images

Will a court consider a pedigreed dog a unique good?

The Right to Obtain Cover In certain situations, buyers and lessees can protect themselves by obtaining **cover**—that is, by purchasing or leasing other goods to substitute for those due under the contract. This option is available when the seller or lessor repudiates the contract or fails to deliver the goods, or when a buyer or lessee has rightfully rejected goods or revoked acceptance. In purchasing or leasing substitute goods, the buyer or lessee must act in good faith and without unreasonable delay [UCC 2–712, 2A–518].

After obtaining substitute goods, the buyer or lessee can recover the following from the seller or lessor:

1. The difference between the cost of cover and the contract price (or lease payments).
2. Incidental damages that resulted from the breach.
3. Consequential damages to compensate for indirect losses (such as lost profits) resulting from the breach that were reasonably foreseeable at the time of contract formation.

Cover A remedy that allows the buyer or lessee, on the seller's or lessor's breach, to obtain substitute goods from another seller or lessor.

Buyers and lessees are not required to cover, and failure to do so will not bar them from using any other remedies available under the UCC. A buyer or lessee who fails to cover, however, may not be able to collect consequential damages that could have been avoided by purchasing or leasing substitute goods.

6. *Houseman v. Dare*, 405 N.J.Super. 538, 966 A.2d 24 (2009).

The Right to Replevy Goods Buyers and lessees also have the right to replevy goods. **Replevin** [7] is an action that a buyer or lessee can use to recover specific goods from a third party, such as a bailee, who is wrongfully withholding them. Under the UCC, the buyer or lessee can replevy goods subject to the contract if the seller or lessor has repudiated or breached the contract. To maintain an action to replevy goods, buyers and lessees usually must show that they are unable to cover for the goods after a reasonable effort [UCC 2–716(3), 2A–521(3)].

Replevin An action that can be used by a buyer or lessee to recover identified goods from a third party, such as a bailee, who is wrongfully withholding them.

The Right to Recover Damages If a seller or lessor repudiates the contract or fails to deliver the goods, the buyer or lessee can sue for damages. For the buyer (or lessee), the measure of recovery is the difference between the contract price (or lease payments) and the market price (or lease payments) at the time the buyer (or lessee) *learned* of the breach. The market price or market lease payments are determined at the place where the seller or lessor was supposed to deliver the goods. The buyer or lessee can also recover incidental and consequential damages, less the expenses that were saved as a result of the breach [UCC 2–713, 2A–519].

Know This

Consequential damages compensate for a loss (such as lost profits) that is not direct but was reasonably foreseeable at the time of the breach.

Example 17.17 Jason & Fils, Inc., contracts to buy a thirty-thousand-gallon industrial tank from Burbank Equipment Corporation for $70,000. Jason & Fils hires Zach's Transport to pick up the tank, but when Zach's arrives at the pickup location, there is no tank. Jason & Fils pays Zach's $7,500 for its services and sues Burbank Equipment to recover.

In this situation, Jason & Fils is entitled to recover the difference between the contract price and the market price of the tank. In addition, Jason & Fils is entitled to incidental damages of at least $7,500 for the cost of transport, as well as any consequential damages that were reasonably foreseeable.

vincent noel/Shutterstock

If a supplier of industrial storage tanks fails to provide a tank when and where specified in the sales contract, can the buyer recover funds paid to a transport company for its shipment?

17–4b When the Seller or Lessor Delivers Nonconforming Goods

When the seller or lessor delivers nonconforming goods, the buyer or lessee has several remedies available under the UCC. The buyer or lessee may reject the goods, revoke acceptance of the goods, or recover damages for accepted goods.

The Right to Reject the Goods If either the goods or the tender of the goods by the seller or lessor fails to conform to the contract *in any respect,* the buyer or lessee can reject the goods in whole or in part [UCC 2–601, 2A–509]. A buyer or lessee who rejects the goods may then obtain cover, cancel the contract, or sue for damages for breach of contract, just as if the seller or lessor had refused to deliver the goods.

Timeliness and Reason for Rejection Required. The buyer or lessee must reject the goods within a reasonable amount of time after delivery and must *seasonably* (timely) notify the seller or lessor [UCC 2–602(1), 2A–509(2)]. If the buyer or lessee fails to reject the goods within a reasonable amount of time, acceptance will be presumed.

When rejecting goods, the buyer or lessee must also designate specific defects that would have been apparent to the seller or lessor on reasonable inspection. Failure to do so precludes the buyer or lessee from using such defects to justify rejection or to establish breach when the seller could have cured the defects if they had been disclosed in a timely fashion [UCC 2–605, 2A–514].

7. Pronounced ruh-*pleh*-vun. Note that outside the UCC, the term *replevin* refers to a prejudgment process that permits the seizure of specific personal property in which a party claims a right or an interest.

Duties of Merchant Buyers and Lessees When Goods Are Rejected. What happens if a *merchant buyer or lessee* rightfully rejects goods and the seller or lessor has no agent or business at the place of rejection? In that situation, the merchant buyer or lessee has a good faith obligation to follow any reasonable instructions received from the seller or lessor with respect to the goods [UCC 2–603, 2A–511]. The buyer or lessee is entitled to be reimbursed for the care and cost entailed in following the instructions. The same requirements hold if the buyer or lessee rightfully revokes acceptance of the goods at some later time [UCC 2–608(3), 2A–517(5)]. (Revocation of acceptance will be discussed shortly.)

If no instructions are forthcoming and the goods are perishable or threaten to decline in value quickly, the buyer can resell the goods in good faith. The buyer can then take the appropriate reimbursement from the proceeds and a selling commission (not to exceed 10 percent of the gross proceeds) [UCC 2–603(1), (2); 2A–511(1), (2)]. If the goods are not perishable, the buyer or lessee may store them for the seller or lessor or reship them to the seller or lessor [UCC 2–604, 2A–512].

Focus Question 4

When can a buyer or lessee revoke acceptance?

Revocation of Acceptance

Acceptance of the goods precludes the buyer or lessee from exercising the right of rejection, but it does not necessarily prevent the buyer or lessee from pursuing other remedies. In certain circumstances, a buyer or lessee is permitted to *revoke* acceptance of the goods.

Revoking Acceptance of a Lot or Commercial Unit. Acceptance of a lot or a commercial unit can be revoked if the nonconformity *substantially* impairs the value of the lot or unit *and* if one of the following factors is present:

1. Acceptance was predicated on the reasonable assumption that the nonconformity would be cured, and it was not cured within a reasonable time [UCC 2–608(1)(a), 2A–517(1)(a)].
2. The buyer or lessee did not discover the nonconformity before acceptance, either because it was difficult to discover before acceptance or because assurances made by the seller or lessor that the goods were conforming kept the buyer or lessee from inspecting the goods [UCC 2–608(1)(b), 2A–517(1)(b)].

Case Example 17.18 Kimberly Accettura purchased a recreational vehicle (RV) from Vacationland, Inc. When Accettura later returned the RV to Vacationland to get a leak fixed, the company notified her that the RV would have to be sent back to the manufacturer for repairs. Before the vehicle could be sent to the manufacturer, Accettura called Vacationland and verbally revoked her purchase. After the RV was repaired, she confirmed her earlier revocation and sued the seller for a return of the purchase price.

Vacationland countered that it had not been given a reasonable opportunity to cure the RV's defect before Accettura revoked. The Illinois Supreme Court rejected this argument, making a clear distinction between a contract in which the buyer knows about a commercial unit's nonconformity [UCC 2-608(1)] and a contract in which the buyer is unaware of the nonconformity [UCC 2-608(2)]. According to the court, the seller's ability to cure is part of the language of the first provision, but not the second. Therefore, because Accettura did not know about the leak when she purchased the RV, she had properly revoked acceptance despite not giving Vacationland time to fix the problem.[8]

welcomia/Shutterstock.com

Under the UCC, what circumstances allow a buyer to revoke the purchase of an RV that has a preexisting defect without giving the seller a chance to fix the defect?

8. *Accettura v. Vacationland, Inc.*, 2019 IL 124285, __ N.E.3d __ (2019).

Notice of Revocation. Revocation of acceptance is not effective until notice is given to the seller or lessor. Notice must occur within a reasonable time after the buyer or lessee either discovers or *should have discovered* the grounds for revocation. Additionally, revocation must occur before the goods have undergone any substantial change (such as spoilage) not caused by their own defects [UCC 2–608(2), 2A–517(4)]. Once acceptance is revoked, the buyer or lessee can pursue remedies just as if the goods had been rejected.

Note that to effectively revoke acceptance, a buyer must "relinquish dominion over the goods." This requires a buyer to return the goods or at least to stop using them, unless the use is necessary to avoid substantial hardship. **Case Example 17.19** Genesis Health Clubs, Inc., contracted with LED Solar & Light Company to furnish replacement lighting for its building. When Genesis experienced problems with the lights, LED Solar offered to fix or replace them or to refund the price. Genesis responded that it wanted a refund and would return all of the lights "in stages so the club would not go dark."

Genesis returned one shipment of the lights but then disputed the way that LED Solar credited its account for the lights. After that, Genesis made no additional returns. In a lawsuit between the parties, a federal district court concluded that Genesis could not recover the purchase price for the lights. A federal appellate court affirmed. Genesis had not effectively revoked acceptance because it did not return the lights (beyond the first shipment) to LED Solar and because it continued to use them.[9]

The Right to Recover Damages for Accepted Goods A buyer or lessee who has accepted nonconforming goods may also keep the goods and recover damages caused by the breach. To do so, the buyer or lessee must notify the seller or lessor of the breach within a reasonable time after the defect was or should have been discovered. Failure to give notice of the defect (breach) to the seller or lessor bars the buyer or lessee from pursuing any remedy [UCC 2–607(3), 2A–516(3)]. In addition, the parties to a sales or lease contract can insert a provision requiring the buyer or lessee to give notice of any defects in the goods within a set period.

When the goods delivered are not as promised, the measure of damages equals the difference between the value of the goods as accepted and their value if they had been delivered as warranted [UCC 2–714(2), 2A–519(4)]. The buyer or lessee is also entitled to incidental and consequential damages when appropriate [UCC 2–714(3), 2A–519(3)]. The UCC also permits the buyer or lessee, with proper notice to the seller or lessor, to deduct all or any part of the damages from the price or lease payments still due under the contract [UCC 2–717, 2A–516(1)].

Is two years after a sale of goods a reasonable time period in which to discover a defect in the goods and notify the seller of a breach? That was the question in the following *Spotlight Case*.

9. *Genesis Health Clubs, Inc. v. LED Solar & Light Co.*, 639 Fed.Appx. 550 (10th Cir. 2016).

Spotlight on Baseball Cards: Case 17.2

Fitl v. Strek

Supreme Court of Nebraska, 269 Neb.51, 690 N.W.2d 605 (2005).

Facts In 1995, James Fitl attended a sports-card show in San Francisco, California, where he met Mark Strek, doing business as Star Cards of San Francisco, an exhibitor at the show. Later, on Strek's representation that a certain 1952 Mickey Mantle Topps baseball card was in near-mint condition, Fitl bought the card from Strek for $17,750. Strek delivered the card to Fitl in Omaha, Nebraska, and Fitl placed it in a safe-deposit box.

In May 1997, Fitl sent the card to Professional Sports Authenticators (PSA), a sports-card grading service. PSA told Fitl that the card was ungradable because it had been discolored and doctored. Fitl complained to Strek, who replied that Fitl should have returned the card within seven days to one month of its receipt— "a typical grace period for the unconditional return of a card." In August,

Continued

Fitl sent the card to ASA Accugrade, Inc. (ASA), another grading service, for a second opinion of the value. ASA also concluded that the card had been refinished and trimmed. Fitl filed a suit in a Nebraska state court against Strek, seeking damages. The court awarded Fitl $17,750, plus his court costs. Strek appealed to the Nebraska Supreme Court.

What is a reasonable time period to discover that a purchased baseball card is not authentic?

Issue Was two years after the sale of the baseball card a reasonable time to discover a defect and notify the seller of a breach?

Decision Yes. The state supreme court affirmed the decision of the lower court.

Reason Section 2–607(3)(a) of the UCC states, "Where a tender has been accepted . . . the buyer must within a reasonable time after he discovers or should have discovered any breach notify the seller of breach or be barred from any remedy." Furthermore, "What is a reasonable time for taking any action depends on the nature, purpose and circumstances of such action." The state supreme court concluded that the buyer (Fitl) had reasonably relied on the seller's (Strek's) representation that the goods were "authentic," which they were not. Fitl had given timely notice when he discovered the defects.

The court reasoned that "the policies behind the notice requirement, to allow the seller to correct a defect, to prepare for negotiation and litigation, and to protect against stale claims at a time beyond which an investigation can be completed, were not unfairly prejudiced by the lack of an earlier notice to Strek. Any problem Strek may have had with the party from whom he obtained the baseball card was a separate matter from his transaction with Fitl, and an investigation into the source of the altered card would not have minimized Fitl's damages."

Critical Thinking

- **What If the Facts Were Different?** *Suppose that Fitl and Strek had included in their deal a written clause requiring Fitl to give notice of any defect in the card within seven days to one month of its receipt. Would the result have been different? Why or why not?*

17–4c Provisions That Affect or Limit Remedies

The parties to a sales or lease contract can vary their respective rights and obligations by contractual agreement. For instance, a seller and buyer can expressly provide for remedies in addition to those provided in the UCC. The parties can also specify remedies in lieu of those provided in the UCC, or they can change the measure of damages. Any agreed-on remedy is in addition to those provided in the UCC unless the parties expressly agree that the remedy is exclusive of all others [UCC 2–719(1), 2A–503(1), (2)].

If this pipe-cutting machine has defective parts, can the buyer insist on replacement of the entire machine?

Exclusive Remedies If the parties state that a remedy is exclusive, then it is the sole remedy. **Example 17.20** Standard Tool Company agrees to sell a pipe-cutting machine to United Pipe & Tubing Corporation. The contract limits United's remedy exclusively to repair or replacement of any defective parts. Thus, repair or replacement of defective parts is the buyer's exclusive remedy under this contract. ■

When circumstances cause an exclusive remedy to fail in its essential purpose, however, it is no longer exclusive, and the buyer or lessee may pursue other remedies available under the UCC [UCC 2–719(2), 2A–503(2)]. In *Example 17.20*, suppose that Standard Tool Company is unable to repair a defective part, and no replacement parts are available. In this situation, because the exclusive remedy failed in its essential purpose, the buyer normally will be entitled to seek other remedies provided by the UCC.

Limitations on Consequential Damages As discussed previously, *consequential damages* are special damages that compensate for indirect losses (such as lost profits) resulting from a breach of contract that were reasonably foreseeable. Under the UCC, parties to a contract can limit or exclude consequential damages, provided the limitation is not unconscionable.

When the buyer or lessee is a consumer, any limitation of consequential damages for personal injuries resulting from consumer goods is *prima facie* (presumptively, or on its face) unconscionable. The limitation of consequential damages is not necessarily unconscionable when the loss is commercial in nature—such as lost profits and property damage [UCC 2–719(3), 2A–503(3)].

Statute of Limitations An action for breach of contract under the UCC must be commenced *within four years after the cause of action accrues*—that is, a buyer or lessee must file the lawsuit within four years after the breach occurs [UCC 2–725(1)]. In addition, a buyer or lessee who has accepted nonconforming goods usually must notify the breaching party of the breach within a reasonable time, or the aggrieved party is barred from pursuing any remedy [UCC 2–607(3)(a), 2A–516(3)].

The parties can agree in their contract to reduce this period to not less than one year, but cannot extend it beyond four years [UCC 2–725(1), 2A–506(1)]. A cause of action accrues for breach of warranty (discussed next) when the seller or lessor tenders delivery. This is the rule even if the aggrieved party is unaware that the cause of action has accrued [UCC 2–725(2), 2A–506(2)].

17–5 Warranties

The UCC has numerous rules governing product warranties as they occur in sales and lease contracts. Article 2 and Article 2A designate several types of warranties that can arise in a sales or lease contract, including warranties of title, express warranties, and implied warranties. If the seller or lessor breaches a warranty, the buyer or lessee can sue to recover damages.

17–5a Warranties of Title

Under the UCC, three types of title warranties—*good title, no liens,* and *no infringements*—can automatically arise in sales and lease contracts.

Good Title In most sales, sellers warrant that they have good and valid title to the goods sold and that transfer of the title is rightful [UCC 2–312(1)(a)]. If the buyer subsequently learns that the seller did not have good title to goods that were purchased, the buyer can sue the seller for breach of this warranty.

Example 17.21 Alexis steals two iPads from Camden and sells them to Emma, who does not know that they are stolen. If Camden discovers that Emma has the iPads, then he has the right to reclaim them from her. When Alexis sold Emma the iPads, Alexis automatically warranted to Emma that the title conveyed was valid and that its transfer was rightful. Because a thief has no title to stolen goods, Alexis breached the warranty of title imposed by the UCC and became liable to Emma for appropriate damages. ■

There is no warranty of good title in lease contracts because title to the goods does not pass to the lessee.

No Liens A **lien** is an encumbrance on (a claim against) property to satisfy a debt or protect a claim for payment of a debt. A second warranty of title shields buyers and lessees who are unaware of any lien against goods at the time the contract is made [UCC 2–312(1)(b), 2A–211(1)]. This warranty protects buyers who unknowingly purchase goods that are subject to a creditor's *security interest* (an interest in the goods that secures payment or performance). If a buyer knows (or has reason to know from the language in the contract) that the goods are subject to a prior claim, then the buyer cannot sue the seller for breach of warranty.[10]

Lien An encumbrance on a property to satisfy a debt or protect a claim for payment of a debt.

10. Note that a *buyer in the ordinary course of business* from a merchant seller generally takes the goods free of the security interest even if the buyer knows of it. For instance, when a merchant has a loan that is secured by all the inventory of the business, this does not prevent a buyer in the ordinary course from obtaining clear title to the goods.

xbrchx/Shutterstock.com

If a person buys a used boat that has a lien on it, but the buyer knows nothing about the lien, what section of the UCC provides a remedy for the buyer if the boat is taken away to satisfy the prior claim?

Example 17.22 Henderson buys a used boat from Loring for cash. A month later, Barish proves that she has a valid security interest in the boat and that Loring, who has missed five payments, is in default. Barish then repossesses the boat from Henderson. Henderson demands his cash back from Loring. Under Section 2–312(1)(b), Henderson has legal grounds to recover from Loring. As a seller of goods, Loring warrants that the goods are delivered free from any security interest or other lien of which the buyer has no knowledge. ■

No Infringements A third type of title warranty is a warranty against infringement of any patent, trademark, or copyright. When the seller or lessor is a merchant, the seller or lessor automatically warrants that the buyer or lessee takes the goods *free of infringements.* In other words, a merchant promises that the goods delivered are free from any copyright, trademark, or patent claims of a third person [UCC 2–312(3), 2A–211(2)]. If a buyer or lessee is subsequently sued by a third party holding copyright, trademark, or patent rights in the goods, then this warranty has been breached.

17–5b Express Warranties

Express Warranty A seller's or lessor's promise as to the quality, condition, description, or performance of the goods being sold or leased.

A seller or lessor can create an **express warranty** by making representations concerning the quality, condition, description, or performance potential of the goods. Under UCC 2–313 and 2A–210, express warranties arise when a seller or lessor indicates any of the following:

1. That the goods conform to any *affirmation* (declaration that something is true) or *promise* of fact that the seller or lessor makes to the buyer or lessee about the goods. Such affirmations or promises are usually made during the bargaining process. **Example 17.23** Vladick, a salesperson at Home Depot, tells a customer, "These drill bits will easily penetrate stainless steel—and without dulling." Vladick's statement is an express warranty. ■
2. That the goods conform to any *description* of them. **Example 17.24** A label reads, "Crate contains one Kawasaki Brute Force 750 4×4i EPS ATV." A contract calls for the delivery of a "wool coat." Both statements create express warranties that the goods sold conform to the descriptions. ■
3. That the goods conform to any *sample* or *model* of the goods shown to the buyer or lessee. **Example 17.25** Melissa orders a stainless steel 6300 Interflow juicer for $1,100 after seeing a dealer demonstrate its use at a health fair. The Interflow is shipped to her. When the juicer arrives, it is an older model, not the 6300 model. This is a breach of an express warranty because the dealer warranted that the juicer would be the same model used in the demonstration. ■

Express warranties can be found in a seller's or lessor's advertisement, e-mail, brochure, or other promotional materials, in addition to being made orally or set forth in a provision of a contract.

Basis of the Bargain To create an express warranty, a seller or lessor does not have to use words such as *warrant* or *guarantee* [UCC 2–313(2), 2A–210(2)]. It is only necessary that a reasonable buyer or lessee would regard the representation of fact as part of the basis of the bargain [UCC 2–313(1), 2A–210(1)]. The UCC does not define *basis of the bargain,* however, and it is a question of fact in each case whether a representation was made at such a time and in such a way that it induced the buyer or lessee to enter into the contract.

Statements of Opinion and Value Only statements of fact create express warranties. If the seller or lessor makes a statement about the supposed value or worth of the goods, or offers an opinion or recommendation about the goods, the seller or lessor is not creating an express warranty [UCC 2–313(2), 2A–210(2)].

Case Example 17.26 Harry's Dairy entered a contract to purchase 3,000 tons of hay from Jeff Good. Harry's Dairy stopped accepting Good's hay because of mold. After Good sued Harry's Dairy for breach of contract, Harry's Dairy countersued, professing that Good had violated an express warranty. This claim was based on a statement that Good made to one of the dairy's representatives when asked about the impact of recent weather on the product. Good said that "the hay had not been exposed to weather that would result in damage or mold to the hay." The Idaho Supreme Court dismissed Harry's Dairy's claim, holding that no express warranty existed because Good's statement was neither an "affirmation of fact" about the possibility of mold nor a "promise" that the hay would not be moldy.[11]

Opinions by Experts. Ordinarily, statements of opinion do not create warranties. If the seller or lessor is an expert, however, and gives an opinion as an expert to a layperson, then a warranty may be created. **Example 17.27** Stephen is an art dealer and an expert in seventeenth-century paintings. If Stephen tells Lauren, a purchaser, that in his opinion a particular painting is by Rembrandt, Stephen has warranted the accuracy of his opinion.

Reasonable Reliance. It is not always easy to determine whether a statement constitutes an express warranty or puffery (seller's talk). The reasonableness of the buyer's or lessee's reliance appears to be the controlling criterion in many cases. For instance, a salesperson's statements that a ladder "will never break" and will "last a lifetime" are so clearly improbable that no reasonable buyer should rely on them.

John Lund/Marc Romanelli/Blend Images/Getty Images

An expert art dealer claims a painting is by Rembrandt. Does his statement create an express warranty? Why or why not?

A reasonable person is more likely to rely on specific statements made in an advertisement than on a statement made orally by a salesperson. **Case Example 17.28** Lennox International, Inc., makes heating, ventilating, and air conditioning (HVAC) systems. T & M Solar and Air Conditioning, Inc., installs HVAC systems in California. T & M became interested in Lennox solar panel systems because Lennox advertised that the systems could run through an existing HVAC system, rather than through an electrical panel. This meant that the systems, unlike traditional solar panel systems, could be installed without modifying the electrical panels in a residence.

Lennox representatives repeatedly assured T & M that their systems would operate as advertised. T & M ordered and paid for six Lennox systems for customers. The systems could not be operated or installed as promised, however, and T & M ultimately had to remove them from customers' homes at its own expense. T & M sued for breach of an express warranty. A federal court found that T & M had ordered the Lennox systems precisely because they could operate through an HVAC system without modification of existing electrical panels. That was sufficient evidence of reasonable reliance to justify a trial.[12]

17–5c Implied Warranties

An express warranty is based on the seller's express promise. In contrast, an **implied warranty** is one that *the law derives* by implication or inference because of the circumstances of a sale. In an action based on breach of implied warranty, it is necessary to show that an implied warranty existed and that the breach of the warranty proximately caused[13] the damage sustained. We look here at some of the implied warranties that arise under the UCC.

Implied Warranty A warranty that arises by law because of the circumstances of a sale and not from the seller's express promise.

11. *Good v. Harry's Dairy, LLC*, __ P.3d. __, 2020 WL 1126649 (Idaho, 2019).
12. *T & M Solar and Air Conditioning, Inc. v. Lennox International, Inc.*, 83 F.Supp.3d 855 (N.D.Cal. 2015).
13. Proximate, or legal, cause exists when the connection between an act and an injury is strong enough to justify imposing liability.

Implied Warranty of Merchantability A warranty that goods being sold or leased are reasonably fit for the general purpose for which they are sold or leased, are properly packaged and labeled, and are of proper quality.

Implied Warranty of Merchantability Every sale or lease of goods made *by a merchant who deals in goods of the kind sold or leased* automatically gives rise to an **implied warranty of merchantability** [UCC 2–314, 2A–212]. Thus, a merchant who is in the business of selling ski equipment makes an implied warranty of merchantability every time she sells a pair of skis. A neighbor selling his skis at a garage sale does not (because he is not in the business of selling goods of this type).

Focus Question 5

What implied warranties arise under the UCC?

Merchantable Goods. Goods that are merchantable are "reasonably fit for the ordinary purposes for which such goods are used." They must be of at least average, fair, or medium-grade quality—quality adequate to pass without objection in the trade or market for goods of the same description. The goods must also be adequately packaged and labeled, and they must conform to the promises or affirmations of fact made on the container or label, if any. The warranty of merchantability may be breached even though the merchant did not know or could not have discovered that a product was defective (not merchantable).

Case Example 17.29 Joy Pipe, USA, L.P., is in the business of selling quality steel couplings for use in oil field drilling operations. Joy Pipe entered into a contract with Fremak Industries (a broker) to purchase grade P-110 steel made in India by ISMT Limited. When the steel arrived, Joy Pipe machined it into couplings, which it then sold to its customers.

Two companies that used these couplings in oil wells had well failures and notified Joy Pipe. Joy Pipe then discovered that the ISMT steel it had purchased was of a much lower grade than P-110, which is what caused the couplings to fail. After Joy Pipe paid another company to locate and replace the nonconforming steel, it sued ISMT for breach of the implied warranty of merchantability. A jury awarded Joy Pipe nearly $3 million in damages. An appellate court affirmed, and also awarded court costs and interest. The court remanded the case back to the trial court to calculate the amount of interest.[14]

Of course, merchants are not absolute insurers against all accidents occurring in connection with their goods. For instance, a bar of soap is not unmerchantable merely because stepping on it could cause a user to slip and fall.

Merchantable Food. The UCC recognizes the serving of food or drink to be consumed on or off the premises as a sale of goods subject to the implied warranty of merchantability [UCC 2–314(1)]. "Merchantable" food means food that is fit to eat.

Courts generally determine whether food is fit to eat on the basis of consumer expectations. The courts assume that consumers should reasonably expect on occasion to find bones in fish fillets, cherry pits in cherry pie, or a nutshell in a package of shelled nuts, for example—because such substances are natural parts of the food. In contrast, consumers would not reasonably expect to find an inchworm in a can of peas or a piece of glass in a soft drink.

In the following *Classic Case*, the court had to determine whether a diner should reasonably expect to find a fish bone in fish chowder.

14. *Joy Pipe, USA, L.P. v. ISMT Limited*, 703 Fed.Appx. 253 (5th Cir. 2017).

Classic Case 17.3

Webster v. Blue Ship Tea Room, Inc.

Supreme Judicial Court of Massachusetts, 347 Mass. 421, 198 N.E.2d 309 (1964).

Facts Blue Ship Tea Room, Inc., was located in Boston in an old building overlooking the ocean. Priscilla Webster, who had been born and raised in New England, went to the restaurant and ordered fish chowder. The chowder was milky in color. After three or four spoonfuls, she felt something lodged in her throat. As a result, she underwent two esophagoscopies (a procedure in which a telescope-like instrument is used to look into the throat). In the second esophagoscopy, a fish bone was found and

Continued

removed. Webster filed a lawsuit against the restaurant in a Massachusetts state court for breach of the implied warranty of merchantability. The jury rendered a verdict for Webster, and the restaurant appealed to the state's highest court.

Issue Does serving fish chowder that contains a bone constitute a breach of an implied warranty of merchantability by the restaurant?

hipokrat/Getty Images

Who is liable for fish bones in seafood chowder?

Decision No. The Supreme Judicial Court of Massachusetts held that Webster could not recover against Blue Ship Tea Room, because no breach of warranty had occurred.

Reason The court, citing UCC Section 2–314, stated that "a warranty that goods shall be merchantable is implied in a contract for their sale if the seller is a merchant with respect to goods of that kind. Under this section the serving for value of food or drink to be consumed either on the premises or elsewhere is a sale. . . . Goods to be merchantable must at least be . . . fit for the ordinary purposes for which such goods are used." The question here was whether a fish bone made the chowder unfit for eating. In the judge's opinion, "the joys of life in New England include the ready availability of fresh fish chowder. We should be prepared to cope with the hazards of fish bones, the occasional presence of which in chowders is, it seems to us, to be anticipated, and which, in the light of a hallowed tradition, do not impair their fitness or merchantability."

Critical Thinking

- **What If the Facts Were Different?** *If Webster had made the chowder herself from a recipe that she had found on the Internet, could she have successfully brought an action against its author for a breach of the implied warranty of merchantability? Explain.*
- **Impact of This Case on Today's Law** *This classic case, phrased in memorable language, was an early application of the UCC's implied warranty of merchantability to food products. The case established the rule that consumers should expect to occasionally find elements of food products that are natural to the product (such as fish bones in fish chowder). Courts today still apply this rule.*

Implied Warranty of Fitness for a Particular Purpose The **implied warranty of fitness for a particular purpose** arises in the sale or lease of goods when a seller or lessor (merchant or nonmerchant) knows *both* of the following:

Implied Warranty of Fitness for a Particular Purpose A warranty that goods sold or leased are fit for the particular purpose for which the buyer or lessee will use the goods.

1. The particular purpose for which a buyer or lessee will use the goods.
2. That the buyer or lessee is relying on the skill and judgment of the seller or lessor to select suitable goods [UCC 2–315, 2A–213].

A "particular purpose" of the buyer or lessee differs from the "ordinary purpose for which goods are used" (merchantability). Goods can be merchantable but unfit for a particular purpose. **Example 17.30** Cheryl needs a gallon of paint to match the color of her living room walls—a light shade of green. She takes a sample to the local hardware store and requests a gallon of paint of that color. Instead, she is given a gallon of bright blue paint. Here, the salesperson has not breached any warranty of implied merchantability—the bright blue paint is of high quality and suitable for interior walls. The salesperson has breached an implied warranty of fitness for a particular purpose, though, because the paint is not the right color for Cheryl's purpose (to match her living room walls).

A seller or lessor need not have actual knowledge of the buyer's or lessee's particular purpose. It is sufficient if the seller or lessor "has reason to know" the purpose. For an implied warranty to be created, however, the buyer or lessee must have relied on the skill or judgment of the seller or lessor in selecting or furnishing suitable goods. For further illustration of how courts analyze implied warranties, see this chapter's *Business Law Analysis* feature.

Implied Warranties

Business Law Analysis

Bariven, S.A. (S.A. stands for Société Anonyme, a French business form), agreed to buy 26,000 metric tons of powdered milk for $123.5 million from Absolute Trading Corp. The powdered milk was to be delivered in shipments from China to Venezuela.

After the first three shipments, China halted dairy exports due to the presence of melamine (a chemical used in plastics and adhesives) in some products. Absolute assured Bariven that its milk was safe, and when China resumed dairy exports, Absolute delivered sixteen more shipments. Tests of samples of the milk revealed that it contained dangerous levels of melamine. Did Absolute breach any implied warranties?

Analysis: Under the UCC, merchants impliedly warrant that the goods they sell or lease are merchantable and, in certain circumstances, fit for a particular purpose. To be merchantable, goods must be "reasonably fit for the ordinary purposes for which such goods are used." They must be at least average, fair, or medium-grade quality—quality that will pass without objection in the trade or market for the goods. For the implied warranty of fitness for a particular purpose to arise, the seller must know (or have reason to know) the purpose for which the buyer will use the goods and that the buyer is relying on the judgment of the seller to select suitable goods.

Result and Reasoning: Absolute Trading breached the implied warranties of merchantability and fitness for a particular purpose. Bariven agreed to buy a substantial quantity of powdered milk from Absolute that was to be delivered in shipments. Absolute assured Bariven that its milk was safe, but tests of samples from the shipments Bariven received revealed that it was contaminated. Therefore, the milk was not of a quality that would pass without objection in the market for the goods. Nor is milk contaminated with melamine "reasonably fit for the ordinary purposes for which such goods are used." The value of the milk as food was impaired because it was potentially lethal and thus not fit to be consumed.

Absolute had reason to know the purpose for which Bariven bought the milk (for human consumption). Absolute also knew that the buyer was relying on it to provide safe milk. In view of the potential hazards and liabilities of consuming the contaminated milk, Absolute was in breach of both of these implied warranties.

Warranties Implied from Prior Dealings or Trade Custom Implied warranties can also arise (or be excluded or modified) as a result of course of dealing or usage of trade [UCC 2–314(3), 2A–212(3)]. In the absence of evidence to the contrary, when both parties to a sales or lease contract have knowledge of a well-recognized trade custom, the courts will infer that both parties intended for that trade custom to apply to their contract.

Example 17.31 Industry-wide custom is to lubricate new cars before they are delivered to buyers. If a dealer fails to lubricate a car, the dealer can be held liable to a buyer for damages resulting from the breach of an implied warranty. (This, of course, would also be negligence on the part of the dealer.)

17–5d Overlapping Warranties

Know This

Express and implied warranties do not necessarily displace each other. More than one warranty can cover the same goods in the same transaction.

Sometimes, two or more warranties are made in a single transaction. Thus, an implied warranty of merchantability, an implied warranty of fitness for a particular purpose, or both can exist in addition to an express warranty. **Example 17.32** A sales contract for a new car states that "this car engine is warranted to be free from defects for 48,000 miles or forty-eight months, whichever occurs first." This statement creates an express warranty against all defects, as well as an implied warranty that the car will be fit for normal use.

The rule under the UCC is that express and implied warranties are construed as *cumulative* if they are consistent with one another [UCC 2–317, 2A–215]. If the warranties are inconsistent, courts apply the following rules to establish which warranty has priority:

1. *Express* warranties displace inconsistent *implied* warranties, except for implied warranties of fitness for a particular purpose.
2. Samples take precedence over inconsistent general descriptions.
3. Exact or technical specifications displace inconsistent samples or general descriptions.

17–5e Warranty Disclaimers

The UCC generally permits warranties to be disclaimed or limited by specific and unambiguous language, provided that the buyer or lessee is protected from surprise. Because each type of warranty is created in a different way, the manner in which a seller or lessor can disclaim warranties varies with the type of warranty.

Express Warranties A seller or lessor can disclaim all oral express warranties by including a statement in the written contract. The disclaimer must be in language that is clear and conspicuous, and is called to the buyer's or lessee's attention [UCC 2–316(1), 2A–214(1)]. This allows the seller or lessor to avoid false allegations that oral warranties were made, and it ensures that only representations made by properly authorized individuals are included in the bargain.

Note, however, that a buyer or lessee must be made aware of any warranty disclaimers or modifications *at the time the contract is formed.* In other words, the seller or lessor cannot modify any warranties or disclaimers made during the bargaining process without the consent of the buyer or lessee.

Implied Warranties Generally, unless circumstances indicate otherwise, the implied warranties of merchantability and fitness are disclaimed by the expressions "as is," "with all faults," or other similar phrases. Both parties must be able to clearly understand from the language used that there are no implied warranties [UCC 2–316(3)(a), 2A–214(3)(a)].

Case Example 17.33 My Custom Shop, Inc. (MCS) bought an eighteen-year-old Ford Ranger truck with 178,000 miles at auction for about $1,300. MCS made several improvements to the vehicle and sold it to Seth Kiewiz for $3,800, verbally promising to replace any malfunctioning parts that it had installed. Both the purchase contract and the "sticker" attached to the truck's window stated that the vehicle was being sold "AS IS," without any warranties. Kiewiz immediately noticed problems with the truck's engine and brakes. After MCS made several failed attempts to resolve these issues, Kiewiz demanded a full refund. MCS refused. Kiewiz sued, claiming breach of the implied warranty of merchantability. A Wisconsin appeals court held that the "AS IS" clauses were valid and, therefore, Kiewiz had no cause of action.[15]

Art Konovalov/Shutterstock.com

A consumer buys a used Ford Ranger truck but is dissatisfied with the vehicle's performance. How will an "AS IS" clause in the sales contract impact the buyer's ability to return the truck for a full refund?

Note that some states have laws that forbid "as is" sales. Other states do not allow disclaimers of warranties of merchantability for consumer goods.

Disclaimer of the Implied Warranty of Merchantability. To specifically disclaim an implied warranty of merchantability, a seller or lessor must mention the word *merchantability* [UCC 2–316(2), 2A–214(2)]. The disclaimer need not be written, but if it is, the writing must be conspicuous [UCC 2–316(2), 2A–214(4)].

15. *Kiewiz v. My Custom Shop, Inc.*, 939 N.W.2d 882, 2020 WL 355376, WI App. 10 (2020).

Know This
Courts generally view warranty disclaimers unfavorably, especially when consumers are involved.

Under the UCC, a term or clause is conspicuous when it is written or displayed in such a way that a reasonable person would notice it. Words are conspicuous when they are in capital letters or are in a larger font size or a different color than the surrounding text.

Disclaimer of the Implied Warranty of Fitness. To specifically disclaim an implied warranty of fitness for a particular purpose, the disclaimer must be in a writing and must be conspicuous. The word *fitness* does not have to be mentioned. It is sufficient if, for instance, the disclaimer states, "THERE ARE NO WARRANTIES THAT EXTEND BEYOND THE DESCRIPTION ON THE FACE HEREOF."

Buyer's or Lessee's Examination or Refusal to Inspect. If a buyer or lessee examines the goods (or a sample or model) as fully as desired, *there is no implied warranty with respect to defects that a reasonable examination would reveal or defects that are found on examination* [UCC 2–316(3)(b), 2A–214(2)(b)]. Therefore, no disclaimer of warranty would be necessary with respect to such defects. Also, if a buyer or lessee refuses to examine the goods at the request of the seller or lessor, there is no implied warranty with respect to reasonably evident defects.

Example 17.34 Janna buys a table at Gershwin's Home Store. No express warranties are made. Gershwin asks Janna to inspect the table before buying it, but she refuses. Had Janna inspected the table, she would have noticed that one of its legs was obviously cracked, which made it unstable. Janna takes the table home and sets a lamp on it. The table later collapses, and the lamp starts a fire that causes significant damage. Janna normally will not be able to hold Gershwin's liable for breach of the warranty of merchantability, because she refused to examine the table as Gershwin requested. Janna therefore assumed the risk that the table was defective. ■

17–5f Lemon Laws

Purchasers of defective automobiles—called "lemons"—may pursue remedies in addition to those provided by the UCC under state *lemon laws*. Basically, state lemon laws provide remedies to consumers who buy automobiles that repeatedly fail to meet standards of quality and performance because they are "lemons."

Although lemon laws vary by state, typically they apply to automobiles under warranty that are defective in a way that significantly affects their value or use. Lemon laws do not necessarily cover used-car purchases (unless the car is covered by a manufacturer's extended warranty) or vehicles that are leased.

Generally, the seller or manufacturer of the automobile is given a number of opportunities to remedy the defect (usually four). If the seller fails to cure the problem despite a reasonable number of attempts (as specified by state law), the buyer is entitled to a new car, replacement of defective parts, or return of all consideration paid.

Typically, buyers must submit their complaint to the arbitration program specified in the manufacturer's warranty before taking the case to court. Buyers who prevail in a lemon-law dispute may also be entitled to reimbursement of their attorneys' fees.

Practice and Review

GFI, Inc., a Hong Kong company, makes audio decoder chips, one of the essential components used in the manufacture of MP3 players. Egan Electronics contracts with GFI to buy 10,000 chips on an installment contract, with 2,500 chips to be shipped every three months, F.O.B. Hong Kong via Air Express. At the time for the first delivery, GFI delivers only 2,400 chips but explains to Egan that even though the shipment is 4 percent short, the chips are of a higher quality than those specified in the contract and are worth

5 percent more than the contract price. Egan accepts the shipment and pays GFI the contract price. At the time for the second shipment, GFI makes a shipment identical to the first. Egan again accepts and pays for the chips. At the time for the third shipment, GFI ships 2,400 of the same chips, but this time GFI sends them via Hong Kong Air instead of Air Express. While in transit, the chips are destroyed. When it is time for the fourth shipment, GFI again sends 2,400 chips, but this time Egan rejects the chips without explanation. Using the information presented in the chapter, answer the following questions.

1. Did GFI have a legitimate reason to expect that Egan would accept the fourth shipment? Why or why not?
2. Does the substitution of carriers for the third shipment constitute a breach of the contract by GFI? Explain.
3. Suppose that the silicon used for the chips becomes unavailable for a period of time and that GFI cannot manufacture enough chips to fulfill the contract but does ship as many as it can to Egan. Under what doctrine might a court release GFI from further performance of the contract?
4. Under the UCC, does Egan have a right to reject the fourth shipment? Why or why not?

Debate This

If a contract specifies a particular carrier, then the shipper must use that carrier or be in breach of the contract—no exceptions should ever be allowed.

Key Terms

conforming goods 409
cover 420
express warranty 426
implied warranty 427
implied warranty of fitness for a particular purpose 429
implied warranty of merchantability 428
installment contract 412
lien 425
perfect tender rule 410
replevin 421
tender of delivery 409

Chapter Summary: Performance and Breach of Sales and Lease Contracts

Obligations of the Seller or Lessor	1. **Tender of delivery**—The seller or lessor must tender *conforming* goods to the buyer or lessee. Tender must take place at a *reasonable hour* and in a *reasonable manner.* 2. **Place of delivery**—If the contract does not indicate where the goods are to be delivered, the place of delivery will be either the seller's place of business, the seller's residence, or the location of the goods. 3. **Delivery via carrier**—In carrier contracts, the seller fulfills the obligation to deliver the goods through either a shipment contract or a destination contract. 4. **The perfect tender rule**—If the goods or tender of delivery fail in any respect to conform to the contract, the buyer or lessee has the right to accept the goods, reject the entire shipment, or accept part and reject part [UCC 2-601, 2A-509]. 5. **Exceptions to the perfect tender rule**—Exceptions may be established by the following: a. Agreement of the parties. b. If the seller or lessor tenders nonconforming goods prior to the performance date and the buyer or lessee rejects them, the seller or lessor may *cure* (repair or replace the goods) within the contract time for performance [UCC 2–508(1), 2A–513(1)]. If the seller or lessor had reasonable grounds to believe that the buyer or lessee would accept the tendered goods, on the buyer's or lessee's rejection the seller or lessor has a reasonable time to substitute conforming goods without liability [UCC 2–508(2), 2A–513(2)].

	c. If the agreed-on means of delivery becomes impracticable or unavailable, the seller must substitute an alternative means (such as a different carrier), if one is available [UCC 2–614(1)]. **d.** If a seller or lessor tenders nonconforming goods in any one installment under an installment contract, the buyer or lessee may reject the installment only if its value is substantially impaired and the nonconformity cannot be cured. The entire installment contract is breached only when one or more nonconforming installments *substantially* impair the value of the *whole* contract [UCC 2–612, 2A–510]. **e.** When performance becomes commercially impracticable owing to circumstances that were not foreseeable when the contract was formed, the perfect tender rule no longer holds [UCC 2–615, 2A–405].
Obligations of the Buyer or Lessee	**1. Payment**—On tender of delivery by the seller or lessor, the buyer or lessee must pay for the goods at the time and place the goods are *received*, unless the sale is made on credit. Payment may be made by any method generally acceptable in the commercial world unless the seller demands cash [UCC 2–310, 2–511]. In lease contracts, the lessee must make lease payments in accordance with the contract [UCC 2A–516(1)]. **2. Right of inspection**—Unless otherwise agreed, the buyer or lessee has an absolute right to inspect the goods before acceptance [UCC 2–513(1), 2A–515(1)]. **3. Acceptance**—The buyer or lessee can manifest acceptance of delivered goods expressly in words or by conduct, or by failing to reject the goods after a reasonable period of time following inspection or after having had a reasonable opportunity to inspect them [UCC 2–606(1), 2A–515(1)]. A buyer will be deemed to have accepted goods on the performance of any act inconsistent with the seller's ownership [UCC 2–606(1)(c)]. **4. Partial acceptance**—The buyer or lessee can make a partial acceptance if some of the goods do not conform to the contract and the seller or lessor failed to cure [UCC 2–601(c), 2A–509(1)]. **5. Anticipatory repudiation**—If, before the time for performance, one party clearly indicates to the other an intention not to perform, under UCC 2–610 and 2A–402, the nonbreaching party may do the following: **a.** Treat the repudiation as a final breach by pursuing a remedy. **b.** Await performance by the repudiating party for a commercially reasonable time. **c.** In either situation, suspend performance. In addition, the breaching party may retract the repudiation by any method that clearly indicates the party's intent to perform.
Remedies of the Seller or Lessor	**1. When the goods are in the possession of the seller or lessor**—The seller or lessor may do the following: **a.** Cancel the contract [UCC 2–703(f), 2A–523(1)(a)]. **b.** Withhold delivery [UCC 2–703(a), 2A–523(1)(c)]. **c.** Resell or dispose of the goods [UCC 2–703(d), 2–706(1), 2A–523(1)(e), 2A–527(1)]. **d.** Sue to recover the purchase price or lease payments due [UCC 2–709(1), 2A–529(1)]. **e.** Sue to recover damages [UCC 2–708, 2A–528]. **2. When the goods are in transit**—The seller or lessor may stop the carrier or bailee from delivering the goods under certain conditions [UCC 2–705, 2A–526]. **3. When the goods are in the possession of the buyer or lessee**—The seller or lessor may do the following: **a.** Sue to recover the purchase price or lease payments due [UCC 2–709(1), 2A–529(1)]. **b.** Reclaim the goods. A seller may reclaim goods received by an insolvent buyer if the demand is made within ten days of the buyer's receipt (reclaiming goods excludes all other remedies) [UCC 2–702(2)]. A lessor may repossess goods if the lessee is in default [UCC 2A–525(2)].
Remedies of the Buyer or Lessee	**1. When the seller or lessor refuses to deliver the goods**—The buyer or lessee may do the following: **a.** Cancel the contract [UCC 2–711(1), 2A–508(1)(a)]. **b.** Recover the goods if the seller or lessor becomes insolvent and the goods are identified to the contract [UCC 2–502, 2A–522]. **c.** Sue to obtain specific performance (when the goods are unique and the remedy at law is inadequate) [UCC 2–716(1), 2A–521(1)]. **d.** Obtain cover [UCC 2–712, 2A–518]. **e.** Replevy the goods (if cover is unavailable) [UCC 2–716(3), 2A–521(3)]. **f.** Sue to recover damages [UCC 2–713, 2A–519]. **2. When the seller or lessor delivers or tenders delivery of nonconforming goods**—The buyer or lessee may do the following: **a.** Reject the goods [UCC 2–601, 2A–509].

b. Revoke acceptance if the nonconformity *substantially* impairs the value of the unit or lot and if one of the following factors is present:

(1) Acceptance was predicated on the reasonable assumption that the nonconformity would be cured, and it was not cured within a reasonable time [UCC 2–608(1)(a), 2A–517(1)(a)].

(2) The buyer or lessee did not discover the nonconformity before acceptance, either because it was difficult to discover before acceptance or because the seller's or lessor's assurance that the goods were conforming kept the buyer or lessee from inspecting the goods [UCC 2–608(1)(b), 2A–517(1)(b)].

c. Accept the goods and recover damages [UCC 2–607, 2–714, 2–717, 2A–519].

3. Provisions that affect or limit remedies—

a. Remedies may be limited in sales or lease contracts by agreement of the parties. If the contract states that a remedy is exclusive, then that is the sole remedy unless the remedy fails in its essential purpose. Sellers and lessors can also limit the rights of buyers and lessees to consequential damages unless the limitation is unconscionable [UCC 2–719, 2A–503].

b. The UCC has a four-year statute of limitations for actions involving breach of contract. By agreement, the parties to a sales or lease contract can reduce this period to not less than one year, but they cannot extend it beyond four years [UCC 2–725(1), 2A–506(1)].

Warranties

1. Warranties of title—Under the UCC, three types of title warranties can automatically arise in sales and lease contracts.

a. In most sales, sellers warrant that they have good and valid title to the goods sold and that transfer of the title is rightful [UCC 2–312(1)(a)].

b. The seller or lessor warrants that the goods are free of any encumbrances, or liens, of which the buyer or lessee is unaware [UCC 2–312(1)(b), 2A–211(1)].

c. Sellers or lessors who are merchants warrant that buyers or lessees take the goods free of infringements [UCC 2–312(3), 2A–211(2)].

2. Express warranties—Under the UCC, an express warranty arises under the UCC when a seller or lessor provides, as part of the basis of the bargain, any of the following [UCC 2–313, 2A–210]:

a. An affirmation or promise of fact.

b. A description of the goods.

c. A sample shown as conforming to the contract goods.

3. Implied warranties—Under the UCC, an implied warranty arises by law because of the circumstances of a sale.

a. An implied warranty of merchantability occurs when a seller or lessor who deals in goods of the kind sold or leased (a merchant) warrants that the goods sold or leased are properly packaged and labeled, are of proper quality, and are reasonably fit for the ordinary purposes for which such goods are used [UCC 2–314, 2A–212].

b. An implied warranty of fitness for a particular purpose arises when the buyer's or lessee's purpose or use is expressly or impliedly known by the seller or lessor, and the buyer or lessee purchases or leases the goods in reliance on the seller's or lessor's skill and judgment [UCC 2–315, 2A–213].

c. Warranties implied from prior dealings or trade custom can arise as a result of course of dealing or usage of trade [UCC 2–314(3), 2A–212(3)].

4. Overlapping warranties—When warranties are consistent with each other, they are considered cumulative under the UCC [UCC 2–317, 2A–215]. If warranties are inconsistent, then express warranties take precedence over implied warranties, except for the implied warranty of fitness for a particular purpose. Also, samples take precedence over general descriptions, and exact or technical specifications displace inconsistent samples or general descriptions.

5. Warranty disclaimers—The effectiveness of disclaimers varies with the type of warranty.

a. Express warranties can be disclaimed if the disclaimer is written in clear language, is conspicuous, and is called to the buyer's or lessee's attention at the time the contract is formed.

b. A disclaimer of the implied warranty of merchantability must specifically mention the word *merchantability*. The disclaimer need not be in writing, but if it is written, it must be conspicuous.

c. A disclaimer of the implied warranty of fitness *must* be in writing and must be conspicuous, though it need not mention the word *fitness*.

d. There is no implied warranty with respect to defects that a reasonable examination would reveal or defects that are found on examination.

6. Lemon laws—State statutes may allow purchasers of defective automobiles to pursue remedies in addition to those provided by the UCC. The seller or manufacturer is given opportunities to remedy the defect. If the seller or manufacturer fails to cure the problem, the buyer is entitled to a new car, replacement of defective parts, or return of all consideration paid.

Issue Spotters

1. Country Fruit Stand orders eighty cases of peaches from Down Home Farms. Without stating a reason, Down Home untimely delivers thirty cases instead of eighty. Does Country have the right to reject the shipment? Explain. (See *Obligations of the Seller or Lessor.*)
2. Brite Images, Inc. (BI), agrees to sell Catalog Corporation (CC) five thousand posters of celebrities, to be delivered on May 1. On April 1, BI repudiates the contract. CC informs BI that it expects delivery. Can CC sue BI without waiting until May 1? Why or why not? (See *Obligations of the Buyer or Lessee.*)

—Check your answers to the *Issue Spotters* against the answers provided in Appendix D.

Business Scenarios and Case Problems

17–1. Remedies. Genix, Inc., has contracted to sell Larson five hundred washing machines of a certain model at list price. Genix is to ship the goods on or before December 1. Genix produces one thousand washing machines of this model but has not yet prepared Larson's shipment. On November 1, Larson repudiates the contract. Discuss the remedies available to Genix in this situation. (See *Remedies of the Seller or Lessor.*)

17–2. Anticipatory Repudiation. Moore contracted in writing to sell her 2010 Hyundai Santa Fe to Hammer for $16,500. Moore agreed to deliver the car on Wednesday, and Hammer promised to pay the $16,500 on the following Friday. On Tuesday, Hammer informed Moore that he would not be buying the car after all. By Friday, Hammer had changed his mind again and tendered $16,500 to Moore. Although Moore had not sold the car to another party, she refused the tender and refused to deliver. Hammer claimed that Moore had breached their contract. Moore contended that Hammer's repudiation had released her from her duty to perform under the contract. Who is correct, and why? (See *Obligations of the Buyer or Lessee.*)

17–3. Spotlight on Apple—Implied Warranties. Alan Vitt purchased an iBook G4 laptop computer from Apple, Inc. Shortly after the one-year warranty expired, the laptop stopped working due to a weakness in the product manufacture. Vitt sued Apple, arguing that the laptop should have lasted "at least a couple of years," which Vitt believed was a reasonable consumer expectation for a laptop. Vitt claimed that Apple's descriptions of the laptop as "durable," "rugged," "reliable," and "high performance" were affirmative statements concerning the quality and performance of the laptop, which Apple did not meet. How should the court rule? Why? [*Vitt v. Apple Computer, Inc.*, 469 Fed.Appx. 605 (9th Cir. 2011)] (See *Warranties.*)

17–4. The Right of Rejection. Erb Poultry, Inc., is a distributor of fresh poultry products in Lima, Ohio. CEME, LLC, does business as Bank Shots, a restaurant in Trotwood, Ohio. CEME ordered chicken wings and "dippers" from Erb, which were delivered and for which CEME issued a check in payment. A few days later, CEME stopped payment on the check. When contacted by Erb, CEME alleged that the products were beyond their freshness date, mangled, spoiled, and the wrong sizes. CEME did not provide any evidence to support the claims or arrange to return the products. Is CEME entitled to a full refund of the amount paid for the chicken? Explain. [*Erb Poultry, Inc. v. CEME, LLC*, 20 N.E.3d 1228 (Ohio App. 2 Dist. 2014)] (See *Remedies of the Buyer or Lessee.*)

17–5. Remedies for Breach. LO Ventures, LLC, doing business as Reefpoint Brewhouse in Racine, Wisconsin, contracted with Forman Awnings and Construction, LLC, for the fabrication and installation of an awning system over an outdoor seating area. After the system was complete, Reefpoint expressed concerns about the workmanship but did not give Forman a chance to make repairs. The brewhouse used the awning for two months and then had it removed so that siding on the building could be replaced. The parties disagreed about whether cracked and broken welds observed after the removal of the system were due to shoddy workmanship. Reefpoint paid only $400 on the contract price of $8,161. Can Reefpoint rescind the contract and obtain a return of its $400? Is Forman entitled to recover the difference between Reefpoint's payment and the contract price? Discuss. [*Forman Awnings and Construction, LLC v. LO Ventures, LLC*, 360 Wis.2d 492, 864 N.W.2d 121 (2015)] (See *Remedies of the Buyer or Lessee.*)

17–6. Business Case Problem with Sample Answer—Remedies of the Buyer or Lessee. M. C. and Linda Morris own a home in Gulfport, Mississippi, that was extensively damaged in Hurricane Katrina. The Morrises contracted with Inside Outside, Inc. (IO), to rebuild their kitchen. When the new kitchen cabinets were delivered, some defects were apparent, and as installation progressed, others were revealed. IO ordered replacement parts to cure the defects. Before the parts arrived, however, the parties' relationship deteriorated, and IO offered to remove the cabinets and refund the price. The Morrises also asked to be repaid for the installation fee. IO refused but emphasized that it was willing to fulfill its contractual obligations. At this point, are the Morrises entitled to revoke their acceptance of the cabinets? Why or why not? [*Morris v. Inside Outside, Inc.*, 185 So.3d 413 (Miss.App. 2016)] (See *Remedies of the Buyer or Lessee.*)

—For a sample answer to Problem 17–6, go to Appendix E.

17–7. Warranty Disclaimers. Charity Bell bought a used Toyota Avalon from Awny Gobran of Gobran Auto Sales, Inc. The odometer showed that the car had been driven 147,000 miles. Bell asked whether it had been in any accidents, and Gobran replied that it was in good condition. The parties signed a warranty disclaimer that the vehicle was sold "as is." Problems with the car arose the same day as the purchase. Gobran made a few ineffectual attempts to repair it before refusing to do more. Meanwhile, Bell obtained a vehicle history report from CARFAX, which showed that the Avalon had been damaged in an accident and that its last reported odometer reading was 237,271.

Was the "as is" disclaimer sufficient to put Bell on notice that the odometer reading could be false and that the car might have been in an accident? Can Gobran avoid any liability that might otherwise be imposed because Bell did not obtain the CARFAX report until after she bought the car? Discuss. [*Gobran Auto Sales, Inc. v. Bell*, 335 Ga.App. 873, 783 S.E.2d 389 (2016)] (See *Warranties.*)

17–8. Implied Warranties. Harold Moore bought a barrel-racing horse named Clear Boggy for $100,000 for his daughter from Betty Roper, who appraises barrel-racing horses. (Barrel racing is a rodeo event in which a horse and rider attempt to complete a cloverleaf pattern around preset barrels in the fastest time.) Clear Boggy was promoted for sale as a competitive barrel-racing horse. On inquiry, Roper represented that Clear Boggy did not have any performance issues or medical problems, and that the only medications the horse had been given were hock injections, a common treatment.

Shortly after the purchase, Clear Boggy began exhibiting significant performance problems, including nervousness, unwillingness to practice, and stalling on the first barrel during runs. Roper then disclosed that the horse had been given shoulder injections prior to the sale and had previously stalled in competition. Moore took the horse to a veterinarian and discovered that it suffered from arthritis, impinged vertebrae, front-left-foot problems, and a right-hind-leg fracture. The vet recommended, and Moore paid for, surgery to repair the hind leg fracture, but Clear Boggy remained unfit for competition. Moore also discovered that the horse had been scratched from competition prior to the sale because it was injured. Can Moore prevail in a lawsuit against Roper for breach of the implied warranty of fitness for a particular purpose? Why or why not? [*Moore v. Roper*, 2018 WL 1123868 (E.D.Okla. 2018)] (See *Warranties.*)

17–9. A Question of Ethics—The IDDR Approach and Buyer's Remedies. Samsung Telecommunications America, LLC, makes Galaxy phones. Daniel Norcia bought a Galaxy S4 in a Verizon store in San Francisco, California. A Verizon employee opened the box, unpacked the phone, and helped Norcia transfer his contacts to the new phone. Norcia took the phone, and its charger and headphones, and left the store. Less than a year later, he filed an action on behalf of himself and other Galaxy S4 buyers in a federal district court against Samsung, alleging that the manufacturer misrepresented the phone's storage capacity and rigged it to operate at a higher speed when it was being tested. [*Norcia v. Samsung Telecommunications America, LLC*, 845 F.3d 1279 (9th Cir. 2017)] (See *Remedies of the Buyer or Lessee.*)

1. Samsung included an arbitration provision in a brochure in the Galaxy S4 box. Would it be ethical of Samsung to assert the arbitration clause?
2. Why would corporate decision makers choose to misrepresent their product? Explain, using the *Discussion* and *Review* steps of the IDDR approach.

Critical Thinking and Writing Assignments

17–10. Business Law Writing. Suppose that you are a collector of antique cars and you need to purchase spare parts for a 1938 engine. These parts are not made anymore and are scarce. You discover that Beem has the spare parts that you need. You contract with Beem to buy the parts and agree to pay 50 percent of the purchase price in advance. You send the payment on May 1, and Beem receives it on May 2. On May 3, Beem, having found another buyer willing to pay substantially more for the parts, informs you that he will not deliver as contracted. That same day, you learn that Beem is insolvent. Write three paragraphs fully discussing any possible remedies that would enable you to take possession of the parts. (See *Remedies of the Buyer or Lessee.*)

17–11. Time-Limited Group Assignment—Warranties. Milan purchased saffron extract, marketed as "America's Hottest New Way to a Flat Belly," online from Dr. Chen. The website stated that recently published studies showed a significant weight loss (more than 25 percent) for people who used pure saffron extract as a supplement *without diet or exercise*. Dr. Chen said that the saffron suppresses appetite by increasing levels of serotonin, which reduces emotional eating. Milan took the extract as directed without any resulting weight loss. (See *Warranties.*)

1. The first group will determine whether Dr. Chen's website made any express warranty on the saffron extract or its effectiveness in causing weight loss.
2. The second group will discuss whether the implied warranty of merchantability applies to the purchase of weight-loss supplements.
3. The third group will decide if Dr. Chen's sale of saffron extract breached the implied warranty of fitness for a particular purpose.
4. The fourth group will determine if current common knowledge that weight loss can only occur if one burns more calories than one consumes makes it impossible to sue any company that offers weight-loss products that require no dieting and no exercise.

Andrey_Popov/Shutterstock.com

18 Negotiable Instruments

Focus Questions

The five *Focus Questions* below are designed to help improve your understanding. After reading this chapter, you should be able to answer the following questions:

1. What requirements must an instrument meet to be negotiable?
2. How does the negotiation of order instruments differ from the negotiation of bearer instruments?
3. What are three basic requirements for attaining the status of a holder in due course (HDC)?
4. What is the difference between signature liability and warranty liability?
5. What four defenses can be used against an ordinary holder that are not effective against an HDC?

"It took many generations for people to feel comfortable accepting paper in lieu of gold or silver."

Alan Greenspan
1926–present
(Chair of the Board of Governors of the Federal Reserve System, 1987–2006)

Most commercial transactions would be inconceivable without negotiable instruments. A **negotiable instrument** is a signed writing that contains an unconditional promise or order to pay an exact amount, either on demand or at a specified future time. The promise can be made to the order of a specific person or to a bearer. Because negotiable instruments originally were (and often still are) paper documents, they are sometimes referred to as *commercial paper*. As indicated in the chapter-opening quotation, it took many years for paper money to be fully accepted as a substitute for gold or silver in commerce.

A negotiable instrument can function as a substitute for cash or as an extension of credit. For a negotiable instrument to operate *practically* as either a substitute for cash or a credit device, or both, it is essential that the instrument be *easily transferable without danger of being uncollectible*. This is a fundamental function of negotiable instruments.

When her bank will not loan Kyra the capital she needs to start a company, her wealthy uncle, Martin, agrees to loan her the funds. Kyra signs a promissory note for $300,000 and promises to pay back the money, with 5 percent interest, exactly two years from today's date. Because the promissory note is a negotiable instrument, it can be sold to another. Therefore, if Martin needs access to the funds before the date set for payment, he can negotiate, or transfer, the promissory note to a third party in exchange for cash. When the note becomes due, Kyra will repay the then-current holder of the note.

18–1 Formation of Negotiable Instruments

The law governing negotiable instruments grew out of commercial necessity. In the medieval world, merchants developed their own set of rules, which eventually became known as the *Lex Mercatoria* (Law Merchant). The Law Merchant was later codified in England and is the forerunner of Article 3 of the Uniform Commercial Code (UCC). Article 3 imposes special requirements for the form and content of negotiable instruments. It also governs their negotiation, or transfer.

Negotiable Instrument A signed writing (record) that contains an unconditional promise or order to pay an exact sum on demand or at a specified future time to a specific person or order, or to bearer.

18–1a Types of Negotiable Instruments

The UCC specifies four types of negotiable instruments: *drafts, checks, promissory notes*, and *certificates of deposit* (CDs). These instruments, which are summarized briefly in Exhibit 18–1, are frequently divided into the two classifications that we will discuss in the following subsections: *orders to pay* (drafts and checks) and *promises to pay* (promissory notes and CDs).

Negotiable instruments may also be classified as either demand instruments or time instruments. A *demand instrument* is payable on demand. In other words, it is payable immediately after it is issued and for a reasonable period of time thereafter. A *time instrument* is payable at a future date.

Note that Section 3–104(b) of the UCC defines *instrument* as a "negotiable instrument."[1] For that reason, whenever the term *instrument* is used in this book, it refers to a negotiable instrument.

Draft Any instrument drawn on a drawee that orders the drawee to pay a certain amount of funds, usually to a third party (the payee), on demand or at a definite future time.

Drafts and Checks (Orders to Pay)

A **draft** is an unconditional written order that involves three parties. The party creating the draft (the **drawer**) orders another party (the **drawee**) to pay funds, usually to a third party (the **payee**). The most common type of draft is a check, but drafts other than checks may be used in commercial transactions.

Drawer The party that initiates a draft (such as a check), thereby ordering the drawee to pay.

Drawee The party that is ordered to pay a draft or check. With a check, a bank or another financial institution is always the drawee.

Payee A person to whom an instrument is made payable.

Time Drafts versus Sight Drafts. A *time draft* is payable at a definite future time. A *sight draft* (or demand draft) is payable on sight—that is, when it is presented to the drawee (usually a bank or another financial institution) for payment. A draft can be both a time and a sight draft. Such a draft is payable at a stated time after sight (a draft that states it is payable ninety days after sight, for instance).

1. Note that all of the references to Article 3 of the UCC in this chapter are to the 1990 version of Article 3, which has been adopted by nearly every state. One-fifth of the states have adopted an amended version of Article 3, issued in 2002.

Exhibit 18–1 Basic Types of Negotiable Instruments

INSTRUMENTS	CHARACTERISTICS	PARTIES
ORDERS TO PAY:		
Draft	An order by one person to another person or to bearer.	*Drawer*—The person who signs or makes the order to pay.
Check	A draft drawn on a bank and payable on demand. (With certain types of checks, such as cashier's checks, the bank is both the drawer and the drawee.)	*Drawee*—The person to whom the order to pay is made. *Payee*—The person to whom payment is ordered.
PROMISES TO PAY:		
Promissory note	A promise by one party to pay funds to another party or to bearer.	*Maker*—The person who promises to pay.
Certificate of deposit	A note issued by a bank acknowledging a deposit of funds made payable to the holder of the note.	*Payee*—The person to whom the promise is made.

Exhibit 18–2 shows a typical time draft. For the drawee to be obligated to honor (pay) the order, the drawee must be obligated to the drawer either by agreement or through a debtor-creditor relationship. **Example 18.1** On January 16, OurTown Real Estate orders $1,000 worth of office supplies from Eastman Supply Company, with payment due in ninety days. Also on January 16, OurTown sends Eastman a draft drawn on its account with the First National Bank of Whiteacre as payment. In this scenario, the drawer is OurTown, the drawee is OurTown's bank (First National Bank of Whiteacre), and the payee is Eastman Supply Company. ■

Acceptance In negotiable instruments law, a drawee's signed agreement to pay a draft when it is presented.

Acceptor A drawee that accepts, or promises to pay, an instrument when it is presented later for payment.

Acceptances. A drawee's written promise to pay a draft when it comes due is called an **acceptance.** Usually, the drawee accepts the instrument by writing the word *accepted* on its face, with a signature and a date. A drawee who has accepted an instrument becomes an **acceptor.**

A *trade acceptance* is a type of draft commonly used in the sale of goods. In this draft, the seller is both the drawer and the payee. The buyer to whom credit is extended is the drawee. **Example 18.2** Jackson Street Bistro buys its restaurant supplies from Osaka Industries. When Jackson requests supplies, Osaka creates a draft ordering Jackson to pay Osaka for the supplies within ninety days. Jackson accepts the draft by signing its face, which obligates it to make the payment. This is a trade acceptance, and Osaka can sell it to a third party at any time before the payment is due. ■

When a draft orders the buyer's bank to pay, it is called a *banker's acceptance*. Banker's acceptances are often used in international trade.

Check A draft drawn by a drawer ordering the drawee bank or other financial institution to pay a certain amount of funds to the payee on demand.

Checks. As mentioned, the most commonly used type of draft is a **check.** Although fewer checks are written today and most transactions are electronic, checks are still more common than promissory notes or other types of negotiable instruments. (For a discussion of mobile payment apps, which are increasingly popular as alternatives to checks, see this chapter's *Adapting the Law to the Online Environment* feature.)

Checks are demand instruments because they are payable on demand. Most commonly, the writer of the check is the drawer, the bank on which the check is drawn is the drawee, and the person to whom the check is made payable is the payee. On certain types of checks, such as *cashier's checks*, the bank is both the drawer and the drawee. A cashier's check functions the same as cash because the bank has committed itself to paying the stated amount on demand.

Exhibit 18–2 A Typical Time Draft

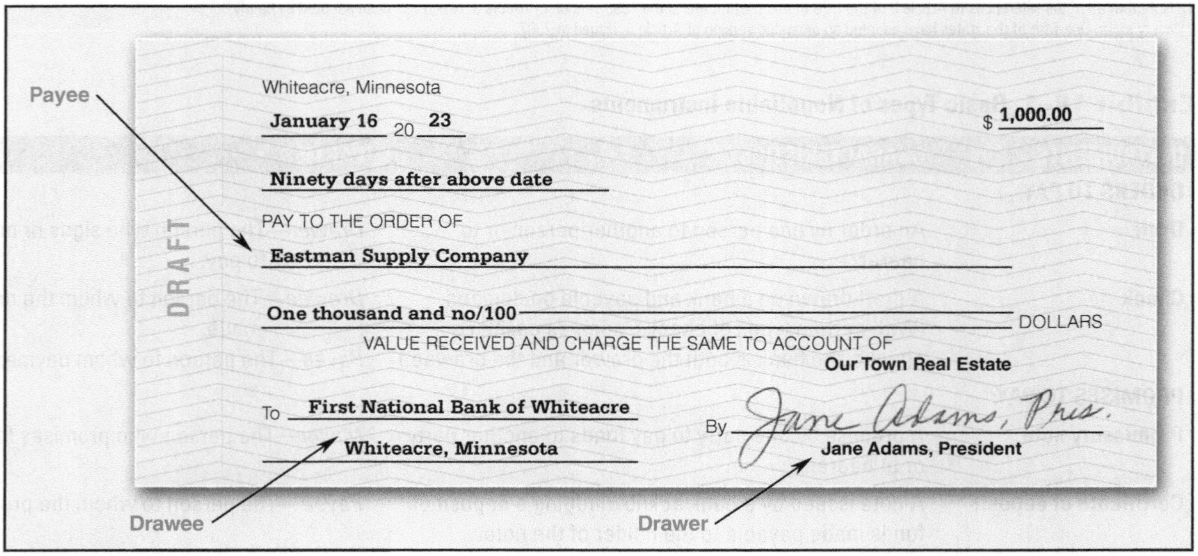

Adapting the Law to the Online Environment

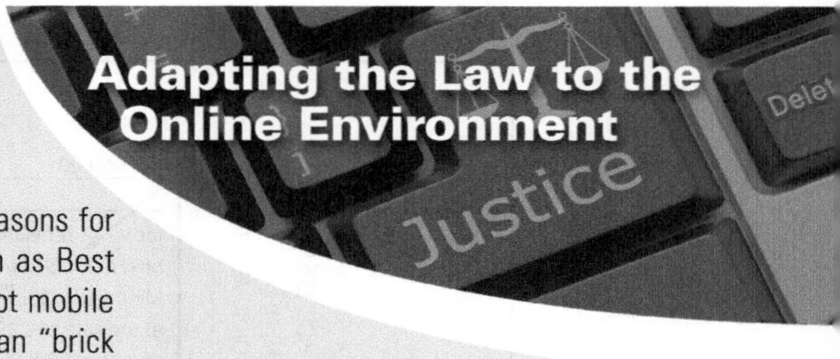

Pay with Your Smartphone

Mobile payment apps allow consumers to pay for goods and services using their smartphones. The funds for these transactions usually come from a bank account or a credit or debit card, or from a software-based system for storing funds called a *digital wallet*.

Certain smartphone apps—in particular, Apple, Inc.'s Apple Pay—communicate wirelessly with special point-of-sale systems using near-field communication technology. A person using the smartphone holds it close to (or "waves" it at) the point-of-sale terminal and authenticates the transaction by holding a fingerprint to the phone's ID touch sensor. Along with Apple Pay, Google Pay and Samsung Pay are the leaders in this field, which is attempting to revolutionize how we make our way down a check-out line.

Digital Mistrust

In major Chinese cities, mobile payments using smartphones have come to dominate daily financial transactions. Such saturation clearly has not yet occurred in the United States. Experts point to several reasons for this. Although large retailers such as Best Buy, Costco, and McDonald's accept mobile payments, the majority of American "brick and mortar" merchants do not. Privacy concerns are also limiting use. Many consumers realize that mobile payments provide corporations with a detailed picture of where they shop, what they purchase, and how much they routinely spend.

The biggest problem, however, appears to be that Americans do not yet trust mobile payments. A survey by Pew Charitable Trusts found that respondents were significantly more worried about security breaches with mobile payment apps than with traditional credit or debit cards.[a] This situation is exacerbated by the patchwork of federal and state regulations that apply to mobile payments. These rules are different for each app, depending on whether it is linked to a credit card company, to a bank, or to a phone company, leaving gaps, ambiguities, and overlap that continue to shackle this burgeoning technology.

Critical Thinking

The Electronic Fund Transfer Act (EFTA)[b] *is a federal law that protects consumers who transfer funds electronically. Among other safeguards, EFTA limits the liability that results from a lost or stolen electronic financial information and requires banks to provide information to consumers concerning potentially fraudulent electronic transactions. EFTA does not cover mobile payments. Should it? Why or why not?*

a. "Are Americans Embracing Mobile Payments?" *www.pewtrusts.org*. The Pew Charitable Trusts: October 3, 2019, Web.

b. Consumer Protection Act Section 902, 15 U.S.C.A Section 1693.

Promissory Notes (Promises to Pay) A **promissory note** is a written promise made by one person (the **maker** of the promise to pay) to another (usually a payee). A promissory note, which is often referred to simply as a *note*, can be made payable at a definite time or on demand. It can name a specific payee or merely be payable to bearer (bearer instruments will be discussed later in this chapter). **Example 18.3** On April 30, Laurence and Margaret sign a writing unconditionally promising to pay "to the order of" the First National Bank of Whiteacre $3,000 (with 5 percent interest) on or before June 29. This writing is a promissory note. (See Exhibit 18–3.)

Promissory notes are used in a variety of credit transactions. Often, a promissory note will carry the name of the transaction involved. A note secured by personal property, such as an automobile, is referred to as a *collateral note* because property pledged as security for the satisfaction of a debt is called *collateral*.[2] A note payable in installments, such as installment payments for a 75-inch smart TV over a twelve-month period, is called an *installment note*.

Promissory Note A written promise made by one person (the maker) to pay a fixed amount of funds to another person (the payee or a subsequent holder) on demand or on a specified date.

Maker One who promises to pay a fixed amount of funds to the holder of a promissory note or a certificate of deposit (CD).

2. To minimize the risk of loss when making a loan, a creditor often requires the debtor to provide some *collateral*, or security, beyond a promise that the debt will be repaid. When this security takes the form of personal property (such as a motor vehicle), the creditor has an interest in the property that is known as a *security interest*.

Exhibit 18–3 A Typical Promissory Note

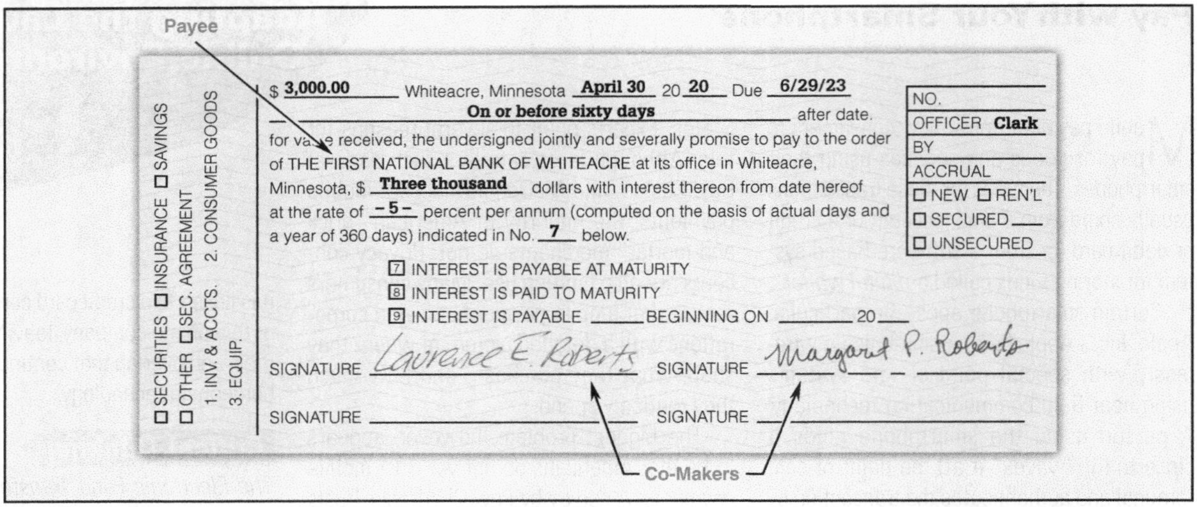
Payee

☐ SECURITIES ☐ INSURANCE ☐ SAVINGS
☐ OTHER ☐ SEC. AGREEMENT
1. INV. & ACCTS. 2. CONSUMER GOODS
3. EQUIP.

$ 3,000.00 Whiteacre, Minnesota April 30 20 20 Due 6/29/23
On or before sixty days after date.
for value received, the undersigned jointly and severally promise to pay to the order of THE FIRST NATIONAL BANK OF WHITEACRE at its office in Whiteacre, Minnesota, $ Three thousand dollars with interest thereon from date hereof at the rate of -5- percent per annum (computed on the basis of actual days and a year of 360 days) indicated in No. 7 below.

NO.
OFFICER Clark
BY
ACCRUAL
☐ NEW ☐ REN'L
☐ SECURED
☐ UNSECURED

7 INTEREST IS PAYABLE AT MATURITY
8 INTEREST IS PAID TO MATURITY
9 INTEREST IS PAYABLE ____ BEGINNING ON ____ 20__

SIGNATURE Laurence E. Roberts SIGNATURE Margaret P. Roberts
SIGNATURE SIGNATURE

Co-Makers

A promissory note is not a debt—it is only the evidence of a debt. **Case Example 18.4** The Bricourts entered an agreement with Wells Fargo Bank to finance the purchase of their home. In doing so, they signed a promissory note to repay Wells Fargo the amount borrowed. The couple failed to make their monthly payments, and Wells Fargo filed a foreclosure action against them. This action did not, however, include the original promissory note, which had been inadvertently lost or destroyed. Instead, Wells Fargo offered a copy of the original note. A Florida appeals court ruled that, given Wells Fargo's good faith efforts to find the original, a copy was sufficient for foreclosure purposes. Even when a promissory note is unavailable, the owner/lender still retains rights and may prove the existence of the note through other evidence.[3]

Certificate of Deposit (CD) A note issued by a bank in which the bank acknowledges the receipt of funds from a party and promises to repay that amount, with interest, to the party on a certain date.

Certificates of Deposit (Promises to Pay) A **certificate of deposit (CD)** is a type of note issued when a party deposits funds with a bank that the bank promises to repay, with interest, on a certain date [UCC 3–104(j)]. The bank is the maker of the note, and the depositor is the payee. **Example 18.5** On February 15, Sara deposits $5,000 with the First National Bank of Whiteacre. The bank issues a CD, in which it promises to repay the $5,000, plus 1.85 percent annual interest, on August 15. (See Exhibit 18–4.)

Because CDs are time deposits, the purchaser-payee typically is not allowed to withdraw the funds before the date of maturity. Banks usually charge a sizable penalty for early withdrawal (except in limited circumstances, such as disability or death). Certificates of deposit are often sold by savings and loan associations, commercial banks, and credit unions. Small CDs are for amounts up to $100,000.

Focus Question 1

What requirements must an instrument meet to be negotiable?

18–1b Requirements for Negotiability

For an instrument to be negotiable, it must meet the following requirements:

1. Be in writing.
2. Be signed by the maker or the drawer.
3. Be an unconditional promise or order to pay.
4. State a fixed amount of money.
5. Be payable on demand or at a definite time.
6. Be payable to order or to bearer, unless the instrument is a check.

3. *Wells Fargo Bank, NA, v. Bricourt,* __ So.3d. __, 2020 WL 698661 (Fla. Dis. Ct. App., 4th Dis., 2020).

Exhibit 18–4 A Sample Certificate of Deposit

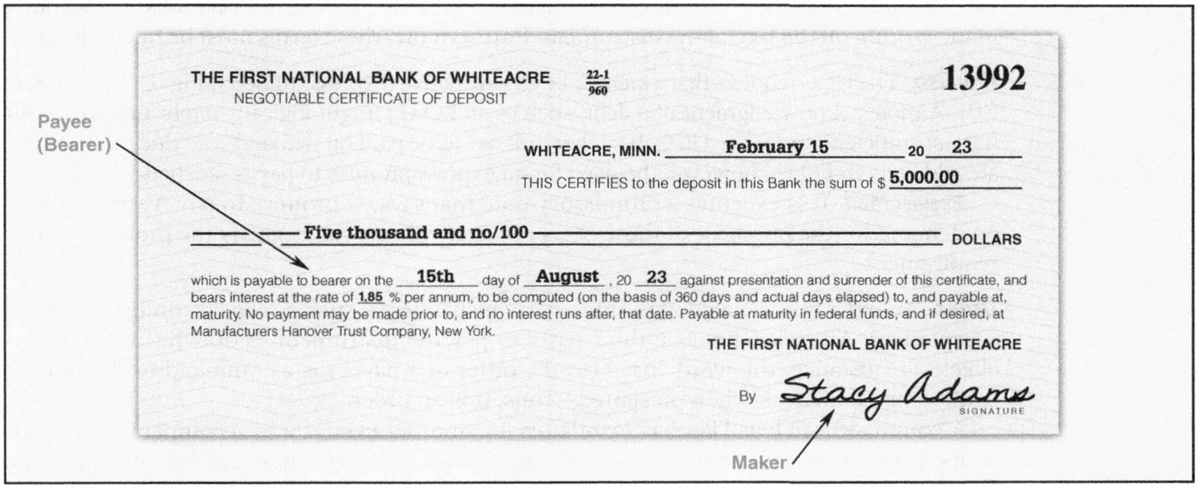

THE FIRST NATIONAL BANK OF WHITEACRE 22-1/960 13992
NEGOTIABLE CERTIFICATE OF DEPOSIT

Payee (Bearer)

WHITEACRE, MINN. February 15 20 23

THIS CERTIFIES to the deposit in this Bank the sum of $ 5,000.00

Five thousand and no/100 DOLLARS

which is payable to bearer on the 15th day of August, 20 23 against presentation and surrender of this certificate, and bears interest at the rate of 1.85 % per annum, to be computed (on the basis of 360 days and actual days elapsed) to, and payable at, maturity. No payment may be made prior to, and no interest runs after, that date. Payable at maturity in federal funds, and if desired, at Manufacturers Hanover Trust Company, New York.

THE FIRST NATIONAL BANK OF WHITEACRE

By Stacy Adams SIGNATURE

Maker

Written Form Negotiable instruments must be in written form (but may be evidenced by an electronic record) [UCC 3–103(a)(6), (9)].[4] This is because negotiable instruments must possess the quality of certainty that only formal, written expression can give. The writing must have the following qualities:

1. The writing must be on material that lends itself to *permanence*. Instruments carved in blocks of ice or etched in sand would not qualify as negotiable instruments. The UCC nevertheless gives considerable leeway as to what can be a negotiable instrument. Courts have found checks and notes written on napkins, menus, tablecloths, shirts, and a variety of other materials to be negotiable.
2. The writing must also have *portability*. Although the UCC does not explicitly state this requirement, if an instrument is not movable, it obviously cannot meet the requirement that it be freely transferable. **Example 18.6** Charles writes on the side of a cow, "I promise to pay $500 to the order of Jason." Technically, this would meet the requirements of a negotiable instrument—except for portability. A cow cannot easily be transferred in the ordinary course of business. Thus, the "instrument" is nonnegotiable.

Karpiyon/Getty Images

Would a promise to pay written on the side of this calf be negotiable? Why or why not?

Signatures For an instrument to be negotiable, it must be signed by (1) the maker, if it is a note or a certificate of deposit, or (2) the drawer, if it is a draft or a check [UCC 3–103(a)(3)]. If a person signs an instrument as an authorized agent of the maker or drawer, the maker or drawer has effectively signed the instrument.

The UCC is quite lenient with regard to what constitutes a signature. Nearly any symbol executed or adopted by a person with the intent to authenticate a written or electronic document can be a signature [UCC 1–201(37)]. A signature can be made by a device, such as a rubber stamp, or by a thumbprint. In addition, it can consist of any name, including a trade name, or a word, mark, or symbol [UCC 3–401(b)]. If necessary, parol evidence is admissible to identify the signer.

The location of the signature on the document is unimportant, although the usual place is the lower right-hand corner. A *handwritten* statement on the body of the instrument, such as "I, Jerome Garcia, promise to pay Elena Greer," is sufficient to act as a signature.

---

4. Under the Uniform Electronic Transactions Act (UETA) and the 2002 amendments to Article 3, an electronic record may be sufficient to constitute a writing. Note, however, that the amendments to Article 3 do not expressly authorize electronic negotiable instruments.

Know This

Negotiable instruments are classified as promises to pay or orders to pay.

Unconditional Promise or Order to Pay For an instrument to be negotiable, it must contain a promise to pay or an express order. The terms of the promise or order must be included in the writing on the face of the instrument. Furthermore, these terms must be unconditional.

Promise. The UCC requires that a *promise* be an affirmative (express) undertaking [UCC 3–103(a)(9)]. A mere acknowledgment of a debt, such as an I.O.U., might logically *imply* a promise, but it is *not* sufficient under the UCC. If such words as "to be paid on demand" or "due on demand" are added to an I.O.U., however, the need for an express promise to pay is satisfied.[5]

Example 18.7 Tess executes a promissory note that says, "I promise to pay Alvarez $1,000 on demand for the purchase of these cases of wine." These words satisfy the promise-to-pay requirement.

Order. An *order* is associated with three-party instruments, such as checks, drafts, and trade acceptances. An order directs a third party to pay the instrument as drawn. In the typical check, for instance, the word "pay" (to the order of a payee) is a command to the drawee bank to pay the check when presented—thus, it is an order.

A command, such as "Pay," is mandatory in an order even if it is accompanied by courteous words, as in "Please pay" or "Kindly pay." Generally, the language used must indicate that a command or order is being given. Stating, "I wish you would pay" does not fulfill this requirement. An order may be addressed to one party or to more than one party, either jointly ("to A *and* B") or alternatively ("to A *or* B") [UCC 3–103(a)(6)].

Unconditionality of Promise or Order. Only *unconditional* promises or orders can be negotiable [UCC 3–106(a)]. A promise or order is conditional (and therefore *not* negotiable) if it states *any* of the following:

1. An express condition to payment.
2. That the promise or order is subject to or governed by another writing or record.
3. That the rights or obligations with respect to the promise or order are stated in another writing or record.

A mere reference to another writing, however, does not make the promise or order conditional [UCC 3–106(a)]. For instance, the words "As per contract" or "This debt arises from the sale of goods X and Y" do not render an instrument nonnegotiable. Similarly, a statement in the instrument that payment can be made only out of a particular fund or source will not render the instrument nonnegotiable [UCC 3–106(b)(ii)].

Case Example 18.8 Sam and Odalis Groome entered into two contracts to buy a pair of alpacas from Alpacas of America, LLC (AOA). To finance the purchases, the buyers signed two notes, one for $18,750 and one for $20,250. Each note included a reference to a contract, a payment schedule, and a security agreement, which provided an interest in the alpacas to secure payment. Within a few months, the Groomes stopped making payments. When AOA sued to collect the unpaid amounts, the Groomes argued that the notes were nonnegotiable because they referred to and were governed by other writings (the contracts). Ultimately, a state appellate court ruled that the Groomes' notes did contain unconditional promises to pay and thus were negotiable.[6]

Terrasprite/Getty Images

Is a note for funds to purchase alpacas negotiable?

In contrast, if the payment is to be made from a fund that does not yet exist, or is conditioned on the occurrence of some future event, the instrument will be nonnegotiable. **Example 18.9** Duffy's note promises to pay Sherman from the trust account that Duffy will establish when he receives the proceeds from his father's estate. This promise is conditional, and the note is nonnegotiable.

In the following case, the court considered the negotiability of a promissory note that included a reference to a mortgage. The makers of the note argued that this reference rendered the note nonnegotiable.

---

5. A certificate of deposit (CD) is an exception in this respect. A CD does not have to contain an express promise, because the bank's acknowledgment of the deposit and the other terms of the instrument clearly indicate a promise by the bank to repay the funds [UCC 3–104(j)].
6. *Alpacas of America, LLC v. Groome*, 179 Wash.App. 391, 317 P.3d 1103 (2014).

Case 18.1

OneWest Bank, FSB[a] v. Nunez

District Court of Appeal of Florida, Fourth District, 41 Fla.L.Weekly. D540, 193 So.3d 13 (2016).

Facts To buy property in Hallandale, Florida, Jose and Jessica Nunez signed a promissory note and mortgage payable to Countrywide Home Loans, Inc. The note contained a reference to the mortgage and described how and under what conditions its payment could be accelerated. Countrywide transferred the note to One-West Bank. The Nunezes defaulted on the payments. OneWest filed a suit in a Florida state court to collect. The Nunezes claimed that OneWest was not entitled to enforce the note because it was not a negotiable instrument. They contended that the reference to the mortgage and the conditions for acceleration destroyed the note's negotiability. The court agreed with the Nunezes and dismissed the complaint. OneWest appealed.

Issue Is a note that refers to a mortgage unconditional?

Decision Yes. A state intermediate appellate court reversed the dismissal of OneWest's complaint. "The mention of the mortgage [and] the . . . rights of acceleration in the promissory note does not destroy the unconditional nature of the note."

Reason The reviewing court looked at Florida's version of UCC 3–106 and determined that the promissory note's reference to the mortgage did not render the note unconditional. The court pointed out that the official comments to UCC 3–106 explain that the inclusion of language regarding collateral and acceleration does not make a note conditional. In addition, the court found several cases from other jurisdictions in which courts had held that notes using exactly the same language as the Nunezes' note were negotiable. Therefore, the court concluded that the note's reference to the Nunez's mortgage and its statement concerning acceleration did not render the note conditional and nonnegotiable.

Critical Thinking

- **What If the Facts Were Different?** *Suppose that the note in this case had stated, "The terms of the mortgage are by this reference made a part hereof." Would the result have been different?*

a. The initials FSB mean Federal Savings Bank.

A Fixed Amount of Money Negotiable instruments must state with certainty a fixed amount of money to be paid at any time the instrument is payable [UCC 3–104(a)]. This requirement ensures that the value of the instrument can be determined with clarity and certainty.

The term *fixed amount* means an amount that is ascertainable from the face of the instrument. A demand note payable with 8 percent interest meets the requirement of a fixed amount because its amount can be determined at the time it is payable or at any time thereafter [UCC 3–104(a)].

Know This
Interest payable on an instrument normally cannot exceed the maximum limit on interest under a state's usury statute.

The rate of interest may also be determined from information that is not contained in the instrument itself but is described by it, such as a formula or a source [UCC 3–112(b)]. For instance, an instrument that is payable at the *legal rate of interest* (a rate of interest fixed by statute) is negotiable. Mortgage notes tied to a variable rate of interest (a rate that fluctuates as a result of market conditions) are also negotiable.

The fixed amount must be *payable in money*. The UCC defines money as "a medium of exchange authorized or adopted by a domestic or foreign government as a part of its currency" [UCC 1–201(24)]. Gold is not a medium of exchange adopted by the U.S. government, so a note payable in gold is nonnegotiable. An instrument payable in the United States with a face amount stated in a foreign currency is negotiable, however, and can be paid in the foreign currency or in the equivalent amount of U.S. dollars [UCC 3–107].

Payable on Demand or at a Definite Time A negotiable instrument must "be payable on demand or at a definite time" [UCC 3–104(a)(2)]. To determine the instrument's value, it is necessary to know when the maker, drawee, or acceptor is required to pay. It is also necessary to know when the obligations of secondary parties, such as *indorsers*,[7] will arise.

Furthermore, it is necessary to know when an instrument is due in order to calculate when the statute of limitations may apply [UCC 3–118(a)]. Finally, with an interest-bearing instrument, it is necessary to know the exact interval during which interest will accrue to determine the instrument's present value.

Presentment The act of presenting an instrument to the party liable on the instrument in order to collect payment. Presentment also occurs when a person presents an instrument to a drawee for a required acceptance.

Payable on Demand. Instruments that are payable on demand include those that contain the words "Payable at sight" or "Payable upon presentment." **Presentment** is a demand made by or on behalf of a person entitled to enforce an instrument to either pay or accept the instrument [UCC 3–501]. Thus, presentment occurs when a person offers the instrument to the appropriate party for payment or acceptance. Presentment can by made by any commercially reasonable means, including oral, written, or electronic communication.

The very nature of the instrument may indicate that it is payable on demand. For instance, a check, by definition, is payable on demand [UCC 3–104(f)]. If no time for payment is specified and the person responsible for payment must pay on the instrument's presentment, the instrument is payable on demand [UCC 3–108(a)]. (See the *Business Law Analysis* feature for further illustration.)

Spotlight Case Example 18.10 National City Bank gave Reger Development, LLC, a line of credit to finance potential development opportunities. Reger signed a promissory note requiring it to "pay this loan in full immediately upon Lender's demand." About a year later, the bank asked Reger to pay down the loan and stated that it would be reducing the amount of cash available through the line of credit. Reger sued, alleging that the bank had breached the terms of the note. The court ruled in the bank's favor. The promissory note was a demand instrument because it explicitly set forth the lender's right to demand payment at any time. Thus, National City had the right to collect payment from Reger at any time on demand.[8]

7. We should note that the UCC uses the spelling *indorse* (*indorsement*, and the like), rather than the more common spelling *endorse* (*endorsement*, and the like). We follow the UCC's spelling here and in other chapters in this text.

8. *Reger Development, LLC v. National City Bank*, 592 F.3d 759 (7th Cir. 2010).

Deciding If an Instrument Is Negotiable

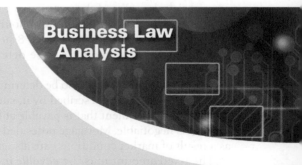

Business Law Analysis

Abby Novel signed a promissory note to her stepfather to obtain funds to manufacture and market a patented jewelry display design. The note read, "Glen Gallwitz 1-8-2016 loaned me $5,000 at 6 percent interest for a total of $10,000.00." The note did not state a time for repayment. More than seven years after Novel signed the note, Gallwitz filed a suit to recover the stated amount. Novel claimed that she did not have to pay because the note was not negotiable—it was incomplete. Is she correct?

Analysis: For an instrument to be negotiable under UCC 3–104, it must meet the following requirements: (1) be in writing, (2) be signed by the maker or the drawer, (3) be an unconditional promise or order to pay, (4) state a fixed amount of money, (5) be payable on demand or at a definite time, and (6) be payable to order or to bearer unless it is a check. When no time for payment is stated on an instrument, the instrument is payable on demand.

Result and Reasoning: Novel is not correct. All of the requirements to establish the instrument as negotiable are met: (1) the instrument is in writing, (2) it is signed by Novel, (3) there are no conditions or promises other than the unconditional promise to pay, (4) the instrument states a fixed amount—$10,000, (5) the instrument does not include a definite repayment date, which means that it is payable on demand, and (6) the instrument is payable to Gallwitz.

Therefore, the instrument is negotiable, and Novel is bound to pay it.

Payable at a Definite Time. If an instrument is not payable on demand, to be negotiable it must be payable at a definite time. An instrument is payable at a definite time if it states *any* of the following:

1. That it is payable on a specified date.
2. That it is payable within a definite period of time (such as thirty days) after being presented for payment.
3. That it is payable on a date or time readily ascertainable at the time the promise or order is issued [UCC 3–108(b)].

The maker or drawee in a time draft is under no obligation to pay until the specified time.

When an instrument is payable by the maker or drawer *on or before* a stated date, it is clearly payable at a definite time. The maker or drawer has the *option* of paying before the stated maturity date, but the payee can still rely on payment being made by the maturity date. **Example 18.11** Ari gives Ernesto an instrument dated May 1, 2022, that indicates on its face that it is payable *on or before* May 1, 2023. This instrument satisfies the definite-time requirement.

In contrast, an instrument that is undated and made payable "one month after date" is clearly nonnegotiable. There is no way to determine the maturity date from the face of the instrument. If the date is uncertain, the instrument is not payable at a definite time. **Example 18.12** An instrument that states, "One year after the death of my grandfather, Jerome Adams, I promise to pay $5,000 to the order of Lucy Harmon. [Signed] Jacqueline Wells," is nonnegotiable. The date on which the instrument becomes payable is uncertain.

Acceleration Clause. An **acceleration clause** allows a payee or other holder of a time instrument to demand payment of the entire amount due, with interest, if a certain event occurs. (A **holder** is any person in possession of an instrument drawn, issued, or indorsed to that person, to that person's order, to bearer, or in blank [UCC 1–201(20)].)

Acceleration Clause A clause that allows a payee or other holder of a time instrument to demand payment of the entire amount due, with interest, if a certain event occurs, such as a default in the payment of an installment when due.

Holder Any person in possession of an instrument drawn, issued, or indorsed to that person, to that person's order, to bearer, or in blank.

Example 18.13 Marta lends $1,000 to Ruth, who makes a negotiable note promising to pay $100 per month (plus interest) for ten months. The note contains an acceleration provision that permits Marta or any holder to immediately demand all the payments plus the interest owed to date if Ruth fails to pay an installment. Ruth fails to make the third payment. Marta accelerates the unpaid balance, and the note becomes due and payable in full. Ruth owes Marta the remaining principal plus any unpaid interest to that date.

Instruments that include acceleration clauses are negotiable because the exact value of the instrument can be ascertained. In addition, the instrument will be payable on a specified date if the event allowing acceleration does not occur [UCC 3–108(b)(ii)]. Thus, the specified date is the outside limit used to determine the value and negotiability of the instrument.

In the following case, a lender invoked an acceleration clause to recover the amount owed on a note. The borrower had defaulted on the payments eight years earlier. Did the lender wait too long to accelerate the debt?

Case 18.2

Collins Asset Group, LLC v. Alialy

Supreme Court of Indiana, 139 N.E.3d 712 (2020).

Facts Alkhemer Alialy executed a promissory note and mortgage to be paid in monthly installments over twenty-five years. The note contained an acceleration clause giving the holder the option to accelerate the debt after a default and to require immediate payment of the full amount owed.

After Alialy stopped making payments, the note was transferred to Collins Asset Group, LLC (CAG). Eight years later, CAG accelerated the debt, demanding payment in full.

Six months passed, and still Alialy did not pay. CAG then filed a suit in an Indiana state court to recover on the note. The court

(Continues)

Continued

dismissed the complaint on the ground that the claim was barred by a six-year statute of limitations for a cause of action on a promissory note. A state intermediate appellate court affirmed the dismissal, finding that CAG did not accelerate the debt within six years of Alialy's initial default and thus waited too long to invoke the acceleration clause. CAG appealed.

Issue Can CAG accelerate the debt on the note and assert its claim for payment?

Decision Yes. The Indiana Supreme Court reversed the judgment of the state intermediate appellate court and remanded the case. "CAG's claim is timely."

Reason The state supreme court explained that a note accompanying a mortgage requires payment in fixed installments over a period of time extending from the note's execution to its maturity date. The note may also include an acceleration clause that gives the lender an option to "fast-forward to the note's maturity date" and demand immediate payment in full if the maker of the note fails to pay an installment.

The court identified two statutes of limitations that apply when a lender sues for payment on a note in Indiana—the state's general statute of limitations and the UCC's statute of limitations. Each statute contains a six-year limit on an action to obtain full payment of the amount owed on an unpaid note. Under either statute, there are multiple dates from which such an action can accrue. One of those dates is when a lender exercises its option to accelerate the debt.

In this case, the court held that "the two statutes provide CAG identical paths to relief. CAG brought its claim against Alialy . . . well within six years of when it accelerated the debt . . .. Thus, CAG's claim to recover the full amount owed on the note is not time-barred."

Critical Thinking

- **Legal Environment** *What advantage does an acceleration clause in a note provide to a creditor?*
- **Economic** *Why would an investor accept a mortgage note on which the maker has already defaulted? Discuss.*

Extension Clause A clause in a time instrument that allows the instrument's date of maturity to be extended into the future.

Extension Clause. The reverse of an acceleration clause is an **extension clause,** which allows the date of maturity to be extended into the future [UCC 3–108(b)(iii), (iv)]. If the right to extend the time of payment is given to the maker or drawer, the interval of the extension must be specified to keep the instrument negotiable. If, however, the holder can extend the time of payment, the extended maturity date need not be specified for the instrument to be negotiable.

Example 18.14 Alek's note reads, "The holder of this note at the date of maturity, January 1, 2022, can extend the time of payment until the following June 1 or later, if the holder so wishes." This note is negotiable. The length of the extension does not have to be specified, because only the holder has the option to extend. After January 1, 2022, the note is, in effect, a demand instrument.

Payable to Order or to Bearer Because one of the functions of a negotiable instrument is to serve as a substitute for cash, freedom to transfer is essential. To ensure a proper transfer, the instrument must be "payable to order or to bearer" at the time it is issued or first comes into the possession of the holder [UCC 3–104(a)(1)]. An instrument is not negotiable unless it meets this requirement.

Order Instrument A negotiable instrument that is payable "to the order of an identified person" or "to an identified person or order."

Order Instruments. An **order instrument** is an instrument that is payable (1) "to the order of an identified person" or (2) "to an identified person or order" [UCC 3–109(b)]. An identified person is the person "to whom the instrument is initially payable" as determined by the intent of the maker or drawer [UCC 3–110(a)]. The identified person, in turn, may transfer the instrument to whomever that person wishes. In this way, the instrument retains its transferability.

Note that with order instruments, the person specified must be identified with *certainty*, because the transfer of the instrument requires the *indorsement*, or signature, of the payee (indorsements will be discussed later in this chapter). An order instrument made "Payable to the order of my nicest cousin," for instance, is not negotiable, because it does not clearly specify the payee.

Bearer Instruments. A **bearer instrument** is an instrument that does not designate a specific payee [UCC 3–109(a)]. The term **bearer** refers to a person in possession of an instrument that is payable to bearer or indorsed in blank (with a signature only, as will be discussed shortly) [UCC 1–201(5), 3–109(a), 3–109(c)]. This means that the maker or drawer agrees to pay anyone who presents the instrument for payment.

Bearer Instrument Any instrument that is not payable to a specific person, including instruments payable to bearer or to cash.

Bearer A person in possession of an instrument payable to bearer or indorsed in blank.

Any instrument containing terms such as the following is a bearer instrument:

1. "Payable to the order of bearer."
2. "Payable to Simon Reed or bearer."
3. "Payable to bearer."
4. "Payable to X" or "Payable to Captain America" (the instrument can be payable to a *nonexistent person*, but not to a company that does not exist).
5. "Pay to the order of cash."

Spotlight Case Example 18.15 Amine Nehme applied for credit at the Venetian Resort Hotel Casino in Las Vegas, Nevada, and was granted $500,000 in credit. He signed a marker—that is, a promise to pay a gambling debt—for $500,000. Nehme quickly lost that amount gambling. The Venetian presented the marker for payment to Nehme's bank, Bank of America, which returned it for insufficient funds. The casino's owner, Las Vegas Sands, LLC, filed a suit against Nehme for failure to pay a negotiable instrument.

The court held that the marker fit the UCC's definitions of negotiable instrument and check. It was a means for payment of $500,000 from Bank of America to the order of the Venetian. It did not state a time for payment and thus was payable on demand. It was also unconditional—that is, it stated no promise by Nehme other than the promise to pay a fixed amount of money.[9]

©nito/Shutterstock.com

Can a gambling marker be a negotiable instrument?

Factors That Do Not Affect Negotiability

Certain ambiguities or omissions will not affect the negotiability of an instrument. The UCC provides the following rules for clearing up ambiguous terms:

1. Unless the date of an instrument is necessary to determine a definite time for payment, the fact that an instrument is *undated* does not affect its negotiability. A typical example is an undated check, which is still negotiable. If a check is not dated, its date is the date of its issue, meaning the date the maker first delivers the check to another person to give that person rights in the check [UCC 3–113(b)].
2. Antedating or postdating an instrument (using a date before or after the actual current date) does not affect the instrument's negotiability [UCC 3–113(a)]. **Example 18.16** Crenshaw draws a check on his account at First Bank, payable to Sirah Imports. He postdates the check by fifteen days. Sirah Imports can immediately negotiate the check, and, unless Crenshaw tells First Bank otherwise, the bank can charge the amount of the check to Crenshaw's account [UCC 4–401(c)].
3. Handwritten terms outweigh typewritten and printed terms (preprinted terms on forms, for instance), and typewritten terms outweigh printed terms [UCC 3–114]. **Example 18.17** Most checks are preprinted "Pay to the order of" followed by a blank line, indicating an order instrument. In handwriting, Chad inserts in the blank, "Anita Delgado or bearer." The handwritten terms will outweigh the printed form, and the check will be a bearer instrument.

Know This

An instrument that purports to be payable both to order and to bearer contains a contradiction in terms. Such an instrument is a bearer instrument.

9. *Las Vegas Sands, LLC v. Nehme*, 632 F.3d 526 (9th Cir. 2011).

4. Words outweigh figures unless the words are ambiguous [UCC 3–114]. This rule is important when the numerical amount and the written amount on a check differ. **Example 18.18** Megan issues a check payable to Reliable Appliance Company. For the amount, she fills in the number "$100" but writes out the words "One thousand and 00/100" dollars. The check is payable in the amount of $1,000.
5. When an instrument does not specify a particular interest rate but simply states "with interest," the interest rate is the *judgment rate of interest* (a rate of interest fixed by statute that is applied to court judgments) [UCC 3–112(b)].
6. A check is negotiable even if a notation on it states that it is "nonnegotiable" or "not governed by Article 3." Any other instrument, in contrast, can be made nonnegotiable if the maker or drawer conspicuously notes on it that it is "nonnegotiable" or "not governed by Article 3" [UCC 3–104(d)].

18–2 Transfer of Instruments

Once issued, a negotiable instrument can be transferred by *assignment* or by *negotiation*. The party receiving the instrument obtains the rights of a holder only if the transfer is by negotiation.

18–2a Transfer by Assignment

Recall that an assignment is a transfer of rights under a contract. Under general contract principles, a transfer by assignment gives the assignee only those rights that the assignor possessed. Any defenses that can be raised against an assignor can normally be raised against the assignee. This same principle applies when a negotiable instrument, such as a promissory note, is transferred by assignment. The transferee is an *assignee* rather than a *holder*.

18–2b Transfer by Negotiation

Negotiation The transfer of an instrument in such form that the transferee (the person to whom the instrument is transferred) becomes a holder.

Negotiation is the transfer of an instrument in such a way that the transferee (the person to whom the instrument is transferred) becomes a holder [UCC 3–201(a)]. Under UCC principles, a transfer by negotiation creates a holder who, at the very least, receives the rights of the previous possessor [UCC 3–203(b)].

Unlike an assignment, a transfer by negotiation can make it possible for a holder to receive more rights in the instrument than the prior possessor had [UCC 3–202(b), 3–305, 3–306]. A holder who receives greater rights is known as a *holder in due course*, a concept we will discuss later in this chapter.

There are two methods of negotiating an instrument so that the receiver becomes a holder. The method used depends on whether the instrument is an *order instrument* or a *bearer instrument*.

Focus Question 2

How does the negotiation of order instruments differ from the negotiation of bearer instruments?

Negotiating Order Instruments An order instrument contains the name of a payee capable of indorsing it, as in "Pay to the order of Lloyd Sorenson." If the instrument is an order instrument, it is negotiated by delivery with any necessary indorsements.

Example 18.19 Welpac Corporation issues a payroll check "to the order of Lloyd Sorenson." Sorenson takes the check to the bank, signs his name on the back (an indorsement), gives it to the teller (a delivery), and receives cash. Sorenson has *negotiated* the check to the bank [UCC 3–201(b)].

Negotiating order instruments requires both delivery and indorsement. If Sorenson had taken the check to the bank and delivered it to the teller without signing it, the transfer would not qualify as a negotiation. In that situation, the transfer would be treated as an assignment, and the bank would become an assignee rather than a holder.

Negotiating Bearer Instruments If an instrument is payable to bearer, it is negotiated by delivery—that is, by transfer into another person's possession. Indorsement is not necessary [UCC 3–201(b)]. The use of bearer instruments thus involves more risk through loss or theft than the use of order instruments.

Example 18.20 Richard writes a check "payable to cash" and hands it to Jessie (a delivery). The check is a bearer instrument, which Richard has issued to Jessie. Jessie places the check in her wallet, and the wallet is subsequently stolen. The thief has possession of the check. At this point, the thief has no rights to the check. If the thief "delivers" the check to an innocent third person, however, negotiation will be complete. All rights to the check will be passed absolutely to that third person, and Jessie will lose all rights to recover the proceeds of the check from that person [UCC 3–306]. Of course, Jessie can attempt to recover the amount from the thief if the thief can be found.

18–2c Indorsements

An indorsement is required whenever an order instrument is negotiated. An **indorsement** is a signature with or without additional words or statements. It is most often written on the back of the instrument itself. If there is no room on the instrument, the indorsement can be on a separate piece of paper that is firmly affixed to the instrument, such as with staples [UCC 3–204(a)].

Indorsement A signature placed on an instrument for the purpose of transferring ownership rights in the instrument.

A person who transfers an instrument by signing (indorsing) it and delivering it to another person is an *indorser*. The person to whom the check is indorsed and delivered is the *indorsee*. **Example 18.21** Luisa receives a graduation check for $100. She can transfer the check to her mother (or to anyone) by signing it on the back. Luisa is an indorser. If Luisa indorses the check by writing "Pay to Avery Perez," Avery is the indorsee.

There are four main categories of indorsements: blank, special, qualified, and restrictive. Note that a single indorsement may have characteristics of more than one category.

Blank Indorsements A **blank indorsement** does not specify a particular indorsee and can consist of a mere signature [UCC 3–205(b)]. **Example 18.22** A check payable "to the order of Alan Luberda" is indorsed in blank if Alan simply writes his signature on the back of the check. A blank indorsement is shown in Exhibit 18–5.

Blank Indorsement An indorsement on an instrument that specifies no indorsee. An order instrument that is indorsed in blank becomes a bearer instrument.

An order instrument indorsed in blank becomes a bearer instrument and can be negotiated by delivery alone, as already discussed. In other words, a blank indorsement converts an order instrument to a bearer instrument, which anybody can cash.

Exhibit 18–5 A Blank Indorsement

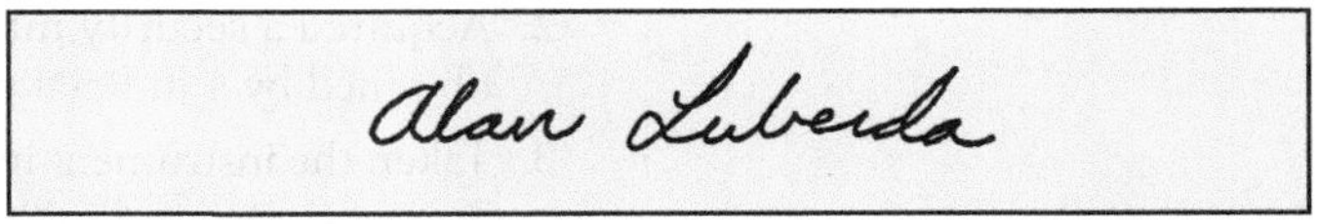

Other Indorsements As mentioned, other types of indorsements include special, qualified, and restrictive indorsements.

- A *special indorsement* identifies the specific person to whom the indorser intends to make the instrument payable. Words such as "Pay to the order of Rick Clay," followed by the signature of the indorser, create a special indorsement.
- A *qualified endorsement* disclaims any contractual liability on the indorsement. Thus, an indorser who does not want to be liable on an instrument can write "Pay to Evelyn Ling without recourse."
- A *restrictive indorsement* requires the indorsee to comply with restrictions, such as "for collection only" or "for deposit" only.

As the use of paper checks has become less common, these types of indorsement have become less important for daily consumer and business transactions in the United States.

18–3 Holder in Due Course (HDC)

Holder in Due Course (HDC)
A holder who acquires a negotiable instrument for value, in good faith, and without notice that the instrument is defective.

Often, whether a holder is entitled to obtain payment will depend on whether the holder is a *holder in due course*. An ordinary holder obtains only those rights that the transferor had in the instrument and normally is subject to any defenses that could be asserted against the transferor. In contrast, a **holder in due course (HDC)** takes an instrument *free* of most of the defenses and claims that could be asserted against the transferor. To become an HDC, a holder must meet certain acquisition requirements.

Example 18.23 Shanna buys a BMW X5 for her business from Heritage Motors in Irvine, California, signing a promissory note for $65,000 as part of the deal. Heritage negotiates the note to Apollo Financial Services, which promises to pay Heritage for it in six months. During the next two months, Shanna has significant problems with the X5 and sues Heritage for breach of contract. She also refuses to make further payments on the note.

Whether Apollo can hold Shanna liable on the note depends on whether it has met the requirements for HDC status. If Apollo has met these requirements and thus has HDC status, it is entitled to payment on the note. If Apollo has not met these requirements, it has the status of an ordinary holder, and Shanna's defense against payment to Heritage will also be effective against Apollo. ■

18–3a Requirements for HDC Status

Focus Question 3
What are three basic requirements for attaining the status of a holder in due course (HDC)?

The basic requirements for attaining HDC status are set forth in UCC 3–302. A holder of a negotiable instrument is an HDC if that person takes the instrument (1) for value, (2) in good faith, and (3) without notice that it is defective. Next, we examine each of these requirements.

Taking for Value An HDC must have given *value* for the instrument [UCC 3–302(a)(2)(i)]. A person who receives an instrument as a gift or inherits it has not met the requirement of value. In these situations, the person becomes an ordinary holder and does not possess the rights of an HDC.

Under UCC 3–303(a), a holder takes an instrument for value if the holder has done any of the following:

1. Performed the promise for which the instrument was issued or transferred.
2. Acquired a security interest or other lien in the instrument, excluding a lien obtained by a judicial proceeding.
3. Taken the instrument in payment of, or as security for, a preexisting claim. **Example 18.24** Zon owes Dwyer $2,000 on a past-due account. If Zon negotiates a $2,000 note signed by Gordon to Dwyer and Dwyer accepts it to discharge the overdue account balance, Dwyer has given value for the instrument. ■
4. Given a negotiable instrument as payment for the instrument. **Example 18.25** Justin issues a six-month, $5,000 negotiable promissory note to Paige. Paige needs cash and does not want to wait for the maturity date to collect. She negotiates the note to her friend Kristen, who pays her $2,000 in cash and writes her a check—a negotiable instrument—for the balance of $3,000. Kristen has given full value for the note. ■
5. Given an irrevocable commitment (such as a letter of credit) as payment for the instrument.

Value Is Distinguishable from Consideration. The concept of *value* in the law of negotiable instruments is not the same as the concept of *consideration* in the law of contracts. Although a promise to give value in the future is valid consideration to support a contract, it does not constitute sufficient value to make the promisor an HDC. If a person promises to perform or give value in the future, that person is not an HDC.

A holder takes an instrument for value *only to the extent that the promise has been performed* [UCC 3–303(a)(1)]. Let's return to *Example 18.23*, in which Heritage Motors negotiates Shanna's promissory note to Apollo Financial Services in return for Apollo's promise to pay in six months. In this example, Apollo is not an HDC. At the time of Shanna's breach of contract lawsuit against Heritage, Apollo has not yet paid Heritage for the note. Thus, it did not take the note for value. If Apollo had paid Heritage for the note at the time of transfer (given value), it would be an HDC and could have held Morrison liable on the note. Exhibit 18–6 illustrates these concepts further.

Exceptions. In a few situations, the holder may pay for the instrument but not acquire HDC status. For instance, when the instrument is purchased at a judicial sale, such as a bankruptcy or creditor's sale, the holder will not be an HDC. Similarly, if the instrument is acquired as a result of taking over a trust or an estate (as administrator), or as part of a corporate purchase of assets, the holder will have only the rights of an ordinary holder [UCC 3–302(c)].

Taking in Good Faith To qualify as an HDC, a holder must take the instrument in *good faith* [UCC 3–302(a)(2)(ii)]. This means that the holder must have acted honestly and observed reasonable commercial standards of fair dealing in the process of acquiring the instrument [UCC 3–103(a)(4)].

The good faith requirement applies only to the *holder*. It is immaterial whether the transferor acted in good faith. Thus, even a person who takes a negotiable instrument from a thief may become an HDC if the person acquired the instrument in good faith and honestly had no reason to be suspicious of the transaction.

Spotlight Case Example 18.26 Cassandra Demery worked as a bookkeeper at Freestyle until the owner, Clinton Georg, discovered that she had embezzled more than $200,000. Georg fired Demery and demanded repayment. Demery went to work for her parents' firm, Metro Fixtures, where she had some authority to write checks. Without specific authorization, she wrote a check for $189,000 to Freestyle on Metro's account and deposited it in Freestyle's account. She told Georg that the check was a loan to her from her family.

Exhibit 18–6 Taking for Value

By exchanging defective goods (a defective BMW X5) for a promissory note, Heritage Motors breached its contract with Shanna. Shanna could assert this breach as a defense if Heritage presented the note to her for payment. Heritage exchanged the note for Apollo Financial Services' promise to pay in six months, however. Because Apollo did not take the note for value, it is not a holder in due course. Thus, Shanna can assert against Apollo the defense of Heritage's breach when Apollo submits the note to Shanna for payment. In contrast, if Apollo had taken the note for value, Shanna could not assert that defense and would be liable to pay the note.

Jacob Wackerhausen/E+/Getty Images; Tupungato/Shutterstock; Wavebreakmedia/Getty Images

When Metro discovered Demery's theft, it filed a suit against Georg and Freestyle. Freestyle argued that it had taken the check in good faith and was an HDC. The Colorado Supreme Court agreed. Demery was the wrongdoer. She had the authority to issue checks for Metro, and Georg had no reason to know that Demery had lied about this check. Therefore, Freestyle was an HDC, and Metro would bear the loss.[10]

Taking without Notice The final requirement for HDC status involves *notice* [UCC 3–302]. Individuals will not qualify for HDC protection if they are *on notice* (knows or has reason to know) that the instrument being acquired is defective in any one of the following ways [UCC 3–302(a)]:

1. It is overdue.
2. It has been dishonored.
3. It is part of a series of which at least one instrument has an uncured (uncorrected) default.
4. It contains an unauthorized signature or has been altered.
5. There is a defense against the instrument or a claim to it.
6. The instrument is so irregular or incomplete as to call its authenticity into question.

Typically, disputes involving the status of an HDC involve persons that acquire negotiable instruments from others. Therefore, taking without notice is a matter of whether the holder has reason to know of a defect in the instrument. Sometimes, however, a person who is a party to the instrument claims HDC status. In the following case, the original payee on promissory notes issued to him when he contributed capital to a business that he co-owned claimed to be an HDC.

10. *Georg v. Metro Fixtures Contractors, Inc.*, 178 P.3d 1209 (Colo. 2008).

Case 18.3

Jarrell v. Conerly

Court of Appeal of Louisiana Fourth Circuit, 240 So.3d 266, La. Ct. App. 4th Cir. (2018).

Facts Jessie Conerly and Ramon Jarrell signed a letter of intent to enter into a business venture and form a limited liability company, K & M, LLC. They planned to buy land from Marion Clay & Gravel, LLC, and extract and sell the natural resources of sand, gravel, and clay from it. Jarrell would own 48 percent of the company and secure $6.8 million in start-up capital for the purpose of buying out the four members of Marion Clay. Jarrell would also receive 50 percent of the profits, provide oversight, and have access to all records and aspects of the operation. Conerly would own 52 percent of K & M, be responsible for daily operational management and oversight, and receive 50 percent of the profits.

After the letter-of-intent agreement, Jarrell began advancing capital to Conerly. Conerly issued four promissory notes (for the principal amounts of $40,000, $20,000, $22,000, and $22,000) naming Jarrell as the payee. Two years later, Jarrell filed a lawsuit in a Louisiana state court against Conerly for failing to pay the balance due on the notes. Conerly claimed several defenses to the notes, including lack of consideration, but the trial court held that Jarrell was an HDC, which precluded Conerly from asserting these defenses. The trial court granted a partial summary judgment to Jarrell in the amount of $104,000. Conerly appealed.

Issue Was Jarrell, the payee on the promissory notes, an HDC of the notes?

Decision No. The state intermediate appellate court held that Jarrell was not an HDC on the four promissory notes. Therefore, Conerly was entitled to present his legitimate defenses. The court reversed the lower court's summary judgment and remanded the case for further proceedings.

Reason According to the court, although a payee on a promissory note *can* be an HDC, that status is not automatic. "When the payee deals with the maker through an intermediary . . . and does not have notices of defenses, such an isolated payee may take as a holder in due course." Normally, however, a payee who has had constant, direct, and meaningful contact with the maker will not be an HDC. A payee in this situation will usually have notices of defenses and claims by virtue of the fact that he has dealt directly with the maker.

In this case, Jarrell had direct and meaningful contact with Conerly, and the notes were relating to financing a company that he helped found, worked for, and partially owned. Given Jarrell's status as a payee, and his personal involvement in the formation and operation of the business venture, Jarrell was not a holder in due course. "Because Jarrell is not a holder in due course, the notes are subject to the defenses advanced by Conerly, such as failure of consideration."

Critical Thinking

- **What If the Facts Were Different?** *If Jarrell had simply invested in K & M, but was not a co-owner and did not interact with Conerly, how might this have affected the outcome of this case?*

What Constitutes Notice? Under UCC 1–201(25), a person is considered to have notice in the following circumstances:

1. The person has actual knowledge of the defect.
2. The person has received a notice or notification concerning the defect (such as a letter from a bank identifying the serial numbers of stolen bearer instruments).
3. The person has reason to know that a defect exists, given all the facts and circumstances known at the time in question.

The holder must also have received notice "at a time and in a manner that gives a reasonable opportunity to act on it" [UCC 3–302(f)]. A purchaser's knowledge of certain facts, such as insolvency proceedings against the maker or drawer of the instrument, does not constitute notice that the instrument is defective [UCC 3–302(b)].

Overdue Instruments. What constitutes notice that an instrument is overdue depends on whether it is a demand instrument or a time instrument.

A purchaser has notice that a *demand instrument* is overdue in two situations. One situation occurs when a person takes the instrument knowing that demand already has been made. The other situation occurs when a person takes a demand instrument an unreasonable length of time after its date. For a check, a "reasonable time" is within ninety days after the date of the check. For all other demand instruments, what will be considered a reasonable time depends on the circumstances [UCC 3–304(a)].

Normally, a *time instrument* is overdue on the day after its due date. Anyone who takes a time instrument after the due date is on notice that it is overdue [UCC 3–304(b)(2)]. Thus, if a promissory note due on May 15 is purchased on May 16, the purchaser is an ordinary holder, not an HDC. If an instrument states that it is "Payable in thirty days," counting begins the day after the instrument is dated. Thus, a note dated December 1 that is payable in thirty days is due by midnight on December 31. If the payment date falls on a Sunday or holiday, the instrument is payable on the next business day.

Dishonored Instruments. To **dishonor** an instrument is to refuse to pay or accept it. Thus, an instrument is dishonored when the party to whom it is presented refuses to pay it. If a holder knows or has reason to know that an instrument has been dishonored, the holder is on notice and cannot claim HDC status [UCC 3–302(a)(2)]. Thus, a person who takes a check clearly stamped "insufficient funds" is put on notice.

Dishonor To refuse to pay or to accept a negotiable instrument that has been presented in a timely and proper manner.

Conversely, if a person purchasing an instrument does not know and has no reason to know that it has been dishonored, the person is *not* put on notice and therefore can become an HDC. **Example 18.27** Leah holds a demand note dated September 1 issued by Apex, Inc., a local business firm. On September 17, she demands payment, and Apex refuses (that is, dishonors the instrument). On September 22, Leah negotiates the note to Brenner, a purchaser who lives in another state. Brenner does not know, and has no reason to know, that the note has been dishonored. Because Brenner is not put on notice, Brenner can become an HDC.

Notice of Claims or Defenses. A holder who has notice of any claim to the instrument or any defense against it cannot become an HDC [UCC 3–302(a)(2)]. A purchaser has notice if the claims or defenses are apparent on the instrument's face or if the purchaser had reason to know of them from facts surrounding the transaction. Instruments with irregularities and incomplete instruments fall under this rule.

Know This
A difference between the handwriting in the body of a check and the handwriting in the signature does not affect the validity of the check.

Any *irregularity* on the face of an instrument (such as an obvious forgery or alteration) that calls into question its validity or ownership will bar HDC status. A good forgery of a signature or the careful alteration of an instrument, however, can go undetected by reasonable examination. In that situation, the purchaser can qualify as an HDC.

In addition, a purchaser cannot become an HDC of an instrument so *incomplete* on its face that an element of negotiability is lacking (for instance, the amount is not filled in) [UCC 3–302(a)(1)]. Minor omissions (such as the omission of the date) are permissible, because these do not call into question the validity of the instrument [UCC 3–113(b)].

18–3b Holder through an HDC

Shelter Principle The principle that the holder of a negotiable instrument who cannot qualify as a holder in due course (HDC), but who derives title through an HDC, acquires the rights of an HDC.

A person who does not qualify as an HDC but who derives title through an HDC can acquire the rights and privileges of an HDC. This rule, which is sometimes called the **shelter principle,** is set out in UCC 3–203(b). Under this rule, anyone—no matter how far removed from an HDC—who can ultimately trace their title back to an HDC may acquire the rights of an HDC. By extending the benefits of HDC status, the shelter principle promotes the marketability and free transferability of negotiable instruments.

There are some limitations on the shelter principle. A holder who participated in fraud or illegality affecting the instrument cannot take advantage of the shelter principle by repurchasing the instrument from a later HDC [UCC 3–203(b)]. Similarly, a holder who had notice of a claim or defense against an instrument cannot gain the benefits of HDC status by later reacquiring the instrument from an HDC.

18–4 Signature and Warranty Liability

Liability on negotiable instruments can arise either from a person's signature or from the warranties that are implied when the person presents the instrument for negotiation. A person who signs a negotiable instrument is potentially liable for payment of the amount stated on the instrument. Unlike signature liability, warranty liability does not require a signature and extends to both signers and nonsigners.

18–4a Signature Liability

The general rule is that every party, except a qualified indorser,[11] who signs a negotiable instrument is either primarily or secondarily liable for payment of that instrument when it comes due. Signature liability is contractual liability—no person will be held contractually liable for an instrument that the person has not signed.

Primary Liability Primary liability is unconditional. A person who is primarily liable on a negotiable instrument is absolutely required to pay the instrument—unless, of course, that

11. A qualified indorser—one who indorses "without recourse"—undertakes no contractual obligation to pay. A qualified indorser merely assumes warranty liability.

person has a valid defense to payment [UCC 3–305]. Only *makers* and *acceptors* of instruments are primarily liable.

The maker of a promissory note unconditionally promises to pay the note. It is the maker's promise to pay that makes the note a negotiable instrument. If the instrument was incomplete when the maker signed it, the maker is obligated to pay it according to its stated terms or according to terms that were agreed on and later filled in to complete the instrument [UCC 3–115, 3–407(a), 3–412].

Example 18.28 Tristan executes a preprinted promissory note to Sharon, without filling in the blank for a due date. If Sharon does not complete the form by adding the date, the note will be payable on demand. If Sharon subsequently fills in a due date that Tristan has authorized, the note is payable on the stated due date. In either situation, Tristan (the maker) is obligated to pay the note.

As mentioned earlier, an acceptor is a drawee, such as a bank, that promises to pay an instrument when it is presented for payment. Once a drawee accepts a draft, the drawee is obligated to pay the draft when it is presented for payment [UCC 3–409(a)]. Failure to pay an accepted draft when presented leads to primary signature liability.

Know This

A drawee is the party ordered to pay a draft or check, such as a bank.

Secondary Liability *Drawers* and *indorsers* are secondarily liable. On a negotiable instrument, secondary liability is *contingent liability* (similar to that of a guarantor in a contract). In other words, a drawer or an indorser will be liable only if the party that is responsible for paying the instrument dishonors it by refusing to pay.

Parties are secondarily liable on a negotiable instrument *only if* the following events occur:[12]

1. The instrument is properly and timely presented.
2. The instrument is dishonored.
3. Timely notice of dishonor is given to the secondarily liable party.

Proper and Timely Presentment. Presentment occurs when a person presents an instrument either to the party liable on the instrument for payment or to a drawee for acceptance. The holder must present the instrument to the appropriate party in a proper and timely fashion and must give reasonable identification if requested [UCC 3–414(f), 3–415(e), 3–501]. The party to whom the instrument must be presented depends on the type of instrument involved. A note or CD is presented to the maker for payment. A draft is presented to the drawee for acceptance, payment, or both. A check is presented to the drawee for payment [UCC 3–501(a), 3–502(b)].

Presentment can be made by any commercially reasonable means, including oral, written, or electronic communication [UCC 3–501(b)]. Ordinarily, it is effective when received. (If presentment takes place after an established cutoff hour, though, it may be treated as occurring the next business day.)

Timeliness is important for proper presentment [UCC 3–414(f), 3–415(e), 3–501(b)(4)]. Failure to present an instrument on time is the most common reason for improper presentment. If the instrument is payable on demand, the holder should present it for payment or acceptance within a reasonable time. The holder of a domestic check must present that check for payment or collection within thirty days of its *date* to hold the drawer secondarily liable. With respect to indorsers, the holder must present a check within thirty days after its indorsement to hold the indorser secondarily liable. The time for proper presentment for various types of instruments is shown in Exhibit 18–7.

simonkr/E+/Getty Images

If this bank customer bought a certificate of deposit, how would she obtain payment for it when it comes due?

12. These requirements are necessary for a secondarily liable party to have signature liability on a negotiable instrument, but they are not necessary for a secondarily liable party to have warranty liability.

Exhibit 18–7 Time for Proper Presentment

TYPE OF INSTRUMENT	FOR ACCEPTANCE	FOR PAYMENT
Time	On or before due date.	On due date.
Demand	Within a reasonable time after date of issue or after secondary party becomes liable on the instrument.	Within a reasonable time.
Check	Not applicable.	Within thirty days of its date, to hold drawer secondarily liable. Within thirty days of indorsement, to hold indorser secondarily liable.

Dishonor. As mentioned, an instrument is dishonored when the required acceptance or payment is refused. It is also dishonored when acceptance or payment cannot be obtained within the prescribed time or when the required presentment is excused (as it would be, for instance, if the maker had died) and the instrument is not properly accepted or paid [UCC 3–502(e), 3–504].

In certain situations, a delay in payment or a refusal to pay an instrument will *not dishonor* the instrument.

1. When presentment is made after an established cutoff hour (not earlier than 2:00 P.M.), a bank can postpone payment until the following business day without dishonoring the instrument [UCC 3–501(b)(4)].
2. When the holder refuses (a) exhibit the instrument, (b) to give reasonable identification, or (c) to sign a receipt for the payment on the instrument, then a bank's refusal to pay does not dishonor the instrument [UCC 3–501(b)(2)].
3. When an instrument is returned because it lacks a proper indorsement, the instrument is not dishonored [UCC 3–501(b)(3)(i)].

Proper Notice of Dishonor. Once an instrument has been dishonored, proper notice must be given to secondary parties (drawers and indorsers) for them to be held liable. **Example 18.29** Oscar writes a check on his account at People's Bank payable to Bess. Bess indorses the check in blank and cashes it at Midwest Grocery, which transfers it to People's Bank for payment. If People's Bank refuses to pay it, Midwest must timely notify Bess to hold her liable.

Notice can be given in any reasonable manner, including an oral, written, or electronic communication, as well as notice written or stamped on the instrument itself. A bank must give any necessary notice before its midnight deadline (midnight of the next banking day after receipt). Notice by any party other than a bank must be given within thirty days following the day of dishonor or the day on which the person who is secondarily liable receives notice of dishonor [UCC 3–503].

Unauthorized Signatures Unauthorized signatures arise in two situations:

1. When a person forges another person's name on a negotiable instrument.
2. When an agent who lacks the authority signs an instrument on behalf of a principal.

The General Rule. The general rule is that an unauthorized signature is wholly inoperative and will not bind the person whose name is signed or forged. **Example 18.30** Parker finds Dolby's checkbook lying in the street, writes a check to himself, and forges Dolby's signature. Banks normally have a duty to determine whether a person's signature on a check is forged. If a bank fails to determine that Dolby's signature is not genuine and cashes the check for Parker, the bank will generally be liable to Dolby for the amount.

The general rule also may apply to agents' signatures. If an agent lacks the authority to sign the principal's name or has exceeded the authority given by the principal, the signature does not bind the principal but will bind the "unauthorized signer" [UCC 3–403(a)].

DNY59/Getty Images

Someone finds a checkbook on the sidewalk, writes a check to himself, and forges the signature of the account holder. Is the bank liable to the true account holder if it cashes the forged check?

Exceptions to the General Rule. There are two exceptions to the general rule that an unauthorized signature will not bind the person whose name is signed:

1. *Ratification.* When the person whose name is signed ratifies (affirms) the signature, that person will be bound [UCC 3–403(a)]. For instance, a mother may ratify her daughter's forgery of the mother's signature so that the daughter will not be prosecuted. A person can ratify an unauthorized signature either expressly (by affirming the signature) or impliedly (by other conduct, such as keeping any benefits received in the transaction or failing to repudiate the signature).
2. *Negligence.* When the negligence of the person whose name was forged substantially contributed to the forgery, a court may not allow the person to deny the effectiveness of an unauthorized signature [UCC 3–115, 3–406, 4–401(d)(2)]. For instance, a person who signs a check but leaves blank the amount and payee's name and then leaves the check in a public place may be unable to deny liability for it.

Special Rules for Unauthorized Indorsements Generally, when an instrument has a forged or unauthorized indorsement, the burden of loss falls on the first party to take the instrument. The reason for this general rule is that the first party to take an instrument is in the best position to prevent the loss.

Example 18.31 Jen steals a check drawn on Universal Bank that is payable to the order of Inga Leed. Jen indorses the check "Inga Leed" and presents the check to Universal Bank for payment. The bank, without asking Jen for identification, pays the check, and Jen disappears. Inga will not be liable on the check, because her indorsement was forged. The bank will bear the loss, which it might have avoided if it had asked Jen for identification.

This general rule has two important exceptions that cause the loss to fall on the maker or drawer. These exceptions arise when an indorsement is made by an imposter or by a fictitious payee.

Imposter Rule. An **imposter** is one who, through deception, induces a maker or drawer to issue an instrument in the name of an impersonated payee. If the maker or drawer believes the imposter to be the named payee at the time of issue, the indorsement by the imposter is not treated as unauthorized when the instrument is transferred to an innocent party. This is because the maker or drawer *intended* the imposter to receive the instrument. In these situations, the unauthorized indorsement of a payee's name can be as effective as if the real payee had signed. The *imposter rule* provides that an imposter's indorsement will be effective—that is, not a forgery—insofar as the drawer or maker is concerned [UCC 3–404(a)].

Imposter One who induces a maker or drawer to issue a negotiable instrument in the name of an impersonated payee. Indorsements by imposters are treated as authorized indorsements under UCC Article 3.

Example 18.32 Carol impersonates Donna and induces Edward to write a check payable to the order of Donna. Carol, continuing to impersonate Donna, negotiates the check to First National Bank as payment on her loan there. As the drawer of the check, Edward is liable for its amount to First National.

Fictitious Payee Rule. When a person causes an instrument to be issued to a payee who will have *no interest* in the instrument, the payee is referred to as a **fictitious payee.** A fictitious

Fictitious Payee A payee on a negotiable instrument whom the maker or drawer did not intend to have an interest in the instrument. Indorsements by fictitious payees are treated as authorized indorsements under UCC Article 3.

payee can be a person or firm that does not exist, or it may be an identifiable party that will not acquire any interest in the instrument. Under the UCC's *fictitious payee rule*, the payee's indorsement is not treated as a forgery, and an innocent holder can hold the maker or drawer liable on the instrument [UCC 3–404(b), 3–405]. Basically, the loss falls on the maker or drawer of the instrument rather than on the third party that accepts it or on the bank that cashes it.

Fictitious payees most often arise in two situations:

1. When a dishonest employee deceives the employer into signing an instrument payable to a party with no right to receive payment on the instrument.
2. When a dishonest employee or agent has the authority to issue an instrument on behalf of the employer and issues a check to a party who has no interest in the instrument.

Case Example 18.33 Braden Furniture Company gave its bookkeeper, Bonnie Manning, general authority to create checks. Over the course of seven years, Manning created more than two hundred unauthorized checks, totaling $470,000, which she deposited in her own account at Union State Bank. Braden Furniture was not a customer of the bank. Most of the checks did not identify a payee (the payee line was left blank). Braden Furniture (the drawer) sued Union State Bank for the loss, claiming that the bank had been negligent in accepting and paying the blank checks. The court, however, held that the fictitious payee rule applied. Therefore, under Alabama's version of the UCC, the loss fell on Braden Furniture, not on Union State Bank.[13]

A furniture company's bookkeeper created several unauthorized business checks for her personal use. How did the fictitious payee rule affect the dispute that arose over who suffered the loss of funds?

18–4b Warranty Liability

In addition to signature liability, transferors make certain implied warranties regarding the instruments that they are negotiating. Warranty liability arises even when a transferor does not sign the instrument [UCC 3–416, 3–417].

Warranty liability is particularly important when a holder cannot hold a party liable on a signature, such as when a person delivers a bearer instrument. *Unlike secondary signature liability, warranty liability is not subject to the conditions of proper presentment, dishonor, or notice of dishonor.*

Warranties fall into two categories: those that arise on the *transfer* of a negotiable instrument and those that arise on *presentment*. Both transfer and presentment warranties attempt to shift liability back to a wrongdoer or to the person who dealt face to face with the wrongdoer and thus was in the best position to prevent the wrongdoing.

Focus Question 4

What is the difference between signature liability and warranty liability?

Transfer Warranties A person who transfers an instrument *for consideration* makes the following five **transfer warranties** to all subsequent transferees and holders who take the instrument in good faith [UCC 3–416]:[14]

1. The transferor is entitled to enforce the instrument.
2. All signatures are authentic and authorized.
3. The instrument has not been altered.

Transfer Warranties Implied warranties made by any person who transfers an instrument for consideration that the person is entitled to enforce the instrument, the signatures are authentic, it has not been altered, there are no defenses, and the transferor is unaware of any bankruptcy proceedings of parties to the instrument.

13. *Braden Furniture Co. v. Union State Bank*, 109 So.3d 625 (Ala. 2012). See also *State of Vermont v. Stewart*, 176 A.3d 1120 (Vt. 2017).
14. An amendment to UCC 3–416(a) adds a sixth warranty "with respect to a remotely created consumer item," such as an electronic check drawn on a consumer account, that is not created by the payor bank and does not contain the drawer's handwritten signature. Under this amendment, which fifteen states have adopted, a bank that accepts and pays the instrument warrants to the next bank in the collection chain that the consumer authorized the item in that amount.

4. The instrument is not subject to a defense or claim of any party that can be asserted against the transferor.
5. The transferor has no knowledge of any bankruptcy proceedings of the maker, the acceptor, or the drawer of the instrument.

Presentment Warranties A person who presents an instrument for payment or acceptance makes the following **presentment warranties** to anyone who in good faith pays or accepts the instrument [UCC 3–417(a), 3–417(d)]:

1. The person obtaining payment or acceptance is entitled to enforce the instrument or is authorized to obtain payment or acceptance on behalf of a person who is entitled to enforce the instrument. (This is, in effect, a warranty that there are no missing or unauthorized indorsements.)
2. The instrument has not been altered.
3. The person obtaining payment or acceptance has no knowledge that the signature of the issuer of the instrument is unauthorized.[15]

The second and third presentment warranties do not apply to makers, acceptors, and drawers when the presenter is an HDC. It is assumed that drawers or makers will recognize their own signatures and that makers or acceptors will recognize whether an instrument has been materially altered.

Presentment warranties generally protect the person to whom the instrument is presented. They often have the effect of shifting liability back to the party that was in the best position to prevent the wrongdoing.

Presentment Warranties Implied warranties made by any person who presents an instrument for payment or acceptance that the person is entitled to enforce the instrument, that the instrument has not been altered, and that the person is unaware of any unauthorized signatures.

18–5 Defenses, Limitations, and Discharge

Defenses can bar collection from persons who would otherwise be primarily or secondarily liable on a negotiable instrument. There are two general categories of defenses—*universal defenses* and *personal defenses*.

18–5a Universal Defenses

A **universal defense** (also called a *real defense*) is valid against *all* holders, including HDCs and holders who take possession through an HDC. Universal defenses include those described next.

Universal Defense A defense that can be used to avoid payment to all holders of a negotiable instrument, including a holder in due course (HDC) or a holder with the rights of an HDC. It is also called a *real defense*.

1. *Forgery of a signature on the instrument*. A forged signature will not bind the person whose name is used. Thus, when an instrument is forged, the person whose name is forged normally has no liability to pay any holder the value of the instrument. If the person whose name is forged ratifies the signature, however, that person may be liable, as discussed earlier.
2. *Fraud in the execution*. If a person is deceived into signing a negotiable instrument by being told that it is something else, *fraud in the execution* is committed against the signer [UCC 3–305(a)(1)]. This defense cannot be raised, however, if reasonable inquiry would have revealed the nature and terms of the instrument.

   Example 18.34 Connor, a salesperson, asks Javier, a customer, to sign a paper. Connor says that it is a receipt for goods that Javier is picking up from the store. In fact, it is a promissory note, but Javier is unfamiliar with English and does

15. Amendments to Article 3 of the UCC provide additional protection for "remotely created" consumer items in the context of presentment also [see Amended UCC 3–417(a)(4)].

not realize this. Here, even if the note is negotiated to an HDC, Javier has a valid defense against payment. (Note that the result might be different if Javier was an English speaker and could have read the words saying it was a promissory note.)

3. *Material alteration*. An alteration is *material* if it changes the obligations of the parties in the instrument *in any way*. Material alterations include completing an incomplete instrument, adding words or numbers, or making any unauthorized changes that affect the obligation of a party [UCC 3–407(a)]. Making any change in the instrument's amount, date, or rate of interest—even if the change is only 1 percent—is material. It is not a material alteration, however, to correct the maker's address or to change the figures on a check so that they agree with the written amount.
   Material alteration is a *complete defense* against an ordinary holder, but only a *partial defense* against an HDC. Thus, an ordinary holder can recover nothing on an instrument that has been materially altered. An HDC can enforce the instrument against the maker or drawer according to its original terms but not for the altered amount.
4. *Discharge in bankruptcy*. Discharge in bankruptcy is an absolute defense on any instrument regardless of the status of the holder, because the purpose of bankruptcy is to settle all of the insolvent party's debts [UCC 3–305(a)(1)].
5. *Minority*. Minority, or infancy, is a universal defense only to the extent that state law recognizes it as a defense to a simple contract [UCC 3–305(a)(1)(i)].
6. *Illegality, mental incapacity, or extreme duress*. When the law declares an instrument to be void because it was issued in connection with illegal conduct, illegality is a universal defense. Similarly, if a court has declared a person who signed the instrument to be mentally incompetent, the instrument is void. If a person was under an immediate threat of force or violence (extreme duress, such as being held at gunpoint), the defense is universal, and the instrument is unenforceable by any holder or HDC [UCC 3–305(a)(1)(ii)].

Personal Defense A defense that can be used to avoid payment to an ordinary holder of a negotiable instrument but not a holder in due course (HDC) or a holder with the rights of an HDC. It is also called a *limited defense*.

Antonio Guillem/Shutterstock.com

If a person makes a gift to another person by writing a note that says, "I promise to pay you $100,000," is the note enforceable? Why or why not?

18–5b Personal Defenses

A **personal defense** (sometimes called a *limited defense*) is used to avoid payment to an ordinary holder of a negotiable instrument. It is not a defense against an HDC or a holder through an HDC. Personal defenses include the following:

1. *Breach of contract or breach of warranty*. When there is a breach of the underlying contract for which the negotiable instrument was issued, the maker of a note can refuse to pay it, or the drawer of a check can stop payment.
2. *Lack or failure of consideration*. The absence of consideration may be a successful personal defense in some instances [UCC 3–303(b), 3–305(a)(2)]. **Example 18.35** Tara gives Clem, as a gift, a note that states, "I promise to pay you $100,000." Clem accepts the note. Because there is no consideration for Tara's promise, a court will not enforce the promise.
3. *Fraud in the inducement (ordinary fraud)*. A person who issues a negotiable instrument based on false statements by the other party will be able to avoid payment to an ordinary holder of that instrument.
4. *Illegality, mental incapacity, or ordinary duress*. If the law declares that an instrument is voidable because of illegality, mental incapacity, or ordinary duress, the defense is personal [UCC 3–305(a)(1)(ii)].

Focus Question 5
What four defenses can be used against an ordinary holder that are not effective against an HDC?

18–5c Discharge from Liability

Discharge from liability on an instrument can come from payment, cancellation, or material alteration. The liability of all parties is discharged when the party primarily liable on the instrument pays to the holder the full amount due [UCC 3–602, 3–603]. Payment by any other party (such as an indorser) discharges only the liability of that party and subsequent parties.

Intentional cancellation by the holder discharges the liability of all parties [UCC 3–604]. Intentionally writing "Paid" across the face of an instrument cancels it, as does intentionally tearing it up. If a holder intentionally crosses out a party's signature, that party's liability and the liability of subsequent indorsers who have already indorsed the instrument are discharged.

Materially altering an instrument may discharge the liability of any party affected by the alteration, as previously discussed [UCC 3–407(b)]. An HDC may be able to enforce a materially altered instrument against its maker or drawer according to the instrument's original terms, however.

Discharge of liability can also occur when a holder impairs another party's right of recourse (right to seek reimbursement) on the instrument [UCC 3–605]. This occurs when, for instance, the holder releases, or agrees not to sue, a party against whom the indorser has a right of recourse.

Practice and Review

Robert Durbin, a student, borrowed funds from a bank for his education and signed a promissory note for their repayment. The bank loaned the funds under a federal program designed to assist students at postsecondary institutions. Under this program, repayment ordinarily begins nine to twelve months after the student borrower fails to carry at least one-half of the normal full-time course load. The federal government guarantees that the note will be fully paid. If the student defaults on the payments, the lender presents the current balance—principal, interest, and costs—to the government. When the government pays the balance, it becomes the lender, and the borrower owes the government directly. After Durbin defaulted on his note, the government paid the lender the balance due and took possession of the note. Durbin then refused to pay the government, claiming that the government was not the holder of the note. The government filed a suit in a federal district court against Durbin to collect the amount due. Using the information presented in the chapter, answer the following questions.

1. Was the note that Durbin signed an order to pay or a promise to pay? Explain.
2. Suppose that the note did not state a specific interest rate but instead referred to a statute that established the maximum interest rate for government-guaranteed student loans. Would the note fail to meet the requirements for negotiability in that situation? Why or why not?
3. How does a party who is not named in a negotiable instrument (in this situation, the government) obtain a right to enforce the instrument?
4. Now suppose that the school Durbin attended closed down before he could finish his education. In court, Durbin argues that this resulted in a failure of consideration: he did not get something of value in exchange for his promise to pay. Assuming that the government is a holder of the promissory note, will this argument likely be successful against it? Why or why not?

Debate This

We should eliminate the status of holder in due course for those who possess negotiable instruments.

Key Terms

acceleration clause 447
acceptance 440
acceptor 440
bearer 449
bearer instrument 449
blank indorsement 451
certificate of deposit (CD) 442
check 440
dishonor 455
draft 439
drawee 439
drawer 439
extension clause 448
fictitious payee 459
holder 447
holder in due course (HDC) 452
imposter 459
indorsement 451
maker 441
negotiable instrument 438
negotiation 450
order instrument 448
payee 439
personal defense 462
presentment 446
presentment warranties 461
promissory note 441
shelter principle 456
transfer warranties 460
universal defense 461

Chapter Summary: Negotiable Instruments

Formation of Negotiable Instruments

1. **Types of negotiable instruments**—The UCC specifies four types of negotiable instruments: drafts, checks, promissory notes, and certificates of deposit (CDs). These instruments fall into two basic classifications:
   a. **Demand instruments versus time instruments**—A demand instrument is payable on demand (when the holder presents it to the maker or drawer). A time instrument is payable at a future date.
   b. **Orders to pay versus promises to pay**—Checks and drafts are orders to pay. Promissory notes and CDs are promises to pay.
2. **Requirements for negotiability**—To be negotiable, an instrument must meet the following requirements.
   a. **Be in writing**—A writing can be on anything that is readily transferable and has a degree of permanence [UCC 3–103(a) (6), (9)].
   b. **Be signed by the maker or drawer**—The signature can be anyplace on the face of the instrument, can be in any form (including a rubber stamp), can consist of any name (including a trade name), and can be made in a representative capacity [UCC 3–103(a)(3), 3–401(b)].
   c. **Be an unconditional promise or order to pay**—
      1. A promise must be more than a mere acknowledgment of a debt [UCC 3–103(a)(6), (9)].
      2. Such words as "pay on demand" meet this criterion.
      3. Only unconditional promises or orders can be negotiable [UCC 3–106(a)].
   d. **State a fixed amount of money**—
      1. An amount is considered a fixed sum if it is ascertainable from the face of the instrument or (for an interest rate) readily determinable by a formula described by the instrument [UCC –104(a), 3–112(b)].
      2. Any medium of exchange recognized as the currency of a government is money [UCC 3–201(24)].
   e. **Be payable on demand or at a definite time**—
      1. Any instrument that is payable on sight, presentation, or issue, or that does not state any time for payment, is a demand instrument [UCC 3—104(a)(2)].
      2. An instrument is payable at a definite time if it states that it is payable on a stated date, within a fixed period after presentment, or on a date or time readily ascertainable at the time of issue [UCC 3–108(a), (b), (c)].
      3. Acceleration clauses allow a payee or other holder of a time instrument to demand payment of the entire amount due, with interest, if a certain event occurs. Extension clauses allow the date of maturity to be extended into the future [UCC 3-108(b)(iii), (iv)].

f. **Be payable to order or bearer—**
   1. An order instrument must identify the payee with certainty.
   2. An instrument that is not payable to an identified person is payable to bearer [UCC 3–109(a)(3)].

3. **Factors that do not affect negotiability**—Certain ambiguities (such as differences between words and figures) or omissions (such as when an instrument is undated) normally will not affect an instrument's negotiability.

Transfer of Instruments

1. **Transfer by assignment**—A transfer by assignment to an assignee gives the assignee only those rights that the assignor possessed. Any defenses against payment that can be raised against an assignor normally can be raised against the assignee.
2. **Transfer by negotiation**—An order instrument is negotiated by indorsement and delivery. A bearer instrument is negotiated by delivery only.
3. **Indorsements**—
   a. Blank indorsements do not specify a particular indorsee and can consist of a mere signature.
   b. Special indorsements contain the signature of the indorser and identify the indorsee.
   c. Qualified indorsements contain language, such as "without recourse," that indicates the indorser is not guaranteeing payment of the instrument.
   d. Restrictive indorsements, such as "For deposit only," require the indorsee to comply with certain instructions regarding the funds involved, but do not prohibit further negotiation of the instrument.

Holder in Due Course (HDC)

1. **Holder**—A person in possession of an instrument drawn, issued, or indorsed to that person, to that person's order, to bearer, or in blank. A holder obtains only those rights that the transferor had in the instrument.
2. **Holder in due course (HDC)**—A holder who, by meeting certain acquisition requirements, takes an instrument free of most defenses and claims to which the transferor was subject.
3. **Requirements for HDC status**—To be an HDC, a holder must take the instrument:
   a. For value—A holder can take an instrument for value in five ways: by performing the promise, acquiring a security interest or other lien in the instrument, taking the instrument as payment (or security) for a preexisting obligation, giving the instrument as payment, or giving an irrevocable commitment as payment [UCC 3–303].
   b. In good faith—A holder can take an instrument in good faith by acting honestly and observing commercial standards of fair dealing.
   c. Without notice—To be an HDC, a holder must not be on notice that the instrument is defective because it is overdue, has been dishonored, is part of a series of which at least one instrument has a uncured defect, contains an unauthorized signature or has been altered, has a defense against it or a claim to it, or is so irregular or incomplete as to call its authenticity into question.
4. **Shelter principle**—A holder who cannot qualify as an HDC has the *rights* of an HDC if the holder derives title through an HDC, unless the holder engaged in fraud or illegality affecting the instrument [UCC 3–203(b)] or had notice of a claim or defense against the instrument.

Signature and Warranty Liability

Liability on negotiable instruments can arise either from a person's signature or from the warranties that are implied when a person presents the instrument for negotiation.

1. **Signature liability**—Every party (except a qualified indorser) who signs a negotiable instrument is either primarily (unconditionally) or secondarily liable for payment of the instrument when it comes due.
   a. Primary liability—Makers and acceptors are primarily liable [UCC 3–115, 3–407, 3–409, 3–412].
   b. Secondary liability—Drawers and indorsers are secondarily liable [UCC 3–412, 3–414, 3–415, 3–501, 3–502, 3–503]. Parties are secondarily liable on an instrument only if presentment is proper and timely, the instrument is dishonored, and they received timely notice of dishonor.

(*Continues*)

2. **Transfer warranties**—Any person who transfers an instrument for consideration makes five warranties to subsequent transferees and holders [UCC 3–416].
   - **a.** The transferor is entitled to enforce the instrument.
   - **b.** All signatures are authentic and authorized.
   - **c.** The instrument has not been altered.
   - **d.** The instrument is not subject to a defense or claim of any party that can be asserted against the transferor.
   - **e.** The transferor has no knowledge of any bankruptcy proceedings against the maker, the acceptor, or the drawer of the instrument.
3. **Presentment warranties**—Any person who presents an instrument for payment or acceptance makes three warranties to any person who in good faith pays or accepts the instrument [UCC 3–417(a), 3–417(d)].
   - **a.** The person is entitled to enforce the instrument or is authorized to act on behalf of a person who is so entitled.
   - **b.** The instrument has not been altered.
   - **c.** The person has no knowledge that the drawer's signature is unauthorized.

Defenses, Limitations, and Discharge

1. **Universal (real) defenses**—The following defenses are valid against all holders, including HDCs and holders with the rights of HDCs [UCC 3–305, 3–403, 3–407]:
   - **a.** Forgery.
   - **b.** Fraud in the execution.
   - **c.** Material alteration.
   - **d.** Discharge in bankruptcy.
   - **e.** Minority—if the contract is voidable under state law.
   - **f.** Illegality, mental incapacity, or extreme duress—if the contract is void under state law.
2. **Personal (limited) defenses**—The following defenses are valid against ordinary holders but not against HDCs or holders with the rights of HDCs [UCC 3–303, 3–305]:
   - **a.** Breach of contract or breach of warranty.
   - **b.** Lack or failure of consideration.
   - **c.** Fraud in the inducement.
   - **d.** Illegality, mental incapacity, or ordinary duress–if the contract is voidable.
3. **Federal limitations on the rights of HDCs**—Rule 433 of the Federal Trade Commission limits the rights of HDCs who purchase instruments arising out of consumer transactions. The rule allows a consumer who is a party to such a transaction to bring any defense the consumer has against the seller against a subsequent holder as well, even if the subsequent holder is an HDC.
4. **Discharge from liability**—All parties to a negotiable instrument will be discharged when the party primarily liable on it pays to the holder the full amount due. Discharge can also occur in other circumstances (if the instrument has been canceled or materially altered, for example) [UCC 3–602 through 3–605].

Issue Spotters

1. Sabrina owes $600 to Yale, who asks Sabrina to sign an instrument for the debt. If written on the instrument by Sabrina, which of the following would prevent its negotiability: "I.O.U. $600," "I promise to pay $600," or an instruction to the bank stating, "I wish you would pay $600 to Yale"? Why? (See *Formation of Negotiable Instruments.*)
2. Rye signs corporate checks for Suchin Corporation. Rye writes a check payable to U-All Company, even though Suchin does not owe U-All anything. Rye signs the check, forges U-All's indorsement, and cashes the check at Viceroy Bank, the drawee. Does Suchin have any recourse against the bank for the payment? Why or why not? (See *Signature and Warranty Liability.*)

—Check your answers to the *Issue Spotters* against the answers provided in Appendix D.

Business Scenarios and Case Problems

18–1. Negotiable Instruments. Muriel Evans writes the following note on the back of an envelope: "I, Muriel Evans, promise to pay Karen Marvin or bearer $100 on demand." Is this a negotiable instrument? Discuss fully. (See *Formation of Negotiable Instruments.*)

18–2. Material Alteration. Williams purchased a used car from Stein for $1,000. Williams paid for the car with a check (written in pencil) payable to Stein for $1,000. Stein, through careful erasures and alterations, changed the amount on the check to read $10,000 and negotiated the check to Boz. Boz took the check for value, in good faith, and without notice of the alteration and thus met the Uniform Commercial Code's requirements for the status of a holder in due course. Can Williams successfully raise the universal (real) defense of material alteration to avoid payment on the check? Explain. (See *Defenses, Limitations, and Discharge.*)

18–3. Indorsements. Angela Brock borrowed $544,000 and signed a note payable to Amerifund Mortgage Services, LLC, to buy a house in Silver Spring, Maryland. The note was indorsed in blank and transferred several times "without recourse" before Brock fell behind on the payments. On behalf of Deutsche Bank National Trust Co., BAC Home Loans Servicing LP initiated foreclosure. Brock filed an action in a Maryland state court to block it, arguing that BAC could not foreclose because Deutsche Bank, not BAC, owned the note. Can BAC enforce the note? Explain. [*Deutsche Bank National Trust Co. v. Brock*, 63 A.3d 40 (Md. 2013)] (See *Transfer of Instruments.*)

18–4. Transfer by Negotiation. Thao Thi Duong signed a note in the amount of $200,000 in favor of Country Home Loans, Inc., to obtain a loan to buy a house in Marrero, Louisiana. The note was indorsed "PAY TO THE ORDER OF [blank space] WITHOUT RECOURSE COUNTRY HOME LOANS, INC." Almost five years later, Duong defaulted on the payments. The Federal National Mortgage Association (Fannie Mae) had come into possession of the note. Fannie Mae wanted to foreclose on the house and sell it to recover the balance due. Duong argued that the words "to the order of [blank space]" in the indorsement made the note an incomplete order instrument and that Fannie Mae thus could not enforce it. What is Fannie Mae's best response to this argument? [*Federal National Mortgage Association v. Thao Thi Duong*, 167 So.3d 920 (La.App. 5 Cir. 2015)] (See *Transfer of Instruments.*)

18–5. Payable to Order or to Bearer. Thomas Caraccia signed a note and mortgage in favor of VirtualBank to obtain funds to buy property in Palm Beach Gardens, Florida. VirtualBank indorsed the note in blank, making it bearer paper, and transferred possession of the note to Bank of America. Bank of America transferred the note to U.S. Bank, which later gave the note back to Bank of America to collect Caraccia's payments on behalf of U.S. Bank. When Caraccia defaulted on the payments, U.S. Bank filed a suit in a Florida state court against him, seeking to enforce the note and foreclose on the property. Caraccia contended that because the note was indorsed in blank and was not in the physical possession of U.S. Bank, the bank could not enforce it. Could the bank successfully argue that although it did not *physically* possess the note, it *constructively* possessed (exercised legal control over) it? Explain. [*Caraccia v. U.S. Bank, National Association*, 41 Fla.L.Weekly. D476, 185 So.3d 1277 (Dist.Ct.App. 2016)] (See *Formation of Negotiable Instruments.*)

18–6. Business Case Problem with Sample Answer—Signature Liability. Guillermo and Guadalupe Albarran and their sons, Ruben and Rolando, owned R Cleaning Impact, Inc. (RCI). Neresh Kumar owned Amba II, Inc., a check-cashing business. The Albarrans cashed checks through Amba on a regular basis, often delivering a stack of employee paychecks to Amba for cashing. Later, the Albarrans' bank refused payment on some of the checks. Kumar learned that some of these items were payable to fictitious payees with fictitious addresses. Others had been filled out for amounts greater than real employees' pay. Meanwhile, RCI became insolvent and closed its account, and Guillermo and Guadalupe filed for bankruptcy. Amba was left with many unpaid checks. Among these parties, who can be held liable for the loss on the unpaid checks? Explain. [*Albarran v. Amba II, Inc.*, 2016 WL 688924 (Md. 2016)] (See *Signature and Warranty Liability.*)

—For a sample answer to Problem 18–6, go to Appendix E.

18–7. Holder in Due Course. Robert Triffin purchased a dishonored payroll check from Fair Law Financial Services (doing business as United Check Cashing) and filed a complaint against the maker seeking to collect on the check. The check was issued by Extensis Group, LLC, to Maria Pagan in the amount of $610. The face of the check clearly stated "THE FACE OF THIS DOCUMENT HAS A COLORED BACKGROUND NOT A WHITE BACKGROUND." But the check that Triffin introduced into evidence had a white background. The check also stated "THE BACK OF THIS DOCUMENT CONTAINS A UNIQUE IDENTITY BARCODE AND AN ARTIFICIAL WATERMARK—HOLD AT AN ANGLE TO VIEW," but Triffin's check did not have this barcode or watermark. Was Triffin an HDC? Why or why not? [*Triffin v. Extensis Group, LLC*, 2018 WL 548613 (N.J.Super.Ct.App.Div. 2018)] (*See Holder in Due Course.*)

18–8. A Question of Ethics—The IDDR Approach and Unconditional Promise or Order to Pay. Carlos Pardo signed a note to obtain $627,500 to buy a house in Stamford, Connecticut. The note was secured by a mortgage. Later, Pardo signed a loan modification agreement that increased the balance due. The modification was not referenced in the note. Deutsche Bank National Trust Company came to possess the note. When Pardo defaulted on the payments, Deutsche Bank filed a suit in a Connecticut state court against him to recover the unpaid balance. Pardo maintained that the bank could not enforce the note. He argued that the bank was not a holder because the note was not a negotiable instrument—the loan modification agreement rendered it conditional. [*Deutsche Bank National Trust Co. v. Pardo,* 170 Conn.App. 642, 155 A.3d 764 (2017)] (See *Formation of Negotiable Instruments.*)

1. Was it ethical of Deutsche Bank to sue to recover the unpaid balance on Pardo's note? Explain, using the steps of the IDDR approach.
2. Is Pardo correct about the status of the note? Was it ethical to make this argument? Discuss.

Critical Thinking and Writing Assignments

18–9. Time-Limited Group Assignment—Negotiability. Peter Gowin was an employee of a granite countertop business owned by Joann Stathis. In November 2022, Gowin signed a promissory note agreeing to pay $12,500 in order to become a co-owner of the business. The note was dated January 15, 2022 (ten months before it was signed), and required him to make installment payments starting in February 2022. Stathis told Gowin not to worry about the note and never requested any payments. Gowin continued to work at the business until 2024, when he quit, claiming that he owned half of the business. Stathis argued that Gowin was not a co-owner because he had never paid the $12,500 into the business. (See *Formation of Negotiable Instruments.*)

1. The first group will argue in favor of Stathis that Gowin did not own any interest in the business.
2. The second group will evaluate the strength of Gowin's argument. Gowin claimed that because compliance with the stated dates was impossible, the note effectively did not state a date for its payment. It therefore was a demand note under UCC 3–108(a). Because no demand for payment had been made, Gowin's obligation to pay had not arisen, and the termination of his ownership interest was improper.
3. The third group will create a list with expanation and examples detailing under what circumstances oral statements by Stathis to Gowin can be enforced or can be used as a defense by Gowin.

19

International and Space Law

Commerce has always crossed national borders, as President Thomas Jefferson noted in the chapter-opening quotation. But technology has fueled dramatic growth in world trade and the emergence of a global business community. Because exchanges of goods, services, and intellectual property on a global level are now routine, students of business law and the legal environment should be familiar with the laws pertaining to international business transactions.

"The merchant has no country."

Thomas Jefferson
1743–1826
(Third president of the United States, 1801–1809)

Suppose that Ryan, a popular Olympic snowboarder, starts an outdoor-wear business and begins manufacturing his own snowboarding gear. The business grows, and Ryan's factory is no longer able to keep up with the demand for his products. Ryan is considering opening a manufacturing plant in Vietnam, where labor costs are lower and there are fewer government regulations. Before he decides, he needs to understand the relevant laws. He also needs to know how the business will be taxed when his goods are imported back into the United States or shipped to other nations. This chapter introduces you to some of the legal considerations involved in doing business globally, including the emerging area of space law.

Focus Questions

The five Focus Questions *below are designed to help improve your understanding. After reading this chapter, you should be able to answer the following questions:*

1. What is the act of state doctrine? In what circumstances is this doctrine applied?
2. Why would a U.S. firm enter into a distribution agreement?
3. What does it mean for the World Trade Organization to grant "normal trade relations status"?
4. What federal law allows U.S. citizens, as well as citizens of foreign nations, to file civil actions in U.S. courts for torts that were committed overseas?
5. What treaty provides a framework for international space law?

19–1 International Law

Laws affecting the international legal environment of business include both international law and national law. **International law** can be defined as a body of law—formed as a result of international customs, treaties, and organizations—that governs relations among or between nations. **National law** is the law of a particular nation, such as Brazil, Germany, Japan, or the United States.

International Law Law—based on international customs, organizations, and treaties—that governs relations among nations.

National Law Law that pertains to a particular nation.

The major difference between international law and national law is that a nation's government authorities can enforce its national law. What government, however, can enforce international law? By definition, a *nation* is a sovereign entity—meaning that there is no higher authority to which that nation must submit.

If a nation violates an international law and persuasive tactics fail, other countries or international organizations have no recourse except to take coercive actions. Coercive actions may include economic sanctions, severance of diplomatic relations, boycotts, and, as a last resort, war against the violating nation. **Example 19.1** North Korea has repeatedly conducted tests of nuclear weapons and ballistic missiles in violation of international law. In response, the United States and the European Union (EU) have imposed numerous economic sanctions against North Korea, including an embargo on imports of oil and exports of coal.

vchal/Shutterstock.com

How have the United States and other countries reacted to North Korea's lack of regard for international law when it comes to testing nuclear missiles?

In essence, international law is the result of centuries-old attempts to reconcile the need of each country to be the final authority over its own affairs with the desire of nations to benefit economically from trade and harmonious relations with one another. Sovereign nations can, and do, voluntarily agree to be governed in certain respects by international law for the purpose of facilitating international trade and commerce, as well as civilized discourse. As a result, a body of international law has evolved.

19–1a Sources of International Law

Basically, there are three sources of international law: international customs, treaties and international agreements, and international organizations.

International Customs One important source of international law consists of the customs that have evolved among nations in their relations with one another. Article 38(1) of the Statute of the International Court of Justice refers to an international custom as "evidence of a general practice accepted as law." The legal principles and doctrines that you will read about shortly are rooted in international customs and traditions that have evolved over time in the international arena.

Treaty A formal international agreement negotiated between two nations or among several nations.

Treaties and International Agreements Treaties and other explicit agreements between or among foreign nations provide another important source of international law. A **treaty** is an agreement or contract between two or more nations that must be authorized and ratified by the supreme power of each nation. Under Article II, Section 2, of the U.S. Constitution, the president has the power "by and with the Advice and Consent of the Senate, to make Treaties, provided two thirds of the Senators present concur."

A *bilateral* agreement, as the term implies, is an agreement formed by two nations to govern their commercial exchanges or other relations with one another. A *multilateral* agreement is formed by several nations. For instance, regional trade associations such as the Andean Common Market (ANCOM), the Association of Southeast Asian Nations (ASEAN), and the European Union (EU) are the result of multilateral trade agreements.

International Organization An organization composed mainly of member nations and usually established by treaty—for instance, the United Nations. More broadly, the term also includes nongovernmental organizations (NGOs), such as the Red Cross.

International Organizations In international law, the term **international organization** generally refers to an organization that is composed mainly of member nations and usually established by treaty. The United States is a member of more than one hundred bilateral and multilateral organizations, including at least twenty through the United Nations.

Adopt Standards. International organizations adopt resolutions, declarations, and other types of standards that often require nations to behave in a particular manner. The General Assembly of the United Nations, for instance, has adopted numerous nonbinding resolutions and declarations that embody principles of international law. Disputes involving these resolutions and declarations may be brought before the International Court of Justice. That court, however, normally has authority to settle legal disputes only when nations voluntarily submit to its jurisdiction.

Create Uniform Rules. International organizations may also create uniform rules. The United Nations Commission on International Trade Law has made considerable progress in establishing uniformity in international law as it relates to trade. One of the commission's most significant creations to date is the 1980 Convention on Contracts for the International Sale of Goods (CISG).

The CISG is similar to Article 2 of the Uniform Commercial Code. It is designed to settle disputes between parties to sales contracts if the parties have not agreed otherwise in their contracts. The CISG governs only sales contracts between trading partners in nations that have ratified the CISG.

19–1b International Principles and Doctrines

Over time, a number of legal principles and doctrines have evolved and have been employed by the courts of various nations to resolve or reduce conflicts that involve a foreign element. The three important legal principles and doctrines discussed next are based primarily on courtesy and respect, and are applied in the interests of maintaining harmonious relations among nations.

The Principle of Comity

Under the principle of **comity,** one nation will defer to and give effect to the laws and judicial decrees of another country, as long as they are consistent with the law and public policy of the accommodating nation. For instance, a U.S. court ordinarily will recognize and enforce a default judgment from an Australian court because the legal procedures in Australia are compatible with those in the United States. Nearly all nations recognize the validity of marriage decrees (at least, those between a man and a woman) issued in another country.

Comity The principle by which one nation defers to and gives effect to the laws and judicial decrees of another nation. This deference is based primarily on respect.

Case Example 19.2 MD Helicopters, Inc., based in Arizona, failed to deliver eight helicopters to the Netherlands (Dutch) National Police Services Agency. The National Police successfully sued MD for breach of contract in Dutch court proceedings. The Netherlands government, representing its police force, then brought a suit in Arizona to compel MD to pay the prescribed damages. The Netherlands based its claim on an Arizona statute that recognizes foreign-country judgments if the relevant laws of that country are "similar" to those of Arizona.

MD countered that no Netherlands *law* addressed the issues relating to its dispute with the National Police. Rather, only Dutch *court decisions* did so. A state appeals court rejected this argument, finding that a party seeking damages would follow essentially the same legal procedures in the Netherlands as in Arizona. Therefore, the court ordered MD to pay the National Police nearly $15 million, as determined by the Dutch court.[1]

Foto11/Shutterstock.com

Under what circumstances would an Arizona court order an Arizona helicopter company to pay damages determined by the ruling of a Dutch court?

The Act of State Doctrine

The **act of state doctrine** provides that the judicial branch of one country will not examine the validity of public acts committed by a recognized foreign government within its own territory.

Act of State Doctrine A doctrine providing that the judicial branch of one country will not examine the validity of public acts committed by a recognized foreign government within its own territory.

Case Example 19.3 Under regulations set by the Liquor Control Board of Ontario (LCBO), Brewers Retails, Inc. (BRI), stores were the only establishments in the province of Ontario, Canada, permitted to sell units of beer larger than a six pack. BRI stores were controlled by two large beer companies, Anheuser-Busch and Molson Coors. Mountain Crest, an independent brewer based in Wisconsin, filed a suit, claiming that the six-pack rule violated U.S. anti-monopoly law.

---

1. *State of Netherlands v. MD Helicopters, Inc.*, 462 P.3d 1038 (Ariz. Ct. App. Div. 1 2020).

Focus Question 1

What is the act of state doctrine? In what circumstances is this doctrine applied?

A federal appeals court held that this legal challenge to the six-pack rule was barred by the act of state doctrine. U.S. courts will not rule on the validity of regulatory decisions made by foreign governments. The court did find, however, that Mountain Crest could sue Anheuser-Busch and Molson Coors for illegally conspiring to bring about the LCBO's monopolistic policy, which clearly harmed Mountain Crest's ability to compete in the Ontario beer market.[2]

When a Foreign Government Takes Private Property. The act of state doctrine can have important consequences for individuals and firms doing business with, and investing in, other countries. This doctrine is frequently employed in situations involving expropriation or confiscation.

Expropriation A government's seizure of a privately owned business or personal property for a proper public purpose and with just compensation.

Confiscation A government's taking of a privately owned business or personal property without a proper public purpose or an award of just compensation.

Expropriation occurs when a government seizes a privately owned business or privately owned goods for a proper public purpose and awards just compensation. When a government seizes private property for an illegal purpose or without just compensation, the taking is referred to as a **confiscation.** The line between these two forms of taking is sometimes blurred because of differing interpretations of what is illegal and what constitutes just compensation.

Example 19.4 Flaherty, Inc., a U.S. company, owns a mine in Brazil. The government of Brazil seizes the mine for public use and claims that the profits that Flaherty realized from the mine in preceding years constitute just compensation. Flaherty disagrees, but the act of state doctrine may prevent the company's recovery in a U.S. court. Note that in a case alleging that a foreign government has wrongfully taken the plaintiff's property, the defendant government has the burden of proving that the taking was an expropriation, not a confiscation.

Doctrine May Immunize a Foreign Government's Actions. When applicable, both the act of state doctrine and the doctrine of *sovereign immunity* (to be discussed next) tend to shield foreign nations from the jurisdiction of U.S. courts. As a result, firms or individuals who own property overseas generally have little legal protection against government actions in the countries in which they operate.

Sovereign Immunity A doctrine that immunizes foreign nations from the jurisdiction of U.S. courts when certain conditions are satisfied.

Case Example 19.5 In 2017, a federal district court ruled that the United States had jurisdiction over an art theft claim against Germany that dated back to the Nazi regime. The plaintiffs, including Alan Philipp, were descendants of Jewish art dealers in Frankfurt who had owned the Welfenschatz collection of medieval art. The plaintiffs argued that the art dealers had been terrorized by the Nazis and forced to sell the collection in 1935 for much less than its market value. (Adolf Hitler had allegedly discussed in letters how Nazis should take action to "save the Welfenschatz.") Germany claimed that the U.S. court did not have jurisdiction, but the federal judge disagreed. The court was convinced by the plaintiffs that Germany was not entitled to sovereign immunity in this case.[3]

TOBIAS SCHWARZ/Getty Images

In the 1930s, Germany's Nazi regime forced a group of Jewish art dealers to sell a famous collection of medieval art. Years later, was Germany entitled to sovereign immunity when Jewish descendants sued to have the artworks returned?

The Doctrine of Sovereign Immunity

When certain conditions are satisfied, the doctrine of **sovereign immunity** immunizes foreign nations from the jurisdiction of U.S. courts. In 1976, Congress codified this rule in the Foreign Sovereign Immunities Act (FSIA).[4] The FSIA exclusively governs the circumstances in which an action may be brought in the United States against a foreign nation, including attempts to attach a foreign nation's property. Because the law is jurisdictional in nature, a plaintiff has the burden of showing that a defendant is not entitled to sovereign immunity.

2. *Mountain Crest SRL, LLC v. Anheuser-Busch InBev SA/NV*, 937 F.3d 1067 (7th Cir. 2019).
3. *Philipp v. Federal Republic of Germany*, 248 F.Supp.3d 59 (D.C.C. 2017).
4. 28 U.S.C. Sections 1602–1611.

When a Foreign State Will Not Be Immune. Section 1605 of the FSIA sets forth the major exceptions to the jurisdictional immunity of a foreign state. A foreign state is not immune from the jurisdiction of U.S. courts in the following situations:

1. When the foreign state has waived its immunity either explicitly or by implication.
2. When the foreign state has engaged in commercial activity within the United States or in commercial activity outside the United States that has "a direct effect in the United States."
3. When the foreign state has committed a tort in the United States or has violated certain international laws.
4. When a foreign state that has been designated "a state sponsor of terrorism" is sued under the FSIA for "personal injury or death that was caused by an act of torture" or a related act of terrorism.

The following case involved an action to attach and execute a judgment against the property of a foreign state that had been held liable for the results of acts of terrorism.

Case 19.1

Rubin v. Islamic Republic of Iran

Supreme Court of the United States, 583 U.S. __, 138 S.Ct. 816, 200 L.Ed.2d 58 (2018).

Facts Hamas, a terrorist organization sponsored by the Islamic Republic of Iran, carried out three suicide bombings in Jerusalem, causing the deaths of five people and injuring nearly two hundred others. Jenny Rubin and other U.S. citizens who were injured or related to those injured obtained a judgment under Section 1605A of the Foreign Sovereign Immunities Act (FSIA) against Iran for $71.5 million in damages.

To collect on the judgment, the plaintiffs sued Iran in a federal district court under Section 1610(g) of the FSIA. The plaintiffs sought to attach and execute against a collection of ancient art owned by Iran that was being housed at the University of Chicago. The court ruled in the defendant's favor, finding that Section 1610(g) did not deprive the art collection of the immunity typically afforded to the property of a foreign sovereign. The plaintiffs appealed. The U.S. Court of Appeals for the Seventh Circuit affirmed. The plaintiffs petitioned the United States Supreme Court.

Issue Does Section 1610(g) apply only when the property of a foreign state is exempt from immunity as provided under other subsections of the statute?

Decision Yes. The United States Supreme Court concluded that Section 1610(g) does not provide "a freestanding basis for parties holding a judgment under Section 1605A to attach and execute against the property of a foreign state." The Court affirmed the judgment of the federal appellate court.

Reason Section 1610(g) provides, "The property of a foreign state against which a judgment is entered under Section 1605A . . . is subject to attachment in aid of execution, and execution, upon that judgment as provided in this section." The Court read "as provided in this section" to refer to Section 1610 as a whole. Thus, Section 1610(g) is not "an independent avenue for abrogation [abolition] of immunity." The subsection governs attachment and execution against property that is exempt from immunity only as provided elsewhere in Section 1610. The holder of a judgment must identify a basis under one of its other provisions to attach and execute against relevant property. For example, Section 1610(a) provides that property used for a commercial activity in the United States is not immune from attachment and execution in seven specific circumstances. Section 1610(b), (d), (e), and (f) set out other circumstances in which certain property of a foreign state "shall not be immune."

Critical Thinking

- **Legal Environment** *Is the Court's interpretation of Section 1610(g) consistent with the purpose of the FSIA? Explain.*
- **Economic** *What practical lesson might be learned from the decision and result in the* Rubin *case? Discuss.*

Exhibit 19–1 Examples of International Principles and Doctrines

The Principle of Comity	The Act of State Doctrine	The Doctrine of Sovereign Immunity
Nations will defer and give effect to the laws and judicial decrees of other nations when those laws are consistent with their own.	**U.S. courts will avoid passing judgment on the validity of public acts committed by a recognized foreign government within its own territory.**	**Foreign nations are immune from U.S. jurisdiction under the Foreign Sovereign Immunities Act when certain circumstances are satisfied. Some major exceptions apply.**
Example: A U.S. court will most likely uphold the validity of a contract created in England, because England's legal procedures are compatible with those in the United States.	***Example:*** A U.S. gas company files a lawsuit against a Saudi Arabian petroleum company, claiming a price-fixing conspiracy. A U.S. court will dismiss the case under the act of state doctrine because Saudi Arabia controls its own natural resources.	***Example:*** A German governmental agency engages in commercial activity in New York. If a party in New York files a lawsuit against the agency, the foreign state is not immune from U.S. jurisdiction.

Application of the Act. When courts apply the FSIA, questions frequently arise as to whether an entity is a "foreign state" and what constitutes a "commercial activity." Under Section 1603 of the FSIA, a *foreign state* includes both a political subdivision of a foreign state and an instrumentality of a foreign state. An *instrumentality* includes any department or agency of any branch of a government.

Section 1603 broadly defines a *commercial activity* as a regular course of commercial conduct, transaction, or act that is carried out by a foreign state within the United States. Section 1603, however, does not describe the particulars of what constitutes a commercial activity. Thus, the courts are left to decide whether a particular activity is governmental or commercial in nature. (This chapter's *Business Law Analysis* feature illustrates how courts decide whether an activity is commercial.) See Exhibit 19–1 for a graphic illustration of the three principles of international law discussed.

Sovereign Immunity Claims

Business Law Analysis

Taconic Plastics, Ltd., is a manufacturer incorporated in Ireland with its principal place of business in New York. Taconic enters into a contract with a German firm, Werner Voss Architects and Engineers, which is acting as an agent for the government of Saudi Arabia. The contract calls for Taconic to supply special materials for tents designed to shelter religious pilgrims visiting holy sites in Saudi Arabia. Most of the material is made in, and shipped from, New York. When the German company does not pay Taconic and files for bankruptcy, Taconic sues the government of Saudi Arabia in a U.S. court, seeking to collect $3 million. Is Saudi Arabia entitled to sovereign immunity?

Analysis: Under the doctrine of sovereign immunity, foreign nations are presumed to be immune from the jurisdiction of U.S. courts unless one of the exceptions in the Foreign Sovereign Immunity Act (FSIA) applies. One of the main exceptions under the FSIA is the commercial activity exception. A government undertaking qualifies as commercial activity when the government acts as a "private player" in the marketplace. Here, the German firm was acting as an agent for Saudi Arabia. The agency relationship allowed Saudi Arabia to "step into the shoes" of a private player—the German construction firm—to complete the tent project.

Result and Reasoning: Based on these facts, Saudi Arabia should not be entitled to sovereign immunity. The government of Saudi Arabia was acting as a private company through its German agent to contract with Taconic in the United States. Also, substantial parts of the contract were performed in the United States because the materials for the tents were made in New York and shipped to Germany. Thus, the U.S. courts should have jurisdiction over this claim against Saudi Arabia.

19–2 Doing Business Internationally

A U.S. domestic firm can engage in international business transactions in a number of ways. The simplest way is for U.S. firms to **export** their goods and services to markets abroad. Alternatively, a U.S. firm can establish foreign production facilities so as to be closer to the foreign market or markets in which its products are sold.

Export The sale of goods and services by domestic firms to buyers located in other countries.

Ethical Issue

Is it ethical (and legal) to brew "imported" beer brands domestically? One-quarter of the beer sold in the United States is imported. Imported beer typically costs more than domestic beer, but the people who buy and drink it believe that its superior taste justifies the higher price. Many consumers are unaware that beers marketed as imported are often made in the United States. For instance, people think of Beck's beer as German, but for a number of years, Beck's has been brewed in St. Louis, Missouri. Foster's beer ads feature Australian countryside scenes, yet Foster's is brewed in Fort Worth, Texas. Killian's Irish Red is brewed in Colorado, not in Ireland. The Japanese beer Sapporo sold in the United States is actually brewed in Canada.

A number of lawsuits have been filed against the owners of imported beer brands made in the United States for misleading country-of-origin labels. One such suit was filed against Anheuser-Busch Companies, LLC, for mislabeling the origin of Beck's beer. The plaintiffs argued that labels, such as "brewed under the German Purity Law" and "originated in Bremen, German," were misleading because the beer was brewed in the United States. The defendants pointed out that each beer bottle stated that it was a "Product of U.S.A." The case was ultimately settled out of court, and the company gave purchasers a right to apply for up to $50 in refunds.[5] Another case was filed in New York against Sapporo U.S.A., Inc., for misleading labels. A federal district court dismissed that action, however, because the beer label clearly stated it was "Brewed and canned [or bottled] by Sapporo Brewing Company, Guelph, Ontario, Canada."[6]

5. *Marty v. Anheuser-Busch Companies, LLC*, 43 F.Supp.3d 1333 (S.D. Fl. 2014), and 2016 WL 397593 (S.D. Fl. 2016).
6. *Bowring v. Sapporo U.S.A., Inc.*, 234 F.Supp.3d 386 (E.D.N.Y. 2017).

19–2a Exporting

Exporting can take two forms: direct and indirect. In *direct exporting*, a U.S. company signs a sales contract with a foreign purchaser that provides for the conditions of shipment and payment for the goods. If sufficient business develops in a foreign country, a U.S. company may set up a specialized marketing organization in that country. This is called *indirect exporting* and may be accomplished through the use of an agency relationship or a distributorship.

Agency Relationships When a U.S. firm prefers to limit its involvement in an international market, it will typically establish an *agency relationship* with a foreign firm. The foreign firm then acts as the U.S. firm's agent and can enter into contracts in the foreign location on behalf of the principal (the U.S. company).

Distribution Agreement
A contract between a seller and a distributor of the seller's products setting out the terms and conditions of the distributorship.

Distributorships When a foreign country represents a substantial market, a U.S. firm may wish to appoint a distributor located in that country. The U.S. firm and the distributor enter into a **distribution agreement.** This is a contract setting out the terms and conditions of the distributorship, such as price, currency of payment, guarantee of supply availability, and method of payment. Disputes concerning distribution agreements may involve jurisdictional or other issues, as well as contract law.

19–2b Manufacturing Abroad

An alternative to direct or indirect exporting is the establishment of foreign manufacturing facilities. The advantages of manufacturing abroad may include lower costs, fewer government regulations, and lower taxes and trade barriers.

Typically, U.S. firms establish manufacturing plants abroad if they believe that doing so will reduce their costs—particularly for labor, shipping, and raw materials. Lower costs will enable the firms to compete more effectively in foreign markets. Japanese manufacturers, such as Canon, Hitachi, and Toyota, have established U.S. plants to avoid import duties that the U.S. Congress may impose on Japanese products entering this country.

A domestic firm may engage in manufacturing abroad by licensing its technology to an existing foreign company. Alternatively, it may establish overseas subsidiaries or participate in joint ventures.

Focus Question 2
Why would a U.S. firm enter into a distribution agreement?

Licensing A U.S. firm may license a foreign manufacturing company to use its copyrighted, patented, or trademarked intellectual property or trade secrets. A licensing agreement with a foreign-based firm is much the same as any other licensing agreement. Its terms require a payment of royalties on some basis—such as so many cents per unit produced or a certain percentage of profits from units sold in a particular geographic territory. **Example 19.6** The Coca-Cola Bottling Company licenses firms worldwide to use (and keep confidential) its secret formula for the syrup used in its soft drink. In return, the foreign firms licensed to make the syrup pay Coca-Cola a percentage of the income earned from the sale of the soft drink. ■

The firm that receives the license can take advantage of an established reputation for quality. The firm that grants the license receives income from the foreign sales of its products and also establishes a global reputation. Once a firm's trademark is known worldwide, the demand for other products manufactured or sold by that firm may increase. Franchising is a well-known form of licensing.

Subsidiaries A U.S. firm can also expand into a foreign market by establishing a wholly owned subsidiary firm in a foreign country. When a wholly owned subsidiary is established, the parent company, which remains in the United States, retains complete ownership of all the facilities in the foreign country, as well as complete authority and control over all phases of the operation.

Joint Ventures A *joint venture* provides another method that a U.S. firm can use to expand into international markets. In a joint venture, the U.S. company owns only part of the operation. The rest is owned either by local owners in the foreign country or by another foreign entity. All of the firms involved in a joint venture share responsibilities, as well as profits and liabilities.

19–2c International Dispute Resolution

International contracts frequently include arbitration clauses. By means of such clauses, the parties agree in advance to be bound by the decision of a specified third party in the event of a dispute.

The New York Convention The United Nations Convention on the Recognition and Enforcement of Foreign Arbitral Awards (often referred to as the *New York Convention*) assists in the enforcement of arbitration clauses, as do provisions in specific treaties among nations. The New York Convention has 164 parties, including the United States. Over two dozen parties have ratified this treaty.

Under the New York Convention, a U.S. court will compel the parties to arbitrate their dispute if all of the following are true:

1. There is a written (or electronically recorded) agreement to arbitrate the matter.
2. The agreement provides for arbitration in a convention signatory nation.
3. The agreement arises out of a commercial legal relationship.
4. One party to the agreement is not a U.S. citizen. In other words, both parties cannot be U.S. citizens.

Spotlight Case Example 19.7 Juridica Investments, Ltd. (JIL), entered into a financing contract with S&T Oil Equipment & Machinery, Ltd., a U.S. company. The contract was signed and performed in Guernsey, which is a British Crown dependency located in the English Channel. The contract included an arbitration clause. When a dispute arose between the parties, JIL initiated arbitration in Guernsey, and S&T filed a suit in a U.S. court. JIL filed a motion to dismiss in favor of arbitration, which the court granted. S&T appealed.

A federal appellate court affirmed and compelled arbitration under the New York Convention. The court explained that all of the necessary requirements for compelling arbitration had been met.[7]

Effect of Choice-of-Law and Forum-Selection Clauses If an international contract does not include an arbitration clause, litigation may occur. When the contract contains forum-selection and choice-of-law clauses, the lawsuit will be heard by a court in the specified forum and decided according to that forum's law.

As you may recall, a **forum-selection clause** indicates what court, jurisdiction, or tribunal will decide any disputes arising under the contract. A **choice-of-law clause** designates the applicable law. Both are useful additions to international contracts.

Forum-Selection Clause A provision in a contract designating the court, jurisdiction, or tribunal that will decide any disputes arising under the contract.

Choice-of-Law Clause A clause in a contract designating the law (such as the law of a particular state or nation) that will govern the contract.

©Roberto Giobbi/Shutterstock.com

How did the New York Convention affect S&T Oil's contract with an investment company?

19–3 Regulation of Specific Business Activities

Doing business abroad can affect the economies, foreign policies, domestic policies, and other national interests of the countries involved. For this reason, nations impose laws to restrict or facilitate international business. Controls may also be imposed by international agreements. Here, we discuss how different types of international activities are regulated.

7. *S&T Oil Equipment & Machinery, Ltd. v. Juridica Investments, Ltd.*, 456 Fed.Appx. 481 (5th Cir. 2012).

19–3a Investment Protections

Firms that invest in foreign nations face the risk that the foreign government may take possession of the investment property. Expropriation, as already mentioned, occurs when property is taken and the owner is paid just compensation. Expropriation generally does not violate observed principles of international law.

Confiscation occurs when property is taken without compensation (or without adequate compensation). Unlike expropriation, confiscation normally violates international law. Few remedies are available for confiscation of property by a foreign government, however. Claims are often resolved by lump-sum settlements after negotiations between the United States and the taking nation.

Because the possibility of confiscation may deter potential investors, many countries guarantee that foreign investors will be compensated if their property is taken. A guaranty can take the form of statutory laws or provisions in international treaties. As further protection for foreign investments, some countries provide insurance for their citizens' investments abroad.

19–3b Export Controls

The U.S. Constitution provides in Article I, Section 9, that "No Tax or Duty shall be laid on Articles exported from any State." Thus, Congress cannot impose export taxes. Congress can, however, use a variety of other methods to restrict or encourage exports, including the following:

Know This
Countries restrict exports for several reasons, including to protect national security, to further foreign policy objectives, and to conserve resources (or raise their prices).

1. *Export quotas.* Congress sets export quotas on various items, such as grain being sold abroad.
2. *Restrictions on technology exports.* Under the Export Administration Act,[8] the flow of technologically advanced products and technical data can be restricted.
3. *Incentives and subsidies.* Incentives and subsidies are used to stimulate some exports and thereby aid domestic businesses. **Example 19.8** The Export Trading Company Act[9] encouraged U.S. banks to invest in export trading companies, which are formed when exporting firms join together to export a line of goods. The Export-Import Bank of the United States has provided financial assistance, primarily in the form of credit guaranties given to commercial banks that, in turn, lend funds to U.S. exporting companies. ■

19–3c Import Controls

Import restrictions include strict prohibitions, quotas, and tariffs. Under the Trading with the Enemy Act,[10] for instance, no goods may be imported from nations that have been designated enemies of the United States. Other laws prohibit the importation of illegal drugs and agricultural products that pose dangers to domestic crops or animals. The import of goods that infringe U.S. patents is also prohibited. The International Trade Commission investigates allegations that imported goods infringe U.S. patents. The commission imposes penalties if necessary.

Quota A set limit on the amount of goods that can be imported.

Quotas A limit on the amount of goods that can be imported is known as a **quota.** At one time, the United States had legal quotas on the number of automobiles that could be imported from Japan. Today, Japan "voluntarily" restricts the number of automobiles exported to the United States. (But Japanese automakers build most cars sold in the United States in U.S. factories.)

---

8. 50 U.S.C. Sections 2401–2420.
9. 15 U.S.C. Sections 4001, 4003.
10. 12 U.S.C. Section 95a.

Tariffs A tax on imports is called a **tariff.** A tariff usually is a percentage of the value of the import, but it can be a flat rate per unit (per barrel of oil, for example). Tariffs raise the prices of imported goods. The effect is to cause some consumers to purchase more domestically manufactured goods.

Tariff A tax on imported goods.

Antidumping Duties The United States has specific laws directed at what it sees as unfair international trade practices. **Dumping,** for instance, is the sale of imported goods at "less than fair value." *Fair value* is usually based on the price of those goods in the exporting country. Foreign firms that engage in dumping in the United States hope to undersell U.S. businesses to obtain a larger share of the U.S. market. To prevent this, an extra tariff—known as an *antidumping duty*—may be assessed on the imports. The duty may be retroactive to cover past dumping.

Dumping The sale of goods in a foreign country at a price below the price charged for the same goods in the domestic market.

Two U.S. government agencies are instrumental in imposing antidumping duties: the International Trade Commission (ITC) and the International Trade Administration (ITA). The ITC assesses the effects of dumping on domestic businesses and then makes recommendations to the president concerning temporary import restrictions. The ITA, which is part of the Department of Commerce, decides whether imports were sold at less than fair value. The ITA's determination establishes the amount of antidumping duties, which equals the difference between the price charged in the United States and the price charged in the exporting country.

In the following case, a Chinese producer and importer challenged the ITC's determination that the import of their products into the United States materially injured the domestic industry.

Case 19.2

Changzhou Trina Solar Energy Co. v. International Trade Commission

United States Court of Appeals, Federal Circuit, 879 F.3d 1377 (2018).

Facts Changzhou Trina Solar Energy Company, a Chinese firm, makes crystalline silicon photovoltaic (CSPV) cells and related products. Trina Solar (U.S.), Inc., imported Changzhou's CSPV products into the United States. The U.S. Department of Commerce found that the imports were subsidized by the Chinese government and sold in the United States at less than fair value. The International Trade Commission (ITC) determined that the domestic CSPV industry was materially injured by the imports from China. Changzhou and Trina challenged this determination in the U.S. Court of International Trade. The court rejected the challenge and sustained the ITC's determination. Changzhou and Trina appealed this decision to the U.S. Court of Appeals for the Federal Circuit.

Issue Was the domestic CSPV industry materially injured by the subsidized, imported products from China?

Decision Yes. The U.S. Court of Appeals for the Federal Circuit affirmed the decision of the lower court. The ITC's explanation of how it determined that the imported products unfairly impacted the domestic industry provided substantial evidence to support imposition of antidumping duties.

Reason The ITC studied the different sources of power in the domestic market—their supply, demand, prices, consumption, and market shares. The ITC considered the domestic CSPV industry's business cycles and financial performance, and the impact of local, state, and federal government incentives and regulations. The ITC reviewed a "variety of evidence" and recognized that other factors "may have" contributed to the decline in domestic prices for CSPV products. But the ITC concluded that the effect of the "unfairly priced and subsidized subject imports" on the domestic industry was "more than inconsequential, immaterial, or unimportant." The imports caused a significant drop in domestic prices for the products, leading U.S. producers to lose revenue. As the imports competed directly with the domestic products and undersold them "at significant margins," the U.S. producers lost market share.

Critical Thinking

- **Economic** *How does the* Changzhou *case illustrate that dumping is an unfair international trade practice? Discuss.*
- **What If the Facts Were Different?** *Suppose that the ITC had not issued detailed findings supported by a variety of evidence, but had only released a statement that the subject imports seemed to have a negative effect on the domestic industry. Would the result have been different? Explain.*

19–3d Minimizing Trade Barriers

Restrictions on imports are also known as *trade barriers*. The elimination of trade barriers is sometimes seen as essential to the world's economic well-being. Various regional trade agreements and associations work to reduce trade barriers among nations.

Focus Question 3

What does it mean for the World Trade Organization to grant a nation "normal trade relations status"?

The World Trade Organization Most of the world's leading trading nations are members of the World Trade Organization (WTO), which was established in 1995. To minimize trade barriers among nations, each member country is required to grant **normal trade relations (NTR) status** to other member countries. This means that each member must treat other members at least as well as it treats the country that receives its most favorable treatment with regard to imports or exports.

Normal Trade Relations (NTR) Status A legal trade status granted to member countries of the World Trade Organization. Each member must treat other members at least as well as it treats the country that receives its most favorable treatment with regard to imports or exports.

The European Union (EU) The European Union (EU) arose out the 1957 Treaty of Rome, which created the Common Market, a free trade zone comprising the nations of Belgium, France, Italy, Luxembourg, the Netherlands, and West Germany. Today, the EU is a single integrated trading unit made up of twenty-seven European nations.

The EU has gone a long way toward creating a new body of law to govern all of the member nations. The EU's council and commission issue regulations, or directives, that define EU law in various areas, such as environmental law, product liability, anticompetitive practices, and corporations. The directives normally are binding on all member countries. Nevertheless, some of the EU's efforts to create uniform laws have been confounded by nationalism. An example is Brexit, which refers to Britain's decision to withdraw from the EU.

The United States–Mexico–Canada Agreement (USMCA) Replacing the North American Free Trade Agreement, the United States–Mexico–Canada Agreement (USMCA) created a regional trading unit consisting of Mexico, Canada, and the United States. The goal of USMCA is to reduce tariffs among these three countries on substantially all goods and to make trade between the three countries as equitable as possible.

USMCA gives the three countries a competitive advantage by retaining tariffs on goods imported from countries outside the USMCA trading unit. Additionally, USMCA requires that 75 percent of automobile components must be manufactured in one of the three countries to qualify for zero tariffs and that 40 to 45 percent of automobile parts must be made by workers who earn at least $16 an hour. The agreement also gives U.S. farmers more access to Canada's dairy market, as well as providing for the free movement of digital products such as music and eBooks between the signatories.

The Central America–Dominican Republic–United States Free Trade Agreement (CAFTA-DR) The Central America–Dominican Republic–United States Free Trade Agreement (CAFTA-DR) was formed by Costa Rica, the Dominican Republic, El Salvador, Guatemala, Honduras, Nicaragua, and the United States. Its purpose is to reduce tariffs and improve market access among all of the signatory nations. Legislatures in all seven countries have approved the CAFTA-DR, despite significant opposition in certain nations.

The Republic of Korea–United States Free Trade Agreement (KORUS FTA) The United States ratified its first free trade agreement with South Korea in 2011. This agreement, called the Republic of Korea–United States Free Trade Agreement (KORUS FTA), is aimed at eliminating 95 percent of each nation's tariffs on industrial and consumer exports. KORUS was expected to boost U.S. exports and benefit U.S. automakers, farmers, ranchers, and manufacturers. To date, however, exports have not increased as much as predicted, and the agreement is likely to be renegotiated.

19–4 U.S. Laws in a Global Context

The internationalization of business raises questions about the extraterritorial application of a nation's laws—that is, the effect of the country's laws outside its boundaries. To what extent do U.S. domestic laws apply to other nations' businesses? To what extent do U.S. domestic laws apply to U.S. firms doing business abroad? Here, we discuss the extraterritorial application of certain U.S. laws, including antitrust laws, tort laws, and laws prohibiting employment discrimination.

19–4a U.S. Antitrust Laws

U.S. antitrust laws have a wide application. They may *subject* firms in foreign nations to their provisions, as well as *protect* foreign consumers and competitors from violations committed by U.S. citizens. Section 1 of the Sherman Act—the most important U.S. antitrust law—provides for the extraterritorial effect of the U.S. antitrust laws.

Any conspiracy that has a *substantial effect* on U.S. commerce is within the reach of the Sherman Act. The law applies even if the violation occurs outside the United States, and foreign governments as well as businesses can be sued for violations.

Example 19.9 A Tokyo-based auto parts supplier, Furukawa Electric Company, and its executives conspired with competitors in an international price-fixing agreement (an agreement to set prices) that lasted more than ten years. As a result of the conspiracy, automobile manufacturers paid noncompetitive and higher prices for parts in cars sold to U.S. consumers.

Because the conspiracy had a substantial effect on U.S. commerce, the United States had jurisdiction to prosecute the case. Ultimately, Furukawa agreed to plead guilty and pay a $200 million fine. The Furukawa executives from Japan also agreed to serve up to eighteen months in a U.S. prison and to cooperate fully with the ongoing investigation. ■

19–4b International Tort Claims

The international application of tort liability has grown in significance and controversy. An increasing number of U.S. plaintiffs have sued foreign (or U.S.) entities for torts that these entities allegedly committed overseas. Often, these cases involve human rights violations by foreign governments. The Alien Tort Statute (ATS),[11] adopted in 1789, allows even foreign citizens to bring civil suits in U.S. courts for injuries caused by violations of international law or a treaty of the United States.

Since 1980, plaintiffs increasingly used the ATS to bring actions against private companies operating in foreign nations, including Colombia, Egypt, Nigeria, and Saudi Arabia. Critics argued that allowing such suits extended the application of the ATS too far. In 2018, the United States Supreme Court limited the application of the ATS when it ruled that foreign corporations could no longer be defendants in suits brought under the ATS.[12]

In the following *Spotlight Case*, the United States Supreme Court considered the parameters of the ATS. The question was whether the statute allows U.S. courts to exercise jurisdiction over a cause of action that occurred outside the United States.

Focus Question 4

What federal law allows U.S. citizens, as well as citizens of foreign nations, to file civil actions in U.S. courts for torts that were committed overseas?

11. 28 U.S.C. Section 1350.
12. *Jesner v. Arab Bank, PLC*, 584 U.S. ____, 138 S.Ct. 1386, 200 L.Ed.2d 612, 2018 WL 1914663 (2018).

Spotlight on International Torts: Case 19.3

Daimler AG v. Bauman

United States Supreme Court, 571 U.S.117, 134 S.Ct. 746, 187 L.Ed.2d 624 (2014).

Facts Barbara Bauman and twenty-one other residents of Argentina filed a suit in a federal district court in California against Daimler AG,[a] a German company. They alleged that Mercedes-Benz (MB) Argentina, a subsidiary of Daimler, had collaborated with state security forces to kidnap, detain, torture, and kill certain MB Argentina workers during Argentina's "dirty war." These workers included the plaintiffs and some of their relatives. Their claims were asserted under the Alien Tort Statute.

©Gil C/Shutterstock.com

Can victims of Argentina's "dirty war" sue a German company in a U.S. court?

Personal jurisdiction was based on the California contacts of Mercedes-Benz USA (MBUSA), a Daimler subsidiary incorporated in Delaware with its principal place of business in New Jersey. MBUSA distributes Daimler-made vehicles to dealerships throughout the United States, including California. The district court dismissed the suit for lack of jurisdiction. The U.S. Court of Appeals for the Ninth Circuit reversed this ruling. Daimler appealed to the United States Supreme Court.

Issue Is there a limit to the authority of a U.S. court to decide a case brought by foreign plaintiffs against a foreign defendant based on events occurring entirely outside of the United States?

Decision Yes. The United States Supreme Court reversed the decision of the appellate court. The federal district court could not exercise jurisdiction over Daimler given the absence of any California connection to the atrocities, perpetrators, or victims described in the complaint.

Reason The Court explained that only a limited set of connections to a state render a defendant subject to jurisdiction there. For a corporation, the "paradigm forum" for the exercise of jurisdiction is the state in which the corporation is "fairly regarded as at home." A corporation may be regarded as at home in the state in which it incorporated and the state in which it has its principal place of business. Both places are unique and easily located. These bases give plaintiffs at least "one clear and certain forum" in which to sue a corporate defendant.

This does not mean that a corporation is subject to jurisdiction *only* in its state of incorporation or principal place of business. In this case, however, the plaintiffs argued for the exercise of jurisdiction in every state in which a corporation engages in "continuous and systematic" business. That argument went too far, according to the Court. Instead, the appropriate question is whether a corporation's connections with a state are so continuous and systematic as to render it at home there. Here, neither Daimler nor MBUSA was incorporated in California, and neither had its principal place of business there.

Critical Thinking

- **Legal Environment** *What are the consequences for Daimler of the decision in this case?*

a. The initials *A.G.* stand for "Automotive Group."

19–4c Antidiscrimination Laws

As you probably know, federal laws in the United States prohibit discrimination on the basis of race, color, national origin, religion, sexual orientation, gender, age, and disability. These laws, as they affect employment relationships, generally apply extraterritorially.

Thus, U.S. employees working abroad for U.S. employers are protected under the Age Discrimination in Employment Act. Similarly, the Americans with Disabilities Act, which requires employers to accommodate the needs of workers with disabilities, applies to U.S. nationals working abroad for U.S. firms.

In addition, the major law regulating employment discrimination—Title VII of the Civil Rights Act—applies extraterritorially to all U.S. employees working for U.S. employers abroad. U.S. employers must abide by U.S. discrimination laws unless to do so would violate the laws of the country where their workplaces are located. This "foreign laws exception" prevents employers from being subjected to conflicting laws.

19–5 Space Law

Space law consists of the international and national laws that govern activities in outer space. For the first fifty years of space exploration, national governments conducted most of those activities. Thus, space law was directed primarily at governments and government activities. More recently, private companies have undertaken some space-related activities and broadened access to outer space for the rest of us. Space law, accordingly, faces new challenges.

Space Law Law consisting of the international and national laws that govern activities in outer space.

19–5a International Space Law

International space law consists of international treaties—primarily negotiated by the United Nations (U.N.)—and U.N. resolutions. These sources recognize fundamentally that activities conducted in outer space and the benefits derived from those activities should improve the welfare of all nations and all humanity.

The major space law treaties were concluded by the U.N. Committee on the Peaceful Uses of Outer Space (COPUOS). COPUOS also administers the treaties and advises the international community on space policy matters.

Exploration and Exploitation The foundation of international space law is the U.N. Treaty on Principles Governing the Activities of States in the Exploration and Use of Outer Space, including the Moon and Other Celestial Bodies.[13] This treaty—generally referred to as the *Outer Space Treaty*—established the framework for later international agreements and U.N. resolutions.

Focus Question 5

What treaty provides a framework for international space law?

The Outer Space Treaty expresses general principles that have been expanded and applied in subsequent treaties. In Article I and Article II, outer space is declared to be free for exploration and use by all nations. The moon, the planets, asteroids, and other celestial bodies are not subject to appropriation by any single nation.[14] In addition, space objects are to be used exclusively for peaceful purposes. No weapons of mass destruction are permitted in outer space under Article IV.[15]

According to Article VI, each nation is responsible for its activities in outer space, whether they are conducted by the government or by a private entity. In fact, the activities of private entities require authorization and supervision by a government. Article VII imposes on each nation liability for damage caused by its space objects. Article VIII provides that each nation retains jurisdiction and control over its space objects and the personnel on them. Finally, Article IX requires that space exploration be conducted so as to avoid "harmful contamination."[16]

Astronauts and Space Objects The Outer Space Treaty was followed by several other agreements, including the following:

- The Agreement on the Rescue of Astronauts, the Return of Astronauts and the Return of Objects Launched into Outer Space (the Rescue Agreement).[17]

Expedition 36, International Space Station (ISS)/NASA

The international space station orbits the earth with crews from different countries. How do international treaties and space law policies affect the way we explore outer space?

13. 18 U.S.T. 2410, T.I.A.S. 6347, 610 U.N.T.S. 205.
14. After the treaty went into effect, the United States and Russia conducted joint space activities.
15. Establishing military bases, testing weapons, and conducting military maneuvers are prohibited.
16. Other articles promote further international cooperation in the exploration and use of space.
17. 19 U.S.T. 7570, T.I.A.S. 6599, 672 U.N.T.S. 119.

- The Convention on International Liability for Damage Caused by Space Objects (the Liability Convention).[18]
- The Convention on Registration of Objects Launched into Outer Space (the Registration Convention).[19]

The Rescue Agreement expands on Articles V and VIII of the Outer Space Treaty. It provides that each nation will undertake to rescue and assist astronauts in distress and return them to their "launching State." All nations are to assist in recovering space objects that return to earth outside the territory of the launching state.

The Liability Convention elaborates on Article VII of the Outer Space Treaty. This agreement provides that a launching state is absolutely liable for personal injury and property damage caused by its space objects on the surface of the earth or to aircraft in flight. Liability for injury or damage in space is subject to a determination of fault. The convention also prescribes procedures for the settlement of claims for damages.

The Registration Convention provides for the mandatory registration of objects launched into outer space. Each launching state is to maintain a registry of the objects that it launches into space. The intent is to assist in the objects' identification. (See this chapter's *Cybersecurity and the Law* feature for insights into a problem that was given little consideration at the time of these international agreements.).

---

18. 24 U.S.T. 2389, T.I.A.S. 7762, 961 U.N.T.S. 187.
19. 28 U.S.T. 695, T.I.A.S. 8480, 1023 U.N.T.S. 15.

Cybersecurity and the Law

Safe Satellites

At the start of the 2020s, about 5,000 human-made satellites orbited the Earth. By the end of the decade, a single aerospace manufacturer—Space X—plans to have launched up to 42,000 satellites. Other companies, including Amazon, Facebook, and OneWeb, have similar plans.

The potential benefits of this vast array include high-speed 5G Internet access to every corner of the planet, improved global navigation systems, and an enhanced ability to monitor meteorological conditions. But space traffic poses potential problems as well, such as high-speed collisions, dead satellites that threaten other spacecraft, and disruption of the work of astronomers. To no one's surprise, the specter of hacking also looms large in the satellite industry's future.

Hacking in Space

According to computer security experts, satellites are particularly susceptible to being hacked. Until recently, satellite engineers have not emphasized cybersecurity in their design and construction plans. To reduce costs, satellite builders often employ less expensive computer components using open-source technology, giving hackers numerous vulnerabilities to exploit. Additionally, a high proportion of satellites already in orbit were launched many years ago, before cybersecurity was a concern. Illegally controlling these defenseless satellites might be as easy as setting up a ground antenna and waiting for one to pass overhead.

Hackers could, for instance, shut down a targeted satellite. Or they could jam the satellite's signals, wreaking havoc on communications and other critical infrastructure systems. Steerable satellites could be hijacked to "attack" other objects, in space or closer to the Earth. Currently, no governmental body in the United States has created cybersecurity guidelines for satellite operations. In this vacuum, it is not clear who would be legally responsible for a security breach in a satellite, nor is there sufficient relevant case law to help American courts determine civil liability for any harm done by a hacked, rogue satellite.

Critical Thinking

Why is international law better suited for satellite regulation than national law?

Space Debris More than 13,000 human-made items larger than four inches are in orbit around the earth. Most of these objects are no longer under any party's control and are classified as *space debris*. In 2009, two orbiting satellites collided for the first time. Fragments generated by such collisions are expected to be a significant source of space debris in the future. As noted previously, the Liability Convention sets out principles of liability to apply in instances of injury or damage in space.

The United Nations has endorsed guidelines to reduce space debris.[20] The guidelines, which reflect the current practices of a number of national and international organizations, apply to the planning, design, manufacture, and operational phases of spacecraft. Among other points, the guidelines suggest that systems should be designed not to release debris during normal operations. They also recognize that some objects no longer in operation should be removed from orbit, if this can be accomplished in a controlled manner.

19–5b U.S. Space Law

In the United States, each government agency that operates or authorizes spacecraft is responsible for complying with U.S. law and international treaties. Federal law, state law, and more than half a century of common practices in space-related industries also affect government and private space activities.

Commercial Spaceflight The Federal Aviation Administration (FAA) regulates private spaceports, as well as the launch and reentry of private spacecraft, under the Commercial Space Launch Act.[21] The FAA is working to establish licensing and safety criteria for private spacecraft. Some states, including Florida, New Mexico, Texas, and Virginia, limit the liability of space tourism providers under state tort law. But state legislatures and, ultimately, courts will need to consider other issues in this context, including insurance requirements and the enforceability of liability waivers.

In addition, Congress has passed legislation aimed at encouraging commercial spaceflight companies. The U.S. Commercial Space Launch Competitiveness Act[22] streamlines regulatory processes and promotes safety standards. In addition, the law provides that if a U.S. citizen or company retrieves minerals or other resources from an asteroid or other space location, that person or company owns them.

Exports of Space Technology Currently, under U.S. regulations, all spacecraft are classified as "defense articles." The defense classification restricts the transfer of space technology and related information to any foreign person or nation under the U.S. Department of State's International Traffic in Arms Regulations.[23] This restriction makes it difficult for U.S. space companies to compete in global space markets.

Property Rights to Space Resources Article II of the Outer Space Treaty bans the national appropriation of territory in space. If the United States cannot appropriate territory in space, then it cannot give U.S. citizens title to property associated with this territory. Under U.S. law, the government must have sovereignty over territory before it can confer title to associated property to its citizens.

Article VIII, however, provides that a state party to the treaty retains jurisdiction over objects on its space registry that are launched into space. In addition, Article IX prohibits interference with space activities. In effect, these provisions confer the protections associated with property rights on private space activities.

---

20. Space Debris Mitigation Guidelines of the Committee on the Peaceful Uses of Outer Space, G.A. Res. 62/217, U.N. GAOR, 50th Sess., U.N.Doc. A/62/20 (Dec. 22, 2007).
21. 51 U.S.C. Sections 50901 *et seq.*
22. Pub. L. No. 114-90, 129 Stat. 704, Nov. 25, 2015.
23. 22 C.F.R. Sections 120.1 *et seq.*

The U.S. Commercial Space Launch Competitiveness Act changed the law somewhat by granting private citizens property rights over asteroid resources that they obtain from space. The act specifically recognizes that the United States is not attempting to assert an exclusive right to or sovereignty over any celestial body.

Practice and Review

Robco, Inc., was a Florida arms dealer. The armed forces of Honduras contracted to purchase weapons from Robco over a six-year period. After the government was replaced and a democracy installed, the Honduran government sought to reduce the size of its military, and its relationship with Robco deteriorated.

Honduras refused to honor the contract by purchasing the inventory of arms, which Robco could sell only at a much lower price. Robco filed a suit in a federal district court in the United States to recover damages for this breach of contract by the government of Honduras. Using the information provided in the chapter, answer the following questions.

1. Should the Foreign Sovereign Immunities Act preclude this lawsuit? Why or why not?
2. Does the act of state doctrine bar Robco from seeking to enforce the contract? Explain.
3. Suppose that before Robco filed its lawsuit, the new government of Honduras enacted a law making it illegal to purchase weapons from foreign arms dealers. What doctrine might lead a U.S. court to dismiss Robco's case in that situation?
4. Now suppose that the U.S. court hears the case and awards damages to Robco, but the government of Honduras has no assets in the United States that can be used to satisfy the judgment. Under which doctrine might Robco be able to collect the damages by asking another nation's court to enforce the U.S. judgment?

Debate This

The U.S. federal courts are accepting too many lawsuits initiated by foreigners that concern matters not relevant to this country.

Key Terms

act of state doctrine 471
choice-of-law clause 477
comity 471
confiscation 472
distribution agreement 476
dumping 479
export 475
expropriation 472
forum-selection clause 477
international law 469
international organization 470
national law 469
normal trade relations (NTR) status 480
quota 478
sovereign immunity 472
space law 483
tariff 479
treaty 470

Chapter Summary: International and Space Law

International Law	1. **Principle of comity**—Under this principle, nations give effect to the laws and judicial decrees of other nations, as long as they are consistent with the law and public policy of the accommodating nation. It is based primarily on respect. 2. **Act of state doctrine**—Under this doctrine, U.S. courts avoid passing judgment on the validity of public acts committed by a recognized foreign government within its own territory. 3. **Doctrine of sovereign immunity**—When certain conditions are satisfied, foreign nations are immune from U.S. jurisdiction under the Foreign Sovereign Immunities Act. Exceptions are made when a foreign state (a) has waived its immunity either explicitly or by implication, (b) has engaged in commercial activity within the United States or that has a direct effect on the United States, (c) has committed a tort within the United States, or (d) has been designated "a state sponsor of terrorism" and is sued for "personal injury or death" caused by an act of terrorism.
Doing Business Internationally	U.S. domestic firms may engage in international business transactions in several ways, including (1) exporting, which may involve foreign agents or distributors, and (2) manufacturing abroad through licensing arrangements, wholly owned subsidiaries, or joint ventures. International business contracts often include arbitration clauses and forum-selection clauses to reduce the uncertainties associated with dispute resolution. The New York Convention assists in the enforcement of arbitration clauses and requires signatory nations to honor private agreements to arbitrate. If the parties have signed a forum-selection clause, the dispute will be tried (or arbitrated) in the specified forum.
Regulation of Specific Business Activities	In the interests of their economies, foreign policies, domestic policies, and other national priorities, nations impose laws that restrict or facilitate international business. Such laws regulate foreign investments, exporting, and importing. Various regional trade agreements and associations, including the World Trade Organization and the European Union, attempt to minimize trade barriers among nations.
U.S. Laws in a Global Context	1. **Antitrust laws**—U.S. antitrust laws may be applied beyond the borders of the United States. Any conspiracy that has a substantial effect on commerce within the United States may be subject to the Sherman Act, even if the violation occurs outside the United States. 2. **International tort claims**—U.S. tort laws may be applied to wrongful acts that take place in foreign jurisdictions under the Alien Tort Statute. This act allows even foreign citizens to bring civil suits in U.S. courts for injuries caused by violations of international law or a treaty of the United States. 3. **Antidiscrimination laws**—The major U.S. laws prohibiting employment discrimination, including Title VII of the Civil Rights Act, the Age Discrimination in Employment Act, and the Americans with Disabilities Act, cover U.S. employees working abroad for U.S. firms—*unless* to apply the U.S. laws would violate the laws of the host country.
Space Law	Space law consists of international and national laws that govern activities in outer space. International treaties and resolutions (mostly through the United Nations) cover space exploration and exploitation, astronauts, space objects, and space debris. National laws in the United States deal with commercial space flights (regulated by the Federal Aviation Administration), space technology, and property rights.

Issue Spotters

1. Café Rojo, Ltd., an Ecuadoran firm, agrees to sell coffee beans to Dark Roast Coffee Company, a U.S. firm. Dark Roast accepts the beans but refuses to pay. Café Rojo sues Dark Roast in an Ecuadoran court and is awarded damages, but Dark Roast's assets are in the United States. Under what circumstances would a U.S. court enforce the judgment of the Ecuadoran court? (See *International Law.*)
2. Gems International, Ltd., is a foreign firm that has a 12 percent share of the U.S. market for diamonds. To capture a larger share, Gems offers its products at a below-cost discount to U.S. buyers (and inflates the prices in its own country to make up the difference). How can this attempt to undersell U.S. businesses be defeated? (See *Regulation of Specific Business Activities.*)

—Check your answers to the *Issue Spotters* against the answers provided in Appendix D.

Business Scenarios and Case Problems

19–1. Doing Business Internationally. Macrotech, Inc., develops an innovative computer chip and obtains a patent on it. The firm markets the chip under the trademarked brand name "Flash." Macrotech wants to sell the chip to Nitron, Ltd., in Pacifica, a foreign country. Macrotech is concerned, however, that after an initial purchase Nitron will duplicate the chip, pirate it, and sell the pirated version to computer manufacturers in Pacifica. To avoid this possibility, Macrotech could establish its own manufacturing facility in Pacifica, but it does not want to do this. How can Macrotech, without establishing a manufacturing facility in Pacifica, protect Flash from being pirated by Nitron? (See *Doing Business Internationally.*)

19–2. Dumping. U.S. pineapple producers alleged that producers of canned pineapple from the Philippines were selling their canned pineapple in the United States for less than its fair market value (dumping). The Philippine producers also exported other products, such as pineapple juice and juice concentrate, which used separate parts of the same pineapple used for the canned pineapple. All these products shared raw material costs, according to the producers' own financial records. To determine fair value and antidumping duties, the plaintiffs argued that a court should calculate the Philippine producers' cost of production and allocate a portion of the shared fruit costs to the canned fruit. The result of this allocation showed that more than 90 percent of the canned fruit sales were below the cost of production. Is this a reasonable approach to determining the production costs and fair market value of canned pineapple in the United States? Why or why not? (See *Regulation of Specific Business Activities.*)

19–3. Sovereign Immunity. Bell Helicopter Textron, Inc., designs, makes, and sells helicopters with distinctive and famous trade dress that identifies them as Bell aircraft. Bell also owns the helicopters' design patents. Bell's Model 206 Series includes the Jet Ranger. Thirty-six years after Bell developed the Jet Ranger, the Islamic Republic of Iran began to make and sell counterfeit Model 206 Series helicopters and parts. Iran's counterfeit versions—the Shahed 278 and the Shahed 285—used Bell's trade dress. The Shahed aircraft was promoted at an international air show in Iran to aircraft customers. Bell filed a suit in a U.S. district court against Iran, alleging violations of trademark and patent laws. Is Iran—a foreign nation—exempt in these circumstances from the jurisdiction of U.S. courts? Explain. [*Bell Helicopter Textron, Inc. v. Islamic Republic of Iran,* 734 F.3d 1175 (C.A.D.C. 2013)] (See *International Law.*)

19–4. Sovereign Immunity. In 1954, the government of Bolivia began expropriating land from Francisco Loza for public projects, including an international airport. The government directed the payment of compensation in exchange for at least some of his land. But the government never paid the full amount. Decades later, his heirs, Genoveva and Marcel Loza, who were both U.S. citizens, filed a suit in a federal district court in the United States against the government of Bolivia, seeking damages for the taking. Can the court exercise jurisdiction? Explain. [*Santivanez v. Estado Plurinacional de Bolivia,* 2013 WL 879983 (11th Cir. 2013)] (See *International Law.*)

19–5. Business Case Problem with Sample Answer—Import Controls. The Wind Tower Trade Coalition is an association of domestic manufacturers of utility-scale wind towers. The coalition filed a suit in the U.S. Court of International Trade against the U.S. Department of Commerce. It challenged the Commerce Department's decision to impose only *prospective* antidumping duties, rather than *retrospective* (retroactive) duties, on imports of utility-scale wind towers from China and Vietnam. The department had found that the domestic industry had not suffered any "material injury" or "threat of material injury" from such imports and that it would be protected by a prospective assessment. Can an antidumping duty be assessed retrospectively? If so, should it be assessed here? Discuss. [*Wind Tower Trade Coalition v. United States,* 741 F.3d 89 (Fed. Cir. 2014)] (See *Regulation of Specific Business Activities.*)

—For a sample answer to Problem 19–5, go to Appendix E.

19–6. The Principle of Comity. Holocaust survivors and the heirs of Holocaust victims filed a suit in a federal district court in the United States against the Hungarian national railway, the Hungarian national bank, and several private Hungarian banks. The plaintiffs alleged that the defendants had participated in expropriating the property of Hungarian Jews who were victims of the Holocaust. The claims arose from events in Hungary seventy years earlier. The plaintiffs had not exhausted remedies available through Hungarian courts. Indeed, they had not even attempted to seek remedies in Hungarian courts, and they did not provide a legally compelling reason for their failure to do so. The defendants asked the court to dismiss the suit. Does the principle of comity support the defendants' request? Explain. [*Fischer v. Magyar Államvasutak Zrt.,* 777 F.3d 847 (7th Cir. 2015)] (See *International Law.*)

19–7. International Law. For fifty years, the Soviet Union made and sold Stolichnaya vodka. At the time, VVO-SPI, a Soviet state enterprise, licensed the Stolichnaya trademark in the United States. When the Soviet Union collapsed, VVO-SPI was purportedly privatized and fell under the control of Spirits International B.V. (SPI). In 2000, a Russian court held that VVO-SPI had not been validly privatized under Russian law. Thus, ownership of the Stolichnaya mark remained with the Soviet Union's successor, the Russian Federation. The Russian Federation assigned the mark to Federal Treasury Enterprise Sojuzplodoimport, OAO (FTE). FTE then filed a suit in a U.S. federal district court against SPI, asserting unlawful misappropriation and commercial exploitation of the mark in violation of federal law. Is the validity of the assignment of the mark to FTE a question to be determined by the court? Why or why not? [*Federal Treasury Enterprise Sojuzplodoimport v. Spirits International B.V.*, 809 F.3d 737 (2d Cir. 2016)] (See *International Law*.)

19–8. Import Controls. Goods exported to a foreign country for repair or alteration can qualify for tariff-free or reduced-tariff treatment when they re-enter the United States. But the goods do not qualify for favorable import-duty treatment if, in the foreign country, they are transformed into commercially different goods. Daimler-Chrysler AG Sprinter vans are marketed in the United States as cargo vans. Pleasure-Way Industries, Inc., bought 144 Sprinter vans and exported them to Canada for conversion into motorhomes. This included the installation of fully plumbed and furnished kitchens, bathrooms, and sleeping quarters. After the conversion, Pleasure-Way sought to import the vehicles back into the United States to market the motorhomes under new model names as upscale leisure vehicles at prices double or triple the price for Sprinter vans. Do the converted vans qualify for favorable import-tariff treatment? Discuss. [*Pleasure-Way Industries, Inc.v. United States*, 878 F.3d 1348 (Fed.Cir. 2018)] (See *Regulation of Specific Business Activities*.)

19–9. A Question of Ethics—The IDDR Approach and Doing Business Internationally. Incorporated under Venezuelan law, a subsidiary of U.S.-based Helmerich & Payne International Drilling Co. supplied oil-drilling rigs to entities that were part of the government of Venezuela. The government fell behind in payment on contracts for the use of the rigs. When the overdue amounts topped $100 million, the government nationalized the rigs and took possession. Helmerich filed a suit in a U.S. federal district court against Venezuela, claiming expropriation of property in violation of international law. Helmerich asserted that the U.S. court had jurisdiction under the Foreign Sovereign Immunities Act (FSIA). [*Bolivarian Republic of Venezuela v. Helmerich & Payne International Drilling Co.*, 581 U.S. __, 137 S.Ct. 1312, 197 L.Ed.2d 663(2017)] (See *International Law*.)

1. Venezuela argued that the FSIA did not apply because Helmerich did not have rights in the rigs, which were the subsidiary's property. Does that fact make Helmerich's claim frivolous and unethical? Explain.
2. Using the IDDR approach, determine whether a company is ethically obligated to become familiar with the political situation before doing business in another country.

Critical Thinking and Writing Assignments

19–10. Time-Limited Group Assignment—Globalization. Assume that you are manufacturing tablet accessories and that your business is becoming more successful. You are now considering expanding operations into another country. (See *Doing Business Internationally*.)

1. One group will explore the costs and benefits of advertising internationally on the Internet.
2. Another group will consider whether to take in a partner from a foreign nation and examine the benefits and risks of doing so.
3. A third group will discuss what problems may arise if you want to manufacture in a foreign location.

Andrey_Popov/Shutterstock.com

20 Banking

Focus Questions

The five Focus Questions *below are designed to help improve your understanding. After reading this chapter, you should be able to answer the following questions:*

1. What type of check does a bank agree in advance to accept when the check is presented for payment?
2. When may a bank properly dishonor a customer's check without being liable to the customer?
3. What is electronic check presentment, and how does it differ from the traditional check-clearing process?
4. What are the four most common types of electronic fund transfers?
5. What role does artificial intelligence (AI) play in digital lending?

"Money is just what we use to keep tally."

Henry Ford
1863–1947
(American automobile manufacturer)

Many people today use debit cards rather than checks for their retail transactions, and payments are increasingly being made via smartphones, tablets, and other mobile devices. Nonetheless, checks remain an integral part of the U.S. economic system and are the most common type of negotiable instrument. Because checks serve as a substitute for cash, we use them to "keep tally," a phrase used by Henry Ford in the chapter-opening quotation.

Many businesses still use checks to pay bills because they facilitate record keeping. But on some occasions, employers have fallen victim to a dishonest employee who embezzles funds using company checks. For instance, assume that Closetmakers, Inc., hired Carter as a bookkeeper. Carter was responsible for maintaining the company checkbook and reconciling it with the monthly statements from TD Financial Bank. He also wrote checks to pay invoices, which Closetmakers' president, Denise, reviewed and signed, but no other employee checked Carter's work.

By the end of his first full month of employment, Carter had forged six checks, amounting to more than $22,000. By the following year, Carter had forged fifty-nine more checks, totaling more than $475,000. A TD Financial employee became suspicious about an item and notified Closetmakers. Carter left work and did not return. Closetmakers sued TD Financial Bank for reimbursement, alleging that it had been negligent in not detecting the forgeries. The bank argued that it was not liable because Closetmakers had been negligent. Who bears the loss resulting from forged checks is one of the many important topics covered in this chapter.

20–1 Checks and the Bank-Customer Relationship

Articles 3 and 4 of the Uniform Commercial Code (UCC) govern issues relating to checks. Article 4 of the UCC governs bank deposits and collections as well as bank-customer relationships. Article 4 also regulates the relationships of banks with one another as they process checks for payment, and it establishes a framework for deposit and checking agreements between a bank and its customers. A check therefore may fall within the scope of Article 3 as a negotiable instrument and yet be subject to the provisions of Article 4 while in the course of collection. If a conflict between Article 3 and Article 4 arises, Article 4 controls [UCC 4–102(a)].

20–1a Checks

A *check* is a special type of draft that is drawn on a bank, ordering the bank to pay a fixed amount of funds on demand [UCC 3–104(f)]. Article 4 defines a *bank* as "a person engaged in the business of banking, including a savings bank, savings and loan association, credit union or trust company" [UCC 4–105(1)]. If any other institution (such as a brokerage firm) handles a check for payment or for collection, the check is *not* covered by Article 4.

A person who writes a check is called the *drawer.* The drawer is a depositor in the bank on which the check is drawn. The person to whom the check is payable is the *payee*. The bank or financial institution on which the check is drawn is the *drawee*. **Example 20.1** When Anita writes a check from her checking account to pay her college tuition, she is the drawer. Her bank is the drawee, and her college is the payee.

Between the time a check is drawn and the time it reaches the drawee, the effectiveness of the check may be altered in some way. For instance, the account on which the check is drawn may no longer have sufficient funds to pay the check. To avoid such problems, a payee may insist on payment by an instrument that has already been accepted by the drawee, such as a cashier's check or a certified check.

Cashier's Checks Checks usually are three-party instruments, but on certain types of checks, the bank can serve as both the drawer and the drawee. For instance, when a bank draws a check on itself, the check is called a **cashier's check** and is a negotiable instrument at the moment it is issued (see Exhibit 20–1) [UCC 3–104(g)]. Normally,

Cashier's Check A check drawn by a bank on itself.

Exhibit 20–1 A Cashier's Check

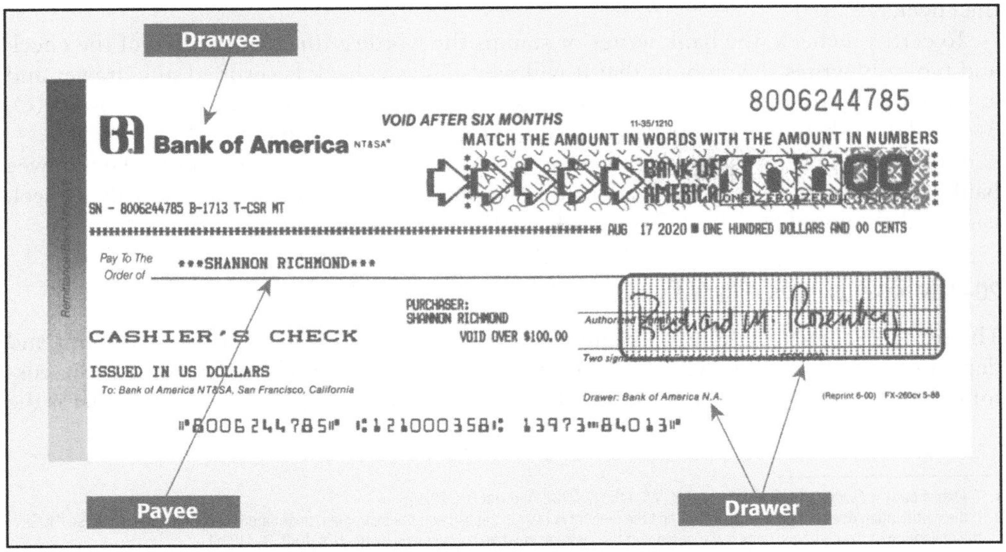

a cashier's check indicates a specific payee. In effect, with a cashier's check, the bank assumes responsibility for paying the check, thus making the check more readily acceptable as a substitute for cash.

Example 20.2 Kramer needs to pay a moving company $8,000 for moving his household goods to his new home in another state. The moving company requests payment in the form of a cashier's check. Kramer goes to a bank (he need not have an account at the bank) and purchases a cashier's check, payable to the moving company, in the amount of $8,000. Kramer has to pay the bank the $8,000 for the check, plus a small service fee. He then gives the check to the moving company.

Cashier's checks are sometimes used in the business community as the near equivalent of cash. Except in very limited circumstances, the issuing bank *must* honor its cashier's checks when they are presented for payment. If a bank wrongfully dishonors a cashier's check, a holder can recover from the bank all expenses incurred, interest, and consequential damages [UCC 3–411]. At the same time, banks may be required to verify the validity of a cashier's check to protect itself and its customers against fraud. **Case Example 20.3** The victim of an elaborate scam, Roy Elizondo unwittingly deposited a counterfeit cashier's check for nearly $500,000 into his Cadence Bank account. The drawee for the cashier's check was Chase Bank. At Elizondo's request, Cadence then completed a wire transfer of $400,000 from his account to the holder of a Japanese bank account.

After the wire transfer had been completed, Chase dishonored the counterfeit cashier's check. Cadence sued Elizondo to recover the $400,000 overdraft. Elizondo countersued, arguing that Cadence had caused the overdraft by failing to verify that the funds from the counterfeit cashier's check had actually been deposited in his account. Had Cadence done so, Elizondo argued, it would have been alerted to the fraud, and the wire transfer never would have been sent. A Texas appeals court agreed, holding that Cadence Bank, not Elizondo, must bear the financial cost of the wire transfer.[1]

Certified Check A check that has been accepted in writing by the bank on which it is drawn. By certifying (accepting) the check, the bank promises to pay the check at the time it is presented.

Certified Checks A **certified check** is a check that has been accepted in writing by the bank on which it is drawn [UCC 3–409(d)]. When a drawee bank *certifies* a check, it immediately charges the drawer's account with the amount of the check and transfers those funds to its own certified check account. In effect, the bank is agreeing in advance to accept that check when it is presented for payment and to make payment from those funds reserved in its certified check account. Essentially, certification prevents the bank from denying liability. It is a promise that sufficient funds are on deposit *and have been set aside* to cover the check.

Focus Question 1

What type of check does a bank agree in advance to accept when the check is presented for payment?

To certify a check, the bank writes or stamps the word *certified* on the face of the check and typically writes the amount that it will pay.[2] Once a check is certified, the drawer and any prior indorsers are completely discharged from liability on the check [UCC 3–414(c), 3–415(d)]. Only the certifying bank is required to pay the instrument.

Either the drawer or the holder (payee) of a check can request certification. The drawee bank is not required to certify the check, however, and the bank's refusal to certify a check is not a dishonor of the check [UCC 3–409(d)].

20–1b The Bank-Customer Relationship

The bank-customer relationship begins when the customer opens a checking account and deposits funds that the bank will use to pay for checks written by the customer. The customer becomes the signatory, or authorized party, on the account. That is, the customer is the

1. *Cadence Bank v. Elizondo*, __ S.W.3d __, 2020 WL 1150126 (Tex. App. 1st Dis. 2020).
2. If the certification does not state an amount, and the amount is later increased and the instrument negotiated to a holder in due course (HDC), the obligation of the certifying bank is the amount of the instrument when it was taken by the HDC [UCC 3–413(b)].

only person from whom the bank should take instructions regarding the account. Essentially, three types of relationships are established at this time between the bank and the customer:

1. A *creditor-debtor relationship* is created when, for instance, a customer makes cash deposits into a checking account. When a customer makes a deposit, the customer becomes a creditor, and the bank a debtor, for the amount deposited.
2. An *agency relationship* arises between the customer and the bank when the customer writes a check. In an agency relationship, one party (an agent) agrees to represent or act for the other party (a principal). In effect, the customer orders the bank to pay the amount on the check. The bank becomes the customer's (principal's) agent and is obligated to honor the customer's request.
3. Finally, a *contractual relationship* exists when certain rights and duties arise. The contractual rights and duties of the bank and the customer depend on the nature of the transaction. For instance, a bank has specific contractual duties when honoring checks, accepting deposits, and transferring funds.

Case Example 20.4 Royal Arcanum Hospital Association of Kings County, Inc., required all of its corporate checks to be signed by two of three corporate officers. These officers were Frank Vassallo, Joseph Rugilio, and William Herrnkind. The three were also named as signatories on the firm's account with Capital One Bank, but the terms of the account did not include the two-signature requirement.

After Vassallo and Rugilio died, Herrnkind opened a new account in the corporate name that expressly permitted checks to be drawn on it with only his signature. Over the next four years, a series of transactions reduced the balance of the account from nearly $200,000 to zero. Royal Arcanum sued Herrnkind and Capital One in a New York state court to recover the funds. The court dismissed the complaint against Capital One, and Royal Arcanum appealed. A state intermediate appellate court affirmed. Capital One was not liable for the payment of unauthorized withdrawals on the firm's corporate accounts because the contract terms never included a two-signature requirement for the transactions.[3]

©Northfoto/Shutterstock.com

Can a customer account require two signatures for any check?

20–2 The Bank's Duty to Honor Checks

Focus Question 2

When may a bank properly dishonor a customer's check without being liable to the customer?

When a banking institution provides checking services, it agrees to honor the checks written by its customers, with the usual stipulation that the account must have sufficient funds available to pay each check [UCC 4–401(a)]. When a drawee bank *wrongfully* fails to honor a check, it is liable to its customer for damages resulting from its refusal to pay [UCC 4–402(b)]. The customer does not have to prove that the bank breached its contractual commitment or was negligent.

The customer's agreement with the bank includes a general obligation to keep sufficient funds on deposit to cover all checks written. The customer is liable to the payee or to the holder of a check in a civil suit if a check is dishonored for insufficient funds. If intent to defraud can be proved, the customer can also be subject to criminal prosecution for writing a bad check.

When the bank properly dishonors a check for insufficient funds, it has no liability to the customer. The bank may rightfully refuse payment on a customer's check in other circumstances as well.

20–2a Overdrafts

When the bank receives an item properly payable from its customer's checking account but the account contains insufficient funds to cover the amount of the check, the bank has two

3. *Royal Arcanum Hospital Association of Kings County, Inc. v. Herrnkind,* 113 A.D.3d 672, 978 N.Y.S.2d 355 (2014).

Overdraft A check that is paid by a bank when the checking account on which the check is written contains insufficient funds to cover the check.

options. It can dishonor the item, or it can pay the item and charge the customer's account, thus creating an **overdraft.** The bank can subtract the amount of the overdraft (plus a service charge) from the customer's next deposit or other customer funds, because a check carries with it an enforceable implied promise to reimburse the bank.

With a joint account, however, the bank cannot hold any joint account owner liable for payment of the overdraft unless that customer signed the check or benefited from its proceeds [UCC 4–401(b)]. **Example 20.5** Aaron and Sarah are married and have a joint bank account. Aaron writes a check to pay the electric bill for their apartment. If the check results in an overdraft, both Aaron and Sarah will be liable, because both obviously benefited from having electricity in their apartment. ■

A bank can expressly agree with a customer to accept overdrafts through an "overdraft protection agreement." If such an agreement is formed, any failure of the bank to honor a check because it would create an overdraft breaches this agreement and is considered a wrongful dishonor [UCC 4–402(a), (b)].

If a bank posts items to a customer's account only once a day, several items of different amounts may accumulate before the posting. Depending on the order in which the items are posted, an overdraft may occur earlier or later in the sequence. If the bank charges its customer a separate fee for honoring each item after an overdraft occurs, the sequencing of items can significantly impact the amount of fees that the customer is charged. At the center of the following case was one bank's decision to switch its sequencing to post items of the highest amount first.

Case 20.1

Legg v. West Bank

Supreme Court of Iowa, 873 N.W.2d 763 (2016).

Facts Darla and Jason Legg had a joint checking account with West Bank in Iowa. When they first opened the account, West Bank provided them with a Deposit Account Agreement stating that the bank had an obligation to exercise good faith and ordinary care in connection with each account. Later, without notifying its customers, the bank changed its posting sequence of transactions from low-to-high to high-to-low check amounts. This sequencing change caused eight overdrafts in the Leggs' account, resulting in eight overdraft fees. Had the bank not changed its sequencing order, the Leggs would have been charged only three overdraft fees. The Leggs filed a suit in an Iowa state court against West Bank, claiming in part that the bank had breached its duty to act in good faith. The bank filed a motion for summary judgment, which the court denied. West Bank appealed.

Issue Could West Bank have breached its duty to act in good faith with the Leggs when it changed its sequencing order?

Decision Yes. The state intermediate appellate court affirmed the lower court's ruling on the Leggs' good faith claim and remanded the case for further proceedings. The court reversed the decision as to the other claims (which included unjust enrichment and usury), however, finding that they should have been dismissed by summary judgment.

Reason A summary judgment is appropriate when there is no genuine issue of material fact and the moving party is entitled to judgment as a matter of law. The court recognized that there were fact issues precluding summary judgment on the good faith claim. "The Leggs could reasonably argue that the change in sequencing of . . . transactions, coupled with the lack of notification, violated the reasonable expectations of customers that the bank act in good faith when exercising its discretion to sequence transactions." Thus, the Leggs were entitled to proceed to trial on that claim. The court also concluded that there were no genuine issues of fact on Leggs' other claims, so the lower court should have granted the bank summary judgment on those claims.

Critical Thinking

- **What If the Facts Were Different?** *Suppose that West Bank's Deposit Account Agreement had not included "an obligation to Depositor to exercise good faith and ordinary care in connection with each account." How might the result have been different?*

20–2b Postdated Checks

A bank may charge a postdated check against a customer's account unless the customer notifies the bank, in a timely manner, not to pay the check until the stated date. (In fact, a check is usually paid without respect to its date.) The notice of postdating must be given in time to allow the bank to act on the notice before it pays the check. A bank that fails to act on the customer's notice and charges the customer's account before the date on the postdated check may be liable for any damages incurred by the customer [UCC 4–401(c)].

20–2c Stale Checks

Commercial banking practice regards a check that is presented for payment more than six months from its date as a **stale check.** A bank is not obligated to pay an uncertified check presented more than six months from its date [UCC 4–404].

Stale Check A check, other than a certified check, that is presented for payment more than six months after its date.

When it receives a stale check for payment, the bank has the option of paying or not paying the check. The bank may consult the customer before paying the check. If a bank pays a stale check in good faith without consulting the customer, the bank has the right to charge the customer's account for the amount of the check.

20–2d Stop-Payment Orders

A **stop-payment order** is an order by a customer to his or her bank not to pay or certify a certain check. Only a customer (or a person authorized to draw on the account) can order the bank not to pay the check when it is presented for payment [UCC 4–403(a)].[4] A customer has no right to stop payment on a check that has been certified or accepted by a bank, however. In addition, the customer-drawer must have a *valid legal ground* for issuing such an order, or the holder can sue the customer-drawer for payment.

Stop-Payment Order An order by a bank customer to the bank not to pay or certify a certain check.

Reasonable Time and Manner The customer must issue the stop-payment order within a reasonable time and in a reasonable manner to permit the bank to act on it [UCC 4–403(a)]. Although a stop-payment order can be given orally over the phone (in most states), it is binding on the bank for only fourteen calendar days unless confirmed in writing. (Recall that an electronic record, such as a stop-payment order submitted via the bank's website, is a writing.) A written or electronic stop-payment order is effective for six months, at which time it may be renewed [UCC 4–403(b)].

Paul Rapson / Alamy

An individual tells his bank to stop payment on a check he wrote to buy a computer. What happens if the bank honors that check?

Bank's Liability for Wrongful Payment If the bank pays the check in spite of a stop-payment order, the bank will be obligated to recredit the customer's account. In addition, if the bank's payment over a stop-payment order causes subsequent checks written on the drawer's account to "bounce" (be returned for nonsufficient funds), the bank will be liable for the resultant costs the drawer incurs. The bank is liable only for the amount of actual damages suffered by the drawer because of the wrongful payment, however [UCC 4–403(c)].

Example 20.6 Mike orders one hundred smartphones from Advanced Communications, Inc., at $100 each. Mike pays in advance with a check for $10,000. Later that day, Advanced Communications tells Mike that it will not deliver the smartphones as arranged. Mike immediately calls the bank and stops payment on the check, which he then confirms in writing. Two days later, in spite of this stop-payment order, the bank inadvertently honors Mike's check to Advanced Communications for the undelivered phones. The bank will be liable to Mike for the full $10,000.

---

4. Note that the right to stop payment is not limited to checks. It extends to any item payable by any bank. (See Official Comment 3 to UCC 4–403.) Also, any person claiming a legitimate interest in the account of a deceased customer may issue a stop-payment order [UCC 4–405].

The result would be different, however, if Advanced Communications had delivered and Mike had accepted ninety phones. Because Mike would have owed Advanced Communications $9,000 for the goods delivered, Mike's actual loss would be only $1,000. Consequently, the bank would be liable to Mike for only $1,000. ■

20–2e Incompetence or Death of a Customer

A customer's mental incompetence or death does not automatically revoke a bank's authority to accept, pay, or collect an item. Only after the bank is notified of the customer's incompetence or death and has reasonable time to act on the notice will the bank's authority be ineffective [UCC 4–405]. Without this provision, banks would constantly be required to verify the continued competence and life of their drawers.

Thus, if a bank is unaware that a customer who wrote a check has been declared incompetent or has died, the bank can pay the item without incurring liability [UCC 4–405]. Even when a bank knows of the death of its customer, for ten days after the *date of death,* it can pay or certify checks drawn on or before the date of death. An exception to this rule is made if a person claiming an interest in the account, such as an heir, orders the bank to stop payment.

20–2f Checks with Forged Drawers' Signatures

When a bank pays a check on which the drawer's signature is forged, generally the bank is liable. A forged signature on a check has no legal effect as the signature of a customer-drawer [UCC 3–403(a)]. A bank may be able to recover at least some of the loss from a customer whose negligence substantially contributed to the forgery, from the forger, or from the holder who cashed the check.

The general rule is that the bank must recredit the customer's account when it pays a check with a forged signature. A bank may contractually shift to the customer the risk of forged checks created electronically or by the use of other nonmanual signatures. For instance, the contract might stipulate that the customer is solely responsible for maintaining security over any signature stamp.

Customer Negligence When the customer's negligence substantially contributed to the forgery, the bank normally will *not* be obligated to recredit the customer's account for the amount of the check [UCC 3–406].[5] To avoid liability for negligence, a customer must examine monthly bank statements and canceled checks promptly and with reasonable care, and report any forged signatures [UCC 4–406].

In addition, the customer has a duty to make sure there are no unauthorized items—such as unfamiliar purchases or suspicious withdrawals—on the account statement. The failure to examine statements and report forged drawer signatures—or any carelessness by the customer that results in a loss to the bank—makes the customer liable for the loss.

Discovery of a forged drawer's signature and notice to the bank must take place within one year from the date that the statement was made available for inspection. Otherwise, the customer loses the legal right to have the bank recredit the account [UCC 4–406(f)].

Sometimes, the same wrongdoer forges a customer's signature on a series of checks. To recover for all the forged, unauthorized items, the customer must discover and report the *first* forged check to the bank within thirty calendar days of the receipt of the bank statement. Failure to notify the bank within this period of time discharges the bank's liability for all similar forged checks and unauthorized items that it pays before notification.

At the center of the following case is the effect of these provisions and of an agreement between the bank and its customer concerning the time periods. The unauthorized item in dispute was not a check but a withdrawal of all of the funds in the account.

5. The customer's liability may be reduced, however, by the amount of the loss caused by negligence on the part of the bank [UCC 3–406(b)].

Case 20.2

Horton v. JPMorgan Chase Bank, N.A.

Court of Appeals of Texas, Dallas, 2018 WL 494776 (2018).

Facts Robbie Horton, a paralegal for Stovall & Associates, P.C., opened an individual checking account with JPMorgan Chase Bank (Chase) and provided a signature card. The terms of the account agreement required Horton to notify Chase, in writing, of any unauthorized item within thirty days of when a statement showing the item was mailed or made available. A failure to provide the notice would prevent a claim based on the item. Two months later, Chase received a second signature card purportedly signed by Horton and Kimberly Stovall, an attorney with Stovall & Associates, to convert the account to a joint account.

Less than a year later, the law firm terminated Horton's employment, and on the same day, Stovall withdrew all of the funds in the joint account. Almost two years after the withdrawal, Horton filed a suit in a Texas state court against Chase, alleging breach of contract. Horton asserted that she had not agreed to the withdrawal by Stovall. Chase filed a motion for summary judgment, which the court granted. Horton appealed.

Issue Were Horton's claims barred by the provisions of the account agreement?

Decision Yes. A state intermediate appellate court affirmed the summary judgment of the trial court. The court pointed out that Chase required thirty days' written notice for any errors in its monthly account statements. Horton did not give such notice.

Reason Under the Uniform Commercial Code (UCC), a bank can only charge a customer's account for an item that is authorized by the customer and in accord with any agreement between the customer and the bank. If a bank sends or makes available an account statement that identifies the items paid, a customer must examine the statement and promptly notify the bank of any unauthorized payment. The UCC "absolutely" bars a customer's claim to recover such a payment if the notice is not provided within one year. These obligations can be varied by agreement.

In this case, the account terms required Horton to review each statement and notify Chase, in writing, of any unauthorized items within thirty days of when the statement was mailed or made available. Without this notice, a claim based on such an item was barred. Chase mailed monthly statements to its customers. The bank also made the statements available online, with images of the items drawn on the account. Horton did not notify Chase, in writing, of any errors regarding her account until she filed her petition twenty months later.

Critical Thinking

- **Legal Environment** *Horton claimed that she had not agreed to the conversion of the account or to the withdrawal of the funds. These contentions did not affect the court's decision. Why not?*
- **Economic** *Why does the UCC "absolutely" limit the time that a customer has to report an altered check or unauthorized signature?*

Bank Negligence In one situation, a bank customer can escape liability, at least in part, for failing to notify the bank of forged checks within the required time period. When the customer can prove that the bank was also negligent—that is, that the bank failed to exercise ordinary care—then the bank, too, will be liable.

Ordinary care means that a bank must observe reasonable banking standards prevalent in its geographical area [UCC3–103]. If the customer can show the bank did not use ordinary care, the loss will be allocated between the bank and the customer on the basis of comparative negligence [UCC 4–406(e)].

Other Parties from Whom the Bank May Recover As noted earlier, a forged signature on a check has no legal effect as the signature of a drawer. Instead, the person who forged the signature is liable [UCC 3–403(a)]. Therefore, when a bank pays a check on which the drawer's signature is forged, the bank has a right to recover from the party who forged the signature (if that person can be found). The bank may also have a right to recover from a party who transferred a check bearing a forged drawer's signature and received payment.

20–2g Checks Bearing Forged Indorsements

A bank that pays a customer's check bearing a forged indorsement must recredit the customer's account or be liable to the customer-drawer for breach of contract. **Example 20.7** Simon issues a $500 check "to the order of Antonio." Juan steals the check, forges Antonio's indorsement, and cashes the check. When the check reaches Simon's bank, the bank pays it and debits Simon's account. The bank must recredit the $500 to Simon's account because it failed to carry out Simon's order to pay "to the order of Antonio" [UCC 4–401(a)].

Eventually, the loss usually falls on the first party to take the instrument bearing the forged indorsement because a forged indorsement does not transfer title. Thus, whoever takes an instrument with a forged indorsement cannot become a holder. In *Example 20.7*, Simon's bank can recover—for breach of warranty—from the bank that cashed the check when Juan presented it [UCC 4–207(a)(2)].

The customer, in any event, has a duty to report forged indorsements promptly. Failure to report forged indorsements within a three-year period after the forged items have been made available to the customer relieves the bank of liability [UCC 4–111].

20–2h Altered Checks

The customer's instruction to the bank is to pay the exact amount on the face of the check to the holder. The bank has a duty to examine each check before making final payment. If the bank fails to detect an alteration, normally it is liable to its customer for the loss because it did not pay as the customer ordered.

The bank's loss is the difference between the original amount of the check and the amount actually paid [UCC 4–401(d)(1)]. **Example 20.8** Hailey writes a check for $11 that is altered to $111. Hailey's account will be charged $11 (the amount the customer ordered the bank to pay). The bank normally will be responsible for the $100 difference.

Customer Negligence As in a situation involving a forged drawer's signature, a customer's negligence can shift the loss when payment is made on an altered check (unless the bank was also negligent). For instance, a person may carelessly write a check and leave large gaps in it where additional numbers and words can be inserted. Similarly, a person who signs a check and leaves the dollar amount for someone else to fill in is barred from protesting when the bank unknowingly and in good faith pays whatever amount is shown [UCC 4–401(d)(2)]. Finally, if the bank can trace its loss on successive altered checks to the customer's failure to discover the initial alteration, the bank can reduce its liability for reimbursing the customer's account [UCC 4–406].

In every situation involving a forged drawer's signature or an alteration, a bank must observe reasonable commercial (banking) standards of care in paying on a customer's checks [UCC 4–406(e)]. The customer's negligence can be used as a defense only if the bank has exercised ordinary care.

Other Parties from Whom the Bank May Recover The bank is entitled to recover the amount of loss from the transferor who presented the check for payment. A transferor, by presenting a check for payment, warrants that the check has not been altered.

There are two exceptions to this rule. First, if the bank is also the drawer (as it is on a cashier's check), it cannot recover from the presenting party if the party is a holder in due course (HDC) acting in good faith [UCC 3–417(a)(2), 4–208(a)(2)]. The reason is that an instrument's drawer is in a better position than an HDC to know whether the instrument has been altered.

Second, an HDC who presents a certified check for payment in good faith will not be held liable under warranty principles if the check was altered before the HDC acquired it [UCC 3–417(a)(2), 4–207(a)(2)]. **Example 20.9** Jordan draws a check for $500 payable to David.

David alters the amount to $5,000. The drawee bank, First National, certifies the check for $5,000. David negotiates the check to Ethan, an HDC. The drawee bank pays Ethan $5,000. On discovering the mistake, the bank cannot recover from Ethan the $4,500 paid by mistake, even though the bank was not in a superior position to detect the alteration. This is in accord with the purpose of certification, which is to obtain the definite obligation of a bank to honor a definite instrument.

20–3 The Bank's Duty to Accept Deposits

A bank has a duty to its customer to accept the customer's deposits of cash and checks. When checks are deposited, the bank must make the funds represented by those checks available within certain time frames. A bank also has a duty to collect payment on any checks payable or indorsed to its customers and deposited by them into their accounts. Cash deposits made in U.S. currency are received into customers' accounts without being subject to further collection procedures.

20–3a Availability Schedule for Deposited Checks

The Expedited Funds Availability Act[6] and Regulation CC[7] (the regulation implementing the act) establish when funds from deposited checks must be made available to the customer. The rules are as follows:

1. Any local check (drawn on a bank in the same area) deposited must be available for withdrawal by check or as cash within one business day from the date of deposit.
2. For nonlocal checks, the funds must be available for withdrawal within not more than five business days.
3. Under the Check Clearing for the 21st Century Act[8] (Check 21, which is the subject of this chapter's *Landmark in the Law* feature), a bank must credit a customer's account as soon as the bank receives the funds.
4. For cash deposits, wire transfers, and government checks, funds must be available on the next business day.
5. The first $100 of any deposit must be available for cash withdrawal on the opening of the next business day after deposit.

A different availability schedule applies to deposits made at *nonproprietary* automated teller machines (ATMs). These are ATMs that are not owned or operated by the bank receiving the deposits. Basically, a five-day hold is permitted on all deposits, including cash deposits, made at nonproprietary ATMs. Other exceptions also exist. For instance, a banking institution has eight days to make funds available in new accounts (those open less than thirty days). A bank that places a longer hold on a deposited check than that specified by the rules must notify the customer.

YinYang/E+/Getty Images

If you deposit a check at your bank that is written on another bank, can you withdraw those funds in cash immediately? Why or why not?

20–3b The Traditional Collection Process

The bank collection process is the process by which a bank that accepts a check for deposit collects the amount from the issuing bank. Usually, deposited checks involve parties that do business at different banks, but sometimes checks are written between customers of the same bank. Either situation is governed by the statutory framework of Article 4 of the UCC.

6. 12 U.S.C. Sections 4001–4010.
7. 12 C.F.R. Sections 229.1–229.42.
8. 12 U.S.C. Sections 5001–5018.

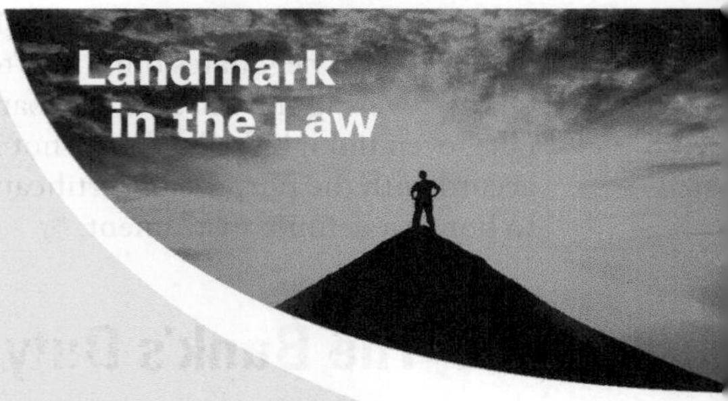

Check Clearing for the 21st Century Act (Check 21)

In the traditional collection process, paper checks had to be processed manually and physically transported before they could be cleared. Although the UCC allowed banks to use *electronic presentment*—that is, to transmit check information electronically instead of sending actual paper checks—this method was not widely adopted because it required agreements among individual banks.

Purpose of Check 21 To streamline the costly and time-consuming collection process and improve the overall efficiency of the nation's payment system, Congress passed the Check Clearing for the 21st Century Act (Check 21), which went into effect in 2004. Check 21 changed the collection process by creating a new negotiable instrument called a *substitute check*. Although the act did not require banks to change their check-collection practices, the creation of substitute checks has facilitated the use of electronic check processing.

Substitute Checks A substitute check is a paper reproduction of the front and back of an original check that contains all of the information required for automated processing. A bank creates substitute checks from digital images of original checks. It can then process the check information electronically or deliver substitute checks to banks that wish to continue receiving paper checks.

The original check can be destroyed after a substitute check is created, helping to prevent the check from being paid twice and reducing expenses. Nevertheless, at least for a while, not all checks will be converted to substitute checks.

Faster Access to Funds The Expedited Funds Availability Act requires the Federal Reserve Board to revise the availability schedule for funds from deposited checks to correspond to reductions in check-processing time. Therefore, as the speed of check processing continues to increase under Check 21, the Federal Reserve Board will reduce the maximum time that a bank can hold funds from deposited checks before making them available to the depositors.

That means, of course, that account holders will have faster access to their deposited funds. But it also means that they will have less *float time*—the time between when a check is written and when the amount is deducted from the account. Consequently, to avoid overdrafts, account holders need to make sure that funds are available to cover checks when they are written.

Application to Today's World *As more financial institutions transfer digital images of checks, the check-processing system becomes more efficient. Customers are increasingly unable to rely on banking float when they are low on funds, so they should make sure that funds are available to cover checks when they are written. Customers cannot opt out of Check 21. Nor can they refuse to accept a substitute check as proof of payment.*

Depositary Bank The first bank to receive a check for payment.

Payor Bank The bank on which a check is drawn (the drawee bank).

Collecting Bank Any bank handling an item for collection, except the payor bank.

Intermediary Bank Any bank to which an item is transferred in the course of collection, except the depositary or payor bank.

Designations of Banks The first bank to receive a check for payment is the **depositary bank.**[9] For instance, when a person deposits a tax-refund check into a personal checking account at the local bank, that bank is the depositary bank. The bank on which a check is drawn (the drawee bank) is the **payor bank.** Any bank except the payor bank that handles a check during some phase of the collection process is a **collecting bank.** Any bank except the payor bank or the depositary bank to which an item is transferred in the course of this collection process is an **intermediary bank.**

During the collection process, any bank can take on one or more of the various roles of depositary, payor, collecting, and intermediary bank. **Example 20.10** A buyer in New York writes a check on her New York bank and sends it to a seller in San Francisco. The seller deposits the check in her San Francisco bank account. The seller's bank is both a *depositary bank* and a *collecting bank*. The buyer's bank in New York is the *payor bank*. As the check travels from San Francisco to New York, any collecting bank handling the item in the collection process (other than the depositary bank and the payor bank) is also called an *intermediary bank*. Exhibit 20–2 illustrates how various banks function in the collection process in the context of this example.

9. All definitions in this section are found in UCC 4–105. The terms *depositary* and *depository* have different meanings in the banking context. A depository bank refers to a *physical place* (a bank or other institution) in which deposits or funds are held or stored.

Exhibit 20–2 The Check-Collection Process

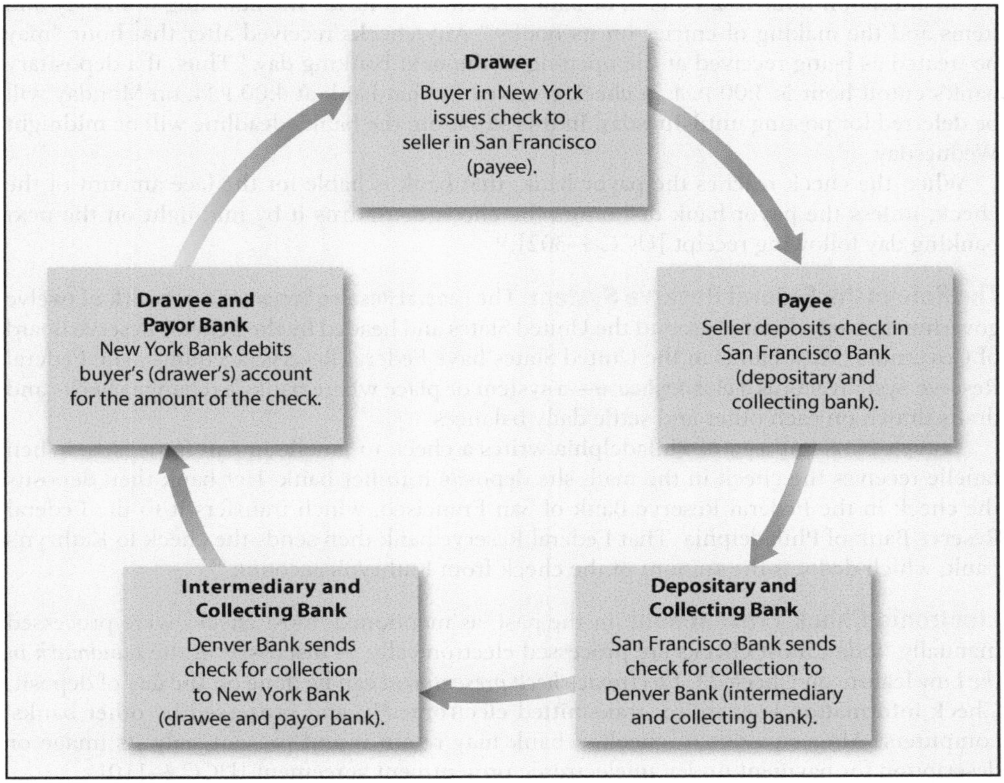

Check Collection Between Customers of the Same Bank An item that is payable by the same bank that receives it (which in this situation is both the depositary bank and the payor bank) is called an "on-us item." Usually, the bank issues a "provisional credit" for on-us items within the same day. If the bank does not dishonor the check by the opening of the second banking day following its receipt, the check is considered paid [UCC 4–215(e)(2)].

Example 20.11 Pam and Jenna have checking accounts at First State Bank. On Monday, Jenna deposits into her checking account a $300 check from Pam. That same day, the bank issues Jenna a provisional (temporary) credit for $300. When the bank opens on Wednesday, Pam's check is considered honored, and Jenna's provisional credit becomes a final payment.

Check Collection between Customers of Different Banks Once a depositary bank receives a check payable to another bank, it must arrange to present the check, either directly or through intermediary banks, to the appropriate payor bank. Each bank in the collection chain must pass the check on before midnight of the next banking day following its receipt [UCC 4–202(b)].[10] A "banking day" is any part of a day that the bank is open to carry on substantially all of its banking functions. Thus, if only a bank's drive-through facilities are open, a check deposited on Saturday will not trigger the bank's midnight deadline until the following Monday.

10. A bank may take a "reasonably longer time" in certain circumstances, such as when the bank's computer system is down due to a power failure, but the bank must show that its action is still timely [UCC 4–202(b)].

The UCC permits what is called *deferred posting*. According to UCC 4–108, "a bank may fix an afternoon hour of 2:00 P.M. or later as a cutoff hour for the handling of money and items and the making of entries on its books." Any checks received after that hour "may be treated as being received at the opening of the next banking day." Thus, if a depositary bank's cutoff hour is 3:00 P.M., a check received by that bank at 4:00 P.M. on Monday will be deferred for posting until Tuesday. In this situation, the bank's deadline will be midnight Wednesday.

When the check reaches the payor bank, that bank is liable for the face amount of the check, unless the payor bank dishonors the check or returns it by midnight on the next banking day following receipt [UCC 4–302].[11]

Federal Reserve System A network of twelve district banks and related branches located around the country and headed by the Federal Reserve Board of Governors. Most banks in the United States have Federal Reserve accounts.

Clearinghouse A system or place where banks exchange checks and drafts drawn on each other and settle daily balances.

The Role of the Federal Reserve System The **Federal Reserve System** is a network of twelve government banks located around the United States and headed by the Federal Reserve Board of Governors. Most banks in the United States have Federal Reserve accounts. The Federal Reserve System acts as a **clearinghouse**—a system or place where banks exchange checks and drafts drawn on each other and settle daily balances.

Example 20.12 Kathryn of Philadelphia writes a check to Janelle in San Francisco. When Janelle receives the check in the mail, she deposits it in her bank. Her bank then deposits the check in the Federal Reserve Bank of San Francisco, which transfers it to the Federal Reserve Bank of Philadelphia. That Federal Reserve bank then sends the check to Kathryn's bank, which deducts the amount of the check from Kathryn's account. ■

Electronic Check Presentment In the past, as mentioned, most checks were processed manually. Today, most checks are processed electronically, as discussed in the *Landmark in the Law* feature on Check 21. *Electronic check presentment* can be done on the day of deposit. Check information is encoded, transmitted electronically, and processed by other banks' computers. After encoding a check, a bank may retain it and present only its image or description for payment under an electronic presentment agreement [UCC 4–110].

Focus Question 3

What is electronic check presentment, and how does it differ from the traditional check-clearing process?

A bank that encodes information for electronic presentment warrants to any subsequent bank or payor that the encoded information is correct [UCC 4–209]. Similarly, a bank that retains a check and presents its image or description for payment warrants that the image or description is accurate.

Regulation CC provides that a returned check must be encoded with the routing number of the depositary bank, the amount of the check, and other information. The regulation further states that a check must still be returned within the deadlines required by the UCC.

20–4 Electronic Fund Transfers

Electronic Fund Transfer (EFT) A transfer of funds through the use of an electronic terminal, smartphone, tablet, telephone, or computer.

An **electronic fund transfer (EFT)** is a transfer of funds through the use of an electronic terminal, smartphone, tablet, computer, or telephone. The law governing EFTs depends on the type of transfer involved. Consumer fund transfers are governed by the Electronic Fund Transfer Act (EFTA).[12] Commercial fund transfers are governed by Article 4A of the UCC.

Although electronic banking offers numerous benefits, it also poses difficulties on occasion. For instance, it is difficult to issue stop-payment orders with electronic banking. Also, fewer records are available to prove or disprove that a transaction took place. The possibilities for tampering with a person's private banking information have increased.

11. A bank may be excused from liability for failing to meet its midnight deadline under certain conditions, such as when there is an electrical outage or equipment failure and the bank has exercised "such diligence as the circumstances require" [UCC 4–109(d)].
12. 15 U.S.C. Sections 1693–1693r. The EFTA amended Title IX of the Consumer Credit Protection Act.

20–4a Types of EFT Systems

Most banks offer EFT services. The following are the most common types of EFT systems used by bank customers:

1. *Automated teller machines (ATMs)*—The machines are connected online to the bank's computers. A customer inserts a plastic card (called an ATM or debit card) issued by the bank and keys in a *personal identification number (PIN)* to access accounts and conduct banking transactions.
2. *Point-of-sale systems*—Online terminals allow consumers to transfer funds to merchants to pay for purchases using a debit card.
3. *Direct deposits and withdrawals*—Customers can authorize the bank to allow another party, such as the government or an employer, to make direct deposits into their accounts. Similarly, customers can request the bank to make automatic payments to a third party at regular, recurrent intervals from the customer's funds (insurance premiums or loan payments, for instance).
4. *Online payment systems*—Many financial institutions permit their customers to access the institution's computer system via the Internet and direct a transfer of funds between accounts or pay a particular bill. Payments can be made on a one-time or a recurring basis.

Know This

The EFTA does not provide for the reversal of an electronic transfer of funds once it has occurred.

Focus Question 4

What are the four most common types of electronic fund transfers?

20–4b Consumer Fund Transfers

The Electronic Fund Transfer Act (EFTA) provides a basic framework for the rights, liabilities, and responsibilities of users of EFT systems. Additionally, the act gave the Federal Reserve Board authority to issue rules and regulations to help implement the act's provisions. The Federal Reserve Board's implemental regulation is called **Regulation E.**

The EFTA governs financial institutions that offer electronic fund transfers involving consumer accounts. The types of accounts covered include checking accounts, savings accounts, and any other asset accounts established for personal, family, or household purposes.

Regulation E A set of rules issued by the Federal Reserve System's Board of Governors to protect users of electronic fund transfer systems.

Disclosure Requirements The EFTA is essentially a disclosure law benefiting consumers. The act requires financial institutions to inform consumers of their rights and responsibilities, including those listed here, with respect to EFT systems.

1. The bank must provide a monthly statement for every month in which there is an electronic transfer of funds. The statement must show the amount and date of the transfer, the names of the retailers or other third parties involved, the location or identification of the terminal, and the fees.
2. If a customer's debit card is lost or stolen and used without permission, the customer will be required to pay no more than $50 if the bank is notified of the loss or theft within two days of learning about it. Otherwise, the liability increases to $500. The customer may be liable for more than $500 if the unauthorized use is not reported within sixty days after it appears on the customer's statement. (If a customer voluntarily gives the debit card to another, who then uses it improperly, the protections just mentioned do not apply.)
3. The customer must discover any error on the monthly statement within sixty days and notify the bank. The bank then has ten days to investigate and must report its conclusions to the customer in writing. If the bank takes longer than ten days, it must return the disputed amount to the customer's account until it finds the error. If there is no error, the customer has to return the disputed funds to the bank.
4. The bank must make receipts available for transactions made through computer terminals, but it is not obligated to do so for telephone transfers.

In the following case, an account holder's daughter initiated hundreds of electronic transfers from her father's accounts to pay her personal bills. He claimed that the transactions were unauthorized. Was the bank liable?

Case 20.3

Binns v. Truist Bank

United States Court of Appeals, Third Circuit, __ F.3d __, 2020 WL 1130639 (2020).

Facts Truist Bank's "Customer Agreements" require a customer to promptly notify the bank of any problems with an account. The agreements also limit the bank's liability for transactions by the same unauthorized party if the customer does not notify the bank within sixty days. A customer cannot commence a legal action based on an unauthorized transaction more than one year from the date of the statement containing the transaction. But the bank may waive the time limit for some transactions without losing the right to impose it for others.

James Binns maintained a commercial account and a personal account with Truist Bank. Without Binns's authorization, his daughter Amy used the routing and account numbers for the commercial account to request hundreds of electronic transfers to pay her personal bills. Truist sent Binns monthly statements detailing the account transactions, but he never reconciled the charges.

Four years after his daughter's first transfer from his commercial account, Binns learned that she had also made withdrawals from his personal account. The bank agreed to waive the required notice and provided a refund for those withdrawals. Binns then reconciled the statements for his commercial account and filed a claim in a federal district court against Truist for reimbursement. The court granted a summary judgment in the bank's favor. Binns appealed.

Issue Did the Customer Agreements bar Binns's claim?

Decision Yes. The U.S. Court of Appeals for the Third Circuit upheld the judgment of the lower court. "The District Court [decided] that the Customer Agreements control, and that they bar Binns's claims. As we agree with the District Court, we will affirm that decision."

Reason The appellate court applied several of the terms in the Customer Agreements to the circumstances in Binns's case. Under those terms, Binns had sixty days from the date of the monthly statement in which his daughter's first unauthorized transaction appeared to file a claim to recover for the entire series of her unauthorized transactions. But Binns did not reconcile his monthly statements or report any unauthorized transactions until four years after the date of the statement that contained the first transaction.

Binns contended that the bank was liable for the unauthorized withdrawals from his commercial account because the bank had permitted his daughter's unauthorized withdrawals from his personal account. He argued that the bank waived the required notice to provide a refund of the withdrawals from the personal account. The court emphasized that the Customer Agreements imposed a duty to investigate on Binns, not the bank, and allowed the bank to waive the notice requirement for some transactions and impose it for others.

Critical Thinking

- **Legal Environment** *On what fact might a court base a decision that the EFTA does not apply in Binns's situation?*
- **What If the Facts Were Different?** *Suppose that Binns had charged the bank with violations of Article 3 of the UCC, which governs negotiable instruments, defined as signed writings that order or promise payments of money. Article 3 allocates loss from a forged signature or alteration on an instrument according to the exercise of ordinary care by a bank and its customer. Would the result have been different? Explain.*

Violations and Damages EFT systems are vulnerable to fraud when someone uses another's card or code or other means to make unauthorized transfers. Unauthorized access to an EFT system constitutes a federal felony, and those convicted may be fined up to $10,000 and sentenced to as long as ten years in prison. Banks must strictly comply with the terms of the EFTA and are liable for any failure to adhere to its provisions.

For a bank's violation of the EFTA, a consumer may recover both actual damages (including attorneys' fees and costs) and punitive damages of not less than $100 and not more than $1,000. Even when a customer has sustained no actual damage, the bank may be liable for legal costs and punitive damages if it fails to follow the proper procedures outlined by the EFTA in regard to error resolution.

Know This

If any part of an electronic fund transfer is covered by the EFTA, the entire transfer is excluded from UCC Article 4A.

20–4c Commercial Fund Transfers

Funds are also transferred electronically "by wire" between commercial parties. In fact, the dollar volume of payments by wire transfer is more than $1 trillion a day—an amount that far exceeds the dollar volume of payments made by other means. The two major wire payment systems are the Federal Reserve's wire transfer network (Fedwire) and the New York Clearing House Interbank Payments Systems (CHIPS).

Commercial wire transfers are governed by Article 4A of the UCC, which has been adopted by most states. Article 4A uses the term *funds transfer* rather than *wire transfer* to describe the overall payment transaction. **Example 20.13** Jellux, Inc., owes $5 million to Perot Corporation. Instead of sending Perot a check or some other instrument that would enable Perot to obtain payment, Jellux instructs its bank, East Bank, to credit $5 million to Perot's account in West Bank. East Bank debits Jellux's East Bank account and wires $5 million to Perot's West Bank account. In more complex transactions, additional banks would be involved. ■

20–5 Banking in the Digital Age

Perhaps the most significant trend in banking today is the emergence of *fintech*. A combination of the words *financial* and *technology*, fintech is an umbrella term used to describe financial services that rely on the technological (the Internet, computers, smartphones) rather than the physical (bank branches, cash, paper checks) to meet consumer needs. Fintech provides levels of speed and convenience that have become the expected norm for the banking industry.

20–5a Online and Mobile Banking

Especially for younger consumers, the notion of visiting a bank branch to make a deposit or writing a paper check has become outdated. Instead, about 90 percent of Americans use *online* and *mobile banking* on a regular basis.

Online banking gives customers access to their bank accounts on the Internet. Online banking programs enable customers to transfer funds between accounts, receive digital payments, manage investments, track loans, and make numerous other transactions on their computers.

Online Banking Traditional banking services, such as account management and transfers, that are provided on the financial institution's Internet website.

Mobile banking takes this level of fintech one step further, giving customers the ability, through apps, to conduct online banking from smartphones and tablets. In addition to the traditional banking services discussed throughout this chapter, mobile banking apps allow users to scan a fingerprint to access their accounts, place temporary holds on credit cards, and view recurring or unauthorized charges in real time. Mobile banking is also crucial for the spread of *open banking*, a particularly innovative variety of fintech that is the subject of this chapter's *Adapting the Law to the Online Environment* feature.

Mobile Banking A version of online banking that is carried out with apps on smartphones or tablets.

Adapting the Law to the Online Environment

Open Banking

Online banking consumers demand that their financial data be protected. These customers, so to speak, want banks to place brick walls around their financial information. *Open banking* takes a wrecking ball to that brick wall—with the customers' consent.

Consumer Benefits

The concept behind open banking is relatively simple: a fintech company shares customer financial data with third parties for the benefit of the customer. Open banking supports the principle that individuals, not banks, own their financial data, and thus individuals should be able to share the data when it benefits them.

Consider MortgageGym, a British fintech company that promises to do the "heavy lifting" for mortgage seekers. First, customers take fifteen minutes to fill out online forms relating to their personal and financial details, as well as their mortgage needs. Then, with the help of another fintech called Experian, MortgageGym obtains the customers' credit rating. Finally, the company does an online search of the United Kingdom's mortgage market. Sixty seconds later, the customers are provided with four of the best mortgage deals available in the country.

Like every other fintech company that provides open banking services in the United Kingdom, MortgageGym operates under the close watch of the Financial Conduct Authority (FCA). Indeed, regulation is a hallmark of open banking worldwide. In the United States, which has yet to embrace the concept, it appears that open banking will be industry driven. As a result, American banks and fintech companies will have to convince consumers not only that open banking adds value to the online banking experience, but also that the financial industry can be trusted not to abuse unfiltered access to its customers' financial data.

Critical Thinking

Why is consumer consent so important to the open banking model?

20–5b Electronic Payment Systems

eBill An electronic version of a paper bill for goods or services that is issued online and can be paid online.

Online and mobile banking facilitate the use of *electronic billing*. An electronic bill, or **eBill,** is simply a digital version of a paper bill. eBills contain the same information as paper bills. The difference is that they can be viewed and paid online. Banks now routinely offer fintech services that enable customers to take advantage of this technology.

Such services include electronic bill payment and presentment (EBPP). One type of EBPP is offered directly by companies that provide goods or services to consumers. Another type allows consumers to pay multiple bills electronically through their banks' online banking system.

Paper checks are still used in about half of all payments made between merchants for goods and services. As corporate America becomes more comfortable with cloud computing, these business-to-business (B2B) payments are increasingly becoming digitized. Many fintech companies have made Internet-based payments systems available for B2B bill paying. Typically, these companies charge a monthly subscription cost plus a small per-unit transaction fee and carry out the payment process automatically, without any additional input from the firms involved in the business dealings.

20–5c Artificial Intelligence (AI) and Fintech

Artificial intelligence (AI) refers to a branch of computer science that gives machines the ability to perform tasks that require human-level intelligence. The role of AI in fintech is sure to increase exponentially over the next decade, but its presence is already being felt. Some banks, for instance, have developed AI-based software that gives customers advice on how their spending and saving habits impact short- and long-term financial goals.

Digital Lending AI is also a crucial component in *digital lending*, the use of fintech to originate and renew loans. The AI program is "taught" the parameters of a financial institution's lending practices, such as which factors determine a potential borrower's creditworthiness. Then the program uses a problem-solving platform called an algorithm to determine whether a loan is warranted, and, if so, on what terms.

Focus Question 5

What role does artificial intelligence (AI) play in digital lending?

Banks that have implemented this strategy, mostly in Europe, report that the time taken to process smaller loans has dropped from twenty days to less than ten minutes. Fintech also has the potential to make the lending process more equitable. The digital mortgage lender Better.com reported a 400 percent increase in loans to single, minority women borrowers in the first year it used an algorithm-based lending program.

Neobanks Increased access to AI is a crucial component in the growth in **neobanks,** or banks that exist only as digital entities. In practical terms, a neobank is an app that helps customers store and manage their money. These financial institutions offer traditional services such as banking and checking accounts, as well as the array of mobile banking options discussed earlier. Additional benefits include no monthly maintenance fees, fewer surprise charges and overdraft problems, and digital lending. The main drawback of neobanks is that, for now, funds deposited with them are not insured by the federal government.

Neobanks Banks that operate exclusively online without traditional physical branch networks.

Practice and Review

RPM Pizza, Inc., issued a check for $96,000 to Systems Marketing for an advertising campaign. A few days later, RPM decided not to go through with the deal and placed a written stop-payment order on the check. RPM and Systems had no further contact for many months. Three weeks after the stop-payment order expired, however, Toby Rierson, an employee at Systems, cashed the check. Bank One Cambridge, RPM's bank, paid the check with funds from RPM's account. Because the check was more than six months old, it was stale. Thus, according to standard banking procedures as well as Bank One's own policies, the signature on the check should have been specially verified, but it was not. RPM filed a suit in a federal district court against Bank One to recover the amount of the check. Using the information presented in the chapter, answer the following questions.

1. How long is a written stop-payment order effective? What else could RPM have done to prevent this check from being cashed?
2. What would have happened if RPM had not had a legitimate reason for stopping payment on the check?
3. What are a bank's obligations with respect to stale checks?
4. Would a court be likely to hold the bank liable for the amount of the check because it failed to verify the signature on the check? Why or why not?

Debate This

To reduce fraud, checks that utilize mechanical or electronic signature systems should not be honored.

Key Terms

cashier's check 491
certified check 492
clearinghouse 502
collecting bank 500
depositary bank 500
eBill 506
electronic fund transfer (EFT) 502
Federal Reserve System 502
intermediary bank 500
mobile banking 505
neobanks 507
online banking 505
overdraft 494
payor bank 500
Regulation E 503
stale check 495
stop-payment order 495

Chapter Summary: Banking

Checks and the Bank-Customer Relationship	1. **Checks**— a. Cashier's check—A check drawn by a bank on itself (the bank is both the drawer and the drawee) and purchased by a customer. In effect, the bank assumes responsibility for paying the check, thus making the check nearly the equivalent of cash. b. Certified check—A check for which the drawee bank certifies in writing that it has set aside funds from the drawer's account to ensure payment of the check on presentation. On certification, the drawer and all prior indorsers are completely discharged from liability on the check. 2. **The bank-customer relationship**—When a customer opens an account, three types of relationships are established with the bank: a creditor-debtor relationship, an agency relationship, and a contractual relationship.
The Bank's Duty to Honor Checks	Generally, a bank has a duty to honor its customers' checks, provided that the customers have sufficient funds on deposit to cover the checks [UCC 4–401(a)]. The bank is liable to its customers for actual damages proved to be due to wrongful dishonor [UCC 4–402(b)]. 1. **Overdraft**—The bank has a right to charge a customer's account for any item properly payable, even if the charge results in an overdraft [UCC 4–401]. 2. **Postdated check**—The bank may charge a postdated check against a customer's account, unless the customer notifies the bank, in a timely manner, not to pay the check until the stated date [UCC 4–401]. 3. **Stale check**—The bank is not obligated to pay an uncertified check presented more than six months after its date, but the bank may do so in good faith without liability [UCC 4–404]. 4. **Stop-payment order**—The customer (or a person authorized to draw on the account) must make a stop-payment order in time for the bank to have a reasonable opportunity to act. Oral orders are binding for only fourteen days unless they are confirmed in writing. Written or electronic orders are effective for six months unless renewed in writing [UCC 4–403(b)]. The bank is liable for wrongful payment over a timely stop-payment order to the extent that the customer suffers a loss. 5. **Incompetence or death of a customer**—So long as the bank does not know of the death or incompetence of a customer, the bank can pay an item without liability. Even with knowledge of a customer's death, a bank can honor or certify checks drawn on or before the date of death (in the absence of a stop-payment order) for ten days after the date of death [UCC 4–405]. 6. **Checks with forged drawers' signatures**—The customer has a duty to examine account statements with reasonable care on receipt and to notify the bank promptly of any forged signatures. On a series of forged signatures by the same wrongdoer, examination and report must be made within thirty calendar days of receipt of the first statement containing a forged item [UCC 4–406]. The customer's failure to comply with these rules releases the bank from liability unless the bank failed to exercise ordinary care, in which case liability may be apportioned according to a comparative negligence standard. Regardless of care or lack of care, the customer is barred from holding the bank liable after one year for forged customer signatures. 7. **Checks bearing forged indorsements**—A bank that pays a customer's check bearing a forged indorsement must recredit the customer's account or be liable to the customer for breach of contract. A customer's failure to report a forged indorsement within a three-year period after the forged items are available to the customer relieves the bank of liability [UCC 4-111]. 8. **Altered checks**—If the bank fails to detect an alteration, normally it is liable to its customer because it did not pay as the customer ordered. Customer negligence can shift the loss.

The Bank's Duty to Accept Deposits	A bank has a duty to accept deposits made by its customers into their accounts. Funds from deposited checks must be made available to customers according to a schedule mandated by the Expedited Funds Availability Act and Regulation CC. A bank also has a duty to collect payment on any checks deposited by its customers. When checks deposited by customers are drawn on other banks, the check-collection process comes into play. **1. Designations of banks**—UCC 4–105 provides the following definitions of banks involved in the collection process: **a.** Depositary bank—The first bank to accept a check for payment. **b.** Payor bank—The bank on which a check is drawn. **c.** Collecting bank—Any bank except the payor bank that handles a check during the collection process. **d.** Intermediary bank—Any bank except the payor bank or the depositary bank to which an item is transferred in the course of the collection process. **2. Check collection between customers of the same bank**—A check payable by the depositary bank that receives it is an "on-us item." If the bank does not dishonor the check by the opening of the second banking day following its receipt, the check is considered paid [UCC 4–215(e)(2)]. **3. Check collection between customers of different banks**—Each bank in the collection process must pass the check on to the next appropriate bank before midnight of the next banking day following its receipt [UCC 4–108, 4–202(b), 4–302]. **4. The role of the Federal Reserve System**—The Federal Reserve System facilitates the check-clearing process by serving as a clearinghouse for checks. **5. Electronic check presentment**—Check information may be encoded, transmitted electronically, and processed by other banks' computers. After encoding a check, a bank may retain it and present only its image or description for payment under an electronic presentment agreement [UCC 4-209, 4–110].
Electronic Fund Transfers	**1. Types of EFT systems**— **a.** Automated teller machines (ATMs). **b.** Point-of-sale systems. **c.** Direct deposits and withdrawals. **d.** Online payment systems. **2. Consumer fund transfers**—Consumer fund transfers are governed by the Electronic Fund Transfer Act (EFTA). The EFTA is basically a disclosure law that sets forth the rights and duties of the bank and the customer with respect to EFT systems. Banks must comply strictly with EFTA requirements. **3. Commercial fund transfers**—Article 4A of the UCC, which has been adopted by almost all of the states, governs fund transfers not subject to the EFTA or other federal or state statutes.
Banking in the Digital Age	**1. Online and mobile banking**— **a.** Online banking provides traditional banking services to customers on computers. **b.** Mobile banking apps offer customers the ability to conduct online banking on smartphones and tablets. **2. Electronic payments systems**— **a.** Electronic bills, or eBills, are digital versions of paper bills that can be viewed and paid online. **b.** Business-to-business (B2B) payments are increasingly being made via electronic means, though paper checks are still common in this segment of the economy. **3. Fintech**, a term that refers to a combination of finance and technology, relies on computerized decision making, or artificial intelligence, to: **a.** Carry out digital lending, in which loan applications are processed by computers rather than bank employees. **b.** Support neobanks, or banks and other financial institutions that operate wholly online, without any physical branches.

Issue Spotters

1. Lyn writes a check for $900 to Mac, who indorses the check in blank and transfers it to Jan. She presents the check to Omega Bank, the drawee bank, for payment. Omega does not honor the check. Is Lyn liable to Jan? Could Lyn be subject to criminal prosecution? Why or why not? (See *The Bank's Duty to Honor Checks.*)

2. Herb steals a check from Kay's checkbook, forges Kay's signature, and transfers the check to Will for value. Unaware that the signature is not Kay's, Will presents the check to First State Bank, the drawee. The bank cashes the check. Two weeks later, Kay discovers the forgery and insists that the bank recredit her account. Can the bank refuse to recredit Kay's account? If not, can the bank recover the amount paid to Will? Why or why not? (See *The Bank's Duty to Honor Checks.*)

—Check your answers to the *Issue Spotters* against the answers provided in Appendix D.

Business Scenarios and Case Problems

20–1. Forged Checks. Roy Supply, Inc., and R. M. R. Drywall, Inc., had checking accounts at Wells Fargo Bank. Both accounts required all checks to carry two signatures—that of Edward Roy and that of Twila June Moore, both of whom were executive officers of both companies. Between January 2018 and March 2019, the bank honored hundreds of checks on which Roy's signature was forged by Moore. On January 31, 2020, Roy and the two corporations notified the bank of the forgeries and then filed a suit in a California state court against the bank, alleging negligence. Who is liable for the amounts of the forged checks? Why? (See *The Bank's Duty to Honor Checks.*)

20–2. Customer Negligence. Gary goes grocery shopping and carelessly leaves his checkbook in his shopping cart. His checkbook, with two blank checks remaining, is stolen by Dolores. On May 5, Dolores forges Gary's name on a check for $100 and cashes the check at Gary's bank, Citizens Bank of Middletown. Gary has not reported the loss of his blank checks to his bank. On June 1, Gary receives his monthly bank statement from Citizens Bank, which includes the forged check, but he does not notice the item, nor does he examine his bank statement. On June 20, Dolores forges Gary's last check. This check is for $1,000 and is cashed at Eastern City Bank, a bank with which Dolores has previously done business. Eastern City Bank puts the check through the collection process, and Citizens Bank honors it. On July 1, on receipt of his bank statement and canceled checks covering June transactions, Gary discovers both forgeries and immediately notifies Citizens Bank. Dolores cannot be found. Gary claims that Citizens Bank must recredit his account for both checks, as his signature was forged. Discuss fully Gary's claim. (See *The Bank's Duty to Honor Checks.*)

20–3. Forged Indorsements. Adley Abdulwahab (Wahab) opened an account on behalf of W Financial Group, LLC, with Wells Fargo Bank. Wahab was one of three authorized signers on the account. Five months later, Wahab withdrew $1,701,250 from W Financial's account to buy a cashier's check payable to Lubna Lateef. Wahab visited a different Wells Fargo branch and deposited the check into the account of CA Houston Investment Center, LLC. Wahab was the only authorized signer on this account. Lateef never received or indorsed the check. W Financial filed a suit to recover the amount. Applying the rules for payment on a forged indorsement, who is liable? [*Jones v. Wells Fargo Bank*, 666 F.3d 955 (5th Cir. 2012)] (See *The Bank's Duty to Honor Checks.*)

20–4. Business Case Problem with Sample Answer—Consumer Fund Transfers. Stephen Patterson held an account with Suntrust Bank in Alcoa, Tennessee. Juanita Wehrman—with whom Patterson was briefly involved in a romantic relationship—stole his debit card and used it for sixteen months (well beyond the length of their relationship) to make unauthorized purchases in excess of $30,000. When Patterson learned what was happening, he closed his account. The bank refused to reimburse him more than $677.46—the amount of unauthorized transactions that had occurred within sixty days of the transmittal of the bank statement that revealed the first unauthorized transaction. Is the bank's refusal justifiable? Explain. [*Patterson v. Suntrust Bank*, 2013 WL 139315 (Tenn.App. 2013)] (See *Electronic Fund Transfers.*)

—For a sample answer to Problem 20–4, go to Appendix E.

20–5. Forged Drawers' Signatures. Victor Nacim had a checking account at Compass Bank. The "Deposit Agreement" required him to report an unauthorized transaction within thirty days of his receipt of the statement on which it appeared to obtain a recredit. When Nacim moved to a new residence, he asked the bank to update the address on his account. Compass continued to mail his statements to his previous address, however, and Nacim did not receive them. In the meantime, Compass officer David Peterson made an unauthorized withdrawal of $34,000 from Nacim's account. A month later, Peterson told Nacim what he had done. The next month, Nacim asked the bank for a recredit. Compass refused on the ground that he reported the withdrawal more than thirty days after the bank mailed the statement on which it appeared—a statement that

Nacim never received. Is Nacim entitled to a recredit? Explain. [*Compass Bank v. Nacim*, 459 S.W.3d 95 (Tex. App.—El Paso 2015)] (See *The Bank's Duty to Honor Checks.*)

20–6. Checks Bearing Forged Indorsements. The law firm of Levy Baldante Finney & Rubenstein, P.C., had a checking account at TD Bank, N.A. The account agreement required notice to the bank of "any problem with a check" within thirty days from when a statement showing the item was mailed. Jack Cohen, a partner at the law firm, stole more than three hundred thousand dollars from the account by fraudulently indorsing twenty-nine checks that had been made payable to clients and other third parties. More than two years after the first item appeared in an account statement, Susan Huffington, the firm's bookkeeper, discovered one of the fraudulently indorsed checks. She reviewed previous statements with images of the back of each check, compiled a list of fraudulently indorsed items, and notified the bank to recredit the account. Is the bank obligated to honor this request? Why or why not? [*Levy Baldante Finney & Rubenstein, P.C. v. Wells Fargo Bank, N.A.*, ___ A.3d ___, 2018 WL 847756 (Pa.Super. 2018)] (See *The Bank's Duty to Honor Checks.*)

20–7. A Question of Ethics—The IDDR Approach and Unauthorized Items. While working as an executive assistant to David Ducote, Michelle Freytag fraudulently obtained a credit card in Ducote's name from Whitney National Bank in New Orleans, Louisiana. Freytag told Whitney to pay the credit card balances with funds from Ducote's bank account. The bank included a "debit memo" of each payment with the monthly account statements sent to Ducote. But Ducote never contacted the bank about any unauthorized items. Freytag's scheme was not discovered until, more than five years later, the bank contacted Ducote to ask about some of the charges to the credit card. [*Ducote v. Whitney National Bank*, 212 So.3d 729 (La.App. 5 Cir. 2017)] (See *The Bank's Duty to Honor Checks.*)

1. Do bank customers in Ducote's position have an ethical duty to examine their account statements? Discuss.
2. Is the bank ethically obligated to recredit Ducote's account? Explain.

Critical Thinking and Writing Assignments

20–8. Critical Legal Thinking. Under the revised Article 4, a bank is no longer required to include the customer's canceled checks when it sends monthly statements to the customer. A bank may simply itemize the checks (by number, date, and amount). It may provide photocopies of the checks as well but is not required to do so. What implications do these rules have for bank customers in terms of liability for unauthorized signatures and indorsements? (See *The Bank's Duty to Honor Checks.*)

20–9. Time-Limited Group Assignment—Death of a Customer. On January 5, Brian drafts a check for $3,000 drawn on Southern Marine Bank and payable to his assistant, Shanta. Brian puts last year's date on the check by mistake. On January 7, before Shanta has had a chance to go to the bank, Brian is killed in an automobile accident. Southern Marine Bank is aware of Brian's death. On January 10, Shanta presents the check to the bank, and the bank honors the check by payment to Shanta. Later, Brian's widow, Joyce, claims that because the bank knew of Brian's death and also because the check was by date over one year old, the bank acted wrongfully when it paid Shanta. Joyce, as executor of Brian's estate and sole heir by his will, demands that Southern Marine Bank recredit Brian's estate for the check paid to Shanta. (See *The Bank's Duty to Honor Checks.*)

1. The first group will determine whether the bank acted wrongfully by honoring Brian's check and paying Shanta.
2. The second group will assess whether Joyce has a valid claim against Southern Marine Bank for the amount of the check paid to Shanta.
3. The third group will assume that the check Brian drafted was on his business account rather than on his personal account and that he had two partners in the business. Would a business partner be in a better position to force Southern Marine Bank to recredit Brian's account than his widow? Why or why not?

oatzpenz studio/Shutterstock.com

21 Security Interests and Creditors' Rights

Focus Questions

The five Focus Questions *below are designed to help improve your understanding. After reading this chapter, you should be able to answer the following questions:*

1. What is required to create a security interest?
2. How can a security interest extend to a debtor's newly acquired inventory?
3. If two parties have perfected security interests in the debtor's collateral, which party has priority on default?
4. When is a creditor required to sell or otherwise dispose of the repossessed collateral?
5. What is a suretyship, and how does it differ from a guaranty?

Secured Transaction Any transaction in which the payment of a debt is guaranteed, or secured, by personal property owned by the debtor or in which the debtor has a legal interest.

"I will pay you some, and, as most debtors do, promise you infinitely."

William Shakespeare
1564–1616
(English dramatist and poet)

When buying or leasing goods, debtors frequently pay some portion of the price now and promise to pay the remainder in the future, as William Shakespeare observed in the chapter-opening quotation. Logically, sellers and lenders do not want to risk nonpayment, so they usually will not sell goods or lend funds unless the payment is somehow guaranteed.

Whenever the payment of a debt is guaranteed, or *secured*, by personal property owned or held by the debtor, the transaction becomes known as a **secured transaction**. Indeed, business as we know it could not exist without laws permitting and governing secured transactions. When Stone Investments, Ltd., wants to buy a Learjet 75 Liberty for executive travel, it borrows funds from Capital Bank. Capital obtains a security interest in the plane to guarantee that Stone will repay the debt.

Article 9 of the Uniform Commercial Code (UCC) governs secured transactions in personal property. Personal property includes accounts, agricultural liens, *chattel paper* (documents or records evidencing a debt secured by personal property), and fixtures (certain property that is attached to land). Personal property also includes other types of intangible property, such as negotiable instruments and patents. Article 9 does not cover creditor-collection devices such as liens and garnishments.

21–1 Creating and Perfecting a Security Interest

A creditor has two main concerns if the debtor **defaults** (fails to pay the debt as promised). The first is whether the debt can be satisfied through the possession and (usually) sale of the collateral. The second concern is whether the creditor will have priority over any other creditors or buyers who may have rights in the same collateral. These two concerns are met through the creation and perfection of a security interest.

Defaults Fails to pay a debt when it is due.

Secured Party A creditor who has a security interest in the debtor's collateral, including a seller, lender, cosigner, or buyer of accounts or chattel paper.

Debtor Under Article 9 of the UCC, any party who owes payment or performance of a secured obligation.

Security Interest Any interest in personal property or fixtures that secures payment or performance of an obligation.

Security Agreement An agreement that creates or provides for a security interest between the debtor and a secured party.

Collateral Under Article 9 of the UCC, the property subject to a security interest.

Financing Statement A document filed by a secured creditor with the appropriate official to give notice to the public of the creditor's security interest in collateral belonging to the debtor named in the statement.

21–1a Definitions

Before we examine the creation and perfection of security interests, you need to understand the UCC's terminology, which is uniformly used by every state. The following is a brief summary of the UCC's definitions relating to secured transactions.

1. A **secured party** is any creditor who has a *security interest* in the *debtor's collateral.* This creditor can be a seller, a lender, a cosigner, or even a buyer of accounts or chattel paper [UCC 9–102(a)(72)].
2. A **debtor** is a person who *owes payment* or other performance of a secured obligation [UCC 9–102(a)(28)].
3. A **security interest** is the *interest* in the collateral (such as personal property or fixtures) that *secures payment or performance of an obligation* [UCC 1–201(37)].
4. A **security agreement** is an *agreement* that *creates* or provides for a *security interest* [UCC 9–102(a)(73)]. In other words, it is the contract in which a debtor agrees to give a creditor the right to take the debtor's property in the event of default.
5. **Collateral** is the *subject* of the *security interest* [UCC 9–102(a)(12)].
6. A **financing statement**—referred to as the UCC-1 form—is the *instrument normally filed to give public notice to third parties* of the *secured party's security interest* [UCC 9–102(a)(39)].

Together, these basic definitions form the concept under which a debtor-creditor relationship becomes a secured transaction relationship (see Exhibit 21–1).

21–1b Requirements to Create a Security Interest

To become a secured party, the creditor must obtain a security interest in the collateral of the debtor. Three requirements must be met for a creditor to have an enforceable security interest:

1. Unless the creditor has possession of the collateral, there must be a written or authenticated security agreement that clearly describes the collateral subject to the security interest and is signed or authenticated by the debtor.
2. The secured party must give something of value to the debtor.
3. The debtor must have "rights" in the collateral.

Focus Question 1

What is required to create a security interest?

Exhibit 21–1 The Secured Transactions Relationship

In a security agreement, a debtor and a creditor agree that the creditor will have a security interest in collateral in which the debtor has rights. In essence, the collateral secures the loan and ensures the creditor of payment should the debtor default.

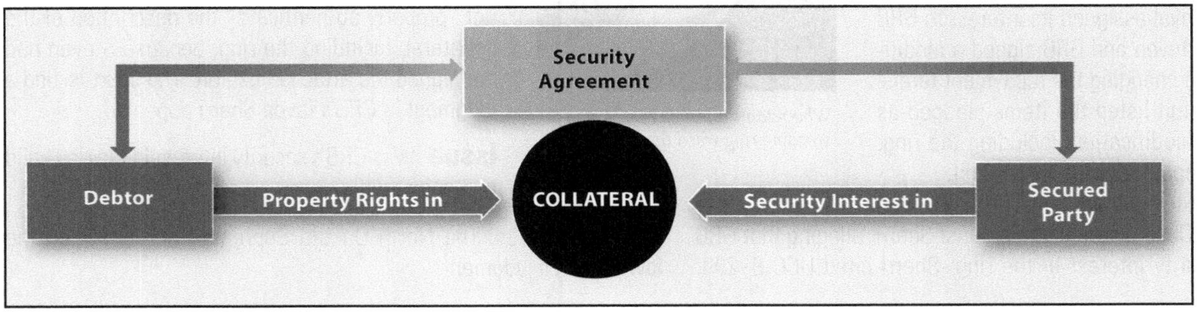

Attachment In a secured transaction, the process by which a secured creditor's interest "attaches" to the collateral and the creditor's security interest becomes enforceable.

Once these requirements have been met, the creditor's rights are said to attach to the collateral. **Attachment** gives the creditor an enforceable security interest in the collateral [UCC 9–203].[1]

Example 21.1 To furnish his new office suite, Bryce applies for a credit card at an office supply store. The application contains a clause stating that the store will retain a security interest in the goods that he buys with the card until he has paid for them in full. This application is a *written security agreement*, which is the first requirement for an enforceable security interest. The goods that Bryce buys with the card are the *something of value* from the secured party (the second requirement). His ownership interest in those goods is the *right* that he has in them (the third requirement). Thus, the requirements for an enforceable security interest are met. When Bryce buys something with the card, the store's rights attach to the purchased goods. ■

Written or Authenticated Security Agreement When the collateral is not in the possession of the secured party, the security agreement must be either written or authenticated. It must also describe the collateral.

Authenticate To sign, execute, or adopt any symbol on an electronic record that verifies the intent to adopt or accept the record.

Here, **authenticate** means to sign, execute, or adopt any symbol on an electronic record that verifies that the person signing has the intent to adopt or accept the record [UCC 9–102(a)(7)(69)]. Authentication provides for electronic filing (the filing process will be discussed later). See this chapter's *Adapting the Law to the Online Environment* feature for a discussion of a type of secured transaction that is performed online.

A security agreement must contain a description of the collateral that reasonably identifies it. Generally, such phrases as "all the debtor's personal property" or "all the debtor's assets" would *not* constitute a sufficient description [UCC 9–108(c)].

If the debtor signs, or otherwise authenticates, a security agreement, does the debtor also have to sign an attached list of the collateral to create a valid security interest? That was the question before the court in the following case.

1. The term *attachment* has a different meaning in secured transactions than in the context of judicial liens, where it refers to a court-ordered seizure of property.

Spotlight on Wedding Rings: Case 21.1

Royal Jewelers, Inc. v. Light

Supreme Court of North Dakota, 2015 ND 44, 859 N.W.2d 921 921 (2015).

Facts Steven Light bought a $55,050 wedding ring for his wife, Sherri Light, on credit from Royal Jewelers, Inc., a store in Fargo, North Dakota. The receipt granted Royal a security interest in the ring. Later, Royal assigned its interest to GRB Financial Corp. Steven and GRB signed a modification agreement changing the repayment terms. An attached exhibit listed the items pledged as security for the modification, including the ring. Steven did not separately sign the exhibit.

A year later, Steven died. Royal and GRB filed a suit in a North Dakota state court against Sherri, alleging that GRB had a valid security interest in the ring. Sherri cited UCC 9–203, under which there is an enforceable interest only if "the debtor has authenticated a security agreement that provides a description of the collateral." Sherri argued that the modification agreement did not "properly authenticate" the description of the collateral, including the ring, because Steven had not signed the attached exhibit. The court issued a judgment in GRB's favor. Sherri appealed.

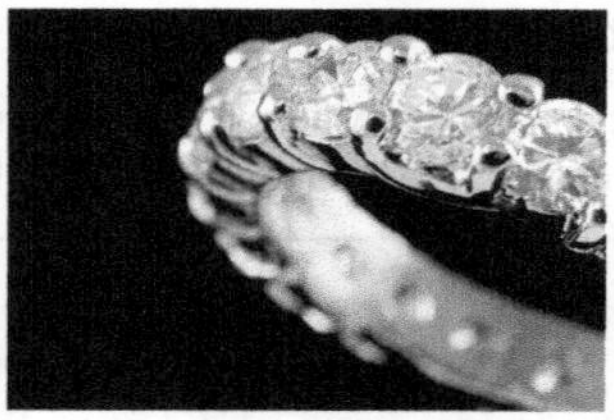

Who retains a security interest in a wedding ring when the buyer dies?

ProArtWork/Getty Images

Issue Was GRB's security interest in the ring valid and enforceable?

Decision Yes. The North Dakota Supreme Court affirmed the lower court's judgment.

Reason The court acknowledged that under UCC 9–203, "a security interest is enforceable against the debtor and third parties with respect to the collateral only if . . . the debtor has authenticated a security agreement that provides a description of the collateral." The court explained, however, that under UCC 9–108(2), collateral may be described in a list attached to the security agreement. In fact, several documents may be considered together to comprise a security agreement. Furthermore, "no authority [requires] a debtor to separately sign an exhibit attached to and referenced in a signed security agreement." Here, Steven had granted a valid security interest in the ring. With Steven's knowledge and consent, Royal had assigned the security interest to GRB. Thus, the lower court "did not err in finding GRB Financial had a valid and enforceable security interest in the ring."

Critical Thinking

- **Ethical** *Under the circumstances, is it ethical for GRB to enforce its security interest in the ring to recover the unpaid amount of the price? Discuss.*

Secured Party Must Give Value The secured party must give something of value to the debtor. Some examples of value include a binding commitment to extend credit or consideration to support a simple contract [UCC 1–204]. Normally, the value given by a secured party is in the form of a direct loan or a commitment to sell goods on credit.

Debtor Must Have Rights in the Collateral The debtor must have rights in the collateral. That means that the debtor must have some ownership interest or right to obtain possession of the collateral. For instance, a retail seller-debtor can give a secured party a security interest not only in existing inventory owned by the retailer but also in *future* inventory to be acquired by the retailer. (A common misconception is that the debtor must have title to the collateral to have rights in it, but this is not a requirement.)

Secured Transactions Online

When you buy something online, you typically must use your credit card or make an electronic fund transfer before the goods that you bought are sent to you. If you are buying an expensive item, such as a car, you are not likely to send funds without being assured that you will receive the item in the condition promised. Enter the concept of escrow.

Escrow Accounts

Escrow accounts are commonly used in real estate transactions, but they are also useful for smaller transactions, particularly those done on the Internet. An escrow account involves three parties—the buyer, the seller, and a trusted third party that collects, holds, and disperses funds according to instructions from the buyer and seller. Escrow services are provided by licensed and regulated escrow companies. For instance, if you buy a car on the Internet, you and the seller will agree on an escrow company to which you will send the funds. When you receive the car and are satisfied with it, the escrow company will release the funds to the seller. This is a type of secured transaction.

Escrow.com

One of the best-known online escrow firms is Escrow.com, which has provided escrow services for billions of dollars in secured transactions. All of its escrow services are offered via its website and provided independently by Internet Escrow Services, one of its operating subsidiaries. Escrow.com is particularly useful for transactions that involve an international buyer or seller. It has become the recommended transaction settlement service for Autotrader, Resale Weekly, Cars.com, eBay Motors, and Flippa.com.

Critical Thinking

How could online escrow services reduce Internet fraud?

21–1c Perfecting a Security Interest

Perfection The legal process by which secured parties protect themselves against the claims of third parties who may wish to have their debts satisfied out of the same collateral. It is usually accomplished by filing a financing statement with the appropriate government official.

Perfection is the legal process by which secured parties protect themselves against the claims of third parties who may wish to have their debts satisfied out of the same collateral. Whether a secured party's security interest is perfected or unperfected can have serious consequences for the secured party.

What if a debtor has borrowed from two different creditors, for instance, using the same property as collateral for both loans? If the debtor defaults on both loans, which of the two creditors has first rights to the collateral? In this situation, the creditor with a perfected security interest will prevail.

Perfection usually is accomplished by filing a financing statement. In some circumstances, however, a security interest becomes perfected even though no financing statement is filed.

SimplyCreativePhotography/Getty Images

When a bank finances the purchase of a tractor, how does it perfect its security interest in that tractor?

Perfection by Filing The most common means of perfection is by filing a *financing statement* with the office of the appropriate government official. A financing statement gives public notice to third parties of the secured party's security interest. The security agreement itself can also be filed to perfect the security interest. The financing statement must provide the names of the debtor and the secured party, and must identify the collateral covered by the financing statement. A uniform financing statement form is used in all states [see UCC 9–521].

Communication of the financing statement to the appropriate filing office, together with the correct filing fee, or the acceptance of the financing statement by the filing officer constitutes a filing [UCC 9–516(a)]. The filing can be accomplished electronically [UCC 9–102(a)(18)]. In fact, most states use electronic filing systems. A financing statement may be filed even before a security agreement is made or a security interest attaches [UCC 9–502(d)].

The Debtor's Name. The UCC requires that a financing statement be filed under the name of the debtor [UCC 9–502(a)(1)]. Filings are indexed by the name of the debtor so that they can be located by subsequent searchers. Slight variations in names normally will not be considered misleading if a search of the filing office's records, using a standard computer search engine routinely used by that office, would disclose the filings [UCC 9–506(c)].[2]

UCC 9–503 sets out some detailed rules for determining when the debtor's name as it appears on a financing statement is sufficient.

1. *Corporations.* For corporations, which are organizations that have registered with the state, the debtor's name on the financing statement must be "the name of the debtor indicated on the public record of the debtor's jurisdiction of organization" [UCC 9–503(a)(1)].
2. *Trusts.* If the debtor is a trust or a trustee for property held in trust, the financing statement must disclose this information and provide the trust's name as specified in its official documents [UCC 9–503(a)(3)].
3. *Individuals and organizations.* For all others, the financing statement must disclose "the individual or organizational name of the debtor" [UCC 9–503(a)(4)(A)]. The word *organization* includes unincorporated associations, such as clubs, churches, joint ventures, and general partnerships. If an organizational debtor does not have a group name, the names of the individuals in the group must be listed.
4. *Trade names.* When the debtor's trade name is not the legal name of the business, providing only the trade name in a financing statement is *not* sufficient for

2. If the name listed in the financing statement is so inaccurate that a search using a standard search engine will not disclose the debtor's name, then the financing statement is deemed seriously misleading under UCC 9–506. See also UCC 9–507, which governs the effectiveness of financing statements found to be seriously misleading.

perfection [UCC 9–503(c)]. The financing statement must also include the owner-debtor's actual name. **Example 21.2** Pete Hanson is a plumber who does business under the name CareFull Plumbing. Hanson obtains a loan from North Bank to purchase some equipment for his business. For North Bank to perfect its security interest in the equipment, the filed financing statement must include the owner's name, Pete Hanson, rather than just his trade name.

If the debtor's name changes, the financing statement remains effective for collateral the debtor acquired before or within four months after the name change. Unless an amendment to the financing statement is filed within this four-month period, a security interest in collateral acquired by the debtor after the four-month period is unperfected [UCC 9–507(b) and (c)]. A one-page uniform financing statement amendment form is available for filing name changes and for other purposes.

Description of the Collateral. Both the security agreement and the financing statement must describe the collateral in which the secured party has a security interest. The security agreement must describe the collateral because no security interest in goods can exist unless the parties agree on which goods are subject to the security interest.

The financing statement must describe the collateral to provide public notice of the fact that certain goods of the debtor are subject to a security interest. Other parties who might later wish to lend funds to the debtor or buy the collateral can thus learn of the security interest by checking with the office in which a financing statement would be filed. For land-related security interests, a legal description of the realty is also required [UCC 9–502(b)].

Sometimes, the descriptions in the two documents vary. The description in the security agreement must be more precise than the description in the financing statement. The UCC permits broad, general descriptions in the financing statement, such as "all assets" or "all personal property," as long as they are accurate [UCC 9–504].

Example 21.3 A security agreement for a commercial loan to Casey Manufacturing lists all of Casey's equipment subject to the loan by serial number. The financing statement for the equipment simply refers to "all equipment owned or hereafter acquired." (This chapter's *Business Law Analysis* feature provides an additional illustration.)

Perfecting a Security Interest

Business Law Analysis

Thomas Tille owned M.A.T.T. Equipment Company. To operate the business, Tille borrowed funds from Union Bank. For each loan, Union filed a financing statement that included Tille's signature and address, the bank's address, and a description of the collateral.

The first loan covered all of Tille's equipment, including "any after-acquired property." The second loan covered a truck crane "whether owned now or acquired later." The third loan covered a "Bobcat mini-excavator." Did these financing statements perfect Union's security interests?

Analysis: In most situations, perfection is accomplished by filing a financing statement with the appropriate official. To effectively perfect a security interest, a financing statement must contain (1) the debtor's signature, (2) the debtor's and creditor's addresses, and (3) a description of the collateral by type or item. Under the UCC, the financing statement can contain broad, general descriptions of the collateral, whereas the security agreement must be more precise.

Result and Reasoning: All of Union Bank's financing statements were sufficient to perfect its security interests in Tille's equipment. Each provided the name and address of the debtor (Tille), and the name and address of the secured party (Union Bank). Each also included a description of the collateral covered by the financing statement. For one loan, it was all of Tille's equipment, including after-acquired property; for another, the truck crane; and for the third, a Bobcat mini-excavator. These descriptions were clearly sufficient to put a prospective creditor on notice that the collateral was the subject of a security interest.

Where to File. Normally, a financing statement must be filed centrally in the appropriate state office, such as the office of the secretary of state, in the state where the debtor is located. An exception occurs when the collateral consists of timber to be cut, fixtures, or items to be extracted—such as oil, coal, gas, and minerals [UCC 9–301(3) and (4), 9–502(b)]. In those circumstances, the financing statement is filed in the county where the collateral is located.

Note that the state in which a financing statement should be filed usually depends on the *debtor's location,* not the location of the collateral (but not for the exception just mentioned) [UCC 9–301]. The debtor's location is determined as follows [UCC 9–307]:

1. For *individual debtors*, it is the state of the debtor's principal residence.
2. For an *organization that is registered with the state*, such as a corporation or limited liability company, it is the state in which the organization is registered. Thus, if a debtor is incorporated in Maryland and has its chief executive office in New York, a secured party would file the financing statement in Maryland.
3. For *all other entities*, it is the state in which the business is located or, if the debtor has more than one office, the place from which the debtor manages its business operations and affairs.

Consequences of an Improper Filing. Improper filing renders the security interest unperfected and reduces the secured party's claim in bankruptcy to that of an unsecured creditor. For instance, if the debtor's name on the financing statement is seriously misleading or if the collateral is not sufficiently described in the financing statement, the filing may not be effective.

Example 21.4 Arthur Mendez Juarez, a strawberry farmer, leases farmland from Morona Fruits, Inc., and borrows funds from Morona for payroll and production expenses. The sublease and other documents set out Juarez's full name, but Juarez generally goes by the name "Mendez" and signs the sublease "Arthur Mendez." To perfect its interests, Morona files financing statements that identify the debtor as "Arthur Mendez."

Later, Juarez contracts to sell strawberries to Frozun Foods, Inc., which advances him funds secured by a financing statement that identifies the debtor as "Arthur Juarez." By the following year, Juarez is unable to pay his debts and owes Morona more than $200,000 and Frozun nearly $50,000. Both Morona and Frozun file a suit against Juarez claiming to have priority under a perfected security interest. In this situation, a properly filed financing statement would identify the debtor's true name (Arthur Juarez). Because a debtor name search for "Arthur Juarez" would not disclose a financing statement in the name of "Arthur Mendez," Morona's financing statement is seriously misleading. Therefore, Frozun's security interest would have priority because its financing statement was recorded properly. ■

Perfection without Filing

A few types of security interests can be perfected without filing a financing statement. One occurs when the collateral is transferred into the possession of the secured party. A second occurs when the security interest can be perfected on attachment (without a filing and without having to possess the goods) [UCC 9–309].

The phrase *perfected on attachment* means that these security interests are automatically perfected at the time of their creation. Two of the more common security interests that are perfected on attachment are a *purchase-money security interest* in consumer goods (discussed shortly) and an assignment of a beneficial interest in a decedent's estate [UCC 9–309(1), (13)].

Pledge A security device in which personal property is transferred into the possession of the creditor as security for the payment of a debt and retained by the creditor until the debt is paid.

Perfection by Possession. In the past, one of the most common means of obtaining financing was to **pledge** certain collateral as security for the debt and transfer the collateral into the creditor's possession. When the debt was paid, the collateral was returned to the debtor.

Article 9 of the UCC retained the common law pledge and the principle that the security agreement need not be in writing to be enforceable if the collateral is transferred to the secured party [UCC 9–310, 9–312(b), 9–313].

Certain items, such as stocks, bonds, negotiable instruments, and jewelry, are commonly transferred into the creditor's possession when they are used as collateral for loans. **Example 21.5** Sheila needs cash to pay for a medical procedure. She obtains a loan for $4,000 from Trent. As security for the loan, she gives him a promissory note on which she is the payee. Even though the agreement to hold the note as collateral was oral, Trent has a perfected security interest and does not need to file a financing statement. No other creditor of Sheila's can attempt to recover the promissory note from Trent in payment for other debts.

For most collateral, however, possession by the secured party is impractical because it denies the debtor the right to use or derive income from the property to pay off the debt. **Example 21.6** Jeb, a farmer, takes out a loan to finance the purchase of a large corn harvester and uses the equipment as collateral. Clearly, the purpose of the purchase would be defeated if Jeb transferred the collateral into the creditor's possession, because he would not be able to use the equipment to harvest his corn.

Perfection by Attachment—The Purchase-Money Security Interest in Consumer Goods. Under the UCC, fourteen types of security interests are perfected automatically at the time they are created [UCC 9–309]. The most common is the **purchase-money security interest (PMSI)** in *consumer goods* (items bought primarily for personal, family, or household purposes).

Purchase-Money Security Interest (PMSI) A security interest that arises when a seller or lender extends credit for part or all of the price of goods purchased by a buyer.

A PMSI in consumer goods is created when a person buys goods on credit. The entity that extends the credit and obtains the PMSI can be either the seller (a store, for instance) or a financial institution that lends the buyer the funds with which to purchase the goods [UCC 9–102(a)(2)].

Automatic Perfection. A PMSI in consumer goods is perfected automatically at the time of a credit sale—that is, at the time the PMSI is created. The seller in this situation does not need to do anything more to perfect the security interest. **Example 21.7** Jami purchases an LG washer and dryer from West Coast Appliance for $2,500. Unable to pay the entire amount in cash, Jami signs a purchase agreement to pay $1,000 down and $100 per month until the balance, plus interest, is fully paid. West Coast Appliance is to retain a security interest in the appliances until full payment has been made. Because the security interest was created as part of a purchase agreement with a consumer, it is a PMSI, and West Coast Appliance's security interest is automatically perfected.

Iakov Filimonov/Dreamstime.com

If this couple buys a washer/dryer set on credit, is a PMSI automatically perfected?

Exceptions to the Rule of Automatic Perfection. There are two exceptions to the rule of automatic perfection for PMSIs:

1. Certain types of security interests that are subject to other federal or state laws may require additional steps to be perfected [UCC 9–311]. Many jurisdictions, for instance, have certificate-of-title statutes that establish perfection requirements for security interests in certain goods, including automobiles, trailers, boats, mobile homes, and farm tractors.

   Example 21.8 Martin purchases a boat at a Florida dealership. Florida has a certificate-of-title statute. Martin obtains financing for his purchase through General Credit Corporation. General Credit Corporation will need to file a certificate of title with the appropriate state official to perfect the PMSI.
2. PMSIs in nonconsumer goods, such as a business's inventory or livestock, are not automatically perfected [UCC 9–324]. These types of PMSIs will be discussed later in this chapter in the context of priorities.

Perfection and the Classification of Collateral Where or how to perfect a security interest sometimes depends on the classification or definition of the collateral. Collateral is generally divided into two classifications: *tangible collateral* (collateral that can be seen, felt, and touched) and *intangible collateral* (collateral that consists of or generates rights). Exhibit 21–2 summarizes the various classifications of collateral and the methods of perfecting a security interest in collateral falling within each of those classifications.[3]

3. There are additional classifications, such as agricultural liens, commercial tort claims, and investment property. For definitions of these types of collateral, see UCC 9–102(a)(5), (a)(13), and (a)(49).

Exhibit 21–2 Selected Types of Collateral and Their Methods of Perfection

TANGIBLE COLLATERAL		METHOD OF PERFECTION
All things that are movable at the time the security interest attaches or that are attached to land, including timber to be cut and growing crops.		
1. Consumer Goods [UCC 9–301, 9–303, 9–309(1), 9–310(a), 9–313(a)]	Goods used or bought primarily for personal, family, or household purposes—for example, household furniture [UCC 9–102(a)(23)].	For purchase-money security interest, attachment (that is, the creation of a security interest) is sufficient. For boats, motor vehicles, and trailers, filing or compliance with a certificate-of-title statute is required. For other consumer goods, general rules of filing or possession apply.
2. Equipment [UCC 9–301, 9–310(a), 9–313(a)]	Goods bought for or used primarily in business (and not part of inventory or farm products)—for example, a delivery truck [UCC 9–102(a)(33)].	Filing or (rarely) possession by secured party.
3. Farm Products [UCC 9–301, 9–310(a), 9–313(a)]	Crops (including aquatic goods), livestock, or supplies produced in a farming operation—for example, ginned cotton, milk, eggs, and maple syrup [UCC 9–102(a)(34)].	Filing or (rarely) possession by secured party.
4. Inventory [UCC 9–301, 9–310(a), 9–313(a)]	Goods held by a person for sale or under a contract of service or lease; raw materials held for production and work in progress [UCC 9–102(a)(48)].	Filing or (rarely) possession by secured party.
INTANGIBLE COLLATERAL		**METHOD OF PERFECTION**
Nonphysical property that exists only in connection with something else.		
1. Chattel Paper [UCC 9–301, 9–310(a), 9–312(a), 9–313(a), 9–314(a)]	A writing or electronic record that evidences both a monetary obligation and a security interest in goods and software used in goods—for example, a security agreement [UCC 9–102(a)(11), (a)(31), and (a)(78)].	Filing or possession or control by secured party.
2. Instruments [UCC 9–301, 9–309(4), 9–310(a), 9–312(a) and (e), 9–313(a)]	A negotiable instrument, such as a check, note, certificate of deposit, draft, or other writing that evidences a right to the payment of money and is not a security agreement or lease, but rather is a type that can ordinarily be transferred (after indorsement, if necessary) by delivery [UCC 9–102(a)(47)].	Normally filing or possession. For the sale of promissory notes, perfection can be by attachment (automatically on the creation of the security interest).
3. Accounts [UCC 9–301, 9–309(2) and (5), 9–310(a)]	Any right to receive payment for property (real or personal), including intellectual licensed property, services, insurance policies, and certain other receivables [UCC 9–102(a)(2) and (a)(46)].	Filing required except for certain assignments that can be perfected by attachment (automatically on the creation of the security interest).
4. Deposit Accounts [UCC 9–104, 9–304, 9–312(b), 9–314(a)]	Any demand, time, savings, passbook, or similar account maintained with a bank [UCC 9–102(a)(29)].	Perfection by control, such as when the secured party is the bank in which the account is maintained or when the parties have agreed that the secured party can direct the disposition of funds in a particular account.

Effective Time Duration of Perfection A financing statement is effective for five years from the date of filing [UCC 9–515]. If a **continuation statement** is filed within six months *prior to* the expiration date, the effectiveness of the original statement is continued for another five years, starting with the expiration date of the first five-year period [UCC 9–515(d), (e)]. The effectiveness of the statement can be continued in the same manner indefinitely. Any attempt to file a continuation statement outside the six-month window will render the continuation ineffective, however, and the perfection will lapse at the end of the five-year period.

If a financing statement lapses, the security interest that had been perfected by the filing becomes unperfected. A purchaser for value can acquire the collateral as if the security interest had never been perfected [UCC 9–515(c)].

Continuation Statement A statement that, if filed within six months prior to the expiration date of the original financing statement, continues the perfection of the security interest for another five years.

21–2 Scope of a Security Interest

A security interest can cover property in which the debtor has either present or future ownership or possessory rights. Therefore, security agreements can cover not only collateral in the present possession or control of the debtor but also proceeds from the sale of collateral, after-acquired property, and future advances, as discussed next.

21–2a Proceeds

Proceeds are whatever cash or property is received when collateral is sold or disposed of in some other way [UCC 9–102(a)(64)]. A security interest in the collateral gives the secured party a security interest in the proceeds acquired from the sale of that collateral.

A security interest in proceeds perfects automatically on the perfection of the secured party's security interest in the original collateral. It remains perfected for twenty days after the debtor receives the proceeds. The parties can agree to extend the twenty-day automatic perfection period in their original security agreement [UCC 9–315(c), (d)]. This is typically done when the collateral is the type that is likely to be sold, such as a retailer's inventory of tablets or smartphones. The UCC also permits a security interest in identifiable cash proceeds to remain perfected after twenty days [UCC 9–315(d)(2)].

Proceeds Under Article 9 of the UCC, whatever is received when collateral is sold or disposed of in some other way.

21–2b After-Acquired Property

After-acquired property is property that the debtor acquired after the execution of the security agreement. The security agreement may provide for a security interest in after-acquired property, such as a debtor's inventory [UCC 9–204(1)]. Generally, the debtor will purchase new inventory to replace the inventory sold. The secured party wants this newly acquired inventory to be subject to the original security interest. Thus, the after-acquired property clause continues the secured party's claim to any inventory acquired thereafter. (This is not to say that the original security interest will always take priority over the rights of all other creditors with regard to this after-acquired inventory, as will be discussed later.)

Example 21.9 Amato buys factory equipment from Bronson on credit, giving as security an interest in all of her equipment—both what she is buying and what she already owns. The security interest with Bronson contains an after-acquired property clause. Six months later, Amato pays cash to another seller of factory equipment for more equipment. Six months after that, Amato goes out of business before she has paid off her debt to Bronson. Bronson has a security interest in all of Amato's equipment, even the equipment bought from the other seller.

After-Acquired Property Property that is acquired by the debtor after the execution of a security agreement.

Focus Question 2

How can a security interest extend to a debtor's newly acquired inventory?

21–2c Future Advances

Often, a debtor will arrange with a bank to have a *continuing line of credit* under which the debtor can borrow funds intermittently. Advances against lines of credit can be subject to a properly perfected security interest in certain collateral.

The security agreement may provide that any future advances made against that line of credit are also subject to the security interest in that collateral [UCC 9–204(c)]. Future advances do not have to be of the same type or otherwise related to the original advance to benefit from this type of **cross-collateralization.**[4] Cross-collateralization occurs when an asset that is not the subject of a loan is used to secure that loan.

Cross-Collateralization The use of an asset that is not the subject of a loan to collateralize that loan.

Example 21.10 Stroh is the owner of a small manufacturing plant with equipment valued at $1 million. He has an immediate need for $50,000 of working capital, so he obtains a loan from Midwestern Bank and signs a security agreement, putting up all of his equipment as security. The bank properly perfects its security interest. The security agreement provides that Stroh can borrow up to $500,000 in the future, using the same equipment as collateral for any future advances. In this situation, Midwestern Bank does not have to execute a new security agreement and perfect a security interest in the collateral each time an advance is made, up to a cumulative total of $500,000. For priority purposes, each advance is perfected as of the date of the *original* perfection.

Baranozdemir/Getty Images

Can equipment be used as collateral for future advances?

21–2d The Floating-Lien Concept

A security agreement that provides for a security interest in proceeds, in after-acquired property, or in collateral subject to future advances by the secured party (or in all three) is often characterized as a **floating lien.** This type of security interest continues in the collateral or proceeds even if the collateral is sold, exchanged, or disposed of in some other way.

A Floating Lien in Inventory Floating liens commonly arise in the financing of inventories. A creditor is not interested in *specific* pieces of inventory, which are constantly changing, so the lien "floats" from one item to another as the inventory changes.

Floating Lien A security interest in proceeds, after-acquired property, or collateral (or all three) subject to future advances by the secured party. The security interest is retained even when the collateral changes in character, classification, or location.

Example 21.11 Cascade Sports, Inc., an Oregon corporation, operates as a cross-country ski dealer and has a line of credit with Portland First Bank to finance its inventory of cross-country skis. Cascade and Portland First enter into a security agreement that provides for coverage of proceeds, after-acquired inventory, present inventory, and future advances. Portland First perfects its security interest in the inventory by filing centrally with the office of the secretary of state in Oregon.

One day, Cascade sells a new pair of the latest cross-country skis and receives a used pair in trade. That same day, Cascade purchases two new pairs of cross-country skis from a local manufacturer for cash. Later that day, to meet its payroll, Cascade borrows $8,000 from Portland First Bank under the security agreement.

Portland First gets a perfected security interest in the used pair of skis under the proceeds clause and a perfected security interest in the two new pairs of skis under the after-acquired property clause. This collateral, as well as other inventory, secures the new funds advanced to Cascade under the future-advances clause. All of this is accomplished under the original perfected security interest. The various items in the inventory have changed, but Portland First still has a perfected security interest in Cascade's inventory. Hence, it has a floating lien in the inventory.

Know This

Secured creditors—perfected or not—have priority over unsecured creditors.

A Floating Lien in a Shifting Stock of Goods The concept of the floating lien can also apply to a shifting stock of goods. The lien can start with raw materials, follow them as they become finished goods and inventories, and continue as the goods are sold and are turned into accounts receivable, chattel paper, or cash.

4. See official Comment 5 to UCC 9–204.

21–3 Priorities, Rights, and Duties

Focus Question 3

If two parties have perfected security interests in the debtor's collateral, which party has priority on default?

When more than one party claims an interest in the same collateral, which has priority? The UCC sets out detailed rules to answer this question. The UCC also defines certain rights and duties of debtors and secured parties.

21–3a General Rules of Priority

General rules govern situations in which security interests conflict. If only one of the conflicting security interests has been perfected, then that security interest has priority. When more than one security interest has been perfected, the first security interest to be perfected (or filed) generally has priority over any security interests that are perfected later. If none of the security interests have been perfected, then the first security interest that attaches has priority.

The UCC's rules of priority can be summarized as follows:

1. *Perfected security interest versus unsecured creditors and unperfected security interests.* When two or more parties have claims to the same collateral, a perfected secured party's interest has priority over the interests of most other parties [UCC 9–322(a)(2)]. This includes priority to the proceeds from a sale of collateral resulting from a bankruptcy (giving the perfected secured party rights that are superior to those of a bankruptcy trustee).
2. *Conflicting perfected security interests.* When two or more secured parties have perfected security interests in the same collateral, the first to perfect (by filing or taking possession of the collateral) generally has priority [UCC 9–322(a)(1)].
3. *Conflicting unperfected security interests.* When two conflicting security interests are unperfected, the first to attach (be created) has priority [UCC 9–322(a)(3)]. This is sometimes called the "first-in-time" rule.

Example 21.12 Rick and his wife and son own a dairy farm called Lost Creek Heifers (LCH) that receives multiple loans through Ag Services, Inc. To obtain the loans, Rick executes a $800,000 promissory note and security agreement in favor of Ag Services. The note lists all of LCH's accounts, equipment, farm products, inventory, livestock, and proceeds as collateral. A year later, Rick and his wife separate, and he signs a separation agreement giving her some cash and land.

The following year, Rick buys out his son's interest in LCH by giving him a promissory note for $100,000. The note lists all of LCH's equipment, inventory, livestock, and proceeds as collateral. Rick also sells a herd of dairy cows for $500,000 and gives his former wife a check for $240,000. LCH files for bankruptcy shortly thereafter. A dispute arises over which party (Ag Services, Rick's son, or Rick's former wife) is entitled to the proceeds from the sale of the cows. In this situation, a court will likely find that because Ag Services' security interest in the proceeds was the first in time to *attach*, Ag Services has first priority to the proceeds.

MaxyM/Shutterstock.com

A family dairy farm operation is sold, and a dispute arises over who has priority to part of the proceeds. What are three rules of priority the court will follow?

The following case involved a priority dispute over the inventory of a car dealership that defaulted on its debts to two creditors—a bank that provided the dealership with a line of credit and a member of the dealership's sales staff who provided funds for the dealership to buy vehicles to sell.

Case 21.2

Lewis v. Chris Carbine, Inc.

Court of Appeal of Louisiana, Fourth Circuit, __ So.3d __, 2020 WL 1056966 (2020).

Facts Chris Carbine, the owner of Chris Carbine, Inc., doing business as Carbine Motor Cars, obtained a line of credit from Whitney Bank. Carbine granted the bank a security interest in the debtor's "present and future" inventory of vehicles and the proceeds from their sale. Whitney perfected its interest.

Later, Carbine entered into a contract with a member of its sales force, Kelly Lewis, who agreed to obtain a personal line of credit with Metairie Bank to provide funds for Carbine to buy vehicles. On the sale of the vehicles, Lewis was to be paid for their cost plus 30 percent of the profit. Carbine bought eight vehicles with funds from Lewis's line of credit and sold two before going out of business and defaulting on its debts.

Lewis filed a suit in a Louisiana state court against Carbine, seeking payment for the two vehicles that were sold and transfer of title to the other six. Whitney petitioned to intervene, seeking to enforce its security interest. The court rendered a summary judgment in favor of the bank. Lewis appealed.

Issue Did Whitney's perfected security interest take priority over Lewis's interest in Carbine's property?

Decision Yes. A state intermediate appellate court affirmed the judgment of the lower court. "Whitney is entitled to summary judgment as a matter of law."

Reason The appellate court explained that to make a security interest in a debtor's property effective against other creditors, a secured party must perfect the interest by filing a UCC financing statement. The purpose of the filing is to notify the public that the security interest exists and to give it priority over other interests if the debtor defaults. Creditors that do not perfect their interests do not realize these benefits.

In this case, Whitney obtained a security interest in all of Carbine's property, including its inventory, as collateral for an extension of a line of credit, and perfected the interest. Lewis had no security interest in the vehicles bought with his funds. He argued that the vehicles did not fall within Whitney's security interest because the bank did not provide the funding for them. The court stated, "This reasoning is frivolous." The vehicles bought with Lewis's funds were "explicitly for Carbine and offered for sale to the public by Carbine on Carbine premises. . . . Moreover, Whitney's UCC financing statements pertaining to those financial arrangements were in the public record."

Critical Thinking

- **Legal Environment** *What might Lewis have done to avoid the result in this case? Discuss.*
- **What If the Facts Were Different?** *Suppose that Lewis had already been reimbursed for the two vehicles that had been sold, and Whitney sought to obtain the funds from Lewis as part of the bank's recovery for Carbine's default on its loan. Would the result have been different? Explain.*

21–3b Exceptions to the General Priority Rules

Under some circumstances, on the debtor's default, the perfection of a security interest will not protect a secured party against certain other third parties having claims to the collateral. For instance, the UCC provides that in some situations a PMSI, properly perfected,[5] will prevail over another security interest in after-acquired collateral, even though the other was perfected first. We discuss some significant exceptions to the general rules of priority next.

Buyers in the Ordinary Course of Business Under the UCC, a person who buys "in the ordinary course of business" takes the goods free from any security interest created by the seller even if the security interest is perfected and the buyer knows of its existence [UCC 9–320(a)]. A *buyer in the ordinary course of business* is a person who in good faith, and without knowledge that the sale violates the rights of another in the goods, buys goods in the

5. Recall that, with some exceptions (such as motor vehicles), a PMSI in *consumer goods* is automatically perfected—no filing is necessary. A PMSI that is *not* in consumer goods must still be perfected.

ordinary course from a person in the business of selling goods of that kind [UCC 1–201(9)].[6] The rationale for this rule is obvious. If buyers could not obtain the goods free and clear of any security interest the merchant had created—for instance, in inventory—the free flow of goods in the marketplace would be hindered.

Example 21.13 Dubbs Auto grants a security interest in its inventory to Heartland Bank for a $300,000 line of credit. Heartland perfects its security interest by filing financing statements with the appropriate state offices. Dubbs uses $9,000 of its credit to buy two used trucks and delivers the certificates of title, which designate Dubbs as the owner, to Heartland.

Later, Dubbs sells one of the trucks to Murdoch and another to Laxton. National City Bank finances both purchases. New certificates of title are issued in the buyers' names, but Heartland receives none of the funds from the sales.

If Heartland sues National City, claiming that its security interest in the vehicles takes priority, it will lose. Because Murdoch and Laxton are buyers in the ordinary course of business, Heartland's security interest in the motor vehicles was extinguished when the vehicles were sold to them. (Dubbs still owes Heartland the $9,000, of course.)

PMSI in Inventory Another important exception to the first-in-time rule has to do with security interests in inventory. (Remember that a PMSI that is *not* in consumer goods must be perfected.) A perfected PMSI in inventory has priority over a conflicting security interest in the same inventory. To maintain this priority, the holder of the PMSI must notify the holder of the conflicting security interest on or before the time the debtor takes possession of the inventory [UCC 9–324(b)].

Buyers of the Collateral The UCC recognizes that there are certain types of buyers whose interests in purchased goods could conflict with those of a perfected secured party on the debtor's default. These include not only buyers in the ordinary course of business (as just discussed), but also buyers of farm products, chattel paper, instruments, documents, or securities. The UCC sets down special rules of priority for these types of buyers.

21–3c Rights and Duties of Debtors and Creditors

The security agreement itself determines most of the rights and duties of the debtor and the secured party. The UCC, however, imposes some rights and duties that are applicable unless the security agreement states otherwise.

Information Requests At the time of filing, a secured party can furnish a copy of the financing statement and request that the filing officer note the file number, date, and hour of the original filing on the copy [UCC 9–523(a)]. The filing officer must send this copy to the person designated by the secured party.

The filing officer must also give information to a person who is contemplating obtaining a security interest from a prospective debtor [UCC 9–523(c), (d)]. If requested, the filing officer must issue a certificate (for a fee) that provides information on possible perfected financing statements with respect to the named debtor.

Release, Assignment, and Amendment A secured party can release all or part of any collateral described in the financing statement, thereby terminating its security interest in that collateral. The release is recorded by filing a uniform amendment form [UCC 9–512, 9–521(b)].

A secured party can also assign all or part of the security interest to a third party (the assignee). The assignee becomes the secured party of record if the assignment is filed by use of a uniform amendment form [UCC 9–514, 9–521(a)].

6. Note that even though a buyer may know about the existence of a perfected security interest, the buyer must not know that purchasing the goods violates the rights of any third party.

If the debtor and the secured party agree, they can amend the filing—to add or substitute new collateral, for example—by filing a uniform amendment form that indicates the file number of the initial financing statement [UCC 9–512(a)]. The amendment does not extend the time period of perfection, but if new collateral is added, the perfection date (for priority purposes) for the new collateral begins on the date the amendment is filed [UCC 9–512(b), (c)].

Confirmation or Accounting Request by Debtor The debtor may believe that the amount of the unpaid debt or the list of collateral subject to the security interest is inaccurate. The debtor has the right to request a confirmation of the unpaid debt or list of collateral [UCC 9–210]. The debtor is entitled to one request without charge every six months.

The secured party must comply with the debtor's confirmation request by authenticating and sending to the debtor an accounting within fourteen days after the request is received. Otherwise, the secured party will be held liable for any loss suffered by the debtor, plus $500 [UCC 9–210, 9–625(f)].

Termination Statement When the debtor has fully paid the debt, if the secured party perfected the security interest by filing, the debtor is entitled to have a termination statement filed. Such a statement demonstrates to the public that the filed perfected security interest has been terminated [UCC 9–513].

Whenever consumer goods are involved, the secured party *must* file a termination statement (or, alternatively, a release). The statement must be filed within one month of the final payment or within twenty days of receiving the debtor's demand, whichever is earlier [UCC 9–513(b)]. When the collateral is not consumer goods, the secured party is not required to file or to send a termination statement unless the debtor demands one [UCC 9–513(c)].

21–4 Default

Article 9 defines the rights, duties, and remedies of the secured party and of the debtor on the debtor's default. If the secured party fails to comply with the specified duties, the debtor is afforded particular rights and remedies under the UCC.

21–4a What Constitutes Default?

What constitutes default is not always clear. In fact, Article 9 does not define the term. Instead, the UCC encourages parties to include in their security agreements the standards under which their rights and duties will be measured [UCC 9–601, 9–603]. In so doing, parties can stipulate the conditions that will constitute a default. Often, these critical terms are shaped by creditors in an attempt to provide themselves with the maximum protection possible. The terms must not, however, run counter to the UCC's provisions regarding good faith and unconscionability.

Any breach of the terms of the security agreement can constitute default. Nevertheless, default occurs most commonly when the debtor fails to meet the scheduled payments or becomes bankrupt.

21–4b Basic Remedies

UCC 9–601(a) and (b) set out rights and remedies for secured parties, and these rights and remedies are *cumulative* [UCC 9–601(c)]. Therefore, a creditor who is unsuccessful in enforcing rights by one method can pursue another method. Generally, a secured party's remedies can be divided into the two basic categories discussed next.

Repossession of the Collateral—The Self-Help Remedy On the debtor's default, a secured party can take peaceful possession of the collateral without the use of judicial process [UCC 9–609(b)]. This provision is often referred to as the "self-help" provision of Article 9.

The UCC does not define *peaceful possession*. The general rule is that the collateral has been taken peacefully if the secured party can take possession without trespassing, assaulting, or breaking and entering.

On taking possession, the secured party may either retain the collateral for satisfaction of the debt [UCC 9–620] or resell the goods and apply the proceeds toward the debt [UCC 9–610].

Marsan/Shutterstock.com

This man is not stealing this car. What UCC remedy might he be exercising instead?

Judicial Remedies Alternatively, a secured party can relinquish the security interest and use any judicial remedy available, such as obtaining a judgment on the underlying debt, followed by execution and levy [UCC 9–601(a)]. (**Execution** is the implementation of a court's decree or judgment. **Levy** is the legal process of obtaining funds through the seizure and sale of nonexempt property, usually done after a writ of execution has been issued.)

Execution The implementation of a court's decree or judgment.

Levy The legal process of obtaining funds through the seizure and sale of nonexempt property, usually done after a writ of execution has been issued.

21–4c Disposition of Collateral

Once default has occurred and the secured party has obtained possession of the collateral, the secured party can:

1. Retain the collateral in full or partial satisfaction of the debt (subject to limitations, discussed next).
2. Sell, lease, license, or otherwise dispose of the collateral in any commercially reasonable manner, and apply the proceeds toward satisfaction of the debt [UCC 9–602(7), 9–603, 9–610(a), 9–613, 9–620]. Any sale is always subject to procedures established by state law.

Retention of Collateral by the Secured Party Parties are sometimes better off if they do not sell the collateral. Therefore, the UCC generally allows secured parties to choose not to sell. A secured party may retain the collateral unless it consists of consumer goods and the debtor has paid 60 percent or more of the purchase price or loan amount (see the discussion of consumer goods for specifics). The general right to retain the collateral is subject to several limitations.

Notice Requirements. The secured party must notify the debtor of its proposal to retain the collateral. Notice is required unless the debtor has signed a statement renouncing or modifying her or his rights *after default* [UCC 9–620(a), 9–621]. If the collateral is consumer goods, the secured party does not need to give any other notice. In all other situations, the secured party must also send notice to any other secured party from whom the secured party has received notice of a claim of interest in the collateral.

Objections. The debtor or other party notified of the retention has the right to object. If, within twenty days after the notice is sent, the secured party receives a written objection, the secured party must sell or otherwise dispose of the collateral. If no written objection is received, the secured party may retain the collateral in full or partial satisfaction of the debtor's obligation [UCC 9–620(a), 9–621].

Focus Question 4

When is a creditor required to sell or otherwise dispose of the repossessed collateral?

Consumer Goods When the collateral is consumer goods and the debtor has paid 60 percent of the purchase price on a PMSI or the loan amount on a non-PMSI, the secured party cannot retain the goods. Instead, the secured party is required to sell or otherwise dispose of the repossessed collateral within ninety days [UCC 9–620(e), (f)]. Failure to comply opens the secured party to an action for conversion or other liability under UCC 9–625(b) and (c). A secured party will not be liable, however, if the consumer-debtor signed a written statement *after default* renouncing or modifying the right to demand the sale of the goods [UCC 9–624].

Disposition Procedures A secured party who does not choose to retain the collateral or who is required to sell it must follow the disposition procedures prescribed in the UCC. The sale can be public or private. The collateral can be disposed of in its present condition or following any commercially reasonable preparation or processing [UCC 9–610(a)].

Cameron Spencer/Getty Images

Is the sale of collateral at auction a reasonable means of disposing of that collateral?

Notice Requirement. The secured party must notify the debtor and other specified parties in writing ahead of time about the sale or disposition of the collateral. If the collateral is consumer goods, the notice must specify the method of intended disposition. Notification is not required if the collateral is perishable, will decline rapidly in value, or is a type customarily sold on a recognized market [UCC 9–611(b), (c)].

Commercially Reasonable Manner. Every aspect of the method, manner, time, and place of disposition must be *commercially reasonable* [UCC 9–610(b)]. If the secured party does not dispose of the collateral in a commercially reasonable manner, the price paid for the collateral at the sale may be negatively affected. In that situation, a court can reduce the amount of any deficiency that the debtor owes to the secured party [UCC 9–626(a)(3)].

The issue in the following case was whether the creditor's disposition of the collateral was commercially reasonable.

Case 21.3

SunTrust Bank v. Monroe

Court of Appeals of Texas, Fort Worth, 2018 WL 651198 (2018).

Facts Liberty Redevelopment Group, LLC, financed the purchase of an Aston Martin for $233,305.46 with a loan from the dealer, Aston Martin of Dallas. Mark Monroe, a Liberty officer and the owner and operator of Delta Bail Bonds, co-signed for the loan. The dealer assigned the loan to SunTrust Bank. Seven months later, Liberty defaulted on the payments. SunTrust repossessed the car and sold it at auction for $115,000.

The bank filed a suit in a Texas state court against Monroe to recover the deficiency between the auction price and the balance of the loan, plus $38,000 in repossession expenses. Monroe responded that the sale was not made in a commercially reasonable manner. A jury agreed with Monroe and found that he owed SunTrust nothing. The bank appealed.

Issue Did the jury reasonably determine that SunTrust did not dispose of the collateral in a commercially reasonable manner?

Decision Yes. A state intermediate appellate court affirmed the lower court's judgment. "Because the jury found that SunTrust did not dispose of the collateral in a commercially reasonable manner, Monroe's liability for a deficiency was limited. . . . The trial court entered a take-nothing judgment. . . . We affirm."

Reason Among the factors that can determine commercial reasonableness are "whether the secured party endeavored to obtain the best price possible; whether the collateral was sold . . . at a propitious [favorable] time; whether the expenses incurred during the sale were reasonable and necessary; . . . what state the collateral was in; and where the sale was conducted." If the sale was at auction, another factor is "whether multiple bids were received."

In this case, Monroe was not informed of the time, date, place, or anything else about the sale. He researched the car's value, which appeared to be between $165,000 and $175,000—much more than the auction price of $115,000. As for the repossession expense, Monroe stated that as a bail bondsman, he had never seen such a high fee. SunTrust did not otherwise show that the sale of the collateral was commercially reasonable. There was no evidence of the vehicle's condition or of an attempt to obtain the best price. And there was no proof that the expenses incurred in the sale were reasonable and necessary.

Critical Thinking

- **Legal Environment** *Is a low price sufficient to establish that a sale of collateral was not made in a commercially reasonable manner? Explain.*
- **Economic** *A jury has broad discretion to identify the value of collateral in a commercially reasonable transaction. What evidence might provide a rational basis for this determination?*

Distribution of Proceeds from the Disposition Proceeds from the disposition of collateral after default on the underlying debt are distributed in the following order:

1. Reasonable expenses incurred by the secured party in repossessing, storing, and reselling the collateral are paid first.
2. The balance of the debt owed to the secured party is then paid.
3. Other lienholders who have made written or authenticated demands are paid.
4. Any surplus goes to the debtor, unless the collateral consists of accounts, payment intangibles, promissory notes, or chattel paper [UCC 9–608(a); 9–615(a), (e)].

Noncash Proceeds Sometimes the secured party receives noncash proceeds from the disposition of collateral after default. Whenever that occurs, the secured party must make a value determination and apply this value in a commercially reasonable manner [UCC 9–608(a)(3), 9–615(c)].

Deficiency Judgment Often, after proper disposition of the collateral, the secured party has not collected all that the debtor still owes. Unless otherwise agreed, the debtor normally is liable for any deficiency, and the creditor can obtain a **deficiency judgment** from a court to collect this amount. Practically speaking, though, debtors who have defaulted on a loan rarely have the cash to pay any deficiency.

Deficiency Judgment A judgment against a debtor for the amount of a debt remaining unpaid after the collateral has been repossessed and sold.

Note that if the underlying transaction was a sale of accounts, chattel paper, or promissory notes, the debtor is *not* liable for any deficiency. Also, the debtor normally is entitled to any surplus from the disposition of these types of collateral [UCC 9–615(e)].

Redemption Rights The debtor or any other secured party can exercise the right of *redemption* of the collateral. Redemption may occur at any time before the secured party disposes of the collateral, enters into a contract for its disposition, or discharges the debtor's obligation by retaining the collateral. The debtor or other secured party exercises the redemption right by tendering performance of all obligations secured by the collateral and by paying the expenses reasonably incurred by the secured party in retaking and maintaining the collateral [UCC 9–623].

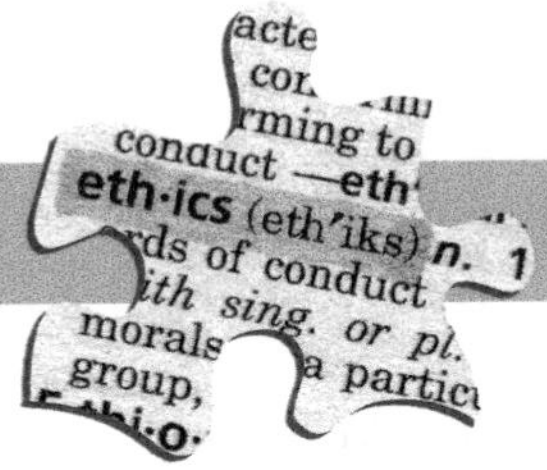

Ethical Issue

How long should a secured party have to seek a deficiency judgment? Because of depreciation, the amount received from the sale of collateral is frequently less than the amount the debtor owes to the secured party. As noted, the secured party can file a suit against the debtor in an attempt to collect the balance due. Article 9 does not contain a statute of limitations provision, so it is not clear how long a secured party has after default to file a deficiency suit against a debtor. If the secured party waits until the debtor becomes solvent again, though, the court may not allow the suit. When creditors have sued debtors for deficiencies owed on repossessed cars, for instance, courts have sometimes applied the four-year limitation period in Article 2 because the transaction was a sale of goods, even though a security interest was involved.[7] Is this fair?

7. See, for example, *Price Automotive II, LLC v. Mass Management, LLC*, 2015 WL 300418 (W.D.Va. 2015).

21–5 Other Laws Assisting Creditors

Both the common law and statutory laws other than Article 9 of the Uniform Commercial Code create rights and remedies for creditors. These remedies are available regardless of whether a creditor is secured or unsecured. Here, we discuss some of these rights and remedies.

21–5a Liens

A *lien* is an encumbrance on (claim against) property to satisfy a debt or protect a claim for the payment of a debt. Creditors' liens may arise under the common law or under statutory law. Statutory liens include *mechanic's liens,* whereas *artisan's liens* were recognized by common law. *Judicial liens* arise when a creditor attempts to collect on a debt before or after a judgment is entered by a court.

Liens can be useful because a lien creditor generally has priority over an unperfected secured party. In other words, if a creditor obtains a lien *before* another party perfects a security interest in the same property, the lienholder has priority. If the lien is obtained *after* another's security interest in the property is perfected, the perfected security interest has priority. Mechanic's and artisan's liens are exceptions to this rule. They normally take priority *even over perfected security interests,* unless a statute provides otherwise.

Mechanic's Lien Sometimes, a person who has contracted for labor, services, or materials to be furnished for making improvements on real property does not immediately pay for the improvements. When that happens, the creditor can place a **mechanic's lien** on the property.

Mechanic's Lien A nonpossessory, filed lien on an owner's real estate for labor, services, or materials furnished for making improvements on the realty.

A mechanic's lien creates a special type of debtor-creditor relationship in which the real estate itself becomes security for the debt. If the property owner fails to pay the debt, the lienholder is technically entitled to foreclose on the real estate and sell it. (*Foreclosure* is the process by which a creditor legally takes a debtor's property to satisfy a debt.) The sale proceeds are then used to pay the debt and the costs of the legal proceedings. The surplus, if any, is paid to the former owner.

In the real world, however, small-amount mechanic's liens are rarely the basis of foreclosure. Rather, these liens simply remain on the books of the state until the property is sold. At closing (when the sale is finalized), the seller agrees to pay all mechanic's liens out of the proceeds of the sale before the seller receives any of the funds. Mechanic's liens for significant amounts, such as when a contractor is owed millions for building an apartment complex, sometimes do lead to foreclosure.[8]

State law governs the procedures that must be followed to create a mechanic's lien. Generally, the lienholder must file a written notice of lien within a specific time period (usually 60 to 120 days) from the last date that labor or materials were provided.

Artisan's Lien When a debtor fails to pay for labor and materials furnished for the repair or improvement of personal property, a creditor can recover payment through an **artisan's lien.**

Artisan's Lien A possessory lien held by a party who has made improvements and added value to the personal property of another party as security for payment for services performed.

Lienholder Must Retain Possession. In contrast to a mechanic's lien, an artisan's lien is *possessory*. The lienholder ordinarily must have retained possession of the property and expressly or impliedly agreed to provide the services on a cash, not a credit, basis. The lien remains in existence as long as the lienholder maintains possession of the property, and the lien is terminated once possession is voluntarily surrendered, unless the surrender is only temporary.

Case Example 21.14 Carrollton Exempted Village School District (in Ohio) hired Clean Vehicle Solutions America, LLC (CVSA, based in New York), to convert ten school buses from diesel to compressed natural gas. The contract price was $660,000. The district paid a

8. See, for example, *Picerne Construction Corp. v. Villas,* 244 Cal.App.4th 1201, 199 Cal.Rptr.3d 257 (2016).

$400,000 deposit and agreed to pay installments of $26,000 to CVSA after the delivery of each converted bus. After the first two buses were delivered, the district refused to continue the contract, claiming that the conversion made the two buses unsafe to drive.

Both parties filed breach of contract lawsuits. CVSA also asserted an artisan's lien over two other buses that it still had in its possession because it had started converting them to natural gas and had spent $65,000 doing so. Regardless of the outcome of the parties' lawsuit, CVSA had an artisan's lien that gave it a priority claim to those two buses as long as they remained in its possession. The buses acted as security for the district's payment of the amount that CVSA had spent converting them to natural gas.[9]

MaxyM/Shutterstock.com

A dispute over payment arose in a contract to convert school buses to natural gas. For the lien on the buses to remain in effect, what must the lienholder do?

Foreclosure on Personal Property. Modern statutes permit the holder of an artisan's lien to foreclose and sell the property subject to the lien to satisfy payment of the debt. As with a mechanic's lien, the holder of an artisan's lien must give notice to the owner of the property prior to foreclosure and sale. The sale proceeds are used to pay the debt and the costs of the legal proceedings, and the surplus, if any, is paid to the former owner.

Judicial Liens When a debt is past due, a creditor can bring a legal action against the debtor to collect the debt. If the creditor is successful, the court awards the creditor a judgment against the debtor (usually for the amount of the debt plus any interest and legal costs incurred). Frequently, however, the creditor is unable to collect the awarded amount.

To ensure that a judgment will be collectible, the creditor can request that certain nonexempt property of the debtor be seized to satisfy the debt. (Under state or federal statutes, certain property is exempt from attachment by creditors.) A court's order to seize the debtor's property is known as a *writ of attachment* if it is issued before a judgment. If the order is issued after a judgment, it is referred to as a *writ of execution.*

Writ of Attachment. In the context of judicial liens, *attachment* is a court-ordered seizure of property before a judgment is secured for a past-due debt. Attachment rights are created by state statutes. Because attachment is a *prejudgment* remedy, it occurs at the time a lawsuit is filed or immediately afterward. The due process clause of the Fourteenth Amendment to the U.S. Constitution requires that the debtor be given notice and an opportunity to be heard before property can be seized.

To use attachment, a creditor must comply with the specific state's statutory restrictions and requirements. The creditor must have an enforceable right to payment of the debt under law and must follow certain procedures. Otherwise, the creditor may be liable for damages for wrongful attachment. The typical procedures for attachment are as follows:

1. The creditor files with the court an *affidavit* (a written statement, made under oath) stating that the debtor has failed to pay. The affidavit must indicate the statutory grounds for seeking attachment.
2. The creditor must post a bond to cover at least the court costs, the value of the property attached, and the value of the loss of use of that property suffered by the debtor.
3. When the court is satisfied that all the requirements have been met, it issues a **writ of attachment.** The writ directs the sheriff or other officer to seize the debtor's nonexempt property. If the creditor prevails at trial, the seized property can be sold to satisfy the judgment.

Writ of Attachment A court order to seize a debtor's nonexempt property prior to a court's final determination of a creditor's rights to the property.

9. *Clean Vehicle Solutions America, LLC v. Carrollton Exempted Village School District Board of Education,* 2015 WL 5459852 (S.D.N.Y. 2015).

Writ of Execution A court order directing the sheriff to seize (levy) and sell a debtor's nonexempt real or personal property to satisfy a court's judgment in the creditor's favor.

Writ of Execution. If the creditor wins a judgment against a debtor and the debtor will not or cannot pay the amount due, the creditor can request a **writ of execution.** A writ of execution is an order that directs the sheriff to seize (levy) and sell any of the debtor's nonexempt real or personal property. The writ applies only to property that is within the court's geographic jurisdiction (usually the county in which the courthouse is located).

The proceeds of the sale are used to pay off the judgment, accrued interest, and the costs of the sale. Any excess is paid to the debtor. The debtor can pay the judgment and redeem the nonexempt property any time before the sale takes place. (Because of exemption laws and bankruptcy laws, many judgments are uncollectible.)

21–5b Garnishment

Garnishment A legal process whereby a creditor collects a debt by seizing property of the debtor that is in the hands of a third party.

An order for **garnishment** permits a creditor to collect a debt by seizing property of the debtor that is being held by a third party. As a result of a garnishment proceeding, for instance, a debtor's employer may be ordered by the court to turn over a portion of the debtor's wages to pay the debt. Many other types of property can be garnished as well, including funds in a bank account, tax refunds, pensions, and trust funds. It is only necessary that the property not be exempt from garnishment and be in the possession of a third party.

Procedures Garnishment can be a prejudgment remedy, requiring a hearing before a court, but it is most often a postjudgment remedy. State law governs garnishment, so the procedure varies.

In some states, the creditor needs to obtain only one order of garnishment, which will then apply continuously to the debtor's wages until the entire debt is paid. In other states, the judgment creditor must go back to court for a separate order of garnishment for each pay period.

Limitations Both federal and state laws limit the amount that can be taken through garnishment proceedings.[10] Federal law provides a framework to protect debtors from suffering unduly when paying judgment debts by setting limits on how much can be garnished per pay period.[11] State laws also provide dollar exemptions, and these amounts are often larger than those provided by federal law. In addition, under federal law, an employer cannot dismiss an employee because the employee's wages are being garnished.

Case Example 21.15 Gwendolyn Berry pleaded guilty to stealing funds from her employers. At sentencing, she was ordered to pay restitution of more than $2 million. To enforce this judgment, the government garnished 50 percent of two investment retirement accounts (IRAs) belonging to Gwendolyn's husband, Michael. A federal appeals court upheld the garnishment, holding that in Texas, where the Berrys lived, a spouse has one-half interest in another spouse's solely managed community property, including IRAs. Therefore, half of Michael's IRA was part of Gwendolyn's garnishable property.

Attempting to reduce the amount of the court order, the Berrys cited a federal law that limits restitution-related garnishments to 25 percent of "weekly earnings." If Michael liquidated his IRA, they argued, that would be same as getting "earnings," and thus the law applied to this case. The court was not convinced, ruling that the definition of earnings—"compensation paid or payable for personable services"—could not be stretched to include cashed-in investments.[12] ■

10. Some states (for example, Texas) do not permit garnishment of wages by private parties except under a child-support order.
11. For instance, the federal Consumer Credit Protection Act, 15 U.S.C. Sections 1601–1693r, provides that a debtor can retain either 75 percent of disposable earnings per week or a sum equivalent to thirty hours of work paid at federal minimum-wage rates, whichever is greater.
12. *United States v. Berry*, 951 F.3d 632 (5th Cir. 2020).

21–5c Creditors' Composition Agreements

Creditors may contract with debtors for discharge of the debtors' liquidated debts (debts that are definite, or fixed, in amount) on payment of a sum less than that owed. These agreements are called **creditors' composition agreements,** or simply *composition agreements,* and usually are held to be enforceable.

Creditors' Composition Agreements Contracts between debtors and creditors in which the creditors agree to discharge the debts on the debtors' payment of a sum less than the amount actually owed.

21–5d Suretyship and Guaranty

When a third person promises to pay a debt owed by another in the event that the debtor does not pay, either a *suretyship* or a *guaranty* relationship is created. Exhibit 21–3 illustrates these relationships. The third person's income and assets become the security for the debt owed.

Suretyship and guaranty provide creditors with the right to seek payment from the third party if the primary debtor defaults on her or his obligations. At common law, there were significant differences in the liability of a surety and a guarantor, as discussed in the following subsections. Today, however, the distinctions outlined here have been abolished in some states.

Focus Question 5

What is a suretyship, and how does it differ from a guaranty?

Surety A contract of strict **suretyship** is a promise made by a third person to be responsible for the debtor's obligation. It is an express contract between the **surety** (the third party) and the creditor. The surety in the strictest sense is primarily liable for the debt of the principal. The creditor need not exhaust all legal remedies against the principal debtor before holding the surety responsible for payment. The creditor can demand payment from the surety from the moment the debt is due.

Suretyship A promise made by a third party to be responsible for a debtor's obligation.

Surety A third party who agrees to be primarily responsible for the debt of another.

Example 21.15 Roberto wants to borrow from the bank to buy a used car. Because Roberto is still in college, the bank will not lend him the funds unless his father, José, who has dealt with the bank before, will cosign the note (add his signature to the note, thereby becoming a surety and thus jointly liable for payment of the debt). When José cosigns the note, he becomes primarily liable to the bank. On the note's due date, the bank can seek payment from either Roberto or José, or both jointly.

Guaranty With a suretyship arrangement, the surety is *primarily* liable for the debtor's obligation. With a guaranty arrangement, the **guarantor**—the third person making the guaranty—is *secondarily* liable. The guarantor can be required to pay the obligation *only after the principal debtor defaults,* and default usually takes place only after the creditor has made an attempt to collect from the debtor.

Guarantor A third party who agrees to be secondarily liable for the debt of another (the debtor) only after the principal debtor defaults.

Exhibit 21–3 Suretyship and Guaranty Relationships

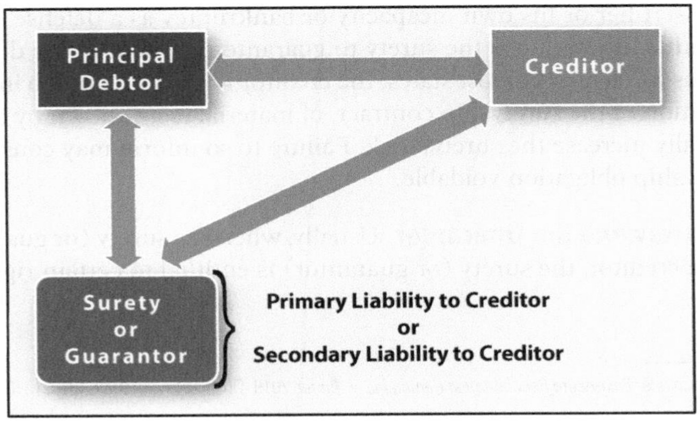

Case Example 21.16 Staff members at Altercare, a nursing home, told resident Connie Turner that her insurance company was covering all costs related to her stay. After Turner left Altercare, however, the nursing home sued to recover an unpaid bill of nearly $8,000. The trial court found that, because the assurances on which she had relied were untrue, Turner did not owe Altercare any repayment. Altercare then tried to recover the costs from Victoria Cox, Turner's granddaughter, who had signed several forms as guarantor of Turner's financial obligations to Altercare. An Ohio appeals court blocked this maneuver, holding that a guarantor could not be held responsible for debts that the debtor was not legally required to pay.[13]

Actions That Release the Surety and Guarantor Basically, the same actions will release a surety or a guarantor from an obligation. In general, the following rules apply to both sureties and guarantors, but for simplicity, we refer just to sureties:

Blend_Images/DigitalVision/Getty Images

Many parents are sureties for their children's student loans. If the student loan is materially modified without the parents' knowledge, can the parents' obligation be completely discharged?

1. *Material modification.* Making any material modification to the terms of the original contract without the surety's consent will discharge the surety's obligation. The extent to which the surety is discharged depends on whether the surety was compensated and the amount of the loss suffered as a result of the modification. For instance, a father who receives no consideration in return for acting as a surety on his daughter's loan will be completely discharged if the loan contract is modified without his consent.
2. *Surrender of property.* If a creditor surrenders the collateral to the debtor or impairs the collateral without the surety's consent, these acts can reduce the obligation of the surety. If the creditor's actions reduce the value of the property used as collateral, the surety is released to the extent of any loss suffered.
3. *Payment or tender of payment.* Naturally, any payment of the principal obligation by the debtor or by another person on the debtor's behalf will discharge the surety from the obligation. Even if the creditor refused to accept payment of the principal debt when it was tendered, the obligation of the surety can be discharged (if the creditor knew about the suretyship).

Defenses of the Surety and the Guarantor Generally, the surety (or guarantor) can also assert any of the defenses available to the principal debtor to avoid liability on the obligation to the creditor. A few exceptions do exist, however. The surety cannot assert the principal debtor's incapacity or bankruptcy as a defense. Nor can the surety assert the statute of limitations as a defense.

Obviously, a surety (or guarantor) may also have her or his own defenses. For instance, the surety can assert her or his own incapacity or bankruptcy as a defense. Furthermore, if the creditor fraudulently induced the surety to guarantee the debt of the debtor, the surety can assert fraud as a defense. In most states, the creditor has a legal duty to inform the surety, before the formation of the suretyship contract, of material facts known by the creditor that would substantially increase the surety's risk. Failure to so inform may constitute fraud and render the suretyship obligation voidable.

Rights of the Surety and the Guarantor Usually, when the surety (or guarantor) pays the debt owed to the creditor, the surety (or guarantor) is entitled to certain rights.

---

13. *Altercare of Canal Winchester Post-Acute Rehabilitation Center, Inc. v. Turner*, 2019 -Ohio- 1011, 2019 WL 1313218 (Ohio Ct. App. 10th Dis. 2019).

The Right of Subrogation. The surety has the legal **right of subrogation,** which means that any right the creditor had against the debtor now becomes the right of the surety. Included are creditor rights in bankruptcy, rights to collateral possessed by the creditor, and rights to judgments secured by the creditor. In short, the surety stands in the shoes of the creditor and may pursue any remedies that were available to the creditor against the debtor.

Right of Subrogation The right of a party to stand in the place of another, giving the substituted party the same legal rights that the original party had.

The Right of Reimbursement. The surety has a **right of reimbursement** from the debtor. Basically, the surety is entitled to receive from the debtor all outlays made on behalf of the suretyship arrangement. Such outlays can include expenses incurred as well as the actual amount of the debt paid to the creditor.

Right of Reimbursement The right of a party to be repaid for costs, expenses, or losses incurred on behalf of another.

The Right of Contribution. When two or more sureties are involved in a suretyship agreement, each is called a **co-surety.** A co-surety who pays more than that co-surety's proportionate share on a debtor's default is entitled to recover the excess amount from the other co-sureties. This is the **right of contribution.** Generally, a co-surety's liability either is determined by agreement between the co-sureties or, in the absence of an agreement, is specified in the suretyship contract itself.

Co-Surety A party who assumes liability jointly with another surety for the payment of a debtor's obligation under a suretyship arrangement.

Right of Contribution The right of a co-surety who pays more than a proportionate share on a debtor's default to recover the excess paid from other co-sureties.

Example 21.17 Two co-sureties—Yasser and Itzhak—are obligated under a suretyship contract to guarantee the debt of Jules. Itzhak's maximum liability is $15,000, and Yasser's is $10,000. Jules owes $10,000 and is in default. Itzhak pays the creditor the entire $10,000.

In the absence of an agreement to the contrary, Itzhak can recover $4,000 from Yasser. The amount of the debt that Yasser agreed to cover is divided by the total amount that Itzhak and Yasser together agreed to cover. The result is multiplied by the amount of the default, yielding the amount that Yasser owes: ($10,000 ÷ $25,000) × $10,000 = $4,000.

Practice and Review

Paul Barton owned a small property-management company, doing business as Brighton Homes. In October, Barton went on a spending spree. First, he bought a Bose surround-sound system for his home from KDM Electronics. The next day, he purchased a Wilderness Systems kayak from Outdoor Outfitters, and the day after that he bought a new Toyota 4-Runner financed through Bridgeport Auto. Two weeks later, Barton purchased six new iMac computers for his office, also from KDM Electronics. Barton bought all of these items under installment sales contracts. Six months later, Barton's property-management business was failing. He could not make the payments due on any of these purchases and thus defaulted on the loans. Using the information presented in the chapter, answer the following questions.

1. For which of Barton's purchases (the surround-sound system, the kayak, the 4-Runner, and the six iMacs) would the creditor need to file a financing statement to perfect its security interest?
2. Suppose that Barton's contract for the office computers mentioned only the name *Brighton Homes.* What would be the consequences if KDM Electronics filed a financing statement that listed only Brighton Homes as the debtor's name?
3. Which of these purchases would qualify as a PMSI in consumer goods?
4. Suppose that after KDM Electronics repossesses the surround-sound system, it decides to keep the system rather than sell it. Can KDM do this under Article 9? Why or why not?

Debate This

A financing statement that does not have the debtor's exact name should still be effective because creditors should always be protected when debtors default.

Key Terms

after-acquired property 521
artisan's lien 530
attachment 514
authenticate 514
collateral 513
continuation statement 521
co-surety 535
creditors' composition agreement 533
cross-collateralization 522
debtor 513
default 512
deficiency judgment 529
execution 527
financing statement 513
floating lien 522
garnishment 532
guarantor 533
levy 527
mechanic's lien 530
perfection 516
pledge 518
proceeds 521
purchase-money security interest (PMSI) 519
right of contribution 535
right of reimbursement 535
right of subrogation 535
secured party 513
secured transaction 512
security agreement 513
security interest 513
surety 533
suretyship 533
writ of attachment 531
writ of execution 532

Chapter Summary: Security Interests and Creditors' Rights

Creating a Security Interest	**1.** Unless the creditor has possession of the collateral, there must be a written or authenticated security agreement that clearly describes the collateral subject to the security interest and is signed or authenticated by the debtor. **2.** The secured party must give value to the debtor. **3.** The debtor must have rights in the collateral.
Perfecting a Security Interest	**1. Perfection by filing**—The most common method of perfection is by filing a financing statement containing the names of the secured party and the debtor and identifying the collateral covered by the financing statement. The financing statement must be filed under the name of the debtor. Trade names normally are not sufficient. **2. Perfection without filing**— **a.** By possession—The debtor can transfer possession of the collateral to the secured party. A *pledge* is an example of this type of transfer. **b.** By attachment—Some types of security interests are perfected automatically when they are created. The most common is the purchase-money security interest (PMSI) in consumer goods. **3. Classification of collateral**—The classification of collateral determines how and where a security interest is perfected (see Exhibit 21–2).
Scope of a Security Interest	A security agreement can cover the following types of property: **1.** *Collateral in the present possession or control of the debtor.* **2.** *Proceeds from a sale, exchange, or disposition of secured collateral.* **3. After-acquired property**—A security agreement may provide that property acquired after execution of the agreement will also be secured by the agreement. This provision is often included in security agreements covering a debtor's inventory. **4. Future advances**—A security agreement may provide that any future advances made against a line of credit will be subject to the initial security interest in the same collateral. **5. The floating-lien concept**—This type of security interest continues in the collateral or proceeds even if the collateral changes in character, classification, or location.
Priorities	**1. General rules**— **a.** Perfected security interest versus unsecured creditors and unperfected security interests—A perfected secured party's interest has priority over the interests of most other parties. **b.** Conflicting perfected security interests—When two or more secured parties have perfected security interests in the same collateral, the first to perfect generally has priority [UCC 9–322(a)(1)]. **c.** Conflicting unperfected security interests—When two conflicting security interests are unperfected, the first to attach (be created) has priority [UCC 9–322(a)(3)].

2. **Exceptions**—
   a. In some instances, a PMSI, properly perfected, will prevail over another security interest in after-acquired collateral, even though the other was perfected first.
   b. A buyer of goods in the ordinary course of the seller's business prevails over a secured party's security interest, even if the security interest is perfected and even if the buyer knows of its existence [UCC 9–320(a)].
   c. A perfected PMSI in inventory has priority over a conflicting security interest in the same inventory.
   d. Exceptions also exist for buyers of farm products, chattel paper, instruments, documents, or securities.

Rights and Duties

1. **Information request**—On request by the filing party, the filing officer must send a statement listing the file number, the date, and the hour of the filing of the financing statement to the person making the request.
2. **Release, assignment, and amendment**—A secured party may (a) release part or all of the collateral described in a filed financing statement, thus ending the creditor's security interest, or (b) assign part or all of the security interest to another party. If the debtor and the secured party agree, they can also amend the filed statement.
3. **Confirmation or accounting request by debtor**—If the debtor requests a confirmation of the unpaid debt or a list of the collateral, the secured party must send the debtor an authenticated accounting within fourteen days.
4. **Termination statement**—When a debt is paid, the secured party generally must file a termination statement. If the financing statement covers consumer goods, the termination statement must be filed by the secured party within one month after the debt is paid or within twenty days of receiving the debtor's demand, whichever is earlier.

Default

Parties can stipulate the conditions that will constitute a default, so long as they do not run counter to the UCC's provisions regarding good faith and unconscionability. Default occurs most commonly when the debtor fails to meet scheduled payments or becomes bankrupt.

1. **Basic Remedies**—The secured party's remedies are the self-help remedy (repossession of the collateral) and judicial remedies (such as obtaining a judgment on the underlying debt, followed by execution and levy).
2. **Disposition of collateral**—On the debtor's default, and once the secured party has possession of the collateral, the secured party may do either of the following:
   a. Retain the collateral in full or partial satisfaction of the debt (subject to limitations).
   b. Sell, lease, license, or otherwise dispose of the collateral in any commercially reasonable manner and apply the proceeds toward satisfaction of the debt [UCC 9–602(7), 9–603, 9–610(a), 9–613, 9–620]. Any sale is subject to procedures established by state law.

Other Laws Assisting Creditors

1. **Mechanic's lien**—A nonpossessory, filed lien on an owner's real estate for labor, services, or materials furnished for making improvements on the realty.
2. **Artisan's lien**—A possessory lien on an owner's personal property for labor performed or value added.
3. **Judicial liens**—
   a. Writ of attachment—A court order to seize a debtor's nonexempt property prior to a court's final determination of a creditor's rights to the property. Attachment is available only if the creditor complies with the applicable state statutes.
   b. Writ of execution—A court order directing the sheriff to seize (levy) and sell a debtor's non-exempt real or personal property to satisfy a court's judgment in the creditor's favor.
4. **Garnishment**—A collection remedy that allows a creditor to collect a debt by seizing property of the debtor that is being held by a third party.
5. **Creditors' composition agreements**—Contracts between debtors and creditors in which the creditors agree to discharge the debts on the debtors' payment of a sum less than the amount actually owed.
6. **Suretyships and guaranty**—Arrangements by which, under contract, a third person agrees to be primarily or secondarily liable for the debt owed by the principal debtor. A creditor can turn to this third person for satisfaction of the debt.

Issue Spotters

1. Liberty Bank loans Michelle $5,000 to buy a car, which is used as collateral to secure the loan. After repaying less than 50 percent of the loan, Michelle defaults. Liberty could repossess and keep the car, but the bank does not want it. What are the alternatives? (See *Priorities, Rights, and Duties.*)
2. Jorge contracts with Midwest Roofing to fix his roof. Jorge pays half of the contract price in advance. Midwest completes the job, but Jorge refuses to pay the rest of the price. What can Midwest do? (See *Other Laws Assisting Creditors.*)

—Check your answers to the *Issue Spotters* against the answers provided in Appendix D.

Business Scenarios and Case Problems

21–1. Priority Disputes. Redford is a seller of electric generators. He purchases a large quantity of generators from a manufacturer, Mallon Corp., by making a down payment and signing an agreement to pay the balance over a period of time. The agreement gives Mallon Corp. a security interest in the generators and the proceeds. Mallon Corp. properly files a financing statement on its security interest. Redford receives the generators and immediately sells one of them to Garfield on an installment contract with payment to be made in twelve equal installments. At the time of the sale, Garfield knows of Mallon's security interest. Two months later, Redford goes into default on his payments to Mallon. Discuss Mallon's rights against purchaser Garfield in this situation. (See *Priorities, Rights, and Duties.*)

21–2. Perfection. Marsh has a prize horse named Arabian Knight. In need of working capital, Marsh borrows $5,000 from Mendez, who takes possession of Arabian Knight as security for the loan. No written agreement is signed. Discuss whether, in the absence of a written agreement, Mendez has a security interest in Arabian Knight. If Mendez does have a security interest, is it a perfected security interest? Explain. (See *Creating and Perfecting a Security Interest.*)

21–3. Guaranty. Timothy Martinez, owner of Koenig & Vits, Inc. (K&V), guaranteed K&V's debt to Community Bank & Trust. The guaranty stated that the bank was not required to seek payment of the debt from any other source before enforcing the guaranty. K&V defaulted. Through a Wisconsin state court, the bank sought payment of $536,739.40, plus interest at the contract rate of 7.5 percent, from Martinez. Martinez argued that the bank could not enforce his guaranty while other funds were available to satisfy K&V's debt. For instance, the debt might be paid out of the proceeds of a sale of corporate assets. Is this an effective defense to a guaranty? Why or why not? [*Community Bank & Trust v. Koenig & Vits, Inc.*, 346 Wis.2d 279 (Wis.App. 2013)] (See *Other Laws Assisting Creditors.*)

21–4. Liens. Daniel and Katherine Balk asked Jirak Construction, LLC, to remodel their farmhouse in Lawler, Iowa. Jirak provided the Balks with an initial estimate of $45,975 for the cost. Over the course of the work, the Balks made significant changes to the plan. Jirak agreed to the changes and regularly advised the Balks about the increasing costs. In mid-project, Jirak provided an itemized breakdown at their request. The Balks paid Jirak $67,000 but refused to pay more. Jirak claimed that they still owed $55,000 in labor and materials. Jirak filed a suit in an Iowa state court against the Balks to collect. Which of the liens discussed in this chapter would be most useful to Jirak in its attempt to collect? How does that type of lien work? Is the court likely to enforce it in this case? Explain. [*Jirak Construction, LLC v. Balk*, 863 N.W.2d 35 (Iowa App. 2015)] (See *Other Laws Assisting Creditors.*)

21–5. Business Case Problem with Sample Answer— Perfection of a Security Interest. G&K Farms, a North Dakota partnership, operated a farm in Texas. G&K was insured under the Supplemental Revenue Assistance Payments Program (SURE), through which the federal government provides financial assistance for crop losses caused by natural disasters. PHI Financial Services, Inc., loaned G&K $6.6 million. PHI filed a financing statement that described the collateral as the debtor's interest in "Government Payments." The document did not refer to the farm's crops. G&K defaulted on the loan. Later, G&K received a SURE payment for crop losses and transferred some of the funds to its law firm, Johnston Law Office, P.C., in payment for services. PHI brought an action against Johnston to recover those funds as partial payment on its loan to G&K. Johnston argued that PHI did not have a perfected security interest in the SURE payment because the financing statement did not identify the crops. Was the description of the collateral in the financing statement sufficient? Why or why not? [*PHI Financial Services, Inc. v. Johnston Law Office, P.C.*, 2016 ND 20, 874 N.W.2d 910 (2016)] (See *Creating and Perfecting a Security Interest.*)

—For a sample answer to Problem 21–5, go to Appendix E.

21–6. Laws Assisting Creditors. Grand Harbour Condominium Owners Association, Inc., obtained a judgment in an Ohio state court against Gene and Nancy Grogg for $45,458.86. To satisfy the judgment, Grand Harbour filed a notice of garnishment with the court, seeking funds held by the Groggs in various banks.

The Groggs disputed Grand Harbour's right to garnish the funds. They claimed that the funds were exempt Social Security and pension proceeds, but they offered no proof of this claim. The banks responded by depositing $23,911.97 with the court. These funds were delivered to Grand Harbour. Later, the Groggs filed a petition for bankruptcy in a federal bankruptcy court. After they were granted a discharge, they filed a "motion to return funds to debtors" but provided no evidence that their debt to Grand Harbour had been included in the discharge. What is Grand Harbour's best argument in response to the Groggs' motion? [*Grand Harbour Condominium Owners Association, Inc. v. Grogg*, 2016 -Ohio- 1386 (Ohio Ct.App. 2016)] (See *Other Laws Assisting Creditors.*)

21–7. Disposition of Collateral. Dustin Mosely financed the purchase of two cars with a loan from Show-Me Credit Union (SMCU). When Mosely stopped making payments on the loan, SMCU notified him that it intended to repossess the cars and dispose of them at a "private or public" sale. After the sale, the creditor filed a suit in a Missouri state court to recover the difference between the sale price and the outstanding debt. Mosely counterclaimed that SMCU had failed to give proper notice before repossessing the vehicles. Public and private sales of collateral are significantly different methods of disposition. Did SMCU's failure to specify the type of sale, either public or private, at which the creditor would dispose of the collateral violate the UCC's notice requirement? Explain. [*Show-Me Credit Union v. Mosely*, 541 S.W.3d 28 (Mo.App.E.D. 2018)] (See *Default.*)

21–8. A Question of Ethics—The IDDR Approach and Defenses of the Guarantor. Woodsmill Park Limited Partnership borrowed $6.2 million secured by real property in Chicago, Illinois. Bill and Brian Bruce and Matthew O'Malley signed guaranties to meet Woodsmill's obligation on the loan. Woodsmill defaulted on the payments. Northbrook Bank & Trust Company filed an action in an Illinois state court against Woodsmill and the Bruces to foreclose on the property. The defendants agreed to resolve the claim in exchange for a deed in lieu of foreclosure and a promise to pay the difference between the value of the property and the unpaid amount of the loan. The parties stipulated, "Nothing in this Agreement shall release or reduce O'Malley's obligations under O'Malley's Guaranty." [*Northbrook Bank & Trust Co. v. Matthew O'Malley*, 2017 IL App (1st) 160438-U (2017)] (See *Other Laws Assisting Creditors.*)

1. What is the effect on O'Malley's guaranty of the agreement between Northbrook, Woodsmill, and the Bruces? Explain.
2. Using the IDDR approach, evaluate the ethics of Northbrook, Woodsmill, and the Bruces in agreeing to the stipulation concerning O'Malley.

Critical Thinking and Writing Assignments

21–9. Business Law Writing. Write a few sentences describing the circumstances in which a creditor would resort to each of the following remedies when trying to collect on debt. (See *Other Laws Assisting Creditors.*)

1. Mechanic's lien
2. Artisan's lien
3. Writ of attachment

21–10. Time-Limited Group Assignment—Validity of a Security Interest. Nick Sabol, doing business in the recording industry as Sound Farm Productions, applied to Morton Community Bank for a $58,000 loan to expand his business. Besides the loan application, Sabol signed a promissory note that referred to the bank's rights in "any collateral." Sabol also signed a letter authorizing Morton Community Bank to execute, file, and record all financing statements, amendments, and other documents required by Article 9 to establish a security interest. Sabol did not sign any other documents, including the financing statement, which contained a description of the collateral. Two years later, without having repaid the loan, Sabol filed for bankruptcy. The bank claimed a security interest in Sabol's sound equipment. (See *Creating and Perfecting a Security Interest.*)

1. The first group will list all the requirements of an enforceable security interest and explain why each of these elements is necessary.
2. The second group will determine if Morton Community Bank had a valid security interest.
3. The third group will discuss whether a bank should be able to execute financing statements on a debtor's behalf without the debtor being present or signing them. Are there are any drawbacks to this practice?

22 Bankruptcy

Focus Questions

The four Focus Questions *below are designed to help improve your understanding. After reading this chapter, you should be able to answer the following questions:*

1. What are the two main goals of bankruptcy?
2. In a Chapter 7 bankruptcy, what happens if a court finds that there was "substantial abuse"? How is the means test used?
3. In a Chapter 11 reorganization, what is the role of the debtor in possession?
4. How does a Chapter 13 bankruptcy differ from bankruptcy under Chapter 7 and Chapter 11?

"Capitalism without bankruptcy is like Christianity without hell."

Frank Borman
1928–present
(U.S. astronaut and businessman)

Many people and businesses in today's economy are struggling to pay their monthly bills. In the old days, debtors were punished and sometimes sent to jail for failing to pay their debts. Today, the law provides debtors with numerous options, including bankruptcy—a last resort in resolving debtor-creditor problems.

As implied by the chapter-opening quotation, bankruptcy is an essential aspect of our capitalistic society. Individuals and businesses in our nation have great opportunities for financial success but may also encounter financial difficulties. For instance, many retail chains (Barney's New York, Forever 21, Sugarfina) have filed for bankruptcy in recent years, in part due to the increase in online shopping. (See this chapter's *Business Web Log* feature for further discussion.) Therefore, every businessperson should have some understanding of the bankruptcy process.

22–1 The Bankruptcy Code

Bankruptcy relief is provided under federal law. Nevertheless, state laws on property, secured transactions, liens, and judgments also play a role in federal bankruptcy proceedings.

Article I, Section 8, of the U.S. Constitution gave Congress the power to establish "uniform laws on the subject of bankruptcies throughout the United States." Federal

Business Web Log

Online Competition, Bankruptcy, and the "Retail Apocalypse"

"The department store is online now," proclaims investment guru Warren Buffet. To the extent that this statement is true, Amazon.com deserves a good deal of the credit—or blame. That Internet technology company has shown a generation of American consumers that is easier, and often cheaper, to shop from home online than it is to visit a brick-and-mortar store. As a result, Amazon is now, among other triumphs, the nation's largest apparel retailer.

Amazon's ascendency helped bring about a "retail apocalypse" in the United States that has seen thousands of retail stores close and hundreds of retail companies file for bankruptcy. To highlight one casualty, the Payless shoe store chain had more than four thousand stores in thirty countries when it first filed for bankruptcy. As part of these proceedings, the Kansas-based company closed nearly seven hundred stores and eliminated about $435 million in debt.

Two years later, still saddled with $470 million in debt, Payless filed for bankruptcy again. This time, management shuttered all remaining stores in the United States and Canada, vowing to strengthen the company's online and international operations. North American consumers now have only one place to buy Payless shoes: on Amazon.com.

Key Point

Any hope for relief from the retail apocalypse ended with the coronavirus pandemic. This public health emergency caused nearly every "nonessential" retail business in the country to close some or all of its physical stores for months, leading to a wave of bankruptcy filings. As consumers became even more accustomed to shopping online, those companies that survived, including retail giants such as Costco and Walmart, were forced to significantly expand their Internet sales capabilities.

bankruptcy legislation was first enacted in 1898 and since then has undergone several modifications, most recently in the Bankruptcy Reform Act.[1] Federal bankruptcy laws are called the Bankruptcy Code or, more simply, the Code.

22–1a Goals of Bankruptcy Law

Focus Question 1

What are the two main goals of bankruptcy?

Bankruptcy law in the United States has two main goals:

1. To protect a debtor by providing a fresh start without creditors' claims.
2. To ensure equitable treatment of creditors who are competing for a debtor's assets.

Thus, the law attempts to balance the rights of the debtor and the creditors.

Although the twin goals of bankruptcy remained the same, the balance between them shifted somewhat after the reform legislation. Because of its significance for creditors and debtors alike, we present the Bankruptcy Reform Act as this chapter's *Landmark in the Law* feature.

Know This

Congress regulates the jurisdiction of the federal courts within the limits set by the U.S. Constitution. Congress can expand or reduce the number of federal courts at any time.

22–1b Bankruptcy Courts

Bankruptcy proceedings are held in federal bankruptcy courts, which are under the authority of U.S. district courts. Rulings by bankruptcy courts can be appealed to the district courts.

A bankruptcy court can conduct a jury trial if the appropriate district court has authorized it and the parties to the bankruptcy consent. Bankruptcy courts follow the Federal Rules of Bankruptcy Procedure rather than the Federal Rules of Civil Procedure. Bankruptcy court judges are appointed for terms of fourteen years.

1. The full title of the act is the Bankruptcy Abuse Prevention and Consumer Protection Act of 2005, Pub. L. No. 109-8, 119 Stat. 23 (April 20, 2005).

The Bankruptcy Abuse Prevention and Consumer Protection Act

When Congress enacted the first Bankruptcy Reform Act in 1978, many claimed that the law made it too easy for debtors to file for bankruptcy protection. The 2005 Bankruptcy Abuse Prevention and Consumer Protection Act (BAPCPA) was passed, in part, in response to businesses' concerns about the rise in personal bankruptcy filings.

From 1978 to 2005, personal bankruptcy filings increased dramatically. Various business groups—including credit-card companies, retailers, and banks—claimed that the bankruptcy process was being abused and that reform was necessary.

More Repayment Plans, Fewer Liquidation Bankruptcies One of the major goals of the BAPCPA is to require consumers to pay as many of their debts as they possibly can instead of having those debts fully discharged in bankruptcy. Before the reforms, the vast majority of bankruptcies were filed under Chapter 7 of the Bankruptcy Code, which permits debtors, with some exceptions, to have *all* of their debts discharged in bankruptcy. Only about 20 percent of personal bankruptcies were filed under Chapter 13 of the Bankruptcy Code.

As you will read later in this chapter, Chapter 13 of the Bankruptcy Code requires the debtor to establish a repayment plan and pay off as many of debts as possible over a maximum period of five years. Under the BAPCPA, more debtors have to file for bankruptcy under Chapter 13.

Other Significant Provisions of the Act The BAPCPA also made a number of other changes. One important provision involves the homestead exemption. Before the passage of the act, some states allowed debtors petitioning for bankruptcy to exempt all of the *equity* (the market value minus the outstanding mortgage owed) in their homes during bankruptcy proceedings. The act leaves these exemptions in place but puts some limits on their use.

Another BAPCPA provision gives child-support obligations priority over other debts and allows enforcement agencies to continue efforts to collect child-support payments.

Application to Today's World *Under the 2005 bankruptcy reforms, fewer debtors are allowed to have their debts discharged in Chapter 7 liquidation proceedings. At the same time, the act makes it more difficult for debtors to obtain a "fresh start" financially—one of the major goals of bankruptcy law in the United States. Today, more debtors are forced to file under Chapter 13.*

Additionally, the bankruptcy process has become more time consuming and costly because it requires more extensive documentation and certification. These changes in the law have left many Americans unable to obtain relief from their debts.

22–1c Types of Bankruptcy Relief

The Bankruptcy Code is contained in Title 11 of the *United States Code* (U.S.C.) and has eight "chapters." Chapters 1, 3, and 5 of the Code include general definitions and provisions governing case administration and procedures, creditors, the debtor, and the estate. These three chapters of the Code normally apply to all types of bankruptcies.

Design Pics Inc/Alamy

Under which chapter of the Code may family farmers seek bankruptcy relief?

Four chapters of the Code set forth the most important types of relief that debtors can seek.

1. Chapter 7 provides for *liquidation* proceedings—that is, the selling of all nonexempt assets and the distribution of the proceeds to the debtor's creditors.
2. Chapter 11 governs reorganizations.
3. Chapter 12 (for family farmers and family fishermen) and Chapter 13 (for individuals) provide for adjustment of the debts of parties with regular income.[2]

---

2. There are no Chapters 2, 4, 6, 8, or 10 in Title 11. Such "gaps" are not uncommon in the *United States Code*. They occur because, when a statute is enacted, chapter numbers (or other subdivisional unit numbers) are sometimes reserved for future use. (A gap may also appear if a law has been repealed.)

Note that a debtor (except for a municipality) need not be insolvent[3] to file for bankruptcy relief under the Bankruptcy Code. Anyone obligated to a creditor can declare bankruptcy.

22–1d Special Treatment of Consumer-Debtors

A **consumer-debtor** is a debtor whose debts result primarily from the purchase of goods for personal, family, or household use. The Bankruptcy Code requires that the clerk of the court give all consumer-debtors written notice of the general purpose, benefits, and costs of each chapter of bankruptcy under which they may proceed. In addition, the clerk must provide consumer-debtors with information on the types of services available from credit counseling agencies. Consumer-debtors are also required to confirm the accuracy of certain information filed with the court (their attorney must do so if they are represented).

Consumer-Debtor One whose debts result primarily from the purchase of goods for personal, family, or household use.

22–2 Chapter 7—Liquidation

Liquidation under Chapter 7 is the most familiar type of bankruptcy proceeding and is often referred to as an *ordinary*, or *straight, bankruptcy.* Put simply, a debtor in a liquidation bankruptcy turns all assets over to a **bankruptcy trustee**, a person appointed by the court to manage the debtor's funds. The trustee sells the nonexempt assets and distributes the proceeds to creditors. With certain exceptions, the remaining debts are then **discharged** (extinguished), and the debtor is relieved of the obligation to pay the debts.

Any "person"—defined as including individuals, partnerships, and corporations[4]—may be a debtor under Chapter 7. Railroads, insurance companies, banks, savings and loan associations, investment companies licensed by the U.S. Small Business Administration, and credit unions *cannot* be Chapter 7 debtors. Other chapters of the Code or other federal or state statutes apply to them. A husband and wife may file jointly for bankruptcy under a single petition.

A straight bankruptcy may be commenced by the filing of either a voluntary or an involuntary **petition in bankruptcy**—the document that is filed with a bankruptcy court to initiate bankruptcy proceedings. If a debtor files the petition, then it is a *voluntary bankruptcy.* If one or more creditors file a petition to force the debtor into bankruptcy, then it is an *involuntary bankruptcy.*

Liquidation The sale of the nonexempt assets of a debtor and the distribution of the funds received to creditors.

Bankruptcy Trustee A person appointed by the court to manage the debtor's funds.

Discharged Extinguished. A discharge in bankruptcy terminates the debtor's obligation to pay debts.

Petition in Bankruptcy The document that is filed with a bankruptcy court to initiate bankruptcy proceedings.

22–2a Voluntary Bankruptcy

To bring a voluntary petition in bankruptcy, a debtor files official forms designated for that purpose in the bankruptcy court. The law now requires that before debtors can file a petition, they must receive credit counseling from an approved nonprofit agency. Debtors filing a Chapter 7 petition must thus include a certificate proving that they have received individual or group counseling from an approved agency within the last 180 days (roughly six months).

A consumer-debtor who is filing a voluntary petition must confirm the accuracy of the petition's contents. The debtor must also state in the petition, at the time of filing, that he or she understands the relief available under other chapters of the Code and has chosen to proceed under Chapter 7.

Attorneys representing consumer-debtors must file an affidavit stating that they have informed the debtors of the relief available under each chapter of the Code. In addition, the attorneys must reasonably attempt to verify the accuracy of the consumer-debtors' petitions and schedules (described next). Failure to do so is considered perjury.

---

3. The inability to pay debts as they come due is known as *equitable* insolvency. A *balance-sheet* insolvency, which exists when a debtor's liabilities exceed assets, is not the test. Thus, it is possible for debtors to petition voluntarily for bankruptcy even though their assets far exceed their liabilities. This situation may occur when a debtor's cash-flow problems become severe.

4. The definition of *corporation* includes unincorporated companies and associations. It also covers labor unions.

Chapter 7 Schedules The voluntary petition contains the following schedules:

1. A list of both secured and unsecured creditors, their addresses, and the amount of debt owed to each.
2. A statement of the financial affairs of the debtor.
3. A list of all property owned by the debtor, including property claimed by the debtor to be exempt.
4. A list of current income and expenses.
5. A certificate of credit counseling (as mentioned previously).
6. Proof of payments received from employers within sixty days prior to the filing of the petition.
7. A statement of the amount of monthly income, itemized to show how the amount is calculated.
8. A copy of the debtor's federal income tax return for the most recent year ending immediately before the filing of the petition.

The official forms must be completed accurately, sworn to under oath, and signed by the debtor. To conceal assets or knowingly supply false information on these schedules is a crime under the bankruptcy laws.

With the exception of tax returns, failure to file the required schedules within forty-five days after the filing of the petition (unless an extension is granted) will result in an automatic dismissal of the petition. The debtor has up to seven days before the date of the first creditors' meeting to provide a copy of the most recent tax returns to the trustee.

Tax Returns during Bankruptcy A debtor may be required to file a tax return at the end of each tax year while the case is pending and to provide a copy to the court. A request for a copy of the debtor's tax return may be made by the court or the **U.S. Trustee**—a government official who performs administrative tasks that a bankruptcy judge would otherwise have to perform. In addition, any *party in interest* (a party, such as a creditor, who has a valid interest in the outcome of the proceedings) may make this request. Debtors may also be required to file tax returns during Chapter 11 and 13 bankruptcies.

U.S. Trustee A government official who performs administrative tasks that a bankruptcy judge would otherwise have to perform.

Substantial Abuse and the Means Test A bankruptcy court can dismiss a Chapter 7 petition if the use of Chapter 7 constitutes a "substantial abuse" of bankruptcy law. The revised Code provides a *means test* to determine a debtor's eligibility for Chapter 7.

Focus Question 2

In a Chapter 7 bankruptcy, what happens if a court finds that there was "substantial abuse"? How is the means test used?

The purpose of the test is to keep higher-income people from abusing the bankruptcy process by filing for Chapter 7, as was thought to have happened in the past. The test forces more people to file for Chapter 13 bankruptcy rather than have their debts discharged under Chapter 7.

The Basic Formula. Debtors wishing to file for bankruptcy must complete the means test to determine whether they qualify for Chapter 7. A debtor's average monthly income in recent months is compared with the median income in the geographic area in which the person lives. (The U.S. Trustee Program provides these data at its website, www.justice.gov/ust.) If the debtor's income is below the median income, the debtor usually is allowed to file for Chapter 7 bankruptcy, as there is no presumption of bankruptcy abuse.

Applying the Means Test to Future Disposable Income. If the debtor's income is above the median income, then further calculations must be made. The goal is to determine whether the person will have sufficient disposable income in the future to repay at least some unsecured debts. As a basis for the calculations, it is presumed that the debtor's recent monthly income will continue for the next sixty months. *Disposable income* is then calculated by subtracting living expenses and interest payments on secured debt, such as mortgage payments, from monthly income.

Living expenses are the amounts allowed under formulas used by the Internal Revenue Service (IRS). The IRS allowances include modest allocations for food, clothing, housing, utilities, transportation (including car payments), health care, and other necessities. (The U.S. Trustee Program's website also provides these amounts.) The allowances do not include expenditures for items such as cell phones and cable television service.

Can the Debtor Afford to Pay Unsecured Debts? Once future disposable income has been estimated, that amount is used to determine whether the debtor will have income that could be applied to unsecured debts. The court may also consider the debtor's bad faith or other circumstances indicating abuse.

Case Example 22.1 John and Sarah Buoy filed for Chapter 7 bankruptcy. For the past three months, John had worked as a supervisor for JB Hunt and had a gross monthly income of $4,900. Sarah was a registered nurse with $6,761 a month in gross income. They had five children. They owed secured debts of $34,321 on a Subaru Impreza and a BMW 328i, on which they intended to continue making loan payments (this is called reaffirmation, as will be discussed later). They owed $123,000 on a mortgage and $19,000 in student loans, and their unsecured debts were $4,900.

An auditor for the U.S. Trustee Program reviewed the Buoys' Chapter 7 schedule and concluded that the family's gross income figures were understated. Because of a mistake in the math, the Buoys had miscalculated their biweekly income by approximately $800 a month (or nearly $650 after taxes). The debtors claimed that they had incurred additional expenses after the petition, including orthodontic braces and another car. Even with those expenses, however, the court found that they would have an additional $400 a month in future disposable income and would receive sizeable tax refunds. In these circumstances, the court concluded that the Buoys could afford to pay their debts and dismissed the Chapter 7 petition for substantial abuse.[5]

Blend Images/Alamy

How does family size affect the calculation and application of the means test?

Additional Grounds for Dismissal

As noted, a debtor's voluntary petition for Chapter 7 relief may be dismissed for substantial abuse or for failure to provide the necessary documents (such as schedules and tax returns) within the specified time. In addition, a motion to dismiss a Chapter 7 filing may be granted in two other situations.

1. If the debtor has been convicted of a violent crime or a drug-trafficking offense, the victim can file a motion to dismiss the voluntary petition.[6]
2. If the debtor fails to pay postpetition domestic-support obligations (which include child and spousal support), the court may dismiss the petition.

Order for Relief

If the voluntary petition for bankruptcy is found to be proper, the filing of the petition will itself constitute an **order for relief**. (An order for relief is the court's grant of assistance to a debtor.) Once a consumer-debtor's voluntary petition has been filed, the clerk of the court (or other appointee) must give the trustee and creditors notice of the order for relief by mail not more than twenty days after the entry of the order.

Order for Relief A court's grant of assistance to a debtor in bankruptcy that relieves the debtor of the immediate obligation to pay debts.

5. *In re Buoy*, 2017 WL 3194755 (N.D. Ohio 2017).
6. Note that the court may not dismiss a case on this ground if the debtor's bankruptcy is necessary to satisfy a claim for a domestic-support obligation.

22–2b Involuntary Bankruptcy

An involuntary bankruptcy occurs when the debtor's creditors force the debtor into bankruptcy proceedings. An involuntary petition cannot be filed against a charitable institution or a farmer (an individual or business that receives more than 50 percent of its gross income from farming operations).

An involuntary petition should not be used as an everyday debt-collection device. The Code provides penalties for the filing of frivolous (unjustified) petitions against debtors. If the court dismisses an involuntary petition, the petitioning creditors may be required to pay the costs and attorneys' fees incurred by the debtor in defending against the petition. If the petition was filed in bad faith, damages can be awarded for injury to the debtor's reputation. Punitive damages may also be awarded.

Requirements For an involuntary action to be filed, the following requirements must be met:

1. If the debtor has twelve or more creditors, three or more of those creditors having unsecured claims totaling at least $16,750 must join in the petition.
2. If the debtor has fewer than twelve creditors, one or more creditors having a claim of $16,750 or more may file.[7]

Order for Relief If the debtor challenges the involuntary petition, a hearing will be held. The bankruptcy court will enter an order for relief if it finds either of the following:

1. The debtor generally is not paying debts as they become due.
2. A general receiver, assignee, or custodian took possession of, or was appointed to take charge of, substantially all of the debtor's property within 120 days before the filing of the involuntary petition.

If the court grants an order for relief, the debtor will be required to supply the same information in the bankruptcy schedules as in a voluntary bankruptcy.

22–2c Automatic Stay

Automatic Stay In bankruptcy proceedings, the suspension of almost all litigation and other actions by creditors against the debtor or the debtor's property. The stay is effective the moment the debtor files a petition in bankruptcy.

The moment a petition, either voluntary or involuntary, is filed, an **automatic stay**, or suspension, of almost all actions by creditors against the debtor or the debtor's property normally goes into effect. Until the bankruptcy proceeding is closed or dismissed, the automatic stay prohibits a creditor from taking any act to collect, assess, or recover a claim against the debtor that arose before the filing of the petition.

If the debtor had two or more bankruptcy petitions dismissed during the prior year, the Code presumes bad faith. In such a situation, the automatic stay does *not* go into effect until the court determines that the petition was filed in good faith.

If a creditor *knowingly* violates the automatic stay (a willful violation), any injured party, including the debtor, is entitled to recover actual damages, costs, and attorneys' fees and may be entitled to punitive damages as well. **Example 22.2** Richard Anderson and his wife file for bankruptcy. One of the debts listed on their Chapter 7 schedule is a Kohl's credit card with a balance of $630. Even after it is notified of the bankruptcy, Recovery Management Systems Corporation (RMSC), a debt collection service, continues to send letters to Richard Anderson in an attempt to collect the balance on the card. In this situation, RMSC is willfully violating the automatic stay. The Andersons are entitled to seek actual damages, costs, attorneys' fees, and even punitive damages for RMSC's conduct. ■ (See this chapter's *Business Law Analysis* feature for further clarification.)

7. 11 U.S.C. Section 303. The amounts stated in this chapter are in accordance with those computed on April 1, 2019. The dollar amounts are adjusted every three years on April 1.

Violations of the Automatic Stay

Business Law Analysis

Michelle Gholston leased a Chevy Impala from EZ Auto Van Rentals. On November 8, Gholston filed for bankruptcy. On November 21, the bankruptcy court notified EZ Auto of Gholston's bankruptcy and the imposition of an automatic stay. Nevertheless, because Gholston had fallen behind on her payments, EZ Auto repossessed the vehicle on November 28.

Gholston's attorney reminded EZ Auto that it could not take this action because of the automatic stay, but the company failed to return the car. As a result of the car's repossession, Gholston suffered damages that included emotional distress, lost wages, attorneys' fees, and car rental expenses. Can Gholston recover from EZ Auto?

Analysis: A debtor may be entitled to recover damages if a creditor knowingly or willfully violates the automatic stay. The test is whether EZ Auto knew about Gholston's bankruptcy at the time it repossessed her car. The bankruptcy court and the debtor's attorney had, in fact, notified EZ Auto about the bankruptcy and the automatic stay a week before the car was repossessed.

Result and Reasoning: Gholston can recover damages because EZ Auto willfully violated the automatic stay. EZ Auto repossessed the car even though it had received notice of the automatic stay from the bankruptcy court. In addition, EZ Auto refused to return the car even after Gholston's attorney had reminded it of the stay. Thus, EZ Auto knew about the automatic stay and violated it willfully. Because Gholston suffered direct damages as a result, she can recover from EZ Auto. She may also be awarded punitive damages for EZ Auto's wrongful conduct.

The Adequate Protection Doctrine Underlying the Code's automatic-stay provision for a secured creditor is a concept known as *adequate protection*. The **adequate protection doctrine**, among other things, protects secured creditors from losing the value of their security interests as a result of the automatic stay. The bankruptcy court can provide adequate protection by requiring the debtor or trustee to make periodic cash payments or a one-time cash payment. If the stay may cause the value of the property to decrease, the court can also require the debtor or trustee to provide additional collateral or replacement liens.

Adequate Protection Doctrine A doctrine that protects secured creditors from losing the value of their security interests (because the collateral depreciates, for instance) as a result of an automatic stay in a bankruptcy proceeding.

Exceptions to the Automatic Stay The Code provides the following exceptions to the automatic stay:

1. Collection efforts can continue for domestic-support obligations, which include any debt owed to or recoverable by a spouse, a former spouse, a child of the debtor, that child's parent or guardian, or a governmental unit.
2. Proceedings against the debtor related to divorce, child custody or visitation, domestic violence, and support enforcement are not stayed.
3. Investigations by a securities regulatory agency can continue.
4. Certain statutory liens for property taxes are not stayed.

Darren Brode/Shutterstock.com

If a collection agency knowingly repossesses a car when there is an automatic stay in effect, what can a debtor do?

Requests for Relief from the Automatic Stay A secured creditor or other party in interest can petition the bankruptcy court for relief from the automatic stay. If a creditor or other party requests relief from the stay, the stay will automatically terminate sixty days after the request, unless the court grants an extension or the parties agree otherwise. The automatic stay on secured property terminates forty-five days after the creditors' meeting unless the debtor redeems or reaffirms certain debts. (Creditors' meetings and reaffirmation will be discussed later in this chapter.)

22–2d Estate in Bankruptcy

Estate in Bankruptcy All of the property owned by a person, including real estate and personal property.

On the commencement of a liquidation proceeding under Chapter 7, an **estate in bankruptcy** is created. The estate consists of all the debtor's interests in property currently held, wherever located. The estate in bankruptcy includes all of the following:

1. *Community property* (property jointly owned by a husband and wife in certain states).
2. Property transferred in a transaction voidable by the trustee.
3. Proceeds and profits from the property of the estate.

Certain after-acquired property to which a debtor becomes entitled *within 180 days after filing* may also become part of the estate. Such after-acquired property includes gifts, inheritances, property settlements (from divorce), and life insurance death proceeds. Generally, though, the filing of a bankruptcy petition fixes a dividing line. Property acquired prior to the filing of the petition becomes property of the estate, and property acquired after the filing of the petition, except as just noted, remains the debtor's.

22–2e The Bankruptcy Trustee

Promptly after the order for relief has been entered, a trustee is appointed. The basic duty of the trustee is to collect the debtor's available estate and reduce it to cash for distribution, preserving the interests of both the debtor and the unsecured creditors. This requires that the trustee be accountable for administering the debtor's estate.

To enable the trustee to accomplish this duty, the Code gives the trustee certain powers. These powers must be exercised within two years after the order for relief has been entered.

Review for Substantial Abuse The trustee is required to review promptly all materials filed by the debtor to determine if there is substantial abuse. Within ten days after the first meeting of the creditors, the trustee must file a statement as to whether the case is presumed to be an abuse under the means test. The trustee must provide all creditors with a copy of this statement.

When there is a presumption of abuse, the trustee must either file a motion to dismiss the petition (or convert it to a Chapter 13 proceeding) or file a statement explaining why a motion would not be appropriate. If the debtor owes a domestic-support obligation (such as child support), the trustee must provide written notice of the bankruptcy to the claim holder (a former spouse, for instance).

Trustee's Powers The trustee has the power to require persons holding the debtor's property at the time the petition is filed to deliver the property to the trustee.[8] To enable the trustee to implement this power, the Code provides that the trustee has rights *equivalent* to those of certain other parties, such as a creditor who has a judicial lien. This power of a trustee, which is equivalent to that of a lien creditor, is known as the *strong-arm power.*

In addition, the trustee has specific *powers of avoidance.* They enable the trustee to set aside (avoid or cancel) a sale or other transfer of the debtor's property and take the property back for the debtor's estate. These powers apply to voidable rights available to the debtor, preferences, and fraudulent transfers by the debtor (as discussed in more detail next). The trustee can also avoid certain statutory liens.

The debtor shares most of the trustee's avoidance powers. Thus, if the trustee does not take action to enforce one of these rights, the debtor in a liquidation bankruptcy can enforce it.

8. Usually, the trustee takes constructive, rather than actual, possession of the debtor's property. For instance, to obtain possession of a business's inventory, a trustee might change the locks on the doors and hire a security guard.

Voidable Rights A trustee steps into the shoes of the debtor. Thus, any reason that a debtor can use to obtain the return of property can be used by the trustee as well. The grounds for recovery include fraud, duress, incapacity, and mutual mistake.

Example 22.3 Ben sells his RV trailer to Inga. Inga gives Ben a check, knowing that she has insufficient funds in her bank account to cover the check. Inga has committed fraud. Ben has the right to avoid that transfer and recover the RV trailer from Inga. If Ben files for bankruptcy relief under Chapter 7, the trustee can exercise the same right to recover the RV trailer from Inga, and the RV trailer becomes part of the debtor's estate.

turtix/Shutterstock.com

Just before filing Chapter 7 bankruptcy, a debtor sells his RV trailer, but the buyer's check is no good. What, if anything, can the trustee do to recover the RV trailer on the debtor's estate's behalf?

Preferences A debtor is not permitted to make a property transfer or a payment that favors—or gives a **preference** to—one creditor over others. The trustee is allowed to recover payments made both voluntarily and involuntarily to one creditor in preference over another.

To have made a recoverable preferential payment, an *insolvent* debtor generally must have transferred property for a *preexisting* debt during the *ninety days* before the filing of the petition in bankruptcy. The transfer must have given the creditor more than the creditor would have received as a result of the bankruptcy proceedings. The Code presumes that the debtor is insolvent during the ninety-day period before filing a petition.

If a **preferred creditor** (one who has received a preferential transfer from the debtor) has sold the property to an innocent third party, the trustee cannot recover the property from the innocent party. The trustee can generally force the preferred creditor to pay the value of the property, however.

Preference In bankruptcy proceedings, a property transfer or payment made by the debtor that favors one creditor over others.

Preferred Creditor In the context of bankruptcy, a creditor who has received a preferential transfer from a debtor.

Insider In bankruptcy proceedings, any individual, partnership, or corporation with a close personal or business relation with the debtor.

Preferences to Insiders. Sometimes, a creditor receiving a preference is an *insider*. An **insider** is any individual (such as a relative or partner), partnership, or corporation with a close relationship with the debtor. In this situation, the avoidance power of the trustee is extended to transfers made within *one year* before filing. (If the transfer was fraudulent, as will be discussed shortly, the trustee can avoid transfers made within *two years* before filing.) However, the trustee must prove that the debtor was insolvent at the time the earlier transfer occurred.

Transfers That Do Not Constitute Preferences. Not all transfers are preferences. To be a preference, the transfer must be made in exchange for something other than current consideration. Most courts do not consider a debtor's payment for services rendered within fifteen days prior to the payment to be a preference. If a creditor receives payment in the ordinary course of business, such as payment of last month's cell phone bill, the trustee in bankruptcy cannot recover the payment. In contrast, a transfer for a preexisting debt, such as a year-old landscaping bill, would be a recoverable preference.

Case Example 22.4 David Tidd operated a business performing small home repairs as well as house-building projects. Tidd and his son regularly purchased supplies for his business on credit from S.W. Collins. Eventually, Tidd filed for Chapter 7 bankruptcy. Within ninety days preceding his petition, Tidd had made four payments for materials to S.W. Collins, totaling $46,000. The trustee filed a motion seeking to avoid this transfer as a preference. The court, however, concluded that the transfer was a substantially contemporaneous exchange of value (current consideration) and not a preference. The payments were made in the ordinary course of business. Therefore, the court found in Tidd's favor and denied the trustee's motion.[9]

9. *In re Tidd,* 2017 WL 4011014 (D.Maine 2017).

Know This
Usually, when property is recovered as a preference, the trustee sells it and distributes the proceeds to the debtor's creditors.

In addition, the Code permits a consumer-debtor to transfer any property to a creditor up to a total value of $6,825 without the transfer constituting a preference. Payments of domestic-support debts do not constitute a preference. Neither do payments required under a plan created by an approved credit-counseling agency.

Fraudulent Transfers A trustee can avoid fraudulent transfers or obligations if (1) they were made within two years of the filing of the petition or (2) they were made with actual intent to hinder, delay, or defraud a creditor. **Case Example 22.5** David Dearmond was a real estate developer who owned interests in two development companies—Briartowne, LLC, and Hillside, LLC. He also owned one-third of Bluffs of Sevier County, LLC, which operated Bluff's Bar & Grill. When Briartowne defaulted on a $623,499 promissory note, SmartBank filed an action against Briartowne, Dearmond, and others.

Five months later, Dearmond sold Boyds Creek Market and Garage, a property he had paid $400,000 for the previous year, to his fiancée, Patricia Harper, for $90,000. Two days after that, Dearmond created two irrevocable trust agreements and transferred all of his interest in Hillside and Bluffs of Sevier County into those trusts. The trusts named Harper as the primary beneficiary. Although SmartBank obtained a judgment against Dearmond (and the other owners of Briartowne), it was unable to collect from these assets.

A year and a half later, Dearmond filed a petition for bankruptcy. The trustee filed a motion seeking to avoid the fraudulent transfers made to benefit Harper. Harper claimed that Dearmond had given her the interest in Hillside as a wedding present. The court concluded that the transfers should be set aside because they were made with actual intent to hinder, delay, or defraud a creditor. Therefore, the trusts no longer owned the properties. The court entered judgment for the trustee in an amount equivalent to the value of the fraudulent transfers.[10]

Jeff Greenberg/Universal Images Group/Getty Images

During bankruptcy proceedings, when can a trustee claim that the sale of a restaurant was a fraudulent transfer?

22–2f Exemptions

An individual debtor is entitled to exempt certain property from the bankruptcy under federal or state exemption schemes.

Federal Exemptions The Bankruptcy Code exempts the following property up to a specified dollar amount that changes automatically every three years:

1. A portion of equity in the debtor's home (not to exceed $170,350[11] under the federal homestead exemption, even if state law would permit a higher amount).
2. Motor vehicles, up to a certain value (usually just one vehicle).
3. Reasonably necessary clothing, household goods and furnishings, and household appliances (the aggregate value not to exceed a specified amount).
4. Jewelry, up to a specified value.
5. Tools of the debtor's trade or profession, up to a specified value.
6. A portion of unpaid but earned wages.
7. Pensions.
8. Public benefits, including public assistance (welfare), Social Security, and unemployment compensation, accumulated in a bank account.
9. Damages awarded for personal injury up to a specified amount.

10. *In re Dearmond*, 2017 WL 4220396 (E.D.Tenn. 2017).
11. The amounts stated in this chapter are in accordance with those computed from the Consumer Price Index as of April 1, 2019.

Property that is *not* exempt under federal law includes bank accounts, cash, family heirlooms, collections of stamps and coins, second cars, and vacation homes.

State Exemptions Individual states have the power to pass legislation precluding debtors from using the federal exemptions within the state. A majority of the states have done this. In those states, debtors may use only state, not federal, exemptions. In the rest of the states, an individual debtor (or a husband and wife filing jointly) may choose either the exemptions provided under state law or the federal exemptions.

Limitations on the Homestead Exemption Probably the most familiar real property exemption is the **homestead exemption**, the purpose of which is to ensure that the debtor will retain some form of shelter. Each state permits the debtor to retain the family home, either in its entirety or up to a specified dollar amount. The Bankruptcy Code limits the amount that can be claimed in bankruptcy under the homestead exemption of any state, however. In general, if the debtor acquired the home within three years and four months preceding the date of filing, the maximum equity exempted is $170,350, even if state law would permit a higher amount.

Homestead Exemption A law permitting a debtor to retain the family home, either in its entirety or up to a specified dollar amount, free from the claims of unsecured creditors or trustees in bankruptcy.

In addition, the state homestead exemption is available only if the debtor has lived in the state for two years before filing the petition. A debtor who has violated securities law, been convicted of a felony, or engaged in certain other intentional misconduct may not be permitted to claim the homestead exemption at all.

StanRohrer/Getty Images

How does the homestead exemption help debtors who go into bankruptcy?

22–2g Creditors' Meeting and Claims

Within a reasonable time after the order of relief has been granted (not more than forty days), the trustee must call a meeting of the creditors listed in the schedules filed by the debtor. The bankruptcy judge does not attend this meeting, but the debtor must attend and submit to an examination under oath. At the meeting, the trustee ensures that the debtor is aware of the potential consequences of bankruptcy and the possibility of filing under a different chapter of the Code.

To be entitled to receive a portion of the debtor's estate, each creditor normally files a *proof of claim* with the bankruptcy court clerk within ninety days of the creditors' meeting. The proof of claim lists the creditor's name and address, as well as the amount that the creditor asserts is owed to the creditor by the debtor.

When the debtor has no assets—called a "no-asset case"—creditors are notified of the debtor's petition for bankruptcy but are instructed not to file a claim. In no-asset cases, the unsecured creditors will receive no payment, and most, if not all, of these debts will be discharged.

22–2h Distribution of Property

The Code provides specific rules for the distribution of the debtor's property to secured and unsecured creditors. If any amount remains after the priority classes of creditors have been satisfied, it is turned over to the debtor.

Distribution to Secured Creditors Secured creditors have priority. The Code requires that consumer-debtors file a statement of intention with respect to the secured collateral. They can choose to pay off the debt and redeem the collateral, claim that it is exempt, reaffirm the debt and continue making payments, or surrender the property to the secured party.

If the collateral is surrendered to the secured party, the secured creditor can either (1) accept the collateral in full satisfaction of the debt or (2) sell the collateral and use the proceeds to pay off the debt. Thus, the secured party has priority over unsecured parties as to the proceeds from the disposition of the collateral. Should the collateral be insufficient to cover the secured debt owed, the secured creditor becomes an unsecured creditor for the difference.

There are limited exceptions to these rules. For instance, certain unsecured creditors can sometimes step into the shoes of secured tax creditors in Chapter 7 liquidation proceedings. In such situations, when the collateral securing the tax claims is sold, the unsecured creditors are paid first. This exception does *not* include holders of unsecured claims for administrative expenses incurred in Chapter 11 cases that are converted to Chapter 7 liquidations. In the following case, the plaintiff argued that it should.

Case 22.1

In re Anderson

United States Court of Appeals, Fourth Circuit, 811 F.3d 166 (2016).

Facts Henry Anderson filed a voluntary petition in a federal bankruptcy court for relief under Chapter 11 of the Bankruptcy Code (which governs reorganizations of the debtor's estate). The Internal Revenue Service (IRS) filed a proof of claim against the bankruptcy estate for unpaid taxes of nearly $1 million. This claim was secured by Anderson's property. Stubbs & Perdue, P.A., served as Anderson's counsel. The court approved compensation of $200,000 to Stubbs for its services. These fees constituted an unsecured claim against the estate for administrative expenses.

Later, Anderson's case was converted to a Chapter 7 liquidation. The trustee accumulated more than $700,000 for distribution to the estate's creditors—but this was not enough to pay the claims of both the IRS and Stubbs. The trustee excluded Stubbs's claim. Stubbs objected. The court dismissed Stubbs's objection. A federal district court upheld the exclusion. Stubbs appealed, arguing that the IRS's claim should be subordinated to Stubbs's claim for fees.

Issue Was Stubbs's claim correctly excluded?

Decision Yes. The U.S. Court of Appeals for the Fourth Circuit affirmed the dismissal of Stubbs's claim.

Reason Under prior law, all holders of administrative expense claims, like Stubbs, did have a right to subordinate secured tax creditors in Chapter 7 liquidations. Then—after Anderson's bankruptcy petition, but before it was converted to a Chapter 7 liquidation—Congress amended the Code to provide greater protection for holders of tax liens. The court in this case applied the law in effect at the time it rendered its decision. Under Section 724(b)(2), "It is clear that Stubbs is not entitled to subordinate the IRS's secured tax claim in favor of its unsecured claim to Chapter 11 administrative expenses."

Critical Thinking

- **Legal Environment** *Why, as a general rule, should a court apply the law that is in effect at the time the court renders its decision?*
- **Ethical** *If Anderson had filed his initial bankruptcy petition under Chapter 7, not under Chapter 11, the result would have been different—Stubbs would have been able to subordinate the IRS claim. Is this fair?*

Distribution to Unsecured Creditors Bankruptcy law establishes an order of priority for classes of debts owed to *unsecured* creditors, and they are paid in the order of their priority. Each class must be fully paid before the next class is entitled to any of the remaining proceeds. If there is any balance remaining after all the creditors are paid, it is returned to the debtor.

In almost all Chapter 7 bankruptcies, the funds will be insufficient to pay all creditors. If there are insufficient proceeds to pay the full amount to all the creditors in a class, the proceeds are distributed *proportionately* to the creditors in that class. Creditors in classes lower in priority receive nothing. Claims for domestic-support obligations, such as child support and alimony, have the highest priority among unsecured claims, so these debts must be paid first. Exhibit 22–1 illustrates the collection and distribution of property in most voluntary bankruptcies.

Exhibit 22–1 Collection and Distribution of Property in Most Voluntary Bankruptcies

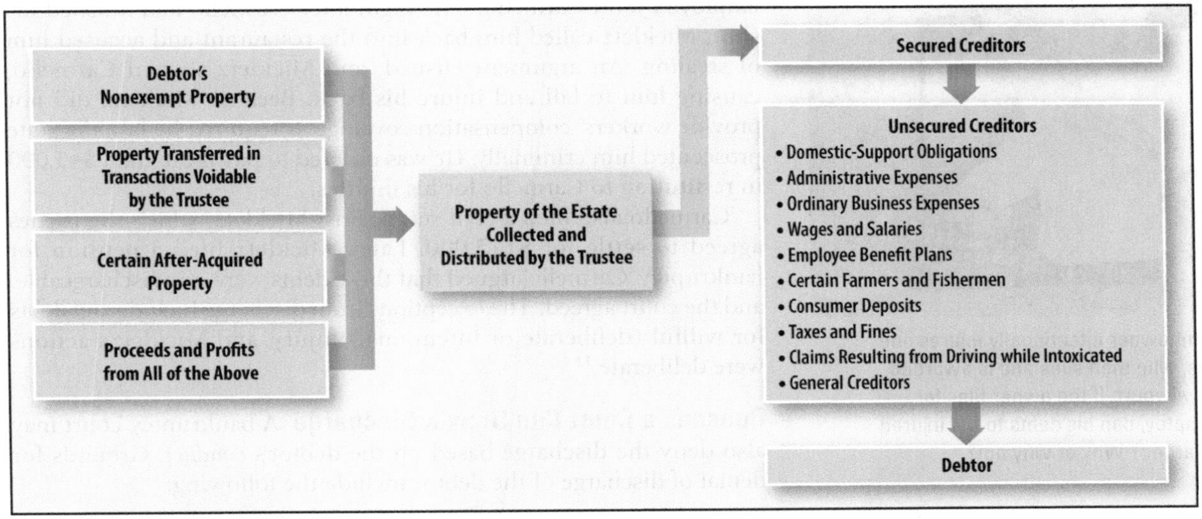

22–2i Discharge

From the debtor's point of view, the primary purpose of liquidation is to obtain a fresh start through the discharge of debts. A discharge voids, or sets aside, any judgment on a discharged debt and prevents any action to collect it. Certain debts, however, are not dischargeable in bankruptcy. Also, certain debtors may not qualify to have all debts discharged in bankruptcy. These situations are discussed next.

Know This

Often, a discharge in bankruptcy—even under Chapter 7—does not free debtors of *all* of their debts.

Debts That Are Not Dischargeable The most important claims that are not dischargeable under Chapter 7 include the following:

1. Claims for back taxes accruing within two years prior to bankruptcy.
2. Claims for amounts borrowed by the debtor to pay federal taxes or any nondischargeable taxes.
3. Claims against property or funds obtained by the debtor under false pretenses or by false misrepresentations.
4. Claims by creditors who were not notified of the bankruptcy. These claims did not appear on the schedules the debtor was required to file.
5. Claims based on fraud or misuse of funds by the debtor or claims involving the debtor's embezzlement or larceny.
6. Domestic-support obligations and property settlements.
7. Claims for amounts due on a retirement loan account.
8. Claims based on willful or malicious conduct by the debtor toward another or toward the property of another.
9. Certain government fines and penalties.
10. Student loans, unless payment of the loans causes an undue hardship for the debtor and the debtor's dependents (such as when paying the loan leaves the debtor unable to maintain a minimal standard of living).
11. Consumer debts of more than $725 for luxury goods or services owed to a single creditor incurred within ninety days of the order for relief.

stockyimages/Shutterstock.com

A pizza restaurant owner intentionally injures one of his employees, who then sues and is awarded damages by a civil court. If the owner files for Chapter 7 bankruptcy, can his debts to the injured worker be discharged? Why or why not?

Case Example 22.6 Anthony Mickletz owned a pizza restaurant that employed John Carmello. One night after Carmello had finished his shift, Mickletz called him back into the restaurant and accused him of stealing. An argument ensued, and Mickletz shoved Carmello, causing him to fall and injure his back. Because Mickletz did not provide workers' compensation coverage as required by law, the state prosecuted him criminally. He was ordered to pay more than $45,000 in restitution to Carmello for his injuries.

Carmello also filed a civil suit against Mickletz, which the parties agreed to settle for $175,000. Later, Mickletz filed a petition for bankruptcy. Carmello argued that these debts were nondischargeable, and the court agreed. The exceptions from discharge include any debts for willful (deliberate or intentional) injury, and Mickletz's actions were deliberate.[12]

Reasons a Court Can Deny a Discharge A bankruptcy court may also deny the discharge based on the debtor's *conduct*. Grounds for denial of discharge of the debtor include the following:

1. The debtor's concealment or destruction of property with the intent to hinder, delay, or defraud a creditor.
2. The debtor's fraudulent concealment or destruction of financial records.
3. The granting of a discharge to the debtor within eight years prior to the filing of the petition.
4. The debtor's failure to complete the required consumer education course.
5. Proceedings in which the debtor could be found guilty of a felony. (Basically, a court may not discharge any debt until the completion of the felony proceedings against the debtor.)

Ethical Issue

Should bankruptcy law provide relief for student loan defaults? At the start of the 2020s, 45 million borrowers owed $1.56 *trillion* in outstanding student loan balances. To alleviate this massive debt, some are suggesting reducing the interest rates that can be charged and imposing student loan debt forgiveness after a certain period of time. Although they are popular with the public, these strategies do raise several questions of ethics. What about those borrowers who have already paid off their student loans? Do they get anything? Also, could it be fair to put taxpayers "on the hook" for such a large amount of unpaid student debt?

Under certain conditions, borrowers can ask a bankruptcy court to discharge their student loan debts. To do so, under the "*Brunner* test," borrowers must show that (1) they cannot, based on current income and expenses, maintain a minimal standard of living; (2) these circumstances are likely to last for a significant amount of time; and (3) they have made good faith efforts at repayment. Applying this standard, a New York bankruptcy judge discharged $220,000 in student loan debt owed by Kevin Rosenberg, who had used to loans to earn an undergraduate history degree and a post-graduate law degree. When he filed for bankruptcy, Rosenberg was making $37,600 a year working in the "outdoor adventure" industry.[13]

12. *In re Mickletz*, 544 Bankr. 804 (E.D. Pa. 2016).
13. *Rosenberg v. Educational Credit Management Corp.*, 2020 WL 1048599 (S.D.N.Y. 2020).

When a discharge is denied under any of the five circumstances previously listed, the debtor's assets are still distributed to the creditors. After the bankruptcy proceeding, however, the debtor remains liable for the unpaid portions of all claims.

A discharge may be revoked (taken back) within one year if it is discovered that the debtor acted fraudulently or dishonestly during the bankruptcy proceeding. If that occurs, a creditor whose claim was not satisfied in the distribution of the debtor's property can proceed with a claim against the debtor.

In the following case, the debtors failed to keep adequate records of financially significant transactions. Was this failure a ground for denial of discharge?

Case 22.2

In re Dykes

United States Court of Appeals, Eighth Circuit, 954 F.3d 1157 (2020).

Facts Daryll and Sharon Dykes filed a petition for Chapter 7 relief in a federal bankruptcy court, reporting just under $400,000 in assets, over $5.6 million in liabilities, and a monthly income insufficient to cover expenses. Both Daryll and Sharon were surgeons, at one time earning more than $1 million per year and living in a $3 million home. They had lost the home to a foreclosure, followed by a loss of their household goods.

In the schedules filed with the bankruptcy petition, the Dykeses did not explain or make an accounting for the "hundreds of thousands of dollars" of lost property, nor did they disclose "substantial" transfers of their assets to their children. Creditors filing claims in the proceeding included the mortgagee who had foreclosed on their home, the homebuilder, and a jeweler.

Before the Dykeses' assets were fully gathered and the estate administered, the bankruptcy court denied a discharge. A Bankruptcy Appellate Panel (BAP) upheld the denial on the basis of undocumented purchases and returns of hundreds of thousands of dollars in watches and jewelry involving the jeweler that had filed a claim.

The Dykeses appealed to the U.S. Court of Appeals for the Eighth Circuit.

Issue Was the Dykeses' failure to keep adequate records of their transactions in watches and jewelry a ground for denial of discharge?

Decision Yes. The U.S. Court of Appeals for the Eighth Circuit agreed with the BAP and affirmed the bankruptcy court's judgment.

Reason The Bankruptcy Code authorizes denial of discharge if a debtor "failed to keep or preserve any recorded information . . . from which the debtor's financial condition . . . might be ascertained, unless such . . . failure . . . was justified under all of the circumstances."

In the Dykeses' case, their failure to keep adequate records meant the bankruptcy court could not determine the extent and effect of their financial transactions. The return of valuable watches and jewelry to the jeweler was "a sudden and large dissipation of assets." The initial purchase and subsequent return of the items had a significant impact on the debtors' financial condition. These transactions could also support or undercut the jeweler's claim. But the only record the debtors provided was a receipt "that utterly failed to substantiate the financial effect of the transaction."

The failure of Dykes, "a well-educated and sophisticated collector of highly valuable watches and jewelry," to keep adequate records was unjustified. The debtors were considering bankruptcy. Their creditors were seeking payment. "In these circumstances, a reasonable person would insist on documenting the impact of this transaction on [the debtors'] financial condition."

Critical Thinking

- **Legal Environment** *In determining whether a debtor's failure to keep adequate records was justified, the Bankruptcy Code requires a determination based on all the circumstances of the case. What factors might a court weigh in making this determination? Discuss.*
- **Economic** *How might the Dykes have established, or at least indicated, the fair market value of the watches and jewelry at the time of their return in order to avoid the result in this case? Explain.*

22–2j Reaffirmation of Debt

Reaffirmation Agreement An agreement between a debtor and a creditor in which the debtor voluntarily agrees to pay a debt dischargeable in bankruptcy.

An agreement to pay a debt dischargeable in bankruptcy is called a **reaffirmation agreement.** A debtor may wish to pay a debt—for instance, a debt owed to a family member, physician, bank, or some other creditor—even though the debt could be discharged in bankruptcy. In addition, a debtor cannot retain secured property while continuing to make payments on the underlying debt without entering into a reaffirmation agreement.

Procedures To be enforceable, reaffirmation agreements must be made before the debtor is granted a discharge. The agreement must be signed and filed with the court (along with disclosure documents, as described next). Court approval is required when the debtor is not represented by an attorney. Even when the debtor is represented by an attorney, court approval may be required if it appears that the reaffirmation will result in undue hardship to the debtor. When court approval is required, a separate hearing will take place. The court will approve the reaffirmation only if it finds that the agreement is consistent with the debtor's best interests and will not result in undue hardship.

Required Disclosures To discourage creditors from engaging in abusive reaffirmation practices, the law provides specific language for disclosures that must be given to debtors entering reaffirmation agreements. Among other things, these disclosures explain that the debtor is not required to reaffirm any debt, but that liens on secured property, such as mortgages and cars, will remain in effect even if the debt is not reaffirmed.

The original disclosure documents must be signed by the debtor, certified by the debtor's attorney, and filed with the court at the same time as the reaffirmation agreement. A reaffirmation agreement that is not accompanied by the original signed disclosures will not be effective.

The reaffirmation agreement must disclose the amount of the debt reaffirmed, the rate of interest, the date payments begin, and the right to rescind. The disclosures also caution the debtor: "Only agree to reaffirm a debt if it is in your best interest. Be sure you can afford the payments you agree to make."

Case Example 22.7 Teresa Chandler took out a loan with Peoples Bank to be paid off in forty-eight installments. After making thirteen timely payments, she missed one on July 7. On July 30, she filed for Chapter 7 bankruptcy. On August 8, she made her fourteenth payment, which People's Bank applied to the missed July 7 payment. She and People's Bank then signed a standard reaffirmation agreement, which was filed with a Kentucky bankruptcy court on September 11. Because of the missed payment, every payment that Chandler made under the reaffirmation agreement was considered one month late, leading to "harassment," extra fees, and penalties.

Chandler filed a complaint alleging that People's Bank had violated the reaffirmation agreement. An appellate court determined that Chandler mistakenly believed the missed July 7 payment to have been forgiven by her declaration of bankruptcy. When a reaffirmation agreement does not specifically differ from the original agreement, the original agreement controls. Therefore, she still owed People's Bank thirty-four payments, not thirty-three. Furthermore, the court noted, as the reaffirmation agreement went into effect on September 11, the bank could not have violated it by any action linked to a payment made on August 8.[14]

22–3 Chapter 11—Reorganization

The type of bankruptcy proceeding used most commonly by corporate debtors is the Chapter 11 *reorganization*. In a reorganization, the creditors and the debtor formulate a plan under which the debtor pays a portion of its debts and the rest of the debts are discharged. The debtor is allowed to continue in business. This type of bankruptcy is generally a corporate reorganization. Nonetheless, any debtor (except a stockbroker or commodities broker) who is eligible for Chapter 7 relief is normally eligible for relief under Chapter 11. Railroads are also eligible.

---

14. *Chandler v. Peoples Bank & Trust Company of Hazard*, 769 Fed.Appx. 242 (6th Cir. 2019).

Congress has established a "fast-track" Chapter 11 procedure for small-business debtors whose liabilities do not exceed $2.56 million and who do not own or manage real estate.[15] The fast track enables a debtor to avoid the appointment of a creditors' committee and also shortens the filing periods and relaxes certain other requirements. Because the process is shorter and simpler, it is less costly.

The same principles that govern the filing of a liquidation (Chapter 7) petition apply to reorganization (Chapter 11) proceedings. The case may be brought either voluntarily or involuntarily. The automatic-stay provision and its exceptions apply in reorganizations as well, as do the provisions regarding substantial abuse and additional grounds for dismissal (or conversion) of bankruptcy petitions.

22–3a Workouts

In some instances, to avoid bankruptcy proceedings, creditors may prefer a private, negotiated adjustment of creditor-debtor relations, known as a **workout**. Often, these out-of-court agreements are much more flexible and thus conducive to a speedy settlement. Speed is critical because delay is one of the most costly elements in any bankruptcy proceeding. Another advantage of workout agreements is that they avoid the various administrative costs of bankruptcy proceedings.

Workout An agreement outlining the respective rights and responsibilities of a borrower and a lender as they try to resolve the borrower's default.

22–3b Best Interests of the Creditors

Once a petition for Chapter 11 has been filed, a bankruptcy court can dismiss or suspend all proceedings in a case at any time if dismissal or suspension would better serve the interests of the creditors. Before taking such an action, the court must give notice and conduct a hearing. The Code also allows a court, after notice and a hearing, to dismiss a reorganization case "for cause" when there is no reasonable likelihood of rehabilitation. Similarly, a court can dismiss a Chapter 11 petition when there is an inability to effect a plan or an unreasonable delay by the debtor that may harm the interests of creditors. A debtor whose petition is dismissed for these reasons can file a subsequent Chapter 11 petition in the future.[16]

22–3c Debtor in Possession

On entry of the order for relief, the debtor in Chapter 11 generally continues to operate the business as a **debtor in possession (DIP)**. The court, however, may appoint a trustee (often referred to as a *receiver*) to operate the debtor's business if gross mismanagement of the business is shown or if appointing a trustee is in the best interests of the estate.

Debtor in Possession (DIP) In Chapter 11 bankruptcy proceedings, a debtor who is allowed to continue in possession of the business and to continue business operations.

The DIP's role is similar to that of a trustee in a liquidation. The DIP is entitled to avoid preferential payments made to creditors and fraudulent transfers of assets. The DIP can also exercise a trustee's strong-arm powers. The DIP has the power to decide whether to cancel or assume prepetition executory contracts (contracts not yet performed) or unexpired leases.

Focus Question 3

In a Chapter 11 reorganization, what is the role of the debtor in possession?

Cancellation of executory contracts or unexpired leases can be of substantial benefit to a Chapter 11 debtor. **Example 22.8** Five years ago, APT Corporation leased an office building for a twenty-year term. Now, APT can no longer pay the rent due under the lease and has filed for Chapter 11 reorganization. In this situation, the debtor in possession can cancel the lease so that APT will not be required to continue paying the substantial rent due for fifteen more years.

15. Note that this figure was temporarily increased to $7.5 million in 2020 to help small-business owners negatively impacted by the the coronavirus pandemic.
16. See 11 U.S.C. Section 1112(b).

22–3d Creditors' Committees

As soon as practicable after the entry of the order for relief, a committee of unsecured creditors is appointed.[17] The committee can consult with the trustee or the debtor concerning the administration of the case or the formulation of the plan. Additional creditors' committees may be appointed to represent special interest creditors. Generally, no orders affecting the estate will be entered without the consent of the committee or a hearing in which the judge is informed of the position of the committee.

As mentioned earlier, businesses with debts of less than $2.56 million that do not own or manage real estate can avoid creditors' committees.[18] In these fast-track proceedings, orders can be entered without a committee's consent.

Know This

Chapter 11 proceedings are typically prolonged and costly. Whether a firm survives depends on its size and its ability to attract new investors despite its Chapter 11 status.

22–3e The Reorganization Plan

A reorganization plan is established to conserve and administer the debtor's assets in the hope of an eventual return to successful operation and solvency. The plan must be fair and equitable and must do the following:

1. Designate classes of claims and interests.
2. Specify the treatment to be afforded the classes. (The plan must provide the same treatment for all claims in a particular class.)
3. Provide an adequate means for execution. (Individual debtors must utilize postpetition assets as necessary to execute the plan.)
4. Provide for payment of tax claims over a five-year period.

The plan need not provide for full repayment to unsecured creditors. Instead, creditors receive a percentage of each dollar owed to them by the debtor.

Filing the Plan Only the debtor may file a plan within the first 120 days after the date of the order for relief. This period may be extended, but not beyond eighteen months from the date of the order for relief. If the debtor does not meet the 120-day deadline or obtain an extension, or if the debtor fails to obtain the required creditor consent (discussed next) within 180 days, any party may propose a plan. If a small-business debtor chooses to avoid a creditors' committee, the time for the debtor's filing is 180 days.

Acceptance and Confirmation of the Plan Once the plan has been developed, it is submitted to each class of creditors for acceptance. For the plan to be adopted, each class must accept it. A class has accepted the plan when a majority of the creditors, representing two-thirds of the amount of the total claim, vote to approve it.

Even when all classes of creditors accept the plan, the court may refuse to confirm it if it is not "in the best interests of the creditors." In addition, confirmation is conditioned on the debtor's certifying that all postpetition domestic-support obligations have been paid in full. For small-business debtors, if the plan meets the listed requirements, the court must confirm the plan within forty-five days (unless this period is extended).

The plan can also be modified upon the request of the debtor, DIP, trustee, U.S. trustee, or holder of an unsecured claim. If an unsecured creditor objects to the plan, specific rules apply to the value of property to be distributed under the plan. Tax claims must be paid over a five-year period.

Cram-Down Provision A provision of the Bankruptcy Code that allows a court to confirm a debtor's Chapter 11 reorganization plan even though only one class of creditors has accepted it.

Even if only one class of creditors has accepted the plan, the court may still confirm the plan under the Code's so-called **cram-down provision**. In other words, the court may

17. If the debtor has filed a plan accepted by the creditors, the trustee may decide not to call a meeting of the creditors.
18. See footnote 15.

confirm the plan over the objections of a class of creditors. Before the court can exercise this right of cram-down confirmation, it must be demonstrated that the plan is fair and equitable.

Discharge The plan is binding on confirmation. Nevertheless, the law provides that confirmation of a plan does not discharge an individual debtor. *For individual debtors, the plan must be completed before discharge will be granted,* unless the court orders otherwise. For all other debtors, the court may order discharge at any time after the plan is confirmed.

On completion of the plan, the debtor is given a reorganization discharge from all claims not protected under the plan. This discharge does not apply to any claims that would be denied discharge under liquidation.

22–4 Bankruptcy Relief under Chapter 13 and Chapter 12

In addition to bankruptcy relief through liquidation (Chapter 7) and reorganization (Chapter 11), the Code also provides for individuals' repayment plans (Chapter 13) and family-farmer and family-fisherman debt adjustments (Chapter 12).

22–4a Individuals' Repayment Plan—Chapter 13

Chapter 13 of the bankruptcy code provides for the "adjustment of debts of an individual with regular income." Individuals (not partnerships or corporations) with regular income who owe fixed unsecured debts of less than $394,725 or fixed secured debts of less than $1,184,200 may take advantage of bankruptcy repayment plans.

Among those eligible are salaried employees and sole proprietors, as well as individuals who live on welfare, Social Security, fixed pensions, or investment income. Many small-business debtors have a choice of filing under either Chapter 11 or Chapter 13. Repayment plans offer some advantages because they are typically less expensive and less complicated than reorganization or liquidation proceedings.

Focus Question 4

How does a Chapter 13 bankruptcy differ from bankruptcy under Chapter 7 and Chapter 11?

Filing the Petition A Chapter 13 repayment plan case can be initiated only by the debtor's filing of a voluntary petition or by court conversion of a Chapter 7 petition (because of a finding of substantial abuse, for instance). Certain liquidation and reorganization cases may be converted to Chapter 13 with the consent of the debtor.[19]

A trustee, who will make payments under the plan, must be appointed. On the filing of a repayment plan petition, an automatic stay takes effect. Although the stay applies to all or part of the debtor's consumer debt, it does not apply to any business debt incurred by the debtor or to any domestic-support obligations.

Good Faith Requirement The Bankruptcy Code imposes the requirement of good faith on a debtor in both the filing of the petition and the filing of the plan. The Code does not define good faith, but if the circumstances as a whole indicate bad faith (such as when a debtor lies about available assets), a court can dismiss a debtor's Chapter 13 petition.

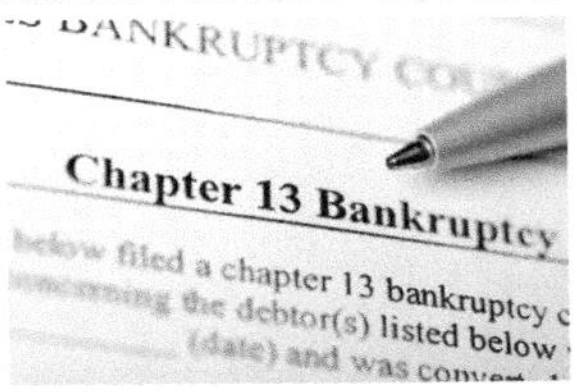

FuzzMartin/E+/Getty Images

How does good faith play a role in Chapter 13 reorganization plans?

The Repayment Plan A plan of rehabilitation by repayment must provide for the following:

1. The turning over to the trustee of future earnings or income of the debtor as necessary for execution of the plan.

19. A Chapter 13 repayment plan may be converted to a Chapter 7 liquidation either at the request of the debtor or, under certain circumstances, "for cause" by a creditor. A Chapter 13 petition may be converted to a Chapter 11 reorganization after a hearing.

2. Full payment through deferred cash payments of all claims entitled to priority, such as taxes.[20]
3. Identical treatment of all claims within a particular class. (The Code permits the debtor to list co-debtors, such as guarantors or sureties, as a separate class.)

The repayment plan may provide either for payment of all obligations in full or for payment of a lesser amount. The debtor applies the means test to determine the amount of disposable income that is available to repay creditors. The debtor is allowed to deduct certain expenses from monthly income to arrive at this amount.

The debtor must begin making payments under the proposed plan within thirty days after the plan has been filed and must continue to make "timely" payments. If the debtor fails to make timely payments or does not commence payments within the thirty-day period, the court can convert the case to a liquidation bankruptcy or dismiss the petition.

The Length of the Plan. The length of the payment plan can be three or five years, depending on the debtor's family income. If the debtor's family income is greater than the median family income in the relevant geographic area under the means test, the term of the proposed plan must be three years.[21] The term may not exceed five years.

Confirmation of the Plan. After the plan is filed, the court holds a confirmation hearing, at which interested parties (such as creditors) may object to the plan. The hearing must be held at least twenty days, but no more than forty-five days, after the meeting of the creditors. The debtor must have filed all prepetition tax returns and paid all postpetition domestic-support obligations before a court will confirm the plan.

The court will confirm a plan with respect to each claim of a secured creditor under any of the following circumstances:

1. If the secured creditors have accepted the plan.
2. If the plan provides that secured creditors retain their liens until there is payment in full or until the debtor receives a discharge.
3. If the debtor surrenders the property securing the claims to the creditors.

Know This

Courts, trustees, and creditors carefully monitor Chapter 13 debtors. If payments are not made, a court can require that the debtor explain why and may allow a creditor to take back the property.

In addition, for a motor vehicle purchased within 910 days before the petition is filed, the plan must provide that a creditor with a purchase-money security interest (PMSI) retains its lien until the entire debt is paid. For PMSIs on other personal property, the payment plan must cover debts incurred within a one-year period preceding the filing.

Discharge After the debtor has completed all payments, the court grants a discharge of all debts provided for by the repayment plan. Generally, all debts are dischargeable except the following:

1. Allowed claims not provided for by the plan.
2. Certain long-term debts provided for by the plan.
3. Certain tax claims and payments on retirement accounts.
4. Claims for domestic-support obligations.
5. Debts related to injury or property damage caused while driving under the influence of alcohol or drugs.

An order granting discharge is final as to the debts listed in the repayment plan. A creditor that willfully continues to attempt to collect on a debt that a court has ordered discharged under Chapter 13 is in violation of the law and can be sanctioned.[22]

---

20. As with a Chapter 11 reorganization plan, full repayment of all claims is not always required.

21. See 11 U.S.C. Section 1322(d) for details on when a court will find that the Chapter 13 plan should extend to a five-year period.

22. See, for example, *In re Vanamann*, 561 Bankr. 106 (D.Nev. 2017).

Under the Bankruptcy Code, a debt constitutes a domestic-support obligation if it is "in the nature of alimony, maintenance, or support." The question in the following case was whether a parent's promise to pay his children's college expenses met this requirement.

Case 22.3

In re Chamberlain

United States Court of Appeals, Tenth Circuit, 721 Fed.Appx. 826, 2018 WL 985737 (2018).

Facts When Stephen and Judith Chamberlain were divorced, their marital settlement agreement included a "College Education" provision. Stephen promised to "pay the costs of tuition, room and board, books, registration fees, and reasonable application fees incident to . . . an undergraduate college education" for each of their three children, Sarah, Kate, and John. Stephen did not meet this obligation.

Judith obtained an order in a Maryland state court to enforce the agreement and initiated an effort to collect. Stephen filed a petition for bankruptcy under Chapter 13. Judith filed a creditor's claim with the bankruptcy court, contending that the college expenses were domestic-support obligations and thus created priority claims that had to be fully paid. The court agreed. Stephen appealed.

Issue Did Stephen's promise to pay for his children's college education qualify as a domestic-support obligation?

Decision Yes. The U.S. Court of Appeals for the Tenth Circuit affirmed the judgment of the bankruptcy court. "Stephen's college expense obligation was 'in the nature of support' as required for a domestic support obligation under the Bankruptcy Code."

Reason The intent of the parties when they entered into their marital settlement agreement and the substance of Stephen's promise indicated that the "College Education" provision involved support. The parties' intent was evidenced by the expression of the obligation in the marital settlement agreement and the parties' testimony in the bankruptcy court. These sources revealed that Stephen and Judith believed a college education was important for their children's growth and maturity, that the couple had long intended to provide for that education, and that they knew this could be accomplished only if Stephen assumed the obligation to pay for it. The function of the promise at the time of the divorce indicated that the obligation was support in "substance." This determination was affected by the parties' relative financial circumstances at the time. In that respect, Stephen was the only parent in a position to pay for their children's college education.

Critical Thinking

- **Legal Environment** *Maryland law arguably does not include postsecondary education expenses in the definition of "child support." Should this state law have governed the court's conclusion in the Chamberlain case? Why or why not?*
- **What If the Facts Were Different?** *Suppose that the marital settlement agreement had obligated Stephen to assume the mortgage debt on the family home. If all other facts were the same, would the result have been different?*

22–4b Family Farmers and Fishermen—Chapter 12

To help relieve economic pressure on small farmers, Congress created Chapter 12 of the Bankruptcy Code. In 2005, Congress extended this protection to family fishermen, modified its provisions somewhat, and made it a permanent chapter in the Bankruptcy Code (previously, it had to be periodically renewed by Congress).

For purposes of Chapter 12, a *family farmer* is one whose gross income is at least 50 percent farm dependent and whose debts are at least 50 percent farm related. The total debt must not exceed $10,000,000. A partnership or a close corporation that is at least 50 percent owned by the farm family can also qualify as a family farmer.[23]

A *family fisherman* is one whose gross income is at least 50 percent dependent on commercial fishing operations and whose debts are at least 80 percent related to commercial fishing. The total debt for a family fisherman must not exceed $2,044,225. As with family farmers, a partnership or close corporation can also qualify.

23. Note that for a corporation or partnership to qualify under Chapter 12, at least 80 percent of the value of the firm's assets must consist of assets related to the farming operation.

Filing the Petition The procedure for filing a family-farmer or family-fisherman bankruptcy plan is similar to the procedure for filing a repayment plan under Chapter 13. The debtor must file a plan not later than ninety days after the order for relief has been entered. The filing of the petition acts as an automatic stay against creditors' and co-obligors' actions against the estate.

A farmer or fisherman who has already filed a reorganization or repayment plan may convert the plan to a Chapter 12 plan. The debtor may also convert a Chapter 12 plan to a liquidation plan.

Content and Confirmation of the Plan The content of a plan under Chapter 12 is basically the same as that of a Chapter 13 repayment plan. Generally, the plan must be confirmed or denied within forty-five days of filing.

The plan must provide for payment of secured debts at the value of the collateral. If the secured debt exceeds the value of the collateral, the remaining debt is unsecured.

For unsecured debtors, the plan must be confirmed if either (1) the value of the property to be distributed under the plan equals the amount of the claim or (2) the plan provides that all of the debtor's disposable income to be received in a three-year period (or longer, by court approval) will be applied to making payments. Completion of payments under the plan discharges all debts provided for by the plan.

Practice and Review

Three months ago, Janet Hart's husband of twenty years died of cancer. Although he had medical insurance, he left Janet with outstanding medical bills of more than $50,000. Janet has worked at the local library for the past ten years, earning $1,500 per month. Since her husband's death, Janet also has received $1,500 in Social Security benefits and $1,100 in life insurance proceeds every month, giving her a monthly income of $4,100. After she pays the mortgage payment of $1,500 and the amounts due on other debts each month, Janet barely has enough left over to buy groceries for her family (she has two teenage daughters at home). She decides to file for Chapter 7 bankruptcy, hoping for a fresh start. Using the information provided in the chapter, answer the following questions.

1. Under the current Bankruptcy Code, what must Janet do before filing a petition for relief under Chapter 7?
2. How much time does Janet have after filing the bankruptcy petition to submit the required schedules? What happens if Janet does not meet the deadline?
3. Assume that Janet files a petition under Chapter 7. Further assume that the median family income in the state in which Janet lives is $49,300. What steps would a court take to determine whether Janet's petition is presumed to be substantial abuse under the means test?
4. Suppose the court determines that no presumption of substantial abuse applies in Janet's case. Nevertheless, the court finds that Janet does have the ability to pay at least a portion of the medical bills out of her disposable income. What would the court likely order in that situation?

Debate This

Rather than being allowed to file Chapter 7 bankruptcy petitions, individuals and couples should always be forced to make an effort to pay off their debts through Chapter 13.

Key Terms

adequate protection doctrine 547
automatic stay 546
bankruptcy trustee 543
consumer-debtor 543
cram-down provision 558
debtor in possession (DIP) 557
discharged 543
estate in bankruptcy 548
homestead exemption 551
insider 549
liquidation 543
order for relief 545
petition in bankruptcy 543
preference 549
preferred creditor 549
reaffirmation agreement 555
U.S. Trustee 544
workout 557

Chapter Summary: Bankruptcy

The Bankruptcy Code	1. **Goals of bankruptcy law**—The law attempts to balance the rights of the debtor and the creditors by giving the debtor a fresh start and ensuring equitable treatment of creditors. 2. **Bankruptcy courts**—Bankruptcy proceedings are held in federal bankruptcy courts (under the authority of U.S. district courts). They follow the Federal Rules of Bankruptcy Procedure. 3. **Types of bankruptcy relief**—Chapter 7 provides for liquidation proceedings, Chapter 11 governs reorganizations, and Chapter 13 (for individuals) and Chapter 12 (for family farmers and family fishermen) provide for adjustment of debts of parties with regular income. 4. **Special treatment of consumer-debtors**—The Bankruptcy Code requires that all consumer-debtors receive written notice of the purpose, benefits, and costs of each chapter of bankruptcy, as well as information on the types of services available from credit counseling agencies.

BANKRUPTCY—A COMPARISON OF CHAPTERS 7, 11, 12, AND 13

Issue	Chapter 7	Chapter 11	Chapters 12 and 13
Who Can Petition	Debtor (voluntary) or creditors (involuntary).	Debtor (voluntary) or creditors (involuntary).	Debtor (voluntary) only.
Who Can Be a Debtor	Any "person" (including partnerships and corporations) except railroads, insurance companies, banks, savings and loan institutions, investment companies licensed by the U.S. Small Business Administration, and credit unions. Farmers and charitable institutions cannot be involuntarily petitioned.	Any debtor eligible for Chapter 7 relief; railroads are also eligible.	*Chapter 12*—Any family farmer (one whose gross income is at least 50 percent farm dependent and whose debts are at least 50 percent farm related) or family fisherman (one whose gross income is at least 50 percent dependent on and whose debts are at least 80 percent related to commercial fishing) or any partnership or close corporation at least 50 percent owned by a family farmer or fisherman, when total debt does not exceed a specified amount ($10,000,000 for farmers and $2,044,225 for fishermen). *Chapter 13*—Any individual (not partnerships or corporations) with regular income who owes fixed (liquidated) unsecured debts of less than $394,175 or fixed secured debts of less than $1,184,200.
Procedure Leading to Discharge	Nonexempt property is sold with proceeds to be distributed (in order) to priority groups. Dischargeable debts are terminated.	Plan is submitted. If it is approved and followed, debts are discharged.	Plan is submitted and must be approved if the value of the property to be distributed equals the amount of the claims or if the debtor turns over disposable income for a three-year or five-year period. If the plan is followed, debts are discharged.
Advantages	On liquidation and distribution, most debts are discharged, and the debtor has an opportunity for a fresh start.	Debtor continues in business. Creditors can either accept the plan, or it can be "crammed down" on them. The plan allows for the reorganization and liquidation of debts over the plan period.	Debtor continues in business or possession of assets. If the plan is approved, most debts are discharged after the specified period.

Issue Spotters

1. After graduating from college, Tina works briefly as a salesperson and then files for bankruptcy. As part of her petition, Tina reveals that her only debts are student loans, taxes accruing within the last year, and a claim against her based on her misuse of funds during her employment. Are these debts dischargeable in bankruptcy? Explain. (See *Chapter 7—Liquidation.*)
2. Ogden is a vice president of Plumbing Service, Inc. (PSI). On May 1, Ogden loans PSI $10,000. On June 1, the firm repays the loan. On July 1, PSI files for bankruptcy. Quentin is appointed trustee. Can Quentin recover the $10,000 paid to Ogden on June 1? Why or why not? (See *Chapter 7—Liquidation.*)

—Check your answers to the *Issue Spotters* against the answers provided in Appendix D.

Business Scenarios and Case Problems

22–1. Voluntary versus Involuntary Bankruptcy. Burke has been a rancher all her life, raising cattle and crops. Her ranch is valued at $500,000, almost all of which is exempt under state law. Burke has eight creditors and a total indebtedness of $70,000. Two of her largest creditors are Oman ($30,000 owed) and Sneed ($25,000 owed). The other six creditors have claims of less than $5,000 each. A drought has ruined all of Burke's crops and forced her to sell many of her cattle at a loss. She cannot pay off her creditors. (See *Chapter 7—Liquidation.*)

1. Under the Bankruptcy Code, can Burke, with a $500,000 ranch, voluntarily petition herself into bankruptcy? Explain.
2. Could either Oman or Sneed force Burke into involuntary bankruptcy? Explain.

22–2. Distribution of Property. Montoro petitioned himself into voluntary bankruptcy. There were three major claims against his estate. One was made by Carlton, a friend who held Montoro's negotiable promissory note for $2,500. Another was made by Elmer, Montoro's employee, who claimed that Montoro owed him three months' back wages of $4,500. The last major claim was made by the United Bank of the Rockies on an unsecured loan of $5,000. In addition, Dietrich, an accountant retained by the trustee, was owed $500, and property taxes of $1,000 were owed to Rock County. Montoro's nonexempt property was liquidated, with proceeds of $5,000. Discuss fully what amount each party will receive, and why. (See *Chapter 7—Liquidation.*)

22–3. Discharge in Bankruptcy. Like many students, Barbara Hann financed her education partially through loans. These loans included three federally insured Stafford Loans of $7,500 each ($22,500 in total). Hann believed that she had repaid the loans, but later, when she filed a Chapter 13 petition, Educational Credit Management Corp. (ECMC) filed an unsecured proof of claim based on the loans. Hann objected. At a hearing at which ECMC failed to appear, Hann submitted correspondence from the lender that indicated the loans had been paid. The court entered an order sustaining Hann's objection. Despite the order, can ECMC resume its effort to collect on Hann's loans? Explain. [*In re Hann,* 711 F.3d 235 (1st Cir. 2013)] (See *Bankruptcy Relief under Chapter 13 and Chapter 12.*)

22–4. Business Case Problem with Sample Answer—Discharge. Michael and Dianne Shankle divorced. An Arkansas state court ordered Michael to pay Dianne alimony and child support, as well as half of the $184,000 in their investment accounts. Instead, Michael withdrew more than half of the investment funds and spent them. Over the next several years, the court repeatedly held Michael in contempt for failing to pay Dianne. Six years later, Michael filed for Chapter 7 bankruptcy, including in the petition's schedule the debt to Dianne of unpaid alimony, child support, and investment funds. Is Michael entitled to a discharge of this debt? Explain. [*In re Shankle,* 554 Fed.Appx. 264 (5th Cir. 2014)] (See *Chapter 7—Liquidation.*)

—For a sample answer to Problem 22–4, go to Appendix E.

22–5. Discharge under Chapter 13. James Thomas and Jennifer Clark married and had two children. They bought a home in Ironton, Ohio, with a loan secured by a mortgage. Later, they took out a second mortgage. On their divorce, the court gave Clark custody of the children and required Clark to pay the first mortgage. The divorce decree also required Thomas and Clark to make equal payments on the second mortgage and provided that Clark would receive all proceeds on the sale of the home. Thomas failed to make any payments, and Clark sold the home. At that point, she learned that Auto Now had a lien on the home because Thomas had not made payments on his car. Clark used all the sale proceeds to pay off the lien and the mortgages. When Thomas filed a petition for a Chapter 13 bankruptcy in a federal bankruptcy court, Clark filed a proof of claim for the mortgage and lien debts. Clark claimed that Thomas should not be able to discharge these debts because they were part of his domestic-support obligations. Are these debts dischargeable? Explain. [*In re Thomas,* 591 Fed.Appx. 443 (6th Cir. 2015)] (See *Bankruptcy Relief under Chapter 13 and Chapter 12.*)

22–6. Liquidation Proceedings. Jeffrey Krueger and Michael Torres, shareholders of Cru Energy, Inc., were embroiled in litigation in a Texas state court. Both claimed to act on Cru's behalf, and each charged the other with attempting to obtain control of Cru through fraud and other misconduct. Temporarily prohibited from participating in Cru's business, Krueger formed Kru, a company with the same business plan and many of the same shareholders as Cru. Meanwhile, to delay state court proceedings, Krueger filed a petition for a Chapter 7 liquidation in a federal bankruptcy court. He did not reveal his interest in Kru to the bankruptcy court. Ownership of Krueger's Cru shares passed to the bankruptcy trustee, but Krueger ignored this. He called a meeting of Cru's shareholders—except Torres—and voted those shares to remove Torres from the board and elect himself chairman, president, chief executive officer, and treasurer. The Cru board then dismissed all of Cru's claims against Krueger in his suit with Torres. Are there sufficient grounds for the bankruptcy court to dismiss Krueger's bankruptcy petition? Discuss. [*In re Krueger*, 812 F.3d 365 (5th Cir. 2016)] (See *Chapter 7—Liquidation*.)

22–7. The Reorganization Plan. Under the "plain language" of the Bankruptcy Code, at least one class of creditors must accept a Chapter 11 plan for it to be confirmed. Transwest Resort Properties, Inc., and four related companies filed a petition for bankruptcy under Chapter 11. The five debtors filed a joint reorganization plan. Several classes of their creditors approved the plan. Grasslawn Lodging, LLC, filed a claim based on its loan to two of the companies, and objected to the plan. Grasslawn further asserted that the Code's confirmation requirement applied on a "per debtor," not a "per plan," basis, and because Grasslawn was the only class member for two of the debtors, the plan in this case did not meet the test. Can the court order a "cram-down"? Why or why not? [*In the Matter of Transwest Resort Properties, Inc.*, 881 F.3d 724 (9th Cir. 2018)] (See *Chapter 11—Reorganization*.)

22–8. A Question of Ethics—The IDDR Approach and Reorganization. Jevic Transportation Corporation filed a petition in a federal bankruptcy court for a Chapter 11 reorganization. A group of former Jevic truck drivers filed a suit and won a judgment against the firm for unpaid wages. This judgment entitled the workers to payment from Jevic's estate ahead of its unsecured creditors. Later, some of Jevic's unsecured creditors filed a suit against some of its other unsecured creditors. The plaintiffs won a judgment on the ground that the firm's payments to the defendants constituted fraudulent transfers and preferences. These parties then negotiated, without the truck drivers' consent, a settlement agreement that called for the workers to receive nothing on their claims while the creditors were to be paid proportionately. [*Czyzewski v Jevic Holding Corp*, 580 U.S. ___, 137 S.Ct. 973, 197 L.Ed.2d 398 (2017)] (See *Chapter 11—Reorganization*.)

1. Was it ethical of the truck drivers to obtain a judgment entitling them to payment ahead of the unsecured creditors? Why or why not?
2. Was it ethical of the unsecured creditors to agree that the workers would receive nothing on their claims? Use the IDDR approach to decide.

Critical Thinking and Writing Assignments

22–9. Time-Limited Group Assignment—Student Loan Debt. Cathy Coleman took out loans to complete her college education. After graduation, Coleman was irregularly employed as a teacher. Eventually, she filed a petition in a federal bankruptcy court under Chapter 13. The court confirmed a five-year plan under which Coleman was required to commit all of her disposable income to paying the student loans. Less than a year later, when Coleman was laid off, she still owed more than $100,000 to Educational Credit Management Corp. Coleman asked the court to discharge the debt on the ground that it would be an undue hardship for her to pay it. (See *Bankruptcy Relief under Chapter 13 and Chapter 12*.)

1. The first group will explain when a debtor normally is entitled to a discharge under Chapter 13.
2. The second group will discuss whether student loans are dischargeable and when "undue hardship" is a legitimate ground for an exception.
3. The third group will outline the goals of bankruptcy law and make an argument, based on these facts and principles, in support of Coleman's request.

Unit Three—Task-Based Simulation

Sonja owns a bakery in San Francisco.

1. **Performance of Sales Contracts.** Sonja orders two new model X23 McIntyre ovens from Western Heating Appliances for $16,000. Sonja and Western Heating agree orally, on the telephone, that Western will deliver the ovens within two weeks and that Sonja will pay for the ovens when they are delivered. Two days later, Sonja receives a fax from Western confirming her order. Before delivery, Sonja learns that she can obtain the same ovens from another company at a much lower price. Sonja wants to cancel her order, but Western refuses. Is the contract enforceable against Sonja? Why or why not?
2. **Banking.** To pay a supplier, Sonja issues a check to Milled Grains Co. that is drawn on United First Bank. A Milled Grains employee, with authorization, indorses the check and transfers it to Milled Grains' financial institution, Second Federal Bank. Second Federal puts the check into the regular bank collection process. If United First refuses to honor the check, who will ultimately suffer the loss? Could Sonja be subject to criminal prosecution if United First refuses to honor the check?
3. **Security Interests.** Sonja wants to borrow $40,000 from Credit National Bank to buy coffee-brewing equipment. If Credit National accepts Sonja's equipment as collateral for the loan, how does it let other potential creditors know of its interest? If Sonja fails to repay the loan, what are Credit National's alternatives with respect to collecting the amount due?
4. **Creditors' Rights.** Sonya borrows $20,000 from Ace Loan Co. to remodel the bakery and gives it to Jones Construction, a contractor, to do the work. The amount covers only half of the cost, but when Jones finishes the work, Sonja fails to pay the rest. Sonja also does not repay Ace for the loan. What can Jones do to collect what it is owed? What can Ace do?

Michal Kalasek/Shutterstock.com

Unit 4 Agency and Employment Law

23 Agency Relationships in Business

Focus Questions

The six Focus Questions below are designed to help improve your understanding. After reading this chapter, you should be able to answer the following questions:

1. What is the difference between an employee and an independent contractor?
2. How do agency relationships arise?
3. What duties do agents and principals owe to each other?
4. How does a person acquire apparent authority to act as someone's agent?
5. When is a principal liable for an agent's negligence?
6. What are some of the ways in which an agency relationship can be terminated?

"[It] is a universal principle in the law of agency, that the powers of the agent are to be exercised for the benefit of the principal only, and not of the agent or of third parties."

Joseph Story
1779–1845
(Associate justice of the United States Supreme Court, 1811–1844)

One of the most common, important, and pervasive legal relationships is that of **agency**. In an agency relationship between two parties, one of the parties, called the *agent*, agrees to represent or act for the other, called the *principal*. The principal has the right to control the agent's conduct in matters entrusted to the agent. Agents must exercise their powers "for the benefit of the principal only," as Justice Joseph Story indicated in the chapter-opening quotation.

Agency relationships are crucial to the business world. Indeed, the only way that some business entities—including corporations and limited liability companies—can function is through their agents. Using agents provides clear benefits to principals, but agents can also create liability for their principals.

Amelia works as the on-site leasing agent for an apartment complex owned by Premier Properties. As part of her job, she signs leases with tenants and accepts rent on behalf of Premier. She also contracts with companies that do routine maintenance and landscaping at the complex. Is Amelia, as an agent, liable if a maintenance worker is injured while working at the apartment complex? Is Premier (the principal) liable if Amelia makes fraudulent statements to tenants? What happens if Amelia signs a contract for a major renovation of the complex that Premier did not authorize? These are just a few of the legal issues that can arise in agency relationships.

23–1 Agency Law

Section 1(1) of the *Restatement (Third) of Agency*[1] defines agency as "the fiduciary relation which results from the manifestation of consent by one person to another that the other shall act in his [or her] behalf and subject to his [or her] control, and consent by the other so to act." In other words, in a principal-agent relationship, the parties have agreed that the agent will act *on behalf and instead of* the principal in negotiating and transacting business with third parties.

Agency A relationship between two parties in which one party (the agent) agrees to represent or act for the other (the principal).

The term **fiduciary** is at the heart of agency law. The term can be used both as a noun and as an adjective. When used as a noun, it refers to a person who, having undertaken a certain enterprise on behalf of another person, has a duty to act for the other person's benefit in all matters related to that enterprise. When used as an adjective, as in "fiduciary relationship," it means that the relationship involves trust and confidence.

Fiduciary As a noun, a person who, having undertaken a certain enterprise on behalf of another person, has a duty to act for the other person's benefit in all matters related to that enterprise. As an adjective, a relationship founded on trust and confidence.

Agency relationships commonly exist between employers and employees. Agency relationships may sometimes also exist between employers and independent contractors who are hired to perform special tasks or services.

23–1a Employer-Employee Relationships

Normally, all employees who deal with third parties are deemed to be agents. A salesperson in a department store, for instance, is an agent of the store's owner (the principal) and acts on the owner's behalf. Any sale of goods made by the salesperson to a customer is binding on the principal. Similarly, most representations of fact made by the salesperson with respect to the goods sold are binding on the principal.

Because employees who deal with third parties are generally deemed to be agents of their employers, agency law and employment law overlap considerably. Agency relationships, however, can exist outside an employer-employee relationship, so agency law has a broader reach than employment law. Additionally, agency law is based on the common law, whereas much employment law is statutory law.

Note that employment laws (state and federal) apply only to the employer-employee relationship. Statutes governing Social Security, withholding taxes, workers' compensation, unemployment compensation, workplace safety, and employment discrimination usually are applicable only if employer-employee status exists.

23–1b Employer–Independent Contractor Relationships

Independent contractors are not employees because, by definition, those who hire them have no control over the details of their physical performance. Section 2 of the *Restatement (Third) of Agency* defines an **independent contractor** as follows:

Independent Contractor One who works for, and receives payment from, an employer but whose working conditions and methods are not controlled by the employer. An independent contractor is not an employee but may be an agent.

> [An independent contractor is] a person who contracts with another to do something for him [or her] but who is not controlled by the other nor subject to the other's right to control with respect to his [or her] physical conduct in the performance of the undertaking. *He [or she] may or may not be an agent.* [Emphasis added.]

Building contractors and subcontractors are independent contractors. A property owner does not control the acts of either of these professionals. Truck drivers who own their equipment and hire themselves out on a per-job basis are independent contractors, whereas truck drivers who drive company trucks on a regular basis are usually employees.

1. The *Restatement (Third) of Agency* is an authoritative summary of the law of agency and is often referred to by judges and other legal professionals.

The relationship between a person or firm and an independent contractor may or may not involve an agency relationship. To illustrate: A homeowner who hires a real estate broker to sell the property has contracted with an independent contractor (the broker). The homeowner also has established an agency relationship with the broker for the specific purpose of selling the property. Insurance agents also operate in this manner, as they are both independent contractors and the agents of the insurance companies for which they sell policies. (Note that an insurance *broker*, in contrast, normally is an agent of the person obtaining insurance and not of the insurance company.)

Focus Question 1

What is the difference between an employee and an independent contractor?

23–1c Determining Employee Status

The courts are frequently asked to determine whether a particular worker is an employee or an independent contractor. How a court decides this issue can have a significant effect on the rights and liabilities of the parties. For instance, employers are required to pay certain taxes, such as Social Security and unemployment insurance taxes, for employees but not for independent contractors. Also, as will be discussed later in the chapter, an employer normally is not legally responsible for the actions of an independent contractor.

Criteria Used by the Courts In determining whether a worker has the status of an employee or an independent contractor, the courts often consider the following questions:

1. How much control can the employer exercise over the details of the work? (If an employer can exercise considerable control over the details of the work, this indicates employee status. The employer's degree of control is perhaps the most important factor weighed by the courts in determining employee status.)
2. Is the worker engaged in an occupation or business distinct from that of the employer? (If so, this points to independent-contractor status.)
3. Is the work usually done under the employer's direction or by a specialist without supervision? (If the work is usually done under the employer's direction, this indicates employee status.)
4. Does the employer supply the tools at the place of work? (If so, this indicates employee status.)
5. For how long is the person employed? (If the person is employed for a long, continuous period, this indicates employee status.)
6. What is the method of payment—by time period or at the completion of the job? (Regular payment by time period, such as once a month, indicates employee status.)
7. What degree of skill is required of the worker? (Independent contractors are more likely to be highly skilled or to have unique skills than to be unskilled, so these types of skills may indicate independent-contractor status.)

Sometimes, workers may benefit from having employee status—for tax purposes and to be protected under certain employment laws, for instance. As mentioned earlier, federal statutes governing employment discrimination apply only when an employer-employee relationship exists. Protection under antidiscrimination statutes provides a significant incentive for workers to claim that they are employees rather than independent contractors.

Employee Status and Overtime According to federal law, employers must pay employees at least one-and-one-half times their regular hourly late for overtime, defined as those hours worked in excess of forty hours per week.[2] Independent contractors are exempt from these overtime rules.

2. Fair Labor Standards Act of 1938, Section 7, 29 U.S.C.A. Section 207(a)(1).

Everyonephoto Studio/shutterstock.com

What factors will a court look at to determine if a pipe welder is an employee or an independent contractor?

Case Example 23.1 Petroplex Pipe & Construction, Inc., hired Joseph Hobbs and Drake Sweeney as pipe welders on various construction projects, classifying them as independent contractors. Petroplex paid Hobbs and Sweeny between $70 and $80 an hour. The two men generally worked from 7 A.M. to 5 P.M., six days a week, as determined by Petroplex. The welders supplied their own trucks and equipment. They also designated themselves as "self-employed" on tax returns and claimed thousands of dollars in deductions for work-related expenses.

After leaving Petroplex, Hobbs and Sweeney filed a suit against the company, alleging that they had been misclassified as independent contractors and deserved significant overtime pay. A federal appellate court determined that, although the issue was not clear cut, as a matter of "economic reality" Hobbs and Sweeney were too dependent on Petroplex to be considered "in business for [themselves]." Petroplex assigned the welders specific tasks at different work sites, set their hours, and determined their wages. Furthermore, for the several years in question, Hobbs and Sweeney worked exclusively for Petroplex. Consequently, the court found that the welders were employees and should be compensated as such.[3]

Criteria Used by the IRS The Internal Revenue Service (IRS) has established its own criteria for determining whether a worker is an independent contractor or an employee. The most important factor in this determination is the degree of control the business exercises over the worker.

The IRS tends to closely scrutinize a firm's classification of its workers because employers can avoid certain tax liabilities by hiring independent contractors instead of employees. Even when a firm classifies a worker as an independent contractor, the IRS may decide that the worker is actually an employee. If the IRS decides that an employee is misclassified, the employer will be responsible for paying any applicable Social Security, withholding, and unemployment taxes due for that employee.

Employee Status and "Works for Hire" Ordinarily, a person who creates a copyrighted work is the owner of it—unless it is a "work for hire." Under the Copyright Act, any copyrighted work created by an employee within the scope of employment at the request of the employer is a "work for hire." The *employer* owns the copyright to the work.

In contrast, when an employer hires an independent contractor—a freelance artist, writer, or computer programmer, for instance—the *independent contractor* normally owns the copyright. An exception is made if the parties agree in writing that the work is a "work for hire."

Case Example 23.2 Over the course of fifty-five years, Stanley Kauffman contributed numerous film reviews and other articles to *The New Republic* (*TNR*) magazine. At no time was Kauffman an employee of *TNR*. After Kauffman died in 2014, forty-four of his articles written for *TNR* in 1999 appeared without permission in an anthology. Kauffman's estate sued for copyright infringement. The publisher of the anthology produced a letter, signed in 2004 by Kauffman and *TNR*'s literary editor, stating that "all articles [Kauffman has] written for *The New Republic* have been 'works for hire'" and therefore belonged to *TNR*.

A federal appellate court ruled that Kauffman, as an independent contractor, retained ownership of the forty-four articles. The legislative intent behind the "work for hire" writing requirement was to make this area of the law more predictable by requiring tangible evidence of the parties' objectives at the time of the agreement. This intent would be frustrated, ruled the court, if parties could enter into a work-for-hire agreement years after the work in question was created.[4]

3. *Hobbs v. Petroplex Pipe and Construction, Inc.*, 946 F.3d. 824 (5th Cir. 2020).
4. *Estate of Kauffman v. Rochester Institute of Technology*, 932 F.3d 74 (2nd Cir. 2019).

Ethical Issues

Does the gig economy take advantage of independent contractors? The gig economy model is based on jobs that are temporary and flexible, performed by independent contractors rather than full-time employees. While workers in the gig economy enjoy a great deal of freedom when it comes to how and when they work, they are not protected by most federal and state labor laws and are not guaranteed a minimum wage or overtime pay. An employer who classifies a worker as an independent contractor avoids paying Social Security and Medicare taxes, which are borne entirely by the worker. By one estimate, businesses reduce their payroll costs by 30 percent when they hire independent contractors rather than employees.

MikeDotta/Shutterstock.com

Why would drivers working for Uber or Lyft want to be reclassified as employees? Why would they want to remain independent contractors?

Finding this situation unfair, California legislators passed a bill designed to extend employee workplace protections to roughly one million gig economy workers in the state. Called AB5, the legislation requires that any worker who performs tasks within the "usual course of the hiring entity's business" must be classified as an employee rather than an independent contractor.[5]

Aimed primarily at large gig-reliant companies such as Uber, Lyft, and Doordash, AB5 has proved controversial. Although appreciative of its protections, many gig workers regret the loss of job freedom that comes with employee status. Furthermore, numerous small businesses located in California will be forced to rely on out-of-state independent contractors or risk closure because of AB5's strain on their limited staffing budgets. "This bill is killing cockroaches with a cannon," said one Los Angeles writer who also operates a small clothing brand.

Focus Question 2

How do agency relationships arise?

23–2 Formation of an Agency

Agency relationships normally are consensual. They come about by voluntary consent and agreement between the parties. Normally, the agreement need not be in writing, and consideration is not required.

A person must have contractual capacity to be a principal. Those who cannot legally enter into contracts directly generally are not allowed to do so indirectly through an agent. (In some states, however, a minor can be a principal.) Any person can be an agent regardless of whether that person has the capacity to enter a contract (including minors).

An agency relationship can be created for any legal purpose. An agency relationship that is created for an illegal purpose or that is contrary to public policy is unenforceable. **Example 23.3** Sharp (as principal) contracts with McKenzie (as agent) to sell illegal narcotics. The agency relationship here is unenforceable because selling illegal narcotics is a felony and is contrary to public policy. ■ Similarly, it is also illegal for physicians and other licensed professionals to employ unlicensed agents to perform professional actions.

Generally, an agency relationship can arise in four ways: by agreement of the parties, by ratification, by estoppel, or by operation of law.

5. "AB-5 Worker Status: Employees and Independent Contractors (2019–2020)." California Legislative Information: September 18, 2019, Web.

23–2a Agency by Agreement

Most agency relationships are based on an express or implied agreement that the agent will act for the principal and that the principal agrees to have the agent so act. An agency agreement can take the form of an express written contract or be created by an oral agreement, such as when a person hires a neighbor to mow his lawn on a regular basis.

An agency agreement can also be implied by conduct. **Spotlight Case Example 23.4** Gilbert Bishop was admitted to Laurel Creek Health Care Center suffering from various physical ailments. During an examination, Bishop told Laurel Creek staff that he could not use his hands well enough to write or hold a pencil, but he was otherwise found to be mentally competent. Bishop's sister offered to sign the admissions forms, but it was Laurel Creek's policy to have the patient's spouse sign the admissions papers if the patient was unable to do so.

Bishop's sister then brought his wife, Anna, to the hospital to sign the paperwork, which included a mandatory arbitration clause. Later, when the family filed a lawsuit against Laurel Creek, the nursing home sought to enforce the arbitration clause. Ultimately, a state appellate court held that Bishop was bound by the contract and the arbitration clause his wife had signed. Bishop's conduct had indicated that he was giving his wife authority to act as his agent in signing the admissions papers.[6]

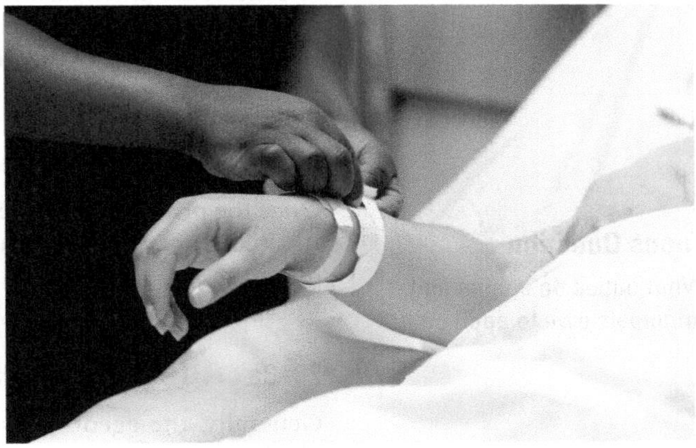
Inez Carter/shutterstock.com

Can a new hospital patient designate someone else to sign all of the paperwork involved in getting admitted to the hospital?

23–2b Agency by Ratification

On occasion, a person who is in fact not an agent (or who is an agent acting outside the scope of authority) may make a contract on behalf of another (a principal). If the principal affirms that contract by word or by action, an agency relationship is created by **ratification.** Ratification involves a question of intent, and intent can be expressed by either words or conduct. The basic requirements for ratification will be discussed later in this chapter.

Ratification A party's act of accepting or giving legal force to a previously unenforceable contract or other obligation entered into on that party's behalf by another party.

23–2c Agency by Estoppel

When a principal causes a third person to believe that another person is the principal's agent, and the third person deals with the supposed agent, the principal is "estopped to deny" the agency relationship. In such a situation, the principal's actions create the *appearance* of an agency that does not in fact exist.

The third person must prove that she or he *reasonably* believed that an agency relationship existed. Facts and circumstances must show that an ordinary, prudent person familiar with business practice and custom would have been justified in concluding that the agent had authority. **Case Example 23.5** Aaron Riedel was experiencing severe back pain when he visited the emergency room at Lodi Community Hospital. The attending emergency room physician, an independent contractor, misdiagnosed Riedel's condition. Riedel filed a suit against Lodi, alleging that the physician's negligence was the proximate cause of his subsequent paraplegia. Lodi hospital argued that it was not liable because the physician was not its employee or agent. An Ohio jury disagreed, awarding Riedel $5.2 million in damages.

A state appellate court affirmed, holding that a hospital can, depending on the circumstances, be liable under the doctrine of agency by estoppel for the negligence of an independent contractor physician. Crucially, the court noted, the public is rarely aware of the technical employment arrangements between a hospital and its staff. In this case, Riedel

6. *Laurel Creek Health Care Center v. Bishop*, 2010 WL 985299 (Ky.App. 2010).

chose Lodi only because it was nearby at the time of his medical emergency. He reasonably expected to be treated by a physician employed by Lodi and to be able to hold Lodi responsible for any resulting negligence.[7]

Note that the acts or declarations of a purported *agent* in and of themselves do not create an agency by estoppel. Rather, it is the deeds or statements of the *principal* that create an agency by estoppel.

23–2d Agency by Operation of Law

The courts may find an agency relationship in the absence of a formal agreement in other situations as well. This can occur in family relationships, such as when one spouse purchases certain necessaries and charges them to the other spouse's account. The courts will often rule that a spouse is liable for necessaries purchased by the other spouse because of either a social policy or a legal duty to supply necessaries to family members.

Agency by operation of law may also occur in emergency situations. If the agent is unable to contact the principal and failure to act would cause the principal substantial loss, the agent may take steps beyond the scope of agency authority. For instance, a railroad engineer may contract on behalf of the railroad for medical care for an injured motorist hit by the train.

23–3 Duties of Agents and Principals

Focus Question 3

What duties do agents and principals owe to each other?

Once the principal-agent relationship has been created, both parties have duties that govern their conduct. Because an agency relationship is *fiduciary* (one of trust), each party owes the other the duty to act with the utmost good faith. In general, for every duty of the principal, the agent has a corresponding right, and vice versa.

23–3a Agent's Duties to the Principal

Generally, the agent owes the principal five duties—performance, notification, loyalty, obedience, and accounting (see Exhibit 23–1).

7. *Riedel v. Akron General Health System*, 2018 -Ohio- 840, 97 N.E.3d 508 (2018).

Exhibit 23–1 Duties of the Agent

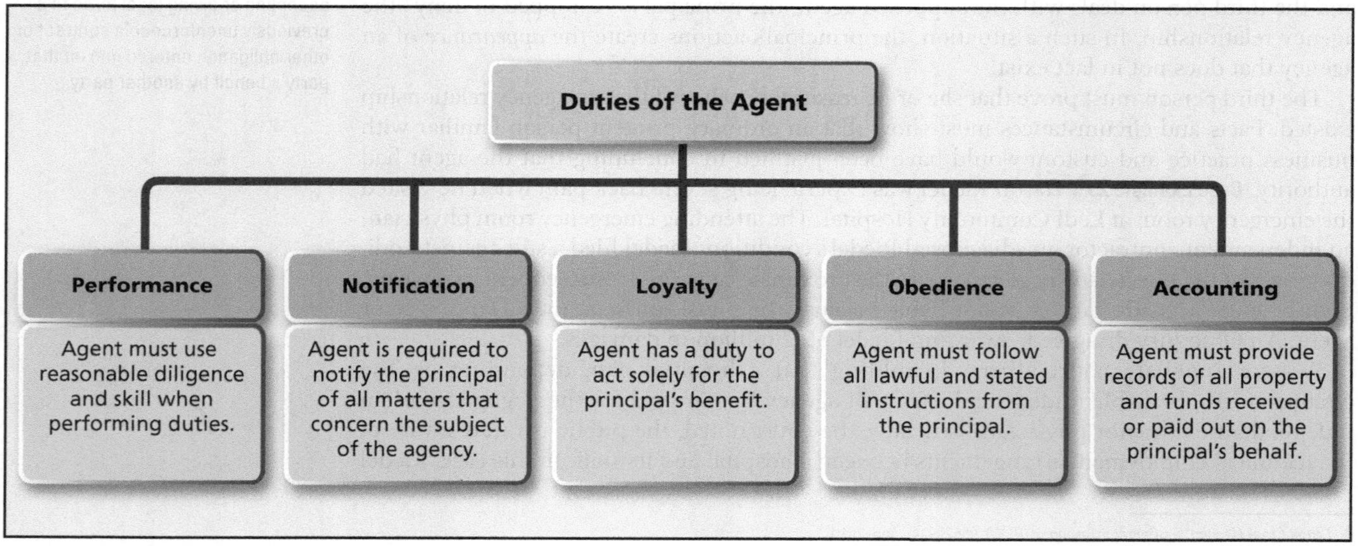

Duties of the Agent
Performance
Agent must use reasonable diligence and skill when performing duties.
Notification
Agent is required to notify the principal of all matters that concern the subject of the agency.
Loyalty
Agent has a duty to act solely for the principal's benefit.
Obedience
Agent must follow all lawful and stated instructions from the principal.
Accounting
Agent must provide records of all property and funds received or paid out on the principal's behalf.

Performance An implied condition in every agency contract is the agent's agreement to use reasonable diligence and skill in performing the work. When an agent fails to do so, liability for breach of contract may result. The degree of skill or care required of an agent is usually that expected of a reasonable person under similar circumstances. Generally, this is interpreted to mean ordinary care. If an agent has claimed to possess special skill, however, failure to exercise that degree of skill constitutes a breach of the agent's duty.

Not all agency relationships are based on contract. In some situations, an agent acts gratuitously—that is, not for monetary compensation. A gratuitous agent cannot be liable for breach of contract, because there is no contract, but it can be subject to tort liability. Once a gratuitous agent has begun to act in an agency capacity, the agent has the duty to continue to perform in that capacity. In addition, a gratuitous agent must perform in an acceptable manner and is subject to the same standards of care and duty to perform as other agents.

Example 23.6 Bryan's friend Alice is a real estate broker. Alice offers to sell Bryan's vacation home at no charge. If Alice never attempts to sell the home, Bryan has no legal cause of action to force her to do so. If Alice does attempt to sell the home, but then performs so negligently that a sale falls through, Bryan can sue Alice for negligence.

Notification An agent is required to notify the principal of all matters that come to the agent's attention concerning the subject matter of the agency. This is the duty of notification, or the duty to inform. **Example 23.7** Lang, an artist, is about to negotiate a contract to sell a series of paintings to Barber's Art Gallery for $25,000. Lang's agent learns that Barber is insolvent and will be unable to pay for the paintings. The agent has a duty to inform Lang of this fact because it is relevant to the subject matter of the agency—the sale of Lang's paintings

Generally, the law assumes that the principal knows of any information acquired by the agent that is relevant to the agency—regardless of whether the agent actually passes on this information to the principal. It is a basic tenet of agency law that notice to the agent is notice to the principal.

Steve Debenport/Getty Images

If a friend who is a licensed real estate broker agrees to sell your house at no charge, can you sue for nonperformance?

Loyalty Loyalty is one of the most fundamental duties in a fiduciary relationship. Basically, the agent has the duty to act *solely for the benefit of the principal* and not in the interest of the agent or a third party. For instance, an agent cannot represent two principals in the same transaction unless both know of the dual capacity and consent to it.

Know This
An agent's disclosure of confidential information could constitute the business tort of misappropriation of trade secrets.

The duty of loyalty also means that any information or knowledge acquired through the agency relationship is considered confidential. It would be a breach of loyalty to disclose such information either during the agency relationship or after its termination. Typical examples of confidential information are trade secrets and customer lists compiled by the principal.

In short, the agent's loyalty must be undivided. The agent's actions must be strictly for the benefit of the principal and must not result in any secret profit for the agent. **Example 23.8** Don contracts with Leo, a real estate agent, to negotiate the purchase of an office building. Leo discovers that the property owner will sell the building only as a package deal with another parcel, so he buys the two properties, intending to resell the building to Don. Leo has breached his fiduciary duty. As a real estate agent, Leo has a duty to communicate all offers to his principal and not to purchase the property secretly and then resell it to his principal. Leo is required to act in Don's best interests and can become the purchaser in this situation only with Don's knowledge and approval.

In the following case, an employer alleged that a former employee had breached his duty of loyalty by planning a competing business while still working for the employer.

Spotlight on Taser International: Case 23.1

Taser International, Inc. v. Ward

Court of Appeals of Arizona, Division 1, 224 Ariz. 389, 231 P.3d 921 (2010).

Facts Taser International, Inc., develops and makes electronic control devices—stun guns—as well as accessories for them, including a personal video and audio recording device called the TASER CAM.

Steve Ward was Taser's vice president of marketing when he began to explore the possibility of developing and marketing devices of his own design, including a clip-on camera. Ward talked to patent attorneys and a product development company and completed most of a business plan.

After he resigned from Taser, Ward formed Vievu, LLC, to market his clip-on camera. Ten months later, Taser announced the AXON, a product that provides an audio-video record of an incident from the visual perspective of the person involved. Taser then filed a suit in an Arizona state court against Ward, alleging that he had breached his duty of loyalty to Taser. The court granted Taser's motion for a summary judgment in the employer's favor. Ward appealed.

Issue Can an employee, while working at a company, research and develop a device to use in competition with the company's products?

Decision No. A state intermediate appellate court agreed with Taser that an employee may not actively compete with his employer before his employment is terminated. But the parties disagreed as to the extent of Ward's pre-termination efforts, creating a genuine issue of material fact that could not be resolved on a motion for summary judgment. The appellate court thus reversed the lower court's decision in Taser's favor and remanded the case for further proceedings.

Reason An agent has a duty to act with good faith and loyalty for the furtherance of the interests of his principal in all matters concerning or affecting the subject of his agency. One aspect of this broad principle is that employees are precluded from actively competing with their employers during the period of employment.

Although an employee may not actively compete prior to termination, the court noted that an employee can take certain actions to prepare for later competition that are not otherwise wrongful. Ward argued that his pre-termination activities did not constitute active competition but were merely lawful preparation for a future business venture. The appellate court concluded that this dispute was one that needed to be resolved by a trial.

Critical Thinking

- **Legal Environment** *Did Ward breach any duties owed to his employer in addition to his alleged breach of the duty of loyalty? Discuss.*
- **What If the Facts Were Different?** *Suppose that Ward's pre-termination activities focused on a product that was not designed to compete with Taser's products. Would these efforts have breached the duty of loyalty? Why or why not?*

Obedience When acting on behalf of a principal, an agent has a duty to follow all lawful and clearly stated instructions of the principal. Any deviation from such instructions is a violation of this duty. During emergency situations, however, when the principal cannot be consulted, the agent may deviate from the instructions without violating this duty. Whenever instructions are not clearly stated, the agent can fulfill the duty of obedience by acting in good faith and in a manner reasonable under the circumstances.

Accounting Unless an agent and a principal agree otherwise, the agent has the duty to keep and make available to the principal an account of all property and funds received and paid out on behalf of the principal. This includes gifts from third parties in connection with the agency. **Example 23.9** Marta is a salesperson for Roadway Supplies. Knife River Construction gives Marta a new tablet as a gift for prompt deliveries of Roadway's paving materials. The tablet belongs to Roadway. ■ The agent has a duty to maintain separate accounts for the principal's funds and for the agent's personal funds, and the agent must not intermingle these accounts.

23–3b Principal's Duties to the Agent

The principal also owes certain duties to the agent (as shown in Exhibit 23–2). These duties relate to compensation, reimbursement and indemnification, cooperation, and safe working conditions.

Compensation In general, when a principal requests services from an agent, the agent reasonably expects payment. The principal therefore has a duty to pay the agent for services rendered. For instance, when an accountant or an attorney is asked to act as an agent, an agreement to compensate the agent for service is implied. The principal also has a duty to pay that compensation in a timely manner.

Unless the agency is gratuitous and the agent does not act in exchange for payment, the principal must pay the agreed-on value for the agent's services. If no amount has been expressly agreed on, the principal owes the agent the customary compensation for such services.

Case Example 23.10 Keith Miller worked as a sales representative for Paul M. Wolff Company, a subcontractor specializing in concrete-finishing services. Sales representatives at Wolff were paid a 15 percent commission on projects that met a 35 percent gross profit threshold. The commission was paid after the projects were completed. When Miller resigned, he asked for commissions on fourteen projects for which he had secured contracts but which had not yet been completed. Wolff refused, so Miller sued.

The court found that "an agent is entitled to receive commissions on sales that result from the agent's efforts," even after the employment or agency relationship ends. Miller had met the gross profit threshold on ten of the unfinished projects, and therefore he was entitled to more than $21,000 in commissions.[8]

Reimbursement and Indemnification Whenever an agent disburses funds at the request of the principal, the principal has the duty to reimburse the agent. The principal must also reimburse the agent for any necessary expenses the agent incurs in the reasonable performance of agency duties. Agents cannot recover for expenses incurred through their own misconduct or negligence, however.

8. *Miller v. Paul M. Wolff Co.*, 178 Wash.App. 957, 316 P.3d 1113 (2014).

Exhibit 23–2 Duties of the Principal

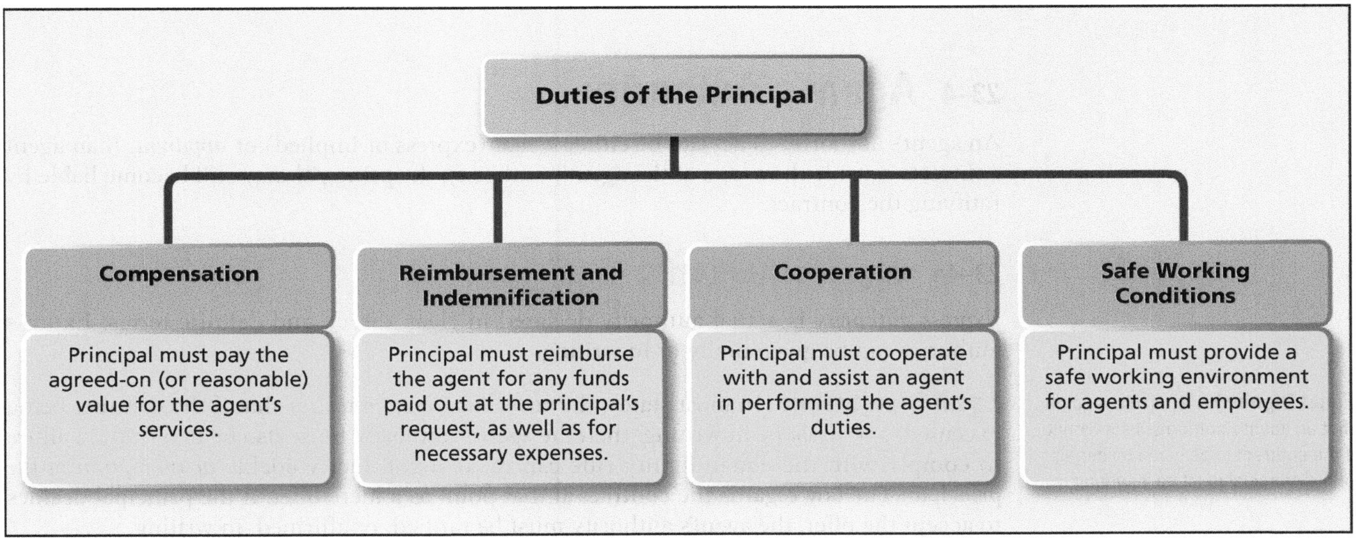

Duties of the Principal
Compensation
Principal must pay the agreed-on (or reasonable) value for the agent's services.
Reimbursement and Indemnification
Principal must reimburse the agent for any funds paid out at the principal's request, as well as for necessary expenses.
Cooperation
Principal must cooperate with and assist an agent in performing the agent's duties.
Safe Working Conditions
Principal must provide a safe working environment for agents and employees.

ESB Professional/Shutterstock.com

A salesperson works for commission based on concrete-finishing services sold. After quitting, is that salesperson still entitled to commissions owed on previous sales?

Subject to the terms of the agency agreement, the principal has the duty to compensate, or *indemnify*, an agent for liabilities incurred because of authorized acts and transactions. For instance, if the principal fails to perform a contract formed by the agent with a third party and the third party then sues the agent, the principal must compensate the agent for any costs incurred in defending against the lawsuit.

Additionally, the principal must indemnify the agent for the value of benefits that the agent confers on the principal. The amount of indemnification is usually specified in the agency contract. If it is not, the courts will look to the nature of the benefits and the type of expenses to determine the amount. Note that this rule applies to acts by gratuitous agents as well. Suppose that a person finds a dog that becomes sick, takes the dog to a veterinarian, and pays for the veterinarian's services. The finder is a gratuitous agent and is entitled to be reimbursed by the dog's owner for those costs.

Cooperation A principal has a duty to cooperate with the agent and to assist the agent in performing agency duties. The principal must do nothing to prevent that performance. When a principal grants an agent an exclusive territory, for instance, the principal creates an exclusive agency and cannot compete with the agent or assign or allow another agent to compete. A principal who does so violates the exclusive agency and can be held liable for the agent's lost profits.

Example 23.11 Penny (the principal) creates an exclusive agency by granting Andrew (the agent) an exclusive territory within which Andrew may sell Penny's organic skin care products. If Penny starts to sell the products herself within Andrew's territory—or permits another agent to do so—Penny has failed to cooperate with the agent. Because she has violated the exclusive agency, Penny can be held liable for Andrew's lost net profits.

Safe Working Conditions A principal is required to provide safe working premises, equipment, and conditions for all agents and employees. The principal has a duty to inspect the working conditions and to warn agents and employees about any hazards. When the agent is an employee, the employer's liability is frequently covered by state workers' compensation insurance, and federal and state statutes often require the employer to meet certain safety standards.

23–4 Agent's Authority

An agent's authority to act can be either *actual* (express or implied) or *apparent*. If an agent contracts outside the scope of the agent's authority, the principal may still become liable by ratifying the contract.

23–4a Express Authority

Express authority is actual authority declared in clear, direct, and definite terms. Express authority can be given orally or in writing.

Equal Dignity Rule A rule requiring that an agent's authority be in writing if the contract to be made on behalf of the principal must be in writing.

Equal Dignity Rule In most states, the **equal dignity rule** requires that if the contract being executed is or must be in writing, then the agent's authority must also be in writing. Failure to comply with the equal dignity rule can make a contract voidable *at the option of the principal*. The law regards the contract at that point as a mere offer. If the principal decides to accept the offer, the agent's authority must be ratified, or affirmed, in writing.

Example 23.12 Parker (the principal) orally asks Austin (the agent) to sell a ranch that Parker owns. Austin finds a buyer and signs a sales contract on behalf of Parker to sell the ranch. Because a contract for an interest in realty must be in writing, the equal dignity rule applies here. Thus, the buyer cannot enforce the contract unless Parker subsequently ratifies Austin's agency status in writing. Once Austin's agency status is ratified, either party can enforce rights under the contract.

Modern business practice allows several exceptions to the equal dignity rule. An executive officer of a corporation normally is not required to obtain written authority from the corporation to conduct *ordinary* business transactions. The equal dignity rule also does not apply when an agent acts in the presence of a principal or when the agent's act of signing is merely a formality. Thus, if the principal negotiates a contract but is called out of town the day it is to be signed and orally authorizes an assistant to act as agent to sign the contract, the oral authorization is normally sufficient.

Power of Attorney Giving an agent a **power of attorney** confers express authority on the agent.[9] The power of attorney is a written document that is usually notarized. (A document is notarized when a **notary public**—an individual authorized by the state to attest to the authenticity of signatures—signs and dates the document and imprints it with a seal of authority.) Most states have statutory provisions for creating a power of attorney.

A power of attorney can be special (permitting the agent to do specified acts only), or it can be general (permitting the agent to transact all business for the principal). Because a general power of attorney grants extensive authority to an agent to act on behalf of the principal in many ways, it should be used with great caution. Ordinarily, a power of attorney terminates on the incapacity or death of the person giving the power.[10]

Power of Attorney Authorization for another to act as one's agent or attorney either in specified circumstances (special) or in all situations (general).

Notary Public A public official authorized to attest to the authenticity of signatures.

23–4b Implied Authority

Agents have the *implied authority* to do what is reasonably necessary to carry out their express authority and accomplish the objectives of the agency. Actual authority can also be implied by custom or inferred from the position the agent occupies.

Example 23.13 Adam is employed by Pete's Supermarket to manage one of its stores. Pete's has not expressly stated that Adam has authority to contract with third persons. Nevertheless, authority to manage a business implies authority to do what is reasonably required (as is customary or can be inferred from a manager's position) to operate the business. It is reasonable to infer that Adam has the authority to form contracts to hire employees, to buy merchandise and equipment, and to advertise the products sold in the store.

23–4c Apparent Authority

Actual authority (express or implied) arises from what the principal manifests *to the agent.* An agent has **apparent authority** when the principal, by either words or actions, causes a *third party* to reasonably believe that an agent has authority to act, even though the agent has no express or implied authority.

Apparent Authority Authority that is only apparent, not real. An agent's apparent authority arises when the principal causes a third party to believe that the agent has authority, even though the agent does not.

Focus Question 4

How does a person acquire apparent authority to act as someone's agent?

Pattern of Conduct Authority usually comes into existence through a principal's pattern of conduct over time. **Spotlight Case Example 23.14** Gilbert Church owned Church Farm, Inc., a horse breeding farm in Illinois managed by Herb Bagley. Church Farm's advertisements for the breeding rights to one of its stallions, Imperial Guard, directed

9. An agent who holds the power of attorney is called an *attorney-in-fact* for the principal. The holder does not have to be an attorney-at-law (and often is not).

10. A *durable* power of attorney, however, continues to be effective despite the principal's incapacity. An elderly person, for example, might grant a durable power of attorney to provide for the handling of property and investments or specific health care needs should the elderly person become incompetent.

all inquiries to "Herb Bagley, Manager." Vern and Gail Lundberg contacted Bagley and executed a preprinted contract giving them breeding rights to Imperial Guard "at Imperial Guard's location." Bagley handwrote a statement on the contract that guaranteed the Lundbergs "six live foals in the first two years." He then signed it "Gilbert G. Church by H. Bagley."

The Lundbergs bred four mares, which resulted in one live foal. Church then moved Imperial Guard from Illinois to Oklahoma. The Lundbergs sued Church for breaching the contract by moving the horse. Church claimed that Bagley was not authorized to sign contracts for Church or to change or add terms, but only to present preprinted contracts to potential buyers. The jury found in favor of the Lundbergs and awarded $147,000 in damages. A state appellate court affirmed. Church was bound by Bagley's actions because Church had allowed circumstances to lead the Lundbergs to believe Bagley had the authority. In other words, Bagley had apparent authority to modify and execute the contract on behalf of Church.[11]

Somogyvari/E+/Getty Images

Can the manager of a horse-breeding farm make guarantees about foals on the owner's behalf?

Apparent Authority and Estoppel A court can apply the doctrine of agency by estoppel, introduced earlier in the chapter, when a principal has given a third party reason to believe that an agent has authority to act. If the third party honestly relies on the principal's representations to the third party's detriment, the principal may be *estopped* (prevented) from denying that the agent had apparent authority.

In the following case, a condominium owner argued that the condominium association that managed the units could not enforce bylaws that some of its own board members had violated. The owner argued, in essence, that the board members were agents acting with apparent authority of the association.

11. *Lundberg v. Church Farm, Inc.*, 502 N.E.2d 806, 151 Ill.App.3d (1986).

Case 23.2

Dearborn West Village Condominium Association v. Makki

Court of Appeals of Michigan, 2019 WL 97152 (2019).

Facts Dearborn West Village Condominium Association manages the Dearborn West Village Condominium complex in Dearborn, Michigan. The complex's bylaws permit a condominium owner to lease his or her unit for single-family residential use, but only if the owner is transferred out of the state by an employer for no longer than two years and first provides a lease to the Association for its review.

Mohamed Makki bought five units and, without meeting the conditions of the bylaws, rented all of the units to third parties. The Association filed a complaint in a Michigan state court against Makki to enforce the bylaws and terminate the rentals. The court issued a judgment in favor of the Association.

Makki appealed, asserting that individual board members who had offered to sell him units they were using as rental properties were acting with apparent authority on behalf of the Association. Thereby, he argued, the Association had waived its right to enforce the leasing restrictions in the bylaws.

Issue Was the Association estopped by the actions of individual board members from enforcing the leasing restrictions?

Decision No. A state intermediate appellate court affirmed the lower court's judgment.

Reason Makki maintained that the actions of individual board members beyond the members' legal authority bound the Association. The appellate court pointed out, however, that "generally, an agent's actions that are outside the scope of the agent's authority do not bind a principal." In other words, estoppel cannot be used to bind a principal in such a situation.

According to the Association's bylaws, its board of directors could not act in ways prohibited by the bylaws, which the board had a duty to enforce. In this case, the board members who leased their units to third parties violated the leasing restrictions in the bylaws and failed to enforce those restrictions. These actions were clearly outside the scope of the authority of the board members and therefore did not bind the Association.

Makki was not in compliance with the leasing restrictions in the Association's bylaws. That one or more of the board members were not in compliance did not obligate the Association to accept or approve Makki's actions in violation of the bylaws.

Critical Thinking

- **Legal Environment** *Normally, modification of the association's bylaws requires the approval of two-thirds of the unit owners. Could Makki have successfully argued that the actions of the board members who violated the bylaws modified them in accord with the freedom to contract? Explain.*
- **Economic** *Why might a condominium complex's bylaws impose restrictions on individual owners' leasing of their units? Why might some of those owners opt to violate the restrictions? Discuss.*

23–4d Emergency Powers

Sometimes, an unforeseen emergency demands action by the agent to protect or preserve the principal's property or rights, but the agent is unable to communicate with the principal. In that situation, the agent has emergency power. **Example 23.15** Rob is an engineer for Pacific Drilling Company. While Rob is acting within the scope of his employment, he is severely injured in an accident on an oil rig many miles from home. Acosta, the rig supervisor, directs Thompson, a physician, to give medical aid to Rob and to charge Pacific for the medical services.

Acosta, an agent, has no express or implied authority to bind the principal, Pacific Drilling, for Thompson's medical services. Because of the emergency situation, however, the law recognizes Acosta as having authority to act appropriately under the circumstances.

23–4e Ratification

Ratification occurs when the principal affirms an agent's *unauthorized act*. When ratification occurs, the principal is bound to the agent's act, and the act is treated as if it had been authorized by the principal *from the outset*. Ratification can be either express or implied.

If the principal does not ratify the contract, the principal is not bound, and the third party's agreement with the agent is viewed as merely an unaccepted offer. Because the third party's agreement is an unaccepted offer, the third party can revoke the offer at any time, without liability, before the principal ratifies the contract.

The requirements for ratification can be summarized as follows:

1. The agent must have acted on behalf of an identified principal who subsequently ratifies the action.
2. The principal must know of all material facts involved in the transaction. If a principal ratifies a contract without knowing all of the facts, the principal can rescind (cancel) the contract.
3. The principal must affirm the agent's act in its entirety.
4. The principal must have the legal capacity to authorize the transaction at the time the agent engages in the act and at the time the principal ratifies. The third party must also have the legal capacity to engage in the transaction.
5. The principal's affirmation (ratification) must occur before the third party withdraws from the transaction.
6. The principal must observe the same formalities when approving the act done by the agent as would have been required to authorize it initially.

Know This

An agent who exceeds his or her authority and enters into a contract that the principal does not ratify may be liable to the third party on the ground of misrepresentation.

23–5 Liability in Agency Relationships

Frequently, a question arises as to which party, the principal or the agent, should be held liable for contracts formed by the agent or for torts or crimes committed by the agent. We look here at these aspects of agency law.

23–5a Liability for Contracts

Liability for contracts formed by an agent depends on how the principal is classified and on whether the actions of the agent were authorized or unauthorized. Principals are classified as disclosed, partially disclosed, or undisclosed.[12]

Disclosed Principal A principal whose identity is known to a third party at the time the agent makes a contract with the third party.

Partially Disclosed Principal A principal whose identity is unknown by a third party, but the third party knows that the agent is or may be acting for a principal at the time the agent and the third party form a contract.

Undisclosed Principal A principal whose identity is unknown by a third party, and the third party has no knowledge that the agent is acting for a principal at the time the agent and the third party form a contract.

A **disclosed principal** is a principal whose identity is known by the third party at the time the contract is made by the agent. A **partially disclosed principal** is a principal whose identity is not known by the third party, but the third party knows that the agent is or may be acting for a principal at the time the contract is made. **Example 23.16** Sarah has contracted with a real estate agent to sell certain property. She wishes to keep her identity a secret, but the agent makes it clear to potential buyers of the property that the agent is acting in an agency capacity. In this situation, Sarah is a partially disclosed principal. An **undisclosed principal** is a principal whose identity is totally unknown by the third party, and the third party has no knowledge that the agent is acting in an agency capacity at the time the contract is made.

Authorized Acts If an agent acts within the scope of authority, normally the principal is obligated to perform the contract regardless of whether the principal was disclosed, partially disclosed, or undisclosed. Whether the agent may also be held liable under the contract, however, depends on the status of the principal.

Disclosed or Partially Disclosed Principal. A disclosed or partially disclosed principal is liable to a third party for a contract made by an agent who is acting within the scope of the agent's authority. (See this chapter's *Business Law Analysis* feature for illustration.) If the

12. *Restatement (Third) of Agency*, Section 1.04(2).

Liability of Disclosed Principals

Business Law Analysis

To display desserts in restaurants, Mario Sclafani ordered refrigeration units from Felix Storch, Inc. Felix faxed a credit application to Sclafani. The application was faxed back with a signature that appeared to be Sclafani's. Felix delivered the units, but Sclafani did not pay for them. Felix sued Sclafani to collect, but Sclafani denied that he had seen the credit application or signed it. Sclafani claimed that he referred all credit questions to "the woman in the office." Who was liable on the contract?

Analysis: First, you need to identify the agent and the principal. In this situation, with respect to the refrigeration-unit contract with Felix, Sclafani was the principal and "the woman in the office" was his agent. Who is liable for contracts formed by an agent depends on how the principal is classified and on whether the actions of the agent were authorized. If the agent acts within the scope of authority, normally the principal is obligated to perform the contract. If the principal is disclosed—that is, if the principal's identity is known by the third party at the time the contract is made—the agent has no contractual liability for the principal's nonperformance.

Result and Reasoning: Sclafani referred all credit questions to "the woman in the office." Sclafani's referral of credit matters to this woman established that she was his agent. He gave her the authority to enter into legally binding credit contracts on his behalf. Thus, whether Sclafani or "the woman in the office" signed Felix's credit application to guarantee payment, Sclafani is bound to the contract. Sclafani was a disclosed principal—Felix knew his identity at the time the contract was made. Therefore, Sclafani is liable on the contract, and his agent is not.

principal is disclosed, an agent has no contractual liability for the nonperformance of the principal or the third party. If the principal is partially disclosed, in most states the agent is also treated as a party to the contract, and the third party can hold the agent liable for contractual nonperformance.[13] This legal doctrine can also be used to protect the partially disclosed principal against the tortious behavior of a negligent third party.

Case Example 23.17 Tomex, a Danish food corporation, hired Mitsui O.S.K. Lines to deliver 53,000 pounds of frozen pork from Chicago to a supermarket chain in the Dominican Republic. Mitsui contracted with ConGlobal Industries, Inc., to provide a refrigerated shipping container for the pork. ConGlobal employees allegedly set the temperature of the container too high, causing the pork to thaw and destroy its value. Tomex's insurer sued ConGlobal for breach of contract. ConGlobal argued that the case should be dismissed because it never had any direct contact with Tomex and did not know that Mistui was acting as Tomex's agent.

The court rejected this argument, reasoning that ConGlobal had to be aware that Mitsui was acting as an agent for some other party, even if it did not know specifically about Tomex. In other words, it was highly unlikely that Mitsui, a shipping company, owned the pork. Under Illinois law, a contract with a "partially disclosed principal" exists when a "third party knows that the agent is contracting on behalf of a principal but does not know the identity of that principal." Therefore, Tomex (the partially disclosed principal) could properly sue ConGlobal (the third party) to enforce a contract entered into by Mitsui (the agent).[14]

Undisclosed Principal. Sometimes, neither the fact of agency nor the identity of the principal is disclosed, but the agent is acting within the scope of authority. In this situation, the undisclosed principal is bound to perform just as if the principal had been fully disclosed at the time the contract was made.

The agent is also liable as a party to the contract. When a principal's identity is undisclosed and the agent is forced to pay the third party, however, the agent is entitled to be indemnified (compensated) by the principal. The principal, although undisclosed, had a duty to perform, and failure to do so will make the principal ultimately liable.

Once the undisclosed principal's identity is revealed, the third party generally can elect to hold either the principal or the agent liable on the contract. At the same time, the undisclosed principal can require the third party to fulfill the contract, except under any of the following circumstances:

1. The undisclosed principal was expressly excluded as a party in the contract.
2. The contract is a negotiable instrument signed by the agent with no indication of signing in a representative capacity.
3. The performance of the agent is personal to the contract, allowing the third party to refuse the principal's performance.

Unauthorized Acts

If an agent has no authority but nevertheless contracts with a third party, the principal cannot be held liable on the contract. It does not matter whether the principal was disclosed, partially disclosed, or undisclosed.

In general, the agent is liable on the contract. **Example 23.18** Scranton signs a contract for the purchase of a truck, purportedly acting as an agent under authority granted by Johnson. In fact, Johnson has not given Scranton any such authority. Johnson refuses to pay for the truck, claiming that Scranton had no authority to purchase it. The seller of the truck is entitled to hold Scranton liable for payment.

---

13. *Restatement (Third) of Agency*, Section 6.02.
14. *Coden Forsikring A/S v. ConGlobal Industries, Inc.*, 315 F.Supp.3d 1085 (N.D.Ill., 2018).

Know This

An agent who signs a negotiable instrument on behalf of a principal may be personally liable on the instrument. Liability depends, in part, on whether the identity of the principal is disclosed and whether the parties intend the agent to be bound by a signature.

If the principal is disclosed or partially disclosed, the agent is liable to the third party only if the third party relied on the agency status. The agent's liability here is based on the breach of an *implied warranty of authority*, not on the breach of contract itself.[15] If the third party knows at the time the contract is made that the agent does not have authority—or if the agent expresses to the third party *uncertainty* as to the extent of the agent's authority—then the agent is not personally liable.

23–5b Liability for Torts and Crimes

Obviously, individuals, including agents, are liable for their own torts and crimes. Whether a principal can also be held liable for an agent's torts and crimes depends on several factors. In some situations, a principal may be held liable for the torts of an agent.

Principal's Tortious Conduct A principal conducting an activity through an agent may be liable for harm resulting from the principal's own negligence or recklessness. Thus, a principal may be liable for giving improper instructions, authorizing the use of improper materials or tools, or establishing improper rules that resulted in the agent's committing a tort.

Example 23.19 Paul knows that Audra is not qualified to drive large trucks. Paul nevertheless tells her to use the company truck to deliver some equipment to a customer. If Audra causes an accident that injures someone, Paul (the principal) will be liable for his own negligence in giving improper instructions to Audra. ■

Principal's Authorization of Agent's Tortious Conduct A principal who authorizes an agent to commit a tort may be liable to persons or property injured thereby, because the act is considered to be the principal's. **Example 23.20** Preston directs his agent, Ames, to cut the corn on specific acreage, which neither of them has the right to do. The harvest is therefore a trespass (a tort), and Preston is liable to the owner of the corn. ■

Note also that an agent acting at the principal's direction can be liable as a tortfeasor (one who commits a tort), along with the principal, for committing the tortious act even if the agent was unaware of the wrongfulness of the act. Assume in *Example 23.20* that Ames, the agent, was unaware that Preston had no right to harvest the corn. Ames can nevertheless be held liable to the owner of the field for damages, along with Preston.

A principal instructs an agent to harvest corn on land that the principal does not own. Is the agent liable to the legal owner of the land?

Liability for Agent's Misrepresentation A principal is exposed to tort liability whenever a third person sustains a loss due to the agent's misrepresentation. The principal's liability depends on whether the agent was actually or apparently authorized to make representations and whether the representations were made within the scope of the agency. The principal is always directly responsible for an agent's misrepresentation made within the scope of the agent's authority.

Example 23.21 Arnett is a demonstrator for Moore's products. Moore sends Arnett to a home show to demonstrate the products and to answer questions from consumers. Moore has given Arnett authority to make statements about the products. If Arnett makes only true representations, all is fine, but if she makes false claims, Moore will be liable for any injuries or damages sustained by third parties in reliance on Arnett's false representations. ■

15. The agent is not liable on the contract because the agent was never intended personally to be a party to the contract.

Liability for Agent's Negligence A principal may also be liable for harm an agent caused to a third party under the doctrine of ***respondeat superior***,[16] a Latin term meaning "let the master respond." This doctrine, which is discussed in this chapter's *Landmark in the Law* feature, is similar to the theory of strict liability. It imposes **vicarious liability**, or indirect liability, on the employer—that is, liability without regard to the personal fault of the employer—for torts committed by an employee in the course or scope of employment.

When an agent commits a negligent act, *both* the agent and the principal are liable. **Example 23.22** BDI Communications hires Pinnacle to provide landscaping services for its property. An herbicide sprayed by Pinnacle employee Hoggatt enters BDI's building through the air-conditioning system and causes Catherine, a BDI employee, to suffer a heart attack. If Catherine sues, both Pinnacle (principal) and Hoggatt (agent) can be held liable for negligence. As Pinnacle's agent, Hoggatt is not excused from responsibility for tortious conduct just because he is working for a principal.

Determining the Scope of Employment. The key to determining whether a principal may be liable for an agent's torts under the doctrine of *respondeat superior* is whether the torts are committed within the scope of employment. In determining whether a particular act

Focus Question 5

When is a principal liable for an agent's negligence?

Respondeat Superior A doctrine under which a principal or an employer is held liable for the wrongful acts committed by agents or employees while acting within the course and scope of agency or employment.

Vicarious Liability Indirect liability imposed on a supervisory party (such as an employer) for the actions of a subordinate (such as an employee) because of the relationship between the two parties.

16. Pronounced ree-*spahn*-dee-uht soo-*peer*-ee-uhr.

The Doctrine of *Respondeat Superior*

The idea that a master (employer) must respond to third persons for losses negligently caused by the master's servant (employee) first appeared in Lord Holt's opinion in *Jones v. Hart* (1698).[a] By the early nineteenth century, this maxim had been adopted by most courts and was referred to as the doctrine of *respondeat superior.*

Theories of Liability The vicarious (indirect) liability of the master for the acts of the servant has been supported primarily by two theories. The first theory rests on the issue of *control,* or *fault*—the master has control over the acts of the servant and is thus responsible for injuries arising out of such service. The second theory is economic in nature—the master receives the benefits or profits of the servant's service and therefore should also suffer the losses. Moreover, the master is better able than the servant to absorb such losses.

The control theory is clearly recognized in the *Restatement (Third) of Agency,* which defines a master as "a principal who employs an agent to perform service in his [or her] affairs and who controls, or has the right to control, the physical conduct of the other in the performance of the service." Accordingly, a servant is defined as "an agent employed by a master to perform service in his [or her] affairs whose physical conduct in his [or her] performance of the service is controlled, or is subject to control, by the master."

Limitations on the Employer's Liability There are limitations on the master's liability for the acts of the servant. As discussed in the text, an employer (master) is responsible only for the wrongful conduct of an employee (servant) that occurs in "the scope of employment." Generally, the act must be of a kind that the servant was employed to do, it must have occurred within "authorized time and space limits," and it must have been "activated, at least in part, by a purpose to serve the master."

Application to Today's World *The courts have accepted the doctrine of respondeat superior for some two centuries. This theory of vicarious liability has practical implications in all situations in which a principal-agent (master-servant, employer-employee) relationship exists. Today, the small-town grocer with one clerk and the multinational corporation with thousands of employees are equally subject to the doctrine.*

a. K.B. 642, 90 Eng.Rep. 1255 (1698).

occurred within the course and scope of employment, the courts consider the following factors:

1. Whether the employee's act was authorized by the employer.
2. The time, place, and purpose of the act.
3. Whether the act was one commonly performed by employees on behalf of their employers.
4. The extent to which the employer's interest was advanced by the act.
5. The extent to which the private interests of the employee were involved.
6. Whether the employer furnished the means or instrumentality (for instance, a truck or a machine) by which the injury was inflicted.
7. Whether the employer had reason to know that the employee would do the act in question and whether the employee had ever done it before.
8. Whether the act involved the commission of a serious crime.

The Distinction between a "Detour" and a "Frolic." A useful insight into the "scope of employment" concept may be gained from the judge's classic distinction between a "detour" and a "frolic" in the case of *Joel v. Morison*.[17] In this case, the English court held that if a servant merely took a detour from his master's business, the master is responsible. If, however, the servant was on a "frolic of his own" and not in any way "on his master's business," the master is not liable.

Example 23.23 While driving his employer's vehicle to call on a customer, Mandel decides to stop at a store—which is one block off his route—to take care of a personal matter. Mandel then negligently runs into a parked vehicle owned by Chan. In this situation, because Mandel's detour from the employer's business is not substantial, he is still acting within the scope of employment, and the employer is liable.

But suppose instead that Mandel decides to pick up a few friends for cocktails in another city and in the process negligently runs into Chan's vehicle. In this situation, the departure from the employer's business is substantial—Mandel is on a "frolic" of his own. Thus, the employer normally is not liable to Chan for damages.

RobertCrum/Getty Images

When can an employer be held liable for an employee's negligence while driving?

Employee Travel Time. The time an employee spends going to and from work or to and from meals is usually considered outside the scope of employment. If travel is part of a person's position, however, as it is for a traveling salesperson or a regional representative of a company, then travel time is normally considered within the scope of employment. Thus, for such an employee, the duration of the business trip, including the return trip home, is within the scope of employment unless there is a significant departure from the employer's business.

What factors determine the liability of an employer for a worker's negligence while driving? This question was at the center of the dispute in the following case.

17. 6 Car. & P. 501, 172 Eng.Rep. 1338 (1834).

Case 23.3

Simon v. Farm Bureau Insurance Co.

Court of Appeals of Louisiana, Third Circuit, __ So.3d __, 2020 WL 1041228 (2020).

Facts Jeff Doughty worked for Beta Land Services, Inc. Doughty received two weeks of mandatory training, after which Beta gave him a computer and required him to be at work between 8 A.M. and 5 P.M. every day. His pay was set at a daily rate for ongoing service. Under his employment contract, Beta retained the right to control his schedule and work, and could cancel the contract at any time without liability for breach.

Doughty was bringing supplies from a Beta field office in Lutcher, Louisiana, to the company's main office in Lafayette when his vehicle rear-ended a vehicle driven by Brock Simon. Simon filed a suit in a Louisiana state court against Doughty; his insurer, Farm Bureau Insurance Co.; and Beta. Simon alleged that at the time of the accident Doughty was Beta's agent, on a mission for the company, rendering Beta vicariously liable for its agent's negligence. Beta argued that Doughty was an independent contractor and that he had not been on a company mission—he had been commuting to the Lafayette office.

The court found that Doughty was an independent contractor and granted Beta's motion for a judgment in its favor. Simon appealed.

Issue Was Beta vicariously liable for Doughty's negligence?

Decision Yes. A state intermediate appellate court reversed the trial court's judgment in Beta's favor. The appellate court issued a judgment in Simon's favor, holding Beta liable for Doughty's actions at the time of the accident.

Reason The appellate court concluded that Doughty was not an independent contractor. The principal factor determining the status of an employment relationship is control over the work. Control by the employer indicates an employer-employee relationship. Here, Beta retained the right to control Doughty's work. This control was evidenced by his required schedule and payment arrangement, and was expressed in the parties' employment contract by the stipulation that Beta could cancel it at any time without liability.

At the time of the accident, Doughty was not acting as an independent contractor but was on a "mission" for Beta. The employer had asked him to go to the company's field office in Lutcher before going to the main office in Lafayette. Doughty's direct performance of a duty imposed by his employer brought his actions within the scope of employment.

In response to the assertion that Doughty was not on a mission for Beta, but on a commute, the court stated, "Doughty was not on his way to work. He was already at work, leaving Beta's field office and returning to its main office to deposit the extra supplies."

Critical Thinking

- **Legal Environment** *If the appellate court had upheld the trial court's finding that Doughty was an independent contractor, would he have been liable to Simon? Explain.*
- **What If the Facts Were Different?** *Suppose that the accident in this case had happened during Doughty's drive home after he had dropped off the supplies. Would the result have been different? Discuss.*

Notice of Dangerous Conditions. The employer is charged with knowledge of any dangerous conditions discovered by an employee and pertinent to the employment situation. **Example 23.24** Brad, a maintenance employee in Martin's apartment building, notices a lead pipe protruding from the ground in the building's courtyard. Brad neglects either to fix the pipe or to inform Martin of the danger. John trips on the pipe and is injured. The employer is charged with knowledge of the dangerous condition regardless of whether or not Brad actually informed him. That knowledge is imputed to Martin by virtue of the employment relationship.

Liability for Agent's Intentional Torts Most intentional torts that employees commit have no relation to their employment. Thus, their employers will not be held liable. Nevertheless, under the doctrine of *respondeat superior*, the employer can be liable for an employee's intentional torts that are committed within the course and scope of employment, just as the

Know This
An agent-employee going to or from work or meals usually is not considered to be within the scope of employment. An agent-employee whose job requires travel, however, is considered to be within the scope of employment for the entire trip, including the return.

employer is liable for negligence. For instance, a department store owner is liable when a security guard who is a store employee commits the tort of false imprisonment while acting within the scope of employment. Similarly, a nightclub owner is liable when a "bouncer" commits the tort of assault and battery while on the job.

In addition, an employer who knows or should know that an employee has a propensity for committing tortious acts is liable for the employee's acts even if they ordinarily would not be considered within the scope of employment. For instance, if the employer hires a bouncer knowing that he has a history of arrests for assault and battery, the employer may be liable if the employee viciously attacks a patron in the parking lot after hours.

An employer may also be liable for permitting an employee to engage in reckless actions that can injure others. **Example 23.25** The owner of Bates Trucking observes an employee smoking while filling containerized trucks with highly flammable liquids. Failure to stop the employee will cause the owner to be liable for any injuries that result if a truck explodes. ■

Liability for Independent Contractor's Torts Generally, an employer is not liable for physical harm caused to a third person by the negligent act of an independent contractor in the performance of the contract. This is because the employer does not have the right to control the details of an independent contractor's performance.

Courts make an exception to this rule when the contract involves unusually hazardous activities, such as blasting operations, the transportation of highly volatile chemicals, or the use of poisonous gases. In such situations, strict liability is imposed, and an employer cannot be shielded from liability merely by using an independent contractor.

Liability for Agent's Crimes Agents are liable for their own crimes. A principal or employer is not liable for an agent's crime even if the crime was committed within the scope of authority or employment, unless the principal participated by conspiracy or other action. In some jurisdictions, under specific statutes, a principal may be liable for an agent's violation in the course and scope of employment. For instance, a principal might be liable when an agent, during work, violates criminal regulations governing sanitation, prices, weights, or the sale of liquor.

23–6 Termination of an Agency

Agency law is similar to contract law in that both an agency and a contract can be terminated *by an act of the parties* or *by operation of law*. Once the relationship between the principal and the agent has ended, the agent no longer has the right (*actual* authority) to bind the principal. For an agent's *apparent* authority to be terminated, third persons may also need to be notified that the agency has been terminated.

Focus Question 6
What are some of the ways in which an agency relationship can be terminated?

23–6a Termination by Act of the Parties

An agency may be terminated by certain acts of the parties. Bases for termination by acts of the parties include lapse of time, achievement of the purpose of the agency, occurrence of a specific event, mutual agreement, and at the option of one party (see Exhibit 23–3).

When an agency agreement specifies the time period during which the agency relationship will exist, the agency ends when that time period expires. If no definite time is stated, then the agency continues for a reasonable time and can be terminated at will by either party. What constitutes a reasonable time depends on the circumstances and the nature of the agency relationship.

The parties can, of course, mutually agree to end their agency relationship. In addition, as a general rule, either party can terminate the agency relationship without the agreement of the other. The act of termination is called *revocation* if done by the principal and *renunciation* if done by the agent. Note, however, that the terminating party may face liability if the termination is wrongful.

Exhibit 23–3 Termination by Act of Parties

METHOD	RULES	ILLUSTRATION
1. Lapse of time	Agency terminates automatically at the end of the stated time.	Page lists her property for sale with Alex, a real estate agent, for six months. The agency ends in six months.
2. Purpose achieved	Agency terminates automatically on the completion of the purpose for which it was formed.	Calvin, a cattle rancher, hires Abe as his agent in the purchase of fifty head of breeding stock. The agency ends when the cattle have been purchased.
3. Occurrence of a specific event	Agency normally terminates automatically on the event's occurrence.	Meredith appoints Allen to handle her business affairs while she is away. The agency terminates when Meredith returns.
4. Mutual agreement	Agency terminates when both parties consent to end the agency relationship.	Linda and Greg agree that Greg will no longer be her agent in procuring business equipment.
5. At the option of one party (*revocation*, if by principal; *renunciation*, if by agent)	Either party normally has a right to terminate the agency relationship. Wrongful termination can lead to liability for breach of contract.	When Patrick becomes ill, he informs Alice that he is revoking her authority to be his agent.

Wrongful Termination Although both parties have the *power* to terminate an agency relationship, they may not always possess the *right* to do so. Wrongful termination can subject the canceling party to a suit for breach of contract. **Case Example 23.26** Smart Trike, Ltd., a Singapore manufacturing company based in Israel, contracted with a New Jersey firm, Piermont Products, LLC, to distribute its products in the United States and Canada. The parties' contract required six months' notice of termination, during which time Smart Trike was to continue paying commissions to Piermont for products that were sold. When Smart Trike terminated the agreement without providing the required notice, Piermont sued for breach of contract. The court held in favor of Piermont. Under the terms of the agreement, Piermont was entitled to receive commissions for products of Smart Trike that it had sold during the six months after the notice of termination.[18]

Agency Coupled with an Interest A special rule applies to an **agency coupled with an interest**, in which the agent has some legal right (an interest) in the property that is the subject of the agency. Because the agent has an additional interest in the property beyond the normal commission for selling it, the agent's position cannot be terminated until the agent's interest ends.

Agency Coupled with an Interest An agency, created for the benefit of the agent, in which the agent has some legal right (interest) in the property that is the subject of the agency

An agency coupled with an interest is not an agency in the usual sense because it is created for the agent's benefit instead of for the principal's benefit. **Example 23.27** Sylvia owns Harper Hills. She needs some cash right away, so she enters into an agreement with Shaquille under which Shaquille will lend her $10,000. In return, she will grant Shaquille a one-half interest in Harper Hills and "the exclusive right to sell" it. The loan is to be repaid out of the sale's proceeds. Shaquille is Sylvia's agent, and their relationship is an agency coupled with an interest. The agency was created when the loan agreement was made for the purpose of securing the loan. Therefore, Shaquille's agency power is irrevocable.

An agency coupled with an interest should not be confused with a situation in which the agent merely derives proceeds or profits from the sale of the subject matter. Many agents are paid a commission for their services, but the agency relationship involved does not constitute an agency coupled with an interest. For instance, a real estate agent who merely receives a commission from the sale of real property does not have a beneficial interest in the property itself.

18. *Smart Trike, MND, PTE, Ltd. v. Piermont Products, LLC*, 147 A.D.3d 477, 48 N.Y.S.3d 23 (2017).

Notice of Termination No particular form is required for notice of agency termination to be effective. If the agent's authority is written, however, it normally must be revoked in writing. The principal can personally notify the agent, or the agent can learn of the termination through some other means.

When an agency is terminated by act of the parties, it is the principal's duty to inform any third parties who know of the existence of the agency that it has been terminated. If the principal knows that a third party has dealt with the agent, the principal is expected to notify that person *directly*.

Although an agent's actual authority ends when the agency is terminated, an agent's *apparent authority* continues until the third party receives notice (from any source) that such authority has been terminated. **Example 23.28** Manning bids on a shipment of steel, and Stone is hired as an agent to arrange transportation of the shipment. When Stone learns that Manning has lost the bid, Stone's authority to make the transportation arrangement terminates. ■

23–6b Termination by Operation of Law

Termination of an agency by operation of law occurs in the circumstances discussed here. Note that when an agency terminates by operation of law, there is no duty to notify third persons.

1. *Death or insanity*. The general rule is that the death or mental incompetence of either the principal or the agent automatically and immediately terminates an ordinary agency relationship. Knowledge of the death is not required. **Example 23.29** Gary sends Tyron to China to purchase a rare painting. Before Tyron makes the purchase, Gary dies. Tyron's agent status is terminated at the moment of Gary's death, even if Tyron does not know that Gary has died. ■ (Some states have enacted statutes that change this common law rule to require an agent's knowledge of the principal's death before termination.)
2. *Impossibility*. When the specific subject matter of an agency is destroyed or lost, the agency terminates. **Example 23.30** Blake employs Pedro to sell Blake's house, but before any sale takes place, the house is destroyed by fire. In this situation, Pedro's agency and authority to sell Blake's house terminate. ■ Similarly, when it is impossible for the agent to perform the agency lawfully because of a change in the law, the agency terminates.
3. *Changed circumstances*. When an event occurs that has such an unusual effect on the subject matter of the agency that the agent can reasonably infer that the principal will not want the agency to continue, the agency terminates. **Example 23.31** Robert hires Miles to sell a tract of land for $40,000. Subsequently, Miles learns that there is oil under the land and that the land is worth $1 million. The agency and Miles's authority to sell the land for $40,000 are terminated. ■
4. *Bankruptcy*. If either the principal or the agent petitions for bankruptcy, the agency is usually terminated. In certain circumstances, as when the agent's financial status is irrelevant to the purpose of the agency, the agency relationship may continue. Insolvency (the inability to pay debts when they become due or when liabilities exceed assets), as distinguished from bankruptcy, does not necessarily terminate the relationship.
5. *War*. When the principal's country and the agent's country are at war with each other, the agency is terminated. In this situation, the agency is automatically suspended or terminated because there is no way to enforce the legal rights and obligations of the parties.

Practice and Review

Lynne Meyer, on her way to a business meeting and in a hurry, stopped by a Buy-Mart store for a new car charger for her smartphone. There was a long line at one of the checkout counters, but a cashier, Valerie Watts, opened another counter and began loading the cash drawer. Meyer told Watts that she was in a hurry and asked Watts to work faster. Watts, however, only slowed her pace. At this point, Meyer hit Watts.

It is not clear whether Meyer hit Watts intentionally or, in an attempt to retrieve the car charger, hit her inadvertently. In response, Watts grabbed Meyer by the hair and hit her repeatedly in the back of the head, while Meyer screamed for help. Management personnel separated the two women and questioned them about the incident. Watts was immediately fired for violating the store's no-fighting policy. Meyer subsequently sued Buy-Mart, alleging that the store was liable for the tort (assault and battery) committed by its employee. Using the information presented in the chapter, answer the following questions.

1. Under what doctrine discussed in this chapter might Buy-Mart be held liable for the tort committed by Watts?
2. What is the key factor in determining whether Buy-Mart is liable under this doctrine?
3. Did Watts's behavior constitute an intentional tort or a tort of negligence? How would this difference affect Buy-Mart's potential liability?
4. Suppose that when Watts applied for the job at Buy-Mart, she disclosed in her application that she had previously been convicted of felony assault and battery. Nevertheless, Buy-Mart hired Watts as a cashier. How might this fact affect Buy-Mart's liability for Watts's actions?

Debate This

The doctrine of respondeat superior should be modified to make agents solely liable for some of their own tortious (wrongful) acts.

Key Terms

agency 569
agency coupled with an interest 589
apparent authority 579
disclosed principal 582
equal dignity rule 578
fiduciary 569
independent contractor 569
notary public 579
partially disclosed principal 582
power of attorney 579
ratification 573
respondeat superior 585
undisclosed principal 582
vicarious liability 585

Chapter Summary: Agency Relationships in Business

Agency Law	In a *principal-agent* relationship, an agent acts on behalf of and instead of the principal in dealing with third parties. 1. **Employer-employee relationships**—An employee who deals with third parties is normally an agent of the employer. 2. **Employer–independent contractor relationships**—An independent contractor is not an employee because the employer has no control over the details of the independent contractor's physical performance. An independent contractor may or may not be an agent.

(Continues)

	3. **Determining employee status**—The criteria used by courts includes the following: a. How much control can the employer exercise over the details of the work? b. Is the worker engaged in an occupation or business distinct from that of the employer? c. Is the work usually done under the employer's direction or by a specialist without supervision? d. Does the employer supply the tools at the place of work? e. For how long is the person employed? f. What is the method of payment—by time period or at the completion of the job? g. What degree of skill is required of the worker?
Formation of an Agency	Agency relationships may be formed by the following methods: 1. **Agreement**—The agency relationship is formed through express consent (oral or written) or implied by conduct. 2. **Ratification**—The principal either by act or by agreement ratifies the conduct of a person who is not in fact an agent. 3. **Estoppel**—The principal causes a third person to believe that another person is the principal's agent, and the third person deals with the supposed agent in the reasonable belief that an agency exists. 4. **Operation of law**—The agency relationship is based on social policy (as in family relationships) or formed in an emergency situation when the agent is unable to contact the principal and failure to act outside the scope of the agent's authority would cause the principal substantial loss.
Duties of Agents and Principals	1. **Duties of the agent**— a. Performance—In performing agency duties, the agent must use reasonable diligence and skill or use the special skills that the agent has claimed to possess. b. Notification—The agent is required to notify the principal of all matters that come to the agent's attention concerning the subject matter of the agency. c. Loyalty—The agent has a duty to act solely for the benefit of the principal and not in the interest of the agent or a third party. d. Obedience—The agent must follow all lawful and clearly stated instructions of the principal. e. Accounting—The agent has a duty to make available to the principal records of all property and funds received and paid out on behalf of the principal. 2. **Duties of the principal**— a. Compensation—Except in a gratuitous agency relationship, the principal must pay the agreed-on value (or reasonable value) for the agent's services. b. Reimbursement and indemnification—The principal must reimburse the agent for all funds disbursed at the request of the principal, as well as for funds disbursed for necessary expenses in the reasonable performance of agency duties. c. Cooperation—A principal must cooperate with and assist an agent in performing agency duties. d. Safe working conditions—A principal must provide safe working conditions for agents and employees.
Agent's Authority	1. **Express authority**—Can be given orally or in writing. Authorization must be in writing if the agent is to execute a contract that must be in writing. 2. **Implied authority**—Authority deemed necessary for the agent to carry out expressly authorized tasks or tasks customarily associated with the agent's position. 3. **Apparent authority**—Exists when the principal, by word or action, causes a third party to reasonably believe that an agent has authority to act, even though the agent has no express or implied authority. 4. **Ratification**—The affirmation by the principal of an agent's unauthorized action or promise. For the ratification to be effective, the principal must be aware of all material facts.

Liability in Agency Relationships	**1. Liability for contracts**—If the principal's identity is disclosed or partially disclosed at the time the agent forms a contract with a third party, the principal is liable to the third party under the contract if the agent acted with proper authority. If the principal's identity is undisclosed at the time of contract formation, the agent is personally liable to the third party, but if the agent acted with proper authority, the principal is also bound by the contract. **2. Liability for torts and crimes**— **a.** A principal conducting an activity through an agent may be liable for harm resulting from the principal's own negligence or recklessness. **b.** Under the doctrine of *respondeat superior*, the principal is liable for any harm caused to another through the agent's torts if the agent was acting within the scope of employment at the time the harmful act occurred. **c.** Liability for agent's intentional torts—Usually, employers are not liable for the intentional torts that their agents commit, unless the acts are committed within the scope of employment, the employer knows or should know that the employee has a propensity for committing tortious acts, or the employer allowed the employee to engage in reckless acts that caused injury to another. **d.** Liability for independent contractor's torts—A principal is not liable for harm caused by an independent contractor's negligence, unless unusually hazardous activities are involved. **e.** Liability for agent's crimes—Agents are responsible for their own crimes, even if the crimes were committed while the agents were acting within the scope of authority or employment. A principal will be liable for an agent's crime only if the principal participated by conspiracy or other action or (in some jurisdictions) if the agent violated certain government regulations in the course of employment.
Termination of an Agency	**1. By act of the parties** (see *Exhibit 23–3*) **a.** Lapse of time. **b.** Purpose achieved. **c.** Occurrence of a specific event. **d.** Mutual agreement. **e.** At the option of one party. Notice to third parties is required when an agency is terminated by act of the parties. **2. By operation of law**— **a.** Death or insanity. **b.** Impossibility. **c.** Changed circumstances. **d.** Bankruptcy. **e.** War.

Issue Spotters

1. Dimka Corporation wants to build a new mall on a specific tract of land. Dimka contracts with Nadine to act as its agent in buying the property. When Nadine learns of the difference between the price that Dimka is willing to pay and the price at which the owner is willing to sell, she wants to buy the land and sell it to Dimka herself. Can she do this? Discuss. (See *Duties of Agents and Principals*.)
2. Davis contracts with Estee to buy a certain horse on her behalf. Estee asks Davis not to reveal her identity. Davis makes a deal with Farmland Stables, the owner of the horse, and makes a down payment. Estee does not pay the rest of the price. Farmland Stables sues Davis for breach of contract. Can Davis hold Estee liable for whatever damages he has to pay? Why or why not? (See *Liability in Agency Relationships*.)

—Check your answers to the *Issue Spotters* against the answers provided in Appendix D.

Business Scenarios and Case Problems

23–1. Ratification by Principal. Springer, who was running for Congress, instructed his campaign staff not to purchase any campaign materials without his explicit authorization. In spite of these instructions, one of his campaign workers contracted with Dubychek Printing Co. to print some promotional materials for Springer's campaign. When the printed materials arrived, Springer did not return them but instead used them during his campaign.

When Springer failed to pay for the materials, Dubychek sued for recovery of the price. Springer contended that he was not liable on the sales contract because he had not authorized his agent to purchase the printing services. Dubychek argued that the campaign worker was Springer's agent and that the worker had authority to make the printing contract. Additionally, Dubychek claimed that even if the purchase was unauthorized, Springer's use of the materials constituted ratification of his agent's unauthorized purchase. Is Dubychek correct? Explain. (See *Formation of an Agency*.)

23–2. Employee versus Independent Contractor. Stephen Hemmerling was a driver for the Happy Cab Co. Hemmerling paid certain fixed expenses and abided by a variety of rules relating to the use of the cab, the hours that could be worked, and the solicitation of fares, among other things. Rates were set by the state. Happy Cab did not withhold taxes from Hemmerling's pay. While driving the cab, Hemmerling was injured in an accident and filed a claim against Happy Cab in a Nebraska state court for workers' compensation benefits. Such benefits are not available to independent contractors. On what basis might the court hold that Hemmerling is an employee? Explain. (See *Agency Law*.)

23–3. Liability for Contracts. Thomas Huskin and his wife entered into a contract to have their home remodeled by House Medic Handyman Service. Todd Hall signed the contract as an authorized representative of House Medic. It turned out that House Medic was a fictitious name for Hall Hauling, Ltd. The contract did not indicate this, however, and Hall did not inform the Huskins about Hall Hauling. When a contract dispute later arose, the Huskins sued Todd Hall personally for breach of contract. Can Hall be held personally liable? Why or why not? [*Huskin v. Hall,* 2012 -Ohio- 653 (Ohio Ct.App. 2012)] (See *Liability in Agency Relationships*.)

23–4. Agent's Authority. Basic Research, LLC, advertised its products on television networks owned by Rainbow Media Holdings, Inc., through an ad agency, Icebox Advertising, Inc. As Basic's agent, Icebox had the express authority to buy ads from Rainbow on Basic's behalf, but the authority was limited to buying ads with cash in advance. Despite this limit, Rainbow sold ads to Basic through Icebox on credit. Basic paid Icebox for the ads, but Icebox did not pass all of the payments on to Rainbow. Icebox filed for bankruptcy. Can Rainbow recoup the unpaid amounts from Basic? Explain. [*American Movie Classics v. Rainbow Media Holdings,* 508 Fed.Appx. 826 (10th Cir. 2013)] (See *Agent's Authority*.)

23–5. Business Case Problem with Sample Answer—Determining Employee Status. Nelson Ovalles worked as a cable installer for Cox Rhode Island Telecom, LLC, under an agreement with a third party, M&M Communications, Inc. The agreement stated that no employer-employee relationship existed between Cox and M&M's technicians, including Ovalles. Ovalles was required to designate his affiliation with Cox on his work van, clothing, and identification badge, but Cox had minimal contact with him and limited power to control the manner in which he performed his duties. Cox supplied cable wire and similar items, but the equipment was delivered to M&M, not to Ovalles. On a workday, while Ovalles was fulfilling a work order, his van rear-ended a car driven by Barbara Cayer. Is Cox liable to Cayer? Explain. [*Cayer v. Cox Rhode Island Telecom, LLC,* 85 A.3d 1140 (R.I. 2014)] (See *Agency Law*.)

—For a sample answer to Problem 23–5, go to Appendix E.

23–6. Agent's Authority. Terry Holden's stepmother, Rosie, was diagnosed with amyotrophic lateral sclerosis (ALS), and Terry's wife, Susan, became Rosie's primary caregiver. Rosie executed a durable power of attorney appointing Susan as her agent. Susan opened a joint bank account with Rosie at Bank of America, depositing $9,643.62 of Rosie's funds. Susan used some of the money to pay for "household expenses to keep us going while we were taking care of her." Rosie died three months later. Terry's father, Charles, as executor of Rosie's estate, filed a petition in a Texas state court against Susan for an accounting. What general duty did Susan owe Rosie as her agent? What does an agent's duty of accounting require? Did Susan breach either of these duties? Explain. [*Holden v. Holden,* 456 S.W.3d 642 (Tex.App.—Tyler 2015)] (See *Agent's Authority*.)

23–7. Agency Relationships. Standard Oil of Connecticut, Inc., sells home heating, cooling, and security systems. Standard schedules installation and service appointments with its customers and then contracts with installers and technicians to do the work. The company requires an installer or technician to complete a project by a certain time but to otherwise "exercise independent judgment and control in the execution of any work." The installers and technicians are licensed and certified by the state. Standard does not train them, provide instruction manuals, supervise them at customers' homes, or inspect their work. The installers and technicians use their own equipment and tools, and they can choose which days they work. Standard pays a set rate per project. According to criteria used by the courts, are these installers and technicians independent contractors or employees? Why? [*Standard Oil of Connecticut, Inc. v. Administrator, Unemployment Compensation Act*, 320 Conn. 611, 134 A.3d 581 (2016)] (See *Agency Law*.)

23–8. Scope of Agent's Authority. Kindred Nursing Centers East, LLC, owns and operates Whitesburg Gardens, a long-term care and rehabilitation facility in Huntsville, Alabama. Lorene Jones was admitted to the facility following knee-replacement surgery. Jones's daughter, Yvonne Barbour, signed the admission forms required by Whitesburg Gardens as her mother's representative in her presence. Jones did not object. The forms included an "Alternative Dispute Resolution Agreement," which provided for binding arbitration in the event of a dispute between "the Resident" (Jones) and "the Facility" (Whitesburg Gardens). Six days later, Jones was transferred to a different facility. After recovering from the surgery, she filed a suit in an Alabama state court against Kindred, alleging substandard care on a claim of negligence. Can Jones be compelled to submit her claim to arbitration? Explain. [*Kindred Nursing Centers East, LLC v. Jones*, 201 So.3d 1146 (Ala. 2016)] (See *Agent's Authority*.)

23–9. Agency Relationships. Jane Westmas was killed when a tree branch cut by Creekside Tree Service, Inc., fell on her while she was walking on a public path through the private property of Conference Point Center on the shore of Lake Geneva in Wisconsin. Conference Point had contracted with Creekside to trim and remove trees from its property, but the owner had no control of (and no right to control) the details of Creekside's work. Jane's husband, John, and her son, Jason, filed a suit in a Wisconsin state court against Creekside, alleging that the service's negligence caused her death. Creekside contended it was immune from the suit under a state statute that provides "no . . . agent of an owner is liable for the death of . . . a person engaging in a recreational activity on the owner's property." Could Creekside be held liable for Jane's death? Why or why not? [*Westmas v. Creekside Tree Service, Inc.*, 2018 WI 12, 379 Wis.2d 471, 907 N.W.2d 68 (2018)] (See *Agency Law*.)

23–10. A Question of Ethics—The IDDR Approach and Agent's Authority. Devin Fink was the manager of Precision Tune Auto Care in Charlotte, North Carolina. Randall Stywall brought her car to the shop to replace the rear shocks. Fink filled out the service order with an estimate of the cost. Later, Stywall returned to pick up her car, and Fink collected payment for the work. When Stywall started to drive away, however, the car bounced as if the shocks had not been replaced. A complaint to Precision's corporate office resulted in the discovery that in fact the work had not been done and Fink had kept the payment. He was charged with larceny against his employer. He argued that he had not committed this crime because the victim was Stywall, not Precision. [*State of North Carolina v. Fink*, 798 S.E.2d 537 (N.C.App. 2017)] (See *Agent's Authority*.)

1. Which agency principles support the charge against Fink? Explain.
2. Using the IDDR approach, determine whether Fink had an ethical duty to offer a defense to the crime with which he was charged. What does Fink's stated defense suggest about his ethics?

Critical Thinking and Writing Assignments

23–11. Critical Legal Thinking. What policy is served by the law that employers do not own the copyrights for works created by independent contractors (unless there is a written "work for hire" agreement)? (See *Agency Law*.)

23–12. Time-Limited Group Assignment—Liability for Independent Contractor's Torts. Dean Brothers Corp. owns and operates a steel-drum manufacturing plant. Lowell Wyden, the plant superintendent, hired Best Security Patrol, Inc. (BSP), a security company, to guard the property and "deter thieves and vandals." Some BSP security guards, as Wyden knew, carried firearms. Pete Sidell, a BSP security guard, was not certified as an armed guard but nevertheless took his gun to work. While working at the Dean plant on October 31, Sidell fired his gun at Tyrone Gaines, in the belief that Gaines was an intruder. The bullet struck and killed Gaines. Gaines's mother filed a lawsuit claiming that her son's death was the result of BSP's negligence, for which Dean was responsible. (See *Liability in Agency Relationships*.)

1. The first group will determine what the plaintiff's best argument is to establish that Dean is responsible for BSP's actions.
2. The second group will discuss Dean's best defense and formulate arguments in support of it.
3. The third group will consider slightly different facts. Suppose that Dean Brothers had an express policy that prohibited all security guards from carrying firearms on its property, which Wyden had conveyed to BSP. Despite knowing about this policy, Sidell had brought his weapon to work, and then fired it, killing Gaines. Could Dean be held responsible for negligence in that situation? Explain.

garagestock/shutterstock.com

24 Employment, Immigration, and Labor Law

Focus Questions

The five Focus Questions *below are designed to help improve your understanding. After reading this chapter, you should be able to answer the following questions:*

1. What is the employment-at-will doctrine?
2. Under the Family and Medical Leave Act, in what circumstances may an employee take family or medical leave?
3. What is the purpose of state workers' compensation laws?
4. What are the two most important federal statutes governing immigration and employment today?
5. What federal statute gave employees the right to engage in collective bargaining and to strike?

"The employer generally gets the employees he deserves."

Sir Walter Gilbey
1831–1914
(English merchant)

Until the early 1900s, most employer-employee relationships were governed by the common law. Even today, private employers have considerable freedom to hire and fire workers under the common law. (This is one reason that employers generally get the employees they deserve, as the chapter-opening quotation observes.)

Numerous statutes and administrative agency regulations now govern the workplace, however. Thus, to a large extent, statutory law has displaced common law doctrines. Note that the distinction made under agency law between employee status and independent-contractor status is important here. The employment laws that will be discussed apply only to the employer-employee relationship. They do not apply to independent contractors.

Suppose that Randall works as an activities director for Valley Manor, a retirement community that offers several independent- and assisted-living options. As director, Randall normally spends his days at the Manor, where he hires and supervises other employees. One day, though, when another employee calls in sick, Randall accompanies residents on an excursion to a local art museum.

During the trip, Randall falls down some cement stairs and breaks his pelvis. He is taken by ambulance to a hospital, where he is told that he will need surgery and likely have a long recovery time. Does Randall qualify for workers' compensation coverage, or did this injury occur outside the scope of his employment? What about the time he will need to take off from work—is Randall entitled to take unpaid medical leave under federal law? If he takes unpaid leave, can he return to his original position afterward? You will learn about these and other important employment-related issues in this chapter.

24–1 Employment at Will

Employment relationships have traditionally been governed by the common law doctrine of **employment at will.** Under this doctrine, either party may terminate the employment relationship at any time and for any reason, unless doing so would violate an employee's statutory or contractual rights.

Employment at Will A common law doctrine under which either party may terminate an employment relationship at any time for any reason, unless it would violate a contract or statute.

Today, the majority of U.S. workers continue to have the legal status of "employees at will." In other words, this common law doctrine is still in widespread use. Only one state (Montana) does not apply it. Nonetheless, federal and state statutes governing employment relationships prevent the doctrine from being applied in a number of circumstances, and the courts have created several exceptions.

Focus Question 1

What is the employment-at-will doctrine?

24–1a Exceptions to the Employment-at-Will Doctrine

Because of the sometimes harsh effects of the employment-at-will doctrine for employees, the courts have carved out various exceptions to it. These exceptions are based on contract theory, tort theory, and public policy.

Exceptions Based on Contract Theory Some courts have held that an *implied* employment contract exists between an employer and an employee. An employee who is fired outside the terms of the implied contract may succeed in an action for breach of contract even though no written employment contract exists. **Example 24.1** Innova Enterprise's employment manual and personnel bulletin both state that, as a matter of policy, workers will be dismissed only for good cause. If the language is clear so that an employee reasonably expects Innova to follow this policy, a court may find that there is an implied contract based on the terms stated in the manual and bulletin. ■ Generally, the employee's reasonable expectations are the key to whether an employment manual creates an implied contractual obligation.

An employer's oral promises to employees regarding discharge policy may also be considered part of an implied contract. If the employer fires a worker in a manner contrary to what was promised, a court may hold that the employer has violated the implied contract and is liable for damages. Most state courts will judge a claim of breach of an implied employment contract by traditional contract standards.

Exceptions Based on Tort Theory In a few situations, the discharge of an employee may give rise to an action for wrongful discharge under tort theories. Abusive discharge procedures may result in a suit for intentional infliction of emotional distress or defamation.

In addition, some courts have permitted workers to sue their employers under the tort theory of fraud. **Example 24.2** Goldfinch, Inc., induces Jarvis to leave a lucrative job and move to another state by offering "a long-term job with a thriving business." In fact, Goldfinch not only is having significant financial problems but also is planning a merger that will result in the elimination of the position offered to Jarvis. If Jarvis takes the job in reliance on Goldfinch's representations and is fired shortly thereafter, she may be able to bring an action against the employer for fraud. ■

Exceptions Based on Public Policy The most common exception to the employment-at-will doctrine is made on the basis that the worker was fired for reasons that violate a fundamental public policy of the jurisdiction. Generally, the public policy involved must be expressed clearly in the jurisdiction's statutory law.

The public-policy exception may also apply to an employee who is discharged for **whistleblowing**—that is, telling government authorities, upper-level managers, or the media that an employer is engaged in some unsafe or illegal activity. Normally, however, whistleblowers seek protection from retaliatory discharge under federal and state statutory laws, such as the Whistleblower Protection Act.[1]

Whistleblowing An employee's disclosure to government authorities, upper-level managers, or the media that the employer is engaged in unsafe or illegal activities.

1. 5 U.S.C. Section 1201.

Once an employee establishes a claim under the Whistleblower Protection Act, that statute is the employee's exclusive remedy. **Case Example 24.3** Dale Yurk was employed at Application Software Technology (AST) Corp. He discovered that AST was planning to reuse and resell software that it had developed for the city of Detroit. Yurk contacted his superiors—including the company's chief executive officer—and told them that he believed the resale infringed on the city's intellectual property rights. Shortly afterward, AST terminated Yurk's employment. Yurk sued AST, alleging that the company had violated both the Whistleblower Protection Act and public policy. A federal district court held that Yurk had stated a claim under the Whistleblower Protection Act and therefore dismissed the public policy claim.[2]

24–1b Wrongful Discharge

Wrongful Discharge An employer's termination of an employee's employment in violation of the law or an employment contract.

Whenever an employer discharges an employee in violation of an employment contract or a statute protecting employees, the employee may bring an action for **wrongful discharge.** For instance, an employee who is terminated in retaliation for some protected activity, such as whistleblowing or participating in an employment-discrimination investigation, can sue for wrongful discharge.

Even if an employer's actions do not violate any provisions in an employment contract or a statute, the employer may still be subject to liability. An employee can sue for wrongful discharge under a common law doctrine such as an agency or tort theory. For instance, if while firing an employee, an employer publicly discloses private facts about that employee's sex life to her co-workers, the employee could claim wrongful discharge based on invasion of privacy. Similarly, if a salesperson is fired because she refuses to participate in falsifying consumers' credit applications as instructed by her employer, she can sue for wrongful discharge as a matter of public policy.[3]

Rawpixel.com/shutterstock.com

What are some of the circumstances under which an employee can bring an action for wrongful discharge against an employer?

24–2 Wages, Hours, and Leave

In the 1930s, Congress enacted several laws regulating the wages and working hours of employees.

1. The Davis-Bacon Act[4] requires contractors and subcontractors working on federal government construction projects to pay "prevailing wages" to their employees.
2. The Walsh-Healey Act[5] applies to U.S. government contracts. It requires that a minimum wage, as well as overtime pay at 1.5 times regular pay rates, be paid to employees of manufacturers or suppliers entering into contracts with agencies of the federal government.
3. The Fair Labor Standards Act (FLSA)[6] extended wage-hour requirements to cover all employers engaged in interstate commerce or in producing goods for interstate commerce. Certain other types of businesses are included as well. The FLSA, as amended, provides the most comprehensive federal regulation of wages and hours today.

Know This
In today's business world, an employment contract may be established or modified via e-mail exchanges.

2. *Yurk v. Application Software Technology Corp.*, 2017 WL 661014 (E.D.Mich. 2017).
3. See *Anderson v. Reeds Jewelers, Inc.*, 2017 WL 1987249 (E.D.Va. 2017).
4. 40 U.S.C. Sections 276a–276a-5.
5. 41 U.S.C. Sections 35–45.
6. 29 U.S.C. Sections 201–260.

24–2a Child Labor

The FLSA prohibits oppressive child labor. Restrictions on child labor differ by age group. Children under fourteen years of age are allowed to do certain types of work. They can deliver newspapers, work for their parents, and be employed in entertainment and (with some exceptions) agriculture. Children aged fourteen and fifteen are allowed to work, but not in hazardous occupations. There are also numerous restrictions on how many hours per day and per week children can work. Working times and hours are not restricted for persons between the ages of sixteen and eighteen, but they cannot be employed in hazardous jobs or in jobs detrimental to their health and well-being. None of these restrictions apply to individuals over the age of eighteen.

24–2b Minimum Wage Requirement

The FLSA provides that a **minimum wage** of $7.25 per hour must be paid to covered, nonexempt employees. More than half of the states (and some cities) also have minimum wage laws. When the state (or city) minimum wage is greater than the federal minimum wage, the employee is entitled to the higher wage.

Minimum Wage The lowest wage, either by government regulation or by union contract, that an employer may pay an hourly worker.

Example 24.4 Seattle, Washington, has one of the highest minimum wages in the country, at about $15 an hour. Various studies have shown that Seattle employees who had low-paying job when this minimum wage went into effect saw their take-home pay increase or stay the same while working *fewer* hours. At the same time, the higher minimum wage discouraged new hires in certain fields and caused employers to offer any new hires fewer hours of work. ■

Ethical Issue

Are employees entitled to receive wages for all the time they spend at work, including times when they are taking a personal break? For some employees, "punching a time clock" means accounting for all of the time that they are not working. These employees must "punch in" when they arrive and "punch out" when they leave for the day, of course, but they also must clock out when they take personal breaks, including bathroom, coffee, and smoking breaks.

The Fair Labor Standards Act does not require that an employer offer personal breaks to its employees. If an employer does offer them, though, employees must be compensated during those breaks. Otherwise, the employer may effectively be in violation of federal minimum wage laws. The issue of unpaid bathroom breaks came to the fore when the U.S. Department of Labor (DOL) filed a lawsuit against American Future Systems, Inc. (doing business as Progressive Business Publications). The DOL alleged that the company had created a compensation system in which none of its six thousand employees were compensated for bathroom breaks. The DOL argued that under federal regulations implementing the FLSA, all workday breaks of twenty minutes or less are compensable time.[7] A federal district court agreed. Because the employees had not been paid for their break time, the court ordered the company to pay past and current employees nearly $2 million in unpaid wages. A federal appellate court affirmed the decision.[8]

---

7. 29 C.F.R. Section 785.18.

8. *Secretary United States Department of Labor v. American Future Systems, Inc.*, 873 F.3d 420 (3d Cir. 2017).

Overtime Provisions and Exemptions Under the FLSA, employees who work more than forty hours per week normally must be paid 1.5 times their regular pay for all hours over forty. The FLSA overtime provisions apply only after an employee has worked more than forty hours per *week*. Thus, employees who work for ten hours a day, four days per week, are not entitled to overtime pay, because they do not work more than forty hours per week.

Certain employees are exempt from the FLSA's overtime provisions. These employees generally include executive, administrative, and professional employees, as well as outside salespersons and those who create computer code. Executive and administrative employees are those whose primary duty is management and who exercise discretion and independent judgment.

Employers are not required to pay overtime wages to exempt employees. Regulations also provide that employers are not required to pay overtime to workers who make salaries of more than $35,568. An employer can voluntarily pay overtime to ineligible employees but cannot waive or reduce the overtime requirements of the FLSA.

The question in the following case was whether an auto dealer's service advisors fit within the FLSA overtime-pay exemption.

Case 24.1

Encino Motorcars, LLC v. Navarro

Supreme Court of the United States, 579 U.S. __, 138 S.Ct. 1134, 200 L.Ed.2d 433 (2018).

Facts Encino Motorcars, LLC, is a Mercedes-Benz dealership. Encino's service advisors meet customers, listen to their concerns about their cars, suggest repair and maintenance services, sell new accessories or parts, record service orders, follow up with customers as the services are performed, and explain the repair and maintenance work when customers return for their vehicles. Some of Encino's service advisors, including Hector Navarro, filed a suit in a federal district court against their employer, alleging that the dealership had violated the Fair Labor Standards Act by failing to pay them overtime. Encino argued that the act's exemption from the overtime-pay requirement for "any salesman, partsman, or mechanic primarily engaged in selling or servicing automobiles" applied to service advisors. The court agreed and dismissed the complaint. The U.S. Court of Appeals for the Ninth Circuit reversed the dismissal. Encino appealed to the United States Supreme Court.

Issue Were Encino's service advisors exempt from the overtime-pay requirement in the FLSA?

Decision Yes. The United States Supreme Court reversed the appellate court's decision and remanded the case. "In sum, we conclude that service advisors are exempt from the overtime-pay requirement of the FLSA because they are salesmen . . . primarily engaged in . . . servicing automobiles."

Reason The Court stated that a service advisor is obviously a "salesman." The ordinary meaning of "salesman" is someone who sells goods or services. And this is precisely what service advisors do—sell services to customers for their vehicles. The Court expanded the job description to include "servicing automobiles," which was defined to mean "the action of maintaining or repairing a motor vehicle, or the action of providing a service." In the eyes of the Court, service advisors do both. The Court acknowledged that service advisors do not physically repair vehicles. But partsmen, too, are "primarily engaged in . . . servicing automobiles," and like service advisors, do not spend most of their time under the hoods of cars. Instead, these employees obtain vehicle parts and provide them to the mechanics. Thus, reasoned the Court, the phrase "primarily engaged in . . . servicing automobiles" must include some individuals who do not repair vehicles but who are integrally involved in the "servicing process." "That description applies to partsmen and service advisors alike."

Critical Thinking

- **Legal Environment** *The salesmen, mechanics, and partsmen identified in the FLSA exemption work irregular hours, sometimes away from their principal work site. Service advisors typically work ordinary, fixed schedules on-site. Should the Court have considered these attributes in making its decision in the Encino case? Discuss.*
- **What If the Facts Were Different?** *Suppose that the FLSA exemption covered "any salesman or mechanic primarily engaged in selling or servicing automobiles" but not "any partsman." Would the result have been different? Explain.*

Interaction of State and Federal Wage and Overtime Laws Note that state legislation may include rules that impact federal wages and overtime laws. For instance, if a state requires employers to give employees one day off per week, an employee who works that day may be entitled to overtime wages.

Case Example 24.5 Christopher Mendoza and Meagan Gordon were Nordstrom employees at different locations in California. Nordstrom had asked both Mendoza and Gordon to fill in for other employees. As a result, both had worked more than six consecutive days without receiving a day off. California state law prohibits employers from causing employees "to work more than six days in seven." The employees filed suit against Nordstrom, Inc., and the case ultimately came before the California Supreme Court.

At issue was whether the law applies on a calendar basis, with each workweek considered a fixed unit, or on a rolling basis. If the rolling basis was used, as Nordstrom argued that it should be, employees could work more than six consecutive days if on average they had one day off per seven. The state's highest court held that Nordstrom had violated California's law. Employees are entitled to one day off each workweek, not one day in seven on a rolling basis. Employees could choose not to take the seventh day off (as they are entitled to do), but employers could not force them to do so, the court said.[9]

24–2c Family and Medical Leave

Focus Question 2

Under the Family and Medical Leave Act, in what circumstances may an employee take family or medical leave?

The Family and Medical Leave Act (FMLA)[10] allows employees to take time off from work for family or medical reasons or in certain situations that arise from military service. A majority of the states have similar legislation. The FMLA does not supersede any state or local law that provides more generous protection.

Coverage and Applicability The FMLA requires employers who have fifty or more employees to provide employees with up to twelve weeks of unpaid family or medical leave during any twelve-month period. The FMLA expressly covers private and public (government) employees who have worked for their employers for at least a year.

An eligible employee may take up to *twelve weeks of leave* within a twelve-month period for any of the following reasons:

1. To care for a newborn baby within one year of birth.
2. To care for an adopted or foster child within one year of the time the child is placed with the employee.
3. To care for the employee's spouse, child, or parent who has a serious health condition.
4. If the employee suffers from a serious health condition and is unable to perform the essential functions of the job.
5. For any qualifying exigency (nonmedical emergency) arising out of the fact that the employee's spouse, son, daughter, or parent is a covered military member on active duty.[11] For instance, an employee can take leave to arrange for child care or to deal with financial or legal matters when a spouse is being deployed overseas.

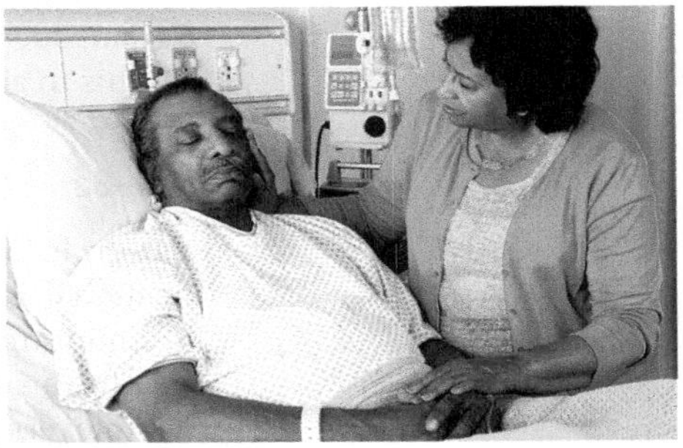
monkeybusinessimages/Getty Images

Under what circumstances can this wife take family leave to care for her sick husband?

In addition, an employee may take up to *twenty-six weeks of military caregiver leave* within a twelve-month period to care for a family member with a serious injury or illness incurred as a result of military duty.[12]

9. *Mendoza v. Nordstrom, Inc.*, 2 Cal.5th 1074, 393 P.3d 375, 216 Cal.Rptr.3d 889 (2017).
10. 29 U.S.C. Sections 2601, 2611–2619, 2651–2654.
11. 29 C.F.R. Section 825.126.
12. 29 C.F.R. Section 825.200.

Benefits and Protections When an employee takes FMLA leave, the employer must continue the worker's health care coverage on the same terms as if the employee had continued to work. On returning from FMLA leave, most employees must be restored to their original position or to a comparable position (with nearly equivalent pay and benefits, for instance).

An important exception allows the employer to avoid reinstating a *key employee*—defined as an employee whose pay falls within the top 10 percent of the firm's local workforce. To justify denying reinstatement, the employer must show that reinstating the key employee would cause "substantial and grievous economic injury" to the employer. The employer must also notify the employee of its intention to deny reinstatement.

Violations An employer that violates the FMLA can be required to provide various remedies, including the following:

1. Damages to compensate an employee for lost benefits, denied compensation, and actual monetary losses (such as the cost of providing for care of the family member) up to an amount equivalent to the employee's wages for twelve weeks (twenty-six weeks for military caregiver leave).
2. Job reinstatement.
3. Promotion, if a promotion has been denied.

A successful plaintiff is also entitled to court costs and attorneys' fees. In addition, if the plaintiff shows the employer acted in bad faith, the plaintiff can receive two times the amount of damages awarded by a judge or jury. Supervisors can also be held personally liable, as employers, for violations of the act.

Employers generally are required to notify employees when an absence will be counted against leave authorized under the act. If an employer fails to provide such notice, and the employee consequently suffers an injury because of the lack of notice, the employer may be sanctioned.

24–3 Health, Safety, Income Security, and Privacy

Under the common law, employees who were injured on the job had to file lawsuits against their employers to obtain recovery. Today, numerous state and federal statutes protect employees and their families from the risk of accidental injury, disease, or death resulting from employment. In addition, the government protects employees' income through programs such as Social Security and unemployment insurance, and protects employees' privacy rights to a certain extent.

24–3a The Occupational Safety and Health Act

At the federal level, the primary legislation protecting employees' health and safety is the Occupational Safety and Health Act,[13] which is administered by the Occupational Safety and Health Administration (OSHA). The act imposes on employers a general duty to keep workplaces safe.

To this end, OSHA has established specific safety standards for various industries that employers must follow. For instance, OSHA regulations require the use of safety guards on certain mechanical equipment and set maximum levels of exposure to substances in the workplace that may be harmful to workers' health.

Case Example 24.6 James Bobo worked at the Tennessee Valley Authority (TVA) nuclear power plant for more than twenty-two years. He eventually contracted asbestos-induced lung cancer. After his death, his wife, Barbara, was diagnosed with malignant mesothelioma. She

13. 29 U.S.C. Sections 553, 651–678.

sued TVA in federal court, alleging that its negligence had resulted in her being exposed to "take-home" asbestos when she washed her husband's work clothes over the years. Although she died prior to trial, her children continued the suit.

At trial, the plaintiffs proved that TVA knew about OSHA regulations—adopted during the time of James's employment—to protect not only workers but also their families. These rules were aimed at preventing asbestos fibers from clinging to an employee's street clothes, skin, or hair and being taken off TVA property. The court held in favor of the plaintiffs and awarded $3.3 million. TVA appealed. A federal appellate court affirmed that TVA was liable for failing to follow OSHA regulations but remanded the case for a recalculation of the damages awarded.[14]

Notices, Records, and Reports The act requires that employers post certain notices in the workplace, maintain specific records, and submit reports. Employers with eleven or more employees are required to keep records of occupational injuries and illnesses. Each record must be made available for inspection when requested by an OSHA compliance officer. Some employers are required to electronically post their workplace injury and illness records from the prior year on OSHA's website.

Whenever a work-related fatality or serious injury requiring hospitalization occurs, employers must report directly to OSHA. The employer must notify OSHA within eight hours if an employee dies and submit a report within twenty-four hours for any inpatient hospitalization, amputation, or loss of an eye. A company that fails to do so will be fined.

Stewart Cohen/Tetra images/Getty Images

Preventing workplace accidents and employee injuries is the goal of the Occupational Safety and Health Act. What are some employer requirements under the act?

Inspections and Employee Complaints OSHA compliance officers may enter and inspect the facilities of any establishment covered by the Occupational Safety and Health Act. Employees may also file complaints of violations and cannot be fired by their employers for doing so. Under the act, an employer cannot discharge an employee who files a complaint or who, in good faith, refuses to work in a high-risk area if bodily harm or death might result.

In the following case, an employer cited for an OSHA violation tried to minimize its own fault by focusing the court's attention on the injured employee's failure to follow workplace safety rules.

14. *Bobo v. Tennessee Valley Authority,* 855 F.3d 1294 (11th Cir. 2017).

Case 24.2

Packers Sanitation Services, Inc. v. Occupational Safety and Health Review Commission

United States Court of Appeals, Eleventh Circuit, 795 Fed.Appx. 814 (2020).

Facts Packers Sanitation Services, Inc., provides cleaning services to a poultry processing facility in Gainesville, Georgia. At the facility is a machine known as a quill puller, which is used to remove chickens' tail feathers. A Packers employee hosing down the quill puller stepped too close to the machine. Its rotating augers caught the employee's glove, pulled in his hand, and amputated a fingertip.

After an investigation, the Occupational Safety and Health Administration cited Packers for failing to appropriately guard the quill puller. Packers contested the citation, arguing that the injured employee had violated a workplace rule requiring each employee to stay at least two feet away from an active quill puller.

(Continues)

Continued

After a hearing, an administrative law judge (ALJ) affirmed the violation. The Occupational Safety and Health Review Commission declined to review the decision. Packers appealed to the U.S. Court of Appeals for the Eleventh Circuit.

Issue Did Packers violate the machine-guarding standard?

Decision Yes. The U.S. Court of Appeals for the Eleventh Circuit upheld the ALJ's determination.

Reason Federal regulations require physical machine guards to protect employees from hazards such as "ingoing nip points." A quill puller's augers form an ingoing nip point. In this case, there was no line or physical barrier marking a safe distance from the machine for an employee tasked with hosing it down. According to the appellate court, "due to operational necessity, it was reasonably predictable that an employee would enter the zone of danger near that nip point." Supervisors walked past the quill puller regularly and could see that it lacked the required physical guards, which showed that Packers was aware of the hazard.

In response to Packers' argument that the employee would have faced no danger if he had followed the two-foot rule, in effect blaming the employee for his injury, the court stated, "Packers misses the mark. The machine-guarding standard would mean little if a company could escape responsibility merely by reminding its employees to stay a safe distance from dangerous machines. After all, common human errors such as neglect, distraction, inattention or inadvertence, which might cause an employee to enter the zone of danger, are part of the basis for the standards in the first place."

Critical Thinking

- **Legal Environment** *As a defense to the citation for an OSHA violation, Packers argued that the injured employee violated the proximity rule. Was this defense relevant to the question before the court? Discuss.*
- **What If the Facts Were Different?** *Suppose that in this case, no accident had taken place. Instead, the employee had refused to clean the unguarded quill puller, and Packers had discharged him. Would the result have been different? Explain.*

24–3b State Workers' Compensation Laws

Workers' Compensation Laws State statutes that establish an administrative process for compensating workers for injuries that arise in the course of their employment, regardless of fault.

Focus Question 3

What is the purpose of state workers' compensation laws?

State **workers' compensation laws** establish an administrative procedure for compensating workers injured on the job. Instead of suing, an injured worker files a claim with the administrative agency or board that administers local workers' compensation claims.

All states require employers to provide workers' compensation insurance, but the specific rules vary by state. Most states have a state fund that employers pay into for workers' compensation coverage. Usually, employers can purchase insurance from a private insurer as an alternative to paying into the state fund. Most states also allow certain employers to be *self-insured*—that is, employers that show an ability to pay claims do not need to buy insurance.

No state covers all employees under its workers' compensation statute. Typically, domestic workers, agricultural workers, temporary employees, and employees of common carriers (companies that provide transportation services to the public) are excluded. Minors are covered.

Requirements for Receiving Workers' Compensation In general, only two requirements must be met for an employee to receive benefits under a state workers' compensation law:

1. The existence of an employment relationship.
2. *An accidental injury that occurred on the job or in the course of employment,* regardless of fault. (An injury that occurs while an employee is commuting to or from work usually is not considered to have occurred on the job or in the course of employment and hence is not covered.)

This chapter's *Business law Analysis* feature illustrates these requirements.

An injured employee must notify the employer promptly (usually within thirty days of the accident). Generally, an employee must also file a workers' compensation claim with the appropriate state agency or board within a certain period (sixty days to two years) from the time the injury is first noticed, rather than from the time of the accident.

Workers' Compensation Claims

Business Law Analysis

As a safety measure, Dynea USA, Inc., required an employee, Tony Schrader, to wear steel-toed boots. One of the boots caused a sore on Schrader's leg. The skin over the sore broke, and within a week, Schrader was hospitalized with a methicillin-resistant staphylococcus aureus (MRSA) infection. He filed a workers' compensation claim. Dynea argued that the MRSA bacteria that caused the infection had been on Schrader's skin before he came to work. Does Schrader's claim meet the requirements to recover workers' compensation benefits?

Analysis: To recover benefits under state workers' compensation laws, an employee must show that an injury (1) was accidental and (2) occurred on the job or in the course of employment. Fault is not an issue. The employee must file a claim with the state agency or board that administers local workers' compensation claims, which Schrader did. The issue here is whether the injury occurred on the job or in the course of employment.

Result and Reasoning: Schrader is entitled to workers' compensation benefits. Dynea required its employees to wear the boots that caused the sore on Schrader's leg, which subsequently became infected with MRSA. Even if the bacteria had been on Schrader's skin before he came to work, it was the rubbing of the boot at work that caused the sore through which the bacteria entered his body. Therefore, the second requirement for the recovery of workers' compensation benefits—that the injury occurred on the job—is fulfilled.

Workers' Compensation versus Litigation An employee's acceptance of workers' compensation benefits bars the employee from suing for injuries caused by the employer's negligence. By barring lawsuits for negligence, workers' compensation laws also prevent employers from raising common law defenses to negligence, such as contributory negligence and assumption of risk. A worker may sue an employer who has *intentionally* injured the worker, however.

24–3c Income Security

Federal and state governments participate in insurance programs designed to protect employees and their families by covering the financial impact of retirement, disability, death, hospitalization, and unemployment. The key federal law on this subject is the Social Security Act.[15]

Social Security The Social Security Act provides for old-age (retirement), survivors', and disability insurance. Hence, the act is often referred to as OASDI. Both employers and employees must contribute under the Federal Insurance Contributions Act (FICA)[16] to help pay for Social Security retirement benefits. Retired workers are then eligible to receive monthly payments from the Social Security Administration, which administers the Social Security Act. Social Security benefits are fixed by statute but increase automatically with increases in the cost of living.

Know This

Social Security covers almost all jobs in the United States. Nine out of ten workers contribute to this protection for themselves and their families.

Medicare Medicare is a federal government health insurance program that is administered by the Social Security Administration for people sixty-five years of age and older and for some under the age of sixty-five who are disabled. Medicare originally had two parts, one pertaining to hospital costs and the other to nonhospital medical costs, such as visits to physicians' offices. It now offers additional coverage options and a prescription drug plan. People who have Medicare hospital insurance can also obtain additional federal medical insurance by paying small monthly premiums, which increase as the cost of medical care increases.

15. 42 U.S.C. Sections 301–1397e.
16. 26 U.S.C. Sections 3101–3125.

www.ssa.gov

Why is the Social Security Act also known as OASDI?

Tax Contributions Under FICA, both employers and employees contribute to Social Security and Medicare, although the contributions are determined differently. The employer withholds the employee's FICA contributions from the employee's wages and ordinarily matches the contributions.

For Social Security, the basis for the contributions is the employee's annual wage base—the maximum amount of the employee's wages that is subject to the tax. The maximum amount subject to the tax is currently $137,700, and the tax rate is 12.4 percent.

The Medicare tax rate is 2.9 percent. Unlike Social Security, Medicare has no cap on the amount of wages subject to the tax. So even if an employee's salary is well above the cap for Social Security, the employee will still owe Medicare tax on the total earned income.

Thus, for Social Security and Medicare together, typically the employer and the employee each pay 7.65 percent—6.2 percent (half of 12.4 percent) for Social Security, up to the maximum wage base, plus 1.45 percent (half of 2.9 percent) for Medicare. Self-employed persons pay both the employer's and the employee's portions of the Social Security and Medicare taxes. Additionally, under the Affordable Care Act, high-income earners are subject to an additional Medicare tax of 0.9 percent (for a total rate of 3.8 percent).

Private Retirement Plans The major federal act regulating employee retirement plans is the Employee Retirement Income Security Act (ERISA).[17] This act empowers a branch of the U.S. Department of Labor to enforce its provisions governing employers that have private pension funds for their employees. ERISA does not require an employer to establish a pension plan. When a plan exists, however, ERISA specifies standards for its management, including establishing rules on how funds must be invested and records kept.

ERISA created the Pension Benefit Guaranty Corporation (PBGC), an independent federal agency, to provide timely and uninterrupted payment of voluntary private pension benefits. The pension plans pay annual insurance premiums (at set rates adjusted for inflation) to the PBGC, which then pays benefits to participants in the event that a plan is unable to do so.

Vesting The creation of an absolute or unconditional right or power.

A key provision of ERISA concerns vesting. **Vesting** gives an employee a legal right to receive pension benefits at some future date when the employee stops working. Before ERISA was enacted, some employees who had worked for companies for as long as thirty years received no pension benefits when their employment terminated because those benefits had not vested. Under ERISA, generally all employee contributions to pension plans vest immediately, and employee rights to employer contributions to a plan vest after five years of employment.

Unemployment Insurance The Federal Unemployment Tax Act (FUTA)[18] created a state-administered system that provides unemployment compensation to eligible individuals. Under this system, employers pay into a fund, and the proceeds are paid out to qualified unemployed workers. The FUTA and state laws require employers that fall under the provisions of the act to pay unemployment taxes at regular intervals. The proceeds from these taxes are then paid out to qualified unemployed workers.

Know This

If an employer does not pay unemployment taxes, a state government can place a lien (claim) on the business's property to secure the debt.

To be eligible for unemployment compensation, a worker must be willing and able to work. Workers who have been fired for misconduct or who have voluntarily left their jobs are not eligible for benefits. Normally, workers must be actively seeking employment to continue receiving benefits.

17. 29 U.S.C. Sections 1001 *et seq.*
18. 26 U.S.C. Sections 3301–3310.

Example 24.7 Martha works for Baily Snowboards in Vermont. One day at work, Martha receives a text from her son saying that he has been taken to the hospital. Martha rushes to the hospital and does not return to work for several days. Bailey hires someone else for Martha's position, and Martha files for unemployment benefits. Martha's claim normally will be denied because she left her job voluntarily and made no effort to maintain contact with her employer. ■

Song_about_summer/shutterstock.com

How does the Federal Unemployment Tax Act benefit employees?

COBRA The Consolidated Omnibus Budget Reconciliation Act (COBRA)[19] enables workers to continue, for a limited time, their health care coverage after they are no longer eligible for their employers' group health insurance plans. The workers—not the employers—pay the premiums for the continued coverage.

COBRA prohibits an employer from eliminating a worker's medical, optical, or dental insurance when the worker's employment is terminated or when a reduction in the worker's hours would affect coverage. Termination of employment may be voluntary or involuntary. Only workers fired for gross misconduct are excluded from protection.

Employers, with some exceptions, must inform an employee of COBRA's provisions when the employee faces termination or a reduction of hours that would affect eligibility for coverage under the employer's health insurance plan. An employer that does not comply with COBRA risks substantial penalties, such as a tax of up to 10 percent of the annual cost of the group plan or $500,000, whichever is less.

Employer-Sponsored Group Health Plans The Health Insurance Portability and Accountability Act (HIPAA)[20] contains provisions that affect employer-sponsored group health plans. HIPAA does not require employers to provide health insurance, but it does establish requirements for those that do. For instance, HIPAA restricts the manner in which covered employers collect, use, and disclose the health information of employees and their families. Employers must designate privacy officials, distribute privacy notices, and train employees to ensure that employees' health information is not disclosed to unauthorized parties.

Failure to comply with HIPAA regulations can result in civil penalties of up to $100 per person per violation (with a cap of $25,000 per year). The employer is also subject to criminal prosecution for certain types of HIPAA violations and can face up to $250,000 in criminal fines and imprisonment for up to ten years if convicted. The consequences for corporate violations of HIPAA are also severe, with maximum annual civil penalties surpassing $1.7 million.

Affordable Care Act The Affordable Care Act[21] (ACA, commonly referred to as Obamacare) requires most employers with fifty or more full-time employees to offer health insurance benefits. Under the act, any business offering health benefits to its employees, even if it is not legally required to do so, may be eligible for tax credits of up to 35 percent to offset the costs.

Under the so-called "50/30 rule," the ACA applies to businesses that employ at least fifty workers for at least thirty hours a week. (The ACA also applies to any mathematical equivalent of fifty workers for thirty hours, so a business that employs a hundred workers for fifteen hours a week falls under ACA requirements.) An employer who fails to provide health benefits as required under the statute can be fined up to $2,000 for each employee. An employer who offers a plan that costs an employee more than 9.5 percent of the employee's income may have to pay a penalty of $3,000 per insured worker.

---

19. 29 U.S.C. Sections 1161–1169.
20. 29 U.S.C.A. Sections 1181 *et seq.*
21. Pub. L. No. 111–148, 124 Stat. 119, March 23, 2010, codified in various sections of 42 U.S.C.

24–3d Employee Privacy Rights

Concerns about the privacy rights of employees have arisen in response to the sometimes invasive tactics used by employers to monitor and screen workers. Perhaps the greatest privacy concern in today's employment arena has to do with electronic monitoring.

dlewis33/Getty Images

Can employees refuse to be video-monitored?

Electronic Monitoring More than half of employers engage in some form of surveillance of their employees. Many employers review employees' e-mail, as well as their social media posts and other Internet messages. Employers may also make video recordings of their employees at work, monitor their telephone conversations, and listen to their voice mail.

Employee Privacy Protection. Employees of private (nongovernment) employers have some privacy protection under tort law and state constitutions. In addition, state and federal statutes may limit an employer's conduct in certain respects. For instance, the Electronic Communications Privacy Act prohibits employers from intercepting an employee's personal electronic communications unless they are made on devices and systems furnished by the employer.

Nonetheless, employers do have considerable leeway to monitor employees in the workplace. In addition, private employers generally are free to use filtering software to block access to certain websites, such as sites containing sexually explicit images. The First Amendment's protection of free speech prevents only *government employers* from restraining speech by blocking websites.

Reasonable Expectation of Privacy. When determining whether an employer is liable for violating an employee's privacy rights, the courts generally weigh the employer's interests against the employee's reasonable expectation of privacy.

Normally, if employees have been informed that their communications are being monitored, they cannot reasonably expect those interactions to be private. In addition, a court will typically hold that employees do not have a reasonable expectation of privacy when using a system (such as an e-mail system) provided by the employer.

If employees are *not* informed that certain communications are being monitored, however, the employer may be held liable for invading their privacy. Most employers that engage in electronic monitoring notify their employees about the monitoring. Nevertheless, notifying employees of a general policy may not sufficiently protect an employer who monitors forms of communications that the policy fails to mention. For instance, notifying employees that their e-mails and phone calls may be monitored does not necessarily protect an employer who also monitors social media posts or text messages.

For a discussion of how some employers are creating their own social media networks, see this chapter's *Adapting the Law to the Online Environment* feature.

Other Types of Monitoring In addition to monitoring their employees' activities electronically, employers also engage in other types of monitoring. These practices, which have included lie-detector tests and drug tests, have often been subject to challenge as violations of employee privacy rights.

Lie-Detector Tests. At one time, many employers required employees or job applicants to take polygraph examinations (lie-detector tests). Today, the Employee Polygraph Protection Act[22] generally prohibits employers from requiring or requesting that employees or job applicants take lie-detector tests. It also prevents employers from asking about the results of a polygraph or taking any negative employment action based on the results.

---

22. 29 U.S.C. Sections 2001 *et seq.*

Social Media in the Workplace Come of Age

What do corporate giant Dell, Inc., and relatively small Nikon Instruments have in common? They—and many other companies—have created internal social media networks using enterprise social networking software and systems, such as Igloo, Slack, Microsoft Teams, and Workplace by Facebook. A glance at the posts on these internal networks reveals that they are quite different from typical posts on Facebook, LinkedIn, and Twitter. Rather than being personal, the tone is businesslike, and the posts deal with workplace concerns such as how a team is solving a problem or how to sell a new product.

Benefits and Pitfalls of Internal Social Media Networks

Internal social media networks offer businesses several advantages. Perhaps the most important is that employees can obtain real-time information about important issues such as production glitches. They can also exchange tips about how to deal with problems, such as difficult customers. News about the company's new products or those of a competitor is available immediately. Furthermore, employees spend much less time sorting through e-mail. Rather than wasting their fellow employees' time by sending mass e-mailings, workers can post messages or collaborate on presentations via the company's internal network.

The downside is that these networks may become polluted with annoying "white noise." If employees start posting comments about what they ate for lunch, for instance, the system will lose much of its utility. Companies can prevent this from happening by establishing explicit guidelines on what can be posted.

Keeping the Data Safe

Another concern is how to keep data and corporate secrets safe. When a company sets up a social media network, it usually decides which employees can see which files and which employees will belong to each specific "social" group within the company. Often, the data created through a social media network are kept on the company's own servers in secure "clouds."

Critical Thinking

What problems might arise if data from an internal social media system are stored on third party servers?

Certain employers are exempt from these prohibitions. Federal, state, and local government employers, as well as certain security service firms, may conduct polygraph tests. In addition, companies that manufacture and distribute controlled substances may perform lie-detector tests. Other employers may use polygraph tests when investigating losses attributable to theft, including embezzlement and the theft of trade secrets.

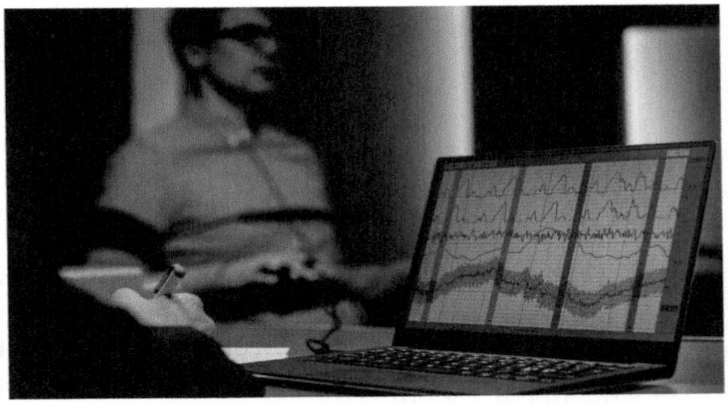
Gorodenkoff/shutterstock.com

Does current federal law allow security service firms to use lie-detector tests?

Drug Testing. In the interests of public safety, many employers, including government employers, require their employees to submit to drug testing. Government (public) employers are constrained in drug testing by the Fourth Amendment to the U.S. Constitution, which prohibits unreasonable searches and seizures. Drug testing of public employees is allowed by statute for transportation workers. Courts normally uphold drug testing of certain employees when drug use in a particular job may threaten public safety. Also, when there is a reasonable basis for suspecting government employees of using drugs, courts often find that drug testing does not violate the Fourth Amendment.

The Fourth Amendment does not apply to drug testing conducted by private employers. Hence, the drug testing of private-sector employees is governed by state law, which varies widely. Many states have statutes that allow drug testing by private employers but place restrictions on when and how the testing may be performed. A collective bargaining agreement may also provide protection against drug testing (or authorize drug testing under certain conditions).

The permissibility of a private employee's drug test often hinges on whether the employer's testing was reasonable. Random drug tests and even "zero-tolerance" policies (which deny a "second chance" to employees who test positive for drugs) have been held to be reasonable.

24–4 Immigration Law

Focus Question 4

What are the two most important federal statutes governing immigration and employment today?

The United States did not have any laws restricting immigration until the late nineteenth century. Today, the most important laws governing immigration and employment are the Immigration Reform and Control Act[23] (IRCA) and the Immigration Act.[24]

Immigration law has become increasingly important in recent years. An estimated 12 million undocumented immigrants now live in the United States. Many of them came to find jobs. Because U.S. employers face serious penalties if they hire undocumented immigrants, businesspersons need to understand our immigration laws.

24–4a Immigration Reform and Control Act (IRCA)

When the IRCA was enacted in 1986, it provided amnesty to certain groups of illegal aliens living in the United States at the time. It also established a system that sanctions employers who hire immigrants lacking work authorization. The IRCA makes it illegal to hire, recruit, or refer for a fee someone not authorized to work in this country. Through Immigration and Customs Enforcement (ICE) officers, the federal government conducts random compliance audits and engages in enforcement actions against employers who hire undocumented immigrants.

I-9 Verification The process of verifying the employment eligibility and identity of a new worker. It must be completed within three days after the worker commences employment.

I-9 Employment Verification To comply with the IRCA, an employer must perform an **I-9 verification** for a new hire, including those hired as "contractors" or "day workers" if they work under the employer's direct supervision. Form I-9, Employment Eligibility Verification, which is available from U.S. Citizenship and Immigration Services, must be completed *within three days* of a worker's commencement of employment. The three-day period is to allow the employer to check the form's accuracy and to review and verify documents establishing the prospective worker's identity and eligibility for employment in the United States.

Documentation Requirements The employer must declare, under penalty of perjury, that an employee produced documents establishing the employee's identity and legal employability. A U.S. passport establishing the person's citizenship is acceptable documentation, as is a document authorizing a foreign citizen to work in the United States, such as a Permanent Resident Card (discussed shortly).

Know This

If an employer had any reason to suspect that a worker's documents were forged or inaccurate at the time of hiring, the employer can be fined for violating the IRCA.

Most legal actions for violations of I-9 rules are brought against employees who provide false information or documentation. If the employee enters false information on an I-9 form or presents false documentation, the employer can fire the worker, who then may be subject to deportation. Nevertheless, employers must be honest when verifying an employee's documentation. If an employer "should have known" that the worker was unauthorized, the employer has violated the rules.

Enforcement U.S. Immigration and Customs Enforcement (ICE) is the largest investigative arm of the U.S. Department of Homeland Security. ICE has a general inspection program that conducts random compliance audits. Other audits may occur if the agency receives a written complaint alleging an employer's violations. Government inspections include a review of an employer's file of I-9 forms. The government does not need a subpoena or a warrant to conduct such an inspection.

---

23. 29 U.S.C. Section 1802.

24. This act amended various provisions of the Immigration and Nationality Act, 8 U.S.C. Sections 1101 *et seq.*

If an investigation reveals a possible violation, ICE will bring an administrative action and issue a Notice of Intent to Fine, which sets out the charges against the employer. The employer has a right to a hearing on the enforcement action if a request is filed within thirty days. This hearing is conducted before an administrative law judge, and the employer has a right to counsel and to discovery. The typical defense in such actions is good faith or substantial compliance with the documentation provisions.

Penalties An employer who violates the law by hiring an unauthorized alien is subject to substantial penalties. The employer may be fined up to $4,568 for each unauthorized employee for a first offense, $11,463 per employee for a second offense, and up to $22,972 for subsequent offenses.

Employers who have engaged in a "pattern or practice of violations" are subject to criminal penalties, which include additional fines and imprisonment for up to ten years. A company may also be barred from future government contracts for violations. In determining the penalty, ICE considers the seriousness of the violation (such as intentional falsification of documents), the employer's past compliance, and whether the employer cooperated with authorities during the investigation.

diego_cervo/Getty Images

What are the penalties for employing an unauthorized immigrant?

24–4b The Immigration Act

Often, U.S. businesses find that they cannot hire enough domestic workers with specialized skills. For this reason, U.S. immigration laws have long made provisions for businesses to hire specially qualified foreign workers.

The Immigration Act placed caps on the number of visas (entry permits) that can be issued to immigrants each year, including employment-based visas. Employment-based visas may be classified as permanent (immigrant) or temporary (nonimmigrant). Employers who wish to hire workers with either type of visa must comply with detailed government regulations.[25]

I-551 Permanent Resident Card A company seeking to hire a noncitizen worker on a permanent basis may do so if the worker is self-authorized—that is, if the worker either is a lawful permanent resident or has a valid temporary Employment Authorization Document. A lawful permanent resident can prove legal status to an employer by presenting an **I-551 Permanent Resident Card**, known as a "green card," or a properly stamped foreign passport.

I-551 Permanent Resident Card A document, known as a "green card," that shows that a foreign-born individual can legally work in the United States.

Many immigrant workers are not already self-authorized, and an employer that wishes to hire them can attempt to obtain labor certification, or green cards, for them. A limited number of new green cards are issued each year. A green card can be obtained only for a person who is being hired for a permanent, full-time position. (A separate authorization system provides for the temporary entry and hiring of nonimmigrant visa workers.)

To gain authorization for hiring a foreign worker, an employer must show that no U.S. worker is qualified, willing, and able to take the job. The government has detailed regulations governing the advertising of positions as well as the certification process. Any U.S. applicants who meet the stated job qualifications must be interviewed for the position. The employer must also be able to show that the qualifications required for the job are a business necessity.

The H-1B Visa Program A relatively common and sometimes controversial temporary visa program is the H-1B visa system. To obtain an H-1B visa, the potential employee must be qualified in a "specialty occupation," meaning that the individual has highly specialized knowledge and has attained a bachelor's or higher degree or its equivalent. Individuals with H-1B visas can stay in the United States for three to six years and can work only for the sponsoring employer.

25. The most relevant regulations can be found at 20 C.F.R. Section 655 (for temporary employment) and 20 C.F.R. Section 656 (for permanent employment).

The recipients of H-1B visas include many high-tech workers. A maximum of sixty-five thousand H-1B visas are set aside each year for new immigrants. That limit is typically reached within the first few weeks of the year. Consequently, technology companies complain that Congress needs to expand the number of H-1B visas available in order to encourage the best and the brightest minds to work in the United States.

An employer who wishes to submit an H-1B application must first file a Labor Condition Application on a form known as ETA 9035. The employer must agree to provide a wage level at least equal to the wages offered to other individuals with similar experience and qualifications. The employer must also show that the hiring will not adversely affect other workers similarly employed. The employer is required to inform U.S. workers of the intent to hire a foreign worker by posting the form. The U.S. Department of Labor reviews the applications and may reject them for omissions or inaccuracies.

H-2, O, L, and E Visas Other specialty temporary visas are available for other categories of employees. H-2A visas provide for workers performing agricultural labor of a seasonal nature. H-2B visas are used for workers in nonagricultural positions. O visas provide entry for persons who have "extraordinary ability in the sciences, arts, education, business or athletics which has been demonstrated by sustained national or international acclaim." L visas allow a company's foreign managers or executives to work inside the United States. E visas permit the entry of certain foreign investors and entrepreneurs.

Focus Question 5

What federal statute gave employees the right to engage in collective bargaining and to strike?

24–5 Labor Law

In the 1930s, in addition to wage-hour laws, the government also enacted the first of several labor laws. These laws protect employees' rights to join labor unions, to bargain with management over the terms and conditions of employment, and to conduct strikes.

24–5a Federal Labor Laws

Federal labor laws governing union-employer relations have developed considerably since the first law was enacted in 1932. Initially, the laws were concerned with protecting the rights and interests of workers. Subsequent legislation placed some restraints on unions and granted rights to employers. We look next at four major federal statutes regulating union-employer relations.

Norris-LaGuardia Act In 1932, Congress protected peaceful strikes, picketing, and boycotts in the Norris-LaGuardia Act.[26] The statute restricted the power of federal courts to issue injunctions against unions engaged in peaceful strikes. In effect, this act established a national policy permitting employees to organize.

National Labor Relations Act One of the foremost statutes regulating labor is the National Labor Relations Act (NLRA), enacted in 1935.[27] This act established the rights of employees to engage in collective bargaining and to strike.

Unfair Labor Practices. The NLRA specifically defined a number of employer practices as unfair to labor:

1. Interference with the efforts of employees to form, join, or assist labor organizations or to engage in concerted activities for mutual aid or protection.
2. An employer's domination of a labor organization or contribution of financial or other support to it.

---

26. 29 U.S.C. Sections 101–110, 113–115.
27. 20 U.S.C. Section 151.

3. Discrimination in the hiring of or awarding of tenure to employees based on union affiliation.
4. Discrimination against employees for filing charges under the act or giving testimony under the act.
5. Refusal to bargain collectively with the duly designated representative of the employees.

FireAtDusk/Getty Images

When were many labor union laws created?

The National Labor Relations Board. The NLRA also created the National Labor Relations Board (NLRB) to oversee union elections and to prevent employers from engaging in unfair and illegal union activities and unfair labor practices.

The NLRB has the authority to investigate employees' charges of unfair labor practices and to file complaints against employers in response to these charges. When violations are found, the NLRB may issue a cease-and-desist order compelling the employer to stop engaging in the unfair practices. Cease-and-desist orders can be enforced by a federal appellate court if necessary. After the NLRB rules on claims of unfair labor practices, its decision may be appealed to a federal court.

Case Example 24.8 Ozburn-Hessey Logistics (OHL) had a discipline policy under which an employee could be fired for accumulating thirteen tardiness and absence "points." Shortly after OHL replaced its push-button clocks with time-screen clocks, employee Laura Keele checked in one minute late. Keele claimed the new, more complex system confused her, causing the delay. Nonetheless, OHL assessed Keele a tardiness point, her thirteenth, and she was fired.

The NLRB filed a complaint against OHL for unfair labor practices, asserting that the upgrade in clocks should have been negotiated with Keele's union. Because it was not, her firing violated federal labor law. An administrative law judge determined that pushing a touchscreen rather than a plastic button did not represent a "significant" change in the terms of Keele's employment. A federal appeals court agreed. OHL's decision to switch clocks did not require collective bargaining, and Keele's firing was not an unfair labor practice.[28] ■

Good Faith Bargaining. Under the NLRA, employers and unions have a duty to bargain in good faith. Bargaining over certain subjects (such as wages, hours, and benefits) is mandatory, and a party's refusal to bargain over these subjects is an unfair labor practice that can be reported to the NLRB. An employer may be required to bargain with the union over the use of hidden video surveillance cameras, for instance.

Workers Protected by the NLRA. To be protected under the NLRA, an individual must be an *employee,* as that term is defined in the statute. Courts have long held that job applicants fall within the definition (otherwise, the NLRA's ban on discrimination in hiring would mean nothing). Additionally, individuals who are hired by a union to organize a company are to be considered employees of the company for NLRA purposes.

Even a temporary worker hired through an employment agency may qualify for protection under the NLRA. The same cannot be said for some faculty at private universities. **Case Example 24.9** A group of non-tenure-track adjunct instructors at the University of Southern California (USC) voted to join a union. USC refused to negotiate with these adjuncts on the ground that, like tenured professors, they were "managers" of university policy who are barred from unionizing, rather than less-powerful "employees," who are permitted to unionize under the NLRA. A federal appeals court ruled against USC in this instance but established guidelines that will make it more difficult for non-tenure-track adjunct faculty at private universities to claim employee status in the future.[29] ■

28. *Ozburn-Hessey Logistics, LLC v. NLRB,* __ Fed.Appx. __, 2020 WL 1199264 (6th Cir. 2020).
29. *University of Southern California v. NLRB, 918 F.3d. 126, 440* U.S.App.D.C. 59 (2019).

Labor Management Relations Act The Labor Management Relations Act (LMRA), also called the Taft-Hartley Act,[30] was passed in 1947 to proscribe certain unfair union practices, such as the *closed shop*. A **closed shop** requires union membership as a condition of employment.

Closed Shop A firm that requires union membership as a condition of employment.

Although the act made the closed shop illegal, it preserved the legality of the union shop. A **union shop** does not require membership as a prerequisite for employment but can, and usually does, require that workers join the union after a specified amount of time on the job.

Union Shop A firm that requires all workers, once employed, to become union members within a specified period of time as a condition of their continued employment.

The LMRA also prohibited unions from refusing to bargain with employers, engaging in certain types of picketing, and *featherbedding*—causing employers to hire more employees than necessary. The act also allowed individual states to pass their own **right-to-work laws,** which make it illegal for union membership to be required for *continued* employment in any establishment. Thus, union shops are technically illegal in the twenty-eight states that have right-to-work laws.

Right-to-Work Laws State laws providing that employees may not be required to join a union as a condition of retaining employment.

Labor-Management Reporting and Disclosure Act The Labor-Management Reporting and Disclosure Act (LMRDA)[31] established an employee bill of rights and reporting requirements for union activities. The act also outlawed the **hot-cargo agreement,** in which employers voluntarily agree with unions not to handle, use, or deal in goods produced by nonunion employees working for other employers.

Hot-Cargo Agreement An illegal agreement in which employers voluntarily agree with unions not to handle, use, or deal in the nonunion-produced goods of other employers.

The LMRDA strictly regulates unions' internal business procedures, including union elections. For instance, it requires a union to hold regularly scheduled elections of officers using secret ballots. Ex-convicts are prohibited from holding union office. Moreover, union officials are accountable for union property and funds. Members have the right to attend and to participate in union meetings, to nominate officers, and to vote in most union proceedings.

The LMRDA holds union officers to a high standard of responsibility and ethical conduct in administering the affairs of their union. **Case Example 24.10** The Services Employees International Union (SEIU) consists of 2.2 million members who work in health care, public services, and property services. United Health Workers (UHW) is affiliated with SEIU and represents 150,000 health care workers in California. The SEIU proposed moving 150,000 long-term care workers from three separate unions, including 65,000 from the UHW, into a new union chartered by the SEIU. The UHW opposed the move.

i4lcocl2/Shutterstock.com

How can labor union officers breach their fiduciary duties to members?

Meanwhile, the UHW officials, while still on the UHW payroll, created and promoted a new union—the National Union of Healthcare Workers (NUHW). The SEIU sued the NUHW and the UHW officials for breach of fiduciary duties. The SEIU claimed that union officials had a duty under the LMRDA to act primarily for the benefit of the union. The court agreed, and a federal appellate court affirmed. Officials who diverted union resources to establish a competing union breached their duty under the LMRDA.[32]

24–5b Union Organization

Typically, the first step in organizing a union at a particular firm is to have the workers sign authorization cards. An **authorization card** usually states that the worker wishes to have a certain union, such as the United Auto Workers, represent the workforce.

Authorization Card A card signed by an employee that gives a union permission to act on the employee's behalf in negotiations with management.

If a majority of the workers sign authorization cards, the union organizers (unionizers) present the cards to the employer and ask for formal recognition of the union. The employer is not required to recognize the union at this point in the process, but it may do so voluntarily on a showing of majority support.

30. 29 U.S.C. Sections 141 *et seq.*
31. 29 U.S.C. Sections 401 *et seq.*
32. *Services Employees International Union v. National Union of Healthcare Workers*, 718 F.3d 1036 (9th Cir. 2013).

Union Elections If the employer does not voluntarily recognize the union—or if less than a majority of the workers sign authorization cards—the union organizers can petition for an election. The organizers present the authorization cards to the NLRB with a petition to hold an election on unionization. For an election to be held, they must demonstrate that at least 30 percent of the workers to be represented support a union or an election on unionization.

Appropriate Bargaining Unit. Not every group of workers can form a single union. The proposed union must represent an *appropriate bargaining unit.* One key requirement of an appropriate bargaining unit is a *mutuality of interest* among all the workers to be represented by the union. Factors considered in determining whether there is a mutuality of interest include the similarity of the jobs of all the workers to be unionized and their physical location.

Election Rules In most instances, the parties agree on the voting unit and other issues. If the parties do not agree, the NLRB holds a pre-election hearing shortly after it receives a petition to resolve issues and determine whether an election should be conducted. Before the hearing, the company must submit a "statement of position" laying out every argument it intends to make against the union. Any argument that the company does not include in its position paper can be excluded from evidence at the hearing. Once the hearing is concluded, an election cannot be scheduled for twenty business days unless the parties agree otherwise.

Voting. If an election is held, the NLRB supervises the election and ensures secret voting and voter eligibility. If the proposed union receives majority support in a fair election, the NLRB certifies the union as the bargaining representative for the employees.

Union Election Campaigns Many disputes between labor and management arise during union election campaigns. Generally, the employer has control over unionizing activities that take place on company property during working hours. An employer may thus limit the campaign activities of union supporters as long as the employer has a legitimate business reason for doing so. The employer may also reasonably limit the times and places that union solicitation occurs so long as the employer is not discriminating against the union. (Can union organizers use company e-mail during campaigns? See this chapter's *Managerial Strategy* feature for a discussion of this topic.)

Union Organizing Using a Company's E-Mail System

When union organizers start an organizing drive, there are certain restrictions on what they can do, particularly within the workplace. Both employers and employees must comply with Section 7 of the National Labor Relations Act (NLRA).

Protected Concerted Activities

Under Section 7, employees have certain rights to communicate among themselves. Section 7 states, "Employees shall have the right to self-organization, . . . and to engage in other concerted activities for the purpose of collective bargaining or other mutual aid or protection."

What about communication via e-mail? Can union organizers use a company-operated e-mail system for organizing purposes? Companies typically provide e-mail systems so that employees can communicate with outsiders and among themselves as part of their jobs. Generally, company policies have prohibited the use of company-owned and -operated e-mail systems for other than job-related communications. Some union organizers have challenged this prohibition.

The NLRB's Perspective Evolves

The National Labor Relations Board (NLRB) has reversed course several times on the issue of employees' use of company e-mail systems, reflecting the changing politics of board members. In the mid-2010s, the NLRB ruled that, if

(Continues)

Continued

an employer provides workers with an e-mail system for work functions, then its employees should have a right under the NLRA to use that same system to discuss any work-related concerns, including union activity.[a]

About five years later, the NLRB heard a case involving a Las Vegas casino that prohibited employees from using company e-mail to discuss working conditions.[b] Upholding the casino's ability to do so, the board broadly revoked the right of workers to conduct union affairs on employer-operated e-mail systems. The NLRB held that businesses have a constitutionally protected right to control or limit the use of their property, which includes digital communications. The prohibition must, however, be nondiscriminatory. That is, a business cannot ban union-related e-mails while allowing communications about other subjects that are not strictly work-related.

a. *Purple Communications, Inc. and Communication Workers of America, AFL-CIO,* Cases 21-CA-095151, 21-RC-091531, and 21-RC-091584, March 16, 2015.

b. *Caesars Entertainment, Inc. and NLRB,* Case 28-CA-060841, December 17, 2019.

Business Questions

1. *Employees meeting around the water cooler or coffee machine have always had the right to discuss work-related matters. Is an employer-provided e-mail system or social media outlet simply a digital water cooler? Why or why not?*
2. *Why might the nondiscrimination component of the NLRB's recent ruling make a ban on union-related e-mails difficult for managers to enforce?*

GaudiLab/Shutterstock.com

When workers wish to organize a union, what types of activities are allowed on the employer's premises? What types of activities are not allowed?

Example 24.11 A union is seeking to organize clerks at a department store owned by Amanti Enterprises. Amanti can prohibit all union solicitation in areas of the store open to the public because that activity could seriously interfere with the store's business. If Amanti allows solicitation for charitable causes in the workplace, however, normally it may not prohibit union solicitation. ■

An employer may campaign among its workers against the union, but the NLRB carefully monitors and regulates the tactics used by management. Otherwise, management might use its economic power to coerce the workers into voting against unionization. If an employer issued threats ("If the union wins, you'll all be fired") or engaged in other unfair labor practices, the NLRB could certify the union even though it lost the election. Alternatively, the NLRB could ask a court to order a new election.

Whether an employer violated its employees' rights under the National Labor Relations Act during a union election campaign was at issue in the following case.

Case 24.3

Contemporary Cars, Inc. v. National Labor Relations Board

United States Court of Appeals, Seventh Circuit 814 F.3d 859 (2016).

Facts Contemporary Cars, Inc., sells and services cars. AutoNation owns this dealership, along with others. The International Association of Machinists began a campaign to organize the company's service technicians. During the election campaign, Contemporary engaged in various activities to monitor and perhaps affect the campaign. AutoNation's vice president, who opposed the union, held group meetings with the service technicians. Afterwards, Bob Berryhill, Contemporary's manager, called individual employees into his office to ask about union activity. He also promised that the dealership was working on finding solutions for various workplace problems the technicians had. In addition, the dealership fired an employee, Anthony Roberts, who was a leader in the union campaign. An administrative law judge ordered Contemporary to stop interfering with its employees' union activities and to reinstate Roberts. The NLRB affirmed the order. The dealership petitioned for a review of the order.

Issue Did Contemporary Cars violate its employees' rights during the union election campaign?

Decision Yes. The U.S. Court of Appeals for the Seventh Circuit affirmed the administrative law judge's order. The dealership and AutoNation violated the National Labor Relations Act (NLRA) by interfering with their employees' protected rights to engage in concerted activity and to organize a union.

Reason Contemporary Cars violated the NLRA by "coercively creating an impression of surveillance of union activity, interrogating employees about union activity, and soliciting and promising to remedy employee grievances." In support of its finding of coercion, the court cited the supervisor's comments on the employees' "rush" to leave work to attend union meetings and the way that management met with individual employees who were "alone and outnumbered by managers." The court pointed out that management's meetings with employees represented "an effort to frustrate the union organizing drive by soliciting and at least implicitly promising to adjust grievances." AutoNation's "overly broad" no-solicitation policy was likely to "chill" concerted activity.

Lastly, the court stated that the dealership's discharge of Roberts was motivated by "anti-union *animus* [hostility]," as evidenced by Berryhill's identification of Roberts as a "troublemaker" and "instigator" of the union campaign. In addition, Roberts had higher productivity, a superior skill rating, and more seniority than technicians who were retained.

Critical Thinking

- **Legal Environment** *What might the dealership have asserted in defense to the charge that its actions violated its employees' rights?*
- **What If the Facts Were Different?** *Suppose that the dealership had taken no steps to change any of the terms or conditions of employment until well after the union election. Would the result have been different in this case? Explain.*

24–5c Collective Bargaining

If the NLRB certifies the union, the union becomes the *exclusive bargaining representative* of the workers. The central legal right of a union is to engage in collective bargaining on the members' behalf. **Collective bargaining** is the process by which labor and management negotiate the terms and conditions of employment, such as wages, benefits, and working conditions. Collective bargaining allows union representatives elected by union members to speak on behalf of the members at the bargaining table.

Collective Bargaining The process by which labor and management negotiate the terms and conditions of employment, including working hours and workplace conditions.

Good Faith Negotiating Once an employer and a union sit down at the conference table, they must negotiate in good faith and make a reasonable effort to come to an agreement. They are not obligated to reach an agreement. They must, however, approach the negotiations with the idea that an agreement is possible. Both parties may engage in hard bargaining, but the bargaining process itself must be geared toward reaching a compromise—not avoiding a compromise.

Although good faith is a matter of subjective intent, a party's actions can be used to evaluate the party's good or bad faith. Excessive delaying tactics may be proof of bad faith, as may insistence on obviously unreasonable contract terms. If an employer (or a union) refuses to bargain in good faith without justification, it has committed an unfair labor practice. Exhibit 24–1 illustrates some differences between good faith and bad faith bargaining.

The Coronavirus Aid, Relief, and Economic Security Act Designed to mitigate the economic impact of the coronavirus pandemic of 2020, the Coronavirus Aid, Relief, and Economic Security (CARES) Act includes several crucial labor law stipulations.[33] To receive federal stimulus loans under CARES, nonunion mid-sized businesses (having between 500 and 10,000 employees) had to agree *not* to oppose the unionization of their workforces during the term of the loan. Furthermore, to be eligible for CARES loans, mid-sized businesses had to *not* "abrogate" (or revoke) existing collective bargaining agreements for the term of the loan plus two years following repayment.

---

33. Pub. L. 116-136, Sections 4003(D)(i)(IX)-(X) (2020).

Exhibit 24–1 Good Faith versus Bad Faith in Collective Bargaining

Good Faith Bargaining	Bad Faith Bargaining
1. Negotiating with the belief that an agreement is possible	1. Excessive delaying tactics
2. Seriously considering the other side's positions	2. Insistence on unreasonable contract terms
3. Making reasonable proposals	3. Rejecting a proposal without offering a counterproposal
4. Being willing to compromise	4. Engaging in a campaign among workers to undermine the union
5. Sending bargainers who have the authority to enter into agreements for the company	5. Constantly shifting positions on disputed contract terms
	6. Sending bargainers who lack authority to commit the company to a contract

24–5d Strikes

Even when labor and management have bargained in good faith, they may be unable to reach a final agreement. When extensive collective bargaining has been conducted and an impasse results, the union may call a strike against the employer to pressure it into making concessions.

Strike An action undertaken by unionized workers when collective bargaining fails. The workers leave their jobs, refuse to work, and (typically) picket the employer's workplace.

In a **strike**, the unionized workers leave their jobs and refuse to work. The workers also typically picket the workplace, standing outside the facility with signs stating their complaints. A strike is an extreme action. Striking workers lose their rights to be paid, and management loses production and may lose customers when orders cannot be filled. Labor law regulates the circumstances and conduct of strikes.

Most strikes take the form of "economic strikes," which are initiated because the union wants a better contract. **Example 24.12** Teachers in Eagle Point, Oregon, engage in an economic strike after contract negotiations with the school district fail to bring an agreement on pay, working hours, and subcontracting jobs. The unionized teachers picket outside the Eagle Point school building. Classes are canceled for a few weeks until the district can find substitute teachers who will fill in during the strike. ■

The Right to Strike The right to strike is guaranteed by the NLRA, within limits. In addition, certain strike activities, such as picketing, are protected by the free speech guarantee of the First Amendment to the U.S. Constitution. Nonworkers have a right to participate in picketing an employer, and workers have the right to refuse to cross a picket line of fellow workers who are engaged in a lawful strike.

Strikers are not allowed to use (or threaten to use) violence against anyone or to prevent others from entering a facility. Furthermore, a strike may be illegal if it contravenes a no-strike clause that was in the previous collective bargaining agreement between the employer and the union.

After a Strike Ends In a typical strike, the employer has a right to hire permanent replacements during the strike. The employer need not terminate the replacement workers when the economic strikers seek to return to work. In other words, striking workers are not guaranteed the right to return to their jobs after the strike if satisfactory replacement workers have been found.

If the employer has not hired replacement workers to fill the strikers' positions, however, then the employer must rehire the economic strikers to fill any vacancies. Employers may not discriminate against former economic strikers, and those who are rehired retain their seniority rights.

Practice and Review

Rick Saldona began working as a traveling salesperson for Aimer Winery in 2009. Sales constituted 90 percent of Saldona's work time. Saldona worked an average of fifty hours per week but received no overtime pay. In June 2019, Saldona's new supervisor, Caesar Braxton, claimed that Saldona had been inflating his reported sales calls and required Saldona to submit to a polygraph test. Saldona reported Braxton to the U.S. Department of Labor, which prohibited Aimer from requiring Saldona to take a polygraph test for this purpose. In August 2019, Saldona's wife, Venita, fell from a ladder and sustained a head injury while employed as a full-time agricultural harvester. Saldona delivered to Aimer's human resources department a letter from his wife's physician indicating that she would need daily care for several months, and Saldona took leave until December 2019. Aimer had sixty-three employees at that time. When Saldona returned to Aimer, he was informed that his position had been eliminated because his sales territory had been combined with an adjacent territory. Using the information presented in the chapter, answer the following questions.

1. Would Saldona have been legally entitled to receive overtime pay at a higher rate? Why or why not?
2. What is the maximum length of time Saldona would have been allowed to take leave to care for his injured spouse?
3. Under what circumstances would Aimer have been allowed to require an employee to take a lie-detector test?
4. Would Aimer likely be able to avoid reinstating Saldona under the *key employee* exception? Why or why not?

Debate This

The U.S. labor market is highly competitive, so state and federal laws that require overtime pay are unnecessary and should be abolished.

Key Terms

authorization card 614
closed shop 614
collective bargaining 617
employment at will 597
hot-cargo agreement 614
I-551 Permanent Resident Card 611
I-9 verification 610
minimum wage 599
right-to-work law 614
strike 618
union shop 614
vesting 606
whistleblowing 597
workers' compensation laws 604
wrongful discharge 598

Chapter Summary: Employment, Immigration, and Labor Law

Employment at Will	Under this common law doctrine, either party may terminate the employment relationship at any time and for any reason ("at will"). 1. **Exceptions to the employment-at-will doctrine**—Courts have made exceptions to the doctrine on the basis of contract theory, tort theory, and public policy. The public policy exception may sometimes apply to whistleblowers. 2. **Wrongful discharge**—Whenever an employer discharges an employee in violation of an employment contract or statutory law protecting employees, the employee may bring a suit for wrongful discharge.

(Continues)

Wages, Hours, and Leave

1. **Davis-Bacon Act**—Requires contractors and subcontractors working on federal government construction projects to pay their employees "prevailing wages."
2. **Walsh-Healey Act**—Requires firms that contract with federal agencies to pay their employees a minimum wage and overtime pay.
3. **Fair Labor Standards Act**—Extended wage and hour requirements to cover all employers whose activities affect interstate commerce plus certain other businesses. The act has specific requirements in regard to child labor, maximum hours, minimum wages, and overtime.
4. **The Family and Medical Leave Act (FMLA)**—Requires employers with fifty or more employees to provide employees with up to twelve weeks of unpaid leave (twenty-six weeks for military caregiver leave) during any twelve-month period. An eligible employee:
   - **a.** May take family leave to care for a newborn baby, an adopted child, or a foster child.
   - **b.** May take medical leave when the employee or the employee's spouse, child, or parent has a serious health condition requiring care.
   - **c.** May take military caregiver leave to care for a family member with a serious injury or illness incurred as a result of military duty.
   - **d.** May take qualifying exigency leave to handle specified nonmedical emergencies when a spouse, parent, or child is in, or called to, active military duty

Health, Safety, Income Security, and Privacy

1. **Occupational Safety and Health Act**—Requires employers to meet specific safety and health standards that are established and enforced by the Occupational Safety and Health Administration (OSHA).
2. **State workers' compensation laws**—Establish an administrative procedure for compensating workers who are injured in accidents that occur on the job, regardless of fault.
3. **Social Security and Medicare**—The Social Security Act provides for old-age (retirement), survivors', and disability insurance. Both employers and employees must make contributions under the Federal Insurance Contributions Act (FICA). The Social Security Administration also administers Medicare, a health insurance program for older or disabled persons.
4. **Private retirement plans**—The federal Employee Retirement Income Security Act (ERISA) establishes standards for the management of employer-provided pension plans.
5. **Unemployment insurance**—The Federal Unemployment Tax Act (FUTA) created a system that provides unemployment compensation to eligible individuals. Employers are taxed to cover the costs.
6. **COBRA**—The Consolidated Omnibus Budget Reconciliation Act (COBRA) requires employers to give employees, on termination of employment, the option of continuing their medical, optical, or dental insurance coverage for a certain period at their own expense.
7. **HIPAA**—The Health Insurance Portability and Accountability Act (HIPAA) establishes requirements for employer-sponsored group health plans. The plans must also comply with various safeguards to ensure the privacy of employees' health information.
8. **Affordable Care Act**—The Affordable Care Act requires most employers with fifty or more full-time employees to offer health insurance benefits. It also provides tax credits to employers who provide benefits even if they are not required to do so.
9. **Employee privacy rights**—Tort law, state constitutions, and federal and state statutes, as well as the U.S. Constitution, provide some protection for employees' privacy rights. Employer practices that have been challenged by employees as violations of their privacy rights include electronic monitoring, lie-detector tests, and drug testing.

Immigration Law

1. **Immigration Reform and Control Act**—Prohibits employers from hiring illegal immigrants. The act is administered by U.S. Citizenship and Immigration Services. Compliance audits and enforcement actions are conducted by U.S. Immigration and Customs Enforcement.
2. **Immigration Act**—Limits the number of legal immigrants entering the United States by capping the number of visas (entry permits) that are issued each year.

Labor Law	1. **Federal labor laws**— a. Norris-LaGuardia Act—Protects peaceful strikes, picketing, and boycotts. b. National Labor Relations Act—Established the rights of employees to engage in collective bargaining and to strike. It also defined specific employer practices as unfair to labor. The National Labor Relations Board (NLRB) was created to administer and enforce the act. c. Labor Management Relations Act—Proscribes certain unfair union practices, such as the closed shop. d. Labor-Management Reporting and Disclosure Act—Established an employee bill of rights and reporting requirements for union activities. 2. **Union organization**—Union campaign activities and elections must comply with the requirements established by federal labor laws and the NLRB. 3. **Collective bargaining**—The process by which labor and management negotiate the terms and conditions of employment (such as wages, benefits, and working conditions). The central legal right of a labor union is to engage in collective bargaining on the members' behalf. 4. **Strikes**—When collective bargaining reaches an impasse, union members may use their ultimate weapon in labor-management struggles—the strike. A strike occurs when unionized workers leave their jobs, refuse to work, and typically picket the employer's workplace.

Issue Spotters

1. Erin, an employee of Fine Print Shop, is injured on the job. For Erin to obtain workers' compensation, does her injury have to have been caused by Fine Print's negligence? Does it matter whether the action causing the injury was intentional? Explain. (See *Health, Safety, Income Security, and Privacy.*)

2. Onyx applies for work with Precision Design Company, which tells her that it requires union membership as a condition of employment. She applies for work with Quality Engineering, Inc., which does not require union membership as a condition of employment but requires employees to join a union after six months on the job. Are these conditions legal? Why or why not? (See *Labor Law.*)

—Check your answers to the *Issue Spotters* against the answers provided in Appendix D.

Business Scenarios and Case Problems

24–1. Unfair Labor Practices. Consolidated Stores is undergoing a unionization campaign. Prior to the union election, management states that the union is unnecessary to protect workers. Management also provides bonuses and wage increases to the workers during this period. The employees reject the union. Union organizers protest that the wage increases during the election campaign unfairly prejudiced the vote. Should these wage increases be regarded as an unfair labor practice? Discuss. (See *Labor Law.*)

24–2. Wrongful Discharge. Denton and Carlo were employed at an appliance plant. Their job required them to do occasional maintenance work while standing on a wire mesh twenty feet above the plant floor. Other employees had fallen through the mesh, and one was killed by the fall. When Denton and Carlo were asked by their supervisor to do work that would likely require them to walk on the mesh, they refused due to their fear of bodily harm or death. Because of their refusal to do the requested work, the two employees were fired. Was their discharge wrongful? If so, under what federal employment law? To what federal agency or department should they turn for assistance? (See *Employment at Will.*)

24–3. Exceptions to the Employment-at-Will Doctrine. Li Li worked for Packard Bioscience, and Mark Schmeizl was her supervisor. In March 2000, Schmeizl told Li Li to call Packard's competitors, pretend to be a potential customer, and request "pricing information and literature." Li Li refused to perform the assignment. She told Schmeizl that she thought the work was illegal and recommended that he contact Packard's legal department. Although a lawyer recommended against the practice, Schmeizl insisted that Li Li perform the calls. Moreover, he later wrote negative performance reviews because she was unable to get the requested information when she called competitors and identified herself as a Packard employee. On June 1, 2000, Li Li was terminated on Schmeizl's recommendation.

Can Li Li bring a claim for wrongful discharge? Why or why not? [*Li Li v. Canberra Industries,* 134 Conn.App. 448, 39 A.3d 789 (2012)] (See *Employment at Will.*)

24–4. Collective Bargaining. SDBC Holdings, Inc., acquired Stella D'oro Biscuit Co., a bakery in New York City. At the time, a collective bargaining agreement existed between Stella D'oro and Local 50 of the Bakery, Confectionary, Tobacco Workers and Grain Millers International Union. During negotiations to renew the agreement, Stella D'oro allowed Local 50 to examine and take notes on the company's financial statement but would not give Local 50 a copy of the statement. Did Stella D'oro engage in an unfair labor practice? Discuss. [*SDBC Holdings, Inc. v. National Labor Relations Board,* 711 F.3d 281 (2d Cir. 2013)] (See *Labor Law.*)

24–5. Business Case Problem with Sample Answer—Unemployment Compensation. Fior Ramirez worked as a housekeeper for Remington Lodging & Hospitality, a hotel in Atlantic Beach, Florida. After her father in the Dominican Republic suffered a stroke, she asked her employer for time off to be with him. Ramirez's manager, Katie Berkowski, refused the request. Two days later, Berkowski received a call from Ramirez to say that she was with her father. He died about a week later, and Ramirez returned to work, but Berkowski told her that she had abandoned her position. Ramirez applied for unemployment compensation. Under the applicable state statute, "an employee is disqualified from receiving benefits if he or she voluntarily left work without good cause." Does Ramirez qualify for benefits? Explain. [*Ramirez v. Reemployment Assistance Appeals Commission,* 135 So.3d 408 (Fla.App. 1 Dist. 2014)] (See *Health, Safety, Income Security, and Privacy.*)

—For a sample answer to Problem 24–5, go to Appendix E.

24–6. Labor Unions. Carol Garcia and Pedro Salgado, bus drivers for Latino Express, Inc., a transportation company, began soliciting signatures from other drivers to certify the Teamsters Local Union No. 777 as the official representative of the employees. Latino Express fired Garcia and Salgado. The two drivers filed a claim with the National Labor Relations Board (NLRB) alleging that the employer had committed an unfair labor practice. Which employer practice defined by the National Labor Relations Act did the plaintiffs most likely charge Latino Express with committing? Is the employer's discharge of Garcia and Salgado likely to be construed as a legitimate act in opposition to union solicitation? If a violation is found, what can the NLRB do? Discuss. [*Ohr v. Latino Express, Inc.,* 776 F.3d 469 (7th Cir. 2015)] (See *Labor Law.*)

24–7. Income Security. Jefferson Partners LP entered into a collective bargaining agreement (CBA) with the Amalgamated Transit Union. Under the CBA, drivers had to either join the union or pay a fair share—85 percent—of union dues, which were used to pay for administrative costs incurred by the union. An employee who refused to pay was subject to discharge. Jefferson hired Tiffany Thompson to work as a bus driver. When told of the CBA requirement, she said that she thought it was unfair. She asserted that it was illegal to compel her to join the union and that it would be illegal to discharge her for not complying. She refused either to join the union or to pay the dues. More than two years later, she was fired on the ground that her continued refusal constituted misconduct. Is Thompson eligible for unemployment compensation? Explain. [*Thompson v. Jefferson Partners LP,* 2016 WL 953038 (Minn. App. 2016)] (See *Health, Safety, Income Security, and Privacy.*)

24–8. Family and Medical Leave. To qualify for leave under the Family and Medical Leave Act (FMLA), an employee must comply with the employer's usual and customary notice requirements, including call-in policies. Robert Stein, an employee of Atlas Industries, Inc., suffered a knee injury at work. Stein took medical leave to have surgery on the knee. Ten weeks into his recovery, Stein's doctor notified Atlas that Stein could return to work with light-duty restrictions in two days. Stein, however, thought he was on leave for several more weeks. Atlas company policy provided that employees who missed three workdays without notification were subject to automatic termination. Stein did not return to work or call in as Atlas expected. Four days later, he was fired. Did Stein's discharge violate the FMLA? Discuss. [*Stein v. Atlas Industries, Inc.,* 730 Fed.Appx. 313, (6th Cir. 2018)] (See *Wages, Hours, and Leave.*)

24–9. A Question of Ethics—The IDDR Approach and Immigration Law. Split Rail Fence Company sells and installs fencing materials in Colorado. U.S. Immigration and Customs Enforcement (ICE) sent Split Rail a list of the company's employees whose documentation did not satisfy the Form I-9 employment eligibility verification requirements. The list included long-term workers who had been involved in company activities, parties, and picnics. They had bank accounts, driver's licenses, cars, homes, and mortgages. At Split Rail's request, the employees orally verified that they were eligible to work in the United States. Unwilling to accept the oral verifications, ICE filed a complaint against Split Rail for its continued employment of the individuals. [*Split Rail Fence Co. v. United States,* 852 F.3d 1228 (10th Cir. 2017)] (See *Immigration Law.*)

1. Using the IDDR approach, identify Split Rail's ethical dilemma. What steps might the company take to resolve it? Explain.
2. Is penalizing employers the best approach to take in attempting to curb illegal immigration? Discuss.

Critical Thinking and Writing Assignments

24–10. Time-Limited Group Assignment—Immigration. Nicole Tipton and Sadik Seferi owned and operated a restaurant in Iowa. Acting on a tip from the local police, agents of Immigration and Customs Enforcement executed search warrants at the restaurant and at an apartment where some restaurant workers lived. The agents discovered six undocumented aliens working at the restaurant and living together. When the I-9 forms for the restaurant's employees were reviewed, none were found for the six aliens. They were paid in cash while other employees were paid by check. Tipton and Seferi were charged with hiring and harboring illegal aliens. (See *Immigration Law.*)

1. The first group will develop an argument that Tipton and Seferi were guilty of hiring and harboring illegal aliens.
2. The second group will assess whether Tipton and Seferi can assert a defense by claiming that they did not know that the workers were unauthorized aliens.
3. The third group will determine the potential penalties that Tipton and Seferi could face for violating the Immigration Reform and Control Act by hiring six unauthorized workers.

25 Employment Discrimination

Focus Questions

The five Focus Questions *below are designed to help improve your understanding. After reading this chapter, you should be able to answer the following questions:*

1. What is required to establish a *prima facie* case of disparate-treatment discrimination?
2. What is a constructive discharge? To which employment discrimination claims does the theory of constructive discharge apply?
3. What federal act prohibits discrimination based on age?
4. What are three defenses to claims of employment discrimination?
5. Why are affirmative action programs often found to be unconstitutional?

"Equal rights for all, special privileges for none."

Thomas Jefferson
1743–1826
(Third president of the United States, 1801–1809)

Out of the civil rights movement of the 1960s grew a body of law protecting employees against discrimination in the workplace. Legislation, judicial decisions, and administrative agency actions restrict employers from discriminating against workers on the basis of race, color, religion, national origin, gender, sexual orientation, age, disability, or military status. A class of persons defined by one or more of these criteria is known as a **protected class.** The laws designed to protect these individuals embody the sentiment expressed by Thomas Jefferson in the chapter-opening quotation.

Suppose that Ellie, a manager at a large accounting firm, is up for promotion. Ellie's job performance reviews were uniformly positive, with one superior calling her an "outstanding professional" with "strong character and integrity." Furthermore, Ellie has recently played a key role in the firm's winning a multi-million-dollar contract with a local professional sports team.

After failing to get the promotion, Ellie learns that she is not popular among some of her coworkers. Specifically, Ellie discovers a series of memos in which the firm's male partners complain that she is too "manly" and needs "a "course at charm school." One partner writes that, to get promoted, Ellie would need to "walk, talk, and dress more femininely and wear make-up." Can Ellie sue for employment discrimination? Are the memos sufficient evidence to prove that she was not promoted because of her gender? These are some of the questions that will be answered in this chapter.

Several federal statutes prohibit *employment discrimination* against members of protected classes. Although this chapter focuses on federal statutes, many states have their own laws that protect employees against discrimination, and some provide more protection to employees than federal laws do.

25–1 Title VII of the Civil Rights Act

Protected Class A group of persons protected by specific laws because of the group's defining characteristics, including race, color, religion, national origin, gender sexual orientation, age, disability, and military status.

The most important statute covering employment discrimination is Title VII of the Civil Rights Act.[1] Title VII prohibits discrimination against employees, applicants, and union members on the basis of race, color, national origin, religion, gender, or sexual orientation at any stage of employment.

Title VII applies to employers with fifteen or more employees and labor unions with fifteen or more members. Title VII also applies to employment agencies, state and local governing units or agencies, and labor unions that operate hiring halls (where members go regularly to be assigned jobs as they become available). A special section of the act prohibits discrimination in most federal government employment. When Title VII applies to an employer, any employee—including an undocumented (alien) worker—can bring an action for employment discrimination.

25–1a The Equal Employment Opportunity Commission

Compliance with Title VII is monitored by the Equal Employment Opportunity Commission (EEOC). A victim of alleged discrimination must file a claim with the EEOC before bringing a suit against the employer. The EEOC may investigate the dispute and attempt to arrange an out-of-court settlement. If a voluntary agreement cannot be reached, the EEOC may file a suit against the employer on the employee's behalf.

Example 25.1 Luis, who is of Puerto Rican heritage, gets a job at an Allison's grocery store in San Diego. A training video instructs employees not to speak Spanish if there is a nonSpanish-speaking customer present. On his third day at Allison's, Luis is reprimanded by a supervisor for speaking Spanish to a Latino customer. Later, Luis is prohibited from speaking Spanish with his coworkers during breaks. He is also harassed by other employees for speaking Spanish at any time.

Luis files a claim with the EEOC because of this treatment. In turn, the EEOC sues Allison's, alleging that its enforcement of an unwritten, blanket "speak-English-only" policy is a form of national origin discrimination under Title VII. ■

sirtravelalot/shutterstock.com

What action can supermarket employees take if they feel they are being discriminated against based on their national origin?

If the EEOC decides not to investigate the claim, the EEOC issues a "right to sue" that allows the victim to bring a personal lawsuit against the employer. The EEOC does not investigate every claim of employment discrimination, regardless of the merits of the claim. Generally, it investigates only "priority cases," such as cases involving retaliatory discharge (firing an employee in retaliation for submitting a claim to the EEOC) and cases involving types of discrimination that are of particular concern to the EEOC.

25–1b Limitations on Class Actions

The United States Supreme Court issued an important decision that limited the rights of employees—as a group, or class—to bring discrimination claims against their employer. The Court held that to bring a class action, employees must prove a company-wide policy of discrimination that had a common effect on all the plaintiffs covered by the action.[2]

1. 42 U.S.C. Sections 2000e–2000e-17.
2. *Wal-Mart Stores, Inc. v. Dukes*, 564 U.S 338 131 S.Ct.2541, 180 L.Ed.2d 374 (2011). See also *Chen-Oster v. Goldman, Sachs & Co.*, 251 F.Supp.3d 579 (S.D.N.Y. 2017).

25–1c Intentional and Unintentional Discrimination

Title VII prohibits both intentional and unintentional discrimination.

Disparate-Treatment Discrimination A form of employment discrimination that results when an employer intentionally discriminates against employees who are members of protected classes.

***Prima Facie* Case** A case in which the plaintiff has produced sufficient evidence of a claim that the case will be decided for the plaintiff unless the defendant produces evidence to rebut the claim.

Intentional Discrimination

Intentional discrimination by an employer against an employee is known as **disparate-treatment discrimination**. Because intent can be difficult to prove, courts have established certain procedures for resolving disparate-treatment cases.

A plaintiff who sues on the basis of disparate-treatment discrimination in hiring must first make out a ***prima facie* case**. *Prima facie* is Latin for "at first sight." Legally, it refers to a fact that is presumed to be true unless contradicted by evidence.

Establishing a* Prima Facie *Case. To establish a *prima facie* case of disparate-treatment discrimination in hiring, a plaintiff must show all of the following:

1. The plaintiff is a member of a protected class.
2. The plaintiff applied and was qualified for the job in question.
3. The plaintiff was rejected by the employer.
4. The employer continued to seek applicants for the position or filled the position with a person not in a protected class.

Focus Question 1

What is required to establish a *prima facie* case of disparate-treatment discrimination?

A plaintiff who can meet these relatively easy requirements has made out a *prima facie* case of illegal discrimination and will win in the absence of a legally acceptable employer defense.

Sometimes, a current or former employee makes a claim of discrimination. When the plaintiff alleges that the employer fired or took some other adverse employment action against him or her, the same basic requirements apply. To establish a *prima facie* case, the plaintiff must show that the firing or adverse treatment was based on discriminatory reasons.

Burden-Shifting Procedure. Once a *prima facie* case has been established, the burden then shifts to the employer-defendant, who must articulate a legal reason for not hiring the plaintiff or for taking some other adverse employment action. If the employer did not have a legal reason for taking the action, the plaintiff wins.

If the employer can articulate a legitimate reason for the action, the burden shifts back to the plaintiff. To prevail, the plaintiff must then show that the employer's reason is a *pretext* (not the true reason) and that the employer's decision was actually motivated by discriminatory intent.

Disparate-Impact Discrimination Discrimination that results from certain employer practices or procedures that, although not discriminatory on their face, have a discriminatory effect.

Unintentional Discrimination

Employers often use interviews and tests to choose among a large number of applicants for job openings. Minimum educational requirements are also common. These practices and procedures may have an unintended discriminatory impact on a protected class. **Disparate-impact discrimination** occurs when a protected group is adversely affected by an employer's practices, procedures, or tests, even though they may not appear to be discriminatory.

In a disparate-impact discrimination case, the complaining party must first show statistically that the employer's practices, procedures, or tests are discriminatory in effect. Once the plaintiff has made out a *prima facie* case, the burden of proof shifts to the employer to show that the practices or procedures in question were justified.

There are two ways of showing that an employer's practices, procedures, or tests are effectively discriminatory—that is, that disparate-impact discrimination exists. These involve the pool of applicants and the rate of hiring.

Pool of Applicants. A plaintiff can prove a disparate impact by comparing the employer's workforce with the pool of qualified individuals available in the local labor market. The plaintiff must show that (1) as a result of educational or other job requirements or hiring procedures, (2) the percentage of nonwhites, women, or members of other protected classes in the employer's workforce (3) does not reflect the percentage of that group in the pool of qualified applicants. A plaintiff who can show a connection between the practice and the disparity has made out a *prima facie* case and need not provide evidence of discriminatory intent.

Rate of Hiring. A plaintiff can also prove disparate-impact discrimination by comparing the employer's selection rates of members and nonmembers of a protected class (for instance, whites and nonwhites). When a job requirement or hiring procedure excludes members of a protected class from an employer's workforce at a substantially higher rate than nonmembers, discrimination occurs, regardless of the balance in the employer's workforce.

The EEOC has devised a test, called the "four-fifths rule," to determine whether an employment selection procedure is discriminatory on its face. Under this rule, a selection rate for protected classes that is less than four-fifths, or 80 percent, of the rate for the group with the highest rate generally is regarded as evidence of disparate impact.

Example 25.2 Shady Cove District Fire Department administers an exam to applicants for the position of firefighter. At the exam session, one hundred white applicants take the test, and fifty pass and are hired. At the same exam session, sixty minority applicants take the test, but only twelve pass and are hired. Because twelve is less than four-fifths (80 percent) of fifty, the test will be considered discriminatory under the EEOC guidelines.

How might the "four-fifths rule" apply to the results of a fire department's entrance exam?

25–1d Discrimination Based on Race, Color, and National Origin

Title VII prohibits employers from discriminating against employees or job applicants on the basis of race, color, or national origin. If an employer's standards for selecting or promoting employees have a discriminatory effect on job applicants or employees in these protected classes, then a presumption of illegal discrimination arises. To avoid liability, the employer must then show that its standards have a substantial, demonstrable relationship to realistic qualifications for the job in question.

Example 25.3 Hai is an instructor at a university in Arkansas. When the university terminates his employment and hires a white male instructor, he files a lawsuit for employment discrimination. Hai is able to make out a *prima facie* case of discrimination because he (1) is a member of a protected class, (2) is qualified for the job, (3) suffered an adverse employment action, and (4) was replaced by a non-Asian instructor.

Nonetheless, the university can avoid liability for discrimination by showing that it discharged Hai for legitimate and nondiscriminatory reasons. For example, if Hai was terminated because he had argued with a university vice president and refused to comply with her instructions, the university is not liable for unlawful discrimination.

Reverse Discrimination

Note that discrimination based on race can also take the form of *reverse discrimination,* or discrimination against "majority" individuals, such as white males. **Case Example 25.4** Montana's Department of Transportation receives federal funds for transportation projects. As a condition of receiving the funds, Montana was required to set up a program to avoid discrimination in awarding contracts to disadvantaged business enterprises (DBEs). DBEs are businesses owned by members of historically disadvantaged groups, such as minorities. Mountain West Holding Company, Inc., installs signs, guardrails, and concrete barriers on highways in Montana and competes against DBEs for contracts.

Mountain West sued the state in federal court for violating Title VII by giving preference to the DBEs. At trial, the court pointed out that any classifications based on race are permissible "only if they are narrowly tailored measures that further compelling governmental interests." Montana thus had the burden of showing that its DBE program met this requirement. To show that the program addressed actual discrimination, the state presented a study that reported disparities in state-awarded contracts and provided anecdotal evidence of a "good ole' boys" network within the state's contracting industry. The district court accepted this evidence and concluded that Montana had satisfied its burden. A federal appellate court reversed, finding that the evidence was insufficient to prove a history of discrimination that would justify the preferences given to DBEs.[3]

Potential Section 1981 Claims Victims of racial or ethnic discrimination may also have a cause of action under 42 U.S.C. Section 1981. This section, which was enacted in 1866 to protect the rights of freed slaves, prohibits discrimination on the basis of race or ethnicity in the formation or enforcement of contracts. Because employment is often a contractual relationship, Section 1981 can provide an alternative basis for a plaintiff's action and is potentially advantageous because it does not place a cap on damages. (There is a cap placed on Title VII damages from small employers, as will be discussed later.)

25–1e Discrimination Based on Religion

Title VII also prohibits government employers, private employers, and unions from discriminating against persons because of their religion. (This chapter's *Adapting the Law to the Online Environment* feature discusses how employers who examine prospective employees' social media posts, including posts concerning religion, might engage in unlawful discrimination.)

Employers cannot treat their employees more or less favorably based on the employees' religious beliefs or practices and cannot require employees to participate in any religious activity (or forbid them from participating in one). **Example 25.5** Jason, a salesperson for TC Chevy, does not attend the weekly prayer meetings of dealership employees for several months. Then he is discharged by his employer. If Jason can show that the dealership required its employees to attend prayer gatherings and fired him for not attending, he has a valid claim of religious discrimination.

Reasonable Accommodation An employer must "reasonably accommodate" the religious practices of its employees, unless to do so would cause undue hardship to the employer's business. This means that an employer may need to make reasonable adjustments to the work environment to allow employees to practice their religion. Reasonable accommodation is required even if an employee's belief is not based on the doctrines of a traditionally recognized religion, such as Christianity or Judaism, or a particular denomination, such as Baptist. The only requirement is that the belief be sincerely held by the employee.

Tatiana Chekryzhova/shutterstock.com

Why is it likely that a hairdresser who is fired for taking a day off on a major Jewish holiday will succeed in a religious discrimination lawsuit against her former employer?

Example 25.6 Tomilina, who is Jewish, works as a hairdresser for Sally's Salon. Two weeks before Yom Kippur, Tomilina asks Sally if she can have a day off on the important Jewish holiday, which always falls on a Saturday. Sally denies the request. Tomilina fails to show up for work on Yom Kippur, and Sally fires her.

When Tomilina sues Sally for religious discrimination, Sally presents two defenses. First, reasonably accommodating Tomilina's request would cause undue hardship, because Saturday is the salon's busiest day of the week, and Sally needs all her employees serving customers. Second, Tomilina is not a religious person, and the day off was really for personal reasons. If Tomilina can show that (a) she was able to reschedule her Saturday appointments, and (b) her religious beliefs are sincere, then she will most likely prevail in her Title VII suit against Sally.

3. *Mountain West Holding Co., Inc. v. State of Montana*, 691 Fed.Appx. 326 (9th Cir. 2017).

Adapting the Law to the Online Environment

Hiring Discrimination Based on Social Media Posts

Human resource officers in most companies routinely check job candidates' social media posts when deciding whom to hire. Certainly, every young person is warned not to post photos that they might later regret having made available to potential employers. But a more serious issue involves standard reviewing of job candidates' social media information. Specifically, do employers discriminate based on such information?

An Experiment in Hiring Discrimination via Online Social Networks

Two researchers at Carnegie-Mellon University conducted an experiment to determine whether social media information posted by prospective employees influences employers' hiring decisions.[a] The researchers created false résumés and social media profiles. They submitted job applications on behalf of the fictional "candidates" to about four thousand U.S. employers. They then compared employers' responses to different groups—for instance, to Muslim candidates versus Christian candidates.

The researchers found that candidates whose public profiles indicated that they were Muslim were less likely to be called for interviews than Christian applicants. The difference was particularly pronounced in parts of the country with more conservative residents. In those locations, Muslims received callbacks only 2 percent of the time, compared with 17 percent for Christian applicants. According to the authors of the study, "Hiring discrimination via online searches of candidates may not be widespread, but online disclosures of personal traits can significantly influence the hiring decisions of a self-selected set of employers."

Job Candidates' Perception of the Hiring Process

Job candidates frequently view the hiring process as unfair when they know that their social media profiles have been used in the selection process. This perception may make litigation more likely. Nevertheless, 70 percent of employers report using social media to recruit job applicants. More than half of those who recruit in this manner admit that they have disqualified applicants based on content found in their social media accounts.[b]

The EEOC Speaks Up

The Equal Employment Opportunity Commission (EEOC) has investigated how prospective employers can use social media to engage in discrimination in the hiring process. Given that the Society for Human Resource Management estimates that more than three-fourths of its members use social media in their employment screening process, the EEOC is interested in regulating this procedure.

Social media sites, examined closely, can provide information to a prospective employer on the applicant's race, color, national origin, disability, religion, and other protected characteristics. The EEOC has reminded employers that such information—whether it comes from social media postings or other sources—may not legally be used to make employment decisions on prohibited bases, such as race, gender, sexual orientation and religion.

Critical Thinking

Can you think of a way a company could use information from an applicant's social media posts without running the risk of being accused of hiring discrimination?

a. A. Acquisti and C. N. Fong, "An Experiment in Hiring Discrimination via Online Social Networks," *Social Service Research Network,* October 26, 2014.

b. Saige Driver, "Keep It Clean: Social Media Screenings Gain in Popularity." *www.businessnewsdaily.com. Business News Daily:* March 23, 2020, Web.

Undue Hardship As mentioned, an employer is not required to make an accommodation that would cause the employer undue hardship. A reasonable attempt to accommodate does not necessarily require the employer to make every change an employee requests or to make a permanent change for an employee's benefit.

Case Example 25.7 Leontine K. Robinson worked as an administrative assistant in the emergency department at the Children's Hospital Boston. The hospital started requiring all employees who worked in or had access to patient-care areas to receive the influenza (flu) vaccine. When Robinson (who had previously received a tetanus vaccine) refused to get the flu vaccine based on her religious beliefs, the hospital terminated her employment. Robinson filed a lawsuit alleging religious discrimination. The hospital argued that allowing Robinson to keep her patient-care position without receiving the vaccine would create an undue hardship. The court agreed and granted a summary judgment for the hospital.[4]

4. *Robinson v. Children's Hospital Boston,* 2016 WL 1337255 (D.Mass. 2016).

25–1f Discrimination Based on Gender

Under Title VII, as well as other federal acts, employers are forbidden from discriminating against employees on the basis of gender. Employers are prohibited from classifying jobs as male or female and from advertising positions as male or female unless they can prove that the gender of the applicant is essential to the job. In addition, employers cannot have separate male and female seniority lists and cannot refuse to promote employees based on gender.

Gender Must Be a Determining Factor Generally, to succeed in a suit for gender discrimination, a plaintiff must demonstrate that gender was a determining factor in the employer's decision to fire or refuse to hire or promote her or him. Typically, this involves looking at all of the surrounding circumstances.

Case Example 25.8 Evangeline Parker received multiple promotions at Reema Consulting Services, Inc. (RCSI). In response, a jealous coworker told other employees that Parker had been promoted because she was having sex with a superior. After this false rumor spread, Parker was informed that she had become ineligible for further advancement and was blamed for "bringing the situation to the workplace."

A trial court barred Parker's gender discrimination lawsuit, finding that RCSI's actions, while reprehensible, were based on her alleged conduct (the affair with her superior), not her gender. A federal appeals court disagreed, emphasizing the continuing power of the cultural stereotype that women use sex to achieve success in the business world. This same stereotype does not apply to successful men. Therefore, the court ruled, gender was a possible determining factor in RCSI's conduct toward Parker, and her lawsuit could proceed.[5] ■

Pregnancy Discrimination The Pregnancy Discrimination Act[6] expanded Title VII's definition of gender discrimination to include discrimination based on pregnancy. Women affected by pregnancy, childbirth, or related medical conditions must be treated the same as other persons not so affected but similar in ability to work. For instance, an employer cannot discriminate against a pregnant woman by withholding benefits available to others under employee benefit programs.

An employer is required to reasonably accommodate a worker who is pregnant. In the following case, an employer accommodated many of its employees who had lifting restrictions due to disabilities. The employer refused to accommodate a pregnant employee with a similar restriction. Did this refusal constitute a violation of the Pregnancy Discrimination Act?

5. *Parker v. Reema Consulting Services, Inc.*, 915 F.3d 297 (4th Cir. 2019).
6. 42 U.S.C. Section 2000e(k).

Case 25.1

Young v. United Parcel Service, Inc.

United States Supreme Court, 575 U.S. 206, 135 S.Ct. 1338 191 L.Ed.2d 279 (2015).

Facts Peggy Young was a driver for United Parcel Service, Inc. (UPS). When she became pregnant, her doctor advised her not to lift more than twenty pounds. UPS required drivers to lift up to seventy pounds and told Young that she could not work under a lifting restriction. She filed a suit in a federal district court against UPS, claiming an unlawful refusal to accommodate her pregnancy-related lifting restriction.

Juanmonino/iStock Unreleased/Getty Images

Is UPS required to offer a pregnant employee a less physically demanding job?

Young alleged that UPS had multiple light-duty-for-injury categories to accommodate individuals whose non-pregnancy-related disabilities created work restrictions similar to hers. UPS responded that, because Young did not fall into any of those categories, it had not discriminated against her. The court issued a summary judgment in UPS's favor. The U.S. Court of Appeals of the Fourth Circuit affirmed the judgment. Young appealed to the United States Supreme Court.

Issue Did Young create a genuine dispute as to whether UPS provided more favorable treatment to employees whose situation could not reasonably be distinguished from hers?

Decision Yes. The United States Supreme Court vacated the judgment of the U.S. Court of Appeals for the Fourth Circuit and remanded the case for further proceedings. On remand, the court must also determine whether Young created a genuine issue of material fact as to whether UPS's stated reasons for treating Young less favorably were a pretext (false reason).

Reason In an action under the Pregnancy Discrimination Act, a plaintiff must show that the employer's policies impose a significant burden on pregnant employees. Thus, to create a genuine issue of material fact in this case, the plaintiff needs to provide evidence that the employer accommodates nonpregnant workers while failing to accommodate pregnant workers.

If Young's allegations are true, she can show that UPS accommodates nonpregnant employees with lifting restrictions and does not accommodate pregnant employees with similar limitations. This showing would establish a *prima facie* case of disparate treatment. In response to UPS's defense, Young can point out the fact that the employer has multiple policies to accommodate nonpregnant employees with lifting restrictions. This fact might suggest that UPS's reasons for not accommodating pregnant employees with lifting restrictions are weak—"to the point that a jury could find that its reasons for failing to accommodate pregnant employees give rise to an inference of intentional discrimination."

Critical Thinking

• **Legal Environment** *Could UPS have succeeded in this case if it had claimed simply that it would be more expensive or less convenient to include pregnant women among those whom it accommodates? Explain.*

Protections Extend to Employees' Post-Pregnancy. An employer must continue to reasonably accommodate medical conditions of an employee related to pregnancy and childbirth, even after the pregnancy has ended. **Case Example 25.9** Professional Ambulance, LLC, hired Allison Mayer as an emergency medical technician (EMT) while she was still breastfeeding an infant. She was supposed to work three twelve-hour shifts a week, but Professional did not provide her with a schedule so that she could arrange child care. Mayer informed Professional that she needed to take short breaks to use a pump to express breast milk (lactation breaks). At first, her supervisor told her to take these breaks in the restroom, but Mayer objected because the conditions were unsanitary. Then the employer made Mayer take lactation breaks in an office that was not private or secure and made Mayer uncomfortable because the male EMTs could hear her pumping.

A few weeks later, Professional fired Mayer, claiming that it was because other employees had complained about her being rude and abusive. The employer refused to provide her with further explanation and replaced her with a male EMT with fewer qualifications. Mayer sued. A federal district court found that Mayer had established a *prima facie* case of discrimination on the basis of pregnancy, childbirth, or related medical conditions.[7]

Wage Discrimination The Equal Pay Act[8] requires equal pay for male and female employees doing similar work at the same establishment. To determine whether the Equal Pay Act has been violated, a court will look to the primary duties of the two jobs—the job content rather than the job description controls. If the wage differential is due to "any factor other than gender," such as a seniority or merit system, then it does not violate the Equal Pay Act.

The Lilly Ledbetter Fair Pay Act[9] made discriminatory wages actionable under federal law regardless of when the discrimination began. Previously, plaintiffs had had to file a complaint within a limited time period. Today, if a plaintiff continues to work for the employer while receiving discriminatory wages, the time period for filing a complaint is basically unlimited.

7. *Mayer v. Professional Ambulance, LLC,* 211 F.Supp.3d 408 (D.R.I. 2016).
8. 29 U.S.C. Section 206(d).
9. Pub. L. No. 111-2, 123 Stat. 5 (January 5, 2009), amending 42 U.S.C. Section 2000e-5[e].

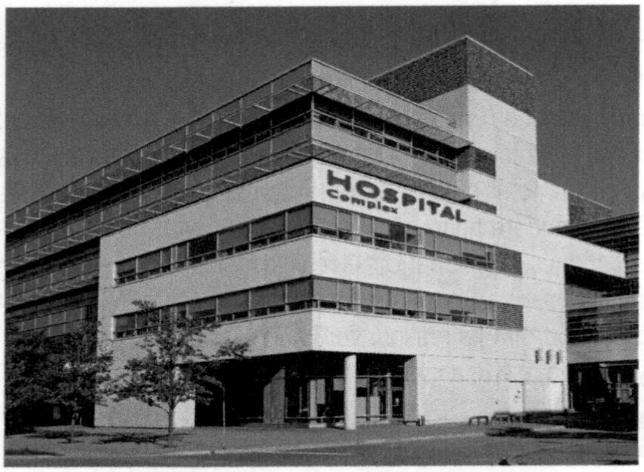

If a hospital does not hire a physician because she identifies as a transgender woman, has the hospital violated Title VII?

Discrimination against Transgender Persons In the past, most courts held that federal law (Title VII) does not protect transgender persons from discrimination. Until 2020, federal courts started interpreting Title VII as applicable to discrimination because of sexual orientation.

Case Example 25.10 Dr. Deborah Fabian applied for a position as an on-call orthopedic surgeon at the Hospital of Central Connecticut. The hospital apparently declined to hire Fabian because she disclosed her identity as a transgender woman. Fabian sued the hospital alleging violations of Title VII of the Civil Rights Act and the Connecticut Fair Employment Practices Act (CFEPA).

The hospital filed a motion for summary judgment, arguing that neither Title VII nor the Connecticut statute prohibits discrimination on the basis of transgender identity. The federal district court rejected this argument, however, finding that discrimination on the basis of transgender identity is discrimination on the basis of gender for Title VII purposes. Fabian was entitled to take her case to a jury and to argue violations of Title VII and the CFEPA.[10]

The Supreme Court on June 15, 2020, in the case *Bostock v. Clayton County* (combined with two other cases), ruled that an employer who fires an individual merely for being gay, lesbian, or transgender violates Title VII. In other words, adverse employment decisions based on gender identity are necessarily a form of gender discrimination and therefore illegal.

Ethical Issue

Should corporations regulate pronoun use in the workplace? The former Nike employee, Jazz Lyles, self-identifies as transmasculine and chooses to be referred to by the pronouns they/them/their. After being repeatedly "misgendered," or denied a preferred gender identity, by coworkers, Lyles left Nike and filed a $1.1 million discrimination lawsuit against the company. Could this situation have been avoided? Along with society at large, corporate America is being asked by many transgender and gender-nonconforming individuals to use pronouns other than he/him/his or she/her/hers. When this doesn't happen, according to one employment attorney, bias takes place in the form of "disbelief, disregard, and disrespect."

For many years prior to 2020, federal law was unsettled concerning the applicability of Title VII to gender identity. As a result, employers were often at a loss for guidance when it came to resolving these disputes, particularly when one employee's religious beliefs clashed with another's gender identity requirements. A solution favored by many human resources experts was a workplace policy based on the concept of respect. That is, employees did not have to "embrace or value" a colleague's choice of pronoun use, but they did have to respect it.

25–1g Constructive Discharge

Constructive Discharge A termination of employment brought about by making the employee's working conditions so intolerable that the employee reasonably feels compelled to leave.

The majority of Title VII complaints involve unlawful discrimination in decisions to hire or fire employees. In some situations, however, employees who leave their jobs voluntarily can claim that they were "constructively discharged" by the employer. **Constructive discharge** occurs when the employer causes the employee's working conditions to be so intolerable that a reasonable person in the employee's position would feel compelled to quit.

10. *Fabian v. Hospital of Central Connecticut*, 172 F.Supp.3d 509 (D.Conn. 2016). See also *Christiansen v. Omnicom Group, Incorporated*, 852 F.3d 195 (2d Cir. 2017).

When constructive discharge is claimed, the employee can pursue damages for loss of income, including back pay. These damages ordinarily are not available to an employee who left a job voluntarily.

Proving Constructive Discharge To prove constructive discharge, an employee must present objective proof of intolerable working conditions. The employee must also show that the employer knew or had reason to know about the conditions, yet failed to correct them within a reasonable period. In addition, courts generally require the employee to show causation—that the employer's unlawful discrimination caused the working conditions to be intolerable. Put in a different way, the employee's resignation must be a foreseeable result of the employer's discriminatory action. Courts weigh the facts on a case-by-case basis.

Focus Question 2

What is a constructive discharge? To which employment discrimination claims does the theory of constructive discharge apply?

Employee demotion is one of the most frequently cited reasons for a finding of constructive discharge, particularly when the employee was subjected to humiliation. **Example 25.11** Khalil's employer humiliates him in front of his coworkers by informing him that he is being demoted to an inferior position. Khalil's coworkers continually insult and harass him about his national origin (he is from Iran). The employer is aware of this discriminatory treatment but does nothing to remedy the situation, despite repeated complaints from Khalil. After several months, Khalil quits his job and files a Title VII claim. In this situation, Khalil would likely have sufficient evidence to maintain an action for constructive discharge in violation of Title VII. ■

Constructive Discharge Applies to All Title VII Discrimination Note that constructive discharge is a theory that plaintiffs can use to establish any type of discrimination claims under Title VII, including race, color, national origin, religion, gender, and sexual orientation. It is most commonly asserted in cases involving sexual harassment. Constructive discharge has also been successfully used in situations involving discrimination based on age or disability.

25–1h Sexual Harassment

Title VII protection against **sexual harassment** in the workplace addresses two types of harassment:

Sexual Harassment The demanding of sexual favors in return for job promotions or other benefits, or language or conduct that is so sexually offensive that it creates a hostile working environment.

1. *Quid pro quo* harassment occurs when sexual favors are demanded in return for job opportunities, promotions, salary increases, or other benefits. *Quid pro quo* is a Latin phrase that is often translated as "something in exchange for something else."
2. *Hostile-environment* harassment occurs when a pattern of sexually offensive conduct runs throughout the workplace and the employer has not taken steps to prevent or discourage it. In this situation, the workplace is permeated with discriminatory intimidation, ridicule, and insult, and this behavior is so severe or pervasive that it alters the conditions of employment.

Harassment by Supervisors For an employer to be held liable for a supervisor's sexual harassment, the supervisor normally must have taken a *tangible employment action* against the employee. A **tangible employment action** is a significant change in employment status or benefits, such as occurs when an employee is fired, refused a promotion, demoted, or reassigned to a position with significantly different responsibilities. Only a supervisor, or another person acting with the authority of the employer, can cause this sort of injury. A constructive discharge also qualifies as a tangible employment action.

Tangible Employment Action A significant change in employment status or benefits, such as occurs when an employee is fired, refused a promotion, or reassigned to a lesser position.

The United States Supreme Court has issued several important rulings in cases alleging sexual harassment by supervisors that established what is known as the "*Ellerth/Faragher* affirmative defense."[11] The defense has two elements:

1. That the employer has taken reasonable care to prevent and promptly correct any sexually harassing behavior (by establishing effective antiharassment policies and complaint procedures, for instance).
2. That the plaintiff-employee unreasonably failed to take advantage of any preventive or corrective opportunities provided by the employer to avoid harm.

An employer that can prove both elements normally will not be liable for a supervisor's harassment.

Retaliation by Employers Employers sometimes retaliate against employees who complain about sexual harassment or other Title VII violations. Retaliation can take many forms. An employer might demote or fire the person, or otherwise change the terms, conditions, and benefits of employment. Title VII prohibits retaliation, and employees can sue their employers on that basis.

In *retaliation claims*, individuals assert that they have suffered a harm as a result of making a charge, testifying, or participating in a Title VII investigation or proceeding. Plaintiffs do not have to prove that the challenged action adversely affected their workplace or employment. Instead, to prove retaliation, plaintiffs must show that the challenged action was one that would likely have dissuaded a reasonable worker from making or supporting a charge of discrimination. Title VII's retaliation protection extends to an employee who speaks out about discrimination during an employer's internal investigation of another employee's complaint.

This chapter's *Business Law Analysis* feature illustrates how courts analyze retaliation claims.

11. *Burlington Industries, Inc. v. Ellerth,* 524 U.S. 742, 118 S.Ct. 2257, 141 L.Ed.2d 633 (1998); and *Faragher v. City of Boca Raton,* 524 U.S. 775, 118 S.Ct. 2275, 141 L.Ed.2d 662 (1998).

Retaliation Claims

Business Law Analysis

Shane Dawson, a male homosexual, worked for Entek International. Some of Dawson's coworkers, including his supervisor, made derogatory comments about his sexual orientation. Dawson's work deteriorated. He filed a complaint with Entek's human resource department. Two days later, he was fired. State law made it unlawful for an employer to discriminate against an individual based on sexual orientation. Can Dawson establish a claim for retaliation?

Analysis: Title VII prohibits retaliation. In retaliation claims, individuals assert that they suffered harm as a result of making a charge, testifying, or participating in a Title VII investigation or proceeding. To prove retaliation, a plaintiff must show that the challenged action was one that would likely have dissuaded a reasonable worker from making or supporting a charge of discrimination.

Result and Reasoning: Dawson can establish a claim for retaliation in his state. Under the applicable state law, it was unlawful for an employer to discriminate against an individual based on sexual orientation. Dawson was subjected to derision on the part of coworkers, including his supervisor, based on his sexual orientation. He filed a complaint with his employer's human resource department. Two days later, he was fired. The fact that the firing occurred so soon after the complaint filing would support a retaliation claim, as would the other circumstances, especially the supervisor's conduct. Also, the discharge would likely have tended to dissuade others from making claims of discrimination. Therefore, it is likely that Dawson offered enough evidence to establish a claim for retaliation.

Harassment by Coworkers and Nonemployees When the harassment of coworkers, rather than supervisors, creates a hostile working environment, an employee may still have a cause of action against the employer. Normally, though, the employer will be held liable only if the employer knew, or should have known, about the harassment and failed to take immediate remedial action.

Occasionally, a court may also hold an employer liable for harassment by *nonemployees* if the employer knew about the harassment and failed to take corrective action. **Example 25.12** Gordon, who owns and manages a Great Bites restaurant, knows that one of his regular customers, Dean, repeatedly harasses Sharon, a waitress. If Gordon does nothing and permits the harassment to continue, he may be liable under Title VII even though Dean is not an employee of the restaurant.

In the following case, a female firefighter claimed that her male coworkers subjected her to a hostile working environment and that the fire department knew about the harassment but failed to act. The city (the defendant) responded that there was no evidence to support this claim.

Case 25.2

Franchina v. City of Providence

United States Court of Appeals, First Circuit, 881 F.3d 32 (2018).

Facts Lori Franchina, a rescue lieutenant with the Providence Fire Department, was assigned to work a shift with firefighter Andre Ferro. During the shift, Ferro subjected her to unprofessional sexual comments and conduct. Based on Franchina's account of Ferro's actions, Chief Curt Varone filed an intra-department complaint, charging Ferro with sexual harassment.

Other firefighters then began to treat Franchina with contempt. She was subjected to insubordination and verbal assaults, and was spit on and shoved, among other things. She submitted forty different complaints of harassment to her superiors. No action was taken against the perpetrators. Franchina filed a suit in a federal district court against the city, asserting that she was subjected to a hostile work environment as a result of her gender in violation of Title VII. The city argued that Franchina presented no evidence to support her claim. A jury issued a verdict in her favor and awarded damages. The city appealed.

Issue Was the evidence sufficient to support the jury's verdict of a hostile work environment?

Decision Yes. The U.S. Court of Appeals for the First Circuit affirmed the judgment. "The abuse Lori Franchina suffered at the hands of the Providence Fire Department is nothing short of abhorrent. . . . Employers should be cautioned that turning a blind eye to blatant discrimination does not generally fare well under anti-discrimination laws like Title VII."

Reason A hostile work environment exists when a workplace is infused with discriminatory insults and behavior so pervasive or severe that it changes the conditions of the victim's employment. In this case, the intimidating remarks and ridicule directed toward Franchina were shown to be motivated by her gender. The male firefighters' repeated use of derogatory, gender-specific epithets—such as *slut, whore, bitch,* and *Frangina* (a combination of her last name and the word *vagina*)—was sufficient evidence of sexual harassment to support the jury's verdict. "This type of sexually based *animus* [hostility] is a hallmark of Title VII."

But there was more. Title VII prohibits subjecting the members of one gender to conditions of employment to which members of the other gender are not exposed. Evidence showed that within the Providence fire department female firefighters were treated as less competent—unless they were perceived as willing to have sex with the male firefighters. Women perceived as willing to have sex with their male coworkers were treated better. "This sampling of evidence demonstrates that the accumulated effect . . . taken together constitutes a hostile work environment."

Critical Thinking

- **Economic** *Because of the constant harassment, Franchina had to be placed on injured-on-duty status. Later, diagnosed with severe post-traumatic stress disorder and unable to work again as a rescue lieutenant, she "retired." What is the appropriate measure of damages for this result? Discuss.*
- **Legal Environment** *What steps might an employer take to avoid the circumstances that occurred in the Franchina case?*

Same-Sex Harassment In *Oncale v. Sundowner Offshore Services, Inc.*,[12] the United States Supreme Court held that Title VII protection extends to individuals who are sexually harassed by members of the same sex. Proving that the harassment in same-sex cases is "based on sex" can be difficult, though. It is usually easier to establish a case of same-sex harassment when the harasser is homosexual.

Sexual-Orientation Harassment Federal law (Title VII) is now interpreted by the Supreme Court to prohibit discrimination or harassment based on a person's sexual orientation. Prior to June 2020, a growing number of states, however, enacted laws that prohibited sexual orientation discrimination in private employment. Some states, such as Michigan, explicitly prohibited discrimination based on a person's gender identity or expression. In addition, many companies and organizations, such as the National Football League, voluntarily established nondiscrimination policies that included sexual orientation.

25–1i Online Harassment

Employees' online activities can create a hostile working environment in many ways. Racial jokes, ethnic slurs, or other comments contained in e-mail, texts, blogs, or social media posts can become the basis for a claim of hostile-environment harassment or other forms of discrimination. Similarly, a worker who regularly sees sexually explicit and offensive images on a coworker's computer screen may claim that they create a hostile working environment.

Employers may be able to avoid liability for online harassment if they take prompt remedial action. **Example 25.13** While working at TriCom, Shonda receives racially harassing tweets from another employee. Shortly afterward, the company issues a warning to the offending employee about the proper use of the Internet at work and holds two meetings to discuss company policy on the use of social media. If Shonda sues TriCom for racial discrimination, a court may find that because the employer took prompt remedial action, TriCom should not be held liable for its employee's racially harassing tweets. ■

25–1j Remedies under Title VII

Employer liability under Title VII may be extensive. If a plaintiff successfully proves that unlawful discrimination occurred, that plaintiff may be awarded reinstatement, back pay, retroactive promotions, and damages. Compensatory damages are available in cases of intentional discrimination. Punitive damages may be recovered against a private employer only if the employer acted with malice or reckless indifference to an individual's rights.

The total amount of compensatory and punitive damages that plaintiffs can recover depends on the size of the employer. For instance, there is a $50,000 cap on damages from employers with one hundred or fewer employees.

25–2 Discrimination Based on Age, Disability, or Military Status

Certain types of employment discrimination that are not banned by Title VII of the Civil Rights Act are prohibited under other statutes. These include discrimination based on age, disability, and military status.

12. 523 U.S. 75, 118 S.Ct. 998, 140 L.Ed.2d 207 (1998).

25–2a Discrimination Based on Age

Focus Question 3

What federal act prohibits discrimination based on age?

Age discrimination is potentially the most widespread form of discrimination, because anyone—regardless of race, color, national origin, or gender—could be a victim at some point in life. The Age Discrimination in Employment Act (ADEA)[13] prohibits employment discrimination on the basis of age against individuals forty years of age or older. The act also prohibits mandatory retirement for nonmanagerial workers. In addition, the act protects federal and private-sector employees from retaliation based on age-related complaints.

For the act to apply, an employer must have twenty or more employees, and the employer's business activities must affect interstate commerce. The EEOC administers the ADEA, but the act also permits private causes of action against employers for age discrimination.

Procedures under the ADEA The burden-shifting procedure under the ADEA differs from the procedure under Title VII. As explained earlier, if the plaintiff in a Title VII case can show that the employer was motivated, at least in part, by unlawful discrimination, the burden of proof shifts to the employer to articulate a legitimate nondiscriminatory reason. Thus, in cases in which the employer has a "mixed motive" for discharging an employee, the employer has the burden of proving that its reason was legitimate.

Under the ADEA, in contrast, a plaintiff must show that the unlawful discrimination was not just a reason but *the* reason for the adverse employment action. In other words, the employee has the burden of establishing "but for" causation—but for the plaintiff's age, the adverse action would not have happened.

Prima Facie *Age Discrimination Case.* To establish a *prima facie* case, the plaintiff must show the following:

1. The plaintiff is a member of the protected age group.
2. The plaintiff was qualified for the position from which he or she was discharged.
3. The plaintiff was discharged because of age discrimination.

Then the burden shifts to the employer to give a legitimate nondiscriminatory reason for the adverse action.

Pretext. If the employer offers a legitimate reason for its action, then the plaintiff must show that the stated reason is only a pretext (a false reason) and that the plaintiff's age was the real reason for the employer's decision.

Case Example 25.14 Jerry Stever was a financial adviser at US Bancorp, Inc. He was terminated at age sixty-eight for "deficient performance." Stever sued US Bancorp in federal court alleging age discrimination and claiming that deficient performance was a pretext. The plaintiff proved that he was in the protected age group (over forty) and was qualified for the position, but he lacked proof that he had been discharged because of his age.

Stever argued that two younger financial advisers had received more favorable treatment from the company than he had. Showing that "similarly situated" younger employees were treated more favorably would have given rise to an inference of discrimination. The court found no evidence of preferential treatment, however. One of the men had generated considerably more revenue than Stever, and the other man differed from Stever in terms of seniority and prior performance. Thus, they were not similarly situated to Stever.

Stever also claimed that his manager had made the comment, "we old dogs had to learn new tricks." The district court found that this single stray remark was not sufficient to demonstrate age discrimination and granted summary judgment to US Bancorp. A federal appellate court affirmed the decision on appeal.[14]

---

13. 29 U.S.C. Sections 621–634.

14. *Stever v. US Bancorp, Inc.*, 690 Fed.Appx. 491 (9th Cir. 2017).

Burlingham/Shutterstock.com

A male bank employee who is over sixty years old is fired for not performing well. If he believes the reason was a pretext, what must he do to establish a *prima facie* case for age discrimination?

State Employees Not Covered by the ADEA Generally, the states are immune from lawsuits brought by private individuals in federal court, unless a state consents to the suit. This immunity stems from the United States Supreme Court's interpretation of the Eleventh Amendment.

State immunity under the Eleventh Amendment is not absolute, however. When fundamental rights are at stake, Congress has the power to abolish state immunity through legislation. For instance, Congress has chosen to subject states to private lawsuits under the Family and Medical Leave Act. State employers are usually immune from suits brought by employees under the ADEA, the Americans with Disabilities Act, and the Fair Labor Standards Act, however.

25–2b Discrimination Based on Disability

The Americans with Disabilities Act (ADA)[15] prohibits disability-based discrimination in workplaces with fifteen or more workers (with the exception of state government employers, who are generally immune). Basically, the ADA requires that employers reasonably accommodate the needs of persons with disabilities unless to do so would cause undue hardship. The ADA Amendments Act broadened the ADA's coverage.[16]

Procedures under the ADA To prevail on a claim under the ADA, a plaintiff must show all of the following:

1. The plaintiff has a disability.
2. The plaintiff is otherwise qualified for the employment in question.
3. The plaintiff was excluded from the employment solely because of the disability.

As in Title VII cases, a plaintiff must pursue the claim through the EEOC before filing an action in court for a violation of the ADA.

The EEOC may decide to investigate and perhaps even sue the employer on behalf of the employee. If the EEOC decides not to sue, then the employee is entitled to sue in court. The EEOC can bring a suit against an employer for disability-based discrimination even though the employee previously agreed to submit any job-related disputes to arbitration.

Plaintiffs in lawsuits brought under the ADA may seek many of the same remedies available under Title VII. These include reinstatement, back pay, a limited amount of compensatory and punitive damages (for intentional discrimination), and certain other forms of relief. Repeat violators may be ordered to pay fines of up to $100,000.

What Is a Disability? The ADA is broadly drafted to cover persons with a wide range of disabilities. Specifically, the ADA defines *disability* to include any of the following:

1. A physical or mental impairment that substantially limits one or more of an individual's major life activities.
2. A record of such an impairment.
3. Being regarded as having such an impairment.

15. 42 U.S.C. Sections 12102–12118.
16. 42 U.S.C. Sections 12103 and 12205a.

Health conditions that have been considered disabilities under the federal law include alcoholism, acquired immune deficiency syndrome (AIDS), blindness, cancer, cerebral palsy, diabetes, heart disease, muscular dystrophy, and paraplegia. Testing positive for the human immunodeficiency virus (HIV) has qualified as a disability, as has morbid obesity. (A morbidly obese person weighs twice the normal weight for the person's height.)

Note that obesity does not qualify as a disability under the ADA unless it involves physical impairment. **Case Example 25.15** Melvin Morriss applied for a machinist position at BNSF Railway. He was offered the position conditioned on a medical review, which was required because the position was considered safety sensitive. BNSF physicians found that Morriss's body mass index, or BMI, exceeded 40, identifying him as seriously obese. (BMI is a typical method of evaluating a person's body fat.) BNSF had a policy of not employing workers with BMIs of 40 or more in safety-sensitive positions. Thus, the company rescinded its offer of employment.

Morriss sued, alleging discrimination on the basis of disability, but the court found that Morriss's obesity was not a physical impairment under the ADA. Morriss was otherwise in good health and did not suffer from any medical condition that caused his obesity or any medical condition associated with obesity. Therefore, the court granted a summary judgment to BNSF Railway. A federal appellate court affirmed.[17]

Association with Disabled Persons. A separate provision in the ADA prevents employers from taking adverse employment actions based on stereotypes or assumptions about individuals who associate with people who have disabilities.[18] **Example 25.16** Joan, an employer, refuses to hire Edward, who has a daughter with a physical disability. She bases her decision on the assumption that, because of his daughter's disability, Edward will miss work too often or be unreliable. Edward can sue Joan for violating the ADA's provisions.

Mitigating Measures. At one time, the courts focused on whether a person was disabled *after* the use of corrective devices or medication. Thus, a severely nearsighted person whose eyesight could be corrected by wearing glasses did not qualify as having a disability. Then Congress amended the ADA to strengthen its protections and prohibit employers from considering mitigating measures, such as medications, when determining if an individual has a disability.

Disability is now determined on a case-by-case basis. A condition may fit the definition of disability in one set of circumstances, but not in another. **Spotlight Case Example 25.17** Larry Rohr, a welding specialist for a power district in Arizona, was diagnosed with type 2 diabetes. If he fails to follow a complex regimen of daily insulin injections and blood tests, as well as a strict diet, his blood sugar will rise to a level that aggravates his disease. Therefore, Rohr's physician forbade him from taking work assignments that involved overnight, out-of-town travel, which were common in his job.

Because of these limitations, the power district asked him to transfer, apply for disability, or take early retirement. Rohr sued for disability discrimination. The lower court granted summary judgment for the employer. Rohr appealed. A federal appellate court reversed. The court held that under the amended ADA, diabetes is a disability if it significantly restricts an individual's eating (a major life activity), as it did for Rohr. Therefore, Rohr was entitled to a trial on his discrimination claim.[19]

17. *Morriss v. BNSF Railway Co.*, 817 F.3d 1104 (8th Cir. 2016).

18. 42 U.S.C. Section 12112(b)(4).

19. *Rohr v. Salt River Project Agricultural Improvement and Power District*, 555 F.3d 850 (9th Cir. 2009).

Disclosure of Confidential Medical Information. ADA provisions also require employers to keep their employees' medical information confidential. An employee who discovers that an employer has disclosed the employee's confidential medical information has a right to sue the employer—even if the employee was not technically disabled. The prohibition against disclosure also applies to other employees acting on behalf of the employer.

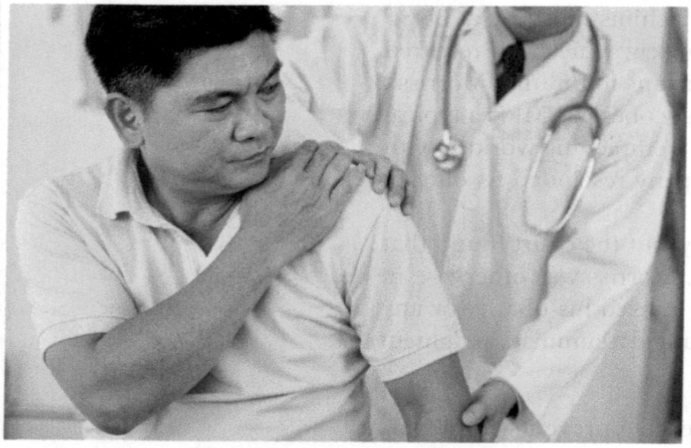

What legal remedy is available to an employee under the ADA if a coworker refers to the employee's injured shoulder in a Facebook post?

Case Example 25.18 George Shoun was working at his job at Best Formed Plastics, Inc., when he fell and injured his shoulder. Another Best Formed employee, Jane Stewart, prepared an accident report for the incident and processed Shoun's workers' compensation claim. As a result of the injury, Shoun had to take several months off work and received workers' compensation.

Stewart posted on her Facebook page a statement about how Shoun's shoulder injury "kept him away from work for 11 months and now he is trying to sue us." Shoun sued Best Formed under the ADA for wrongfully disclosing confidential information about his medical condition to other people via Facebook. He claimed the action resulted in loss of employment and impairment of his earning capacity. The court allowed Shoun's claim to go forward to trial.[20]

Reasonable Accommodation The ADA does not require that employers accommodate the needs of job applicants or employees with disabilities who are not otherwise qualified for the work. If a job applicant or an employee with a disability can perform essential job functions with a reasonable accommodation, however, the employer must make the accommodation.

Required modifications may include installing ramps for a wheelchair, establishing more flexible working hours, creating or modifying job assignments, and creating or improving training materials and procedures. Generally, employers should give primary consideration to employees' preferences in deciding what accommodations should be made.

Undue Hardship. Employers who do not accommodate the needs of persons with disabilities must demonstrate that the accommodations will cause "undue hardship" in terms of being significantly difficult or expensive for the employer. Usually, the courts decide whether an accommodation constitutes an undue hardship on a case-by-case basis by looking at the employer's resources in relation to the specific accommodation.

Example 25.19 Bryan, who uses a wheelchair, works for a cell phone company that provides parking for its employees. Lockhart informs company supervisors that the parking spaces are so narrow that he is unable to extend the ramp that allows him to get in and out of his van. Bryan requests that the company reasonably accommodate his needs by paying a monthly fee for him to use a larger parking space in an adjacent lot. In this situation, a court would likely find that it would not be an undue hardship for the employer to pay for additional parking for Bryan.

Before reaching conclusions about the necessity and reasonableness of an accommodation, a court must determine that the part of a job affected by the accommodation is an essential function of the job. In the following case, the court addressed this issue.

20. *Shoun v. Best Formed Plastics, Inc.*, 28 F.Supp.3d 786 (N.D.Ind. 2014).

Case 25.3

Kassa v. Synovus Financial Corp.

United States Court of Appeals, Eleventh Circuit, 800 Fed.Appx. 804 (2020).

Facts Tony Kassa, who suffers from bipolar disorder and intermittent explosive disorder, worked for Synovus Financial Corporation in the company's Network Operation Center (NOC). Kassa's supervisor, Diana Young, knew about his disorders and granted his request to take short breaks when he became frustrated as long as his area was covered and he could be reached if necessary.

As part of a corporate restructuring, Kassa was transferred to the Automated Teller Machine (ATM) team to handle customer service calls. Worried about the possible effects that his disorders might have during calls, Kassa asked his new supervisor, Wes Mason, if he could take a short break whenever he was having an episode. The request was not granted. Several months later, after a "rude and unprofessional" comment during a call, Kassa was terminated.

He filed a suit in a federal district court against Synovus, alleging discrimination under the Americans with Disabilities Act for the employer's failure to provide him with a reasonable accommodation for his disability. The court, after concluding that the plaintiff had failed to show that Synovus had withheld reasonable accommodation, granted the company's motion for summary judgment. Kassa appealed to the U.S. Court of Appeals for the Eleventh Circuit.

Issue Did Synovus violate the ADA by denying Kassa's request to take short breaks?

Decision Yes. The U.S. Court of Appeals for the Eleventh Circuit vacated the lower court's summary judgment in Synovus's favor on Kassa's failure-to-accommodate claim and remanded the case for further proceedings.

Reason An employer's failure to provide a reasonable accommodation for the known physical or mental limitations of an otherwise qualified individual with a disability is a violation of the ADA, unless doing so would impose an undue hardship on the employer.

An accommodation is reasonable only if it enables the employee to perform an essential function of the job. In Kassa's case, the appellate court found that answering customer service calls was an essential function of his job. He testified that answering customer service calls was "just about all" he did in his position. And sometimes he was the only one available to take the calls.

The court also found that Kassa's request to take short breaks was a reasonable accommodation for his disability. He could control his anger by taking short breaks, which would enable him to answer calls. In his position on the NOC team, his supervisor had allowed him to take short breaks with positive results.

But when Kassa was transferred to Mason's team, the accommodations stopped. The court concluded, "Because an employer's failure to provide a reasonable accommodation is itself a violation of the ADA, Synovus is unentitled to summary judgment."

Critical Thinking

- **Legal Environment** *Could Synovus have successfully claimed that Kassa's short breaks created an undue hardship? Explain.*
- **What If the Facts Were Different?** *Suppose that instead of asking to take a short break whenever he had an episode, Kassa had asked if he could take customer service calls only from technicians, work nights, or work from home. Would the result have been different? Discuss.*

Job Applications and Preemployment Physical Exams. Employers must modify their job-application process so that those with disabilities can compete for jobs with those who do not have disabilities. For instance, a job announcement might be modified to allow job applicants to respond by e-mail or letter, as well as by telephone, so that it does not discriminate against potential applicants with hearing impairments.

Employers are restricted in the kinds of questions they may ask on job application forms and during preemployment interviews. Furthermore, they cannot require persons with disabilities to submit to preemployment physicals unless such exams are required of all other applicants. Employers can condition an offer of employment on the applicant's successfully passing a medical examination, but can disqualify the applicant only if the medical problems discovered would render the applicant unable to perform the job.

Know This

Preemployment screening procedures must be applied equally in regard to all job applicants.

Substance Abuse. Drug addiction is a disability under the ADA because it is a substantially limiting impairment. The act does not protect those who are actually using illegal drugs. The ADA protects only persons with *former* drug addictions—those who have completed or are now in a supervised drug-rehabilitation program. Individuals who have used drugs casually in the past are not protected under the act. They are not considered addicts and therefore do not have a disability (addiction).

People suffering from alcoholism are protected by the ADA. Of course, employers have the right to prohibit the use of alcohol in the workplace and can require that employees not be under the influence of alcohol while working. Employers can also fire or refuse to hire people who are alcoholics if (1) they pose a *substantial risk of harm* either to themselves or to others, and (2) the risk cannot be reduced by reasonable accommodation.

Health Insurance Plans. Workers with disabilities must be given equal access to any health insurance provided to other employees and cannot be excluded from coverage for preexisting health conditions. An employer can put a limit, or cap, on health care payments under its group health policy, but such caps must be "applied equally to all insured employees" and must not "discriminate on the basis of disability."

25–2c Discrimination Based on Military Status

The Uniformed Services Employment and Reemployment Rights Act (USERRA) prohibits discrimination against persons who have served in the military.[21] In effect, the USERRA makes military service and status a protected class and gives members of this class a right to sue an employer for violations.

Broad Application and Provisions The USERRA covers *all* employers, public and private, large and small. Even an employer with only one employee is subject to its provisions. The act also applies to United States employers operating in foreign countries.

Under the USERRA, military plaintiffs can sue not only the employer but also individual employees who were acting in an official capacity for the employer. In other words, these employees—supervisors, for instance—can be held personally liable for violations. Additionally, there is no statute of limitations for bringing a lawsuit. The cause of action could have arisen ten weeks or ten years before the suit was filed.

The USERRA specifies that veterans can be terminated from their employment only "for cause." The employer is obligated to give employees a list of all the behaviors that would trigger a for-cause termination.

DanielBendjy/E+/Getty Images

Are reserve and former members of the military considered a protected class? Why or why not?

***Prima Facie* Case of Discrimination under the USERRA** To establish a *prima facie* case under the USERRA, the plaintiff must establish that the employer took an adverse employment action based in part on the employee's connection with the military. If another similarly situated person who did not serve in the military or engage in a protected activity was treated more favorably than the plaintiff, the employer has violated the USERRA.

Case Example 25.20 Baldo Bello, a staff sergeant with the United States Marine Corps Reserve, was employed by the Village of Skokie as a police officer. Police officers in Skokie normally have nine regular days off (RDO) per month and eight sick days per year. Skokie officers who are in the Reserve receive two weeks of paid leave for annual training each summer, but they do not receive pay for the required weekend military training.

During his first four years as an officer in Skokie, Bello always requested RDOs to cover his weekend training drills. After that, he started requesting military leave for the two to four days of drills per month, in addition to his nine RDO days. Skokie at first granted Bello

21. Pub. L. No. 103–353, codified at 38 U.S.C. Sections 4301–4335.

Exhibit 25–1 Coverage of Employment Discrimination Laws

TITLE VII OF THE CIVIL RIGHTS ACT	AGE DISCRIMINATION IN EMPLOYMENT ACT	AMERICANS WITH DISABILITIES ACT (AS AMENDED)	UNIFORMED SERVICES EMPLOYMENT AND REEMPLOYMENT RIGHTS ACT
Prohibits discrimination based on race, color, national origin, religion, gender, sexual orientation, and pregnancy; prohibits sexual harassment.	Prohibits discrimination against persons over forty years of age.	Prohibits discrimination against persons who have a mental or physical impairment that substantially limits a major life activity, who have a record of such an impairment, who are regarded as having such an impairment, or who are associated with a disabled person.	Prohibits discrimination against persons who have served in the military.
Applies to employers with fifteen or more employees.	Applies to employers with twenty or more employees.	Applies to employers with fifteen or more employees.	Applies to all employers, even if they have only one employee.

military leave for monthly drills but later began to deny the requests. When Skokie officials told Bello that he needed to schedule his RDOs to cover his weekend military training, he filed suit in a federal district court alleging violations of the USERRA. Skokie filed a motion for summary judgment, which the court denied. The court found that Bello was meeting his employer's legitimate expectations. He was therefore entitled to a trial on the issue of whether Skokie had treated his leave requests less favorably than requests from other employees.[22]

Plaintiffs May Be Entitled to Promotions Under the USERRA, returning service members are to be reemployed in the jobs that they would have attained had they not been absent for military service. Reinstatement could affect their seniority, status, pay, and other rights and benefits (such as health and pension plans). In essence, this means that a returning service member who successfully sues an employer for violations of the USERRA could receive not only damages and reinstatement but also a promotion.

Exhibit 25–1 illustrates the coverage of the employment discrimination laws discussed in this chapter.

25–3 Defenses to Employment Discrimination

The first line of defense for an employer charged with employment discrimination is to assert that the plaintiff has failed to meet the initial burden of proving that discrimination occurred. Once a plaintiff succeeds in proving discrimination, the burden shifts to the employer to justify the discriminatory practice.

Possible justifications include that the discrimination was the result of a business necessity, a bona fide occupational qualification, or a seniority system. In addition, as noted earlier, an employer that has an effective antiharassment policy and takes prompt remedial action when harassment occurs may be shielded from liability for sexual harassment under Title VII.

Focus Question 4
What are three defenses to claims of employment discrimination?

25–3a Business Necessity

An employer may defend against a claim of disparate-impact (unintentional) discrimination by asserting that a practice that has a discriminatory effect is a **business necessity.** **Example 25.21** EarthFix, Inc., an international consulting agency, requires its applicants to be fluent in at least two languages. If requiring a second language is shown to have a discriminatory effect,

Business Necessity A defense to an allegation of employment discrimination in which the employer demonstrates that an employment practice that discriminates against members of a protected class is related to job performance.

22. *Bello v. Village of Skokie*, 151 F.Supp.3d 849 (N.D.Ill. 2015).

EarthFix can argue that this requirement is necessary for its workers to perform the job at a required level of competence. If EarthFix can demonstrate a definite connection between multilingual fluency and job performance, it normally will succeed in this business necessity defense.

25–3b Bona Fide Occupational Qualification

Bona Fide Occupational Qualification (BFOQ) An identifiable characteristic reasonably necessary to the normal operation of a particular business. Such characteristics can include gender, national origin, and religion, but not race.

Another defense applies when discrimination against a protected class is essential to a job—that is, when a particular trait is a **bona fide occupational qualification (BFOQ).** Race, however, can never be a BFOQ.

Generally, courts have restricted the BFOQ defense to instances in which the employee's gender is essential to the job. For instance, a women's clothing store might legitimately hire only female sales attendants if part of an attendant's job involves assisting clients in the store's dressing rooms. Similarly, the Federal Aviation Administration can legitimately impose age limits for airline pilots—but an airline cannot impose weight limits only on female flight attendants.

25–3c Seniority Systems

Seniority System A system in which those who have worked longest for an employer are first in line for promotions, salary increases, and other benefits, and are last to be laid off if the workforce must be reduced.

An employer with a history of discrimination may have no members of protected classes in upper-level positions. Nevertheless, the employer may have a defense against a discrimination suit if promotions or other job benefits have been distributed according to a fair *seniority system.* In a **seniority system,** workers with more years of service are promoted first or laid off last.

Case Example 25.22 Charee Stanley worked as a flight attendant for ExpressJet Airlines, Inc. A practicing Muslim, Stanley requested that she be excused from preparing and serving alcohol during flights for religious reasons. ExpressJet refused this accommodation, which would have been at odds with a collective bargaining agreement (CBA) between the airline and its employees. The CBA gave senior flight attendants the ability to choose work assignments, including whether to serve alcohol.

Because of her short tenure with the airline, Stanley was frequently the junior attendant on a particular flight. Consequently, she was required by the CBA to serve alcohol if her senior partner declined to do so. A federal appeals court ruled that ExpressJet would violate this seniority system if it granted Stanley's accommodation request, and therefore her religious discrimination claim was preempted by the CBA.[23]

principalli/iStock/Getty Images

If this job candidate makes material misrepresentations on her application and is hired, can her employer use after-acquired evidence to shield itself from a discrimination lawsuit?

25–3d After-Acquired Evidence of Employee Misconduct

In some situations, employers have attempted to avoid liability for employment discrimination on the basis of *after-acquired evidence* of an employee's misconduct—that is, evidence that the employer discovered after the employee had filed a lawsuit. **Example 25.23** Pratt Legal Services fires Lucy, who then sues Pratt for employment discrimination. During pretrial investigation, Pratt discovers that Lucy made material misrepresentations on her job application. Had Pratt known of these misrepresentations, it would have had grounds to fire Lucy.

23. *Stanley v. ExpressJet Airlines, Inc.*, ___Fed.Appx.__, 2020 WL 1698963 (6th Cir. 2020).

After-acquired evidence of wrongdoing cannot shield an employer entirely from liability for discrimination. It may, however, be used to limit the amount of damages for which the employer is liable.

25–4 Affirmative Action

Federal statutes and regulations providing for equal opportunity in the workplace were designed to reduce or eliminate discriminatory practices with respect to hiring, retaining, and promoting employees. **Affirmative action** programs go further and attempt to "make up" for past patterns of discrimination by giving members of protected classes preferential treatment in hiring or promotion. During the 1960s, all federal and state government agencies, private companies that contracted to do business with the federal government, and institutions that received federal funding were required to implement affirmative action policies.

Affirmative Action Job-hiring policies that give special consideration to members of protected classes in an effort to overcome present effects of past discrimination.

Title VII of the Civil Rights Act neither requires nor prohibits affirmative action. Thus, most private firms have not been required to implement affirmative action policies, though many have voluntarily done so. Affirmative action programs have been controversial, however, particularly when they have resulted in reverse discrimination.

25–4a Equal Protection Issues

Focus Question 5

Why are affirmative action programs often found to be unconstitutional?

Because of their inherently discriminatory nature, affirmative action programs may violate the equal protection clause of the Fourteenth Amendment to the U.S. Constitution. Any federal, state, or local affirmative action program that uses racial or ethnic classifications as the basis for making decisions is subject to strict scrutiny (the highest standard to meet) by the courts.

Today, an affirmative action program normally is constitutional only if it attempts to remedy past discrimination and does not make use of quotas or preferences. Furthermore, once such a program has succeeded in the goal of remedying past discrimination, it must be changed or eliminated.

Know This

The Fourteenth Amendment prohibits any state from denying any person "the equal protection of the laws." This prohibition applies to the federal government through the due process clause of the Fifth Amendment.

25–4b State Laws Prohibiting Affirmative Action Programs

Some states, including California, Maryland, Michigan, New Hampshire, Oklahoma, Virginia, and Washington, have enacted laws that prohibit affirmative action programs at public institutions (colleges, universities, and state agencies) within their borders. The United States Supreme Court has recognized that states have the power to enact such bans. **Case Example 25.24** Michigan voters passed an initiative to amend the state's constitution to prohibit publicly funded colleges from granting preferential treatment to any group on the basis of race, sex, color, ethnicity, or national origin. The law also prohibited Michigan from considering race and gender in public hiring and contracting decisions.

A group that supports affirmative action programs in education sued the state's attorney general and others, claiming that the initiative deprived minorities of equal protection and violated the U.S. Constitution. A federal appellate court agreed that the law violated the equal protection clause, but the United States Supreme Court reversed. The Court did not rule on the constitutionality of any specific affirmative action program but held that a state has the inherent power to ban affirmative action within that state.[24]

24. *Schuette v. Coalition to Defend Affirmative Action, Integration and Immigrant Rights*, 572 U.S. 291, 134 S.Ct. 1623, 188 L.Ed.2d 613 (2014).

Practice and Review

Amaani Lyle, an African American woman, took a job as a scriptwriters' assistant at Warner Brothers Television Productions. She worked for the writers of *Friends*, a popular, adult-oriented television series. One of her essential job duties was to type detailed notes for the scriptwriters during brainstorming sessions in which they discussed jokes, dialogue, and story lines. The writers then combed through Lyle's notes after the meetings for script material.

During the meetings, the three male scriptwriters told lewd and vulgar jokes and made sexually explicit comments and gestures. They often talked about their personal sexual experiences and fantasies, and some of these conversations were later used in episodes of *Friends*. During the meetings, Lyle never complained that she found the writers' conduct offensive.

After four months, Lyle was fired because she could not type fast enough to keep up with the writers' conversations during the meetings. She filed a suit against Warner Brothers alleging sexual harassment and claiming that her termination was based on racial discrimination. Using the information presented in the chapter, answer the following questions.

1. Would Lyle's claim of racial discrimination be for intentional (disparate-treatment) or unintentional (disparate-impact) discrimination? Explain.
2. Can Lyle establish a *prima facie* case of racial discrimination? Why or why not?
3. When she was hired, Lyle was told that typing speed was extremely important to her position. At the time, she maintained that she could type eighty words per minute, so she was not given a typing test. It later turned out that Lyle could type only fifty words per minute. What impact might typing speed have on Lyle's lawsuit?
4. Lyle's sexual harassment claim was based on the hostile work environment created by the writers' sexually offensive conduct at meetings that she was required to attend. The writers, however, argued that their behavior was essential to the "creative process" of writing *Friends*, a show that routinely contained sexual innuendos and adult humor. Which defense discussed in the chapter might Warner Brothers assert using this argument?

Debate This

Members of minority groups and women no longer need special legislation to protect them from employment discrimination.

Key Terms

affirmative action 645
bona fide occupational qualification (BFOQ) 644
business necessity 643
constructive discharge 632
disparate-impact discrimination 626
disparate-treatment discrimination 626
***prima facie* case** 626
protected class 625
seniority system 644
sexual harassment 633
tangible employment action 633

Chapter Summary: Employment Discrimination

Title VII of the Civil Rights Act	Title VII prohibits employment discrimination based on race, color, national origin, religion, sexual orientation, or gender. 1. **Procedures**—An employee alleging discrimination must file a claim with the Equal Employment Opportunity Commission (EEOC). The EEOC may sue the employer on the employee's behalf. If it does not, the EEOC may allow the employee to sue the employer directly. 2. **Types of discrimination**—Title VII prohibits both intentional (disparate-treatment) and unintentional (disparate-impact) discrimination. Disparate-impact discrimination occurs when an employer's practices, tests, or procedures, such as requiring a certain level of education, have the effect of discriminating against a protected class. Title VII extends to discriminatory practices, such as various forms of harassment, in the online environment. 3. **Remedies for discrimination under Title VII**—Remedies include reinstatement, back pay, and retroactive promotions. Damages (both compensatory and punitive) may be awarded for intentional discrimination.
Discrimination Based on Age, Disability, or Military Status	1. **The Age Discrimination in Employment Act (ADEA)**—Prohibits employment discrimination on the basis of age against individuals forty years of age or older. Procedures for bringing a case under the ADEA are similar to those for bringing a case under Title VII. 2. **The Americans with Disabilities Act (ADA)**—Prohibits employment discrimination against persons with disabilities who are otherwise qualified to perform the essential functions of the jobs for which they apply. a. To prevail on a claim, a plaintiff must have a disability, must be otherwise qualified for the employment in question, and must have been excluded from it solely because of the disability. Procedures and remedies under the ADA are similar to those in Title VII cases. b. The ADA defines the term *disability* as a physical or mental impairment that substantially limits one or more of an individual's major life activities, a record of such impairment, or being regarded as having such an impairment. c. Employers are required to reasonably accommodate the needs of qualified persons with disabilities through such measures as modifying the physical work environment and permitting more flexible work schedules. 3. **The Uniformed Services Employment and Reemployment Rights Act (USERRA)**—Prohibits discrimination against persons who have served in the military. The USERRA applies to *all* employers regardless of their size.
Defenses to Employment Discrimination	As defenses to claims of employment discrimination, employers may assert that the discrimination was required for reasons of business necessity, to meet a bona fide occupational qualification, or to maintain a legitimate seniority system. Evidence of prior employee misconduct acquired after the employee has been fired is not a defense to discrimination.
Affirmative Action	Affirmative action programs attempt to "make up" for past patterns of discrimination by giving members of protected classes preferential treatment in hiring or promotion. Such programs are subject to strict scrutiny by the courts and are often struck down for violating the Fourteenth Amendment.

Issue Spotters

1. Ruth is a supervisor for a Subs & Suds restaurant. Tim is a Subs & Suds employee. The owner announces that some employees will be discharged. Ruth tells Tim that if he has sex with her, he can keep his job. Is this sexual harassment? Why or why not? (See *Title VII of the Civil Rights Act.*)
2. Koko, a person with a disability, applies for a job at Lively Sales Corporation for which she is well qualified, but she is rejected. Lively continues to seek applicants and eventually fills the position with a person who does not have a disability. Could Koko succeed in a suit against Lively for discrimination? Explain. (See *Discrimination Based on Age, Disability, or Military Status.*)

—Check your answers to the *Issue Spotters* against the answers provided in Appendix D.

Business Scenarios and Case Problems

25–1. Title VII Violations. Discuss fully whether either of the following actions would constitute a violation of Title VII of the Civil Rights Act.

1. Tennington, Inc., is a consulting firm with ten employees. These employees travel on consulting jobs in seven states. Tennington has an employment record of hiring only white males. (See *Title VII of the Civil Rights Act.*)
2. Novo Films, Inc., is making a film about Africa and needs to employ approximately one hundred extras for this picture. To hire these extras, Novo advertises in all major newspapers in Southern California. The ad states that only African Americans need apply. (See *Defenses to Employment Discrimination.*)

25–2. Religious Discrimination. Gina Gomez, a devout Roman Catholic, worked for Sam's Department Stores, Inc., in Phoenix, Arizona. Sam's considered Gomez a productive employee because her sales exceeded $200,000 per year. The store gave its managers the discretion to grant unpaid leave to employees but prohibited vacations or leave during the holiday season—October through December. Gomez felt that she had a "calling" to go on a "pilgrimage" in October to a location in Bosnia where some persons claimed to have had visions of the Virgin Mary. The Catholic Church had not designated the site an official pilgrimage site, the visions were not expected to be stronger in October, and tours were available at other times. The store managers denied Gomez's request for leave, but she had a nonrefundable ticket and left anyway. Sam's terminated her employment, and she could not find another job. Can Gomez establish a *prima facie* case of religious discrimination? Explain. (See *Title VII of the Civil Rights Act.*)

25–3. Spotlight on Dress Code Policies—Discrimination Based on Gender. Burlington Coat Factory Warehouse, Inc., had a dress code that required male sales clerks to wear business attire consisting of slacks, shirt, and necktie. Female sales clerks, by contrast, were required to wear a smock so that customers could readily identify them. Karen O'Donnell and other female employees refused to wear the smock. Instead, they reported to work in business attire and were suspended. After numerous suspensions, the female employees were fired for violating Burlington's dress code policy. All other conditions of employment, including salary, hours, and benefits, were the same for female and male employees. Was the dress code policy discriminatory? Why or why not? [*O'Donnell v. Burlington Coat Factory Warehouse, Inc.,* 656 F.Supp. 263 (S.D.Ohio 1987)] (See *Title VII of the Civil Rights Act.*)

25–4. Age Discrimination. Beginning in 1986, Paul Rangel was a sales professional for pharmaceutical company Sanofi-Aventis U.S., LLC (S-A). Rangel had satisfactory performance reviews until 2006, when S-A issued new expectations guidelines with sales call quotas and other standards that he failed to meet. After two years of negative performance reviews, Rangel—who was then more than forty years old—was terminated as part of a nationwide reduction of sales professionals who had not met the expectations guidelines. This sales force reduction also included younger workers. Did S-A engage in age discrimination? Discuss. [*Rangel v. Sanofi Aventis U.S. LLC,* 507 Fed.Appx. 782 (10th Cir. 2013)] (See *Discrimination Based on Age, Disability, or Military Status.*)

25–5. Discrimination Based on Disability. Cynthia Horn worked for Knight Facilities Management–GM, Inc., in Detroit, Michigan, as a janitor. When Horn developed a sensitivity to cleaning products, her physician gave her a "no exposure to cleaning solutions" restriction. Knight discussed possible accommodations with Horn. She suggested that restrooms be eliminated from her cleaning route or that she be provided with a respirator. Knight explained that she would be exposed to cleaning solutions in any situation and concluded that there was no work available within her physician's restriction. Has Knight violated the Americans with Disabilities Act by failing to provide Horn with the requested accommodations? Explain. [*Horn v. Knight Facilities Management–GM, Inc.,* 556 Fed.Appx. 452 (6th Cir. 2014)] (See *Discrimination Based on Age, Disability, or Military Status.*)

25–6. Business Case Problem with Sample Answer—Sexual Harassment. Jamel Blanton, a male employee at a Pizza Hut restaurant operated by Newton Associates, Inc., in San Antonio, Texas, was subjected to sexual and racial harassment by the general manager, who was female. Newton had a clear, straightforward antidiscrimination policy and complaint procedure. The policy provided that in such a situation, an employee should complain to the harasser's supervisor. Blanton alerted a shift leader and an assistant manager about the harassment, but they were subordinate to the general manager and did not report the harassment to higher-level management. When Blanton finally complained to a manager with authority over the general manager, the employer investigated and fired the general manager within four days. Blanton filed a suit in a federal district court against Newton, seeking to impose liability on the employer for the general manager's actions. What is Newton's best defense? Discuss. [*Blanton v. Newton Associates, Inc.,* 593 Fed.Appx. 389 (5th Cir. 2015)] (See *Title VII of the Civil Rights Act.*)

—For a sample answer to Problem 25–6, go to Appendix E.

25–7. Discrimination Based on Disability. Dennis Wallace was a deputy sheriff for Stanislaus County, California, when he injured his left knee. After surgery, he was subject to limits on prolonged standing, walking, and running. The county assigned him to work as a bailiff. The sergeants who supervised him rated his performance above average. Less than a year later, without consulting those supervisors, the county placed him on an unpaid leave of absence, under the mistaken belief that he could not safely perform the essential functions of the job. Wallace filed an action in a California state court against the county, alleging discrimination based on disability. Under state law, discriminatory intent is shown by evidence that an actual or perceived disability was a "substantial motivating factor or reason" for an employer's adverse employment action. An employee is not required to show that the action was motivated by animosity or ill will. Could Wallace likely prove the "substantial motivating factor or reason" element? Explain. [*Wallace v. County of Stanislaus*, 245 Cal.App.4th 109, 199 Cal.Rptr.3d 462 (5 Dist. 2016)] (See *Discrimination Based on Age, Disability, or Military Status.*)

25–8. Discrimination Based on Gender. The Fresno County Office of Education hired Aileen Rizo as a math consultant. She had previously worked as a middle and high school math teacher, earning about $50,000 a year. Fresno based the salary of its new hires on the individual's prior salary, according to the county's Standard Operating Procedure (SOP). When Rizo learned that she was being paid less than comparable male employees for the same work, she filed a complaint. The county responded that all salaries were set under the SOP. Rizo filed a suit against Jim Yovino, the Fresno superintendent, claiming a violation of the Equal Pay Act. She asserted that under the Equal Pay Act, an employer should not be able to justify a wage differential between men and women on the basis of prior salary. Yovino argued that basing pay on a prior salary was permissible under an exception in the act for "any factor other than gender." Did the county violate the Equal Pay Act? Discuss. [*Rizo v. Yovino*, 887 F.3d 453 (9th Cir. 2018)] (See *Title VII of the Civil Rights Act.*)

25–9. A Question of Ethics—The IDDR Approach and Unintentional Discrimination. McLane Company is a supply-chain services company that distributes goods to retailers. McLane requires employees with physically demanding jobs to have physical evaluations, both when they start work and when they return after medical leave. After working in a physically demanding job for McLane for eight years, Damiana Ochoa took maternity leave. When she returned to work, she failed the physical evaluation and was fired. She filed a discrimination complaint with the Equal Employment Opportunity Commission (EEOC). The agency issued a subpoena—an order to appear in court—seeking the names and contact information of McLane employees who had been asked to have evaluations throughout the company's national operations. [*McLane Co. v. E.E.O.C.*, 581 U.S.___, 137 S.Ct. 1159, 197 L.Ed.2d 500 (2017)] (See *Title VII of the Civil Rights Act.*)

1. On what legal ground might McLane legitimately refuse to comply with the EEOC's subpoena? What practical factors could affect the choice not to comply? Discuss.
2. Using the IDDR approach, consider whether McLane has an ethical duty to comply with the subpoena.

Critical Thinking and Writing Assignments

25–10. Critical Legal Thinking. Why has the federal government limited the application of the statutes discussed in this chapter to firms with a specified number of employees, such as fifteen or twenty? Should these laws apply to all employers regardless of size? Why or why not? (See *Title VII of the Civil Rights Act.*)

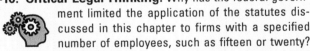

25–11. Time-Limited Group Assignment—Discrimination Based on Race. Two African American plaintiffs sued the producers of the reality television series *The Bachelor* and *The Bachelorette* for racial discrimination. The plaintiffs claimed that the shows had never featured a person of color in the lead role. Plaintiffs also alleged that the producers had failed to provide people of color who auditioned for lead roles with the same opportunities to compete as white people who auditioned. (See *Title VII of the Civil Rights Act.*)

1. The first group will assess whether the plaintiffs can establish a *prima facie* case of disparate-treatment discrimination.
2. The second group will consider what the plaintiffs would have to show to establish disparate-impact discrimination.
3. The third group will assume that the plaintiffs established a *prima facie* case and that the burden has shifted to the employer to articulate a legal reason for not hiring the plaintiffs. What legitimate reasons might the employer assert for not hiring the plaintiffs in this situation? Should the law require television producers to hire persons of color for lead roles in reality television shows? Explain your answer.

Unit Four—Task-Based Simulation

iStockphoto.com/KLH49

Two brothers, Ray and Paul Ashford, start a business—Ashford Brothers, Inc.—manufacturing a new type of battery system for hybrid automobiles. The batteries hit the market at the perfect time and are in great demand.

1. **Agency.** Loren, one of Ashford's salespersons, anxious to make a sale, intentionally quotes a price to a customer that is $500 lower than Ashford has authorized for the product. The customer purchases the product at the quoted price. When Ashford learns of the deal, it claims that it is not legally bound to the sales contract because it has not authorized Loren to sell the product at that price. Is Ashford bound to the contract? Discuss fully.
2. **Workers' Compensation.** One day, Gina, an Ashford employee, suffered a serious burn when she accidentally spilled some acid on her hand. The accident occurred because another employee, who was suspected of using illegal drugs, carelessly bumped into her. Gina's hand required a series of skin grafts before it healed sufficiently to allow her to return to work. Gina wants to obtain compensation for her lost wages and medical expenses. Can she do that? If so, how?
3. **Drug Testing.** After Gina's injury, Ashford decides to conduct random drug tests on all of its employees. Several employees claim that the testing violates their privacy rights and bring a lawsuit. What factors will the court consider in deciding whether the random drug testing is legally permissible?
4. **COBRA.** Ashford provides health insurance for its two hundred employees, including Dan. For personal medical reasons, Dan takes twelve weeks' leave. During this period, can Dan continue his coverage under Ashford's health insurance plan? After Dan returns to work, Ashford closes Dan's division and terminates the employees, including Dan. Can Dan continue his coverage under Ashford's health insurance plan after the termination? Explain.
5. **Sexual Harassment.** Aretha, another employee at Ashford, is disgusted by the sexually offensive behavior of several male employees. She has complained to her supervisor on several occasions about the behavior, but the supervisor merely laughs at her concerns. Aretha decides to bring a legal action against the company for sexual harassment. Does Aretha's complaint concern *quid pro quo* harassment or hostile-environment harassment? What federal statute protects employees from sexual harassment? What remedies are available under that statute? What procedures must Aretha follow in pursuing her legal action?

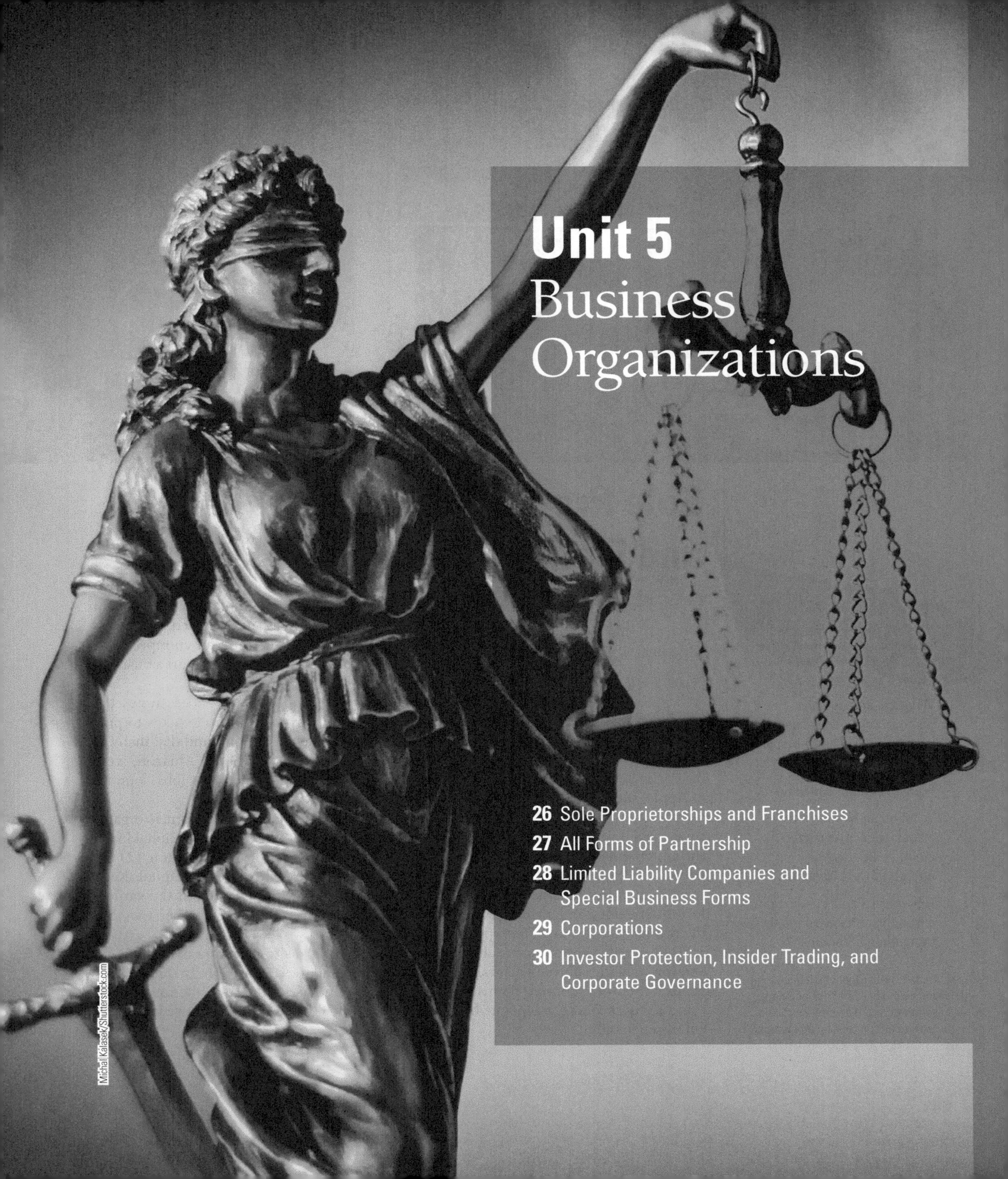

Michal Kalasek/Shutterstock.com

Unit 5 Business Organizations

26 Sole Proprietorships and Franchises

Focus Questions

The four *Focus Questions* below are designed to help improve your understanding. After reading this chapter, you should be able to answer the following questions:

1. What advantages and disadvantages are associated with the sole proprietorship?
2. What is required by the Franchise Rule, and why?
3. What might happen if a franchisor exercises too much control over the operations of a franchise?
4. When will a court decide that a franchisor has wrongfully terminated a franchise?

Entrepreneur One who initiates and assumes the financial risk of a new business enterprise and undertakes to provide or control its management.

"Why not go out on a limb? Isn't that where the fruit is?"

Frank Scully
1892–1964
(American author)

Many Americans would agree with Frank Scully's comment in the chapter-opening quotation that to succeed in business one must "go out on a limb." Certainly, an entrepreneur's primary motive for "going out on a limb" to start a business enterprise is to make profits.

An **entrepreneur** is one who initiates and assumes the financial risks of a new enterprise and undertakes to provide or control its management. Keep in mind that many of the biggest corporations today, such as Apple, Alphabet (Google), and Amazon, were originally very small companies. Jeff Bezos, founder of Amazon, and Steve Jobs, founder of Apple, started their companies in their garages.

One of the first decisions an entrepreneur must make is which form of business organization will be most appropriate for the new endeavor. In selecting an organizational form, the entrepreneur will consider a number of factors, including (1) ease of creation, (2) the liability of the owners, (3) tax considerations, and (4) the ability to raise capital. Keep these factors in mind as you read the chapters in this unit and learn about the various forms of business organization. In considering these business forms, remember, too, that the primary motive of an entrepreneur is to make profits.

Traditionally, entrepreneurs have used three major forms to structure their business enterprises—the sole proprietorship, the partnership, and the corporation. In this chapter, we examine sole proprietorships. We also discuss franchises. Although the franchise is not, strictly speaking, a separate business organizational form, it is widely used today by entrepreneurs.

26–1 Sole Proprietorships

The simplest form of business is a **sole proprietorship**. In this form, the owner is the business. Thus, anyone who does business without creating a separate business organization has a sole proprietorship.

Sole Proprietorship The simplest form of business organization, in which the owner is the business. The owner reports business income as personal income and is legally responsible for all debts and obligations incurred by the business.

More than two-thirds of all U.S. businesses are sole proprietorships. Sole proprietors can own and manage any type of business, from an informal home office or Web-based undertaking to a large restaurant or construction firm. Most sole proprietorships are small enterprises, however. About 99 percent of the sole proprietorships in the United States have revenues of less than $1 million per year.

26–1a Advantages of the Sole Proprietorship

Focus Question 1
What advantages and disadvantages are associated with the sole proprietorship?

A major advantage of the sole proprietorship is that the proprietor owns the entire business and has a right to receive all of the profits (because of assuming all of the risk). In addition, starting a sole proprietorship is often easier and less costly than starting any other kind of business, as few legal formalities are involved. Generally, no documents need to be filed with the government to start a sole proprietorship.[1]

Taxes A sole proprietor pays only personal income taxes (including Social Security and Medicare taxes) on the business's profits. The profits are reported as personal income on the proprietor's personal income tax return. In other words, the business itself need not file an income tax return. Sole proprietors are allowed to establish retirement accounts that are tax-exempt until the funds are withdrawn. Like any form of business enterprise, a sole proprietorship can be liable for other taxes, such as those collected and applied to the disbursement of unemployment compensation.

Flexibility A sole proprietorship also offers more flexibility than does a partnership or a corporation. The sole proprietor is free to make any decision concerning the business—including whom to hire, when to take a vacation, and what kind of business to pursue. The sole proprietor can sell or transfer all or part of the business to another party at any time without seeking approval from anyone else. In contrast, approval is typically required from partners in a partnership and from shareholders in a corporation.

In the following case, a sole proprietor sold his cabinet and furniture business to another sole proprietor, and later filed a claim to recover for a customer's breach of contract. Considering that the seller no longer owned the business, on what basis did he have standing to pursue the claim?

1. Sole proprietorships may need to comply with certain zoning requirements, obtain a business license or other appropriate license from the state, and the like.

Case 26.1

Port Orchard Airport, Inc. v. Wagner

Court of Appeals of Washington, Division 2, __ Wash.App. __, __ P.3d __, 2020 WL 901452 (2020).

Facts Shannon Wagner was the owner of Northwest Cabinets & Furniture, a sole proprietorship, in Port Orchard, Washington, when he sold the business and its assets to Claire Misenar. Those assets included the business's books and records, computers and software, fixtures and furniture, phone system, phone number, trade name and all other intellectual property, domain name, social media accounts, and inventory. Wagner continued to work for the business, and within two years, Wagner and Misenar were married.

(Continues)

Continued

Later, Wagner filed a breach of contract claim in a Washington state court against Port Orchard Airport, Inc., for work performed by Northwest Cabinets & Furniture after Wagner had sold the business and married Misenar. A jury awarded damages, but the court found that Wagner was not the owner of the business, concluded that he lacked standing to assert the claim, and granted Port Orchard's motion to dismiss. Wagner appealed.

Issue Did Wagner have standing to pursue the claim against Port Orchard?

Decision Yes. A state intermediate appellate court reversed the trial court's order dismissing Wagner's claim and remanded the case with instructions to the trial court to reinstate the jury verdict in Wagner's favor.

Reason The trial court concluded that Northwest Cabinets & Furniture was Misenar's separate property. The appellate court disagreed.

Misenar bought the business, a sole proprietorship, from Wagner. The appellate court recognized, "When an individual does business as a sole proprietorship, the individual and the sole proprietorship are legally indistinguishable. An individual does not create a separate legal entity by doing business as a sole proprietor." The court reasoned that because Northwest Cabinets & Furniture was a sole proprietorship, it was inseparable from Misenar.

To have standing to assert a claim, a party must have a "real" interest in the case. In the state of Washington, all property acquired during marriage is community property. Wagner and Misenar were married. Therefore, Wagner had a community property interest in Northwest Cabinets & Furniture. And a community property interest is a sufficiently real interest to confer standing.

Critical Thinking

- **Legal Environment** *The trial court ruled that Wagner could have been an agent for "the business." Why, in the view of the appellate court, did this ruling make no sense?*
- **What If the Facts Were Different?** *Suppose that instead of Wagner, Misenar had pursued the claim in the case against Port Orchard. Would the result have been different? Discuss.*

26–1b Disadvantages of the Sole Proprietorship

The major disadvantage of the sole proprietorship is that the proprietor alone bears the burden of any losses or liabilities incurred by the business enterprise. In other words, the sole proprietor has unlimited liability, or legal responsibility, for all obligations incurred in doing business.

Sawat Banyenngam/Shutterstock.com

Can a person who owns a trucking business as a sole proprietorship avoid liability for the business's tax debts?

Case Example 26.1 Richard Casias registered his business, Casias Trucking, as a sole proprietorship with the New Mexico Taxation and Revenue Department. Several years later, Casias began presenting Casias Trucking as a limited liability company (LLC) to the public. He did not, however, follow the proper procedures in registering this change with the Department.

An audit revealed that Casias Trucking owed about $200,000 in back taxes, interest, and penalties. When the bulk of this amount went unpaid, the Department placed a tax lien on Casias's personal property. Casias argued that the tax liability did not rest with him, but with Casias Trucking LLC. A state appeals court ruled that, because Casias had failed to properly register Casias Trucking as an LLC with the Department, it remained a sole proprietorship. Therefore, Casias was personally liable for Casias Trucking's debts.[2]

This chapter's *Adapting the Law to the Online Environment* feature further demonstrates how difficult it is for a sole proprietor to escape liability for acts taken on behalf of the business entity.

2. *Casias v. New Mexico Taxation and Revenue Department*, 2019 WL 1599167 (N.M. Ct. App. 2019).

Adapting the Law to the Online Environment

"Doing Business As" a Sole Proprietor

Suppose Jane Smith wants to start a face-mask manufacturing business as a sole proprietor. Jane finds the name "Jane Smith's Face Masks" uninspiring. She would rather call her new venture "Masks Almighty." She thinks this name will make for more effective online marketing. Because the business name is different from her name, in many states Jane will be required to file a "Doing Business As" (DBA) statement, which provides notice to the public of the true owner of the enterprise.

Simple, Inexpensive, and Separate

Even if it were not legally required, many sole proprietors would file for DBAs, known in some jurisdictions as Fictitious Business Names (FBNs). For the most part, DBAs are simple and inexpensive to create. As with the case of Jane Smith, they allow the sole proprietor to match the name to the product or service provided in a marketing-friendly way. DBAs also provide privacy and a degree of separation for sole proprietors who might not want their personal names easily connected to their businesses.

Regulations for DBAs vary from state to state. In most instances, the sole proprietor must go online and check a state database to ensure that the new trade name is not already being used. In many, though not all, states, the entire DBA process can be completed on the Internet, with costs as low as $45 and approval waiting times as short as one week.

The DBA Effect

The fact that the name of the business owner and the name of the business are different does not change the basic rule that, with a sole proprietorship, the owner is the business. A federal court felt the need to drive this legal point home to David Ruiz after a restaurant that Ruiz owned as a sole proprietor showed a televised boxing match without paying a licensing fee. When the licensor sued, Ruiz said that he had leased the restaurant, Cotija Mex Grill, to Enrique Hernandez before the night of the match. Therefore, Ruiz claimed, he was not responsible for the incident.

"It is unclear," said the court, "how Ruiz could lease Cotija to Hernandez when Cotija, as a sole proprietorship, is legally indistinct from Ruiz." Because Ruiz and the restaurant, with its DBA, were a single legal entity, the court ruled, Ruiz could be held liable for Cotija Mex Grill's wrongdoing.[a]

Critical Thinking

After filing (often online) a DBA or FBN, the sole proprietor must publish the statement in a newspaper to notify the public. For the most part, online DBA notification is not an option. Should it be? Explain your answer.

a. *G & G Closed Circuit Events, LLC, v. Gonzalez Ruiz*, 379 F.Supp. 3d 1061 (S.D. Cal. 2019).

Personal Assets at Risk Because of the sole proprietor's unlimited liability, creditors can go after personal assets to satisfy any business debts. Although sole proprietors may obtain insurance to protect the business, liability can easily exceed policy limits. This unlimited liability is a major factor to be considered in choosing a business form.

Example 26.2 Sheila operates a golf shop near a world-class golf course as a sole proprietorship. One of Sheila's employees fails to secure a display of golf clubs, and they fall on Dean, a professional golfer, and seriously injure him. If Dean sues Sheila's shop and wins, Sheila's personal liability could easily exceed the limits of her insurance policy. Sheila could lose not only her business, but also her house, her car, and any other personal assets that can be attached to pay the judgment.

Lack of Continuity and Limited Ability to Raise Capital The sole proprietorship also has the disadvantage of lacking continuity after the death of the proprietor. When the owner dies, so does the business—it is automatically dissolved.

Another disadvantage is that in raising capital, the proprietor is limited to personal funds and any loans that can be obtained for the business. Lenders may be unwilling to make loans to sole proprietorships, particularly start-ups, because the sole proprietor risks unlimited personal liability and may not be able to pay.

26–2 Franchises

Instead of setting up a completely independent business, many entrepreneurs opt to purchase a franchise. A **franchise** is an arrangement in which the owner of intellectual property—such as a trademark, a trade name, or a copyright—licenses others to use it in the selling of goods or services. A **franchisee** (a purchaser of a franchise) is generally legally independent of the **franchisor** (the seller of the franchise). At the same time, the franchisee is economically dependent on the franchisor's integrated business system. In other words, a franchisee can operate as an independent businessperson and choose any business form but still obtain the advantages of a regional or national organization. Today, franchising companies and their franchisees account for a significant portion of all retail sales in this country. Well-known franchises include McDonald's, 7-Eleven, and Holiday Inn.

Franchise Any arrangement in which the owner of a trademark, trade name, or copyright licenses another to use that trademark, trade name, or copyright in the selling of goods or services.

Franchisee One receiving a license to use another's (the franchisor's) trademark, trade name, or copyright in the sale of goods and services.

Franchisor One licensing another (the franchisee) to use the owner's trademark, trade name, or copyright in the selling of goods or services.

26–2a Types of Franchises

Many different kinds of businesses sell franchises, and numerous types of franchises are available. Generally, though, most franchises fall into one of three classifications: distributorships, chain-style business operations, or manufacturing or processing-plant arrangements.

Distributorships In a *distributorship*, a manufacturer (the franchisor) licenses a dealer (the franchisee) to sell its product. Often, a distributorship covers an exclusive territory. Automobile dealerships and beer distributorships are examples of this type of franchise.

Example 26.3 Black Snow Beer Company distributes its beer brands through a network of authorized wholesale distributors, each with an assigned territory. Marik signs a distributorship contract for the area from Gainesville to Ocala, Florida. If the contract states that Marik is the exclusive distributor in that area, then no other franchisee may distribute Black Snow beer in that region. ■

alaincouillaud/E+/Getty Images

If a brand of beer is sold through authorized wholesale distributors only, can a potential distributor of the beer obtain an exclusive territory?

Chain-Style Business Operations In a *chain-style business operation*, a franchise operates under a franchisor's trade name and is identified as a member of a select group of dealers that engage in the franchisor's business. The franchisee is generally required to follow standardized or prescribed methods of operation. In addition, the franchisee may be required to obtain materials and supplies exclusively from the franchisor.

McDonald's and most other fast-food chains are examples of chain-style franchises. This type of franchise is also common in service-related businesses, including real estate brokerage firms such as Century 21 and tax-preparing services such as H&R Block, Inc.

Manufacturing or Processing-Plant Arrangements In a *manufacturing or processing-plant arrangement*, the franchisor transmits to the franchisee the essential ingredients or formula to make a particular product. The franchisee then markets the product either at wholesale or at retail in accordance with the franchisor's standards. Examples of this type of franchise are Pepsi-Cola and other soft-drink bottling companies.

Know This

Because a franchise involves the licensing of a trademark, a trade name, or a copyright, the law governing intellectual property may apply in some situations.

26–2b Laws Governing Franchising

Because a franchise relationship is primarily a contractual relationship, it is governed by contract law. If the franchise exists primarily for the sale of products manufactured by the franchisor, the law governing sales contracts as expressed in Article 2 of the Uniform Commercial Code applies.

Additionally, the federal government and most states have enacted laws governing certain aspects of franchising. Generally, these laws are designed to protect prospective franchisees from dishonest franchisors and to prohibit franchisors from terminating franchises without good cause.

Federal Regulation of Franchising The federal government regulates franchising through laws that apply to specific industries and through the Franchise Rule, created by the Federal Trade Commission (FTC).

Industry-Specific Standards. Congress has enacted laws that protect franchisees in certain industries, such as automobile dealerships and service stations. These laws protect the franchisee from unreasonable demands and bad-faith terminations of the franchise by the franchisor.

An automobile manufacturer-franchisor cannot make unreasonable demands of dealer-franchisees or set unrealistically high sales quotas, for instance. If an automobile manufacturer-franchisor terminates a franchise because of a dealer-franchisee's failure to comply with unreasonable demands, the manufacturer may be liable for damages.[3]

Similarly, federal law prescribes the conditions under which a franchisor of service stations can terminate a franchise.[4] In addition, federal antitrust laws sometimes apply to prohibit certain types of anticompetitive agreements involving service-station franchises.

The Franchise Rule. The FTC's Franchise Rule requires franchisors to disclose certain material facts that a prospective franchisee needs in order to make an informed decision concerning the purchase of a franchise.[5] Those who violate the Franchise Rule are subject to substantial civil penalties, and the FTC can sue on behalf of injured parties to recover damages.

Focus Question 2
What is required by the Franchise Rule, and why?

The rule requires the franchisor to make numerous written disclosures to prospective franchisees (see Exhibit 26–1). All representations made to a prospective franchisee must have a reasonable basis. For instance, if a franchisor provides projected earnings figures, the franchisor must indicate whether the figures are based on actual data or hypothetical

Exhibit 26–1 The FTC's Franchise Rule Requirements

REQUIREMENTS	EXPLANATION
Written (or electronic) disclosures	The franchisor must make numerous disclosures, such as the range of goods and services included, as well as the value and estimated profitability of the franchise. Disclosures can be delivered on paper or electronically. Prospective franchisees must be able to download or save any electronic disclosure documents.
Reasonable basis for any representations	To prevent deception, all representations made to a prospective franchisee must have a reasonable basis at the time they are made.
Projected earnings figures	If a franchisor provides projected earnings figures, the franchisor must indicate whether the figures are based on actual data or hypothetical examples. The Franchise Rule does not require franchisors to provide potential earnings figures, however.
Actual data	If a franchisor makes sales or earnings projections based on actual data for a specific franchise location, the franchisor must disclose the number and percentage of its existing franchises that have achieved this result.
Explanation of terms	Franchisors are required to explain termination, cancellation, and renewal provisions of the franchise contract to potential franchisees before the agreement is signed.

3. Automobile Dealers' Franchise Act of 1965, also known as the Automobile Dealers' Day in Court Act, 15 U.S.C. Sections 1221 *et seq.*
4. Petroleum Marketing Practices Act (PMPA) of 1979, 15 U.S.C. Sections 2801 *et seq.*
5. 16 C.F.R. Part 436.

examples. If a franchisor makes sales or earnings projections based on actual data for a specific franchise location, the franchisor must disclose the number and percentage of its existing franchises that have achieved this result. The Franchise Rule does not require franchisors to provide potential earnings figures, however.

State Regulation of Franchising State legislation varies but generally is aimed at protecting franchisees from unfair practices and bad-faith terminations by franchisors.

State Disclosures. A number of states have laws similar to the federal rules requiring franchisors to provide presale disclosures to prospective franchisees.[6] Many state laws also require that a disclosure document (known as the Franchise Disclosure Document, or FDD) be registered or filed with a state official. State laws may also require that a franchisor submit advertising aimed at prospective franchisees to the state for approval.

To protect franchisees, a state law may require the disclosure of information such as the actual costs of operation, recurring expenses, and profits earned, along with data substantiating these figures. State deceptive trade practices acts may also apply and may prohibit certain actions on the part of franchisors.

When can an automobile manufacturer franchisor terminate the franchise of an authorized dealer for failing to sufficiently hire and train personnel?

Requirements for Termination. To prevent arbitrary or bad-faith terminations, state law may prohibit termination without "good cause" or require that certain procedures be followed in terminating a franchising relationship.

Case Example 26.4 TS & A Motors (TSA) entered into a franchise agreement to become an authorized dealership for the sale and service of Kia automobiles. Under this agreement, TSA was required to employ a "sufficient number of competent personnel" and provide regular training for its parts and service department employees.

Over a period of nearly five years, TSA consistently failed to fill the positions mandated by the franchise agreement or to provide the necessary training for staffers. Finally, Kia canceled TSA's franchise. TSA sued, claiming that Kia had not given it enough time under state law to fix issues caused by "an unprecedented tight labor market for automobile service workers." The Supreme Court of New Hampshire ruled that Kia had good cause for termination, considering the "continuing nature" of TSA's staffing problems and Kia's patience while giving the franchisee multiple chances to solve these problems.[7]

26–3 The Franchise Contract

The franchise relationship is defined by a contract between the franchisor and the franchisee. The franchise contract specifies the terms and conditions of the franchise and spells out the rights and duties of both parties. If either party fails to perform the contractual duties, that party may be subject to a lawsuit for breach of contract. Generally, statutes and case law governing franchising emphasize the importance of good faith and fair dealing in franchise relationships.

6. These states include California, Florida, Hawaii, Illinois, Indiana, Maryland, Michigan, Minnesota, New York, North Dakota, Oregon, Rhode Island, South Dakota, Texas, Utah, Virginia, Washington, and Wisconsin.
7. *TS & A Motors, LLC v. Kia Motors America, Inc.*, 172 N.H. 94, 208 A.3d 429 (2019).

Because each type of franchise relationship has its own characteristics, franchise contracts tend to differ. Nonetheless, certain major issues typically are addressed in a franchise contract.

26–3a Payment for the Franchise

The franchisee ordinarily pays an initial fee or lump-sum price for the franchise license (the privilege of being granted a franchise). This fee is separate from the various products that the franchisee purchases from or through the franchisor. The franchise agreement may also require the franchisee to pay a percentage of advertising costs and certain administrative expenses.

In some industries, the franchisor relies heavily on the initial sale of the franchise for realizing a profit. In other industries, the continued dealing between the parties brings profit to both. Generally, the franchisor receives a stated percentage of the annual (or monthly) sales or volume of business done by the franchisee.

Eric Glenn/shutterstock.com

What are some of the payments that franchisees typically make to franchisors?

26–3b Business Premises

The franchise agreement may specify whether the premises for the business must be leased or purchased outright. Sometimes, a building must be constructed or remodeled to meet the terms of the agreement. The agreement usually specifies whether the franchisor supplies equipment and furnishings for the premises or whether this is the responsibility of the franchisee.

26–3c Location of the Franchise

Typically, the franchisor determines the territory to be served. Some franchise contracts give the franchisee exclusive rights, or "territorial rights," to a certain geographic area. Other franchise contracts, though they define the territory allotted to a particular franchise, either specifically state that the franchise is nonexclusive or are silent on the issue of territorial rights.

Many franchise cases involve disputes over territorial rights, and the implied covenant of good faith and fair dealing often comes into play in this area of franchising. If the franchise contract does not grant exclusive territorial rights to a franchisee and the franchisor allows a competing franchise to be established nearby, the franchisee may suffer a significant loss in profits. In this situation, a court may hold that the franchisor's actions breached an implied covenant of good faith and fair dealing.

26–3d Quality Control by the Franchisor

The day-to-day operation of the franchise business normally is left up to the franchisee. Nonetheless, the franchise agreement may specify that the franchisor will provide some degree of supervision and control so that it can protect the franchise's name and reputation.

Means of Control When the franchise prepares a product, such as food, or provides a service, such as motel accommodations, the contract often states that the franchisor will establish certain standards for the facility. Typically, the contract states that the franchisor is permitted to make periodic inspections to ensure that the standards are being maintained.

As a means of controlling quality, franchise agreements also typically limit the franchisee's ability to sell the franchise to another party. **Example 26.5** Mark Keller, an authorized Jaguar franchise, contracts to sell its dealership to Henrique Autos West. A Jaguar franchise generally cannot be sold without Jaguar Cars' permission. Prospective franchisees must meet Jaguar's customer satisfaction standards. If Henrique Autos fails to meet those standards, Jaguar can refuse to allow the sale and can terminate the franchise.

Focus Question 3

What might happen if a franchisor exercises too much control over the operations of a franchise?

Degree of Control As a general rule, the validity of a provision permitting the franchisor to establish and enforce certain quality standards is unquestioned. The franchisor has a legitimate interest in maintaining the quality of the product or service to protect its name and reputation.

If a franchisor exercises too much control over the operations of its franchisees, however, the franchisor risks potential liability. A franchisor may also occasionally be held liable—under the doctrine of *respondeat superior*—for the tortious acts of the franchisees' employees. (This chapter's *Cybersecurity and the Law* feature looks at the issue of control in the context of security breaches.)

Know This

Under the doctrine of *respondeat superior*, an employer may be liable for the torts of employees if they occur within the scope of employment, without regard to the personal fault of the employer.

26–3e Pricing Arrangements

Franchises provide the franchisor with an outlet for the firm's goods and services. Depending on the nature of the business, the franchisor may require the franchisee to purchase certain supplies from the franchisor at an established price.[8] A franchisor cannot, however, set the prices at which the franchisee will resell the goods, because such price setting may be a violation of state or federal antitrust laws, or both. A franchisor can suggest retail prices but cannot mandate them.

8. Although a franchisor can require franchisees to purchase supplies from it, requiring a franchisee to purchase exclusively from the franchisor may violate federal antitrust laws.

Cybersecurity and the Law

Brinker International, Inc.

The news that Brinker International, Inc., was the defendant in a cybersecurity class-action lawsuit did not attract much attention outside the business world.[a] The reason: Brinker, a franchisor, has only a fraction of the name recognition of its main franchise, Chili's Grill & Bar. But when the payment systems at a number of Chili's restaurants were hacked, Brinker was the entity sued, underscoring a growing dilemma for franchisors in the era of large-scale data breaches.

Attacking the Franchise

Because of the massive number of credit card transactions they process, franchises are a common target of hackers. In case after case involving franchises such as Dairy Queen, UPS, Wendy's, and Goodwill, hackers have used malware to infiltrate the franchise's point-of-sale (POS) system. Even though the franchisee usually has actual control over the POS terminals, the focus in the wake of a data breach is almost always the franchisor.

In some instances, the Franchise Disclosure Document (FDD) will contain specific provisions that detail the responsibilities and obligations for both franchisors and franchisees with regard to data protection. Many FDDs are vague when it comes to cybersecurity, however, leaving the impression that the franchisor, which generally has control over the franchisee's information technology (IT) systems, must provide security for those systems. Furthermore, as far as plaintiffs' attorneys are concerned, the "deep pockets" of the franchisor hold more promise for a large settlement that do the relatively limited resources of any individual franchisee. So, as was the case with Brinker, after a data breach of a franchisee, the blame and potential liability almost always end up with the franchisor.

Critical Thinking

Suppose a franchisor has two choices when it comes to cybersecurity provisions in its FDD. The franchisor can either (a) assume control and responsibility for a franchisee's privacy security system, or (b) avoid this control and responsibility, leaving point-of-sale security in the hands of the franchisee. Which is the better choice? Why?

a. See *In re Brinker Data Incident Litigation*, Case No. 3:18-cv-686-J-32MCR (M.D. Fla. 2020).

26–4 Franchise Termination

The duration of the franchise is a matter to be determined between the parties. Sometimes, a franchise will start out for a short period, such as a year, so that the franchisor can determine whether it wants to stay in business with the franchisee. At other times, the duration of the franchise contract correlates with the term of the lease for the business premises, and both are renewable at the end of that period.

26–4a Grounds for Termination

Usually, the franchise agreement specifies that termination must be "for cause" and then defines the grounds for termination. Cause might include, for instance, the death or disability of the franchisee, insolvency of the franchisee, breach of the franchise agreement, or failure to meet specified sales quotas.

In the following case, a franchisee contended that its franchisor did not have good cause to terminate the franchise.

Case 26.2

S&P Brake Supply, Inc. v. Daimler Trucks North America, LLC

Montana Supreme Court, 2018 MT 25, 390 Mont. 243, 411 P.3d 1264 (2018).

Facts S&P Brake Supply, Inc., was the sole authorized dealer of Western Star Trucks in Yellowstone County, Montana. S&P operated its franchise under an agreement with Daimler Trucks North America, LLC. The agreement required S&P to sell a certain number of trucks in its "area of responsibility" (AOR) (Yellowstone County). Over a three-year period, S&P sold only two trucks. Daimler advised its franchisee to use more effective marketing strategies and hire more sales staff, among other things.

The next year, primarily because of S&P's failure to meet its sales goals, Daimler notified S&P that the franchise was being terminated. S&P filed an objection with the Montana Department of Justice, Motor Vehicle Division. The department issued a decision in Daimler's favor. S&P filed a petition in a state court for review. The court upheld the department's decision. S&P appealed to the Montana Supreme Court.

Issue Did Daimler have good cause to terminate S&P's franchise?

Decision Yes. The Montana Supreme Court affirmed the judgment of the lower court. The court did not err by upholding the department's decision.

Reason The evidence showed, and the department found, that "S&P's sales were deficient no matter which way one analyzed the data." Year after year, S&P failed to meet its sales goals, which were based on market factors and the population of Yellowstone County. In addition to this failure, of the seven Western Star trucks registered in the county during the last four years of S&P's franchise, S&P had sold only two of them. That the majority of Western Star trucks in S&P's AOR were bought elsewhere indicated that the franchisee was not reaching and serving local customers. Compared to the sales performance of other Western Star dealers in the region, S&P's share of its market was low. This comparison relied on national truck registration data. S&P argued that an analysis of its performance should have been based solely on evidence related to Yellowstone County. Because S&P was the only dealer in the county, however, limiting the evidence would not allow a comparison to other dealers, and there would be no meaningful basis for evaluating the lone franchisee's performance.

Critical Thinking

- **Economic** *The department concluded that S&P's failure to use more effective marketing strategies and to hire more sales staff breached the franchise agreement. S&P argued that these were not material breaches because the agreement's fundamental purpose was to sell trucks. Is S&P correct? Discuss.*
- **Legal Environment** *Considering that S&P was the only Western Star truck dealer in Yellowstone County, did discontinuing the franchise injure the public interest? Explain.*

Notice Requirements Most franchise contracts provide that notice of termination must be given. If no set time for termination is specified, then a reasonable time, with notice, is implied. A franchisee must be given reasonable time to wind up the business—that is, to do the accounting and return the copyright or trademark or any other property of the franchisor.

Opportunity to Cure a Breach A franchise agreement may state that the franchisee may attempt to cure an ordinary, curable breach within a certain period of time after notice so as to postpone, or even avoid, the termination of the contract. Even when a contract contains a notice-and-cure provision, however, a franchisee's breach of the duty of honesty and fidelity may be enough to allow the franchisor to terminate the franchise.

Spotlight Case Example 26.6 Milind and Minaxi Upadhyaya entered into a franchise contract with 7-Eleven, Inc., to operate a store in Pennsylvania. The contract included a notice-and-cure provision. Under 7-Eleven's usual contract, franchisees lease the store and equipment, and receive a license to use 7-Eleven's trademarks and other intellectual property. 7-Eleven receives a percentage of the store's gross profit (net sales less the cost of goods sold).

Tupungato/Shutterstock.com

Why did a court prevent 7-Eleven franchisees from curing a breach of their franchise agreement?

A 7-Eleven manager noticed a high rate of certain questionable transactions at the Upadhyayas' store and began investigating. The investigation continued for nearly two years and revealed that the store had been misreporting its sales to 7-Eleven so as to conceal sales proceeds. Evidence indicated that nearly one-third of the store's sales transactions had not been properly recorded.

7-Eleven sent a "non-curable" notice of material breach and termination of the franchise to the Upadhyayas. The franchisees argued that they had not been given an opportunity to cure the breach. The court found there was sufficient evidence of fraud to warrant immediate termination without an opportunity to cure.[9]

26–4b Wrongful Termination

Because a franchisor's termination of a franchise often has adverse consequences for the franchisee, much franchise litigation involves claims of wrongful termination. Generally, the termination provisions of contracts are more favorable to the franchisor. This means that the franchisee, who normally invests a substantial amount of time and funds to make the franchise operation successful, may receive little or nothing for the business on termination. The franchisor owns the trademark and hence the business.

It is in this area that statutory and case law become important. The federal and state laws discussed earlier attempt, among other things, to protect franchisees from arbitrary or unfair termination of their franchises by the franchisors.

Focus Question 4

When will a court decide that a franchisor has wrongfully terminated a franchise?

26–4c The Importance of Good Faith and Fair Dealing

Generally, both statutory law and case law emphasize the importance of good faith and fair dealing in terminating a franchise relationship. In determining whether a franchisor has acted in good faith when terminating a franchise agreement, the courts generally try to balance the rights of both parties.

If a court perceives that a franchisor has arbitrarily or unfairly terminated a franchise, the franchisee will be provided with a remedy for wrongful termination. When a franchisor's decision to terminate a franchise was made in the normal course of the franchisor's business operations, however, that weighs in favor of the franchisor. In that situation, a court generally will not consider termination wrongful as long as reasonable notice of termination was given to the franchisee.

The importance of good faith and fair dealing in a franchise relationship is underscored by the consequences of the franchisor's acts in the following case.

9. *7-Eleven, Inc. v. Upadhyaya*, 926 F.Supp.2d 614 (E.D.Penn. 2013).

Spotlight on Holiday Inns: Case 26.3

Holiday Inn Franchising, Inc. v. Hotel Associates, Inc.

Court of Appeals of Arkansas, 2011 Ark.App. 147, 382 S.W.3d 6 (2011).

Facts Buddy House was in the construction business. For decades, he collaborated on projects with Holiday Inn Franchising, Inc. Their relationship was characterized by good faith—many projects were undertaken without written contracts. At Holiday Inn's request, House inspected a hotel in Wichita Falls, Texas, to estimate the cost of getting it into shape. Holiday Inn wanted House to renovate the hotel and operate it as a Holiday Inn. House estimated that recovering the cost of renovation would take him more than ten years, so he asked for a franchise term longer than Holiday Inn's usual ten years. Holiday Inn refused but said that if he ran the hotel "appropriately," the term would be extended at the end of ten years. House bought the hotel, renovated it, and operated it as Hotel Associates, Inc. (HAI), generating substantial profits. He refused offers to sell it for as much as $15 million.

Before the ten years had passed, Greg Aden, a Holiday Inn executive, developed a plan to license a different local hotel as a Holiday Inn instead of renewing House's franchise license. Aden stood to earn a commission from licensing the other hotel. No one informed House of Aden's plan. When the time came, HAI applied for an extension of its franchise, and Holiday Inn asked for major renovations. HAI spent $3 million to comply with this request. Holiday Inn did not renew the term for HAI, however, and granted a franchise to the other hotel instead. HAI sold its hotel for $5 million and filed a suit against Holiday Inn, asserting fraud. The court awarded HAI compensatory and punitive damages. Holiday Inn appealed.

Issue Did Holiday Inn's failure to inform House that it intended to grant the franchise to a different local hotel constitute fraud?

Decision Yes. A state intermediate appellate court affirmed the lower court's judgment.

Reason The court recognized that a failure to volunteer information normally does not constitute fraud. But silence can amount to fraud when parties are in a relationship of trust and there is an "inequality" of knowledge between them—for instance, when one party has information that the other party is justified in assuming does not exist.

In this case, House's relationship with Holiday Inn was characterized by "honesty, trust, and the free flow of pertinent information." With respect to the Wichita Falls hotel, Holiday Inn assured HAI that its franchise would be renewed after ten years if it ran the hotel "appropriately." House was thus justified in assuming that his franchise was not in jeopardy.

Holiday Inn, however, knew of Aden's plan to license a different facility in the same area and did not inform House. In these circumstances, the failure to inform was fraud. Even Holiday Inn personnel, including Aden, admitted that House should have been informed. The appellate court also upheld the lower court's award of compensatory damages and increased the amount of punitive damages, citing Holiday Inn's "degree of reprehensibility."

Critical Thinking

- **Legal Environment** *Why should House and HAI have been advised of Holiday Inn's plan to grant a franchise to a different hotel in their territory?*

Practice and Review

Carlos Del Rey decided to open a fast-food Mexican restaurant and signed a franchise contract with a national chain called La Grande Enchilada. Under the franchise agreement, Del Rey purchased the building, and La Grande Enchilada supplied the equipment. The contract required the franchisee to strictly follow the franchisor's operating manual and stated that failure to do so would be grounds for terminating the franchise contract. The manual set forth detailed operating procedures and safety standards, and provided that a La Grande Enchilada representative would inspect the restaurant monthly to ensure compliance.

Nine months after Del Rey began operating his restaurant, a spark from the grill ignited an oily towel in the kitchen. No one was injured, but by the time firefighters put out the fire, the kitchen had sustained

extensive damage. The cook told the fire department that the towel was "about two feet from the grill" when it caught fire, which was in compliance with the franchisor's manual that required towels to be at least one foot from the grills. Nevertheless, the next day La Grande Enchilada notified Del Rey that his franchise would terminate in thirty days for failure to follow the prescribed safety procedures. Using the information presented in the chapter, answer the following questions.

1. What type of franchise was Del Rey's La Grande Enchilada restaurant?
2. If Del Rey operates the restaurant as a sole proprietorship, who bears the loss for the damaged kitchen? Explain.
3. Assume that Del Rey files a lawsuit against La Grande Enchilada, claiming that his franchise was wrongfully terminated. What is the main factor a court would consider in determining whether the franchise was wrongfully terminated?
4. Would a court be likely to rule that La Grande Enchilada had good cause to terminate Del Rey's franchise in this situation? Why or why not?

Debate This

All franchisors should be required by law to provide a comprehensive estimate of the profitability of a prospective franchise based on the experiences of their existing franchisees.

Key Terms

entrepreneur 652
franchise 656
franchisee 656
franchisor 656
sole proprietorship 653

Chapter Summary: Sole Proprietorships and Franchises

Sole Proprietorships	The sole proprietorship is the simplest form of business organization. Anyone who does business without creating a separate business entity is a sole proprietor. The owner is the business. The owner pays personal income taxes on all profits and is personally liable for all business debts.
Franchises	**1. Types of franchises—** **a.** Distributorships (for example, automobile dealerships). **b.** Chain-style business operations (for example, fast-food chains). **c.** Manufacturing or processing-plant arrangements (for example, soft-drink bottling companies). **2. Laws governing franchising—**Franchises are governed by contract law. They are also governed by federal and state statutory laws, as well as agency regulations.

The Franchise Contact	The franchise relationship is defined by a contract between the franchisor and the franchisee. The contract normally spells out the following terms: 1. **Payment for the franchise**—Ordinarily, the contract requires the franchisee (purchaser) to pay an initial fee or lump-sum price for the franchise license. 2. **Business premises**—The contract may specify whether the business premises will be leased or purchased by the franchisee and which party will provide the equipment and furnishings. 3. **Location of the franchise**—The franchisor typically specifies the territory to be served by the franchisee. 4. **Quality control**—The franchisor may require the franchisee to abide by certain standards of quality relating to the product or service offered. 5. **Pricing arrangements**—The franchisor may require the franchisee to purchase certain supplies from the franchisor at an established price but cannot set retail resale prices.
Franchise Termination	Usually, the contract specifies the duration and conditions of termination of the franchise arrangement. Both federal and state statutes attempt to protect franchisees from franchisors who unfairly or arbitrarily terminate franchises.

Issue Spotters

1. Frank plans to open a sporting goods store and to hire Gogi and Hap. Frank will invest only his own funds. He expects that he will not make a profit for at least eighteen months and will make only a small profit in the three years after that. He hopes to expand eventually. Would a sole proprietorship be an appropriate form for Frank's business? Why or why not? (See *Sole Proprietorships.*)
2. Thirsty Bottling Company and U.S. Beverages, Inc. (USB), enter into a franchise agreement that states that the franchise may be terminated at any time "for cause." Thirsty fails to meet USB's specified sales quota. Does this constitute "cause" for termination? Why or why not? (See *Franchise Termination.*)

—Check your answers to the *Issue Spotters* against the answers provided in Appendix D.

Business Scenarios and Case Problems

26–1. Franchising. Maria, Pablo, and Vicky are recent college graduates who would like to go into business for themselves. They are considering purchasing a franchise. If they enter into a franchising arrangement, they would have the support of a large company that could answer any questions they might have. Also, a firm that has been in business for many years would be experienced in dealing with some of the problems that novice businesspersons might encounter. These and other attributes of franchises can lessen some of the risks of the marketplace. What other aspects of franchising—positive and negative—should Maria, Pablo, and Vicky consider before committing themselves to a particular franchise? (See *Franchises.*)

26–2. Control of a Franchise. National Foods, Inc., sells franchises to its fast-food restaurants, known as Chicky-D's. Under the franchise agreement, franchisees agree to hire and train employees strictly according to Chicky-D's standards. In addition, Chicky-D's regional supervisors must approve all new hires and policies, which they generally do. Chicky-D's reserves the right to terminate a franchise for violating the franchisor's rules. After several incidents of racist comments and conduct by Tim, a recently hired assistant manager at a Chicky-D's, Sharon, a counterperson at the restaurant, resigns. Sharon files a suit against National. National files a motion for summary judgment, arguing that it is not liable for harassment by franchise employees. Will the court grant National's motion? Why or why not? (See *The Franchise Contract.*)

26–3. Spotlight on McDonald's—Franchise Termination. C.B. Management, Inc., had a franchise agreement with McDonald's Corp. to operate McDonald's restaurants in Cleveland, Ohio. The agreement required C.B. to make monthly payments of certain percentages of the gross sales to McDonald's. If any payment was more than thirty days late, McDonald's had the right to terminate the franchise. The agreement also stated that even if McDonald's accepted a late payment, that would not "constitute a waiver of any subsequent breach." McDonald's sometimes accepted C.B.'s late payments, but when C.B. defaulted on the payments in July, McDonald's gave notice of thirty days to comply or surrender possession of the restaurants. C.B. missed the deadline. McDonald's demanded that C.B. vacate the restaurants, but C.B. refused. McDonald's alleged that C.B. had violated the franchise agreement. C.B. claimed that McDonald's had breached the implied covenant of good faith and fair dealing. Which party should prevail, and why? [*McDonald's Corp. v. C.B. Management Co.*, 13 F.Supp.2d 705 (N.D.Ill. 1998)] (See *Franchise Termination.*)

26–4. Business Case Problem with Sample Answer—Quality Control. JTH Tax, Inc., doing business as Liberty Tax Service, provides tax preparation and related loan services throughout the United States in more than two thousand company-owned and franchised stores. Liberty's agreement with its franchisees reserved the right to control their ads. In company operations manuals, Liberty provided step-by-step instructions, directions, and limitations to its franchisees regarding their ads. Liberty retained the right to unilaterally modify the steps at any time. The California Attorney General filed a suit in a California state court against Liberty, alleging misleading or deceptive ads by its franchisees regarding refund anticipation loans and e-refund checks. Can Liberty be held liable? Discuss. [*People v. JTH Tax, Inc.*, 212 Cal.App.4th 1219, 151 Cal.Rptr.3d 728 (1 Dist. 2013)] (See *The Franchise Contract.*)

—For a sample answer to Problem 26–4, go to Appendix E.

26–5. Quality Control. The franchise agreement of Domino's Pizza, LLC, sets out operational standards, including safety requirements, for a franchisee to follow but provides that the franchisee is an independent contractor. Each franchisee is free to use its own means and methods. For example, Domino's does not know whether a franchisee's delivery drivers are complying with vehicle safety requirements. MAC Pizza Management, Inc., operates a Domino's franchise. A vehicle driven by Joshua Balka, a MAC delivery driver, hydroplaned due to a bald tire and wet pavement, and struck the vehicle of Devavaram and Ruth Christopher, killing Ruth and injuring Devavaram. Is Domino's liable for negligence? Explain. [*Domino's Pizza, LLC v. Reddy*, 2015 WL 1247349 (Tex.App.—Beaumont 2015)] (See *The Franchise Contract.*)

26–6. Franchise Termination. Executive Home Care Franchising, LLC, sells in-home health-care franchises. Clint, Massare, and Greer Marshall entered into a franchise agreement with Executive Home Care. The agreement provided that the franchisees' failure to comply with the agreement's terms would likely cause irreparable harm to the franchisor, entitling it to an injunction. About two years later, the Marshalls gave up their franchise. They returned thirteen boxes of documents, stationery, operating manuals, marketing materials, and other items—everything in their possession that featured Executive Home Care trademarks. They quit operating out of the franchised location. They transferred the phone number back to the franchisor and informed their clients that they were no longer associated with Executive Home Care. They continued to engage in the home health-care business, however, under the name "Well-Being Home Care Corp." Is Executive Home Care entitled to an injunction against the Marshalls and their new company? Discuss. [*Executive Home Care Franchising, LLC v. Marshall Health Corp.*, 642 Fed.Appx. 181 (3d Cir. 2016)] (See *Franchise Termination.*)

26–7. Location of the Franchise. Chrysler, LLC, awarded a Chrysler-Jeep franchise in Billings, Montana, to Lithia Motors, Inc. Lithia exceeded the sales goals and other expectations expressed in the franchise agreement. Later, Chrysler approved an application by Rimrock Chrysler, Inc., to open an additional Chrysler-Jeep franchise less than a mile from Lithia's location. Lithia's agreement was silent on the issue of territorial rights, but the dealer protested Chrysler's approval of Rimrock's application. Could Chrysler's actions be considered a breach of the franchisor's deal with Lithia? Discuss. [*Rimrock Chrysler, Inc. v. State of Montana Department of Justice, Motor Vehicle Division*, 2018 MT 24, 390 Mont. 235, 411 P.3d 1278 (2018)] (See *The Franchise Contract.*)

26–8. A Question of Ethics—The IDDR Approach and Sole Proprietorships. Tom George was the sole owner of Turbine Component Super Market, LLC (TCSM), when its existence was terminated by the state of Texas. A TCSM creditor, Turbine Resources Unlimited, filed and won a suit in a Texas state court against George for breach of contract. The plaintiff sought to collect the amount of the judgment through a sale of George's property. Instead of turning his assets over to the court, however, George tried to hide them by reforming TCSM. Without telling the court, he paid an unrelated debt with $100,000 of TCSM's funds. George claimed that the funds were a loan and that he was merely an employee of TCSM. [*Mitchell v. Turbine Resources Unlimited, Inc.*, 523 S.W.3d 189 (Tex.App.—Houston [14th Dist.] 2017)] (See *Sole Proprietorships.*)

1. Is it more likely that the court will recognize TCSM as an LLC or a sole proprietorship? Why?
2. Using the *Discussion* step of the IDDR approach, consider whether the owner of a business has an ethical obligation to represent the character and purpose of the organization truthfully.

Critical Thinking and Writing Assignments

26–9. Business Law Writing. Jordan Mendelson is interested in purchasing a franchise in a meal-preparation business. Customers will come to the business to assemble gourmet dinners and then take the prepared meals to their homes for cooking. The franchisor requires each store to use a specific layout and provides the recipes for various dinners, but the franchisee is not required to purchase the food products from the franchisor. What general factors should Mendelson consider before entering into a contract to buy such a franchise? Is location important? Are there any laws that Mendelson should consider, given that this franchise involves food preparation and sales? Should Mendelson operate this business as a sole proprietorship? Why or why not? (See *The Franchise Contract*.)

26–10. Time-Limited Group Assignment—Franchise Termination. Walid Elkhatib, an Arab American, bought a Dunkin' Donuts franchise in Illinois. Ten years later, Dunkin' Donuts began offering breakfast sandwiches with bacon, ham, or sausage through its franchises. Elkhatib refused to sell these items at his store on the ground that his religion forbade the handling of pork. Elkhatib then opened a second franchise, at which he also refused to sell pork products. The next year, at both locations, Elkhatib began selling meatless sandwiches. He also opened a third franchise. When he proposed to relocate this franchise, Dunkin' Donuts refused to approve the new location and informed him that it would not renew any of his franchise agreements because he did not carry the full sandwich line. Elkhatib filed a lawsuit against Dunkin' Donuts. (See *Franchise Termination*.)

1. The first group will argue on behalf of Elkhatib that Dunkin' Donuts wrongfully terminated his franchises.
2. The second group will take the side of Dunkin' Donuts and justify its decision to terminate the franchises.
3. The third group will assess whether Dunkin' Donuts acted in good faith in its relationship with Elkhatib. It will also consider whether Dunkin' Donuts should be required to accommodate Elkhatib's religious beliefs and allow him to not serve pork in these three locations.

27 All Forms of Partnership

Focus Questions

The five Focus Question *below are designed to help impove your understanding. After reading this chapter, you should be able to answer the following questions:*

1. What are the three essential elements of a partnership?
2. What are the fiduciary duties of partners in a general partnership?
3. What is dissociation? What happens when a partner dissociates from a partnership?
4. What advantages do limited liability partnerships offer to businesspersons that are not offered by general partnerships?
5. What are the key differences between the rights and liabilities of general partners and those of limited partners?

"All men's gains are the fruit of venturing."

Herodotus
Fifth Century B.C.E.
(Greek historian)

Historically, the two most common forms of business organization selected by two or more persons going into business together have been the partnership and the corporation. A *partnership* arises from an agreement, express or implied, between two or more persons to carry on a business for profit. Partners are co-owners of a business and have joint control over its operation and the right to share in its profits. As the chapter-opening quotation indicates, all gains are the "fruit of venturing," and partnerships—to the extent that they encourage business ventures—contribute to those gains.

Suppose that, after graduating with a fine arts degree, Coralee starts an online business that sells handmade jewelry and crafts. Her business grows, and she hires employees. Then she meets an app developer, Derek, who wants to invest in her business. He also wants to work with her to create an app that will enable people to easily place orders for her goods from their smartphones and from devices such as Alexa and Google Home.

Coralee agrees to give Derek a 25 percent share of her business profits in exchange for the cash he is contributing and for building the app. Although they sign a contract to that effect, the contract does not identify a particular business form. Is Derek now Coralee's partner? Does Derek have a right to control any aspects of Coralee's business? If Derek never creates the app, or if the app does not function properly, does Coralee still have to give him 25 percent of the profits? Is she liable for his actions? In this chapter, you will learn the answers to questions such as these.

27–1 Basic Partnership Concepts

The traditional partnership is an ordinary, or *general*, partnership. General partnerships are governed both by common law concepts—in particular, those relating to agency—and by statutory law. As in so many other areas of business law, the National Conference of Commissioners on Uniform State Laws has drafted uniform laws for partnerships, and these uniform laws have been widely adopted by the states.

27–1a Agency Concepts and Partnership Law

When two or more persons agree to do business as partners, they enter into a special relationship with one another. To an extent, their relationship is similar to an agency relationship because each partner is deemed to be the agent of the other partners and of the partnership. Thus, the common law agency concepts apply. Specifically, each partner is charged with knowledge of, and responsibility for, acts done within the scope of the partnership relationship. In their relationships with one another, partners, like agents, are bound by fiduciary ties.

In one important way, however, partnership law is distinct from agency law. A partnership is based on a voluntary contract between two or more competent persons who agree to commit financial capital, labor, and skill to a business with the understanding that profits and losses will be shared. In a nonpartnership agency relationship, the agent usually does not have an ownership interest in the business and is not obliged to bear a portion of the ordinary business losses.

Know This

Two or more persons are required to form a partnership. Other forms of business can be organized by a single individual.

27–1b The Uniform Partnership Act

The Uniform Partnership Act (UPA) governs the operation of partnerships *in the absence of an express agreement*. In other words, the partners are free to establish rules for their partnership that differ from those stated in the UPA. The majority of the states have adopted the most recent version of the UPA (completed in 1997 and last amended in 2013).

27–1c Definition of a Partnership

The UPA defines a **partnership** as "an association of two or more persons to carry on as co-owners a business for profit" [UPA 101(6)]. Note that the UPA's definition of *person* includes corporations, so a corporation can be a partner in a partnership [UPA 101(10)]. The *intent* to associate is a key element of a partnership, and a person cannot join a partnership unless all of the other partners consent [UPA 401(i)].

Partnership An agreement by two or more persons to carry on, as co-owners, a business for profit.

27–1d Essential Elements of a Partnership

Parties sometimes find themselves in conflict over whether their business enterprise is a legal partnership, especially when there is no formal, written partnership agreement. In determining whether a partnership exists, courts usually look for three essential elements, which are implicit in the UPA's definition of a general partnership:

1. A sharing of profits and losses.
2. A joint ownership of the business.
3. An equal right to be involved in the management of the business.

If the evidence in a particular case is insufficient to establish all three factors, the UPA provides a set of guidelines to be used.

Focus Question 1

What are the three essential elements of a partnership?

The court in the following case considered these and other factors to determine whether a partnership existed between two participants in a new restaurant venture.

Case 27.1

Harun v. Rashid

Texas Court of Appeals, Dallas, 2018 WL 329292 (2018).

Facts Mohammed Harun was interested in opening a new restaurant, Spice-N-Rice, in Irving, Texas, but lacked the financial resources. He asked Sharif Rashid if Rashid was interested in funding the venture. Rashid said that he was and provided $60,000. Rashid also helped negotiate a lease for the restaurant, was a signatory on its bank account, dealt with contractors, paid for advertising, and bought furniture, equipment, and supplies. In addition, Rashid hired a bookkeeper to perform the restaurant's accounting.

When the bookkeeper expressed concern about Harun's reporting of Spice-N-Rice's income on his tax return, Harun removed Rashid from the bank account and locked him out of the restaurant's premises. Rashid filed a suit in a Texas state court against Harun and Spice-N-Rice, alleging the existence of a partnership and a breach of fiduciary duty. Harun denied that he and Rashid had ever been partners. The court ruled that a partnership existed and awarded damages to Rashid. The defendant appealed.

Issue Were Harun and Rashid partners in Spice-N-Rice?

Decision Yes. A state intermediate appellate court affirmed the lower court's award to Rashid of actual damages of $36,000 (the difference between Rashid's investment of $60,000 and the amount Harun had repaid), punitive damages of $36,000, and attorneys' fees of $79,768, plus interest and costs.

Reason The court listed several factors that can indicate the existence of a partnership in a business. These included the parties' sharing, or right to share, the profits, losses, and liabilities of the business, and the parties' participation, or right to participate, in control of the business. Another factor is an agreement to contribute, or the actual contribution of, money or property to the business.

Rashid presented evidence of his investment and participation in the opening and operation of Spice-N-Rice, including an agreement with Harun to share in its profits and losses. His payment of the restaurant's bills, his hiring of and communicating with the bookkeeper, and his access to the business's bank account were further indications of his partnership in the venture. The appellate court stated, "We conclude the trial court's finding a partnership existed between Harun and Rashid is supported by more than a scintilla [small amount] of evidence." The parties' status as partners supported the lower court's award of damages to Rashid for a breach of fiduciary duty.

Critical Thinking

- **Legal Environment** *Harun's income tax return and other documents prepared by the bookkeeper on behalf of Spice-N-Rice identified the business as a sole proprietorship. Should the appellate court have reversed the finding of a partnership on this basis? Explain.*
- **What If the Facts Were Different?** *Suppose that the appellants had complained that there was a lack of evidence of an agreement between Harun and Rashid to share losses. Would the result have been different? Why or why not?*

The Sharing of Profits and Losses The sharing of *both profits and losses* from a business creates a presumption (legal inference) that a partnership exists. **Case Example 27.1** David Tubb, representing Superior Shooting Systems, Inc., entered into an agreement with Aspect International, Inc., to create a business that would make and sell ammunition to the public. Their contract stated that both companies would participate in the business and split the profits equally, but it did not say explicitly that they would share the losses. It also did not specify what type of entity the business would be. A dispute arose between the two companies, and the matter ended up in court.

A Texas appellate court held that the two corporations had created a partnership even though there was no express agreement to share in losses. They had agreed to share control and ownership of the business and to split the profits equally. They would therefore also have to share the losses equally.[1]

A court will *not presume* that a partnership exists, however, if shared profits are received as payment of any of the following [UPA 202(c)(3)]:

1. A debt by installments or interest on a loan.
2. Wages of an employee or payment for the services of an independent contractor.
3. Rent to a landlord.
4. An annuity to a surviving spouse or representative of a deceased partner.
5. A sale of the goodwill of a business or property.

Jacob Lund/shutterstock.com

What factors can an investor present in court to show that the investor entered into a partnership with a restaurant owner?

Example 27.2 A debtor, Mason, owes a creditor, Alice, $5,000 on an unsecured debt. They agree that Mason will pay 10 percent of his monthly business profits to Alice until the loan with interest has been paid. Although Mason and Alice are sharing profits from the business, they are not presumed to be partners.

Joint Property Ownership Joint ownership of property does not in and of itself create a partnership [UPA 202(c)(1), (2)]. The parties' intentions are key. **Example 27.3** Chiang and Burke jointly own farmland and lease it to a farmer for a share of the profits from the farming operation in lieu of fixed rental payments. This arrangement normally would not make Chiang, Burke, and the farmer partners.

Equal Management Rights In general, every partner in a partnership has an equal say in managing the partnership's affairs. In other words, each partner has a single vote in the management decisions, regardless of that partner's proportional interest in the business (unless the partners have agreed otherwise).

27–1e Entity versus Aggregate Theory of Partnerships

At common law, a partnership was treated only as an aggregate of individuals and never as a separate legal entity. Thus, at common law a lawsuit could never be brought by or against the firm in its own name. Each individual partner had to sue or be sued.

Today, in contrast, a majority of the states follow the UPA and treat a partnership as an entity for most purposes. For instance, a partnership usually can sue or be sued, collect judgments, and have all accounting procedures performed in the name of the partnership entity [UPA 201, 307(a)]. As an entity, a partnership may hold the title to real or personal property in its name rather than in the names of the individual partners. Additionally, federal procedural laws permit the partnership to be treated as an entity in lawsuits in federal courts and bankruptcy proceedings.

27–1f Tax Treatment of Partnerships

Modern law does treat a partnership as an aggregate of the individual partners rather than as a separate legal entity in one situation—for federal income tax purposes. The partnership is a pass-through entity and not a taxpaying entity.

1. *Tubb v. Aspect International, Inc.*, 2017 WL 192919 (Tex.App.—Tyler 2017).

Pass-Through Entity A business entity that has no tax liability. The entity's income is passed through to the owners, and they pay taxes on the income.

Information Return A tax return submitted by a partnership that reports the business's income and losses. The partnership itself does not pay taxes on the income received by the partnership.

A **pass-through entity** is a business entity that has no tax liability—the entity's income is passed through to the owners of the entity, who pay income taxes on it. Thus, the income or losses the partnership incurs are "passed through" the entity framework and attributed to the partners on their individual tax returns. The partnership itself pays no taxes and is responsible only for filing an **information return** with the Internal Revenue Service.

A partner's profit from the partnership (whether distributed or not) is taxed as individual income to the individual partner. Similarly, partners can deduct a share of the partnership's losses on their individual tax returns (in proportion to their partnership interests).

27–2 Formation and Operation

A partnership is a voluntary association of individuals. As such, it is formed by the agreement of the partners.

27–2a The Partnership Agreement

As a general rule, agreements to form a partnership can be *oral, written,* or *implied by conduct.* Some partnership agreements, however, such as one authorizing the transfer of interests in real property, must be in writing to be legally enforceable. (Recall that a writing may be an electronic record.)

Articles of Partnership A written agreement that sets forth each partner's rights and obligations with respect to the partnership.

A partnership agreement, called **articles of partnership,** can include any terms that the parties wish, unless the terms are illegal or contrary to public policy or statute [UPA 103]. The terms commonly included in a partnership agreement are listed in Exhibit 27–1.

The rights and duties of partners are governed largely by the specific terms of their partnership agreement. In the absence of provisions to the contrary in the partnership agreement, the law imposes certain rights and duties, as discussed in the following subsections. The character and nature of the partnership business generally influence the application of these rights and duties.

Exhibit 27–1 Common Terms Included in a Partnership Agreement

TERM	DESCRIPTION
Basic Structure	**1.** Name of the partnership and names of the partners. **2.** Location of the business and the state law under which the partnership is organized. **3.** Purpose and duration of the partnership.
Capital Contributions	**1.** Amount of capital that each partner is contributing. **2.** The agreed-on value of any real or personal property that is contributed instead of cash. **3.** How losses and gains on contributed capital will be allocated, and whether contributions will earn interest.
Sharing of Profits and Losses	**1.** Percentage of the profits and losses of the business that each partner will receive. **2.** When distributions of profit will be made and how net profit will be calculated.
Management and Control	**1.** How management responsibilities will be divided among the partners. **2.** Name(s) of the managing partner(s) and whether other partners have voting rights.
Dissociation and Dissolution	**1.** Events that will cause the dissociation of a partner or dissolve the firm, such as the retirement, death, or incapacity of any partner. **2.** How partnership property will be valued and apportioned on dissociation and dissolution. **3.** Whether an arbitrator will determine the value of partnership property on dissociation and dissolution, and whether that determination will be binding.

27–2b Duration of the Partnership

The partnership agreement can specify the duration of the partnership by stating that it will continue until a certain date or the completion of a particular project. A partnership that is specifically limited in duration is called a *partnership for a term.* Generally, withdrawing prematurely (before the expiration date) from a partnership for a term constitutes a breach of the agreement. The responsible partner can be held liable for any resulting losses [UPA 602(b)(2)].

If no fixed duration is specified, the partnership is a *partnership at will.* A partnership at will can be dissolved at any time without liability.

27–2c Partnership by Estoppel

When a third person has reasonably and detrimentally relied on a representation that a nonpartner was part of a partnership, a court may conclude that a **partnership by estoppel** exists.

Partnership by Estoppel A partnership imposed by a court when nonpartners have held themselves out to be partners, or have allowed themselves to be held out as partners, and others have detrimentally relied on their misrepresentations.

Liability Imposed A partnership by estoppel may arise when a person who is not a partner holds himself or herself out as a partner and makes representations that third parties rely on. In this situation, a court may impose liability—but not partnership rights—on the alleged partner.

Case Example 27.4 Sanitation District No. 1 (SD1) contracted with DCI Properties to upgrade the sewage systems of several counties in Northern Kentucky. DCI contracted with Coppage Construction Company to provide the labor, goods, and services for the construction project. After a series of disputes, DCI terminated its contract with Coppage. In a lawsuit against SD1, Coppage alleged that it had extended credit, consisting of goods and services, to DCI based on its belief that DCI and SD1 were partners.

The trial court dismissed the claim, holding that SD1 and DC1 were not partners and that SD1 therefore could not be liable to Coppage for any damages resulting from DCI's actions. A state appeals court reversed, noting that SD1 had assured Coppage that it was backing the project financially. Indeed, on one occasion, SD1—not DCI—had made a payment to Coppage. Even if there was no express partnership between DCI and SD1, the court ruled, Coppage should be given the chance to argue there was an "apparent" partnership under the doctrine of partnership by estoppel.[2]

Nonpartner as Agent A partnership by estoppel may also be imposed when a partner represents, expressly or impliedly, that a nonpartner is a member of the firm. In this situation, the nonpartner may be regarded as an agent whose acts are binding on the partnership [UPA 308].

27–2d Rights of Partners

The rights of partners in a partnership relate to the following areas: management, interest in the partnership, compensation, inspection of books, accounting, and property.

Management Rights In a general partnership, all partners have equal rights in managing the partnership [UPA 401(f)]. Unless the partners agree otherwise, each partner has one vote in management matters *regardless of the proportional size of that partner's interest in the firm.* In a large partnership, partners often agree to delegate daily management responsibilities to a management committee made up of one or more of the partners.

---

2. *Coppage Construction Company, Inc. v. Sanitation District No. 1,* __ S.W.3d __, 2019 WL 6795706 (Ky. Ct. App. 2019).

The majority rule controls decisions in ordinary matters connected with partnership business, unless otherwise specified in the agreement. Decisions that significantly change the nature of the partnership or its ordinary course of business, however, require the *unanimous* consent of the partners [UPA 301(2), 401(i), (j)]. For instance, unanimous consent is likely required for a partnership to admit new partners, to amend the partnership agreement, or to enter a new line of business.

Interest in the Partnership Each partner is entitled to the proportion of business profits and losses designated in the partnership agreement. If the agreement does not apportion profits (indicate how the profits will be shared), the UPA provides that profits will be shared equally. If the agreement does not apportion losses, losses will be shared in the same ratio as profits [UPA 401(b)].

Example 27.5 The partnership agreement for Rick and Brent provides for capital contributions of $60,000 from Rick and $40,000 from Brent. If the agreement is silent as to how Rick and Brent will share profits or losses, they will share both profits and losses equally. In contrast, if the agreement provides for profits to be shared in the same ratio as capital contributions, 60 percent of the profits will go to Rick, and 40 percent will go to Brent. Unless the agreement provides otherwise, losses will be shared in the same ratio as profits. ■

Compensation Devoting time, skill, and energy to partnership business is a partner's duty and generally is not a compensable service. Rather, as mentioned, a partner's income from the partnership takes the form of a distribution of profits according to the partner's share in the business.

Partners can, of course, agree otherwise. For instance, the managing partner of a law firm often receives a salary—in addition to a share of profits—for performing special administrative or managerial duties.

Inspection of Books Partnership books and records must be accessible to all partners. Each partner has the right to receive full and complete information concerning the conduct of all aspects of partnership business [UPA 403]. Partners have a duty to provide the information to the firm, which has a duty to preserve it and keep accurate records.

The partnership's books must be kept at the firm's principal business office (unless partners agree otherwise) and cannot be removed without the consent of all of the partners. Every partner is entitled to inspect all books and records on demand and can make copies of the materials. The personal representative of a deceased partner's estate has the same right of access to partnership books and records as the decedent would have had [UPA 403].

junpiiiiiiiiiii/shutterstock.com
Where are partnership books and records normally kept?

Accounting of Partnership Assets or Profits An accounting of partnership assets or profits is required to determine the value of each partner's share in the partnership. An accounting can be performed voluntarily, or it can be compelled by court order. Under UPA 405(b), a partner has the right to bring an action for an accounting during the term of the partnership, as well as on the partnership's dissolution.

Property Rights Property acquired by a partnership is the property of the partnership and not of the partners individually [UPA 203]. Partnership property includes all property that was originally contributed to the partnership and anything later purchased by the partnership or in the partnership's name (except in rare circumstances) [UPA 204].

A partner may use or possess partnership property only on behalf of the partnership [UPA 401(g)]. A partner is *not* a co-owner of partnership property and has no right to sell, mortgage, or transfer it.

Because partnership property is owned by the partnership as an entity and not by the individual partners, the property cannot be used to satisfy the personal debts of individual partners. A partner's creditor, however, can petition a court for a **charging order** to attach the partner's *interest* in the partnership (her or his proportionate share of any profits that are distributed) to satisfy the partner's obligation. (A partner can also assign her or his right to a share of the partnership profits to another to satisfy a debt.)

Charging Order In partnership law, an order granted by a court to a judgment creditor that entitles the creditor to attach a partner's interest in the partnership.

27–2e Duties and Liabilities of Partners

The duties and liabilities of partners are basically derived from agency law. Each partner is an agent of every other partner and acts as both a principal and an agent in any business transaction within the scope of the partnership agreement.

Each partner is also a general agent of the partnership in carrying out the usual business of the firm "or business of the kind carried on by the partnership" [UPA 301(1)]. Thus, every act of a partner concerning partnership business, or "business of the kind," and every contract signed in the partnership's name bind the firm.

Fiduciary Duties The fiduciary duties a partner owes to the partnership and to the other partners are the duty of care and the duty of loyalty [UPA 404(a)]. Under the UPA, a partner's *duty of care* involves refraining from "grossly negligent or reckless conduct, intentional misconduct, or a knowing violation of law" [UPA 404(c)]. A partner is not liable to the partnership for simple negligence or honest errors in judgment in conducting partnership business.

Focus Question 2

What are the fiduciary duties of partners in a general partnership?

The *duty of loyalty* requires a partner to account to the partnership for "any property, profit, or benefit" derived by the partner from the partnership's business or the use of its property [UPA 404(b)]. A partner must also refrain from competing with the partnership in business or dealing with the firm as an adverse party.

The duty of loyalty can be breached by self-dealing, misusing partnership property, disclosing trade secrets, or usurping a partnership business opportunity, as the following *Classic Case* illustrates.

Classic Case 27.2

Meinhard v. Salmon

Court of Appeals of New York, 249 N.Y. 458, 164 N.E. 545 (1928).

Facts Walter Salmon negotiated a twenty-year lease for the Hotel Bristol in New York City. To pay for the conversion of the building into shops and offices, Salmon entered into an agreement with Morton Meinhard, who was to assume half of the cost. Salmon and Meinhard agreed to share the profits and losses from the joint venture (a *joint venture* is similar to a partnership but typically is created for a single project, whereas a partnership usually involves an ongoing business). Salmon was to have the sole power to manage the building, however.

olaser/E+/Getty Images

What fiduciary duties does a partner have with respect to renewing a hotel lease?

Less than four months before the end of the lease term, the building's owner approached Salmon about a project to raze the converted structure and construct a new building. Salmon agreed and signed a new lease in the name of his own business, Midpoint Realty Company, without telling Meinhard. When Meinhard learned of the

(Continues)

Continued

deal, he filed a suit against Salmon. The court ruled in Meinhard's favor, and Salmon appealed.

Issue Did Salmon breach his fiduciary duty of loyalty to Meinhard?

Decision Yes. The Court of Appeals of New York held that Salmon had breached his fiduciary duty by failing to inform Meinhard of the business opportunity and secretly taking advantage of it for himself. The court therefore granted Meinhard an interest "measured by the value of half of the entire lease."

Reason The court stated, "Joint adventurers, like copartners, owe to one another, while the enterprise continues, the duty of the finest loyalty." Salmon's conduct excluded Meinhard from any chance to compete and from any chance to enjoy the opportunity for benefit. As a partner, Salmon was bound by his "obligation to his copartners in such dealings not to separate his interest from theirs, but, if he acquires any benefit, to communicate it to them." Salmon was also the managing co-adventurer, and thus the court found that "for him and for those like him the rule of undivided loyalty is relentless and supreme."

Critical Thinking

- **What If the Facts Were Different?** *Suppose that Salmon had disclosed the proposed deal to Meinhard, who had said that he was not interested. Would the result in this case have been different? Explain.*
- **Impact of This Case on Today's Law** *This case involved a joint venture, not a partnership. At the time, a member of a joint venture had only the duty to refrain from actively subverting the rights of the other members. The decision in this case imposed the highest standard of loyalty on joint-venture members. The duty is now the same in both joint ventures and partnerships. Courts today frequently quote the eloquent language used in this opinion when describing the standard of loyalty that applies to partnerships.*

Breach and Waiver of Fiduciary Duties A partner's fiduciary duties may not be waived or eliminated in the partnership agreement. In fulfilling these duties, each partner must act consistently with the obligation of good faith and fair dealing [UPA 103(b), 404(d)]. The agreement can specify acts that the partners agree will violate a fiduciary duty.

Note that partners may pursue their own interests without automatically violating these duties [UPA 404(e)]. The key is disclosing the interest to the other partners. **Example 27.6** Jayne, a partner at Jacoby & Meyers, owns a shopping mall. Jayne may vote against a partnership proposal to open a competing mall, provided that she has fully disclosed her interest in the existing shopping mall to the other partners at the firm. Partners cannot make secret profits or put self-interest before their duty to the interest of the partnership, however.

Authority of Partners The UPA affirms general principles of agency law that pertain to the authority of a partner to bind a partnership in contract. If a partner acts within the scope of this authority, the partnership is legally bound to honor the partner's commitments to third parties.

A partner may also subject the partnership to tort liability under agency principles. When a partner is carrying on partnership business with third parties in the usual way, both the partner and the firm share liability. The partnership will not be liable, however, if the third parties *know* that the partner had no authority to commit the partnership.

Limitations on Authority. A partnership may limit the capacity of a partner to act as the firm's agent or transfer property on its behalf by filing a "statement of partnership authority" in a designated state office [UPA 105, 303]. Such limits on a partner's authority normally are effective only with respect to third parties who are notified of the limitations. (An exception is made in real property transactions when the statement of authority has been recorded with the appropriate state office.)

The Scope of Implied Powers. The agency concepts relating to apparent authority, actual authority, and ratification also apply to partnerships. *The extent of implied authority is generally broader for partners than for ordinary agents.*

In an ordinary partnership, the partners can exercise all implied powers reasonably necessary and customary to carry on that particular business. Some customarily implied powers include the authority to make warranties on goods in a retail sales business and the power to enter into contracts consistent with the firm's ordinary course of business.

Example 27.7 Jamie, a partner in a firm that operates a retail tire store, regularly promises that "each tire will be warranted for normal wear for 40,000 miles." Because Jamie has authority to make warranties, the partnership is bound to honor them. Jamie would not, however, have the authority to sell the partnership's office equipment, fixtures, or other property without the consent of all of the other partners.

Kzenon/Alamy Stock Photo

A partner in a tire store tells customers that every tire comes with a specific type of warranty. How could the partner's words affect the partnership as a whole?

Liability of Partners One significant disadvantage associated with a traditional partnership is that partners are *personally* liable for the debts of the partnership. In most states, the liability is essentially unlimited because the acts of one partner in the ordinary course of business subject the other partners to personal liability [UPA 305].

Joint Liability. Each partner in a partnership is jointly liable for the partnership's obligations. **Joint liability** means that a third party must sue all of the partners as a group, but each partner can be held liable for the full amount.[3]

Joint Liability In partnership law, the partners' shared liability for partnership obligations and debts. A third party must sue all of the partners as a group, but each partner can be held liable for the full amount.

If, for instance, a third party sues one individual partner on a partnership contract, that partner has the right to demand that the other partners be sued as well. In fact, if the third party does not name all of the partners in the lawsuit, the assets of the partnership cannot be used to satisfy the judgment. With joint liability, the partnership's assets must be exhausted before creditors can reach the partners' individual assets.

Joint and Several Liability. In the majority of the states, under UPA 306(a), partners are jointly and severally (separately or individually) liable for all partnership obligations. **Joint and several liability** means that a third party has the option of suing all of the partners together (jointly) or one or more of the partners separately (severally).

Joint and Several Liability In partnership law, a doctrine under which a plaintiff may sue, and collect a judgment from, all of the partners together (jointly) or one or more of the partners separately (severally, or individually). Partners can be held liable even if they did not participate in, ratify, or know about the conduct that gave rise to the lawsuit.

All the partners in a partnership can be held liable even if a particular partner did not participate in, know about, or ratify the conduct that gave rise to the lawsuit. Normally, though, the partnership's assets must be exhausted before a creditor can enforce a judgment against a partner's personal assets [UPA 307(d)]. In addition, a partner who commits a tort may be required to indemnify (reimburse) the partnership for any damages it pays unless the tort was committed in the ordinary course of the partnership's business.

A judgment against one partner severally (separately) does not extinguish the others' liability. (Similarly, a release of one partner does not discharge the partners' several liability.) Those not sued in the first action may be sued subsequently, unless the court in the first action held that the partnership was not liable.

If a plaintiff is successful in a suit against a partner or partners, the plaintiff may collect on the judgment only against the assets of those partners named as defendants. **Example 27.8** Brian and Julie are partners. If Tom sues Brian for a debt on a partnership contract and wins, Tom can collect the amount of the judgment against Brian only. If Tom cannot collect enough from Brian, however, Tom can later sue Julie for the difference.

Liability of Incoming Partners. A partner newly admitted to an existing partnership is not personally liable for any partnership obligations incurred before the person became a partner [UPA 306(b)]. The new partner's liability to existing creditors of the partnership is limited to the amount of the partner's capital contribution to the firm.

3. Under the prior version of the UPA, which is still in effect in a few states, partners were subject to joint liability on partnership debts and contracts, but not on partnership debts arising from torts.

Example 27.9 Smartclub, an existing partnership with four members, admits a new partner, Alex. He contributes $100,000 to the partnership. Smartclub has debts amounting to $600,000 at the time Alex joins the firm. Although Alex's capital contribution of $100,000 can be used to satisfy Smartclub's prior obligations, Alex is not personally liable for debts incurred before he became a partner. If, however, the partnership incurs additional debts after Alex becomes a partner, he will be personally liable for those amounts, along with all other partners.

27–3 Dissociation and Termination

Dissociation The severance of the relationship between a partner and a partnership.

Focus Question 3

What is dissociation? What happens when a partner dissociates from a partnership?

Dissociation occurs when a partner ceases to be associated in the carrying on of the partnership business. Dissociation normally entitles the partner to have his or her interest purchased by the partnership. It also terminates the partner's actual authority to act for the partnership and to participate with the partners in running the business.

Once dissociation occurs, the partnership normally may continue to do business without the dissociating partner.[4] If the partners no longer wish to (or are unable to) continue the business, the partnership may be terminated (dissolved).

27–3a Events That Cause Dissociation

Under UPA 601, a partner can be dissociated from a partnership in any of the following ways:

Billion Photos/shutterstock.com

A partner who is convicted of a crime can be dissociated from a partnership. What other events can cause a partner's dissociation?

1. By the partner's voluntarily giving notice of an "express will to withdraw." (When a partner gives notice of intent to withdraw, the remaining partners must decide whether to continue the partnership business. If they decide not to continue, the voluntary dissociation of a partner will dissolve the firm [UPA 801(1)].)
2. By the occurrence of an event agreed to in the partnership agreement.
3. By a unanimous vote of the other partners under certain circumstances.
4. By order of a court or arbitrator if the partner has engaged in wrongful conduct that affects the partnership business. The court can order dissociation if a partner breached the partnership agreement or violated a duty owed to the partnership or to the other partners. Dissociation may also be ordered if the partner engaged in conduct that makes it "not reasonably practicable to carry on the business in partnership with the partner" [UPA 601(5)].
5. By the partner's declaring bankruptcy, assigning his or her interest in the partnership for the benefit of creditors, becoming physically or mentally incapacitated, or dying.

Wrongful Dissociation A partner always has the *power* to dissociate from the firm, but may not have the *right* to do so. If the partner lacks the right to dissociate, then the dissociation is considered wrongful under the law [UPA 602]. When a partner's dissociation is in breach of the partnership agreement, for instance, it is wrongful.

4. Under the previous version of the UPA, when a partner withdrew from a partnership, the partnership was considered dissolved, its business had to be wound up, and the proceeds had to be distributed to creditors and among the partners. The new UPA dramatically changed the law governing partnership breakups and does not require that a partnership be dissolved just because one partner has left the firm.

Example 27.10 Jensen & Whalen's partnership agreement states that it is a breach of the agreement for any partner to assign partnership property to a creditor without the consent of the other partners. If Janis, a partner, makes such an assignment, she not only has breached the agreement but also has wrongfully dissociated from the partnership.

A partner who wrongfully dissociates is liable to the partnership and to the other partners for damages caused by the dissociation. This liability is in addition to any other obligation to the partnership or to the partners.

Effects of Dissociation Dissociation (rightful or wrongful) terminates some of the rights of the dissociated partner, requires that the partnership purchase the dissociated partner's interest, and alters the liability of the parties to third parties.

Rights and Duties. On dissociation, a partner loses the right to participate in the management and conduct of the partnership business [UPA 603]. The partner's duty of loyalty also ends. A partner's duty of care continues only with respect to events that occurred before dissociation, unless the partner participates in *winding up* the partnership's business (discussed shortly).

Example 27.11 Tanya, a partner who leaves an accounting firm, Bubb & Ferngold, can immediately compete with that firm for new clients. She must exercise care in completing ongoing client transactions, however, and must account to Bubb & Ferngold for any fees received from the former clients based on those transactions.

Buyouts. According to the rules of UPA 701, the partnership interest of a dissociated partner must be purchased by the partnership. The **buyout price** is based on the amount that would have been distributed to the partner if the partnership had been wound up on the date of dissociation. Offset against the price are any amounts owed by the partner to the partnership, including any damages to the firm if the dissociation was wrongful.

Buyout Price The amount payable to a partner on dissociation from a partnership, based on the amount distributable to that partner if the partnership had been wound up on that date and offset by any damages for wrongful dissociation.

Liability to Third Parties. For two years after a partner dissociates from a continuing partnership, the partnership may be bound by the acts of the dissociated partner based on apparent authority [UPA 702]. In other words, if a third party reasonably believed at the time of a transaction that the dissociated partner was still a partner, the partnership may be liable. In addition, a dissociated partner may be liable for partnership obligations entered into during a two-year period following dissociation [UPA 703].

To avoid this possible liability, a partnership should notify its creditors, customers, and clients of a partner's dissociation. Also, either the partnership or the dissociated partner can file a *statement of dissociation* in the appropriate state office to limit the dissociated partner's authority to ninety days after the filing [UPA 704].

27–3b Partnership Termination

The same events that cause dissociation can result in the end of the partnership if the remaining partners no longer wish to (or are unable to) continue the business. A partner's departure will not necessarily end the partnership, though. The partnership can continue if the remaining partners consent.

The termination of a partnership is referred to as **dissolution**, which essentially means the commencement of the winding up process. **Winding up** is the actual process of collecting, liquidating, and distributing the partnership assets. If the partners entered into a *buy-sell agreement* (discussed shortly) at the time they formed the partnership, that agreement will govern the specific procedures used.

Dissolution The formal disbanding of a partnership or a corporation. Partnerships can be dissolved by acts of the partners, by operation of law, or by judicial decree.

Winding Up The second of two stages in the termination of a partnership or corporation, in which the firm's assets are collected, liquidated, and distributed, and liabilities are discharged.

Dissolution Dissolution of a partnership generally can be brought about by acts of the partners, by operation of law, or by judicial decree [UPA 801]. Any partnership (including one for a fixed term) can be dissolved by the partners' agreement. Similarly, if the partnership agreement states that it will dissolve on a certain event, such as a partner's death or bankruptcy, then the occurrence of that event will dissolve the partnership. A partnership for a fixed term or a particular undertaking is dissolved by operation of law at the expiration of the term or on the completion of the undertaking.

Case Example 27.12 Will Sukenik and Irvin Fine formed PDC Office Park as general partners. Under the partnership agreement, on the death of one partner, the other had thirty days to elect to continue the partnership. Fine died, but Sukenik failed to take this step. A third party that owned a limited interest in PDC convinced a trial court that the partnership must be dissolved and its assets liquidated. Although Sukenik tried numerous delaying tactics to block this dissolution, including a breach of contract suit against the third party, a state appeals court ruled that the terms of the partnership were clear and must be respected.[5] ■

Illegality or Impracticality. Any event that makes it unlawful for the partnership to continue its business will result in dissolution [UPA 801(4)]. Under the UPA, a court may order dissolution when it becomes obviously impractical for the firm to continue—for instance, if the business can only be operated at a loss [UPA 801(5)]. Even when one partner has brought a court action seeking to dissolve a partnership, the partnership continues to exist until it is legally dissolved by the court or by the parties' agreement.

Case Example 27.13 Members of the Russell family began operating Russell Realty Associates (RRA) as a partnership. Eddie Russell had decision-making authority over the partnership's business, which involved buying, holding, leasing, and selling investment properties. After several years, Eddie and his sister, Nina Russell, became involved in disputes, and Nina began to routinely question Eddie's business decisions. Because of their disagreements, RRA experienced two years of delays before it could sell one piece of property. Although the firm continued to profit, Eddie filed a complaint seeking a judicial dissolution of the partnership, which the court granted. Nina appealed.

The Virginia Supreme Court affirmed the lower court's decision that Russell Realty must be judicially dissolved. The partners' relationship had deteriorated to the point where the partnership was unable to function effectively. As a result, the firm had incurred substantial and unnecessary added costs, which frustrated the partnership's economic purpose and made it impracticable to continue.[6] ■

Sherry V Smith/shutterstock.com

Why might a court judicially dissolve a golf club partnership in response to a lawsuit brought by one of the partners?

Good Faith. Each partner must exercise good faith during the dissolution of a partnership. Some state statutes allow partners injured by another partner's bad faith to file a tort claim for wrongful dissolution.

Case Example 27.14 Attorneys Randall Jordan and Mary Helen Moses formed a two-member partnership for an indefinite term. Jordan ended the partnership three years later and asked the court for declarations concerning the partners' financial obligations. Moses, who had objected to ending the partnership, filed a claim against Jordan for wrongful dissolution and for appropriating $180,000 in fees that should have gone to the partnership.

Ultimately, the court held in favor of Moses. A claim for wrongful dissolution of a partnership may be based on damages

5. *810 Properties, LLP, et al., v. Will Sukenik, et al.*, 2020 -Ohio- 1623, 2020 WL 1951507 (Ohio Ct. App. 2020).
6. *Russell Realty Associates v. Russell*, 724 S.E.2d 690 (Va.Sup.Ct. 2012).

arising from the excluded partner's loss of "an existing, or continuing, business opportunity" or of income and material assets. Because Jordan had attempted to appropriate partnership assets through dissolution, Moses could sue for wrongful dissolution.[7]

Winding Up and Distribution of Assets After dissolution, the partnership continues for the limited purpose of the winding up process. The partners cannot create new obligations on behalf of the partnership. They have authority only to complete transactions begun but not finished at the time of dissolution and to wind up the partnership's business [UPA 803, 804(1)].

What happens when the partners cannot agree on the method for a distribution of the partnership assets during the winding up process? That was the question before the court in the following case.

7. *Jordan v. Moses*, 291 Ga. 39, 727 S.E.2d 460 (2012).

Case 27.3

Guenther v. Ryerson

Idaho Supreme Court, 166 Idaho 315, 458 P.3d 184 (2020).

Facts Joseph Guenther and Michelle Ryerson bought real property on Lost Sage Lane in Boise, Idaho, and formed a partnership, West Foothills TIC, to develop a vineyard for profit. There was no written partnership agreement and no allocation of contributions or responsibility for liabilities. Both parties commingled their personal funds with partnership funds, investing a considerable amount in the development of the vineyard and the construction of a house.

When they decided not to continue to operate the business as partners, Guenther filed an action in an Idaho state court to dissolve the partnership. He sought to buy Ryerson's interest in the Lost Sage Lane property and continue to live there and work the vineyard. Ryerson asked the court to liquidate the partnership's assets by sale. She claimed that this was the only way to determine the true value of the property. Guenther argued that a different means of winding up the partnership's business would be more equitable. The court issued an order that required the property to be sold on the open market. Guenther appealed.

Issue Is a sale of partnership assets on the open market required in this case?

Decision Yes. The Idaho Supreme Court held that the property of the Guenther and Ryerson partnership must be sold on the open market for its fair market value, and remanded the case for further proceedings.

Reason Idaho's version of the Uniform Partnership Act requires a partnership, in winding up its business, to discharge its debts, obligations, and other liabilities, settle and close its business, and marshal and distribute its assets. The act further requires that, unless the partnership agreement provides otherwise, "all distributions made to the partners must be paid in money."

In the view of the state's highest court, "the plain language" of the act is "unambiguous." During the winding up of the business of a partnership, a distribution to a partner must be paid in money. A distribution to a partner in any form other than money would contradict the plain language of the act and would not be allowed. Thus, before being distributed to the partners, the firm's assets must be reduced to cash.

The court found the application of these requirements to the facts of this case to be "fairly straightforward." Guenther and Ryerson had no written partnership agreement, and they had not otherwise provided for, or agreed to, a distribution of their partnership's property in any form other than cash. Therefore, under the state's partnership statutes, the Lost Sage Lane property must be reduced to cash before being distributed to the partners.

Critical Thinking

- **Legal Environment** *Could the partnership in this case have avoided the liquidation of its assets during the winding up process? Explain.*
- **Economic** *How should the lower court, on remand, structure the sale of the partnership's Lost Sage Lane property? Discuss.*

Duties and Compensation. Winding up includes collecting and preserving partnership assets, discharging liabilities (paying debts), and accounting to each partner for the value of that partner's interest in the partnership. Partners continue to have fiduciary duties to one another and to the firm during this process. UPA 401(h) provides that a partner is entitled to compensation for services in winding up partnership affairs (and reimbursement for expenses incurred in the process) above and apart from a share in the partnership profits.

Know This
Secured creditors have priority over unsecured creditors in any assets that serve as collateral for a partnership's debts.

Creditors' Claims. Both creditors of the partnership and creditors of the individual partners can make claims on the partnership's assets. In general, partnership creditors and the partners' personal creditors share proportionately in the partners' assets, which include their interests in the partnership.

A partnership's assets are distributed according to the following priorities [UPA 807]:

1. Payment of debts, including those owed to partner and nonpartner creditors.
2. Return of capital contributions and distribution of profits to partners.

If the partnership's liabilities are greater than its assets, the partners bear the losses—in the absence of a contrary agreement—in the same proportion in which they shared the profits (rather than, for instance, in proportion to their contributions to the partnership's capital).

Partnership Buy-Sell Agreements Before entering into a partnership, partners may agree on how the assets will be valued and divided in the event that the partnership dissolves. Such an agreement may eliminate costly negotiations or litigation later.

Buy-Sell Agreement An agreement made at the time of partnership formation providing for one or more of the partners to buy out the other or others, in the event the firm is dissolved. It is also called a *buyout agreement*.

The agreement may provide for one or more partners to buy out the other or others, should the situation warrant. This is called a **buy-sell agreement,** or simply a *buyout agreement*. Alternatively, the agreement may specify that one or more partners will determine the value of the interest being sold and that the other or others will decide whether to buy or sell.

Under UPA 701(a), if a partner's dissociation does not result in a dissolution of the partnership, a buyout of the partner's interest is mandatory. The UPA contains an extensive set of buyout rules that apply when the partners do not have a buy-sell agreement. Basically, a withdrawing partner receives the same amount through a buyout that the partner would receive if the business were winding up [UPA 701(b)].

27–4 Limited Liability Partnerships

Focus Question 4
What advantages do limited liability partnerships offer to businesspersons that are not offered by general partnerships?

The **limited liability partnership (LLP)** is a hybrid form of business designed mostly for professionals who normally do business as partners in a partnership. Almost all of the states have enacted LLP statutes.

The major advantage of the LLP is that it allows a partnership to continue as a pass-through entity for tax purposes but limits the personal liability of the partners. The LLP is especially attractive for professional service firms and family businesses. All of the "Big Four" accounting firms—the four largest international accountancy and professional services firms—are organized as LLPs, including Ernst & Young, LLP, and Pricewaterhouse-Coopers, LLP.

Limited Liability Partnership (LLP) A hybrid form of business organization that is used mainly by professionals who normally do business as partners in a partnership. An LLP is a pass-through entity for tax purposes, but a partner's personal liability for the malpractice of other partners is limited.

27–4a Formation of an LLP

LLPs must be formed and operated in compliance with state statutes, which may include provisions of the UPA. The appropriate form must be filed with a central state agency, usually the secretary of state's office, and the business's name must include either "Limited Liability Partnership" or "LLP" [UPA 1001, 1002]. An LLP must file an annual report with the state to remain qualified as an LLP in that state [UPA 1003].

In most states, it is relatively easy to convert a traditional partnership into an LLP because the firm's basic organizational structure remains the same. Additionally, all of the statutory and common law rules governing partnerships still apply (apart from those modified by the LLP statute). Normally, LLP statutes are simply amendments to a state's already existing partnership law.

27–4b Liability in an LLP

An LLP allows professionals, such as attorneys and accountants, to avoid personal liability for the malpractice of other partners. Partners in an LLP are still liable for their own wrongful acts, such as negligence, of course. Also liable is the partner who supervised the individual who committed a wrongful act. (This supervisory liability generally applies to all types of partners and partnerships, not just LLPs.)

Robert Daly/Caiaimage/Getty Images

What advantage do limited liability partnerships offer to professionals, such as attorneys?

Example 27.15 Five lawyers operate a law firm as a limited liability partnership. One of the attorneys, Dan, is sued for malpractice and loses. The firm's malpractice insurance is insufficient to pay the judgment. If the firm had been organized as a general partnership, the personal assets of the other attorneys could be used to satisfy the obligation. Because the firm is organized as an LLP, however, no other partner at the law firm can be held *personally* liable for Dan's malpractice, unless that partner acted as Dan's supervisor. In the absence of a supervisor, only Dan's personal assets can be used to satisfy the judgment. ■

Although LLP statutes vary from state to state, generally each state statute limits the liability of partners in some way. For instance, Delaware law protects each innocent partner from the "debts and obligations of the partnership arising from negligence, wrongful acts, or misconduct." The UPA more broadly exempts partners in an LLP from personal liability for any partnership obligation, "whether arising in contract, tort, or otherwise" [UPA 306(c)].

Liability outside the State of Formation When an LLP formed in one state wishes to do business in another state, it may be required to register in the second state—for instance, by filing a Statement of Foreign Qualification [UPA 1102]. Because state LLP statutes are not uniform, a question sometimes arises as to which law applies if the LLP statutes in the two states provide different liability protection. Most states apply the law of the state in which the LLP was formed, which is also the rule under UPA 1101.

Sharing Liability among Partners When more than one partner in an LLP is negligent, there is a question as to how liability is to be shared. Is each partner jointly and severally liable for the entire result, as a general partner would be in most states?

Some states provide instead for proportionate liability—that is, for separate determinations of the negligence of the partners. **Example 27.16** Accountants Zach and Lyla are partners in an LLP, with Zach supervising Lyla. Lyla negligently fails to file a tax return for a client, Centaur Tools. Centaur files a suit against Zach and Lyla. Under a proportionate liability statute, Zach will be liable for no more than his portion of the responsibility for the missed tax deadline. In a state that does not allow for proportionate liability, Zach can be held liable for the entire loss. ■

Focus Question 5

What are the key differences between the rights and liabilities of general partners and those of limited partners?

27–5 Limited Partnerships

A **limited partnership (LP)** limits the liability of *some* of its owners. Limited partnerships originated in medieval Europe and have been in existence in the United States since the early 1800s. Today, most states and the District of Columbia have adopted laws based on the Revised Uniform Limited Partnership Act (RULPA).

Limited Partnership (LP) A partnership consisting of one or more general partners and one or more limited partners.

General Partner In a limited partnership, a partner who assumes responsibility for the management of the partnership and has full liability for all partnership debts.

Limited Partners In a limited partnership, a partner who contributes capital to the partnership but has no right to participate in its management and has no liability for partnership debts beyond the amount of her or his investment.

Certificate of Limited Partnership The document that must be filed with a designated state official to form a limited partnership.

Know This

A limited partner is liable only to the extent of any contribution made to the partnership, but can lose this limited liability by participating in management.

Limited partnerships differ from general partnerships in several ways.[8] A limited partnership consists of at least one **general partner** and one or more **limited partners.** A general partner assumes management responsibility for the partnership and so has full responsibility for the partnership and for all of its debts. Limited partners contribute cash or other property and own an interest in the firm but do not undertake any management responsibilities and are not personally liable for partnership debts beyond the amount of their investment. A limited partner can forfeit limited liability by taking part in the management of the business.

27–5a Formation of an LP

In contrast to the informal, private, and voluntary agreement that usually suffices for a general partnership, the formation of a limited partnership is a public and formal proceeding. The partners must strictly follow statutory requirements. See Exhibit 27–2 for a comparison of the characteristics of general and limited partnerships.

Not only must a limited partnership have at least one general partner and one limited partner, but the partners must also sign a **certificate of limited partnership.** The certificate must include certain information, such as the name, mailing address, and capital contribution of each general and limited partner. The certificate must be filed with the designated state official—under the RULPA, the secretary of state. The certificate is usually open to public inspection.

27–5b Liabilities of Partners in an LP

General partners, unlike limited partners, are personally liable to the partnership's creditors. Thus, at least one general partner is necessary in a limited partnership so that someone has personal liability. This policy can be circumvented in states that allow a corporation to be

8. Under the UPA, a general partnership can be converted into a limited partnership and vice versa [UPA 902, 903]. The UPA also provides for the merger of a general partnership with one or more general or limited partnerships under rules that are similar to those governing corporate mergers [UPA 905].

Exhibit 27–2 A Comparison of General Partnerships and Limited Partnerships

CHARACTERISTIC	GENERAL PARTNERSHIP (UPA)	LIMITED PARTNERSHIP (RULPA)
Creation	By agreement of two or more persons to carry on a business as co-owners for profit.	By agreement and by filing a certificate of limited partnership with the secretary of state. There must be at least one general partner and one limited partner.
Sharing of Profits and Losses	By agreement. In the absence of agreement, profits are shared equally by the partners, and losses are shared in the same ratio as profits.	Profits are shared as stated in the certificate. Losses are also shared, up to the amount of the limited partners' capital contributions. In the absence of a provision in the certificate, profits and losses are shared on the basis of percentages of capital contributions.
Liability	Unlimited personal liability of all partners.	Unlimited personal liability of all general partners; limited partners liable only to the extent of their capital contributions.
Capital Contribution	No minimum or mandatory amount; set by agreement.	Set by agreement.
Management	By agreement. In the absence of agreement, all partners have an equal voice.	Only the general partner (or the general partners). Limited partners have no voice. A limited partner who participates in management will be just as liable as a general partner to third parties.
Duration	A fixed term can be set by the agreement. If no duration is specified, the partners can continue to do business even when a partner dissociates from the partnership.	As specified in the certificate. An LP may be dissolved by a court or by the general partner's bankruptcy, retirement, mental incompetence, or death. Death of a limited partner does not terminate the partnership, unless the deceased is the only remaining limited partner.

the general partner in a partnership. Because the corporation has limited liability by virtue of corporate laws, if a corporation is the general partner, no one in the limited partnership has personal liability.

The liability of limited partners, as mentioned, is limited to the capital that they contribute or agree to contribute to the partnership [RULPA 502]. Limited partners enjoy this limited liability only so long as they do not participate in management [RULPA 303].

A limited partner who participates in management will be just as liable as a general partner to any creditor who transacts business with the limited partnership. Liability arises when the creditor believes, based on the limited partner's conduct, that the limited partner is a general partner [RULPA 303]. The extent of review and advisement a limited partner can engage in before being exposed to liability is not always clear, however.

Ethical Issue

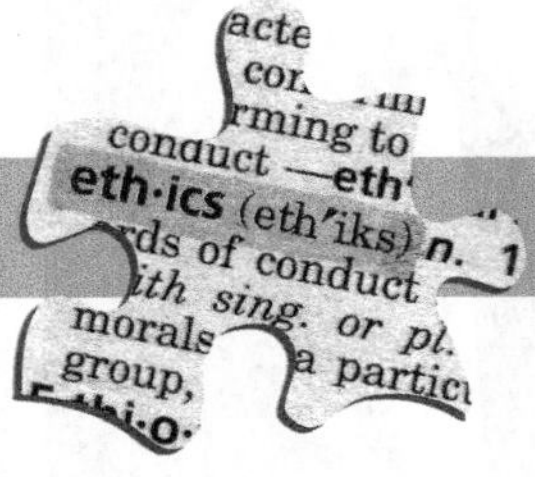

Should an innocent general partner be jointly liable for fraud? When general partners in a limited partnership jointly engage in fraud, there is usually no question that they are jointly liable. But if one general partner engages in fraud and the other is unaware of the wrongdoing, is it fair to make the innocent partner share in the liability? Many states' limited partnership laws protect innocent general partners from suits for fraud brought by limited partners. The law is less clear, however, in some other situations.

For example, Robert Bisno and James Coxeter formed two limited partnerships to develop property in Berkeley, California. Without Coxeter's knowledge, Bisno took almost $500,000 from one of the partnerships to buy a personal home. He also made material misrepresentations to potential investors. One of those investors, George Miske—after purchasing an interest in the limited partnership—discovered the fraud and brought suit. Coxeter argued that Miske was a limited partner, not an innocent third party. Under the state's limited partnership law, that meant Coxeter should be protected from liability.

The court disagreed. The fraud at issue had induced Miske to purchase the limited partnership interest. Therefore, at the time the fraud was perpetrated by Bisno, Miske was an innocent third party. As a result, Coxeter, though innocent of any wrongdoing, was jointly liable.[9]

27–5c Dissociation and Dissolution in an LP

A general partner has the power to voluntarily dissociate, or withdraw, from a limited partnership unless the partnership agreement specifies otherwise. A limited partner can withdraw from the partnership by giving six months' notice *unless* the partnership agreement specifies a term, which most do. Also, some states have passed laws prohibiting the withdrawal of limited partners.

Events That Cause Dissolution A limited partnership can be dissolved by court decree [RULPA 802]. In addition, a general partner's voluntary dissociation from the firm normally will lead to dissolution unless all partners agree to continue the business. Similarly, the bankruptcy, retirement, death, or mental incompetence of a general partner will cause the dissociation of that partner and the dissolution of the limited partnership unless the other members agree to continue the firm [RULPA 801].

Bankruptcy of a limited partner, however, does not dissolve the partnership unless it causes the bankruptcy of the firm. Death or an assignment of the interest of a limited partner does not dissolve a limited partnership [RULPA 702, 704, 705].

9. *Miske v. Bisno*, 204 Cal.App.4th 1249, 139 Cal.Rptr.3d 626 (2012). See also *In re Barlaam*, 2014 WL 3398381 (9th Cir. 2014).

Distribution of Assets On dissolution, creditors' claims, including those of partners who are creditors, take first priority. After that, partners and former partners receive unpaid distributions of partnership assets and, except as otherwise agreed, amounts representing returns of their capital contributions and proportionate distributions of profits [RULPA 804].

Kevin Winter/Getty Images

Can a limited partner in actor Kevin Costner's limited partnership force the sale of the entity?

Valuation of Assets Disputes commonly arise about how the partnership's assets should be valued and distributed on dissolution and whether the business should be sold. **Spotlight Case Example 27.17** Actor Kevin Costner was a limited partner in Midnight Star Enterprises, LP, which runs a casino, bar, and restaurant in South Dakota. There were two other limited partners, Carla and Francis Caneva, who owned a small percentage of the partnership (3.25 units each) and received salaries for managing its operations. Another company owned by Costner, Midnight Star Enterprises, Limited (MSEL), was the general partner. Costner thus controlled a majority of the partnership (93.5 units).

When communications broke down between the partners, MSEL asked a court to dissolve the partnership. MSEL's accountant determined that the firm's fair market value was $3.1 million. The Canevas presented evidence that a competitor would buy the business for $6.2 million. The Canevas wanted the court to force Costner to either buy the business for that price or sell it on the open market to the highest bidder. Ultimately, the state's highest court held in favor of Costner. A partner cannot force the sale of a limited partnership when the other partners want to continue the business. The court also accepted the $3.1 million buyout price of MSEL's accountant and ordered Costner to pay the Canevas the value of their 6.5 partnership units.[10]

10. *In re Dissolution of Midnight Star Enterprises, LP*, 2006 S.D. 98, 724 N.W.2d 334 (2006).

Practice and Review

Grace Tarnavsky and her sons, Manny and Jason, bought a ranch known as the Cowboy Palace in March 2019. The three orally agreed to share the business for five years. Grace contributed 50 percent of the investment, and each son contributed 25 percent. Manny agreed to handle the livestock, and Jason agreed to do the bookkeeping. The Tarnavskys took out joint loans and opened a joint bank account into which they deposited the ranch's proceeds and from which they made payments for property, cattle, equipment, and supplies.

In September 2021, Manny severely injured his back while baling hay and became permanently unable to handle livestock. Manny therefore hired additional laborers to tend the livestock, causing the Cowboy Palace to incur significant debt. In September 2022, Al's Feed Barn filed a lawsuit against Jason to collect $32,400 in unpaid debts. Using the information presented in the chapter, answer the following questions.

1. Was this relationship a partnership for a term or a partnership at will?
2. Did Manny have the authority to hire additional laborers to work at the ranch after his injury? Why or why not?
3. Under the UPA, can Al's Feed Barn bring an action against Jason individually for the Cowboy Palace's debt? Why or why not?
4. Suppose that after his back injury in 2021, Manny sent his mother and brother notice indicating his intent to withdraw from the partnership. Can he still be held liable for the debt to Al's Feed Barn? Why or why not?

Debate This

A partnership should automatically end when one partner dissociates from the firm.

Key Terms

articles of partnership 672
buy-sell agreement 682
buyout price 679
certificate of limited partnership 684
charging order 675
dissociation 678
dissolution 679
general partner 684
information return 672
joint and several liability 677
joint liability 677
limited liability partnership (LLP) 682
limited partners 684
limited partnership (LP) 683
partnership 669
partnership by estoppel 673
pass-through entity 672
winding up 679

Chapter Summary: All Forms of Partnership

Basic Partnership Concepts	1. **Agency concepts and partnership law**—A partnership is similar to an agency relationship except that partners have an ownership interest in the business and are obliged to bear a portion of ordinary business losses. 2. **The Uniform Partnership Act (UPA)**—Governs the operation of partnerships in the absence of an express agreement. 3. **Definition of a partnership**—An agreement by two or more persons to carry on, as co-owners, a business for profit. 4. **Essential elements of a partnership**—A sharing of profits and losses, a joint ownership of the business, and an equal right to be involved in the management of the business. 5. **Entity versus aggregate theory of partnerships**—A majority of the states follow the UPA and treat a partnership as an entity for most purposes. 6. **Tax treatment of partnerships**—Partnerships are treated as an aggregate of the individual partners rather than as a separate legal entity for federal income tax purposes. The partnership is a pass-through entity and not a tax-paying entity.
Formation and Operation	1. **The partnership agreement**—Also called articles of partnership, the written agreement sets forth each partner's rights and obligations with respect to the partnership. 2. **Duration of the partnership**—A partnership specifically limited in duration is called a partnership for a term. If no fixed duration is specified, the partnership is called a partnership at will. 3. **Partnership by estoppel**—Imposed by a court when a third person has reasonably and detrimentally relied on a representation that a nonpartner was part of a partnership. 4. **Rights of partners**—Rights include (a) management, (b) interest in the partnership, (c) compensation, (d) inspection of books, (e) accounting, and (f) property. 5. **Duties and liabilities of partners**— a. Fiduciary duties (duty of care and duty of loyalty) may not be waived. Each partner must act consistently with good faith and fair dealing. b. A partner has the authority to bind the partnership in a contract. A partner may also subject the partnership to tort liability under agency principles. The extent of implied authority is generally broader for partners than for ordinary agents. c. In a traditional partnership, partners are personally liable for the debts of the partnership.
Dissociation and Termination	1. **Events that cause dissociation**— a. A partner's voluntarily giving notice of an "express will to withdraw." b. The occurrence of an event agreed to in the partnership agreement. c. Unanimous vote of the other partners under certain circumstances. d. The order of a court or arbitrator if the partner engaged in wrongful conduct that affects the business. e. The partner's declaring bankruptcy, assigning his or her interest in the partnership for the benefit of creditors, becoming physically or mentally incapacitated, or dying. 2. **Partnership termination**—Referred to as dissolution. Winding up is the actual process of collecting, liquidating, and distributing the partnership assets. A buy-sell agreement provides for one or more of the partners to buy out the other or others, and may specify how the assets will be valued in the event the firm is dissolved.

(Continues)

Limited Liability Partnerships (LLPs)	1. **Formation**—The appropriate form must be filed with a state agency, usually the secretary of state's office. Typically, an LLP is formed by professionals who work together as partners in a partnership. Under most state LLP statutes, it is relatively easy to convert a traditional partnership into an LLP. 2. **Liabilities of partners**—LLP statutes vary, but under the UPA, professionals generally can avoid personal liability for acts committed by other partners. Partners in an LLP continue to be liable for their own wrongful acts and for the wrongful acts of those whom they supervise.
Limited Partnerships (LPs)	1. **Formation**—A certificate of limited partnership must be filed with the secretary of state's office or other designated state official. The certificate must include information about the business. The partnership consists of one or more general partners and one or more limited partners. 2. **Liabilities of partners**—General partners have unlimited liability for partnership obligations. Limited partners are liable only to the extent of their contributions. Limited partners have no voice in management. If they do participate in management, they risk having general-partner liability. 3. **Dissociation and dissolution**—A limited partnership can be dissolved by court decree. In addition, a general partner's voluntary dissociation, bankruptcy, death, or mental incompetence will cause the dissociation of that partner and the partnership's dissolution unless all partners agree to continue the business. The death or assignment of the interest of a limited partner does not dissolve the partnership. Bankruptcy of a limited partner also does not dissolve the partnership unless it causes the bankruptcy of the firm.

Issue Spotters

1. Darnell and Eliana are partners in D&E Designs, an architectural firm. When Darnell dies, his widow claims that as Darnell's heir, she is entitled to take his place as Eliana's partner or to receive a share of the firm's assets. Is she right? Why or why not? (See *Dissociation and Termination.*)

2. Finian and Gloria are partners in F&G Delivery Service. When business is slow, without Gloria's knowledge, Finian leases the delivery vehicles as moving vans. Because the delivery vehicles would otherwise be sitting idle in a parking lot, can Finian keep the income that results from leasing the vehicles? Explain your answer. (See *Formation and Operation.*)

—Check your answers to the *Issue Spotters* against the answers provided in Appendix D.

Business Scenarios and Case Problems

27–1. Partnership Formation. Daniel is the owner of a chain of shoe stores. He hires Rubya to be the manager of a new store, which is to open in Grand Rapids, Michigan. Daniel, by written contract, agrees to pay Rubya a monthly salary and 20 percent of the profits. Without Daniel's knowledge, Rubya represents himself to Classen as Daniel's partner, showing Classen the agreement to share profits. Classen extends credit to Rubya. Rubya defaults. Discuss whether Classen can hold Daniel liable as a partner. (See *Formation and Operation.*)

27–2. Limited Partnership. Dorinda, Luis, and Elizabeth form a limited partnership. Dorinda is a general partner, and Luis and Elizabeth are limited partners. Discuss fully whether each of the separate events below constitutes a dissolution of the limited partnership. (See *Limited Partnerships.*)

1. Luis assigns his partnership interest to Ashley.
2. Elizabeth is petitioned into involuntary bankruptcy.
3. Dorinda dies.

27–3. Winding Up. Dan and Lori Cole operated a Curves franchise exercise facility in Angola, Indiana, as a partnership. The firm leased commercial space from Flying Cat, LLC, for a renewable three-year term. The Coles renewed the lease for a second three-year term. Two years later, however, the Coles divorced. By the end of the second term, the Coles owed Flying Cat more than $21,000 on the lease. Without telling the landlord about the divorce, Lori signed another extension. More rent went unpaid. Flying Cat obtained a judgment in an Indiana state court against the partnership for almost $50,000. Can Dan be held liable? Why or why not? [*Curves for Women Angola v. Flying Cat, LLC,* 983 N.E.2d 629 (Ind.App. 2013)] (See *Dissociation and Termination.*)

27–4. Business Case Problem with Sample Answer—Partnerships. Karyl Paxton asked Christopher Sacco to work with her interior design business, Pierce Paxton Collections, in New Orleans. At the time, they were in a romantic relationship. Sacco was involved in every aspect of the business—bookkeeping, marketing, and design—but was not paid a salary. He was reimbursed, however, for expenses charged to his personal credit card, which Paxton also used. Sacco took no profits from the firm, saying that he wanted to "grow the business" and "build sweat equity." When Paxton and Sacco's personal relationship soured, she fired him. Sacco objected, claiming that they were partners. Is Sacco entitled to 50 percent of the profits of Pierce Paxton Collections? Explain. [*Sacco v. Paxton,* 133 So.3d 213 (La.App. 2014)] (See *Formation and Operation.*)

—For a sample answer to Problem 27–4, go to Appendix E.

27–5. Formation. Leisa Reed and Randell Thurman lived together in Spring City, Tennessee. Randell and his father, Leroy, formed a cattle-raising operation and opened a bank account in the name of L&R Farm. Within a few years, Leroy quit the operation. Leisa and Randell each wrote a personal check for $5,000 to buy his cattle. Leisa picked up supplies, fed and administered medicine to cattle, collected hay, and participated in the bookkeeping for L&R. Later, checks drawn on her personal account for $12,000 to buy equipment and $35,000 to buy cattle were deposited into the L&R account. After several years, Leisa decided that she no longer wanted to associate with Randell, but they could not agree on a financial settlement. Was Leisa a partner in L&R? Is she entitled to half of the value of L&R's assets? Explain. [*Reed v. Thurman,* 2015 WL 1119449 (Tenn.App. 2015)] (See *Formation and Operation.*)

27–6. Formation and Operation. FS Partners is a general partnership whose partners are Jerry Stahlman, a professional engineer, and Fitz & Smith, Inc., a corporation in the business of excavating and paving. Timothy Smith signed the partnership agreement on Fitz & Smith's behalf and deals with FS matters on Fitz & Smith's behalf. Stahlman handles the payment of FS's bills, including its tax bills, and is the designated partner on FS's federal tax return. FS was formed to buy and develop twenty acres of unoccupied, wooded land in York County, Pennsylvania. The deed to the property lists the owner as "FS Partners, a general partnership." When the taxes on the real estate were not paid, the York County Tax Claim Bureau published notice that the property would be sold at a tax sale. The bureau also mailed a notice to FS's address of record and posted a notice on the land. Is this sufficient notice of the tax sale? Discuss. [*FS Partners v. York County Tax Claim Bureau,* 132 A.3d 577 (Pa. 2016)] (See *Formation and Operation.*)

27–7. Dissociation and Termination. Marc Malfitano and seven others formed Poughkeepsie Galleria as a partnership to own and manage a shopping mall in New York. The partnership agreement stated that "all decisions to be made by the Partners shall be made by the casting of votes" with "no less than fifty-one percent" of the partners "required to approve any matter." The agreement also provided that the partnership would dissolve on "the election of the Partners" or "the happening of any event which makes it unlawful for the business . . . to be carried on." Later, Malfitano decided to dissociate from the firm and wrote to the other partners, "I hereby elect to dissolve the Partnership." Did Malfitano have the power and the right to dissociate from Poughkeepsie Galleria? Could he unilaterally dissolve the partnership? Can the other partners continue the business? Which, if any, of these actions violate the partnership agreement? Discuss. [*Congel v. Malfitano,* 101 N.E.3d 341, 2018 WL 1473551 (N.Y.S.2d 2018)] (See *Dissociation and Termination.*)

27–8. A Question of Ethics—The IDDR Approach and a Partner's Fiduciary Duty. Floyd Finch and Bruce Campbell were partners in a law firm. They did not have a written partnership agreement, but they shared the firm's expenses and profits equally. The partnership operated on a cash basis, using billing software to track time spent on client matters. Instead of using the software, however, Finch would review e-mails and other work product to create and generate bills months or years after the work had been performed. As a result, large amounts of the firm's accounts receivable were uncollectible. Upset over the lost revenue, Campbell filed a claim in a Missouri state court against Finch. Campbell argued that failing to bill clients in a timely manner was a breach of a partner's fiduciary duty. He alleged that Finch was trying to lower his income because he was involved in divorce proceedings. Finch responded that billing clients was a matter of partnership management and operation reserved to the judgment of each partner. [*Finch v. Campbell,* 541 S.W.3d 616 (Mo.App.W.D. 2017)] (See *Formation and Operation.*)

1. Is Finch's billing practice a breach of ethics? Explain, using the IDDR approach.
2. Finch asserted that there must be self-dealing for a partner's act to be a breach of fiduciary duty. Is he correct? Discuss.

Critical Thinking and Writing Assignments

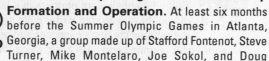

27–9. Business Law Writing. Sandra Lerner and Patricia Holmes were friends. One evening, while applying nail polish to Lerner, Holmes layered a raspberry color over black to produce a new color, which Lerner liked. Later, the two created other colors with names like "Bruise," "Smog," and "Oil Slick," and titled their concept "Urban Decay." Lerner and Holmes started a firm to produce and market the polishes but never discussed the sharing of profits and losses. They agreed to build the business and then sell it. Together, they did market research, worked on a logo and advertising, obtained capital, and hired employees. Then Lerner began scheming to edge Holmes out of the firm. (See *Formation and Operation.*)

1. Lerner claimed that there was no partnership agreement because there was no agreement on how to divide profits. Was Lerner right? Why or why not?
2. Suppose that Lerner, but not Holmes, had contributed a significant amount of personal funds to developing and marketing the new nail polish. Would this entitle Lerner to receive more of the profit? Explain.
3. Did Lerner violate her fiduciary duty? Why or why not?

27–10. Time-Limited Group Assignment—Partnership Formation and Operation. At least six months before the Summer Olympic Games in Atlanta, Georgia, a group made up of Stafford Fontenot, Steve Turner, Mike Montelaro, Joe Sokol, and Doug Brinsmade agreed to sell Cajun food at the games and began making preparations. On May 19, the group (calling themselves Prairie Cajun Seafood Catering of Louisiana) applied for a business license with the county health department.

Ted Norris sold members of the group a mobile kitchen in return for an $8,000 check drawn on the "Prairie Cajun Seafood Catering of Louisiana" account and two promissory notes, one for $12,000 and the other for $20,000. The notes, which were dated June 12, listed only Fontenot "d/b/a Prairie Cajun Seafood" as the maker (*d/b/a* is an abbreviation for "doing business as").

On July 31, Fontenot and his friends signed a partnership agreement, which listed specific percentages of profits and losses. They drove the mobile kitchen to Atlanta, but business was disastrous. When the notes were not paid, Norris filed a suit in a Louisiana state court against Fontenot, seeking payment. (See *Formation and Operation.*)

1. The first group will discuss the elements of a partnership and determine whether there was a partnership among Fontenot and the others.
2. The second group will determine who can be held liable on the notes and why.
3. The third group will discuss the concept of "d/b/a," or "doing business as." Does a person who uses this designation when signing checks or promissory notes avoid liability on the checks or notes?

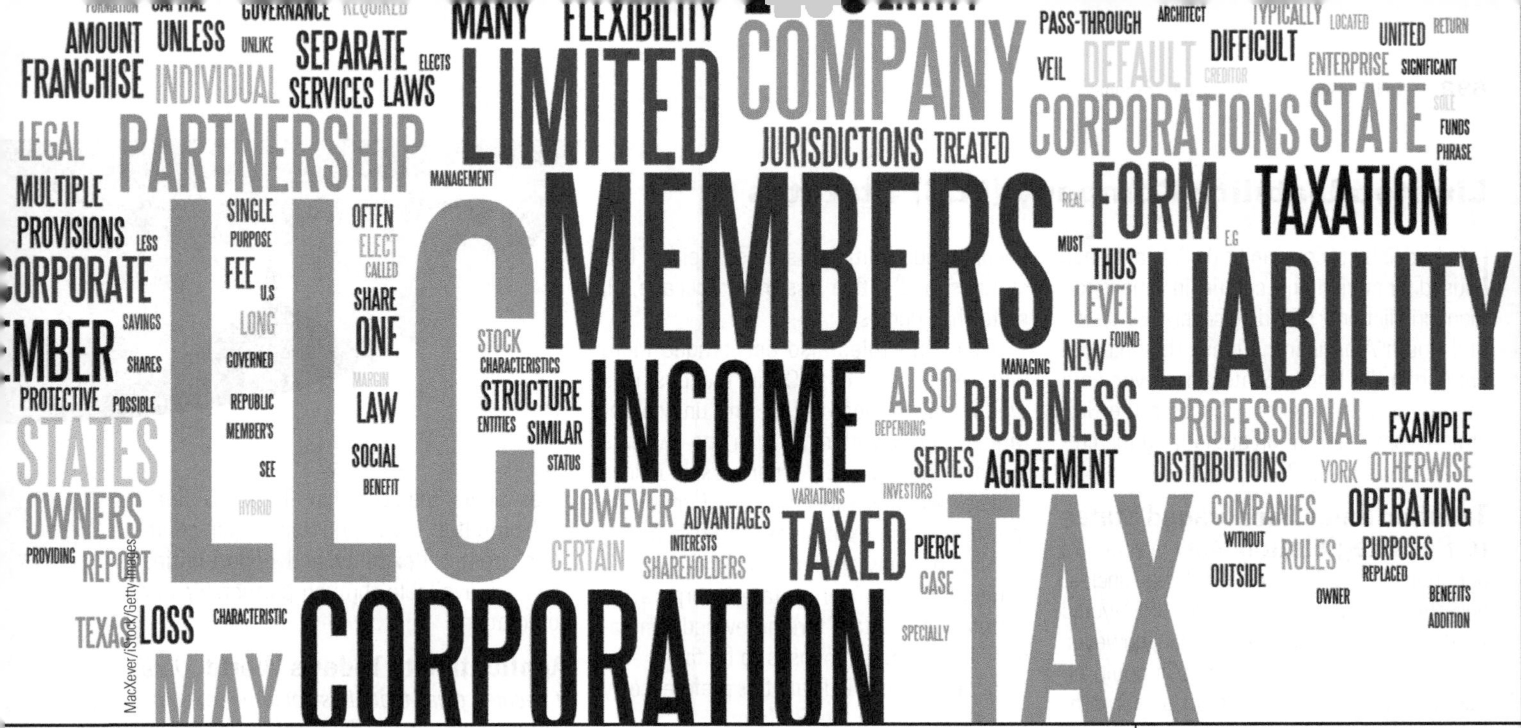

MacXever/iStock/Getty Images

Limited Liability Companies and Special Business Forms

28

Our government allows entrepreneurs to choose from a variety of business organizational forms. Many businesspersons would agree with the chapter-opening quotation that in business "to play it safe is not to play." Because risk is associated with the potential for higher profits, businesspersons are motivated to choose organizational forms that limit their liability while allowing them to take risks that may lead to greater profits.

> "To play it safe is not to play."
>
> **Robert Altman**
> 1925–2006
> (American film director)

A relatively new and increasingly common form of business organization is the *limited liability company (LLC)*. LLCs have become the organizational form of choice among many small businesses. Other special business forms outlined in this chapter include joint ventures, syndicates, joint stock companies, business trusts, and cooperatives.

Focus Questions

The four Focus Questions *below are designed to help improve your understanding. After reading this chapter, you should be able to answer the following questions:*

1. What advantages do limited liability companies offer to businesspersons that are not offered by sole proprietorships or partnerships?
2. What are the two options for managing limited liability companies?
3. What happens when a member dissociates from an LLC?
4. What is a joint venture? How is it similar to a partnership? How is it different?

28–1 The Limited Liability Company

A **limited liability company (LLC)** is a hybrid business form that combines the limited liability aspects of a corporation and the tax advantages of a partnership. This chapter's *Landmark in the Law* feature discusses the evolution of laws authorizing LLCs in the United States.

LLCs are governed by state LLC statutes, which vary, of course, from state to state. In an attempt to create more uniformity, the National Conference of Commissioners on Uniform State Laws (NCCUSL) issued the Uniform Limited Liability Company Act (ULLCA). Fewer than one-fifth of the states have adopted it, however. Thus, the law governing LLCs remains far from uniform.

Nevertheless, some provisions are common to most state statutes. We base our discussion of LLCs on these common elements.

Limited Liability Company (LLC) A hybrid form of business enterprise that offers the limited liability of a corporation and the tax advantages of a partnership.

Limited Liability Company (LLC) Statutes

Limited liability companies (LLCs) have been used for more than a century in various foreign jurisdictions, including several European and South American nations. They did not emerge in the United States, however, until the late 1970s. Wyoming became the first state to pass legislation authorizing the creation of LLCs in 1977.

Taxation Rules Encouraged States to Pass Legislation After Wyoming's adoption of its LLC statute, it still was unclear how the Internal Revenue Service (IRS) would treat LLCs for tax purposes. In 1988, however, the IRS ruled that Wyoming LLCs could be taxed as partnerships instead of corporations, providing that certain requirements were met. This ruling was favorable toward LLCs because it meant that, like a partnership, an LLC could pass through profits to its owners without paying taxes on them. Before the ruling, only one other state—Florida, in 1982—had authorized LLCs. The 1988 ruling encouraged additional states to enact LLC statutes, and within less than a decade, all states had done so.

Other IRS rules also encouraged more widespread use of LLCs in the business world. Under these rules, any unincorporated business with more than one owner is automatically taxed as a partnership unless it indicates otherwise on the tax form or fits into one of the exceptions. The exceptions involve publicly traded companies, companies formed under a state incorporation statute, and certain foreign-owned companies. If a business chooses to be taxed as a corporation, it can indicate this preference by checking a box on the IRS form.

Foreign Entities May Be LLC Members Another factor that has encouraged the creation of LLCs in this country is that foreign investors are allowed to become LLC members. In an era increasingly characterized by global business efforts and investments, the LLC often offers U.S. firms and potential investors from other countries greater flexibility and opportunities than are available through partnerships or corporations.

Application to Today's World *Once it became clear that LLCs could be taxed as partnerships, the LLC form of business organization was widely adopted. Members could avoid the personal liability associated with the partnership form of business as well as the double taxation of the corporate form of business. Today, LLCs are a common form of business organization.*

28–1a The Nature of the LLC

LLCs share many characteristics with corporations. Like corporations, LLCs are creatures of the state. In other words, they must be formed and operated in compliance with state law. Like shareholders in a corporation, the owner of an LLC—called a **member**—enjoys limited liability [ULLCA 303].

Member A person who has ownership interests in a limited liability company.

Limited Liability of Members Members of LLCs are shielded from personal liability in most situations. In other words, the liability of members is normally limited to the amount of their investments.

An exception arises when a member has significantly contributed to an LLC's tortious conduct.

Case Example 28.1 JGR Technologies, LLC, provided various Internet-related services for the Missouri Radio Ozarks Network (ORN). Following a fee dispute between the two companies, Luke Baugh, a JGR employee, "seized' several Internet domain names owned by ORN that were associated with its radio stations, including kuku.com. Baugh then sold kuku.com to a foreign buyer for $50,000.

A trial court found Baugh and three JGR members liable for the tort of conversion, which occurs when someone intentionally interferes with another's personal property. The JGR members appealed on the ground that they were shielded by law from liability for the acts of Baugh on behalf of the LLC. A state appellate court noted that a great deal of evidence had been presented at trial showing the extent to which the three LLC members "participated in

Know This

A uniform law is a "model" law. It does not become the law of any state until the state legislature adopts it, either in part or in its entirety.

or directed" Baugh's tortious conduct. Consequently, the appeals court affirmed the trial court's ruling. The members were personally liable and, along with Baugh, owed ORN $50,000 in damages, plus interest.[1]

When Liability May Be Imposed The members of an LLC, like the shareholders in a corporation, can lose their limited personal liability in certain circumstances. For instance, when an individual guarantees payment of a business loan to the LLC, that individual is personally liable for the business's obligation. In addition, if an LLC member fails to comply with certain formalities, such as by commingling personal and business funds, a court can impose personal liability.

Under various principles of corporate law, courts may hold the owners of a business liable for its debts. On rare occasions, for instance, courts ignore the corporate structure ("pierce the corporate veil") to expose the shareholders to personal liability when it is required to achieve justice. Similarly, courts will sometimes pierce the veil of an LLC to hold its members personally liable. Note, however, that courts have reserved piercing the veil of an LLC for circumstances that are clearly extraordinary. There must normally be some flagrant disregard of the LLC formalities, as well as fraud or malfeasance on the part of the LLC member.

Case Example 28.2 Tom and Shannon Brown purchased a new home in Hattiesburg, Mississippi, from Ray Richard and Nick Welch. Richard had hired Waldron Properties, LLC (WP), to build the home. Several years later, cracks began to develop in the walls of the Browns' home as a result of defects in the construction of the foundation. The Browns sued Murray Waldron, the sole member of WP, for breach of warranty under the state's New Home Warranty Act (NHWA). Because Waldron had signed the notice required by the NHWA that the Browns had received when they bought the home, they claimed that Waldron was liable personally.

The trial court found that WP (the LLC), not Waldron individually, was the builder of the Browns' home. The Browns appealed. They contended that even if WP was the builder, the court should pierce the veil of the LLC and hold Waldron personally liable. A state appellate court affirmed the lower court's ruling. The Browns had not entered into a contract with either Waldron or WP. There was not sufficient evidence that Waldron had disregarded LLC formalities or had engaged in fraud or other misconduct to justify piercing the LLC's veil to hold him personally liable.[2]

Other Similarities to Corporations Like corporations, LLCs are legal entities apart from their members. As a legal person, an LLC can sue or be sued, enter into contracts, and hold title to property [ULLCA 201]. The terminology used to describe LLCs formed in other states or nations is also similar to the terminology used in corporate law. For instance, an LLC formed in one state but doing business in another state is referred to in the second state as a *foreign LLC*.

28–1b The Formation of the LLC

LLCs are creatures of statute and thus must follow state statutory requirements.

Articles of Organization To form an LLC, **articles of organization** must be filed with a central state agency—usually the secretary of state's office [ULLCA 202].[3] Typically, the articles must include the name of the business, its principal address, the name and address of a registered agent, the members' names, and information on how the LLC

Articles of Organization The document filed with a designated state official by which a limited liability company is formed.

1. *Missouri Ozarks Radio, Network, Inc. v. Baugh*, 598 S.W.3d 154 (Mo.Ct.App. 2020).
2. *Brown v. Waldron*, 186 So.3d 955 (Miss.App. 2016).
3. In addition to requiring the filing of articles of organization, a few states require that a notice of the intention to form an LLC be published in a local newspaper.

Monkey Business Images/Shutterstock.com

Many hotel chains are franchised as limited liability companies. What is the document required to form an LLC?

will be managed [ULLCA 203]. The business's name must include the words *Limited Liability Company* or the initials *LLC* [ULLCA 105(a)]. Although a majority of the states permit one-member LLCs, some states require at least two members.

Preformation Contracts Businesspersons sometimes enter into contracts on behalf of a business organization that is not yet formed. For instance, persons forming a corporation may enter into contracts during the process of incorporation but before the corporation becomes a legal entity. These contracts are referred to as *preincorporation contracts*. Once the corporation is formed, it can adopt the preincorporation contract (by means of a *novation,* which substitutes a new contract for the old contract) and enforce the contract terms.

In dealing with the preorganization contracts of LLCs, courts may apply the well-established principles of corporate law relating to preincorporation contracts. That is, when the promoters of an LLC enter preformation contracts, the LLC, once formed, can adopt the contracts through novation and then enforce them.

Spotlight Case Example 28.3 607 South Park, LLC, entered into an agreement to sell a hotel to 607 Park View Associates, Ltd., which then assigned the rights to the purchase to another company, 02 Development, LLC. At the time, 02 Development did not yet exist—it was legally created several months later. 607 South Park subsequently refused to sell the hotel to 02 Development, and 02 Development sued for breach of the purchase agreement.

A California appellate court ruled that LLCs should be treated the same as corporations with respect to preorganization contracts. Although 02 Development did not exist when the agreement was executed, once it came into existence, it could enforce any preorganization contract made on its behalf.[4]

28–1c Jurisdictional Requirements

A significant difference between LLCs and corporations involves federal jurisdictional requirements. Under federal law, a corporation is deemed to be a citizen of the state where it is incorporated and maintains its principal place of business.[5] Federal law does not mention the citizenship of partnerships, LLCs, and other unincorporated associations, but the courts have tended to regard these entities as citizens of every state of which their members are citizens.

The state citizenship of LLCs may come into play when a party sues an LLC based on diversity of citizenship. Remember that when parties to a lawsuit are from different states, a federal court can exercise diversity jurisdiction if the amount in controversy exceeds $75,000. *Total* diversity of citizenship must exist, however.

Example 28.4 Jen, a citizen of New York, wishes to bring a lawsuit against Skycel, an LLC formed under the laws of Connecticut. One of Skycel's members also lives in New York. Jen will not be able to bring the action against Skycel in federal court on the basis of diversity jurisdiction because the defendant LLC is also considered a citizen of New York. The same would be true if Jen was filing a suit against multiple defendants and one of the defendants lived in New York.

4. *02 Development, LLC v. 607 South Park, LLC,* 159 Cal.App.4th 609, 71 Cal.Rptr.3d 608 (2008).
5. 28 U.S.C. Section 1332.

28–1d Advantages of the LLC

The LLC offers many advantages to businesspersons, which is why this form of business organization has become increasingly popular.

Focus Question 1

What advantages do limited liability companies offer to businesspersons that are not offered by sole proprietorships or partnerships?

Limited Liability A key advantage of the LLC is that the liability of members is limited to the amount of their investments. The LLC as an entity can be held liable for any loss or injury caused by the wrongful acts or omissions of its members. The members themselves generally are not personally liable.

In the following case, an LLC member, who was also the LLC's manager, alleged that he was not personally liable for the firm's failure to meet its obligations to a creditor.

Case 28.1

Nesset, Inc. v. Jones

Court of Appeals of Iowa, __ N.W.2d __, 2020 WL 1879582 (2020).

Facts Larry Nesset, the owner of Nesset, Inc., doing business as Weber Paint and Glass, subcontracted to complete various remodeling projects for the renovation of the hundred-year-old Sokol building in Cedar Rapids, Iowa, owned by Green Development, LLC.

When Green Development's general contractor, Miles Wilson, bowed out, Nesset began to deal directly with Charles Jones, member and manager of the LLC. Nesset and Jones did not enter into a written contract.

Disputes soon arose between Jones and Nesset concerning the quality of certain work. Months passed, and some of Weber's invoices to Green Development remained unpaid. In text messages and letters, Jones affirmed his intent to pay the past due bills. These communications were not written on LLC letterhead and did not include Jones's title.

Ultimately, Nesset filed a petition in an Iowa state court against Jones and the LLC to collect on the debt, alleging breach of contract. Jones answered that any contractual relationship Weber had would have been with Green Development, not with Jones personally.

The court issued a judgment in Nesset's favor, holding Jones personally liable for $17,708.33, plus interest and attorney's fees. Jones appealed.

Issue Did the trial court mistakenly hold Jones personally liable for Green Development's breach?

Decision Yes. A state intermediate appellate court reversed the trial court's ruling on the question of Jones's personal liability for his LLC's debt. "The record does not support the [trial] court's conclusion that Jones is individually liable."

Reason The appellate court explained that an LLC is an entity distinct from its members. Normally, a member or manager is not liable for the debts or other liabilities of the firm solely because he or she acts as a member or manager.

Under exceptional circumstances, a court will pierce the veil of an LLC and hold a member or manager personally liable. This can occur if the LLC is undercapitalized, does not keep separate books or records, commingles its finances with those of an individual, pays an individual's debts, is used to commit an illegal act such as fraud, or is otherwise "merely a sham."

In this case, Nesset failed to show that the circumstances warranted imposing personal liability on Jones as a member of Green Development. Nesset acknowledged that Jones acted as the LLC's representative when he took over the general contracting duties from Wilson. When Weber's invoices were paid, Jones made the payments on Green Development's account. Nesset offered no evidence that the LLC was undercapitalized, lacked separate books or finances, was promoting any fraud or illegality, or was a sham. Furthermore, "Nothing about the casual nature of Jones's text messages undermines the financial soundness or legitimacy of his LLC structure."

Critical Thinking

- **Legal Environment** *Besides the "exceptional circumstances" noted by the court in the Nesset case, in what situations might an LLC's member or manager be personally liable for the liability of the company? Explain.*
- **Economic** *Why does the law allow—and even encourage—limits on the liability of a business organization's owners and managers for the organization's actions? Discuss.*

Flexibility in Taxation Another advantage of the LLC is its flexibility in regard to taxation. An LLC that has *two or more members* can choose to be taxed either as a partnership or as a corporation. A corporate entity normally must pay income taxes on its profits, and the shareholders must then pay personal income taxes on any of those profits that are distributed as dividends. An LLC that wants to distribute profits to its members may prefer to be taxed as a partnership to avoid the "double taxation" that is characteristic of the corporate entity.

Unless an LLC indicates that it wishes to be taxed as a corporation, the Internal Revenue Service (IRS) automatically taxes it as a partnership. This means that the LLC, as an entity, pays no taxes. Rather, as in a partnership, profits are "passed through" the LLC to the members, who then personally pay taxes on the profits.

If an LLC's members want to reinvest profits in the business rather than distribute the profits to members, however, they may prefer to be taxed as a corporation. Corporate income tax rates also may be lower than personal tax rates.

An LLC that has only *one member* cannot be taxed as a partnership. For federal income tax purposes, one-member LLCs are automatically taxed as sole proprietorships unless they indicate that they wish to be taxed as corporations. With respect to state taxes, most states follow the IRS rules.

Management and Foreign Investors One more advantage of the LLC for businesspersons is the flexibility it offers in terms of business operations and management, as will be discussed shortly. Foreign investors are allowed to become LLC members, so organizing as an LLC can enable a business to attract investors from other countries.

Focus Question 2

What are the two options for managing limited liability companies?

28–1e Disadvantages of the LLC

The main disadvantage of the LLC is that state LLC statutes are not uniform. Therefore, businesses that operate in more than one state may not receive consistent treatment. Generally, most states apply to a foreign LLC (an LLC formed in another state) the law of the state where the LLC was formed. Difficulties can arise, though, when one state's court must interpret and apply another state's laws.

Exhibit 28–1 Management of an LLC

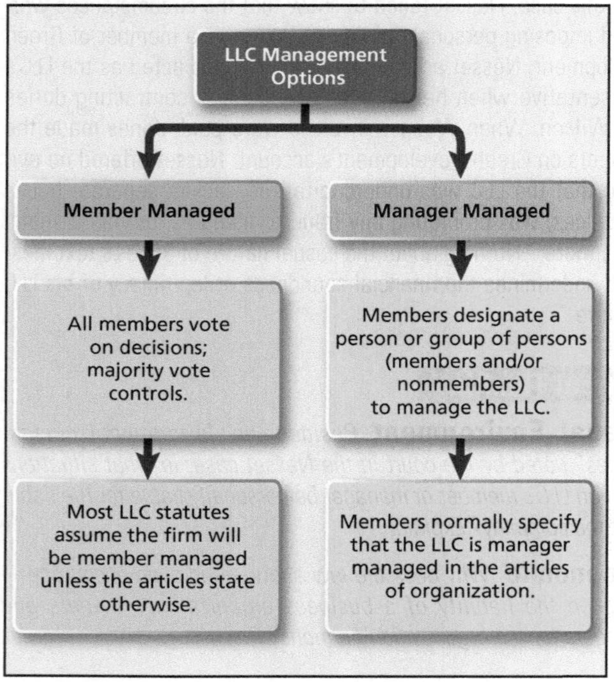

28–2 LLC Operation and Management

The members of an LLC have considerable flexibility in operating and managing the business. Here, we discuss management options for an LLC, the fiduciary duties owed, and the operating agreement and general operating procedures.

28–2a Management of an LLC

Basically, LLC members have two options for managing the firm, as shown in Exhibit 28–1. It can be either a member-managed LLC or a manager-managed LLC. Most LLC statutes and the ULLCA provide that unless the articles of organization specify otherwise, an LLC is assumed to be member managed [ULLCA 203(a)(6)].

In a *member-managed* LLC, all of the members participate in management, and decisions are made by majority vote [ULLCA

404(a)]. In a *manager-managed* LLC, the members designate a person or group of persons to manage the firm. The management group may consist of only members, both members and nonmembers, or only nonmembers.

However an LLC is managed, its managers need to be aware of the firm's potential liability under employment-discrimination laws. Those laws may sometimes extend to individuals who are not members of a protected class, as discussed in this chapter's *Managerial Strategy* feature.

28–2b Fiduciary Duties

Under the ULLCA, managers in a manager-managed LLC owe fiduciary duties (the duty of loyalty and the duty of care) to the LLC and to its members, just as corporate directors and officers owe fiduciary duties to the corporation and to its shareholders [ULLCA 409(a), (h)]. Because not all states have adopted the ULLCA, some state statutes provide that managers owe fiduciary duties only to the LLC and not to its members.

To whom a fiduciary duty is owed may seem insignificant at first glance, but it can have a dramatic effect on the outcome of litigation. In North Carolina and Virginia, for instance,

Can a Person Who Is Not a Member of a Protected Class Sue for Discrimination?

Under federal law and the laws of most states, discrimination in employment based on race, color, religion, national origin, gender, sexual orientation, age, or disability is prohibited. Persons who are members of these protected classes can sue if they are subjected to discrimination.

But can a person subjected to discrimination bring a lawsuit if he is not a member of a protected class, even though managers and other employees believe that he is? This somewhat unusual situation occurred in New Jersey.

A New Jersey Case

Myron Cowher worked at Carson & Roberts Site Construction & Engineering, Inc. For more than a year, at least two of his supervisors directed almost daily barrages of anti-Semitic remarks at him. They believed that he was Jewish, although his actual background was German-Irish and Lutheran.

Cowher brought a suit against the supervisors and the construction company, claiming a hostile work environment. The trial court, however, ruled that he did not have standing to sue under New Jersey law because he was not Jewish and, thus, was not a member of a protected class. Cowher appealed.

The appellate court disagreed with the trial court. The court ruled that if Cowher could prove that the discrimination "would not have occurred but for the perception that he was Jewish," his claim was covered by New Jersey's antidiscrimination law.[a] In the appellate court's view, the nature of the discriminatory remarks—and not the actual characteristics of the plaintiff—determines whether the remarks are actionable.

Perception and Reality

Corey Dickson, an obese bus driver, had been teased by coworkers about his weight. Under New Jersey law, Dickson did not quality as disabled because his obesity was not caused by a medical condition. Still, Dickson brought a hostile work environment claim against his employer, arguing that, as in the *Cowher* case, his coworkers perceived him to be a member of a protected class even though technically he was not. An appellate court dismissed the lawsuit, holding that Dickson's coworkers perceived that he was obese, not disabled, and obesity alone did not make him a member of a protected class.[b]

Business Questions

1. *Should a manager for an LLC respond to employee complaints of discrimination any differently than a manager at a corporation, a partnership, or a sole proprietorship? Why or why not?*

2. *How can a company, whether an LLC or some other business form, reduce the possibility of discrimination lawsuits?*

---

a. *Cowher v. Carson & Roberts*, 425 N.J.Super. 285, 40 A.3d 1171 (2012).

b. *Dickson v. Community Bus Lines, Inc.*, 206 A.3d 429, 458 N.J.Super. 522 (2019).

Rawpixel.com/Shutterstock.com

When can a person who is not a member of a protected class sue a company for discrimination?

Operating Agreement An agreement in which the members of a limited liability company set forth the details of how the business will be managed and operated.

LLC statutes do not explicitly state that managers owe fiduciary duties to members.[6] Thus, in those two states, a manager-member owes fiduciary duties only to the LLC and not to its members.[7] In contrast, laws in Idaho and Kentucky provide that a manager-member owes fiduciary duties to the LLC's members and that the members can sue the manager for breaching fiduciary duties.[8]

28–2c The LLC Operating Agreement

The members of an LLC can decide how to operate the various aspects of the business by forming an **operating agreement** [ULLCA 103(a)]. In many states, an operating agreement is not required for an LLC to exist, and if there is one, it need not be in writing. Generally, though, LLC members should protect their interests by creating a written operating agreement.

Operating agreements typically contain provisions relating to the following areas:

1. Management and how future managers will be chosen or removed. (Although most LLC statutes are silent on this issue, the ULLCA provides that members may choose and remove managers by majority vote [ULLCA 404(b)(3)].)
2. How profits will be divided.
3. How membership interests may be transferred.
4. Whether the dissociation of a member, such as by death or departure, will trigger dissolution of the LLC.
5. Whether formal members' meetings will be held.
6. How voting rights will be apportioned. (If the agreement does not cover voting, LLC statutes in most states provide that voting rights are apportioned according to each member's capital contributions. Some states provide that, in the absence of an agreement to the contrary, each member has one vote.)
7. How a buyout price will be calculated in the event of a member's dissociation.

If a dispute arises and there is no agreement covering the topic under dispute, the state LLC statute will govern the outcome. For instance, most LLC statutes provide that if the members have not specified how profits will be divided, they will be divided equally among the members. When an issue is not covered by an operating agreement or by an LLC statute, the courts often apply principles of partnership law.

Sometimes, as in the following case, an operating agreement and the state's LLC statutes are applied together to determine the outcome of a dispute between the members of an LLC.

6. North Carolina General Statutes Section 57C-3-22(b); and Virginia Code Section 13.1-1024.1.
7. See, for instance, *Atkinson v. Lackey*, 2015 WL 867181 (N.C.Super. 2015).
8. Idaho Code Sections 30-25-101 *et seq.*; and Kentucky Revised Statutes Section 275.170.

Case 28.2

Schaefer v. Orth

Wisconsin Court of Appeals, 382 Wis.2d 271, 915 N.W.2d 730 (2018).

Facts Jason Schaefer and Randy Orth created Grilled Cheese, LLC, to own and operate a "Tom and Chee" franchise, a casual restaurant specializing in grilled cheese sandwiches and soups. The operating agreement provided that Schaefer would be responsible for the restaurant's day-to-day operations, for which the LLC would pay him a monthly salary and bonuses. Orth would be responsible for the LLC's business and financial decisions and would not receive any compensation. The restaurant reported a profit only in its first full month of operations. Five months later, when Schaefer was not paid his salary and bonuses, he quit.

Later, Orth closed the restaurant and worked to wind up the business. Both parties lost all the funds they had invested in the LLC. Schaefer filed a suit in a Wisconsin state court against Orth, claiming breach of contract for Orth's failure to pay Schaefer's salary. The court directed a verdict in Orth's favor. Schaefer appealed.

Issue Was Orth personally liable to Schaefer for his unpaid salary and bonuses?

Decision No. A state intermediate appellate court affirmed the lower court's judgment. "The evidence presented at trial does not permit a legal conclusion that Orth was personally liable to Schaefer for" his unpaid salary and bonuses.

Reason At trial, both Orth and Schaefer testified that the LLC, not Orth, was responsible for paying Schaefer's compensation. The agreement's "unambiguous language" supported this testimony. A section titled "Distributions" provided that Schaefer's salary and bonuses were to be paid before other "distributions" to the members. All "distributions" were to be made from the funds of the LLC. Similarly, a section titled "Profits" stated, "The LLC shall, as the first priority, allocate Profit to Schaefer to the extent, if any, [of] compensation accruing in his favor." The agreement defined "profit" as the profit of the LLC.

Furthermore, under Wisconsin's LLC statutes, "the . . . obligations . . . of a limited liability company . . . shall be solely the . . . obligations . . . of the limited liability company." A member of an LLC "is not personally liable for any . . . obligation . . . of the limited liability company, except that a member or manager may become personally liable by his or her acts or conduct other than as a member or manager." Here, there was no evidence that Orth acted outside his capacity as a member or manager when Schaefer was not paid his salary and bonuses.

Critical Thinking

- **Economic** *The operating agreement stated that an "aggrieved party may pursue all redress permitted by law," including attorneys' fees. Under this provision, would Schaefer be entitled to an award of attorneys' fees even though the trial court granted Orth's motion for a directed verdict? Discuss.*
- **Legal Environment** *Could Schaefer have sued the LLC to recover his unpaid salary and bonuses? Explain.*

28–3 Dissociation and Dissolution of an LLC

Recall that in a partnership, *dissociation* occurs when a partner ceases to be associated in the carrying on of the business. The same concept applies to LLCs. Like a partner in a partnership, a member of an LLC has the *power* to dissociate at any time but may not have the *right* to dissociate.

Under the ULLCA, the events that trigger a member's dissociation from an LLC are similar to the events causing a partner to be dissociated under the Uniform Partnership Act (UPA). These include voluntary withdrawal, expulsion by other members or by court order, bankruptcy, incompetence, and death. Generally, if a member dies or otherwise dissociates from an LLC, the other members may continue to carry on the LLC's business, unless the operating agreement provides otherwise.

28–3a The Effects of Dissociation

Focus Question 3
What happens when a member dissociates from an LLC?

A member who dissociates from an LLC loses the right to participate in management and the right to act as an agent for the LLC. The member's duty of loyalty to the LLC also terminates, and the duty of care continues only with respect to events that occurred before dissociation.

Generally, the dissociated member also has a right to have his or her interest in the LLC bought out by the other members. The LLC's operating agreement may contain provisions establishing a buyout price. If it does not, the member's interest is usually purchased at a fair value. In states that have adopted the ULLCA, the LLC must purchase the interest at fair value within 120 days after the dissociation.

If the member's dissociation violates the LLC's operating agreement, it is considered legally wrongful, and the dissociated member can be held liable for damages caused by the dissociation. **Example 28.5** Chadwick and Barrel are members of an LLC. Chadwick manages the accounts, and Barrel, who has many connections in the community and is a skilled investor, brings in the business. If Barrel wrongfully dissociates from the LLC, the LLC's business will suffer, and Chadwick can hold Barrel liable for the loss of business resulting from her withdrawal.

28–3b Dissolution

Regardless of whether or not a member's dissociation was wrongful, normally the dissociated member has no right to force the LLC to dissolve. The remaining members can opt to either continue or dissolve the business.

Members can also stipulate in their operating agreement that certain events will cause dissolution, or they can agree that they have the power to dissolve the LLC by vote. As with partnerships, a court can order an LLC to be dissolved in certain circumstances. For instance, a court might order dissolution when the members have engaged in illegal or oppressive conduct, or when it is no longer feasible to carry on the business.

Case Example 28.6 Charles Timmons was a member of Lake City Golf Club, a limited liability company operated by another member, Claude Ste. Marie. Timmons became disenchanted with Ste. Marie's management of the club's finances and filed a suit against Lake City. The settlement agreement from this action granted Timmons $1,750,000 to be paid by Lake City in installments. When Lake City was unable to make these payments, Timmons sued again. This time, an arbitrator decided that, given its precarious financial situation, Lake City must be judicially dissolved. A trial court eventually found that Timmons was owed about $1,850,000 of the proceeds from this dissolution, an amount upheld on appeal.[9] (See this chapter's *Business Law Analysis* feature for an illustration of when a court will not dissolve an LLC.)

A judge's exercise of discretion to order the dissolution of an LLC was disputed in the following case.

9. *Timmons v. Lake City Golf, LLC*, 293 So.3d 596 (Fla.Dis.Ct.App. 2020).

Case 28.3

Reese v. Newman

District of Columbia Court of Appeals, 131 A.3d 880 (2016).

Facts Allison Reese and Nicole Newman, the owners of ANR Construction Management, LLC, could not reconcile their difference of opinion over the company's direction. Newman told Reese that she was going to dissolve and wind up the firm. Reese wanted Newman to dissociate from ANR, so that Reese could continue the business. This dispute led to Newman's filing a suit in a District of Columbia court against Reese.

Following a trial, a jury found grounds for both ANR's dissolution and Newman's dissociation. The court chose to exercise its discretion under the state statutes governing the dissociation of members and the dissolution of LLCs. The court ordered dissolution. Reese appealed.

Issue Did the trial judge have the discretion to choose either the dissociation of a member or the dissolution of the LLC?

Decision Yes. A state intermediate appellate court affirmed the lower court's order. The trial court acted within its discretion in ordering dissolution rather than dissociation.

Reason Reese argued that the statutes did not allow for any exercise of discretion by the judge but instead required the court to order Newman's dissociation based on the jury's findings. The appellate court disagreed. The court applied the plain language rule to construe the language of the two statutes. Both the dissociation statute and the dissolution statute used the word "shall" ("shall be dissociated" and "shall be dissolved"), which the court reasoned was not a command. The court interpreted the effect as meaning "when both grounds for dissociation of a member and dissolution of the LLC exist, the trial judge has discretion to choose either alternative."

Critical Thinking

- **Legal Environment** *Newman alleged that after she delivered her notice to dissolve ANR, Reese locked her out of the LLC's bank accounts, blocked her access to the LLC's files and e-mail, and ended her salary and health benefits. Do these allegations, if proved, support or refute the court's decision to dissolve the firm? Explain.*

28–3c Winding Up

When an LLC is dissolved, any members who did not wrongfully dissociate may participate in the winding up process. To wind up the business, members must collect, liquidate, and distribute the LLC's assets.

Members may preserve the assets for a reasonable time to optimize their returns, and they continue to have the authority to perform reasonable acts in conjunction with winding up. In other words, the LLC will be bound by the reasonable acts of its members during the winding up process.

Once all the LLC's assets have been sold, the proceeds are distributed. Debts to creditors are paid first (including debts owed to members who are creditors of the LLC). The members' capital contributions are returned next. Any remaining amounts are then distributed to members in equal shares or according to their operating agreement.

When Will a Court Order the Dissolution of an LLC?

Business Law Analysis

Walter Van Houten and John King formed 1545 Ocean Avenue, LLC, with each managing 50 percent of the business. Its purpose was to renovate an existing building and construct a new commercial building. Van Houten and King quarreled over many aspects of the work on the properties. King claimed that Van Houten paid the contractors too much for the work performed. As the projects neared completion, King demanded that the LLC be dissolved and that Van Houten agree to a buyout. Because the parties could not agree on a buyout, King sued for dissolution. The trial court enjoined (prevented) further work on the projects until the dispute was settled.

As the ground for dissolution, King cited the fights over management decisions. There was no claim of fraud or frustration of purpose. The trial court ordered that the LLC be dissolved, and Van Houten appealed. Should either of the owners be forced to dissolve the LLC before the completion of its purpose—that is, before the building projects are finished?

Analysis: The issue here is whether disagreements over management decisions are a sufficient reason for a court to dissolve an LLC. Normally, the grounds for dissolution are specified in the operating agreement. If not, then a court will consider several factors. Usually, the petitioning member must establish that (1) the management of the entity is unable or unwilling to reasonably permit or promote the stated purpose of the entity to be realized or achieved, or (2) continuing the entity is financially unfeasible.

A court will not dissolve a LLC merely because events have not turned out exactly as the LLC's owners originally envisioned or because the LLC has failed to be profitable. Dissolution is reserved for situations in which the LLC's management has become so dysfunctional or its business purpose so thwarted that it is no longer practicable to operate the business. For instance, when there is a voting deadlock among members or the defined purpose of the entity has become impossible to fulfill, a court will order dissolution.

Result and Reasoning: Here, there was disagreement about the work being done (and the price), but the project was moving toward completion. Thus, there is no reason that the purpose of the LLC should not be fulfilled. Also, there is no evidence that the entity is financially unfeasible. Therefore, a court is not likely to order dissolution of the LLC.

28–4 Special Business Forms

Focus Question 4

What is a joint venture? How is it similar to a partnership? How is it different?

Besides the business forms already discussed in this unit, several other forms can be used to organize a business. For the most part, these special business forms are hybrid organizations—that is, they combine features of other organizational forms, such as partnerships and corporations. These forms include joint ventures, syndicates, joint stock companies, business trusts, and cooperatives.

28–4a Joint Ventures

Joint Venture A joint undertaking by two or more persons or business entities to combine their efforts or their property for a single transaction or project or for a related series of transactions or projects. A joint venture is generally treated like a partnership for tax and other legal purposes.

In a **joint venture**, two or more persons or business entities combine their efforts or their property for a single transaction or project or for a related series of transactions or projects. For instance, when several contractors combine their resources to build and sell houses in a single development, their relationship is a joint venture. Unless otherwise agreed, joint venturers share profits and losses equally.

Joint ventures range in size from very small activities to multimillion-dollar joint actions carried out by some of the world's largest corporations. Large organizations often investigate new markets or new ideas by forming joint ventures with other enterprises. **Example 28.7** BMW enters into a joint venture with JLR's Range Rover Division. Under the agreement, the companies work together and use the S63, a twin-turbo V8 engine, to manufacture certain automobiles. ■

Similarities to Partnerships The joint venture resembles a partnership and is taxed like a partnership. For this reason, most courts apply the same principles to joint ventures as they apply to partnerships. Joint venturers owe each other the same fiduciary duties, including the duty of loyalty, that partners owe each other. Thus, if one of the venturers secretly buys land that was supposed to be acquired by the joint venture, the other joint venturers may be awarded damages for the breach of loyalty. Joint venturers have some authority as agents to enter into contracts for business purposes that will bind the joint venture.

A joint venturer can be held personally liable for the venture's debts (because joint venturers share losses as well as profits). Like partners, joint venturers have equal rights to manage the activities of the enterprise, but they can agree to give control of the operation to one of the members.

Know This

A partnership involves a continuing relationship of the partners. A joint venture is often a one-time association.

Differences from Partnerships Joint ventures differ from partnerships in several important ways. A joint venture is typically created for a single project or series of transactions, whereas a partnership usually (though not always) involves an ongoing business. Thus unlike most partnerships, a joint venture normally terminates when the project or the transaction for which it was formed has been completed.

Because the activities of a joint venture are more limited than the business of a partnership, the members of a joint venture are presumed to have less power to bind their co-venturers. Accordingly, the members of a joint venture have less implied and apparent authority than the partners in a partnership (each of whom is treated as an agent of the other partners).

28–4b Syndicates

Syndicate A group of individuals or firms that join together to finance a project. A syndicate is also called an *investment group*.

In a **syndicate**, or *investment group*, several individuals or firms join together to finance a particular project. Syndicates can finance projects such as the construction of a shopping center or the purchase of a professional basketball franchise. The form of such groups varies considerably. A syndicate may be organized as a corporation or as a general or limited partnership. In some instances, the members do not have a legally recognized business arrangement but merely purchase and own property jointly.

28–4c Joint Stock Companies

A **joint stock company** is a true hybrid of a partnership and a corporation. It has many characteristics of a corporation in that (1) its ownership is represented by transferable shares of stock, (2) it is managed by directors and officers of the company or association, and (3) it can have a perpetual existence.

Most of its other features, however, are more characteristic of a partnership, and it is usually treated like a partnership. Like a partnership, a joint stock company is formed by agreement (not statute). Property is usually held in the names of the members, who are called shareholders, and they have personal liability. In a joint stock company, however, shareholders are not considered to be agents of one another, as they are in a partnership.

Joint Stock Company A hybrid form of business organization that combines characteristics of a corporation and a partnership. Usually, a joint stock company is regarded as a partnership for tax and other legal purposes.

28–4d Business Trusts

A **business trust** is created by a written trust agreement that sets forth the interests of the beneficiaries and obligations and powers of the trustee. This form of organization was started in Massachusetts in an attempt to obtain the limited liability advantage of a corporation while avoiding restrictions on real property ownership. With a business trust, legal ownership and management of the trust's property stay with one or more of the trustees, and the profits are distributed to the beneficiaries.

A business trust resembles a corporation in many respects. Beneficiaries of the trust, for instance, are not personally responsible for the trust's debts or obligations. In fact, in a number of states, business trusts must pay corporate taxes.

Business Trust A form of business organization, created by a written trust agreement, that resembles a corporation. Legal ownership and management of the trust's property stay with the trustees, and the profits are distributed to the beneficiaries, who have limited liability.

Cooperative An association, which may or may not be incorporated, that is organized to provide an economic service to its members. Unincorporated cooperatives are often treated like partnerships for tax and other legal purposes.

28–4e Cooperatives

A **cooperative** (co-op) is an association that is organized to provide an economic service to its members (or shareholders). It may or may not be incorporated. Most cooperatives are organized under state statutes for cooperatives, general business corporations, or LLCs. Co-ops range in size from small, local consumer cooperatives to national businesses such as Ace Hardware and Land O'Lakes, a well-known producer of dairy products.

Generally, an incorporated cooperative distributes dividends, or profits, to its owners on the basis of their transactions with the cooperative rather than on the basis of the amount of capital they contributed. Members of incorporated cooperatives have limited liability, as do shareholders of corporations and members of LLCs. Cooperatives that are unincorporated are often treated like partnerships, and members have joint liability for the cooperative's acts.

The cooperative form of business is generally adopted by groups of individuals who wish to pool their resources to gain some advantage in the marketplace. *Consumer purchasing co-ops*, for instance, are formed to obtain lower prices through quantity discounts. *Seller marketing co-ops* are formed to control the market and thereby enable members to sell their goods at higher prices.

RiverNorthPhotography/iStock Unreleased/Getty Images

Most people believe that cooperatives are small enterprises, but not all are. Ace Hardware is a nationwide co-op that was formed over eighty years ago. What is the benefit of forming a co-op?

Practice and Review

The city of Papagos, Arizona, had a deteriorating bridge in need of repair on a prominent public roadway. The city posted notices seeking proposals for an artistic bridge design and reconstruction. Davidson Masonry, LLC—owned and managed by Carl Davidson and his wife, Marilyn Rowe—decided to submit a bid for a decorative concrete project that incorporated artistic metalwork. They contacted Shana Lafayette, a local sculptor who specialized in large-scale metal creations, to help them design the bridge. The city selected their bridge design and awarded them the contract for a commission of $184,000.

Davidson Masonry and Lafayette then entered into an agreement to work together on the bridge project. Davidson Masonry agreed to install and pay for concrete and structural work, and Lafayette agreed to install the metalwork at her expense. They agreed that overall profits would be split, with 25 percent going to Lafayette and 75 percent going to Davidson Masonry. Lafayette designed numerous metal salmon sculptures that were incorporated into colorful decorative concrete forms designed by Rowe, while Davidson performed the structural engineering. The group worked together successfully until the completion of the project. Using the information presented in the chapter, answer the following questions.

1. Would Davidson Masonry automatically be taxed as a partnership or a corporation? Explain.
2. Is Davidson Masonry member managed or manager managed?
3. When Davidson Masonry and Lafayette entered into an agreement to work together, what kind of special business form was created? Explain.
4. Suppose that during construction, Lafayette entered into an agreement to rent space in a warehouse that was close to the bridge so that she could work on her sculptures near the location where they would be installed. She entered into the contract without the knowledge or consent of Davidson Masonry. In this situation, would a court be likely to hold that Davidson Masonry was bound by the contract? Why or why not?

Debate This

Because LLCs are essentially just partnerships with limited liability for members, all partnership laws should apply.

Key Terms

articles of organization 693
business trust 703
cooperative 703
joint stock company 703
joint venture 702
limited liability company (LLC) 691
member 692
operating agreement 698
syndicate 702

Chapter Summary: Limited Liability Companies and Special Business Forms

The Limited Liability Company	A limited liability company (LLC) is a hybrid form of business enterprise that offers the limited liability of a corporation and the tax advantages of a partnership. 1. **Formation**—Articles of organization must be filed with the appropriate state office—usually the office of the secretary of state—setting forth the name of the business, its principal address, the name and address of a registered agent, the names of the owners (called *members*), and information on how the LLC will be managed. 2. **Advantages and disadvantages of the LLC**—Advantages of the LLC include limited liability, the option to be taxed as a partnership or as a corporation, and flexibility in deciding how the business will be managed and operated. The LLC also allows foreign investors to be members. The main disadvantage is the absence of uniformity in state LLC statutes.
LLC Operation and Management	1. **Management**—An LLC can be member managed or manager managed. The management group may consist of members only, both members and nonmembers, or nonmembers only. 2. **Fiduciary duties**—In some states, managers in a manager-managed LLC owe fiduciary duties (the duty of loyalty and the duty of care) to the LLC and to its members. 3. **Operating agreement**—When an LLC is formed, the members decide, in an operating agreement, how the business will be managed and what rules will apply to the organization.
Dissociation and Dissolution of an LLC	Members of an LLC have the power to dissociate from the LLC at any time, but they may not have the right to dissociate. Dissociation does not always result in the dissolution of an LLC. The remaining members can choose to continue the business. Dissociated members have a right to have their interest purchased by the other members. If the LLC is dissolved, the business must be wound up and the assets sold. Creditors are paid first, and then members' capital investments are returned. Any remaining proceeds are distributed to members.
Special Business Forms	1. **Joint venture**—An organization created by two or more persons in contemplation of a single transaction or project or a related series of transactions or projects. A joint venture is similar to a partnership in many respects. 2. **Syndicate**—An investment group that undertakes to finance a particular project. A syndicate may be organized as a corporation or as a general or limited partnership. 3. **Joint stock company**—A business form similar to a corporation in some respects (transferable shares of stock, management by directors and officers, perpetual existence) but otherwise resembling a partnership. 4. **Business trust**—A business form created by a written trust agreement that sets forth the interests of the beneficiaries and the obligations and powers of the trustees. Beneficiaries are not personally liable for the debts or obligations of the business trust, which is similar to a corporation in many respects. 5. **Cooperative**—An association organized to provide an economic service, without profit, to its members. A co-op may or may not be incorporated.

Issue Spotters

1. Gabriel, Harry, and Ida are members of Jeweled Watches, LLC. What are their options with respect to the management of their firm? (See *LLC Operation and Management.*)
2. Greener Delivery Company and Hiway Trucking, Inc., form a business trust. Insta Equipment Company and Jiffy Supply Corporation form a joint stock company. Kwik Mart, Inc., and Luscious Produce, Inc., form an incorporated cooperative. What do these forms of business organization have in common? (See *Special Business Forms.*)

—Check your answers to the *Issue Spotters* against the answers provided in Appendix D.

Business Scenarios and Case Problems

28–1. Limited Liability Companies. John, Lesa, and Trevor form a limited liability company. John contributes 60 percent of the capital, and Lesa and Trevor each contribute 20 percent. Nothing is decided about how profits will be divided. John assumes that he will be entitled to 60 percent of the profits, in accordance with his contribution. Lesa and Trevor, however, assume that the profits will be divided equally. A dispute over the profits arises, and ultimately a court has to decide the issue. What law will the court apply? In most states, what will result? How could this dispute have been avoided in the first place? Discuss fully. (See *The Limited Liability Company.*)

28–2. Special Business Forms. Faraway Corp. supplies business equipment. Faraway is considering entering into two contracts, one with a joint stock company east of the Mississippi River and the other with a business trust formed by a number of sole proprietors on the West Coast. Both contracts require Faraway to make large capital outlays in order to supply the businesses with restaurant equipment. In both business organizations, at least two shareholders or beneficiaries are personally wealthy, but each organization has limited financial resources. The owner-managers of Faraway are not familiar with either form of business organization. Because each form resembles a corporation, they are concerned about whether they will be able to collect payments from the wealthy members of the business organizations in the event that either organization breaches the contract by failing to make the payments. Discuss fully Faraway's concern. (See *Special Business Forms.*)

28–3. Jurisdiction. Joe, a resident of New Jersey, wants to open a restaurant. He asks his friend Kay, who is an experienced attorney and a New Yorker, for her business and legal advice in exchange for a 20 percent ownership interest in the restaurant. Kay helps Joe negotiate a lease for the restaurant premises and advises Joe to organize the business as a limited liability company (LLC). Joe forms Café Olé, LLC, and, with Kay's help, obtains financing. Then, the night before the restaurant opens, Joe tells Kay that he is "cutting her out of the deal." The restaurant proves to be a success. Kay wants to file a suit in a federal district court against Joe and the LLC. Can a federal court exercise jurisdiction over the parties based on diversity of citizenship? Explain. (See *The Limited Liability Company.*)

28–4. Business Case Problem with Sample Answer—LLC Operation. James Williford, Patricia Mosser, Marquetta Smith, and Michael Floyd formed Bluewater Logistics, LLC, to bid on construction contracts after Hurricane Katrina struck the Gulf Coast. Under Mississippi law, every member of a member-managed LLC is entitled to participate in managing the business. The operating agreement provided for a "supermajority" 75 percent vote to remove a member who "has either committed a felony or under any other circumstances that would jeopardize the company status" as a contractor. After Bluewater had completed more than $5 million in contracts, Smith told Williford that she, Mosser, and Floyd were exercising their "supermajority" vote to fire him. No reason was provided. Williford sued Bluewater and the other members. Did Smith, Mosser, and Floyd breach the state LLC statute, their fiduciary duties, or the Bluewater operating agreement? Discuss. [*Bluewater Logistics, LLC v. Williford*, 55 So.3d 148 (Miss. 2011)] (See *LLC Operation and Management.*)

—For a sample answer to Problem 28–4, go to Appendix E.

28–5. Jurisdictional Requirements. Fadal Machining Centers, LLC, and MAG Industrial Automation Centers, LLC, sued a New Jersey–based corporation, Mid-Atlantic CNC, Inc., in federal district court. Ten percent of MAG was owned by SP MAG Holdings, a Delaware LLC. SP MAG had six members, including a Delaware limited partnership called Silver Point Capital Fund and a Delaware LLC called SPCP Group III. In turn, Silver Point and SPCP Group had a common member, Robert O'Shea, who was a New Jersey citizen. Assuming that the amount in controversy exceeds $75,000, does the district court have diversity jurisdiction? Why or why not? [*Fadal Machining Centers, LLC v. Mid-Atlantic CNC, Inc.*, 464 Fed.Appx. 672 (9th Cir. 2012)] (See *The Limited Liability Company.*)

28–6. Jurisdictional Requirements. Siloam Springs Hotel, LLC, operates a Hampton Inn in Siloam Springs, Arkansas. Siloam bought insurance from Century Surety Co. to cover the hotel. When guests suffered injuries due to a leak of carbon monoxide from the heating element of an indoor swimming pool, Siloam filed a claim with Century. Century denied coverage. Siloam disputed the denial. Century asked a federal district court to resolve the dispute. In asserting that the federal court had jurisdiction, Century noted that the amount in controversy exceeded $75,000 and that the parties had complete diversity of citizenship: Century is "a corporation organized under the laws of Ohio, with its principal place of business in Michigan," and Siloam is "a corporation organized under the laws of Oklahoma, with its principal place of business in Arkansas." Can the court exercise diversity jurisdiction in this case? Discuss. [*Siloam Springs Hotel, L.L.C. v. Century Surety Co.*, 781 F.3d 1233 (10th Cir. 2015)] (See *The Limited Liability Company.*)

28–7. Special Business Forms. Randall and Peggy Norman operated a dairy farm in Pine River, Minnesota. About ten years after the operation was begun, the cows started to experience health issues. Over the next eighteen years, the herd suffered many serious health problems. Eventually, stray electrical voltage—which can use cow hooves as an unintended pathway, causing health issues—was detected. By then, milk production in the Normans' herd had declined from 27 percent above the state average to 20 percent below it. The Normans filed a suit in a Minnesota state court against Crow Wing Cooperative Power & Light Company, a member-owned electrical cooperative that provided electricity to the Normans' farm. If Crow Wing is found to have acted negligently, can its members be held jointly liable for the cooperative's acts? Explain. [*Norman v. Crow Wing Cooperative Power & Light Co.,* 2016 WL 687472 (Minn.App. 2016)] (See *Special Business Forms.*)

28–8. Limited Liability. Vision Metals, Inc., owned and operated a pipe manufacturing facility that caused groundwater contamination. The Texas Commission on Environmental Quality (TCEQ) issued a plan that obligated Vision to treat the water and monitor the treatment. Later, Vision sold the property to White Lion Holdings, LLC. Bernard Morello, the sole member of White Lion, knew of the environmental obligations accompanying the property. When White Lion failed to comply with the TCEQ plan, the agency filed a suit in a Texas state court against Morello, asserting violations of the state's environmental rules. Morello was charged with personally removing the facility's treatment plant and monitoring system. Considering the nature of an LLC, what is Morello's best argument that he is not liable? Is this argument likely to succeed? Explain. [*State of Texas v. Morello,* 61 Tex.Sup.Ct.J. 381, 547 S.W.3d 881 (2018)] (See *Limited Liability Companies.*)

28–9. A Question of Ethics—The IDDR Approach and LLC Operation and Management. Q Restaurant Group Holdings, LLC, owns and operates Q-BBQ restaurants. Michael Lapidus managed the restaurants and conducted the day-to-day operations. This included bargaining with the restaurants' vendors, buying the supplies, keeping the books and records of account, and handling the company's money. Lapidus dealt with the staff and made the hiring and firing decisions. He was expected to use his best efforts to grow the profitability of the restaurants. The LLC discovered, however, that Lapidus was misappropriating and converting company funds to his own use. He was also exposing the LLC to liability by mistreating female employees and vendors. When the members voted to terminate Lapidus, he changed the passwords on the Q-BBQ social media accounts, interfered with the employees during their work hours, and refused to return company property in his possession. [*Q Restaurant Group Holdings, LLC v. Lapidus,* 2017 IL App (2d) 170804-U, 2017 WL 6550606 (2017)] (See *LLC Operation and Management.*)

1. What action should the LLC take against Lapidus? Consider the ethics of the options, using the IDDR approach.
2. Suppose that Lapidus was in the midst of a contentious divorce, experiencing severe financial problems, and undergoing psychological distress as a consequence. Could these issues excuse his conduct at work? Discuss.

Critical Thinking and Writing Assignments

28–10. Time-Limited Group Assignment—Fiduciary Duties. Newbury Properties Group owns, manages, and develops real property. Jerry Stoker and the Stoker Group, Inc. (the Stokers), also develop real property. Newbury entered into agreements with the Stokers concerning a large tract of property in Georgia. The parties formed Bellemare, LLC, to develop various parcels of the tract for residential purposes. The operating agreement of Bellemare indicated that "no Member shall be accountable to the LLC or to any other Member with respect to any other business or activity even if the business or activity competes with the LLC's business." Later, when the Newbury group contracted with other parties to develop parcels within the tract in competition with Bellemare, LLC, the Stokers sued, alleging breach of fiduciary duty. (See *LLC Operation and Management.*)

1. The first group will discuss and outline the fiduciary duties that the members of an LLC owe to each other.
2. The second group will determine whether the terms of an operating agreement can alter these fiduciary duties.
3. The last group will decide in whose favor the court should rule in this situation.

10'000 Hours/DigitalVision/Getty Images

29 Corporations

Focus Questions

The five Focus Questions below are designed to help improve your understanding. After reading this chapter, you should be able to answer the following questions:

1. What is a close corporation?
2. What four steps are involved in bringing a corporation into existence?
3. In what circumstances might a court disregard the corporate entity ("pierce the corporate veil") and hold the shareholders personally liable?
4. What are the duties of corporate directors and officers?
5. What is a voting proxy?

Corporation A legal entity formed in compliance with statutory requirements that is distinct from its shareholder-owners.

"A corporation is an artificial being, invisible, intangible, and existing only in contemplation of law."

John Marshall
1755–1835
(Chief Justice of the United States Supreme Court, 1801–1835)

A **corporation** is a creature of statute—a legal entity created and recognized by state law. As John Marshall indicated in the chapter-opening quotation, a corporation is an artificial being, existing only in law and neither tangible nor visible. Its existence generally depends on state law. Each state has its own body of corporate law, and these laws are not entirely uniform.

The Model Business Corporation Act (MBCA) is a codification of modern corporate law that has been influential in shaping state corporation statutes. Today, the majority of state statutes are guided by the most recent version of the MBCA, often referred to as the Revised Model Business Corporation Act (RMBCA).

Keep in mind, however, that there is considerable variation among the laws of states that have used the MBCA or the RMBCA as a basis for their statutes. In addition, several states do not follow either act. Consequently, individual state corporation laws should be relied on to determine corporate law, rather than the MBCA or RMBCA.

29–1 Nature and Classification

A corporation is a legal entity created and recognized by state law. This business entity can have one or more owners (called shareholders), and it operates under a name distinct from the names of its owners. Both individuals and other businesses can be shareholders. The corporation substitutes itself for its shareholders when conducting corporate business and incurring liability. Its authority to act and the liability for its actions, however, are separate and apart from the shareholders who own it.

A corporation is recognized under U.S. law as a person—an artificial *legal person,* as opposed to a *natural person.* As a "person," it enjoys many of the same rights and privileges under state and federal law that U.S. citizens enjoy. For instance, corporations possess the same right of access to the courts as citizens and can sue or be sued. The constitutional guarantees of due process, free speech, and freedom from unreasonable searches and seizures also apply to corporations.

29–1a Corporate Personnel

In a corporation, the responsibility for the overall management of the firm is entrusted to a *board of directors*, whose members are elected by the shareholders. The board of directors hires *corporate officers* and other employees to run the corporation's daily business operations.

When an individual purchases a share of stock (an equity interest) in a corporation, that person becomes a shareholder and thus an owner of the corporation. Unlike the members of a partnership, the body of shareholders can change constantly without affecting the continued existence of the corporation. A shareholder can sue the corporation, the corporation can sue a shareholder, and in certain situations, a shareholder can sue "on behalf of" the corporation.

monkeybusinessimages/iStock/Getty Images

Who hires corporate officers?

29–1b The Limited Liability of Shareholders

The major advantage of the corporate form is the limited liability of its owners (shareholders). Corporate shareholders' liability is limited to the amount of their investments. Shareholders usually are not otherwise liable for the debts of the corporation. To enable the firm to obtain credit, however, shareholders in small companies sometimes voluntarily assume personal liability, as guarantors, for corporate obligations.

29–1c Corporate Earnings and Taxation

When a corporation earns profits, it can either pass them on to its shareholders in the form of a **dividend** or retain them as profits. These **retained earnings**, if invested properly, will yield higher corporate profits in the future and cause the price of the company's stock to rise. Individual shareholders can then reap the benefits in the capital gains that they receive when they sell their stock.

Dividend A distribution of corporate profits to the corporation's shareholders in proportion to the number of shares held.

Retained Earnings The portion of a corporation's profits that has not been paid out as dividends to shareholders.

Whether a corporation retains its profits or passes them on to the shareholders as dividends, those profits are subject to income taxation by various levels of government. Failure to pay taxes can lead to severe consequences. The state can suspend the entity's corporate status until the taxes are paid or even dissolve the corporation for failing to pay taxes.

Another important aspect of corporate taxation is that corporate profits can be subject to double taxation. The company pays tax on its profits, and then if the profits are passed on to the shareholders as dividends, the shareholders must also pay income tax on them. The corporation normally does not receive a tax deduction for dividends it distributes to shareholders. This double-taxation feature is one of the major disadvantages of the corporate business form.

Currently, the federal government taxes corporate income at a flat rate of 21 percent. This relatively low rate is good for corporate profits but does not affect the potential for double taxation.

29–1d Torts and Criminal Acts

Under modern criminal law, a corporation may be held liable for the criminal acts of its agents and employees. Although corporations cannot be imprisoned, they can be fined. (Of course, corporate directors and officers can be imprisoned, and many have been in recent years.) In addition, under sentencing guidelines for crimes committed by corporate employees (white-collar crimes), corporations can face fines amounting to hundreds of millions of dollars.

A corporation is also liable for the torts committed by its agents or officers within the course and scope of their employment. The doctrine of *respondeat superior* applies to corporations in the same way as it does to other agency relationships. A claim against a corporate employer based on *respondeat superior* requires a showing that the individual who committed the tort was an employee acting in the course of employment. The question in the following case was whether the identity of the employee had to be established as well.

Case 29.1

Wulf v. Bravo Brio Restaurant Group, Inc.

Court of Appeals of Ohio, Twelfth District, Butler County, 2019-Ohio-3434, 142 N.E.3d 123 (2019).

Facts Roland Wulf went to dinner at the Bravo Cucina Italiana restaurant in West Chester, Ohio. He was walking down an aisle between dining booths and the kitchen food counter to the restroom when someone backed into him. Wulf lost his balance, fell to the floor, and fractured a hip.

He filed a complaint in an Ohio state court against the owner of the restaurant, Bravo Brio Restaurant Group, Inc. Wulf alleged that his injuries resulted from the negligence of a Bravo waitress and that Bravo Brio, her corporate employer, was liable under the doctrine of *respondeat superior.* Wulf described the waitress—in her twenties, 5 feet 6 inches tall, slender, with brown hair, in a Bravo uniform, and not wearing glasses—and testified that she had admitted working for the restaurant and had apologized. But he could not specifically identify her.

The trial court concluded that Wulf's failure to identify the waitress was fatal to his claim and granted Bravo Brio's motion for summary judgment. Wulf appealed.

Issue Did the trial court err in requiring that the waitress be specifically identified as a prerequisite to applying the doctrine of *respondeat superior*?

Decision Yes. A state intermediate appellate court reversed the judgment of the trial court and remanded the case for further proceedings. Wulf did not need to establish the waitress's identity to proceed with his claim against Bravo Brio.

Reason The appellate court set out the principles for the application of the doctrine of *respondeat superior* in a case involving an employee's negligence.

For the employer to be liable, the employee's negligent acts must occur during the performance of work subject to the employer's control. The employee's acts must also be within the scope of the employment. That is all that an injured plaintiff needs to prove for the doctrine to apply—the employee was negligent and acting within the scope of employment. As the court pointed out, "There is no requirement that the employee be named as a party to the suit in order to prove his [or her] negligent acts."

The court found no cases requiring that the identity of the employee be established to apply the doctrine. The court added, "We see no reason why a claim of *respondeat superior* should be dependent upon the plaintiff establishing the identity of the negligent employee, as long as the plaintiff establishes that the negligent individual was an employee in the course of employment." Thus, in the *Wulf* case, specific identification of the waitress was not required because Wulf saw her Bravo uniform and she acknowledged working for the restaurant.

Critical Thinking

- **Legal Environment** *What issues of fact must be resolved concerning Wulf's claim for Bravo Brio to be held liable under the doctrine of* respondeat superior? *Discuss.*
- **Economic** *Why should a corporation be held liable for torts committed by its employees during the course of their employment?*

29–1e Classification of Corporations

Corporations can be classified in several ways. The classification of a corporation normally depends on its location, purpose, and ownership characteristics, as described in the following subsections.

Domestic, Foreign, and Alien Corporations A corporation is referred to as a **domestic corporation** by its home state (the state in which it incorporates). A corporation formed in one state but doing business in another is referred to in the second state as a **foreign corporation**. A corporation formed in another country (say, Mexico) but doing business in the United States is referred to in the United States as an **alien corporation**.

Domestic Corporation In a given state, a corporation that is organized under the law of that state.

Foreign Corporation In a given state, a corporation that does business in that state but is not incorporated there.

Alien Corporation A corporation formed in another country but doing business in the United States.

A corporation does not have an automatic right to do business in a state other than its state of incorporation. In some instances, it must obtain a *certificate of authority* in any state in which it plans to do business. Once the certificate has been issued, the corporation generally can exercise in that state all of the powers conferred on it by its home state. If a foreign corporation does business in a state without obtaining a certificate of authority, the state can impose substantial fines and sanctions on the corporation, and sometimes even on its officers, directors, or agents.

Note that most state statutes specify certain activities, such as soliciting orders via the Internet, that are not considered doing business within the state. Thus, a foreign corporation normally does not need a certificate of authority to sell goods or services via the Internet or by mail.

Courts are often asked to determine what constitutes "doing business" in a state for jurisdictional purposes. **Case Example 29.1** South Carolina resident Bud Fidrych severely injured his thumb at The Boscolo-Milano hotel in Milan, Italy. Fidrych subsequently filed a negligence lawsuit in a federal district court in South Carolina against Marriott International, Inc., a Delaware corporation that was affiliated with The Boscolo.

The district court established that, although Marriott did not own or operate any hotels in South Carolina, it had ninety franchisees and licensees in the state. Additionally, Marriott's booking website was accessible to South Carolinians, just as it was accessible to anyone with online access. Finally, as a foreign corporation, Marriott had obtained the necessary certificate of authority to operate in South Carolina.

These minimal contacts did not, the district court ruled, make Marriott "at home" in South Carolina for jurisdictional purposes. Therefore, Fidrych's lawsuit could not proceed. A federal appeals court agreed. As the court noted, under South Carolina law, obtaining a certificate of authority does not automatically indicate that a foreign corporation conducts "sufficient activities" in the state to be subject to a lawsuit in the state's courts.[1]

MariaX/Shutterstock.com

What factors will a court consider when determining whether a hotel chain has "sufficient activities" in a state to be subject to a negligence lawsuit there?

Public and Private Corporations A **public corporation** is one formed by the government to meet some political or governmental purpose. Cities and towns that incorporate are common examples. In addition, many federal government organizations—such as the U.S. Postal Service, the Tennessee Valley Authority, and AMTRAK—are public corporations.

Public Corporation A corporation owned by a federal, state, or municipal government to meet a political or governmental purpose.

Note that a public corporation is not the same as a *publicly held* corporation (often called a *public company*). A **publicly held corporation** is any corporation whose shares are publicly traded in securities markets, such as the New York Stock Exchange or the NASDAQ. (The NASDAQ is an electronic stock exchange founded by the National Association of Securities Dealers.)

Publicly Held Corporation A corporation whose shares are publicly traded in securities markets, such as the New York Stock Exchange or the NASDAQ.

Private corporations, in contrast, are created either wholly or in part for private benefit. Most corporations are private. Although private corporations may serve a public purpose, as a public electric or gas utility does, they are owned by private persons rather than by the government.[2]

1. *Fidrych v. Marriott International, Inc.*, 952 F.3d 124 (4th Cir. 2020).
2. The United States Supreme Court first recognized the property rights of private corporations and clarified the distinction between public and private corporations in the landmark case *Trustees of Dartmouth College v. Woodward*, 17 U.S. (4 Wheaton) 518, 4 L.Ed. 629 (1819).

Nonprofit Corporations Corporations that are formed without a profit-making purpose are called *nonprofit* or *not-for-profit corporations.* Private hospitals, educational institutions, charities, and religious organizations, for instance, are frequently organized as nonprofit corporations. The nonprofit corporation is a convenient form of organization that allows various groups to own property and to form contracts without exposing the individual members to personal liability.

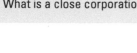

Close Corporation A corporation whose shareholders are limited to a small group of persons, often family members.

Close Corporations Most corporate enterprises in the United States fall into the category of close corporations. A **close corporation** is one whose shares are held by relatively few persons, often members of a family. Close corporations are also referred to as *closely held, family,* or *privately held* corporations.

Usually, the members of the small group constituting a close corporation are personally known to one another. Because the number of shareholders is so small, there is no trading market for the shares. In practice, close corporations often operate somewhat like partnerships. The statutes in many states allow them to depart significantly from certain formalities required by traditional corporation law.[3]

Focus Question 1
What is a close corporation?

Under the RMBCA, close corporations have considerable flexibility in determining their operating rules [RMBCA 7.32]. If all of a corporation's shareholders agree in writing, the corporation can operate without directors and bylaws. In addition, a close corporation need not hold annual or special shareholders' or directors' meetings, issue stock certificates, or keep formal records of shareholders' and directors' decisions.[4]

Management of Close Corporations. Management of a close corporation resembles that of a sole proprietorship or a partnership in that a single shareholder or a tightly knit group of shareholders usually hold the positions of directors and officers. As a corporation, however, the firm must meet all specific legal requirements set forth in state statutes.

To prevent a majority shareholder from dominating a close corporation, a close corporation may require that more than a simple majority of the directors approve any action taken by the board. In a larger corporation, such a requirement would typically apply only to extraordinary actions (such as selling all the corporate assets) and not to ordinary business decisions.

Rawpixel.com/Shutterstock.com

How is a close corporation usually managed?

Transfer of Shares in Close Corporations. By definition, a close corporation has a small number of shareholders. Thus, the transfer of one shareholder's shares to someone else can cause serious management problems. The other shareholders may find themselves required to share control with someone they do not know or like.

To avoid this situation, the corporation could restrict the transferability of shares to outside persons. Shareholders could be required to offer their shares to the corporation or the other shareholders before selling them to an outside purchaser. In fact, a few states have statutes that prohibit the transfer of close corporation shares unless certain persons—including shareholders, family members, and the corporation—are first given the opportunity to purchase the shares for the same price.

Misappropriation of Close Corporation Funds. Sometimes, a majority shareholder in a close corporation takes advantage of the position by misappropriating company funds. In such situations, the normal remedy for the injured minority shareholders is to have their shares appraised and to be paid the fair market value for them.

3. For example, in some states (such as Maryland), a close corporation need not have a board of directors.
4. Shareholders cannot agree, however, to eliminate certain rights of shareholders, such as the right to inspect corporate books and records and the right to bring lawsuits on behalf of the corporation.

S Corporations A close corporation that meets the qualifying requirements specified in Subchapter S of the Internal Revenue Code can operate as an **S corporation**. (A corporation will automatically be taxed under Subchapter C unless it elects S corporation status.) If a corporation has S corporation status, it can avoid the imposition of income taxes at the corporate level while retaining many of the advantages of a corporation, particularly limited liability. Among the numerous requirements for S corporation status, the following are the most important:

S Corporation A close business corporation that has most corporate attributes, including limited liability, but qualifies under the Internal Revenue Code to be taxed as a partnership.

1. The corporation must be a domestic corporation.
2. The corporation must not be a member of an affiliated group of corporations.
3. The shareholders must be individuals, estates, or certain trusts. Partnerships and nonqualifying trusts cannot be shareholders. Corporations can be shareholders under certain circumstances.
4. The corporation must have no more than one hundred shareholders.
5. The corporation must have only one class of stock, although all shareholders do not have to have the same voting rights.
6. No shareholder of the corporation may be a nonresident alien.

An S corporation is treated differently from a regular corporation for tax purposes. It is taxed like a partnership, so the corporate income passes through to the shareholders, who pay personal income tax on it. This treatment enables the S corporation to avoid the double taxation that is imposed on regular corporations. In addition, the shareholders' tax brackets may be lower than the tax bracket that the corporation would have been in if the tax had been imposed at the corporate level.

In spite of these benefits, the S corporation has lost much of its appeal. The newer limited liability business forms (such as LLCs, LPs, and LLPs) offer similar tax advantages and greater flexibility.

Know This

The shareholders of professional corporations generally must be licensed professionals.

Professional Corporations Professionals such as physicians, lawyers, dentists, and accountants can incorporate. Professional corporations typically are identified by the letters *S.C.* (service corporation), *P.C.* (professional corporation), or *P.A.* (professional association). In general, the laws governing the formation and operation of professional corporations are similar to those governing ordinary business corporations. There are some differences in terms of liability, however.

Benefit Corporation A for-profit corporation that seeks to have a material positive impact on society and the environment. It is available by statute in a number of states.

For liability purposes, some courts treat a professional corporation somewhat like a partnership and hold each professional liable for any malpractice committed by others in the firm within the scope of the firm's business. With the exception of malpractice or a breach of duty to clients or patients, a shareholder in a professional corporation generally cannot be held liable for torts committed by other professionals at the firm.

Benefit Corporations A growing number of states have enacted legislation that creates a new corporate form called a *benefit corporation*. A **benefit corporation** is a for-profit corporation that seeks to have a material positive impact on society and the environment. Benefit corporations differ from traditional corporations in the following ways:

wavebreakmedia/Shutterstock.com

Benefit corporations strive to have a positive impact on society. How do they differ from traditional, for-profit corporations?

1. *Purpose*. Although the corporation is designed to make a profit, its purpose is to benefit the public as a whole (rather

than just to provide long-term shareholder value, as in ordinary corporations). The directors of a benefit corporation must, during the decision-making process, consider the impact of their decisions on society and the environment.

2. *Accountability.* Shareholders of a benefit corporation determine whether the company has achieved a material positive impact. Shareholders also have a right of private action, called a *benefit enforcement proceeding,* enabling them to sue the corporation if it fails to pursue or create public benefit.

3. *Transparency.* A benefit corporation must issue an annual benefit report on its overall social and environmental performance that uses a recognized third-party standard to assess its performance. The report must be delivered to the shareholders and posted on a public website.

In the following case, a benefit corporation took an action that it believed would have a positive impact on those it was established to serve. Two of those affected by the action disagreed and filed a suit to challenge the action.

Case 29.2

Greenfield v. Mandalay Shores Community Association

California Court of Appeal, Second District, Division 6, 21 Cal.App.5th 896, 230 Cal.Rptr.3d 827 (2018).

Facts Mandalay Shores is a beach community in California's Oxnard Coastal Zone, where nonresidents have vacationed for decades, renting homes on a short-term basis. Robert and Demetra Greenfield owned a single-family residence at Mandalay Shores that they rented to families for periods of less than thirty days. Mandalay Shores Community Association is a mutual benefit corporation established for the development of the community. The association adopted a resolution banning short-term rentals (STRs), claiming that it was necessary to reduce parking, noise, and trash problems. Homeowners who rented their homes "for less than 30 consecutive days" were subjected to fines of up to $5,000 per offense.

The Greenfields filed a suit in a California state court against the association, contending that the STR ban violated the California Coastal Act. The court denied the plaintiffs' request for a preliminary injunction to stay the enforcement of the association's resolution. The Greenfields appealed.

Issue Did the association violate California state law when it adopted the STR ban?

Decision Yes. A state intermediate appellate court reversed the lower court's denial of the Greenfields' motion and ordered the issuance of a preliminary injunction.

Reason The California Coastal Act is meant to "maximize public access to and along the coast and maximize public recreational opportunities to the coastal zone consistent with sound resources conservation principles and constitutionally protected right of private property owners." A coastal development permit is required to undertake a "development" in the coastal zone. A development includes any "change in the density or intensity of use of land."

The STR ban affects 1,400 housing units on beach properties that have long been used as STRs. It changes the intensity of use and access to single-family residences in the Oxnard Coastal Zone. Thus, its imposition is subject to a decision by the city and the Coastal Commission, not by a homeowners' association. In effect, the court ruled that the association had "erected a monetary barrier to the beach," and it had "no right to do so."

Critical Thinking

- **Legal Environment** *Did the STR ban adopted by the association comport with or contravene its status as a benefit corporation? Discuss.*
- **What If the Facts Were Different?** *Suppose that instead of adopting an STR ban on its own, the association had petitioned the city and the Coastal Commission to impose one. Would the result have been different? Explain.*

29–2 Formation and Powers

Incorporating a business is much simpler today than it was at one time. Many states allow businesses to incorporate via the Internet.

29–2a Promotional Activities

In the past, preliminary steps were taken to organize and promote a business prior to incorporating. Contracts were made with investors and others on behalf of the future corporation. Today, due to the relative ease of forming a corporation in most states, persons incorporating a business rarely, if ever, engage in preliminary promotional activities.

Nevertheless, businesspersons need to understand that they are personally liable for any preincorporation contracts made with investors, accountants, or others on behalf of the future corporation. Liability continues until the corporation is formed and explicitly assumes the contract by novation.

29–2b Incorporation Procedures

Each state has its own set of incorporation procedures, which most often are listed on the secretary of state's website. Generally, however, all incorporators follow four basic steps, discussed next.

Focus Question 2

What four steps are involved in bringing a corporation into existence?

Select the State of Incorporation Because state corporate laws differ, individuals may look for the states that offer the most advantageous tax or other provisions. Many corporations, for instance, have chosen to incorporate in Delaware because it has historically had the least restrictive laws, along with provisions that favor corporate management. For reasons of convenience and cost, though, businesses often choose to incorporate in the state in which the corporation's business will primarily be conducted.

Secure an Appropriate Corporate Name The choice of a corporate name is subject to state approval to ensure against duplication or deception. In today's online world, what matters most is to secure a corporate name that can be used as a domain name. A new corporation's name cannot be the same as (or deceptively similar to) the name of an existing corporation. Therefore, the incorporators usually must perform a search to confirm that the corporate name they choose is available as a domain name. State approval of the name may also be required. In addition, all states require the corporation name to include the word *Corporation, Incorporated, Company,* or *Limited,* or an abbreviation of one of these terms.

Prepare the Articles of Incorporation The primary document needed to incorporate a business is the **articles of incorporation**. The articles include basic information about the corporation and serve as a primary source of authority for its future organization and business functions. The person or persons who execute (sign) the articles are the *incorporators*. Articles of incorporation vary widely depending on the jurisdiction and the size and type of the corporation. Generally, though, the articles *must* include the following information [RMBCA 2.02]:

Articles of Incorporation The document that is filed with the appropriate state official, usually the secretary of state, when a business is incorporated and that contains basic information about the corporation.

1. The name of the corporation.
2. The number of shares of stock the corporation is authorized to issue [RMBCA 2.02(a)]. (Large corporations often also state a par value for each share, such as $0.20 per share, and specify the various types or classes of stock authorized for issuance.)
3. The name and street address of the corporation's initial registered agent and registered office. The registered agent is the person who can receive legal documents (such as orders to appear in court) on behalf of the corporation. The registered office is usually the main corporate office.
4. The name and address of each incorporator.

In addition, the articles *may* set forth other information, such as the names and addresses of the initial members of the board of directors and the duration and purpose of the corporation. A corporation has perpetual existence unless the articles state otherwise.

As to the corporation's purpose, a corporation can be formed for any lawful purpose, and the RMBCA does not require the articles to include a specific statement of purpose. Consequently, the articles often include only a general statement of purpose. By not mentioning specifics, the corporation avoids the need for future amendments to the corporate articles [RMBCA 2.02(b)(2)(i), 3.01]. Similarly, the articles do not provide much detail about the firm's operations, which are spelled out in the company's *bylaws* (discussed shortly).

File the Articles of Incorporation Once the articles of incorporation have been prepared and signed by the incorporators, they are sent to the appropriate state official. They are most often filed with the secretary of state's office, along with the required filing fee. In most states, the secretary of state then stamps the articles as "Filed" and returns a copy of the articles to the incorporators. Once this occurs, the corporation officially exists.

Bylaws The internal rules of management adopted by a corporation at its first organizational meeting.

29–2c First Organizational Meeting to Adopt Bylaws

After incorporation, the first organizational meeting must be held. If the articles of incorporation named the initial board of directors (as is typical), then the directors, by majority vote, call the meeting. If the articles did not name the directors, then the incorporators hold the meeting to elect the directors and conduct any other necessary business.

oneinchpunch/Shutterstock.com

What are some of the important functions of a corporation's first organizational meeting?

Usually, the most important function of the first organizational meeting is the adoption of the **bylaws**, which are the corporation's internal rules of management. The bylaws cannot conflict with the state corporate statute or the articles of incorporation [RMBCA 2.06].

Under the RMBCA, the shareholders may amend or repeal the bylaws. The board of directors may also amend or repeal the bylaws, unless the articles of incorporation or provisions of the state corporate statute reserve this power to the shareholders exclusively [RMBCA 10.20]. The bylaws typically describe such matters as voting requirements for shareholders, the election and replacement of the board of directors, and the manner and time of holding shareholders' and board meetings.

Know This

Unlike the articles of incorporation, bylaws do not need to be filed with a state official.

29–2d Improper Incorporation

The procedures for incorporation are very specific. If they are not followed precisely, others may be able to challenge the existence of the corporation. Errors in the incorporation procedures can become important when, for instance, a third party who is attempting to enforce a contract or bring a suit for a tort injury learns of them.

***De Jure* Corporations** If a corporation has substantially complied with all conditions precedent to incorporation, the corporation is said to have *de jure* (rightful and lawful) existence. In most states and under the RMBCA 2.03(b), the secretary of state's filing of the articles of incorporation is conclusive proof that all mandatory statutory provisions have been met.

Sometimes, the incorporators fail to comply with all statutory mandates. If the defect is minor, such as an incorrect address listed on the articles of incorporation, most courts will overlook the defect and find that a *de jure* corporation exists.

***De Facto* Corporations** If a defect in formation is substantial, such as a corporation's failure to hold an organizational meeting to adopt bylaws, the outcome will vary depending on the court. Some states, including Mississippi, New York, Ohio, and Oklahoma, recognize the common law doctrine of *de facto* corporation. In those states, the courts will treat a corporation as a legal corporation despite the defect in its formation if all three of the following requirements are met:

1. A state statute exists under which the corporation can be validly incorporated.
2. The parties have made a good faith attempt to comply with the statute.
3. The parties have already undertaken to do business as a corporation.

Many states' courts, however, have interpreted their states versions of the RMBCA as abolishing the common law doctrine of *de facto* corporation. These states include Alaska, Arizona, Minnesota, New Mexico, Oregon, South Dakota, Tennessee, Utah, and Washington, as well as the District of Columbia. In those states, if there is a substantial defect in complying with the statutory mandates, the corporation does not legally exist, and the incorporators are personally liable.

Corporation by Estoppel Sometimes, a business association holds itself out to others as being a corporation when it has made no attempt to incorporate. In those situations, the firm normally will be estopped (prevented) from denying corporate status in a lawsuit by a third party. The estoppel doctrine most commonly applies when a third party contracts with an entity that claims to be a corporation but has not filed articles of incorporation. It may also be applied when a third party contracts with a person claiming to be an agent of a corporation that does not, in fact, exist.

When justice requires, the courts treat an alleged corporation as if it were an actual corporation for the purpose of determining the rights and liabilities in a particular circumstance. Recognition of corporate status does not extend beyond the resolution of the problem at hand.

Case Example 29.2 55 Day Spa, Inc., signed a three-year lease to rent premises owned by Ilan Weiss, who represented himself as a managing member of TY Builders II, LLC. Three months later, 55 Day Spa informed Weiss that it would be vacating the premises. Weiss, who had since incorporated and operated as TY Builders II, Inc., filed an action to recover damages for breach of contract. 55 Day Spa moved for the lawsuit to be dismissed, arguing that because TY Builders II, Inc., did not exist when the lease was signed, the corporation could not enforce the terms of the lease.

A New York trial court found that 55 Day Spa had recognized TY Builders as a valid business operation when it agreed to lease the property and when it took possession of the property. Therefore, it should not be allowed to use Weiss's lack of proper incorporation as an excuse to break the contract. A state appellate court agreed, holding that, pursuant to the doctrine of corporation by estoppel, TY Builders II, Inc., should be "deemed to exist" for the purpose of Weiss's contract with 55 Day Spa.[5]

Subbotina Anna/Shutterstock.com

Why would a court estop (prevent) a day spa owner from breaking a lease with a corporation that did not legally exist when the two parties signed the contract?

29–2e Corporate Financing

Securities Generally, stocks, bonds, or other items that represent an ownership interest in a corporation or a promise of repayment of debt by a corporation.

Part of the process of corporate formation involves financing. Corporations normally are financed by the issuance and sale of corporate securities. **Securities**—stocks and bonds—evidence the right to participate in earnings and the distribution of corporate property or the obligation to pay funds.

5. *TY Bldrs. II, Inc. v. 55 Day Spa, Inc.*, 167 A.D.3d 679, 90 N.Y.S.3d 47 (2018).

Bond Securities that evidence a corporate (or government) debt.

Bonds A **bond** (a *debenture* or *debt security*) represents the borrowing of funds. Bonds are issued by business firms and by governments at all levels as evidence of the funds they are borrowing from investors.

Bonds normally have a designated *maturity date*—the date when the principal, or face, amount of the bond is returned to the bondholder. Bondholders also receive fixed-dollar interest payments, usually semiannually, during the period of time before maturity. For that reason, bonds are sometimes referred to as *fixed-income securities.* Because debt financing represents a legal obligation on the part of the corporation, various features and terms of a particular bond issue are specified in a lending agreement.

Of course, not all debt is in the form of debt securities. For instance, some debt is in the form of accounts payable and notes payable, which typically are short-term debts. Bonds are simply a way for the corporation to split up its long-term debt so that it can be more easily marketed.

Stocks Securities that evidence an ownership (equity) interest in a corporation, measured in units of shares.

Common Stock Shares of ownership in a corporation that give the owner a proportionate interest in the corporation with regard to control, earnings, and net assets. Common stock is lowest in priority with respect to payment of dividends and distribution of the corporation's assets on dissolution.

Preferred Stock Stock that has priority over common stock as to payment of dividends and distribution of assets on the corporation's dissolution.

Stocks Issuing stock is another way that corporations can obtain financing. **Stocks**, or *equity securities,* represent the purchase of ownership in the business firm. The true ownership of a corporation is represented by **common stock**. Common stock provides a proportionate interest in the corporation with regard to (1) control (voting rights), (2) earnings, and (3) net assets. A shareholder's interest is generally proportionate to the number of shares the shareholder owns out of the total number of shares issued.

An issuing firm is not obligated to return a principal amount per share to each holder of its common stock, nor does the firm have to guarantee a dividend. Indeed, some corporations never pay dividends. Holders of common stock are investors who assume a *residual* position in the overall financial structure of a business. They benefit when the market price of the stock increases. In terms of receiving payment for their investments, they are last in line.

Preferred stock is stock with *preferences*. Holders of preferred stock usually have priority over holders of common stock as to dividends and payment on dissolution of the corporation, but may not have the right to vote. Although holders of preferred stock have a stronger position than common shareholders with respect to dividends and claims on assets, they will not share in the full prosperity of the firm if it grows successfully over time. Preferred stockholders do receive fixed dividends periodically, however, and they may benefit to some extent from changes in the market price of the shares.

Venture Capital Financing provided by professional, outside investors (venture capitalists) to new business ventures.

Venture Capital Start-up businesses and high-risk enterprises often obtain venture capital financing. **Venture capital** is capital provided to new business ventures by professional, outside investors (*venture capitalists,* usually groups of wealthy investors and securities firms). Venture capital investments are high risk—the investors must be willing to lose their invested funds—but offer the potential for well-above-average returns at some point in the future.

To obtain venture capital financing, the start-up business typically gives up a share of its ownership to the venture capitalists. In addition to funding, venture capitalists may provide managerial and technical expertise, and they nearly always are given some control over the new company's decisions. Many Internet-based companies, such as Amazon and Google, were initially financed by venture capital.

Private Equity Capital Funds invested in an existing corporation by a private equity firm, usually to purchase and reorganize it.

Private Equity Capital Private equity firms pool funds from wealthy investors and use this **private equity capital** to invest in existing corporations. Usually, a private equity firm buys an entire corporation and then reorganizes it. Sometimes, divisions of the purchased company are sold off to pay down debt. Ultimately, the private equity firm may sell shares in the reorganized (and perhaps more profitable) company to the public in an *initial public offering* (IPO). In this way, the private equity firm can make profits by selling its ownership rights in the company to the public.

Crowdfunding **Crowdfunding** is a cooperative activity in which people network and pool funds and other resources via the Internet to assist a cause or invest in a venture. Sometimes, crowdfunding is used to raise funds for charitable purposes, such as disaster relief, but increasingly it is being used to finance budding entrepreneurs. Basic crowdfunding websites include NextSeed and StartEngine.

Crowdfunding A cooperative activity in which people network and pool funds and other resources via the Internet to assist a cause (such as disaster relief) or invest in a venture (business).

Current Securities and Exchange Commission rules allow companies to offer and sell securities through crowdfunding. The rules, which took effect relatively recently, removed a decades-old ban on public solicitation for private investments. In essence, this means that companies can advertise investment opportunities to the public, which will encourage more crowdfunding in the future. The new rules are intended to help smaller companies raise capital while providing investors with additional protections.

29–2f Corporate Powers

When a corporation is created, the express and implied powers necessary to achieve its purpose also come into existence. Corporations cannot engage in acts that are beyond their powers, nor can a corporation's owners (shareholders) avoid liability if they misuse the corporate entity for their own personal benefit.

Express Powers The express powers of a corporation are found in its articles of incorporation, in the law of the state of incorporation, and in the state and federal constitutions. Corporate bylaws also establish express powers of the corporation. Because state corporation statutes frequently provide default rules that apply if the company's bylaws are silent on an issue, it is important that the bylaws set forth the specific operating rules of the corporation. In addition, after the bylaws are adopted, the corporation's board of directors will pass resolutions that grant or restrict corporate powers.

On occasion, the U.S. government steps in to challenge what a corporation may consider one of its express powers. This chapter's *Cybersecurity and the Law* feature discusses steps taken by the U.S. government that threaten the ability of corporations to protect cloud-based data.

Implied Powers When a corporation is created, it acquires certain implied powers. Barring express constitutional, statutory, or other prohibitions, the corporation has the implied power to perform all acts reasonably appropriate and necessary to accomplish its corporate purposes. For this reason, a corporation has the implied power to borrow funds within certain limits, to lend funds, and to extend credit to those with whom it has a legal or contractual relationship.

Most often, the president or chief executive officer of the corporation will execute the necessary papers on behalf of the corporation. In so doing, a corporate officer has the implied power to bind the corporation in matters directly connected with the *ordinary* business affairs of the enterprise. There is a limit to what a corporate officer can do, though. A corporate officer does not have the authority to bind the corporation to an action that will greatly affect the corporate purpose or undertaking, such as the sale of substantial corporate assets.

***Ultra Vires* Doctrine** The term *ultra vires* means "beyond the powers." In corporate law, acts of a corporation that are beyond its express and implied powers are ***ultra vires* acts**.

***Ultra Vires* Acts** Acts of a corporation that are beyond its express and implied powers to undertake (the Latin phrase means "beyond the powers").

In the past, most cases dealing with *ultra vires* acts involved contracts made for unauthorized purposes. Now, however, most private corporations are organized for "any legal business" and not for a specific purpose, so the *ultra vires* doctrine has declined in importance. Today, cases that allege *ultra vires* acts usually involve nonprofit corporations or municipal (public) corporations.[6]

6. See, for instance, *Xcel Energy Services, Inc. v. Federal Energy Regulatory Commission*, 815 F.3d 947 (D.C.Cir. 2016).

The CLOUD Act

Cybersecurity and the Law

The case pending before the United States Supreme Court involved a battle of wills between the U.S. government and Microsoft Corporation in its role as a cloud service provider (CSP). The federal government had issued a warrant requiring Microsoft to produce e-mails related to a criminal narcotics investigation. The e-mails were stored in a Microsoft cloud storage location in Ireland. Microsoft refused to comply with the warrant, arguing that the reach of the U.S. government stopped at the U.S. border, and sought to have the warrant invalidated.

Microsoft initially lost its case in a New York district court but won on appeal in the U.S. Appeals Court for the Second Circuit. The U.S. Justice Department then filed an appeal with the Supreme Court, which agreed to hear the case.[a]

Before the case could come to trial, however, Congress resolved the issue by enacting the Clarifying Lawful Overseas Use of Data (CLOUD) Act.[b] This legislation provides the U.S. government with access to cloud-based data held by U.S. CSPs regardless of where in the world the data are physically stored. For purposes of the law, cloud-based data includes e-mails, texts, instant messages, remote or backup data storage, wireless calls, and other forms of business information.

The U.S. Department of Justice heralded passage of the CLOUD Act as critical to global investigations of terrorism, cybercrime, and the sexual exploitation of children.

Qualified Foreign Governments

The CLOUD Act also creates a framework for the United State to enter into treaties that would give qualified foreign governments (QFGs) access to cloud data stored by the "Big Five" American CSPs—Amazon, Apple, Facebook, Google, and Microsoft. For U.S. businesses, the potential consequences of this provision are significant.

Suppose that a U.S. company called Ramway, Inc., uses Google to store its digital data in the cloud. A QFG suspects that Ramway is involved in criminal activity. Without involving U.S. courts, Google can give the QFG access to Ramway's digital data as part of that government's criminal investigation. Ramway may never even be aware of the QFG's request, or of Google's compliance with it. The CLOUD Act does not require the CSP or foreign government to disclose data requests to the targeted CSP customer.

Domestically, the Big Five CSPs receive more than 175,000 requests for information linked to criminal investigations from U.S. law enforcement agencies each year.

Critical Thinking

What type of American businesses are impacted by the CLOUD Act? What steps should these businesses take in response to the CLOUD Act?

a. *United States v. Microsoft Corp.*, 548 U.S. __, 138 S.Ct. 1186, 200 L.Ed.2d 610 (2018).
b. 18 U.S.C. Section 2703.

Under Section 3.04 of the RMBCA, shareholders can seek an injunction from a court to prevent (or stop) the corporation from engaging in *ultra vires* acts. The attorney general in the state of incorporation can also bring an action to obtain an injunction against the *ultra vires* transactions or seek dissolution of the corporation.

29–2g Piercing the Corporate Veil

Piercing the Corporate Veil The action of a court to disregard the corporate entity and hold the shareholders personally liable for corporate debts and obligations.

Occasionally, the owners use a corporate entity to perpetrate a fraud, circumvent the law, or in some other way accomplish an illegitimate objective. In these situations, the court will ignore the corporate structure by **piercing the corporate veil** and exposing the shareholders to personal liability [RMBCA 2.04].

Generally, courts pierce the veil when corporate privilege is abused for personal benefit or when the corporate business is treated so carelessly that it is indistinguishable from that of a controlling shareholder. In short, when the facts show that great injustice would result from a shareholder's use of a corporation to avoid individual responsibility, a court will look behind the corporate structure to the individual shareholder. The shareholder/owner is then required to assume personal liability to creditors for the corporation's debts.

Factors That Lead Courts to Pierce the Corporate Veil The following are some of the factors that frequently cause the courts to pierce the corporate veil:

1. A party is tricked or misled into dealing with the corporation rather than the individual.
2. The corporation is set up to never make a profit or always be insolvent, or it is too thinly capitalized—that is, it has insufficient capital at the time of formation to meet its prospective debts or other potential liabilities.
3. Statutory corporate formalities, such as holding required corporation meetings, are not followed.
4. Personal and corporate interests are **commingled** to such an extent that the corporation has no separate identity.

Focus Question 3

In what circumstances might a court disregard the corporate entity ("pierce the corporate veil") and hold the shareholders personally liable?

Commingled Mixed to such a degree that the individual parts (such as funds or goods) no longer have separate identities.

The courts may use the same criteria in deciding whether to pierce the veil of an LLC. **Case Example 29.3** Timothy Hunsaker was the sole member of Breawick, LLC, a construction company in Ohio. Cheryl Denny hired Breawick to build a house. During the course of construction, many disagreements arose, and Hunsaker eventually quit working before the house was finished. Denny had to hire another company to repair Hunsaker's flaws and finish the house. Denny then filed a claim against Breawick and Hunsaker for breach of contract and other offenses. She claimed, among other things, that Hunsaker had altered the building plans without her consent and demanded payments beyond those specified in the contract.

The trial court found that Breawick had breached its contract with Denny by charging excessive amounts without her approval and failing to perform in a "workmanlike" manner. His acts were so egregious under Ohio law that the court was willing to "pierce the corporate veil" and hold Hunsaker personally liable for the amount Denny spent to finish the house after he quit. An appellate court affirmed. Hunsaker had drawn funds from Breawick's bank account to pay for personal expenses and had taken no steps to distinguish himself from the business entity. The appeals court concluded that Breawick was Hunsaker's "alter ego" and had no separate existence of its own. "A member of a limited liability company may be held personally liable" if it is shown that the member's behavior merits disregarding, or piercing, the company's limited liability structure.[7] (See this chapter's *Business Law Analysis* feature, which illustrates a situation in which a court may decide not to pierce the corporate veil.)

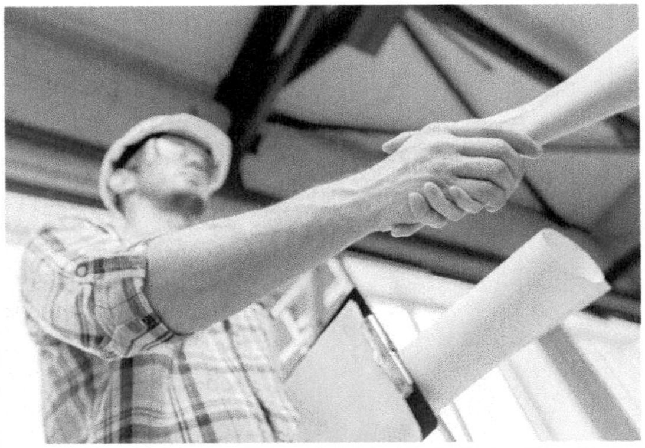
Syda Productions/Shutterstock.com

When can a homebuilder who operates as the sole member of an LLC be held personally liable for the LLC's obligations?

A Potential Problem for Close Corporations The potential for corporate assets to be used for personal benefit is especially great in a close corporation. In such a corporation, the separate status of the corporate entity and the shareholders must be carefully preserved. Certain practices invite trouble for a close corporation, such as the commingling of corporate and personal funds or the shareholders' continuous personal use of corporate property (for instance, vehicles).

Typically, courts are reluctant to hold shareholders in close corporations personally liable unless there is some evidence of fraud or wrongdoing. **Spotlight Case Example 29.4** Pip, Jimmy, and Theodore

7. *Denny v. Breawick, LLC,* 137 N.E.3d 578, 2019 -Ohio- 2066 (Ohio Ct.App. 2019).

Piercing the Corporate Veil

Business Law Analysis

Country Contractors, Inc., contracted to provide excavation services for Westside Storage of Indianapolis, Inc., but did not complete the job and later filed for bankruptcy. Stephen Songer and Jahn Songer were Country's sole shareholders. The Songers had not misused the corporate form to engage in fraud. The firm had not been undercapitalized, personal and corporate funds had not been commingled, and Country had kept accounting records and minutes of its annual board meetings. Are the Songers personally liable for Country's failure to complete its contract?

Analysis:

A hallmark of the corporate form of business organization is that shareholders are not personally liable for the debts of the corporation. If the corporation fails, the shareholders can lose their investments, but that is generally the limit of their liability. A court may pierce the corporate veil to hold the shareholders personally liable in certain instances of fraud, undercapitalization, or failure to observe corporate formalities. But these situations are exceptions.

Result and Reasoning: The Songers are not personally liable for Country's failure to complete its contract with Westside Storage. They had not misused the corporate form to engage in misconduct, the firm had not been undercapitalized, and personal and corporate funds had not been commingled. In addition, Country had kept accounting records and minutes of its annual board meetings, thus observing the formalities required by law. These circumstances fall under none of the exceptions to the limit on shareholders' liability for corporate obligations. Thus, as shareholders, the Songers are not personally liable for the failure of their company to complete its job.

Brennan are brothers and shareholders of Brennan's, Inc., which owns and operates New Orleans's famous Brennan's Restaurant. As a close corporation, Brennan's, Inc., did not hold formal corporate meetings with agendas and minutes, but it did maintain corporate books, hold corporate bank accounts, and file corporate tax returns.

The Brennan brothers retained attorney Edward Colbert to represent them in a family matter, and the attorney's bills were sent to the restaurant and paid from the corporate account. Later, when Brennan's, Inc., sued Colbert for malpractice, Colbert argued that the court should pierce the corporate veil because the Brennan brothers did not observe corporate formalities. The court refused to do so, however, because there was no evidence of fraud or other wrongdoing by the Brennan brothers. There is no requirement for small, close corporations to operate with the formality usually expected of larger corporations.[8]

29–3 Directors and Officers

Corporate directors and officers play different roles in the corporation. It is important to understand the rights, duties, and liabilities of directors and officers.

29–3a Directors

The board of directors is the ultimate authority in every corporation. Directors have responsibility for all policymaking decisions necessary to the management of corporate affairs. The board selects and removes the corporate officers, determines the capital structure of the corporation, and declares dividends.

8. *Brennan's, Inc. v. Colbert*, 85 So.3d 787 (La.App.4th Cir. 2012).

Directors are sometimes inappropriately characterized as *agents* because they act on behalf of the corporation. No *individual* director, however, can act as an agent to bind the corporation. As a group, directors collectively control the corporation in a way that no agent is able to control a principal.

Few qualifications are legally required for directors. Only a handful of states impose minimum age and residency requirements. A director may be a shareholder, but this is not necessary (unless the articles of incorporation or bylaws require it).

Election of Directors Subject to statutory limitations, the number of directors is set forth in the corporation's articles or bylaws. Historically, the minimum number of directors has been three, but today many states permit fewer. Normally, the incorporators appoint the first board of directors at the time the corporation is created. The initial board serves until the first annual shareholders' meeting. Subsequent directors are elected by a majority vote of the shareholders.

Directors usually serve for a term of one year—from annual meeting to annual meeting. Most state statutes permit longer and staggered terms. A common practice is to elect one-third of the board members each year for a three-year term. In this way, there is greater management continuity.

A director can be removed *for cause*—that is, for failing to perform a required duty—either as specified in the articles or bylaws or by shareholder action. When a vacancy occurs or a new position is created through amendment of the articles or bylaws, how the vacancy is filled depends on state law or the provisions of the bylaws. Usually, either the shareholders or the board itself can fill the vacant position by an election. The board cannot attempt to manipulate the election in order to reduce the shareholders' influence, however. If it does, the shareholders can challenge the election in court.

Know This
The articles of incorporation may provide that a director can be removed only for cause.

Compensation of Directors In the past, corporate directors rarely were compensated. Today, they are often paid at least nominal sums and may receive more substantial compensation in large corporations because of the time, the work, the effort, and especially the risk involved. Most states permit the corporate articles or bylaws to authorize compensation for directors. In fact, the RMBCA states that unless the articles or bylaws provide otherwise, the board of directors itself may set directors' compensation [RMBCA 8.11].

In many corporations, directors are also chief corporate officers (president or chief executive officer, for instance) and receive compensation in their managerial positions. A director who is also an officer of the corporation is referred to as an **inside director**, whereas a director who does not hold a management position is an **outside director**. Typically, a corporation's board of directors includes both inside and outside directors.

Inside Director A person on the board of directors who is also an officer of the corporation.

Outside Director A person on the board of directors who does not hold a management position in the corporation.

Board of Directors' Meetings The board of directors conducts business by holding formal meetings with recorded minutes. The dates of regular meetings are usually established in the articles or bylaws or by board resolution, and ordinarily no further notice is required. Special meetings can be called as well, with notice sent to all directors. Today, most states allow directors to participate in board meetings from remote locations via telephone, Web conferencing, Zoom, or Skype, provided that all the directors can simultaneously hear each other during the meeting [RMBCA 8.20].

Normally, a majority of the board of directors constitutes a quorum [RMBCA 8.24]. (A **quorum** is the minimum number of members of a body of officials or other group that must be present in order for business to be validly transacted.) Some state statutes, including those of Delaware and New York, specifically allow corporations to set a quorum at less than a majority but not less than one-third of the directors.

Quorum The number of members of a decision-making body that must be present before business may be transacted.

Once a quorum is present, the directors transact business and vote on issues affecting the corporation. Each director present at the meeting has one vote.[9] Ordinary matters generally require a simple majority vote, but certain extraordinary issues may require a greater-than-majority vote.

hxdbzxy/Shutterstock.com

What are the two committees most commonly formed by a large corporation's board of directors?

Committees of the Board of Directors When a board of directors has a large number of members and must deal with myriad complex business issues, meetings can become unwieldy. Therefore, the boards of large publicly held corporations typically create committees of directors and delegate certain tasks to these committees. Committees focus on individual subjects and increase the efficiency of the board.

Two of the most common types of committees are the *executive committee* and the *audit committee.* An executive committee handles interim management decisions between board meetings. It is limited to making decisions about ordinary business matters and does not have the power to declare dividends, amend the bylaws, or authorize the issuance of stock. The Sarbanes-Oxley Act requires all publicly held corporations to have an audit committee. The audit committee is responsible for the selection, compensation, and oversight of the independent public accountants that audit the firm's financial records.

Rights of Directors A corporate director must have certain rights to function properly in that position and make informed policy decisions for the company.

1. *Right to participation.* Directors are entitled to participate in all board of directors' meetings and to be notified of these meetings. Because the dates of regular board meetings are usually specified in the bylaws, no notice of these meetings is required. If special meetings are called, however, notice is required unless waived by the director.
2. *Right of inspection.* Each director can access the corporation's books and records, facilities, and premises. Inspection rights are essential for directors to make informed decisions and to exercise the necessary supervision over corporate officers and employees. This right of inspection is almost absolute and cannot be restricted (by the articles, bylaws, or any act of the board).
3. *Right to indemnification.* When directors become involved in litigation by virtue of their positions or actions, they may have a right to be indemnified (reimbursed) for legal costs, fees, and damages incurred. Most states allow corporations to indemnify and purchase liability insurance for corporate directors [RMBCA 8.51].

Case Example 29.5 NavLink, Inc., a Delaware corporation, provides high-end data management for customers and governments in Saudi Arabia, Qatar, Lebanon, and the United Arab Emirates. NavLink's co-founders, George Chammas and Laurent Delifer, serve on its board of directors. Chammas and Delifer were concerned about the company's 2015 annual budget and three-year operating plan. Despite repeated requests, Chammas was never given the minutes from several board meetings in 2015. Chammas and Delifer believed that the other directors were withholding information and holding secret "pre-board meetings" at which plans and decisions were being made without them. They filed a lawsuit in a Delaware state court seeking inspection rights.

The court ordered NavLink to provide the plaintiffs with board meeting minutes and with communications from NavLink's secretary regarding the minutes. The plaintiffs were also

9. Except in Louisiana, which allows a director to authorize another person to cast a vote in the director's place under certain circumstances.

entitled to inspect corporate documents and communications concerning NavLink's 2015 budget and three-year plan.[10]

29–3b Corporate Officers and Executives

Corporate officers and other executive employees are hired by the board of directors. At a minimum, most corporations have a president, one or more vice presidents, a secretary, and a treasurer. In most states, an individual can hold more than one office, such as president and secretary, and can be both an officer and a director of the corporation. In addition to carrying out the duties articulated in the bylaws, corporate and managerial officers act as agents of the corporation, and the ordinary rules of agency normally apply to their employment.

Corporate officers and other high-level managers are employees of the company, so their rights are defined by employment contracts. The board of directors, though, normally can remove corporate officers at any time with or without cause. If the directors remove an officer in violation of an employment contract, however, the corporation may be liable for breach of contract.

Know This

Shareholders own the corporation, and directors make policy decisions, but the officers who run the corporation's daily business often have significant decision-making power.

29–3c Duties and Liabilities of Directors and Officers

Directors and officers are considered fiduciaries of the corporation because their relationship with the corporation and its shareholders is one of trust and confidence. As fiduciaries, directors and officers owe ethical—and legal—duties to the corporation and to the shareholders as a whole. These fiduciary duties include the duty of care and the duty of loyalty.

Focus Question 4

What are the duties of corporate directors and officers?

Duty of Care Directors and officers must exercise due care in performing their duties. The standard of due care generally requires a director or officer to act in good faith (honestly) and to exercise the care that an ordinarily prudent person would exercise in similar circumstances. In addition, directors and officers are expected to act in what they consider to be the best interests of the corporation [RMBCA 8.30]. Directors and officers whose failure to exercise due care results in harm to the corporation or its shareholders can be held liable for negligence (unless the *business judgment rule* applies, as discussed shortly).

Duty to Make Informed and Reasonable Decisions. Directors and officers are expected to be informed on corporate matters and to conduct a reasonable investigation of the relevant situation before making a decision. They must do what is necessary to keep adequately informed: attend meetings and presentations, ask for information from those who have it, read reports, and review other written materials. They cannot make decisions on the spur of the moment without adequate research.

Although directors and officers are expected to act in accordance with their own knowledge and training, they are also normally entitled to rely on information given to them by certain other persons. Most states and Section 8.30(b) of the RMBCA allow a director to make decisions in reliance on information furnished by competent officers and employees. The director may also rely on information provided by professionals (such as attorneys and accountants) and by committees of the board of directors on which the director does not serve.

Duty to Exercise Reasonable Supervision. Directors are also expected to exercise a reasonable amount of supervision when they delegate work to corporate officers and employees. **Example 29.6** Dale, a corporate bank director, has not attended a board of directors' meeting for five years. In addition, Dale never inspects any of the corporate books or records and generally fails to supervise the efforts of the bank president and the loan committee. Meanwhile,

10. *Chammas v. NavLink, Inc.*, 2016 WL 767714 (Del.Ch.Ct. 2016).

Brennan, the bank president, makes various improper loans and permits large overdrafts. In this situation, Dale can be held liable to the corporation for losses resulting from the unsupervised actions of the bank president and the loan committee.

The Business Judgment Rule. Directors and officers are expected to exercise due care and to use their best judgment in guiding corporate management, but they are not insurers of business success. Under the **business judgment rule**, a corporate director or officer will not be liable to the corporation or to its shareholders for honest mistakes of judgment or bad business decisions made in good faith.

Business Judgment Rule A rule under which courts will not hold corporate officers and directors liable for honest mistakes of judgment and bad business decisions that were made in good faith.

Courts give significant deference to the decisions of corporate directors and officers, and consider the reasonableness of a decision at the time it was made, *without the benefit of hindsight.* Thus, corporate decision makers are not subjected to second-guessing by shareholders or others in the corporation.

When the Rule Applies. The business judgment rule will apply as long as the director or officer did the following:

1. Took reasonable steps to become informed about the matter.
2. Had a rational basis for the decision.
3. Did not have a conflict between personal interests and the interests of the corporation.

Case Example 29.7 iStar, Inc., promised to award shares of company stock to employees for their performance if its stock averaged a certain price per share over a specific period. The stock price rose 300 percent, but the performance target was missed. The board changed the basis for an award from performance to service—any employee who had been with iStar for a certain period of time was entitled to an award. The board then issued additional shares to pay the awards.

Two iStar shareholders, Albert and Lena Oliveira, demanded that the board cancel the awards and filed a suit on the company's behalf to seek damages. The board declined to file the suit. The Oliveiras then sued Jay Sugarman, the board chairman, and the other iStar directors, alleging a breach of fiduciary duty. The court held in favor of the directors and dismissed the suit. The Oliveiras' "bald allegations of impropriety are plainly insufficient to overcome the presumption of the business judgment rule."[11]

Hero Images Inc./Alamy Stock Photo

How did the business judgment rule help iStar employees receive a stock award for their tenure with the company?

The Rule Provides Broad Protections. The business judgment rule provides broad protections to corporate decision makers. In fact, most courts will apply the rule unless there is evidence of bad faith, fraud, or a clear breach of fiduciary duties. Consequently, if there is a reasonable basis for a business decision, a court is unlikely to interfere with that decision, even if the corporation suffers as a result. The business judgment rule does not apply, however, when a director engages in fraud, dishonesty, or other intentional or reckless misconduct. For instance, if a director acts without board approval, ignores board rules, and personally mistreats other directors, shareholders, and employees, the business judgment rule may not protect that director.

Duty of Loyalty *Loyalty* can be defined as faithfulness to one's obligations and duties. In the corporate context, the duty of loyalty requires directors and officers to subordinate their personal interests to the welfare of the corporation. Directors cannot use corporate funds or

11. *Oliveira v. Sugarman*, 226 Md.App. 524, 130 A.3d 1085 (2016).

confidential corporate information for personal advantage and must refrain from self-dealing. For instance, a director should not personally take advantage of a business opportunity that is offered to the corporation and is in the corporation's best interest.

Cases dealing with the duty of loyalty typically involve one or more of the following:

1. Competing with the corporation.
2. Usurping (taking over) a corporate opportunity.
3. Having an interest that conflicts with the interest of the corporation.
4. Engaging in insider trading (using information that is not public to make a profit trading securities).
5. Authorizing a corporate transaction that is detrimental to minority shareholders.
6. Selling control over the corporation.

The following *Classic Case* illustrates the conflict that can arise between a corporate official's personal interests and the duty of loyalty.

Classic Case 29.3

Guth v. Loft, Inc.

Supreme Court of Delaware, 23 Del.Ch. 255, 5 A.2d 503 (1939).

Facts In 1930, Charles Guth became the president of Loft, Inc., a candy and restaurant chain. At the time, Guth and his family owned Grace Company, which made syrups for soft drinks in a plant in Baltimore, Maryland. Coca-Cola Company supplied Loft with cola syrup. Unhappy with what he felt was Coca-Cola's high price, Guth entered into an agreement with Roy Megargel to acquire the trademark and formula for Pepsi-Cola and form Pepsi-Cola Corporation.

BrooklynScribe/Shutterstock.com

Pepsi-Cola got its start when the head of Loft Candy Company usurped a corporate opportunity.

Neither Guth nor Megargel could finance the new venture, and Grace Company was insolvent. Without the knowledge of Loft's board of directors, Guth used Loft's capital, credit, facilities, and employees to further the Pepsi enterprise. At Guth's direction, a Loft employee made the concentrate for the syrup, which was sent to Grace Company to add sugar and water. Loft charged Grace Company for the concentrate but allowed forty months' credit. Grace charged Pepsi for the syrup but also granted substantial credit. Grace sold the syrup to Pepsi's customers, including Loft, which paid on delivery or within thirty days. Loft also paid for Pepsi's advertising.

Finally, losing profits at its stores as a result of switching from Coca-Cola, Loft filed a suit in a Delaware state court against Guth, Grace, and Pepsi, seeking their Pepsi stock and an accounting. The court entered a judgment in the plaintiff's favor. The defendants appealed to the Delaware Supreme Court.

Issue Did Guth violate his duty of loyalty to Loft, Inc., by acquiring the Pepsi-Cola trademark and formula for himself without the knowledge of Loft's board of directors?

Decision Yes. The Delaware Supreme Court upheld the judgment of the lower court. The state supreme court was "convinced that the opportunity to acquire the Pepsi-Cola trademark and formula, goodwill and business belonged to [Loft], and that Guth, as its president, had no right to appropriate the opportunity to himself."

Reason The court pointed out that the officers and directors of a corporation stand in a fiduciary relationship to that corporation and to its shareholders. Corporate officers and directors must protect the corporation's interest at all times. They must also "refrain from doing anything that works injury to the corporation." In other words, corporate officers and directors must provide undivided and unselfish loyalty to the corporation, and "there should be no conflict between duty and self-interest." Whenever an opportunity is presented to the corporation, officers and directors with knowledge of that opportunity cannot seize it for themselves. "The corporation may elect to claim all of the benefits of the transaction for itself, and the law will impress a trust in favor of the corporation upon the property, interest, and profits required."

(Continues)

Continued

Guth clearly created a conflict between his self-interest and his duty to Loft—the corporation of which he was president and director. Guth illegally appropriated the Pepsi-Cola opportunity for himself and thereby placed himself in the position of competing with the company for which he worked.

Critical Thinking

• **What If the Facts Were Different?** *Suppose that Loft's board of directors had approved Pepsi-Cola's use of its personnel and equipment. Would the court's decision have been different? Discuss.*

• **Impact of This Case on Today's Law** *This early Delaware decision was one of the first to set forth a test for determining when a corporate officer or director has breached the duty of loyalty. The test has two basic parts—whether the opportunity was reasonably related to the corporation's line of business, and whether the corporation was financially able to undertake the opportunity. The court also considered whether the corporation had an interest or expectancy in the opportunity and recognized that when the corporation had "no interest or expectancy, the officer or director is entitled to treat the opportunity as his own."*

Disclosure of Conflicts of Interest Corporate directors often have many business affiliations, and a director may sit on the board of more than one corporation. Of course, directors are precluded from entering into or supporting businesses that operate in direct competition with corporations on whose boards they serve. Their fiduciary duty requires them to make a full disclosure of any potential conflicts of interest that might arise in any corporate transaction [RMBCA 8.60].

In addition, a corporation sometimes enters into a contract or engages in a transaction in which an officer or director has a personal interest. The director or officer must make a *full disclosure* of that interest and must abstain from voting on the proposed transaction.

Example 29.8 Southwood Corporation needs office space. Alden, one of its five directors, owns the building adjoining the corporation's main office building. He negotiates a lease with Southwood for the space, making a full disclosure to Southwood and the other four directors. The lease arrangement is fair and reasonable, and it is unanimously approved by the other four directors. In this situation, Alden has not breached his duty of loyalty to the corporation, and thus the lease contract is valid. If it were otherwise, directors would be prevented from ever transacting business with the corporations they serve. ■

Liability of Directors and Officers Directors and officers are exposed to liability on many fronts. They are, of course, liable for their own crimes and torts. They also may be held liable for the crimes and torts committed by corporate employees under their supervision.

Additionally, if shareholders perceive that the corporate directors are not acting in the best interests of the corporation, they may sue the directors on behalf of the corporation. (This is known as a *shareholder's derivative suit,* which will be discussed later in this chapter.) Directors and officers can also be held personally liable under a number of statutes, such as those enacted to protect consumers or the environment.

29–4 Shareholders

Know This
Shareholders normally are not agents of the corporation.

The acquisition of a share of stock makes a person an owner and shareholder in a corporation. Shareholders thus own the corporation, but they generally are not responsible for its daily management. Although they have no legal title to corporate property, such as buildings and equipment, they do have an equitable (ownership) interest in the firm.

29–4a Shareholders' Powers

Shareholders must approve fundamental changes affecting the corporation before the changes can be implemented. Hence, shareholders are empowered to amend the articles of incorporation and bylaws, approve a merger or the dissolution of the corporation, and approve the sale of all or substantially all of the corporation's assets. Some of these powers are subject to prior board approval. Shareholder approval may also be requested (though it is not required) for certain other actions, such as to approve an independent auditor.

Shareholders have the power to elect or remove members of the board of directors. As mentioned earlier, the incorporators normally choose the first directors, who serve until the first shareholders' meeting. From that time on, the selection and retention of directors are exclusively shareholder functions.

Directors usually serve their full terms. If the shareholders judge them unsatisfactory, they are simply not reelected. Shareholders have the inherent power, however, to remove a director from office for cause (such as for breach of duty or misconduct) by a majority vote. Some state statutes (and some corporate articles) permit removal of directors without cause by the vote of a majority of the shareholders entitled to vote.

29–4b Shareholders' Meetings

Shareholders' meetings must occur at least annually. In addition, special meetings can be called to deal with urgent matters. A corporation must notify its shareholders of the date, time, and place of an annual or special shareholders' meeting at least ten days, but not more than sixty days, before the meeting date [RMBCA 7.05].[12] Notice of a special meeting must include a statement of the purpose of the meeting, and business transacted at the meeting is limited to that purpose.

Focus Question 5
What is a voting proxy?

Proxies It is usually not practical for owners of only a few shares of stock of publicly traded corporations to attend shareholders' meetings. Therefore, the law allows stockholders to either vote in person or appoint another person as their agent to vote their shares at the meeting. The agent's formal authorization to vote the shares is called a **proxy** (from the Latin *procurare,* meaning "to manage, take care of"). Proxy materials are sent to all shareholders before shareholders' meetings.

Proxy In corporate law, formal authorization to serve as an agent for corporate shareholders and vote their shares in a certain manner.

Management often solicits proxies, but any person can solicit proxies to concentrate voting power. Proxies have been used by groups of shareholders as a device for taking over a corporation. Proxies normally are revocable (that is, they can be withdrawn), unless they are specifically designated as irrevocable. Under RMBCA 7.22(c), proxies last for eleven months, unless the proxy agreement provides for a longer period.

Shareholder Proposals When shareholders want to change a company policy, they can put their idea up for a shareholder vote. They can do this by submitting a shareholder proposal to the board of directors and asking the board to include the proposal in the proxy materials that are sent to all shareholders before meetings.

Rules for Proxies and Shareholder Proposals The Securities and Exchange Commission (SEC), which regulates the purchase and sale of securities, has special provisions relating to proxies and shareholder proposals. SEC Rule 14a-8 provides that all shareholders who own stock worth at least $1,000 are eligible to submit proposals for inclusion in corporate proxy materials. The corporation is required to include information on whatever proposals will be considered at the shareholders' meeting along with proxy materials.

12. A shareholder can waive the requirement of written notice by signing a waiver form or, in some states, by attending a meeting without protesting the lack of notice.

Under the SEC's e-proxy rules,[13] all public companies must post their proxy materials on the Internet and notify shareholders how to find that information. Although the law requires proxy materials to be posted online, public companies may still choose among several options—including paper documents and DVDs sent by mail—for delivering the materials to shareholders.

Ethical Issue

Should proxy advisory firms be more heavily regulated by the SEC? Hundreds of shareholder proposals are put forward each year, making it difficult for institutional investors, such as mutual funds, to stay current. As a result, these investors rely on *proxy advisory firms* for recommendations on how to vote at corporate annual meetings. Given that institutional investors hold nearly 80 percent of American shares, proxy advisory firms have a significant influence on the success or failure of many shareholder proposals. Supporters of these firms believe that this influence acts as a positive check on "egregious management behavior" in a way that individual investors could never hope to accomplish.

At the same time, just two firms—Institutional Shareholder Services (ISS) and Glass Lewis—control about 97 percent of the proxy advisory market. Given the widespread practice of "robo-voting," in which institutional investors automatically follow proxy advisor advice, this dominance gives ISS and Glass Lewis, by one estimate, control of nearly 38 percent of all shareholder votes in the United States. Furthermore, critics believe that proxy advisory firms generally favor shareholder proposals that advocate environmental and social agendas, regardless of the proposals' impact on corporate profits or shareholder value. In recent years, the SEC has tried to curb the influence of the proxy industry by subjecting it to anti-fraud regulations that punish false or misleading statements and by requiring more transparency regarding the motives behind proxy voting advice.

29–4c Shareholder Voting

Shareholders exercise ownership control through the power of their votes. Corporate business matters are presented in the form of *resolutions,* which shareholders vote to approve or disapprove. Each common shareholder is entitled to one vote per share. The articles of incorporation can exclude or limit voting rights, particularly for certain classes of shares. For instance, owners of *preferred stock* usually are denied the right to vote.

Quorum Requirements For shareholders to act during a meeting, a quorum must be present. Generally, a quorum exists when shareholders holding more than 50 percent of the outstanding shares are present, but state laws often permit the articles of incorporation to set higher or lower quorum requirements.

Know This
Once a quorum is present, a vote can be taken even if some shareholders leave without casting their votes.

Voting Requirements Once a quorum is present, voting can proceed. If a state statute requires specific voting procedures, the corporation's articles or bylaws must be consistent with the statute.

Normally, a majority vote of the shares represented at the meeting is required to pass resolutions. At times, more than a simple majority vote is required, either by a state statute or by the corporate articles. Extraordinary corporate matters, such as a merger, consolidation, or dissolution of the corporation, require approval by a higher percentage of all corporate shares entitled to vote [RMBCA 7.27].

---

13. 17 C.F.R. Parts 240, 249, and 274.

Case Example 29.9 The board of directors of Tesla, Inc., approved an incentive-laden compensation plan for Elon Musk, the electric car company's chief executive officer (CEO). The board then called a special meeting of Tesla stockholders to vote on the plan. Because CEO compensation is not considered an "extraordinary" corporate matter, failure to vote would not be counted as a "no" but rather, it would have no effect on the proceedings. With a quorum established, 73 percent of the shares *present* at the meeting voted in favor of the plan. This tally represented only 47 percent of *all* shares, not counting those controlled by Musk and his wife.

franz12/Shutterstock.com

Why did a court accept a stockholder vote to increase the salary of a Tesla executive even though fewer than half of all eligible shares voted "yes" on the matter?

In response to a lawsuit filed by an unhappy shareholder, a Delaware court rejected the argument that the vote was invalid because it did not represent the majority view of all disinterested stockholders. Under state law, as long as a majority of shares entitled to vote are present at a shareholder's meeting, and the majority of those shares vote "yes," the result is valid. The court did, however, allow the shareholder to challenge Musk's compensation—which could be as high at $56 billion—on the grounds that it was unfairly excessive.[14]

Cumulative Voting Most states permit, and some require, shareholders to elect directors by *cumulative voting*. This voting method is designed to allow minority shareholders to be represented on the board of directors.[15]

With cumulative voting, each shareholder is entitled to a total number of votes equal to the number of board members to be elected multiplied by the number of voting shares the shareholder owns. The shareholder can cast all of these votes for one candidate or split them among several candidates. All candidates stand for election at the same time.

Example 29.10 Nak Corporation has 10,000 shares issued and outstanding. The minority shareholders hold 3,000 shares, and the majority shareholders hold the other 7,000 shares. Three members of the board are to be elected. The majority shareholders' nominees are Acevedo, Barkley, and Craycik. The minority shareholders' nominee is Drake. Can Drake be elected by the minority shareholders?

If cumulative voting is allowed, the answer is yes. Together, the minority shareholders have 9,000 votes (3 directors to be elected times 3,000 shares held by minority shareholders equals 9,000 votes). All of these votes can be cast to elect Drake. The majority shareholders have 21,000 votes (3 times 7,000 equals 21,000), but these votes have to be distributed among their three nominees. No matter how the majority shareholders cast their 21,000 votes, they will not be able to elect all three directors if the minority shareholders cast all of their 9,000 votes for Drake, as illustrated in Exhibit 29–1.

In contrast, in "regular" voting, each candidate is elected by a simple majority. A shareholder cannot give more than one vote per share to any single nominee.

14. *Tornetta v. Musk*, 2019 WL 4566943 (Del.Ch. 2019).

15. See, for instance, California Corporations Code Section 708. Under RMBCA 7.28, however, no cumulative voting rights exist unless the articles of incorporation provide for them.

Exhibit 29–1 Results of Cumulative Voting

BALLOT	MAJORITY SHAREHOLDERS' VOTES			MINORITY SHAREHOLDERS' VOTES	DIRECTORS ELECTED
	Acevedo	**Barkley**	**Craycik**	**Drake**	
1	10,000	10,000	1,000	9,000	Acevedo/Barkley/Drake
2	9,001	9,000	2,999	9,000	Acevedo/Barkley/Drake
3	6,000	7,000	8,000	9,000	Barkley/Craycik/Drake

Other Voting Techniques Before a shareholders' meeting, a group of shareholders can agree in writing to vote their shares together in a specified manner. Such agreements, called *shareholder voting agreements,* usually are held to be valid and enforceable. As noted earlier, a shareholder can also appoint a voting agent and vote by proxy.

29–4d Rights of Shareholders

Shareholders possess numerous rights in addition to the right to vote their shares, and we examine several here.

Stock Certificate A certificate issued by a corporation evidencing the ownership of a specified number of shares in the corporation.

Stock Certificates In the past, shareholders had a right to a **stock certificate** that evidenced ownership of a specified number of shares in the corporation. Only a few jurisdictions still require physical stock certificates, however. Shareholders there have the right to demand that the corporation issue certificates (or replace those that were lost or destroyed). Stock is intangible personal property, however, and the ownership right exists independently of the certificate itself.

In most states today and under RMBCA 6.26, boards of directors may provide that shares of stock will be uncertificated, or "paperless"—that is, no physical stock certificates will be issued. Notice of shareholders' meetings, dividends, and operational and financial reports are distributed according to the ownership lists recorded in the corporation's books.

Preemptive Rights The rights of a shareholder in a corporation to have the first opportunity to purchase a new issue of that corporation's stock in proportion to the amount of stock already owned by the shareholder.

Preemptive Rights Sometimes, the articles of incorporation grant preemptive rights to shareholders [RMBCA 6.30]. With **preemptive rights**, a shareholder receives a preference over all other purchasers to subscribe to or purchase a prorated share of a new issue of stock. Generally, preemptive rights apply only to additional, newly issued stock and must be exercised within a specified time period (usually thirty days).

A shareholder who is given preemptive rights can purchase a percentage of the new shares being issued that is equal to the percentage of shares already held in the company. This allows each shareholder to maintain proportionate control, voting power, and financial interest in the corporation.

Example 29.11 Alisha is a shareholder who owns 10 percent of a company. Because she has preemptive rights, she can buy 10 percent of any new issue (to maintain her 10 percent position). Thus, if the corporation issues one thousand more shares, Alisha can buy one hundred of them. ■

Preemptive rights are most important in close corporations because each shareholder owns a relatively small number of shares but controls a substantial interest in the corporation. Without preemptive rights, it would be possible for a shareholder to lose proportionate control over the firm.

Dividends As mentioned, a *dividend* is a distribution of corporate profits or income ordered by the directors and paid to the shareholders in proportion to their shares in the corporation. Dividends can be paid in cash, property, stock of the corporation that is paying the dividends, or stock of other corporations.[16] On one occasion, a distillery declared and paid a "dividend" in bonded whiskey.

State laws vary, but each state determines the general circumstances and legal requirements under which dividends are paid. State laws also control the sources of revenue to be used. All states allow dividends to be paid from the undistributed net profits earned by the corporation, for instance, and a number of states allow dividends to be paid out of any surplus.

16. Technically, dividends paid in stock are not dividends. They maintain each shareholder's proportionate interest in the corporation.

Illegal Dividends. Dividends are illegal if they are improperly paid from an unauthorized account, or if their payment causes the corporation to become insolvent (unable to pay its debts as they come due). Whenever dividends are illegal or improper, the board of directors can be held personally liable for the amount of the payment.

Directors' Failure to Declare a Dividend. When directors fail to declare a dividend, shareholders can ask a court to compel the directors to do so. To succeed, the shareholders must show that the directors have acted so unreasonably in withholding the dividend that their conduct is an abuse of their discretion. The mere fact that the firm has sufficient earnings or surplus available to pay a dividend is not enough to compel directors to distribute funds that, in the board's opinion, should not be distributed. There must be a clear abuse of discretion.

Inspection Rights Shareholders in a corporation enjoy both common law and statutory inspection rights. The RMBCA provides that every shareholder is entitled to examine specified corporate records for a *proper purpose,* provided the request is made in advance. The shareholder can inspect in person or have an attorney, accountant, or other authorized agent do so. In some states, a shareholder must have held shares for a minimum period of time immediately preceding the demand to inspect or must hold a minimum number of outstanding shares.

The power of inspection is fraught with potential abuses, and the corporation is allowed to protect itself from them. For instance, a corporation can properly deny a shareholder access to corporate records to prevent harassment or to protect trade secrets or other confidential corporate information.

Case Example 29.12 Trading Block Holdings, Inc., offers online brokerage services. On April 1, some Trading Block shareholders, including Sunlitz Holding Company, sent a letter (through an attorney) asking to inspect specific items in the corporation's books and records. This letter indicated that the purpose was to determine the company's financial condition, how it was being managed, and whether its financial practices were appropriate. The letter also stated that the shareholders wanted to know whether Trading Block's management had engaged in any self-dealing that had negatively impacted the company as a whole.

On April 30, Trading Block responded with a letter stating that the plaintiffs were on a "fishing expedition" and did not have a proper purpose for inspecting the corporate records. Eventually, the shareholders filed a motion to compel inspection in an Illinois state court. The trial court denied the plaintiffs' motion. On appeal, the reviewing court reversed. The court held that the plaintiffs' allegations of self-dealing constituted a proper purpose for their inspection request.[17]

WAYHOME studio/Shutterstock.com

How might a shareholder's right to inspect corporate books help or hurt a corporation?

Transfer of Shares Corporate stock represents an ownership right in intangible personal property. The law generally recognizes the right to transfer stock to another person unless there are valid restrictions on its transferability, such as frequently occur with close corporation stock. Restrictions must be reasonable and can be set out in the bylaws or in a shareholder agreement.

When shares are transferred, a new entry is made in the corporate stock book to indicate the new owner. Until the corporation is notified and the entry is complete, all rights—including voting rights and the right to dividend distributions—remain with the currently recorded owner.

17. *Sunlitz Holding Co. v. Trading Block Holdings, Inc.,* 17 N.E.3d 715, 384 Ill.Dec. 733 (4 Dist. 2014).

29–4e The Shareholder's Derivative Suit

Shareholder's Derivative Suit A suit brought by a shareholder to enforce a corporate cause of action against a third person.

When the corporation is harmed by the actions of a third party, the directors can bring a lawsuit in the name of the corporation against that party. If the corporate directors fail to bring a lawsuit, shareholders can do so "derivatively" in what is known as a **shareholder's derivative suit**.

The right of shareholders to bring a derivative action is especially important when the wrong suffered by the corporation results from the actions of corporate directors or officers. For obvious reasons, the directors and officers would probably be unwilling to take any action against themselves.

Written Demand Required Before shareholders can bring a derivative suit, they must submit a written demand to the corporation, asking the board of directors to take appropriate action [RMBCA 7.40]. The directors then have ninety days in which to act. Only if they refuse to do so can the derivative suit go forward. In addition, a court will dismiss a derivative suit if the majority of directors or an independent panel determines in good faith that the lawsuit is not in the best interests of the corporation [RMBCA 7.44].

Damages Recovered Go into Corporate Funds When shareholders bring a derivative suit, they are not pursuing rights or benefits for themselves personally but are acting as guardians of the corporate entity. Therefore, if the suit is successful, any damages recovered normally go into the corporation's treasury, not to the shareholders personally.

Example 29.13 Zeon Corporation is owned by two shareholders, each holding 50 percent of the corporate shares. One of the shareholders wants to sue the other for misusing corporate assets. In this situation, the plaintiff-shareholder will have to bring a shareholder's derivative suit (not a suit in the plaintiff's own name) because the alleged harm was suffered by Zeon, not by the plaintiff personally. Any damages awarded will go to the corporation, not to the plaintiff-shareholder.

29–4f Duties of Majority Shareholders

In some instances, a majority shareholder is regarded as having a fiduciary duty to the corporation and to the minority shareholders. This occurs when a single shareholder (or a few shareholders acting in concert) owns a sufficient number of shares to exercise *de facto* (actual) control over the corporation. In these situations, which commonly involve close corporations, majority shareholders owe a fiduciary duty to the minority shareholders.

When a majority shareholder breaches the fiduciary duty to a minority shareholder, the minority shareholder can sue for damages. A breach of fiduciary duties by those who control a close corporation normally constitutes what is known as *oppressive conduct*. A common example of a breach of fiduciary duty occurs when the majority shareholders "freeze out" the minority shareholders and exclude them from certain benefits of participating in the firm.

Example 29.14 Brodie, Jordan, and Barbara form a close corporation to operate a machine shop. Brodie and Jordan own 75 percent of the shares in the company, but all three are directors. After disagreements arise, Brodie asks the company to purchase his shares, but his requests are refused. A few years later, Brodie dies, and his wife, Ella, inherits his shares. Jordan and Barbara refuse to perform a valuation of the company, deny Ella access to the corporate information she requests, do not declare any dividends, and refuse to elect Ella as a director. In this situation, the majority shareholders have violated their fiduciary duty to Ella.

29–5 Major Business Forms Compared

When deciding which form of business organization would be most appropriate, businesspersons normally take into account several factors, including ease of creation, the liability of the owners, tax considerations, and the need for capital. Each major form of business organization offers distinct advantages and disadvantages with respect to these and other factors. Exhibit 29–2 summarizes the essential advantages and disadvantages of each of the forms of business organization discussed in this unit.

Exhibit 29–2 Major Forms of Business Compared

CHARACTERISTIC	SOLE PROPRIETORSHIP	GENERAL PARTNERSHIP	CORPORATION
Method of Creation	Created at will by owner.	Created by agreement of the parties.	Authorized by the state under the state's corporation law.
Legal Position	Not a separate entity; owner is the business.	A general partnership is a separate legal entity in most states.	Always a legal entity separate and distinct from its owners—a legal fiction for the purposes of owning property and being a party to litigation.
Liability	Unlimited liability.	Unlimited liability.	Limited liability of shareholders—shareholders are not liable for the debts of the corporation.
Duration	Determined by owner; automatically dissolved on owner's death.	Terminated by agreement of the partners, but can continue to do business even when a partner dissociates from the partnership.	Can have perpetual existence.
Transferability of Interest	Interest can be transferred, but individual's proprietorship then ends.	Although partnership interest can be assigned, assignee does not have full rights of a partner.	Shares of stock can be transferred.
Management	Completely at owner's discretion.	Each partner has a direct and equal voice in management unless expressly agreed otherwise in the partnership agreement.	Shareholders elect directors, who set policy and appoint officers.
Taxation	Owner pays personal taxes on business income.	Each partner pays pro rata share of income taxes on net profits, whether or not they are distributed.	Double taxation—corporation pays income tax on net profits, with no deduction for dividends, and shareholders pay income tax on disbursed dividends they receive.
Organizational Fees, Annual License Fees, and Annual Reports	None or minimal.	None or minimal.	All required.
Transaction of Business in Other States	Generally no limitation.	Generally no limitation.[a]	Normally must qualify to do business and obtain certificate of authority.

a. A few states have enacted statutes requiring that foreign partnerships qualify to do business within those states.

(Continues)

Exhibit 29–2 Major Forms of Business Compared—Continued

CHARACTERISTIC	LIMITED PARTNERSHIP	LIMITED LIABILITY COMPANY	LIMITED LIABILITY PARTNERSHIP
Method of Creation	Created by agreement to carry on a business for profit. At least one party must be a general partner and the other(s) limited partner(s). Certificate of limited partnership is filed to be recognized by the state.	Created by an agreement of the member-owners of the company. Articles of organization are filed to be recognized by the state.	Created by agreement of the partners. A statement of qualification for the limited liability partnership is filed to be recognized by the state.
Legal Position	Treated as a legal entity.	Treated as a legal entity.	Generally, treated same as a general partnership.
Liability	Unlimited liability of all general partners. Limited partners are liable only to the extent of capital contributions.	Member-owners' liability is limited to the amount of capital contributions or investments.	Varies, but under the Uniform Partnership Act, liability of a partner for acts committed by other partners is limited.
Duration	By agreement in certificate, or by termination of the last general partner or last limited partner.	Unless a single-member LLC, can have perpetual existence (same as a corporation).	Remains in existence until cancellation or revocation.
Transferability of Interest	Interest can be assigned (same as a general partnership), but if assignee becomes a member with consent of other partners, certificate must be amended.	Member interests are freely transferable.	Interest can be assigned the same as in a general partnership.
Management	General partners have equal voice, or determined by agreement. Limited partners may not retain limited liability if they actively participate in management.	Member-owners can fully participate in management or can designate a group of persons to manage on behalf of the members.	Same as a general partnership.
Taxation	Generally taxed as a partnership.	LLC is not taxed, and members are taxed personally on profits passed through the LLC.	Same as a general partnership.
Organizational Fees, Annual License Fees, and Annual Reports	Organizational fee required; usually not others.	Organizational fee required. Others vary with states.	Fees are set by each state for filing statements of qualification, statements of foreign qualification, and annual reports.
Transaction of Business in Other States	Generally no limitations.	Generally no limitations, but may vary depending on state.	Must file a statement of foreign qualification before doing business in another state.

Practice and Review

William Sharp was the sole shareholder and manager of Chickasaw Club, Inc., an S corporation that operated a popular nightclub of the same name in Columbus, Georgia. Sharp maintained a corporate checking account but paid the club's employees, suppliers, and entertainers in cash out of the club's proceeds. Sharp owned the property on which the club was located. He rented it to the club but made mortgage payments out of the club's proceeds and often paid other personal expenses with Chickasaw corporate funds.

At 12:45 A.M. on July 31, eighteen-year-old Aubrey Lynn Pursley, who was already intoxicated, entered the Chickasaw Club. Chickasaw employees did not check Pursley's identification to verify her age, as required by a city ordinance. Pursley drank more alcohol at Chickasaw and was visibly intoxicated when she left the club at 3:00 A.M. with a beer in her hand. Shortly afterward, Pursley lost control of her car, struck a tree, and was killed. Joseph Dancause, Pursley's stepfather, filed a tort lawsuit against Chickasaw Club and William Sharp. Using the information presented in the chapter, answer the following questions.

1. Under what theory might the court in this case make an exception to the limited liability of shareholders and hold Sharp personally liable for the damages? What factors would be relevant to the court's decision?
2. Suppose that Chickasaw's articles of incorporation failed to describe the corporation's purpose or management structure as required by state law. Would the court be likely to rule that Sharp is personally liable to Dancause on that basis? Why or why not?
3. Suppose that the club extended credit to its regular patrons in an effort to maintain a loyal clientele, although neither the articles of incorporation nor the corporate bylaws authorized this practice. Would the corporation likely have the power to engage in this activity? Explain.
4. How would the court classify Chickasaw Club, Inc.—domestic or foreign, public or private?

Debate This

The sole shareholder of an S corporation should not be able to avoid liability for the torts of employees.

Key Terms

alien corporation 711
articles of incorporation 715
benefit corporation 713
bond 718
business judgment rule 726
bylaws 716
close corporation 712
commingle 721
common stock 718
corporation 708
crowdfunding 719
dividend 709
domestic corporation 711
foreign corporation 711
inside director 723
outside director 723
piercing the corporate veil 720
preemptive rights 732
preferred stock 718
private equity capital 718
proxy 729
public corporation 711
publicly held corporation 711
quorum 723
retained earnings 709
S corporation 713
securities 717
shareholder's derivative suit 734
stocks 718
stock certificate 732
***ultra vires* acts** 719
venture capital 718

Chapter Summary: Corporations

Nature and Classification	A corporation is a legal entity distinct from its owners. Formal statutory requirements, which vary somewhat from state to state, must be followed in forming a corporation. Under U.S. law, a corporation is recognized as an artificial legal person and enjoys the same rights that U. S. citizens enjoy. **1. Corporate personnel**—Shareholders, whose liability is limited to the amount of their investments, own the corporation. They elect a board of directors to govern the corporation. The board of directors hires corporate officers and other employees to run the firm's daily business. **2. Corporate taxation**—The corporation pays income tax on net profits, and shareholders pay income tax on the disbursed dividends that they receive from the corporation (double-taxation feature). **3. Torts and criminal acts**—The corporation is liable for the torts committed by its agents or officers within the course and scope of their employment (under the doctrine of *respondeat superior*). A corporation can be held liable (and be fined) for the criminal acts of its agents and employees. **4. Domestic, foreign, and alien corporations**—A corporation is referred to as a *domestic corporation* within its home state (the state in which it incorporates), as a *foreign corporation* by any state that is not its home state, and as an *alien corporation* if it originates in another country but does business in the United States. **5. Public and private corporations**—A public corporation is formed by a government (for example, a city or town). A private corporation is formed wholly or in part for private benefit. Most corporations are private corporations. **6. Nonprofit corporations**—Corporations formed without a profit-making purpose. **7. Close corporations**—Corporations owned by a relatively small number of individuals, often members of the same family. Transfer of shares is usually restricted. **8. S corporations**—Small domestic corporations that receive special tax treatment under Subchapter S of the Internal Revenue Code. Shareholders enjoy limited liability while avoiding double taxation. **9. Professional corporations**—Corporations formed by professionals (such as physicians and lawyers). For liability purposes, some courts disregard the corporate form and treat the shareholders as partners. **10. Benefit corporations**—Corporations formed to benefit the public as a whole and have a material positive impact on society and the environment.
Formation and Powers	**1. Promotional activities**—A person who enters contracts on behalf of the future corporation is personally liable on all preincorporation contracts until the corporation is formed and assumes the contracts by novation. **2. Incorporation procedures**—Procedures vary among the states, but the basic steps are as follows: **a.** Select a state of incorporation. **b.** Secure an appropriate corporate name. **c.** Prepare the articles of incorporation. The articles must include the corporate name, the number of shares of stock the corporation is authorized to issue, the names and addresses of the registered office and agent, and the name and address of each incorporator. **d.** File the articles with the secretary of state. The state's filing of the articles authorizes the corporation to conduct business. **3. First organizational meeting**—The main function of the meeting is to adopt the bylaws, or internal rules of the corporation, but other business, such as election of the board of directors, may also take place. **4. Improper incorporation**—A corporation that has complied with the conditions for incorporation has *de jure* status. A minor defect in formation generally does not affect this status. If a defect is substantial, courts in some states may hold that the corporation has *de facto* status and treat it as a corporation despite the defect. **5. Corporation by estoppel**—If a firm is not incorporated but represents itself to be a corporation and is sued as such by a third party, it may be held to be a corporation by estoppel.

6. **Corporate financing**—Corporations normally are financed by the issuance and sale of securities. *Bonds* are debt securities representing funds borrowed by the firm, and *stocks* are equity securities representing ownership in the firm.
7. **Corporate powers**—
   a. Express and implied powers—The express powers of a corporation are found in its articles of incorporation, in the law of the state of incorporation, and in the state and federal constitutions. Barring express constitutional, statutory, or other prohibitions, the corporation has the implied power to perform all acts reasonably appropriate and necessary to accomplish its corporate purposes.
   b. ***Ultra vires* doctrine** —Any act of a corporation that is beyond its express or implied powers is an *ultra vires* act and may lead to a lawsuit by the shareholders or the state attorney general.
8. **Piercing the corporate veil**—To avoid injustice, courts may "pierce the corporate veil" and hold a shareholder personally liable. This usually occurs when the facts show that great injustice would result from the use of a corporation to avoid individual responsibility.

Directors and Officers

1. **Directors**—Directors are responsible for all policymaking decisions necessary to the management of corporate affairs. Directors are elected by the shareholders and usually serve a one-year term. Compensation is usually specified in the corporate articles or bylaws. The board conducts business by holding formal meetings with recorded minutes. Directors' rights include the rights of participation, inspection, and indemnification.
2. **Corporate officers and executives**—Corporate officers and other executive employees are normally hired by the board of directors and have the rights defined by their employment contracts.
3. **Duty of care**—Directors and officers are obligated to act in good faith, to use prudent business judgment in the conduct of corporate affairs, and to act in the corporation's best interests. A director who fails to exercise this duty of care can be answerable to the corporation and to the shareholders.
4. **The business judgment rule**—This rule immunizes directors and officers from liability for honest mistakes of judgment or bad business decisions made in good faith.
5. **Duty of loyalty**—Directors and officers have a fiduciary duty to subordinate their own interests to those of the corporation in matters relating to the corporation.
6. **Conflicts of interest**—To fulfill their duty of loyalty, directors and officers must make a full disclosure of any potential conflicts between their personal interests and those of the corporation.
7. **Liability**—Directors and officers are liable for their own crimes and torts, and may be liable for the crimes and torts committed by corporate employees under their supervision.

Shareholders

1. **Shareholders' powers**—Shareholders must approve all fundamental changes affecting the corporation and elect the board of directors.
2. **Shareholders' meetings**—Shareholders' meetings must occur at least annually. Special meetings can be called when necessary. Notice of the date, time, and place of the meeting (and its purpose, if it is specially called) must be sent to shareholders. Shareholders may vote by proxy and may submit proposals to be included in the proxy materials sent to shareholders before meetings.
3. **Shareholder voting**—Shareholder voting requirements and procedures are as follows:
   a. A minimum number of shareholders (a quorum) must be present at a meeting for business to be conducted. Resolutions are usually passed by simple majority vote.
   b. Cumulative voting may be required or permitted. Cumulative voting gives minority shareholders a better chance to be represented on the board of directors.
   c. A shareholder voting agreement (in which shareholders agree to vote their shares together) is usually held to be valid and enforceable.
4. **Rights of shareholders**—Shareholders have numerous rights, which may include preemptive rights, the right to dividends, inspection rights, the right to transfer shares, and the right to sue on behalf of the corporation (bring a shareholder's derivative suit).
5. **Duties of shareholders**—A majority shareholder may be regarded as having a fiduciary duty to the corporation and to minority shareholders. A breach of fiduciary duties by those who control a close corporation normally constitutes oppressive conduct.

Issue Spotters

1. Name Brand, Inc., is a small business. Twelve members of a single family own all of its stock. Ordinarily, corporate income is taxed at the corporate and shareholder levels. How can Name Brand avoid this double taxation of income? (See *Nature and Classification*.)
2. Wonder Corporation has an opportunity to buy stock in XL, Inc. The directors decide that instead of buying the stock in the name of the corporation, they will buy it for themselves. Yvon, a Wonder shareholder, learns of the purchase and wants to sue the directors on Wonder's behalf. Can she do it? Explain. (See *Shareholders*.)

—Check your answers to the *Issue Spotters* against the answers provided in Appendix D.

Business Scenarios and Case Problems

29–1. Preincorporation. Cummings, Okawa, and Taft are recent college graduates who want to form a corporation to manufacture and sell personal computers. Peterson tells them he will set in motion the formation of their corporation. First, Peterson makes a contract with Owens for the purchase of a piece of land for $20,000. Owens does not know of the prospective corporate formation at the time the contract is signed. Second, Peterson makes a contract with Babcock to build a small plant on the property being purchased. Babcock's contract is conditional on the corporation's formation. Peterson secures all necessary capitalization and files the articles of incorporation. Discuss whether the newly formed corporation, Peterson, or both are liable on the contracts with Owens and Babcock. Is the corporation automatically liable to Babcock on formation? Explain. (See *Formation and Powers*.)

29–2. Conflicts of Interest. Oxy Corp. is negotiating with the Wick Construction Co. for the renovation of the Oxy corporate headquarters. Wick, the owner of the Wick Construction Co., is also one of the five members of Oxy's board of directors. The contract terms are standard for this type of contract. Wick has previously informed two of the other directors of his interest in the construction company. Oxy's board approves the contract by a three-to-two vote, with Wick voting with the majority. Discuss whether this contract is binding on the corporation. (See *Directors and Officers*.)

29–3. Spotlight on Smart Inventions—Piercing the Corporate Veil. Thomas Persson and Jon Nokes founded Smart Inventions, Inc., to market household consumer products. The success of their first product, the Smart Mop, continued with later products, which were sold through infomercials. Persson and Nokes were the firm's officers and equal shareholders, with Persson responsible for product development and Nokes in charge of day-to-day activities. By 1998, they had become dissatisfied with each other's efforts. Nokes represented the firm as financially "dying," and "in a grim state, . . . worse than ever." He offered to buy all of Persson's shares for $1.6 million, and Persson accepted.

On the day that they signed the agreement to transfer the shares, Smart Inventions began marketing a new product—the Tap Light. It was an instant success, generating millions of dollars in revenues. In negotiating with Persson, Nokes had intentionally kept the Tap Light a secret. Persson sued Smart Inventions, asserting fraud and other claims. Under what principle might Smart Inventions be liable for Nokes's fraud? Is Smart Inventions liable in this case? Explain. [*Persson v. Smart Inventions, Inc.,* 125 Cal.App.4th 1141, 23 Cal.Rptr.3d 335 (2 Dist. 2005)] (See *Formation and Powers*.)

29–4. Business Case Problem with Sample Answer—Piercing the Corporate Veil. Scott Snapp contracted with Castlebrook Builders, Inc., which was owned by Stephen Kappeler, to remodel a house. Kappeler estimated that the remodeling would cost around $500,000. Eventually, however, Snapp paid Kappeler more than $1.3 million. Snapp filed a suit in an Ohio state court against Castlebrook, alleging breach of contract and fraud, among other things. During the trial, it was revealed that Castlebrook had issued no shares of stock and had commingled personal and corporate funds. The minutes of the corporate meetings all looked exactly the same. In addition, Kappeler could not provide an accounting for the Snapp project. In particular, he could not explain evidence of double and triple billing nor demonstrate that the amount Snapp paid had actually been spent on the remodeling project. Are these sufficient grounds to pierce the corporate veil? Explain. [*Snapp v. Castlebrook Builders, Inc.,* 2014 -Ohio- 163, 7 N.E.3d 574 (2014)] (See *Formation and Powers*.)

—For a sample answer to Problem 29–4, go to Appendix E.

29–5. Torts. Jennifer Hoffman took her cell phone to a store owned by R&K Trading, Inc., for repairs. Later, Hoffman filed a suit in a New York state court against R&K, Verizon Wireless, Inc., and others, seeking to recover damages for a variety of torts, including infliction of emotional distress and negligent hiring and supervision. She alleged that an R&K employee, Keith Press, had examined her phone in a back room, accessed private photos of her stored on her phone, and disseminated the photos to the public. Hoffman testified that "after the incident, she learned from another R&K employee that personal information and pictures had been removed from the phones of other customers." Can R&K be held liable for the torts of its employees? Explain. [*Hoffman v. Verizon Wireless, Inc.*, 5 N.Y.S.3d 123, 125 A.D.3d 806 (2015)] (See *Nature and Classification.*)

29–6. Piercing the Corporate Veil. In New York City, 2406-12 Amsterdam Associates, LLC, brought an action in a New York state court against Alianza Dominicana and Alianza, LLC, to recover unpaid rent. The plaintiff asserted cause to pierce the corporate veil, alleging that Alianza Dominicana had made promises to pay its rent while discreetly forming Alianza, LLC, to avoid liability for it. According to 2406-12, Alianza, LLC, was 90 percent owned by Alianza Dominicana, had no employees, and had no function but to hold Alianza Dominicana's assets away from its creditors. The defendants filed a motion to dismiss the plaintiff's claim. Assuming that 2406-12's allegations are true, are there sufficient grounds to pierce Alianza, LLC's corporate veil? Discuss. [*2406-12 Amsterdam Associates, LLC v. Alianza, LLC*, 136 A.D.3d 512, 25 N.Y.S.2d 167 (1 Dept. 2016)] (See *Formation and Powers.*)

29–7. Rights of Shareholders. FCR Realty, LLC, and Clifford B. Green & Sons, Inc., were co-owned by three brothers—Frederick, Clifford Jr., and Richard Green. Each brother was a shareholder of the corporation. Frederick was a controlling shareholder, as well as president. Each brother owned a one-third interest in the LLC. Clifford believed that Frederick had misused LLC and corporate funds to pay nonexistent debts and liabilities and had diverted LLC assets to the corporation. He also contended that Frederick had disbursed about $1.8 million in corporate funds to Frederick's own separate business. Clifford hired an attorney and filed an action on behalf of the two companies against Frederick for a breach of fiduciary duty. Frederick argued that Clifford lacked the knowledge necessary to adequately represent the companies' interest because he did not understand financial statements. Can Clifford maintain the action against Frederick? If so, and if the suit is successful, who recovers the damages? Explain. [*FCR Realty, LLC v. Green*, 2016 WL 571449 (Conn.Super. 2016)] (See *Shareholders.*)

29–8. Certificate of Authority. Armour Pipe Line Company assigned leases to its existing oil wells in Texas to Sandel Energy, Inc. The assignment included royalties for the oil produced from the wells. Armour specified that the assignment "does not pertain to production attributable to these leases from any new wells," reserving for itself an interest in those royalties. Later, Armour—a foreign corporation in Texas—forfeited its certificate of authority to do business in the state. More than three years later, the certificate was reissued. Meanwhile, new wells were drilled on the leases. Sandel filed a suit in a Texas state court against Armour, claiming that the reservation of a royalty interest in those wells was "ineffective" because of the temporary forfeiture. When and why does a corporation need a certificate of authority? Is Armour entitled to the royalties from the new wells? Discuss. [*Armour Pipeline Co. v. Sandel Energy, Inc.*, 546 S.W.3d 455 (Tex.App.—Houston (14th Dist.) 2018)] (See *Nature and Classification.*)

29–9. A Question of Ethics—The IDDR Approach and Duties of Directors and Officers. Hewlett-Packard Company (HP) hired detectives to secretly monitor the phones and e-mail accounts of its directors to find the sources of leaks of company information to the media. When the government learned of the monitoring, criminal charges were brought against HP's then-chairwoman and general counsel. Mark Hurd, HP's chief executive officer, was found free of wrongdoing. The scandal had the effect of bolstering Hurd's reputation for integrity, and he became both chairman and CEO. In congressional testimony, press releases, and investor briefings, Hurd proclaimed HP's integrity and its intent to enforce violations of its corporate code of ethics, the Standards of Business Conduct (SBC). Hurd's statements concerning HP's commitment to ethics and compliance with the SBC reassured investors and the public, and kept HP's stock prices from falling.

Meanwhile, an independent contractor for HP accused Hurd of sexual harassment. An investigation by HP's board found no harassment, but revealed that Hurd had lied about his personal relationship with the woman and falsified expense reports to cover it up. Hurd resigned, causing the price of HP stock to drop. A group of shareholders sued HP claiming that Hurd's unethical behavior while promoting HP's commitment to ethics constituted fraud. [*Retail Wholesale and Department Store Union Local 338 Retirement Fund v. Hewlett-Packard Co.*, 845 F.3d 1268 (9th Cir. 2017)] (See *Directors and Officers.*)

1. Using the *Discussion* step of the IDDR approach, consider whether Hurd's conduct constituted an ethical violation against HP and its shareholders.
2. Using the *Review* step of the IDDR approach, evaluate HP's decision to monitor its directors' phones.

Critical Thinking and Writing Assignments

29–10. Time-Limited Group Assignment—Shareholders' Duties. Milena Weintraub and Larry Griffith were shareholders in Grand Casino, Inc., which operated a casino in South Dakota. Griffith owned 51 percent of the stock and Weintraub 49 percent. Weintraub managed the casino, which Griffith typically visited once a week. At the end of 2012, an accounting audit showed that the cash on hand was less than the amount posted in the casino's books. Later, more shortfalls were discovered. In October 2014, Griffith did a complete audit. Weintraub was unable to account for $200,500 in missing cash. Griffith kept all of the casino's most recent profits, including Weintraub's $90,447.20 share, and, without telling Weintraub, sold the casino for $400,000 and kept all of the proceeds. Weintraub filed a suit against Griffith, asserting a breach of fiduciary duty. Griffith countered with evidence of Weintraub's misappropriation of corporate cash. (See *Shareholders*.)

1. The first group will discuss the duties that these parties owed to each other and determine whether Weintraub or Griffith, or both, breached those duties.
2. The second group will decide how this dispute should be resolved and who should pay what to whom to reconcile the finances.
3. The third group will discuss whether Weintraub or Griffin violated any ethical duties to each other or to the corporation.

Freedomz/Shutterstock.com

Investor Protection, Insider Trading, and Corporate Governance

30

"You are remembered for the rules you break."

General Douglas MacArthur
1880–1964
(U.S. Army general)

Focus Questions

The four Focus Questions *below are designed to help improve your understanding. After reading this chapter, you should be able to answer the following questions:*

1. What is meant by the term *securities?*
2. What is insider trading? Why is it prohibited?
3. What are some of the features of state securities laws?
4. What certification requirements does the Sarbanes-Oxley Act impose on corporate executives?

After the stock market crash of 1929, Congress enacted legislation to regulate securities markets. **Securities** generally include any instruments representing corporate ownership (stock) or debts (bonds). The goal of regulation was to provide investors with more information to help them make buying and selling decisions about securities and to prohibit deceptive, unfair, and manipulative practices.

Securities Generally, any instruments representing corporate ownership (stock) or debt (bonds).

Today, the sale and transfer of securities are heavily regulated by federal and state statutes and by government agencies. The Securities and Exchange Commission (SEC) is the main independent regulatory agency that administers securities regulations. The SEC continually updates its rules in response to legislation, such as the Dodd-Frank Wall Street Reform and Consumer Protection Act.[1]

Despite all efforts to regulate the securities markets, people continue to break the rules and are often remembered for it, as observed in the chapter-opening quotation. Consider what happened to Jun Ying, who was an executive with Equifax when the consumer credit reporting agency experienced a massive data breach affecting 145 million Americans. Acting on this sensitive information before it became public, Ying sold about $1 million in shares of Equifax stock. When news of the hack reached global financial markets, the stock's value dropped 15 percent. Yin was convicted of insider trading and scolded by a federal prosecutor for thinking of "his own financial gain before the millions of people exposed in this data breach even knew they were victims."

In this chapter, we explore securities regulations and laws on insider trading so that you understand how to avoid breaking the rules. We also discuss corporate governance and accountability.

1. Pub. L. No. 111-203, July 21, 2010, 124 Stat. 1376; 12 U.S.C. Sections 5301 *et seq.*

30–1 Securities Act of 1933

Focus Question 1

What is meant by the term *securities?*

The Securities Act of 1933[2] governs initial sales of stock by businesses. The act was designed to prohibit various forms of fraud and to stabilize the securities industry by requiring that all essential information concerning the issuance of securities be made available to the investing public. Basically, the purpose of the 1933 act is to require disclosure. The act provides that all securities transactions must be registered with the SEC unless they qualify for an exemption.

National Archives

During the stock market crash of 1929, hordes of investors crowded Wall Street to find out the latest news. How did the "crash" affect stock trading in the years thereafter?

30–1a What Is a Security?

Section 2(1) of the Securities Act contains a broad definition of *securities*, which generally include the following:[3]

1. Instruments and interests commonly known as securities, such as preferred and common stocks, treasury stocks, bonds, debentures, and stock warrants.
2. Any interests, such as stock options, puts, calls, or other types of privilege on a security or on the right to purchase a security or a group of securities on a national security exchange.
3. Notes, instruments, or other evidence of indebtedness, including certificates of interest in a profit-sharing agreement and certificates of deposit.
4. Any fractional undivided interest in oil, gas, or other mineral rights.
5. Investment contracts, which include interests in limited partnerships and other investment schemes.

Investment Contract In securities law, a transaction in which a person invests in a common enterprise reasonably expecting profits that are derived primarily from the efforts of others.

The *Howey* Test In interpreting the act, the United States Supreme Court has held that an **investment contract** is any transaction in which a person (1) invests (2) in a common enterprise (3) reasonably expecting profits (4) derived *primarily* or *substantially* from others' managerial or entrepreneurial efforts.[4] Known as the *Howey* test, this definition continues to guide the determination of what types of contracts can be considered securities.

The following case centered on an alleged *Ponzi scheme*—a fraudulent investment operation that pays returns to investors with funds from later investors rather than with profits earned by legitimate means. In reaching its decision, the court had to apply the *Howey* test to determine whether the agreements in question met the definition of investment contracts and were, therefore, securities.

2. 15 U.S.C. Sections 77–77aa.
3. 15 U.S.C. Section 77b(1). Amendments in 1982 added stock options.
4. *Securities and Exchange Commission v. W. J. Howey Co.*, 328 U.S. 293, 66 S.Ct. 1100, 90 L.Ed. 1244 (1946).

Case 30.1

Securities and Exchange Commission v. Scoville

United States Court of Appeals, Tenth Circuit, 913 F.3d 1204 (2019).

Facts Internet traffic exchange businesses sell visits to a buyer's website to make it look more popular than it really is so that it will rank higher in search results displayed by Google and other search engines. Charles Scoville operated an exchange through his company Traffic Monsoon, LLC. Its primary product was Adpacks—bundled Internet advertising services that entitled buyers to a certain number of visits to their websites but also gave them the opportunity to share in the company's revenue. Buyers were offered the possibility of high rates of return on the amounts they paid for the Adpacks. The company represented that the returns came from the sales of all of its advertising services. In fact, the returns on the purchases of Adpacks were paid with money from later Adpack sales.

The Securities and Exchange Commission filed an action in a federal district court against Scoville, alleging that he had violated federal securities laws by operating Traffic Monsoon as a Ponzi scheme in which the business paid returns to its investors financed, not by the success of the business, but with funds acquired from later investors. Before the trial, the court enjoined the defendant from continuing to operate his business. Scoville appealed, arguing that Adpacks were not securities.

Issue Did the Adpacks meet the requirements of the *Howey* test?

Decision Yes. The U.S. Court of Appeals for the Tenth Circuit affirmed the district court's decision to enjoin Scoville from continuing to operate his business.

Reason The appellate court pointed out that the Securities Act of 1933 regulates investments "in whatever form they are made and by whatever name they are called." The court alluded to "the virtually limitless scope of human ingenuity, especially in the creation of countless and variable schemes devised by those who seek the use of the money of others on the promise of profits."

As defined by the Securities Act of 1933, an investment contract is a security. In the *Howey* case, the United States Supreme Court defined an investment contract as a contract, transaction, or scheme whereby a person invests money in a common enterprise and is led to expect profits solely from the efforts of the promoter or a third party. Thus, under *Howey*, there are three requirements that distinguish an investment contract from other business deals: (1) an investment, (2) in a common enterprise, (3) with a reasonable expectation of profits to be derived from the entrepreneurial or managerial efforts of others.

Here, the appellate court reasoned, an Adpack was an investment, offering its buyer the opportunity to share in Traffic Monsoon's revenue. An Adpack involved a common enterprise—the sale of Internet advertising services. And an Adpack provided its buyer with a reasonable expectation of profit derived from others' entrepreneurial or managerial efforts—Traffic Monsoon's success was expected to depend "significantly" on its efforts to sell its advertising services.

Accordingly, "the district court did not err in concluding that Adpacks meet *Howey's* three-part test and, therefore, qualify as investment contracts and, thus, as securities subject to regulation under the federal securities laws."

Critical Thinking

- **Legal Environment** *Scoville argued that the Adpacks were not investment contracts because there was no guarantee that buyers would receive a return on their investment. Should the court have ruled in Scoville's favor based on this argument? Explain.*
- **Economic** *The return on an investment in an Adpack was not based on any underlying business activity. Instead, money from new investors was used to pay earlier investors. Is this a legitimate business model? Discuss.*

Many Types of Securities For our purposes, it is probably convenient to think of securities in their most common forms—stocks and bonds issued by corporations. Bear in mind, though, that securities can take many forms, including interests in whiskey, cosmetics, worms, beavers, boats, vacuum cleaners, muskrats, and cemetery lots. Almost any stake in the ownership or debt of a company can be considered a security. Investment contracts in condominiums, franchises, limited partnerships in real estate, and oil or gas or other mineral rights have qualified as securities as well.

30–1b Registration Statement

Section 5 of the Securities Act of 1933 broadly provides that a security must be *registered* before being offered to the public unless it qualifies for an exemption. The issuing corporation must file a *registration statement* with the SEC and must provide all investors with a *prospectus*. In principle, the registration statement and the prospectus supply sufficient information to enable unsophisticated investors to evaluate the financial risk involved.

A **prospectus** is a written disclosure document that describes the security being sold, the financial operations of the issuing corporation, and the investment risk attaching to the security. The prospectus also serves as a selling tool for the issuing corporation. The SEC allows an issuer to deliver its prospectus to investors electronically.[5]

Prospectus A written document required by securities laws when a security is being sold. The prospectus describes the security, the financial operations of the issuing corporation, and the risk attaching to the security.

5. Basically, an electronic prospectus must meet the same requirements as a printed prospectus. The SEC has special rules that address situations in which the graphics, images, or audio files in a printed prospectus cannot be reproduced in electronic form. 17 C.F.R. Section 232.304.

Know This

The purpose of the Securities Act of 1933 is disclosure. The SEC does not consider whether a security is worth the investment price.

Contents of the Registration Statement The registration statement must be written in plain English and must fully describe the following:

1. The securities being offered for sale, including their relationship to the issuer's other securities.
2. The corporation's properties and business (including a financial statement certified by an independent public accounting firm).
3. The management of the corporation, including managerial compensation, stock options, pensions, and other benefits. Any interests of directors or officers in any material transactions with the corporation must be disclosed.
4. How the corporation intends to use the proceeds of the sale.
5. Any pending lawsuits or special risk factors.

All companies, both domestic and foreign, must file their registration statements electronically so that they can be posted on the SEC's EDGAR (Electronic Data Gathering, Analysis, and Retrieval) database. The EDGAR database includes material on initial public offerings, proxy statements, corporations' annual reports, registration statements, and other documents that have been filed with the SEC. Investors can access the database online to obtain information that they can use to make investment decisions.

The Registration Process The registration statement does not become effective until after it has been reviewed and approved by the SEC (unless it is filed by a *well-known seasoned issuer,* as will be discussed shortly). The process includes several stages, and the 1933 act restricts the types of activities that an issuer can engage in at each stage.

Prefiling Period. During the *prefiling period* (before the registration statement is filed), the issuer normally cannot sell or offer to sell the securities. Once the registration statement has been filed, a waiting period begins while the SEC reviews the registration statement for completeness.[6]

Waiting Period. During the *waiting period,* or *quiet period,* the securities can be offered for sale but cannot legally be sold. Only certain types of offers are allowed during this period.

All issuers can now distribute a *preliminary prospectus,* which contains most of the information that will be included in the final prospectus but often does not include a price. Most issuers can also distribute a *free-writing prospectus.*[7] A **free-writing prospectus** is any type of written, electronic, or graphic offer that describes the issuer or its securities. The free-writing prospectus must include a legend indicating that the issuer has filed a registration statement (including a prospectus) with the SEC and that these documents can be obtained at the SEC website.

Free-Writing Prospectus A written, electronic, or graphic communication associated with the offer to sell a security and used during the waiting period to supplement other information about the security.

Posteffective Period. Once the SEC has reviewed and approved the registration statement and the waiting period is over, the registration is effective, and the *posteffective period* begins. The issuer can now offer and sell the securities without restrictions. If the company issued a preliminary or free-writing prospectus to investors, it must provide those investors with a final prospectus either before or at the time they purchase the securities. The issuer can require investors to download the final prospectus from a website if it notifies them of the appropriate Internet address.

6. The waiting period must last at least twenty days but always extends much longer because the SEC invariably requires numerous changes and additions to the registration statement.
7. See SEC Rules 164 and 433.

Well-Known Seasoned Issuers A *well-known seasoned issuer* (WKSI) is a firm that has issued at least $1 billion in securities in the last three years or has outstanding stock valued at $700 million or more in the hands of the public.[8] WKSIs have greater flexibility than other issuers. They can file registration statements the day they announce a new offering and are not required to wait for SEC review and approval. They can also use a free-writing prospectus at any time, even during the prefiling period.

Know This

The issuer of an exempt security does not have to disclose the same information as other issuers.

30–1c Exempt Securities

Certain types of securities are exempt from the registration requirements of the Securities Act because they are low-risk investments or are regulated by other statutes.[9] Exempt securities maintain their exempt status forever and can also be resold without being registered. Exempt securities include the following:

- Government-issued securities.
- Bank and financial institution securities.
- Short-term notes and drafts (negotiable instruments that have a maturity date that does not extend beyond nine months).
- Securities of nonprofit, educational, and charitable organizations.
- Securities issued by common carriers (railroads and trucking companies).
- Insurance policies, endowments, and annuity contracts.
- Securities issued in a corporate reorganization in which one security is exchanged for another or in a bankruptcy proceeding.
- Securities issued in stock dividends and stock splits.

Exhibit 30–1 Exempt Transactions under the 1933 Securities Act

Exempt Transactions

Regulation A

Securities issued by an issuer that has offered less than $50 million in securities during any twelve-month period if the issuer meets specific requirements:

- Tier 1 for offerings of up to $20 million in a twelve-month period. (Unlimited number of investors, both accredited and unaccredited.)
- Tier 2 for offerings of up to $50 million with additional review requirements in a twelve-month period. (Unlimited number of investors, but unaccredited investors may not invest more than 10 percent of their annual income or net worth.)

Regulation D

- **Rule 504:** Noninvestment company offerings up to $5 million in any twelve-month period.
- **Rule 506:** Private noninvestment company offerings in unlimited amounts that are not generally advertised or solicited. Unlimited number of accredited investors and thirty-five unaccredited investors.

Unregistered Restricted Securities

Restricted securities must be registered before resale *unless* they qualify for a safe harbor under Rule 144 or 144A.

30–1d Exempt Transactions

The Securities Act of 1933 also exempts certain transactions from registration requirements (see Exhibit 30–1 for a summary of these exemptions). The transaction exemptions are very broad and can enable an issuer to avoid the high cost and complicated procedures associated with registration. For instance, private (nonpublic) offerings that involve a small number of investors generally are exempt. Securities offered and sold only to residents of the state in which the issuing firm is incorporated and does business are also exempt. In addition, crowdfunding is allowed without SEC registration, as discussed in this chapter's *Adapting the Law to the Online Environment* feature.

Note, however, that even when a transaction is exempt from the registration requirements, the offering is still subject to the antifraud provisions of the 1933 act (and the 1934 act).

Regulation A Offerings Securities issued by an issuer that has offered less than $50 million in securities during any twelve-month period are

8. Securities Offering Reform, codified at 17 C.F.R. Sections 200, 228, 229, 230, 239, 240, 243, 249, and 274.
9. 15 U.S.C. Section 77c.

Adapting the Law to the Online Environment

Investment Crowdfunding—Regulations and Restrictions

Today, small entrepreneurs can gain access to public funds through crowdfunding without filing a registration statement with the Securities and Exchange Commission (SEC). Generally, crowdfunding refers to raising small sums of money from a large number of individuals via the Internet. Crowdfunding as a way for businesses to raise equity capital was made possible by the Jumpstart Our Business Startups Act, or JOBS Act—specifically, by Title III, also known as the Crowdfund Act.[a]

Restrictions on Those Who Invest

The Crowdfund Act imposes certain restrictions on investors. The aggregate amount sold to any investor cannot exceed the greater of $2,200 or 5 percent of the investor's annual income or net worth if that net worth is less than $107,000. For those investors with higher incomes or net worth, the limit is 10 percent.

Other Restrictions

Companies seeking investment funds through crowdfunding cannot offer shares directly to investors. They must go through an online fundraising platform registered with the SEC. Some companies that provide such platforms take an active role in the crowdfunding process, drafting paperwork and soliciting investors. Others take a more hands-off approach. An increasing number of approved crowdfunding portals are available. They usually impose a fee of 5 to 10 percent of the funds raised.

Of course, a potential start-up entrepreneur does not simply create a video and ask people to send money via the Internet. Paperwork must be filed prior to the start of a crowdfunding campaign, and detailed financial statements must be available for potential investors. At the beginning of the COVID-19 outbreak, the SEC made it easier for small businesses that might not ordinarily be eligible for crowdfunding to take advantage of these procedures for a much-needed infusion of capital.

Critical Thinking

What alternatives are there to crowdfunding for a start-up business?

a. 17 C.F.R. Parts 200, 227, 232, 239, 240, and 249 (2016).

exempt from registration.[10] Under Regulation A,[11] the issuer must file with the SEC a notice of the issue and an offering circular, which must also be provided to investors before the sale. This is a much simpler and less expensive process than full registration.

There are two types of public offerings under this regulation:

- Tier 1, for securities offerings of up to $20 million in a twelve-month period.
- Tier 2, for securities offerings of up to $50 million in a twelve-month period. (Legislation has been proposed that would raise the Tier 2 limit to $75 million.)

An issuer of $20 million or less of securities can elect to proceed under either Tier 1 or Tier 2. Both tiers are subject to certain basic requirements, and Tier 2 offerings are subject to additional requirements. Purchasers under Tier 2 who are not *accredited investors* cannot purchase shares that cost more than 10 percent of their annual income or net worth. (An **accredited investor** is a sophisticated investor, such as a bank, an insurance company, and a person whose income or net worth exceeds a certain amount.)

Accredited Investor In the context of securities offerings, a sophisticated investor, such as a bank, insurance company, investment company, the issuer's executive officers and directors, and a person whose income or net worth exceeds certain limits.

Important Rule Changes. Note that the cap for Regulation A—which, as noted, is now $50 million—was $5 million until 2015. At that time, the SEC approved rule changes (commonly known as Reg A+) to make it easier for small and mid-sized businesses to raise capital. This chapter's *Landmark in the Law* feature discusses these important changes.

10. 15 U.S.C. Section 77c(b).
11. 17 C.F.R. Sections 230.251–230.263.

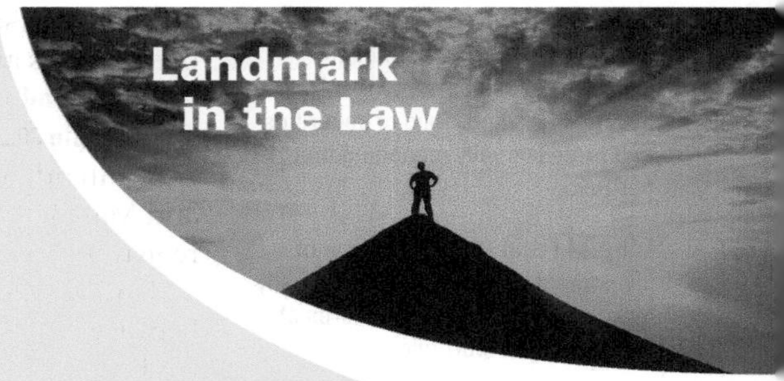

Changes to Regulation A: "Reg A+"

Under the Securities Act of 1933, before offering or selling securities, a corporation must register the securities with the SEC unless the securities qualify for an exemption.

Traditionally, most of the exempt transactions have involved offers and sales made to *accredited investors* (sophisticated investors, such as banks, insurance companies, and people whose income or net worth exceeds a certain amount). As a result, members of the general public were unable to invest in smaller, growth-stage companies and start-ups.

In addition, small businesses and start-ups were at a relative disadvantage in raising capital through initial public offerings (IPOs) if they could not qualify for an exemption or afford the cost of SEC registration. Start-ups were forced to seek financing from other sources, often giving up some degree of control in the business in exchange for funds.

Legislation Led to Amended Rules Congress passed the Jumpstart Our Business Startups Act (JOBS Act)[a] to encourage small business growth and to bolster employment. The goal was to provide more funding and reduce the regulatory hurdles for companies trying to go public. In 2015, the SEC adopted final rules (Regulation A+ or Reg A+) to implement the JOBS Act. These rules establish an IPO process that is less expensive and complicated than the procedures associated with normal SEC registration.

Reg A+ Provides Benefits Reg A+ expands the number of issuers that qualify for exemption by raising the limit from $5 to $50 million. It also creates a two-tier system—one for companies seeking to raise less than $20 million, and another for those seeking to raise between $20 and $50 million. Small and mid-sized businesses can now raise up to $50 million a year selling stock by using a simple, streamlined, and cost-efficient process.

Moreover, anyone in the world can invest in Reg A+ offerings, not just accredited investors, although some restrictions apply to certain offerings.[b] Companies can also advertise their stock to the general public. (This is not possible with transactions exempted under Regulation D)

Application to Today's Law *The SEC's changes to Regulation A offer average investors enhanced opportunities to invest in companies that they believe in and hope to profit from financially. Reg A+ also helps start-ups and growing companies reach a bigger pool of potential investors and still retain control of their operations. Because it provides a simpler, lower-cost IPO process for small businesses, Reg A+ is likely to decrease the significance of all the other exemptions over time.*

a. Pub. L. No. 112-106, April 5, 2012, 126 Stat 306.

b. For Tier 2 offerings, nonaccredited investors cannot invest more than 10 percent of their annual income or net worth.

Example 30.1 Myomo, Inc., is a company based in Massachusetts that makes robotic medical devices for people with upper-body paralysis. The company relied on venture capital funding for a number of years but decided to take advantage of the amended Regulation A when it became available. Seeking to raise $15 million, Myomo became the first company to issue an initial public offering under Regulation A+.

Boston Globe/Getty Images

How did Myomo, Inc., in Massachusetts, benefit from rule changes to Regulation A offerings?

Testing the Waters. Before preparing a Regulation A offering circular, companies are allowed to "test the waters" for potential interest. To *test the waters* means to determine potential interest without actually selling any securities or requiring any commitment on the part of those who express interest.

Small Offerings—Regulation D The SEC's Regulation D contains exemptions from registration requirements (Rules 504 and 506) for offers that either involve a small dollar amount or are made in a limited manner.

Rule 504. Rule 504 is the exemption used by most small businesses. It provides that noninvestment company offerings up to $5 million in any twelve-month period are exempt. Noninvestment companies are firms that are not engaged primarily in the business of investing

Investment Company A company that acts on the behalf of many smaller shareholders-owners by buying a large portfolio of securities and professionally managing that portfolio.

Mutual Fund A specific type of investment company that continually buys or sells to investors shares of ownership in a portfolio.

or trading in securities. (In contrast, an **investment company** is a firm that buys a large portfolio of securities and professionally manages it on behalf of many smaller shareholders-owners. A **mutual fund** is a type of investment company.)

Example 30.2 Zeta Enterprises is a limited partnership that develops commercial property. Zeta intends to offer $600,000 of its limited partnership interests for sale between June 1 and May 31. According to the definition of a security, this offering would be subject to the registration and prospectus requirements of the 1933 Securities Act.

Under Rule 504, however, the sales of Zeta's interests are exempt from these requirements because Zeta is a noninvestment company making an offering of less than $1 million in a twelve-month period. Therefore, Zeta can sell its limited partnership interests without filing a registration statement with the SEC or issuing a prospectus to any investor.

Rule 506—Private Placement Exemption. Rule 506 exempts private noninvestment company offerings in unlimited amounts if these offerings are not generally solicited or advertised. This exemption is often referred to as the *private placement exemption* because it exempts "transactions not involving any public offering."[12] The offering can involve an unlimited number of accredited investors and no more than thirty-five unaccredited investors. The issuer must believe that each unaccredited investor has sufficient knowledge or experience in financial matters to be capable of evaluating the investment's merits and risks.[13]

Know This

Investors can be "sophisticated" by virtue of their education and experience or by virtue of investing through knowledgeable, experienced representatives.

The private placement exemption is perhaps most important to firms that want to raise funds through the sale of securities without registering them. **Example 30.3** Citco Corporation needs to raise capital to expand its operations. Citco decides to make a private $10 million offering of its common stock directly to two hundred accredited investors and thirty highly sophisticated, but unaccredited, investors. Citco provides all of these investors with a prospectus and material information about the firm, including its most recent financial statements.

As long as Citco notifies the SEC of the sale, this offering will likely qualify for the private placement exemption. The offering is nonpublic and not generally advertised. There are fewer than thirty-five unaccredited investors, and each of them possesses sufficient knowledge and experience to evaluate the risks involved. The issuer has provided all purchasers with the necessary material information. Thus, Citco will not be required to comply with the registration requirements of the Securities Act.

Resales and Safe Harbor Rules

Most securities can be resold without registration. The Securities Act provides exemptions for resales by most persons other than issuers or underwriters. Thus, the average investor who sells shares of stock does not have to file a registration statement with the SEC.

Different rules apply to resales of *restricted securities*—securities acquired in an unregistered private sale. Resales of restricted securities trigger the registration requirements unless the party selling them complies with Rule 144 or Rule 144A. These rules are sometimes referred to as "safe harbors."

Rule 144. Rule 144 exempts restricted securities from registration on resale if all of the following conditions are met:

1. There is adequate current public information about the issuer. ("Adequate current public information" refers to the reports that certain companies are required to file under the 1934 Securities Exchange Act.)

---

12. 15 U.S.C. Section 77d(2).

13. 17 C.F.R. Section 230.506.

2. The person selling the securities has owned them for at least six months, if the issuer is subject to the reporting requirements of the 1934 act. If the issuer is not subject to the 1934 act's reporting requirements, the seller must have owned the securities for at least one year.
3. The securities are sold in certain limited amounts in unsolicited brokers' transactions.
4. The SEC is notified of the resale.[14]

Rule 144A. Rule 144A allows the resale of unregistered securities that, at the time of issue, are not of the same class as securities listed on a national securities exchange or quoted in a U.S. automated interdealer quotation system.[15] The securities may be sold only to qualified institutional buyers (institutions, such as insurance companies and banks, that hold and manage at least $100 million in securities). The seller must take reasonable steps to ensure that the buyer knows that the seller is relying on the exemption under Rule 144A.

Know This

Securities do not have to be held for a specific period (six months) to be exempt from registration on a resale under Rule 144A, as they do under Rule 144.

30–1e Violations of the 1933 Act

It is a violation of the Securities Act to intentionally defraud investors by misrepresenting or omitting facts in a registration statement or prospectus. Liability may also be imposed on those who are negligent with respect to the preparation of these publications. Selling securities before the effective date of the registration statement or under an exemption for which the securities do not qualify also results in liability.

Remedies Criminal violations are prosecuted by the U.S. Department of Justice. Violators may be fined anywhere from $10,000 to $2 million, depending on circumstances, and imprisoned for up to five years.

The SEC is authorized to seek civil sanctions against those who willfully violate the 1933 act. It can request an injunction to prevent further sales of the securities involved or ask the court to grant other relief, such as an order to a violator to refund profits. Parties who purchase securities and suffer harm as a result of false or omitted statements may also bring suits in a federal court to recover their losses and other damages.

Defenses There are three basic defenses to charges of violations under the 1933 act. A defendant can avoid liability by proving any of the following:

1. The statement or omission was not material.
2. The plaintiff knew about the misrepresentation at the time of purchasing the stock.
3. The defendant exercised *due diligence* in preparing the registration and reasonably believed at the time that the statements were true and there were no omissions of material facts.

In most instances, a defendant must disclose any conflicts of interest when that defendant substantially benefits from recommending to clients specific investment purchases. **Case Example 30.4** Dennis Malouf worked for UASNM, Inc., an investment advice firm. Malouf steered his clients to purchase securities from a branch office of the financial service company Raymond James. The owner of this Raymond James branch earned commissions from these trades, making it easier for him to pay off a large sum of money he owed Malouf. UASNM compliance procedures required Malouf to disclose this conflict of interest. He failed to do so.

14. 17 C.F.R. Section 230.144.
15. 17 C.F.R. Section 230.144A.

Rido/Shutterstock.com

Under what circumstances can an investment advisor be held responsible for false or misleading statements made by another party regarding the trade of securities?

The SEC found that Malouf had engaged in a deceptive scheme under the 1933 Act and banned him from the securities industry for life. Malouf countered that it was not his duty to warn UASNM's clients of the conflict of interest. Rather, that responsibility lay with UASNM's compliance officer. An appeals court rejected this attempt to shift the blame, holding that—clearly—Malouf had known he was required to report his conflict of interest to the compliance officer and had failed to do so.[16]

30–2 Securities Exchange Act of 1934

The 1934 Securities Exchange Act provides for the regulation and registration of securities exchanges, brokers, dealers, and national securities associations, such as the National Association of Securities Dealers (NASD). Unlike the 1933 act, which is a one-time disclosure law, the 1934 act provides for continuous periodic disclosures by publicly held corporations to enable the SEC to regulate subsequent trading.

The Securities Exchange Act applies to companies that have assets in excess of $10 million and either two thousand or more shareholders or five hundred or more shareholders who are unaccredited. These corporations are referred to as *Section 12 companies* because they are required to register their securities under Section 12 of the 1934 act. Section 12 companies must file reports with the SEC annually and quarterly, and sometimes even monthly if specified events occur (such as a merger). Other provisions in the 1934 act require all securities brokers and dealers to be registered, to keep detailed records of their activities, and to file annual reports with the SEC.

The act also authorizes the SEC to engage in market surveillance to deter undesirable market practices such as fraud, market manipulation (attempts at illegally influencing stock prices), and misrepresentation. In addition, the act provides for the SEC's regulation of proxy solicitations for voting.

30–2a Section 10(b), SEC Rule 10b-5, and Insider Trading

Section 10(b) is an especially important section of the Securities Exchange Act. This section proscribes the use of any manipulative or deceptive mechanism in violation of SEC rules and regulations. Among the rules that the SEC has promulgated pursuant to Section 10(b) is **SEC Rule 10b-5,** which prohibits the commission of fraud in connection with the purchase or sale of any security.

SEC Rule 10b-5 A rule of the Securities and Exchange Commission that prohibits the commission of fraud in connection with the purchase or sale of any security.

SEC Rule 10b-5 applies to almost all cases concerning the trading of securities, whether on organized exchanges, in over-the-counter markets, or in private transactions. Generally, the rule covers just about any form of security, and the securities need not be registered under the 1933 act for the 1934 act to apply.

Know This

A required element in any fraud claim is reliance. The innocent party must justifiably have relied on the misrepresentation.

Private parties can sue for securities fraud under the 1934 act and SEC Rule 10b-5. The basic elements of a securities fraud action are as follows:

1. A *material misrepresentation* (or omission) in connection with the purchase and sale of securities.
2. *Scienter* (a wrongful state of mind).

16. *Malouf v. Securities & Exchange Commission,* 933 F.3d 1248 (10th Cir. 2019), applying the United States Supreme Court's ruling in *Lorenzo v. Securities & Exchange Commission,* __ U.S. __, 139 S.Ct. 1094, 203 L.Ed.2d 484 (2019), which contemplated similar issues involving a violation of SEC Rule 10b-5.

3. *Reliance* by the plaintiff on the material misrepresentation.
4. An *economic loss*.
5. *Causation*, meaning that there is a causal connection between the misrepresentation and the loss.

Insider Trading One of the major goals of Section 10(b) and SEC Rule 10b-5 is to prevent so-called **insider trading,** which occurs when persons buy or sell securities on the basis of information that is not available to the public. Corporate directors, officers, and majority shareholders, among others, often have advance inside information about events that can affect the future market value of the corporate stock. Obviously, acting on this information would give them a trading advantage over the general public and other shareholders.

Focus Question 2

What is insider trading? Why is it prohibited?

Insider Trading The purchase or sale of securities on the basis of information that has not been made available to the public.

The 1934 act defines inside information and extends liability to those who take advantage of such information in their personal transactions when they know that the information is unavailable to those with whom they are dealing. Section 10(b) of the act and SEC Rule 10b-5 apply to anyone who has access to or receives information of a nonpublic nature on which trading is based—not just to corporate "insiders."

Disclosure under SEC Rule 10b-5 Any material omission or misrepresentation of material facts in connection with the purchase or sale of a security may violate not only the Securities Act of 1933 but also the antifraud provisions of Section 10(b) of the 1934 act and SEC Rule 10b-5. The key to liability (which can be civil or criminal) under Section 10(b) and SEC Rule 10b-5 is whether the insider's information is *material*.

The following are some examples of material facts calling for disclosure under SEC Rule 10b-5:

1. Fraudulent trading in the company's stock by a broker-dealer.
2. A dividend change (whether up or down).
3. A contract for the sale of corporate assets.
4. A new discovery, a new process, or a new product.
5. A significant change in the firm's financial condition.
6. Potential litigation against the company.

fizkes/Shutterstock.com

What are some examples of material facts that should be disclosed according to SEC Rule 10b-5?

Note that any one of these facts, by itself, is not *automatically* considered a material fact. Rather, it will be regarded as a material fact if it is significant enough that it would likely affect an investor's decision as to whether to purchase or sell the company's securities.

Example 30.5 Sheen, Inc., is the defendant in a class-action product liability suit that its attorney, Paula, believes that the company will lose. Paula has advised Sheen's directors, officers, and accountants that the company will likely have to pay a substantial damages award. Sheen plans to make a $5 million offering of newly issued stock before the date when the trial is expected to end. Sheen's potential liability and the financial consequences to the firm are material facts that must be disclosed, because they are significant enough to affect an investor's decision as to whether to purchase the stock.

The following is a *Classic Case* interpreting materiality under SEC Rule 10b-5.

Classic Case 30.2

Securities and Exchange Commission v. Texas Gulf Sulphur Co.

United States Court of Appeals, Second Circuit, 401 F.2d 833 (1968).

Facts On November 12, 1963, the Texas Gulf Sulphur Company (TGS) drilled a hole that appeared to yield a core with an exceedingly high mineral content, although further drilling would be necessary to establish whether there was enough ore to be mined commercially. TGS kept secret the results of the core sample.

After learning of the ore discovery, officers and employees of the company made substantial purchases of TGS's stock or accepted stock options (rights to purchase stock).

Dyzi0/Shutterstock.com

After sample drilling revealed potential mineral deposits, company executives made large stock purchases. Did they violate insider trading laws?

On April 11, 1964, an unauthorized report of the mineral find appeared in the newspapers. On the following day, April 12, TGS issued a press release that played down the discovery and stated that it was too early to tell whether the ore find would be significant.

Later on, TGS announced a strike of at least 25 million tons of ore. The news led to a substantial increase in the price of TGS stock. The Securities and Exchange Commission (SEC) brought a suit in a federal district court against the officers and employees of TGS for violating the insider-trading prohibition of SEC Rule 10b-5. The officers and employees argued that the prohibition did not apply. They reasoned that the information on which they had traded was not material, as the find had not been commercially proved.

The trial court held that most of the defendants had not violated SEC Rule 10b-5, and the SEC appealed.

Issue Did the officers and employees of TGS violate SEC Rule 10b-5 by buying the stock, even though they did not know the full extent and profit potential of the ore discovery at the time of their purchases?

Decision Yes. The U.S. Court of Appeals for the Second Circuit reversed the lower court's decision and remanded the case for further proceedings, holding that the employees and officers had violated SEC Rule 10b-5's prohibition against insider trading.

Reason For SEC Rule 10b-5 purposes, the test of materiality is whether the information would affect the judgment of reasonable investors. Reasonable investors include speculative as well as conservative investors. "A major factor in determining whether the . . . discovery [of the ore] was a material fact is the importance attached to the drilling results by those who knew about it. . . . The timing by those who knew of it of their stock purchases and their purchases of short-term calls [rights to buy shares at a specified price within a specified time period]—purchases in some cases by individuals who had never before purchased calls or even TGS stock—virtually compels the inference that the insiders were influenced by the drilling results. . . . We hold, therefore, that all transactions in TGS stock or calls by individuals apprised of the drilling results . . . were made in violation of Rule 10b-5."

Critical Thinking

- **What If the Facts Were Different?** *Suppose that further drilling had revealed that there was not enough ore at this site for it to be mined commercially. Would the defendants still have been liable for violating SEC Rule 10b-5? Why or why not?*
- **Impact of This Case on Today's Law** *This landmark case affirmed the principle that the test of whether information is "material," for SEC Rule 10b-5 purposes, is whether it would affect the judgment of reasonable investors. The corporate insiders' acquisition of stock and stock options indicated that they were influenced by the results—in other words, that the information about the drilling results was material. The courts continue to cite this case when applying SEC Rule 10b-5 to cases of alleged insider trading.*

Outsiders and SEC Rule 10b-5 The traditional insider-trading case involves true insiders—corporate officers, directors, and majority shareholders who have access to (and trade on) inside information. Increasingly, liability under Section 10(b) of the 1934 act and SEC Rule 10b-5 is being extended to certain "outsiders"—persons who trade on inside information acquired indirectly. Two theories have been developed under which outsiders may be held liable for insider trading: the *tipper/tippee theory* and the *misappropriation theory.*

Tipper/Tippee Theory. Anyone who acquires inside information as a result of a corporate insider's breach of a fiduciary duty can be liable under SEC Rule 10b-5. This liability extends to a **tippee** (an individual who receives "tips" from insiders) and even remote tippees (tippees of tippees).

Tippee A person who receives inside information.

The key to liability under this theory is that the inside information must be obtained as a result of someone's breach of a fiduciary duty to the corporation whose shares are involved in the trading. The tippee is liable under this theory only if the following requirements are met:

1. There is a breach of a duty not to disclose inside information.
2. The disclosure is made in exchange for personal benefit.
3. The tippee knows (or should know) of this breach and benefits from it.

Case Example 30.6 Eric McPhail was a member of the same country club as an executive at American Superconductor. While they were golfing, the executive shared information with McPhail about the company's expected earnings, contracts, and other major developments, trusting that McPhail would keep the information confidential. Instead, McPhail repeatedly tipped six of his other golfing buddies at the country club, and they all used the nonpublic information to their advantage in trading. In this situation, the executive breached his duty not to disclose the information, which McPhail knew. McPhail (the tippee) is liable under SEC Rule 10b-5, and so are his other golfing buddies (remote tippees). All traded on inside information to their benefit.[17]

Misappropriation Theory. Liability for insider trading may also be established under the misappropriation theory. Under this theory, an individual who wrongfully obtains (misappropriates) inside information and trades on it for personal gain should be held liable because, in essence, that individual stole information rightfully belonging to another.

The misappropriation theory has been controversial because it significantly extends the reach of SEC Rule 10b-5 to outsiders who ordinarily would *not* be deemed fiduciaries of the corporations in whose stock they trade. It is not always wrong to disclose material, nonpublic information about a company to another person. Nevertheless, a person who obtains the information and trades securities on it can be liable.

kali9/E+/Getty Images

A golfer obtains inside information while playing with an executive of a listed company. The golfer then tells his friends about this valuable information. When can friends be liable for insider trading under securities law?

Case Example 30.7 Robert Bray, a real estate developer, first met Patrick O'Neill, an executive at Eastern Bank, at the Oakley Country Club, and the two men became good friends. One day, Bray told O'Neill that he needed cash to fund a project and asked O'Neill if he had any "bank stock tips" for him. O'Neill mentioned a few names of local banks. Then Bray wrote the word "Wainwright" on a napkin and slid it across the bar to O'Neill.

O'Neill, who knew that Eastern Bank was in the process of buying Wainwright Bank, told Bray, "this could be a good one." The next day, Bray bought 25,000 shares of Wainwright stock, and he bought another 31,000 shares a few weeks later. Then, Eastern publicly announced that it was buying Wainwright, and the stock price doubled. Bray eventually sold the stock at a profit of $300,000.

The SEC prosecuted Bray for insider trading using the misappropriation theory. He was convicted after a jury trial. On appeal, the conviction was affirmed. Bray and O'Neill had been good friends for many years. The jury could reasonably have concluded that Bray not only knew that he had traded on material, nonpublic information, but also knew that O'Neill owed Eastern a duty of loyalty and confidentiality.[18]

17. Three of the defendants in this case agreed to settle with the SEC and return the trading profits. See SEC press release 2014-134, "SEC Charges Group of Amateur Golfers in Insider Trading Ring."
18. *United States v. Bray*, 853 F.3d 18 (1st Cir. 2017).

Minimizing the Personal-Benefits Test. Following precedent, courts have consistently held that, under Section 10(b) and SEC Rule 10b-5, tippers/insiders are not guilty of securities fraud unless they disclose material information in exchange for a personal benefit. This is the so-called personal-benefits test.

The importance of the personal-benefits test was lessened significantly by the U.S. Court of Appeals for the Second Circuit in a case in which tippers were convicted on federal wire fraud charges. The court ruled that, under federal criminal law, prosecutors are not required to prove that tippers received any personal benefit in exchange for sharing material information with tippees.[19] Without the need to prove that defendants received a personal benefit, the federal government has a strong incentive to treat insider trading broadly as a white-collar crime rather than specifically as a violation of the 1934 Act.

Insider Reporting and Trading—Section 16(b) Section 16(b) of the 1934 act provides for the recapture by the corporation of all profits realized by an insider on a purchase and sale, or sale and purchase, of the corporation's stock within any six-month period.[20] It is irrelevant whether the insider actually uses inside information—all such **short-swing profits** must be returned to the corporation.

Short-Swing Profits Profits earned by a purchase and sale, or sale and purchase, of the same security within a six-month period.

In this context, *insiders* means officers, directors, and large stockholders of Section 12 corporations. (Large stockholders are those owning at least 10 percent of the class of equity securities registered under Section 12 of the 1934 act.) To discourage such insiders from using nonpublic information about their companies for their personal benefit in the stock market, the SEC requires them to file reports concerning their ownership and trading of the corporation's securities.

Section 16(b) applies not only to stock but also to stock warrants, options, and securities convertible into stock. In addition, the courts have fashioned complex rules for determining profits. Note, however, that the SEC exempts a number of transactions under Rule 16b-3.[21]

Exhibit 30–2 compares the effects of SEC Rule 10b-5 and Section 16(b). Because of these and other effects, corporate insiders are wise to seek specialized counsel before trading in the corporation's stock.

19. *United States v. Blaszczak*, 947 F.3d. 19 (2nd Cir. 2019).
20. A person who expects the price of a particular stock to decline can realize profits by "selling short"—selling at a high price and repurchasing later at a lower price to cover the "short sale."
21. 17 C.F.R. Section 240.16b-3.

Exhibit 30–2 Comparison of Coverage, Application, and Liability under SEC Rule 10b-5 and Section 16(b)

AREA OF COMPARISON	SEC RULE 10b-5	SECTION 16(b)
What is the subject matter of the transaction?	Any security (does not have to be registered).	Any security (does not have to be registered).
What transactions are covered?	Purchase or sale.	Short-swing purchase and sale or short-swing sale and purchase.
Who is subject to liability?	Almost anyone with inside information under a duty to disclose—including officers, directors, controlling shareholders, and tippees.	Officers, directors, and shareholders who own 10 percent or more of the relevant class of securities.
Is omission or misrepresentation necessary for liability?	Yes.	No.
Are there any exempt transactions?	No.	Yes, there are a number of exemptions.
Who may bring an action?	A person transacting with an insider, the SEC, or a purchaser or seller damaged by a wrongful act.	A corporation or a shareholder by derivative action.

The Private Securities Litigation Reform Act The disclosure requirements of SEC Rule 10b-5 had the unintended effect of deterring the disclosure of forward-looking information. **Example 30.8** BT Company announces that its projected earnings in a future time period will be a certain amount, but the forecast turns out to be wrong. The earnings are, in fact, much lower, and the price of BT's stock is affected negatively. The shareholders then file a suit against BT, claiming that its directors violated SEC Rule 10b-5 by disclosing misleading financial information.

To encourage companies to make earnings projections, Congress passed the Private Securities Litigation Reform Act (PSLRA) in 1995.[22] The PSLRA provides a "safe harbor" for publicly held companies that make forward-looking statements, such as financial forecasts. Those who make such statements are protected against liability for securities fraud if they include "meaningful cautionary statements identifying important factors that could cause actual results to differ materially from those in the forward-looking statement."[23]

The PSLRA also affects the level of detail required in securities fraud complaints. Plaintiffs must specify each purportedly misleading statement and say how it led them to a mistaken belief.

30–2b Regulation of Proxy Statements

Section 14(a) of the Securities Exchange Act of 1934 regulates the solicitation of proxies (authorization to vote shares) from shareholders of Section 12 companies. The SEC regulates the content of proxy statements. Whoever solicits a proxy must fully and accurately disclose in the proxy statement all of the facts that are pertinent to the matter on which the shareholders are to vote. SEC Rule 14a-9 is similar to the antifraud provisions of SEC Rule 10b-5. Remedies for violations range from injunctions to prevent a vote from being taken to monetary damages.

30–2c Violations of the 1934 Act

As mentioned earlier, violations of Section 10(b) of the Securities Exchange Act and SEC Rule 10b-5, including insider trading, may be subject to criminal or civil liability.

***Scienter* Requirement** For either criminal or civil sanctions to be imposed, *scienter* must exist—that is, the violator must have had an intent to defraud or knowledge of engaging in misconduct. *Scienter* can be proved by showing that the defendant made false statements or wrongfully failed to disclose material facts. In some situations, *scienter* can even be proved by showing that the defendant was consciously reckless as to the truth or falsity of the relevant statements.

Case Example 30.9 Etsy, Inc., a Brooklyn-based company, operates a website that connects buyers and sellers of handmade and vintage goods. When Etsy went public, it filed a prospectus and registration statement that set forth its commitment to working solely with "responsible, small-batch manufacturing partners" that adhere to Etsy's ethical expectations. Further, it described the company as "a mindful, transparent, and humane business." The statement also explained the company's methods for safeguarding against counterfeit goods and goods that infringe on another's copyright or trademark rights.

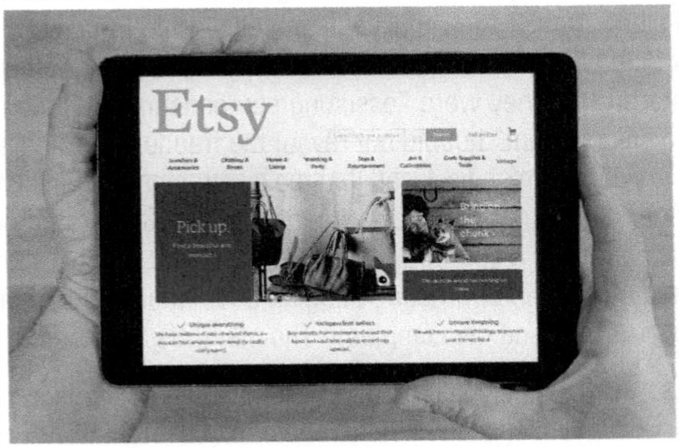

M4OS Photos/Alamy Stock Photo

Did Etsy violate the 1933 act by omitting material facts on its registration statement? Why or why not?

22. Pub. L. No. 104-67, 109 Stat. 737 (codified in scattered sections of Title 15 of the *United States Code*).
23. 15 U.S.C. Sections 77z-2, 78u-5.

Saleh Altayyar and several other investors sued Etsy, alleging that it had misrepresented or omitted material facts in its registration statement. The plaintiffs claimed that Etsy had made false and misleading statements about its values and that nearly 5 percent of its goods were counterfeit or infringing. Etsy argued that it had exercised due diligence and reasonably believed that the statements were true and contained no omissions of material facts. A federal district court in New York ruled in Etsy's favor and dismissed the case. The court found that the plaintiffs did not establish *scienter*. "The plaintiffs may disagree with the defendants' opinions [statements about the company], but disagreement does not render the opinions false."[24]

In filing a complaint, the plaintiff must state facts giving rise to an inference of *scienter*—knowledge that an action was illegal or that statements were false. The dispute in the following case was whether, as part of an allegation of securities fraud under Section 10(b) of the 1934 act, the plaintiffs adequately alleged the required elements of the claim, including *scienter.*

24. *Altayyar v. Etsy, Inc.*, 242 F.Supp.3d 161 (E.D.N.Y. 2017).

Case 30.3

Singer v. Reali

United States Court of Appeals, Fourth Circuit, 883 F.3d 425 (2018).

Facts TranS1, Inc., a medical device company, sold the "System," a spinal surgical procedure. TranS1's financial success hinged on reimbursement by health insurers and government health care programs of the claims of the surgeons who used the System. When the American Medical Association designated the System to be "experimental," surgeons could no longer count on being reimbursed for its use. TranS1 then coached surgeons to file fraudulent claims that would allow for full reimbursement. The company's officers publicly stated that they were "assisting surgeons in obtaining appropriate reimbursement" but did not reveal the fraudulent scheme.

When TranS1 disclosed that the government was investigating the firm, the value of its stock dropped. Phillip Singer and other shareholders filed a suit in a federal district court against Kenneth Reali and other TranS1 officers, alleging a violation of Section 10(b). The court dismissed the complaint. The plaintiffs appealed.

Issue Did the complaint sufficiently allege the misrepresentation, *scienter*, and causation elements of the claim?

Decision Yes. The U.S. Court of Appeals for the Fourth Circuit vacated the judgment of the district court and remanded the case.

Reason The misrepresentation element requires a deceptive, material misstatement or omission by a defendant with a duty to disclose. To allege *scienter*, a plaintiff must show that the defendant acted with an intent to deceive. The causation element requires a direct connection between the defendant's fraud and the plaintiff's loss. In this case, the complaint asserted that TranS1's declaration that it was assisting surgeons in obtaining reimbursement established a duty to disclose the allegedly fraudulent scheme. The company violated this duty by failing to make the disclosure. This was material because a reasonable investor would consider the scheme important in deciding whether to buy or sell TranS1 stock.

The complaint's allegation that the officers knew of the "clearly illegal" scheme when the company violated its duty to disclose gave rise to "a strong inference" of the defendants' intent to deceive. And the complaint's statement that after TranS1 publicly revealed the government's investigation, the value of the company's stock dropped "is wholly adequate" to allege the cause of the plaintiffs' loss.

Critical Thinking

- **Legal Environment** *In documents available to the public, TranS1 included general warnings about "the risks of regulatory scrutiny and litigation." Did this satisfy the company's duty to disclose its allegedly fraudulent scheme? Why or why not?*
- **Economic** *If the plaintiffs can prove the elements of their claim, what should be the measure of their damages? Explain.*

***Scienter* Not Required for Section 16(b) Violations** Violations of Section 16(b) include the sale by insiders of stock acquired less than six months before the sale (or less than six months after the sale if selling short). These violations are subject to civil sanctions. Liability under Section 16(b) is strict liability. Neither *scienter* nor negligence is required.

Criminal Penalties For violations of Section 10(b) and Rule 10b-5, an individual may be fined up to $5 million, imprisoned for up to twenty years, or both. A partnership or a corporation may be fined up to $25 million. The Sarbanes-Oxley Act increased the penalties for securities fraud. Section 807 of the act provides that for a *willful* violation of the 1934 act, the violator may be imprisoned for up to twenty-five years in addition to being fined.

For a defendant to be convicted in a criminal prosecution under the securities laws, there can be no reasonable doubt that the defendant was aware of acting wrongfully. A jury is not allowed merely to speculate that the defendant may have acted willfully.

Case Example 30.10 Kim Hannan had several clients that he had acquired from his former employment as a financial advisor. He also owned several small businesses. Hannan's lavish lifestyle and his method of raising funds from his clients aroused the suspicion of his girlfriend, Pamela Crawford, who lodged an anonymous complaint with the SEC. State investigators determined that Hannan, through deception, had convinced his clients to provide him with $1.6 million to fund not only his failed businesses but also his gambling sprees and other personal expenses. An Ohio jury found Hannan guilty on fifty-one counts of securities fraud, and he was sentenced to twenty years in prison.

Hannan appealed, arguing that prosecutors had not proved his intent to deceive his clients and that "misfortune does not constitute fraud." Evidence from his trial, however, showed that Hannan had solicited funds from his clients by telling them that his businesses were flourishing, when the opposite was true. In fact, Hannan was operating a Ponzi scheme in which he paid old investors with funds from new investors. Furthermore, he never informed clients that he was using their investments for personal expenses. An appeals court found that Hannan had "intentionally made false representations" that misled his clients. The court affirmed his conviction accordingly.[25]

Civil Sanctions The SEC can also bring suit in a federal district court against anyone violating or aiding in a violation of the 1934 act or SEC rules by purchasing or selling a security while in the possession of material nonpublic information.[26] The violation must occur on or through the facilities of a national securities exchange or through a broker or dealer. A court may assess a penalty for as much as triple the profits gained or the loss avoided by the guilty party. In addition, the Insider Trading and Securities Fraud Enforcement Act increased the number of persons who may be subject to civil liability for insider trading and gave the SEC authority to pay monetary rewards to informants.[27]

Private parties may also sue violators of Section 10(b) and Rule 10b-5. A private party may obtain rescission (cancellation) of a contract to buy securities or damages to the extent of the violator's illegal profits. Those found liable have a right to seek contribution from those who share responsibility for the violations, including accountants, attorneys, and corporations. For violations of Section 16(b), a corporation can bring an action to recover the short-swing profits.

30–2d Online Securities Fraud

A problem facing the SEC today is how to enforce the antifraud provisions of the securities laws in the online environment. Internet-related forms of securities fraud include many types of investment scams. Spam, online newsletters and bulletin boards, chat rooms, blogs,

25. *State of Ohio v. Hannan*, 2020 -Ohio- 755, 2020 WL 1028925 (Ohio Ct.App. 2020).
26. The Insider Trading Sanctions Act of 1984, 15 U.S.C. Section 78u(d).
27. 15 U.S.C. Section 78u-1.

social media, and tweets can all be used to spread false information and perpetrate fraud. For a relatively small cost, fraudsters can even build sophisticated Web pages to facilitate their investment scams.

Investment Newsletters Hundreds of online investment newsletters provide information on stocks. Legitimate online newsletters can help investors gather valuable information, but some e-newsletters are used for fraud. The law allows companies to pay the people who write these newsletters to tout their securities, but the newsletters are required to disclose who paid for the advertising. Many newsletters do not follow that law, however. Thus, an investor reading an online newsletter may believe that the information is unbiased, when in fact the fraudsters will directly profit by convincing investors to buy or sell particular stocks.

Zoonar GmbH/Alamy

How do social media, such as Twitter and Facebook, complicate securities fraud?

Social Media Social media sites have presented a particularly difficult problem for the SEC. Using sites such as Twitter and Facebook, anonymous fraudsters can quickly disseminate information to millions of people at little or no cost. Again, their aim is to convince others to trade in specific stocks. It can be difficult for the SEC to access social media accounts to investigate potential violations. The government must subpoena the sites to determine the user behind particular messages. In addition, social media sites are constantly being updated and changed, which adds another wrinkle for enforcement.

Still, the SEC can take steps to protect investors against deceptive behavior in this arena. For instance, the agency temporarily suspended the ability of twenty-three companies to sell shares in the wake of the COVID-19 outbreak of 2020. These companies had used social media to make false or misleading claims about their products' ability to "prevent, detect, or cure coronavirus." SEC officials worried that such claims were being used to "pump up" the value of a stock, which would then be "dumped" by the fraudulent promoters before the inevitable reality-based market correction.

30–3 State Securities Laws

Focus Question 3

What are some of the features of state securities laws?

Every state has its own corporate securities laws, or "blue sky laws," that regulate the offer and sale of securities within its borders. (The phrase *blue sky laws* dates to a 1917 decision by the United States Supreme Court in which the Court declared that the purpose of such laws was to prevent "speculative schemes which have no more basis than so many feet of 'blue sky.'")[28] Article 8 of the Uniform Commercial Code, which has been adopted by all of the states, also imposes various requirements relating to the purchase and sale of securities.

30–3a Requirements under State Securities Laws

State securities laws apply mainly to intrastate transactions (transactions within one state). Typically, state laws have disclosure requirements and antifraud provisions, many of which are patterned after Section 10(b) of the Securities Exchange Act and SEC Rule 10b-5. State laws also provide for the registration of securities offered or issued for sale within the state and impose disclosure requirements.

---

28. *Hall v. Geiger-Jones Co.*, 242 U.S. 539, 37 S.Ct. 217, 61 L.Ed. 480 (1917).

Case Example 30.11 Randall Fincke was the founder, director, and officer of Access Cardiosystems, Inc., a small start-up company that sold portable automated external heart defibrillators. Fincke prepared a business plan stating that Access's "patent counsel" had advised him that Access's product did not infringe any patents. This statement was false—patent counsel never offered Access any opinion on the question of infringement.

Fincke gave this plan to potential investors, including Joseph Zimmel, who bought $1.5 million in Access shares. When the company later filed for Chapter 11 bankruptcy protection, Zimmel filed a complaint with the federal bankruptcy court, alleging that Fincke had violated the Massachusetts blue sky law. The court awarded Zimmel $1.5 million in damages, and the award was affirmed on appeal. Fincke had solicited investors by means of a false statement of material fact, in violation of the fraud provisions in the state's securities laws.[29]

Methods of registration, required disclosures, and exemptions from registration vary among states. Unless an exemption from registration is applicable, issuers must register or qualify their stock with the appropriate state official, often called a *corporations commissioner*. Additionally, most state securities laws regulate securities brokers and dealers.

30–3b Concurrent Regulations

Since the adoption of the 1933 and 1934 federal securities acts, the state and federal governments have regulated securities concurrently. Issuers must comply with both federal and state securities laws, and exemptions from federal law are not exemptions from state laws.

The dual federal and state system has not always worked well, particularly during the early 1990s, when the securities markets underwent considerable expansion. Today, most duplicate regulations have been eliminated, and the SEC has exclusive power to regulate most national securities activities. In addition, the National Conference of Commissioners on Uniform State Laws substantially revised the Uniform Securities Act to coordinate state and federal securities regulation and enforcement efforts. A majority of the states have adopted this most recent version of the Uniform Securities Act.[30]

Know This

Federal securities laws do not take priority over state securities laws.

30–4 Corporate Governance

Corporate governance can be narrowly defined as the relationship between a corporation and its shareholders. Some argue for a broader definition—that corporate governance specifies the rights and responsibilities among different participants in the corporation, such as the board of directors, managers, shareholders, and other stakeholders, and spells out the rules and procedures for making decisions on corporate affairs. Regardless of the way it is defined, effective corporate governance requires more than just compliance with laws and regulations.

Corporate Governance A set of policies specifying the rights and responsibilities of the various participants in a corporation and spelling out the rules and procedures for making corporate decisions.

Effective corporate governance is essential in large corporations because corporate ownership (by shareholders) is separated from corporate control (by officers and managers). Under these circumstances, officers and managers may attempt to advance their own interests at the expense of the shareholders. The well-publicized corporate scandals in the first decade of the 2000s clearly illustrated the reasons for concern about managerial opportunism.

29. *In re Access Cardiosystems, Inc.*, 776 F.3d 30 (1st Cir. 2015).
30. At the time this book went to press, some form of the Uniform Securities Act had been adopted in thirty-nine states and the District of Columbia.

30–4a Promoting Accountability

Effective corporate governance standards are designed to address problems and to motivate officers to make decisions that promote the financial interests of the company's shareholders. Generally, corporate governance entails corporate decision-making structures that monitor employees (particularly officers) to ensure that they are acting for the benefit of the shareholders. Firms that are more accountable to shareholders typically report higher profits, higher sales growth, higher firm value, and other economic advantages.

Corporate governance involves, at a minimum:

1. Audited reporting of the corporation's financial progress, so that managers can be evaluated.
2. Legal protections for shareholders so that violators of the law who attempt to take advantage of shareholders can be punished for misbehavior and victims can recover damages for any associated losses.

Governance and Corporate Law State corporation statutes set up the legal framework for corporate governance. Under the corporate law of Delaware, where most major companies incorporate, all corporations must have certain structures of corporate governance in place. The most important structure, of course, is the board of directors, because the board makes the major decisions about the future of the corporation.

The Board of Directors Under corporate law, a corporation must have a board of directors elected by the shareholders. Directors are responsible for ensuring that the corporation's officers are operating wisely and in the exclusive interest of shareholders. The directors receive reports from the officers and give them managerial direction. In reality, though, corporate directors devote a relatively small amount of time to monitoring officers.

Ideally, shareholders would monitor the directors' supervision of the officers. In practice, however, it can be difficult for shareholders to monitor directors and hold them responsible for corporate failings. Although the directors can be sued for failing to do their jobs effectively, directors are rarely held personally liable.

The Audit Committee. A crucial committee of the board of directors is the *audit committee,* which oversees the corporation's accounting and financial reporting processes, including both internal and outside auditors. Unless the committee members have sufficient expertise and are willing to spend the time to carefully examine the corporation's bookkeeping methods, however, the audit committee may be ineffective.

The audit committee also oversees the corporation's "internal controls." These controls, carried out largely by the company's internal auditing staff, are measures taken to ensure that reported results are accurate. For instance, internal controls help to determine whether a corporation's debts are collectible. If the debts are not collectible, it is up to the audit committee to make sure that the corporation's financial officers do not simply pretend that payment will eventually be made.

The Compensation Committee. Another important committee of the board of directors is the *compensation committee.* This committee monitors and determines the compensation of the company's officers. As part of this process, it is responsible for assessing the officers' performance and for designing a compensation system that will better align the officers' interests with those of the shareholders.

Ethical Issue

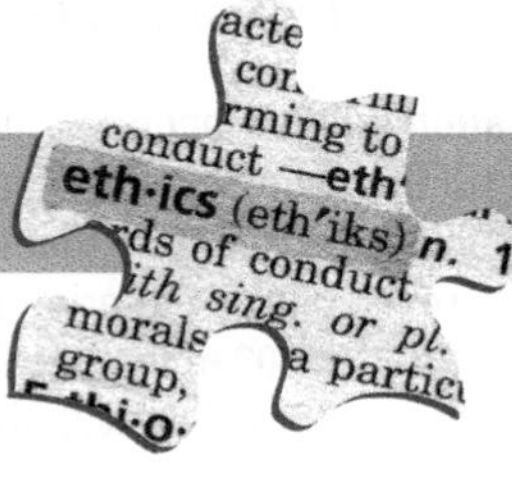

Does corporate America need gender quotas for boards of directors? Driven by pressure from institutional investors—as well as changes in the society at large—the nation's 500 largest corporations increased the number of women on their boards of directors by 37 percent during the last half of the 2010s. At the same time, California became the first state to legally compel the presence of women on corporate boards. Under California law, every publicly traded company based in the state must have at least one female director or be fined $100,000. Companies with five board members must have at least two female directors, and those with six board members must have at least three female directors. Larger corporations face fines of $300,000 for every seat that should be filled by a woman but is not.[31]

Given that the average director salary in California is about $180,000, complying with this law will be a hardship for some smaller firms. Still, the legislator who sponsored the law lauded its twin goals of "advancing gender equality" and enhancing "the economic well-being of the state." Opponents of the law counter that it is "patronizing" to women and also violates the equal protection clause of the U.S. Constitution by perpetuating gender-based discrimination. In addition, critics point out that a number of European countries have had gender quotas for corporate boards of directors in place for years, with no measurable impact on corporate financial performance or the expected "trickle-down" effect of increased hiring of female executives.

30–4b The Sarbanes-Oxley Act

In 2002, following a series of corporate scandals, Congress passed the Sarbanes-Oxley Act,[32] which addresses certain issues relating to corporate governance. Generally, the act attempts to increase corporate accountability by imposing strict disclosure requirements and harsh penalties for violations of securities laws. The act requires chief corporate executives to take responsibility for the accuracy of financial statements and reports that are filed with the SEC.

Additionally, the act requires that certain financial and stock-transaction reports be filed with the SEC earlier than was required under the previous rules. The act also created a new entity, called the Public Company Accounting Oversight Board, to regulate and oversee public accounting firms. Other provisions of the act established private civil actions and expanded the SEC's remedies in administrative and civil actions.

Because of the importance of this act for corporate leaders and for those dealing with securities transactions, we highlight some of its key provisions relating to corporate accountability in Exhibit 30–3.

More Internal Controls and Accountability The Sarbanes-Oxley Act introduced direct *federal* corporate governance requirements for public companies (companies whose shares are traded in the public securities markets). The law addressed many of the corporate governance procedures discussed here and created new requirements in an attempt to make the system work more effectively. The requirements deal with independent monitoring of company officers by both the board of directors and auditors.

---

31 "SB-826 Corporations: Boards of Directors." *www.leginfo.legislature.ca.gov.* California Legislative Information: September 30, 2018, Web.

32. 15 U.S.C. Sections 7201 *et seq.*

Exhibit 30–3 Some Key Provisions of the Sarbanes-Oxley Act Relating to Corporate Accountability

Certification Requirements—Under Section 906 of the Sarbanes-Oxley Act, the chief executive officers (CEOs) and chief financial officers (CFOs) of most major companies listed on public stock exchanges must certify financial statements that are filed with the SEC. CEOs and CFOs must certify that filed financial reports "fully comply" with SEC requirements and that all of the information reported "fairly represents in all material respects, the financial conditions and results of operations of the issuer."

Under Section 302 of the act, CEOs and CFOs of reporting companies are required to certify that a signing officer reviewed each quarterly and annual filing with the SEC and that none contained untrue statements of material fact. Also, the signing officer or officers must certify that they have established an internal control system to identify all material information and that any deficiencies in the system were disclosed to the auditors.

Effectiveness of Internal Controls on Financial Reporting—Under Section 404(a), all public companies are required to assess the effectiveness of their internal control over financial reporting. Section 404(b) requires independent auditors to report on management's assessment of internal controls, but companies with a public float (price times total shares publicly owned) of less than $75 million are exempted from this requirement.

Loans to Directors and Officers—Section 402 prohibits any reporting company, as well as any private company that is filing an initial public offering, from making personal loans to directors and executive officers (with a few limited exceptions, such as for certain consumer and housing loans).

Protection for Whistleblowers—Section 806 protects whistleblowers—employees who report ("blow the whistle" on) securities violations by their employers—from being fired or in any way discriminated against by their employers.

Blackout Periods—Section 306 prohibits certain types of securities transactions during "blackout periods"—periods during which the issuer's ability to purchase, sell, or otherwise transfer funds in individual account plans (such as pension funds) is suspended.

Enhanced Penalties for—

- *Violations of Section 906 Certification Requirements*—A CEO or CFO who certifies a financial report or statement filed with the SEC knowing that the report or statement does not fulfill all of the requirements of Section 906 will be subject to criminal penalties of up to $1 million in fines, ten years in prison, or both. *Willful* violators of the certification requirements may be subject to $5 million in fines, twenty years in prison, or both.
- *Violations of the 1934 Securities Exchange Act*—Penalties for securities fraud under the 1934 act were increased. Individual violators may be fined up to $5 million, imprisoned for up to twenty years, or both. *Willful* violators may be imprisoned for up to twenty-five years in addition to being fined.
- *Destruction or Alteration of Documents*—Anyone who alters, destroys, or conceals documents or otherwise obstructs any official proceeding will be subject to fines, imprisonment for up to twenty years, or both.
- *Other Forms of White-Collar Crime*—The act stiffened the penalties for certain criminal violations, such as federal mail and wire fraud, and ordered the U.S. Sentencing Commission to revise the sentencing guidelines for white-collar crimes.

Statute of Limitations for Securities Fraud—Section 804 provides that a private right of action for securities fraud may be brought no later than two years after the discovery of the violation or five years after the violation, whichever is earlier.

Sections 302 and 404 of Sarbanes-Oxley require high-level managers (the most senior officers) to establish and maintain an effective system of internal controls. The system must include "disclosure controls and procedures" to ensure that company financial reports are accurate and timely and to document financial results prior to reporting.

Senior management must reassess the system's effectiveness annually. Some companies had to take expensive steps to bring their internal controls up to the new federal standard. After the act was passed, hundreds of companies reported that they had identified and corrected shortcomings in their internal control systems.

Exemptions for Smaller Companies The Sarbanes-Oxley Act initially required all public companies to have an independent auditor file a report with the SEC on management's assessment of internal controls. Later, however, Congress enacted an exemption for smaller companies in an effort to reduce compliance costs. Public companies with a market capitalization, or public float (price times total shares publicly owned), of less than $75 million no longer need to have an auditor report on management's assessment of internal controls.

Certification and Monitoring Requirements Section 906 requires that chief executive officers (CEOs) and chief financial officers (CFOs) certify that the information in the corporate financial statements "fairly represents in all material respects, the financial conditions and results of operations of the issuer." This requirement makes officers directly accountable for the accuracy of their financial reporting and avoids any "ignorance defense" if shortcomings are later discovered.

The act also includes requirements to improve directors' monitoring of officers' activities. All members of the corporate audit committee for public companies must be outside directors. The audit committee must have a written charter that sets out its duties and provides for performance appraisal. At least one "financial expert" must serve on the audit committee, which must hold executive meetings without company officers present. In addition to reviewing the internal controls, the committee also monitors the actions of the outside auditor.

Focus Question 4

What certification requirements does the Sarbanes-Oxley Act impose on corporate executives?

Practice and Review

Dale Emerson served as the chief financial officer for Reliant Electric Company, a distributor of electricity serving portions of Montana and North Dakota. Reliant was in the final stages of planning a takeover of Dakota Gasworks, Inc., a natural gas distributor that operated solely within North Dakota. On a weekend fishing trip with his uncle, Ernest Wallace, Emerson mentioned that he had been putting in a lot of extra hours at the office planning a takeover of Dakota Gasworks. When he returned from the fishing trip, Wallace purchased $20,000 worth of Reliant stock. Three weeks later, Reliant made a tender offer to Dakota Gasworks stockholders and purchased 57 percent of Dakota Gasworks stock. Over the next two weeks, the price of Reliant stock rose 72 percent before leveling out. Wallace sold his Reliant stock for a gross profit of $14,400. Using the information presented in the chapter, answer the following questions.

1. Would registration with the SEC be required for Dakota Gasworks securities? Why or why not?
2. Did Emerson violate Section 10(b) of the Securities Exchange Act of 1934 and SEC Rule 10b-5? Why or why not?
3. What theory or theories might a court use to hold Wallace liable for insider trading?
4. Under the Sarbanes-Oxley Act, who would be required to certify the accuracy of the financial statements Reliant filed with the SEC?

Debate This

Insider trading should be legalized.

Key Terms

accredited investor 748
corporate governance 761
free-writing prospectus 746
insider trading 753
investment company 750
investment contract 744
mutual fund 750
prospectus 745
SEC Rule 10b-5 752
securities 743
short-swing profits 756
tippee 755

Chapter Summary: Investor Protection, Insider Trading, and Corporate Governance

Securities Act of 1933

Prohibits fraud and stabilizes the securities industry by requiring disclosure of all essential information relating to the issuance of securities to the investing public.

1. **Registration requirements**—Securities, unless exempt, must be registered with the SEC before being offered to the public.
   a. The *registration statement* must include detailed financial information about the securities being offered for sale; the issuing corporation's properties, business, and management; the intended use of the proceeds of the sale of the securities being issued; and any pending lawsuits or special risk factors.
   b. The issuer must provide investors with a *prospectus* that describes the security being sold, the financial operations of the issuing corporation, and the investment risk attaching to the security.
2. **Exemptions**—The SEC has exempted certain offerings from the requirements of the Securities Act of 1933. Exemptions may be determined on the basis of the size of the issue, whether the offering is private or public, and whether advertising is involved.

Securities Exchange Act of 1934

Provides for the regulation and registration of securities exchanges, brokers, dealers, and national securities associations. Maintains a continuous disclosure system for publicly held corporations to enable the SEC to regulate subsequent trading. Applies to companies that have assets in excess of $10 million and either two thousand or more shareholders or five hundred or more shareholders who are unaccredited (Section 12 companies).

1. **SEC Rule 10b-5 [under Section 10(b) of the 1934 act]**—This rule prohibits the commission of fraud in connection with the purchase or sale of any security.
   a. Applies to almost all trading of securities—a firm's securities do not have to be registered under the 1933 act for the 1934 act to apply.
   b. Applies to insider trading by corporate officers, directors, majority shareholders, and any persons receiving inside information (information not available to the public) who base their trading on this information. Liability for insider trading may be based on the tipper/tippee or the misappropriation theory.
   c. May be violated by omitting or misrepresenting "material facts" related to the purchase or sale of a security.
   d. Liability for violations can be civil or criminal.
2. **Insider trading [under Section 16(b) of the 1934 act]**—To prevent corporate insiders from taking advantage of inside information, the 1934 act requires officers, directors, and shareholders owning 10 percent or more of the issued stock of a corporation to turn over to the corporation all short-term profits (called *short-swing profits*) realized from the purchase and sale or sale and purchase of corporate stock within any six-month period.
3. **Regulation of proxies**—Section 14(a) of the 1934 act regulates the solicitation of proxies from shareholders of Section 12 companies.
4. **Online securities fraud**—The SEC today faces the problem of enforcing the antifraud provisions of the securities laws in the online environment. Internet-related forms of securities fraud include fraudulent newsletters and social media posts.

State Securities Laws

Regulate the offer and sale of securities within state borders (also known as *blue sky laws*). States regulate securities concurrently with the federal government. The Uniform Securities Act promotes coordination of state and federal securities regulation and enforcement efforts.

Corporate Governance

Involves a set of policies specifying the rights and responsibilities of the various participants in a corporation and spelling out the rules and procedures for making decisions on corporate affairs. Corporate governance is necessary in large corporations because corporate ownership (by the shareholders) is separated from corporate control (by officers and managers). This separation of corporate ownership and control can often result in conflicting interests. Corporate governance standards address such issues.

1. **Promoting accountability**—Measures designed to ensure that officers and other employees are acting in the best interests of shareholders include audits of the corporation's financial health and oversight by a board of directors.
2. **Sarbanes-Oxley Act**—This act attempts to increase corporate accountability by imposing strict disclosure requirements and harsh penalties for violations of securities laws.

Issue Spotters

1. When a corporation wishes to issue certain securities, it must provide sufficient information for an unsophisticated investor to evaluate the financial risk involved. Specifically, the law imposes liability for making a false statement or omission that is "material." What sort of information would an investor consider material? (See *Securities Exchange Act of 1934.*)

2. Lee is an officer of Magma Oil, Inc. Lee knows that a Magma geologist has just discovered a new deposit of oil. Can Lee take advantage of this information to buy and sell Magma stock? Why or why not? (See *Securities Exchange Act of 1934.*)

—Check your answers to the *Issue Spotters* against the answers provided in Appendix D.

Business Scenarios and Case Problems

30–1. Registration Requirements. Langley Brothers, Inc., a corporation incorporated and doing business in Kansas, decides to sell common stock worth $1 million to the public. The stock will be sold only within the state of Kansas. Joseph Langley, the chair of the board, says the offering need not be registered with the Securities and Exchange Commission. His brother, Harry, disagrees. Who is right? Explain. (See *Securities Act of 1933.*)

30–2. Insider Trading. David Gain is the chief executive officer (CEO) of Forest Media Corp., which is interested in acquiring RS Communications, Inc. To initiate negotiations, Gain meets with RS's CEO, Gill Raz, on Friday, July 12. Two days later, Gain phones his brother, Mark, who buys 3,800 shares of RS stock on the following Monday. Mark discusses the deal with their father, Jordan, who buys 20,000 RS shares on Thursday. On July 25, the day before the RS bid is due, Gain phones his parents' home, and Mark buys another 3,200 RS shares. Over the next few days, Gain periodically phones Mark and Jordan, both of whom continued to buy RS shares. On August 5, RS refuses Forest's bid and announces that it is merging with another company. The price of RS stock rises 30 percent, increasing the value of Mark's and Jordan's shares by nearly $660,000 and $400,000, respectively. Is Gain guilty of insider trading? What is required to impose sanctions for this offense? Could a court hold Gain liable? Why or why not? (See *Securities Exchange Act of 1934.*)

30–3. Violations of the 1934 Act. Matrixx Initiatives, Inc., makes and sells over-the-counter pharmaceutical products. Its core brand is Zicam, which accounts for 70 percent of its sales. Matrixx received reports that some consumers had lost their sense of smell (a condition called *anosmia*) after using Zicam Cold Remedy. Four product liability suits were filed against Matrixx, seeking damages for anosmia. In public statements relating to revenues and product safety, however, Matrixx did not reveal this information.

James Siracusano and other Matrixx investors filed a suit in a federal district court against the company and its executives under Section 10(b) of the Securities Exchange Act of 1934 and SEC Rule 10b-5, claiming that the statements were misleading because they did not disclose the information about the product liability suits. Matrixx argued that to be material, information must consist of a statistically significant number of adverse events that require disclosure. Because Siracusano's claim did not allege that Matrixx knew of a statistically significant number of adverse events, the company contended that the claim should be dismissed. What is the standard for materiality in this context? Should Siracusano's claim be dismissed? Explain. [*Matrixx Initiatives, Inc. v. Siracusano,* 563 U.S. 27, 131 S.Ct. 1309, 179 L.Ed.2d 398 (2011)] (See *Securities Exchange Act of 1934.*)

30–4. Business Case Problem with Sample Answer—Disclosure under SEC Rule 10b-5. Dodona I, LLC, invested $4 million in two securities offerings from Goldman, Sachs & Co. The investments were in collateralized debt obligations (CDOs). Their value depended on residential mortgage-backed securities (RMBSs), whose value in turn depended on the performance of subprime residential mortgages. Before marketing the CDOs, Goldman had noticed several "red flags" relating to investments in the subprime market, in which it had invested heavily.

To limit its risk, Goldman began betting against subprime mortgages, RMBSs, and CDOs, including the CDOs it had sold to Dodona. In other words, Goldman made investments based on the assumption that subprime mortgages and the securities instruments built upon them would decrease in value. In an internal e-mail, one Goldman official commented that the company had managed to "make some lemonade from some big old lemons." Nevertheless, Goldman's marketing materials provided only boilerplate statements about the risks of investing in the securities. The CDOs were later downgraded to junk status, and Dodona suffered a major loss while Goldman profited. Assuming that Goldman did not affirmatively misrepresent any facts about the CDOs, can Dodona still recover under SEC Rule 10b-5? If so, how? [*Dodona I, LLC v. Goldman, Sachs & Co.,* 847 F.Supp.2d 624 (S.D.N.Y. 2012)] (See *Securities Exchange Act of 1934.*)

—For a sample answer to Problem 30–4, go to Appendix E.

30–5. Violations of the 1933 Act. Three shareholders of iStorage sought to sell their stock through World Trade Financial Corp. The shares were *restricted securities*—that is, securities acquired in an unregistered, private sale. Restricted securities typically bear a "restrictive" legend clearly stating that they cannot be resold in the public marketplace. This legend had been wrongly removed from the iStorage shares, however. Information about the company that was publicly available included the fact that, despite a ten-year life, it had no operating history or earnings. In addition, it had net losses of about $200,000, and its stock was thinly traded. Without investigating the company or the status of its stock, World Trade sold more than 2.3 million shares to the public on behalf of the three customers. Did World Trade violate the Securities Act of 1933? Discuss. [*World Trade Financial Corp. v. Securities and Exchange Commission*, 739 F.3d 1243 (9th Cir. 2014)] (See *Securities Act of 1933*.)

30–6. Securities Act of 1933. Big Apple Consulting USA, Inc., provided small publicly traded companies with a variety of services, including marketing, business planning, and website development and maintenance. CyberKey Corp. sold customizable USB drives. CyberKey falsely informed Big Apple that CyberKey had been awarded a $25 million contract with the Department of Homeland Security (DHS). Big Apple used this information in aggressively promoting CyberKey's stock and was compensated for the effort in the form of CyberKey shares. When the Securities and Exchange Commission (SEC) began to investigate, Big Apple sold its shares for $7.8 million. The SEC filed an action in a federal district court against Big Apple, alleging a violation of the Securities Act of 1933. Can liability be imposed on a seller for a false statement that was made by someone else? Explain. [*U.S. Securities and Exchange Commission v. Big Apple Consulting USA, Inc.*, 783 F.3d 786 (11th Cir. 2015)] (See *Securities Act of 1933*.)

30–7. The Securities Exchange Act of 1934. Dilean Reyes-Rivera was the president of Global Reach Trading (GRT), a corporation registered in Puerto Rico. His brother Jeffrey was the firm's accountant. Along with GRT sales agents and other promoters, the brothers solicited funds from individuals by promising to invest the funds in low-risk, short-term, high-yield securities. The investors were guaranteed a rate of return of up to 20 percent. Through this arrangement, more than 230 persons provided the brothers with about $22 million. This money was not actually invested. Instead, the funds received from later investors were used to pay "returns" to earlier investors. The Reyes-Riveras spent $4.6 million of the proceeds to buy luxury vehicles, houses, furniture, jewelry, and trips for themselves. What is this type of scheme called? What are the potential consequences? Discuss. [*United States v. Reyes-Rivera*, 812 F.3d 79 (1st Cir. 2016)] (See *Securities Exchange Act of 1934*.)

30–8. Securities Fraud. First Solar, Inc., is one of the world's largest producers of photovoltaic solar panel modules. When First Solar revealed to the market that the company had discovered defects in its products, the price of the company's stock fell, causing the shareholders to suffer an economic loss. Mineworkers' Pension Scheme and other First Solar shareholders filed a suit in a federal district court against the firm and its officers, alleging a violation of Section 10(b). The plaintiffs contended that for more than two years, First Solar had wrongfully concealed its discovery, misrepresented the cost and scope of the defects, and reported false information on financial statements. On these facts, can the plaintiffs successfully plead the causation element of a securities fraud action under Section 10(b)? Explain. [*Mineworkers' Pension Scheme. v. First Solar Inc.*, 881 F.3d 750 (9th Cir. 2018)] (See *Securities Exchange Act of 1934*.)

30–9. A Question of Ethics—The IDDR Approach and InsiderTrading. Nan Huang was a senior data analyst for Capital One Financial Corporation. In violation of the company's confidentiality policies, Huang downloaded and analyzed confidential information regarding purchases made with Capital One credit cards at more than 200 consumer retail companies and used that information to conduct more than 2,000 trades in the securities of those companies. Capital One terminated Huang due to his violation of the company's policies. The next day, Huang boarded a flight to his home country of China. Four days later, the Securities and Exchange Commission filed a complaint against Huang, alleging violations of Section 10(b) and Rule 10b-5. [*Securities and Exchange Commission v. Huang*, 684 Fed. Appx. 167 (3d Cir. 2017)] (See *Securities Exchange Act of 1934*.)

1. Evaluate the ethics of Huang's actions, as an employee of Capital One, using the IDDR approach.
2. When Capital One learned what Huang had done, was the company ethically obligated to terminate him? Explain.

Critical Thinking and Writing Assignments

30–10. Time-Limited Group Assignment—Violations of Securities Laws. Karel Svoboda, a credit officer for Rogue Bank, evaluated and approved his employer's extensions of credit to clients. These responsibilities gave Svoboda access to nonpublic information about the clients' earnings, performance, acquisitions, and business plans from confidential memos, e-mail, and other sources. Svoboda devised a scheme with Alena Robles, an independent accountant, to use this information to trade securities. Pursuant to their scheme, Robles traded in the securities of more than twenty different companies and profited by more than $2 million. Svoboda also executed trades for his own profit of more than $800,000, despite their agreement that Robles would do all of the trading. Aware that their scheme violated Rogue Bank's policy, they attempted to conduct their trades in such a way as to avoid suspicion. When the bank questioned Svoboda about his actions, he lied, refused to cooperate, and was fired. (See *Securities Exchange Act of 1934*.)

1. The first group will determine whether Svoboda or Robles committed any crimes.
2. The second group will decide whether Svoboda or Robles is subject to civil liability. If so, who could file a suit and on what ground? What are the possible sanctions?
3. A third group will identify any defenses that Svoboda or Robles could raise and determine whether the defenses would be likely to succeed.

Unit Five—Task-Based Simulation

Devonyu/iStock/Getty Images

John leases an office and buys computer equipment. Initially, to pay for the lease and the equipment, he goes into the business of designing applications for smartphones. He also has an idea for a new software product that he hopes will be more profitable than designing apps. Whenever he has time, he works on the software.

1. **Selecting a Business Organization.** After six months, Mary and Paul come to work in the office to help develop John's idea. John continues to pay the rent and other expenses, including salaries for Mary and Paul. John does not expect to make a profit until the software is developed, which could take months. Even then, there may be very little profit unless the product is marketed successfully. If the software is successful, though, John believes that the firm will be able to follow up with other products. In choosing a form of business organization for this firm, what are the important considerations? What are the advantages and disadvantages of each basic option?

2. **Corporate Nature and Classification.** It is decided that the organizational form for this firm should provide limited liability for the owners. The owners will include John, Mary, Paul, and some members of their respective families. Limited liability is one of the features of the corporate form. Ordinarily, however, corporate income is taxed at both the corporate level and the shareholder level. Which corporate form could the firm use to avoid this double taxation? Which other forms of business organization provide limited liability? What factors, other than liability and taxation, influence a firm's choice among these forms?

3. **Duties of Corporate Directors.** The firm is incorporated as Digital Software, Inc. (DSI). The software is developed and marketed successfully, and DSI prospers. John, Mary, and Paul become directors of DSI. At a board meeting, Paul proposes a marketing strategy for DSI's next product, and John and Mary approve it. Implementing the strategy causes DSI's profits to drop. If the shareholders accuse Paul of breaching his fiduciary duty to DSI, what is Paul's most likely defense? If the shareholders accuse John and Mary of the same breach, what is their best defense? In either case, if the shareholders file a suit, how is a court likely to rule?

4. **Securities Regulation.** Mary and Paul withdraw from DSI to set up their own firm. To obtain operating capital, they solicit investors, who agree to become "general partners." Mary and Paul designate themselves "managing partners." The investors are spread over a wide area geographically and learn about Mary and Paul's business only through contact from Mary and Paul. Are Mary and Paul truly soliciting partners, or are they selling securities? What are the criteria for determining whether an investment is a security? What are the advantages and disadvantages of selling securities versus soliciting partners?

Michal Kalasek/Shutterstock.com

Unit 6 Government Regulation

hafakot/Shutterstock.com

31 Antitrust Law and Promoting Competition

Focus Questions

The six *Focus Questions* below are designed to help improve your understanding. After reading this chapter, you should be able to answer the following questions:

1. What is a monopoly? What is market power? How do these concepts relate to each other?
2. What rule do courts apply to price-fixing agreements, and why?
3. What two types of activities are prohibited by Section 2 of the Sherman Act?
4. What are the four major provisions of the Clayton Act, and what types of activities do these provisions prohibit?
5. What agencies of the federal government enforce the federal antitrust laws?
6. When will a U.S. court apply the Sherman Act to foreign persons or entities?

"Competition is not only the basis of protection to the consumer but is the incentive to progress."

Herbert Hoover 1874–1964
(Thirty-first president of the United States, 1929–1933)

The laws regulating economic competition in the United States are referred to as *antitrust laws*. They include the Sherman Antitrust Act of 1890,[1] the Clayton Act,[2] and the Federal Trade Commission Act,[3] passed by Congress to further curb anticompetitive and unfair business practices. Congress later amended these acts to broaden and strengthen their coverage.

The basis of antitrust legislation is our society's desire to foster competition. As President Herbert Hoover said in the chapter-opening quotation, competition not only protects the consumer, but also provides "the incentive to progress." Consumers and society as a whole benefit when producers strive to develop better products that they can sell at lower prices to beat the competition.

How do antitrust laws promote competition? Suppose that Select Seafood Company is one of five major producers of prepackaged seafood in the United States. Casey Bowman, Select's chief executive officer, has been meeting with leaders of the other four producers for the last several years. They discuss market developments, supply issues, and other matters of common interest. But what if they were to agree eventually to work together to control the price of packaged seafood in the United States? Such a price-fixing agreement would be illegal because it would harm competition. If the government found out about it, the firms could be prosecuted under the laws discussed in this chapter.

1. 15 U.S.C. Sections 1–7.
2. 15 U.S.C. Sections 12–27.
3. 15 U.S.C. Sections 41–58.

31–1 The Sherman Antitrust Act

Today's **antitrust laws** are the direct descendants of common law actions intended to limit *restraints of trade* (agreements between or among firms that have the effect of reducing competition in the marketplace). Such actions date to the fifteenth century in England.

Antitrust Laws Laws protecting commerce from unlawful restraints and anticompetitive practices.

After the U.S. Civil War (1861–1865), the American public became increasingly concerned about declining competition in the marketplace. Large corporate enterprises were attempting to reduce or eliminate competition by legally tying themselves together in contracts to create *business trusts* (unincorporated organizations with limited liability). The most powerful of these organizations was the Standard Oil trust.

In 1890, Congress passed "An Act to Protect Trade and Commerce against Unlawful Restraints and Monopolies"—commonly known as the Sherman Antitrust Act or, more simply, as the Sherman Act. The Sherman Act became (and still is) one of the government's most powerful weapons in the effort to maintain a competitive economy. The act and the role of the Standard Oil trust in its passage are examined in this chapter's *Landmark in the Law* feature.

31–1a Major Provisions of the Sherman Act

Sections 1 and 2 contain the main provisions of the Sherman Act:

1. Every contract, combination in the form of trust or otherwise, or conspiracy, in restraint of trade or commerce among the several States, or with foreign nations, is hereby declared to be illegal [and is a felony punishable by a fine and/or imprisonment].

The Sherman Antitrust Act

The author of the Sherman Antitrust Act, Senator John Sherman, was the brother of the famous Civil War general William Tecumseh Sherman and a recognized financial authority. Sherman had been concerned for years about diminishing competition in U.S. industry and the emergence of monopolies, such as the Standard Oil trust.

The Standard Oil Trust By 1890, the Standard Oil trust had become the foremost petroleum refining and marketing combination in the United States. Streamlined, integrated, and centrally controlled, Standard Oil maintained an indisputable monopoly over the industry. The trust controlled 90 percent of the U.S. market for refined petroleum products, making it impossible for small producers to compete.

The increasing consolidation in U.S. industry, and particularly the Standard Oil trust, came to the attention of the public in March 1881. Henry Demarest Lloyd, a young journalist from Chicago, published an article in the *Atlantic Monthly* entitled "The Story of a Great Monopoly." The article argued that the U.S. petroleum industry was dominated by one firm—Standard Oil. Lloyd's article was so popular that the issue was reprinted six times. It marked the beginning of the U.S. public's growing concern over monopolies.

The Passage of the Sherman Antitrust Act The common law regarding trade regulation was not always consistent. Certainly, it was not very familiar to the members of Congress. The public concern over large business trusts was familiar, however. In 1888, 1889, and again in 1890, Senator Sherman introduced in Congress bills designed to destroy the large combinations of capital that, he felt, were creating imbalance within the nation's economy.

In 1890, the Fifty-First Congress finally enacted the bill into law. Generally, the act prohibits business combinations and conspiracies that restrain trade and commerce, as well as certain monopolistic practices. According to its author, the Sherman Act "does not announce a new principle of law, but applies old and well-recognized principles of the common law."[a]

Application to Today's World *The Sherman Antitrust Act remains very relevant to today's world. The U.S. Department of Justice and state attorneys general investigate many complaints and prosecute a number of corporations for Sherman Act violations each year.*

a. 21 *Congressional Record* 2456 (1890).

Focus Question 1

What is a monopoly? What is market power? How do these concepts relate to each other?

2. Every person who shall monopolize, or attempt to monopolize, or combine or conspire with any other person or persons, to monopolize any part of the trade or commerce among the several States, or with foreign nations, shall be deemed guilty of a felony [and is similarly punishable].

31–1b Differences between Section 1 and Section 2

The two sections of the Sherman Act are quite different. Violation of Section 1 requires two or more persons, as a person cannot contract or combine or conspire alone. Thus, the essence of the illegal activity is *the act of joining together.* Section 2, though, can apply either to one person or to two or more persons because it refers to "every person." Thus, unilateral conduct can result in a violation of Section 2.

It follows that the cases brought under Section 1 of the Sherman Act differ from those brought under Section 2. Section 1 cases are often concerned with finding an agreement (written or oral) that leads to a restraint of trade. Section 2 cases deal with the structure of a monopoly that already exists in the marketplace.

Monopoly A market in which there is a single seller or a very limited number of sellers.

Monopoly Power The ability of a monopoly to dictate what takes place in a given market.

Market Power The power of a firm to control the market price of its product. A monopoly has the greatest degree of market power.

The term **monopoly** generally is used to describe a market in which there is a single seller or a very limited number of sellers. Whereas Section 1 focuses on agreements that are restrictive—that is, agreements that have a wrongful purpose—Section 2 addresses the misuse of **monopoly power** in the marketplace. Monopoly power exists when a firm has an extreme amount of **market power**—the power to affect the market price of its product.

Both Section 1 and Section 2 seek to curtail market practices that result in undesired monopoly pricing and output behavior. For a case to be brought under Section 2, however, the "threshold" or "necessary" amount of monopoly power must already exist. We illustrate the different requirements for violating these two sections of the Sherman Act in Exhibit 31–1.

31–1c Jurisdictional Requirements

The Sherman Act applies only to restraints that have a substantial impact on interstate commerce. Generally, any activity that substantially affects interstate commerce falls within the scope of the Sherman Act. The Sherman Act also extends to U.S. nationals abroad who are engaged in activities that have an effect on U.S. foreign commerce.

Federal courts have exclusive jurisdiction over antitrust cases brought under the Sherman Act. State laws regulate local restraints on competition, and state courts decide claims brought under those laws.

In the following case, the defendants argued that their bid-rigging scheme did not fall under the Sherman Act because the proof of a connection between the scheme and interstate commerce fell short.

Exhibit 31–1 Required Elements of a Sherman Act Violation

SECTION 1 VIOLATION REQUIREMENTS	SECTION 2 VIOLATION REQUIREMENTS
1. An agreement between two or more parties that 2. unreasonably restrains competition and 3. affects interstate commerce.	1. The possession of monopoly power in the relevant market, and 2. the willful acquisition or maintenance of that power as distinguished from growth or development as a consequence of a superior product, business acumen, or historic accident.

Case 31.1

United States v. Vega-Martínez

United States Court of Appeals, First Circuit, 949 F.3d 43 (2020).

Facts Private bus companies owned by Luciano Vega-Martínez and others provided busing for students to public schools in Caguas, Puerto Rico. The municipality announced that it would hold an auction for four-year school bus transportation contracts. Instead of submitting competing bids, the bus company owners met and agreed to divide up the routes among themselves. For each route, they designated a "winner" whose noncompetitive "low" bid would not be outbid by the others.

Unaware of the bid rigging, the municipality awarded the routes to the "low bidders." When the scheme was revealed, two years into the four-year term of the contracts, the federal government charged the owners of the bus companies with conspiracy to restrain trade in violation of the Sherman Act. A jury convicted the defendants, and a federal district court sentenced them to prison terms and ordered restitution.

Vega-Martínez appealed, contending that the bid rigging did not fall under the Sherman Act because there was insufficient proof of a connection between the scheme and interstate commerce.

Issue Did the defendants' conduct take place in the flow of interstate commerce, or did it substantially affect interstate commerce?

Decision Yes. The U.S. Court of Appeals for the First Circuit affirmed the trial court's determination. The appellate court also upheld the defendants' convictions, their prison sentences, and the trial court's order for restitution.

Reason The appellate court recognized that the Sherman Act "reaches only activities in the flow of interstate commerce or that, while wholly local in nature, would substantially affect interstate commerce if successful." Bid rigging is a form of price fixing. In such cases, there is "almost surely" an impact on the relevant market and therefore an effect on interstate commerce.

Here, the government provided sufficient evidence to establish a connection between the defendants' activities and interstate commerce "beyond a reasonable doubt." The federal government provided the funds used to pay the conspirators. In the court's estimation, the defendants' "grab" of those funds was alone sufficient to establish an interstate connection, "given that the funds flowed in interstate commerce."

But there was more. The buses that the defendants planned to use for their routes were all bought in Florida. This meant that they "flowed" in interstate commerce. If the prices for the buses increased substantially, the demand for buses would be affected. The court noted, for example, that if the municipality merged bus routes or reduced the services in other ways, the result might be fewer buses bought by local companies from Florida or other states.

"The evidence in total was sufficient to establish a nexus with interstate commerce."

Critical Thinking

- **Legal Environment** *Could the defendants have successfully argued that their agreement to rig bids and allocate the market for public school bus transportation was reasonable, or that it could be justified on an economic or business basis? Explain.*
- **Economic** *Following the discovery of the bid-rigging scheme, Caguas held a presumably fair auction to award new school bus transportation contracts. Could the bids in the second auction provide a basis for determining the restitution amounts? Discuss.*

31–2 Section 1 of the Sherman Act

The underlying assumption of Section 1 of the Sherman Act is that society's welfare is harmed if rival firms are permitted to join in an agreement that consolidates their market power or otherwise restrains competition. The types of trade restraints that Section 1 of the Sherman Act prohibits generally fall into two broad categories: *horizontal restraints* and *vertical restraints*, both of which will be explained shortly. First, though, we look at the rules that the courts may apply when assessing the anticompetitive impact of alleged restraints on trade.

31–2a *Per Se* Violations versus the Rule of Reason

Some restraints are so blatantly and substantially anticompetitive that they are deemed a ***per se* violation**—illegal *per se* (on their face, or inherently)—under Section 1. Other agreements, however, even though they result in enhanced market power, do not *unreasonably*

***Per Se* Violation** A restraint of trade that is so anticompetitive that it is deemed inherently (*per se*) illegal.

Rule of Reason A test used to determine whether an anticompetitive agreement constitutes a reasonable restraint on trade. Courts consider such factors as the purpose of the agreement, its effect on competition, and whether less restrictive means could have been used.

restrain trade. Using what is called the **rule of reason**, the courts analyze anticompetitive agreements that allegedly violate Section 1 of the Sherman Act to determine whether they actually constitute reasonable restraints on trade.

Why the Rule of Reason Was Developed The need for a rule-of-reason analysis of some agreements in restraint of trade is obvious—if the rule of reason had not been developed, almost any business agreement could conceivably be held to violate the Sherman Act. Justice Louis Brandeis effectively phrased this sentiment in *Chicago Board of Trade v. United States,* a case decided in 1918:

> Every agreement concerning trade, every regulation of trade, restrains. To bind, to restrain, is of their very essence. The true test of legality is whether the restraint imposed is such as merely regulates and perhaps thereby promotes competition or whether it is such as may suppress or even destroy competition.[4]

Factors Courts Consider under the Rule of Reason When analyzing an alleged Section 1 violation under the rule of reason, a court will consider the following factors:

1. The purpose of the agreement.
2. The parties' ability to implement the agreement to achieve that purpose.
3. The effect or potential effect of the agreement on competition.
4. Whether the parties could have relied on less restrictive means to achieve their purpose.

Dmitry Kalinovsky/Shutterstock.com

Does forcing consumers to buy bundles of cable and satellite channels constitute an antitrust violation?

Spotlight Case Example 31.1 A group of consumers sued NBC Universal, the Walt Disney Company, and other broadcasters, as well as cable and satellite distributors, for antitrust violations. The consumers claimed that the bundling together of high-demand and low-demand television channels in cable and satellite programming packages violates the Sherman Act. Bundling forces consumers to pay for channels they do not watch to have access to channels they watch regularly.

The consumers argued that the defendants, through their control of high-demand programming, exercised market power that made it impossible for any distributor to offer unbundled programs. A federal appellate court ruled in favor of the defendants and dismissed the case. The court reasoned that the bundling of channels does not injure competition and thus does not violate the Sherman Act.[5]

31–2b Horizontal Restraints

Horizontal Restraint Any agreement that restrains competition between rival firms competing in the same market.

The term **horizontal restraint** is encountered frequently in antitrust law. A horizontal restraint is any agreement that in some way restrains competition between rival firms competing in the same market. Horizontal restraints may include price fixing, group boycotts, market divisions, and trade associations.

Price-Fixing Agreement An agreement between competitors to fix the prices of products or services at a certain level.

Price Fixing Any **price-fixing agreement**—an agreement among competitors to fix prices—constitutes a *per se* violation of Section 1. The agreement on price need not be explicit. As long as it restricts output or artificially fixes price, it violates the law.

Classic Case Example 31.2 Independent oil producers in Texas and Louisiana were caught between falling demand due to the Great Depression of the 1930s and increasing supply from newly discovered oil fields in the region. In response to these conditions, a group of major

4. 246 U.S. 231, 38 S.Ct. 242, 62 L.Ed. 683 (1918).
5. *Brantley v. NBC Universal, Inc.*, 675 F.3d 1192 (9th Cir. 2012).

refining companies agreed to buy "distress" gasoline (excess supplies) from the independents so as to dispose of it in an "orderly manner." Although there was no explicit agreement as to price, it was clear that the purpose of the agreement was to limit the supply of gasoline on the market and thereby raise prices.

Focus Question 2

What rule do courts apply to price-fixing agreements, and why?

There may have been good reasons for the agreement. Nonetheless, the United States Supreme Court recognized the potentially adverse effects that such an agreement could have on open and free competition. The Court held that the reasonableness of a price-fixing agreement is never a defense. Any agreement that restricts output or artificially fixes price is a *per se* violation of Section 1.[6]

Price-fixing cartels (groups) are commonplace in today's business world, particularly among global companies. International price-fixing cartels have been alleged in numerous industries, including air freight, auto parts, computer monitors, digital commerce, and pharmaceuticals. The U.S. government actively pursues companies that it suspects of being involved in price-fixing cartels.

Case Example 31.3 After Amazon released the Kindle e-book reader, it began selling e-book downloads at $9.99 (lower than the actual cost) and made up the difference by selling more Kindles. When the iPad entered the e-book scene, Apple and some book publishers agreed to use Apple's "agency" model, which Apple was already using for games and apps. The agency model allowed the book publishers to set their own prices, while Apple kept 30 percent as a commission.

The U.S. government sued Apple and the publishers for price fixing. Because the publishers involved in the arrangement chose prices that were relatively similar, the government argued that price fixing was evident and "would not have occurred without the conspiracy among the defendants." Ultimately, a federal appellate court held that Apple's agreement with publishers was a *per se* illegal price-fixing conspiracy. As a result, Apple was ordered to pay $400 million to consumers and $50 million in attorneys' fees.[7]

Group Boycotts A **group boycott** is an agreement by two or more sellers to refuse to deal with (that is, to boycott) a particular person or firm. Because they involve concerted action, group boycotts have been held to constitute *per se* violations of Section 1 of the Sherman Act. To prove a violation of Section 1, the plaintiff must demonstrate that the boycott or joint refusal to deal was undertaken with the intention of eliminating competition or preventing entry into a given market. Most boycotts are illegal. A few types of boycotts, such as group boycotts against a supplier for political reasons, may be protected under the First Amendment right to freedom of expression, however.

Group Boycott An agreement by two or more sellers to refuse to deal with a particular person or firm.

Market Divisions It is a *per se* violation of Section 1 of the Sherman Act for competitors to divide up territories or customers. **Example 31.4** Bell TV Basics, Hall Servo Supplies, and Prime Electronics compete against each other in the states of Kansas, Nebraska, and Oklahoma. The three firms agree that Bell will sell products only in Kansas, Hall will sell only in Nebraska, and Prime will sell only in Oklahoma. This concerted action violates Section 1 of the Sherman Act. It reduces marketing costs and allows all three firms (assuming there is no other competition) to raise the price of the goods they sell in their respective states.

The same violation would take place if the three firms divided up their customers by class rather than region. They might agree that Bell would sell only to institutional purchasers (such as governments and schools) in all three states, Hall only to wholesalers, and Prime only to retailers. The result would be the same.

Grzegorz Czapski/Shutterstock.com

Is it legal for three separate manufacturers of smart televisions to agree to divide up their sales into three separate geographical areas?

6. *United States v. Socony-Vacuum Oil Co.*, 310 U.S. 150, 60 S.Ct. 811, 84 L.Ed. 1129 (1940).
7. *United States v. Apple, Inc.*, 791 F.3d 290 (2d Cir. 2015). Apple had previously agreed to settle the case for these amounts if its appeal was unsuccessful.

Trade Associations Businesses in the same general industry or profession frequently organize trade associations to pursue common interests. A trade association may engage in various joint activities, such as exchanging information, representing the members' business interests before governmental bodies, conducting advertising campaigns, and setting regulatory standards to govern the industry or profession.

Generally, the rule of reason is applied to many of these horizontal actions. If a court finds that a trade association practice or agreement that restrains trade is sufficiently beneficial both to the association and to the public, it may deem the restraint reasonable.

Concentrated Industry An industry in which a single firm or a small number of firms control a large percentage of market sales.

In concentrated industries, however, trade associations can be, and have been, used as a means to facilitate anticompetitive actions, such as fixing prices or allocating markets. A **concentrated industry** is one in which either a single firm or a small number of firms control a large percentage of market sales. When trade association agreements have substantially anticompetitive effects, a court will consider them to be in violation of Section 1 of the Sherman Act.

31–2c Vertical Restraints

Vertical Restraint A restraint of trade created by an agreement between firms at different levels in the manufacturing and distribution process.

Vertically Integrated Firm A firm that carries out two or more functional phases (manufacturing, distribution, and retailing, for instance) of the chain of production.

A **vertical restraint** of trade results from an agreement between firms at different levels in the manufacturing and distribution process. In contrast to horizontal relationships, which occur at the same level of operation, vertical relationships encompass the entire chain of production. The chain of production normally includes the purchase of inventory, basic manufacturing, distribution to wholesalers, and eventual sale of a product at the retail level. When a single firm carries out two or more of the separate functional phases, it is considered to be a **vertically integrated firm**.

Even though firms operating at different functional levels are not in direct competition with one another, they are in competition with other firms. Thus, agreements between firms standing in a vertical relationship may affect competition. Some vertical restraints are *per se* violations of Section 1. Others are judged under the rule of reason.

Territorial or Customer Restrictions In arranging for the distribution of its products, a manufacturing firm often wishes to insulate dealers from direct competition with other dealers selling the product. To do so, it may institute territorial restrictions or attempt to prohibit wholesalers or retailers from reselling the product to certain classes of buyers, such as competing retailers.

May Have Legitimate Purpose. A firm may have legitimate reasons for imposing such territorial or customer restrictions. For instance, an electronics manufacturer may wish to prevent a dealer from reducing costs and undercutting rivals by offering the manufacturer's products without promotion or customer service. In this situation, the cost-cutting dealer reaps the benefits (sales of the product) paid for by other dealers who undertake promotion and arrange for customer service. By not providing customer service (and relying on a nearby dealer to provide the service), the cost-cutting dealer may also harm the manufacturer's reputation.

Judged under the Rule of Reason. Territorial and customer restrictions were once considered *per se* violations of Section 1. In 1977, however the United States Supreme Court held that they should be judged under the rule of reason. **Classic Case Example 31.5** The Supreme Court case involved GTE Sylvania, Inc., a manufacturer of television sets. Sylvania limited the number of retail franchises that it granted in any given geographic area. It also required each franchise to sell only Sylvania products from that location.

Sylvania retained sole discretion to increase the number of retailers in an area. When the company decided to open a new franchise, it terminated the franchise of Continental T.V., Inc. Continental sued, claiming that Sylvania's vertically restrictive franchise system violated

Section 1. The Supreme Court found that "vertical restrictions promote interbrand competition by allowing the manufacturer to achieve certain efficiencies in the distribution of his products." Therefore, Sylvania's vertical system, which was not price restrictive, did not constitute a *per se* violation of Section 1 of the Sherman Act.[8]

The decision in the *Continental* case marked a definite shift from rigid characterization of these kinds of vertical restraints to a more flexible, economic analysis under the rule of reason. A firm may have legitimate reasons for imposing territorial or customer restrictions, and not all such restrictions harm competition.

Resale Price Maintenance Agreements An agreement between a manufacturer and a distributor or retailer in which the manufacturer specifies what the retail prices of its products must be is referred to as a **resale price maintenance agreement**. Such agreements were also once considered to be *per se* violations of the Sherman Act.

Resale Price Maintenance Agreement An agreement between a manufacturer and a retailer in which the manufacturer specifies what the retail prices of its products must be.

Today, however, both *maximum* resale price maintenance agreements and *minimum* resale price maintenance agreements are judged under the rule of reason.[9] The setting of a maximum—or a minimum—price that retailers and distributors can charge for a manufacturer's products may sometimes increase competition and benefit consumers.

31–3 Section 2 of the Sherman Act

Focus Question 3

What two types of activities are prohibited by Section 2 of the Sherman Act?

Section 1 of the Sherman Act prohibits certain concerted activities that restrain trade. In contrast, Section 2 condemns "every person who shall monopolize, or attempt to monopolize." Thus, two distinct types of behavior are subject to sanction under Section 2: *monopolization* and *attempts to monopolize*.

One tactic that may be involved in either offense is **predatory pricing**. Predatory pricing involves an attempt by one firm to drive its competitors from the market by selling its product at prices substantially *below* the normal costs of production. Once the competitors are eliminated, the firm will presumably attempt to recapture its losses and go on to earn higher profits by driving prices up far above their competitive levels.

Predatory Pricing The pricing of a product below cost with the intent to drive competitors out of the market.

31–3a Monopolization

The United States Supreme Court has defined the offense of **monopolization** as involving two elements:

Monopolization The possession of monopoly power in the relevant market and the willful acquisition or maintenance of that power, as distinguished from growth or development as a consequence of a superior product, business acumen, or historic accident.

1. The possession of monopoly power in the relevant market.
2. "The willful acquisition or maintenance of [that] power as distinguished from growth or development as a consequence of a superior product, business acumen, or historic accident."[10]

To establish a violation of Section 2, a plaintiff must prove both of these elements—monopoly power and an intent to monopolize.

Defining Monopoly Power The Sherman Act does not define *monopoly*. In economic theory, monopoly refers to control of a single market by a single entity. It is well established in antitrust law, however, that a firm may be deemed a monopolist even though it is not the sole seller in a market.

8. *Continental T.V., Inc. v. GTE Sylvania, Inc.*, 433 U.S. 36, 97 S.Ct. 2549, 53 L.Ed.2d 568 (1977).
9. The United States Supreme Court ruled that maximum resale price agreements should be judged under the rule of reason in *State Oil Co. v. Khan*, 522 U.S. 3, 118 S.Ct. 275, 139 L.Ed.2d 199 (1997). In *Leegin Creative Leather Products, Inc. v. PSKS, Inc.*, 551 U.S. 877, 127 S.Ct. 2705, 168 L.Ed.2d 623 (2007), the Supreme Court found that the rule of reason also applies to minimum resale price agreements.
10. *United States v. Grinnell Corp.*, 384 U.S. 563, 86 S.Ct. 1698, 16 L.Ed.2d 778 (1966).

Additionally, size alone does not determine whether a firm is a monopoly. For instance, a "mom and pop" grocery located in an isolated town is a monopolist if it is the only grocery serving that particular market. Size in relation to the market is what matters, because monopoly involves the power to affect prices.

Proving Monopoly Power Monopoly power may be proved by direct evidence that the firm used its power to control prices and restrict output. Usually, though, there is not enough evidence to show that the firm was intentionally controlling prices, so the plaintiff has to offer indirect, or circumstantial, evidence of monopoly power.

To prove monopoly power indirectly, the plaintiff must show that the firm has a dominant share of the relevant market and that there are significant barriers for new competitors entering that market. A plaintiff must also show that the relevant market is a market capable of being monopolized. **Case Example 31.6** Global distribution systems (GDSs) are electronic networks that travel agents use to book flights for their clients. Sabre Holding Corporation dominates the GDS market to the extent that travel agents have little choice but to use its platforms. Taking advantage of this position, Sabre negotiated highly favorable agreements with the airlines. US Airways, Inc., a Sabre client, sued the company for illegally monopolizing the travel-agent GDS market in violation of Section 2. A district court dismissed the lawsuit, noting that Sabre was the only company that offered its specific services to travel agents. Thus, it could not, wrongly monopolize a market that was limited to its own customers.

A federal appellate court disagreed, holding that "a single brand of a product or service" can be a relevant market for antitrust purposes when no substitute exists for that product or service. In other words, it was possible that travel agents—and airlines—were unfairly "locked into" working with Sabre. Therefore, the court ruled US Airways (which later merged with American Airlines) should be given the chance to prove that Sabre was operating as an illegal monopoly in this instance.[11]

VGstockstudio/Shutterstock.com

Under what circumstances can a company that offers a single product or service, such as booking networks for travel agents, be considered a "relevant market" under Section 2 of the Sherman Act?

Relevant Market Before a court can determine whether a firm has a dominant market share, it must define the relevant market. The relevant market consists of two elements: a relevant product market and a relevant geographic market.

Relevant Product Market. The relevant product market includes all products that, although produced by different firms, have identical attributes—for example, tea. It also includes reasonably interchangeable products. Products are considered reasonably interchangeable if consumers treat them as acceptable substitutes (coffee may be substituted for tea, for instance).

Establishing the relevant product market is often a key issue in monopolization cases because the way the market is defined may determine whether a firm has monopoly power. When the product market is defined narrowly, the degree of a firm's market power appears greater. **Example 31.7** White Whale Apps acquires Springleaf Apps, its main competitor in nationwide Android-based mobile phone apps. White Whale maintains that the relevant product market consists of all online retailers of mobile phone apps. The Federal Trade Commission (FTC), however, argues that the relevant product market consists of retailers that sell only apps for Android mobile phones. Under the FTC's narrower definition, White Whale can be seen to have a dominant share of the relevant product market. Thus, the FTC can take appropriate actions against White Whale.

11. *US Airways, Inc. v. Sabre Holdings Corp.*, 938 F.3d 43 (2nd Cir. 2019).

Relevant Geographic Market. The second component of the relevant market is the market's geographic extent. For products that are sold nationwide, the geographic market encompasses the entire United States. If transportation costs are significant or a producer and its competitors sell in only a limited area (one in which customers have no access to other sources of the product), the geographic market is limited to that area. A national firm may thus compete in several distinct areas and have monopoly power in one area but not in another.

Generally, the geographic market is that section of the country within which a firm can increase its price a bit without attracting new sellers or losing many customers to alternative suppliers outside that area. Of course, the Internet and e-commerce are changing the notion of the size and limits of a geographic market. It may become difficult to perceive any geographic market as local, except for products that are not easily transported, such as concrete.

The Intent Requirement Monopoly power, in and of itself, does not constitute the offense of monopolization under Section 2 of the Sherman Act. The offense also requires an *intent* to monopolize.

Know This

Section 2 of the Sherman Act essentially condemns the act of monopolizing, not the possession of monopoly power.

A dominant market share may be the result of business acumen or the development of a superior product. It may simply be the result of a historic accident. In these situations, the acquisition of monopoly power is not an antitrust violation. Indeed, it would be contrary to society's interest to condemn every firm that acquired a position of power because it was well managed and efficient, and marketed a product desired by consumers.

In contrast, if a firm possesses market power as a result of carrying out some purposeful act to acquire or maintain that power through anticompetitive means, then it is in violation of Section 2. In most monopolization cases, intent may be inferred from evidence that the firm had monopoly power and engaged in anticompetitive behavior.

Unilateral Refusals to Deal As discussed previously, joint refusals to deal (group boycotts) are subject to close scrutiny under Section 1 of the Sherman Act. A single manufacturer acting unilaterally, though, normally is free to deal, or not to deal, with whomever it wishes.

Nevertheless, in some instances, a unilateral refusal to deal will violate Section 2 of the Sherman Act. These instances occur only if (1) the firm refusing to deal has—or is likely to acquire—monopoly power and (2) the refusal is likely to have an anticompetitive effect on a particular market.

Example 31.8 Clark Industries, the owner of three of the four major downhill ski areas in Blue Hills, Idaho, refuses to continue participating in a jointly offered six-day "all Blue Hills" lift ticket. Clark's refusal to cooperate with its smaller competitor is a violation of Section 2 of the Sherman Act. Because Clark owns three-fourths of the local ski areas, it has monopoly power. Thus, its unilateral refusal to deal has an anticompetitive effect on the market.

Attempted Monopolization An action by a firm that involves anticompetitive conduct, the intent to gain monopoly power, and a "dangerous probability" of success in achieving monopoly power.

Vstock/iStock/Getty Images

The dominant owner of ski facilities in a particular area refuses to participate with a smaller competitor in offering an all-area lift ticket. Why is this a violation of antitrust laws?

31–3b Attempts to Monopolize

Section 2 also prohibits **attempted monopolization** of a market, which requires proof of the following three elements:

1. Anticompetitive conduct.
2. The specific intent to exclude competitors and garner monopoly power.
3. A "dangerous" probability of success in achieving monopoly power. The probability is not dangerous unless the alleged offender possesses some degree of market power. Only *serious* threats of monopolization are condemned as violations.

The chapter's *Adapting the Law to the Online Environment* feature explores widespread concerns that the country's largest technology companies have grown too big for antitrust regulators to ignore.

31–4 The Clayton Act

Focus Question 4

What are the four major provisions of the Clayton Act, and what types of activities do these provisions prohibit?

In 1914, Congress attempted to strengthen federal antitrust laws by enacting the Clayton Act. The act was aimed at specific anticompetitive or monopolistic practices that the Sherman Act did not cover. The substantive provisions of the act deal with four distinct forms of business behavior, which are declared illegal but not criminal. In each instance, the act states that the behavior is illegal only if it tends to substantially lessen competition or to create monopoly power. The major offenses under the Clayton Act are set out in Sections 2, 3, 7, and 8 of the act.

Adapting the Law to the Online Environment

Big Tech's Monopoly Problem

Traditionally, the tripwire for antitrust action has been price. In other words, a company begins to draw scrutiny from federal regulators when its market power grows to a point that would allow it to harm consumers by charging unfairly high prices for its goods or services.

Today's largest tech companies (Big Tech), however, provide many of their most popular services at a zero price, in exchange for data rather than money. Thus, consumers do not pay to search the Internet on Google, or to stay in touch with friends on Facebook, or to download many free apps from Apple.

Yet these Big Tech companies are being investigated by the U.S. Department of Justice and the Federal Trade Commission for violating antitrust law. Why?

Dominating Many Markets

The answer lies in concerns about size and anticompetitive tendencies. Alphabet, the parent company of Google, has acquired more than two hundred startups—including YouTube, Android, and Waze—and dominates the online advertising and mapping industries. Facebook was allowed to purchase its two main social networking rivals, Instagram and WhatsApp, without any antitrust consequences. Amazon owns one of the biggest e-commerce marketplaces in the world and also sells products on it.

Smaller competitors have filed numerous lawsuits against Big Tech for anticompetitive practices, such as knowingly violating patents, engaging in unfair business negotiations, and manipulating results on search engines.

Amazon, in particular, has come under criticism for its ability to "out-discount" its competitors and become the dominant force in any market it enters. Notoriously, Amazon engaged in a price war with Diapers.com, dropping the price of Amazon diapers to the point at which the smaller company could no longer compete and was acquired—by Amazon.

Forced Breakups?

Politicians and antimonopoly activists have devised several strategies to limit the reach of Big Tech. One proposed law would ban companies with market values of more than $100 billion from acquiring any other companies.

Another possible law would prohibit any company with annual global revenues of more than $25 billion from owning a platform and doing business on that platform. Such a restriction would require Amazon to "spin off" its brands, such as Amazon Basics, and would require Apple to sell its apps, such as Mail and Maps. For the industry's fiercest critics, there is only one solution: forced breakups, turning these few giant tech companies into many smaller companies, as happened to the telephone industry in the 1980s.

Critical Thinking

Given that consumers seem to benefit from the free or low-cost services provided by Big Tech, should these companies have limits placed on them by federal antitrust regulators? Explain your answer.

31–4a Section 2—Price Discrimination

Section 2 of the Clayton Act prohibits **price discrimination**, which occurs when a seller charges different prices to competing buyers for identical goods or services. Congress strengthened this section by amending it in 1936 with the passage of the Robinson-Patman Act. As amended, Section 2 prohibits price discrimination that cannot be justified by differences in production costs, transportation costs, or cost differences due to other reasons.

Price Discrimination A seller's act of charging competing buyers different prices for identical products or services.

Requirements To violate Section 2, the seller must be engaged in interstate commerce, the goods must be of like grade and quality, and the goods must have been sold to two or more purchasers. In addition, the effect of the price discrimination must be to substantially lessen competition, tend to create a monopoly, or otherwise injure competition. Without proof of an actual injury resulting from the price discrimination, the plaintiff cannot recover damages.

Price discrimination claims can arise from discounts, offsets, rebates, or allowances given to one buyer over another. Giving favorable credit terms, delivery, or freight charges to only some buyers can also lead to allegations of price discrimination. For instance, in some circumstances, offering goods to different customers at the same price but including free delivery only for some of the customers may violate Section 2.

Defenses There are several statutory defenses to liability for price discrimination.

1. *Cost justification.* If the seller can justify the price reduction by demonstrating that a particular buyer's purchases saved the seller costs in producing and selling the goods, the seller will not be liable for price discrimination.
2. *Meeting competitor's prices.* If the seller charged the lower price in a good-faith attempt to meet an equally low price of a competitor, the seller will not be liable for price discrimination. **Example 31.9** Rogue, Inc., is a retail dealer of Mercury Marine outboard motors in Shady Cove, Oregon. Mercury Marine also sells its motors to other dealers in the Shady Cove area. When Rogue discovers that Mercury is selling its outboard motors at a substantial discount to Rogue's largest competitor, it files a price discrimination lawsuit. Mercury Marine can defend itself by showing that the discounts given to Rogue's competitor were made in good faith to meet the low price charged by another manufacturer of marine motors. ■
3. *Changing market conditions.* A seller may lower its price on an item in response to changing conditions affecting the market for or the marketability of the goods concerned. Sellers are allowed to readjust their prices to meet the realities of the market without liability for price discrimination. Thus, if an advance in technology makes a particular product less marketable than it was previously, a seller can lower the product's price.

State Laws Concerning Price Discrimination Some states have enacted statutes to prohibit price discrimination, which can apply in addition to the Clayton Act. For instance, a state statute may apply when a business sells goods or services at different prices to buyers in different locations within the state. Some of these laws protect specific businesses, such as auto dealerships, from discriminatory wholesale or incentive pricing.

Other state laws protect businesses and consumers from economic injuries caused by wrongful business practices. These include unfair competition statutes. In the following case, a state court considered whether an allegation of age-based price discrimination in violation of the state's civil rights statute could support a claim for a violation of the state's unfair competition statute.

Case 31.2

Candelore v. Tinder, Inc.

California Court of Appeal, Second District, Division 3, 19 Cal.App.5th 1138, 228 Cal.Rptr.3d 336 (2018).

Facts Tinder, Inc., owns and operates the dating app Tinder. The free version of Tinder presents users with photos of potential dates. When a photo appears on the device's screen, the user can swipe right to express approval, or swipe left to express disapproval. The premium service, Tinder Plus, allows users to access additional features of the app for a monthly fee. Tinder charges consumers who are age thirty and older $19.99 per month for Tinder Plus, while it charges consumers under the age of thirty only $9.99 or $14.99 per month for the Tinder Plus features.

On behalf of consumers who were over age thirty when they subscribed to Tinder Plus, Allan Candelore filed a suit in a California state court against Tinder, Inc. Candelore alleged age-based price discrimination in violation of California's civil rights statute, which prohibits arbitrary discrimination by businesses on the basis of personal characteristics, and the state's unfair competition law (UCL). The court concluded that the company's age-based pricing model was justified by public policies that promote "profit maximization by the vendor, a legitimate goal in our capitalistic economy." Candelore appealed.

Issue Can an allegation of age-based price discrimination in violation of the state's civil rights statute support a claim for a violation of the state's unfair competition statute?

Decision Yes. A state intermediate appellate court reversed the judgment of the lower court. "Tinder's alleged discriminatory pricing model violates the public policy embodied in the [civil rights statute, and] the UCL . . . provides an independent basis for relief on the facts alleged."

Reason Society's interest in increasing the use, of a premium online dating app by persons under thirty is not compelling enough to justify discriminatory age-based pricing. Users over thirty who are less economically advantaged could be excluded from enjoying the same premium app. Maximizing profits can be an acceptable business objective that can be advanced by price discrimination. But this goal is no excuse for a prohibited discriminatory policy. Tinder's pricing model discriminates against users over the age of thirty. The complaint alleges a sufficient claim for age discrimination in violation of the state's civil rights statute. The UCL prohibits unfair competition, which includes any unlawful, unfair, or fraudulent business practice. The violation of any law can serve as the basis for a violation of the UCL. Because the complaint adequately states a claim for a violation of the civil rights statute, the allegations are sufficient to state a claim under the UCL.

Critical Thinking

- **Legal Environment** *A California statute provides for the waiver of fees at state university campuses for senior citizens. What distinguishes this differential treatment from the discriminatory practice at issue in the* Candelore *case?*
- **Economic** *Instead of personal characteristics such as age, could a business like Tinder use economic distinctions to broaden its user base and increase profits? Discuss.*

31–4b Section 3—Exclusionary Practices

Under Section 3 of the Clayton Act, sellers or lessors cannot condition the sale or lease of goods on the buyer's or lessee's promise not to use or deal in the goods of the seller's competitor. In effect, this section prohibits two types of vertical agreements involving exclusionary practices—*exclusive-dealing contracts* and *tying arrangements*.

Exclusive-Dealing Contract An agreement under which a seller forbids a buyer to purchase products from the seller's competitors.

Exclusive-Dealing Contracts

A contract under which a seller forbids a buyer to purchase products from the seller's competitors is called an **exclusive-dealing contract**. A seller is prohibited from making an exclusive-dealing contract under Section 3 if the effect of the contract is "to substantially lessen competition or tend to create a monopoly."

Classic Case Example 31.10 In a case decided by the United States Supreme Court in 1949, Standard Oil Company, the largest gasoline seller in the nation at that time, made exclusive-dealing contracts with independent stations in seven western states. The contracts involved 16 percent of all retail outlets, with sales amounting to approximately 7 percent of all retail sales in that market. The market was substantially concentrated because the seven largest gasoline suppliers all used exclusive-dealing contracts with their independent retailers. Together, these suppliers controlled 65 percent of the market.

The Court looked at market conditions after the arrangements were instituted and found that market shares were extremely stable and entry into the market was apparently restricted. Because competition was "foreclosed in a substantial share" of the relevant market, the Court held that Section 3 of the Clayton Act had been violated.[12]

Note that since the Supreme Court's 1949 decision, a number of subsequent decisions have called the holding in this case into doubt.[13]

Today, it is clear that to violate antitrust law, an exclusive-dealing agreement (or a tying arrangement, discussed next) must qualitatively and substantially harm competition. To prevail, a plaintiff must present affirmative evidence that the performance of the agreement will foreclose competition and harm consumers.

Tying Arrangements When a seller conditions the sale of a product (the tying product) on the buyer's agreement to purchase another product (the tied product) produced or distributed by the same seller, a **tying arrangement** results. The legality of a tying arrangement (or *tie-in sales agreement*) depends on many factors, particularly the purpose of the agreement and its likely effect on competition in the relevant markets (the market for the tying product and the market for the tied product).

Tying Arrangement A seller's act of conditioning the sale of a product or service on the buyer's agreement to purchase another product or service from the seller.

Section 3 of the Clayton Act has been held to apply only to commodities, not to services. Some tying arrangements, however, can also be considered agreements that restrain trade in violation of Section 1 of the Sherman Act. Thus, cases involving tying arrangements of services have been brought under Section 1 of the Sherman Act. Although earlier cases condemned tying arrangements as illegal *per se,* courts now evaluate tying agreements under the rule of reason.

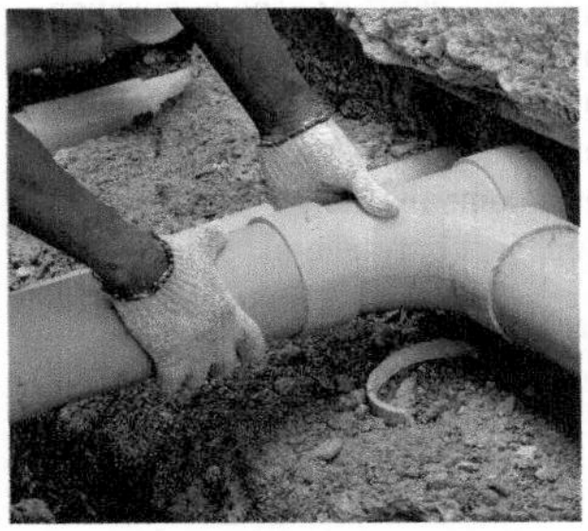

NarisaFotoSS/Shutterstock.com

Why might a private electric company succeed in a lawsuit against a city that has "tied" its water and natural gas services?

Case Example 31.11 The city of LaGrange, Georgia, was the only provider of water and natural gas services to much of unincorporated Troup County. LaGrange passed an ordinance requiring that all new construction in this area install gas appliances in order to receive water service from the city. In response, Diverse Power, a local, private electric company, filed a suit against LaGrange, alleging that the ordinance constituted an unlawful tying arrangement. That is, Troup County residents who needed water (the tying product) were forced to use natural gas (the tied product) instead of electricity offered by Diverse Power.

LaGrange did not deny that it had created a tying arrangement. Rather, the city argued that, as a government entity, it was exempt from federal antitrust law. Disagreeing, a federal appellate court noted that, by this logic, LaGrange could pass an anticompetitive ordinance covering any product—from natural gas service to the "purchase of Goodyear tires"—as long as it was tied to the city's legal water-services monopoly. Not wishing to grant LaGrange "powers so unlimited," the court allowed Diverse Power's lawsuit to proceed.[14]

31–4c Section 7—Mergers

Under Section 7 of the Clayton Act, a person or business organization cannot hold stock or assets in another entity "where the effect ... may be to substantially lessen competition." Section 7 is the statutory authority for preventing mergers or acquisitions that could result in monopoly power or a substantial lessening of competition in the marketplace.

Market Concentration A crucial consideration in most merger cases is the **market concentration** of a product or business. Determining market concentration involves allocating percentage market shares among the various companies in the relevant market. When a small number of companies control a large share of the market, the market is concentrated.

Market Concentration The degree to which a small number of firms control a large percentage of a relevant market.

12. *Standard Oil Co. of California v. United States,* 337 U.S. 293, 69 S.Ct. 1051, 93 L.Ed. 1371 (1949).
13. See, for instance, *Illinois Tool Works, Inc. v. Independent Ink, Inc.,* 547 U.S. 28, 126 S.Ct. 1281, 164 L.Ed.2d 26 (2006); and *Stop & Shop Supermarket Co. v. Blue Cross & Blue Shield of Rhode Island,* 373 F.3d 57 (1st Cir. 2004).
14. *Diverse Power, Inc. v. City of LaGrange, Georgia,* 934 F.3d 1270 (11th Cir. 2019).

Example 31.12 If the four largest grocery stores in Chicago account for 80 percent of all retail food sales, the market is concentrated in those four firms. If one of these stores absorbs the assets and liabilities of another, so that the other ceases to exist, the result is a merger that further concentrates the market and possibly diminishes competition. ■

Competition is not necessarily diminished solely as a result of market concentration, and courts will consider other factors in determining whether a merger will violate Section 7. One factor of particular importance in evaluating the effects of a merger is whether the merger will make it more difficult for *potential* competitors to enter the relevant market.

Horizontal Merger A merger between two firms that are competing in the same market.

Horizontal Mergers A merger between firms that compete with each other in the same market is called a **horizontal merger**. If a horizontal merger creates an entity with a significant market share, the merger will be presumed illegal because it increases market concentration. The Federal Trade Commission (FTC) and the U.S. Department of Justice (DOJ) have established guidelines for determining which mergers will actually be challenged. The guidelines focus on whether a merger will substantially lessen competition.

When analyzing the legality of a horizontal merger, the courts also consider three other factors: the overall concentration of the relevant product market, the relevant market's history of tending toward concentration, and whether the merger is apparently designed to establish market power or to restrict competition.

Vertical Merger The acquisition by a company at one stage of production of a company at a higher or lower stage of production (such as a company merging with one of its suppliers or retailers).

Vertical Mergers A **vertical merger** occurs when a company at one stage of production acquires a company at a higher or lower stage of production. An example of a vertical merger is a company merging with one of its suppliers or retailers.

Whether a vertical merger is illegal generally depends on several factors, such as whether the merger would produce a firm controlling an undue proportion of the relevant market. The courts also analyze the concentration of firms in the market, barriers to entry into the market, and the apparent intent of the merging parties. A vertical merger is unlawful if it prevents competitors of either merging firm from competing in a segment of the market that otherwise would be open to them, resulting in a substantial lessening of competition.

31–4d Section 8—Interlocking Directorates

Section 8 of the Clayton Act deals with *interlocking directorates*—that is, the practice whereby individuals serve as directors on the boards of two or more competing companies simultaneously. Specifically, no person may be a director in two or more competing corporations at the same time if either of the corporations has capital, surplus, or undivided profits aggregating more than $38,204,000 or competitive sales of $3,820,400 or more. (The FTC adjusts the threshold amounts each year. The amounts given here are those announced by the FTC in 2020.)

The reasoning behind the FTC's prohibition of interlocking directorates is that if two competing businesses share the same officers and directors, the firms are unlikely to compete with one another, or to compete aggressively. If directors or officers do not comply with this prohibition, they may be liable under the Clayton Act.

Focus Question 5

What agencies of the federal government enforce the federal antitrust laws?

31–5 Enforcement and Exemptions

The federal agencies that enforce the federal antitrust laws are the U.S. Department of Justice (DOJ) and the Federal Trade Commission (FTC). The FTC was established in 1914 by the Federal Trade Commission Act. Section 5 of that act condemns all forms of anticompetitive behavior that are not covered under other federal antitrust laws.

31–5a Enforcement by Federal Agencies

Only the DOJ can prosecute violations of the Sherman Act, which may be either criminal or civil offenses. Violations of the Clayton Act are not crimes, but the act can be enforced by either the DOJ or the FTC through civil proceedings.

The DOJ or the FTC may ask the courts to impose various remedies, including **divestiture** (making a company give up one or more of its operating functions) and dissolution. A meatpacking firm, for instance, might be forced to divest itself of control or ownership of butcher shops.

Divestiture A company's sale of one or more of its divisions' operating functions under court order as part of the enforcement of the antitrust laws.

The FTC has sole authority to enforce violations of Section 5 of the Federal Trade Commission Act. FTC actions are effected through administrative orders, but if a firm violates an FTC order, the FTC can seek court sanctions for the violation.

Know This

Section 5 of the Federal Trade Commission Act is broader than the other antitrust laws. It covers nearly all anticompetitive behavior, including conduct that does not violate either the Sherman Act or the Clayton Act.

31–5b Actions by Private Parties

A private party who has been injured as a result of a violation of the Sherman Act or the Clayton Act can sue for **treble damages** (three times the actual damages suffered) and attorneys' fees. In some instances, private parties may also seek injunctive relief to prevent antitrust violations. A party wishing to sue under the Sherman Act must prove the following:

Treble Damages Damages that, by statute, are three times the amount of actual damages suffered.

1. The antitrust violation either caused or was a substantial factor in causing the injury that was suffered.
2. The unlawful actions of the accused party affected business activities of the plaintiff that were protected by the antitrust laws.

Additionally, a great deal of case law has established that to pursue antitrust lawsuits, private parties must present some evidence suggesting that an illegal agreement was made.[15]

A private party can bring an action under Section 2 of the Sherman Act based on the attempted enforcement of a fraudulently obtained patent. Such an action is called a *Walker Process* claim.[16] To prevail, the plaintiff must first show that the defendant obtained the patent by committing fraud against the U.S. Patent and Trademark Office and enforced the patent with knowledge of the fraud. The plaintiff must then establish all the other elements of a Sherman Act monopolization claim—anticompetitive conduct, an intent to monopolize, and a dangerous probability of achieving monopoly power.

In the following case, a respiratory filter maker was accused of patent infringement. The maker sought a declaratory judgment of noninfringement, asserting a *Walker Process* claim. One of the primary issues was whether attorneys' fees were an appropriate basis for damages.

15. See *Viamedia, Inc. v. Comcast Corp.*, 951 F.3d. 429 (7th Cir. 2020).
16. The name of the claim comes from the title of the case in which the claim originated—*Walker Process Equipment v. Food Machine and Chemical Corp.*, 382 U.S. 172, 86 S.Ct. 347, 15 L.Ed.2d 247 (1965).

Case 31.3

TransWeb, LLC v. 3M Innovative Properties Co.

United States Court of Appeals, Federal Circuit, 812 F.3d 1295 (2016).

Facts TransWeb, LLC, manufactures respirator filters made of nonwoven fibrous material to be worn by workers at contaminated work sites. At a filtration industry exposition, TransWeb's founder, Kumar Ogale, handed out samples of TransWeb's filter material. At the time, 3M Innovative Products Company was experimenting with filter materials. At the expo, 3M employees obtained the TransWeb samples.

(Continues)

Continued

More than a year later, 3M obtained patents for its filter products and filed a suit against TransWeb, claiming infringement. 3M asserted that it had not received the TransWeb samples until after its patent application had been filed. The suit was dismissed.

TransWeb then filed a suit in a federal district court, seeking a declaratory judgment of noninfringement and asserting a *Walker Process* claim. A jury found that 3M had obtained its patents through fraud, that its assertion of the patents against TransWeb violated antitrust law, and that TransWeb was entitled to attorneys' fees as damages. TransWeb had incurred $7.7 million in fees defending against 3M's infringement suit. The court trebled this to $23 million. 3M appealed.

Issue Can a court award treble damages based on the amount of attorneys' fees that the plaintiff incurred?

Decision Yes. The U.S. Court of Appeals for the Federal Circuit affirmed the lower court's judgment and award of trebled attorneys' fees.

Reason The court reasoned that 3M's unlawful act was the bringing of a suit based on a patent known to be fraudulently obtained. What made this act unlawful under the antitrust laws was its attempt to gain a monopoly based on this fraudulently obtained patent. "TransWeb's attorney fees flow directly from this unlawful aspect of 3M's act." Thus, the court concluded, they "are an antitrust injury that can properly serve as the basis for antitrust damages."

Critical Thinking

- **Legal Environment** *How would TransWeb's injury have been "shared by all consumers in the relevant markets" if TransWeb had not sued until after it had been driven out of those markets by 3M's actions?*
- **Ethical** *What does 3M's conduct suggest about its corporate ethics?*

31–5c Exemptions from Antitrust Laws

There are many legislative and constitutional limitations on antitrust enforcement. Most are statutory or judicially created exemptions applying to the areas listed in Exhibit 31–2. One of the most significant exemptions covers joint efforts by businesspersons to obtain legislative, judicial, or executive action. Under this exemption, for instance, Blu-ray producers can jointly lobby Congress to change the copyright laws without being held liable for attempting to restrain trade.

31–6 U.S. Antitrust Laws in the Global Context

Focus Question 6

When will a U.S. court apply the Sherman Act to foreign persons or entities?

U.S. antitrust laws have a broad application. Not only may persons in foreign nations be subject to their provisions, but the laws may also be applied to protect foreign consumers and competitors from violations committed by U.S. business firms. Consequently, *foreign persons*—a term that by definition includes foreign governments—may sue under U.S. antitrust laws in U.S. courts.

31–6a The Extraterritorial Application of U.S. Antitrust Laws

The United States is a major proponent of free competition in the global economy. Accordingly, Section 1 of the Sherman Act provides for the extraterritorial effect of the U.S. antitrust laws. Any conspiracy that has a *substantial effect* on U.S. commerce is within the reach of the Sherman Act. The violation may even occur outside the United States, and foreign persons, including governments, can be sued for violation of U.S. antitrust laws.

Before U.S. courts will exercise jurisdiction and apply antitrust laws, it must be shown that the alleged violation had a substantial effect on U.S. commerce. U.S. jurisdiction is automatically invoked, however, when a *per se* violation occurs. If a domestic firm, for instance, joins a foreign cartel to control the production, price, or distribution of goods, and this cartel has a *substantial effect* on U.S. commerce, a *per se* violation may arise. Hence, both the domestic firm and the foreign cartel could be sued for violation of the U.S. antitrust laws.

Exhibit 31–2 Exemptions to Antitrust Enforcement

EXEMPTION	SOURCE AND SCOPE
Labor	Clayton Act—Permits unions to organize and bargain without violating antitrust laws and specifies that strikes and other labor activities normally do not violate any federal law.
Agricultural associations	Clayton Act and Capper-Volstead Act—Allow agricultural cooperatives to set prices.
Fisheries	Fishery Cooperative Marketing Act—Allows the fishing industry to set prices.
Insurance companies	McCarran-Ferguson Act—Exempts the insurance business in states in which the industry is regulated.
Exporters	Webb-Pomerene Act—Allows U.S. exporters to engage in cooperative activity to compete with similar foreign associations. Export Trading Company Act—Permits the U.S. Department of Justice to exempt certain exporters.
Professional baseball	The United States Supreme Court has held that professional baseball is exempt because it is not "interstate commerce."
Oil marketing	Interstate Oil Compact—Allows states to set quotas on oil to be marketed in interstate commerce.
Defense activities	Defense Production Act—Allows the president to approve, and thereby exempt, certain activities to further the military defense of the United States.
Small businesses' cooperative research	Small Business Administration Act—Allows small firms to undertake cooperative research.
State actions	The United States Supreme Court has held that actions by a state are exempt if the state clearly articulates and actively supervises the policy behind its action.
Regulated industries	Industries (such as airlines) are exempt when a federal administrative agency (such as the Federal Aviation Administration) has primary regulatory authority.
Businesspersons' joint efforts to seek government action	Cooperative efforts by businesspersons to obtain legislative, judicial, or executive action are exempt unless it is clear that an effort is "objectively baseless" and is an attempt to make anticompetitive use of government processes.

Likewise, if a foreign firm doing business in the United States enters into a price-fixing or other anticompetitive agreement to control a portion of U.S. markets, a *per se* violation may exist. This may be true even if a foreign law directly conflicts with U.S. antitrust law.

Case Example 31.13 Science Products, Inc., and The Ranis Company, Inc., were U.S. companies that imported large amounts of vitamin C. These companies filed a lawsuit against four Chinese manufacturers that collectively controlled over 60 percent of the world's vitamin C market, alleging a conspiracy to fix prices and manipulate output in the United States in violation of the Sherman Act.

The defendants did not dispute these allegations. Instead, they claimed that they had acted in accordance with Chinese government regulations, and that their actions were therefore beyond the reach of the American legal system. An appellate court agreed and overturned the decision of the district court, which had ruled in favor of the plaintiffs and awarded them approximately $147 million in damages. The United States Supreme Court, in turn, reversed the appellate court, stating that American judges should "carefully consider" a foreign country's laws and views but should not allow those factors to fully decide the matter. In this case, the Court found that evidence of the defendants' price fixing was persuasive, regardless of the policy goals of the Chinese government.[17]

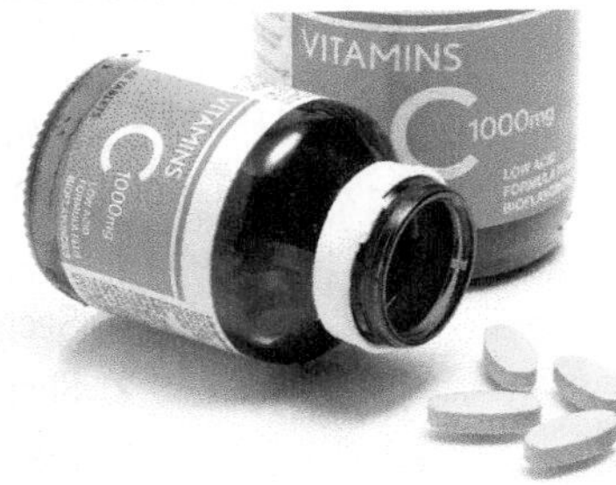

Wutthichai/Shutterstock.com

Can a Chinese company that is required by its government to fix the prices of vitamin C in the United States be exempted from U.S. antitrust law? Why or why not?

17. *Animal Science Products, Inc. v. Hebei Welcome Pharmaceutical Co., Ltd.*, 585 U.S. __, 138 S.Ct. 1865, 201 L.Ed.2d 225 (2018).

31–6b The Application of Foreign Antitrust Laws

Large U.S. companies increasingly must be concerned about the application of foreign antitrust laws as well. The European Union (EU), in particular, has stepped up its enforcement actions against antitrust violators. The EU's laws promoting competition are stricter in many respects than those of the United States and define more conduct as anticompetitive. Microsoft, Apple, and Amazon have been investigated, and sometimes fined, by the EU's Competitive Commission, but the main target of European antitrust efforts has been Google.

After years of investigations, the EU found that Google had (1) abused its dominant position in the search engine market by promoting its own services over those of its rivals, (2) used its ownership of the Android operating system to illegally keep other smartphone manufacturers out of the market, and (3) forced websites that want to use Google's search bar to favor ads run by Google's advertising clients. The EU imposed a combined $9.5 billion in antitrust fines against Google because of these infractions.

Along with Facebook, Google has also been the focus of billions of dollars in lawsuits under a set of European privacy rules called the General Data Protection Regulation (GDPR). These rules are designed to limit the amount of personal data that large technology companies can collect without the consent of users.

In the past, the EU was sometimes faulted for unfairly victimizing technology companies from the United States. Today, the EU's efforts are viewed as potential models for American antitrust efforts in this field, discussed earlier in the chapter.

Practice and Review

The Internet Corporation for Assigned Names and Numbers (ICANN) is a nonprofit entity that organizes Internet domain names. It is governed by a board of directors elected by various groups with commercial interests in the Internet. One of ICANN's functions is to authorize an entity to serve as a registrar for certain top-level domains (TLDs). ICANN entered into an agreement with VeriSign to provide registry services for the ".com" TLD in accordance with ICANN's specifications. VeriSign complained that ICANN was restricting the services that VeriSign could make available as a registrar, blocking new services, imposing unnecessary conditions on those services, and setting the prices at which the services were offered. VeriSign claimed that ICANN's control of the registry services for domain names violated Section 1 of the Sherman Act. Using the information presented in the chapter, answer the following questions.

1. Should ICANN's actions be judged under the rule of reason or be deemed a *per se* violation of Section 1 of the Sherman Act? Explain.
2. Should ICANN's actions be viewed as a horizontal or a vertical restraint of trade? Explain.
3. Does it matter that ICANN's directors are chosen by groups with commercial interests in the Internet? Why or why not?
4. If the dispute is judged under the rule of reason, what might be ICANN's defense for having a standardized set of registry services that must be used?

Debate This

The Internet and the rise of e-commerce have rendered our antitrust concepts and laws obsolete.

Key Terms

antitrust laws 773
attempted monopolization 781
concentrated industry 778
divestiture 787
exclusive-dealing contract 784
group boycott 777
horizontal merger 786
horizontal restraint 776
market concentration 785
market power 774
monopolization 779
monopoly 774
monopoly power 774
***per se* violation** 775
predatory pricing 779
price discrimination 783
price-fixing agreement 776
resale price maintenance agreement 779
rule of reason 776
treble damages 787
tying arrangement 785
vertically integrated firm 778
vertical merger 786
vertical restraint 778

Chapter Summary: Antitrust Law and Promoting Competition

The Sherman Antitrust Act (1890)	1. **Major provisions**— a. Section 1—Prohibits contracts, combinations, and conspiracies in restraint of trade. (1) Horizontal restraints subject to Section 1 include price-fixing agreements, group boycotts (joint refusals to deal), horizontal market divisions, and certain trade association agreements. (2) Vertical restraints subject to Section 1 include territorial or customer restrictions and resale price maintenance agreements. b. Section 2—Prohibits monopolies and attempts to monopolize. 2. **Jurisdictional requirements**—The Sherman Act applies only to activities that have a significant impact on interstate commerce and those that affect U.S. foreign commerce. 3. **Interpretive rules**— a. *Per se* rule—Applied to restraints on trade that are so inherently anticompetitive that they cannot be justified and are deemed illegal as a matter of law. b. Rule of reason—Applied when an anticompetitive agreement may be justified by legitimate benefits. Under the rule of reason, the lawfulness of a trade restraint will be determined by the purpose and effects of the restraint.
The Clayton Act (1914)	Aimed at specific anticompetitive or monopolistic acts not covered by the Sherman Act. The major provisions are as follows: 1. **Section 2**—As amended in 1936 by the Robinson-Patman Act, prohibits a seller engaged in interstate commerce from price discrimination that substantially lessens competition. 2. **Section 3**—Prohibits exclusionary practices, such as exclusive-dealing contracts and tying arrangements, when the effect may be to substantially lessen competition. 3. **Section 7**—Prohibits mergers when the effect may be to substantially lessen competition or to tend to create a monopoly. a. A horizontal merger will be presumed unlawful if the entity created by the merger will have a significant market share. b. A vertical merger will be unlawful if the merger prevents competitors of either merging firm from competing in a segment of the market that otherwise would be open to them, resulting in a substantial lessening of competition. 4. **Section 8**—Prohibits interlocking directorates.
Enforcement and Exemptions	1. **Enforcement by federal agencies**—The U.S. Department of Justice and the Federal Trade Commission enforce the federal antitrust laws. 2. **Actions by private parties**—Private parties who have been injured as a result of violations of the Sherman Act or Clayton Act may bring civil suits, and, if successful, they may be awarded treble damages and attorneys' fees. 3. **Exemptions from antitrust laws**—See Exhibit 31–2 for a list of significant exemptions.

U.S. Antitrust Laws in the Global Context	1. **Extraterritorial application of U.S. laws**—U.S. antitrust laws can be applied in foreign nations to protect foreign consumers and competitors. Foreign governments and persons can also bring actions under U.S. antitrust laws. Section 1 of the Sherman Act applies to any conspiracy that has a substantial effect on U.S. commerce. 2. **Application of foreign laws**—Many other nations also have laws that promote competition and prohibit trade restraints, and some are more restrictive than U.S. laws. These foreign antitrust laws are increasingly being applied to U.S. firms.

Issue Spotters

1. Under what circumstances would Pop's Market, a small store in a small, isolated town, be considered a monopolist? If Pop's is a monopolist, is it in violation of Section 2 of the Sherman Act? Why or why not? (See *Section 2 of the Sherman Act.*)
2. Maple Corporation conditions the sale of its syrup on buyers' agreement to buy Maple's pancake mix. What factors would a court consider to decide whether this arrangement violates the Clayton Act? (See *The Clayton Act.*)

—Check your answers to the *Issue Spotters* against the answers provided in Appendix D.

Business Scenarios and Case Problems

31–1. Sherman Act. An agreement that is blatantly and substantially anticompetitive is deemed a *per se* violation of Section 1 of the Sherman Act. Under what rule is an agreement analyzed if it appears to be anticompetitive but is not a *per se* violation? In making this analysis, what factors will a court consider? (See *Section 1 of the Sherman Act.*)

31–2. Tying Arrangement. John Sheridan owned a Marathon gas station franchise. He sued Marathon Petroleum Co. under Section 1 of the Sherman Act and Section 3 of the Clayton Act, charging it with illegally tying the processing of credit card sales to the gas station. As a condition of obtaining a Marathon dealership, dealers had to agree to let the franchisor process credit cards. They could not shop around to see if credit card processing could be obtained at a lower price from another source. The district court dismissed the case for failure to state a claim. Sheridan appealed. Is there a tying arrangement? If so, does it violate the law? (See *The Clayton Act.*)

31–3. Spotlight on Digital Music—Price Fixing. Together, EMI, Sony BMG Music Entertainment, Universal Music Group Recordings, Inc., and Warner Music Group Corp. produced, licensed, and distributed 80 percent of the digital music sold in the United States. The companies formed MusicNet to sell music to online services that sold the songs to consumers. MusicNet required all of the services to sell the songs at the same price and subject to the same restrictions. Digitization of music became cheaper, but MusicNet did not change its prices. Did MusicNet violate the antitrust laws? Explain. [*Starr v. Sony BMG Music Entertainment*, 592 F.3d 314 (2d Cir. 2010)] (See *Section 1 of the Sherman Act.*)

31–4. Business Case Problem with Sample Answer—Price Discrimination. Dayton Superior Corp. sells its products in interstate commerce to several companies, including Spa Steel Products, Inc. The purchasers often compete directly with each other for customers. From 2005 to 2007, one of Spa Steel's customers purchased Dayton Superior's products from two of Spa Steel's competitors. According to the customer, Spa Steel's prices were always 10 to 15 percent higher for the same products. As a result, Spa Steel lost sales to at least that customer and perhaps others. Spa Steel wants to sue Dayton Superior for price discrimination. Which requirements for such a claim under Section 2 of the Clayton Act does Spa Steel satisfy? What additional facts will it need to prove? [*Dayton Superior Corp. v. Spa Steel Products, Inc.*, 2012 WL 113663 (N.D.N.Y. 2012)] (See *The Clayton Act.*)

—For a sample answer to Problem 31–4, go to Appendix E.

31–5. Section 1 of the Sherman Act. The National Collegiate Athletic Association (NCAA) and the National Federation of State High School Associations (NFHS), in an effort to enhance player safety and reduce technology-driven home runs and other big hits, set a standard for nonwood baseball bats to ensure that aluminum and composite bats performed like wood bats. Marucci Sports, LLC, makes nonwood bats. Under the new standard, four of Marucci's eleven products were decertified for use in high school and collegiate games. Marucci filed suit against the NCAA and the NFHS under Section 1 of the Sherman Act. At trial, Marucci's evidence focused on injury to its own business. Did the NCAA and NFHS's standard restrain trade in violation of the Sherman Act? Explain. [*Marucci Sports, LLC v. National Collegiate Athletic Association*, 751 F.3d 368 (5th Cir. 2014)] (See *Section 1 of the Sherman Act.*)

31–6. Mergers. St. Luke's Health Systems, Ltd., operated an emergency clinic in Nampa, Idaho. Saltzer Medical Group, P.A., had thirty-four physicians practicing at its offices in Nampa. Saint Alphonsus Health System, Inc., operated the only hospital in Nampa. St. Luke's acquired Saltzer's assets and entered into a five-year professional service agreement with the Saltzer physicians. This affiliation resulted in a combined share of two-thirds of the Nampa adult primary care provider market. Together, the two entities could impose a significant increase in the prices charged patients and insurers, and correspondence between the parties indicated that they would. Saint Alphonsus filed a suit against St. Luke's to block the merger. Did this affiliation violate antitrust law? Explain. [*Saint Alphonsus Medical Center-Nampa Inc. v. St. Luke's Health System, Ltd.*, 778 F.3d 775 (9th Cir. 2015)] (See *The Clayton Act.*)

31–7. Section 1 of the Sherman Act. Manitou North America, Inc., makes and distributes telehandlers (forklifts with extendable telescopic booms) to dealers throughout the United States. Manitou agreed to make McCormick International, LLC, its exclusive dealer in the state of Michigan. Later, Manitou entered into an agreement with Gehi Company, which also makes and sells telehandlers. The companies agreed to allocate territories within Michigan among certain dealers for each manufacturer, limiting the dealers' selection of competitive products to certain models. Under this agreement, McCormick was precluded from buying or selling Gehi telehandlers. What type of trade restraint did the agreement between Manitou and Gehi represent? Is this a violation of antitrust law? If so, who was injured, and how were they injured? Explain. [*Manitou North America, Inc. v. McCormick International, LLC*, 2016 WL 439354 (2016)] (See *Section 1 of the Sherman Act.*)

31–8. Tying Arrangements. PRC-Desoto International, Inc., makes and distributes more than 90 percent of the aerospace sealant used in military and commercial aircraft. Packaging Systems, Inc., buys the sealant in wholesale quantities, repackages it into special injection kits, and sells the kits on the retail market to aircraft maintenance companies. PRC-Desoto bought one of the two main manufacturing companies of injection kits and announced a new policy to prohibit the repackaging of its sealant for resale. Packaging Systems was forced to buy both the sealant and the kits from PRC-Desoto. Due to the anti-repackaging constraint, the reseller could no longer meet its buyers' needs for pre-filled injection kits. Does this policy represent an unlawful tying arrangement? Explain. [*Packaging Systems, Inc. v. PRC-Desoto International, Inc.*, 2018 WL 735978 (C.D.Cal. 2018)] (See *The Clayton Act.*)

31–9. A Question of Ethics—The IDDR Approach and Section 2 of the Sherman Act. Apple, Inc., controls which apps—such as ringtones, instant messaging, and video—can run on iPhone software. Apple's App Store is a website where iPhone users can find, buy, and download the apps. Apple prohibits third-party developers from selling iPhone apps through channels other than the App Store, threatening to cut off sales by any developer who violates this prohibition. Apple also discourages iPhone owners from downloading unapproved apps, threatening to void iPhone warranties if they do. Seven iPhone app buyers filed a complaint in a federal district court against Apple. The plaintiffs alleged that the firm monopolized the market for iPhone apps. [*In re Apple iPhone Antitrust Litigation*, 846 F.3d 313 (9th Cir. 2017)] (See *Section 2 of the Sherman Act.*)

1. Using the *Decision* step of the IDDR approach, provide reasons why Apple might attempt to protect iPhone software by setting narrow boundaries on the sales of related apps and aggressively enforcing them.
2. Explain why Apple's actions in this case might be considered unethical.

Critical Thinking and Writing Assignments

31–10. Business Law Writing. Write two paragraphs explaining some ways in which antitrust laws might place too great a burden on commerce in the global marketplace. (See *Section 2 of the Sherman Act.*)

31–11. Time-Limited Group Assignment—Antitrust Violations. Residents of the city of Madison, Wisconsin, became concerned about overconsumption of liquor near the campus of the University of Wisconsin (UW). The city took action by imposing conditions on area bars to discourage reduced-price "specials" that were believed to encourage high-volume and dangerous drinking. Later, the city began to draft an ordinance to ban all drink specials. Bar owners responded by announcing that they had "voluntarily" agreed to discontinue drink specials on Friday and Saturday nights after 8:00 P.M. The city put its ordinance on hold. Several UW students filed a lawsuit against the local bar owners' association alleging violations of antitrust law. (See *Section 1 of the Sherman Act.*)

1. The first group will identify the grounds on which the plaintiffs might base their claim for relief and formulate an argument on behalf of the plaintiffs.
2. The second group will determine whether the defendants are exempt from the antitrust laws.
3. The third group will decide how the court should rule in this dispute and provide reasons for its answer.

32 Consumer and Environmental Law

Focus Questions

The six Focus Questions *below are designed to help improve your understanding. After reading this chapter, you should be able to answer the following questions:*

1. When will advertising be deemed deceptive?
2. What law protects consumers against contaminated and misbranded foods and drugs?
3. What does Regulation Z require, and how does it relate to the Truth in Lending Act?
4. What does an environmental impact statement contain, and who must file one?
5. What are three main goals of the Clean Water Act?
6. What is Superfund? What categories of people are liable under Superfund?

"The good of the people is the greatest law."

Marcus Tullius Cicero
106–43 B.C.E. (Roman politician and orator)

Congress has enacted a substantial amount of legislation to protect "the good of the people," to borrow Cicero's phrase from the chapter-opening quotation. All statutes, agency rules, and common law judicial decisions that attempt to protect the interests of consumers are classified as *consumer law.* Similarly, all laws and regulations designed to protect and preserve the environment are categorized as environmental law.

Sources of consumer protection exist at all levels of government. Numerous federal laws have been passed to define the duties of sellers and the rights of consumers. Exhibit 32–1 indicates some of the areas of consumer law that are regulated by statutes.

The Federal Trade Commission (FTC) is one of many federal agencies that work to protect consumers. One FTC action, for instance, involved Luminosity, a popular "brain-training" app made by Lumos Labs, Inc. Lumos advertised that playing the app's games led to better performance in school, sports, and work—in addition to helping prevent Alzheimer's disease and other forms of dementia. According to the ads, people who played ten minutes a day three times a week would realize their full potential in every aspect of life.

Lumos could not provide scientific evidence to support these claims, however. As a result, the FTC concluded that the advertising was deceptive in violation of consumer protection laws and filed an action against the company. Ultimately, Lumos was ordered to pay a $2 million fine and to stop running the deceptive ads.

Exhibit 32–1 Selected Areas of Consumer Law Regulated by Statutes

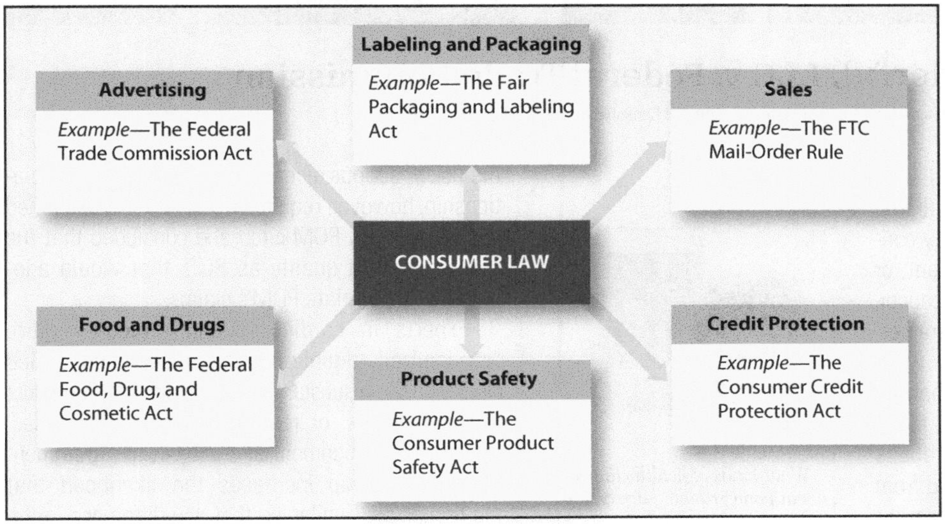

32–1 Advertising, Marketing, Sales, and Labeling

Focus Question 1

When will advertising be deemed deceptive?

Nearly every agency and department of the federal government has an office of consumer affairs. Most states have one or more such offices, including the offices of state attorneys general, to assist consumers. Many of the complaints received by these offices involve consumers who say they were misled by sellers' advertising, marketing, sales, or labeling tactics.

32–1a Deceptive Advertising

Deceptive Advertising Advertising that misleads consumers, either by making unjustified claims about a product or by omitting a material fact concerning the product.

One of the most important federal consumer protection laws is the Federal Trade Commission Act.[1] The act created the Federal Trade Commission (FTC) to carry out the broadly stated goal of preventing unfair and deceptive trade practices, including deceptive advertising.

Generally, **deceptive advertising** involves a claim that would mislead a reasonable consumer. Vague generalities and obvious exaggerations (that a reasonable person would not believe to be true) are permissible. These claims are known as *puffery*. **Case Example 32.1** Sheila Cruz and others sued Anheuser-Busch Companies, LLC, for falsely advertising its "Bud Light Lime-A-Rita" beverages as "light." She argued that the word "light" was misleading because the drinks contained more calories than light beer (Bud Light). The court dismissed Cruz's case, and a federal appellate court affirmed. The Lime-A-Rita beverages were described and advertised as "Margaritas with a Twist," so no reasonable consumer would believe they were the same as light beer. They also contained fewer calories than traditional tequila margaritas. Thus, the court concluded that the label was not misleading.[2] ■ When a claim has the appearance of authenticity, however, it may create problems.

Bryan Steffy/Getty Images

Was Anheuser-Busch's advertisement for a "light" alcoholic beverage deceptive? Why or why not?

Claims That Appear to Be Based on Factual Evidence Advertising that *appears* to be based on factual evidence but that in fact cannot be scientifically supported will be deemed deceptive. For instance, advertising that uses a phrase such as "scientifically proven" or "clinical studies show" may appear to be factual. But if no actual data support the claims, then the advertising is deceptive.

The following *Spotlight Case* involved an advertising claim based on limited scientific evidence.

1. 15 U.S.C. Sections 41–58
2. *Cruz v. Anheuser-Busch Companies, LLC*, 682 Fed.Appx. 583 (9th Cir. 2017).

Spotlight Case 32.1

POM Wonderful, LLC v. Federal Trade Commission

United States Court of Appeals, District of Columbia Circuit, 777 F.3d 478 (2015).

Facts POM Wonderful, LLC, makes and sells pomegranate-based products. In ads, POM touted medical studies claiming to show that daily consumption of its products could treat, prevent, or reduce the risk of heart disease, prostate cancer, and erectile dysfunction. These ads mischaracterized the scientific evidence.

The Federal Trade Commission (FTC) charged POM with, and held POM liable for, making false, misleading, and unsubstantiated representations in violation of the FTC act. POM was barred from running future ads asserting that its products treat or prevent any disease unless "randomized, controlled, human clinical trials" (RCTs) demonstrated statistically significant results. POM petitioned the U.S. Court of Appeals for the District of Columbia Circuit to review this injunctive order.

gresei/iStock/Getty Images

What kinds of health claims about pomegranate juice can its producer make?

Issue Can an advertising claim based on limited scientific evidence be deemed deceptive?

Decision Yes. The U.S. Court of Appeals for the District of Columbia Circuit enforced the FTC's order. "An advertiser who makes express representations about the level of support for a particular claim must possess the level of proof claimed in the ad and must convey that information to consumers in a non-misleading way."

Reason POM's ads conveyed the impression that clinical studies had established the ability of its products to treat, prevent, or reduce the risk of serious disease. To establish such a relationship, however, requires RCTs. The FTC examined the studies that POM cited and concluded that the studies did not qualify as RCTs that would adequately substantiate POM's claims.

Experts in cardiology and urology require "randomized, double-blinded, placebo-controlled clinical trials to substantiate any claim that a product treats, prevents, or reduces the risk of disease." The random assignment of a subject to a treatment or control group increases the likelihood that the groups are similar, so that any difference in the outcome between the groups can be attributed to the treatment. When a study is double-blinded, the participants and the investigators do not know who is in which group, making bias less likely to affect the results. The existence of the control group allows investigators to distinguish the effects of a tested product from other effects, such as those due to the act of being treated (the placebo effect).

Critical Thinking

- **Ethical** *POM claimed that, for ethical reasons, RCTs should not be required to substantiate disease-related claims about food products. It argued that, for instance, "doctors cannot . . . ethically deprive a control group of patients of all Vitamin C for a decade to determine whether Vitamin C helps prevent cancer." Is this a valid argument? Why or why not?*

Bait-and-Switch Advertising Advertising a product at an attractive price and then telling consumers that the advertised product is not available or is of poor quality and encouraging them to purchase a more expensive item.

Bait-and-Switch Advertising The FTC has issued rules that govern specific advertising techniques.[3] Some retailers systematically advertise merchandise at low prices to get customers into their stores and then tell the customers that the merchandise is unavailable or of poor quality and encourage them to purchase a more expensive item instead. This practice, known as **bait-and-switch advertising,** is a form of deceptive advertising.

The low price is the "bait" to lure the consumer into the store. The salesperson is instructed to "switch" the consumer to a different, more expensive item. According to the FTC, bait-and-switch advertising occurs if the seller refuses to show the advertised item or fails to have reasonable quantities of it available. It also occurs if the seller fails to promise to deliver the advertised item within a reasonable time or discourages employees from selling the item.

3. 16 C.F.R. Section 288.

Example 32.2 Signs on the front of Shockoe Tire Store advertise tires for sale for $30 each. When consumers come in looking for the $30 tires, salespeople tell them the tires are sold out and try to convince them to buy more expensive tires instead. Under FTC guidelines, Shockoe's bait-and-switch sales tactics are deceptive advertising.

Online Deceptive Advertising Deceptive advertising occurs in the online environment as well. The FTC actively monitors online advertising and has identified numerous websites that have made false or deceptive claims for products and services.

The FTC issues guidelines to help online businesses comply with the laws prohibiting deceptive advertising. Current guidelines include the following basic requirements:

1. All advertisements—both online and offline—must be truthful and not misleading.
2. The claims made in an ad must be substantiated—that is, advertisers must have evidence to back up their claims.
3. Ads cannot be unfair, which the FTC defines as "likely to cause substantial consumer injury that consumers could not reasonably avoid and that is not outweighed by the benefit to consumers or competition."
4. Ads must disclose relevant limitations and qualifying information underlying the claims.
5. Required disclosures must be "clear and conspicuous." Because consumers may not read an entire Web page, an online disclosure should be placed as close as possible to the claim being qualified. Generally, hyperlinks to a disclosure are recommended only for lengthy disclosures. If hyperlinks are used, they should be obvious and should be placed as close as possible to the information they qualify.

Know This

Changes in technology often require changes in the law.

The FTC creates additional guidelines as needed to respond to new issues that arise with online advertising.

Federal Trade Commission Actions The FTC receives complaints from many sources, including competitors of alleged violators, consumers, trade associations, Better Business Bureaus, and government organizations and officials. When the agency receives numerous and widespread complaints about a particular problem, it often will investigate.

Formal Complaint. If the FTC concludes that a given advertisement is unfair or deceptive, it sends a formal complaint to the alleged offender. The company may agree to settle the complaint without further proceedings. If not, the FTC can conduct a hearing before an administrative law judge in which the company can present its defense. The agency also can file lawsuits in federal court seeking injunctions, civil penalties, and other forms of relief.

Example 32.3 The popular online dating service Match.com allows users to maintain free profiles on its website. These users cannot, however, respond to other members without paying a subscription fee. The FTC sued the corporate parent of Match.com for engaging in deceptive advertising practices designed to "trick" nonpaying members into purchasing access to the site. According to the FTC's complaint, Match.com sent millions of fake "You caught his eye" e-mails to users who had only free accounts, suggesting that another member was romantically interested in them. At least 500,000 users, the agency estimates, were convinced to buy paid subscriptions after being flattered by these fraudulent e-mails.

vectorfusionart/Shutterstock.com

According to an FTC lawsuit, how did one of the nation's most popular online dating services fraudulently entice consumers to purchase access to its website?

Cease-and-Desist Order An administrative or judicial order prohibiting a person or business firm from conducting activities that an agency or court has deemed illegal.

Counteradvertising New advertising that is undertaken to correct earlier false claims that were made about a product.

Multiple Product Order An order requiring a firm that has engaged in deceptive advertising to cease and desist from false advertising in regard to all the firm's products.

FTC Orders and Remedies. If the FTC succeeds in proving that an advertisement is unfair or deceptive, it usually issues a **cease-and-desist order** requiring the company to stop the challenged advertising. In some circumstances, the FTC may also require **counteradvertising,** in which the company advertises anew—in print, on the Internet, on radio, or on television—to inform the public about the earlier misinformation. The FTC sometimes institutes a **multiple product order,** which requires a firm to cease and desist from false advertising in regard to all of its products, not just the product that was the subject of the action.

Damages When Consumers Are Injured. When a company's deceptive ad involves wrongful charges to consumers, the FTC may seek other remedies, including restitution. **Case Example 32.4** The FTC sued the University of Phoenix (UOP), a for-profit university, and its parent corporation over a deceptive advertising campaign that focused on prospective students' career prospects. Titled "Let's Get To Work," the campaign's social media, television, and radio advertisements made it appear that the school was working with high-profile employers such as Yahoo!, Microsoft, Twitter, and Adobe to find jobs for UOP graduates.

In reality, none of these "corporate partners" had any connection with UOP. Conceding wrongdoing, UOP agreed to settle with the FTC for $191 million. While $50 million of this amount went to the FTC as a fine, the remaining $141 million was used to pay off the debts of UOP students who had been misled by the deceptive advertisements.[4] ■

32–1b False Advertising Claims under the Lanham Act

The Lanham Act protects trademarks, as discussed earlier in this text. The act also covers false advertising claims. To state a successful claim for false advertising under this act, a business must establish each of the following elements:

1. An injury to a commercial interest in reputation or sales.
2. Direct causation of the injury by false or deceptive advertising by a competing company.
3. A loss of business from buyers who were deceived by the advertising.

32–1c State Laws Concerning False Advertising

State consumer-fraud statutes also prohibit false, misleading, and deceptive advertising. Recovery under a state law typically requires proof of the following elements:

1. The defendant committed a deceptive or unfair act.
2. The act was committed in the course of trade or commerce.
3. The defendant intended that others rely on the deception.
4. The plaintiff suffered actual damages proximately caused by the deception.

At issue in the following case was a plaintiff's claim under Illinois's consumer fraud statute.

4. *Federal Trade Commission v. The University of Phoenix, Inc.*, 2:19-CV-05772 (D. Ariz. 2019).

Case 32.2

Haywood v. Massage Envy Franchising, LLC

United States Court of Appeals, Seventh Circuit, 887 F.3d 329 (2018).

Facts Massage Envy, LLC, is a franchisor based in Arizona that grants licenses to independently owned and operated entities for the use of its name, trademark, and standardized operations. Massage Envy's website advertises its services, including an "Introductory 1-hour Massage Session." At the bottom of the home page, a link to "pricing and promotional details" leads to a page with disclaimers. One disclaimer, titled "Session," explains that a "session includes massage or facial and time for consultation and dressing."

Kathy Haywood, a resident of Illinois, scheduled an appointment through the website. At the session, for which Haywood paid with a gift card, she received a massage that lasted no more than fifty minutes. Citing Massage Envy's online ad, Haywood filed a suit in a federal district court against the company, alleging unfair and deceptive business practices in violation of the Illinois Consumer Fraud and Deceptive Business Practices Act (ICFA). The court dismissed the claim. Haywood appealed.

Issue Did Haywood fail to establish the causation required by the state's consumer fraud statute?

Decision Yes. The U.S. Court of Appeals for the Seventh Circuit affirmed the dismissal. "The district court did not abuse its discretion in dismissing the complaint."

Reason To succeed on a claim under the state's ICFA, a plaintiff must establish: (1) a deceptive act or promise by the defendant, (2) the defendant's intent that the plaintiff rely on the act or promise, (3) the commission of the act or making of the promise in the course of trade or commerce, and (4) actual damage as a result. In other words, the deceptive act or promise must have been the "but-for" cause of the damage.

Here, the court found that Haywood failed to establish causation. The court noted the lack of a contention in the complaint that Haywood's belief about the length of the massage caused her to make her appointment. "The only reasonable conclusion is that Massage Envy's representations regarding the one-hour massage session were not the but-for cause of any alleged injury." According to the court, "the only reasonable and plausible inference" is that the gift card influenced Haywood to book the massage, not Massage Envy's alleged deception.

Critical Thinking

- **Economic** *A fraud injury can be measured in two ways. As a loss of the benefit of the bargain, damages consist of the difference between the value of what was promised and the value of what was received. Under the out-of-pocket rule, the measure is the difference between the price paid and the market value of what was received. If Haywood had established her claim, which of these methods would have applied? Why?*
- **What If the Facts Were Different?** *Suppose that reliance was not an element of a consumer fraud claim under the ICFA. Would the result in this case have been different? Explain.*

32–1d Marketing

In addition to regulating advertising practices, Congress has passed several laws to protect consumers against other marketing practices.

Telephone Solicitation The Telephone Consumer Protection Act (TCPA)[5] prohibits telephone solicitation using an automatic telephone dialing system or a prerecorded voice. The act is enforced by the Federal Communications Commission (FCC). In addition, most states have statutes regulating telephone solicitation.

The TCPA has long been considered lacking when it comes to protecting consumers against unsolicited *robocalls*—calls or texts generated by computerized autodialing technology and placed by a telemarketer. By the end of the 2010s, American were receiving between 5 and 6 billion unsolicited robocalls each month. In response, Congress passed the TRACED Act, an amendment to the TCPA that broadens the definition of prohibited robocalls and requires telephone providers to offer consumers more effective robocall-blocking options.[6] The amendment also gives the FCC the ability to impose substantial fines on individuals or businesses entities.

Fraudulent Telemarketing The FTC's Telemarketing Sales Rule (TSR)[7] requires a telemarketer to identify the seller's name, describe the product being sold, and disclose all material facts related to the sale (such as the total cost of the goods being sold). The TSR makes it

5. 47 U.S.C. Sections 227 *et seq.*
6. Pallone-Thune Telephone Robocall Abuse Criminal Enforcement and Deterrence Act, 47 U.S.C. Section 227(b).
7. 16 C.F.R. Sections 310.1–310.8.

illegal for telemarketers to misrepresent information or facts about their goods or services. A telemarketer must also remove a consumer's name from its list of potential contacts if the customer so requests.

An amendment to the TSR established the national Do Not Call Registry. Telemarketers must refrain from calling consumers who have placed their names on the list. Significantly, the TSR applies to any offer made to consumers in the United States—even if the offer comes from a foreign firm. Thus, the TSR helps to protect consumers from illegal cross-border telemarketing operations.

Case Example 32.5 Jason Abraham formed Instant Response Systems, LLC (IRS), to sell medical alert monitoring systems to the elderly. IRS employed telemarketers to make sales calls to people sixty-four years old and older. Some of these consumers were on the Do Not Call Registry. The telemarketers, using company-supplied scripts, falsely told consumers that they were calling in response to a request for information about IRS's medical alert services. Consumers who did not order the IRS system were still billed for it, receiving follow-up letters and calls accusing them of nonpayment. When they objected, IRS employees resorted to threats.

How did the Telemarketing Sales Rule affect a dispute between a medical-alert service and the Federal Trade Commission?

Atstock Productions/Shutterstock.com

The FTC sued IRS and Abraham for violating the Telemarketing Sales Rule and won. IRS's telemarketers had made false and misleading statements to consumers, and had used threats to force them to make payments. IRS had also called individuals on the Do Not Call Registry without permission. The court ordered Abraham to pay more than $3.4 million (the amount of revenues he had received through the company's unlawful scheme). The court also permanently enjoined (prohibited) Abraham from marketing medical alert systems in the future.[8] ■

32–1e Sales

Various statutes protect consumers by requiring the disclosure of certain terms in sales transactions and providing rules governing such matters as unsolicited merchandise, door-to-door sales, and mail-order sales. The FTC has regulatory authority in this area, as do some other federal agencies.

"Cooling-Off" Laws Laws that allow buyers of goods sold in certain transactions to cancel their contracts within three business days.

Many states and the FTC have **"cooling-off" laws** that permit the buyers of goods sold in certain transactions to cancel their contracts within three business days. The FTC rule also requires that consumers be notified in Spanish of this right if the oral negotiations for the sale were in that language. The contracts that fall under these cancellation rules include trade show sales contracts, contracts for home equity loans, Internet purchase contracts, and home (door-to-door) sales contracts. In addition, certain states have passed laws allowing consumers to cancel contracts for things such as dating services, gym memberships, and weight loss programs.

The FTC's Mail, Internet, or Telephone Order Merchandise Rule[9] protects consumers who purchase goods via mail, Internet, or phone. Merchants must ship orders within the time promised in their advertisements and must notify consumers when orders cannot be shipped on time. If the seller does not give an estimated shipping time, it must ship within thirty days. Merchants must also issue a refund within a specified period of time when a consumer cancels an order.

8. *Federal Trade Commission v. Instant Response Systems, LLC*, 2015 WL 1650914 (E.D.N.Y. 2015).
9. 16 C.F.R. Sections 435.1–435.2.

32–1f Labeling

In general, labels must be accurate, and they must use words that are understood by the ordinary consumer. In some instances, labels must specify the raw materials used in the product, such as the percentage of cotton, nylon, or other fibers used in a garment. In other instances, the product must carry a warning, such as those required on cigarette packages and advertising.[10]

Automobile Fuel Economy Labels The Energy Policy and Conservation Act (EPCA)[11] requires automakers to attach an information label to every new car. This label must include the Environmental Protection Agency's fuel economy estimate for the vehicle. **Spotlight Case Example 32.6** Gaetano Paduano bought a new Honda Civic Hybrid in California. The information label on the car included the fuel economy estimate from the Environmental Protection Agency (EPA). Honda's sales brochure added, "Just drive the Hybrid like you would a conventional car and save on fuel bills."

When Paduano discovered that the car's fuel economy was less than half of the EPA's estimate, he sued Honda for deceptive advertising. The automaker claimed that the federal law (the EPCA) preempted the state's deceptive advertising law, but the court held in Paduano's favor, finding that the federal statute did not preempt a claim for deceptive advertising made under state law.[12]

Food Labeling Because the quality and safety of food are so important to consumers, several statutes deal specifically with food labeling. The Fair Packaging and Labeling Act requires that food product labels identify (1) the product, (2) the net quantity of the contents, (3) the manufacturer, and (4) the packager or distributor.[13] The act includes additional requirements concerning descriptions on packages, savings claims, components of nonfood products, and standards for the partial filling of packages.

Nutritional Content. Food products must bear labels detailing the food's nutritional content, including the number of calories and the amounts of various nutrients. The Nutrition Labeling and Education Act requires food labels to provide standard nutrition facts and regulates the use of such terms as *fresh* and *low fat*.

The U.S. Food and Drug Administration (FDA) and the U.S. Department of Agriculture (USDA) are the primary agencies that issue regulations on food labeling. These rules are published in the *Federal Register* and updated annually. For instance, current rules require labels on fresh and frozen fruits and vegetables to indicate where the food originated so that consumers can know if their food was imported.

Product Identification Issues. FDA regulations define dairy products as coming from milk-producing animals such as cows and goats. Yet supermarkets are filled with drinks made from non-dairy sources such as almonds and cashews that are labeled "milk." A similar phenomenon exists in the meat industry, with a proliferation of plant- and soy-based products mimicking the shape and taste of animal meat. Representatives of the traditional dairy and beef industries believe that labeling these alternative food sources as "milk" and "burgers" risks confusing consumers.

A number of states and the federal government are considering legislation that would ban the use of words such as *milk* and *burger* on the labels of products that are not derived from animal sources. Critics of this regulatory trend reject the idea that consumers are unsure whether almond milk comes from a cow or an Impossible Burger is made with beef. Any

---

10. 15 U.S.C. Sections 1331 *et seq.*
11. 49 U.S.C. Section 32908(b)(1).
12. *Paduano v. American Honda Motor Co.*, 169 Cal.App. 4th 1453, 88 Cal.Rptr.3d 90 (2009).
13. 15 U.S.C. Sections 4401–4408.

confusion that might exist, these observers point out, can be cleared up by the nutritional content label.

Case Example 32.7 A group of California consumers brought a class action lawsuit against Blue Diamond Growers, claiming that the company mislabeled its almond beverages as "almond milk." The plaintiffs insisted that the product should be labeled "imitation milk" because it resembles dairy milk to a degree that is confusing to consumers. A federal appeals court dismissed this lawsuit, finding that a "reasonable consumer" is not going to be deceived into thinking that almond milk is a substitute for or an equivalent to dairy milk. As long as Blue Diamond accurately labels and advertises its almond milk, the court held, it is not "misleading" under federal or state law.[14]

Amarita/Shutterstock.com

Why did an appeals court reject the argument that labeling an almond beverage "milk" was misleading to consumers?

Caloric Content of Restaurant Foods. The health care reform bill enacted in 2010 (the Affordable Care Act) included provisions aimed at combating the problem of obesity in the United States. All restaurant chains with twenty or more locations are now required to post the caloric content of the foods on their menus so that customers will know how many calories the foods contain.[15] Foods offered through vending machines must also be labeled so that their caloric content is visible to would-be purchasers.

In addition, restaurants must post guidelines on the number of calories that an average person requires daily so that customers can determine what portion of a day's calories a particular food will provide. The hope is that consumers, armed with this information, will consider the number of calories when they make their food choices. The federal law on menu labeling supersedes all previous state and local laws.

Know This

The U.S. Food and Drug Administration is authorized to obtain, among other things, orders for the recall and seizure of certain products.

32–2 Protection of Health and Safety

Although labeling laws promote consumer health and safety, there is a significant distinction between regulating the information dispensed about a product and regulating the actual content of the product. The classic example is tobacco products. Producers of tobacco products are required to warn consumers about the hazards associated with the use of their products, but the sale of tobacco products has not been subjected to significant restrictions or banned outright despite the obvious dangers to health. We now examine various laws that regulate the actual products made available to consumers.

Focus Question 2

What law protects consumers against contaminated and misbranded foods and drugs?

32–2a Food and Drugs

The most important legislation regulating food and drugs is the Federal Food, Drug, and Cosmetic Act (FDCA).[16] The act protects consumers against adulterated (contaminated) and misbranded foods and drugs.

The FDCA established food standards, specified safe levels of potentially hazardous food additives, and provided guidelines for advertising and labeling food products. The FDCA also created a reportable food registry, established record-keeping requirements, required the registration of all food facilities, and provided for inspections. Most of these statutory requirements are monitored and enforced by the FDA.

---

14. *Painter v. Blue Diamond Growers*, 757 Fed.Appx. 517 (9th Cir. 2018).
15. See Section 4205 of the Patient Protection and Affordable Care Act, Pub. L. No.111-148, March 23, 2010, 124 Stat. 119.
16. 21 U.S.C. Section 301.

Some foods considered safe by the FDCA in the United States are prohibited in Europe, however. For instance, products containing ingredients such as olestra (often in potato chips) and brominated vegetable oils (in certain sports drinks) are banned in the European Union. Many foreign nations also ban the use of certain chemicals and food colorings that are commonly found in U.S. food products.

Tainted Foods In the last several years, many people in the United States have contracted food poisoning from eating foods that were contaminated—often with *Salmonella* or *E.coli* bacteria. **Example 32.8** Hundreds of people across the United States were sickened by eating contaminated food at the popular restaurant chain Chipotle Mexican Grill. Causes of illness in these outbreaks included *E.coli* and *Salmonella*, as well as the highly contagious norovirus. ■ In response, Congress enacted the Food Safety Modernization Act (FSMA),[17] which provides greater government control over the U.S. food safety system.

The goal of the modernization act was to shift the focus of federal regulators from responding to incidents of contamination to preventing them. The act also gives the FDA authority to directly recall any food products that it suspects are tainted, rather than relying on the producers to recall items.

The FSMA requires any party that manufactures, processes, packs, distributes, receives, holds, or imports food products to pay a fee and register with the U.S. Department of Health and Human Services. (There are some exceptions for small farmers.) Owners and operators of such facilities are required to analyze and identify food safety hazards, implement preventive controls, monitor effectiveness, and take corrective actions. The act also places more restrictions on importers of food and requires them to verify that imported foods meet U.S. safety standards.

Drugs and Medical Devices The FDA is also responsible under the FDCA for ensuring that drugs are safe and effective before they are marketed to the public. It is the responsibility of the company seeking to market a drug to test it and submit evidence that it is safe and effective. The FDA has established extensive procedures that drug manufacturers must follow. The FDA also has the authority to regulate medical devices, such as pacemakers, and to withdraw from the market any such device that is mislabeled.[18]

The FDA has been criticized for failing to recognize the addictive qualities of prescription opioids such as Oxycontin and fentanyl, which have been linked to hundreds of thousands of opioid overdose deaths. **Case Example 32.9** Pharmaceutical Manufacturing Research Services, Inc. (PMRS), sought approval from the FDA to advertise a new prescription opioid drug as being less prone to abuse and addiction than other opioids. The company claimed that its product contained a purplish dye that would "create a visual deterrent" to intravenous injection. Furthermore, the drug's label would recommend a maximum daily dose below industry standards.

The FDA denied approval on the grounds that PMRS had not provided any evidence that, based on its physical and chemical properties, the drug actually carried less potential for abuse. A federal appeals court upheld the FDA's decision, finding that a proposed label heralding PMRS's product as "the safest opioid" on the market would be false or misleading.[19] ■

32–2b Consumer Product Safety

The Consumer Product Safety Act[20] created a comprehensive regulatory scheme over consumer safety matters and established the Consumer Product Safety Commission (CPSC).

---

17. Pub. L. No. 111-353, 124 Stat. 3885 (January 4, 2011). This statute affected numerous parts of Title 21 of the U.S.C.
18. 21 U.S.C. Sections 352(o), 360(j), 360(k), and 360c–360k.
19. *Pharmaceutical Manufacturing Research Services, Inc. v. Food & Drug Administration*, __ F.3d. __, 2020 WL 2090081 (D.C. Cir., 2020).
20. 15 U.S.C. Section 2051.

The CPSC's Authority The CPSC conducts research on the safety of individual products and maintains a clearinghouse on the risks associated with various products. The Consumer Product Safety Act authorizes the CPSC to do the following:

1. Set safety standards for consumer products.
2. Ban the manufacture and sale of any product that the commission believes poses an "unreasonable risk" to consumers. (Products banned by the CPSC have included various types of fireworks, cribs, and toys, as well as many products containing asbestos or vinyl chloride.)
3. Remove from the market any products it believes to be imminently hazardous. The CPSC frequently works with manufacturers to voluntarily recall defective products from stores. **Example 32.10** In cooperation with the CPSC, the Scandinavian company IKEA recalled nearly 1 million three-drawer Kullen dressers after it became clear that these pieces of furniture easily tipped over, posing an unacceptable danger to small children. (The dressers had been linked to the deaths of at least nine children, along with dozens of injuries.) ■
4. Require manufacturers to report any products already sold or intended for sale that have proved to be hazardous.
5. Administer other product-safety legislation, including the Child Protection and Toy Safety Act[21] and the Federal Hazardous Substances Act.[22]

buzbuzzer/iStock Unreleased/Getty Images

Why would IKEA want to cooperate with the Consumer Product Safety Commission?

Notification Requirements The Consumer Product Safety Act imposes notification requirements on distributors of consumer products. Distributors must immediately notify the CPSC when they receive information that a product "contains a defect which . . . creates a substantial risk to the public" or "an unreasonable risk of serious injury or death."

32–2c Health Care Reforms

The health care reforms (Obamacare) enacted in 2010 gave Americans new rights and benefits with regard to health care.[23] These laws prohibit certain insurance company practices, such as denial of coverage for preexisting conditions.

Expanded Coverage for Children and Seniors The reforms enabled more children to obtain health-insurance coverage and allowed young adults (under age twenty-six) to remain covered by their parents' health-insurance policies. The legislation also ended lifetime limits and most annual limits on care, and gave patients access to recommended preventive services (such as cancer screenings, vaccinations, and well-baby checks) without cost. Under most standard health care plans, Medicare recipients receive a 75 percent discount on the cost of name-brand and generic drugs.

Controlling Costs of Health Insurance In an attempt to control the rising costs of health insurance, the laws placed restrictions on insurance companies. Insurance companies must spend at least 85 percent of all premium dollars collected from large employers (80 percent of premiums collected from individuals and small employers) on benefits and quality improvement. If insurance companies do not meet these goals, they must provide rebates to consumers. Additionally, states can require insurance companies to justify their premium increases to be eligible to participate in the health-insurance exchanges mandated by the law.

21. 15 U.S.C. Section 1262(e).
22. 15 U.S.C. Sections 1261–1273.
23. Patient Protection and Affordable Health Care Act, Pub. L. No. 111-148, March 23, 2010, 124 Stat. 119; and Health Care and Education Reconciliation Act, Pub. L. No. 111-152, March 30, 2010, 124 Stat. 1029.

32–3 Credit Protection

Credit protection is one of the most important aspects of consumer protection legislation. A large percentage of U.S. consumers have credit cards, and many carry a balance on these cards and other revolving debt, which amounts to over a trillion dollars of such debt nationwide. The Consumer Financial Protection Bureau oversees the credit practices of banks, mortgage lenders, and credit card companies.

32–3a Truth in Lending Act

A key statute regulating the credit and credit card industries is the Truth in Lending Act (TILA), the name commonly given to Title 1 of the Consumer Credit Protection Act (CCPA), as amended.[24] The TILA is basically a *disclosure law.* It is administered by the Federal Reserve Board and requires sellers and lenders to disclose credit terms or loan terms (such as the annual percentage rate, or APR, and any finance charges) so that individuals can shop around for the best financing arrangements.

Application TILA requirements apply only to persons who, in the ordinary course of business, lend funds, sell on credit, or arrange for the extension of credit. Thus, sales or loans made between two consumers do not come under the act. Additionally, this law protects only debtors who are *natural* persons (as opposed to the artificial "person" of a corporation) and does not extend to other legal entities.

Disclosure The TILA's disclosure requirements are found in **Regulation Z,**[25] issued by the Federal Reserve Board of Governors. If the contracting parties are subject to the TILA, the requirements of Regulation Z apply to any transaction involving an installment sales contract that calls for payment to be made in more than four installments. Transactions subject to Regulation Z typically include installment loans, retail installment sales, car loans, home-improvement loans, and certain real estate loans, if the amount of financing is less than $58,300.

Regulation Z A set of rules issued by the Federal Reserve Board of Governors to implement the provisions of the Truth in Lending Act.

Focus Question 3

What does Regulation Z require, and how does it relate to the Truth in Lending Act?

Equal Credit Opportunity The Equal Credit Opportunity Act (ECOA) amended the TILA. The ECOA prohibits the denial of credit solely on the basis of race, religion, national origin, color, gender, marital status, or age. The act also prohibits credit discrimination on the basis of whether an individual receives certain forms of income, such as public-assistance benefits.

Courts tend to interpret the ECOA's protections broadly, particularly when the lending institution is perceived to have treated a credit applicant unfairly. **Case Example 32.11** Chase Bank USA rejected Jeffrey Chen's application for a credit card, citing his previous "unsatisfactory relationship with the bank" as the only reason for the denial. Chen filed suit against Chase for violating the ECOA. Chase moved for the action to be dismissed because Chen could not show that he had been the victim of discrimination based on any of the factors identified in the ECOA.

Investigating the legislative record of the ECOA, a federal court found that Congress intended for the law not only to discourage discriminatory practices but also to provide educational and informational benefits to consumers. Under this latter requirement, "instead of being told only that they do not meet a particular creditor's standards," rejected credit applicants must be given specific reasons for the denial. Because Chase clearly failed to provide Chen with this information, the court ruled that Chen's action under the ECOA could proceed.[26]

Know This

The Federal Reserve Board is part of the Federal Reserve System, which influences the lending and investing activities of commercial banks and the cost and availability of credit.

24. 15 U.S.C. Sections 1601–1693r. The TILA was amended in 1980 by the Truth-in-Lending Simplification and Reform Act and again in 2009 by the Credit Card Accountability Responsibility and Disclosure Act.
25. 12 C.F.R. Sections 226.1–226.30.
26. *Chen v. Chase Bank USA, N.A.*, 393 F.Supp.3d 850 (N.D. Cal. 2019).

Hire Image Picture Library/Alamy Stock Photo

What are some basic TILA provisions that benefit credit card holders?

Credit Card Rules The TILA also contains provisions regarding credit cards. One provision limits the liability of a cardholder to $50 per card for unauthorized charges made before the creditor was notified that the card was lost. If a consumer received an *unsolicited* credit card in the mail that was later stolen, the company that issued the card cannot charge the consumer for any unauthorized charges.

Another provision requires credit card companies to disclose the balance computation method that is used to determine the outstanding balance and to state when finance charges begin to accrue. Other provisions set forth procedures for resolving billing disputes with the credit card company. These procedures may be used if, for instance, a cardholder wishes to withhold payment for a faulty product purchased with a credit card.

Amendments to Credit Card Rules Amendments to TILA's credit card rules added the following protections:

1. A company may not retroactively increase the interest rates on existing card balances unless the account is sixty days delinquent.
2. A company must provide forty-five days' advance notice to consumers before changing its credit card terms.
3. Monthly bills must be sent to cardholders twenty-one days before the due date.
4. The interest rate charged on a customer's credit card balance may not be increased except in specific situations, such as when a promotional rate ends.
5. A company may not charge fees for being over the credit card's limit except in specified situations.
6. When the customer has balances at different interest rates, payments in excess of the minimum amount due must be applied first to the balance with the highest rate (for instance, a higher interest rate is commonly charged for cash advances).
7. A company may not compute finance charges based on the previous billing cycle (a practice known as double-cycle billing, which hurts consumers because they are charged interest for the previous cycle even if they have paid the bill in full).

32–3b Fair Credit Reporting Act

The Fair Credit Reporting Act (FCRA)[27] protects consumers against inaccurate credit reporting and requires that lenders and other creditors report correct, relevant, and up-to-date information. The act provides that consumer credit reporting agencies may issue credit reports to users only for specified purposes. Legitimate purposes include the extension of credit, the issuance of insurance policies, and in response to the consumer's request.

Consumer Notification and Inaccurate Information Any time a consumer is denied credit or insurance on the basis of a credit report, the consumer must be notified of that fact. The same notice must be sent to consumers who are charged more than others ordinarily would be for credit or insurance because of their credit reports.

Under the FCRA, consumers can request the source of any information used by the credit agency, as well as the identity of anyone who has received an agency's report. Consumers are also permitted to have access to the information contained about them in a credit reporting agency's files.

27. 15 U.S.C. Sections 1681 *et seq.*

A consumer who discovers that the agency's files contain inaccurate information should report the problem to the agency. On the consumer's written (or electronic) request, the agency must conduct a systematic examination of its records. Any unverifiable or erroneous information must be deleted within a reasonable period of time.

teekid/E+/Getty Images

Which law attempts to protect consumers against inaccurate credit information?

Remedies for Violations A credit reporting agency that fails to comply with the act is liable for actual damages, plus additional damages not to exceed $1,000 and attorneys' fees.[28] Creditors and other companies that use information from credit reporting agencies may also be liable for violations of the FCRA. Punitive damages may be awarded for *willful* violations. An insurance company's failure to notify new customers that they are paying higher insurance rates as a result of their credit scores is considered a willful violation of the FCRA.[29]

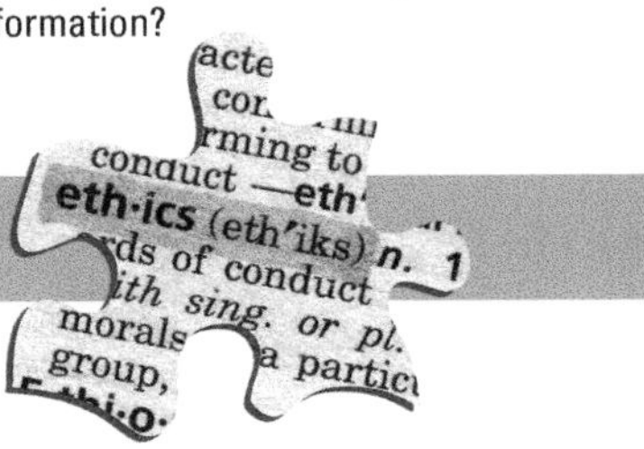

Ethical Issue

Can a company that provides background checks willfully violate the Fair Credit Reporting Act? After graduating from college with a bachelor's degree, Richard Williams applied for a job in his hometown with Rent-A-Center as an account representative. As part of the application process, he agreed to a drug test (which he passed) and a criminal-background check. Rent-A-Center contracted with First Advantage LNS Screening Solutions, Inc., a credit reporting agency that provides various background checks.

First Advantage reported to Rent-A-Center that a Richard Williams had a sale-of-cocaine record in another part of the state. Williams disputed the report. First Advantage admitted that Richard Williams is a common name and that it had not obtained three identifiers of that record. When First Advantage investigated, it determined that the criminal record was for a different person with the same name. It removed that criminal record from Williams's report. By then, however, it was too late, as Rent-A-Center had hired someone else.

Williams continued applying for a multitude of jobs. Eventually, another prospective employer ran a background check through First Advantage. This time, First Advantage reported to the employer that Williams had been convicted of aggravated battery on a pregnant woman. Again, it turned out to be a different Richard Williams, but by then, the employer had rejected Williams and hired someone else. Williams sued First Advantage in a federal district court for willfully violating the FCRA. After a jury trial, he was awarded $250,000 in compensatory damages and $3.3 million in punitive damages. First Advantage filed a motion for a new trial, which the court denied. Evidence supported the jury's finding that First Advantage had willfully violated the FCRA and that the damages awarded were appropriate and not unconstitutionally excessive.[30]

32–3c Fair and Accurate Credit Transactions Act

Congress passed the Fair and Accurate Credit Transactions (FACT) Act to combat identity theft.[31] The act established a national fraud alert system so that consumers who suspect that they have been or may be victimized by identity theft can place an alert in their credit files. The act also requires the major credit reporting agencies to provide consumers with a free copy of their credit reports every twelve months.

28. 15 U.S.C. Section 1681n.
29. This was the holding of the United States Supreme Court in *Safeco Insurance Co. of America v. Burr,* 551 U.S. 47, 127 S.Ct. 2201, 167 L.Ed.2d 1045 (2007).
30 *Williams v. First Advantage LSN Screening Solutions, Inc.,* 238 F.Supp.3d 1333 (N.D.Fla. 2017).
31. Pub. L. No. 108-159, 117 Stat. 1952 (December 4, 2003).

Another provision requires account numbers on credit card receipts to be truncated (shortened) so that merchants, employees, and others who have access to the receipts cannot obtain a consumer's name and full credit card number. The act also mandates that financial institutions work with the FTC to identify "red flag" indicators of identity theft and to develop rules for disposing of sensitive credit information.

32–3d Fair Debt Collection Practices Act

The Fair Debt Collection Practices Act (FDCPA)[32] attempts to curb abuses by collection agencies. The act applies only to specialized debt-collection agencies and attorneys who regularly attempt to collect debts on behalf of someone else, usually for a percentage of the amount owed. Creditors attempting to collect debts are not covered by the act unless, by misrepresenting themselves, they cause the debtors to believe that they are collection agencies.

Requirements Under the FDCPA, a collection agency may not do any of the following:

1. Contact the debtor at the debtor's place of employment if the debtor's employer objects.
2. Contact the debtor at inconvenient or unusual times (such as three o'clock in the morning), or at any time if the debtor is being represented by an attorney.
3. Contact third parties other than the debtor's parents, spouse, or financial adviser about payment of a debt unless a court authorizes such action.
4. Harass or intimidate the debtor (by using abusive language or threatening violence, for instance) or make false or misleading statements (such as posing as a police officer).
5. Communicate with the debtor at any time after receiving notice that the debtor is refusing to pay the debt, except to advise the debtor of further action to be taken by the collection agency.

The FDCPA also requires a collection agency to include a *validation notice* whenever it initially contacts a debtor for payment of a debt or within five days of that initial contact. The notice must state that the debtor has thirty days in which to dispute the debt and to request a written verification of the debt from the collection agency. The debtor's request for debt validation must be in writing.

The question before the court in the following case concerned what constitutes a misleading statement in violation of the FDCPA.

32. 15 U.S.C. Section 1692.

Case 32.3

Manuel v. Merchants and Professional Bureau, Inc.

United States Court of Appeals, Fifth Circuit, 956 F.3d 822 (2020).

Facts Silvia Manuel owed Texas Orthopedics, Sports and Rehabilitation Associates $250. The debt was transferred to Merchants and Professional Bureau, Inc., for collection.

After six years had passed with no effort to collect, Merchants sent Manuel four collection letters. By that time, a four-year Texas statute of limitations barred any suit to collect the debt. In other words, the debt was not legally enforceable. But the collection letters did not disclose this fact, instead making vague references to a "special offer" and possible "additional collection efforts."

Manuel filed a suit in a federal district court against Merchants, claiming that the collection letters were false and misleading under the Fair Debt Collection Practices Act (FDCPA). The court issued a summary judgment in Manuel's favor. She had agreed not to seek actual damages and thus was awarded the maximum $1,000 statutory damages.

Merchants appealed, arguing that its silence concerning the legal enforceability of the old debt was not in itself misleading.

Issue Did Merchants' collection letters misrepresent the legal enforceability of Manuel's debt?

Decision Yes. The U.S. Court of Appeals for the Fifth Circuit affirmed the judgment of the lower court.

Reason The appellate court reasoned that, when "read as a whole," the letters from Merchants were misleading. The letters did not notify Manuel that Texas has a statute of limitations, explain how that statute could affect collection of the debt, or even specify when the debt had been incurred. "If they had," stated the court, "they might give a consumer at least some inkling that the debt might be too old to be legally enforceable."

The letters referred vaguely to a "special offer," implying that it would expire soon, and to "additional collection efforts" that could be made if the debt was not paid. Neither the terms of the offer nor the possible collection efforts were set out. According to the court, "the combined effect of the letters' vague language and their silence as to the debt's time-barred nature leaves [a] consumer with the impression that the debt is enforceable, and that if payment is not levied quickly then adverse collection efforts will follow."

The FDCPA requires clarity. Ambiguous language in a collection letter can violate the act. The court read Merchants' letters to be "examples of careful and crafted ambiguity." In sum, the court concluded, the letters "misrepresent the legal enforceability of the underlying debt in violation" of the FDCPA.

Critical Thinking

- **Legal Environment** *How might Merchants have phrased its debt collection letters to meet the standards of the FDCPA? Explain.*
- **Economic** *Why would a debt collector use carefully crafted, ambiguous language in an attempt to collect an old debt? Discuss.*

Enforcement The Federal Trade Commission is primarily responsible for enforcing the FDCPA. A debt collector who fails to comply with the act is liable for actual damages, plus additional damages not to exceed $1,000 and attorneys' fees.

Debt collectors who violate the act are exempt from liability if they can show that the violation was not intentional and resulted from a bona fide error. The "bona fide error" defense typically has been applied to mistakes of fact or clerical errors.

32–4 Protecting the Environment

We now turn to a discussion of the various ways in which businesses are regulated by the government in the interest of attempting to protect the environment. Environmental protection is not without a price. For many businesses, the costs of complying with environmental regulations are high, and for some, they may seem too high.

32–4a Federal Regulation

Congress has enacted a number of statutes to control the impact of human activities on the environment. Some of these laws have been passed in an attempt to improve the quality of air and water. Other laws specifically regulate toxic chemicals, including pesticides, herbicides, and hazardous wastes.

Environmental Regulatory Agencies The primary agency regulating environmental law is the Environmental Protection Agency (EPA). Other federal agencies with authority to regulate specific environmental matters include the Department of the Interior, the Department of Defense, the Department of Labor, the Food and Drug Administration, and the Nuclear Regulatory Commission.

Focus Question 4

What does an environmental impact statement contain, and who must file one?

State and local agencies also play an important role in enforcing federal environmental legislation. In addition, most federal environmental laws provide that private parties can sue to enforce environmental regulations if government agencies fail to do so. Typically, a threshold hurdle in such suits is meeting the requirements for standing to sue.

Environmental Impact Statement (EIS) A formal analysis required for any major federal action that will significantly affect the quality of the environment to determine the action's impact and explore alternatives.

Environmental Impact Statements All agencies of the federal government must take environmental factors into consideration when making significant decisions. The National Environmental Policy Act (NEPA)[33] requires that an **environmental impact statement (EIS)** be prepared for every major federal action that significantly affects the quality of the environment (see Exhibit 32–2). An EIS must analyze the following:

1. The impact that the action will have on the environment.
2. Any adverse effects on the environment and alternative actions that might be taken.
3. Irreversible effects the action might generate.

Note that an EIS must be prepared for every major federal action. An action qualifies as "major" if it involves a substantial commitment of resources (monetary or otherwise). An action is "federal" if a federal agency has the power to control it. **Example 32.12** Development of a ski resort by a private developer on federal land may require an EIS. Construction or operation of a nuclear plant, which requires a federal permit, necessitates an EIS, as does creation of a dam as part of a federal project. ■

If an agency decides that an EIS is unnecessary, it must issue a statement supporting this conclusion. Private individuals, consumer interest groups, businesses, and others who believe that a federal agency's actions threaten the environment often use EISs as a means of challenging those actions.

32–4b Common Law Actions

Even before there were statutes and regulations explicitly protecting the environment, the common law recognized that individuals have the right not to have their environment contaminated by others. Common law remedies against environmental pollution originated centuries ago in England. Those responsible for operations that created dirt, smoke, noxious odors, noise, or toxic substances were sometimes held liable under common law theories of nuisance or negligence. Today, individuals who have suffered harm from pollution continue to rely on the common law to obtain damages and injunctions against business polluters.

33. 42 U.S.C. Sections 4321–4370d.

Exhibit 32–2 Environmental Impact Statements

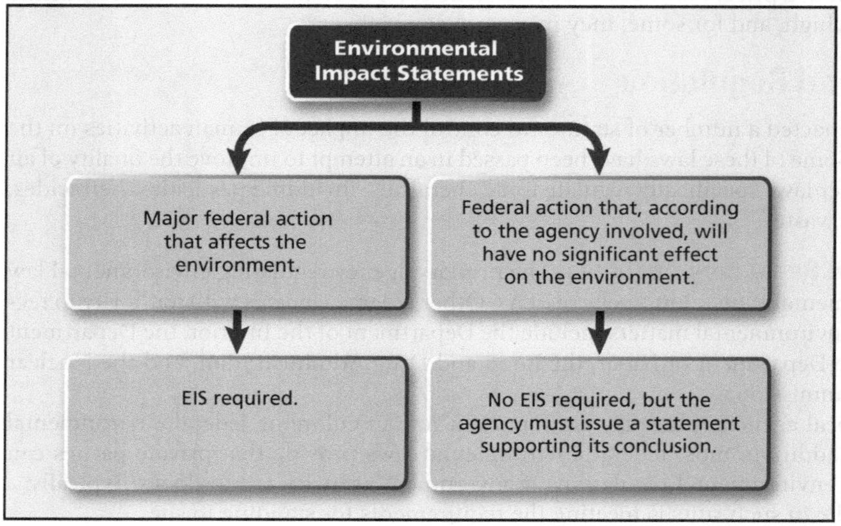

Nuisance Under the common law doctrine of **nuisance,** persons may be held liable if they use their property in a manner that unreasonably interferes with others' rights to use or enjoy their own property. In these situations, the courts commonly balance the harm caused by the pollution against the costs of stopping it.

Nuisance A common law doctrine under which persons may be held liable for using their property in a manner that unreasonably interferes with others' rights to use or enjoy their own property.

Courts have often denied injunctive relief on the ground that the hardships that would be imposed on the polluter and on the community are relatively greater than the hardships suffered by the plaintiff. **Example 32.13** Hewitt's Factory causes neighboring landowners to suffer from smoke, soot, and vibrations. If the factory is the core of the local economy, a court may leave it in operation and award monetary damages to the injured parties. Damages may include compensation for any decline in the value of their property caused by Hewitt's operation.

To obtain relief from pollution under the nuisance doctrine, a property owner may have to identify a distinct harm (a "private" nuisance) separate from that affecting the general public. Under the common law—which is still followed in some states—individuals must establish a private nuisance to have standing to sue. A public authority (such as a state's attorney general), though, can sue to stop or reduce a "public" nuisance.

AP Images/David J. Phillip

How can a local factory that is considered a "nuisance" by nearby property owners be held liable for noise or air pollution?

Negligence and Strict Liability An injured party may sue a business polluter under the negligence and strict liability theories discussed in the torts chapter. A negligence action is based on a business's alleged failure to use reasonable care toward a party whose injury was foreseeable and was caused by the lack of reasonable care. For instance, employees might sue an employer whose failure to use proper pollution controls contaminated the air and caused the employees to suffer respiratory illnesses.

Businesses that engage in ultrahazardous activities—such as the transportation of radioactive materials—are strictly liable for any injuries the activities cause. In a strict liability action, the injured party does not need to prove that the business failed to exercise reasonable care.

Lawsuits for personal injuries caused by exposure to a toxic substance, such as asbestos, radiation, or hazardous waste, have given rise to a growing body of tort law known as **toxic torts**. These torts may be based on a theory of negligence or strict liability.

Toxic Torts A civil wrong arising from exposure to a toxic substance, such as asbestos, radiation, or hazardous waste.

32–5 Air and Water Pollution

The United States has long recognized the need to protect our natural resources. During the industrial revolution, factories began discharging substances into our air and water. Over time, it became clear that many of these substances were harmful to our environment, and the government began regulating.

32–5a Air Pollution

Federal involvement with air pollution goes back to the 1950s and 1960s, when Congress authorized funds for air pollution research and enacted the Clean Air Act.[34] The Clean Air Act provides the basis for issuing regulations to control multistate air pollution. It covers both mobile sources of pollution (such as automobiles and other vehicles) and stationary sources of pollution (such as electric utilities and industrial plants).

Mobile Sources of Air Pollution Regulations governing air pollution from automobiles and other mobile sources specify pollution standards and establish time schedules for meeting the standards. The EPA periodically updates the pollution standards to reduce the amount of emissions allowed in light of new developments and data.

34. 42 U.S.C. Sections 7401 *et seq.*

The most recent federal guidelines for mobile sources of air pollution were passed in 2020.[35] Under Part II of the Safer Affordable Fuel Efficient Vehicles (SAFE) Rule, American automakers must reduce emissions in new passenger cars and light trucks by 1.5 percent each year through 2026, starting with model year 2021. Similarly, SAFE Part II requires automakers to improve the fuel efficiency of their fleets by 1.5 percent per year through 2026, also starting in 2021.

Stationary Sources of Air Pollution The Clean Air Act authorizes the EPA to establish air-quality standards for stationary sources, such as manufacturing plants. The standards are aimed at controlling hazardous air pollutants—those likely to cause death or a serious, irreversible, or incapacitating condition, such as cancer or neurological or reproductive damage.

The act recognizes that the primary responsibility in this area rests with state and local governments. Thus, the EPA sets primary and secondary levels of ambient standards—that is, the maximum permissible levels of certain pollutants—and the states formulate plans to achieve those standards. Different standards apply depending on whether the sources of pollution are located in clean areas or polluted areas and whether they are existing sources or major new sources.

Hazardous Air Pollutants. The Clean Air Act requires the EPA to list all regulated hazardous air pollutants on a prioritized schedule. In all, nearly two hundred substances, including asbestos, benzene, beryllium, cadmium, and vinyl chloride, have been classified as hazardous. They are emitted from stationary sources by a variety of business activities, including smelting (melting ore to produce metal), dry cleaning, house painting, and commercial baking.

Maximum Achievable Control Technology. The Clean Air Act does not establish specific emissions standards for each hazardous air pollutant. Instead, the act requires *major new sources* of pollutants to use pollution-control equipment that represents the *maximum achievable control technology,* or MACT, to reduce emissions. The EPA issues guidelines as to what equipment meets this standard.[36]

Greenhouse Gases Although greenhouse gases, such as carbon dioxide (CO_2), are generally thought to contribute to global climate change, the Clean Air Act does not specifically mention CO_2 emissions. Therefore, the EPA did not regulate CO_2 emissions until 2009, after the Supreme Court ruled that it had the authority to do so.

Classic Case Example 32.14 Environmental groups and several states, including Massachusetts, sued the EPA in an effort to force the agency to regulate CO_2 emissions. When the case reached the United States Supreme Court, the EPA argued that the plaintiffs lacked standing. The agency claimed that because climate change has widespread effects, an individual plaintiff cannot show the particularized harm required for standing. The agency also maintained that it did not have authority under the Clean Air Act to address global climate change and regulate CO_2.

The Court, however, ruled that Massachusetts had standing because its coastline, including state-owned lands, faced a threat from the rising sea levels that may result from climate change. The Court also held that the Clean Air Act's broad definition of air pollution gives the EPA authority to regulate CO_2 and requires the EPA to regulate any air pollutants that might "endanger public health or welfare." Accordingly, the Court ordered the EPA to determine

35. "The Safer Affordable Fuel Efficient (SAFE) Vehicles Final Rule for Model Years 2021-2026." *www.epa.gov.* United States Environmental Protection Agency: April 30, 2020, Web.

36. The EPA has also issued rules to regulate hazardous air pollutants emitted by landfills. See 40 C.F.R. Sections 60.750–60.759.

whether CO_2 was a pollutant that endangered the public health.[37] The EPA went on to conclude that greenhouse gases, including CO_2 emissions, do constitute a public danger and began regulating them in 2011.

Does the Environmental Protection Agency have the power to regulate CO_2 emissions from power plants?

Violations of the Clean Air Act For violations of emission limits under the Clean Air Act, the EPA can assess civil penalties of up to $101,439 per day. Additional fines of up to $7,500 per day can be assessed for other violations, such as failing to maintain the required records. To penalize those who find it more cost-effective to violate the act than to comply with it, the EPA is authorized to obtain a penalty equal to the violator's economic benefits from noncompliance. Persons who provide information about violators may be paid up to $10,000. Private individuals can also sue violators.

32–5b Water Pollution

Water pollution stems mostly from industrial, municipal, and agricultural sources. Pollutants entering streams, lakes, and oceans include organic wastes, heated water, sediments from soil runoff, nutrients (including fertilizers and human and animal wastes), and toxic chemicals and other hazardous substances.

Federal regulations governing the pollution of water can be traced back to the 1899 Rivers and Harbors Appropriation Act.[38] These regulations prohibited ships and manufacturers from discharging or depositing refuse in navigable waterways without a permit. In 1948, Congress passed the Federal Water Pollution Control Act (FWPCA),[39] but its regulatory system and enforcement powers proved to be inadequate.

The Clean Water Act In 1972, amendments to the FWPCA—known as the Clean Water Act (CWA)—established the following goals: (1) make waters safe for swimming, (2) protect fish and wildlife, and (3) eliminate the discharge of pollutants into the water. The amendments set specific time schedules, which were extended by amendment and by the Water Quality Act.[40] Under these schedules, the EPA limits the discharge of various types of pollutants based on the technology available for controlling them.

Focus Question 5
What are three main goals of the Clean Water Act?

Permit System for Point-Source Emissions. The CWA established a permit system, called the National Pollutant Discharge Elimination System (NPDES), for regulating discharges from "point sources" of pollution. Point sources include industrial facilities, municipal facilities (such as sewer pipes and sewage treatment plants), and agricultural facilities.[41] Under this system, industrial, municipal, and agricultural polluters must apply for permits before discharging wastes into surface waters.

NPDES permits can be issued by the EPA, authorized state agencies, and Indian tribes, but only if the discharge will not violate water-quality standards (either federal or state standards). Special requirements must be met to discharge toxic chemicals and residue from oil spills. NPDES permits must be renewed every five years.

Storm Water. Although the NPDES system initially focused mainly on industrial wastewater, it was later expanded to cover storm water discharge. **Case Example 32.15** The Maryland Department of the Environment (MDE) issued separate storm sewer system (MS4) discharge permits to various counties in Maryland. A number of environmental organizations,

37. *Massachusetts v. Environmental Protection Agency,* 549 U.S. 497, 127 S.Ct. 1438, 167 L.Ed.2d 248 (2007).
38. 33 U.S.C. Sections 401–418.
39. 33 U.S.C. Sections 1251–1387.
40. This act amended 33 U.S.C. Section 1251.
41. 33 U.S.C. Section 1342.

including Anacosta Riverkeeper, sued the MDE, claiming that its MS4 permits did not comply with federal law. They argued that the MS4 permits allowed permit holders to discharge chemicals and other substances into the Chesapeake Bay at levels exceeding the daily maximum load set by the EPA. A state trial court ruled in the MDE's favor, and the plaintiffs appealed.

A state appellate court reviewed the requirements of the state's MS4 permit system and determined that it complied with the Clean Water Act. Although Maryland's storm water management system was not perfect, the court concluded that it was a reasonable attempt to control and restore the state's water quality. The court reasoned that municipal storm water discharge is highly intermittent and includes relatively high flows that occur over short periods. The fact that the discharges sometimes exceeded the daily maximum load did not mean that the MS4 permits violated the Clean Water Act.[42]

What law governs discharge of pollutants into water?

Standards for Equipment. Regulations generally specify that the *best available control technology*, or BACT, be installed. The EPA issues guidelines as to what equipment meets this standard. Essentially, the guidelines require the most effective pollution-control equipment available.

New sources must install BACT equipment before beginning operations. Existing sources are subject to timetables for the installation of BACT equipment and must immediately install equipment that utilizes the *best practical control technology*, or BPCT. The EPA also issues guidelines as to what equipment meets this standard.

Violations of the Clean Water Act Because point-source water pollution control is based on a permit system, the permits are the key to enforcement. States have primary responsibility for enforcing the permit system, subject to EPA monitoring.

Discharging emissions into navigable waters without a permit, or in violation of pollution limits under a permit, violates the CWA. Violators are subject to a variety of civil and criminal penalties. Depending on the violation, civil penalties can be as high as $55,800 per violation per day.

Criminal penalties, which apply only if a violation was intentional, range from a fine of $2,500 per day and imprisonment for up to one year to a fine of $1 million and fifteen years' imprisonment. Injunctive relief and damages can also be imposed. The polluting party can be required to clean up the pollution or pay for the cost of doing so.

Drinking Water The Safe Drinking Water Act[43] requires the EPA to set maximum levels for pollutants in public water systems. Public water system operators must come as close as possible to meeting the EPA's standards by using the best available technology that is economically and technologically feasible. Each supplier of drinking water must send an annual statement describing the source of its water to every household it supplies. The statement must disclose the level of any contaminants in the water and any possible health concerns associated with the contaminants.

32–6 Toxic Chemicals and Hazardous Waste

Today, the control of toxic chemicals used in agriculture and in industry has become increasingly important. If not properly disposed of, these chemicals may present a substantial danger to human health and the environment—for instance, by contaminating public drinking water resources.

---

42. *Maryland Department of the Environment v. Anacosta Riverkeeper*, 447 Md. 88, 134 A.3d 892 (2016).
43. 42 U.S.C. Sections 300f to 300j-25.

32–6a Pesticides and Herbicides

The Federal Insecticide, Fungicide, and Rodenticide Act (FIFRA)[44] regulates the use of pesticides and herbicides. These substances must be (1) registered before they can be sold, (2) certified and used only for approved applications, and (3) used in limited quantities when applied to food crops. The act gives the EPA authority to oversee the sale and use of these substances and to determine whether, and at what levels, a substance may be harmful.

It is a violation of FIFRA to sell a pesticide or herbicide that is unregistered or has had its registration canceled or suspended. It is also a violation to sell a pesticide or herbicide with a false or misleading label, or to destroy or deface any labeling required under the act.

Criminal penalties for commercial dealers include imprisonment for up to one year and a fine of up to $50,000. Farmers and other private users of pesticides or herbicides who violate the act are subject to a $1,000 fine and incarceration for up to thirty days. Note that a state can also regulate the sale and use of federally registered pesticides.

32–6b Toxic Substances

The Toxic Substances Control Act[45] regulates chemicals and chemical compounds that are known to be toxic, such as asbestos and polychlorinated biphenyls (PCBs). The act also controls the introduction of new chemical compounds by requiring investigation of any possible harmful effects from these substances.

The act authorizes the EPA to require that manufacturers, processors, and other organizations planning to use chemicals first determine their effects on human health and the environment. The EPA can regulate substances that could pose an imminent hazard or an unreasonable risk of injury to health or the environment. The EPA may require special labeling, limit the use of a substance, set production quotas, or prohibit the use of a substance altogether.

32–6c Resource Conservation and Recovery Act

The Resource Conservation and Recovery Act (RCRA)[46] was passed in reaction to concern over the effects of hazardous waste materials on the environment. The RCRA required the EPA to determine which forms of solid waste should be considered hazardous and to establish regulations to monitor and control hazardous waste disposal.

The act authorized the EPA to issue technical requirements for facilities that store and treat hazardous waste. The act also required all producers of hazardous waste materials to label and package properly any hazardous waste to be transported. Amendments to the RCRA decreased the use of land containment in the disposal of hazardous waste and required smaller generators of hazardous waste to comply with the act.

32–6d Superfund

Focus Question 6

What is Superfund? What categories of people are liable under Superfund?

The Comprehensive Environmental Response, Compensation, and Liability Act (CERCLA),[47] commonly known as Superfund, regulates the clean-up of disposal sites in which hazardous waste is leaking into the environment. CERCLA, as amended, has four primary elements:

1. It established an information-gathering and analysis system that enables the government to identify chemical dump sites and determine the appropriate action.

44. 7 U.S.C. Sections 135–136y.
45. 15 U.S.C. Sections 2601–2692.
46. 42 U.S.C. Sections 6901 *et seq.*
47. 42 U.S.C. Sections 9601–9675.

2. It authorized the EPA to respond to hazardous substance emergencies and to arrange for the clean-up of a leaking site directly if the persons responsible for the problem fail to clean up the site.
3. It created a Hazardous Substance Response Trust Fund (also called Superfund) to pay for the clean-up of hazardous sites using funds obtained through taxes on certain businesses.
4. It allowed the government to recover the cost of clean-up from persons who were responsible (even remotely) for hazardous substance releases.

Potentially Responsible Parties Superfund provides that when a release or a potential release of hazardous chemicals from a site occurs, the following persons may be held responsible for cleaning up the site:

1. A person who generated the wastes disposed of at the site.
2. A person who transported the waste to the site.
3. The person who owned or operated the site at the time of the disposal.
4. The current owner or operator of the site.

Potentially Responsible Party (PRP) A party liable for the costs of cleaning up a hazardous waste disposal site under the Comprehensive Environmental Response, Compensation, and Liability Act.

A person falling within one of these categories is referred to as a **potentially responsible party (PRP)**. If the PRPs do not clean up the site, the EPA can clean up the site and recover the costs from the PRPs.

Strict Liability of PRPs Superfund imposes strict liability on PRPs, and that liability cannot be avoided through transfer of ownership. Thus, selling a site where hazardous wastes were disposed of does not relieve the seller of liability, and the buyer also becomes liable for the clean-up. Liability also extends to businesses that merge with or buy corporations that have violated CERCLA.

Joint and Several Liability Liability under Superfund is usually joint and several—that is, a person who generated *only a fraction of the hazardous waste* disposed of at the site may nevertheless be liable for *all* of the clean-up costs. CERCLA authorizes a party who has incurred clean-up costs to bring a "contribution action" against any other person who is liable or potentially liable for a percentage of the costs.

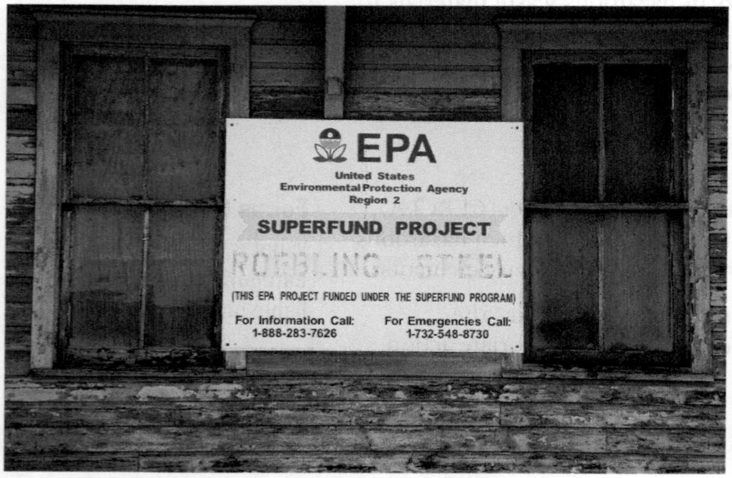

XenLights/Alamy

Who is liable for the clean-up of leaking hazardous waste?

Minimizing Liability One way for a business to minimize its potential liability under Superfund is to conduct environmental compliance audits of its own operations regularly. That is, the business can investigate its own operations and property to determine whether any environmental hazards exist.

The EPA encourages companies to conduct self-audits and promptly detect, disclose, and correct wrongdoing. Companies that do so are subject to lighter penalties for violations of environmental laws. (Fines may be reduced by as much as 75 percent.)

In addition, under EPA guidelines, the EPA will waive all fines if a small company corrects environmental violations within 180 days after being notified of the violations (or 360 days if pollution-prevention techniques are involved). The policy does not apply to criminal violations of environmental laws, though, or to violations that pose a significant threat to public health, safety, or the environment.

Defenses There are a few defenses to liability under CERCLA. The most important is the *innocent landowner defense*, which may protect a landowner who acquired the property after it was used for hazardous waste disposal.

To succeed in this defense, landowners must show that at the time the property was acquired, they had no reason to know that it had been used for hazardous waste disposal. These owners must show that at the time of the purchase, they undertook all appropriate investigation into the previous ownership and uses of the property to determine whether there was reason to be concerned about hazardous substances. In effect, this defense protects only property owners who took precautions and investigated the possibility of environmental hazards at the time they bought the property.

Practice and Review

Residents of Lake Caliopa, Minnesota, began noticing an unusually high number of lung ailments among the local population. Several concerned citizens pooled their resources and commissioned a study to compare the frequency of these health conditions in Lake Caliopa with national averages. The study concluded that residents of Lake Caliopa experienced four to seven times the rate of frequency of asthma, bronchitis, and emphysema as the population nationwide.

During the study period, citizens began expressing concerns about the large volume of smog emitted by the Cotton Design apparel manufacturing plant on the outskirts of town. The plant had a production facility two miles east of town beside the Tawakoni River and employed seventy workers. Just downstream on the Tawakoni River, the city of Lake Caliopa operated a public waterworks facility, which supplied all city residents with water.

After conducting its own investigation, the Minnesota Pollution Control Agency ordered Cotton Design to install new equipment to control air and water pollution. Later, citizens brought a lawsuit in a Minnesota state court against Cotton Design for various respiratory ailments allegedly caused or compounded by smog from Cotton Design's factory. Using the information presented in the chapter, answer the following questions.

1. Under the common law, what would each plaintiff be required to identify in order to be given relief by the court?
2. What standard for limiting emissions into the air does Cotton Design's pollution-control equipment have to meet?
3. If Cotton Design's emissions violated the Clean Air Act, how much can the EPA assess in fines per day?
4. What information must the city send to every household that it supplies with water?

Debate This

Laws against bait-and-switch advertising should be abolished because no consumer is ever forced to buy anything.

Key Terms

bait-and-switch advertising 796
cease-and-desist order 798
"cooling-off" laws 800
counteradvertising 798
deceptive advertising 795
environmental impact statement (EIS) 810
multiple product order 798
nuisance 811
potentially responsible party (PRP) 816
Regulation Z 805
toxic tort 811

Chapter Summary: Consumer and Environmental Law

CONSUMER LAW	
Advertising, Marketing, Sales, and Labeling	1. **Deceptive advertising**—Generally, an advertising claim will be deemed deceptive if it would mislead a reasonable consumer. a. Bait-and-switch advertising—Advertising a lower-priced product (the bait) to lure consumers into the store and then telling them the product is unavailable or of poor quality and urging them to buy a higher-priced product (the switch) instead; prohibited by the FTC. b. Online deceptive advertising—The FTC has issued guidelines to help online businesses comply with the laws prohibiting deceptive advertising. c. FTC actions against deceptive advertising—(1) A formal complaint is sent to the alleged offender. (2) A cease and-desist order is generally issued, requiring the advertiser to stop the challenged advertising. (3) Counteradvertising may be required, so that the advertiser can correct the earlier misinformation. (4) Restitution may be sought. 2. **False advertising claims under the Lanham Act**—A successful claim for false advertising requires that a business establish (a) an injury to a commercial interest in reputation or sales, (b) direct causation of the injury by false or deceptive advertising by a competing company, and (c) a loss of business from buyers who were deceived by the advertising. 3. **Marketing**—Telemarketers are prohibited from using automatic dialing systems and prerecorded voices. Telemarketers must identify the seller, describe the product being sold, and disclose all material facts related to the sale. 4. **Sales**—"Cooling-off" laws permit buyers of goods sold in certain sales transactions (such as trade shows and door-to-door sales) to cancel their contracts within three business days. 5. **Labeling**—Manufacturers must comply with the labeling requirements for their specific products. In general, all labels must be accurate and not misleading.
Protection of Health and Safety	1. **Food and drugs**—The federal Food, Drug, and Cosmetic Act protects consumers against adulterated and misbranded foods and drugs. The act establishes food standards, specifies safe levels of potentially hazardous food additives, and provides guidelines for advertising and labeling food products. 2. **Consumer product safety**—The Consumer Product Safety Act seeks to protect consumers from injury from hazardous products. The Consumer Product Safety Commission has the power to set safety standards for consumer products, ban the manufacture and sale of products that pose unreasonable risk, and remove products that are deemed imminently hazardous from the market.
Credit Protection	1. **Truth in Lending Act, or TILA**—A disclosure law that requires sellers and lenders to disclose credit terms or loan terms in certain transactions, including retail installment sales and loans, car loans, home-improvement loans, and certain real estate loans. Additionally, the TILA provides for the following: a. Equal credit opportunity—Creditors are prohibited from discriminating on the basis of race, religion, marital status, gender, national origin, color, or age. b. Credit card protection—Liability of cardholders for unauthorized charges is limited to $50, providing that notice requirements are met. Consumers are not liable for unauthorized charges made on unsolicited credit cards. The act also sets out procedures to be used in settling disputes between credit card companies and their cardholders.

	2. **Fair Credit Reporting Act**—Entitles consumers to request verification of the accuracy of a credit report and to have unverified or false information removed from their files. 3. **Fair and Accurate Credit Transactions Act**—Combats identity theft by establishing a national fraud alert system. It requires account numbers to be truncated and credit reporting agencies to provide one free credit report per year to consumers. 4. **Fair Debt Collection Practices Act**—Prohibits debt collectors from using unfair debt-collection practices, such as contacting the debtor at the debtor's place of employment if the employer objects or at unreasonable times, contacting third parties about the debt, and harassing the debtor.
ENVIRONMENTAL LAW	
Protecting the Environment	1. **Federal regulation**— a. The Environmental Protection Agency (EPA) is the primary agency regulating environmental law and administers most federal environmental policies and statutes. b. An environmental impact statement (EIS) is required for every major federal action. An EIS must analyze the action's impact on the environment, its adverse effects and possible alternatives, and its irreversible effects on environmental quality. 2. **Common law actions**— a. Nuisance—A common law doctrine under which persons may be held liable if their use of their property unreasonably interferes with others' rights to use their own property. b. Negligence and strict liability—Parties may recover damages for injuries sustained as a result of a firm's pollution-causing activities if they can demonstrate that the harm was a foreseeable result of the firm's failure to exercise reasonable care (negligence). Businesses engaging in ultrahazardous activities are liable for whatever injuries the activities cause, regardless of whether they exercise reasonable care.
Air and Water Pollution	1. **Air pollution**—Regulated under the authority of the Clean Air Act and its amendments. 2. **Water pollution**—Regulated under the authority of the Rivers and Harbors Appropriation Act and the Federal Water Pollution Control Act, as amended by the Clean Water Act.
Toxic Chemicals and Hazardous Waste	Pesticides and herbicides, toxic substances, and hazardous waste are regulated under the authority of the Federal Insecticide, Fungicide, and Rodenticide Act; the Toxic Substances Control Act; and the Resource Conservation and Recovery Act, respectively. The Comprehensive Environmental Response, Compensation, and Liability Act (CERCLA), or Superfund, regulates clean-up of hazardous waste disposal sites.

Issue Spotters

1. United Pharmaceuticals, Inc., has developed a new drug that it believes will be effective in the treatment of patients with AIDS. The drug has had only limited testing, but United wants to make the drug widely available as soon as possible. To market the drug, what must United prove to the U.S. Food and Drug Administration? (See *Protection of Health and Safety*.)

2. ChemCorp generates hazardous wastes from its operations. Disposal Trucking Company transports those wastes to Eliminators, Inc., which owns a site for hazardous waste disposal. Eliminators sells the property on which the disposal site is located to Fluid Properties, Inc. If the Environmental Protection Agency cleans up the site, from whom can it recover the cost? (See *Toxic Chemicals and Hazardous Waste*.)

—Check your answers to the *Issue Spotters* against the answers provided in Appendix D.

Business Scenarios and Case Problems

32–1. Environmental Laws. Fruitade, Inc., is a processor of a soft drink called Freshen Up. Fruitade uses returnable glass bottles, which it cleans with a special acid to allow for further beverage processing. The acid is diluted with water and then allowed to pass into a navigable stream. Fruitade crushes its broken bottles and throws the crushed glass into the stream. Discuss fully any environmental laws that Fruitade may have violated. (See *Air and Water Pollution*.)

32–2. Credit Protection. Maria Ochoa receives two new credit cards on May 1. She has solicited one of them from Midtown Department Store, and the other arrives unsolicited from High-Flying Airlines. During the month of May, Ochoa makes numerous credit card purchases from Midtown Department Store, but she does not use the High-Flying Airlines card. On May 31, a burglar breaks into Ochoa's home and steals both credit cards, along with other items.

Ochoa notifies Midtown Department Store of the theft on June 2, but she fails to notify High-Flying Airlines. Using the Midtown credit card, the burglar makes a $500 purchase on June 1 and a $200 purchase on June 3. The burglar then charges a vacation flight on the High-Flying Airlines card for $1,000 on June 5. Ochoa receives the bills for these charges and refuses to pay them. Discuss Ochoa's liability in these situations. (See *Credit Protection.*)

32–3. Spotlight on McDonald's—Food Labeling. A McDonald's Happy Meal® consists of an entrée, a small order of French fries, a small drink, and a toy. In the early 1990s, McDonald's Corp. began to aim its Happy Meal marketing at children aged one to three. In 1995, McDonald's began making nutritional information for its food products available in documents known as "McDonald's Nutrition Facts." The documents list the food items that the restaurant serves and provide a nutritional breakdown, but the Happy Meal is not included.

Marc Cohen filed a suit in an Illinois state court against McDonald's. Cohen alleged, among other things, that McDonald's had violated a state law prohibiting consumer fraud and deceptive business practices by failing to follow the Nutrition Labeling and Education Act (NLEA). The NLEA generally requires that standard nutrition facts be listed on food labels. The act, however, sets out different, less detailed requirements for products specifically intended for children under the age of four. Does it make sense to have different requirements for children of this age? Why or why not? Should a state court impose regulations when the NLEA has not done so? Explain. [*Cohen v. McDonald's Corp.*, 347 Ill.App.3d 627, 808 N.E.2d 1, 283 Ill.Dec. 451 (1 Dist. 2004)] (See *Advertising, Marketing, Sales, and Labeling.*)

32–4. Environmental Impact Statements. The U.S. Forest Service (USFS) proposed a travel management plan (TMP) for the Beartooth Ranger District in the Pryor and Absaroka Mountains in the Custer National Forest of southern Montana. The TMP would convert unauthorized user-created routes within the wilderness to routes authorized for motor vehicle use. It would also permit off-road "dispersed vehicle camping" within 300 feet of the routes, with some seasonal restrictions. The TMP would ban cross-country motorized travel outside the designated routes. Is an environmental impact statement required before the USFS implements the TMP? If so, what aspects of the environment should the USFS consider in preparing it? Discuss. [*Pryors Coalition v. Weldon*, 551 Fed.Appx. 426 (9th Cir. 2014)] (See *Protecting the Environment.*)

32–5. Business Case Problem with Sample Answer—Deceptive Advertising. Innovative Marketing, Inc. (IMI), sold "scareware"—computer security software. IMI's Internet ads redirected consumers to sites where they were told that a scan of their computers had detected dangerous files—viruses, spyware, and "illegal" pornography. In fact, no scans were conducted. Kristy Ross, an IMI cofounder and vice president, reviewed and edited the ads. She was also aware of the many complaints that consumers had made about them. An individual can be held liable under the Federal Trade Commission Act's prohibition of deceptive acts or practices if the person (1) participated directly in the deceptive practices or had the authority to control them and (2) had or should have had knowledge of them. Were IMI's ads deceptive? If so, can Ross be held liable? Explain. [*Federal Trade Commission v. Ross*, 743 F.3d 886 (4th Cir. 2014)] (See *Advertising, Marketing, Sales, and Labeling.*)

—For a sample answer to Problem 32–5, go to Appendix E.

32–6. The Clean Water Act. ICG Hazard, LLC, operated the Thunder Ridge surface coal mine in Leslie County, Kentucky, under a National Pollutant Discharge Elimination System permit issued by the Kentucky Division of Water (KDOW). As part of the operation, ICG discharges selenium into the surrounding water. Selenium is a naturally occurring element that endangers aquatic life at a certain concentration. KDOW knew when it issued the permit that mines in the area may produce selenium but did not specify discharge limits for the element in ICG's permit. Instead, the agency imposed a one-time monitoring requirement, which ICG met. Does ICG's discharge of selenium violate the Clean Water Act? Explain. [*Sierra Club v. ICG Hazard, LLC*, 781 F.3d 281 (6th Cir. 2015)] (See *Air and Water Pollution.*)

32–7. Debt Collection. Zakia Mashiri owns a home in San Diego, California. She is a member of the Westwood Club Homeowners' Association (HOA), which charges each member an annual fee. When Mashiri failed to pay the fee, the law firm of Epsten Grinnell & Howell sent her a letter demanding payment. The letter read, "Failure to pay your . . . account in full within thirty-five days from the date of this letter will result in a lien . . . against your property." Mashiri asked for validation of the debt. Within two weeks of receiving it, she sent the HOA a check for the fee. Meanwhile, the law firm filed a lien against her property. Mashiri filed a lawsuit in a federal district court against the law firm, alleging a violation of the Fair Debt Collection Practices Act. On what provision of the act did Mashiri likely base her allegation? Will she succeed in her lawsuit against the law firm? Explain your answer. [*Mashiri v. Epsten Grinnell & Howell*, 845 F.3d 984 (9th Cir. 2017)] (See *Credit Protection.*)

32–8. False Advertising. Rainbow School, Inc., has run a childcare facility in Fayetteville, North Carolina, for over twenty years. In addition to using the word "rainbow" in its name, the school uses rainbow imagery on its logo. Rainbow Early Education Holding, LLC, operates child-care facilities in several states. Early Education opened a branch in Fayetteville near the school under the name "Rainbow Child Care Center" that also used rainbow imagery on its logo. The school filed a suit in a federal district court against Early Education, alleging a violation of the Lanham Act. The parties entered into a settlement agreement that required Early Education to stop using the word "rainbow" in connection with its Fayetteville facility. The court issued an injunction to enforce the agreement. Early Education continued to use the word "rainbow" in domain names, links, and meta tags associated with its Fayetteville facility's website. Rainbow imagery was used in a mailer inviting residents to the "nearest Rainbow Child Care Center." Did Early Education violate the Lanham Act? Explain. [*Rainbow School, Inc. v. Rainbow Early Education Holding LLC,* 887 F.3d 610 (4th Cir. 2018)] (See *Advertising, Marketing, Sales, and Labeling.*)

32–9. A Question of Ethics—The IDDR Approach and Consumer Protection. In Richland, Washington, Robert Ingersoll planned his wedding to include about a hundred guests, a photographer, a caterer, a wedding cake, and flowers. Ingersoll had been a customer of Arlene's Flowers and Gifts for more than nine years and had spent several thousand dollars at the shop. When he approached Arlene's owner, Baronelle Stutzman, to buy flowers for his wedding, she refused because Ingersoll and his fiancé, Curt Freed, were a same-sex couple. Deeply offended, Ingersoll and Freed dropped their wedding plans and married in a modest ceremony. [*Arlene's Flowers, Inc. v. State of Washington,* __U.S.__, 138 S.Ct. 2671, 201 L.Ed.2d 1067 (2018)] (See *Advertising, Marketing, Sales, and Labeling.*)

1. Federal and state laws attempt to protect consumers from unfair trade practices, including discriminatory requirements, related to consumer transactions. Using the *Review* step of the IDDR approach, consider whether it would be ethically fair to hold Stutzman personally liable for a violation of these laws.
2. Using the *Discussion* step of the IDDR approach, consider actions that Ingersoll and Freed as consumers might take in response to Arlene's—Stutzman's—discriminatory rejection of their offer to do business.

Critical Thinking and Writing Assignments

32–10. Time-Limited Group Assignment—Consumer Protections. Many states have enacted laws that go even further than federal laws to protect consumers against deceptive and false advertising. These laws vary tremendously from state to state. (See *Advertising, Marketing, Sales, and Labeling.*)

1. The first group will decide whether having different laws is fair to sellers, who may be prohibited from engaging in a practice in one state that is legal in another.
2. The second group will consider how these different laws might affect a business.
3. A third group will determine whether it is fair that residents of one state have more protection than residents of another.

TRMK/Shutterstock.com

33 Liability of Accountants and Other Professionals

Focus Questions

The five Focus Questions *below are designed to help improve your understanding. After reading this chapter, you should be able to answer the following questions:*

1. Under what common law theories may professionals be liable to clients?
2. What are the rules concerning an auditor's liability to third parties?
3. How might an accountant violate the Securities Act?
4. What crimes might an accountant commit under the Internal Revenue Code?
5. What is protected by the attorney-client privilege?

"A member should observe the profession's technical and ethical standards . . . and discharge professional responsibility to the best of the member's ability."

Article V, Code of Professional Conduct
American Institute of Certified Public Accountants

Professionals, such as accountants, attorneys, physicians, and architects, are increasingly faced with the threat of liability. In part, this is because the public has become more aware that professionals are required to deliver competent services and adhere to certain standards of performance within their professions.

The standard of due care to which the members of the American Institute of Certified Public Accountants are expected to adhere is set out in the chapter-opening quotation. Investors rely heavily on the opinions of certified public accountants when making decisions about whether to invest in a company.

The failure of several major companies and leading public accounting firms in the past twenty years has focused attention on the importance of abiding by professional accounting standards. Numerous corporations—from American International Group (AIG, the world's largest insurance company), to Goldman Sachs, Lehman Brothers, now-defunct Theranos, and Japan-based Toshiba—have been accused of engaging in accounting fraud. These companies may have reported fictitious revenues, concealed liabilities or debts, or artificially inflated their assets.

33–1 Potential Liability to Clients

Under the common law, professionals may be liable to clients for breach of contract, negligence, or fraud.

Focus Question 1

Under what common law theories may professionals be liable to clients?

33–1a Liability for Breach of Contract

Accountants and other professionals face liability under the common law for any breach of contract. A professional owes a duty to a client to honor the terms of their contract and to perform the contract within the stated time period. If the professional fails to perform as agreed, then the contract has been breached, and the client has the right to pursue recovery of damages.

Possible damages include expenses incurred by the client in securing another professional to provide the contracted-for services and any other reasonable and foreseeable losses that arise from the professional's breach. For instance, if the client had to pay penalties for failing to meet deadlines, the court may order the professional to pay an equivalent amount in damages to the client.

33–1b Liability for Negligence

Accountants and other professionals may also be held liable under the common law for negligence in the performance of their services. Recall that the following elements must be proved to establish negligence:

1. A duty of care existed.
2. That duty of care was breached.
3. The plaintiff suffered an injury.
4. The injury was proximately caused by the defendant's breach of the duty of care.

Negligence cases against professionals often focus on the standard of care exercised by the professional. All professionals are subject to standards of conduct established by codes of professional ethics, by state statutes, and by judicial decisions. They are also governed by the contracts they enter into with their clients.

In performing their contracts, professionals must exercise the established standards of care, knowledge, and judgment generally accepted by members of their professional group. Here, we look at the duty of care owed by two groups of professionals that frequently perform services for business firms: accountants and attorneys.

Accountant's Duty of Care Accountants play a major role in a business's financial system. Accountants establish and maintain financial records, as well as design, control, and audit record-keeping systems. They also prepare statements that reflect an individual's or a business's financial status, give tax advice, and prepare tax returns.

Generally, an accountant must possess the skills that an ordinarily prudent accountant would have and must exercise the degree of care that an ordinarily prudent accountant would exercise. The level of skill expected of accountants and the degree of care that they should exercise in performing their services are reflected in the standards discussed next.

GAAP and GAAS. When performing their services, accountants in the United States must comply with **generally accepted accounting principles (GAAP)** and **generally accepted auditing standards (GAAS)**. The Financial Accounting Standards Board (FASB, usually pronounced "faz-bee") determines what accounting conventions, rules, and procedures constitute GAAP at a given point in time. GAAS, established by the American Institute of Certified Public Accountants, set forth the professional qualities and judgment that an auditor should exercise

Generally Accepted Accounting Principles (GAAP) The conventions, rules, and procedures developed by the Financial Accounting Standards Board to define accepted accounting practices at a particular time.

Generally Accepted Auditing Standards (GAAS) Standards established by the American Institute of Certified Public Accountants to define the professional qualities and judgment that should be exercised by an auditor in performing an audit.

in performing an audit. Normally, an accountant who conforms to generally accepted standards and acts in good faith will not be held liable to the client for incorrect judgment.

A violation of GAAP or GAAS is considered *prima facie* evidence of negligence on the part of the accountant. Compliance with GAAP and GAAS, however, does not *necessarily* relieve an accountant from potential legal liability. An accountant may be held to a higher standard of conduct established by state statute or by judicial decisions.

International Financial Reporting Standards (IFRS). A set of accounting standard used in many nations around the world.

IFRS. Although U.S. companies use GAAP, many other countries rely on a different set of accounting rules known as **International Financial Reporting Standards (IFRS).** There has been some discussion of eventually replacing GAAP with IFRS, which are considered simpler and more straightforward. For the time being, however, companies in the United States will continue to comply with GAAP.

Defalcation Embezzlement or misappropriation of funds.

Auditor An accountant qualified to perform audits (systematic inspections) of a business's financial records.

Discovering Improprieties. An accountant is not required to discover every impropriety, **defalcation** [1] (embezzlement), or fraud in a client's books. If, however, the impropriety, defalcation, or fraud has gone undiscovered because of the accountant's negligence or failure to perform an express or implied duty, the accountant will be liable for any resulting losses suffered by the client. Therefore, an accountant who uncovers suspicious financial transactions and fails to investigate the matter fully or to inform the client of the discovery can normally be held liable to the client for the resulting loss.

GaudiLab/Shutterstock.com

Suppose an accountant uncovers evidence that a partner has been embezzling funds from a client law firm. What steps should the accountant take? What are the possible ramifications if the accountant fails to take these steps?

Audits. One of the most important tasks that an accountant may perform for a business is an audit. An *audit* is a systematic inspection, by analyses and tests, of a business's financial records. An accountant qualified to perform audits is often called an **auditor**. After performing an audit, the auditor issues an opinion letter stating whether the financial statements fairly present the business's financial position.

The purpose of an audit is to provide the auditor with evidence to support an opinion on the reliability of the business's financial statements. A normal audit is not intended to uncover fraud or other misconduct. Nevertheless, an accountant may be liable for failing to detect misconduct if a normal audit would have revealed it. Also, if an auditor agreed to examine the records for evidence of fraud or other obvious misconduct and then failed to detect it, the auditor may be liable.

Qualified Opinions and Disclaimers. In issuing an opinion letter, an auditor may *qualify* the opinion or include a *disclaimer.* In a disclaimer, the auditor basically states that there is insufficient information to issue an opinion. A qualified opinion or a disclaimer must be specific and must identify the reason for the qualification or disclaimer.

Example 33.1 Richard performs an audit of Lacey Corporation. In the opinion letter, Richard qualifies his opinion by stating that there is uncertainty about how a lawsuit against the firm will be resolved. In this situation, Richard will not be liable if the outcome of the suit is unfavorable for the firm. Richard could still be liable, however, for failing to discover other problems that an audit in compliance with GAAS rules would have revealed. ■

Unaudited Financial Statements. Sometimes, accountants are called on to prepare unaudited financial statements. (A financial statement is considered unaudited if incomplete auditing procedures have been used in its preparation or if insufficient procedures have been used to justify an opinion.) Lesser standards of care are typically required in this situation.

1. This term, pronounced deh-fal-*kay*-shun, is derived from the Latin *de* ("off") and *falx* ("sickle"—a tool used for cutting grain or tall grass). As used here, the term refers to the act of an embezzler.

Nevertheless, accountants may be liable for omissions from unaudited statements. Accountants may be subject to liability for failing, in accordance with standard accounting procedures, to designate a balance sheet as "unaudited." An accountant will also be held liable for failure to disclose to a client any facts or circumstances that give reason to believe that misstatements have been made or that a fraud has been committed.

Defenses to Negligence. If an accountant is found guilty of negligence, the client can collect damages for losses that arose from the accountant's negligence. An accountant facing a claim of negligence, however, has several possible defenses, including the following:

1. The accountant was not negligent.
2. If the accountant was negligent, this negligence was not the proximate cause of the client's losses.
3. The client was also negligent (depending on whether state law allows contributory negligence as a defense).

Example 33.2 Coopers & Peterson, LLP, provides accounting services for Bandon Steel Mills, Inc. (BSM). Coopers advises BSM to report a certain transaction as a $12.3 million gain on its financial statements. Later, BSM plans to make a public offering of its stock. The SEC reviews its financial statements and determines that certain errors in the accounting treatment of the transaction have to be corrected before the sale.

Because of the delay, the public offering does not occur on May 2, when BSM's stock is selling for $16 per share. Instead, it takes place on June 13, when, due to unrelated factors, the price has fallen to $13.50. If BSM files a lawsuit against Coopers, claiming that the negligent accounting resulted in the stock's being sold at a lower price, BSM is unlikely to prevail. Although the accounting firm's negligence may have delayed the stock offering, the negligence was not the proximate cause of the decline in the stock price. Thus, Coopers would not be liable for damages based on the price decline.

branex/iStock/Getty Images

Assume that the accounting firm for this steel manufacturer makes an error in a financial statement. If the initial public offering is delayed and the stock price falls in the meantime, is the accounting firm liable for the lower price?

Attorney's Duty of Care

The conduct of attorneys is governed by rules established by each state and by the American Bar Association's Model Rules of Professional Conduct. All attorneys owe a duty to provide competent and diligent representation.

Attorneys are required to be familiar with well-settled principles of law applicable to a case and to find relevant law that can be discovered through a reasonable amount of research. They must also investigate and discover facts that could materially affect clients' legal rights.

Normally, an attorney's performance is expected to be that of a reasonably competent general practitioner of ordinary skill, experience, and capacity. An attorney who holds himself or herself out as having expertise in a particular area of law (such as intellectual property) is held to a higher standard of care in that area of the law than attorneys without such expertise.

Misconduct. Typically, a state's rules of professional conduct for attorneys provide that committing a criminal act that reflects adversely on the attorney's "honesty or trustworthiness, or fitness as a lawyer in other respects" is professional misconduct. The rules often further provide that a lawyer should not engage in conduct involving "dishonesty, fraud, deceit, or misrepresentation." Under these rules, state authorities can discipline attorneys for many types of misconduct.

Case Example 33.3 Evangalos Argyrakis, a Nebraska attorney, pleaded guilty to a felony for repeatedly punching his eighty-three-year-old father in the face. He was sentenced to three years' probation. The state judiciary began an inquiry into whether Argyrakis had been convicted of a "crime of violence," which would trigger severe sanctions under Nebraska's rules of professional conduct for attorneys. Argyrakis denied the allegation, insisting that his father had been the "aggressor" in the incident. In addition, Argyrakis blamed his behavior on mental health issues for which he had recently started receiving treatment.

The Nebraska Supreme Court was unmoved by Argyrakis's claims of self-defense and mental health problems. In the court's view, by falling back on such excuses, Argyrakis showed that he had not accepted responsibility for his actions. The court also found that Argyrakis had clearly been convicted of a crime of violence. Given the need to maintain public confidence in the integrity of the legal profession, the court decided that it had no alternative but to disbar Argyrakis, thus prohibiting him from the further practice of law in the state.[2]

Malpractice Professional negligence, or failure to exercise reasonable care and professional judgment, that results in injury, loss, or damage to those relying on the professional.

Liability for Malpractice. An attorney who fails to exercise reasonable care and professional judgment breaches the duty of care and can be held liable for **malpractice** (professional negligence). In malpractice cases—as in all cases involving allegations of negligence—the plaintiff must prove that the attorney's breach of the duty of care actually caused the plaintiff to suffer some injury.

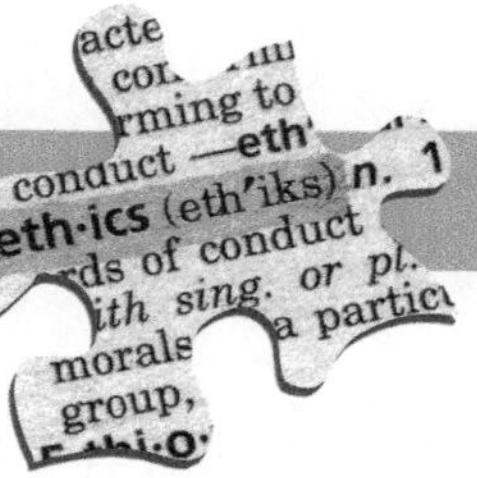

Ethical Issue

What are an attorney's responsibilities with respect to protecting data stored on the cloud? To achieve both cost savings and better security, more and more attorneys are storing their data, including confidential client information, on the cloud. Sometimes, professionals assume that once their data have migrated to the cloud, they no longer have to be concerned with keeping the information secure. But cloud computing is simply the virtualization of the computing process. In other words, the professional is still ultimately responsible for the information.

Attorneys' obligations for their clients' information are spelled out in the American Bar Association's Model Rules of Professional Conduct, which serve as the basis for the ethics rules for attorneys adopted by most states. Comment 17 to Model Rule 1.6 states, "The lawyer must take reasonable precautions to prevent the [client's] information from coming into the hands of unintended recipients." Thus, lawyers have an ethical duty to safeguard confidential client information, whether it is stored as documents in a filing cabinet or as electromagnetic impulses on a server that might be located anywhere. (Note that Rule 1.6 does not require an attorney to *guarantee* that a breach of confidentiality will never occur.)

Certainly, it is harder to maintain control over information stored on the cloud. The attorney who "owns" the data probably does not even know the location of the server where the information is stored. Furthermore, a provider of cloud computing services may move data from one server to another. Nevertheless, attorneys should be aware of jurisdictional issues and make sure that their cloud computing service provider is complying with data protection regulations and privacy notification requirements wherever the provider's servers are located.

Case Example 33.4 June De Line consulted with attorney Carol Johnston on estate and wealth-preservation matters, especially with respect to a home June owned in La Jolla, California. With Johnston's assistance, June sought to effect a "base transfer" in which she would sell the La Jolla home and buy a home in Los Angeles while retaining the La Jolla home's relatively low assessment value, meaning that her property taxes would not increase. She would also be able to leave the home to her daughter Grace at the same assessment.

2. *State ex. Rel. Counsel for Discipline of Nebraska Supreme Court v. Argyrakis*, 305 Neb. 396, 940 N.W.2d 279 (2020).

Rules for the base transfer were not adequately observed in the purchase, however, so June (and Grace) did not receive the expected tax benefits.

Grace sued Johnston in a California state court for malpractice. The court dismissed this suit, holding that Johnston owed no duty of care to Grace because Grace was not Johnston's client. Grace appealed, arguing that she was owed a duty of care as her mother's intended beneficiary. An appeals court upheld the lower court's decision, noting that it remained uncertain whether (1) June would keep the Los Angeles house for the rest of her life, (2) June would transfer the house to Grace on her death, or (3) California's property tax laws would remain the same until June's death. Therefore, the court ruled, any injury that a nonclient such as Grace might suffer because of Johnston's alleged malpractice was not "reasonably foreseeable" and could not be the basis for legal action.[3]

Katarzyna Bialasiewicz/Dreamstime.com

What must a plaintiff prove when when claiming that an attorney has committed malpractice?

33–1c Liability for Fraud

Recall that fraud, or fraudulent misrepresentation, involves the following elements:

1. A misrepresentation of a material fact.
2. An intent to deceive.
3. Justifiable reliance by the innocent party on the misrepresentation.

In addition, to obtain damages, the innocent party must have been injured. Both actual and constructive fraud are potential sources of legal liability for an accountant or other professional.

Actual Fraud A professional may be held liable for *actual fraud* when (1) the professional intentionally misstates a material fact to mislead a client, and (2) the client is injured as a result of justifiably relying on the misstated fact. A material fact is one that a reasonable person would consider important in deciding whether to act.

The connection between the fraudulent conduct of an accountant and the tax liability of a defrauded business owner was at issue in the following case.

3. *De Line v. Katten Muchin Rosenman LLP,* __ Cal.App.2d __, 2020 WL 598099 (2020).

Case 33.1

Suarez v. Fernandez

Court of Appeals of Texas, Dallas, __ S.W.3d __, 2019 WL 1922732 (2019).

Facts Susanna Fernandez, Julian Ochoa, Francisco Bravo, and Rogelio Montoya formed El Hoyo, Inc., to operate a restaurant. Juan Suarez was the accountant for the corporation.

In the seventh year of El Hoyo's operation, during an audit of the restaurant's records, the Internal Revenue Service (IRS) informed Fernandez that she had an outstanding personal tax liability of $105,397. She contacted Bravo and Montoya, who told her to speak with Suarez. Her attempts to see Suarez were unsuccessful.

Fernandez filed a suit in a Texas state court against Suarez, asserting fraud and seeking actual damages and exemplary, or punitive, damages. She claimed that Suarez had fraudulently used her identity to process credit card payments for goods sold by the restaurant, kept the proceeds without paying the taxes, and thereby made her personally liable for the unpaid amount. Suarez did not respond to the complaint.

After a hearing, the trial court rendered a default judgment in favor of Fernandez, awarding the plaintiff the amount of the unpaid

(Continues)

Continued

taxes as damages and $400,000 in exemplary damages. Suarez filed an appeal.

Issue Was there sufficient proof of a causal connection between Suarez's fraud and Fernandez's injuries?

Decision Yes. A state intermediate appellate court affirmed the trial court's judgment and award of actual damages. "We conclude the evidence was legally sufficient to support the trial court's actual damage award."

Reason Fernandez was the only witness at the hearing in the trial court. She testified that Suarez had told her that El Hoyo had a taxpayer ID number and a machine to process credit card payments through the corporation's merchant account. However, the IRS informed her during its audit that all of the credit card payments had been processed under her name and Social Security number. Credit card income for food and drinks at the restaurant led to her outstanding tax liability of $105,397.

Before this revelation, Fernandez had no idea that credit card payments to the restaurant were being processed under her name instead of through a corporate account. She had not given permission for this use of her name and Social Security number. When Fernandez had confronted Bravo and Montoya, they had said they knew nothing about the set-up and had told her to ask Suarez. She had attempted to see Suarez several times, but he had completely avoided her.

Fernandez's unopposed testimony was sufficient to prove that her personal tax liability for credit card payments to the restaurant resulted from Suarez's misrepresentation. The appellate court remanded the case for a redetermination of the amount of exemplary damages, however, which were limited under a state statute to "two times the amount of economic damages."

Critical Thinking

- **Legal Environment** *In light of the fact that Suarez did not respond to Fernandez's complaint at the trial level, should any restrictions be placed on his appeal? Discuss.*
- **Economic** *What might Fernandez and El Hoyo have done to thwart Suarez's fraud? Explain.*

Constructive Fraud Conduct that is treated as fraud under the law even when there is no proof of intent to defraud, usually because of the existence of a special relationship or fiduciary duty.

Constructive Fraud Professionals may sometimes be held liable for **constructive fraud** whether or not they acted with fraudulent intent. Liability arises because the professional has a duty to the client and violates that duty by making a material misrepresentation. The client must be injured as a result of justifiably relying on the professional's misstatements to obtain damages.

Constructive fraud may be found when accountants are grossly negligent in performing their duties. **Example 33.5** Paula, an accountant, is conducting an audit of ComCo, Inc. Paula accepts the explanations of Ron, a ComCo officer, regarding certain financial irregularities, despite evidence that contradicts those explanations and indicates that the irregularities may be illegal. Paula's conduct could be characterized as an intentional failure to perform a duty in reckless disregard of the consequences of such failure. This would constitute gross negligence and could be held to be constructive fraud. ■

33–2 Potential Liability to Third Parties

Traditionally, accountants and other professionals owed a duty only to those with whom they had a direct contractual relationship—that is, those with whom they were in *privity of contract.* A professional's duty was solely to the client. Violations of statutes, fraud, and other intentional or reckless acts of wrongdoing were the only exceptions to this general rule.

Today, numerous third parties—including investors, shareholders, creditors, corporate managers and directors, and regulatory agencies—rely on the opinions of auditors when making decisions. In view of this extensive reliance, many courts have all but abandoned the privity requirement in regard to accountants' liability to third parties.

In this section, we focus primarily on the potential liability of auditors to third parties. The majority of courts now hold that auditors can be held liable to third parties for negligence, but the standard for the imposition of this liability varies.

33–2a The *Ultramares* Rule

Focus Question 2

What are the rules concerning an auditor's liability to third parties?

The traditional rule regarding an accountant's liability to third parties is based on privity of contract and was enunciated by Chief Judge Benjamin Cardozo (of the New York Court of Appeals) in 1931. **Classic Case Example 33.6** Fred Stern & Company hired the public accounting firm of Touche, Niven & Company to review Stern's financial records and prepare a balance sheet for the year ending December 31, 1923.[4] Touche prepared the balance sheet and supplied Stern with thirty-two certified copies. According to the certified balance sheet, Stern had a net worth (assets less liabilities) of $1,070,715.26.

In reality, however, Stern's liabilities exceeded its assets. The company's records had been falsified by insiders at Stern so that assets exceeded liabilities, resulting in a positive net worth. In reliance on the certified balance sheets, Ultramares Corporation loaned substantial amounts to Stern. After Stern was declared bankrupt, Ultramares brought an action against Touche for negligence in an attempt to recover damages.

The New York Court of Appeals (that state's highest court) refused to impose liability on Touche. The court concluded that Touche's accountants owed a duty of care only to those persons for whose "primary benefit" the statements were intended. In this case, the statements were intended only for the benefit of Stern. The court held that in the absence of privity or a relationship "so close as to approach that of privity," a party could not recover from an accountant.[5]

The Requirement of Privity The requirement of privity has since been referred to as the *Ultramares* rule, or the New York rule. It continues to be used in some states. **Spotlight Case Example 33.7** Toro Company supplied equipment and credit to Summit Power Equipment Distributors and required Summit to submit audited reports indicating its financial condition. Accountants at Krouse, Kern & Company prepared the reports, which allegedly contained mistakes and omissions regarding Summit's financial condition.

Toro extended large amounts of credit to Summit in reliance on the audited reports. When Summit was unable to repay the loans, Toro brought a negligence action against the accounting firm and proved that accountants at Krouse had known the reports would be used by Summit to induce Toro to extend credit. Nevertheless, under the *Ultramares* rule, the court refused to hold the accounting firm liable because the firm was not in privity with Toro.[6]

blackred/Getty Images

To what extent is an accounting firm liable for incorrect balance-sheet information that is distributed to the public?

"Near Privity" Modification The *Ultramares* rule was modified somewhat in a 1985 New York case, *Credit Alliance Corp. v. Arthur Andersen & Co.*[7] In that case, the court held that if a third party has a sufficiently close relationship or *nexus* (link, or connection) with an accountant, then the *Ultramares* privity requirement may be satisfied without the establishment of an accountant-client relationship. The rule enunciated in the *Credit Alliance* case is often referred to as the "near privity" rule. Only a minority of states have adopted this rule.

33–2b The *Restatement* Rule

The *Ultramares* rule has been severely criticized. Because much of the work performed by auditors is intended for use by persons who are not parties to the contract, many argue that auditors should owe a duty to these third parties. As support for this position has grown, there has been an erosion of the *Ultramares* rule to expose accountants to liability to third parties in some situations.

4. Banks, creditors, stockholders, purchasers, and sellers often rely on a balance sheet as a basis for making decisions relating to a company's business.
5. *Ultramares Corp. v. Touche*, 255 N.Y. 170, 174 N.E. 441 (1931).
6. *Toro Co. v. Krouse, Kern & Co.*, 827 F.2d 155 (7th Cir. 1987).
7. 66 N.Y.2d 812, 489 N.E.2d 249, 498 N.Y.S.2d 362 (1985).

The majority of courts have adopted the position taken by the *Restatement (Third) of Torts,* which states that accountants are subject to liability for negligence not only to their clients but also to foreseen or *known* users—or classes of users—of their reports or financial statements. Under the *Restatement (Third) of Torts,* an accountant's liability extends to the following:

1. Persons for whose benefit and guidance the accountant "intends to supply the information or knows that the recipient intends to supply it."
2. Persons whom the accountant "intends the information to influence or knows that the recipient so intends."

Example 33.8 Steve, an accountant, prepares a financial statement for Tech Software, Inc., a client, knowing that Tech Software will submit the statement when it applies for a loan from First National Bank. If Steve makes negligent misstatements or omissions in the statement, he may be held liable to the bank because he knew that the bank would rely on his work product when deciding whether to make the loan.

33–2c The "Reasonably Foreseeable Users" Rule

A small minority of courts hold accountants liable to any users whose reliance on an accountant's statements or reports was *reasonably foreseeable.* This standard has been criticized as extending liability too far and exposing accountants to massive liability.

Exhibit 33–1 summarizes the three different views of accountants' liability to third parties. The majority of courts have concluded that the *Restatement*'s approach is the most reasonable because it allows accountants to control their exposure to liability. Liability is "fixed by the accountants' particular knowledge at the moment the audit is published," not by the foreseeability of the harm that might occur to a third party after the report is released.

33–2d Liability of Attorneys to Third Parties

Like accountants, attorneys may be held liable under the common law to third parties who rely on legal opinions to their detriment. Generally, an attorney is not liable to a nonclient unless there is fraud (or malicious conduct) by the attorney. The liability principles stated in the *Restatement (Third) of Torts,* however, may apply to attorneys as well as to accountants.

33–3 Liability of Accountants under Federal Laws

Accountants also face potential liability under federal statutes, several of which merit special discussion. These include the Sarbanes-Oxley Act, the Securities Act of 1933, the 1934 Securities Exchange Act, and the Private Securities Litigation Reform Act.

Exhibit 33–1 Three Basic Rules of Accountant's Liability to Third Parties

RULE	DESCRIPTION	APPLICATION
***Ultramares* rule**	Liability is imposed only if the accountant is in privity, or near privity, with the third party.	A minority of courts apply this rule.
***Restatement* rule**	Liability is imposed only if the third party's reliance is foreseen, or known, or if the third party is among a class of foreseen, or known, users.	The majority of courts have adopted this rule.
"Reasonably foreseeable users" rule	Liability is imposed if the third party's use was reasonably foreseeable.	A small minority of courts use this rule.

33–3a The Sarbanes-Oxley Act

The Sarbanes-Oxley Act imposes a number of strict requirements on both domestic and foreign public accounting firms. These requirements apply to firms that provide auditing services to companies ("issuers") whose securities are sold to public investors. The act defines an *issuer* as a company that (1) has securities that are registered under Section 12 of the Securities Exchange Act of 1934, (2) is required to file reports under Section 15(d) of the 1934 act, or (3) files—or has filed—a registration statement that has not yet become effective under the Securities Act of 1933.

The Public Company Accounting Oversight Board The Sarbanes-Oxley Act increased government oversight of public accounting practices by creating the Public Company Accounting Oversight Board, which reports to the Securities and Exchange Commission. The board oversees the audit of public companies that are subject to securities laws. The goal is to protect public investors and to ensure that public accounting firms comply with the provisions of the act. The act defines *public accounting firms* as firms "engaged in the practice of public accounting or preparing or issuing audit reports." The key provisions relating to the duties of the oversight board and the requirements relating to public accounting firms are summarized in Exhibit 33–2.

Exhibit 33–2 Key Provisions of the Sarbanes-Oxley Act Relating to Public Accounting Firms

AUDITOR INDEPENDENCE

To help ensure that auditors remain independent of the firms that they audit, Title II of the Sarbanes-Oxley Act does the following:

1. Makes it unlawful for Registered Public Accounting Firms (RPAFs) to perform both audit and nonaudit services for the same company at the same time. Nonaudit services include the following:
    - Bookkeeping or other services related to the accounting records or financial statements of the audit client.
    - Financial information systems design and implementation.
    - Appraisal or valuation services.
    - Fairness opinions.
    - Management functions.
    - Broker or dealer, investment adviser, or investment banking services.
2. Requires preapproval for most auditing services from the issuer's (the corporation's) audit committee.
3. Requires audit partner rotation by prohibiting RPAFs from providing audit services to an issuer if either the lead audit partner or the audit partner responsible for reviewing the audit has provided such services to that corporation in each of the prior five years.
4. Requires RPAFs to make timely reports to the audit committees of the corporations. The report must indicate all critical accounting policies and practices to be used; all alternative treatments of financial information within generally accepted accounting principles that have been discussed with the corporation's management officials, the ramifications of the use of such alternative treatments, and the treatment preferred by the auditor; and other material written communications between the auditor and the corporation's management.
5. Makes it unlawful for an RPAF to provide auditing services to an issuer if the corporation's chief executive officer, chief financial officer, chief accounting officer, or controller was previously employed by the auditor and participated in any capacity in the audit of the corporation during the one-year period preceding the date that the audit began.

DOCUMENT INTEGRITY AND RETENTION

1. The act provides that anyone who destroys, alters, or falsifies records with the intent to obstruct or influence a federal investigation or in relation to bankruptcy proceedings can be criminally prosecuted and sentenced to a fine, imprisonment for up to twenty years, or both.
2. The act requires accountants who audit or review publicly traded companies to retain all working papers related to the audit or review for a period of five years (amended to seven years). Violators can be sentenced to a fine, imprisonment for up to ten years, or both.

As part of an audit, the board may compel persons to testify in an investigative interview. Under the board's rules, any person compelled to testify "may be accompanied, represented and advised by counsel." The board can limit attendance at the interview to the person being examined, that person's counsel, and other persons that the board determines are "appropriate."

Whether the board infringed a witness's right to counsel under its own rules was at issue in the following case.

Case 33.2

Laccetti v. Securities and Exchange Commission

United States Court of Appeals, District of Columbia Circuit, 885 F.3d 724 (2018).

Facts The Public Company Accounting Oversight Board investigated an audit by the Ernst & Young accounting firm. The investigation focused on Mark Laccetti, who was the Ernst & Young partner in charge of the audit. As part of the investigation, the board interviewed Laccetti. During the interview, the board allowed him to be accompanied by an Ernst & Young attorney. But the board denied his request to also be accompanied by an accounting expert who would assist his counsel. Ultimately, the board found that Laccetti had violated the board's rules and auditing standards. The board suspended him from the accounting profession for two years and fined him $85,000. The Securities and Exchange Commission (SEC) upheld the sanctions. Laccetti appealed.

Issue Did the board act unlawfully when it barred Laccetti from bringing an accounting expert to assist his legal counsel during the investigative interview?

Decision Yes. The U.S. Court of Appeals for the District of Columbia Circuit vacated the SEC's order against Laccetti and remanded the case. "The Board infringed [Laccetti's] right to counsel by unreasonably barring the accounting expert from assisting his counsel at the interview."

Reason Laccetti's request was denied because the board did not want Ernst & Young to monitor the investigation. The court reasoned that this rationale "suffers from three independent flaws." First, the explanation was arbitrary and capricious—"given the presence of the Ernst & Young attorney at the interview," the rationale "makes no sense." Second, the board could have told Laccetti to bring an accounting expert who was not affiliated with Ernst & Young, but the board did not do this. Third, the board's rules prevent it from denying Laccetti the use of an expert to assist his counsel at the interview. A lawyer educated only in the law may not fully serve a client during the proceeding without guidance from an expert. If this assistance is denied, the client's right to counsel is "substantially qualified." In this light, "an expert is an extension of counsel." Furthermore, the board directs its staff to permit the presence of "a technical consultant" at an investigative interview.

Critical Thinking

- **Legal Environment** *If the board were to open a new disciplinary proceeding against Laccetti and re-interview him, what would it have to do to comply with the court's decision?*
- **What If the Facts Were Different?** *Suppose that the board's rules guaranteed a witness's right to counsel but expressly excluded "technical consultants and experts" during an investigative interview. Would the result have been different? Explain.*

Working Papers The documents used and developed by an accountant during an audit, such as notes, computations, and memoranda.

Requirements for Maintaining Working Papers Performing an audit for a client involves an accumulation of **working papers**—the documents used and developed during the audit. These include notes, computations, memoranda, copies, and other papers that make up the work product of an accountant's services to a client.

Under the common law, which in this instance has been codified in a number of states, working papers remain the accountant's property. It is important for accountants to retain such records in the event that they need to defend against lawsuits for negligence or other actions in which their competence is challenged. The client also has a right to access an accountant's working papers because they reflect the client's financial situation. On a client's request, an accountant must return to the client any of the client's records or journals, and failure to do so may result in liability.

Section 802(a)(1) of the Sarbanes-Oxley Act required accountants to maintain working papers relating to an audit or review for five years from the end of the fiscal period in which the audit or review was concluded. The requirement was subsequently extended to seven years. A knowing violation of this requirement will subject the accountant to a fine, imprisonment for up to ten years, or both.

33–3b The Securities Act of 1933

The Securities Act requires issuers to file registration statements with the Securities and Exchange Commission (SEC) prior to an offering of securities.[8] Accountants frequently prepare and certify the financial statements that are included in the issuer's registration statement.

Focus Question 3

How might an accountant violate the Securities Act?

Liability under Section 11 Section 11 of the 1933 Securities Act imposes civil liability on accountants for misstatements and omissions of material facts in registration statements. Accountants may be liable if a financial statement they prepared for inclusion "contained an untrue statement of a material fact or omitted to state a material fact required to be stated therein or necessary to make the statements therein not misleading."[9]

An accountant's liability for a misstatement or omission of a material fact in a registration statement extends to anyone who acquires a security covered by the registration statement. A purchaser of a security need only demonstrate having suffered a loss on the security. Proof of reliance on the materially false statement or misleading omission ordinarily is not required. Nor is there a requirement of privity between the accountant and the security purchaser.

Due Diligence A required standard of care that certain professionals, such as accountants, must meet to avoid liability for securities violations.

The Due Diligence Standard. Section 11 imposes a duty on accountants to use **due diligence** in preparing the financial statements included in registration statements. Thus, after a purchaser has proved a loss on a security, the accountant has the burden of showing that due diligence was exercised in the preparation of the financial statements.

To prove due diligence, accountants must demonstrate that they followed generally accepted standards and did not commit negligence or fraud. Specifically, to avoid liability, accountants must show that they did the following:

1. Conducted a reasonable investigation.
2. Had reasonable grounds to believe and did believe, at the time the registration statement became effective, that the statements therein were true and that there was no omission of a material fact that would be misleading.[10]

In particular, the due diligence standard places a burden on accountants to verify information furnished by a corporation's officers and directors. Merely asking questions is not always sufficient to satisfy the requirement. Accountants may be held liable for failing to detect danger signals in documents furnished by corporate officers that required further investigation.

8. Many securities and transactions are expressly exempted from the 1933 Securities Act.
9. 15 U.S.C. Section 77k(a).
10. 15 U.S.C. Section 77k(b)(3).

Other Defenses to Liability. Besides proving that they have acted with due diligence, accountants can raise the following defenses to Section 11 liability:

1. There were no misstatements or omissions.
2. The misstatements or omissions were not of material facts.
3. The misstatements or omissions had no causal connection to the plaintiff's loss.
4. The plaintiff-purchaser invested in the securities knowing of the misstatements or omissions.

Hero Images/Getty Images

Which federal agency can bring criminal actions against professionals who commit willful violations under Section 12(2) of the Securities Act of 1933?

Liability under Section 12(2) Section 12(2) of the 1933 Securities Act imposes civil liability for fraud in relation to offerings or sales of securities.[11] Liability arises when an oral statement to an investor or a written prospectus[12] includes an untrue statement or omits a material fact. Some courts have applied Section 12(2) to accountants who aided and abetted (assisted) the seller or the offeror of the securities in violating Section 12(2).

Those who purchase securities and suffer harm as a result of a false or omitted statement, or some other violation, may bring a suit in a federal court to recover their losses and other damages. The U.S. Department of Justice brings criminal actions against those who commit willful violations. The penalties include fines of up to $10,000, imprisonment for up to five years, or both. The SEC is authorized to seek an injunction against a willful violator to prevent further violations. The SEC can also ask a court to grant other relief, such as an order to a violator to refund profits derived from an illegal transaction.

33–3c The Securities Exchange Act of 1934

Under Sections 18 and 10(b) of the Securities Exchange Act and SEC Rule 10b-5, an accountant may be found liable for fraud. A plaintiff has a substantially heavier burden of proof under the 1934 act than under the 1933 act because an accountant does not have to prove due diligence to escape liability under the 1934 act.

Liability under Section 18 Section 18 of the 1934 act imposes civil liability on an accountant who makes or causes to be made in any application, report, or document a statement that at the time and in light of the circumstances was false or misleading with respect to any material fact.[13]

Section 18 liability is narrow in that it applies only to applications, reports, documents, and registration statements filed with the SEC. This remedy is further limited in that it applies only to sellers and purchasers. Under Section 18, a seller or purchaser must prove one of the following:

1. That the false or misleading statement affected the price of the security.
2. That the purchaser or seller relied on the false or misleading statement in making the purchase or sale and was not aware of the inaccuracy of the statement.

---

11. 15 U.S.C. Section 77l.
12. A *prospectus* contains financial disclosures about the corporation for the benefit of potential investors.
13. 15 U.S.C. Section 78r(a).

Good Faith Defense. Accountants will not be liable for violating Section 18 if they acted in good faith in preparing the financial statement. To demonstrate good faith, they must show that they had no knowledge that the financial statement was false and misleading. In addition, they must have had no intent to deceive, manipulate, defraud, or seek unfair advantage over another party.

Note that "mere" negligence in preparing a financial statement does not lead to liability under the 1934 act. This differs from the 1933 act, under which an accountant is liable for *all* negligent acts.

Other Defenses. In addition to the good faith defense, accountants can escape liability by proving that the buyer or seller of the security in question knew that the financial statement was false and misleading. Also, the statute of limitations may be asserted as a defense to liability under the 1934 act.

Liability under Section 10(b) and Rule 10b-5 Accountants additionally face potential legal liability under the antifraud provisions contained in the Securities Exchange Act and SEC Rule 10b-5. The scope of these antifraud provisions is very broad and allows private parties to bring civil actions against violators.

Prohibited Conduct. Section 10(b) makes it unlawful for any person, including an accountant, to use, in connection with the purchase or sale of any security, any manipulative or deceptive device or contrivance in contravention of SEC rules and regulations.[14] Rule 10b-5 further makes it unlawful for any person, by use of any means or instrumentality of interstate commerce, to do the following:

1. Employ any device, scheme, or artifice (pretense) to defraud.
2. Make any untrue statement of a material fact or omit a material fact necessary to ensure that the statements made were not misleading, in light of the circumstances.
3. Engage in any act, practice, or course of business that operates or would operate as a fraud or deceit on any person, in connection with the purchase or sale of any security.[15]

Extent of Liability. Accountants may be held liable only to sellers or purchasers of securities under Section 10(b) and Rule 10b-5. Privity is not necessary for a recovery.

An accountant may be found liable not only for fraudulent misstatements of material facts in written material filed with the SEC, but also for any fraudulent oral statements or omissions made in connection with the purchase or sale of any security. In some situations, accountants may also have the duty to correct misstatements that they discover in previous financial statements. For plaintiffs to succeed in recovering damages under these antifraud provisions, they must prove intent (*scienter*) to commit the fraudulent or deceptive act. Ordinary negligence is not enough.

33–3d The Private Securities Litigation Reform Act

The Private Securities Litigation Reform Act made some changes to the potential liability of accountants and other professionals in securities fraud cases. Among other things, the act imposed a statutory obligation on accountants. An auditor must use adequate procedures in

14. 15 U.S.C. Section 78j(b)
15. 17 C.F.R. Section 240.10b-5.

an audit to detect any illegal acts of the company being audited. If something illegal is detected, the auditor must disclose it to the company's board of directors, the audit committee, or the SEC, depending on the circumstances.[16]

Proportionate Liability The act provides that, in most situations, a party is liable only for the proportion of damages for which that party is responsible.[17] An accountant who participates in, but is unaware of, illegal conduct may not be liable for the entire loss caused by the illegality.

Example 33.9 Nina, an accountant, helps the president and owner of Midstate Trucking company draft financial statements. The statements misrepresent Midstate's financial condition, but Nina is not aware of the fraud. Nina might be held liable, but the amount of her liability could be proportionately less than the entire loss.

Andrey_Popov/Shutterstock.com

If an accountant is unaware of a company officer's fraud, will he still be held fully liable for any losses caused by the misstatements?

Aiding and Abetting The act also made it a separate crime to aid and abet a violation of the Securities Exchange Act. Aiding and abetting might include knowingly participating in such an act, assisting in it, or keeping quiet about it. If an accountant knowingly aids and abets a primary violator, the SEC can seek an injunction or monetary damages.

Example 33.10 Smith & Jones, an accounting firm, performs an audit for ABC Sales Company that is so inadequate as to constitute gross negligence. ABC uses the materials provided by Smith & Jones as part of a scheme to defraud investors. When the scheme is uncovered, the SEC can bring an action against Smith & Jones for aiding and abetting on the ground that the firm knew or should have known of the material misrepresentations that were in its audit and on which investors were likely to rely.

33–4 Potential Criminal Liability

An accountant may be found criminally liable for violations of securities laws and tax laws. In addition, most states make it a crime to (1) knowingly certify false reports, (2) falsify, alter, or destroy books of accounts, and (3) obtain property or credit through the use of false financial statements.

33–4a Criminal Violations of Securities Laws

Accountants may be subject to criminal penalties for *willful* violations of U.S. securities laws. If convicted under the 1933 Securities Act, as noted earlier, they face imprisonment for up to five years and/or a fine of up to $10,000. Under the Sarbanes-Oxley Act, if an accountant's false or misleading certified audit statement is used in a securities filing, the accountant may be held criminally liable. The accountant may be fined up to $5 million, imprisoned for up to twenty years, or both.

16. 15 U.S.C. Section 78j-1.
17. 15 U.S.C. Section 78u-4(g).

33–4b Criminal Violations of Tax Laws

Focus Question 4

What crimes might an accountant commit under the Internal Revenue Code?

The Internal Revenue Code makes it a felony to willfully make false statements in a tax return or to willfully aid or assist others in preparing a false tax return. Felony violations are punishable by a fine of $100,000 ($500,000 in the case of a corporation) and imprisonment for up to three years.[18] This provision applies to anyone who prepares tax returns for others for compensation—not just to accountants.[19]

For a *negligent* understatement of a client's tax liability, the tax preparer is subject to a penalty of $1,000 or 50 percent of the income the preparer derived from the faulty return, whichever is greater. For a *willful* understatement of tax liability or reckless or intentional disregard of rules or regulations, the penalty is the greater of either $5,000 or 75 percent of the income so derived.[20] A tax preparer may also be subject to penalties for failing to furnish the taxpayer with a copy of the return, failing to sign the return, or failing to furnish the appropriate tax identification numbers.

In addition, a tax preparer may be fined $1,000 per document for aiding and abetting another's understatement of tax liability (the penalty is increased to $10,000 in corporate cases).[21] The tax preparer's liability is limited to one penalty per taxpayer per tax year.

33–5 Confidentiality and Privilege

Professionals are restrained by the ethical tenets of their professions to keep all communications with their clients confidential.

33–5a Attorney-Client Relationships

The confidentiality of attorney-client communications is protected by law, which confers a privilege on such communications. This privilege exists because of the client's need to fully disclose the facts of the case to the attorney.

Focus Question 5

What is protected by the attorney-client privilege?

To encourage frankness, confidential attorney-client communications relating to representation are normally held in strictest confidence and protected by law. The attorney and the attorney's employees may not discuss the client's case with anyone—even under court order—without the client's permission. The client holds the privilege, and only the client may waive it—by disclosing privileged information to someone outside the privilege, for instance.

Note, however, that the SEC has implemented rules requiring attorneys who become aware that a client has violated securities laws to report the violation to the SEC. Because reporting a client's misconduct can be a breach of the attorney-client privilege, these rules have created potential conflicts for some attorneys.

Once an attorney-client relationship arises, all communications between the parties are privileged. The question in the following case was whether communications between an attorney and an individual *before* that individual was informed that the attorney was *not* his counsel were privileged.

---

18. 26 U.S.C. Section 7206(2).
19. 26 U.S.C. Section 7701(a)(36).
20. 26 U.S.C. Section 6694.
21. 26 U.S.C. Section 6701.

Case 33.3

Commonwealth of Pennsylvania v. Schultz

Superior Court of Pennsylvania, 133 A.3d 294 (2016).

Facts An investigation into allegations of sexual misconduct involving minors and Jerry Sandusky, a former defensive coordinator for the Pennsylvania State University football team, led a grand jury to subpoena Gary Schultz. Schultz, a retired vice president of the university, had overseen the campus police at the time of the alleged events.

Before testifying, Schultz met with Cynthia Baldwin, counsel for Penn State. He told her that he did not have any documents relating to the two incidents, believing this disclosure to be in the strictest confidence between attorney and client. Baldwin, however, saw her role as counsel only for Penn State, representing Schultz as an agent of the university, not personally. She did not explain this to him, and she appeared with him during his testimony.

Later, a file was found in Schultz's office containing notes pertaining to the two incidents. When Baldwin was called to testify, she revealed what he had told her at their meeting. On the basis of this testimony, the grand jury charged Schultz with the crimes of perjury, obstruction of justice, and conspiracy. Before a trial was held on these charges, Schultz filed a motion to preclude Baldwin's testimony and quash (suppress) the charges, arguing that her testimony violated the attorney-client privilege. The court denied the motion. Schulz appealed.

Issue Could an attorney who represented Penn State University testify about statements that Schultz made to her at a time when he believed that the attorney was representing him?

Decision No. A state intermediate appellate court reversed the order of the lower court regarding Schultz's pretrial motion. Baldwin was precluded from testifying about Schultz's privileged communications with her, and the charges of perjury, obstruction of justice, and conspiracy against Schultz were quashed.

Reason Baldwin claimed that she had offered only limited representation to Schultz before and during a grand jury investigation. She argued that attorneys who represent corporations are allowed to divulge communications made by persons in the firm because they represent the entity, not the individual. The court concluded that this situation was different because Baldwin had not informed Schultz that she was not his personal attorney. Baldwin had neglected to adequately explain the distinction between personal representation and agency representation to Schultz. Therefore, all communications between Schultz and Baldwin were protected by the attorney-client privilege and could not be divulged to third parties or to the court.

Critical Thinking

- **What If the Facts Were Different?** *Suppose that a hearing had been held on the question of the attorney-client privilege before Baldwin testified. Would the result have been different?*

33–5b Accountant-Client Relationships

In a few states, accountant-client communications are privileged by state statute. In these states, accountant-client communications may not be revealed even in court or in court-sanctioned proceedings without the client's permission.

The majority of states, however, abide by the common law, which provides that, if a court so orders, accountants must disclose information about their clients to the court. Physicians and other professionals may similarly be compelled to disclose in court information given to them in confidence by patients or clients.

Communications between professionals and their clients—other than those between attorneys and their clients—are not privileged under federal law. In cases involving federal law, state-provided rights to confidentiality of accountant-client communications are not recognized. Thus, in those cases, an accountant must provide all information requested in a court order.

Practice and Review

Superior Wholesale Corporation planned to purchase Regal Furniture, Inc., and wished to determine Regal's net worth. Superior hired Lynette Shuebke, of the accounting firm Shuebke Delgado, to review an audit that had been prepared by Norman Chase, the accountant for Regal. Shuebke advised Superior that Chase had performed a high-quality audit and that Regal's inventory on the audit dates was stated accurately on the general ledger. As a result of these representations, Superior went forward with its purchase of Regal.

After the purchase, Superior discovered that the audit by Chase had been materially inaccurate and misleading, primarily because the inventory had been grossly overstated on the balance sheet. Later, a former Regal employee who had begun working for Superior exposed an e-mail exchange between Chase and former Regal chief executive officer Buddy Gantry. The exchange revealed that Chase had cooperated in overstating the inventory and understating Regal's tax liability. Using the information presented in the chapter, answer the following questions.

1. If Shuebke's review was conducted in good faith and conformed to generally accepted accounting principles, could Superior hold Shuebke Delgado liable for negligently failing to detect material omissions in Chase's audit? Why or why not?
2. According to the rule adopted by the majority of courts to determine accountants' liability to third parties, could Chase be liable to Superior? Explain.
3. Generally, what requirements must be met before Superior can recover damages under Section 10(b) of the Securities Exchange Act of 1934 and SEC Rule 10b-5? Can Superior meet these requirements?
4. Suppose that a court determined that Chase had aided Regal in willfully understating its tax liability. What is the maximum penalty that could be imposed on Chase?

Debate This

Only the largest publicly held companies should be subject to the Sarbanes-Oxley Act.

Key Terms

auditor 824
constructive fraud 828
defalcation 824
due diligence 833
generally accepted accounting principles (GAAP) 823
generally accepted auditing standards (GAAS) 823
International Financial Reporting Standards (IFRS) 824
malpractice 826
working papers 832

Chapter Summary: Liability of Accountants and Other Professionals

Potential Liability to Clients	1. **Breach of contract**—A professional who fails to fulfill contractual obligations can be held liable for breach of contract and resulting damages. 2. **Negligence**—An accountant, attorney, or other professional, in performing professional duties, must use the care, knowledge, and judgment generally used by professionals in the same or similar circumstances. Failure to do so is negligence. An accountant's violation of generally accepted accounting principles or generally accepted auditing standards is *prima facie* evidence of negligence. 3. **Fraud**—Intentionally misrepresenting a material fact to a client, when the client relies on the misrepresentation, is fraud. Gross negligence in performance of duties is constructive fraud.

Potential Liability to Third Parties	An accountant may be liable for negligence to any third person the accountant knows or should have known will benefit from the accountant's work. The standard for imposing this liability varies, but generally courts follow one of the following rules (see Exhibit 33–1): 1. ***Ultramares* rule**—Liability will be imposed only if the accountant is in privity, or near privity, with the third party. 2. ***Restatement* rule**—Liability will be imposed only if the third party's reliance is foreseen or known, or if the third party is among a class of foreseen or known users. The majority of courts have adopted this rule. 3. **"Reasonably foreseeable users" rule**—Liability will be imposed if the third party's reliance was reasonably foreseeable.
Liability of Accountants under Federal Laws	1. **The Sarbanes-Oxley Act**—The act imposes requirements on public accounting firms that provide auditing services to companies whose securities are sold to public investors. It created the Public Company Accounting Oversight Board, which oversees the audit of public companies that are subject to securities laws. The act requires accountants to maintain working papers relating to an audit or review for seven years from the end of the fiscal period in which the audit or review was concluded. 2. **The Securities Act of 1933**— a. Section 11—An accountant who makes a false statement or omits a material fact in audited financial statements required for registration of securities under the act may be liable to anyone who acquires securities covered by the registration statement. The accountant's defense is basically the use of due diligence and the reasonable belief that the work was complete and correct. The burden of proof is on the accountant. Willful violations of this act may be subject to criminal penalties. b. Section 12(2)—An accountant may be liable when a prospectus or other communication presented to an investor contained an untrue statement or omitted a material fact. 3. **The Securities Exchange Act of 1934**— a. Section 18—Accountants may be held liable for false and misleading applications, reports, and documents filed with the SEC. The burden is on the plaintiff, and the accountant has numerous defenses, including good faith and lack of knowledge that what was submitted was false. Negligence alone does not lead to liability under the 1934 act. b. Section 10(b) and Rule 10b-5—Provisions allow private parties to bring civil actions against violators. Accountants may be held liable only to sellers or purchasers of securities. Privity is not necessary for recovery. 4. **The Private Securities Litigation Reform Act**—An auditor must use adequate procedures to detect any illegal acts of the company being audited and disclose any illegalities detected. Parties are liable only for the proportion of damages for which they are responsible.
Potential Criminal Liability	1. Willful violations of the Securities Act of 1933 and the Securities Exchange Act of 1934 may be subject to criminal penalties. 2. Willfully making false statements in a tax return or willfully aiding or assisting in the preparation of a false tax return is a felony. Aiding and abetting an individual's understatement of tax liability is a separate crime.
Confidentiality and Privilege	Communications other than those between attorneys and clients are not privileged under federal law. 1. **Attorney-client relationships**—Communications relating to representation are normally held in the strictest confidence and protected by law. Only the client may waive the privilege. The SEC, however, has implemented rules requiring attorneys who learn that a client has violated securities laws to report the violation to the SEC. 2. **Accountant-client relationships**—The majority of states follow the common law. If a court so orders, an accountant must disclose information about the client to the court.

Issue Spotters

1. Dave, an accountant, prepares a financial statement for Excel Company, a client, knowing that Excel will use the statement to obtain a loan from First National Bank. Dave makes negligent omissions in the statement that result in a loss to the bank. Can the bank successfully sue Dave? Why or why not? (See *Potential Liability to Third Parties.*)
2. Nora, an accountant, prepares a financial statement as part of a registration statement that Omega, Inc., files with the Securities and Exchange Commission before making a public offering of securities. The statement contains a misstatement of material fact that is not attributable to Nora's fraud or negligence. Pat relies on the misstatement, buys some of the securities, and suffers a loss. Can Nora be held liable to Pat? Explain. (See *Liability of Accountants under Federal Laws.*)

—Check your answers to the *Issue Spotters* against the answers provided in Appendix D.

Business Scenarios and Case Problems

33–1. The *Ultramares* Rule. Larkin, Inc., retains Howard Perkins to manage its books and prepare its financial statements. Perkins, a certified public accountant, lives in Indiana and practices there. After twenty years, Perkins has become a bit bored with generally accepted accounting principles (GAAP) and has adopted more creative accounting methods. Now, though, Perkins has a problem. He is being sued by Molly Tucker, one of Larkin's creditors. Tucker alleges that Perkins either knew or should have known that Larkin's financial statements would be distributed to various individuals. Furthermore, she asserts that these financial statements were negligently prepared and seriously inaccurate. What are the consequences of Perkins's failure to follow GAAP? Under the traditional *Ultramares* rule, can Tucker recover damages from Perkins? Explain. (See *Potential Liability to Third Parties.*)

33–2. The *Restatement* Rule. The accounting firm of Goldman, Walters, Johnson & Co. prepared financial statements for Lucy's Fashions, Inc. After reviewing the financial statements, Happydays State Bank agreed to loan Lucy's Fashions $35,000 for expansion. When Lucy's Fashions declared bankruptcy under Chapter 11 six months later, Happydays State Bank filed an action against Goldman, Walters, Johnson & Co., alleging negligent preparation of financial statements. Assuming that the court has abandoned the *Ultramares* approach, what is the result? What are the policy reasons for holding accountants liable to third parties with whom they are not in privity? (See *Potential Liability to Third Parties.*)

33–3. Accountant's Liability under Rule 10b-5. In early 2018, Bennett, Inc., offered a substantial number of new common shares to the public. Harvey Helms had a long-standing interest in Bennett because his grandfather had once been president of the company. On receiving Bennett's prospectus, Helms was dismayed by the pessimism it embodied, so he decided to delay purchasing stock in the company. Later, Helms asserted that the prospectus prepared by the accountants had been overly pessimistic and had contained materially misleading statements. Discuss fully how successful Helms would be in bringing a suit under Rule 10b-5 against Bennett's accountants. (See *Liability of Accountants under Federal Laws.*)

33–4. Professional's Liability. Soon after Teresa DeYoung's husband died, her mother-in-law also died, leaving an inheritance of more than $400,000 for DeYoung's children. DeYoung hired John Ruggiero, an attorney, to ensure that her children would receive it. Ruggiero advised her to invest the funds in his real estate business. She declined. A few months later, $300,000 of the inheritance was sent to Ruggiero. Without telling DeYoung, he deposited the $300,000 in his account and began to use the funds in his real estate business. Nine months later, $109,000 of the inheritance was sent to Ruggiero. He paid this to DeYoung. She asked about the remaining amount. Ruggiero lied to hide his theft. Unable to access these funds, DeYoung's children changed their college plans to attend less expensive institutions. Nearly three years later, DeYoung learned the truth. Can she bring a suit against Ruggiero? If so, on what ground? If not, why not? Did Ruggiero violate any standard of professional ethics? Discuss. [*DeYoung v. Ruggiero,* 2009 VT 9, 971 A.2d 627 (2009)] (See *Potential Liability to Clients.*)

33–5. Professional Malpractice. Jeffery Guerrero hired James McDonald, a certified public accountant, to represent him and his business in an appeal to the Internal Revenue Service. The appeal concerned audits that showed Guerrero owed more taxes. When the appeal failed, McDonald assisted in preparing materials for an appeal to the Tax Court, which was not successful. Guerrero then sued McDonald for professional negligence in the preparation of his evidence for the court. Specifically, Guerrero claimed that he would have won the case if McDonald had adequately prepared witnesses and had presented all the arguments that could have been made on his behalf. Guerrero contended that McDonald was liable for all of the additional taxes he was required to pay. Is Guerrero's claim likely to result in liability on McDonald's part? What factors would the court consider? [*Guerrero v. McDonald*, 302 Ga.App. 164, 690 S.E.2d 486 (2010)] (See *Potential Liability to Clients.*)

33–6. Business Case Problem with Sample Answer—Potential Liability to Third Parties. In 2006, twenty-seven parties became limited partners in two hedge funds that had invested with Bernard Madoff and his investment firm. The partners' investment adviser gave them various investment information, including a memorandum indicating that an independent certified public accountant, KPMG, LLP, had audited the hedge funds' annual reports. Since 2004, KPMG had also prepared annual reports addressed to the funds' "partners." Each report stated that KPMG had investigated the funds' financial statements, had followed generally accepted auditing principles, and had concluded that the statements fairly summarized the funds' financial conditions. Moreover, KPMG used the information from its audits to prepare individual tax statements for each fund partner.

In 2008, Madoff was charged with securities fraud for running a massive Ponzi scheme. In a 2009 report, the Securities and Exchange Commission identified numerous "red flags" that should have been discovered by investment advisers and auditors. Unfortunately, they were not, and the hedge funds' partners lost millions of dollars. Is KPMG potentially liable to the funds' partners under the *Restatement (Third) of Torts?* Why or why not? [*Askenazy v. Tremont Group Holdings, Inc.*, 2012 WL 440675 (Mass.Super. 2012)] (See *Potential Liability to Third Parties.*)

—For a sample answer to Problem 33–6, go to Appendix E.

33–7. Attorney's Duty of Care. Luis and Maria Rojas contracted to buy a house in Westchester County, New York, from Andrew and Karen Paine. The house was on property designated as "Lot No. 8" on a subdivision map filed in the county clerk's office. The Paines had acquired the property in two parts by the transfer of two separate deeds. At the closing, they delivered a deed stating that it covered "the same property." In fact, however, the legal description attached to the deed covered only the portion of Lot No. 8 described in one of the two previous deeds. Attorney Paul Herrick represented the Rojases in the deal with the Paines. When the Rojases sought to sell the property two years later, the title search revealed that they owned only part of Lot No. 8, and the buyer refused to go through with the sale. Is Herrick liable for malpractice? Explain. [*Rojas v. Paine*, 125 A.D.3d 745, 4 N.Y.S.3d 223 (2 Dept. 2015)] (See *Potential Liability to Clients.*)

33–8. Attorney Misconduct. Solomons One, LLC, was formed to develop waterfront property in Maryland. Vernon Donnelly was a member of the LLC and served as the company's counsel. The state denied Solomons's request for a permit to build a pier. Donnelly appealed the denial. Meanwhile, he assigned Solomons's potential right to build a pier to a trust, appointed himself trustee, and changed his fee arrangement with the company. These steps were taken without Solomons's authorization, but there was no financial harm to the LLC and no additional evidence that Donnelly engaged in dishonesty or deceit. On learning of Donnelly's actions, however, a majority of the LLC members voted to terminate his representation. Despite the vote, he pursued the pier case until the LLC ultimately gained the right to build a pier. Donnelly had not previously been disciplined for misconduct. Should he be disciplined in this case? Why or why not? [*Attorney Grievance Commission of Maryland v. Donnelly*, 458 Md. 237, 182 A.3d 743 (2018)] (See *Potential Liability to Clients.*)

33–9. A Question of Ethics—The IDDR Approach and Attorney Misconduct. Brandy Sutton was the sole owner of the law firm Pendleton & Sutton in Lawrence, Kansas. Sutton offered a retirement plan as a benefit to the members of her staff. Employees could contribute up to 3 percent of their salaries. Sutton withheld the contributions from the employees' paychecks, which indicated that the amounts were deposited into the plan. For a period of years, however, she failed to make the deposits, using the funds to cover her professional expenses instead. An associate attorney with the firm discovered the discrepancy and filed a complaint with the state disciplinary office. In response, Sutton argued that the misconduct was caused by financial difficulties, including "several items" involving the associate who filed the complaint. Sutton expressed remorse, and within sixteen months properly funded all of the employees' accounts. [*In the Matter of Sutton*, 307 Kan. 95, 405 P.3d 1205 (2017)] (See *Potential Liability to Clients.*)

1. When a business experiences financial difficulties, can it withhold amounts owed to its employees to pay more immediate obligations? Consider this question from an ethical perspective, using the IDDR approach.
2. Should a sanction be imposed on Sutton in this case? If so, what should it be? Possibilities include suspension from the practice of law for a limited time or an indefinite period, and probation. Explain.

Critical Thinking and Writing Assignments

33–10. Time-Limited Group Assignment—Attorney-Client Privilege. Napster, Inc., offered a service that allowed its users to browse digital music files on other users' computers and download selections for free. Music industry principals sued Napster for copyright infringement, and the court ordered Napster to remove files that were identified as infringing from its service. When Napster failed to comply, it was shut down.

A few months later, Bertelsmann, a German corporation, loaned Napster $85 million to fund its anticipated transition to a licensed digital music distribution system. The terms allowed Napster to spend the loan on "general, administrative and overhead expenses." In an e-mail, Napster's chief executive officer referred to a "side deal" under which Napster could use up to $10 million of the loan to pay litigation expenses. Napster failed to launch the new system before declaring bankruptcy. The plaintiffs filed a suit against Bertelsmann, alleging that its loan had prolonged Napster's infringement. The plaintiffs asked the court to order the disclosure of all attorney-client communications related to the loan. (See *Confidentiality and Privilege.*)

1. The first group will identify the principle that Bertelsmann could assert to protect these communications and outline the purpose of this protection.
2. The second group will decide whether this principle should protect a client who consults an attorney for advice that will help the client commit fraud.
3. A third group will determine whether the court should grant the plaintiffs' request.

Unit Six—Task-Based Simulation

StockPhoto.com/Yuri_Arcurs

Alpha Software, Inc., and Beta Products Corporation—both small firms—are competitors in the business of software research, development, and production.

1. **Antitrust Law.** Alpha and Beta form a joint venture to research, develop, and produce new software for a particular line of computers. Does this business combination violate the antitrust laws? If so, is it a *per se* violation, or is it subject to the rule of reason? Alpha and Beta decide to merge. After the merger, Beta is the surviving firm. What aspect of this firm's presence in the market will be assessed to decide whether this merger is in violation of any antitrust laws?

2. **Consumer Law.** To market its products profitably, Beta considers a number of advertising and labeling proposals. One proposal is that Beta suggest in its advertising that one of its software products has a certain function, even though the product does not actually have that capability. Another suggestion is that Beta sell half of a certain program in packaging that misleads the buyer into believing the entire program is included. To obtain the entire program, customers would need to buy a second product. Can Beta implement these suggestions or otherwise market its products in any way it likes? If not, why not?

3. **Environmental Law.** The production part of Beta's operations generates hazardous waste. Gamma Transport Company transports the waste to Omega Waste Corporation, which owns and operates a hazardous waste disposal site. At the site, some containers leak hazardous waste, and the Environmental Protection Agency (EPA) cleans it up. From whom can the EPA recover the cost of the cleanup?

4. **Liability of Accountants.** Beta hires a certified public accountant, Aaron Schleger, to prepare its financial reports and issue opinion letters based on those reports. One year, Beta falls into serious financial trouble, but this is not reflected in Schleger's reports and opinion letters. Relying on Schleger's portrayal of the company's fiscal health, Beta borrows substantial amounts to develop a new product. The bank, in lending funds to Beta, relies on an opinion letter from Schleger, and Schleger is aware of the bank's reliance. Assuming that Schleger was negligent but did not engage in intentional fraud, what is his potential liability in this situation? Discuss fully.

Unit 7
Property and Its Protection

Michal Kalasek/Shutterstock.com

Nomad_Soul/Shutterstock.com

34 Personal Property and Bailments

Focus Questions

The four Focus Questions *below are designed to help improve your understanding. After reading this chapter, you should be able to answer the following questions:*

1. What is real property? What is personal property?
2. What are the three necessary elements for an effective gift?
3. How does lost property differ from mislaid property? Does a finder of such property acquire title to it?
4. What are the three elements of a bailment?

"The great . . . end . . . of men's uniting into commonwealths, and putting themselves under government, is the preservation of their property."

John Locke
1632–1704
(English political philosopher)

Property consists of the legally protected rights and interests a person has in anything with an ascertainable value that is subject to ownership. For instance, digital property has become quite valuable in today's world. When a couple divorces, they might dispute who owns the virtual world assets they have acquired, their Internet accounts, or the data stored on their devices. Property would have little value, however, if the law did not define owners' rights to use their property, to sell or dispose of it, and to prevent trespass on it. Indeed, John Locke, as indicated in the chapter-opening quotation, considered the preservation of property to be the primary reason for the establishment of government.

In this chapter, we first examine the differences between personal and real property. We then look at the methods of acquiring ownership of personal property and consider issues relating to mislaid, lost, and abandoned personal property. In the remainder of the chapter, we discuss bailment relationships. A *bailment* is created when personal property is temporarily delivered into the care of another without a transfer of title, such as when a person takes an item of clothing to the dry cleaners.

34–1 Personal Property versus Real Property

Real Property Land and everything permanently attached to it, such as trees and buildings.

Property is divided into real property and personal property. **Real property** (sometimes called *realty* or *real estate*) consists of land and everything permanently attached to it, including structures and anything permanently attached to the structures. Everything else is **personal property,** or *personalty*. Attorneys sometimes refer to personal property as **chattel,** a term used under the common law to denote all forms of personal property.

Personal Property Property that is movable. Any property that is not real property.

Chattel Personal property.

Personal property can be tangible or intangible. *Tangible* personal property, such as an 8K TV, heavy construction equipment, or a car, has physical substance. *Intangible* personal property represents some set of rights and interests but has no physical substance. Stocks and bonds, patents, trademarks, and copyrights—as well as digital property—are examples of intangible personal property.

Both personal property and real property can be owned by an individual person or by some other entity, such as an organization. When two or more persons own real or personal property together, concurrent ownership exists. (The different types of concurrent ownership will be discussed in the real property chapter.)

Focus Question 1
What is real property? What is personal property?

34–1a Why Is the Distinction Important?

The distinction between real and personal property is important for several reasons. How property is taxed and what is required to transfer or acquire the property is determined by whether the property is classified as real or personal.

Taxation The two types of property are usually subject to different types of taxes. Generally, each city and county assesses property taxes on real property. Typically, the tax rate is based on the market value of the real property and the various services provided by the city and county in which the property is located. For instance, higher taxes may be imposed on real property located within the city limits to pay for schools, roads, and libraries.

Businesses often also pay taxes on the personal property they own, use, or lease, including office or farm equipment and supplies. Individuals may pay sales tax when purchasing personal property, but generally they are not required to pay annual taxes on personal property that is not used for business.

Acquisition Another reason for distinguishing between real and personal property has to do with the way the property is acquired or transferred. Personal property can be transferred with a minimum of formality—such as by selling goods on eBay or at a garage sale. In contrast, real property transfers generally involve a written sales contract and a *deed* that is recorded with the state.

Similarly, establishing ownership rights is simpler for personal property than for real property. **Example 34.1** If Mia gives Shawn an iPad as a gift, Shawn does not need to have any paperwork evidencing title, as he would if she had given him real property. ■ The ways to acquire ownership of personal property will be discussed shortly.

34–1b Conversion of Real Property to Personal Property

Sometimes, real property can be turned into personal property by detaching it from the land. For instance, the trees, bushes, and plants growing on land are considered part of the real property (with the exception of crops that must be planted every year, such as wheat). If the property is sold, all the vegetation growing on the land normally is transferred to the new owner of the real property.

Once the items are severed (removed) from the land, however, they become personal property. If the trees are cut from the land, the timber is personal property. If apples, grapes, or raspberries are picked from trees or vines growing on real property, they become personal property. Similarly, if land contains minerals (including oil) or other natural resources (such as marble), the resources are part of the real property. But once removed, they become personal property.

Conversely, personal property may be converted into real property by permanently attaching it to the real property. Personal property that is affixed to real property in a permanent way, such as tile installed in a house, is known as a *fixture*.

monkeybusinessimages/ iStock/Getty Images

What is the most common way to acquire ownership rights in personal property?

34–2 Acquiring Ownership of Personal Property

The most common way of acquiring personal property is by purchasing it. (Today, even virtual property is often purchased—see this chapter's *Adapting the Law to the Online Environment* feature for a discussion.)

We reviewed the purchase and sale of goods (which are personal property) in earlier chapters. Often, property is acquired by will or inheritance, as we will discuss in a later chapter. Here, we look at additional ways in which ownership of personal property can be acquired, including acquisition by possession, production, gifts, accession, and confusion.

34–2a Possession

Sometimes, a person can become the owner of personal property merely by possessing it. An example of acquiring ownership by possession is the capture of wild animals. Wild animals belong to no one in their natural state, and the first person to take possession of a wild animal normally owns it. A hunter who kills a deer, for instance, has assumed ownership of it (unless the hunter acted in violation of the law). Those who find lost or abandoned property can also acquire ownership rights through mere possession of the property, as will be discussed later in this chapter.

34–2b Production

Production—the fruits of labor—is another means of acquiring ownership of personal property. For instance, writers, inventors, and manufacturers produce personal property and thereby acquire title to it. (In some situations, as when a researcher is hired to develop a new product, the researcher-producer may not own what is produced.)

The Exploding World of Digital Property

Adapting the Law to the Online Environment

Using the same blockchain technology as do cryptocurrencies such as Bitcoin, online enthusiasts can now create one-of-a-kind digital merchandise. Known as NFTs (non-fungible tokens), these digital assets have single owners and, like real-world goods, can be bought or sold based on their relative scarcity and worth. CryptoKitties, an online game involving the breeding of digital cats, showed the potential of this market when an NFT named Dragon—created by one of the game's players—sold for approximately $170,000.

If the prospect of paying real funds for virtual cartoon cats seems disconcerting, remember that property does not have to be tangible. Property consists of a bundle of rights in anything that has an ascertainable value and is subject to ownership. This definition encompasses virtual pets, land, and art, as well as all the intangible products used in virtual worlds such as Entropia Universe and Fortnite.

Digital Goods Have Value, Too

Digital goods include virtual goods. More importantly, they include digital books, music libraries, and movie downloads, as well as domain names and expensively created websites. This digital property has real value. Some digital music libraries, for example, cost thousands of dollars.

Who Keeps the Digital Goods?

The growing value of digital goods raises some legal questions. For instance, what are the respective rights of the creator/owner of a virtual-world website and the players at that site? What happens when a husband and wife decide to divorce after they have purchased virtual real estate or digital goods (or a beloved virtual cat) with real-world dollars? The couple—or a court—will have to figure out a way to divide the goods. Property and divorce laws will have to adapt to take this emerging world of digital property into account.

Critical Thinking

How might a couple who enjoy purchasing digital goods together avoid property division issues in the event of a divorce?

34–2c Gifts

A **gift** is another fairly common means of acquiring and transferring ownership of real and personal property. A gift is essentially a *voluntary* transfer of property ownership for which no consideration is given. The absence of consideration is what distinguishes a gift from a contractual obligation to transfer ownership of property.

Gift A voluntary transfer of property made without consideration, past or present.

For a gift to be effective, the following three elements are required:

1. Donative intent on the part of the *donor* (the one giving the gift).
2. Delivery.
3. Acceptance by the *donee* (the one receiving the gift).

Until these three requirements are met, no effective gift has been made. **Example 34.2** Your aunt tells you that she *intends* to give you a new BMW for your next birthday. This is simply a promise to make a gift. It is not considered a gift until the BMW is delivered and accepted.

Focus Question 2

What are the three necessary elements for an effective gift?

Ethical Issue

Who owns the engagement ring? Often, when two people decide to marry, one party (traditionally the man in an opposite-sex relationship) gives the other an engagement ring. What if the engagement is called off? Etiquette authorities routinely counsel that if the woman breaks the engagement, she should return the ring, but if the man calls the wedding off, the woman is entitled to keep the ring. When the party who gave the ring (the donor) sues for its return after a breakup, the courts are split.

Courts in a majority of states, including Kansas, Michigan, New York, and Ohio, hold that an engagement ring is not a real gift. Rather, it is a "conditional gift" that becomes final only if the marriage occurs. If the marriage does not take place, the ring is returned to the donor regardless of who broke the engagement. This position is similar to the law of ancient Rome, which mandated that when an engagement was broken, the woman had to return the ring, as a penalty, regardless of who was at fault. Some judges, however, disagree with the conditional-gift theory and contend that an engagement ring is a gift and, as such, it belongs to the donee, even if the engagement is broken.

Donative Intent When a gift is challenged in court, the court will determine whether donative intent exists by looking at the language of the donor and the surrounding circumstances. A court may look at the relationship between the parties and the size of the gift in relation to the donor's other assets. When a person has given away a suspiciously large amount of assets, the court will scrutinize the transaction closely to determine the donor's mental capacity and to look for indications of fraud or duress.

Spotlight Case Example 34.3 Over a period of three months, Jean Knowles Goodman, who was eighty-five years old, gave Steven Atwood several checks that totaled $56,100. Atwood was a veterinarian who had cared for Goodman's dogs for nearly twenty years, and he and Goodman had become friends. Shortly after writing the last check, Goodman was hospitalized and diagnosed with dementia (loss of brain function) and alcohol dependency.

The guardian who was appointed to represent Goodman filed a lawsuit to invalidate the gifts, claiming that Goodman had lacked mental capacity

Grzegorz Czapski/Shutterstock.com

If a close relative tells you that she intends to give you a BMW, has she gifted you the car? Why or why not?

and donative intent. At trial, a psychiatrist who had examined Goodman testified on behalf of Atwood that while Goodman lacked the capacity to care for herself, she would have understood that she was giving away her funds. Therefore, the court concluded that Goodman had donative intent to make the gifts to Atwood.[1]

Delivery The gift must be delivered to the donee. Delivery may be accomplished by means of a third person who is the agent of either the donor or the donee. Naturally, no delivery is necessary if the gift is already in the hands of the donee. Delivery is obvious in most cases, but some objects cannot be relinquished physically. Then the question of delivery depends on the surrounding circumstances.

Constructive Delivery A symbolic delivery of property that cannot be physically delivered.

Constructive Delivery. When the object itself cannot be physically delivered, a symbolic, or constructive, delivery will be sufficient. **Constructive delivery** confers the right to take possession of the object in question. **Example 34.4** Angela wants to make a gift of various rare coins that she has stored in a safe-deposit box. She obviously cannot deliver the box itself to the donee, and she does not want to take the coins out of the bank. Angela can simply deliver the key to the box to the donee and authorize the donee's access to the box and its contents. This action constitutes a constructive delivery of the contents of the box.

Constructive delivery is always necessary for gifts of intangible property, such as stocks, bonds, insurance policies, and contracts. What will be delivered are documents that represent rights and are not, in themselves, the true property. (See this chapter's *Business Law Analysis* feature for an illustration.)

1. *Goodman v. Atwood*, 78 Mass.App.Ct. 655, 940 N.E.2d 514 (2011).

Effective Gift of a Brokerage Account

Business Law Analysis

John Weider opened a brokerage account with Quick and Reilly, Inc., in the name of his son James. Twelve years later, when the balance was $52,085, John closed the account and transferred the funds to a joint account in John's name and the name of his other son, James's brother. James did not learn of the existence of the account in his name until the transfer, when he received a tax form for the account's final year. James filed a suit in a Connecticut state court against Quick and Reilly, alleging breach of contract and seeking to recover the account's principal and interest. What are the elements of a valid gift? Did John's opening of the account in James's name with Quick and Reilly constitute a gift to James?

Analysis: A gift is a transfer of property without consideration. To make a valid gift, the donor must have "donative intent" (an intent that title to the property will pass to the donee). The donor must also hand over control of the property to the recipient of the gift. The three requirements for an effective gift are (1) the donor's donative intent, (2) delivery of the property, and (3) the donee's acceptance.

Result and Reasoning: John's use of James's name to open the account may indicate donative intent. But the most significant element in this situation is delivery, which requires the donor to part with possession of the property and relinquish control. Delivery may be actual or constructive. Notice to James of the account's existence might have been sufficient to constitute constructive delivery, but in this scenario, James never received actual delivery of the funds in the account. As for constructive delivery, James was not even aware of the existence of the account (or his right to the funds) until after the funds had been withdrawn and the account had been closed. Without actual or constructive delivery, there is no way for James to prove that the account constituted a valid gift.

Relinquishing Dominion and Control. An effective delivery also requires giving up complete control and **dominion** (ownership rights) over the subject matter of the gift. The outcome of disputes often turns on whether control has actually been relinquished. The Internal Revenue Service carefully examines transactions between relatives, especially when one claims to have given income-producing property to another who is in a lower marginal tax bracket. Unless complete control over the property has been relinquished, the "donor"—not the family member who received the "gift"—will have to pay taxes on the income from that property.

Dominion Ownership rights in property, including the right to possess and control the property.

In the following *Classic Case,* the court focused on the requirement that a donor must relinquish complete control and dominion over property given to the donee before a gift can be effectively delivered.

Classic Case 34.1

In re Estate of Piper

Missouri Court of Appeals, 676 S.W.2d897 (1984).

Facts Gladys Piper died intestate (without a will) in 1982. At her death, she owned miscellaneous personal property worth $5,000 and had in her purse $200 in cash and two diamond rings. Wanda Brown, Piper's niece, took the contents of the purse, allegedly to preserve the items for the estate. Clara Kaufmann, a friend of Piper's, filed a claim against the estate for $4,800. From October 1974 until Piper's death, Kaufmann had taken Piper to the doctor, beauty shop, and grocery store. Kaufmann had also written Piper's checks to pay her bills and had helped her care for her home.

doram/iStock/Getty Images

How can two diamond rings have been gifted if they remained in the owner's purse after her death?

Kaufmann maintained that Piper had promised to pay her for these services and had given her the diamond rings as a gift. A Missouri state trial court denied her request for payment. The court found that her services had been voluntary. Kaufmann then filed a petition for delivery of personal property—the rings—which was granted by the trial court. Brown, other heirs, and the administrator of Piper's estate appealed.

Issue Had Gladys Piper made an effective gift of the rings to Clara Kaufmann?

Decision No. The state appellate court reversed the judgment of the trial court on the ground that Piper had never delivered the rings to Kaufmann.

Reason Kaufmann claimed that the rings belonged to her by reason of a "consummated gift long prior to the death of Gladys Piper." Two witnesses testified at the trial that Piper had told them that she was going to wear the rings until she died but that the rings belonged to Kaufmann. The appellate court, however, found "no evidence of any actual delivery." The court pointed out that the essentials of a gift are (1) a present intention to make a gift on the part of the donor, (2) a delivery of the property by the donor to the donee, and (3) an acceptance by the donee. Here, the evidence showed only an intent to make a gift. Because there was no delivery—either actual or constructive—no valid gift was made.

Critical Thinking

- **What If the Facts Were Different?** *Suppose that Gladys Piper had told Clara Kaufmann that she was giving the rings to Clara but wished to keep them in her possession for a few more days. Would this have affected the court's decision in this case? Explain.*
- **Impact of This Case on Today's Law** *This case clearly illustrates the delivery requirement when making a gift. Assuming that Piper did, indeed, intend for Kaufmann to have the rings, it was unfortunate that Kaufmann had no right to receive them after Piper's death. Yet the alternative could lead to perhaps even more unfairness. The policy behind the delivery requirement is to protect property owners and their heirs from fraudulent claims based solely on parol evidence. If not for this policy, a person could easily claim that a gift had been made when, in fact, it had not.*

Acceptance The final requirement of a valid gift is acceptance by the donee. This rarely presents any problem, as most donees readily accept their gifts. The courts generally assume acceptance unless the circumstances indicate otherwise.

Gifts *Inter Vivos* and Gifts *Causa Mortis* A gift made during one's lifetime is termed a **gift *inter vivos.*** A **gift *causa mortis*** (a so-called *deathbed gift*) is made in contemplation of imminent death. To be effective, a gift *causa mortis* must meet not only the three requirements discussed earlier—donative intent, delivery, and acceptance—but also some additional conditions.

Gift *Inter Vivos.* A gift made during one's lifetime and not in contemplation of imminent death, in contrast to a gift *causa mortis.*

Gift *Causa Mortis* A gift made in contemplation of imminent death. The gift is revoked if the donor does not die as contemplated.

Automatically Revoked if Donor Recovers. A gift *causa mortis* does not become absolute until the donor dies from the contemplated event, and it is automatically revoked if the donor survives. **Example 34.5** Yang, who is about to undergo surgery to remove a cancerous tumor, delivers an envelope to Chao, a close business associate. The envelope contains a letter saying, "I want to give you this check for $1 million in the event of my death from this operation." Chao cashes the check. The surgeon performs the operation and removes the tumor. Yang recovers fully. Several months later, Yang dies from a heart attack that is totally unrelated to the operation.

If the administrator of Yang's estate tries to recover the $1 million, she will normally succeed. The gift *causa mortis* to Chao is automatically revoked if Yang recovers. The *specific event* that was contemplated in making the gift was death from a particular operation. Because Yang's death was not the result of this event, the gift is revoked, and the $1 million passes to Yang's estate.

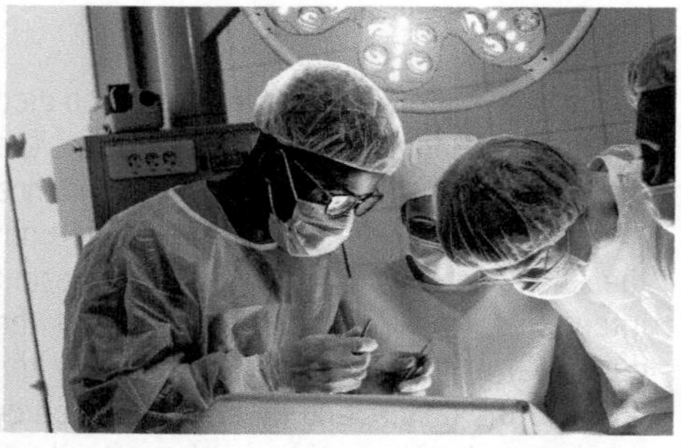

UfaBizPhoto/shutterstock.com

Before undergoing surgery, a patient gives a large gift to a friend in the event of the patient's death from the surgery. What is the effect on the gift if the patient recovers?

Automatically Revoked if Donee Dies. A gift *causa mortis* is also revoked if the prospective donee dies before the donor. Therefore, even if Yang in Example 34.5 had died during the operation, the gift would have been revoked if Chao had died a few minutes earlier. In that event, the $1 million would have passed to Yang's estate, and not to Chao's heirs.

34–2d Accession

Accession means "something added." Accession occurs when someone adds value to an item of personal property by the use of either labor or materials.

Accession The addition of value to personal property by the use of labor or materials.

Generally, there is no dispute about who owns the property after an accession occurs, especially when the accession is accomplished with the owner's consent. **Example 34.6** Harvey buys all the materials necessary to customize his Corvette. He hires Zach, a customizing specialist, to come to his house to perform the work. Harvey pays Zach for the value of the labor, obviously retaining title to the property.

If an improvement is made wrongfully—without the permission of the owner—the owner retains title to the property and normally does not have to pay for the improvement. This is true even if the accession increases the value of the property substantially. **Example 34.7** Colton steals a truck and puts expensive new tires on it. If the rightful owner later recovers the truck, the owner obviously will not be required to compensate Colton, a thief, for the value of the new tires.

34–2e Confusion

Confusion The mixing together of goods belonging to two or more owners to such an extent that the separately owned goods cannot be identified.

Confusion is the commingling (mixing together) of goods to such an extent that one person's personal property cannot be distinguished from another's. Confusion frequently occurs with *fungible goods,* such as grain or oil, which consist of identical units.

If confusion occurs as a result of agreement, an honest mistake, or the act of some third party, the owners share ownership and will share any loss in proportion to their ownership interests in the property. **Example 34.8** Five farmers in a small Iowa community enter into a cooperative arrangement. Each fall, the farmers harvest the same amount of number 2–grade yellow corn and store it in silos that are held by the cooperative. Each farmer thus owns one-fifth of the total corn in the silos. If a fire burns down one of the silos, each farmer will bear one-fifth of the loss. If goods are confused due to an intentional wrongful act, then the innocent party ordinarily acquires title to the whole.

34–3 Mislaid, Lost, and Abandoned Property

As already mentioned, one of the methods of acquiring ownership of property is to possess it. Simply finding something and holding on to it, however, does not necessarily give the finder any legal rights in the property. Different rules apply, depending on whether the property was mislaid, lost, or abandoned. Exhibit 34-1 summarizes the distinctions among these types of property, which are discussed in the following subsections.

34–3a Mislaid Property

Property that has been *voluntarily* placed somewhere by the owner and then inadvertently forgotten is **mislaid property.** A person who finds mislaid property does not obtain title to it. Instead, the owner of the place where the property was mislaid becomes the caretaker of the property because it is highly likely that the true owner will return.[2] **Example 34.9** Maya goes to a movie theater. While paying for popcorn at the concessions stand, she sets her iPhone on the counter and then leaves it there. The phone is mislaid property, and the theater owner is entrusted with the duty of reasonably caring for it.

Mislaid Property Property that the owner has voluntarily parted with and then has inadvertently forgotten.

Lost Property Property that the owner has involuntarily parted with and then cannot find or recover.

34–3b Lost Property

Property that is *involuntarily* left is **lost property.** A finder of the property can claim title to the property against the whole world—*except the true owner.*[3] If the true owner is identified and demands that the lost property be returned, the finder must return it. In contrast, if a third party attempts to take possession of the lost property, the finder will have a better title than the third party.

Example 34.10 Kayla works in a large library at night. As she crosses the courtyard on her way home, she finds a gold bracelet set with what seem to be precious stones. She takes the bracelet to a jeweler to have it appraised.

Serhii Bobyk/Shutterstock.com

When a person leaves a smartphone at a movie theater, is it mislaid, lost, or abandoned property?

2. For a classic English case establishing this principle, see *Armory v. Delamirie*, 93 Eng.Rep. 664 (K.B. [King's Bench] 1722).
3. The finder of mislaid property is an involuntary bailee.

Exhibit 34–1 Mislaid, Lost, and Abandoned Property

Mislaid Property	Property that is placed somewhere voluntarily by the owner and then inadvertently forgotten. A finder of mislaid property will not acquire title to the goods, and the owner of the place where the property was mislaid becomes a caretaker of the mislaid property.
Lost Property	Property that is involuntarily left by the owner. A finder of lost property can claim title to the property against the whole world except the true owner.
Abandoned Property	Property that has been discarded by the true owner, who has no intention of reclaiming title to the property in the future. A finder of abandoned property can claim title to it against the whole world, including the original owner.

Focus Question 3

How does lost property differ from mislaid property? Does a finder of such property acquire title to it?

While pretending to weigh the bracelet, the jeweler's employee removes several of the stones. If Kayla brings an action to recover the stones from the jeweler, she normally will win, because she found lost property and holds title against everyone *except the true owner.*

Conversion of Lost Property When a finder of lost property knows the true owner and fails to return the property to that person, the finder has committed the tort of *conversion* (the wrongful taking of another's property). **Example 34.11** Mike finds a bicycle lying on the sidewalk in front of his house. He knows that the bicycle belongs to Geneva. If Mike does not return the bicycle, he can be held liable for conversion. Many states require the finder to make a reasonably diligent search to locate the true owner of lost property.

Estray Statutes Statutes defining finders' rights in property when the true owners are unknown.

Estray Statutes Many states have **estray statutes,** which encourage and facilitate the return of property to its true owner and reward the finder for honesty if the property remains unclaimed. These laws provide an incentive for finders to report their discoveries by making it possible for them, after a specified period of time, to acquire legal title to the property they have found.

Generally, the item must be lost property, not merely mislaid property, for estray statutes to apply. Estray statutes usually require the finder or the county clerk to advertise the property in an attempt to help the owner recover it.

Spotlight Case Example 34.12 Drug smugglers often enter the United States illegally from Canada via a frozen river that flows through Van Buren, Maine. When two railroad employees walking near the railroad tracks in Van Buren found a duffel bag that contained $165,580 in cash, they reported their find to U.S. Customs agents, who took custody of the bag and cash. A drug-sniffing dog gave a positive alert on the bag for the scent of drugs. The federal government filed a lawsuit claiming title to the property under criminal forfeiture laws (because the property was involved in illegal drug transactions).

The two employees argued that they were entitled to the $165,580 under Maine's estray statute. That statute required finders to (1) provide written notice to the town clerk within seven days after finding the property, (2) post a public notice in the town, and (3) advertise in the town's newspaper for one month. Because the employees had not fulfilled these requirements, the court ruled that they had not acquired title to the property. Thus, the federal government had a right to seize the cash.[4]

Abandoned Property Property that has been discarded by the owner, who has no intention of reclaiming it.

34–3c Abandoned Property

Property that has been *discarded* by the true owner, who has *no intention* of reclaiming title to it, is **abandoned property.** Someone who finds abandoned property acquires title to it that is good against the whole world, *including the original owner.* If a person finds abandoned property while trespassing on the property of another, however, the owner of the land, not the finder, will acquire title to the property.

An owner of lost property who eventually gives up any further attempt to find it is frequently held to have abandoned the property. **Example 34.13** As Alekis is hiking in the redwoods, her expensive watch falls off her wrist. She retraces her route and searches for the watch but cannot find it. She finally gives up her search and returns home some five hundred miles away. When Frye later finds the watch, he acquires title to it that is good even against Alekis. By completely giving up her search, Alekis abandoned the watch just as effectively as if she had intentionally discarded it.

Joshua Resnick/shutterstock.com

If a hiker loses an expensive watch, when is it considered abandoned property?

4. *United States v. One Hundred Sixty-Five Thousand Five Hundred Eighty Dollars ($165,580) in U.S. Currency*, 502 F.Supp.2d 114 (D.Me. 2007).

Companion pets—including dogs—are personal property. Because a dog is personal property, a court may be tasked with determining whether a dog's owner abandoned it by leaving it with a friend, as in the following case.

Case 34.2

Zephier v. Agate

Court of Appeals of Minnesota, 2020 WL 1845251 (2020).

Facts Dannielle Zephier, who lived in Minnesota, had a pet dog named Oliver. On moving to California to attend school, where her housing situation did not allow dogs, Zephier arranged with Derrick Agate, a close friend in Minnesota, to care for Oliver. Over the next several years, Agate and Zephier communicated often, and she sometimes returned to visit the dog. Eventually, however, Agate refused to allow any more visits. After her attempts to contact Agate and reclaim Oliver were unsuccessful, Zephier filed a suit in a Minnesota state court to recover the dog.

The court, applying the common law of abandonment, found that Zephier had abandoned Oliver and denied her recovery. Zephier appealed.

Issue Did the trial court err by concluding that Zephier had abandoned Oliver?

Decision Yes. A state intermediate appellate court reversed the lower court's judgment, allowing Zephier to recover Oliver.

Reason A Minnesota state statute "lays out a clear, concise process to obtain ownership of abandoned tangible personal property." The statute imposes a time period for abandonment and requires notice to the prior owner of the property before ownership can transfer to the possessor. Six months must pass before the property can be deemed abandoned. Thirty days' notice that the time has elapsed, and that ownership will be transferred at the end of the thirty days, must then be given to the prior owner "personally or by certified mail."

Notice gives the prior owner an opportunity to retrieve her property before she loses all claim to it. This notice is central to the application of the statute. The appellate court reasoned that "because permitting the common law to persist would render the notice provisions of the statute superfluous, the statute necessarily abrogates [overrides] the common law."

In this case, at the trial, Agate admitted that he had not told Zephier that he considered her to have abandoned Oliver, nor had he notified her to either take Oliver or lose her right to ownership. And Zephier testified that she had no knowledge or notice that Agate believed she had abandoned Oliver. "Because Agate failed to provide this statutory notice, Zephier remains the legal owner of Oliver."

Critical Thinking

- **Legal Environment** *Suppose someone else's snow blower is left in your garage for an extended period of time. You've given its owner permission to leave it there indefinitely. Under the statute applied in the* Zephier *case, could you become the owner of the snow blower? Explain.*
- **Economic** *Why is a possessor of abandoned property allowed to obtain ownership rights to it? Discuss.*

34–4 Bailments

Many routine personal and business transactions involve bailments. A **bailment** is formed by the delivery of personal property without transfer of title by one person, called a **bailor**, to another, called a **bailee**. Usually, a bailment is formed for a particular purpose—for instance, to loan, lease, store, repair, or transport the property. What distinguishes a bailment from a sale or a gift is that there is no passage of title and no intent to transfer title. On completion of the purpose, the bailee is obligated to return the bailed property in the same or better condition to the bailor or a third person or to dispose of it as directed.

Although bailments typically arise by contract, not all of the elements of a contract must necessarily be present for a bailment to be created. **Example 34.14** If Amy lends her bicycle to a friend, a bailment is created, but not by contract, because there is no consideration. Many commercial bailments, such as the delivery of clothing to the cleaners for dry cleaning, are based on contract, though.

Bailment A situation in which the personal property of one person (a bailor) is entrusted to another (a bailee), who is obligated to return the bailed property to the bailor or dispose of it as directed.

Bailor One who entrusts goods to a bailee.

Bailee One to whom goods are entrusted by a bailor.

Focus Question 4

What are the three elements of a bailment?

34–4a Elements of a Bailment

Not all transactions involving the delivery of property from one person to another create a bailment. For such a transfer to become a bailment, the following three elements must be present:

1. Personal property.
2. Delivery of possession without title.
3. Agreement that the property will be returned to the bailor or otherwise disposed of according to its owner's directions.

Olena Yakobchuk/Shutterstock.com

A passenger checks her luggage onto an airplane. Has a bailment been created? Why or why not?

Personal Property Requirement Only personal property, not real property or persons, can be the subject of a bailment. **Example 34.15** When Jai checks her bags at the airport, a bailment of Jai's luggage is created because the luggage is personal property. When Jai boards the plane as a passenger, no bailment is created. Although bailments commonly involve *tangible* items—jewelry, cattle, automobiles, and the like—*intangible* personal property, such as promissory notes and shares of stock, may also be bailed.

Delivery of Possession *Delivery of possession* means the transfer of possession of the property to the bailee. For delivery to occur, the bailee must be given exclusive possession and control over the property, and the bailee must *knowingly* accept the personal property.[5] In other words, the bailee must *intend* to exercise control over it.

If either delivery of possession or knowing acceptance is lacking, there is no bailment relationship. **Example 34.16** Sophia goes to a five-star restaurant and checks her coat at the door. She forgets that there is a $20,000 diamond necklace in the coat pocket. In accepting the coat, the bailee does not *knowingly* also accept the necklace. Thus, a bailment of the coat exists—because the restaurant has exclusive possession and control over the coat and has knowingly accepted it—but not a bailment of the necklace.

Physical versus Constructive Delivery. Either *physical* or *constructive* delivery will result in the bailee's exclusive possession of and control over the property. As discussed earlier, in the context of gifts, constructive delivery is a substitute, or symbolic, delivery. What is delivered to the bailee is not the actual property bailed (such as a car) but something so related to the property (such as the car keys) that the requirement of delivery is satisfied.

Involuntary Bailments. In certain situations, a bailment is found despite the apparent lack of the requisite elements of control and knowledge. One instance occurs when the bailee acquires the property accidentally or by mistake—as in finding someone else's lost or mislaid property. A bailment is created even though the bailor did not voluntarily deliver the property to the bailee. Such bailments are called *constructive* or *involuntary* bailments.

Example 34.17 Several corporate managers attend a meeting at the law office of Jacobs & Matheson. One of the corporate officers, Gustafson, inadvertently leaves his briefcase at the office at the conclusion of the meeting. In this situation, a court may find that an involuntary bailment has been created, even though Gustafson has not voluntarily delivered the briefcase and the law firm has not intentionally accepted it. If an involuntary bailment exists, the firm is responsible for taking care of the briefcase and returning it to Gustafson.

Bailment Agreement A bailment agreement can be express or implied. Although a written contract is not required for bailments of less than one year (that is, the Statute of Frauds does not apply), it is a good idea to have one, especially when valuable property is involved.

The bailment agreement expressly or impliedly provides for the return of the bailed property to the bailor or to a third person, or for the disposal of the property by the bailee. It is assumed that the bailee will return the identical goods originally given by the bailor. In certain types of bailments, such as bailments of fungible goods, however, the property returned need only be equivalent property.

5. The requirements outlined in this sentence apply to *voluntary bailments*, not to *involuntary bailments*.

Example 34.18 A bailment is created when Holman stores his grain (fungible goods) in Joe's Warehouse. At the end of the storage period, however, the warehouse is not obligated to return to Holman exactly the same grain that he stored. As long as the warehouse returns grain of the same *type, grade,* and *quantity,* the warehouse—the bailee—has performed its obligation.

34–4b Ordinary Bailments

Bailments are either *ordinary* or *special (extraordinary).* There are three types of ordinary bailments. They are distinguished according to *which party receives a benefit from the bailment.* This factor will dictate the rights and liabilities of the parties, and the courts use it to determine the standard of care required of the bailee in possession of the personal property.

The three types of ordinary bailments are as follows:

1. *Bailment for the sole benefit of the bailor.* This is a gratuitous bailment (a bailment that involves no consideration) for the convenience and benefit of the bailor. Basically, the bailee is caring for the bailor's property as a favor. Therefore, the bailee owes only a slight duty of care and will be liable only if grossly negligent in caring for the property.
   Example 34.19 Allen asks his friend Sumi to store his car in her garage while he is away. If Sumi agrees to do so, a gratuitous bailment will be created, because the bailment will be for the sole benefit of the bailor (Allen). If the car is damaged while in Sumi's garage, Sumi will not be responsible for the damage unless it is caused by her gross negligence.
2. *Bailment for the sole benefit of the bailee.* This type of bailment typically occurs when one person lends an item to another person (the bailee) solely for the bailee's convenience and benefit. Because the bailee is borrowing the item for personal benefit, the bailee owes a duty to exercise the utmost care and will be liable for even slight negligence.
   Example 34.20 Allen asks to borrow Sumi's boat so that he can go sailing over the weekend. The bailment of the boat is for Allen's (the bailee's) sole benefit. If Allen fails to pay attention and runs the boat aground, damaging its hull, he is liable for the costs of repairing the boat.
3. *Bailment for the mutual benefit of the bailee and the bailor.* This is the most common kind of bailment and involves some form of compensation for storing property or holding property while it is being serviced. It is a contractual bailment and may be referred to as a *bailment for hire* or a *commercial bailment.* In this type of bailment, the bailee owes a duty to exercise a reasonable degree of care.
   Example 34.21 Allen leaves his car at Quick Lube for an oil change. Because Quick Lube will be paid to change Allen's oil, this is a mutual-benefit bailment. If Quick Lube fails to put the correct amount of oil back into Allen's car and the engine is damaged as a result, Quick Lube will be liable for failure to exercise reasonable care.

Subbotina Anna/Shutterstock.com

What kind of bailment is created when someone lends a sailboat to a friend for the weekend? Who is responsible for the repair costs if the friend damages the sailboat? Why?

Rights of the Bailee

Certain rights are implicit in the bailment agreement. Generally, the bailee has the right to take possession of the property and to use it to accomplish the purpose of the bailment. Bailees also have a right to receive compensation (unless otherwise agreed), and to limit their liability for the bailed goods. These rights are present (with some limitations) in varying degrees in all bailment transactions.

Right of Possession. A hallmark of the bailment agreement is that the bailee acquires the *right to control and possess the property temporarily.* The bailee's right of possession permits the bailee to recover damages from any third person for damage or loss of the property.

Example 34.22 No-Spot Dry Cleaners sends all suede leather garments to Cleanall Company for special processing. If Cleanall loses or damages any leather goods, No-Spot has the right to recover against Cleanall. ■ In addition, if the bailed property is stolen, the bailee has a legal right to regain possession of it.

Right to Use Bailed Property. The extent to which bailees can use the property entrusted to them depends in part on the terms of the bailment contract. When no provision is made, the extent of use depends on how necessary it is for the goods to be at the bailee's disposal for the ordinary purpose of the bailment to be carried out.

Example 34.23 If Lauren borrows a car to drive Devin to the airport, she, as the bailee, will obviously be expected to use the car. In contrast, if Devin drives his own car to the airport and places it in long-term storage nearby, the storage company, as the bailee, will not be expected to use the car. The ordinary purpose of a storage bailment does not include use of the property. The bailee will, however, be expected to use or move the car if necessary in an emergency (such as a hurricane or flood) to protect it from harm. ■

Right of Compensation. Except in a gratuitous bailment, a bailee has a right to be compensated as provided for in the bailment agreement. The bailee also has a right to be reimbursed for services rendered and costs incurred in keeping the bailed property (even in a gratuitous bailment).

To enforce the right of compensation, the bailee has a right to place a *possessory lien* on the bailed property until full payment has been made. A lien on bailed property is referred to as a **bailee's lien,** or an *artisan's lien.* If the bailor refuses to pay or cannot pay the charges, in most states the bailee is entitled to foreclose on the lien and sell the property to recover the amount owed.

Bailee's Lien A possessory (artisan's) lien that a bailee entitled to compensation can place on the bailed property to ensure payment for the services provided.

Example 34.24 Liam leaves his car at Annette's Automotive for repairs. Annette's informs Liam that the car needs a new transmission, and Liam authorizes Annette's to perform the work. When Liam returns to pick up the car, he refuses to pay the amount due for the transmission work. Annette's has a right to keep the car and place a lien on it until Liam pays for the repairs. If Liam continues to refuse to pay, Annette's can follow the state statutory process for foreclosing on the lien by selling the car to recover what is owed. ■

Right to Limit Liability. In ordinary bailments, bailees have the right to limit their liability, provided that both of the following are true:

1. *The limitations are called to the attention of the bailor.* It is essential that the bailor be informed of the limitation in some way. **Example 34.25** A sign in Nikolai's garage states that Nikolai will not be responsible "for loss due to theft, fire, or vandalism." Whether the sign will constitute notice will depend on the size of the sign, its location, and any other circumstances affecting the likelihood that customers will see it. (In most cases, the owner will still be held liable.) ■
2. *The limitations are not against public policy.* Even when the bailor knows of the limitation, courts consider certain types of disclaimers of liability to be against public policy and therefore illegal. The courts carefully scrutinize *exculpatory clauses,* which limit a party's liability for the party's own wrongful acts. In bailments, especially mutual-benefit bailments, exculpatory clauses are often held to be illegal. **Example 34.26** A receipt from Al's Parking Garage expressly disclaims liability for any damage to parked cars, regardless of the cause. Because the bailee (the garage) has attempted to exclude liability for the bailee's own negligence, the clause will likely be deemed unenforceable because it is against public policy. ■

Duties of the Bailee

The bailee's duties are based on a mixture of tort law and contract law and include two basic responsibilities:

1. To take appropriate care of the property.
2. To surrender the property to the bailor or dispose of it in accordance with the bailor's instructions at the end of the bailment.

The Duty of Care. The bailee must exercise reasonable care in preserving the bailed property. What constitutes reasonable care in a bailment situation normally depends on the nature and specific circumstances of the bailment.

The courts determine the appropriate standard of care on the basis of the type of bailment involved. As mentioned earlier, in a bailment for the sole benefit of the bailor, the bailee need exercise only a slight degree of care. In a mutual-benefit bailment, courts normally impose a reasonable standard of care. In a bailment for the sole benefit of the bailee, the bailee must exercise great care. Exhibit 34-2 illustrates these concepts.

Determining whether a bailee exercised an appropriate degree of care is usually a question of fact for the jury or (in a nonjury trial) the judge. A bailee's failure to exercise appropriate care in handling the bailor's property results in tort liability.

Case Example 34.27 Toll Processing Services bought a secondhand pickle line, equipment used to remove impurities and rust from steel, but had nowhere to put it. Kastalon, Inc., a company that services pickle lines, agreed to store the machinery until Toll Processing filed a reconditioning purchase order. Kastalon would then perform any necessary repairs on the pickle line and return it to Toll Processing. No specific time frame for this process was discussed, but both sides assumed that the storage would last several months. After more than two years, not having heard from Toll Processing, a Kastalon employee assumed that the other company had gone out of business.

Based on this assumption and the pickle line's state of disrepair, Kastalon had it scrapped. Six months later, Toll Processing learned of this and sued Kastalon for negligence. A lower court dismissed the case, holding that Kastalon, the bailee, had met its duty of care by reasonably concluding that, after more than two and a half years with no contact, Toll Processing had abandoned the pickle line. An appeals court reversed, citing the lower court's failure to determine whether Kastalon had taken reasonable steps to protect the bailed property. Why, for example, didn't someone from Kastalon simply contact Toll Processing to learn its intentions regarding the pickle line?[6]

Duty to Return Bailed Property. At the end of the bailment, the bailee normally must hand over the bailed property to the bailor or to someone the bailor designates, or must otherwise dispose of it as directed. Failure to give up possession at the time the bailment ends is a breach of contract and can result in a tort lawsuit for conversion or negligence.

A bailee may be liable for conversion if the goods being held are delivered to the wrong person. Hence, the bailee should verify that the person (other than the bailor) to whom the goods are given is authorized to take possession.

Case Example 34.28 SANY America, Inc., loaned a crane to Turner Brothers, LLC, a construction contractor, for demonstration purposes. SANY wanted to sell the crane to Turner and continued to allow Turner to use it during their negotiations, but the parties never came to an agreement on a price. After the negotiations ended, SANY asked Turner for the crane's location to arrange retrieval. Before SANY retrieved the crane from Turner, however, it was severely damaged while being operated at Turner's construction site.

Humannet/Shutterstock.com

Why did an appeals court overrule a lower court's decision that a bailee had exercised reasonable care when it destroyed steel production machinery owned by a bailor?

6. *Toll Processing Services, LLC v. Kastalon, Inc.*, 880 F. 3d 820 (7th Cir. 2018).

Exhibit 34–2 Degree of Care Required of a Bailee

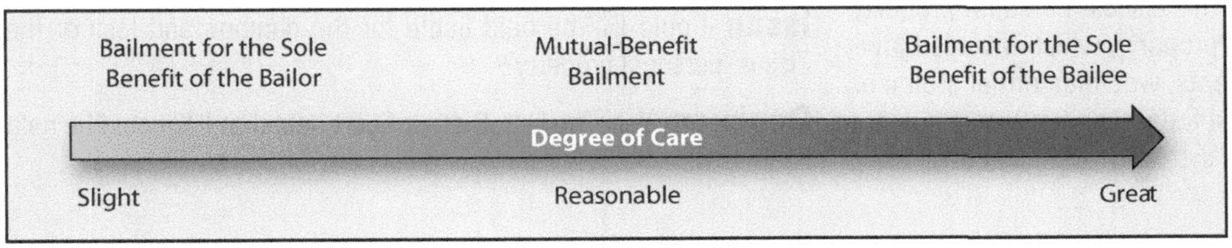

Know This

A finder who appropriates the personal property of another, knowing who the true owner is, can be held liable for the tort of conversion.

Turner removed the inoperable crane from the site at its own expense and then notified SANY that it expected compensation for the transportation expenses. In addition, Turner refused to return the crane to SANY and began billing SANY for daily storage costs. SANY sued for conversion, and Turner counterclaimed. A federal district court held that the parties' transaction was a bailment. Because Turner had wrongfully retained the crane after SANY demanded its return, SANY was entitled to summary judgment for conversion.[7]

Lost or Damaged Property. If the bailed property has been lost or is returned damaged, a court will presume that the bailee was negligent. The bailee's obligation is excused, however, if the property was destroyed, lost, or stolen through no fault of the bailee (or claimed by a third party with a superior claim). In other words, the bailee can rebut the presumption of negligence by showing that due care was exercised.

Case Example 34.29 Hornbeck Offshore Service engaged R&R Marine, Inc., to repair the ship *Erie Service* at R&R's shipyard on Lake Sabine in Port Arthur, Texas. While repairs were being made, a tropical storm warning was issued for Port Arthur. R&R's personnel left the shipyard without securing or preparing the *Erie Service* for the storm. During the night, rain and water from Lake Sabine swamped the vessel. R&R's insurer, National Liability & Fire Insurance Company, asked a federal district court to declare that it was not required to pay the salvage cost. Hornbeck filed a counterclaim with the court alleging that R&R had been negligent. The lower court issued a decision in Hornbeck's favor, and R&R appealed.

A federal appellate court affirmed the lower court's ruling. The ship had been delivered to R&R afloat, R&R had full custody of the vessel, and it sank while in R&R's care. This gave rise to a presumption of negligence. The severity of the weather conditions in Port Arthur had been foreseeable, and R&R showed no evidence that it had exercised ordinary care. The court held that R&R—not the insurer—was liable for the salvage cost because R&R had been negligent in failing to protect the ship from damage from the storm.[8]

Photomarine/Shutterstock.com

A bailee did not secure a ship to the dock when it was in the bailee's care. If the ship is damaged during a storm as a result, will the bailee be liable? Why or why not?

In the following case, the court had to determine whether a constructive bailment existed with respect to the personal property of tenants who were evicted. If so, was the landlord-bailor negligent for removing the tenants' personal property and leaving it outside?

7. *SANY America, Inc. v. Turner Brothers, LLC*, 2016 WL 1452341 (D.Mass. 2016).
8. *National Liability & Fire Insurance Co. v. R&R Marine, Inc.*, 756 F.3d 825 (5th Cir. 2014).

Case 34.3

Zissu v. IH2 Property Illinois, L.P.

United States District Court, Northern District of Illinois, Eastern Division, 157 F.Supp.3d 797 (2016).

Facts Pavel and Aise Zissu lived in an apartment in Chicago, Illinois, owned by IH2 Property Illinois, L.P. IH2 obtained an order from an Illinois state court allowing it to evict the Zissus. IH2 entered the apartment and moved the Zissus' personal property outside, placing it on the curb. The property, which included jewelry, furniture, and personal documents, was then either stolen or damaged. The Zissus filed a suit in a federal district court against IH2. The tenants alleged that IH2's taking possession of their property had constituted a bailment, and that the company had been negligent in its care of the bailed property. IH2 filed a motion to dismiss the suit.

Issue Could IH2 be held liable for the damage and loss of the Zissus' personal property?

Decision Yes. The U.S. District Court held that IH2 could be held liable and denied IH2's motion to dismiss.

Reason A constructive, or implied, bailment "may be found where the property of one person is voluntarily received by another for some purpose other than that of obtaining ownership." IH2's taking possession of the apartment's contents—the Zissus' personal property—created a constructive bailment. A duty of care arises when a landlord chooses to act as a bailee with respect to a tenant's property. The Zissus alleged sufficient facts to state a claim for negligence.

Critical Thinking

• **What If the Facts Were Different?** *Suppose that instead of putting the Zissus' personal property outside, IH2 had taken it to a storage facility. Would the result have been different? Why or why not?*

Duties of the Bailor The duties of a bailor are essentially the same as the rights of a bailee. A bailor has a duty to compensate the bailee as agreed and to reimburse the bailee for costs incurred by the bailee in keeping the bailed property. A bailor also has an all-encompassing duty to provide the bailee with goods or chattels that are free from known defects that could cause injury to the bailee.

Bailor's Duty to Reveal Defects. The bailor's duty to reveal defects to the bailee translates into two rules:

1. In a mutual-benefit bailment, the bailor must notify the bailee of all known defects and any hidden defects that the bailor knows of or could have discovered with reasonable diligence and proper inspection.
2. In a bailment for the sole benefit of the bailee, the bailor must notify the bailee of any known defects.

The bailor's duty to reveal defects is based on a negligence theory of tort law. A bailor who fails to give the appropriate notice is liable to the bailee and to any other person who might reasonably be expected to come into contact with the defective article.

Example 34.30 Rentco (the bailor) rents a tractor to Hal Iverson. Unknown to Rentco, the brake mechanism on the tractor is defective at the time the bailment is made. Rentco could have discovered the defect on reasonable inspection. Iverson uses the defective tractor without knowledge of the brake problem and is injured, along with two other field workers, when the tractor rolls downhill out of control after failing to stop. In this situation, Rentco is liable for the injuries sustained by Iverson and the other workers because it negligently failed to discover the defect and notify Iverson. ■

Warranty Liability for Defective Goods. A bailor can also incur *warranty liability* (discussed in an earlier chapter) based on contract law for injuries resulting from the bailment of defective articles. Property that is leased from a bailor must be *fit for the intended purpose of the bailment.* Warranties of fitness arise by law in sales contracts and leases, and courts have held that these warranties apply to bailments "for hire." Article 2A of the Uniform Commercial Code (UCC) extends the implied warranties of merchantability and fitness for a particular purpose to bailments that include rights to use the bailed goods.[9]

34–4c Special Types of Bailments

A business is likely to engage in some special types of bailment transactions in which the bailee's duty of care is *extraordinary* and the bailee's liability for loss or damage to the property is absolute. These situations usually involve common carriers and hotel operators. Warehouse companies have a higher duty of care than ordinary bailees but are not subject to strict

9. UCC 2A–212, 2A–213.

liability. Like carriers, warehouse companies are subject to extensive regulation under federal and state laws, including Article 7 of the UCC.

Common Carriers *Common carriers* are publicly licensed to transport goods or passengers on regular routes at set rates. They are legally bound to carry all passengers or freight as long as there is enough space, the fee is paid, and there are no reasonable grounds to refuse service. Common carriers differ from private carriers, which operate transportation facilities for only a select clientele. A private carrier is not required to provide service to every person or company making a request.

Strict Liability Applies. The delivery of goods to a common carrier creates a bailment relationship between the shipper (bailor) and the common carrier (bailee). Unlike ordinary bailees, the common carrier is held to a standard of care based on *strict liability,* rather than reasonable care, in protecting the bailed personal property. This means that the common carrier is absolutely liable, regardless of due care, for all loss or damage to goods except when damage was caused by a natural disaster or war.

Limitations on Liability. Common carriers cannot contract away their liability for damaged goods. Subject to government regulations, however, they are permitted to limit their dollar liability to an amount stated on the shipment contract or rate filing.

Example 34.31 A jewelry store (Martinez Daughters) uses UPS to ship a diamond ring worth $200,000. The owner of the jewelry store, Julie Martinez, arranges for the shipment on UPS's website, which requires her to click on two on-screen boxes to agree to "My UPS Terms and Conditions." In these terms, UPS and its insurer limit their liability and the amount of insurance coverage on packages to $50,000 and refuse to ship items worth more than $50,000. Both UPS and its insurer disclaim liability *entirely* for such items. Nevertheless, Martinez purchases $50,000 in insurance for the package.

If the ring is subsequently lost in shipping, the jewelry store cannot recover any amount from UPS under the insurance policy. UPS's disclaimer of liability is enforceable, and the jewelry store breached the contract by indicating that the shipment was worth less than $50,000.

manley099/iStock/Getty Images

A jewelry storeowner ships a $200,000 diamond ring knowing that the shipper's maximum shipment value is only $50,000. What happens if the ring never arrives at its destination?

Warehouse Companies *Warehousing* is the business of storing property for compensation. Like ordinary bailees, warehouse companies are liable for loss or damage to property resulting from negligence. But because a warehouse company is a professional bailee, it is expected to exercise a high degree of care to protect and preserve the goods.

Limitations on Liability. A warehouse company can limit the dollar amount of its liability. Under the UCC, however, it must give the bailor the option of paying a higher storage rate for an increase in the liability limit.[10]

Warehouse Receipts. Warehouse companies often issue *documents of title*—in particular, *warehouse receipts.*[11] A warehouse receipt describes the bailed property and the terms of the bailment contract. It can be negotiable or nonnegotiable, depending on how it is written. It is negotiable if its terms provide that the warehouse company will deliver the goods "to the bearer" of the receipt or "to the order of" a person named on the receipt.[12]

---

10. UCC 7–204(1), (2).

11. A *document of title* is defined in UCC 1-201(15) as any "document which in the regular course of business or financing is treated as adequately evidencing that the person in possession of it is entitled to receive, hold, and dispose of the document and the goods it covers." A *warehouse receipt* is a document of title issued by a person engaged for hire in the business of storing goods for hire.

12. UCC 7–104.

The warehouse receipt represents the goods (that is, it indicates title) and hence has value and utility in financing commercial transactions. **Example 34.32** Ossip delivers 6,500 cases of canned corn to Chaney, the owner of a warehouse. Chaney issues a negotiable warehouse receipt payable "to bearer" and gives it to Ossip. Ossip sells and delivers the warehouse receipt to Better Foods, Inc. Better Foods is now the owner of the corn and has the right to obtain the cases by simply presenting the warehouse receipt to Chaney.

Hotel Operators At common law, hotel owners were strictly liable for the loss of any cash or property that guests brought into their rooms. Today, state statutes continue to apply strict liability to hotel operators for any loss or damage to their guests' personal property. In many states, however, hotel operators can avoid strict liability by providing a safe in which to keep guests' valuables and notifying guests that a safe is available.

In addition, state statutes often limit the liability of hotels with regard to articles that are not kept in the safe and may limit the availability of damages in the absence of negligence. Most statutes require that the hotel post these limitations on the doors of the rooms or otherwise notify guests. The failure of the hotel to follow the state statutory requirements can lead to liability.

Example 34.33 A guest at Crown Place hotel is traveling with jewelry valued at $1 million. She puts the jewelry in the safe in her room, but someone comes into the room and removes the jewelry from the safe without the use of force. The woman sues the hotel, which claims that it is not liable under the state statute. If Crown Place did not comply with statutory requirements that it post the legal limitations in the guest rooms, it will not be protected from liability. Crown Place will be strictly liable for the loss of the woman's jewelry.

Practice and Review

Vanessa Denai owned forty acres of land in rural Louisiana. On the property were a 1,600-square-foot house and a metal barn. Denai met Lance Finney, who had been seeking a small plot of rural property to rent. After several meetings, Denai invited Finney to live on a corner of her land in exchange for Finney's assistance in cutting wood and tending her property. Denai agreed to store Finney's sailboat in her barn.

With Denai's consent, Finney constructed a concrete and oak foundation on Denai's property and purchased a 190-square-foot dome from Dome Baja for $3,395. The dome was shipped by Doty Express, a transportation company licensed to serve the public. When it arrived, Finney installed the dome frame and fabric exterior so that the dome was detachable from the foundation. A year after Finney installed the dome, Denai wrote Finney a note stating, "I've decided to give you four acres of land surrounding your dome as drawn on this map." This gift violated no local land-use restrictions. Using the information presented in the chapter, answer the following questions.

1. Is the dome real property or personal property? Explain.
2. Is Denai's gift of land to Finney a gift *causa mortis* or a gift *inter vivos?*
3. What type of bailment relationship was created when Denai agreed to store Finney's boat? What degree of care was Denai required to exercise in storing the boat?
4. What standard of care applied to the shipment of the dome by Doty Express?

Debate This

Common carriers should not be able to limit their liability.

Key Terms

Chapter Summary: Personal Property and Bailments

PERSONAL PROPERTY	
Personal Property versus Real Property	Personal property (personalty or chattel) includes all property not classified as real property (realty). Personal property can be tangible (such as a car) or intangible (such as stocks or bonds). The two types of property are usually subject to different types of taxes. In addition, acquiring or transferring real property requires a greater degree of formality than acquiring or transferring personal property.
Acquiring Ownership of Personal Property	The most common way of acquiring ownership in personal property is by purchasing it. The following are additional methods of acquiring personal property: **1. Possession**—Property may be acquired by possession if no other person has title to the property (for instance, capturing wild animals). **2. Production**—Any item produced by an individual (with minor exceptions) becomes the property of that individual. **3. Gifts**—A gift is effective under the following conditions: **a.** There is evidence of *intent* to make a gift of the property in question. **b.** The gift is *delivered* (physically or constructively) to the donee or the donee's agent. **c.** The gift is *accepted* by the donee. **4. Accession**—When value is added to personal property by the use of labor or materials, the owner of the original property generally retains title to the property and benefits from the added value. **5. Confusion**—If confusion of fungible goods occurs as a result of agreement, an honest mistake, or the act of some third party, the owners share ownership as tenants in common. If goods are confused due to an intentional wrongful act, the innocent party ordinarily acquires title to the whole.
Mislaid, Lost, and Abandoned Property	The finder of property acquires different rights depending on whether the property was mislaid, lost, or abandoned. **1. Mislaid property**—Property that is placed somewhere voluntarily by the owner and then inadvertently forgotten. The finder does not acquire title. **2. Lost property**—Property that the owner has involuntarily parted with and then cannot find or recover. The finder can claim title to the property against the whole world except the true owner. **3. Abandoned property**—Property that is discarded by the owner, who has no intention of reclaiming it in the future. The finder can claim title to the property against the whole world, including the original owner.
BAILMENTS	
Elements of a Bailment	**1. Personal property**—Bailments involve only personal property. **2. Delivery of possession without title**—For an effective bailment to exist, the bailee (the one receiving the property) must be given exclusive possession and control over the property. In a voluntary bailment, the bailee must knowingly accept the personal property. **3. The bailment agreement**—The agreement expressly or impliedly provides for the return of the bailed property to the bailor or a third party, or for the disposal of the bailed property by the bailee.

Ordinary Bailments	**1. Types of bailments—** **a.** Bailment for the sole benefit of the bailor—A gratuitous bailment undertaken for the sole benefit of the bailor (for example, as a favor to the bailor). **b.** Bailment for the sole benefit of the bailee—A gratuitous loan of an article to a person (the bailee) solely for the bailee's benefit. **c.** Mutual-benefit (contractual) bailment—This is the most common kind of bailment and involves compensation between the bailee and bailor for the service provided. **2. Rights of a bailee (duties of a bailor)—** **a.** The right of possession—Allows a bailee to sue any third persons for damage or loss of the bailed property. **b.** The right to use the property—Allowed to the extent necessary to carry out the purpose of the bailment. **c.** The right to be compensated and reimbursed for expenses—In the event of nonpayment, the bailee has the right to place a possessory (bailee's) lien on the bailed property until fully compensated. **d.** The right to limit liability—An ordinary bailee can limit liability for loss or damage, provided proper notice is given and the limitation is not against public policy. In special bailments, limitations on liability for negligence or on types of losses usually are not allowed, but limitations on the monetary amount of liability are permitted. **e.** Duty to reveal defects—A bailor must notify the bailee of any known defects and, in mutual-benefit bailments, hidden defects as well. **f.** Warranty liability—A bailor can incur warranty liability for injuries resulting from the bailment of defective articles. **3. Duties of a bailee (rights of a bailor)—** **a.** Bailees must exercise appropriate care over property entrusted to them. What constitutes appropriate care normally depends on the nature and circumstances of the bailment. See Exhibit 34–2. **b.** Bailed goods in a bailee's possession must be either returned to the bailor or disposed of according to the bailor's directions. A bailee's failure to return the bailed property creates a presumption of negligence and constitutes a breach of contract or the tort of conversion.
Special Types of Bailments	**1. Common carriers**—Carriers that are publicly licensed to provide transportation services to the general public are held to a standard of care based on strict liability. **2. Warehouse companies**—Because a warehouse company is a professional bailee, it is expected to exercise a high degree of care to protect and preserve the bailed goods. Warehouse companies often issue documents of title (warehouse receipts) for goods, which may be negotiable or nonnegotiable. **3. Hotel operators**—Operators of hotels are subject to strict liability for any loss or damage to their guests' personal property. State statutes may limit liability if the hotel provides a safe and properly notifies its guests.

Issue Spotters

1. While walking to work, Bill finds an expensive ring lying on the curb. Bill gives the ring to his son, Hunter. Two weeks later, Martin Avery, the true owner of the ring, discovers that Bill found the ring and demands that Hunter return it. Who is entitled to the ring, and why? (See *Mislaid, Lost, and Abandoned Property*.)

2. Rosa de la Mar Corporation ships a load of goods via Southeast Delivery Company. The load of goods is lost in a hurricane in Florida. Who suffers the loss? Explain your answer. (See *Bailments*.)

—Check your answers to the *Issue Spotters* against the answers provided in Appendix D.

Business Scenarios and Case Problems

34–1. Duties of the Bailee. Discuss the standard of care traditionally required of the bailee for the bailed property in each of the following situations, and determine whether the bailee breached that duty. (See *Bailments*.)

1. Ricardo borrows Steve's lawn mower because his own lawn mower needs repair. Ricardo mows his front yard. To mow the backyard, he needs to move some hoses and lawn furniture. He leaves the mower in front of his house while doing so. When he returns to the front yard, he discovers that the mower has been stolen.
2. Alicia owns a valuable speedboat. She is going on vacation and asks her neighbor, Maureen, to store the boat in one stall of Maureen's double garage. Maureen consents, and the boat is moved into the garage. Maureen needs some grocery items for dinner and drives to the store. She leaves the garage door open while she is gone, as is her custom, and the speedboat is stolen during that time.

34–2. Gifts. Jaspal has a severe heart attack and is taken to the hospital. He is aware that he is not expected to live. Because he is a bachelor with no close relatives nearby, Jaspal gives his car keys to his close friend Friedrich, telling Friedrich that he is expected to die and that the car is Friedrich's. Jaspal survives the heart attack, but two months later he dies from pneumonia. Sam, Jaspal's uncle and the executor of his estate, wants Friedrich to return the car. Friedrich refuses, claiming that the car was a gift from Jaspal. Discuss whether Friedrich will be required to return the car to Jaspal's estate. (See *Acquiring Ownership of Personal Property*.)

34–3. Lost Property. Sara Simon misplaced her Galaxy cell phone in Manhattan, Kansas. Days later, Shawn Vargo contacted her, claiming to have bought the phone from someone else. He promised to mail it to Simon if she would wire $100 to him through a third party, Mark Lawrence. When Simon spoke to Lawrence about the wire transfer, she referred to the phone as hers and asked, "Are you going to send my phone to me?" Simon paid, but she did not get the phone. Instead, Lawrence took it to a Best Buy store and traded it in for credit. Charged with the theft of lost property, Lawrence claimed that he did not know Simon was the owner of the phone. Was Simon's phone lost, mislaid, or abandoned? What is the finder's responsibility with respect to this type of property? Can Lawrence successfully argue that he did not know the phone was Simon's? Explain. [*State of Kansas v. Lawrence,* 347 P.3d 240 (Kan.App. 2015)] (See *Mislaid, Lost, and Abandoned Property*.)

34–4. Bailments. Christie's Fine Art Storage Services, Inc. (CFASS), is in the business of storing fine works of art at its warehouse in Brooklyn, New York. The warehouse is next to the East River in a flood zone. Boyd Sullivan owns works of art by Alberto Vargas, including *Beauty and the Beast* and *Miss Universe.* Sullivan contracted to store the works at CFASS's facility under an agreement that limited the warehouser's liability for damage to the goods to $200,000. A few months later, as Hurricane Sandy approached, CFASS was warned, along with the other businesses in the flood zone, of the potential for damage from the storm. CFASS e-mailed its clients that extra precautions were being taken. Despite this assurance, Sullivan's works were left exposed on a ground floor and sustained severe damage in the storm. Who is most likely to suffer the loss? Why? [*Sullivan v. Christie's Fine Art Storage Services, Inc.,* 2016 WL 427615 (Sup. N.Y. County 2016)] (See *Bailments*.)

34–5. Duties of the Bailee. James Heal owned a vehicle salvage yard in Homestead, Iowa. Brian Anderson contracted with Heal to run the business. Anderson cleaned up the property, removed trash, installed heat and fixed the plumbing in the buildings, and brought in tools and equipment. He used his own resources to rebuild the aging inventory. Anderson reinvested all of the profits in the business. When Anderson sold a 2004 Ford F-150 that he had bought with his own money for his own use, however, Heal pocketed the proceeds and locked Anderson out of the business. Heal filed a suit in an Iowa state court against Anderson, alleging breach of contract, and obtained an injunction to keep him off the property. Do these circumstances create a bailment? What is the appropriate standard of care if there is a bailment? Discuss. [*Heal v. Anderson,* 900 N.W.2d 617 (Iowa App. 2017)] (See *Bailments*.)

34–6. The Nature of Personal Property. American Multi-Cinema, Inc. (AMC), owns movie theaters. To determine the amount of taxes it owed to Texas, AMC subtracted its cost of goods sold (COGS) from its total revenue. AMC included the cost of showing movies in its COGS. In other words, it treated showing movies as a "good." Texas, however, refused to allow AMC to claim this cost. AMC protested, arguing it was in the business of showing movies. Specifically, AMC sold its "product"—the right to watch films in its theaters—to moviegoers. The state countered that this right is intangible "non-property," arguing that an AMC customer exits a theater with memories but not a copy of the film. Thus, AMC's product is not considered a "good" for the purpose of COGS. Does the right to watch a film in a movie theater constitute property? Discuss. [*American Multi-Cinema, Inc. v. Hegar,* 2017 WL 74416 (Tex.App.— Austin 2017)] (See *Personal Property versus Real Property*.)

34–7. Business Case Problem with Sample Answer— Duties of the Bailee. KZY Logistics, LLC, transported a load of Mrs. Ressler's Food Products from New Jersey to California. When KZY's driver delivered the cargo, the customer rejected it—its temperature was higher than expected, making it unsafe. Mrs. Ressler's filed a suit against KZY in a federal district court. KZY contended that the temperature in its refrigerated trailer was proper and that Mrs. Ressler's had delivered a "hot" product for transport. KZY supplemented its allegations with temperature readings from the unit during the time in question. In transporting the cargo, what level of care did KZY owe Mrs. Ressler's? Did KZY meet this standard? Explain. [*Mrs. Ressler's Food Products v. KZY Logistics, LLC,* 675 Fed.Appx. 136 (3d Cir. 2017)] (See *Bailments.*)

—For a sample answer to Problem 34–7, go to Appendix E.

34–8. Bailor's Duty to Reveal Defects. Anastasio Guerra agreed to loan his pick-up truck to Gina Mandujano so that she could go grocery shopping in exchange for her making him lunch. When Mandujano drove out of the store's parking lot, the truck's power steering failed. Her wrist was caught in the spokes of the steering wheel, and she was severely injured. Guerra knew that there was a problem with his truck's steering, but he thought he had fixed the problem by replenishing the steering fluid. He did not believe that the issue was dangerous and had not told Mandujano. What type of bailment existed between Guerra and Mandujano? What standard of care did the bailor owe the bailee? Was the duty breached? Who is liable for the cost of Mandujano's injury? Explain. [*Mandujano v. Guerra,* 2018 WL 1611458 (Md. 2018)] (See *Bailments.*)

34–9. A Question of Ethics—The IDDR Approach and Abandoned Property. Mansoor Akhtar lived rent-free in the basement of Anila Dairkee's duplex in Minneapolis, Minnesota, for more than a year. When Dairkee asked Akhtar to move out, he refused. She changed the locks and advised him to remove his property from the duplex. But he did not. About a year later, while Dairkee was staying in New York, her father had the basement cleaned out. When Dairkee returned four months later, she learned that her father had disposed of Akhtar's property. Akhtar filed a suit in a Minnesota state court against Dairkee, alleging that she had wrongfully disposed of his property. [*Akhtar v Dairkee,* 2017 WL 1210140 (Minn.App. 2017)] (See *Mislaid, Lost, and Abandoned Property.*)

1. Dairkee contended that Akhtar had abandoned his property. Is she correct? Explain.
2. Using the *Review* step of the IDDR approach, consider whether Dairkee's handling of Akhtar's property was ethical.

Critical Thinking and Writing Assignments

34–10. Time-Limited Group Assignment—Bailments. On learning that Sébastien planned to travel abroad, Roslyn asked him to deliver $25,000 in cash to her family in Mexico. During a customs inspection at the border, Sébastien told the customs inspector that he carried less than $10,000. The officer discovered the actual amount of cash that Sébastien was carrying, seized it, and arrested Sébastien. Roslyn asked the government to return what she claimed were her funds, arguing that the arrangement with Sébastien was a bailment and that she still held title to the cash. (See *Bailments.*)

1. The first group will argue that Roslyn is entitled to the cash.
2. The second group will take the position of the government and develop an argument that Roslyn's agreement with Sébastien does not qualify as a bailment.
3. The third group will assume that a bailment was created, identify what type of bailment it was, and explain the degree of care required of the bailee.

35 Real Property and Landlord-Tenant Law

Focus Questions

The four Focus Questions *below are designed to help improve your understanding. After reading this chapter, you should be able to answer the following questions:*

1. What is a fixture, and how does it relate to real property rights?
2. What is the difference between a joint tenancy and a tenancy in common?
3. What are the requirements for acquiring property by adverse possession?
4. What are the duties of the landlord and the tenant with respect to the use and maintenance of leased property?

"The right of property is the most sacred of all the rights of citizenship."

Jean-Jacques Rousseau
1712–1778
(French writer and philosopher)

From earliest times, property has provided a means for survival. Primitive peoples lived off the fruits of the land, eating the vegetation and wildlife. Later, as the vegetation was cultivated and the wildlife domesticated, property provided farmland and pasture.

Throughout history, property has continued to be an indicator of family wealth and social position. Indeed, an individual's right to ownership of property has become, in the words of Jean-Jacques Rousseau, one of the "most sacred of all the rights of citizenship."

In this chapter, we examine the nature of real property and the ways in which it can be owned and transferred. We even consider whether the buyer of a haunted house can rescind the sale in this chapter's *Spotlight Case*. We also discuss leased property and landlord-tenant relationships.

35–1 The Nature of Real Property

Real property consists of land and the buildings, plants, and trees that are on it. Real property also includes subsurface and airspace rights, as well as personal property that has become permanently attached to the real property. Whereas personal property is movable, real property—also called *real estate* or *realty*—is immovable.

35–1a Land and Structures

Land includes the soil on the surface of the earth and the natural or artificial structures that are attached to it. It further includes all the waters contained on or under the surface and much, but not necessarily all, of the airspace above it. The exterior boundaries of land extend down to the center of the earth and up to the farthest reaches of the atmosphere (subject to certain qualifications).

35–1b Airspace and Subsurface Rights

The owner of real property has rights to the airspace above the land, as well as to the soil and minerals underneath it. Limitations on either airspace rights or subsurface rights normally must be indicated on the document that transfers title at the time of purchase. When no such limitations, or *encumbrances,* are noted, a purchaser generally can expect to have an unlimited right to possession of the property.

Airspace Rights Disputes concerning airspace rights may involve the right of commercial and private planes to fly over property and the right of individuals and governments to seed clouds and produce rain artificially. Flights over private land normally do not violate property rights unless the flights are so low and so frequent that they directly interfere with the owner's enjoyment and use of the land. Leaning walls or buildings and projecting eave spouts or roofs may also violate the airspace rights of an adjoining property owner.

RSnapshotPhotos/Shutterstock.com

Who owns airspace above residential land?

Subsurface Rights In many states, land ownership may be separated, in that the surface of a piece of land and the subsurface may have different owners. Subsurface rights can be extremely valuable, as these rights include the ownership of minerals, oil, and natural gas. Subsurface rights would be of little value, however, if the owner could not use the surface to exercise those rights. Hence, a subsurface owner has a right (called a *profit*, to be discussed later in this chapter) to go onto the surface of the land to, for instance, discover and mine minerals.

When ownership is separated into surface and subsurface rights, the owner of one set of rights can pass title without the consent of the other owner. Of course, conflicts can arise between the surface owner's use of the property and the subsurface owner's need to extract minerals, oil, or natural gas. In that situation, one party's interest may become subservient (secondary) to the other party's interest either by statute or by case law.

If the owners of the subsurface rights excavate (dig), they are absolutely liable if their excavation causes the surface to collapse. Many states have statutes that also make the excavators liable for any damage to structures on the land. Typically, these statutes provide precise requirements for excavations of various depths.

35–1c Plant Life and Vegetation

Plant life, both natural and cultivated, is also considered to be real property. In many instances, the natural vegetation, such as trees, adds greatly to the value of the realty. When a parcel of land is sold and the land has growing crops on it, the sale includes the crops, unless otherwise specified in the sales contract. When crops are sold by themselves, however, they are considered to be personal property, or goods. Consequently, the sale of crops is a sale of goods and thus is governed by the Uniform Commercial Code (UCC) rather than by real property law.[1]

---

1. See UCC 2–107(2).

Focus Question 1

What is a fixture, and how does it relate to real property rights?

Fixture An item of personal property that has become so closely associated with real property that it is legally regarded as part of that real property.

35–1d Fixtures

Certain personal property can become so closely associated with the real property to which it is attached that the law views it as real property. Such property is known as a **fixture**—an item *affixed* to realty, meaning that it is attached to the real property in a permanent way. The item may be embedded in the land or permanently attached to the property or to another fixture on the property by means of cement, mortar, bolts, nails, roots, or screws. An item, such as a statue, may even sit on the land without being attached, as long as the owner intends the property to be a fixture.

Fixtures are included in the sale of land if the sales contract does not provide otherwise.[2] The sale of a house includes the land and the house and any detached garage on the land, as well as the cabinets, plumbing, and windows. Because these are permanently affixed to the property, they are considered to be a part of it. Certain items, such as drapes and window-unit air conditioners, are difficult to classify. Thus, a contract for the sale of a house or commercial realty should indicate which items of this sort are included in the sale.

Example 35.1 Rosemary & Sage Farm has an eight-tower center-pivot irrigation system that is bolted to a cement slab and connected to an underground well. The bank holds a mortgage note on the farm secured by "all buildings, improvements, and fixtures." Later, when Rosemary & Sage files for bankruptcy, a dispute arises between the bank and another creditor over the irrigation system. In this situation, a court is likely to find that the irrigation system is a fixture because it is firmly attached to the land and integral to the operation of the farm. Therefore, the bank's security interest will have priority over the other creditor's interest.

Songbird839/iStock/Getty Images

Under what circumstances is an industrial-quality irrigation system considered a fixture?

35–2 Ownership Interests and Leases

Ownership of real property is abstract and differs from ownership of personal property. No one can actually possess or *hold* a piece of land, the airspace above it, the earth below it, and all the water contained on it. The legal system therefore recognizes certain rights and duties that constitute ownership interests in real property.

Traditionally, ownership interests in real property were referred to as *estates in land*, which include fee simple estates, life estates, and leasehold estates. We examine estates in land, forms of concurrent ownership, and certain other interests in real property in the following subsections.

As you will see, ownership of real property (as well as personal property) can be viewed as a bundle of rights, including the right to possess the property and to dispose of it by sale, gift, lease, or other means. A person can own either the whole bundle of rights (a fee simple) or only a part of the rights. When only some of the rights are transferred, the effect is to limit the ownership rights of both the transferor of the rights and the recipient.

Fee Simple An ownership interest in land in which the owner has the greatest possible aggregation of rights, privileges, and power.

35–2a Ownership in Fee Simple

One who possesses the entire bundle of rights is said to hold the property in **fee simple** (usually referring to *fee simple absolute*), which is the most complete form of ownership. Owners in fee simple are entitled to use, possess, or dispose of the property as they choose during their lifetimes. The owners have the rights of *exclusive* possession and use of the property. They can give the property away, sell it, or lease it.

Duration On the fee simple owner's death, the interests in the property descend (pass down) to the owner's heirs, even in the absence of a will. Thus, a fee simple is potentially infinite in duration and is assigned forever to individuals and their heirs without limitation or condition.

2. Trade fixtures, which are items installed by a tenant for a commercial purpose (such as a walk-in cooler for a restaurant), are an exception and do not become part of the landowner's real property.

Limitations on Use The rights that accompany a fee simple include the right to use the land for whatever purpose the owner sees fit. Of course, other laws, including applicable zoning regulations, noise regulations, and environmental laws, may limit the owner's ability to use the property in certain ways. A fee simple owner cannot build a manufacturing plant on the property if doing so would violate applicable city or county rules and regulations, for instance. Also, a person who uses property in a manner that unreasonably interferes with others' right to use or enjoy their own property can be liable for the tort of *nuisance*.

Spotlight Case Example 35.2 Nancy and James Biglane owned and lived in a building in Natchez, Mississippi. Next door to the couple's property was the Under the Hill Saloon, a popular bar that featured live music. During the summer, the Saloon, which had no air-conditioning, opened its windows and doors, and live music echoed up and down the street.

Although the Biglanes installed extra insulation, thicker windows, and air-conditioning units in their building, the noise from the Saloon kept them awake at night. Eventually, the Biglanes sued the owners of the Saloon for nuisance. The court held that the noise from the bar unreasonably interfered with the Biglanes' right to enjoy their property and prohibited the Saloon from opening its windows and doors while playing music.[3]

35–2b Life Estates

A **life estate** is an estate that lasts for the life of some specified individual. A **conveyance**, or transfer of real property, "to Alex Munson for his life" creates a life estate. In a life estate, the life tenant's ownership rights cease to exist on the life tenant's death.

Life tenants have the right to use the land provided that they commit no **waste** (injury to the land). In other words, a life tenant cannot use the land in a manner that would adversely affect its value. **Example 35.3** Julian, a life tenant on Blazin Acres, can use the land to harvest crops. If mines and oil wells are already on the land, Julian can extract minerals and oil from it, but he cannot drill new oil wells or excavate mines on the property.

Life tenants also have the right to create liens, *easements* (discussed shortly), and leases, but none can extend beyond the life of the tenants. In addition, with a few exceptions, owners of life estates have an exclusive right to possession during their lifetimes.

Along with these rights, life tenants also have some duties. They must keep the property in repair and pay property taxes. In short, the owners of life estates have the same rights as a fee simple owner, except that life tenants must maintain the value of the property during their tenancy. Also, life tenants cannot sell the property or leave it to their heirs.

The distinction between a life estate and a fee simple determined the result in the following case.

Life Estate An interest in land that exists only for the duration of the life of a specified individual, usually the holder of the estate.

Conveyance The transfer of title to real property from one person to another by deed or other document.

Waste The use of real property in a manner that damages or destroys its value.

3. *Biglane v. Under the Hill Corp.*, 949 So.2d 9 (Miss.Sup.Ct. 2007).

Case 35.1

In the Matter of the Estate of Nelson

North Dakota Supreme Court, 2018 ND 118, 910 N.W.2d 856, (2018).

Facts When Sidney Solberg died, 100 mineral acres—that is, the right to all of the minerals under a certain 100 acres—and other real property in his estate were distributed to his widow, Lillian, for her life. The remainder interest (the right of ownership after Lillian's interest ended) was conveyed to their four children, including Glenn Solberg.

Later, Lillian married Lyle Nelson. When Lillian passed away, a codicil (addition) to her will allegedly gave the 100 mineral acres to Glenn. The codicil also purported to create for Glenn an option to buy the other real property she had inherited from Sidney. When Lyle Nelson died, Glenn filed a claim in a North Dakota state court against

(Continues)

Continued

Nelson's estate. Glenn claimed that under the terms of the codicil to Lillian's will, he was entitled to the ownership of the 100 mineral acres and the right to buy the other property. The court dismissed Glenn's claim. He appealed to the state supreme court.

Issue Did Lillian's interest in the 100 mineral acres and the option property terminate with her death?

Decision Yes. The North Dakota Supreme Court affirmed the dismissal of Glenn's claim. "The [lower] court properly concluded that, with certainty, it would be impossible for Glenn Solberg to obtain the relief he requested from the Lyle Nelson Estate."

Reason The owner of a life estate has an interest in the possession and use of the property of the estate for the duration of the life that determines the period of the right. The owner may transfer her interest, but the transferee's interest in the property cannot exceed the duration of the life estate. Lillian had a life estate in the 100 mineral acres and the other property measured by the duration of her own life. As the owner of the estate, she could transfer an interest in the property only during her life, and that interest would end when her life ended. Lillian's attempt to convey her interests to Glenn in the codicil to her will was thus invalid.

On Lillian's death, her life estate ended, and the 100 mineral acres and the other property became the property of her four children as the holders of the remainder interest. Glenn could not recover the property from the Nelson estate because the estate did not have an interest in the property.

Critical Thinking

- **What If the Facts Were Different?** *Suppose that Sidney Solberg had disposed of his entire estate in fee simple before his death. Would the result have been different? Discuss.*

35–2c Concurrent Ownership

Concurrent Ownership Joint ownership.

Persons who share ownership rights simultaneously in particular property (including real property and personal property) are said to have **concurrent ownership**. There are two principal types of concurrent ownership: *tenancy in common* and *joint tenancy*. Concurrent ownership rights can also be held in a *tenancy by the entirety* or as *community property*, but these types of concurrent ownership are less common.

Tenancy in Common Joint ownership of property in which each party owns an undivided interest that passes to the party's heirs at death.

Tenancy in Common The term **tenancy in common** refers to a form of co-ownership in which each of two or more persons owns an undivided interest in the property. The interest is undivided because each tenant shares rights in the whole property. On the death of a tenant in common, that tenant's interest in the property passes to the tenant's heirs.

Example 35.4 Four friends purchase a condominium unit in Hawaii together as tenants in common. This means that each of them has a one-fourth ownership interest in the whole. If one of the four owners dies a year after the purchase, his ownership interest passes to his heirs (his wife and children, for instance) rather than to the other tenants in common. ■

Unless the co-tenants have agreed otherwise, a tenant in common can transfer ownership interest in the property to anyone without the consent of the remaining co-owners. In most states, it is presumed that a co-tenancy is a tenancy in common unless there is specific language indicating the intent to establish a joint tenancy (discussed next).

Joint Tenancy Joint ownership of property in which each co-owner owns an undivided portion of the property. On the death of one of the joint tenants, that tenant's interest automatically passes to the surviving joint tenant(s).

Joint Tenancy In a **joint tenancy**, each of two or more persons owns an undivided interest in the property, but a deceased joint tenant's interest passes to the surviving joint tenant or tenants.

Right of Survivorship. The right of a surviving joint tenant to inherit a deceased joint tenant's ownership interest—referred to as a *right of survivorship*—distinguishes a joint tenancy from a tenancy in common. **Example 35.5** Jerrold and Eva are married and purchase a house as joint tenants. The title to the house clearly expresses the intent to create a joint tenancy because it says "to Jerrold and Eva as joint tenants with right of survivorship." Jerrold has three children from a prior marriage. If Jerrold dies, his interest in the house automatically passes to Eva rather than to his children from the prior marriage. ■

Termination of a Joint Tenancy. Joint tenants can transfer their rights by sale or gift to another without the consent of the other joint tenants. Doing so terminates the joint tenancy. A person who purchases property from a joint tenant or receives it as a gift becomes a tenant in common, not a joint tenant. **Example 35.6** Three brothers, Brody, Saul, and Jacob, own land as joint tenants. Brody is experiencing financial difficulties and sells his interest in the property to Beth. The sale terminates the joint tenancy, and now Beth, Saul, and Jacob hold the property as tenants in common.

A joint tenant's interest can also be levied against (seized by court order) to satisfy the tenant's judgment creditors. If this occurs, the joint tenancy terminates, and the remaining owners hold the property as tenants in common. (Judgment creditors can also seize the interests of tenants in a tenancy in common.)

Focus Question 2

What is the difference between a joint tenancy and a tenancy in common?

Tenancy by the Entirety A less common form of shared ownership of real property by married persons is a **tenancy by the entirety**. It differs from a joint tenancy in that neither spouse may separately transfer interest in the property unless the other spouse consents. In some states in which statutes give the wife the right to convey her property, this form of concurrent ownership has effectively been abolished. A divorce, either spouse's death, or mutual agreement will terminate a tenancy by the entirety.

Tenancy by the Entirety Joint ownership of property by a married couple in which neither spouse can transfer any interest in the property without the consent of the other.

Community Property A limited number of states[4] allow married couples to own property as **community property**. If property is held as community property, each spouse technically owns an undivided one-half interest in the property. This type of ownership applies to most property acquired by either spouse during the course of the marriage. It generally does *not* apply to property acquired prior to the marriage or to property acquired by gift or inheritance as separate property during the marriage. After a divorce, community property is divided equally in some states and according to the discretion of the court in other states.

Community Property A form of concurrent property ownership in which each spouse owns an undivided one-half interest in property acquired during the marriage.

35–2d Leasehold Estates

A **leasehold estate** is created when a real property owner or lessor (landlord) agrees to convey the right to possess and use the property to a lessee (tenant) for a certain period of time. The tenant has a *qualified* right to exclusive possession. It is qualified because the landlord has a right to enter onto the premises to ensure that no waste (damage or destruction) is being committed.

The *temporary* nature of possession under a lease is what distinguishes a tenant from a purchaser, who acquires title to the property. The tenant can use the land—for instance, by harvesting crops—but cannot injure it by such activities as cutting down timber for sale or extracting oil.

Leasehold Estate An interest in real property that gives a tenant a qualified right to possess and/or use the property for a limited time under a lease.

Fixed-Term Tenancy A **fixed-term tenancy**, also called a *tenancy for years*, is created by an express contract by which property is leased for a specified period of time. Signing a one-year lease to occupy an apartment, for instance, creates a fixed-term tenancy. Note that the term need not be specified by date and can be conditioned on the occurrence of an event, such as leasing a cabin for the summer or an apartment in New Orleans during Mardi Gras.

At the end of the period specified in the lease, the lease ends (without notice), and possession of the property returns to the lessor. If the tenant dies during the period of the lease, the lease interest passes to the tenant's heirs as personal property. Often, leases include renewal or extension provisions.

Fixed-Term Tenancy A type of tenancy under which property is leased for a specified period of time, such as a month, a year, or a period of years. It is also called a *tenancy for years*.

4. These states include Alaska, Arizona, California, Idaho, Louisiana, Nevada, New Mexico, Texas, Washington, and Wisconsin. Puerto Rico allows property to be owned as community property as well.

Periodic Tenancy A lease interest for an indefinite period involving payment of rent at fixed intervals, such as week to week, month to month, or year to year.

Periodic Tenancy A **periodic tenancy** is created by a lease that does not specify how long it is to last but does specify that rent is to be paid at certain intervals. This type of tenancy is automatically renewed for another rental period unless properly terminated. **Example 35.7** Kayla enters into a lease with Capital Properties. The lease states, "Rent is due on the tenth day of every month." This provision creates a periodic tenancy from month to month. ■ This type of tenancy can also extend from week to week or from year to year.

Under the common law, to terminate a periodic tenancy, the landlord or tenant must give at least one period's notice to the other party. If the tenancy extends from month to month, for instance, one month's notice must be given prior to the last month's rent payment. Today, however, many states' statutes require a different period for notice of termination in a periodic tenancy.

Tenancy at Will A type of tenancy that either the landlord or the tenant can terminate without notice.

Tenancy at Will With a **tenancy at will**, either party can terminate the tenancy without notice. This type of tenancy can arise if a landlord allows a person to live on the premises without paying rent or rents property to a tenant "for as long as both agree." Tenancies at will are rare today because most state statutes require a landlord to provide some period of notice to terminate a tenancy. States may also require a landowner to have sufficient cause to end a residential tenancy.

Tenancy at Sufferance A tenancy that arises when a tenant wrongfully continues to occupy leased property after the lease has terminated.

Tenancy at Sufferance The mere possession of land without right is called a **tenancy at sufferance**. A tenancy at sufferance is not a true tenancy because it is created when a tenant *wrongfully* retains possession of property. Whenever a tenancy for years or a periodic tenancy ends and the tenant continues to retain possession of the premises without the owner's permission, a tenancy at sufferance is created.

35–2e Nonpossessory Interests—Easements, Profits, and Licenses

Nonpossessory Interest In the context of real property, an interest that involves the right to use land but not the right to possess it.

Easement A nonpossessory right, established by express or implied agreement, to make limited use of another's property without removing anything from the property.

Profit In real property law, the right to enter onto another's property and remove something of value from that property.

In contrast to the types of property interests just described, some interests in land do not include any rights to possess the property. Such an interest is known as a **nonpossessory interest** and includes easements, profits, and licenses.

An **easement** is the right of a person to make limited use of another person's real property without taking anything from the property. An easement, for instance, can be the right to walk or drive across another's property. In contrast, a **profit**[5] is the right to go onto land owned by another and take away some part of the land itself or some product of the land. **Example 35.8** Steve owns The Dunes. Steve gives Carmen the right to go there to remove all the sand and gravel that she needs for her cement business. Carmen has a profit. ■

Easements and profits can be classified as either *appurtenant* or *in gross*. Because easements and profits are similar and the same rules apply to both, we discuss them together.

Easement or Profit Appurtenant An easement or profit *appurtenant* arises when the owner of one piece of land has a right to go onto or remove something from an adjacent piece of land owned by another. The land that is benefited by the easement or profit is called the *dominant estate*, and the land that is burdened is called the *servient estate*.

Because easements appurtenant are intended to *benefit the land*, they run (are conveyed) with the land when it is transferred. **Example 35.9** Taylor has a right to drive his car across Green's land, which is adjacent to Taylor's land. This right-of-way over Green's property is an easement appurtenant to Taylor's property and can be used only by Taylor. If Taylor sells his land, the easement runs with the land to benefit the new owner. ■

Easement or Profit in Gross In an easement or profit *in gross*, the right to use or take things from another's land is given to one who does not own an adjacent tract of land. These easements or profits are intended to *benefit a particular person or business*, not a particular piece of land, and cannot be transferred.

5. As used here, the term *profit* does not refer to the profits made by a business firm. Rather, it means a gain or an advantage.

Example 35.10 Avery owns a parcel of land with a marble quarry. Avery conveys (transfers) to Classic Stone Corporation the right to come onto her land and remove up to five hundred pounds of marble per day. Classic Stone owns a profit in gross and cannot transfer this right to another. ■ Similarly, when a utility company is granted an easement to run its power lines across another's property, it obtains an easement in gross.

Know This An easement appurtenant requires two adjacent pieces of land owned by two different persons, but an easement in gross needs only one piece of land owned by someone other than the owner of the easement.

Creation of an Easement or Profit Most easements and profits are created by an express grant in a contract, a deed, or a will. This allows the parties to include terms defining the extent and length of time of use. In some situations, an easement or profit can also be created without an express agreement.

An easement or profit may arise by *implication* when the circumstances surrounding the division of a parcel of property imply its existence. **Example 35.11** Mathews divides a parcel of land that has only one well for drinking water. If Mathews conveys the half without a well to Dean, a profit by implication arises because Dean needs drinking water. ■

An easement or profit may also be created by *necessity*. An easement by necessity does not require a division of property for its existence. A person who rents an apartment, for instance, has an easement by necessity in the private road leading up to the apartment building.

An easement or profit may arise by *prescription* when one person uses another person's land without the landowner's consent. The use must be apparent and continue for the length of time required by the applicable statute of limitations. (In much the same way, title to property may be obtained by *adverse possession,* discussed later in this chapter.)

Case Example 35.12 From 1993 to 2016, Charles and Mary Fee used a roadway located on the property of their neighbors Richard and Gail Cheatham to haul livestock to and from a nearby highway and for deliveries of products such as feed, fertilizer, and lime. In July 2016, Richard told the Fees that the road was now off limits and erected a gate to block their passage. The Fees filed a lawsuit claiming that they had a right to access the roadway by prescriptive easement. A Kentucky statute holds that such an easement is created if the use is "unobstructed, open, peaceable, [and] continuous" without express permission of the landowner for at least fifteen years.

The trial court ruled in favor of the Cheathams based on its mistaken view that the relevant time period started when the gate was erected in July 2016. A state appellate court corrected this error, noting that the Fees had used the roadway for more than twenty years *before* the gate was built. Given Richard's testimony that he had seen the Fees' vehicles on the roadway "every now and then" at least once a year during that entire time, the appeals court found that the Fees had met the statutory requirements for easement by prescription.[6] ■

Gerard Koudenburg/Shutterstock.com

Why was a landowner's admission that he had seen a neighbor's truck using a road on his property crucial for establishing the neighbor's easement by prescription?

Termination of an Easement or Profit An easement or profit can be terminated in several ways. The simplest way is to deed it back to the owner of the land that is burdened by it. Similarly, if the owner of an easement or profit becomes the owner of the property burdened by it, then it is merged into the property.

Another way to terminate an easement or profit is to abandon it and create evidence of intent to relinquish the right to use it. Mere nonuse will not extinguish an easement or profit *unless the nonuse is accompanied by an overt act showing the intent to abandon.*

License In the context of real property, a **license** is the revocable right to enter onto another person's land. It is a personal privilege that arises from the consent of the owner of the land and can be revoked by the owner. A ticket to attend a movie at a theater or a concert is an example of a license.

License In the context of real property, a revocable right or privilege to enter onto another person's land.

In essence, a license grants a person the authority to enter the land of another and perform a specified act or series of acts without obtaining any permanent interest in the land. When a person with a license exceeds the authority granted and undertakes an action that is not permitted, the property owner can sue that person in tort law for trespass.

6. *Fee v. Cheatham,* 2019 WL 2712604 (Ky. Ct. App. 2019).

Case Example 35.13 Richard and Mary Orman purchased real property owned at one time by Sandra Curtis. Part of the garage extended nine feet onto Curtis's neighboring property. In an agreement on file with the deed, Curtis had given the Ormans permission to use the garage as long as it continued to be used as a garage. After the Ormans moved in, they converted the garage's workshop into guest quarters but continued to use the garage as a garage.

A dispute arose over the driveway shared by Curtis and the Ormans, which straddled the property line. The Ormans filed a suit claiming that Curtis left "junk objects" near the driveway that impeded their access. Curtis countered that the permission she had given the buyers to use the garage was a license. She claimed that the Ormans, by converting the workshop into living quarters, had exceeded their authority under the license, which she could therefore revoke. The court looked at the agreement's wording, which clearly gave the Ormans the right to use the garage but did not mention the workshop. The court concluded that because the Ormans were continuing to use the garage as a garage, Curtis could not revoke their right to do so.[7]

Exhibit 35–1 illustrates the various interests in property discussed in this chapter.

35–3 Transfer of Ownership

Ownership interests in real property are frequently transferred (conveyed) by sale, and the terms of the transfer are specified in a real estate sales contract.

Real property ownership can also be transferred by deed, by will or inheritance, by adverse possession, or by eminent domain. When ownership rights in real property are transferred, the type of interest being transferred and the conditions of the transfer normally are set forth in a *deed* executed by the person who is conveying the property.

35–3a Real Estate Sales Contracts

In some ways, a sale of real estate is similar to a sale of goods, because it involves a transfer of ownership, often with specific warranties. A sale of real estate, however, is a more complicated transaction that involves certain formalities that are not required in a sale of goods. In part because of these complications, real estate brokers or agents who are licensed by the state generally assist the buyers and sellers during a real estate sales transaction.

Exhibit 35–1 Interests in Real Property

Ownership Interests	1. *Fee simple*—The most complete form of ownership. 2. *Life estate*—An estate that lasts for the life of a specified individual. 3. *Concurrent ownership*—Ownership by two or more persons who hold title to property together. Types of concurrent ownership are as follows: a. Tenancy in common b. Joint tenancy c. Tenancy by the entirety d. Community property
Leasehold Estates	1. Fixed-term tenancy (tenancy for years) 2. Periodic tenancy 3. Tenancy at will 4. Tenancy at sufferance
Nonpossessory Interests	1. Easements 2. Profits 3. Licenses

7. *Orman v. Curtis*, 54 Misc.3d 1206(A), 50 N.Y.S.3d 27 (2017).

Usually, the parties to a sale of real estate enter into a detailed contract setting forth their agreement. A contract for a sale of land includes such terms as the purchase price, the type of deed the buyer will receive, the condition of the premises, and any items that will be included.

A buyer who does not pay cash for the property must obtain financing through a mortgage loan. Real estate sales contracts can be made contingent on the buyer's ability to obtain financing at or below a specified rate of interest. The contract may also be contingent on certain events, such as the completion of a land survey or the property's passing one or more inspections. Normally, the buyer is responsible for having the premises inspected for physical or mechanical defects and for insect infestation.

Implied Warranties in the Sale of New Homes Most states recognize a warranty—the **implied warranty of habitability**—in the sale of new homes. Because the warranty is implied, it need not be included in the contract of sale or the deed to be effective.

Implied Warranty of Habitability An implied promise by a seller of a new house that the house is fit for human habitation. Also, the implied promise by a landlord that rented residential premises are habitable.

Under this warranty, the seller of a new home essentially warrants that it is in reasonable working order and is of reasonably sound construction. Thus, the seller is in effect a guarantor of the home's fitness. In some states, the warranty protects not only the first purchaser but any subsequent purchaser as well.

Seller's Duty to Disclose Hidden Defects In most jurisdictions, courts impose on sellers a duty to disclose any known defect that materially affects the value of the property and that the buyer could not reasonably discover. Failure to disclose such a material defect gives the buyer the right to rescind the contract and to sue for damages based on fraud or misrepresentation. The buyer generally must bring such a suit within a specified time.

Example 35.14 Matthew partially renovates a house in Louisiana and sells it to the Morelands for $68,000. Two months after the Morelands move in, they discover rotten wood behind the tile in the bathroom and experience problems with the plumbing. A state statute specifies that the Morelands have one year from the date of the sale or the discovery of the defect to file a lawsuit. Therefore, the Morelands must file suit within twelve months of discovering the defects (which would be fourteen months from the date of the sale).

In the following *Spotlight Case*, the court had to decide whether the buyer of a "haunted" house had the right to rescind the sales contract.

RuslanDashinsky/E+/Getty Images

If this homeowner discovers numerous defects in her recently purchased house, can she wait years to attempt to rescind the contract?

Spotlight on Sales of Haunted Houses: Case 35.2

Stambovsky v. Ackley

Supreme Court, Appellate Division, New York, 572 N.Y.S.2d 672, 169 A.D.2d 254 (1991).

Facts Jeffrey Stambovsky signed a contract to buy Helen Ackley's house in Nyack, New York. After the contract was signed, Stambovsky discovered that the house was widely reputed to be haunted. The Ackley family claimed to have seen poltergeists on numerous occasions over the previous nine years. The Ackleys had been interviewed about the house in both a national publication (*Reader's Digest*) and the local newspaper. The house was included on a walking tour of Nyack, New York, as "a riverfront Victorian (with ghost)."

When Stambovsky learned of the house's reputation, he sued to rescind the contract, alleging that Ackley and her real estate agent had made material misrepresentations when they failed to disclose Ackley's belief that the house was haunted. Ackley argued that she was under no duty to disclose to the buyer the home's haunted reputation. The trial court dismissed Stambovsky's case, and Stambovsky appealed.

Issue Was the failure to inform Stambovsky that the house was supposedly haunted a material misrepresentation that would allow him to rescind the contract?

(Continues)

Continued

Decision Yes. The New York appellate court found that the seller did have a duty to disclose. The court allowed Stambovsky to rescind the contract.

Reason Ackley and her family had created the house's reputation as haunted and had profited from that reputation over a number of years. That reputation harmed the resale value of the home, however. Because the Ackleys had created the impairment and knew that it was not likely to be discovered by a purchaser from out of town, they had an obligation to disclose it. They should have brought the impairment to the attention of all prospective buyers, including Stambovsky. Even though the Ackleys did not actively mislead Stambovsky, they allowed him to sign the contract knowing that he was unaware of the home's haunted reputation. Because they unfairly took advantage of his ignorance, they could not enforce the contract.

pixeldigits/iStock/Getty Images

When will a buyer of a house that is allegedly haunted have the right to rescind the deal?

Critical Thinking

- **Ethical** *Assuming that Ackley's behavior was unethical, was it unethical because she failed to tell Stambovsky something about the house that he did not know, or was it unethical because of the nature of the information she omitted? What if Ackley had failed to mention that the roof leaked or that the well was dry—conditions that a buyer would normally investigate? Explain your answer.*

35–3b Deeds

Deed A document by which title to real property is passed.

Possession and title to land are passed from person to person by means of a **deed**—the instrument of conveyance of real property. Unlike a contract, a deed does not have to be supported by legally sufficient consideration. To be valid, a deed must include the following elements:

1. The names of the grantor (the giver or seller) and the grantee (the donee or buyer).
2. Words evidencing the intent to convey the property (such as, "I hereby bargain, sell, grant, or give"). No specific words are necessary. If the deed does not specify the type of estate being transferred, it is presumed to transfer the property in fee simple absolute.
3. A legally sufficient description of the land. The description must include enough detail to distinguish the property being conveyed from every other parcel of land. The property can be identified by reference to an official survey or recorded plat map, or each boundary can be described by metes and bounds. *Metes and bounds* is a system of measuring boundary lines by the distance between two points, often using physical features of the local geography—for instance, "beginning at the southwesterly intersection of Court and Main Streets, then West 40 feet to the fence, then South 100 feet, then Northeast approximately 120 feet back to the beginning."
4. The signature of the grantor' (and often the grantor's spouse).
5. Delivery of the deed.

Know This

Gifts of real property are common, and they require deeds even though there is no consideration for the gift.

Different types of deeds provide different degrees of protection against defects of title. A defect of title exists, for instance, if an undisclosed third person has an ownership interest in the property.

Warranty Deed A deed that provides the greatest amount of protection for the grantee. The grantor promises that he or she has title to the property conveyed in the deed, that there are no undisclosed encumbrances on the property, and that the grantee will enjoy quiet possession of the property.

Warranty Deeds

A **warranty deed** contains the greatest number of *covenants,* or promises, of title and thus provides the greatest protection against defects of title. In most states, special language is required to create a general warranty deed. Warranty deeds commonly include the following covenants:

1. A covenant that the grantor has the title to, and the power to convey, the property.
2. A covenant of quiet enjoyment (a warranty that the buyer's possession of the land will not be disturbed).

3. A covenant that transfer of the property is made without knowledge of adverse claims of third parties.

Generally, the warranty deed makes the grantor liable for all defects of title during the time that the property was held by the grantor and previous titleholders. **Example 35.15** Mandal sells a two-acre lot and office building by warranty deed to Flash Technologies, LLC. Subsequently, Perkins shows that he has better title to the property than Mandal had and evicts Flash Technologies. Here, Flash Technologies can sue Mandal for breaching the covenant of quiet enjoyment. Flash Technologies can recover the purchase price of the land, plus any other damages incurred as a result.

Special Warranty Deeds A **special warranty deed**, or *limited warranty deed,* in contrast, warrants only that grantors, or sellers, held good title during their ownership of the property. In other words, the grantor does not warrant that there were no defects of title when the property was held by previous owners.

Special Warranty Deed A deed that warrants only that the grantor held good title during the grantor's ownership of the property and does not warrant that there were no defects of title when the property was held by previous owners.

If the special warranty deed discloses all liens and other encumbrances, the seller will not be liable to the buyer if a third person subsequently interferes with the buyer's ownership. If the third person's claim arises out of, or is related to, some act of the seller, though, the seller will be liable to the buyer for damages.

Quitclaim Deeds A **quitclaim deed** offers the least amount of protection against defects of title. Basically, a quitclaim deed conveys to the grantee whatever interest the grantor had. Therefore, if the grantor had no interest, then the grantee receives no interest.

Quitclaim Deed A deed that conveys only whatever interest the grantor had in the property and therefore offers the least amount of protection against defects of title.

Quitclaim deeds are often used when sellers, or grantors, are uncertain as to the extent of their rights in the property. These deeds may also be used to release a party's interest in a particular parcel of property, such as in divorce settlements or business dissolutions when the grantors are dividing up their interests in real property.

Recording Statutes Every state has a **recording statute**, which allows a deed to be recorded for a fee. Deeds are recorded in the county where the property is located. Recording a deed gives notice to the public that a certain person is now the owner of a particular parcel of real estate. By putting everyone on notice as to the true owner, recording a deed prevents the previous owners from fraudulently conveying the land to other purchasers. Thus, prospective buyers can check the public records to see whether there have been earlier transactions creating interests or rights in specific parcels of real property.

Recording Statute A statute that allows deeds, mortgages, and other real property transactions to be recorded so as to provide notice to future purchasers or creditors of an existing claim on the property.

35–3c Will or Inheritance

Property that is transferred on an owner's death is passed either by will or by state inheritance laws. If the owner of land dies with a will, the land passes in accordance with the terms of the will. If the owner dies without a will, state inheritance statutes prescribe how and to whom the property will pass.

35–3d Adverse Possession

A person who wrongfully possesses the real property of another (by occupying or using it) may eventually acquire title to it through adverse possession. **Adverse possession** is a means of obtaining title to land without delivery of a deed and without the consent of—or payment to—the true owner. Thus, adverse possession is a method of *involuntarily* transferring title to the property from the true owner to the adverse possessor.

Adverse Possession The acquisition of title to real property through open occupation, without the consent of the owner, for a period of time specified by state statute. The occupation must be actual, exclusive, open, continuous, and in opposition to all others, including the owner.

Essentially, when one person possesses the property of another for a certain statutory period, that person acquires title to the land. The statutory period varies from three to thirty years, depending on the state, with ten years being the most common.

Focus Question 3

What are the requirements for acquiring property by adverse possession?

Requirements for Adverse Possession For property to be held adversely, four elements must be satisfied:

1. *Possession must be actual and exclusive.* The possessor must physically occupy the property. This requirement is clearly met if the possessor lives on the property, but it may also be met if the possessor builds fences, erects structures, plants crops, or even grazes animals on the land.
2. *Possession must be open, visible, and notorious,* not secret or clandestine. The possessor must occupy the land for all the world to see. The obviousness requirement ensures that the true owner is on notice that someone is possessing the owner's property wrongfully.
3. *Possession must be continuous and peaceable for the required period of time.* This requirement means that the possessor must not be interrupted in the occupancy by the true owner or by the courts. *Continuous* does not mean constant. It simply means that the possessor has continuously occupied the property in some fashion for the statutory time. *Peaceable* means that no force was used to possess the land.
4. *Possession must be hostile and adverse.* In other words, the possessor cannot be living on the property with the owner's permission and must claim the property as against the whole world. (See this chapter's *Business Law Analysis* feature for an illustration.)

When Possession of Property Is Not "Adverse"

Business Law Analysis

The McKeag family operated a marina on their lakefront property in Bolton, New York. For more than forty years, the McKeags used a section of property belonging to their neighbors, the Finleys, as a beach for the marina's customers. The McKeags also stored a large float on the beach during the winter months, built their own retaining wall, and planted bushes and flowers there.

The McKeags prevented others from using the property, including the Finleys. Nevertheless, the families always had a friendly relationship, and one of the Finleys gave the McKeags permission to continue using the beach. He also reminded them of his ownership several times, to which they said nothing. The McKeags also asked for permission to mow grass on the property and once apologized for leaving a jet ski there. Can the McKeags establish adverse possession over the statutory period of ten years?

Analysis: There are four requirements to acquire title to property through adverse possession. The possession must be (1) actual and exclusive, (2) open and obvious, (3) continuous for the required period of time, and (4) hostile and adverse.

Result and Reasoning: The McKeags satisfied the first three requirements for adverse possession:

1. Their possession was actual and exclusive because they used the beach and prevented others from doing so, including the Finleys.
2. Their possession was open and visible because they made improvements to the beach and regularly kept their belongings there.
3. Their possession was continuous and peaceable for the required ten years. They possessed the property for more than four decades, and they even kept a large float there during the winter months.

Nevertheless, the McKeags' possession was *not* hostile and adverse, which is the fourth requirement. The Finleys provided substantial evidence that they had given the McKeags permission to use the beach. Rather than reject the Finleys' permission as unnecessary, the McKeags sometimes said nothing and other times seemingly affirmed that the property belonged to the Finleys (by asking permission to mow grass, for instance). Thus, because the McKeags did not satisfy all four requirements, they cannot establish adverse possession.

A claim of adverse possession was at the center of the following case, which involved a dispute between the owners of neighboring properties.

Case 35.3

A2 Creative Group, LLC v. Anderson

Missouri Court of Appeals, Western District, 596 S.W.3d 214 (2020).

Facts Gary and Cristina Worden owned the Main Street Inn, a bed and breakfast, in Parkville, Missouri. A stone wall ran the length of the property behind the Inn. A driveway and walkway along the wall was used to access the service entrance to the Inn for the delivery of supplies and equipment. The Wordens also maintained the landscaping on their side of the wall—for example, they cut the grass, planted flowers, put down paver and edging stones, and removed dying trees.

After owning the Inn for eleven years, the Wordens sold the business to A2 Creative Group, LLC, whose principals, Jason and Kathy Ayers, lived in the Inn and had been operating it for the sellers. At about the same time, Soheil Anderson, owner of the property on the other side of the stone wall, obtained a survey of her property. The survey revealed that a 400-square-foot tract on the Inn's side of the stone wall was actually Anderson's property.

A2 filed a petition in a Missouri state court against Anderson to establish its title to the tract based on a claim of adverse possession. The trial court ruled in favor of A2, concluding that its possession of the disputed property was "(1) hostile; (2) actual; (3) open and notorious; (4) exclusive; and (5) continuous for at least 10 years," the requisite period for adverse possession under Missouri's statute.

Anderson appealed, claiming that A2 had not proved that its possession was exclusive and continuous.

Issue Was A2's possession exclusive and continuous?

Decision Yes. A state intermediate appellate court affirmed the trial court's judgment.

Reason With respect to exclusivity, the appellate court concluded that "A2 and the Wordens demonstrated visible acts of ownership over the premises." A2 and the Wordens possessed the land for themselves, and not for others, and they wholly excluded the true owner, Anderson, from the property. The evidence that A2 and the Wordens maintained and used the tract for themselves, and not for their neighbor, was sufficient to demonstrate that their possession of the property was exclusive.

The appellate court also concluded that A2 had proved the "continuous" element of adverse possession. The court explained that the requisite ten years of possession must be consecutive, and once the time has run, "the possessor is vested with title and the record owner is divested." To meet the ten-year requirement and succeed on a claim for adverse possession, a possessor can add its time of possession to that of its predecessors. In this case, "there was evidence of occupancy, upkeep, and no intent to abandon the disputed property" by A2 and the Wordens for the required period.

Critical Thinking

- **Legal Environment** *Would an adverse possessor satisfy the element of "exclusive" on showing only that disputed property was not jointly possessed with the previous owner? Explain.*
- **What If the Facts Were Different?** *Suppose that for a year during the Wordens' ownership of the Inn, they closed it for remodeling. Would the result in this case have been different? Discuss.*

Purpose of the Doctrine There are a number of public-policy reasons for the adverse possession doctrine. These include society's interest in resolving boundary disputes, determining title when title to property is in question, and ensuring that real property remains in the stream of commerce. More fundamentally, the doctrine punishes owners who do not take action when they see adverse possession and rewards possessors for putting land to productive use.

35–3e Eminent Domain

No ownership rights in real property can ever really be absolute. Even ownership in fee simple absolute is limited by a superior ownership. In the United States, the government has an ultimate ownership right in all land. This right, known as **eminent domain**,

Eminent Domain The power of a government to take land from private citizens for public use on the payment of just compensation.

is sometimes referred to as the *condemnation power* of government to take land for public use. It gives the government the right to acquire possession of real property in the manner directed by the U.S. Constitution and the laws of each state whenever the public interest requires it. Property normally may be taken only for public use, not for private benefit.

Condemnation Proceedings The judicial procedure by which the government exercises its power of eminent domain. It generally involves two phases: a taking and a determination of fair value.

The power of eminent domain generally is invoked through **condemnation proceedings** that occur before a judge. For instance, when a new public highway is to be built, the government must decide where to build it and how much land it needs. After the government determines that a particular parcel of land is necessary for public use, it will first offer to buy the property. If the owner refuses the offer, the government brings a judicial (*condemnation*) proceeding to obtain title to the land.

Condemnation proceedings usually involve two distinct phases—the first to establish the government's right to take the property, and the second to determine the fair value of the property.

Taking The taking of private property by the government for public use through the power of eminent domain.

dmadig/E+/Getty Images

Why does the U.S. Constitution require that a government taking, such as the acquisition of private land for a gas pipeline, be for "public use"?

The Taking When the government takes land owned by a private party for public use, it is referred to as a **taking**. Under the *takings clause* of the Fifth Amendment to the U.S. Constitution, the government may take private property for public use with just compensation to the property owner. State constitutions contain similar provisions. In the first phase of condemnation proceedings, the government must prove that it needs to acquire privately owned property for a public use.

Example 35.16 Franklin County, Iowa, engages Bosque Systems to build a liquefied natural gas pipeline across the property of more than two hundred landowners. Some property owners consent to this use and accept Bosque's offer of compensation. Others refuse the firm's offer. A court will likely deem Bosque's pipeline to be a public use. Therefore, the government can exert its eminent domain power to "take" the land, provided that it pays just compensation to the property owners.

The Compensation The U.S. Constitution and state constitutions require that the government pay just compensation to the landowner when invoking its condemnation power. Just compensation means fair value. In the second phase of the condemnation proceeding, the court determines the fair value of the land, which usually is approximately equal to its market value.

Economic Development The United States Supreme Court has ruled that the power of eminent domain can be used to further "economic development."[8] This ruling may apply in cases where, for instance, a city government decides that it is in the public interest to have a larger parking lot for a privately owned sports stadium or to have a manufacturing plant located in the city to create more jobs. The government may condemn certain tracts of existing housing or business property and then convey the land to the privately owned stadium or manufacturing plant.

Such actions may bring in private developers and businesses that provide jobs and increase tax revenues, thus revitalizing communities. Opponents of the practice, however, dispute that the land is being taken for "public use," as required by the Fifth Amendment. The Supreme Court recognizes the right of individual states to pass laws that prohibit takings for economic development, and most states have done so. Still, some states do allow takings for the redevelopment of economically stressed neighborhoods and, controversially, the promotion of recreational activities.

---

8. See *Kelo v. City of New London, Connecticut*, 545 U.S. 469, 125 S.Ct. 2655, 162 L.Ed.2d 439 (2005).

Ethical Issue

Should eminent domain be used to take private land for recreational uses? Across the country, state and local governments are showing a willingness to take land for hiking paths, bike trails, and other recreational purposes. Public officials and nature enthusiasts argue that this use of eminent domain is justified because of the many benefits these projects bestow on the community. Bike trails, for instance, reduce automobile traffic and provide transportation options for low-income residents. Supporters also point to the general physical and emotional rewards of recreational activities for those who take part.

Others—particularly those who own the land in question—have a different view of the situation. Farmers in Mahoning County, Ohio, went to court to fight a park service's efforts to take control of an abandoned railway that runs through their property. The farmers argued that the proposed recreational bike path would cut their farms in half, making it difficult for livestock and heavy machinery to move freely. They also worried about liability if trail users wandered onto their property and were injured. Plaintiffs in Iowa and Massachusetts have taken similar legal actions to keep recreational trails off private land. A Wisconsin legislator, defending his state's ban on the use of eminent domain for such purposes, says, "Somebody else's recreational opportunity should not be forced on my property."

35–4 Landlord-Tenant Relationships

A landlord-tenant relationship is established by a lease contract. In most states, statutes require leases for terms exceeding one year to be in writing. The lease should describe the property and indicate the length of the term, the amount of the rent, and how and when it is to be paid.

State or local law often dictates permissible lease terms, particularly in residential leases. For instance, a statute or ordinance might prohibit the leasing of a structure that is not in compliance with local building codes. As in other areas of law, the National Conference of Commissioners on Uniform State Laws has issued a model act to create more uniformity in the laws governing landlord-tenant relationships. The Uniform Residential Landlord and Tenant Act (URLTA), which was issued in 1972, has been adopted in some form by many states. A revised version of the act was issued in 2015.

Know This

Sound business practice dictates that a lease for commercial property should be written carefully and should clearly define the parties' rights and obligations.

35–4a Rights and Duties

The rights and duties of landlords and tenants generally pertain to four broad areas of concern—the possession, use, and maintenance of the leased property and, of course, rent.

Focus Question 4

What are the duties of the landlord and the tenant with respect to the use and maintenance of leased property?

Possession A landlord is obligated to give a tenant possession of the property that the tenant has agreed to lease. After obtaining possession, the tenant retains the property exclusively until the lease expires, unless the lease states otherwise.

Quiet Enjoyment. The covenant of quiet enjoyment mentioned previously also applies to leased premises. Under this covenant, the landlord promises that during the lease term, neither the landlord nor anyone having a superior title to the property will disturb the tenant's use and enjoyment of the property. This covenant forms the essence of the landlord-tenant relationship, and if it is breached, the tenant can terminate the lease and sue for damages.

Eviction A landlord's act of depriving a tenant of possession of the leased premises.

Constructive Eviction A form of eviction that occurs when a landlord fails to perform adequately any of the duties required by the lease, thereby making the tenant's further use and enjoyment of the property exceedingly difficult or impossible.

Eviction. If the landlord deprives the tenant of possession of the leased property or interferes with the tenant's use or enjoyment of it, an **eviction** occurs. A **constructive eviction** occurs when the landlord wrongfully performs or fails to perform any of the duties the lease requires, thereby making the tenant's further use and enjoyment of the property exceedingly difficult or impossible. Examples of constructive eviction include a landlord's failure to provide heat in the winter, electricity, or other essential utilities.

Use of the Premises The tenant normally may make any use of the leased property, provided the use is legal and does not injure the landlord's interest. The parties are free to limit by agreement the uses to which the property may be put.

Maintenance of the Premises Tenants are responsible for any damage to the premises that they cause, intentionally or negligently, and may be held liable for the cost of returning the property to the physical condition it was in when the lease began. Unless the parties have agreed otherwise, tenants are not responsible for ordinary wear and tear and the property's consequent depreciation in value.

In some jurisdictions, landlords of residential property are required by statute to maintain the premises in good repair. Landlords must also comply with any applicable state statutes and city ordinances regarding maintenance and repair of buildings.

Know This

Options that may be available to a tenant on a landlord's breach of the implied warranty of habitability include repairing the defect and deducting the cost from the rent, canceling the lease, and suing for damages.

In addition, the implied warranty of habitability discussed earlier may apply to *residential* leases. The warranty requires a landlord who leases residential property to ensure that the premises are habitable—that is, a safe and suitable place for people to live. Also, the landlord must make repairs to maintain the premises in that condition for the lease's duration.

Generally, this warranty applies to major, or *substantial,* physical defects that the landlord knows or should know about and has had a reasonable time to repair—such as a large hole in the roof or a broken heating system. **Example 35.17** The Galprins own a house within the city limits of Redmond. A city regulation states that a residence must be connected to the city sewer system before anyone, including tenants, can live in the residence. The Galprins' house is not connected to the city system. Thus, it is not legally habitable, and they cannot lease it to tenants. ■

Rent *Rent* is the tenant's payment to the landlord for the tenant's occupancy or use of the landlord's real property. Usually, tenants must pay the rent even if they refuse to occupy the property or move out, as long as the refusal or the move is unjustified and the lease is in force. **Example 35.18** Lifetime Insurance Agency enters into a lease with Mallory for a suite of offices in Mallory's building. Lifetime's revenue is less than managers had projected, however, and the rent is now more than they want to pay. Lifetime vacates the offices before the end of the lease. In terms of the landlord-tenant relationship, the move is unjustified, and the lease remains in force. Lifetime must continue to pay the rent. ■

Under the common law, if the leased premises were destroyed by fire or flood, the tenant still had to pay rent. Today, however, if an apartment building is destroyed, most states' laws do not require tenants to continue to pay rent.

In some situations, such as when a landlord breaches the implied warranty of habitability, a tenant may be allowed to withhold rent as a remedy. When rent withholding is authorized under a statute, the tenant usually must put the amount withheld into an *escrow account.* The funds are held in the name of the tenant and are returned to the tenant if the landlord fails to make the premises habitable.

Commercial Lease Terms State statutes often allow tenants and landlords more flexibility in negotiating the terms of a commercial lease. **Case Example 35.19** Constellation-F, LLC, leased warehouse space to World Trading 23, Inc., a retailer of drones and remote-controlled toys. By the terms of the agreement, World Trading's rent would increase by 150 percent if it still occupied the warehouse after the lease expired. When World Trading overstayed its lease by more than two months, Constellation sued to recover the holdover rent at the higher rate.

The trial court ruled in World Trading's favor after determining that the holdover rate was too high and therefore, under California law, an unenforceable penalty for breach of contract. A state appeals court reversed, reasoning that World Trading had chosen to accept the lease agreement with full understanding of the consequences of remaining on the premises after the expiration date. Because this choice was in no way coerced, World Trading was required to meet its obligations under the contract and pay Constellation the holdover rent.[9]

intararit/Shutterstock.com

Why did a California court require a retailer to pay what seemed to be unreasonably high rent for several months' use of a warehouse?

35–4b Transferring Rights to Leased Property

Either the landlord or the tenant may wish to transfer the rights to leased property during the term of the lease. If a landlord transfers complete title to the leased property to another, the tenant becomes the tenant of the new owner. The new owner may collect subsequent rent but must abide by the terms of the existing lease.

Assignment Tenants who transfer their entire interest in the leased property to a third person have agreed to an *assignment* of the lease. Many leases require the landlord's written consent for an assignment to be valid. The landlord can nullify (avoid) an assignment made without the required consent and evict the assignee. State statutes may specify that the landlord may not unreasonably withhold consent, however. Also, a landlord who knowingly accepts rent from the assignee may be held to have waived the consent requirement.

When an assignment is valid, the assignee acquires all of the tenant's rights under the lease. Nevertheless, an assignment does not release the original tenant (the assignor) from the obligation to pay rent should the assignee default. In addition, if the assignee exercises an option under the original lease to extend the term, the assignor remains liable for the rent during the extension, unless the landlord agrees otherwise.

Subleases The tenant's transfer of all or part of the premises for a period shorter than the lease term is a **sublease**. Many leases also require the landlord's written consent for a sublease. If the landlord's consent is required, a sublease without such permission is ineffective. Also, like an assignment, a sublease does not release tenants from their obligations under the lease.

Sublease A tenant's transfer of all or part of the leased premises to a third person for a period shorter than the lease term.

Example 35.20 Derek, a student, leases an apartment for a two-year period. Although Derek had planned on attending summer school, he decides to accept a job offer in Europe for the summer months instead. Derek therefore obtains his landlord's consent to sublease the apartment to Ava. Ava is bound by the same terms of the lease as Derek, and the landlord can hold Derek liable if Ava violates the lease terms.

35–4c Termination of the Lease

Usually, a lease terminates when its term ends. The tenant surrenders the property to the landlord, who retakes possession. If the lease states the time it will end, the landlord is not required to give the tenant notice. The lease terminates automatically.

A lease can also be terminated in several other ways. If the tenant purchases the leased property from the landlord during the term of the lease, for instance, the lease will be terminated. The parties may also agree to end a tenancy before it would otherwise terminate. In addition, the tenant may *abandon* the premises—move out completely with no intention of returning before the lease term expires.

At common law, a tenant who abandoned leased property was still obligated to pay the rent for the full term of the lease. The landlord could let the property stand vacant and charge the tenant for the remainder of the term. This is still the rule in some states. In most states today, however,

9. *Constellation-F, LLC, v. World Trading 23, Inc.*, 45 Cal.App.5th 22, 258 Cal.Rptr.3d 341 (2020).

landlords have a duty to *mitigate* their damages—that is, to make a reasonable attempt to lease the property to another party. Consequently, the tenant's liability for unpaid rent is restricted to the period of time that the landlord would reasonably need to lease the property to another tenant. Damages may also be allowed for the landlord's costs in leasing the property again.

Practice and Review

Vern Shoepke bought a two-story home in Roche, Maine. The warranty deed did not specify what covenants would be included in the conveyance. The property was adjacent to a public park that included a popular Frisbee golf course. (Frisbee golf is a sport similar to golf but using Frisbees.) Wayakichi Creek ran along the north end of the park and along Shoepke's property. The deed allowed Roche citizens the right to walk across a five-foot-wide section of the lot beside Wayakichi Creek as part of a two-mile public trail system. Teenagers regularly threw Frisbee golf discs from the walking path behind Shoepke's property over his yard to the adjacent park. Shoepke habitually shouted and cursed at the teenagers, demanding that they not throw the discs over his yard.

Two months after moving into his Roche home, Shoepke leased the second floor to Lauren Slater for nine months. The lease agreement did not specify that Shoepke's consent would be required to sublease the second floor. After three months of tenancy, Slater sublet the second floor to a local artist, Javier Indalecio. Over the remaining six months, Indalecio's use of oil paints damaged the carpeting in Shoepke's home. Using the information presented in the chapter, answer the following questions.

1. What is the term for the right of Roche citizens to walk across Shoepke's land on the trail?
2. What covenants would most courts infer were included in the warranty deed that Shoepke received when he bought his house?
3. Can Shoepke hold Slater financially responsible for the damage to the carpeting caused by Indalecio? Explain.
4. Could the fact that teenagers continually throw Frisbees over Shoepke's yard outside the second-floor windows arguably be a breach of the covenant of quiet enjoyment? Why or why not?

Debate This

Under no circumstances should a local government be able to condemn property in order to sell it later to real estate developers for private use.

Key Terms

Chapter Summary: Real Property and Landlord-Tenant Law

The Nature of Real Property	Real property (also called real estate or realty) includes land and structures, subsurface and airspace rights, plant life and vegetation, and fixtures.
Ownership Interests and Leases	1. **Fee simple**—The most complete form of ownership. Owners can use, possess, or dispose of the property as they choose during their lifetimes and pass on the property to their heirs at death. 2. **Life estate**—An estate that lasts for the life of a specified individual, during which time the individual is entitled to possess, use, and benefit from the estate. The life tenant cannot use the land in a manner that would adversely affect its value. The life tenant's ownership rights cease to exist at death. 3. **Concurrent ownership**—When two or more persons hold title to property together, concurrent ownership exists. a. A *tenancy in common* exists when two or more persons own an undivided interest in property. On a tenant's death, that tenant's property interest passes to the heirs. b. A *joint tenancy* exists when two or more persons own an undivided interest in property, with a right of survivorship. On the death of a joint tenant, that tenant's property interest transfers to the remaining tenant(s), not to the heirs of the deceased. c. A *tenancy by the entirety* is a form of co-ownership between married persons that is similar to a joint tenancy, except that a spouse cannot separately transfer interest unless the other spouse consents. d. *Community property* is a form of co-ownership between married persons in which each spouse technically owns an undivided one-half interest in property acquired during the marriage. This type of ownership exists in only a few states. 4. **Leasehold estates**—A leasehold estate is an interest in real property that is held for only a limited period of time, as specified in the lease agreement. Types of tenancies relating to leased property include the following: a. Fixed-term tenancy (tenancy for years)—Tenancy for a period of time stated by express contract. b. Periodic tenancy—Tenancy for a period determined by the frequency of rent payments. It is automatically renewed unless proper notice is given. c. Tenancy at will—Tenancy for as long as both parties agree. No notice of termination is required. d. Tenancy at sufferance—Possession of land without legal right. 5. **Nonpossessory interest**—An interest that involves the right to use real property but not to possess it. Easements, profits, and licenses are nonpossessory interests.
Transfer of Ownership	1. **By sales contract**—A contract for the sale of land includes the purchase price, the type of deed the buyer will receive, the condition of the premises, and any items that will be included. It is often contingent on the buyer's ability to obtain financing and on certain events, such as satisfactory inspections. 2. **By deed**—When real property is sold or transferred as a gift, title to the property is conveyed by means of a deed. A deed must meet specific legal requirements. A *warranty deed* provides the most extensive protection against defects of title. A *quitclaim deed* conveys to the grantee only whatever interest the grantor had in the property. A deed may be recorded in the manner prescribed by *recording statutes* in the appropriate jurisdiction to give third parties notice of the owner's interest. 3. **By will or inheritance**—If the owner dies after having made a valid will, the land passes as specified in the will. If the owner dies without having made a will, the heirs inherit according to state inheritance statutes. 4. **By adverse possession**—When a person possesses the property of another for a statutory period of time (ten years is the most common), that person acquires title to the property, provided the possession is actual and exclusive, open and visible, continuous and peaceable, and hostile and adverse (without the permission of the owner). 5. **By eminent domain**—The government can take land for public use, with just compensation, when the public interest requires the taking.

Landlord-Tenant Relationships	The landlord-tenant relationship is created by a lease agreement. State or local laws may dictate whether the lease must be in writing and what lease terms are permissible. 1. **Rights and duties**—The rights and duties of landlords and tenants that arise under a lease agreement generally pertain to the following areas: a. Possession—The tenant has an exclusive right to possess the leased premises. Under the covenant of quiet enjoyment, the landlord promises that during the lease term, neither the landlord nor anyone having superior title to the property will disturb the tenant's use and enjoyment of the property. b. Use of the premises—Unless the parties agree otherwise, the tenant may make any legal use of the property. c. Maintenance of the premises—Tenants are responsible for any damage that they cause. Landlords must comply with laws that set specific standards for the maintenance of real property. The implied warranty of habitability requires that landlords furnish and maintain residential premises in a habitable condition (that is, in a condition safe and suitable for human life). d. Rent—The tenant must pay the rent as long as the lease is in force, unless the tenant justifiably refuses to occupy the property or withholds the rent because of the landlord's failure to maintain the premises properly. 2. **Transferring rights to leased property**— a. If the landlord transfers complete title to the leased property, the tenant becomes the tenant of the new owner. The new owner may collect the rent but must abide by the existing lease. b. Generally, in the absence of an agreement to the contrary, tenants may assign their rights (but not their duties) under a lease contract to a third person. Tenants may also sublease leased property to a third person, but the original tenant is not relieved of any obligations to the landlord under the lease. In either situation, the landlord's consent may be required, but statutes may prohibit the landlord from unreasonably withholding consent.

Issue Spotters

1. Bernie sells his house to Consuela under a warranty deed. Later, Delmira appears, holding a better title to the house than Consuela has. Delmira wants Consuela off the property. What can Consuela do? (See *Transfer of Ownership.*)
2. Grey owns a commercial building in fee simple. Grey transfers temporary possession of the building to Haven Corporation. Can Haven transfer possession for even less time to Idyll Company? Explain. (See *Landlord-Tenant Relationships.*)

—Check your answers to the *Issue Spotters* against the answers provided in Appendix D.

Business Scenarios and Case Problems

35–1. Property Ownership. Twenty-two years ago, Lorenz was a wanderer. At that time, he decided to settle down on an unoccupied, three-acre parcel of land that he did not own. People in the area told him that they had no idea who owned the property. Lorenz built a house on the land, got married, and raised three children while living there. He fenced in the land, installed a gate with a sign above it that read "Lorenz's Homestead," and removed trespassers. Lorenz is now confronted by Joe Reese, who has a deed in his name as owner of the property. Reese, claiming ownership of the land, orders Lorenz and his family off the property. Discuss who has the better "title" to the property. (See *Transfer of Ownership.*)

35–2. Deeds. Wiley and Gemma are neighbors. Wiley's lot is extremely large, and his present and future use of it will not involve the entire area. Gemma wants to build a single-car garage and driveway along the present lot boundary. Because the placement of her existing structures makes it impossible for her to comply with an ordinance requiring buildings to be set back fifteen feet from an adjoining property line, Gemma cannot build the garage. Gemma contracts to purchase ten feet of Wiley's property along their boundary line for $3,000. Wiley is willing to sell but will give Gemma only a quitclaim deed, whereas Gemma wants a warranty deed. Discuss the differences between these deeds as they would affect the rights of the parties if the title to this ten feet of land later proves to be defective. (See *Transfer of Ownership.*)

35–3. Implied Warranty of Habitability. Sarah has rented a house from Frank. The house is only two years old, but the roof leaks every time it rains. The water that has accumulated in the attic has caused stucco to fall off ceilings in the upstairs bedrooms, and one ceiling has started to sag. Sarah has complained to Frank and asked him to have the roof repaired. Frank says that he has caulked the roof, but the roof still leaks. Frank claims that because Sarah has sole control of the leased premises, she has the duty to repair the roof. Sarah insists that repairing the roof is Frank's responsibility. Discuss fully who is responsible for repairing the roof and, if the responsibility belongs to Frank, what remedies are available to Sarah. (See *Landlord-Tenant Relationships.*)

35–4. Rent. Flawlace, LLC, leased unfinished commercial real estate in Las Vegas, Nevada, from Francis Lin to operate a beauty salon. The lease required Flawlace to obtain a "certificate of occupancy" from the city to commence business. This required the installation of a fire protection system. The lease did not allocate responsibility for the installation to either party. Lin voluntarily undertook to install the system. After a month of delays, Flawlace moved out. Three months later, the installation was complete, and Lin leased the premises to a new tenant. Did Flawlace owe rent for the three months between the time that it moved out and the time that the new tenant moved in? Explain. [*Tri-Lin Holdings, LLC v. Flawlace, LLC,* 2014 WL 1101577 (Nev. Sup.Ct. 2014)] (See *Landlord-Tenant Relationships.*)

35–5. Landlord-Tenant Relationships. Bhanmattie Kumar was walking on a sidewalk in Flushing, New York, when she tripped over a chipped portion of the sidewalk and fell. The defective sidewalk was in front of a Pretty Girl store—one of a chain of apparel stores headquartered in Brooklyn—on premises leased from PI Associates, LLC. Kumar filed a claim in a New York state court against PI, seeking to recover damages for her injuries. PI filed a cross-claim against Pretty Girl. On what basis would the court impose liability on PI? In what situation would Pretty Girl be the liable party? Is there any circumstance in which Kumar could be at least partially responsible for her injury? Discuss. [*Bhanmattie Rajkumar Kumar v. PI Associates, LLC,* 125 A.D.3d 609, 3 N.Y.S.3d 372 (2 Dept. 2015)] (See *Landlord-Tenant Relationships.*)

35–6. Business Case Problem with Sample Answer—Joint Tenancies. Arthur and Diana Ebanks owned three properties in the Cayman Islands in joint tenancy. With respect to joint tenancies, Cayman law is the same as U.S. law. When the Ebanks divorced, the decree did not change the tenancy in which the properties were held. On the same day as the divorce filing, Arthur executed a will providing that "any property in my name and that of another as joint tenants ... will pass to the survivor, and I instruct my Personal Representative to make no claim thereto." Four years later, Arthur died. His brother Curtis, the personal representative of his estate, asserted that Arthur's interest in the Cayman properties was part of the estate. Diana said that the sole interest in the properties was hers. To whom do the Cayman properties belong? Why? [*Ebanks v. Ebanks,* 41 Fla. L. Weekly D291, 198 So.3d 716 (2 Dist. 2016)] (See *Ownership Interests and Leases.*)

—For a sample answer to Problem 35–6, go to Appendix E.

35–7. Eminent Domain. In Tarrytown, New York, Citibank operated a branch that included a building and a parking lot with thirty-six spaces. Tarrytown leased twenty-one of the spaces from Citibank for use as public parking. When Citibank closed the branch and decided to sell the building, the public was denied access to the parking lot. After a public hearing, the city concluded that it should exercise its power of eminent domain to acquire the twenty-one spaces to provide public parking. Is this an appropriate use of the power of eminent domain? Suppose that Citibank opposes the plan and alternative sites are available. Should Tarrytown be required to acquire those sites instead of Citibank's property? In any event, what is Tarrytown's next step? Explain. [*Citibank, N.A. v. Village of Tarrytown,* 149 A.D.3d 931, 52 N.Y.S.3d 398 (2 Dept. 2017)] (See *Transfer of Ownership.*)

35–8. Transfer of Ownership. Craig and Sue Shaffer divided their real property into two lots. They enclosed one lot with a fence and sold it to the Murdocks. The other lot was sold to the Cromwells. All of the parties orally agreed that the fence marked the property line. Over the next three decades, each lot was sold three more times. Houses were built, and the lots were landscaped, including lilac bushes planted against the fence. Later, one of the owners removed the fence, and another built a shed next to where it had been. On the lot with the shed, the Talbots erected a carport abutting the lilac bushes. The Nielsons bought the adjacent lot from the Parkers and measured it according to the legal description in the deed. They discovered that the Talbots' carport encroached on the Nielsons' property by about thirteen feet. Are the Nielsons entitled to damages for their "lost" property from any party? Explain. [*Nielson v. Talbot,* 163 Idaho 480, 415 P.3d 348 (2018)] (See *Transfer of Ownership.*)

35–9. A Question of Ethics—The IDDR Approach to Easements. Two organizations, Class A Investors Post Oak, LP, and Cosmopolitan Condominium VP, L.P., owned adjacent pieces of property in Houston, Texas. Each owner organization planned to build a high-rise tower on its lot. The organizations signed an agreement that granted each of them an easement in the other's property to "facilitate the development." Cosmopolitan built its residential high-rise first. Later, Class A began moving forward with its plan for a mixed-use high-rise. Cosmopolitan objected that the proposed tower would "be vastly oversized for its proposed location; situated perilously close to [Cosmopolitan's] building; create extraordinary traffic hazards; impede fire protection and other emergency vehicles in the area, and substantially interfere with the use and enjoyment of [Cosmopolitan's] property." [*Cosmopolitan Condominium Owners Association v. Class A Investors Post Oak, LP*, 2017 WL 1520448 (Tex.App.—Houston 2017)] (See *Ownership Interests*.)

1. On what basis can Class A proceed with its plan? Explain, using the IDDR approach.
2. On what ethical ground might Cosmopolitan continue to oppose its neighbor's project? Discuss.

Critical Thinking and Writing Assignments

35–10. Time-Limited Group Assignment—Adverse Possession. The Wallen family owned a cabin on Lummi Island in the state of Washington. A driveway ran from the cabin across their property to South Nugent Road. Floyd Massey bought the adjacent lot and built a cabin on it in 1985. To gain access to his property, Massey used a bulldozer to extend the driveway, without the Wallens' permission but also without their objection. In 2010, the Wallens sold their property to Wright Fish Company. Massey continued to use and maintain the driveway without permission or objection. In 2016, Massey sold his property to Robert Drake. Drake and his employees continued to use and maintain the driveway without permission or objection, although Drake knew it was located largely on Wright's property. In 2018, Wright sold its lot to Robert Smersh. The next year, Smersh told Drake to stop using the driveway. Drake filed a suit against Smersh, claiming an easement by prescription (which is created by meeting the same requirements as adverse possession). (See *Transfer of Ownership*.)

1. The first group will decide whether Drake's use of the driveway meets all of the requirements for adverse possession (easement by prescription).
2. The second group will determine how the court should rule in this case and why. Does it matter that Drake knew the driveway was located largely on Wright's (and then Smersh's) property? Should it matter?
3. The third group will evaluate the underlying policy and fairness of adverse possession laws. Should the law reward persons who take possession of someone else's land for their own use? Does it make sense to punish owners who allow someone else to use their land without complaint?
4. The fourth team will consider how the laws governing adverse possession (easement by prescription) vary from state to state. To acquire title through adverse possession, a person might be required to possess the property for five years in one state, for instance, and for twenty years in another. Are there any legitimate reasons for such regional differences? Would it be better if all states had the same requirements? Explain your answers.

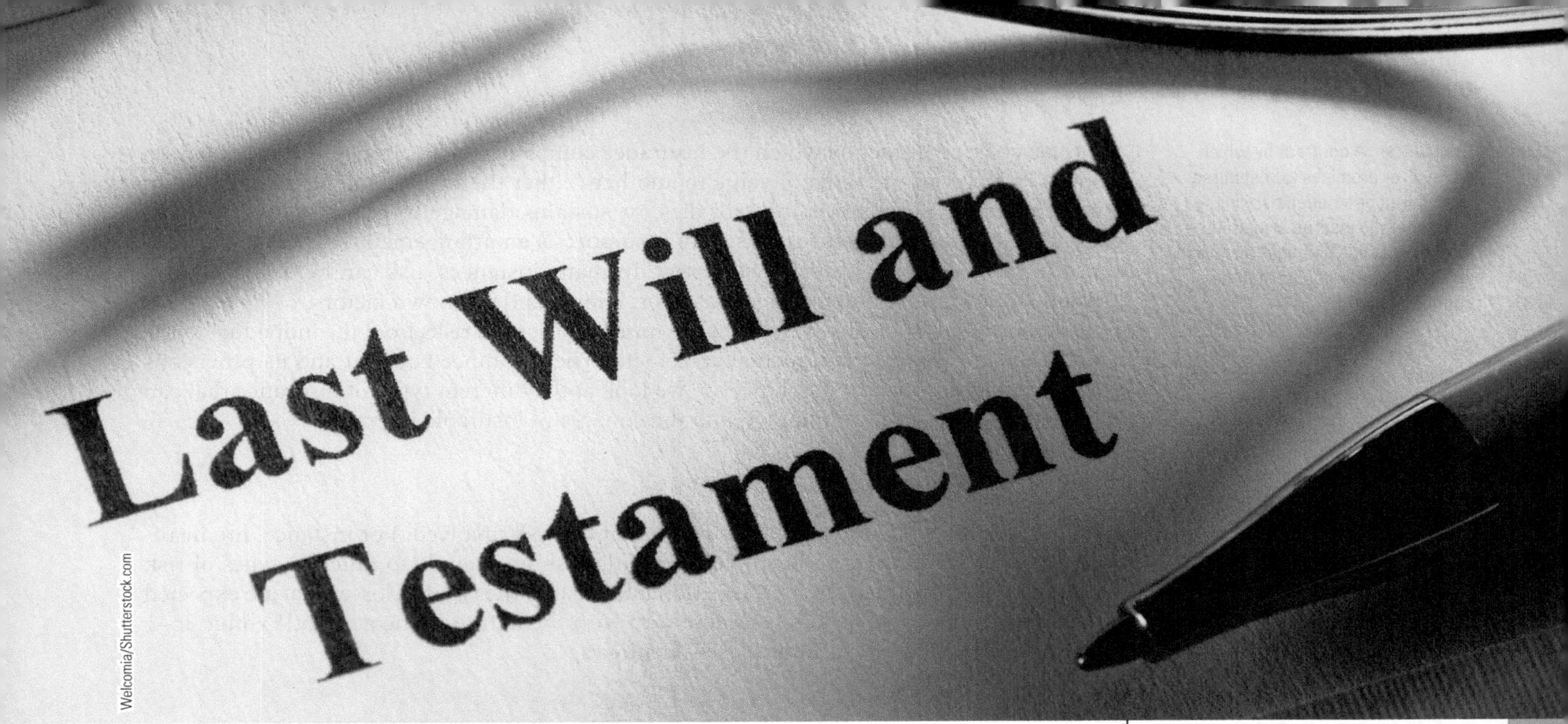

Welcomia/Shutterstock.com

36

Insurance, Wills, and Trusts

Most individuals insure their real and personal property (as well as their lives). As Calvin Coolidge asserted in the chapter-opening quotation, insurance is "all common sense"—by insuring our property, we protect ourselves against damage and loss. In the first part of this chapter, we focus on insurance, which is a foremost concern of all property owners.

"Insurance is part charity and part business, but all common sense."

Calvin Coolidge
1872–1933
(Thirtieth president of the United States, 1923–1929)

In the remainder of the chapter, we examine how property is transferred on the death of its owner. Certainly, the laws governing such transfers are a necessary corollary to the concept of private ownership of property. Our laws require that on death, title to the property of the decedent (the one who has died) must be delivered in full somewhere. This can be done through wills, trusts, or state laws prescribing distribution of property among heirs or next of kin.

In today's world, a person's property may include digital assets and social media. We discuss this aspect of estate planning later in the chapter.

36–1 Insurance

Many precautions may be taken to protect against the hazards of life. For instance, an individual may wear a seat belt to protect against injuries from automobile accidents and install smoke detectors to guard against injury from fire. Of course, no one can predict whether an accident or a fire will ever occur, but individuals and businesses must establish plans to protect their personal and financial interests should some event threaten to undermine their security.

Focus Questions

The four Focus Questions *below are designed to help improve your understanding. After reading this chapter, you should be able to answer the following questions:*

1. What is an insurable interest? When must an insurable interest exist?
2. What are the basic requirements for executing a will?
3. What is the difference between a *per stirpes* distribution and a *per capita* distribution of an estate to the grandchildren of the deceased?
4. What are the four essential elements of a trust?

Insurance A contract by which the insurer promises to reimburse the insured or a beneficiary in the event that the insured is injured, dies, or sustains damage to property as a result of particular, stated contingencies.

Risk Management In the context of insurance, the transfer of certain risks from the insured to the insurance company by contractual agreement.

Risk A prediction concerning potential loss based on known and unknown factors.

Insurance is a contract by which the insurance company (the insurer) promises to pay an amount or to give something of value to another (either the insured or the beneficiary) in the event that the insured is injured, dies, or sustains damage to property as a result of particular, stated contingencies. Basically, insurance is an arrangement for *transferring and allocating risk*—that is, for **risk management**. In many instances, **risk** can be described as a prediction concerning potential loss based on known and unknown factors.

Risk management normally involves the transfer of certain risks from the individual to the insurance company by a contractual agreement. The insurance contract and its provisions will be examined shortly. First, however, we look at the different types of insurance that can be obtained, insurance terminology, and the concept of insurable interest.

36–1a Classifications of Insurance

Insurance is classified according to the nature of the risk involved. For instance, fire insurance, casualty insurance, life insurance, and title insurance apply to different types of risk and protect different interests. This is reasonable because the types of losses that are expected and that are foreseeable or unforeseeable vary with the nature of the activity. Exhibit 36–1 presents a list of selected insurance classifications.

Exhibit 36–1 Selected Insurance Classifications

TYPE OF INSURANCE	COVERAGE
Accident	Covers expenses, losses, and suffering incurred by the insured because of accidents causing physical injury and any consequent disability; sometimes includes a specified payment to heirs of the insured if death results from an accident.
All-risk	Covers all losses that the insured may incur except those that are specifically excluded. Typical exclusions are war, pollution, earthquakes, and floods.
Automobile	May cover damage to automobiles resulting from specified hazards or occurrences (such as fire, vandalism, theft, or collision); normally provides protection against liability for personal injuries and property damage resulting from the operation of the vehicle.
Casualty	Protects against losses incurred by the insured as a result of being held liable for personal injuries or property damage sustained by others.
Disability	Replaces a portion of the insured's monthly income from employment in the event that illness or injury causes a short- or long-term disability. Benefits typically last a set period of time, such as six months or five years.
Fire	Covers losses incurred by the insured as a result of fire.
Floater	Covers movable property, as long as the property is within the territorial boundaries specified in the contract.
Homeowners'	Protects homeowners against some or all risks of loss to their residences and the residences' contents or liability arising from the use of the property.
Key-person	Protects a business in the event of the death or disability of a key employee.
Liability	Protects against liability imposed on the insured as a result of injuries to the person or property of another.
Life	Covers the death of the policyholder. On the death of the insured, the insurer pays the amount specified in the policy to the insured's beneficiary.
Major medical	Protects the insured against major hospital, medical, or surgical expenses.
Malpractice	Protects professionals (physicians, lawyers, and others) against malpractice claims brought against them by their patients or clients; a form of liability insurance.
Term life	Provides life insurance for a specified period of time (term) with no cash surrender value; usually renewable.

36–1b Insurance Terminology

An insurance contract is called a **policy**, the consideration paid to the insurer is called a **premium**, and the insurance company is sometimes called an **underwriter**. The parties to an insurance policy are the *insurer* (the insurance company) and the *insured* (the person covered by its provisions or the holder of the policy).

Insurance contracts are usually obtained through an *agent,* who typically works for the insurance company, or through a *broker,* who is ordinarily an *independent contractor.* When a broker deals with an applicant for insurance, the broker is, in effect, the applicant's agent and not an agent of the insurance company. In contrast, an insurance agent is an agent of the insurance company, not of the applicant. Thus, the agent owes fiduciary duties to the insurance company, but not to the person who is applying for insurance. As a general rule, the insurance company is bound by the acts of its agents when they act within the scope of the agency relationship.

Policy In insurance law, the contract between the insurer and the insured.

Premium In insurance law, the price paid by the insured for insurance protection for a specified period of time.

Underwriter In insurance law, the insurer, or the one assuming a risk in return for the payment of a premium.

36–1c Insurable Interest

Individuals can insure anything in which they have an **insurable interest**. Without an insurable interest, there is no enforceable insurance contract, and a transaction to purchase insurance coverage would have to be treated as a wager.

Insurable interest An interest that exists when a person benefits from the preservation of the health or life of the insured or the property to be insured.

Life Insurance In regard to life insurance, a person must have a reasonable expectation of benefit from the continued life of another in order to have an insurable interest in that person's life. The insurable interest must exist *at the time the policy is obtained.* The benefit may be pecuniary (monetary), or it may be founded on the relationship between the parties (by blood or affinity).

Focus Question 1

What is an insurable interest? When must an insurable interest exist?

Key-person insurance is a type of life insurance obtained by an organization on the life of a person (such as a talented executive) who is important to that organization. Because the organization expects to experience some financial gain from the continuation of the key person's life or some financial loss from the key person's death, the organization has an insurable interest.

Property Insurance In regard to real and personal property, an insurable interest exists when the insured derives a pecuniary (monetary) benefit from the preservation and continued existence of the property. Put another way, a person has an insurable interest in property when the person would sustain a financial loss from its destruction. For property insurance, the insurable interest must exist at the time the loss occurs but need not exist when the policy is purchased.

The existence of an insurable interest is a primary concern in determining liability under an insurance policy. **Spotlight Case Example 36.1** ABM Industries, Inc., leased office and storage space in the World Trade Center (WTC) in New York City in 2001. ABM also ran the building's heating, ventilation, and air-conditioning systems, and maintained all of the WTC's common areas. At the time, ABM employed more than eight hundred workers at the WTC. Zurich American Insurance Company insured ABM against losses resulting from "business interruption" caused by direct physical loss or damage "to property owned, controlled, used, leased or intended for use" by ABM.

ihsanyildizli/E+/Getty Images

After the World Trade Center was destroyed on September 11, 2001, should the company providing maintenance have been reimbursed by its insurance company for all of its income losses?

After the terrorist attacks on September 11, 2001, ABM filed a claim with Zurich to recover for the loss of all income derived from ABM's WTC operations. Zurich argued that ABM's recovery should be limited to the income lost as a result of the destruction of ABM's office and storage space and supplies. A court, however, ruled that ABM was entitled to compensation for the loss of all of its WTC operations. The court reasoned that the "policy's scope expressly includes real or personal property that the insured 'used,' 'controlled,' or 'intended for use.'" Because ABM's income depended on "the common areas and leased premises in the WTC complex," it had an insurable interest in that property at the time of the loss.[1]

In the following case, the plaintiff sought to retain his insurable interest in a home he no longer owned.

Case 36.1

Breeden v. Buchanan

Court of Appeals of Mississippi, 164 So.3d 1057 (2015).

Facts Donald Breeden and Willie Buchanan were married in Marion County, Mississippi. They lived in a home in Sandy Hook. Nationwide Property & Casualty Insurance Company insured the home under a policy bought by Breeden that named him as the insured. The policy provided that the spouse of the named insured was covered as an insured. After eight years of marriage, Breeden and Buchanan divorced. Breeden transferred his interest in the home to Buchanan as part of the couple's property settlement. Less than a year later, a fire completely destroyed the home. A claim was filed with Nationwide. Nationwide paid Buchanan. Breeden filed a suit in a Mississippi state court against Buchanan and Nationwide, asserting claims for breach of contract and bad faith, and seeking to recover the proceeds under the policy. The court dismissed the suit. Breeden appealed.

satori13/iStock/Getty Images

A year after a couple divorces, fire destroys their house. Who should obtain the insurance proceeds?

Issue Did Breeden's one-time right to the proceeds continue after he transferred his interest in the home to his spouse on their divorce?

Decision No. A state intermediate appellate court affirmed the lower court's dismissal of Breeden's suit. Buchanan, not Breeden, was entitled to the proceeds of the claim filed with Nationwide.

Reason Breeden's claims against Nationwide were based on the insurance policy. The policy provided that the spouse of the named insured who resided at the premises was also covered. At the beginning of the policy period, both Breeden and Buchanan had an insurable interest in the home because they were married and lived together in it. Later, Breeden transferred his interest in the insured property to Buchanan as part of a property settlement agreement on their divorce. This occurred several months before the fire that caused the loss of the property. For this reason, the lower court ruled that Breeden did not have an "insurable interest" in the property at the time of the loss and thus had no right to the proceeds of the policy. Because Breeden had no insurable interest in the property, Nationwide did not breach the insurance contract or act in bad faith by failing to pay Breeden the insurance proceeds. Based on these circumstances, "there was simply nothing further that Nationwide owed under the insurance policy."

Critical Thinking

- **Economic** *Why is an insurable interest required for the enforcement of an insurance contract?*

36–1d The Insurance Contract

An insurance contract is governed by the general principles of contract law, although the insurance industry is heavily regulated by the states.[2] Customarily, a party offers to purchase insurance by submitting an application to the insurance company. The company can either accept or reject the offer. For the contract to be binding, consideration (in the form of a premium) must be given, and the parties forming the contract must have the required contractual capacity to do so.

1. *Zurich American Insurance Co. v. ABM Industries, Inc.*, 397 F.3d 158 (2d Cir. 2005).
2. The states were given authority to regulate the insurance industry by the McCarran-Ferguson Act of 1945, 15 U.S.C. Sections 1011–1015.

Application The filled-in application form for insurance is usually attached to the policy and made a part of the insurance contract. The person applying for insurance normally is bound by any false statements that appear in the application (subject to certain exceptions). Because the insurance company evaluates the risk factors based on the information included in the insurance application, misstatements or misrepresentations can void a policy. This is particularly true if the insurance company can show that it would not have extended insurance if it had known the true facts.

Know This
The federal government has the power to regulate the insurance industry under the commerce clause of the U.S. Constitution. Instead of exercising this power itself, Congress allows the states to regulate insurance.

Effective Date The effective date of an insurance contract—the date on which the insurance coverage begins—is important. In some situations, the insurance applicant is not protected until a formal written policy is issued. In other situations, the applicant is protected between the time the application is received and the time the insurance company either accepts or rejects it. Four facts should be kept in mind:

1. As stated earlier, a broker is an agent of the applicant, not an agent of the insurance company. Therefore, if a person hires a broker to obtain insurance, and the broker fails to procure a policy, the applicant normally is not insured.
2. A person who seeks insurance from an insurance company's agent is usually protected from the moment the application is made, provided—for life insurance—that some form of premium has been paid. Usually, the agent will write a memorandum, or **binder**, indicating that a policy is pending and stating its essential terms.
3. If the parties agree that the policy will be issued and delivered at a later time, the contract is not effective until the policy is issued and delivered. Thus, any loss sustained between the time of application and the delivery of the policy is not covered.
4. Parties may agree that a life insurance policy will be binding at the time the insured pays the first premium, or the policy may be expressly contingent on the applicant's passing a physical examination. If the applicant pays the premium and passes the examination, then the policy coverage is continuously in effect.

Binder A written, temporary insurance policy.

If the applicant pays the premium but dies before having the physical examination, the policy may still be effective. Then, in order to collect, the applicant's estate normally must show that the applicant *would have passed* the examination.

Coinsurance Clauses Often, when taking out fire insurance policies, property owners insure their property for less than full value because most fires do not result in a total loss. To encourage owners to insure their property for an amount as close to full value as possible, fire insurance policies commonly include a coinsurance clause.

Typically, a *coinsurance clause* provides that if an owner insures the property up to a specified percentage—usually 80 percent—of its value, the owner will recover any loss up to the face amount of the policy. If the insurance is for less than the specified percentage, the owner is responsible for a proportionate share of the loss.

Coinsurance applies only in instances of partial loss. The amount of the recovery is calculated by using the following formula:

$$\text{Loss} \times \left(\frac{\text{Amount of Insurance Coverage}}{\text{Coinsurance Percentage} \times \text{Property Value}} \right) = \text{Amount of Recovery}$$

Example 36.2 Madison, who owns property valued at \$200,000, takes out a policy in the amount of \$100,000. If Madison then suffers a loss of \$80,000, her recovery will be \$50,000. Madison will be responsible for (coinsure) the balance of the loss, or \$30,000, which is the amount of loss (\$80,000) minus the amount of recovery (\$50,000).

$$\$80{,}000 \times \left(\frac{\$100{,}000}{0.8 \times \$200{,}000}\right) = \$50{,}000$$

If Madison had taken out a policy in the amount of 80 percent of the value of the property, or $160,000, then according to the same formula, she would have recovered the full amount of the loss.

Incontestability Clause A clause in a policy for life or health insurance stating that after the policy has been in force for a specified length of time (usually two or three years), the insurer cannot contest statements made in the policyholder's application.

Incontestability Clauses Statutes commonly require that a policy for life or health insurance include an **incontestability clause**. Under this clause, after the policy has been in force for a specified length of time—often two or three years—the insurer cannot contest statements made in the application. Once a policy becomes incontestable, the insurer cannot later avoid a claim on the basis of, for instance, fraud on the part of the insured, unless the clause provides an exception for that circumstance.

Some important provisions and clauses that are frequently included in insurance contracts are described in Exhibit 36–2.

Interpreting the Insurance Contract The courts recognize that most people do not have the special training necessary to understand the intricate terminology used in insurance policies. Therefore, when disputes arise, the courts will interpret the words used in an insurance contract according to their ordinary meanings in light of the nature of the coverage involved.

When there is an ambiguity in the policy, the provision generally is interpreted *against the insurance company.* Also, when it is unclear whether an insurance contract actually exists because the written policy has not been delivered, the uncertainty normally is resolved against the insurance company. The court presumes that the policy is in effect unless the company can show otherwise. Similarly, an insurer must make sure that the insured is adequately notified of any change in coverage under an existing policy.

Disputes over insurance often focus on the application of exclusions in the policy. **Case Example 36.3** Kevon Taylor walked into Cole's Place, a Louisville, Kentucky, nightclub, and began shooting. Six of the patrons injured in this attack sued Cole's Place for negligence. The nightclub filed a claim with its insurer, United Specialty Insurance Company (USIC), to provide a defense against the lawsuits. USIC refused, based in part on an exclusion in Cole's Place's liability policy stating that coverage did not apply to "bodily injury . . . arising out of or resulting from [any] assault or battery."

Exhibit 36–2 Insurance Contract Provisions and Clauses

TYPE OF CLAUSE	DESCRIPTION
Antilapse clause	An antilapse clause provides that the policy will not automatically lapse if no payment is made on the date due. Ordinarily, under such a provision, the insured has a *grace period* of thirty or thirty-one days within which to pay an overdue premium before the policy is canceled.
Appraisal clause	Insurance policies frequently provide that if the parties cannot agree on the amount of a loss covered under the policy or the value of the property lost, an appraisal, or estimate, by an impartial and qualified third party can be demanded.
Arbitration clause	Many insurance policies include clauses that call for arbitration of any disputes that arise between the insurer and the insured concerning the settlement of claims.
Incontestability clause	An incontestability clause provides that after a policy has been in force for a specified length of time—usually two or three years—the insurer cannot contest statements made in the application.
Multiple insurance policies clause	Many insurance policies include a clause providing that if the insured has multiple insurance policies that cover the same property and the amount of coverage exceeds the loss, the loss will be shared proportionately by the insurance companies.

During the litigation of the dispute, USIC argued that the terms *assault* and *battery* in the policy should be given their ordinary meaning. Cole's Place countered that the terms should be given their legal meaning. An appeals court reasoned that, whether in common parlance or under criminal law, what happened at the nightclub was obviously an "assault or battery." Therefore, the language in the policy excluding coverage for such actions was clear and unambiguous, and USIC was not required to defend Cole's Place.[3]

Cancellation The insured can cancel a policy at any time, and the insurer can cancel under certain circumstances. When an insurance company can cancel its insurance contract, the policy or a state statute usually requires that the insurer give advance written notice of the cancellation to the insured. The same requirement applies when only part of a policy is canceled. Any premium paid in advance may be refundable on the policy's cancellation. The insured may also be entitled to a life insurance policy's cash surrender value.

Cristi Lucaci/Shutterstock.com

What exclusions might be in a nightclub's liability policy?

The insurer may cancel an insurance policy for various reasons, depending on the type of insurance. Following are some examples:

1. Automobile insurance can be canceled for nonpayment of premiums or suspension of the insured's driver's license.
2. Property insurance can be canceled for nonpayment of premiums or for other reasons, including the insured's fraud or misrepresentation, gross negligence, or conviction for a crime that increases the risk assumed by the insurer.
3. Life and health policies can be canceled because of false statements made by the insured in the application, but the cancellation must take place before the effective date of an incontestability clause.

An insurer cannot cancel—or refuse to renew—a policy for discriminatory reasons or other reasons that violate public policy. Also, an insurer cannot cancel a policy because the insured has appeared as a witness in a case brought against the company.

Duties and Obligations of the Parties Both parties to an insurance contract are responsible for the obligations they assume under the contract. In addition, both the insured and the insurer have an implied duty to act in good faith.

Duties of the Insured. Good faith requires the party who is applying for insurance to reveal everything necessary for the insurer to evaluate the risk. The applicant must disclose all material facts, including all facts that an insurer would consider in determining whether to charge a higher premium or to refuse to issue a policy altogether. Many insurance companies today require that an applicant give the company permission to access other information, such as private medical records and credit ratings, for the purpose of evaluating the risk.

Once the insurance policy is issued, the insured has three basic duties under the contract:

1. To pay the premiums as stated in the contract.
2. To notify the insurer within a reasonable time if an event occurs that gives rise to a claim.
3. To cooperate with the insurer during any investigation or litigation.

Duties of the Insurer. Once the insurer has accepted the risk, and some event occurs that gives rise to a claim, the insurer has a *duty to investigate* to determine the facts. When a policy provides insurance against third party claims, the insurer is obligated to make reasonable efforts to settle such a claim.

If a settlement cannot be reached, then regardless of the claim's merit, the insurer has a *duty to defend* any suit against the insured. Usually, a policy provides that in this situation the

3. *United Specialty Insurance Company v. Cole's Place, Inc.*, 936 F.3d 386 (6th Cir. 2019).

insured must cooperate in the defense and attend hearings and trials if necessary. An insurer has a duty to provide or pay an attorney to defend its insured when a complaint alleges facts that could, if proved, impose liability on the insured within the policy's coverage.

Spotlight Case Example 36.4 Dentist Robert Woo installed implants for one of his employees, Tina Alberts, whose family raised potbellied pigs. As a joke, while Alberts was anesthetized, Woo installed a set of "flippers" (temporary partial bridges) shaped like boar tusks and took photos. A month later, Woo's staff showed the photos to Alberts at a party. Alberts refused to return to work. She filed a suit against Woo for battery.

Woo's insurance company refused to defend him in the suit, and he ended up paying Alberts $250,000 to settle her claim. Woo then sued the insurance company and won. The court held that the insurance company had a duty to defend Woo under the professional liability provision of his policy because Woo's practical joke took place during a routine dental procedure.[4]

Bad-Faith Actions. Although insurance law generally follows contract law, most states now recognize a "bad-faith" tort action against insurers. Thus, if an insurer in bad faith denies coverage of a claim, the insured may recover in tort in an amount exceeding the policy's coverage limits and may also recover punitive damages. Some courts have held insurers liable for bad-faith refusals to settle claims for reasonable amounts within the policy limits.

Defenses against Payment An insurance company can raise any of the defenses that would be valid in an ordinary action on a contract, as well as some defenses that do not apply in ordinary contract actions.

1. *Fraud or misrepresentation.* If the insurance company can show that the policy was procured by fraud or misrepresentation, it may have a valid defense for not paying on a claim. (The insurance company may also have the right to disaffirm or rescind the insurance contract.)
2. *Lack of an insurable interest.* An absolute defense exists if the insurer can show that the insured lacked an insurable interest—thus rendering the policy void from the beginning.
3. *Illegal actions of the insured.* Improper actions, such as those that are against public policy or that are otherwise illegal, can also give the insurance company a defense against the payment of a claim or allow it to rescind the contract.

Case Example 36.5 Charles Pendleton, an antique vehicle collector, bought a 1956 Mercedes-Benz and insured it with Foremost Insurance Company. Two weeks later, Pendleton filed a claim saying that the car had been destroyed in a collision with a Ford truck on an icy road. Foremost refused to pay the claim because it believed that Pendleton was lying about how the car was destroyed. Foremost sued, seeking a court declaration releasing it from liability.

At trial, Foremost provided enough evidence to show that Pendleton had towed the antique, inoperative Mercedes onto an icy road and then pushed it into a tree using the truck. A jury found that Pendleton had intentionally destroyed the Mercedes and issued a verdict in favor of Foremost. Pendleton appealed, but the reviewing court affirmed the jury's verdict. The insurance company did not have to pay for the damage to the Mercedes.[5]

Charlie Edward/Shutterstock.com

Is an insurer of an antique car liable for damages when the insured lies about how the damage occurred? Why or why not?

An insurance company can be prevented, or estopped, from asserting some defenses that are usually available. For instance, an insurance company normally cannot escape payment on the death of an insured on the ground

4. *Woo v. Fireman's Fund Insurance Co.*, 161 Wash.2d 43, 164 P.3d 454 (2007).
5. *Foremost Insurance Co. v. Charles Pendleton*, 675 Fed.Appx. 457 (5th Cir. 2017).

that the person's age was stated incorrectly on the application. Also, incontestability clauses prevent the insurer from asserting certain defenses.

36–2 Wills

Not only do the owners of property want to protect it during their lifetime through insurance coverage, but they typically also wish to transfer it to their loved ones at the time of their death. Often, they accomplish this by making wills. A **will** carries out the maker's final wishes regarding property distribution after death. It is a formal instrument that must follow exactly the requirements of state law to be effective. A will is referred to as a *testamentary disposition* of property, and one who dies after having made a valid will is said to have died **testate**.

Will An instrument made by a testator directing what is to be done with the testator's property after death.

Testate Having left a will at death.

A will can serve other purposes besides the distribution of property. It can appoint a guardian for minor children or incapacitated adults. It can also appoint a personal representative to settle the affairs of the deceased. Exhibit 36–3 presents excerpts from the

Exhibit 36–3 Excerpts from Michael Jackson's Will

LAST WILL OF MICHAEL JOSEPH JACKSON	
I, MICHAEL JOSEPH JACKSON, a resident of the State of California, declare this to be my last Will, and do hereby revoke all former wills and codicils made by me.	
I	I declare that I am not married. My marriage to DEBORAH JEAN ROWE JACKSON has been dissolved. I have three children now living, PRINCE MICHAEL JACKSON, JR., PARIS MICHAEL KATHERINE JACKSON and PRINCE MICHAEL JOSEPH JACKSON, II. I have no other children, living or deceased.
II	It is my intention by this Will to dispose of all property which I am entitled to dispose of by will. I specifically refrain from exercising all powers of appointment that I may possess at the time of my death.
III	I give my entire estate to the Trustee or Trustees then acting under that certain Amended and Restated Declaration of Trust executed on March 22, 2002 by me as Trustee and Trustor which is called the MICHAEL JACKSON FAMILY TRUST, giving effect to any amendments thereto made prior to my death. All such assets shall be held, managed and distributed as a part of said Trust according to its terms and not as a separate testamentary trust. If for any reason this gift is not operative or is invalid, or if the aforesaid Trust fails or has been revoked, I give my residuary estate to the Trustee or Trustees named to act in the MICHAEL JACKSON FAMILY TRUST, as Amended and Restated on March 22, 2002, and I direct said Trustee or Trustees to divide, administer, hold and distribute the trust estate pursuant to the provisions of said Trust * * * . * * * *
IV	I direct that all federal estate taxes and state inheritance or succession taxes payable upon or resulting from or by reason of my death (herein "Death Taxes") attributable to property which is part of the trust estate of the MICHAEL JACKSON FAMILY TRUST, including property which passes to said trust from my probate estate shall be paid by the Trustee of said trust in accordance with its terms. Death Taxes attributable to property passing outside this Will, other than property constituting the trust estate of the trust mentioned in the preceding sentence, shall be charged against the taker of said property. * * *
VIII	If any of my children are minors at the time of my death, I nominate my mother, KATHERINE JACKSON as guardian of the persons and estates of such minor children. If KATHERINE JACKSON fails to survive me, or is unable or unwilling to act as guardian, I nominate DIANA ROSS as guardian of the persons and estates of such minor children.

will of Michael Jackson, the "King of Pop," who died from cardiac arrest at the age of fifty. Jackson held a substantial amount of tangible and intangible property, including the publishing rights to most of the Beatles' music catalogue. The will is a "pour-over" will, meaning that it transfers all of Jackson's property (that is not already held in the name of the trust) into the Michael Jackson Family Trust (trusts are discussed later in this chapter). Jackson's will also appoints his mother, Katherine Jackson, as the guardian of his three minor children.

36–2a Terminology of Wills

Testator One who makes and executes a will.

Executor A person appointed by a testator in a will to administer the testator's estate.

Administrator One who is appointed by a court to administer a person's estate if the decedent died without a valid will or if the executor named in the will cannot serve.

Intestate As a noun, one who has died without having created a valid will. As an adjective, the state of having died without a will.

Intestacy laws State statutes that specify how property will be distributed when a person dies intestate (without a valid will).

Devise A gift of real property by will, or the act of giving real property by will.

Bequest A gift of personal property by will (from the verb *to bequeath*).

Legacy A gift of personal property under a will.

Devisee One designated in a will to receive a gift of real property.

Legatee One designated in a will to receive a gift of personal property.

A person who makes out a will is known as a **testator** (from the Latin *testari*, "to make a will"). The court responsible for administering any legal problems surrounding a will is called a *probate court*.

When a person dies, a personal representative administers the estate and settles all of the decedent's affairs. An **executor** is a personal representative named in the will, whereas an **administrator** is a personal representative appointed by the court for a decedent who dies without a will. The court will also appoint an administrator if the will does not name an executor or if the named person lacks the capacity to serve as an executor.

A person who dies without having created a valid will is said to have died **intestate**. In this situation, state **intestacy laws** (sometimes referred to as *laws of descent*) prescribe the distribution of the property among heirs or next of kin (relatives). If no heirs or kin can be found, title to the property will be transferred to the state.

A gift of real estate by will is generally called a **devise**, and a gift of personal property by will is called a **bequest**, or **legacy**. The recipient of a gift by will is a **devisee** or a **legatee**, depending on whether the gift was a devise or a legacy.

36–2b Types of Gifts

Gifts by will can be specific, general, or residuary. If a decedent's assets are not sufficient to cover all the gifts identified in the will, an abatement is necessary.

Specific and General Devises A *specific* devise or bequest (legacy) describes particular property (such as "Eastwood Estate" or "my gold pocket watch") that can be distinguished from all the rest of the testator's property.

A *general* devise or bequest (legacy) does not single out any particular item of property to be transferred by will. For instance, "I devise all my lands" is a general devise. A general bequest may specify the property's value in monetary terms (such as "two diamonds worth $10,000") or simply state a dollar amount (such as "$30,000 to my nephew, Carleton").

Residuary Clause Sometimes, a will provides that any assets remaining after the estate's debts have been paid and specific gifts have been made are to be distributed in a specific way through a *residuary clause*. Residuary clauses are often used when the exact amount to be distributed cannot be determined until all of the other gifts and payouts have been made. If the testator has not indicated what party or parties should receive the residuary of the estate, the residuary passes according to state laws of intestacy.

Abatement If the assets of an estate are insufficient to pay in full all general bequests provided for in the will, an *abatement* takes place. In an abatement, the legatees receive reduced benefits. **Example 36.6** Julie's will leaves $15,000 each to her children, Tamara and Stan. On Julie's death, only $10,000 is available to honor these bequests. By abatement, each child will receive $5,000. ■ If bequests are more complicated, abatement may be more complex. The testator's intent, as expressed in the will, controls.

36–2c Requirements for a Valid Will

A will must comply with statutory formalities designed to ensure that the testator understood the actions taken at the time the will was made. These formalities are intended to help prevent fraud. Unless they are followed, the will is declared void, and the decedent's property is distributed according to the laws of intestacy of that state, as discussed later in this chapter.

Although the required formalities vary among jurisdictions, most states have certain basic requirements for executing a will. The National Conference of Commissioners on Uniform State Laws has issued the Uniform Probate Code (UPC) to govern various aspects of wills, inheritance, and estates. Almost half of the states have enacted some part of the UPC and incorporated it into their own probate codes.

For a valid will, most states require proof of (1) the testator's capacity, (2) testamentary intent, (3) a written document, (4) the testator's signature, and (5) the signatures of persons who witnessed the testator's signing of the will.

monkeybusinessimages/iStock/Getty Images

If this couple leaves a sum of money to each of their children, but there are not enough assets to pay the amounts specified in the will, what happens?

Focus Question 2

What are the basic requirements for executing a will?

Testamentary Capacity and Intent To have testamentary capacity, a testator must be of legal age and sound mind *at the time the will is made.* The minimum legal age for executing a will in most states and under the UPC is eighteen years [UPC 2–501]. Thus, the will of a twenty-one-year-old decedent written when the person was sixteen is invalid if, under state law, the legal age for executing a will is eighteen.

The concept of "being of sound mind" refers to the testator's ability to formulate and to comprehend a personal plan for the disposition of property. Persons who have been declared incompetent in a legal proceeding do not meet the sound mind requirement.

Related to the requirement of capacity is the concept of intent. A valid will is one that represents the maker's intention to transfer and distribute property in a certain manner. Generally, a testator must:

1. Know the nature of the act (of making a will).
2. Comprehend and remember the "natural objects of his or her bounty"—that is, the people to whom the testator would naturally leave the estate (such as family members and friends).
3. Know the nature and extent of the property involved.
4. Understand the distribution of assets called for by the will.

Undue Influence. When it can be shown that the decedent's plan of distribution was the result of fraud or of undue influence, the will is declared invalid. A court may sometimes infer undue influence when the named beneficiary was in a position to influence the making of the will. If the testator ignored blood relatives and named as a beneficiary a nonrelative who was in constant close contact with the testator, for instance, a court might infer undue influence.

Case Example 36.7 Laura and Marvin Farmer had four children—Gary, Rita, Roger, and Sharon. The year that Marvin died, Laura underwent triple bypass surgery and moved in with Sharon, who lived nearby.

Sharon took control of most of Laura's daily life. She refused to allow her brothers and sister to visit their mother. She convinced Laura that they stole from her and wanted to put her in a nursing home. Neither of these beliefs was true, but they affected Laura's decision making. Laura revoked her will—which named all four of her children as beneficiaries—and executed a new will leaving most of her estate to Sharon. After Laura died, Sharon offered the new will for probate. Her siblings contested the will. Sharon argued that it was the product of Laura's "free and independent judgment." The court dismissed the siblings' claim and affirmed the will. Gary, Rita, and Roger appealed.

A state intermediate appellate court vacated the lower court's decision and remanded the case. Sharon had not presented "clear and convincing evidence" that Laura had exercised "free and independent judgment" in making the second will. Thus, the will was not valid, because Laura's intent was in doubt. It was possible that Sharon had exercised undue influence over Laura.[6]

Disinheritance. Although a testator must be able to remember the persons who would naturally be heirs to the estate, there is no requirement that testators give their estates to the natural heirs. A testator may decide to disinherit, or leave nothing to, an individual for various reasons. Most states have laws that attempt to prevent accidental disinheritance, however. There are also laws that protect minor children from loss of the family residence. Therefore, the testator's intent to disinherit needs to be clear.

Spotlight Case Example 36.8 In 1975, William Melton executed a will that, among other things, stated that his daughter, Vicki Palm, was to receive nothing. In 1979, he added a handwritten note to the will, saying that his friend Alberta Kelleher was to receive a small portion of his estate.

In 1995, Melton sent a signed, handwritten letter to Kelleher. The letter said that Melton wanted to put "something in writing" leaving Kelleher his "entire estate." Melton also said, "I *do not* want my brother Larry J. Melton or Vicki Palm or any of my other relatives to have one penny of my estate."

stockcreations/Shutterstock.com

Can a father disinherit his daughter?

When Melton died in 2008, Kelleher had already passed away, and Melton's daughter, Vicki Palm, was his only natural heir. The state of Nevada argued that it should receive everything because Palm had been disinherited. Nevertheless, the trial court applied the state's intestacy laws and distributed the entire estate to Palm. The state appealed. The Nevada Supreme Court reversed the judgment of the lower court. It held that the disinheritance clause was clear and enforceable and that Melton's estate should therefore go to the state of Nevada.[7]

One method of disinheritance is to include an *in terrorem* clause in a will to provide that anyone who challenges the admission of the will to probate will be disinherited and receive nothing under the will.[8] The enforcement of an *in terrorem* clause prompted an appeal in the following case.

6. *In re Estate of Laura Copeland Farmer*, 2017 WL 1830096 (Tenn.App. 2017).
7. *In re Estate of Melton*, 272 P.3d 668 (Nev.Sup.Ct. 2012).
8. *In terrorem* clauses vary from state to state. In some states, they are not enforceable. Under the UPC, an *in terrorem* clause will stand as long as the challenger does not have probable cause for bringing the challenge.

Case 36.2

In the Matter of the Estate of Thorn

Court of Appeals of Kansas, __ Kan.App.2d __, 461 P.3d 84 (2020).

Facts James Thorn experienced health-related issues, resulting in several hospital stays. During this time, he visited Jennifer Stultz, an experienced estate-planning attorney, to draft and execute a will.

Thorn had two daughters, Kimberly Tolley and Jamea Wilson. He expressed concerns to Stultz that Wilson was irresponsible—several creditors had outstanding judgments against her. He wanted her share of the estate held in trust, to be paid at $500 per month, protected from her creditors.

Thorn was also concerned that Wilson might contest his will. After a discussion with Stultz, he agreed to add an *in terrorem* clause that would disinherit anyone who contested the will unless that person had probable cause to do so. The witnesses to Thorn's execution of his will were Scott Lawrence, Stultz's administrative assistant, and Virginia Rowsey, the manager of the facility where Thorn was living.

Less than two months later, Thorn died. Tolley petitioned a Kansas state court to admit Thorn's will to probate. Wilson filed an objection, claiming in part that Thorn lacked testamentary capacity. The court admitted the will to probate and enforced the *in terrorem* clause. Wilson appealed.

Issue Did the court properly admit Thorn's will to probate and enforce the *in terrorem* clause?

Decision Yes. A state intermediate court affirmed the trial court's judgment.

Reason Thorn objected to the trial's court finding of capacity. The appellate court, however, cited the testimony of Stultz, an experienced lawyer, which indicated that Thorn had capacity at the time the will was discussed, drafted, and executed. Lawrence and Rowsey, the witnesses, corroborated Stultz's observations. Because Wilson did not show that the trial court ignored contrary evidence or that its decision was based on "bias, passion, or prejudice," she failed to show that it erred in admitting Thorn's will to probate.

As to probable cause, the court defined the term as "the existence, at the time of the initiation of the proceeding, of evidence which would lead a reasonable person, properly informed and advised, to conclude that there is a substantial likelihood that the contest or attack will be successful." Wilson argued that "all reasonable persons would conclude that the competency of James Thorn . . .was at issue" but was not able to support that position.

Wilson claimed that she had not had enough time to obtain "all the relevant medical information" before entering her objection to admission of the will. She did not explain *why* she could not have obtained the records before entering her objection, however. Furthermore, she had made no attempt to contact the witnesses as to their testimony, which was directly contrary to her claim of lack of capacity. The appellate court reasoned that she had failed "to frame her argument within the probable cause standard" to challenge the will.

The court concluded that "the record contains substantial competent evidence to support the . . . finding Wilson lacked probable cause to object to the admission of the Will to probate." Under the *in terrorem* clause, because she contested Thorn's will without probable cause, Wilson was disinherited.

Critical Thinking

- **Legal Environment** *Besides an* in terrorem *clause, what is an effective method to disinherit a person who would otherwise have a right to a decedent's estate? Discuss.*
- **Ethical** *Was Thorn's addition of an* in terrorem *clause to his will ethical? Explain.*

Writing Requirements Generally, a will must be in writing. The writing itself can be informal as long as it substantially complies with the statutory requirements. In some states, a will can be handwritten in crayon or ink. It can be written on a sheet or scrap of paper, on a paper bag, or on a piece of cloth. A will that is completely in the handwriting of the testator is called a **holographic will** (sometimes referred to as an *olographic will*).

Holographic Will A will written entirely in the testator's handwriting.

A **nuncupative will** is an oral will made before witnesses. Oral wills are not permitted in most states. Where authorized by statute, such wills are generally valid only if made during the last illness of the testator and are therefore sometimes referred to as *deathbed wills*. Normally, only personal property can be transferred by a nuncupative will. Statutes may also permit members of the military to make nuncupative wills when on active duty.

Nuncupative Will An oral will (often called a *deathbed will*) made before witnesses. Usually, such wills are limited to transfers of personal property.

Signature Requirements A fundamental requirement is that the testator's signature must appear on the will, generally at the end. Each jurisdiction dictates by statute and court decision what constitutes a signature. Initials, an X or other mark, and words such as "Mom" have all been upheld as valid when it was shown that the testators *intended* them to be signatures.

Witness Requirements A will usually must be attested (sworn to) by two, and sometimes three, witnesses. The number of witnesses, their qualifications, and the manner in which the witnessing must be done are generally set out in a statute. A witness can be required to be disinterested—that is, not a beneficiary under the will. The UPC, however, allows even interested witnesses to attest to a will [UPC 2–505]. There are no age requirements for witnesses, but they must be mentally competent.

The purpose of the witnesses is to verify that the testator actually executed (signed) the will and had the requisite intent and capacity at the time. A witness does not have to read the contents of the will. Usually, the testator and all witnesses sign in the sight or the presence of one another. The UPC does not require all parties to sign in the presence of one another, however, and deems it sufficient if the testator acknowledges having signed [UPC 2–502]. The UPC also provides an alternative to traditional witnesses—the signature may be acknowledged by the testator before a notary public.

36–2d Revocation of Wills

A testator can revoke a will at any time, either by a physical act or by a subsequent writing. Wills can also be revoked by operation of law. Revocation can be partial or complete, and must follow certain strict formalities.

Sorapop Udomsri/Shutterstock.com

Is tearing up a will a legally recognized method of revoking that will?

Revocation by a Physical Act A testator can revoke a will by *intentionally* burning, tearing, canceling, obliterating, or otherwise destroying it.[9] A testator can also revoke a will by intentionally having someone else destroy it in the testator's presence and at the testator's direction.

In some states, a testator can partially revoke a will by the physical act of crossing out some provisions in the will. Then, those portions that are crossed out are dropped, and the remaining parts of the will are valid. In no circumstances, however, can a provision be crossed out and an additional or substitute provision written in its place. Such altered portions require reexecution (re-signing) and reattestation (rewitnessing).

To revoke a will by physical act, it is necessary to follow the mandates of a state statute exactly. When a state statute prescribes the specific methods for revoking a will by physical act, only those methods can be used to revoke the will.

Codicil A written supplement or modification to a will. A codicil must be executed with the same formalities as a will.

Revocation by a Subsequent Writing A will may be wholly or partially revoked by a **codicil**, a written instrument separate from the will that amends or revokes provisions in the will. A codicil eliminates the necessity of redrafting an entire will merely to add to it or amend it. It can also be used to revoke an entire will. The codicil must be executed with the same formalities required for a will, and it must refer expressly to the will. In effect, it updates a will, because the will is "incorporated by reference" into the codicil.

A new will (second will) can be executed that may or may not revoke the first or a prior will, depending on the language used. To revoke a prior will, the second will must use language specifically revoking other wills, such as "This will hereby revokes all prior wills." If the express *declaration of revocation* is missing, then both wills are read together. If there are any discrepancies between the wills, the second will controls.

Revocation by Operation of Law Revocation by *operation of law* occurs when marriage, divorce or annulment, or the birth of a child takes place after a will has been executed.

Marriage and Divorce. In most states, when a testator marries after executing a will that does not include the new spouse, the spouse can still receive a share of the testator's estate. On the testator's death, the surviving spouse can receive the amount that would have been received had the testator died intestate (intestacy laws will be discussed shortly). The rest of the estate is passed under the will [UPC 2–301, 2–508].

If, however, a new spouse is otherwise provided for in the will (or by transfer of property outside the will), the new spouse will not be given an intestate amount. Also, if the parties had a valid *prenuptial agreement* (a contract made prior to marriage), its provisions dictate what the surviving spouse receives.

Divorce or annulment does not necessarily revoke the entire will. Rather, a divorce or an annulment occurring after a will has been executed revokes those dispositions of property made under the will to the former spouse [UPC 2–508].

9. The destruction cannot be inadvertent. The testator must have the intent to revoke the will.

Children. If a child is born after a will has been executed, that child may be entitled to a portion of the estate. Most state laws allow a child of the deceased to receive some portion of a parent's estate even if no provision is made in the parent's will. This is true *unless it is clear from the will's terms that the testator intended to disinherit the child* (see *Spotlight Case Example 36.8*). Under the UPC, the rule is the same.

36–2e Probate Procedures and Estate Planning

To **probate** a will means to establish its validity and to carry the administration of the estate through a court process. Probate laws vary from state to state. Typically, the procedure depends on the size and complexity of the decedent's estate.

Probate The process of proving and validating a will and settling all matters pertaining to an estate.

People commonly engage in estate planning in an attempt to avoid formal probate procedures and to maximize the value of their estate by reducing taxes and other expenses. Individuals should also consider formulating online asset estate plans, as discussed in this chapter's *Adapting the Law to the Online Environment* feature.

Informal Probate For smaller estates, most state statutes provide for the distribution of assets without formal probate proceedings. Faster and less expensive methods are then used. Property can be transferred by *affidavit* (a written statement taken before a person who has authority to affirm it). Problems or questions can be handled during an administrative hearing. Some state statutes allow car titles, savings and checking accounts, and certain other property to be transferred simply by filling out forms.

Online Asset Estate Planning

Adapting the Law to the Online Environment

The scams are devious and upsetting. Perpetrators will steal information from a deceased person's Facebook profile and then use it to set up a new account. Or they will simply hack into the deceased person's account and take it over. These "zombie" profiles are used to send friend requests that lead to fake advertising sites, used to sell counterfeit products and harvest credit card numbers.

Online Executors

To protect against such scams, Facebook allows the accounts of users who have died to be "memorialized"—making the profile an inactive space for remembrance—or deactivated entirely. However, a Facebook profile is only one part of a person's online existence, which includes not only other social media activities but also e-mails, passwords for money-management and other important accounts, and blogs. As a result, estate planning may now require an online executor to manage the deceased's social media profiles and much more.

Access Versus Privacy

To provide legal guidelines for this process, the Uniform Law Commission developed the Revised Uniform Fiduciary Access to Digital Assets Act (RUFADAA),[a] which has been enacted by most states. RUFADAA gives online executors certain powers to manage digital assets, but it also provides privacy protections for the owners of the assets. Thus, for instance, an online executor does not have authority over e-mails and social media posts unless by express consent. To access other types of digital assets, the online executor may have to petition a probate court and explain why the asset is part of the estate.

To negotiate the many restrictions imposed by the RUFADAA, individuals must be thorough in managing their online estates. Experts suggest creating a document listing usernames and passwords and providing explicit directions telling online executors how to proceed with each account. What should be done with stored photos? Should they be shared with family and friends, or deleted? Should blogs be archived and saved? What about old tweets? These few examples illustrate the scope of an estate planning challenge that will only become more complex as we experience more aspects of our lives online.

a. "Fiduciary Access to Digital Assets Act, Revised." *www.uniformlaws.org*. Uniform Law Commission: visited May 29, 2020, Web.

Critical Thinking

In an earlier version of the RUFADAA, an online executor had the same rights to the deceased person's Internet accounts as did the deceased person when alive. Why do you think these guidelines met strong opposition?

A majority of states also provide for *family settlement agreements,* which are private agreements among the beneficiaries. Once a will is admitted to probate, the family members can agree among themselves on how to distribute the decedent's assets. Although a family settlement agreement speeds the settlement process, a court order is still needed to protect the estate from future creditors and to clear title to the assets involved.

Formal Probate For larger estates, formal probate proceedings normally are undertaken, and the probate court supervises every aspect of the process. Additionally, in some situations—such as when a guardian for minor children must be appointed—more formal probate procedures cannot be avoided.

Formal probate proceedings may take several months or several years to complete, depending on the size and complexity of the estate and whether the will is contested. As a result, a sizable portion of the decedent's assets (as much as 10 percent) may go toward payment of court costs and fees charged by attorneys and personal representatives.

Will Substitutes Various instruments, such as living trusts and life insurance plans, that may be used to avoid the formal probate process.

Property Transfers outside the Probate Process Often, people can avoid the cost of probate by employing various **will substitutes**. Examples include *living trusts* (discussed later in this chapter), life insurance policies, and individual retirement accounts (IRAs) with named beneficiaries.

One way to transfer property outside the probate process is to make gifts to children or others while one is still living. Another way is to own property in a joint tenancy. As previously discussed, in a joint tenancy, when one joint tenant dies, the other joint tenant or tenants automatically inherit the deceased tenant's share of the property. This is true even if the deceased tenant has provided otherwise in a will. Not all alternatives to formal probate administration are suitable to every estate, however.

36–2f Intestacy Laws

As mentioned, each state regulates by statute how property will be distributed when a person dies intestate (without a valid will). Intestacy laws attempt to carry out the likely intent and wishes of the decedent. These laws assume that deceased persons would have intended that their natural heirs (spouses, children, grandchildren, or other family members) inherit their property. Therefore, intestacy statutes set out rules and priorities under which these heirs inherit the property. If no heirs exist, the state will assume ownership of the property. The rules of descent vary widely from state to state.

Surviving Spouse and Children Usually, state statutes provide that the estate must be used first to satisfy the debts of the decedent. Then, the remaining assets pass to the surviving spouse and to the children. A surviving spouse usually receives only a share of the estate—one-half if there is also a surviving child and one-third if there are two or more children. Only if no children or grandchildren survive the decedent will a surviving spouse be entitled to the entire estate.

New Africa/Shutterstock.com

When a person dies without a will (intestate), how do states distribute the property of the deceased person?

Example 36.9 Allen dies intestate and is survived by his wife, Beth, and his children, Duane and Tara. Allen's property passes according to intestacy laws. After his outstanding debts are paid, Beth will receive the family home (either in fee simple or as a life estate) and ordinarily a one-third interest in all other property. The remaining real and personal property will pass to Duane and Tara in equal portions. ■

Under most state intestacy laws and under the UPC, in-laws do not share in an estate. Thus, if a child dies before the parents, the child's spouse will not receive an inheritance on the parents' death. For instance, if Duane had died before his father (Allen) in *Example 36.9*, Duane's spouse would not inherit Duane's share of Allen's estate.

When There Is No Surviving Spouse or Child When there is no surviving spouse or child, the order of inheritance is grandchildren, then brothers and sisters, and, in some states, parents of the decedent. These relatives are usually called *lineal descendants.*

If there are no lineal descendants, then *collateral heirs*—nieces, nephews, aunts, and uncles of the decedent—make up the next group to share. If there are no survivors in any of these groups, most statutes provide for the property to be distributed among the next of kin of the collateral heirs.

Stepchildren, Adopted Children, and Illegitimate Children Under intestacy laws, stepchildren are not considered kin. Legally adopted children, however, are recognized as lawful heirs of their adoptive parents (as are children who are in the process of being adopted at the time of the parents' death).

Statutes vary from state to state in regard to the inheritance rights of illegitimate children (children born out of wedlock). In some states, an illegitimate child has the right to inherit only from the mother and her relatives, unless the father's paternity has been established by a legal proceeding. In the majority of states, however, a child born of any union that has the characteristics of a formal marriage relationship (such as unmarried parents who cohabit) is considered to be legitimate.

Under the revised UPC, a child is the child of both natural (biological) parents, regardless of their marital status, as long as each natural parent has openly treated the child as such [UPC 2–114]. Although illegitimate children may have inheritance rights in most states, their rights are not necessarily identical to those of legitimate children.

Focus Question 3

What is the difference between a *per stirpes* distribution and a *per capita* distribution of an estate to the grandchildren of the deceased?

Grandchildren Usually, a decedent's will provides for how the estate will be distributed to descendants of deceased children—that is, to the decedent's grandchildren. If a will does not include such a provision—or if a person dies intestate—the question arises as to what share the grandchildren of the decedent will receive. Each state uses one of two methods of distributing the assets of intestate decedents—*per stirpes* or *per capita.*

Per Stirpes *Distribution.* Under the ***per stirpes***[10] method, within a class or group of distributees (such as grandchildren), the children of a descendant take the share that their deceased parent *would have been* entitled to inherit. Thus, grandchildren with no siblings inherit all of their parent's share, while grandchildren with siblings divide their parent's share.

Example 36.10 Michael, a widower, has two children, Scott and Jonathan. Scott has two children (Becky and Holly), and Jonathan has one child (Paul). Scott and Jonathan die before their father, and then Michael dies. If Michael's estate is distributed *per stirpes,* Becky and Holly each receive one-fourth of the estate (dividing Scott's one-half share). Paul receives one-half of the estate (taking Jonathan's one-half share). ■ Exhibit 36–4 illustrates the *per stirpes* method of distribution.

Per Stirpes A method of distributing an intestate's estate so that each heir in a certain class (such as grandchildren) takes the share to which the heir's deceased ancestor (such as a mother or father) would have been entitled.

Per Capita *Distribution.* An estate may also be distributed on a ***per capita***[11] basis, which means that each person in a class or group takes an equal share of the estate. In *Example 36.10,* if Michael's estate is distributed *per capita,* Becky, Holly, and Paul each receive a one-third share. Exhibit 36–5 illustrates the *per capita* method of distribution.

Per Capita A method of distributing an intestate's estate so that each heir in a certain class (such as grandchildren) receives an equal share.

36–3 Trusts

A **trust** is any arrangement through which property is transferred from one person to a trustee to be administered for the transferor's or another party's benefit. It can also be defined as a right of property held by one party for the benefit of another. A trust can be created for any purpose that is not illegal or against public policy, and it can be express or implied.

Trust An arrangement in which title to property is held by one person (a trustee) for the benefit of another (a beneficiary).

10. *Per stirpes* is a Latin term meaning "by the roots" or "by stock." When used in estate law, it means proportionally divided among beneficiaries according to their deceased ancestor's share.

11. *Per capita* is a Latin term meaning "per person" or "for each head." When used in estate law, it means equally divided among beneficiaries.

Exhibit 36–4 ***Per Stirpes*** **Distribution**

Under this method of distribution, an heir takes the share that his or her deceased parent would have been entitled to inherit had the parent lived. This may mean that a class of distributees—the grandchildren in this example—will not inherit in equal portions. Note that Becky and Holly receive only one-fourth of Michael's estate while Paul inherits one-half.

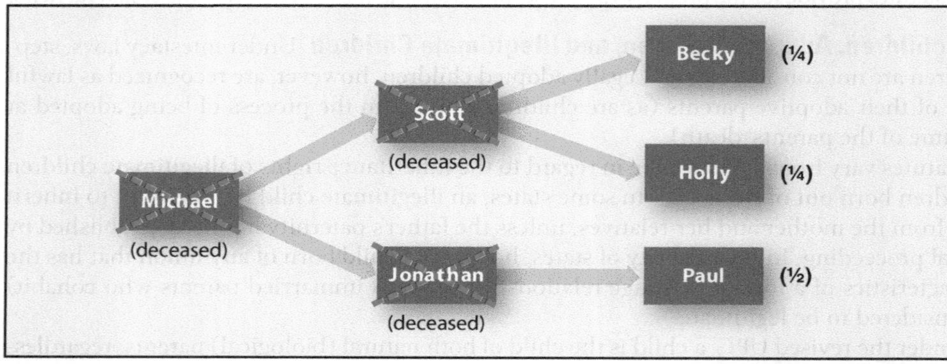

Exhibit 36–5 ***Per Capita*** **Distribution**

Under this method of distribution, all heirs in a certain class—in this example, the grandchildren—inherit equally. Note that Becky and Holly in this situation each inherit one-third, as does Paul.

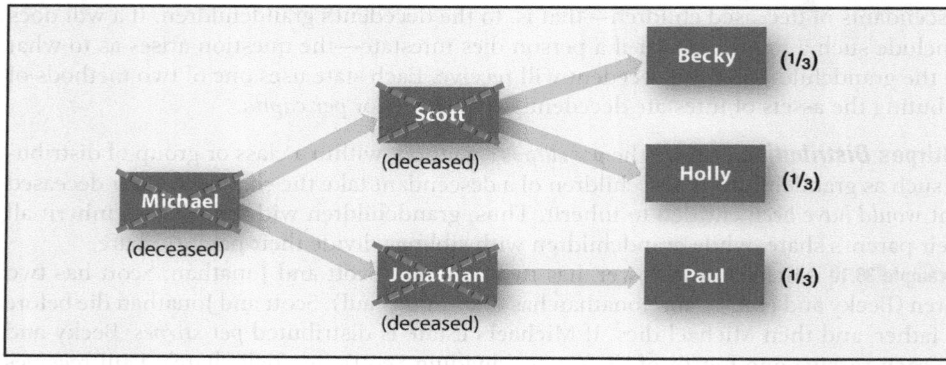

Focus Question 4

What are the four essential elements of a trust?

The essential elements of a trust are as follows:

1. A designated beneficiary.
2. A designated trustee.
3. A fund sufficiently identified to enable title to pass to the trustee.
4. Actual delivery by the *grantor* (or *settlor,* the person creating the trust) to the trustee with the intention of passing title.

36–3a Express Trusts

An express trust is created or declared in explicit terms, usually in writing. There are many types of express trusts, each with its own special characteristics.

Living (*Inter Vivos*) Trust A trust created by the grantor (settlor) and effective during the grantor's lifetime.

Living Trusts A **living (*inter vivos*) trust**—*inter vivos* is Latin for "between or among the living"—is a trust created by a grantor while the grantor is still alive. Living trusts have become a popular estate-planning option because at the grantor's death, assets held in a living trust can pass to the heirs without going through probate.

Note, however, that living trusts do not shelter assets from estate taxes. Furthermore, the grantor may have to pay income taxes on trust earnings, depending on whether the trust is revocable or irrevocable.

Revocable Living Trusts. Living trusts can be revocable or irrevocable. In a *revocable* living trust, which is the most common type, the grantor retains control over the trust property. The grantor deeds the property to the trust but retains the power to amend, alter, or revoke the trust.

Grantors may also serve as trustees or co-trustees and can arrange to receive income earned by the trust assets during their lifetimes. Because grantors are in control of the funds, they are required to pay income taxes on the trust earnings. Unless the trust is revoked, the principal of the trust is transferred to the trust beneficiary or beneficiaries on the grantor's death.

Example 36.11 James Cortez owns and operates a large farm. After his wife dies, James contacts his attorney to create a living trust for the benefit of his three children, Alicia, Emma, and Jayden. The attorney prepares the documents creating the trust. James then executes a deed conveying the farm to the trust and transfers the farm's bank accounts into the name of the trust.

The trust designates James as the trustee and names his son, Jayden, as the *successor trustee,* who will take over the management of the trust when James dies or becomes incapacitated. Each of the children and James (as *income beneficiaries*) will receive income from the trust while James is alive. When James dies, the farm will pass to them without having to go through probate. By holding the property in a revocable living trust, James retains control over the farm during his life (and can make changes to the trust at any time). This trust arrangement is illustrated in Exhibit 36–6.

The following case involved a revocable living trust that included the phrase, "death of each." The resolution of the dispute turned on whether, in the context, "each" meant "either" or "both."

Case 36.3

Dowdy v. Dowdy

District Court of Appeal of Florida, Second District, 41 Fla.L.Weekly D85, 182 So.3d 807 (2016).

Facts Betty and Dennis Dowdy created the Dowdy Family Trust. The property of the trust comprised two parcels of real estate. The trust document identified Betty and Dennis as the settlors, the initial trustees, and the initial beneficiaries. The trust document provided for the revocation or amendment of the trust and for distributions to the settlors. It also appointed one of each settlor's children as co-successor trustees and, following the settlors' deaths, provided for liquidation and distribution to all of their children.

Dennis had three children, and Betty had two—they did not have any children in common. After Dennis died, Betty amended the trust to remove Dennis's children as successor trustees and as beneficiaries. Betty also sold the trust's property.

kodachrome25/E+/Getty Images

If a married couple holds this house in a revocable family trust, can one spouse sell the property after the other spouse dies?

Dennis's son, Michael, who was named as a co-successor trustee in the trust document along with Betty's daughter, Deborah, learned of the sale and filed a petition in a Florida state court against Betty. Michael maintained that Betty's amendment was invalid because it had been executed after Dennis's death. He argued that when Dennis died, the trust became irrevocable, and he succeeded Dennis as co-trustee. The court ordered Betty to deposit the proceeds of the sale with the court pending its construction of the trust. Betty appealed.

Issue When a husband and a wife create a revocable family trust in which both are trustees, does the death of one spouse mean that the surviving spouse can no longer amend the trust terms?

(Continues)

Continued

Decision No. The state intermediate appellate court reversed the order of the lower court. The court found that Michael's petition had no likelihood of success and that he thus was not entitled to the injunction preventing Betty from using the proceeds of the sale of trust property.

Reason Article III of the trust provided that successor trustees (one child of each spouse) would be appointed "in the event of the death of each of the Initial Trustees." Michael argued that the phrase "death of each" meant the death of *either* initial trustee, thereby making him a co-trustee with Betty upon his father's death. The court rejected this argument, holding that the succession of trustees occurred only upon the death of *both* initial trustees. The court reasoned that "the phrase 'death of each' must mean the death of both. Otherwise, the article's direction to liquidate the trust estate and immediately distribute it" to the beneficiaries "or the survivor" would make no sense. "Indeed, upon the death of one settlor it would altogether nullify the survivor's status as beneficiary." Under the appellate court's interpretation of the trust, Betty had been the sole trustee and beneficiary of the trust at all times since her husband's death. As such, she had sole authority and discretion to sell the remaining trust property for her own benefit.

Critical Thinking

- **What If the Facts Were Different?** *Suppose that the Dowdy Family Trust had provided for a specific child to become co-trustee on the death of that child's parent—Deborah to succeed Betty, for example. How would the result have been different?*

Exhibit 36–6 A Revocable Living Trust Arrangement

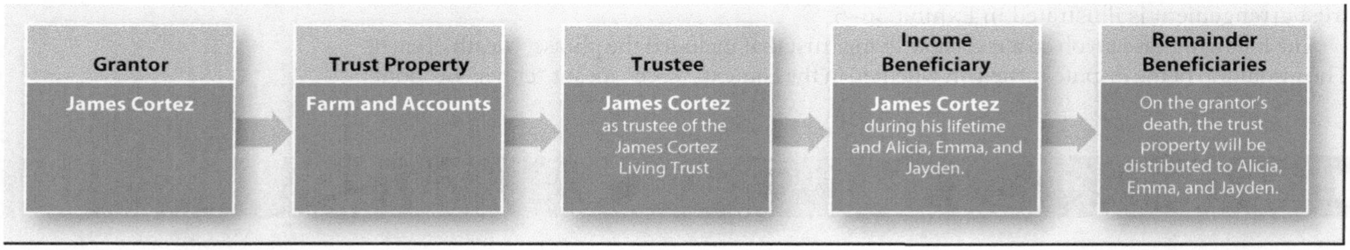

Irrevocable Living Trusts. In an *irrevocable* living trust, the grantor permanently gives up control over the property to the trustee. The grantor executes a trust deed, and legal title to the trust property passes to the named trustee. The trustee has a duty to administer the property as directed by the grantor for the benefit and in the interest of the beneficiaries.

The trustee must preserve the trust property and make it productive. If required by the terms of the trust agreement, the trustee must pay income to the beneficiaries in accordance with the terms of the trust. Because the grantors have, in effect, given over the property for the benefit of the beneficiaries, they are no longer responsible for paying income taxes on the trust earnings.

Testamentary Trust A trust that is created by will and therefore does not take effect until the death of the testator.

Testamentary Trusts A **testamentary trust** is created by will and comes into existence on the grantor's death. Although a testamentary trust has a trustee who maintains legal title to the trust property, the trustee's actions are subject to judicial approval. This trustee can be named in the will or be appointed by the court (if not named in the will). The legal responsibilities of the trustee are the same as in a living trust.

If a court finds that the will setting up a testamentary trust is invalid, then the trust will also be invalid. The property that was supposed to be in the trust will then pass according to intestacy laws, not according to the terms of the trust.

Charitable Trust A trust in which the property held by the trustee must be used for a charitable purpose, such as the advancement of health, education, or religion.

Charitable Trusts A **charitable trust** is an express trust designed for the benefit of a segment of the public or the public in general. It differs from other types of trusts in that the identities of the beneficiaries are uncertain and it can be established to last indefinitely. Usually, to be deemed a charitable trust, a trust must be created for charitable, educational, religious, or scientific purposes.

Spendthrift Trusts A **spendthrift trust** is created to provide for the maintenance of a beneficiary by preventing the beneficiary from being careless with the bestowed funds. Unlike the beneficiaries of other trusts, the beneficiary in a spendthrift trust is not permitted to transfer or assign the right to the trust's principal or future payments from the trust. Essentially, beneficiaries can withdraw only a certain portion of the total amount to which they are entitled at any one time. The majority of states allow spendthrift trust provisions that prohibit creditors from attaching such trusts.

Spendthrift Trust A trust in which only a certain portion of the total amount is given to the beneficiary at any one time; most states prohibit creditors from attaching assets of the trust.

Totten Trusts A **Totten trust**[12] is created when a grantor deposits funds in the grantor's name with instructions that on the grantor's death, whatever is in that account should go to a specific beneficiary. This type of trust is revocable at will until the depositor dies or completes the gift (by delivering the funds to the intended beneficiary, for instance). The beneficiary has no access to the funds until the depositor's death, when the beneficiary obtains property rights to the balance on hand.

Totten Trust A trust created when a grantor deposits funds in the grantor's own name for a specific beneficiary, who will receive the funds on the depositor's death. The trust is revocable at will until the depositor dies or completes the gift.

36–3b Implied Trusts

Sometimes, a trust will be imposed (implied) by law, even in the absence of an express trust. Implied trusts include constructive trusts and resulting trusts.

Constructive Trusts A **constructive trust** is an equitable trust imposed by a court in the interests of fairness and justice. In a constructive trust, the owner of the property is declared to be a trustee for the parties who are, in fairness, actually entitled to the benefits that flow from the property.

Constructive Trust An equitable trust that is imposed in the interests of fairness and justice when someone wrongfully holds legal title to property.

Courts often impose constructive trusts when someone who is in a confidential or fiduciary relationship with another person, such as a guardian to a ward, has breached a duty to that person. A court may also impose a constructive trust when someone wrongfully holds legal title to property—because the property was obtained through fraud or in breach of a legal duty, for instance.

Case Example 36.12 When Yvonne Ryan died, her daughter Ruby Revell—as a beneficiary of a trust set up by Ryan's mother—was entitled to 50 percent of the trust's assets. Revell was unaware that the trust existed. The same could not be said for Bret Lovett, who was working for Revell on an unrelated matter. Without telling her why, Lovett had Revell initial an "Agreement" under which he would receive 85 percent of the value of any real property "left behind" by her mother that he was able to recover for Revell.

Revell later fired Lovett, but he continued to misrepresent himself as Revell's attorney. Without Revell's knowledge, Lovett convinced the trustee to sell property controlled by the trust. He then conspired to place the proceeds from the sale—Revell's inheritance—in an escrow account from which he paid himself 85 percent, about $96,000. Given the level of bad faith involved, a court voided the escrow account and found that Lovett had been holding the proceeds from the sale of the property in a constructive trust for Revell's benefit.[13]

Resulting Trusts A **resulting trust** arises from the conduct of the parties. When circumstances raise an inference that one party holds legal title to the property for the benefit of another, a court may infer a resulting trust.

Resulting Trust An implied trust that arises when one party holds the legal title to another's property only for that other's benefit.

Example 36.13 Gabriela wants to put one acre of land she owns on the market for sale. Because she is going out of the country for two years and will not be able to deed the property

12. This type of trust derives its unusual name from the case *In re Totten*, 179 N.Y. 112, 71 N.E. 748 (1904).
13. *Revell v. Burlison Law Group*, 2020 WL 1227140 (Cal. Ct. App. 2020).

to a buyer during that period, she conveys (transfers) the property to her good friend Oswald. Oswald can then attempt to sell the property while Gabriela is gone.

The transaction in which Gabriela conveyed the property to Oswald was intended to be neither a sale nor a gift. Consequently, Oswald will hold the property in a resulting trust for the benefit of Gabriela. When Gabriela returns, Oswald will be required either to deed the property back to her or, if the property has been sold, to turn over the proceeds (held in trust) to her.

36–3c The Trustee

The *trustee* is the person holding the trust property. Anyone legally capable of holding title to, and dealing in, property can be a trustee. If a trust fails to name a trustee, or if a named trustee cannot or will not serve, the trust does not fail—an appropriate court can appoint a trustee.

Trustee's Duties A trustee must act with honesty, good faith, and prudence in administering the trust and must exercise a high degree of loyalty toward the trust beneficiary. The general standard of care is the degree of care prudent individuals would exercise in their personal affairs.[14] The duty of loyalty requires that the trustee act in the exclusive interest of the beneficiary.

Hero Images/Getty Images
What are some specific duties of a trustee?

A trustee's specific duties include the following:

1. Maintain clear and accurate accounts of the trust's administration.
2. Furnish complete and correct information to the beneficiary.
3. Keep trust assets separate from the trustee's own assets.
4. Pay to an income beneficiary the net income of the trust assets at reasonable intervals.
5. Limit the risk of loss from investments by reasonable diversification, and dispose of assets that do not represent prudent investments. (Prudent investment choices might include federal, state, or municipal bonds and some corporate bonds and stocks.)

Trustee's Powers When creating a trust, a grantor may set forth the trustee's powers and performance. State law governs in the absence of specific terms in the trust, and the states often restrict the trustee's investment of trust funds.

Typically, statutes confine trustees to investments in conservative debt securities such as government, utility, and railroad bonds. Frequently, though, a grantor gives a trustee discretionary investment power. In that circumstance, any statute may be considered only advisory, with the trustee's decisions subject in most states to the prudent person rule.

Of course, a trustee is responsible for carrying out the purposes of the trust. A trustee who fails to comply with the terms of the trust or the controlling statute is personally liable for any loss.

Allocations between Principal and Income Often, a grantor will provide one beneficiary with a life estate and another beneficiary with the remainder interest in a trust. A farmer, for instance, may create a testamentary trust providing that the farm's income be paid to the surviving spouse and that on the surviving spouse's death, the farm be given to their children. In this situation, the surviving spouse has a *life estate* in the farm's income, and the children have a *remainder interest* in the farm (the principal).

When a trust is set up in this manner, questions may arise as to how the receipts and expenses for the farm's management and the trust's administration should be allocated

14. Revised Uniform Principal and Income Act, Section 2(a)(3); *Restatement (Third) of Trusts (Prudent Investor Rule)*, Section 227. This rule is in force in the majority of states by statute and in a small number of states under the common law.

between income and principal. When a trust instrument does not provide instructions, a trustee must refer to applicable state law.

The general rule is that ordinary receipts and expenses are chargeable to the income beneficiary, whereas extraordinary receipts and expenses are allocated to the principal beneficiaries.[15] The receipt of rent from trust realty would be ordinary, as would the expense of paying the property's taxes. The cost of long-term improvements and proceeds from the property's sale would be extraordinary.

36–3d Trust Termination

The terms of a trust should expressly state the event on which the grantor wishes it to terminate—for instance, the beneficiary's or the trustee's death. If the trust instrument does not provide for termination on the beneficiary's death, the beneficiary's death will not end the trust. Similarly, without an express provision, a trust will not terminate on the trustee's death.

Typically, a trust instrument specifies a termination date. For instance, a trust created to educate the grantor's child may provide that the trust ends when the beneficiary reaches the age of twenty-five. If the trust's purpose is fulfilled before that date, a court may order the trust's termination. If no date is specified, a trust will terminate when its purpose has been fulfilled. Of course, if a trust's purpose becomes impossible or illegal, the trust will terminate.

15. Revised Uniform Principal and Income Act, Sections 3, 6, 8, and 13; *Restatement (Second) of Trusts,* Section 233.

Practice and Review

In June 2018, Bernard Ramish set up a $48,000 trust fund through West Plains Credit Union to provide tuition for his nephew, Nathan Covacek, to attend Tri-State Polytechnic Institute. The trust was established under Ramish's control and went into effect that August. In December, Ramish suffered a brain aneurysm that caused frequent, severe headaches but no other symptoms. In August 2019, Ramish developed heat stroke and collapsed on the golf course at La Prima Country Club.

After recuperating at the clubhouse, Ramish quickly wrote his will on the back of a wine list. It stated, "My last will and testament: Upon my death, I give all of my personal property to my friend Bernard Eshom and my home to Lizzie Johansen." He signed the will at the bottom in the presence of five men in the La Prima clubhouse, and all five men signed as witnesses.

A week later, Ramish suffered a second aneurysm and died in his sleep. He was survived by his mother (Dorris Ramish), his nephew (Nathan Covacek), his son-in-law (Bruce Lupin), and his granddaughter (Tori Lupin). Using the information presented in the chapter, answer the following questions.

1. Does Ramish's testament on the back of the wine list meet the requirements for a valid will?
2. Suppose that after Ramish's first aneurysm in 2018, Covacek contacted an insurance company to obtain a life insurance policy on Ramish's life. Would Covacek have had an insurable interest in his uncle's life? Why or why not?
3. What would the order of inheritance have been if Ramish had died intestate?
4. What will most likely happen to the trust fund established for Covacek on Ramish's death?

Debate This

Any changes to existing, fully witnessed wills should also have to be witnessed.

Key Terms

Chapter Summary: Insurance, Wills, and Trusts

INSURANCE	
Classifications	See Exhibit 36–1 for a list of types of insurance.
Terminology	1. **Policy**—The insurance contract. 2. **Premium**—The consideration paid to the insurer for a policy. 3. **Underwriter**—The insurance company. 4. **Parties**—Include the insurer (the insurance company), the insured (the person covered by insurance), and an agent (a representative of the insurance company) or a broker (ordinarily an independent contractor). Certain types of insurance also include a beneficiary (a person to receive proceeds under the policy) other than the insured.
Insurable Interest	An insurable interest exists whenever an individual or entity benefits from the preservation of the health or life of the insured or the property to be insured. For life insurance, an insurable interest must exist at the time the policy is issued. For property insurance, an insurable interest must exist at the time of the loss.
The Insurance Contract	1. **Laws governing**—The general principles of contract law are applied. The insurance industry is also heavily regulated by the states. 2. **Application**—An insurance applicant is bound by any false statements that appear in the application (subject to certain exceptions), which is part of the insurance contract. Misstatements or misrepresentations may be grounds for voiding the policy. 3. **Effective date**—Coverage on an insurance policy can begin when a *binder* (a written memorandum indicating that a formal policy is pending and stating its essential terms) is written; when the policy is issued and delivered; depending on the terms of the contract, when certain conditions are met (such as payment of the premium). 4. **Provisions and clauses**—See Exhibit 36–2 for specific provisions. Words will be given their ordinary meanings, and any ambiguity in the policy will be interpreted against the insurance company. When the written policy has not been delivered and it is unclear whether an insurance contract actually exists, the uncertainty will be resolved against the insurance company. The court will presume that the policy is in effect unless the company can show otherwise. 5. **Cancellation**—The insured can cancel a policy at any time, and the insurer can cancel under certain circumstances. 6. **Duties and obligations of the parties**— a. Duties of the insured—Once the policy has been issued, the insured must pay the premiums, notify the insurer within a reasonable time if an event gives rise to a claim, and cooperate with the insurer during any investigation or litigation. b. Duties of the insurer—The insurer has a duty to investigate any event that gives rise to a claim and is obligated to make reasonable efforts to settle any third-party claims. The insurer also has a duty to defend any suit against the insured. 7. **Defenses against payment to the insured**—Defenses include misrepresentation or fraud by the applicant, lack of an insurable interest, and the illegal actions of the insured.

WILLS	
Terminology	1. **Testator**—A person who makes out a will. 2. **Executor**—A person named in a will to settle the affairs of a decedent. 3. **Administrator**—A personal representative appointed by the court to settle the affairs of an intestate decedent. 4. **Intestate**—One who dies without a valid will. 5. **Devise**—A gift of real estate by will; may be general or specific. The recipient of a devise is a *devisee.* 6. **Bequest, or legacy**—A gift of personal property by will; may be general or specific. The recipient of a bequest (legacy) is a *legatee.*
Requirements for a Valid Will	1. The testator must have testamentary capacity (be of legal age and sound mind at the time the will is made). 2. Testators must have the necessary intent to transfer and distribute their property. 3. A will must be in writing (except for nuncupative wills). A holographic will is completely in the handwriting of the testator. 4. A will must be signed by the testator. What constitutes a signature varies from jurisdiction to jurisdiction. 5. A nonholographic will (an attested will) must be witnessed in the manner prescribed by state statute.
Revocation of Wills	1. **By physical act of the maker**—Intentionally burning, tearing up, canceling, obliterating, or otherwise destroying a will. 2. **By subsequent writing**— a. Codicil—A formal, separate document to amend or revoke an existing will. b. Second will or new will—A new, properly executed will expressly revoking the existing will. 3. **By operation of law**— a. Marriage—Generally revokes part of a will written before the marriage. b. Divorce or annulment—Revokes dispositions of property made under a will to a former spouse. c. Subsequently born child—Most states allow the child to receive a portion of the estate.
Probate Procedures and Estate Planning	To probate a will means to establish its validity and to carry the administration of the estate through a state court process. Probate procedures may be informal or formal, depending on the size of the estate and other factors, such as whether a guardian for minor children must be appointed.
Intestacy Laws	1. Intestacy laws vary widely from state to state. Usually, the law provides that the surviving spouse and children inherit the property of the decedent (after the decedent's debts are paid). The spouse usually inherits the entire estate if there are no children, one-half of the estate if there is one child, and one-third of the estate if there are two or more children. 2. If there is no surviving spouse or child, then, in order, lineal descendants (grandchildren, brothers and sisters, and—in some states—parents of the decedent) inherit. If there are no lineal descendants, then collateral heirs (nieces, nephews, aunts, and uncles of the decedent) inherit. 3. Each state uses one of two methods to distribute assets of the decedent. Under the *per stirpes* method, within a class or group of distributees (such as grandchildren), the children of a descendant take the share that their deceased parent *would have been* entitled to inherit (see Exhibit 36–4). Under the *per capita* method, each person in a class or group takes an equal share of the estate (see Exhibit 36–5).
TRUSTS	
Definition and Elements	A trust is any arrangement through which property is transferred from one person to a trustee to be administered for the transferor's or another party's benefit. The essential elements of a trust are (1) a designated beneficiary, (2) a designated trustee, (3) a fund sufficiently identified to enable title to pass to the trustee, and (4) actual delivery by the grantor to the trustee with the intention of passing title.
Express Trusts	Express trusts are created by explicit terms, usually in writing, and include the following: 1. **Living** (*inter vivos*) **trust**—A trust created by a grantor during the grantor's lifetime. 2. **Testamentary trust**—A trust that is created by will and comes into existence on the death of the grantor. 3. **Charitable trust**—A trust designed for the benefit of a public group or the public in general. 4. **Spendthrift trust**—A trust created to provide for a beneficiary by allowing the beneficiary to withdraw only a certain amount at any one time. 5. **Totten trust**—A trust created when the grantor deposits funds in the grantor's own name as a trustee for a specific beneficiary.

(Continues)

Implied Trusts	Implied trusts, which are imposed by law in the interests of fairness and justice, include the following: 1. **Constructive trust**—Arises by operation of law when a person wrongfully takes title to property. A court may require the owner to hold the property in trust for those who, in equity, are entitled to the benefits from the trust. 2. **Resulting trust**—Arises from the conduct of the parties when an apparent intention to create a trust is present.
Trustee	A trustee must act with honesty, good faith, and prudence in administering the trust, and must exercise a high degree of loyalty toward the trust beneficiary.
Termination	Typically, a trust instrument specifies a termination date. If no date is specified, a trust will terminate when its purpose has been fulfilled.

Issue Spotters

1. Sheila makes out a will leaving her property in equal thirds to Toby and Uma, her children, and Velda, her niece. Two years later, Sheila is adjudged mentally incompetent, and that same year, she dies. Can Toby and Uma have Sheila's will revoked on the ground that she did not have the capacity to make a will? Why or why not? (See *Wills*.)

2. When Ralph dies, he has not made a will and is survived by many relatives—a spouse, children, adopted children, sisters, brothers, uncles, aunts, cousins, nephews, and nieces. What determines who inherits what? (See *Wills*.)

—Check your answers to the *Issue Spotters* against the answers provided in Appendix D.

Business Scenarios and Case Problems

36–1. Timing of Insurance Coverage. On October 10, Joleen Vora applied for a $50,000 life insurance policy with Magnum Life Insurance Co. She named her husband, Jay, as the beneficiary. Joleen paid the insurance company the first year's premium on making the application. Two days later, before she had a chance to take the physical examination required by the insurance company and before the policy was issued, Joleen was killed in an automobile accident. Jay submitted a claim to the insurance company for $50,000. Can Jay collect? Explain. (See *Insurance*.)

36–2. Wills and Intestacy Laws. Benjamin is a widower who has two married children, Edward and Patricia. Patricia has two children, Perry and Paul. Edward has no children. Benjamin makes a will leaving his property equally to Edward and Patricia. The will provides that should a child predecease him, the grandchildren are to take *per stirpes*. The will is witnessed by Patricia and by Benjamin's lawyer and is signed by Benjamin in their presence. Benjamin dies, and Patricia has predeceased him. Edward claims the will is invalid. (See *Wills*.)

1. Discuss whether the will is valid.
2. Discuss the distribution of Benjamin's estate if the will is invalid.
3. Discuss the distribution of Benjamin's estate if the will is valid.

36–3. Undue Influence. Louise Kane executed a will that left her entire estate to her grandson. When her grandson died, Louise executed a new will that named her great-grandson as her sole beneficiary and specifically disinherited her son, Tommy. At the time, Tommy's ex-wife was living with Louise. After Louise died, Tommy filed a suit, claiming that her will was the product of undue influence on the part of his ex-wife. Several witnesses testified that Louise had been mentally competent when she executed her will. Does undue influence appear likely based on these facts? Why or why not? (See *Wills*.)

36–4. Insurance Provisions and Clauses. Darling's Rent-a-Car carried property insurance on its cars under a policy issued by Philadelphia Indemnity Insurance Co. The policy listed Darling's as the "insured." Darling's rented a car to Joshuah Farrington. In the rental contract, Farrington agreed to be responsible for any damage to the car and declined the optional insurance. Later, Farrington collided with a moose. Philadelphia paid Darling's for the damage to the car and sought to collect this amount from Farrington. Farrington argued that he was an "insured" under Darling's policy. How should "insured" be interpreted in this case? Why? [*Philadelphia Indemnity Insurance Co. v. Farrington*, 37 A.3d 305 (Me. 2012)] (See *Insurance*.)

36–5. Requirements of a Will. Sherman Hemsley was a well-known actor from the 1970s. Most notably, he played George Jefferson on the television shows *All in the Family* and *The Jeffersons*. He was born to Arsena Chisolm and William Thornton. Thornton was married to another woman, and Hemsley never had a relationship with his father or that side of the family. Hemsley never married and had no children. He lived with Flora Bernal, his business manager. Diagnosed with cancer, Hemsley executed a will naming Bernal the sole beneficiary of his estate. At the signing, Hemsley indicated that he knew he was executing his will and that he had deliberately chosen Bernal, but he did not discuss his relatives or the nature of his property with his attorney or the witnesses. After his death, the Thorntons challenged the will. Was Hemsley of sound mind? Discuss. [*In re Estate of Hemsley*, 460 S.W.3d 629 (Tex.App.—El Paso 2014)] (See *Wills*.)

36–6. Business Case Problem with Sample Answer—Wills. Andrew Walker executed a will giving a certain parcel of real estate in fee simple to his three children from a previous marriage—Mark Walker, Michelle Peters, and Andrea Knox—with a "life use" in the property granted to his current spouse, Nora Walker. A year later, Andrew, who suffered from asbestosis, was discharged from a hospital to spend his last days at home. He told Nora that he wished to execute a new will to change the disposition of the property to devise half of it to her. Nora recorded his wish and took her notes to the office of attorney Frederick Meagher to have the document drafted. Meagher did not see Nora's notes, he did not talk to Walker, no one from his office was present at the signing of the document, and, when Walker signed it, he did not declare that it was his will, as required by state law. Is the document a valid will? Explain. [*In re Estate of Walker,* 124 A.D.3d 970, 2 N.Y.S.3d 628 (3 Dept. 2015)] (See *Wills.*)

—For a sample answer to Problem 36–6, go to Appendix E.

36–7. Defenses against Insurance Payment. American National Property and Casualty Co. issued an insurance policy to Robert Houston, insuring certain residential property and its contents against fire and other hazards. Twenty months later, Houston issued a quitclaim deed to the property to John and Judy Sykes, reserving a life estate for himself. Houston died two years after that, but John continued to renew the American policy in Houston's name. When a fire substantially damaged the property, John filed a claim with the insurer on behalf of Houston, whom John said was out of town and unavailable. On learning that Houston had died seven years earlier, American refused to pay, claiming that it had no liability. Who will suffer the loss under these circumstances? Why? How might this loss have been avoided? Explain. [*American National Property and Casualty Co. v. Sykes,* 2016 WL 390069 (S.D.Miss. E.Div. 2016)] (See *Insurance.*)

36–8. Testamentary Intent. When Larry Neal died, Gary, his brother and his estate's executor, applied to a Texas state court to probate Larry's will. The will provided, "I do give and bequeath to my niece, Valorie Jean (Neal) White, all my personal effects and all my tangible personal property, including automobiles, hangars, aircraft, fly-drive vehicles, patents, companies, and all other things owned by me at the time of my death," including bank accounts, securities, and other "intangibles." Gary interpreted this provision to entitle Valorie to all of Larry's personal and real property. Larry's daughter, Lori, objected, arguing that under the terms of the will, Larry's personal property passed to Valorie and his real property passed by intestacy to her and Larry's sons. Did Larry's will devise his real property to Valorie? Discuss. [*Estate of Neal,* 2018 WL 283780 (Tex.App.—Fort Worth 2018)] (See *Wills.*)

36–9. A Question of Ethics—The IDDR Approach and Bad Faith. Bernd Moving Systems owned a warehouse in Yakima, Washington. American Guarantee & Liability Insurance Co. insured Bernd under a policy that included coverage of "Personal property of others in your care, custody and control." Before storing property in the warehouse, William and Colleen Merriman were told that their goods would be fully insured. Later, a fire destroyed the warehouse and the Merrimans' property. American Guarantee did not inform them of Bernd's coverage, however. Instead, they were advised to file a claim under their homeowner's insurance because there would most likely be no coverage under Bernd's policy. [*Merriman v. American Guarantee & Liability Insurance Co.,* 198 Wash. App. 594, 396 P.3d 351 (Div. 3 2017)] (See *Insurance.*)

1. On what grounds might the Merrimans base a legal action against American Guarantee?
2. Are there sufficient grounds to argue that the insurer acted unethically? Discuss.

Critical Thinking and Writing Assignments

36–10. Time-Limited Group Assignment—Intestacy Laws. Three and a half years after Lauren and Warren Woodward were married, they were informed that Warren had leukemia. At the time, the couple had no children, and physicians told the Woodwards that the leukemia treatment might leave Warren sterile. The couple arranged for Warren's sperm to be collected and placed in a sperm bank for later use.

Two years after Warren died, Lauren gave birth to twin girls who had been conceived through artificial insemination using his sperm. The following year, Lauren applied for Social Security survivor benefits for the two children. Her application was rejected on the ground that she had not established that the twins were the husband's children within the meaning of the Social Security Act. Woodward then filed a paternity action in Massachusetts, and the probate court determined that Warren Woodward was the twins' father. She then filed an action in court to determine the inheritance rights of the twins. (See *Wills.*)

1. The first group will outline how a court should decide the inheritance rights of children conceived from the sperm of a deceased individual and his surviving spouse.
2. The second group will decide if children conceived after a parent's death (by means of artificial insemination or *in vitro* fertilization) still inherit under intestate succession laws, and will explain why or why not.
3. The third group will consider the inheritance rights of a child who was conceived by means of artificial insemination, *in vitro* fertilization, or a surrogate. Should they be different from the rights of a child conceived in the traditional manner? Assuming the biological parent is not part of the child's life, should the child still be able to inherit from the biological parent? Why or why not?

Unit Seven—Task-Based Simulation

StockPhoto.com/proxyminder

Dave graduates from State University with an engineering degree and goes into business as a self-employed computer programmer.

1. **Ownership of Personal Property.** To advertise his services on the Internet, Dave creates and produces a short digital video. Venture Films, Inc., sees the video and hires Dave to program the special effects for a short sequence in a Venture Films movie. Their contract states that all rights to the sequence belong to Venture Films. What belongs to Dave: the digital video, the movie sequence, both, or neither? Explain.
2. **Landlord-Tenant Law.** Dave leases an office in Carl's Riverside Plaza office building for a two-year term. What is Dave's obligation for the rent if he moves out before the end of the term? If Dave dies during the term, who is entitled to possession of the office? What is Dave's obligation for the rent if Carl sells the building to Commercial Investments, Inc., before Dave's lease is up?
3. **Real Property Deeds.** At the end of the lease term, Dave buys the office building from Carl, who gives Dave a warranty deed. Commercial Investments later challenges Dave's ownership of the building and presents its own allegedly valid deed. What will it mean if a court rules that Dave owns the building in fee simple? If Commercial Investments is successful, can Dave recover anything from Carl? Explain.
4. **Insurance.** Dave's programming business expands, and he hires Mary as an employee. Mary becomes invaluable to the business, and Dave obtains a key-person insurance policy on her life. She dies six years later. If the insurance company discovers that Dave understated Mary's age when applying for the policy (which includes an incontestability clause), can the insurer legitimately refuse payment? If Mary had resigned to start her own programming firm one year before she died, could Dave have collected payment under the policy? Why or why not?
5. **Wills and Trusts.** Over time, Dave acquires other commercial property, which eventually becomes the most lucrative part of his business. Dave wants his adult children, Frank and Terry, to get the benefit of this property when he dies. Dave does not think that Frank and Terry can manage the property, however, because they have their own careers and live in other states. How can Dave provide for them to get the benefit of the property under someone else's management? In his will, Dave designates Hal, his attorney, as executor. What does an executor do?

Appendix A

How to Brief Cases and Analyze Case Problems

How to Brief Cases

To fully understand the law with respect to business, you need to be able to read and understand court decisions. To make this task easier, you can use a method of case analysis that is called *briefing*. There is a fairly standard procedure that you can follow when you "brief" any court case. You must first read the case opinion carefully. When you feel you understand the case, you can prepare a brief of it.

Although the format of the brief may vary, typically it will present the essentials of the case under headings such as those listed below.

1. **Citation**. Give the full citation for the case, including the name of the case, the date it was decided, and the court that decided it.
2. **Facts**. Briefly indicate (a) the reasons for the lawsuit; (b) the identity and arguments of the plaintiff(s) and defendant(s), respectively; and (c) the lower court's decision—if appropriate.
3. **Issue**. Concisely phrase, in the form of a question, the essential issue before the court. (If more than one issue is involved, you may have two—or even more—questions here.)
4. **Decision**. Indicate here—with a "yes" or "no," if possible—the court's answer to the question (or questions) in the Issue section above.
5. **Reason**. Summarize as briefly as possible the reasons given by the court for its decision (or decisions) and the case or statutory law relied on by the court in arriving at its decision.

For a case-specific example of what should be included under each of the above headings when briefing a case, see the review of the sample court case presented in the appendix to Chapter 1 of this text.

Analyzing Case Problems

In addition to learning how to brief cases, students of business law and the legal environment also find it helpful to know how to analyze case problems. Part of the study of business law and the legal environment usually involves analyzing case problems, such as those included in this text at the end of each chapter.

For each case problem in this book, we provide the relevant background and facts of the lawsuit and the issue before the court. When you are assigned one of these problems, your job will be to determine how the court should decide the issue, and why. In other words, you will need to engage in legal analysis and reasoning. Here, we offer some suggestions on how to make this task less daunting. We begin by presenting a sample case problem:

> While Janet Lawson, a famous pianist, was shopping in Quality Market, she slipped and fell on a wet floor in one of the aisles. The floor had recently been mopped by one of the store's employees, but there were no signs warning customers that the floor in that area was wet. As a result of the fall, Lawson injured her right arm and was unable to perform piano concerts for the next six months. Had she been able to perform the scheduled concerts, she would have earned approximately $60,000 over that period of time. Lawson sued Quality Market for this amount, plus another $10,000 in medical expenses. She claimed that the store's failure to warn customers of the wet floor constituted negligence and therefore the market was liable for her injuries. Will the court agree with Lawson? Discuss.

Understand the Facts

This may sound obvious, but before you can analyze or apply the relevant law to a specific set of facts, you must clearly understand those facts. In other words, you should read through the case problem carefully—more than once, if necessary—to make sure you understand the identity of the plaintiff(s) and defendant(s) in the case and the progression of events that led to the lawsuit.

In the sample case problem just given, the identity of the parties is fairly obvious. Janet Lawson is the one bringing the suit; therefore, she is the plaintiff. Lawson is bringing the suit against Quality Market, so it is the defendant. Some of the case problems you work on may have multiple plaintiffs or defendants. Often, it is helpful to use abbreviations for the parties. To indicate a reference to a plaintiff, for example, the *pi* symbol—π—is often used, and a defendant is denoted by a *delta*—Δ—a triangle.

The events leading to the lawsuit are also fairly straightforward. Lawson slipped and fell on a wet floor, and she contends that Quality Market should be liable for her injuries because it was negligent in not posting a sign warning customers of the wet floor.

When you are working on case problems, realize that the facts should be accepted as they are given. For instance, in our sample problem, it should be accepted that the floor was wet and that there was no sign. In other words, avoid making conjectures, such as "Maybe the floor wasn't too wet," or "Maybe an employee was getting a sign to put up," or "Maybe someone stole the sign." Questioning the facts as they are presented only adds confusion to your analysis.

Legal Analysis and Reasoning

Once you understand the facts given in the case problem, you can begin to analyze the case. The **IRAC method** is a helpful tool to use in the legal analysis and reasoning process. IRAC is an acronym for **I**ssue, **R**ule, **A**pplication, **C**onclusion. Applying this method to our sample problem would involve the following steps:

1. First, you need to decide what legal **issue** is involved in the case. In our sample case, the basic issue is whether Quality Market's failure to warn customers of the wet floor constituted negligence. Negligence is a *tort*—a civil wrong. In a tort lawsuit, the plaintiff seeks to be compensated for another's wrongful act. A defendant will be deemed negligent if he or she breached a duty of care owed to the plaintiff and the breach of that duty caused the plaintiff to suffer harm.
2. Once you have identified the issue, the next step is to determine what **rule of law** applies to the issue. To make this determination, you will want to carefully review the text discussion relating to the issue involved in the problem. Our sample case problem involves the tort of negligence. The applicable rule of law is the tort law principle that business owners owe a duty to exercise reasonable care to protect their customers (*business invitees*). Reasonable care, in this context, includes either removing—or warning customers of—*foreseeable* risks about which the owner *knew* or *should have known*. Business owners need not warn customers of "open and obvious" risks, however. If a business owner breaches this duty of care (fails to exercise the appropriate degree of care toward customers), and the breach of duty causes a customer to be injured, the business owner will be liable to the customer for the customer's injuries.
3. The next—and usually the most difficult—step in analyzing case problems is the **application** of the relevant rule of law to the specific facts of the case you are studying. In our sample problem, applying the tort law principle just discussed presents few difficulties. An employee of the store had mopped the floor in the aisle where Lawson slipped and fell, but no sign was present indicating that the floor was wet. That a customer might fall on a wet floor is clearly a foreseeable risk. Therefore, the failure to warn customers about the wet floor was a breach of the duty of care owed by the business owner to the store's customers.
4. Once you have completed Step 3 in the IRAC method, you should be ready to draw your **conclusion**. In our sample problem, Quality Market is liable to Lawson for her injuries because the market's breach of its duty of care caused Lawson's injuries.

The fact patterns in the case problems presented in this text are not always as simple as those presented in our sample problem. Often, a case has more than one plaintiff or defendant. A case may also involve more than one issue and have more than one applicable rule of law. Furthermore, in some case problems the facts may indicate that the general rule of law should not apply. Suppose that a store employee told Lawson about the wet floor and advised her not to walk in that aisle, but Lawson decided to walk there anyway. This fact could alter the outcome of the case because the store could then raise the defense of *assumption of risk*. Nonetheless, a careful review of the chapter should always provide you with the knowledge you need to analyze the problem thoroughly and arrive at accurate conclusions.

Appendix B

The Constitution of the United States

One of the primary sources of American law is the U.S. Constitution, which is the supreme law of the land. As such, it is the basis of all law in the United States. A law in violation of the U.S. Constitution, if challenged, will be declared unconstitutional and will not be enforced, no matter what its source.

The U.S. Constitution is available on many websites, including https://www.usa.gov/history.

Appendix C

The Uniform Commercial Code

One of the most important uniform acts is the Uniform Commercial Code (UCC), which was created through the joint efforts of the National Conference of Commissioners on Uniform State Laws (NCCUSL) and the American Law Institute. The UCC was first issued in 1952 and has been adopted in all fifty states (at least in part), the District of Columbia, and the Virgin Islands. The UCC facilitates commerce among the states by providing a uniform, yet flexible, set of rules governing commercial transactions. Because of its importance in the area of commercial law, we cite the UCC frequently in this text.

To view sections of the UCC, see the American Law Institute website at https://www.ali.org/ or the Uniform Law Commission website at http://www.uniformlaws.org/. Articles 1, 2, and 2A are the most pertinent to students of *Business Law Today*.

Appendix D

Answers to the *Issue Spotters*

Chapter 1

1. No. The U.S. Constitution is the supreme law of the land and applies to all jurisdictions. A law in violation of the Constitution (in this question, the First Amendment to the Constitution) will be declared unconstitutional.
2. Yes. Administrative rulemaking starts with the publication of a notice of the rulemaking in the *Federal Register*. Among other details, this notice states where and when the proceedings, such as a public hearing, will be held. Proponents and opponents can offer their comments and concerns regarding the pending rule. After reviewing all the comments from the proceedings, the agency's decision makers consider what was presented and draft the final rule.

Chapter 2

1. Even if commercial speech is neither related to illegal activities nor misleading, it may be restricted if a state has a substantial interest that cannot be achieved by less restrictive means. In this situation, the state's interest in energy conservation is substantial, but it could be achieved by less restrictive means. That would be the utilities' defense against the enforcement of this state law.
2. Yes. The tax would limit the liberty of some persons, such as out-of-state businesses, so it is subject to a review under the equal protection clause. Protecting local businesses from out-of-state competition is not a legitimate government objective. Thus, such a tax would violate the equal protection clause.

Chapter 3

1. When a corporation decides to respond to what it sees as a moral obligation to correct for past discrimination by adjusting pay differences among its employees, an ethical conflict is raised between the firm and its employees and between the firm and its shareholders. This dilemma arises directly out of the effect such a decision has on the firm's profits. If satisfying this obligation increases profitability, then the dilemma is easily resolved in favor of "doing the right thing."
2. Maybe. On the one hand, it is not the company's "fault" when a product is misused. Also, keeping the product on the market is not a violation of the law, and stopping sales would hurt profits. On the other hand, suspending sales could reduce suffering and could prevent negative publicity that might occur if sales continued.

Chapter 4

1. Tom could file a motion for a directed verdict. This motion asks the judge to direct a verdict for Tom on the ground that Sue presented no evidence that would justify granting her relief. The judge grants the motion if there is insufficient evidence to raise an issue of fact.
2. Yes. Submission of the dispute to mediation or nonbinding arbitration is mandatory, but compliance with the decision of the mediator or arbitrator is voluntary.

Chapter 5

1. Probably. To recover on the basis of negligence, the injured party as a plaintiff must show that the truck's owner owed the plaintiff a duty of care, that the owner breached that duty, that the plaintiff was injured, and that the breach caused the injury. In this problem, the owner's actions breached the duty of reasonable care. The billboard falling on the plaintiff was the direct cause of the injury, not the plaintiff's own negligence. Thus, liability turns on whether the plaintiff can connect the breach of duty to the injury. This involves the test of proximate cause—the question of foreseeability. The consequences to the injured party must have been a foreseeable result of the owner's carelessness.
2. The company might defend against this electrician's claim by asserting that the electrician should have known of the risk and, therefore, the company had no duty to warn. According to the problem, the danger is common knowledge in the electrician's field and should have been apparent to this electrician, given his years of training and experience. In other words, the company most likely had no need to warn the electrician of the risk.

   The firm could also raise comparative negligence. Both parties' negligence, if any, could be weighed and the liability distributed proportionately. The defendant could furthermore assert assumption of risk, claiming that the electrician voluntarily entered into a dangerous situation, knowing the risk involved.

Chapter 6

1. Yes. Those who make, sell, or lease goods are liable for the harm or damages caused by those goods to a consumer, user, or bystander. The maker of component parts may also be liable. In this situation, Rim Corporation makes tires that Superior installs on its vehicles before selling them to dealers. Thus, Superior is the manufacturer, and Rim is the maker of component parts. A manufacturer is liable for its failure to exercise due care to any person who sustains an injury proximately caused by a negligently made (defective) product. Superior's failure to inspect and test the tires it installs is a failure to use due care. Thus, Superior is liable to the injured buyer, Uri. Rim Corporation may also be liable.
2. Bensing can assert the defense of preemption. An injured party may not be able to sue the manufacturer of defective products that are subject to comprehensive federal regulatory schemes (such as medical devices and vaccinations). In this situation, it is likely that a court would conclude that the federal regulations pertaining to drug labeling preempt Ohio's common law rules. Therefore, Bensing would not be liable to Rothfus for defective labeling if it complied with federal law.

Chapter 7

1. Yes, Roslyn has committed theft of trade secrets. Lists of suppliers and customers cannot be patented, copyrighted, or trademarked, but the information they contain is protected against appropriation by others as trade secrets. Most likely, Roslyn signed a contract agreeing not to use this information outside her employment by Organic. But even without this contract, Organic could make a convincing case against its ex-employee for a theft of trade secrets.
2. This is patent infringement. A software maker in this situation might best protect its product, save litigation costs, and profit from its patent by the use of a license. In the context of this problem, a license would grant permission to sell a patented item. (A license can be limited to certain purposes and to the licensee only.)

Chapter 8

1. Karl may have committed trademark infringement. Search engines compile their results by looking through websites' key-word fields. A site that appropriates the key words of other sites with more frequent hits will appear in the same search engine results as the more popular sites. But using another's trademark as a key word without the owner's permission normally constitutes trademark infringement. Of course, some uses of another's trademark as a meta tag may be permissible if the use is reasonably necessary and does not suggest that the owner authorized or sponsored the use.
2. Yes. This may be an instance of trademark dilution. Dilution occurs when a trademark is used, without permission, in a way that diminishes the distinctive quality of the mark. Dilution does not require proof that consumers are likely to be confused by the use of the unauthorized mark. The products involved do not have to be similar. Dilution does require, however, that a mark be famous when the dilution occurs.

Chapter 9

1. Yes. With respect to the gas station, Dana has obtained goods by false pretenses. She might also be charged with the crimes of larceny and forgery, and most states have special statutes covering illegal use of credit cards.
2. Yes. The Counterfeit Access Device and Computer Fraud and Abuse Act provides that a person who accesses a computer online, without permission, to obtain classified data—such as consumer credit files in a credit agency's database—is subject to criminal prosecution. The crime has two elements: accessing the computer without permission and taking data. It is a felony if done for private financial gain. Penalties include fines and imprisonment for up to twenty years. The victim of the theft can also bring a civil suit against the criminal to obtain damages and other relief.

Chapter 10

1. Under the objective theory of contracts, if a reasonable person would have thought that Joli had accepted Kerin's offer when she signed and returned the letter, then a contract was made, and Joli is obligated to buy the book. This depends, in part, on what was said in the letter and what was said in response. For instance, did the letter contain a valid offer, and did the response constitute a valid acceptance? Under any circumstances, the issue is not whether either party subjectively believed that a contract had been made.
2. No. This contract, although not fully executed, is for an illegal purpose and therefore is void. A void contract gives rise to no legal obligation on the part of any party. A contract that is void is no contract. There is nothing to enforce.

Chapter 11

1. No. Revocation of an offer may be implied by conduct inconsistent with the offer. When Fidelity Corporation rehired Monica, and Ron learned of the hiring, the offer was revoked. His acceptance was too late.
2. First, it might be noted that the Uniform Electronic Transactions Act (UETA) does not apply unless the parties to a contract agree to use e-commerce in their transaction. In this deal, of course, the parties used e-commerce. The UETA removes barriers to e-commerce by giving the same legal effect to e-records and e-signatures as to paper documents and signatures. The UETA itself does not include rules for e-commerce transactions, however.

Chapter 12

1. Yes. Under the doctrine of promissory estoppel, the promisee is entitled to payment of $5,000 from the promisor on graduation. There was a promise on which the promisee relied, the reliance was substantial and definite (the promisee went to college for the full term, incurring considerable expense, and will likely graduate), and it would only be fair to enforce the promise.
2. No. Generally, an exculpatory clause (a clause attempting to absolve a party of negligence or other wrongs) is not enforced if the party seeking its enforcement is involved in a business that is important to the public as a matter of practical necessity, such as an airline. Because of the essential nature of such services, the party would have an advantage in bargaining strength and could insist that anyone contracting for its services agree not to hold it liable.

Chapter 13

1. Yes. Rescission may be granted on the basis of fraudulent misrepresentation. The elements of fraudulent misrepresentation include intent to deceive, or *scienter*. *Scienter* exists if a party makes a statement recklessly, without regard to whether it is true or false, or if a party says or implies that a statement is made on some basis such as personal knowledge or personal investigation when it is not.
2. The court might conclude that under the doctrine of promissory estoppel, the employer is estopped from claiming the lack of a written contract as a defense. The oral contract may be enforced because the employer made a promise on which the employee justifiably relied in moving to New York, the reliance was foreseeable, and injustice can be avoided only by enforcing the promise. If the court strictly enforces the Statute of Frauds, however, the employee may be without a remedy.

Chapter 14

1. Yes. Generally, if a contract clearly states that a right is not assignable, no assignment will be effective, but there are exceptions. Assignment of the right to receive monetary payment cannot be prohibited.
2. This is a novation. Novation substitutes a new party for an original party by agreement of all the parties. The requirements are a previous valid obligation, an agreement of all the parties to a new contract, extinguishment of the old obligation, and a new, valid contract. Novation revokes and discharges the previous obligation. Here, C&D delegated its duties under its contract with Ace to Dean, with Ace's consent. Ace's obligation to pay C&D for the execution of those duties is discharged, but its obligation under the new contract to pay Dean for those services will not be discharged until Dean is paid. The novation did, however, discharge C&D's obligation under the contract.

Chapter 15

1. A nonbreaching party is entitled to the benefit of the bargain under the contract. Here, the innocent party is entitled to be put in the position she would have been in if the contract had been fully performed. The measure of the benefit is the cost to complete the work ($500). These are compensatory damages.
2. No. To recover damages that flow from the consequences of a breach but that are caused by circumstances beyond the contract (consequential damages), the breaching party must know, or have reason to know, that special circumstances will cause the nonbreaching party to suffer the additional loss. That was not the situation in this problem.

Chapter 16

1. A shipment of nonconforming goods constitutes an acceptance and a breach, unless the seller reasonably notifies the buyer that the nonconforming shipment does not constitute an acceptance and is offered only as an accommodation. Thus, since there was no notification in this problem, the shipment was both an acceptance and a breach.
2. Yes. In a transaction between merchants, the requirement of a writing is satisfied if one of them sends to the other a signed written confirmation that indicates the terms of the agreement, and the merchant receiving it has reason to know of its contents. If the merchant who receives the confirmation does not object in writing within ten days after receipt, the writing will be enforceable against him or her even though he or she has not signed anything.

Chapter 17

1. Yes. A seller is obligated to deliver goods in conformity with a contract in every detail. This is the perfect tender rule. The exception of the seller's right to cure does not apply here because the seller delivered too little too late to take advantage of this exception.
2. Yes. When anticipatory repudiation occurs, a buyer (or lessee) can resort to any remedy for breach even if the buyer tells the seller (the repudiating party in this problem) that the buyer will wait for the seller's performance.

Chapter 18

1. A statement that "I.O.U." money (or anything else) or an instruction to a bank stating, "I wish you would pay," would render any instrument nonnegotiable. To be negotiable, an instrument must contain an express promise to pay. An I.O.U. is only an acknowledgment of indebtedness. An order stating, "I wish you would pay," is not sufficiently precise.

2. No. When a drawer's employee provides the drawer with the name of a fictitious payee (a payee whom the drawer does not actually intend to have any interest in an instrument), a forgery of the payee's name is effective to pass good title to subsequent transferees.

Chapter 19

1. Under the principle of comity, a U.S court would defer and give effect to foreign laws and judicial decrees that are consistent with U.S. law and public policy.
2. The practice described in this problem is known as dumping, which is regarded as an unfair international trade practice. Dumping is the sale of imported goods at "less than fair value." Based on the price of those goods in the exporting country, an extra tariff—known as an antidumping duty—can be imposed on the imports.

Chapter 20

1. Yes, to both questions. In a civil suit, a drawer (Lyn) is liable to a payee (Jan) or to a holder of a check that is not honored. If intent to defraud can be proved, the drawer (Lyn) can also be subject to criminal prosecution for writing a bad check.
2. The general rule is that the bank must recredit a customer's account when it pays on a forged signature. The bank has no right to recover from a holder who, without knowledge, cashes a check bearing a forged drawer's signature. Thus, the bank in this problem can collect from neither its customer nor the party who cashed the check. The bank's only recourse is to look for the thief.

Chapter 21

1. When collateral consists of consumer goods, and the debtor has paid less than 60 percent of the debt or the purchase price, the creditor has the option of disposing of the collateral in a commercially reasonable manner. This generally requires notice to the debtor of the place, time, and manner of sale. A debtor can waive the right to notice, but only after default. Before the disposal, a debtor can redeem the collateral by tendering performance of all of the obligations secured by the collateral and by paying the creditor's reasonable expenses in retaking and maintaining the collateral.
2. The creditor (Midwest) can place a mechanic's lien on the debtor's property. If the debtor does not pay what is owed, the property can be sold to satisfy the debt. The only requirements are that the lien be filed within a specific time from the time of the work, depending on the state statute, and that notice of the foreclosure and sale be given to the debtor in advance.

Chapter 22

1. No. Besides the claims listed in this problem, the debts that cannot be discharged in bankruptcy include amounts borrowed to pay back taxes, goods obtained by fraud, debts that were not listed in the petition, domestic support obligations, certain cash advances, and others.
2. Yes. A debtor's payment to a creditor made for a preexisting debt, within ninety days (one year in the case of an insider or fraud) of a bankruptcy filing, can be recovered if it gives a creditor more than he or she would have received in the bankruptcy proceedings. A trustee can recover this preference using his or her specific avoidance powers.

Chapter 23

1. No. Nadine, as an agent, is prohibited from taking advantage of the agency relationship to obtain property that the principal (Dimka Corporation) wants to purchase. This is the duty of loyalty that arises with every agency relationship.
2. Yes. A principal has a duty to indemnify (reimburse) an agent for liabilities incurred because of authorized and lawful acts and transactions and for losses suffered because of the principal's failure to perform his or her duties.

Chapter 24

1. Workers' compensation laws establish a procedure for compensating workers who are injured on the job. Instead of suing to collect benefits, an injured worker notifies the employer of the injury and files a claim with the appropriate state agency. The right to recover is normally determined without regard to negligence or fault, but intentionally inflicted injuries are not covered. Unlike the potential for recovery in a lawsuit based on negligence or fault, recovery under a workers' compensation statute is limited to the specific amount designated in the statute for the employee's injury.
2. A closed shop (a company that requires union membership as a condition of employment) is illegal. A union shop (a company that does not require union membership as a condition of employment but requires workers to join the union after a certain time on the job) is illegal in a state with a right-to-work law, which makes it illegal in that state to require union membership for continued employment.

Chapter 25

1. Yes. One type of sexual harassment occurs when a request for sexual favors is a condition of employment and the person making the request is a supervisor or acts with the authority of the employer. A tangible employment action, such as a promise of continued employment, may also lead to the employer's liability for the supervisor's conduct. That the injured employee is a male and the supervisor a female, instead of the other way around, would not affect the outcome. Same-gender harassment is also actionable.

2. Yes, Koko can succeed in a discrimination suit if she can show that she was not hired solely because of her disability. The other elements for a discrimination suit based on a disability are that the plaintiff (1) has a disability and (2) is otherwise qualified for the job. Both of these elements appear to be satisfied in this scenario.

Chapter 26

1. When a business is relatively small and is not diversified, employs relatively few people, has modest profits, and is not likely to expand significantly or require extensive financing in the immediate future, the most appropriate form for doing business may be a sole proprietorship.
2. Yes. Failing to meet a specified sales quota can constitute a breach of a franchise agreement. If the franchisor is acting in good faith, "cause" may also include the death or disability of the franchisee, the insolvency of the franchisee, and a breach of another term of the franchise agreement.

Chapter 27

1. No. A widow (or widower) has no right to take a dead partner's place. A partner's death causes dissociation, after which the partnership must purchase the dissociated partner's partnership interest. Therefore, the surviving partners must pay the decedent's estate (for his widow) the value of the deceased partner's interest in the partnership.
2. No. Under the partners' fiduciary duty, a partner must account to the partnership for any personal profits or benefits derived without the consent of all the partners in connection with the use of any partnership property. Here, the leasing partner may not keep the funds.

Chapter 28

1. The members of a limited liability company (LLC) may designate a group to run their firm. In that situation, the firm would be a manager-managed LLC. The group may include only members, only nonmembers, or members and nonmembers. If, instead, all members participate in management, the firm would be a member-managed LLC. In fact, unless the members agree otherwise, all members are considered to participate in the management of the firm.
2. Although there are differences, all of these forms of business organization resemble corporations. A joint stock company, for example, is owned by shareholders, is managed by directors and officers, and has perpetual existence. A business trust, like a corporation, distributes profits to persons who are not personally responsible for the debts of the organization, and management of the business is in the hands of trustees, just as the management of a corporation is in the hands of directors and officers. An incorporated cooperative, which is subject to state laws covering nonprofit corporations, distributes profits to its owners.

Chapter 29

1. Yes. Small businesses that meet certain requirements can qualify as S corporations, created specifically to permit small businesses to avoid double taxation. The six requirements of an S corporation are (1) the firm must be a domestic corporation; (2) the firm must not be a member of an affiliated group of corporations; (3) the shareholders must be individuals, estates, or qualified trusts (or corporations in some cases); (4) the firm must have no more than one hundred shareholders; (5) there can be only one class of stock; and (6) no shareholder can be a nonresident alien.
2. Yes. A shareholder can bring a derivative suit on behalf of a corporation if some wrong is done to the corporation. Normally, any damages recovered go into the corporate treasury.

Chapter 30

1. The average investor is concerned not with minor inaccuracies but with facts that if disclosed would tend to deter him or her from buying the securities. These include material facts that have an important bearing on the condition of the issuer and its business—such as liabilities, loans to officers and directors, customer delinquencies, and pending lawsuits.
2. No. The Securities Exchange Act of 1934 extends liability to officers and directors in their personal transactions for taking advantage of inside information when they know it is unavailable to the persons with whom they are dealing.

Chapter 31

1. Size alone does not determine whether a firm is a monopoly—size in relation to the market is what matters. A small store in a small, isolated town is a monopolist if it is the only store serving that market. Monopoly involves the power to affect prices and output. If a firm has sufficient market power to control prices and exclude competition, that firm has monopoly power. Monopoly power in itself is not a violation of Section 2 of the Sherman Act. The offense also requires an intent to acquire or maintain that power through anticompetitive means.
2. This agreement is a tying arrangement. The legality of a tying arrangement depends on the purpose of the agreement, the agreement's likely effect on competition in the relevant markets (the market for the tying product and the market for the tied product), and other factors. Tying arrangements for commodities are subject to Section 3 of the Clayton Act. Tying arrangements for services can be agreements in restraint of trade in violation of Section 1 of the Sherman Act.

Chapter 32

1. Under an extensive set of procedures established by the U.S. Food and Drug Administration, which administers the federal Food,

Drug, and Cosmetic Act, drugs must be shown to be effective as well as safe before they may be marketed to the public. In general, manufacturers are responsible for ensuring that the drugs they offer for sale are free of any substances that could injure consumers.

2. The Comprehensive Environmental Response, Compensation, and Liability Act (CERCLA) regulates the cleanup of hazardous waste disposal sites. Any potentially responsible party can be charged with the entire cost of cleaning up a site. Potentially responsible parties include the party that generated the waste (ChemCorp), the party that transported the waste to the site (Disposal), the party that owned or operated the site at the time of the disposal (Eliminators), and the current owner or operator of the site (Fluid). A party held responsible for the entire cost may be able to recoup some of it in a lawsuit against other potentially responsible parties.

Chapter 33

1. Yes. In these circumstances, when the accountant knows that the bank will use the statement, the bank is a foreseeable user. A foreseeable user is a third party within the class of parties to whom an accountant may be liable for negligence.
2. No. In the circumstances described, the accountant will not be held liable to a purchaser of the securities. Although an accountant may be liable under securities laws for including untrue statements in or omitting material facts from financial statements, due diligence is a defense to liability. Due diligence requires an accountant to conduct a reasonable investigation and to reasonably believe that the financial statements are accurate. The problem scenario specifies that the misstatement of material fact in Omega's financial statement was not attributable to any fraud or negligence on Nora's part. Therefore, Nora can show that she used due diligence and will not be held liable to Pat.

Chapter 34

1. The ring is classified as lost property because it was discovered under circumstances indicating that the owner had not voluntarily placed it where it was found. The general rule is that the finder of the lost property has the right to possession (and eventual title) over all others *except* the true owner of the lost property. Therefore, Martin, as the true owner of the ring, is entitled to repossess the ring from Hunter.
2. Rosa de la Mar Corporation, the shipper, suffers the loss. A common carrier is liable for damage caused by the willful acts of third persons or by an accident. Other losses must be borne by the shipper (or the recipient, depending on the terms of their contract). In this situation, this shipment was lost due to an act of God.

Chapter 35

1. This is a breach of the warranty deed's covenant of quiet enjoyment. Consuela can sue Bernie and recover the purchase price of the house, plus any damages.
2. Yes. An owner of a fee simple has the most rights possible—he or she can give the property away, sell it, transfer it by will, use it for almost any purpose, possess it to the exclusion of all the world, or, as in this case, transfer possession for any period of time. The party to whom possession is transferred can also transfer her or his interest (usually only with the owner's permission) for any lesser period of time.

Chapter 36

1. No. To have testamentary capacity, a testator must be of legal age and sound mind *at the time the will is made*. Generally, the testator must (1) know the nature of the act, (2) comprehend and remember the "natural objects of his or her bounty," (3) know the nature and extent of her or his property, and (4) understand the distribution of assets called for by the will. In this situation, Sheila had testamentary capacity at the time she made the will. The fact that she was ruled mentally incompetent two years after making the will does not provide sufficient grounds to revoke it.
2. The estate will pass according to the state's intestacy laws. Intestacy laws set out how property is distributed when a person dies without a will. Their purpose is to carry out the likely intent of the decedent. The laws determine which of the deceased's natural heirs (including, in this order, the surviving spouse, lineal descendants, parents, and collateral heirs) inherit his or her property.

Appendix E

Sample Answers for *Business Case Problems with Sample Answer*

1–6. Sample Answer—Reading Citations.

The court's opinion in the case *Friends of Buckingham v. State Air Pollution Control Board* can be found in volume 947 of the Federal Reporter, third series, on page 68. The Federal Reporter contains the decisions of all the United States Courts of Appeals, including, as is the case here, the Fourth Circuit Court of Appeals. Also, this case was decided (though not necessarily filed) in 2020.

2–3. Sample Answer—Freedom of Speech.

No, Wooden's conviction was not unconstitutional. Certain speech is not protected under the First Amendment. Speech that violates criminal laws—threatening speech, for example— is not constitutionally protected. Other unprotected speech includes fighting words, or words that are likely to incite others to respond violently. And speech that harms the good reputation of another, or defamatory speech, is not protected under the First Amendment.

In his e-mail and audio notes to the alderwoman, Wooden referred to a sawed-off shotgun, domestic terrorism, and the assassination and murder of various politicians. He compared the alderwoman to the biblical character Jezebel, referring to her as a "bitch in the Sixth Ward." These references caused the alderwoman to feel threatened. The First Amendment does not protect such threats, which in this case violated a state criminal statute. There was nothing unconstitutional about punishing Wooden for this unprotected speech.

In the actual case on which this problem is based, Wooden appealed his conviction, arguing that it violated his right to freedom of speech. Under the principles set out above, the Missouri Supreme Court affirmed the conviction.

3–6. Sample Answer—Business Ethics.

It seems obvious from the facts stated in this problem that Hratch Ilanjian behaved unethically. Ethics, of course, involves questions relating to the fairness, justness, rightness, or wrongness of an action. Business ethics focuses on how businesspersons apply moral and ethical principles in making their decisions and whether those decisions are right or wrong.

In this problem, Ilanjian misrepresented himself to Vicken Setrakian, the president of Kenset Corporation, leading Setrakian to believe that Ilanjian was an international businessman who could help turn around Kenset's business in the Middle East. Ilanjian insisted that Setrakian provide him with confidential business documents. Then, claiming that they had an agreement, Ilanjian demanded full and immediate payment. He threatened to disclose the confidential information to a Kenset supplier if payment was not forthcoming. Kenset denied that they had a contract. In the ensuing litigation, during discovery, Ilanjian was uncooperative. Each of these acts was unethical.

In the actual case on which this problem is based, a trial court concluded that there was no contract, ordered the return of the confidential documents, and enjoined Ilanjian from using the information. The U.S. Court of Appeals for the Third Circuit affirmed.

4–6. Sample Answer—Corporate Contacts.

No, the defendants' motion to dismiss the suit for lack of personal jurisdiction should not be granted. A corporation normally is subject to jurisdiction in a state in which it is doing business. A court applies the minimum-contacts test to determine whether it can exercise jurisdiction over an out-of-state corporation. This requirement is met if the corporation sells its products within the state or places them in the "stream of commerce" with the intention of selling them in the state.

In this problem, the state of Washington filed a suit in a Washington state court against LG Electronics, Inc., and nineteen other foreign companies that participated in the global market for cathode ray tube (CRT) products. The state alleged a conspiracy to raise prices and set production levels in the market for CRTs in violation of a state consumer protection statute. The defendants filed a motion to dismiss the suit for lack of personal jurisdiction. For many years, however, these companies had sold CRTs in high volume in the United States, including the state of Washington. In other words, the corporations had purposefully established minimum contacts in the state of Washington. This is a sufficient basis for a Washington state court to assert personal jurisdiction over the defendants.

In the actual case on which this problem is based, the trial court dismissed the suit for lack of personal jurisdiction. On appeal, a state intermediate appellate court reversed based on the reasoning stated above.

5–4. Sample Answer—Negligence.

Negligence requires proof that (a) the defendant owed a duty of care to the plaintiff, (b) the defendant breached that duty, (c) the defendant's breach caused the plaintiff's injury, and (d) the plaintiff suffered a legally recognizable injury. With respect to the duty of care, a business owner has a duty to use reasonable care to protect business invitees. This duty includes an obligation to discover and correct or warn of unreasonably dangerous conditions that the owner of the premises should reasonably foresee might endanger an invitee. Some risks are so obvious that an owner need not warn of them. But even if a risk is obvious, a business owner may not be excused from the duty to protect the business's customers from foreseeable harm.

Because Lucario was the Weatherford's business invitee, the hotel owed her a duty of reasonable care to make its premises safe for her use. The balcony ran nearly the entire width of the window in Lucario's room. She could have reasonably believed that the window was a means of access to the balcony. The window/balcony configuration was dangerous, however, because the window opened wide enough for an adult to climb out, but the twelve-inch gap between one side of the window and the balcony was unprotected. This unprotected gap opened to a drop of more than three stories to a concrete surface below.

Should the hotel have anticipated the potential harm to a guest who opened the window in Room 59 and attempted to access the balcony? The hotel encouraged guests to "step out onto the balcony" to smoke. The dangerous window/ balcony configuration could have been remedied at a minimal cost. These circumstances could be perceived as creating an "unreasonably dangerous" condition. And it could be concluded that the hotel created or knew of the condition and failed to take reasonable steps to warn of it or correct it. Of course, the Weatherford might argue that the window/ balcony configuration was so obvious that the hotel was not liable for Lucario's fall.

In the actual case on which this problem is based, the court concluded that the Weatherford did not breach its duty of care to Lucario. On McMurtry's appeal, a state intermediate appellate court held that this conclusion was in error, vacated the lower court's judgment in favor of the hotel on this issue, and remanded the case.

6–4. Sample Answer—Product Liability.

Here, the accident was caused by Jett's inattention, not by the texting device in the cab of his truck. In a product-liability case based on a design defect, the plaintiff has to prove that the product was defective at the time it left the hands of the seller or lessor. The plaintiff must also show that this defective condition made it "unreasonably dangerous" to the user or consumer. If the product was delivered in a safe condition and subsequent mishandling made it harmful to the user, the seller or lessor normally is not liable. To successfully assert a design defect, a plaintiff has to show that a reasonable alternative design was available and that the defendant failed to use it.

The plaintiffs could contend that the defendant manufacturer of the texting device owed them a duty of care because injuries to vehicle drivers and passengers, and others on the roads, were reasonably foreseeable due to the product's design that (1) required the driver to divert his eyes from the road to view an incoming text from the dispatcher, and (2) permitted the receipt of texts while the vehicle was moving. But manufacturers are not required to design a product incapable of distracting a driver. The duty owed by a manufacturer to the user or consumer of a product does not require guarding against hazards that are commonly known or obvious or protecting against injuries that result from a user's careless conduct. That is what happened here.

In the actual case on which this problem is based, the court reached the same conclusion, based on the reasoning stated above, and an intermediate appellate court affirmed the judgment.

7–5. Sample Answer—Patents.

One ground on which the denial of Raymond Gianelli's patent application in this problem could be reversed on appeal is that the design of his "Rowing Machine" is *not obvious* in light of the design of the "Chest Press Apparatus for Exercising Regions of the Upper Body."

To obtain a patent, an applicant must demonstrate to the satisfaction of the U.S. Patent and Trademark Office (PTO) that the invention, discovery, process, or design is novel, useful, and not obvious in light of current technology. In this problem, the PTO denied Gianelli's application for a patent for his "Rowing Machine"—an exercise machine on which a user *pulls* on handles to perform a rowing motion against a selected resistance to strengthen the back muscles. The PTO considered the device obvious in light of a patented "Chest Press Apparatus for Exercising Regions of the Upper Body"—a chest press exercise machine on which a user *pushes* on handles to overcome a selected resistance. But it can be easily argued that it is *not* obvious to modify a machine with handles designed to be *pushed* into one with handles designed to be *pulled.* In fact, anyone who has used exercise machines knows that a way to cause injury is to use a machine in a manner not intended by the manufacturer.

In the actual case on which this problem is based, the U.S. Court of Appeals for the Federal Circuit reversed the PTO's denial of Gianelli's application for a patent based on the reasoning stated above.

8–5. Sample Answer—Social Media.

As stated in the text, law enforcement can use social media to detect and prosecute suspected criminals. But there must be an authenticated connection between the suspects and the posts. To make this connection, law enforcement officials can present the testimony or certification of authoritative representatives of the social media site or other experts. The posts can be traced from the pages on which they are displayed and the accounts of the "owners" of the pages to the posters through Internet Protocol (IP) addresses. An IP address can reveal the e-mail address, and even the mailing address, of an otherwise anonymous poster.

The custodians of Facebook, for example, can verify Facebook pages and posts because they maintain those items as business records in the course of regularly conducted business activities. From those sources, the prosecution in Hassan's case could have tracked the IP address to discover his identity.

In the actual case on which this problem is based, on Hassan's appeal of his conviction, the U.S. Court of Appeals for the Fourth Circuit affirmed.

9–3. Sample Answer—White-Collar Crime.

Yes, the acts committed by Matthew Simpson and the others constituted wire and mail fraud. Federal law makes it a crime to devise any scheme that uses the U.S. mail, commercial carriers (such as FedEx or UPS), or wire (such as telegraph, telephone, television, the Internet, or e-mail) with the intent to defraud the public.

Here, as stated in the facts, Simpson and his cohorts created and operated a series of corporate entities to defraud telecommunications companies, creditors, credit reporting agencies, and others. Through these entities, Simpson and the others used routing codes and spoofing services to make long distance calls appear to be local. They stole other firms' network capacity and diverted payments to themselves. They leased goods and services without paying for them. And they assumed false identities, addresses, and credit histories, and issued false bills, invoices, financial statements, and credit references, in order to hide their association with their entities and with each other. Through the use of this "scheme," the perpetrators defrauded telecommunications companies and other members of the public in order to gain goods and services for themselves. They used wire services—the Internet and, presumably, phones and other qualifying services—to further the scheme.

In the actual case on which this problem is based, a federal district court convicted Simpson of participating in a wire and mail fraud conspiracy (and other crimes). On appeal, the U.S. Court of Appeals for the Fifth Circuit affirmed the conviction.

10–5. Sample Answer—Implied Contracts.

Yes, Allstate was liable under the homeowner's policy. A contract that is implied from the conduct of the parties. This type of contract differs from an express contract in that the conduct of the parties, rather than their words, creates and defines the terms of the contract. For an implied contract to exist, a party must furnish a service or property (which includes money), the party must expect to receive something in return for that property or service, and the other party must know or should know of that expectation and had a chance to reject the property or service but did not. Of course, a contract may be a mix of express and implied terms.

In this problem, the homeowner's policy was a mix of express and implied terms. As for the elements showing the existence of the implied terms, the payments for the premiums on the policy continued after Ralph's death, but the amounts were paid from Douglas's account. Undoubtedly, Douglas expected to receive coverage under the policy in return for his payments. The insurer Allstate must have known that Douglas expected the coverage—insurance has long been Allstate's business, and the company obviously understands the relationship between the payments of premiums and the expectation of insurance coverage. And Allstate had the opportunity to cancel the homeowner's policy—as it had with Ralph's auto insurance, which was canceled—but did not terminate it.

In the actual case on which this problem is based, the court issued a judgment in Allstate's favor on the implied contract issue. The U.S. Court of Appeals for the Sixth Circuit reversed this judgment—"A reasonable fact-finder could determine that [Allstate's] continuation of the premium payments constituted a contract implied in fact with Douglas."

11–6. Sample Answer—Requirement of the Offer.

No, TCP is not correct—the bonus plan was not too indefinite to be an offer. One of the requirements for an effective offer is that its terms must be reasonably definite. This enables a court to determine whether a breach has occurred and award an appropriate remedy. Generally, the offer's terms include an identification of the parties and the object or subject of the contract, the consideration to be paid, and the time of performance.

In this problem, TCP provided its employees, including Bahr, with the details of a bonus plan. A district sales manager such as Bahr who achieved 100 percent year-over-year sales growth and a 42 percent gross margin would earn 200 percent of his or her base salary. TCP added that it retained absolute discretion to modify the plan. Bahr exceeded the goal and expected a bonus commensurate with her performance. TCP paid her less than half what its plan promised, however. In the ensuing litigation, TCP claimed that the bonus plan was too indefinite to constitute an offer, but this was not, in fact, the case. The plan provided clear criteria to determine an employee's eligibility for a certain amount within a specific time. A court asked to apply the plan would have little or no doubt as to the amount an employee would be entitled to. The term that reserved discretion to TCP to modify the plan did not sufficiently undercut the clarity of the offer to prevent the formation of a contract.

In the actual case on which this problem is based, the trial court concluded that the reservation of discretion to revoke a plan makes an offer too indefinite and issued a judgment in TCP's favor. A state intermediate appellate court reversed this judgment, holding that TCP's plan was a sufficiently definite offer.

12–4. Sample Answer—Agreements That Lack Consideration.

Yes, there was consideration to support the Telephone Deal. Consideration can consist of a promise, a performance, or a forbearance (refraining from an action that one has a legal right to undertake).

In this problem, Mark Garnett, an owner of Arkansas-Missouri Forest Products, LLC (Ark-Mo), and Stuart Lerner, an owner of Blue Chip Manufacturing (BCM), agreed to engage in wood-pallet enterprises together, with Ark-Mo to have a 30 percent ownership interest in their future projects. When Lerner formed Blue Chip Recycling, LLC (BCR), to manage a pallet repair facility in California, however, he allocated only a 5 percent interest to Ark-Mo. Garnett objected. In a "Telephone

Deal," Lerner promised that Ark-Mo would receive a 30 percent interest in their future projects in the Midwest. Garnett then agreed to forego an ownership interest in BCR.

Acting on Ark-Mo's behalf, Garnett could have accepted the 5 percent allocation in BCR, but he refrained from doing so. Instead, he accepted Lerner's promise of a 30 percent share in their future projects in the Midwest and made no more demands regarding BCR. In other words, Garnett gave up the opportunity to have an ownership interest in BCR in exchange for Lerner's agreement that Ark-Mo would have a 30 percent ownership interest in certain future projects.

In the actual case on which this problem is based, Ark-Mo filed a suit in a Missouri state court against Lerner, alleging breach of contract. The court issued a judgment in Lerner's favor. A state intermediate appellate court reversed, in part on the reasoning stated here. "Valid legal consideration supported the Telephone Deal."

13–5. Sample Answer—Fraudulent Misrepresentation.

Yes, the facts in this problem evidence fraud. There are three elements to fraud: (1) the misrepresentation of a material fact, (2) an intent to deceive, and (3) an innocent party's justifiable reliance on the misrepresentation. To collect damages, the innocent party must suffer an injury.

Here, Pervis represented to Pauley that no further commission would be paid by Osbrink. This representation was false—despite Pervis's statement to the contrary, Osbrink continued to send payments to Pervis. Pervis knew the representation was false, as shown by the fact that she made it more than once during the time that she was continuing to receive payments from Osbrink. Each time Pauley asked about commissions, Pervis replied that she was not receiving any. Pauley's reliance on her business associate's statements was justified and reasonable. And for the purpose of recovering damages, Pauley suffered an injury in the amount of her share of the commissions that Pervis received as a result of the fraud.

In the actual case on which this problem is based, Pauley filed a suit in a Georgia state court against Pervis, who filed for bankruptcy in a federal bankruptcy court to stay the state action. The federal court held Pervis liable on the ground of fraud for the amount of the commissions that were not paid to Pauley and denied Pervis a discharge of the debt.

14–5. Sample Answer—Conditions of Performance.

The requirement that the contractor obtain an engineer's certificate of final completion before the final payment will be made is a condition precedent. In most contracts, promises of performance are not expressly conditioned—they are absolute and must be performed to avoid a breach of the contract. In some situations, however, performance is contingent on the occurrence of a certain event. If the condition is not satisfied, the obligations of the parties are discharged. A condition that must be fulfilled before a party's performance can be required is a condition precedent.

In this problem, H&J Ditching was hired to excavate and grade land for a residential construction project. Cornerstone Community Bank financed the project. As the work progressed, H&J received payments totaling 90 percent of the price on its contract. But the last payment was not forthcoming when H&J believed it was due. The contractor filed a suit in a Tennessee state court against the bank to recover the final payment. The bank responded that H&J did not receive the payment because it had failed to obtain an engineer's certificate of final completion, a condition under its contract. H&J argued that it had completed all the work it contracted to do.

H&J is not entitled to the final payment on the contract because it did not comply with the condition to obtain the engineer's certificate. This condition preceded the bank's obligation under the contract to make the final payment. Even assuming that H&J "completed all the work it contracted to do," the final payment need not be made without the certificate.

In the actual case on which this problem is based, the trial court issued a judgment in the bank's favor. A state intermediate appellate court affirmed. "No certificate of substantial completion was ever issued, a condition precedent to final payment."

15–5. Sample Answer—Limitation-of-Liability Clauses.

Yes, the limitation-of-liability agreement that Eriksson signed is likely to be enforced in her parents' suit against Nunnink, their daughter's riding coach. And this would likely result in a judgment against them unless they can establish "direct, willful and wanton negligence" on Nunnink's part. A limitation-of-liability clause affects the availability of certain remedies. Under basic contract principles, to be enforceable, these clauses must be clear and unambiguous.

In this problem, Eriksson, a young horseback-riding competitor, signed an agreement that released Nunnink from all liability except for damages caused by Nunnink's "direct, willful and wanton negligence." During an event, Eriksson's horse struck a hurdle, causing her to fall from the horse. The horse fell on her, resulting in her death. Her parents filed a suit against Nunnink for wrongful death. The limitation-of-liability clause signed by Eriksson, however, was straightforward, clear, and unambiguous, and therefore enforceable. Nunnink would be liable only if Eriksson's death was caused by Nunnink's gross negligence. The facts do not state that Eriksson's parents proved that Nunnink was grossly negligent.

In the actual case on which this problem is based, the trial court issued a judgment in Nunnink's favor. A state intermediate appellate court affirmed the judgment on the basis explained here.

16–5. Sample Answer—Goods and Services Combined.

A court will apply common law principles to a dispute over a contract that involves both goods and services when the court finds the services to be the dominant feature of the agreement. In contrast, a court will rule that the UCC should be applied when it finds the goods to be the dominant aspect of the deal. In either situation, the applicable law covers both the goods and services parts of the contract.

In this problem, because the trial court applied common law contract principles to rule in National's favor on both parties' claims, the court must have concluded that the services part of the contract was the dominant aspect.

In the actual case on which this problem is based, a state intermediate appellate court affirmed the lower court's ruling in National's favor. The appellate court recognized that the contract was a hybrid involving goods and services and reasoned that the lower court must have found the services portion of the agreement to be the dominant factor. But the parties did not provide a trial transcript or a copy of the contract, so the appellate court could only affirm the lower court's order.

17–6. Sample Answer—Remedies of the Buyer or Lessee.

No, at this point the Morrises are not entitled to revoke their acceptance of the cabinets that IO delivered. Under the UCC, acceptance of a lot or a commercial unit can be revoked if a nonconformity substantially impairs the value of the lot or unit and acceptance was based on the reasonable assumption that the nonconformity would be cured, and it has not been cured within a reasonable period of time. One of the corollaries to this rule is, of course, that the seller must be given a reasonable time within which to effect a cure.

Here, the Morrises contracted with IO to rebuild the kitchen in their home on the Gulf coast of Mississippi after it was extensively damaged in a hurricane. As part of the deal, IO delivered new cabinets. Some defects were apparent, and as installation progressed, others emerged. IO ordered replacement parts to cure the defects and later offered to remove the cabinets and refund the price. The Morrises asked to be reimbursed for the installation fee as well. IO refused this request, but at all times, the seller emphasized that it was willing to fulfill its contractual obligations. The buyers then attempted to revoke their acceptance of the cabinets—before the replacement parts arrived and without attempting to negotiate any other accommodation.

In the actual case on which this problem is based, the Morrises filed a suit in a Mississippi state court against IO. The court dismissed the complaint and entered a judgment in the defendant's favor. A state intermediate appellate court affirmed. "The Morrises were not entitled to recovery because they revoked acceptance of the cabinets before giving IO a reasonable opportunity to cure the defects."

18–6. Sample Answer—Signature Liability.

The parties who can be held liable for the loss on the unpaid checks in the *Albarran* case are R. Cleaning Impact, Inc. (RCI), and its owners, Guillermo, Guadalupe, Ruben, and Rolando Albarran.

Generally, when an indorsement is forged or unauthorized, the burden of loss falls on the first party to take the instrument with the forged or unauthorized indorsement. But this rule has an important exception that causes the loss to fall on the drawer of the check rather than the first party to take it—the fictitious payee rule. This rule applies when a person causes an instrument to be issued to a payee (fictitious or real) who will have no interest in it. In that situation, the payee's indorsement is not treated as a forgery, and an innocent holder can hold the maker or drawer liable on the instrument.

In this problem, Amba, a check-cashing service, and the Albarrans and their sons, owners of a cleaning company, established a regular check-cashing relationship between their respective businesses. The Albarrans often delivered a stack of their employees' paychecks for cashing through Amba. Later, the Albarrans' bank began refusing payment on some of the checks. Amba learned that the unpaid items were payable to fictitious payees with fictitious addresses, or for amounts more than the actual employees' pay. Under normal circumstances, Amba would be most likely to suffer the loss. But under the fictitious payee rule, RCI or its owners, as the drawers of the checks, could be held liable. Because RCI is insolvent, and its accounts are closed, and Guillermo and Guadalupe filed for bankruptcy protection, the parties most likely to be assessed with liability are Ruben and Rolando.

In the actual case on which this problem is based, Amba filed a suit in a Maryland state court against the Albarrans to recover the amount of the unpaid checks. The defendants did not respond. The court entered a default judgment against them. On the defendants' later motion, the court vacated the award of damages with respect to the parents, because they had filed for bankruptcy, but not the sons, who remained liable. A state intermediate appellate court affirmed.

19–5. Sample Answer—Import Controls.

Yes, an antidumping duty can be assessed retrospectively (retroactively). But it does not seem likely that such a duty should be assessed here.

In this problem, the Wind Tower Trade Coalition (an association of domestic manufacturers of utility-scale wind towers) filed a suit in the U.S. Court of International Trade against the U.S. Department of Commerce. Wind Tower challenged the Commerce Department's decision to impose only *prospective* antidumping duties on imports of utility-scale wind towers from China and Vietnam. The Commerce Department had found that the domestic industry had not suffered any "material injury" or "threat of material injury" and that it would be protected by a prospective assessment. Because the domestic industry had not suffered discernible injury, any retrospective duties collected would not be payable to members of the industry. Thus, it does not seem likely that retroactive duties should be imposed.

In the actual case on which this problem is based, the court denied the plaintiff's request for an injunction. On appeal, the U.S. Court of Appeals for the Federal Circuit affirmed the denial, holding that the lower court acted within its discretion in determining that retrospective duties were not appropriate.

20–4. Sample Answer—Consumer Fund Transfers.

Yes, the bank's refusal to reimburse Patterson more than $677.46 was justified. Under the Electronic Fund Transfer Act (EFTA), if a customer's debit card is lost or stolen and used without her or his permission, the customer does not have to pay more than $50. But for this limit to apply, the customer must notify the bank of the loss or theft within two days of learning about it. Otherwise, the liability increases to $500. The customer may be liable for more than $500 if the unauthorized use is not reported within sixty days after it appears on the customer's statement.

In this problem, Stephen Patterson held an account with SunTrust Bank. He was briefly involved in a romantic relationship with Juanita Wehrman, who stole his debit card and used it for sixteen months (well beyond the length of their relationship), spending more than $30,000. When Patterson learned what was happening, he closed his account. But, of course, sixteen months is much more than sixty days, and the bank refused to reimburse him more than $677.46. This was the amount of unauthorized transactions that occurred within sixty days of the transmittal of the bank statement that revealed the first unauthorized transaction.

In the actual case on which this problem is based, Patterson filed suit in a Tennessee state court against the bank to recover the rest of the spent funds. The court upheld the bank's refusal, and a state intermediate appellate court affirmed.

21–5. Sample Answer—Perfection of a Security Interest.

Yes, the description in PHI's financing statement was sufficient to perfect the creditor's security interest in the SURE payment. A financing statement must describe the collateral in which a secured party has a security interest in order to provide public notice of the fact that certain property of the debtor is subject to a security interest. The UCC permits broad, general descriptions in a financing statement, such as "all assets."

In this problem, G&K Farms was insured under the federal Supplemental Revenue Assistance Payments Program (SURE), which provides financial assistance for crop losses caused by natural disasters. PHI loaned G&K $6.6 million and filed a financing statement that described the collateral as G&K's interest in "Government Payments." The statement did not refer specifically to the farm's crops. G&K defaulted on the loan. When G&K received a SURE payment for crop losses and transferred some of the funds to its law firm, Johnston Law Office, PHI sought to recover the funds as a partial payment on its loan. Johnston argued that PHI did not have a perfected security interest in the SURE payment because PHI's financing statement did not identify the farm's crops.

Johnston's argument is faulty because the debtor's crops were not the collateral at issue. The government's SURE payment was the disputed collateral, and PHI's financing statement sufficiently described it with the general reference to "Government Payments." PHI's security interest was perfected.

In the actual case on which this problem is based, PHI filed its suit against Johnston in a North Dakota state court, which entered a judgment in the creditor's favor. The North Dakota Supreme Court affirmed on the issue highlighted in this problem based on the reasoning stated here.

22–4. Sample Answer—Discharge.

No, Michael is not entitled to a discharge of the debt to Dianne. The debt, comprising unpaid alimony, child support, and investment funds, qualifies as an exception to discharge. As far as a debtor is concerned, the primary purpose of a liquidation proceeding is to obtain a fresh start through a discharge of debts. But certain debts are not dischargeable in bankruptcy. These debts include domestic-support obligations and property settlements provided for in a divorce decree and claims based on willful or malicious conduct by the debtor toward another.

In this problem, on Michael and Dianne's divorce, a court ordered Michael to pay Dianne alimony and child support, as well as half of the $184,000 in their investment accounts. Instead of complying with the order, Michael withdrew half of the investment funds and spent them on himself. Meanwhile, the court repeatedly held him in contempt for failing to pay Dianne alimony, child support, and half of the investment funds. These items are nondischargeable because they are domestic-support obligations and part of the property settlement provided for in the parties' divorce decree. The unpaid investment funds also constitute a claim based on willful and malicious conduct. Michael deliberately defied multiple contempt orders, leaving Dianne uncompensated and thereby inflicting harm on her.

In the actual case on which this problem is based, the court concluded that Michael's conduct was willful and malicious and that the debt to Dianne listed in the petition's schedule was therefore nondischargeable. On Michael's appeal, the U.S. Court of Appeals for the Fifth Circuit affirmed.

23–5. Sample Answer—Determining Employee Status.

No, Cox is not liable to Cayer for the injuries or damages that she sustained in the accident with Ovalles. Generally, an employer is not liable for physical harm caused to a third person by the negligent act of an independent contractor in the performance of a contract. This is because the employer does not have the right to control the details of the performance. In determining whether a worker has the status of an independent contractor, how much control the employer can exercise over the details of the work is the most important factor weighed by the courts.

In this problem, Ovalles worked as a cable installer for Cox under an agreement with M&M. The agreement disavowed any employer-employee relationship between Cox and M&M's installers. Ovalles was required to designate his affiliation with Cox on his van, clothing, and an I.D. badge. But Cox had minimal contact with Ovalles and limited power to control the manner in which he performed his work. Cox supplied cable wire and other equipment, but these items were delivered to M&M, not Ovalles. These facts indicate that Ovalles was an independent contractor, not an employee. Thus, Cox was not liable to Cayer for the harm caused to her by Ovalles when his van rear-ended her car.

In the actual case on which this problem is based, the court issued a judgment in Cox's favor. The Rhode Island Supreme Court affirmed, applying the principles stated above to arrive at the same conclusion.

24–5. Sample Answer—Unemployment Compensation.

Yes, Ramirez qualifies for unemployment compensation. Generally, to be eligible for unemployment compensation, a worker must be willing and able to work. Workers who have been fired for misconduct or who have voluntarily left their jobs are not eligible for benefits. In the facts of this problem, the applicable state statute disqualifies an employee from receiving benefits if he or she voluntarily leaves work without "good cause."

The issue is whether Ramirez left her job for "good cause." When her father in the Dominican Republic had a stroke, she asked her employer for time off to be with him. Her employer refused the request. But Ramirez left to be with her father and called to inform her employer. It seems likely that this family emergency would constitute "good cause," and Ramirez's call and return to work after her father's death indicated that she did not disregard her employer's interests.

In the actual case on which this problem is based, the state of Florida denied Ramirez unemployment compensation. On Ramirez's appeal, a state intermediate appellate court reversed based on the reasoning stated above.

25–6. Sample Answer—Sexual Harassment.

Newton's best defense to Blanton's assertion of liability is the "*Ellerth/Faragher* affirmative defense." To establish this defense, an employer must show that it has taken reasonable care to prevent and promptly correct any sexually harassing behavior and that the plaintiff unreasonably failed to take advantage of any opportunity provided by the employer to avoid the harm.

In this problem, Blanton was subjected to sexual harassment by the general manager at their place of employment, a Pizza Hut restaurant operated by Newton. Blanton alerted low-level supervisors about the harassment, but they, like Blanton, were subordinate to the general manager and had no authority over her. Newton had a clear, straightforward antidiscrimination policy and complaint procedure, which provided that an employee should complain to the harasser's supervisor in such a situation. Once Blanton finally complained to a manager with authority over the general manager, Newton promptly and effectively responded to Blanton's complaint. His delay in reporting the harassment to the appropriate authority can be construed as an unreasonable failure to take advantage of the opportunity provided by the employer to avoid the harm.

In the actual case on which this problem is based, Blanton filed suit against Newton seeking to hold it liable for the general manager's actions. A jury found that the plaintiff had been harassed as he claimed, but it also found that the defendant had proved the *Ellerth/Faragher* affirmative defense. The court issued a judgment in the employer's favor, and the U.S. Court of Appeals for the Fifth Circuit affirmed.

26–4. Sample Answer—Quality Control.

Yes, Liberty can be held liable for the statements in its franchisees' ads. The validity of a provision permitting the franchisor to establish and enforce certain quality standards is unquestioned. The franchisor has a legitimate interest in maintaining the quality of the product or service to protect its name and reputation. If a franchisor exercises too much control over the operations of its franchisees, however, the franchisor risks potential liability. A franchisor may occasionally be held liable under the doctrine of *respondeat superior* for the tortious acts of a franchisee or the franchisees' employees.

In this problem, Liberty's agreement with its franchisees reserved the right to control their ads. In operations manuals, Liberty provided its franchisees with step-by-step instructions, directions, and limitations regarding their ads and retained the right to unilaterally modify the steps at any time. This seems to give the franchisor a great deal of control over its franchisees' marketing, which under the principles stated above, points to the franchisor's liability for the franchisees' misleading or deceptive ads.

In the actual case on which this problem is based, the trial court issued a judgment in California's favor. Liberty appealed. A state intermediate appellate court affirmed. "Liberty retained the right to control, and in fact did seek to control, its franchisees' advertising and other marketing activities beyond that necessary to protect its marks and goodwill."

27–4. Sample Answer—Partnerships.

Yes, Sacco is entitled to 50 percent of the profits of Pierce Paxton Collections. The requirements for establishing a partnership are (1) a sharing of profits and losses, (2) a joint ownership of the business, and (3) an equal right to be involved in the management of the business.

The effort and time that Sacco expended in the business constituted a sharing of losses. His proprietary interest in the assets of the partnership consisted of his share of the profits, which he expressly left in the business to "grow the company" and "build sweat equity" for the future. He was involved in every aspect of the business. Although he was not paid a salary, he was reimbursed for business expenses charged to his personal credit card, which Paxton also used. These facts arguably meet the requirements for establishing a partnership.

In the actual case on which this problem is based, Sacco filed a suit in a Louisiana state court against Paxton, and the court awarded Sacco 50 percent of the profits. A state intermediate appellate court affirmed based generally on the reasoning stated above.

28–4. Sample Answer—LLC Operation.

No. One Bluewater member could not unilaterally "fire" another member without providing a reason. Part of the attractiveness of an LLC as a form of business enterprise is its flexibility. The members can decide how to operate the business through an operating agreement. For example, the agreement can set forth procedures for choosing or removing members or managers.

Here, the Bluewater operating agreement provided for a "super majority" vote to remove a member under circumstances that would jeopardize the firm's contractor status. Thus, one Bluewater member could not unilaterally "fire" another member without providing a reason. In fact, a majority of the members could not terminate the other's interest in the firm without providing a reason. Moreover, the only acceptable reason would be a circumstance that undercut the firm's status as a contractor.

The flexibility of the LLC business form relates to its framework, not to its members' capacity to violate its operating agreement. In the actual case on which this problem is based, Smith attempted to "fire" Williford without providing a reason. In Williford's suit, the court issued a judgment in his favor.

29–4. Sample Answer—Piercing the Corporate Veil.

Yes, there are sufficient grounds in the facts of this problem to support piercing the corporate veil and holding Kappeler personally liable to Snapp. First, in a case in which a plaintiff seeks to pierce a corporate veil, fraud or some other injustice must have taken place. In that situation, a court will consider whether the following factors were present: (1) a party was tricked or misled into dealing with the corporation rather than the individual; (2) the corporation had insufficient capital to meet its prospective debts or other potential liabilities; (3) corporate formalities, such as holding required corporate meetings, were not followed; and (4) personal and corporate interests were commingled.

In this problem, the amount that Snapp ultimately paid the builder exceeded the original estimate by nearly $1 million—and the project was still unfinished. Kappeler could not provide an accounting for the Snapp project— he could not explain double and triple charges nor whether the amount that Snapp paid had actually been spent on the project. These facts support a conclusion of fraud, and they also suggest that Kappeler may have tricked or misled Snapp into dealing with Castlebrook, the corporation, rather than with Kappeler as an individual. Castlebrook had issued no shares of stock, which points to insufficient capitalization. The minutes of the corporate meetings "all looked exactly the same," indicating that, in fact, the required corporate meetings had not been held. Finally, Kappeler had commingled personal and corporate funds.

In the actual case on which this problem is based, Snapp filed suit against the builder seeking to pierce the corporate veil. The court did so and held Kappeler personally liable. A state intermediate appellate court affirmed.

30–4. Sample Answer—Disclosure under SEC Rule 10b-5.

Yes. Even if Goldman did not affirmatively misrepresent any facts about the CDOs, Dodona can recover if Goldman failed to disclose material facts. An omission is regarded as material if it is significant enough that it would have affected an investor's decision concerning the securities. Here, Dodona might recover by showing that Goldman did not fully disclose the risks of investing in the CDOs. Goldman may have misled Dodona by providing only boilerplate statements about investments that it knew were particularly risky.

31–4. Sample Answer—Price Discrimination.

Spa Steel satisfies most of the requirements for a price discrimination claim under Section 2 of the Clayton Act. Dayton Superior is engaged in interstate commerce, and it sells goods of like grade and quality to at least three purchasers. Moreover, Spa Steel can show that, because it sells Dayton Superior's products at a higher price, it lost business and thus suffered an injury. To recover, however, Spa Steel will also need to prove that Dayton Superior charged Spa Steel's competitors a lower price for the same product. Spa Steel cannot recover if its prices were higher for reasons related to its own business, such as having higher overhead or seeking a larger profit.

32–5. Sample Answer—Deceptive Advertising.

Yes, Ross can be held personally liable for a violation of the Federal Trade Commission Act's prohibition of deceptive acts or practices. Generally, deceptive advertising occurs if a reasonable consumer would be misled by the advertising claim. Advertising that appears to be based on factual evidence but that in fact cannot be supported will be deemed deceptive. An individual can be held personally liable under the act if the person (1) participated directly in the deceptive practices or had the authority to control them and (2) had or should have had knowledge of them.

In this problem, the facts indicate that IMI's ads were deceptive. Consumers were misled by the ads, which appeared to be based on factual evidence but were not supportable— the ads claimed that a scan of the consumers' computers had detected dangerous files, such as viruses, when in fact no scans were conducted. The issue is whether Ross can be held individually liable for these violations. She was an IMI co-founder and vice president, reviewed and edited the ads, and was aware of the many complaints about them. Thus, under the Federal Trade Commission Act, Ross met the standard for personal liability—she knew of the deceptive practices, she had the authority to control them, and she directly participated in them.

In the actual case on which this problem is based, the Federal Trade Commission filed suit against Ross, and a federal district court held her jointly and severally liable. On appeal, the U.S. Court of Appeals for the Fourth Circuit affirmed.

33–6. Sample Answer—Potential Liability to Third Parties.

KPMG is potentially liable to the hedge funds' partners under the *Restatement (Second) of Torts.* Under Section 552 of the *Restatement,* an auditor owes a duty to "persons for whose benefit and guidance the accountant intends to supply . . . information."

In this case, KPMG prepared annual reports on the hedge funds and addressed them to the funds' "Partners." Additionally, KPMG knew who the partners were because it prepared individual tax forms for them each year. Thus, KPMG's annual reports were for the partners' benefit and guidance. The partners relied on the reports, including their representations that they complied with generally accepted accounting principles.

As a result, they lost millions of dollars, which exposes KPMG to possible liability under Section 552.

34–7. Sample Answer—Duties of the Bailee.

KZY owed Mrs. Ressler's a duty to exercise reasonable care. From an ethical perspective, KZY appears to have met this standard.

A bailee must exercise reasonable care in preserving bailed property. What constitutes reasonable care depends on the nature and circumstances of the bailment. A bailment for the mutual benefit of the bailee and the bailor involves compensation. The bailee must exercise ordinary care—the care that a reasonably careful person would use under the circumstances. A bailee who fails to exercise reasonable care will be liable for ordinary negligence. If bailed property is returned damaged, a bailee will be presumed to have been negligent. The bailee is excused, however, if the property was damaged through no fault of the bailee.

In this problem, KZY transported a load of Mrs. Ressler's Food Products. When KZY delivered the cargo, the customer rejected it because its temperature was higher than expected, making it unsafe. In Mrs. Ressler's suit against KZY, the defendant asserted that the temperature in its trailer was proper and that Mrs. Ressler's delivered a "hot" product for transport. KZY provided temperature readings from the refrigerated unit during the time in question. This would be a complete defense to a claim that the bailee was negligent in failing to maintain a proper temperature during the transport.

KZY's ethical duty was the same as the bailee's legal duty of care. In handling Mrs. Ressler's cargo, KZY was ethically bound to exercise the care that a reasonably careful person would use under the circumstances. If the temperature readings from the refrigerated unit would absolve the bailee from liability for negligence, the proof would also refute any charge that KZY had acted unethically.

In the actual case on which this problem is based, KZY failed to file a timely response to Mrs. Ressler's suit, and the court entered a default judgment against the defendant. The U.S. Court of Appeals for the Third Circuit reversed the lower court's decision. "KZY alleged a *prima facie* meritorious defense to the action" and "there was no direct evidence that KZY acted in bad faith."

35–6. Sample Answer—Joint Tenancies.

Under the law of the Cayman Islands, and according to Arthur's will, the three disputed Cayman properties became Diana's sole property when Arthur died. In a joint tenancy, each of two or more persons owns an undivided interest in the property. A deceased joint tenant's interest passes to the surviving joint tenant or tenants. The right of a surviving joint tenant to inherit a deceased joint tenant's ownership interest is referred to as a right of survivorship.

In this problem, Arthur and Diana owned three properties in the Cayman Islands in a joint tenancy. (For this purpose, Cayman law is the same as U.S. law.) When the couple divorced, the decree did not change the tenancy. Later, Arthur died. His will provided that any property he held in joint tenancy "will pass to the survivor, and I instruct my Personal Representative to make no claim thereto." Despite this provision, his brother Curtis, personal representative of his estate, asserted that Arthur's interest in the properties were part of the estate. Diana said that the properties were entirely hers. Clearly, Diana is correct. Under the applicable principles of ownership of property by joint tenancy, as the sole surviving joint tenant, Arthur's interest in the properties passed to her. And under the terms of Arthur's will, his interest passed to her (and Curtis was "to make no claim thereto.")

A joint tenant can transfer any personal rights to the property without the consent of the other joint tenants. The new owner becomes a tenant in common, however, not a joint tenant. Or a joint tenant's interest can be levied against to satisfy the tenant's judgment creditors. In either case, the joint tenancy terminates, and the remaining owners hold the property as tenants in common. Neither of these situations occurred in the facts of this problem, however.

In the actual case on which this problem is based, Curtis asked the Florida state court that issued the couple's divorce to declare that Arthur's interest in the Cayman properties were part of his estate. The court ruled in the estate's favor and ordered Diana to sell the properties or buy Arthur's interest in them. A state intermediate appellate court reversed the order.

36–6. Sample Answer—Wills.

No, the document that Walker signed was not a valid will. A will is a person's final declaration of how his or her property is to be disposed of after death. It is a formal instrument that must follow exactly the requirements of state law. These formalities are intended to help prevent fraud. Unless they are followed, the will is void. Generally, a will must be attested to by two or three witnesses in a specified manner. The testator typically must either sign the will in the witnesses' presence or acknowledge that the signature on the document is his or hers. In some states, at the signing, the testator must declare that the document is his or her will.

Here, Andrew told Nora that he wished to change the disposition of his property provided for in a prior will by devising half of it to her in a new will. She noted his wish and took her notes to the office of attorney Meagher to have the document drafted. Meagher did not see Nora's notes, he did not talk to Walker, no one from his office was present at the signing of the document, and, when Walker signed it, he did not declare that it was his will, as required by state law. These facts indicate that formalities required by state law for the execution of a will were not followed strictly, undercutting the validity of the document as a will.

In the actual case on which this problem is based, Nora submitted this document to a New York state court as Walker's will. His children objected. The court denied the admission of the will to probate. "In light of the uncertainty surrounding the [will's] drafting and execution," a state intermediate appellate court affirmed.

Glossary

A

Abandoned Property Property that has been discarded by the owner, who has no intention of reclaiming it.

Acceleration Clause A clause that allows a payee or other holder of a time instrument to demand payment of the entire amount due, with interest, if a certain event occurs, such as a default in the payment of an installment when due.

Acceptance The act of voluntarily agreeing, through words or conduct, to the terms of an offer, thereby creating a contract. In negotiable instruments law, a drawee's signed agreement to pay a draft when it is presented.

Acceptor A drawee that accepts, or promises to pay, an instrument when it is presented later for payment.

Accession The addition of value to personal property by the use of labor or materials.

Accord and Satisfaction A common means of settling a disputed claim, whereby a debtor offers to pay a lesser amount than the creditor purports to be owed.

Accredited Investor In the context of securities offerings, sophisticated investors, such as banks, insurance companies, investment companies, the issuer's executive officers and directors, and persons whose income or net worth exceeds certain limits.

Actionable Capable of serving as the basis of a lawsuit. An actionable claim can be pursued in a lawsuit or other court action.

Act of State Doctrine A doctrine providing that the judicial branch of one country will not examine the validity of public acts committed by a recognized foreign government within its own territory.

Actual Malice The deliberate intent to cause harm that exists when a person makes a statement with either knowledge of its falsity or reckless disregard of the truth. It is required to establish defamation against public figures.

Actus Reus A guilty (prohibited) act. It is one of the two essential elements required to establish criminal liability.

Adequate Protection Doctrine A doctrine that protects secured creditors from losing the value of their security (because the collateral depreciates, for instance) as a result of an automatic stay in a bankruptcy proceeding.

Adhesion Contract A standard-form contract in which the stronger party dictates the terms.

Adjudicate To render a judicial decision. Adjudication is the trial-like proceeding in which an administrative law judge hears and resolves disputes involving an administrative agency's regulations.

Administrative Agency A federal, state, or local government agency created by the legislature to perform a specific function, such as to make and enforce rules pertaining to the environment.

Administrative Law The body of law created by administrative agencies in order to carry out their duties and responsibilities.

Administrative Law Judge (ALJ) One who presides over an administrative agency hearing and has the power to administer oaths, take testimony, rule on questions of evidence, and make determinations of fact.

Administrative Process The procedure used by administrative agencies in fulfilling their three basic functions: rulemaking, enforcement, and adjudication.

Administrator One who is appointed by a court to administer a person's estate if the decedent died without a valid will or if the executor named in the will cannot serve.

Adverse Possession The acquisition of title to real property through open occupation, without the consent of the owner, for a period of time specified by a state statute. The occupation must be actual, exclusive, open, continuous, and in opposition to all others, including the owner.

Affirmative Action Job-hiring policies that give special consideration to members of protected classes in an effort to overcome present effects of past discrimination.

After-Acquired Property Property that is acquired by the debtor after the execution of a security agreement.

Agency A relationship between two parties in which one party (the agent) agrees to represent or act for the other (the principal).

Agency Coupled with an Interest An agency, created for the benefit of the agent, in which the agent has some legal right (interest) in the property that is the subject of the agency

Age of Majority The age (eighteen years, in most states) at which a person is granted by law the rights and responsibilities of an adult.

Agreement A mutual understanding or meeting of the minds between two or more individuals regarding the terms of a contract.

Alien Corporation A corporation formed in another country but doing business in the United States.

Alienation The transfer of title to real property (which "alienates" the real property from the former owner).

Allege To state, recite, assert, or charge.

Alternative Dispute Resolution (ADR) The resolution of disputes in ways other than those involved in the traditional judicial process, such as negotiation, mediation, and arbitration.

Answer Procedurally, a defendant's response to the plaintiff's complaint.

Anticipatory Repudiation An assertion or action by a party indicating that the party will not perform a contractual obligation.

Antitrust Law Laws protecting commerce from unlawful restraints and anticompetitive practices.

Apparent Authority Authority that is only apparent, not real. An agent's apparent authority arises when the principal causes a third party to believe that the agent has authority, even though she or he does not.

Appropriation In tort law, the use by one person of another person's name, likeness, or other identifying characteristic without permission and for the benefit of the user.

Arbitration Clause A clause in a contract that provides that, in the event of a dispute, the parties will submit the dispute to arbitration rather than litigate the dispute in court.

Arbitration The settling of a dispute by submitting it to a disinterested third party (other than a court), who renders a decision.

Arson The intentional burning of a building.

Articles of Incorporation The document that is filed with the appropriate state official, usually the secretary of state, when a business is incorporated and that contains basic information about the corporation.

Articles of Organization The document filed with a designated state official by which a limited liability company is formed.

Articles of Partnership A written agreement that sets forth each partner's rights and obligations with respect to the partnership.

Artisan's Lien A possessory lien held by a party who has made improvements and added value to the personal property of another party as security for payment for services performed.

Assault Any word or action intended to make another person fearful of immediate physical harm—a reasonably believable threat.

Assignee A party to whom the rights under a contract are transferred, or assigned.

Assignment The transfer to another of all or part of one's rights arising under a contract.

Assignor A party who transfers (assigns) rights under a contract to another party (the *assignee*).

Assumption of Risk A defense to negligence that bars a plaintiff from recovering for injuries or damage suffered as a result of risks that were known and voluntarily assumed.

Attachment In a secured transaction, the process by which a secured creditor's interest "attaches" to the collateral and the creditor's security interest becomes enforceable.

Attempted Monopolization An action by a firm that involves anticompetitive conduct, the intent to gain monopoly power, and a "dangerous probability" of success in achieving monopoly power.

Auditor An accountant qualified to perform audits (systematic inspections) of a business's financial records.

Authenticate To sign, execute, or adopt any symbol on an electronic record that verifies the intent to adopt or accept the record.

Authorization Card A card signed by an employee that gives a union permission to act on the employee's behalf in negotiations with management.

Automatic Stay In bankruptcy proceedings, the suspension of almost all litigation and other actions by creditors against the debtor or the debtor's property. The stay is effective the moment the debtor files a petition in bankruptcy.

Award The monetary compensation given to a party at the end of a trial or other proceeding.

B

Bailee One to whom goods are entrusted by a bailor.

Bailee's Lien A possessory (artisan's) lien that a bailee entitled to compensation can place on the bailed property to ensure payment for the services provided.

Bailment A situation in which the personal property of one person (a bailor) is entrusted to another (a bailee), who is obligated to return the bailed property to the bailor or dispose of it as directed.

Bailor One who entrusts goods to a bailee.

Bait-and-Switch Advertising Advertising a product at an attractive price and then telling the consumer that the advertised product is not available or is of poor quality and encouraging her or him to purchase a more expensive item.

Bankruptcy Court A federal court of limited jurisdiction that handles only bankruptcy proceedings, which are governed by federal bankruptcy law.

Bankruptcy Trustee A person appointed by the court to manage the debtor's funds.

Battery Physical contact with another that is unexcused, harmful or offensive, and intentionally performed.

Bearer A person in possession of an instrument payable to bearer or indorsed in blank.

Bearer Instrument Any instrument that is not payable to a specific person, including instruments payable to bearer or to cash.

Benefit Corporation A for-profit corporation that seeks to have a material positive impact on society and the environment. It is available by statute in a number of states.

Bequest A gift of personal property by will (from the verb *to bequeath*).

Beyond a Reasonable Doubt The standard of proof used in criminal cases.

Bilateral Contract A type of contract that arises when a promise is given in exchange for a return promise.

Bilateral Mistake A mistake that occurs when both parties to a contract are mistaken about the same material fact.

Bill of Rights The first ten amendments to the U.S. Constitution.

Binder A written, temporary insurance policy.

Binding Authority Any source of law that a court *must* follow when deciding a case.

Blank Indorsement An indorsement on an instrument that specifies no indorsee. An order instrument that is indorsed in blank becomes a bearer instrument.

Bona Fide Occupational Qualification (BFOQ) An identifiable characteristic reasonably necessary to the normal operation of a particular business. Such characteristics can include gender, national origin, and religion, but not race.

Bond A security that evidences a corporate (or government) debt.

Botnet A network of compromised computers connected to the Internet that can be used to generate spam, relay viruses, or cause servers to fail.

Breach of Contract The failure, without legal excuse, of a promisor to perform the obligations of a contract.

Brief A written summary or statement prepared by one side in a lawsuit to explain its case to the judge.

Browse-Wrap Terms Terms or conditions of use presented when an online buyer downloads a product but to which the buyer does not have to agree before installing or using the product.

Burglary The unlawful entry or breaking into a building with the intent to commit a felony.

Business Ethics The application of moral principles and values in a business context.

Business Invitees Persons, such as customers or clients who are invited onto business premises by the owner of those premises for business purposes.

Business Judgment Rule A rule under which courts will not hold corporate officers and directors liable for honest mistakes of judgment and bad business decisions that were made in good faith.

Business Necessity A defense to an allegation of employment discrimination in which the employer demonstrates that an employment practice that discriminates against members of a protected class is related to job performance.

Business Tort Wrongful interference with another's business rights and relationships.

Business Trust A form of business organization, created by a written trust agreement, that resembles a corporation. Legal ownership and management of the trust's property stay with the trustees, and the profits are distributed to the beneficiaries, who have limited liability.

Buyout Price The amount payable to a partner on dissociation from a partnership, based on the amount distributable to that partner if the partnership had been wound up on that date and offset by any damages for wrongful dissociation.

Buy-Sell Agreement An agreement made at the time of partnership formation providing for one or more of the partners to buy out the other or others, in the event the firm is dissolved. It is also called a *buyout agreement*.

Bylaws The internal rules of management adopted by a corporation at its first organizational meeting.

C

Case Law The rules of law announced in court decisions. Case law interprets statutes, regulations, and constitutional provisions, and governs all areas not covered by statutory or administrative law.

Case on Point A previous case involving factual circumstances and issues that are similar to those in the case before the court.

Cashier's Check A check drawn by a bank on itself.

Categorical Imperative An ethical guideline developed by Immanuel Kant under which an action is evaluated in terms of what would happen if everybody else in the same situation, or category, acted the same way.

Causation in Fact An act or omission without which an event would not have occurred.

Cease-and-Desist Order An administrative or judicial order prohibiting a person or business firm from conducting activities that an agency or court has deemed illegal.

Certificate of Deposit (CD) A note issued by a bank in which the bank acknowledges the receipt of funds from a party and promises to repay that amount, with interest, to the party on a certain date.

Certificate of Limited Partnership The document that must be filed with a designated state official to form a limited partnership.

Certification Mark A mark used by one or more persons, other than the owner, to certify the region, materials, mode of manufacture, quality, or other characteristic of specific goods or services.

Certified Check A check that has been accepted in writing by the bank on which it is drawn. By certifying (accepting) the check, the bank promises to pay the check at the time it is presented.

Charging Order In partnership law, an order granted by a court to a judgment creditor that entitles the creditor to attach a partner's interest in the partnership.

Charitable Trust A trust in which the property held by the trustee must be used for a charitable purpose, such as the advancement of health, education, or religion.

Chattel Personal property.

Check A draft drawn by a drawer ordering the drawee bank or financial institution to pay a certain amount of funds to the payee on demand.

Checks and Balances The system under which the powers of the federal government are divided among three separate branches—the executive, legislative, and judicial branches—each of which exercises a check on the actions of the others.

Choice-of-Law Clause A clause in a contract designating the law (such as the law of a particular state or nation) that will govern the contract.

Citation A reference to a publication in which a legal authority—such as a statute or a court decision—or other source can be found.

Civil Law The branch of law dealing with the definition and enforcement of all private or public rights, as opposed to criminal matters.

Civil Law System A system of law derived from Roman law that is based on codified laws (rather than on case precedents).

Clearinghouse A system or place where banks exchange checks and drafts drawn on each other and settle daily balances.

Click-On Agreement An agreement that arises when an online buyer clicks on "I agree" or otherwise indicates assent to be bound by the terms of an offer.

Close Corporation A corporation whose shareholders are limited to a small group of persons, often family members.

Closed Shop A firm that requires union membership as a condition of employment.

Cloud Computing The delivery to users of on-demand services from third-party servers over a network.

Codicil A written supplement or modification to a will. A codicil must be executed with the same formalities as a will.

Collateral Under Article 9 of the UCC, the property subject to a security interest.

Collateral Promise A secondary promise to a primary transaction, such as a promise made by one person to pay the debts of another if the latter fails to perform. A collateral promise normally must be in writing to be enforceable.

Collecting Bank Any bank handling an item for collection, except the payor bank.

Collective Bargaining The process by which labor and management negotiate the terms and conditions of employment, including working hours and workplace conditions.

Collective Mark A mark used by members of a cooperative, association, union, or other organization to certify the region, materials, mode of manufacture, quality, or other characteristic of specific goods or services.

Comity The principle by which one nation defers to and gives effect to the laws and judicial decrees of another nation. This recognition is based primarily on respect.

Commerce Clause The provision in Article I, Section 8, of the U.S. Constitution that gives Congress the power to regulate interstate commerce.

Commercial Impracticability A doctrine that may excuse the duty to perform a contract when performance becomes much more difficult or costly due to forces that neither party could have controlled or foreseen at the time the contract was formed.

Commingled Mixed to such a degree that the individual parts (such as funds or goods) no longer have separate identities.

Common Law The body of law developed from custom or judicial decisions in English and U.S. courts, not attributable to a legislature.

Common Stock Shares of ownership in a corporation that give the owner a proportionate interest in the corporation with regard to control, earnings, and net assets. Common stock is lowest in priority with respect to payment of dividends and distribution of the corporation's assets on dissolution.

Community Property A form of concurrent property ownership in which each spouse owns an undivided one-half interest in property acquired during the marriage.

Comparative Negligence A rule in tort law, used in the majority of states, that reduces the plaintiff's recovery in proportion to the plaintiff's degree of fault, rather than barring recovery completely.

Compelling Government Interest A test of constitutionality that requires the government to have convincing reasons for passing any law that restricts fundamental rights, such as free speech, or distinguishes between people based on a suspect trait.

Compensatory Damages A monetary award equivalent to the actual value of injuries or damage sustained by the aggrieved party.

Complaint The pleading made by a plaintiff alleging wrongdoing on the part of the defendant. When filed with a court, the complaint initiates a lawsuit.

Computer Crime Any violation of criminal law that involves knowledge of computer technology for its perpetration, investigation, or prosecution.

Concentrated Industry An industry in which a single firm or a small number of firms control a large percentage of market sales.

Concurrent Conditions Conditions that must occur or be performed at the same time—they are mutually dependent. No obligations arise until these conditions are simultaneously performed.

Concurrent Jurisdiction Jurisdiction that exists when two different courts have the power to hear a case.

Concurrent Ownership Joint ownership.

Concurring Opinion A court opinion by one or more judges or justices who agree with the majority but want to make or emphasize a point that was not made or emphasized in the majority's opinion.

Condemnation Proceedings The judicial procedure by which the government exercises its power of eminent domain. It generally involves two phases: a taking and a determination of fair value.

Condition A qualification, provision, or clause in a contractual agreement, the occurrence or nonoccurrence of which creates, suspends, or terminates the obligations of the contracting parties.

Condition Precedent A condition in a contract that must be met before a party's promise becomes absolute.

Condition Subsequent A condition in a contract that, if it occurs, operates to terminate a party's absolute promise to perform.

Confiscation A government's taking of a privately owned business or personal property without a proper public purpose or an award of just compensation.

Conforming Goods Goods that conform to contract specifications.

Confusion The mixing together of goods belonging to two or more owners to such an extent that the separately owned goods cannot be identified.

Consequential Damages Foreseeable damages that result from a party's breach of contract but are caused by special circumstances beyond the contract itself.

Consideration The value given in return for a promise or performance in a contractual agreement.

Constitutional Law The body of law derived from the U.S. Constitution and the constitutions of the various states.

Constructive Delivery A symbolic delivery of property that cannot be physically delivered.

Constructive Discharge A termination of employment brought about by making the employee's working conditions so intolerable that the employee reasonably feels compelled to leave.

Constructive Eviction A form of eviction that occurs when a landlord fails to perform adequately any of the duties required by the lease, thereby making the tenant's further use and enjoyment of the property exceedingly difficult or impossible.

Constructive Fraud Conduct that is treated as fraud under the law even when there is no proof of intent to defraud, usually because of the existence of a special relationship or fiduciary duty.

Constructive Trust An equitable trust that is imposed in the interests of fairness and justice when someone wrongfully holds legal title to property.

Consumer-Debtor One whose debts result primarily from the purchase of goods for personal, family, or household use.

Continuation Statement A statement that, if filed within six months prior to the expiration date of the original financing statement, continues the perfection of the security interest for another five years.

Contract A set of promises constituting an agreement between parties, giving each a legal duty to the other and the right to seek a remedy for the breach of the promises or duties.

Contractual Capacity The capacity required by the law for a party who enters into a contract to be bound by that contract.

Contributory Negligence A rule in tort law, used in only a few states, that completely bars the plaintiff from recovering any damages if the harm suffered is partly the plaintiff's own fault.

Conversion Wrongfully taking or retaining possession of an individual's personal property and placing it in the service of another.

Conveyance The transfer of title to real property from one person to another by deed or other document.

Cookie A small file sent from a website and stored in a user's Web browser to track the user's Web browsing activities.

"Cooling-Off" Laws Laws that allow buyers of goods sold in certain transactions to cancel their contracts within three business days.

Cooperative An association, which may or may not be incorporated, that is organized to provide an economic service to its members. Unincorporated cooperatives are often treated like partnerships for tax and other legal purposes.

Copyright The exclusive right of an author or originator of a literary or artistic production to publish, print, sell, or otherwise use that production for a statutory period of time.

Corporate Governance A set of policies specifying the rights and responsibilities of the various participants in a corporation and spelling out the rules and procedures for making corporate decisions.

Corporate Social Responsibility (CSR) The idea that corporations can and should act ethically and be accountable to society for their actions.

Corporation A legal entity formed in compliance with statutory requirements that is distinct from its shareholder-owners.

Cost-Benefit Analysis A decision-making technique that involves weighing the costs of a given action against the benefits of that action.

Co-Surety A party who assumes liability jointly with another surety for the payment of a debtor's obligation under a suretyship arrangement.

Counteradvertising New advertising that is undertaken to correct earlier false claims that were made about a product.

Counterclaim A claim made by a defendant in a civil lawsuit against the plaintiff. In effect, the defendant is suing the plaintiff.

Counteroffer An offeree's response to an offer in which the offeree rejects the original offer and at the same time makes a new offer.

Course of Dealing Prior conduct between the parties to a contract that establishes a common basis for their understanding.

Course of Performance The conduct that occurs under the terms of a particular agreement, which indicates what the parties to that agreement intended the agreement to mean.

Covenant Not to Compete A contractual promise of one party to refrain from conducting business similar to that of another party for a certain period of time and within a specified geographical area.

Covenant Not to Sue An agreement to substitute a contractual obligation for another legal action based on a valid claim.

Cover A remedy that allows the buyer or lessee, on the seller's or lessor's breach, to obtain substitute goods from another seller or lessor.

Cram-Down Provision A provision of the Bankruptcy Code that allows a court to confirm a debtor's Chapter 11 reorganization plan even though only one class of creditors has accepted it.

Creditors' Composition Agreements A contract between debtors and creditors in which the creditors agree to discharge the debts on the debtor's payment of a sum less than the amount actually owed.

Crime A wrong against society proclaimed in a statute and, if committed, punishable by society through fines, imprisonment, or death.

Criminal Law The branch of law that defines and punishes wrongful actions committed against the public.

Cross-Collateralization The use of an asset that is not the subject of a loan to collateralize that loan.

Cost-Benefit Analysis A decision-making technique that involves weighing the costs of a given action against the benefits of that action.

Crowdfunding A cooperative activity in which people network and pool funds and other resources via the Internet to assist a cause (such as disaster relief) or invest in a venture (business).

Cure The right of a party who tenders nonconforming performance to correct his or her performance within the contract period.

Cyber Crime A crime that occurs in the online environment.

Cyber Fraud Any misrepresentation knowingly made over the Internet with the intention of deceiving another for the purpose of obtaining property or funds.

Cyberlaw An informal term used to refer to all laws governing electronic communications and transactions, particularly those conducted via the Internet.

Cybersquatting The act of registering a domain name that is the same as, or confusingly similar to, the trademark of another and then offering to sell that domain name back to the trademark owner.

Cyberterrorist Criminals who use technology and the Internet to cause fear, violence, and extreme financial harm.

Cyber Tort A tort committed via the Internet.

D

Damages A monetary award sought as a remedy for a breach of contract or a tortious action.

Debtor in Possession (DIP) In Chapter 11 bankruptcy proceedings, a debtor who is allowed to continue in possession of the business and to continue business operations.

Debtor Under Article 9 of the UCC, any party who owes payment or performance of a secured obligation.

Deceptive Advertising Advertising that misleads consumers, either by making unjustified claims about a product or by omitting a material fact concerning the product.

Deed A document by which title to real property is passed.

Defalcation Embezzlement or misappropriation of funds.

Defamation Anything published or publicly spoken that causes injury to another's good name, reputation, or character.

Default Failure to pay a debt when it is due.

Default Judgment A judgment entered by a court against a defendant who has failed to appear in court to answer or defend against the plaintiff's claim.

Defendant One against whom a lawsuit is brought or the accused person in a criminal proceeding.

Defense A reason offered by a defendant in an action or lawsuit as to why the plaintiff should not prevail.

Deficiency Judgment A judgment against a debtor for the amount of a debt remaining unpaid after the collateral has been repossessed and sold.

Delegatee A party to whom contractual obligations are transferred, or delegated.

Delegation of Duties The transfer to another of a contractual duty.

Delegator A party who transfers (delegates) obligations under a contract to another party (the *delegatee*).

Depositary Bank The first bank to receive a check for payment.

Deposition The testimony of a party to a lawsuit or a witness taken under oath before a trial.

Destination Contract A contract for the sale of goods in which the seller is required or authorized to ship the goods by carrier and tender delivery of the goods at a particular destination. The seller assumes liability for any losses or damage to the goods until they are tendered at the destination specified in the contract.

Devise A gift of real property by will, or the act of giving real property by will.

Devisee One designated in a will to receive a gift of real property.

Disaffirmance The legal avoidance, or setting aside, of a contractual obligation.

Discharge The termination of an obligation, such as occurs when the parties to a contract have fully performed their contractual obligations. In bankruptcy proceedings, the termination of a debtor's obligation to pay debts.

Disclosed Principal A principal whose identity is known to a third party at the time the agent makes a contract with the third party.

Discovery A method by which the opposing parties obtain information from each other to prepare for trial.

Dishonor To refuse to pay or to accept a negotiable instrument that has been presented in a timely and proper manner.

Disparagement of Property An economically injurious falsehood about another's product or property.

Disparate-Impact Discrimination Discrimination that results from certain employer practices or procedures that, although not discriminatory on their face, have a discriminatory effect.

Disparate-Treatment Discrimination A form of employment discrimination that results when an employer intentionally discriminates against employees who are members of protected classes.

Dissenting Opinion A court opinion that presents the views of one or more judges or justices who disagree with the majority's decision.

Dissociation The severance of the relationship between a partner and a partnership.

Dissolution The formal disbanding of a partnership or a corporation. Partnerships can be dissolved by acts of the partners, by operation of law, or by judicial decree.

Distributed Network A network that can be used by persons located (distributed) around the country or the globe to share computer files.

Distribution Agreement A contract between a seller and a distributor of the seller's products setting out the terms and conditions of the distributorship.

Diversity of Citizenship A basis for federal court jurisdiction over a lawsuit between citizens of different states or a U.S. citizen and a citizen of a different country.

Divestiture A company's sale of one or more of its divisions' operating functions under court order as part of the enforcement of the antitrust laws.

Dividend A distribution of corporate profits to the corporation's shareholders in proportion to the number of shares held.

Docket The list of cases entered on a court's calendar and thus scheduled to be heard by the court.

Document of Title A paper exchanged in the regular course of business that evidences the right to possession of goods (for example, a bill of lading or a warehouse receipt).

Domain Name The series of letters and symbols used to identify a site operator on the Internet (an Internet address).

Domestic Corporation In a given state, a corporation that is organized under the law of that state.

Dominion Ownership rights in property, including the right to possess and control the property.

Double Jeopardy The Fifth Amendment requirement that prohibits a person from being tried twice for the same criminal offense.

Draft Any instrument drawn on a drawee that orders the drawee to pay a certain amount of funds, usually to a third party (the payee), on demand or at a definite future time.

Dram Shop Act A state statute that imposes liability on those who sell or serve alcohol, for injuries resulting from accidents caused by intoxicated persons when the sellers or servers contributed to the intoxication.

Drawee The party that is ordered to pay a draft or check. With a check, a bank or a financial institution is always the drawee.

Drawer The party that initiates a draft (such as a check), thereby ordering the drawee to pay.

Due Diligence A required standard of care that certain professionals, such as accountants, must meet to avoid liability for securities violations.

Due Process Clause The provisions in the Fifth and Fourteenth Amendments that guarantee that no person shall be deprived of life, liberty, or property without due process of law. State constitutions often include similar clauses.

Dumping The sale of goods in a foreign country at a price below the price charged for the same goods in the domestic market.

Duress Unlawful pressure causing a person to perform an act that the person would not otherwise perform.

Duty-Based Ethics An ethical philosophy rooted in the idea that every person (and every business) has certain duties to others, including both humans and the planet.

Duty of Care The duty of all persons, as established by tort law, to exercise a reasonable amount of care in their dealings with others. Failure to exercise due care, which is normally determined by the reasonable person standard, constitutes the tort of negligence.

E

Easement A nonpossessory right, established by express or implied agreement, to make limited use of another's property without removing anything from the property.

eBill An electronic version of a paper bill for goods or services that is issued online and can be paid online.

E-Contract A contract that is formed electronically.

E-Evidence A type of evidence that consists of computer-generated or electronically recorded information.

Electronic Fund Transfer (EFT) A transfer of funds through the use of an electronic terminal, smartphone, tablet, telephone, or computer.

Emancipation In regard to minors, the act of being freed from parental control.

Embezzlement The fraudulent appropriation of funds or other property by a person who was entrusted with the funds or property.

Eminent Domain The power of a government to take land from private citizens for public use on the payment of just compensation.

E-Money Prepaid funds stored on microchips in laptops, smartphones, tablets, and other devices.

Employment at Will A common law doctrine under which either party may terminate an employment relationship at any time for any reason, unless it would violate a contract or statute.

Employment Contract A contract between an employer and an employee in which the terms and conditions of employment are stated.

Enabling Legislation A statute enacted by Congress that authorizes the creation of an administrative agency and specifies the name, composition, purpose, and powers of the agency being created.

Entrapment A defense in which a defendant claims to have been induced by a public official to commit a crime that otherwise would not have been committed.

Entrepreneur One who initiates and assumes the financial risk of a new business enterprise and undertakes to provide or control its management.

Environmental Impact Statement (EIS) A formal analysis required for any major federal action that will significantly affect the quality of the environment to determine the action's impact and explore alternatives.

Equal Dignity Rule A rule requiring that an agent's authority be in writing if the contract to be made on behalf of the principal must be in writing.

Equal Protection Clause The provision in the Fourteenth Amendment that requires state governments to treat similarly situated individuals in a similar manner.

Equitable Maxims General propositions or principles of law that have to do with fairness (equity).

E-Signature An electronic sound, symbol, or process attached to or logically associated with a record and adopted by a person with the intent to sign the record.

Establishment Clause The provision in the First Amendment that prohibits the government from establishing any state-sponsored religion or enacting any law that promotes religion or favors one religion over another.

Estate in Bankruptcy All of the property owned by a person, including real estate and personal property.

Estopped Barred, impeded, or precluded.

Estray Statute A statute defining finders' rights in property when the true owners are unknown.

Ethical Reasoning A reasoning process in which an individual links his or her moral convictions or ethical standards to the situation at hand.

Ethics Moral principles and values applied to social behavior.

Eviction A landlord's act of depriving a tenant of possession of the leased premises.

Exclusionary Rule A rule that prevents evidence that is obtained illegally or without a proper search warrant from being admissible in court.

Exclusive-Dealing Contract An agreement under which a seller forbids a buyer to purchase products from the seller's competitors.

Exclusive Jurisdiction Jurisdiction that exists when a case can be heard only in a particular court or type of court.

Exculpatory Clause A clause that releases a contractual party from liability in the event of monetary or physical injury, no matter who is at fault.

Executed Contract A contract that has been fully performed by both parties.

Execution The implementation of a court's decree or judgment.

Executor A person appointed by a testator in a will to administer the testator's estate.

Executory Contract A contract that has not yet been fully performed.

Export The sale of goods and services by domestic firms to buyers located in other countries.

Express Contract A contract in which the terms of the agreement are stated in words, oral or written.

Express Warranty A seller's or lessor's promise as to the quality, condition, description, or performance of the goods being sold or leased.

Expropriation A government's seizure of a privately owned business or personal property for a proper public purpose and with just compensation.

Extension Clause A clause in a time instrument that allows the instrument's date of maturity to be extended into the future.

Extrinsic Evidence Any evidence not contained in the contract itself, which may include the testimony of the parties, additional agreements or communications, or other information relevant to determining the parties' intent.

F

Federal Form of Government A system of government in which the states form a union and the sovereign power is divided between the central government and the member states.

Federal Question A question that pertains to the U.S. Constitution, an act of Congress, or a treaty and provides a basis for federal jurisdiction in a case.

Federal Reserve System A network of twelve district banks and related branches located around the country and headed by the Federal Reserve Board of Governors. Most banks in the United States have Federal Reserve accounts.

Fee Simple An ownership interest in land in which the owner has the greatest possible aggregation of rights, privileges, and power.

Felony A serious crime—such as arson, murder, rape, or robbery—that carries the most severe sanctions, ranging from more than one year in a state or federal prison to the death penalty.

Fictitious Payee A payee on a negotiable instrument whom the maker or drawer did not intend to have an interest in the instrument. Indorsements by fictitious payees are treated as authorized indorsements under UCC Article 3.

Fiduciary As a noun, a person who, having undertaken a certain enterprise on behalf of another person, has a duty to act for the other person's benefit in all matters related to that enterprise. As an adjective, a relationship founded on trust and confidence.

Filtering Software A computer program that is designed to block access to certain websites, based on their content. The software blocks the retrieval of a site whose URL or key words are on a list within the program.

Financing Statement A document filed by a secured creditor with the appropriate official to give notice to the public of the creditor's security interest in collateral belonging to the debtor named in the statement.

Firm Offer An offer (by a merchant) that is irrevocable without the necessity of consideration for a stated period of time or, if no definite period is stated, for a reasonable time (neither period to exceed three months).

Fixed-Term Tenancy A type of tenancy under which property is leased for a specified period of time, such as a month, a year, or a period of years. It is also called a *tenancy for years*.

Fixture An item of personal property that has become so closely associated with real property that it is legally regarded as part of that real property.

Floating Lien A security interest in proceeds, after-acquired property, or collateral subject to future advances by the secured party (or all three). The security interest is retained even when the collateral changes in character, classification, or location.

Forbearance The act of refraining from an action that one has a legal right to undertake.

Foreign Corporation In a given state, a corporation that does business in that state but is not incorporated there.

Forgery The fraudulent making or altering of any writing in a way that changes the legal rights and liabilities of another.

Formal Contract An agreement that by law requires a specific form for its validity.

Forum-Selection Clause A provision in a contract designating the court, jurisdiction, or tribunal that will decide any disputes arising under the contract.

Franchise Any arrangement in which the owner of a trademark, trade name, or copyright licenses another to use that trademark, trade name, or copyright in the selling of goods or services.

Franchisee One receiving a license to use another's (the franchisor's) trademark, trade name, or copyright in the sale of goods and services.

Franchisor One licensing another (the franchisee) to use the owner's trademark, trade name, or copyright in the selling of goods or services.

Fraudulent Misrepresentation Any misrepresentation, either by misstatement or by omission of a material fact, knowingly made with the intention of deceiving another and on which a reasonable person would and does rely to that person's detriment.

Free Exercise Clause The provision in the First Amendment that prohibits the government from interfering with people's religious practices or forms of worship.

Free-Writing Prospectus A written, electronic, or graphic communication associated with the offer to sell a security and used during the waiting period to supplement other information about the security.

Frustration of Purpose A court-created doctrine under which a party to a contract will be relieved of the duty to perform when the objective purpose of performance no longer exists due to reasons beyond that party's control.

Full Faith and Credit Clause A provision in Article IV, Section 1, of the U.S. Constitution that ensures that rights established under deeds, wills, contracts, and similar instruments in one state will be honored by other states and that judicial decisions will be honored and enforced in all states.

Fungible Goods Goods that are alike by physical nature, agreement, or trade usage.

G

Garnishment A legal process whereby a creditor collects a debt by seizing property of the debtor that is in the hands of a third party.

General Damages In a tort case, an amount awarded to compensate individuals for the nonmonetary aspects of the harm suffered, such as pain and suffering. Not available to companies.

Generally Accepted Accounting Principles (GAAP) The conventions, rules, and procedures developed by the Financial Accounting Standards Board to define accepted accounting practices at a particular time.

Generally Accepted Auditing Standards (GAAS) Standards established by the American Institute of Certified Public Accountants to define the professional qualities and judgment that should be exercised by an auditor in performing an audit.

General Partner In a limited partnership, a partner who assumes responsibility for the management of the partnership and has full liability for all partnership debts.

Gift A voluntary transfer of property made without consideration, past or present.

Gift *Causa Mortis* A gift made in contemplation of imminent death. The gift is revoked if the donor does not die as contemplated.

Gift *Inter Vivos* A gift made during one's lifetime and not in contemplation of imminent death, in contrast to a gift *causa mortis*.

Good Samaritan Statute A state statute stipulating that persons who provide emergency services to, or rescue, someone in peril cannot be sued for negligence unless they act recklessly and cause further harm.

Goodwill In the business context, the valuable reputation of a business viewed as an intangible asset.

Grand Jury A group of citizens who decide, after hearing the state's evidence, whether a reasonable basis (probable cause) exists for believing that a crime has been committed and that a trial ought to be held.

Group Boycott An agreement by two or more sellers to refuse to deal with a particular person or firm.

Guarantor A third party who agrees to be secondarily liable for the debt of another (the debtor) only after the principal debtor defaults.

H

Hacker A person who uses computers to gain unauthorized access to data.

Historical School A school of legal thought that looks to the past to determine what the principles of contemporary law should be.

Holder Any person in possession of an instrument drawn, issued, or indorsed to that person, to that person's order, to bearer, or in blank.

Holder in Due Course (HDC) A holder who acquires a negotiable instrument for value, in good faith, and without notice that the instrument is defective.

Holographic Will A will written entirely in the testator's handwriting.

Homestead Exemption A law permitting a debtor to retain the family home, either in its entirety or up to a specified dollar amount, free from the claims of unsecured creditors or trustees in bankruptcy.

Horizontal Merger A merger between two firms that are competing in the same market.

Horizontal Restraint Any agreement that restrains competition between rival firms competing in the same market.

Hot-Cargo Agreement An illegal agreement in which employers voluntarily agree with unions not to handle, use, or deal in the nonunion-produced goods of other employers.

I

I-9 Verification The process of verifying the employment eligibility and identity of a new worker. It must be completed within three days after the worker commences employment.

I-551 Permanent Resident Card A document, known as a "green card," that shows that a foreign-born individual can legally work in the United States.

Identification In a sale of goods, the express designation of the goods provided for in the contract.

Identity Theft The illegal use of someone else's personal information to access the victim's financial resources.

Implied Contract A contract formed in whole or in part from the conduct of the parties.

Implied Warranty A warranty that arises by law because of the circumstances of a sale and not from the seller's express promise.

Implied Warranty of Fitness for a Particular Purpose A warranty that goods sold or leased are fit for the particular purpose for which the buyer or lessee will use the goods.

Implied Warranty of Habitability An implied promise by a seller of a new house that the house is fit for human habitation. Also, the implied promise by a landlord that rented residential premises are habitable.

Implied Warranty of Merchantability A warranty that goods being sold or leased are reasonably fit for the general purpose for which they are sold or leased, are properly packaged and labeled, and are of proper quality.

Impossibility of Performance A doctrine under which a party to a contract is relieved of the duty to perform when performance becomes objectively impossible or totally impracticable.

Imposter One who induces a maker or drawer to issue a negotiable instrument in the name of an impersonated payee. Indorsements by imposters are treated as authorized indorsements under UCC Article 3.

Incidental Beneficiary A third party who benefits from a contract even though the contract was not formed for that purpose. An incidental beneficiary has no rights in the contract and cannot sue to have it enforced.

Incidental Damages Damages that compensate for expenses directly incurred because of a breach of contract, such as those incurred to obtain performance from another source.

Incontestability Clause A clause in a policy for life or health insurance stating that after the policy has been in force for a specified length of time (usually two or three years), the insurer cannot contest statements made in the policyholder's application.

Independent Contractor One who works for, and receives payment from, an employer but whose working conditions and methods are not controlled by the employer. An independent contractor is not an employee but may be an agent.

Indictment A charge by a grand jury that a reasonable basis (probable cause) exists for believing that a crime has been committed and that a trial should be held.

Indorsement A signature placed on an instrument for the purpose of transferring ownership rights in the instrument.

Informal Contract A contract that does not require a specific form or method of creation to be valid.

Information A formal accusation or complaint (without an indictment) issued in certain types of actions (usually criminal actions involving lesser crimes) by a government prosecutor.

Information Return A tax return submitted by a partnership that reports the business's income and losses. The partnership itself does not pay taxes on the income received by the partnership.

Innocent Misrepresentation A misrepresentation that occurs when a person makes a false statement of fact that he or she believes is true.

Inside Director A person on the board of directors who is also an officer of the corporation.

Insider In bankruptcy proceedings, any individual, partnership, or corporation with a close personal or business relation with the debtor.

Insider Trading The purchase or sale of securities on the basis of information that has not been made available to the public.

Installment Contract A contract that requires or authorizes delivery in two or more separate lots to be accepted and paid for separately.

Insurable Interest A property interest in goods being sold or leased that is sufficiently substantial to permit a party to insure against damage to the goods.

Insurance A contract by which the insurer promises to reimburse the insured or a beneficiary in the event that the insured is injured, dies, or sustains damage to property as a result of particular, stated contingencies.

Intangible Property Property that cannot be seen or touched but exists only conceptually, such as corporate stocks. Such property is not governed by Article 2 of the UCC.

Integrated Contract A written contract that constitutes the final expression of the parties' agreement. Evidence extraneous to the contract that contradicts or alters the meaning of the contract in any way is inadmissible.

Intellectual Property Property resulting from intellectual and creative processes.

Intended Beneficiary A third party for whose benefit a contract is formed. An intended beneficiary can sue the promisor if the contract is breached.

Intentional Tort A wrongful act knowingly committed.

Intermediary Bank Any bank to which an item is transferred in the course of collection, except the depositary or payor bank.

International Financial Reporting Standards (IFRS) A set of accounting standards used in many nations around the world.

International Law Law—based on international customs, organizations, and treaties—that governs relations among nations.

International Organization An organization composed mainly of member nations and usually established by treaty—for instance, the United Nations. More broadly, the term also includes nongovernmental organizations (NGOs), such as the Red Cross.

Internet Service Provider (ISP) A business or organization that offers users access to the Internet and related services.

Interpretive Rules Nonbinding rules or policy statements issued by an administrative agency that explains how it interprets and intends to apply the statutes it enforces.

Interrogatories A series of written questions for which written answers are prepared by a party to a lawsuit, usually with the assistance of the party's attorney, and then signed under oath.

Intestacy Laws State statutes that specify how property will be distributed when a person dies intestate (without a valid will).

Intestate As a noun, one who has died without having created a valid will. As an adjective, the state of having died without a will.

Investment Company A company that acts on the behalf of many smaller shareholders-owners by buying a large portfolio of securities and professionally managing that portfolio.

Investment Contract In securities law, a transaction in which a person invests in a common enterprise reasonably expecting profits that are derived primarily from the efforts of others.

J

Joint and Several Liability In partnership law, a doctrine under which a plaintiff may sue, and collect a judgment from, all of the partners together (jointly) or one or more of the partners separately (severally, or individually). Partners can be held liable even if they did not participate in, ratify, or know about the conduct that gave rise to the lawsuit.

Joint Liability In partnership law, the partners' shared liability for partnership obligations and debts. A third party must sue all of the partners as a group, but each partner can be held liable for the full amount.

Joint Stock Company A hybrid form of business organization that combines characteristics of a corporation and a partnership. Usually, a joint stock company is regarded as a partnership for tax and other legal purposes.

Joint Tenancy Joint ownership of property in which each co-owner owns an undivided portion of the property. On the death of one of the joint tenants, that tenant's interest automatically passes to the surviving joint tenant(s).

Joint Venture A joint undertaking by two or more persons or business entities to combine their efforts or their property for a single transaction or project or for a related series of transactions or projects. A joint venture is generally treated like a partnership for tax and other legal purposes.

Judicial Review The process by which a court decides on the constitutionality of legislative enactments and actions of the executive branch.

Jurisdiction The authority of a court to hear and decide a specific case.

Jurisprudence The science or philosophy of law.

Justiciable Controversy A controversy that is not hypothetical or academic but real and substantial. It is a requirement that must be satisfied before a court will hear a case.

L

Larceny The wrongful taking and carrying away of another person's personal property with the intent to permanently deprive the owner of the property.

Latent Defect A defect that is not obvious or cannot readily be ascertained.

Law A body of enforceable rules governing relationships among individuals and between individuals and their society.

Lease Under Article 2A of the UCC, a transfer of the right to possess and use goods for a period of time in exchange for payment.

Lease Agreement An agreement in which one person (the lessor) agrees to transfer the right to the possession and use of property to another person (the lessee) in exchange for rental payments.

Leasehold Estate An interest in real property that gives a tenant a qualified right to possess and/or use the property for a limited time under a lease.

Legacy A gift of personal property under a will.

Legal Positivism A school of legal thought centered on the assumption that there is no law higher than the laws created by a national government. Laws must be obeyed, even if they are unjust, to prevent anarchy.

Legal Realism A school of legal thought that holds that the law is only one factor to be considered when deciding cases, and that social and economic circumstances should also be taken into account.

Legal Reasoning The process of reasoning by which a judge harmonizes his or her opinion with the judicial decisions in previous cases.

Legatee One designated in a will to receive a gift of personal property.

Legislative Rules Administrative agency rules that carry the same weight as a congressionally enacted statute.

Lessee A person who acquires the right to the possession and use of another's goods in exchange for rental payments.

Lessor A person who transfers the right to the possession and use of goods to another in exchange for rental payments.

Levy The legal process of obtaining funds through the seizure and sale of nonexempt property, usually done after a writ of execution has been issued.

Liability The state of being legally responsible (liable) for something, such as a debt or obligation.

Libel Defamation in writing or another permanent form (such as a digital recording).

License An agreement by the owner of intellectual property to permit another to use a trademark, copyright, patent, or trade secret for certain limited purposes. In the context of real property, a revocable right or privilege to enter onto another person's land.

Lien An encumbrance on a property to satisfy a debt or protect a claim for payment of a debt.

Life Estate An interest in land that exists only for the duration of the life of a specified individual, usually the holder of the estate.

Limited Liability Company (LLC) A hybrid form of business enterprise that offers the limited liability of a corporation and the tax advantages of a partnership.

Limited Liability Partnership (LLP) A hybrid form of business organization that is used mainly by professionals who normally do business as partners in a partnership. An LLP is a pass-through entity for tax purposes, but a partner's personal liability for the malpractice of other partners is limited.

Limited Partner In a limited partnership, a partner who contributes capital to the partnership but has no right to participate in its management and has no liability for partnership debts beyond the amount of her or his investment.

Limited Partnership (LP) A partnership consisting of one or more general partners and one or more limited partners.

Liquidated Damages An amount, stipulated in a contract, that the parties to the contract believe to be a reasonable estimation of the damages that will occur in the event of a breach.

Liquidated Debt A debt whose amount has been ascertained, fixed, agreed on, settled, or exactly determined.

Liquidation The sale of the nonexempt assets of a debtor and the distribution of the funds received to creditors.

Litigation The process of resolving a dispute through the court system.

Living (*Inter Vivos*) Trust A trust created by the grantor (settlor) and effective during his or her lifetime.

Long Arm Statute A state statute that permits a state to exercise jurisdiction over nonresident defendants.

Lost Property Property that the owner has involuntarily parted with and then cannot find or recover.

M

Mailbox Rule A common law rule that acceptance takes effect, and thus completes formation of the contract, at the time the offeree sends or delivers the acceptance via the communication mode expressly or impliedly authorized by the offeror.

Majority Opinion A court opinion that represents the views of the majority (more than half) of the judges or justices deciding the case.

Maker One who promises to pay a fixed amount of funds to the holder of a promissory note or a certificate of deposit (CD).

Malpractice Professional negligence, or failure to exercise reasonable care and professional judgment, that results in injury, loss, or damage to those relying on the professional.

Malware Malicious software programs, such as viruses and worms, that are designed to cause harm to a computer, network, or other device.

Market Concentration The degree to which a small number of firms control a large percentage of a relevant market.

Market Power The power of a firm to control the market price of its product. A monopoly has the greatest degree of market power.

Market-Share Liability A theory under which liability is shared among all firms that manufactured and distributed a particular product during a certain period of time. This form of liability sharing is used only when the specific source of the harmful product is unidentifiable.

Mechanic's Lien A nonpossessory, filed lien on an owner's real estate for labor, services, or materials furnished for making improvements on the realty.

Mediation A method of settling disputes outside the courts by using the services of a neutral third party, who acts as a communicating agent between the parties and assists them in negotiating a settlement.

Members Persons who have ownership interest in a limited liability company.

Mens Rea A wrongful mental state ("guilty mind"), or intent. It is one of the two essential elements required to establish criminal liability.

Merchant Under the UCC, a person who deals in goods of the kind involved in the sales contract or who holds herself or himself out as having skill or knowledge peculiar to the practices or goods being purchased or sold.

Metadata Data that are automatically recorded by electronic devices and provide information about who created a file and when, and who accessed, modified, or transmitted the file. It can be described as data about data.

Meta Tags Key words in a document that can serve as an index reference to the document. On the Web, search engines return results based, in part, on the tags in Web documents.

Minimum Wage The lowest wage, either by government regulation or by union contract, that an employer may pay an hourly worker.

Mirror Image Rule A common law rule that requires that the terms of the offeree's acceptance adhere exactly to the terms of the offeror's offer for a valid contract to be formed.

Misdemeanor A lesser crime than a felony, punishable by a fine or incarceration in jail for up to one year.

Mislaid Property Property that the owner has voluntarily parted with and then has inadvertently forgotten.

Mitigation of Damages The requirement that a plaintiff do whatever is reasonable to minimize the damages caused by the defendant's breach of contract.

Mobile Banking A version of online banking that is carried out with apps on smartphones or tablets.

Money Laundering Engaging in financial transactions to conceal the identity, source, or destination of illegally gained funds.

Monopolization The possession of monopoly power in the relevant market and the willful acquisition or maintenance of that power, as distinguished from growth or development as a consequence of a superior product, business acumen, or historic accident.

Monopoly A market in which there is a single seller or a very limited number of sellers.

Monopoly Power The ability of a monopoly to dictate what takes place in a given market.

Moral Minimum The minimum level of ethical behavior expected by society, which is usually defined as compliance with the law.

Motion for a Directed Verdict A motion for the judge to take the decision out of the hands of the jury and to direct a verdict for the party making the motion on the ground that the other party has not produced sufficient evidence to support a claim.

Motion for a New Trial A motion asserting that the trial was so fundamentally flawed (because of error, newly discovered evidence, prejudice, or another reason) that a new trial is necessary to prevent a miscarriage of justice.

Motion for Judgment *n.o.v.* A motion requesting the court to grant judgment in favor of the party making the motion on the ground that the jury's verdict was unreasonable and erroneous.

Motion for Judgment on the Pleadings A motion by either party to a lawsuit at the close of the pleadings requesting the court to decide the issue solely on the pleadings without proceeding to trial. The motion will be granted only if no facts are in dispute.

Motion for Summary Judgment A motion requesting the court to enter a judgment without proceeding to trial. The motion can be based on evidence outside the pleadings and will be granted only if no facts are in dispute.

Motion to Dismiss A pleading in which a defendant admits the facts as alleged by the plaintiff but asserts that the plaintiff's claim to state a cause of action has no basis in law.

Multiple Product Order An order requiring a firm that has engaged in deceptive advertising to cease and desist from false advertising in regard to all the firm's products.

Mutual Fund A specific type of investment company that continually buys or sells to investors shares of ownership in a portfolio.

N

National Law Law that pertains to a particular nation (as opposed to international law).

Natural Law The oldest school of legal thought, based on the belief that the legal system should reflect universal ("higher") moral and ethical principles that are inherent in human nature.

Necessaries Necessities required to maintain a standard of living, such as food, shelter, clothing, and medical attention.

Negligence The failure to exercise the standard of care that a reasonable person would exercise in similar circumstances.

Negligent Misrepresentation A misrepresentation that occurs when a person makes a false statement of fact because he or she did not exercise reasonable care or use the skill and competence required by her or his business or profession.

Negotiable Instrument A signed writing (record) that contains an unconditional promise or order to pay an exact sum on demand or at a specified future time to a specific person or order, or to bearer.

Negotiation A process in which parties attempt to settle their dispute informally, with or without attorneys to represent them. In negotiable instruments law, the transfer of an instrument in such form that the transferee (the person to whom the instrument is transferred) becomes a holder.

Neobanks Banks that operate exclusively online without traditional physical branch networks.

Nominal Damages A small monetary award (often one dollar) granted to a plaintiff when no actual damage was suffered.

Nonpossessory Interest In the context of real property, an interest that involves the right to use land but not the right to possess it.

Normal Trade Relations (NTR) Status A legal trade status granted to member countries of the World Trade Organization. Each member must treat other members at least as well as it treats the country that receives its most favorable treatment with regard to imports or exports.

Notary Public A public official authorized to attest to the authenticity of signatures.

Novation The substitution, by agreement, of a new contract for an old one, with the rights under the old one being terminated.

Nuisance A common law doctrine under which persons may be held liable for using their property in a manner that unreasonably interferes with others' rights to use or enjoy their own property.

Nuncupative Will An oral will (often called a *deathbed will*) made before witnesses. Usually, such wills are limited to transfers of personal property.

O

Objective Theory of Contracts The view that contracting parties shall be bound only by terms that can be objectively inferred from promises made.

Obligee One to whom an obligation is owed.

Obligor One who owes an obligation to another.

Offer A promise or commitment to perform or refrain from performing some specified act in the future.

Offeree A person to whom an offer is made.

Offeror A person who makes an offer.

Online Banking Traditional banking services, such as account management and transfers, that are provided on the financial institution's Internet website.

Online Dispute Resolution (ODR) The resolution of disputes with the assistance of organizations that offer dispute-resolution services via the Internet.

Operating Agreement An agreement in which the members of a limited liability company set forth the details of how the business will be managed and operated.

Option Contract A contract under which the offeror cannot revoke the offer for a stipulated time period (because the offeree has given consideration for the offer to remain open).

Order for Relief A court's grant of assistance to a debtor in bankruptcy that relieves the debtor of the immediate obligation to pay debts.

Order Instrument A negotiable instrument that is payable "to the order of an identified person" or "to an identified person or order."

Ordinance A regulation enacted by a city or county legislative body that becomes part of that state's statutory law.

Outcome-Based Ethics An ethical philosophy that focuses on the consequences of any given action in order to maximize benefits and minimize harms.

Output Contract An agreement in which a seller agrees to sell and a buyer agrees to buy all or up to a stated amount of what the seller produces.

Outside Director A person on the board of directors who does not hold a management position at the corporation.

Outsourcing The practice by which a company hires an outside firm or individual to perform work rather than hiring employees to do it.

Overdraft A check that is paid by a bank when the checking account on which the check is written contains insufficient funds to cover the check.

P

Parol Evidence Rule A rule of contracts under which a court will not receive into evidence prior or contemporaneous external agreements that contradict the terms of the parties' written contract.

Partially Disclosed Principal A principal whose identity is unknown by a third party, but the third party knows that the agent is or may be acting for a principal at the time the agent and the third party form a contract.

Partnering Agreement An agreement between a seller and a buyer who frequently do business with each other concerning the terms and conditions that will apply to all subsequently formed electronic contracts.

Partnership An agreement by two or more persons to carry on, as co-owners, a business for profit.

Partnership by Estoppel A partnership imposed by a court when nonpartners have held themselves out to be partners, or have allowed themselves to be held out as partners, and others have detrimentally relied on their misrepresentations.

Pass-Through Entity A business entity that has no tax liability. The entity's income is passed through to the owners, and they pay taxes on the income.

Past Consideration Something given or some act done in the past, which cannot ordinarily be consideration for a later bargain.

Patent A property right granted by the federal government that gives an inventor an exclusive right to make, use, and sell an invention for a limited time.

Payee A person to whom an instrument is made payable.

Payor Bank The bank on which a check is drawn (the drawee bank).

Peer-to-Peer (P2P) Networking The sharing of resources among multiple computers or other devices without the requirement of a central network server.

Penalty A sum specified in a contract not as a measure of compensation for its breach but rather as a punishment for a default. The agreement as to the amount will not be enforced, and recovery will be limited to the actual damages.

Per Capita A method of distributing an intestate's estate so that each heir in a certain class (such as grandchildren) receives an equal share.

***Per Curiam* Opinion** A court opinion that does not indicate which judge or justice authored the opinion.

Perfection The legal process by which secured parties protect themselves against the claims of third parties who may wish to have their debts satisfied out of the same collateral. It is usually accomplished by filing a financing statement with the appropriate government official.

Perfect Tender Rule The legal right of a buyer or lessee of goods to insist on perfect tender by the seller or lessor. If the goods fail to conform to the contract, the buyer may accept the goods, reject the goods, or accept part and reject part of the goods tendered.

Performance The fulfillment of one's duties under a contract—the normal way of discharging one's contractual obligations.

Periodic Tenancy A lease interest for an indefinite period involving payment of rent at fixed intervals, such as week to week, month to month, or year to year.

***Per Se* Violation** A restraint of trade that is so anticompetitive that it is deemed inherently (*per se*) illegal.

Personal Defense A defense that can be used to avoid payment to an ordinary holder of a negotiable instrument but not a holder in due course (HDC) or a holder with the rights of an HDC. It is also called a *limited defense*.

Personal Property Property that is movable. Any property that is not real property.

Per Stirpes A method of distributing an intestate's estate so that each heir in a certain class (such as grandchildren) takes the share to which her or his deceased ancestor (such as a mother or father) would have been entitled.

Persuasive Authority Any legal authority or source of law that a court may look to for guidance but need not follow when making its decision.

Petition in Bankruptcy The document that is filed with a bankruptcy court to initiate bankruptcy proceedings.

Petty Offense The least serious kind of criminal offense, such as a traffic or building-code violation.

Phishing A form of identity theft in which the perpetrator sends e-mails purporting to be from legitimate businesses to induce recipients to reveal their personal financial data, passwords, or other information.

Piercing the Corporate Veil The action of a court to disregard the corporate entity and hold the shareholders personally liable for corporate debts and obligations.

Plaintiff One who initiates a lawsuit.

Plea Bargaining The process by which a criminal defendant and the prosecutor work out an agreement to dispose of the criminal case, subject to court approval.

Pleadings Statements by the plaintiff and the defendant that detail the facts, charges, and defenses of a case.

Pledge A security device in which personal property is transferred into the possession of the creditor as security for the payment of a debt and retained by the creditor until the debt is paid.

Plurality Opinion A court opinion that is joined by the largest number of the judges or justices hearing the case, but less than half of the total number.

Police Powers Powers possessed by the states as part of their inherent sovereignty. These powers may be exercised to protect or promote the public order, health, safety, morals, and general welfare.

Policy In insurance law, the contract between the insurer and the insured.

Potentially Responsible Party (PRP) A party liable for the costs of cleaning up a hazardous waste disposal site under the Comprehensive Environmental Response, Compensation, and Liability Act.

Power of Attorney Authorization for another to act as one's agent or attorney either in specified circumstances (special) or in all situations (general).

Precedent A court decision that furnishes an example or authority for deciding subsequent cases involving identical or similar facts.

Predatory Pricing The pricing of a product below cost with the intent to drive competitors out of the market.

Predominant-Factor Test A test courts use to determine whether a contract is primarily for the sale of goods or for the sale of services.

Preemption A doctrine under which certain federal laws preempt, or take precedence over, conflicting state or local laws.

Preemptive Right The right of a shareholder in a corporation to have the first opportunity to purchase a new issue of that corporation's stock in proportion to the amount of stock already owned by the shareholder.

Preference In bankruptcy proceedings, a property transfer or payment made by the debtor that favors one creditor over others.

Preferred Creditor In the context of bankruptcy, a creditor who has received a preferential transfer from a debtor.

Preferred Stock Stock that has priority over common stock as to payment of dividends and distribution of assets on the corporation's dissolution.

Premium In insurance law, the price paid by the insured for insurance protection for a specified period of time.

Prenuptial Agreement An agreement made before marriage that defines each partner's ownership rights in the other partner's property. Prenuptial agreements must be in writing to be enforceable.

Presentment The act of presenting an instrument to the party liable on the instrument in order to collect payment. Presentment also occurs when a person presents an instrument to a drawee for a required acceptance.

Presentment Warranties Implied warranties made by any person who presents an instrument for payment or acceptance that the person is entitled to enforce the instrument, that the instrument has not been altered, and that the person is unaware of any unauthorized signatures.

Price Discrimination A seller's act of charging competing buyers different prices for identical products or services.

Price-Fixing Agreement An agreement between competitors to fix the prices of products or services at a certain level.

***Prima Facie* Case** A case in which the plaintiff has produced sufficient evidence of a claim that the case will be decided for the plaintiff unless the defendant produces evidence to rebut the claim.

Primary Source of Law A source that establishes the law on a particular issue, such as a constitution, a statute, an administrative rule, or a court decision.

Principle of Rights The belief that human beings have certain fundamental rights.

Private Equity Capital Funds invested in an existing corporation by a private equity firm, usually to purchase and reorganize it.

Privilege A special right, advantage, or immunity that enables a person or a class of persons to avoid liability for defamation.

Privileges and Immunities Clause Article IV, Section 2, of the U.S. Constitution requires states not to discriminate against one another's citizens. A resident of one state, when in another state, cannot be denied the privileges and immunities of that state.

Privity of Contract The relationship that exists between the promisor and the promisee of a contract.

Probable Cause Reasonable grounds for believing that a search or seizure should be conducted.

Probate The process of proving and validating a will and settling all matters pertaining to an estate.

Probate Court A state court of limited jurisdiction that conducts proceedings relating to the settlement of a deceased person's estate.

Procedural Law Law that establishes the methods of enforcing the rights established by substantive law.

Proceeds Under Article 9 of the UCC, whatever is received when collateral is sold or disposed of in some other way.

Product Liability The legal liability of manufacturers, sellers, and lessors of goods for injuries or damage caused by the goods to consumers, users, or bystanders.

Profit In real property law, the right to enter onto another's property and remove something of value from that property.

Promise A declaration that binds a person who makes it (the promisor) to do or not do a certain act.

Promisee A person to whom a promise is made.

Promisor A person who makes a promise.

Promissory Estoppel A doctrine that can be used to enforce a promise when the promisee has justifiably relied on the promise and when justice will be better served by enforcing the promise.

Promissory Note A written promise made by one person (the maker) to pay a fixed amount of funds to another person (the payee or a subsequent holder) on demand or on a specified date.

Prospectus A written document required by securities laws when a security is being sold. The prospectus describes the security, the financial operations of the issuing corporation, and the risk attaching to the security.

Protected Class A group of persons protected by specific laws because of the group's defining characteristics, including race, color, religion, national origin, gender, age, disability, and military status.

Proximate Cause Legal cause. It exists when the connection between an act and an injury is strong enough to justify imposing liability.

Proxy In corporate law, formal authorization to serve as an agent for corporate shareholders and vote their shares in a certain manner.

Public Corporation A corporation owned by a federal, state, or municipal government to meet a political or governmental purpose.

Publicly Held Corporation A corporation whose shares are publicly traded in securities markets, such as the New York Stock Exchange or the NASDAQ.

Puffery A salesperson's exaggerated claims concerning the quality of property offered for sale. Such claims involve opinions rather than facts and are not legally binding promises or warranties.

Punitive Damages Monetary damages that may be awarded to a plaintiff to punish the defendant and deter similar conduct in the future.

Purchase-Money Security Interest (PMSI) A security interest that arises when a seller or lender extends credit for part or all of the price of goods purchased by a buyer.

Q

Qualified Indorsement An indorsement on a negotiable instrument in which the indorser disclaims any contract liability on the instrument. The notation "without recourse" is commonly used to create a qualified indorsement.

Quantum Meruit A Latin phrase meaning "as much as he or she deserves." The expression describes the extent of compensation owed under a quasi contract.

Quasi Contract An obligation or contract imposed by law (a court), in the absence of an agreement, to prevent the unjust enrichment of one party.

Question of Fact In a lawsuit, an issue that involves only disputed facts, and not what the law is on a given point.

Question of Law In a lawsuit, an issue involving the application or interpretation of a law.

Quitclaim Deed A deed that conveys only whatever interest the grantor had in the property and therefore offers the least amount of protection against defects of title.

Quorum The number of members of a decision-making body that must be present before business may be transacted.

Quota A set limit on the amount of goods that can be imported.

R

Ratification A party's act of accepting or giving legal force to a previously unenforceable contract or other obligation entered into on that party's behalf by another party.

Reaffirmation Agreement An agreement between a debtor and a creditor in which the debtor voluntarily agrees to pay a debt dischargeable in bankruptcy.

Real Property Land and everything permanently attached to it, such as trees and buildings.

Reasonable Person Standard The standard of behavior expected of a hypothetical "reasonable person." It is the standard against which negligence is measured and that must be observed to avoid liability for negligence.

Record Information that is either inscribed on a tangible medium or stored in an electronic or other medium and is retrievable in visual form.

Recording Statute A statute that allows deeds, mortgages, and other real property transactions to be recorded so as to provide notice to future purchasers or creditors of an existing claim on the property.

Reformation A court-ordered correction of a written contract so that it reflects the true intentions of the parties.

Regulation E A set of rules issued by the Federal Reserve System's Board of Governors to protect users of electronic fund transfer systems.

Regulation Z A set of rules issued by the Federal Reserve Board of Governors to implement the provisions of the Truth in Lending Act.

Release An agreement in which one party gives up the right to pursue a legal claim against another party.

Remedy The relief given to an innocent party to enforce a right or compensate for the violation of a right.

Replevin An action that can be used by a buyer or lessee to recover identified goods from a third party, such as a bailee, who is wrongfully withholding them.

Reply Procedurally, a plaintiff's response to a defendant's answer.

Requirements Contract An agreement in which a buyer agrees to purchase and a seller agrees to sell all or up to a stated amount of what the buyer needs or requires.

Resale Price Maintenance Agreement An agreement between a manufacturer and a retailer in which the manufacturer specifies what the retail prices of its products must be.

Rescission A remedy whereby a contract is canceled and the parties are returned to the positions they occupied before the contract was made.

Respondeat Superior A doctrine under which a principal or an employer is held liable for the wrongful acts committed by agents or employees while acting within the course and scope of agency or employment.

Restitution An equitable remedy under which persons are restored to their original position prior to loss or injury, or placed in the position they would have been in had the breach not occurred.

Restrictive Indorsement An indorsement on a negotiable instrument that requires the indorsee to comply with certain instructions regarding the funds involved.

Resulting Trust An implied trust that arises when one party holds the legal title to another's property only for that other's benefit.

Retained Earnings The portion of a corporation's profits that has not been paid out as dividends to shareholders.

Revocation The withdrawal of a contract offer by the offeror. Unless an offer is irrevocable, it can be revoked at any time prior to acceptance without liability.

Right of Contribution The right of a co-surety who pays more than his or her proportionate share on a debtor's default to recover the excess paid from other co-sureties.

Right of Reimbursement The right of a party to be repaid for costs, expenses, or losses incurred on behalf of another.

Right of Subrogation The right of a party to stand in the place of another, giving the substituted party the same legal rights that the original party had.

Right-to-Work Laws State laws providing that employees may not be required to join a union as a condition of retaining employment.

Risk A prediction concerning potential loss based on known and unknown factors.

Risk Management In the context of insurance, the transfer of certain risks from the insured to the insurance company by contractual agreement.

Robbery The act of forcefully and unlawfully taking personal property of any value from another.

Royalties Payments made by a licensee to a licensor as part of an agreement for the ongoing use of the licensor's trademarked asset.

Rulemaking The process by which an administrative agency formally adopts a new regulation or amends an old one.

Rule of Four A rule of the United States Supreme Court under which the Court will not issue a writ of *certiorari* unless at least four justices approve of the decision to issue the writ.

Rule of Reason A test used to determine whether an anticompetitive agreement constitutes a reasonable restraint on trade. Courts consider such factors as the purpose of the agreement, its effect on competition, and whether less restrictive means could have been used.

S

Sale The passing of title to property from the seller to the buyer for a price.

Sales Contracts Contracts for the sale of goods.

Scienter Knowledge on the part of a misrepresenting party that material facts have been falsely represented or omitted with an intent to deceive.

S Corporation A close business corporation that has most corporate attributes, including limited liability, but qualifies under the Internal Revenue Code to be taxed as a partnership.

Search Warrant An order granted by a public authority, such as a judge, that authorizes law enforcement personnel to search particular premises or property.

Seasonably Within a specified time period or, if no period is specified, within a reasonable time.

Secondary Source of Law A publication that summarizes or interprets the law, such as a legal encyclopedia, a legal treatise, or an article in a law review.

SEC Rule 10b-5 A rule of the Securities and Exchange Commission that prohibits the commission of fraud in connection with the purchase or sale of any security.

Secured Party A creditor who has a security interest in the debtor's collateral, including a seller, lender, cosigner, or buyer of accounts or chattel paper.

Secured Transaction Any transaction in which the payment of a debt is guaranteed, or secured, by personal property owned by the debtor or in which the debtor has a legal interest.

Securities Generally, stocks, bonds, or other items that represent an ownership interest in a corporation or a promise of repayment of debt by a corporation.

Security Agreement An agreement that creates or provides for a security interest between the debtor and a secured party.

Security Interest Any interest in personal property or fixtures that secures payment or performance of an obligation.

Self-Defense The legally recognized privilege to do what is reasonably necessary to protect oneself, one's property, or someone else against injury by another.

Self-Incrimination Giving testimony in a trial or other legal proceeding that could expose the person testifying to criminal prosecution.

Seniority System A system in which those who have worked longest for an employer are first in line for promotions, salary increases, and other benefits, and are last to be laid off if the workforce must be reduced.

Service Mark A trademark that is used to distinguish the services (rather than the products) of one person or company from those of another.

Service of Process The delivery of the complaint and summons to a defendant.

Sexual Harassment The demanding of sexual favors in return for job promotions or other benefits, or language or conduct that is so sexually offensive that it creates a hostile working environment.

Shareholder's Derivative Suit A suit brought by a shareholder to enforce a corporate cause of action against a third person.

Shelter Principle The principle that the holder of a negotiable instrument who cannot qualify as a holder in due course (HDC), but who derives title through an HDC, acquires the rights of an HDC.

Shipment Contract A contract for the sale of goods in which the seller is required or authorized to ship the goods by carrier. The seller assumes liability for any losses or damage to the goods until they are delivered to the carrier.

Short-Swing Profits Profits earned by a purchase and sale, or sale and purchase, of the same security within a six-month period.

Shrink-Wrap Agreement An agreement whose terms are expressed in a document located inside a box in which goods (usually software) are packaged.

Slander Defamation in oral form.

Slander of Quality (Trade Libel) The publication of false information about another's product, alleging that it is not what its seller claims.

Slander of Title The publication of a statement that denies or casts doubt on another's legal ownership of property, causing financial loss to that property's owner.

Small Claims Court A special court in which parties can litigate small claims without an attorney.

Smart Card A card containing a microprocessor with security programming that is typically used for financial transactions, personal identification, and other purposes.

Social Media Forms of communication through which users create and share information, ideas, messages, and other content via the Internet.

Sole Proprietorship The simplest form of business organization, in which the owner is the business. The owner reports business income as personal income and is legally responsible for all debts and obligations incurred by the business.

Sovereign Immunity A doctrine that immunizes foreign nations from the jurisdiction of U.S. courts when certain conditions are satisfied.

Sovereignty The power of a state to do what is necessary to govern itself. Individual state sovereignty is determined by the U.S. Constitution.

Space Law Law consisting of the international and national laws that govern activities in outer space.

Spam Bulk, unsolicited (junk) e-mail.

Special Damages In a tort case, an amount awarded to compensate the plaintiff for quantifiable monetary losses, such as medical expenses, property damage, and lost wages and benefits (now and in the future).

Special Indorsement An indorsement on an instrument that identifies the specific person to whom the indorser intends to make the instrument payable.

Special Warranty Deed A deed that warrants only that the grantor held good title during the grantor's ownership of the property and does not warrant that there were no defects of title when the property was held by previous owners.

Specific Performance An equitable remedy in which a court orders the parties to perform as promised in the contract. This remedy normally is granted only when the legal remedy (monetary damages) is inadequate.

Spendthrift Trust A trust in which only a certain portion of the total amount is given to the beneficiary at any one time; most states prohibit creditors from attaching assets of the trust.

Stakeholders Groups that are affected by corporate decisions. Stakeholders include employees, customers, creditors, suppliers, and the community in which the corporation operates.

Stale Check A check, other than a certified check, that is presented for payment more than six months after its date.

Standing to Sue The legal requirement that an individual must have a sufficient stake in a controversy in order to bring a lawsuit.

Stare Decisis A common law doctrine under which judges are obligated to follow the precedents established in prior decisions.

Statute of Frauds A state statute that requires certain types of contracts to be in writing to be enforceable.

Statute of Repose A statute that places outer time limits on product liability actions. Such statutes cut off absolutely the right to bring an action after a specified period of time following some event (often the product's manufacture or purchase) other than the occurrence of an injury.

Statutory Law The body of law enacted by legislative bodies (as opposed to constitutional law, administrative law, or case law).

Stocks Securities that evidence an ownership (equity) interest in a corporation, measured in units of shares.

Stock Certificate A certificate issued by a corporation evidencing the ownership of a specified number of shares in the corporation.

Stock Option A right to buy a given number of shares of stock at a set price, usually within a specified time period.

Stop-Payment Order An order by a bank customer to the bank not to pay or certify a certain check.

Stored-Value Card A card bearing a magnetic strip that holds magnetically encoded data providing access to stored funds.

Strict Liability Liability regardless of fault, which is imposed on those engaged in abnormally dangerous activities, on persons who keep dangerous animals, and on manufacturers or sellers that introduce into commerce defective and unreasonably dangerous goods.

Strike An action undertaken by unionized workers when collective bargaining fails. The workers leave their jobs, refuse to work, and (typically) picket the employer's workplace.

Sublease A tenant's transfer of all or part of the leased premises to a third person for a period shorter than the lease term.

Substantive Law Law that defines, describes, regulates, and creates legal rights and obligations.

Summary Jury Trial (SJT) A method of settling disputes by holding a trial in which the jury's verdict is not binding but instead guides the parties toward reaching an agreement during the mandatory negotiations that immediately follow.

Summons A document informing defendants that a legal action has been commenced against them and that they must appear in court on a certain date to answer the plaintiff's complaint.

Supremacy Clause The provision in Article VI of the U.S. Constitution that the Constitution, laws, and treaties of the United States are "the supreme Law of the Land."

Surety A third party who agrees to be primarily responsible for the debt of another.

Suretyship A promise made by a third party to be responsible for a debtor's obligation.

Symbolic Speech Nonverbal expressions of beliefs. Symbolic speech, which includes gestures, movements, and articles of clothing, is given substantial protection by the courts.

Syndicate A group of individuals or firms that join together to finance a project. A syndicate is also called an *investment group*.

T

Taking The taking of private property by the government for public use through the power of eminent domain.

Tangible Employment Action A significant change in employment status or benefits, such as occurs when an employee is fired, refused a promotion, or reassigned to a lesser position.

Tangible Property Property that has physical existence and can be distinguished by the senses of touch and sight.

Tariff A tax on imported goods.

Tenancy at Sufferance A tenancy that arises when a tenant wrongfully continues to occupy leased property after the lease has terminated.

Tenancy at Will A type of tenancy that either the landlord or the tenant can terminate without notice.

Tenancy by the Entirety Joint ownership of property by a married couple in which neither spouse can transfer any interest in the property without the consent of the other.

Tenancy in Common Joint ownership of property in which each party owns an undivided interest that passes to his or her heirs at death.

Tender An unconditional offer to perform an obligation by a person who is ready, willing, and able to do so.

Tender of Delivery A seller's or lessor's act of placing conforming goods at the disposal of the buyer or lessee and providing whatever notification is reasonably necessary to enable the buyer or lessee to take delivery.

Testamentary Trust A trust that is created by will and therefore does not take effect until the death of the testator.

Testate Having left a will at death.

Testator One who makes and executes a will.

Third Party Beneficiary One who is not a party to the contract but who stands to benefit from the contract's performance.

Tippee A person who receives inside information.

Toll To temporarily suspend the running of a prescribed time period, such as a statute of limitations.

Tolling A legal doctrine that allows for the temporary suspension of the running of a prescribed time period, such as a statute of limitations.

Tort A wrongful act (other than a breach of contract) that results in harm or injury to another and leads to civil liability.

Tortfeasor One who commits a tort.

Totten Trust A trust created when a grantor deposits funds in the grantor's own name for a specific beneficiary, who will receive the funds on the depositor's death. The trust is revocable at will until the depositor dies or completes the gift.

Toxic Tort A civil wrong arising from exposure to a toxic substance, such as asbestos, radiation, or hazardous waste.

Trade Dress The image and overall appearance of a product.

Trade Name A name that a business uses to identify itself and its brand. A trade name is directly related to a business's reputation and goodwill, and is protected under trademark law.

Trade Secret A formula, device, idea, process, or other information used in a business that gives the owner a competitive advantage in the marketplace.

Trademark A distinctive word, symbol, sound, or design that identifies the manufacturer as the source of particular goods and distinguishes its products from those made or sold by others.

Trademark Dilution The unauthorized use of a distinctive and famous mark in a way that impairs the mark's distinctiveness or harms its reputation.

Transfer Warranties Implied warranties made by any person who transfers an instrument for consideration that the person is entitled to enforce the instrument, the signatures are authentic, it has not been altered, there are no defenses, and the transferor is unaware of any bankruptcy proceedings of parties to the instrument.

Transferred Intent A legal principle under which a person who intends to harm one individual, but unintentionally harms a different individual, can be liable to the second victim for an intentional tort.

Traveler's Check A check that is payable on demand, drawn on or payable through a financial institution, and designated as a traveler's check.

Treaty A formal international agreement negotiated between two nations or among several nations.

Treble Damages Damages that, by statute, are three times the amount of actual damages suffered.

Trespass to Land Entry onto, above, or below the surface of land owned by another without the owner's permission or legal authorization.

Trespass to Personal Property Wrongfully taking or harming the personal property of another or otherwise interfering with the lawful owner's possession of personal property.

Triple Bottom Line A measure that includes a corporation's profits, its impact on people, and its impact on the planet.

Trust An arrangement in which title to property is held by one person (a trustee) for the benefit of another (a beneficiary).

Trust Indorsements An indorsement to a person who is to hold or use funds for the benefit of the indorser or a third person. It is also known as an *agency indorsement*.

Tying Arrangement A seller's act of conditioning the sale of a product or service on the buyer's agreement to purchase another product or service from the seller.

Typosquatting A form of cybersquatting that relies on mistakes, such as typographical errors, made by Internet users when entering information into a Web browser.

U

Ultra Vires Acts Acts of a corporation that are beyond its express and implied powers to undertake (the Latin phrase means "beyond the powers").

Unconscionable Unscrupulous or grossly unfair. An unconscionable contract or clause is void on the basis of public policy because one party was forced to accept terms that are unfairly burdensome and that unfairly benefit the other party.

Underwriter In insurance law, the insurer, or the one assuming a risk in return for the payment of a premium.

Undisclosed Principal A principal whose identity is unknown by a third party, and the third party has no knowledge that the agent is acting for a principal at the time the agent and the third party form a contract.

Undue Influence Persuasion that is less than actual force but more than advice and that induces a person to act according to the will or purposes of the dominating party.

Unenforceable Contract A valid contract rendered unenforceable by some statute or law.

Uniform Law Model laws developed by the National Conference of Commissioners on Uniform State Laws for the states to consider enacting into statute.

Unilateral Contract A type of contract that results when an offer can be accepted only by the offeree's performance.

Unilateral Mistake A mistake that occurs when one party to a contract is mistaken as to a material fact.

Union Shop A firm that requires all workers, once employed, to become union members within a specified period of time as a condition of their continued employment.

Universal Defense A defense that can be used to avoid payment to all holders of a negotiable instrument, including a holder in due course (HDC) or a holder with the rights of an HDC. It is also called a *real defense*.

Unliquidated Debt A debt that is uncertain in amount.

Unreasonably Dangerous Product A product that is so defective that it is dangerous beyond the expectation of an ordinary consumer, or a product for which a less dangerous alternative was feasible but the manufacturer failed to produce it.

Usage of Trade Any practice or method of dealing that is so regularly observed in a place, vocation, or trade that parties justifiably expect it will be observed in their transaction.

U.S. Trustee A government official who performs administrative tasks that a bankruptcy judge would otherwise have to perform.

Usury Charging an illegal rate of interest.

Utilitarianism An approach to ethical reasoning in which an action is evaluated in terms of its consequences for those whom it will affect. A "good" action is one that results in the greatest good for the greatest number of people.

V

Valid Contract A contract that results when the elements necessary for contract formation (agreement, consideration, capacity, and legality) are present.

Venture Capital Financing provided by professional, outside investors (venture capitalists) to new business ventures.

Venue The geographic district in which a legal action is tried and from which the jury is selected.

Vertically Integrated Firm A firm that carries out two or more functional phases (manufacturing, distribution, and retailing, for instance) of the chain of production.

Vertical Merger The acquisition by a company at one stage of production of a company at a higher or lower stage of production (such as a company merging with one of its suppliers or retailers).

Vertical Restraint A restraint of trade created by an agreement between firms at different levels in the manufacturing and distribution process.

Vesting The creation of an absolute or unconditional right or power.

Vicarious Liability Indirect liability imposed on a supervisory party (such as an employer) for the actions of a subordinate (such as an employee) because of the relationship between the two parties.

Virus A software program that can replicate itself over a network and spread from one device to another, altering files and interfering with normal operations.

Void Contract A contract having no legal force or binding effect.

Voidable Contract A contract that may be legally avoided at the option of one or both of the parties.

Voir Dire A part of the jury selection process in which the attorneys question prospective jurors about their backgrounds, attitudes, and biases to ascertain whether they can be impartial jurors.

Voluntary Consent Knowledge of and genuine assent to the terms of a contract.

W

Warranty Deed A deed that provides the greatest amount of protection for the grantee. The grantor promises that she or he has title to the property conveyed in the deed, that there are no undisclosed encumbrances on the property, and that the grantee will enjoy quiet possession of the property.

Waste The use of real property in a manner that damages or destroys its value.

Whistleblowing An employee's disclosure to government authorities, upper-level managers, or the media that the employer is engaged in unsafe or illegal activities.

White-Collar Crime Nonviolent crime committed by individuals or business entities to obtain a personal or business advantage.

Will An instrument made by a testator directing what is to be done with her or his property after death.

Will Substitutes Various instruments, such as living trusts and life insurance plans, that may be used to avoid the formal probate process.

Winding Up The second of two stages in the termination of a partnership or corporation, in which the firm's assets are collected, liquidated, and distributed, and liabilities are discharged.

Workers' Compensation Laws State statutes that establish an administrative process for compensating workers for injuries that arise in the course of their employment, regardless of fault.

Working Papers The documents used and developed by an accountant during an audit, such as notes, computations, and memoranda.

Workout An agreement outlining the respective rights and responsibilities of a borrower and a lender as they try to resolve the borrower's default.

Worm A software program that automatically replicates itself over a network but does not alter files and is usually invisible to the user until it has consumed system resources.

Writ of Attachment A court order to seize a debtor's nonexempt property prior to a court's final determination of a creditor's rights to the property.

Writ of *Certiorari* A writ from a higher court asking a lower court for the record of a case.

Writ of Execution A court order directing the sheriff to seize (levy) and sell a debtor's nonexempt real or personal property to satisfy a court's judgment in the creditor's favor.

Wrongful Discharge An employer's termination of an employee's employment in violation of the law or an employment contract.

Table of Cases

For your convenience and reference, here is a list of all the cases mentioned in this text, including those within the footnotes, features, and case problems. The summarized cases in the chapters of this text are given special emphasis by having their titles appear in **boldface**.

A

B

C

D

E

F

G

H

I

J

K

L

M

N

O

P

Q

R

S

T

U

V

W

Index

A

B

C

D

F

G

H

I

J

K

L

M

N

P

Q

R

T

U